EXPANSION AND COEXISTENCE

EXPANSION AND COEXISTENCE

Soviet Foreign Policy, 1917–73

Second Edition

Adam B. Ulam

HOLT, RINEHART AND WINSTON, INC.

New York   Chicago   San Francisco   Atlanta
Dallas   Montreal   Toronto   London   Sydney

Published in the United States of America in 1974
by Praeger Publishers
A Division of Holt, Rinehart and Winston
200 Park Avenue, New York, N.Y. 10017

This is the second edition of the book published in 1968.

Library of Congress Cataloging in Publication Data

Ulam, Adam Bruno, 1922–
  Expansion and coexistence: Soviet foreign policy, 1917–1973.

  Includes bibliographical references.
  1. Russia—Foreign relations—1917–1945. 2. Russia—Foreign relations—1945–

I. Title.
DK266.U49 1974   327.47   73-8181

ISBN 0–275–33270–5
ISBN 0–03–038696–9

Printed in the United States of America

90123 090 98765

PREFACE
TO THE SECOND EDITION

When the first edition of this book appeared in 1968, the "new look" of Soviet foreign policy was just in the making. The invasion of Czechoslovakia had just taken place; the Kremlin was still puzzled—as was the rest of the world—by the Chinese Cultural Revolution, uncertain over how to respond both to the dangers and to the opportunities it presented for Soviet foreign policy. America's intervention in Vietnam had already ceased to be a cause of apprehension for Moscow, but the rulers of the U.S.S.R. were still undecided on how to exploit the attrition of U.S. power and prestige that resulted from America's disastrous policies in Southeast Asia. What the developments of the past few years have meant and what they portend for the future is discussed in the last, largely new, two chapters of this book. It is clear that 1971–72 marked the opening of a new phase in Soviet foreign policy—a departure from the old pattern at least as significant as what took place after Stalin's death in 1953, when his successors undertook a fresh assessment of the international situation. It is important that the possible consequences of this new posture of the U.S.S.R. in world affairs be carefully assessed. As for my own approach, I repeat what I said in the Preface of the first edition: "The student of Soviet affairs has as his first task to be neither hopeful nor pessimistic but simply to state the facts and tendencies of Russian politics. It is when he begins to see in certain political trends the inevitabilities of the future and when he superimposes upon them his own conclusions about the desirable policies of America toward the U.S.S.R. that he is courting trouble. To be sure, complete detachment is impossible, and the reader will occasionally find *hints* as to various Western sins of commission and omission in dealing with the U.S.S.R."

I have found no reason to change any interpretations and material in the bulk of the 1968 edition, but I have added certain facts that have recently come to light and that bear on Sino-Soviet relations between 1945 and 1960.

I should like to restate my gratitude to the Russian Research Center at Harvard, within whose congenial precincts I have done most of my work. I am especially indebted, as must be many scholars in this field, to two of its directors now, alas, no longer with us, the late Clyde Kluckhohn and Merle Fainsod. I recall with pleasure and gratitude many talks on Soviet foreign policy that I have had with my colleagues at the Center, especially Melvin Croan, now of the University of Wisconsin; Marshall Goldman, of Wellesley College; and Mark Pinon, now of the University of Tel Aviv. Along with many others, I have been a beneficiary of the Center's efficient organization, which is due largely to the labors of its successive administrative assistants Helen Parsons and Mary Towle. Karl Spiellmann helped me with the materials. Elisabeth Sifton was a vigilant editor of the first edition; Denise Rathbun, of this one.

Cambridge, Massachusetts
August, 1973

CONTENTS

EXPANSION AND COEXISTENCE

I

THE SOURCES

1. *The Inheritance of the Past*

In the early part of November 1917, a *coup d'état* delivered political power in Russia into the hands of the Bolshevik Party. To a contemporary or to a pedantic historian, almost every word in the preceding sentence would have appeared inaccurate or calling for qualification. There was no *coup d'état* in the classical sense of the phrase, meaning the totality of the government being seized by a unified group of conspirators. Armed revolts in several urban centers, notably in the two capitals, Petrograd and Moscow, had destroyed what remained of the fading authority of the previous regime. Though the new executive, the Council of Commissars, was composed exclusively of members of the Bolshevik Party, it claimed to rule on behalf of the Congress of Soviets of Workers' and Soldiers' Deputies, an extra-legal and haphazardly elected body that was by no means exclusively Bolshevik and that was to be the legislative organ only until the convocation of the really representative assembly of the peoples of Russia: the Constituent Assembly. Again, "political power" is a most imperfect expression. Parts of the country were under foreign occupation. Large areas of what had been the Russian empire refused to recognize the authority of the new rulers in Petrograd and Moscow. The nature and extent of the Bolsheviks' control was subject to debate and dissension even within their own ranks. Few among them thought of themselves as rulers in the traditional sense of the word; they were agents of a world revolution-in-the-making; their concern for affairs in Moscow or the situation of the Russian army was hardly greater than their attention to events in Vienna or opportunities for revolutionary developments among German soldiers.

Yet, as we now know—and it was forcibly brought to the awareness of the Bolsheviks themselves within a few months—the immediate and the most important consequence was that they became the rulers of Russia, heirs of the Tsars. What was the nature of this inheritance?

The Russian empire entered the ranks of the Great Powers early in the eighteenth century during the reign of Peter the Great. The almost continuous wars of the century enabled Russia to push Turkey out of Europe except for the Balkans. The two previous claimants to the domination of the east, Poland and Sweden, were by the middle of the century reduced to the status of third-rate powers; at its end, Poland ceased to exist, and the major part of the territories of the once great Polish Lithuanian state, which at one point early in the 1600's had threatened to turn Russia proper into a satellite state, went to the empire of the Tsars. Unlike the expansion of many European powers in the eighteenth century, Russia's was not only political but also, and predominantly, ethnic in character. Most of the territory Russia claimed from Poland was inhabited by Ukrainian and Byelorussian peasants close to the Great Russians in their language, professing for the most part the Orthodox religion, and among whom no upper or middle class had as yet arisen to claim a national distinctness. In Asia proper, beyond the Urals, Russian expansion ever since the sixteenth century had encountered but sparse nomadic tribes, and, finally, a treaty toward the end of the seventeenth century with China had legally secured the vast areas of eastern Siberia.

The conditions of the late eighteenth century were, then, favorable to the creation of that type of Russian nationalism which with amazing tenacity survived till the Revolution and, its makers would have been shocked to foresee, was to make its quite explicit resurgence under Stalin. In its territorial extent, Russia was the largest country in Europe. There was no power to check her expansion into Asia to the shores of the Pacific, at least not until the end of the nineteenth century and the emergence of modern Japan. In the south, Russia's territorial drive around the Black Sea encountered the two moribund empires Turkey and Persia, neither of which alone was capable of stopping the progress of Russian arms and influence.

Many elements of Russia's great historical fortune in the eighteenth century were to weigh heavily on her destiny well into our days. She became an Asiatic as well as a European power. The process of modernization that accompanied her emergence on the world stage was primarily the work of the government, largely designed to increase the state's military potential, and it was almost totally unaccompanied by the emergence of that middle class which in the West was already becoming the main vehicle of progress and/or revolution.

Even more important was the birth of the nationalism that colored so much Russian history in the nineteenth and twentieth centuries. "That which stops growing begins to rot," said a minister of Catherine the Great. The tendency toward territorial expansion and nationalism went hand in hand in the history of most major European states, but already in the beginnings of Russian imperialism we begin to encounter some fairly unique elements of this association. Predating Peter's reign and going back to the earliest days of Muscovy, there is the notion of the historical mission of the Russian nation as the representative and defender of eastern Christianity as against Catholicism and also (and especially) as against Islam. The concrete expression of this mission was the goal of expelling Turkey from Europe and regaining Constantinople and the Straits for Christendom.

From the beginning, this expansionist nationalism was not free of certain compensatory elements, to use a modern term. Russia's vast territories and her military power were felt by her rulers to offset her acknowledged cultural and social backwardness as compared with the West. Applying a historical parallel with caution, there is at least a shadow of resemblance between late eighteenth-century Russia, and her German-descended dynasty and her largely German civil and military bureaucracy, pursuing national and religious expansion, and the first generation of Bolsheviks, so many of them of Jewish, Polish, and other non-Russian origin, devising plans of political and ideological conquest. If one probes deeply enough, even in the eighteenth century one finds the seed of the populist rationale of imperialism that was used quite openly though incongruously by Tsarist Russia in the nineteenth century and that has been a cornerstone of the official Soviet position: Russia's partitions of Poland were represented as a legitimate reclamation of Russian-speaking peasants suffering from national as well as religious oppression at the hands of their Polish landlords.

In brief, it was not entirely historical fancy and propagandistic needs of the moment that made Stalin in the 1930's abjure the dogmatic Marxian classification of imperial Russia and claim continuity with certain elements in the policies of Ivan the Terrible[1] and Peter the Great. It was also a belated acknowledgment that November 1917 had not wiped the slate clean, that underneath the new language, for all the new cult and the new ruling class, there were some fundamental links with the imperial past.

The modern era in Russian history is dated from 1815—the end of the

---

[1] Here, one may say, Stalin injected certain personal predilections.

Napoleonic wars—when the empire emerged as the first power on the Continent and an arbiter of Europe's destinies at the Congress of Vienna.[2]

The settlement in Vienna included one provision that was to weigh heavily on Russian foreign policy and, indeed, on domestic policy, too. Russia emerged as the main beneficiary of a new partition of Poland, her share now including territories purely Polish in population, with Warsaw, the country's former capital. This purely Polish territory (but not the largely non-Polish areas of the old Polish state annexed to Russia in the eighteenth century) now received autonomous status, being joined to Russia through the person of the emperor, in this case Alexander I. The autocrat of Russia was to be a constitutional monarch of Poland (just as he was in Finland, acquired previously from Sweden), a situation which, granting the past history of the two countries, was bound to prove untenable. From our perspective, it is also easy to see that the Polish question was bound to tie the hands of Russian policy-makers for decades to come. The empire acquired a vested interest in suppressing nascent European nationalisms in subjugated or divided countries. A common interest in preventing the restoration of Polish independence tied Russian policies to those of Austria-Hungary and, especially, of Prussia, a situation from which the empire was not fully emancipated until the end of the century. By then, however, Prussia had established the German empire, which replaced Russia as the main power on the Continent.

Not until the Soviet period was Russian foreign policy to bear so pronounced an ideological character as it did during the forty years between the Treaty of Vienna and the death of Emperor Nicholas I in 1855. Its aims were to freeze the status quo in Europe not only insofar as the territories of the powers were concerned but also the general social and political order. This attitude recalled again a refrain that will be repeated in Russian history—a reaction to internal developments which in the opinion of its rulers represented a threat both to the territorial cohesion of the empire and to its autocratic system. Once an enlightened autocrat who had toyed with the ideas of abolition of serfdom and bestowal of the rudiments of constitutionalism, Alexander I became, after 1815, increasingly suspicious of liberal ideas. Nicholas I, on his accession in 1825, was greeted by an attempted *coup d'état*—the Decembrist revolt—which was a delayed echo of the French Revolution and the Napoleonic wars. It was the first example of the infectiousness and explosive power of Western ideas of liberty. (The nucleus of the plot was among aristocratic Guards officers who had imbibed of the culture of France and England.) The iron curtain that was designed

---

[2] This date would be disputed by Soviet historians. In their Marxian classification scheme, the modern "capitalist" period of Russian history begins with the emancipation of serfs in the 1860's, the previous period, going far into the past, being classified as "feudal."

to keep out Western ideas and institutions (it included such modern features as the establishment of a secret police with a network of informers, and absurdly detailed censorship of literature and what there was of the press) was accompanied by an aggressive foreign policy which in Nicholas' reign attempted to range Russia's power on the side of conservatism and repression in any part of Europe. The Polish uprising of 1830, which was suppressed and followed by the abolition of Poland's autonomous status, led to a convention of 1833 in which the monarchs of Russia, Austria, and Prussia promised mutual help in the case of not only external but also internal threats to their power. The great revolutionary years of the Continent, 1830 and 1848, found the Russian empire ready to intervene militarily on the side of reaction in places as distant as Belgium and Italy. This intervention finally materialized in 1849 when, at the request of the Habsburg monarchy, Russian troops helped to crush the Hungarian national revolt. A bit more than a hundred years later, Russian troops were to re-enter Hungary to suppress a popular uprising and to re-establish a regime dependent upon a foreign power.

It was seen by the more perceptive observers at the end of Nicholas' reign that the ideological encrustation of the regime and what might be called the Russian national interest were in clear conflict. Russia's economic and social development lagged far behind the West, then in the full throes of the industrial revolution. Eventually even the military strength of the autocracy was to suffer because of its clinging to obsolete policies, while its support of receding reaction was to leave the empire isolated in the international arena. With the defeat in the Crimean War, the ideological phase of Tsarist Russia's foreign policy came to an end. The natural sympathy of the emperors and of the majority of the bureaucrats who in their name ruled the empire until World War I was bound to remain on the side of reaction and, in international politics, on the side of states that professed monarchical and conservative principles. But, after 1856, those considerations were no longer the *decisive* element in Russia's foreign policy.

The sixty-nine years that separate the death of Nicholas I from the world war display many themes of continuity with the Soviet period. The historian's retrospect is of course conditioned by the catastrophic collapse of the empire in 1917. Yet he must grant that those years, with their uneven progress, punctuated by violence and revolution, laid a foundation for modern Russia that was to prove strong enough to survive a military defeat and a ruinous civil war. The immediate post-Nicholas period was one of great internal reforms which, it is not too much to say, transformed Russia from a backwater of Europe into a modern civilized country. It is perhaps hard to swallow this conclusion when one keeps in mind that even at the end of the generation of reforms, at the assassination of Alexander

II in 1881, Russia possessed no national parliament and no responsible government. But the same period saw the abolition of serfdom, the institution of a modern judicial system, and a score of hardly less fundamental changes. Even the period of reaction that followed it and lasted until the Revolution of 1905 saw tremendous progress in the economic sphere. Beginning far behind the countries of the West, Russia soon approached a rate of industrial growth equal to that of the leaders: the United States and Germany. It was this race to catch up with the modern world—Russia's great economic and cultural dynamism set against the lingering traces of social and political backwardness—that set the stage for the revolutionary drama.

An analyst of foreign policy taking a retrospective look in 1914 to the 1880's and 1890's would have found the country's resources and commitments overextended. It was, to be sure, an age of imperialism, and the rounding out of earlier conquests in the Caucasus, Central Asia, and the Far East was a logical development which did not involve Russia in a conflict with a major power. But further territorial ambitions in Persia and Afghanistan brought an aggravation of Russo-British tension, a constant feature of international politics until the Anglo-Russian Entente of 1907. The fate of the two buffer states was again to be a source of conflict and intrigue between Soviet Russia and Great Britain and to continue to be so until the latter's Asiatic empire passed into history. Nor had the Crimean War put a stop to the Russian pressure upon the Turkish empire. The struggle for spheres of influence in the Balkans and the feeling, wide-spread in Russia, that the Balkan Slavs were, because of their ethnic background and Orthodox religion, entitled to special protection by the great Slavic power involved the country in this veritable cauldron of European politics, which was eventually to provide the occasion for the world war and catastrophe.

The same retrospective look would have revealed dangerous tendencies in the whole rationale of Russian foreign policy. The principle of legitimism and conservatism as the basis for intervention in the affairs of others had become obsolete and unavailing by the middle of the nineteenth century. But in its place, militant nationalism provided a rationale for a pushful foreign policy. The most farseeing of the imperial statesmen, such as Sergei Witte, the great advocate of industrial development in the 1890's and prime minister after the 1905 Revolution, realized very clearly that Russia could only lose by an overambitious and expansionist policy. The empire was already vast. There was a multitude of internal problems calling for solution and peaceful development. Foreign adventures and wars were bound to aggravate the internal sores, illuminate the still existing social and political weaknesses of the regime. It could not escape attention that each of Russia's wars and defeats, minor though they were by our contemporary standards, was followed by the heightening of internal tensions. The defeat in the Crimea opened a period of reforms but also of revolutionary currents which in a sense never subsided until 1914. In the Balkan war of 1877–78, Russia defeated Turkey, but the subsequent pressure of the Great Powers at the Congress of Berlin robbed her of most of the fruits of the victory; the revolutionary wave crested and in three years brought the assassination of Alexander II at the hands of the terrorists of the People's Will. In the beginning of the twentieth century, Russia's ambition to dominate Manchuria and northern China finally encountered resistance, and the Russo-Japanese War vividly revealed the empire's weakness and internal instability. The previous defeats had been followed by revolutionary currents, this one by a full-fledged revolution from which the monarchy and the established order of Russian society never really recovered.

Yet this lesson, which was not lost upon Stalin in 1939—that an oppressive political system risks more than military defeat in a war—continued to be ignored by the majority of the empire's policy-makers. In fact, a strange fatalism appears to have enveloped the internal-external policy nexus of the empire. An aggressive foreign policy was believed to be a remedy for the internal ills. In the 1870's, it was a wave of national enthusiasm, in which the critics of the regime shared, which pushed Alexander II into the Balkan war on behalf of the "brother Slavs." In the beginning of the twentieth century, the prospect of a conflict with an upstart Asiatic state was considered lightheartedly by the Tsar's ministers. It would be a splendid little war that would go far to relieve the internal pressures for reforms and a constitutional regime.

The Soviet period will show us a regime being capable for the most part of distinguishing between propaganda and policy in its foreign relations, perceiving that its ideology and the national interest are not always synonymous. It is clear that Soviet sophistication and skill in such matters was largely a product of the lessons learned from the Tsarist period. If, in Nicholas I's reign, Tsarist statesmen conceived their duty to preserve the political status quo and expanded their country's resources and prestige in that enterprise, then in the following period an opposite but equally dangerous principle guided their activity. It would be an exaggeration to say that Tsarist Russia, still the bastion of autocracy in the late nineteenth century, conducted a revolutionary foreign policy. But certainly it was a foreign policy designed to overturn the existing territorial status quo, favoring what might anachronistically be called "wars of liberation" of the Balkan Slavs against their Turkish overlords, and professing sympathy with the alleged plight of the Slavic inhabitants of the Austro-Hungarian empire. Conscious Panslavism, the desire to unite all Slavic nations under Russian leadership, was not a mainspring of Russian foreign policy, much as it enjoyed a vogue in certain intellectual circles. But it was an undertone of the diplomatic struggle with Austria-Hungary, now Russia's main rival in the Balkans, and it was an eloquent extension of the theme of Russian nationalism and its age-long struggle against Germany's eastern expansion. Like future Soviet solicitude for the victims of colonial oppression, the Tsarist concern for the Slavs had a paradoxical and ironic aspect. Tsarist Russia—the "prisonhouse of nationalities" as Lenin called it—was the main beneficiary of the suppression of Polish independence. The rising national consciousness among another Slavic people, the Ukrainians, was also being suppressed by the government in St. Petersburg. Many of the "oppressed" Slavs, such as the Czechs, Slovenes, and Croats under Habsburg rule, enjoyed political freedoms and a standard of living above those which were the lot of the *Russian* people. Even the Slavic nations in the Balkans, upon being granted statehood, were endowed with constitutions and parliamentary government, something which was not introduced in Russia until 1905–6. Those paradoxes were not obscured, as during the Soviet period, by a superbly functioning propaganda machine and a world-wide movement that adopted Russia's cause as its own.

The complicated strains of Russia's foreign and internal problems culminated in the 1890's in her alliance with France. On the face of it, the alliance was as yet another paradox. The bastion of autocracy in Europe was linked in a diplomatic and military agreement with the state that epitomized republican and democratic principles. It meant a breach and possible war with the one power that next to Russia stood for the legitimist and conservative political outlook: imperial Germany, with whose ruling house the Romanovs had age-long connections. Yet, for both states, the alliance represented a successful effort to break out of international isolation. The chronic conflict with Austria-Hungary had finally led to severance of the Russo-German alliance. Another nineteenth-century rival of the empire, Great Britain, was also at the time in conflict with France over a variety of colonial problems. The Franco-Russian alliance was a prelude to impressive investments and loans from France which at times, as after the 1905 Revolution, were to save the Tsarist regime from virtual bankruptcy. But to the more conservative and farseeing of the Russian statesmen, the alliance promised no benefits. It involved Russia in the explosive Franco-German confrontation, and it made probable an eventual military struggle with the greatest power on the Continent. The wisest among them deplored any undertaking to expand Russia's foreign commitments.

The alliance brought the empire no benefit in those periodic crises which every few years for a generation before 1914 threatened to trigger off a world war. There was no obligation—indeed no possibility—for France to intervene on Russia's side in the Russo-Japanese War. Had not another war come to pass within a few years, Russia's defeat might well be described now in history books as a blessing in disguise. The war and the 1905

Revolution once more exposed the social and political weaknesses—now catastrophic—of her society. A program of reforms began to transform Russia into a constitutional state. Even more important were wide-reaching reforms in the countryside and the settling of Russian peasants in Siberia, which promised both to cure rural overpopulation and to create a rural middle class as a barrier to revolution. But in 1914, one of the recurrent international crises this time did not end in a conference and a patched-up agreement but plunged the Russian empire into war.

Russia entered the war in fulfillment of her obligations to a small Slavic country, Serbia, that was being threatened by Austria-Hungary. To many, not least of all in the liberal and progressive camp, the war was a welcome event. It ranged Russia on the side of the progressive and democratic powers, Great Britain and France, and it was bound to lead to the transformation of the monarchy into a fully constitutional regime. The wave of strikes that had swept over Russia since 1912 subsided upon the declaration of war. There were spontaneous patriotic demonstrations in the major cities and professions of loyalty to the emperor, who appeared to symbolize the national resolve to break finally with the pro-German and absolutist tradition of his house and to bring Russia into the camp of progress and democracy. It was only at the two extremes of the political spectrum—at the reactionary right and, at the left, among the handful of Bolsheviks—that the war was viewed as an irremediable catastrophe for the monarchy and as an opening for revolution.[3]

Many years later, in the beginning of his drive to industrialize his country in a hurry and at a prodigious human cost, Stalin was to render a characteristic verdict on the record of the Tsarist period. Old Russia, he said, for all her vast extent and resources, was continually beaten by foreign enemies. The French and English in the Crimean War, the Japanese, and then Germany in the Great War continually triumphed over the empire, because of its economic and technological backwardness and because of the obsolescence of its social system. This capsule judgment was hardly fair: the history of the empire was certainly also one of many military triumphs and of a vast territorial expansion. But Stalin's judgment summarizes an important lesson the Bolsheviks drew from the history of their predecessors, who had allowed their commitments to outrun the military and economic potential of the state. The fateful decision to enter the world war was a consequence of a tangle of moral and treaty obligations and of nationalist and Panslavist sentiments outraged by the pressure on a small Slavic country. Yet the Tsarist statesmen must also have had in mind the internal lessons of the Russo-Japanese War, which, though so much smaller in scope,

---

[3] Also among a few elder statesmen such as Witte and his fellow negotiator of the Russo-Japanese Treaty, Baron Rosen.

had led their regime close to collapse. The authoritarian regime found itself a captive not only of its international obligations but also of its own ideology, although both pointed in a direction that threatened the very principle of authoritarianism itself. For all its more extensive ideological character and mission, the Soviet regime has eschewed such categorical commitments.

It is easy to see also that Stalin's verdict implied an approval of the expansionist aims of pre-Revolutionary Russia. Had they been more frank, the Soviet statesmen might have repeated the device of their eighteenth-century predecessor: "That which stops growing begins to rot." Those instruments and rationalizations of imperial Russia's expansion— the ethnic argument, Panslavism, even the Orthodoxy—were all to find their place in the arsenal of Soviet Russia's foreign policy. By 1945, the goal the Tsars' governments had striven for but never achieved was ful- filled by their successors: eastern Europe was under the full domination of Russia. The ethnic frontiers of Germany were pushed back to where they had been in the Middle Ages. Though committed officially to atheism, Stalin's government repressed the Greek Catholic rite in eastern Galicia and extended its efforts on behalf of the Orthodox Church, just as Nicholas I's government had done in the empire's western domains in the 1830's and 1840's. The potential sources of irredentism were removed when all the Ukrainians and Byelorussians were included in the U.S.S.R. These facts are eloquent in themselves as evidence of the strong continuity be- tween the old and the new regime.

2. *Marxism*

The existence of continuities does not mean that Lenin's and Stalin's Russia sought simply, under new slogans, the territorial and political aims of the Tsars. The people who captured power in November 1917 were sincere Marxists. No matter how unorthodox from the point of view of their ideology was their hurrying the historical process and attempting to introduce socialism into a relatively backward country, they believed that they were acting in the spirit if not according to the letter of their faith. Their mentality was shaped by the doctrines promulgated in the nineteenth century by Marx and Engels and by the circumstances of their long activity as socialists. Thus, what might be called the Marxist element of Soviet Russia's policies has at least three elements. There is first the canon of the doctrine: the thought of Marx and Engels. Then there is the historical experience of the Bolsheviks in their struggles with other sections of the Russian socialist and revolutionary movement. And there is finally the lesson of the years of war and revolution, 1914–17, when many previous tenets and strategies gave way to bold improvisations and new theories which we associate with the term Leninism. Impossible though a neat separation of these three components is, it must be attempted, for otherwise it is difficult to see how a doctrine shaped by the circumstances of the mid-nineteenth century came to be the guiding light of twentieth-century policies.

For the fundamental point to be kept in mind about Marxism is that it is a doctrine shaped by the circumstances and attitudes of the *mid-nineteenth century in the West*. What might be called pure Marxism could offer but little in the way of guidelines for *Russia*'s foreign policies in the *twentieth* century and not much more for the strategy of an international revolutionary movement conceived almost exactly one hundred years after the birth of Karl Marx.

A careful reading of the *Communist Manifesto* will bear out the fact that Marx and Engels expected revolutions to take place in advanced industrial countries and as a consequence of an internal breakdown of the economic and political system. As to foreign policies a socialist country might pursue, Marx and Engels have nothing to say. This omission is not fortuitous, any more than the relative lack of indications in their work as to exactly how the economy of the socialist country should work. The socialist revolution will occur in every country as it reaches a high level of industrialization. It will not be substantially affected by any developments on the international scene. In the *Manifesto* itself, there is an explicit statement that the materials of international politics—frontiers, militarism, religious differences, and the like—are of decreasing importance. The progress of economy and civilization makes nationalism itself of ever diminishing effect on the destiny of peoples. With the economy becoming world-wide, the interests of the two hostile classes, capitalists and workers, also begin to transcend national frontiers. The implication is clear that not only the workers but also the capitalists "have no country," in the sense that no national loyalties can take precedence over what the given class in the given country conceives to be its economic interest.

Thus the very internationalism of the doctrine is based paradoxically on the assumption that considerations of international politics have become and will continue to be less important. If the capitalists of England and France find their trade mutually profitable, then no considerations of national honor, no territorial dispute will impel them to go to war. And by the same token, socialist France and England will find no reason for war or rivalry: their respective working classes will realize that the fullest development of their internal resources is the only way to the improvement of their countries' economic, and hence general, welfare. War and with it much of international politics will simply become obsolete. As to the possibility of a cataclysmic struggle between socialist and nonsocialist nations, that, in the canon of Marxism, is excluded almost by definition. In the first place, the implication is that capitalism, repressive as it is *internally*, is in international politics a force for peace. (It is the drastic modification of this analysis which is at the root of Lenin's philosophy of international affairs.) In the second place, the countries entering socialism will be industrially and thus potentially also militarily far advanced, hence with little to fear from those nations whose obsolete feudal economy and political organization would impel them to warlike and expansionist drives. In brief, Marx's is a socialist version of what was in his time the enlightened liberal theory on the future of international politics—the product of the century of rationalism, of material and scientific progress, and of unbounded optimism in civilized man's ability to eliminate the terrors and distress of the past.

Such in general is the main view of Marxian theory of the problem of international politics in the future. But it is necessary immediately to inject an important qualification. As publicists and observers of the contemporary political scene, both Marx and Engels wrote voluminously about diplomatic and military problems of the day, and, from their insights and arguments, there emerges a body of observations which, though not contesting their main theory, still represent a different dimension of their thinking on international problems.[4]

In addition, Marx and Engels thought of themselves as politicians and as leaders (at least in the intellectual sphere) called upon to advise on the day-to-day strategy of the international socialist movement. In this capacity, Marx and Engels sympathized with most of the revolutionary and national emancipation movements of their day. This sympathy appears most natural to us, as does the whole nexus between the concepts of Marxism and revolution. Yet, in fact, few of the other socialist system-makers of the nineteenth century were revolutionaries in the sense of advocating *violent* overthrow of existing forms of society. The deterministic character of Marxism would again lead us to believe that it discourages the notion that violence can prevail against the forces of history as expressed in society's economic development. But the founders of the movement were not only socialists but also revolutionaries, and those two strains coexisted and sometimes clashed within Marxism. The approval of various revolutionary movements

---

[4] We might describe the relationship between Marx's primary and secondary views on international politics by using the analogy of a student of the international situation who both hopes and believes that in the long run the United Nations must become the decisive factor in the world. At the same time his comments about actual conditions indicate that he is well aware that nationalism, national sovereignty, and the inability of the United Nations to resolve the most basic and dangerous conflicts are facts of life of the present day.

in nineteenth-century Europe, even when some of them bore a most unsocialist mark, was often rationalized in terms of international considerations. Thus, Polish nationalism was warmly supported by Marx, even though at the time its source was found mostly among the Polish upper and middle classes and the Polish proletariat was virtually nonexistent,[5] because Polish nationalism and the abortive Polish uprisings were directed at the three powers—Prussia, Austria, and especially Russia—that were the bulwark of European reaction and barriers to the development everywhere on the Continent of modern economic and social conditions which would eventually lead to socialism. Hence, there was excellent revolutionary logic in this virtual alliance between socialists and nationalist-minded Polish landlords. The doctrine of the desirability of [some!] "wars of national liberation" was not an invention of Khrushchev's; it is at least as old as the *Communist Manifesto*.

Of almost equal antiquity, and coming from the same source, is the tactic of what might be called revolutionary patience: the support of a revolutionary movement, even if its strategy and ideology are clearly antithetical to those of Marxism, if this movement is effective in disrupting the traditional pattern of politics in the given country. Marx and Engels viewed with admiration the struggle of the Russian Populists against Tsarism, much as the ideology and the means of struggle employed by the Populists (in some cases individual terrorism) were obsolete and erroneous by the lights of Marxism. The indulgence of the fathers of Marxism extended so far that at times they discouraged the idea of forming a specific Marxist party in Russia, believing that the chances of discrediting or overthrowing the Russian autocracy would only be compromised by internal rivalry within the revolutionary camp.

Nineteenth-century Russia was a logical target for the international revolutionary movement because of her backwardness and her role as the main supporter of reaction. But, for a militant Marxist, Great Britain, the most advanced capitalist state, was hardly less so. Yet, despite the prophecies and assumptions of Marx's doctrine, revolutionary socialism made but insignificant inroads within the British working class, while trade-unionist and reformist tendencies were in full sway. A revolutionary socialist's main source of hope insofar as Great Britain was concerned was the revolutionary stirrings in Ireland, though again they had nothing socialist about them. For, in a sense, the fathers of Marxism recognized a danger in taming the class struggle through trade unionism and parliamentary institutions and looked with sympathy upon any revolutionary

[5] A meeting in favor of Polish independence was the occasion of the creation of the First International in 1864.

opening, any movement or social problem, that could not be contained within a constitutional and peaceful framework, that would disrupt the state sufficiently to enable revolution to challenge the bourgeoisie.

That the tactics of international socialism have to be flexible, that no weapon—the national or religious question, or even parliamentarism—is to be scorned in weakening capitalism and the status quo is, then, implicit in the thinking of Marx and Engels. Their commitment to violent revolution per se was never absolute. Marx, some years before his death, granted that in a few states like Great Britain, the United States, and Holland, socialism might come through peaceful means. Engels, who lived to observe electoral successes of the German Social Democratic Party, enlarged this prognosis still further. In the most advanced European countries, capitalists were on the defensive: the extension of franchise was making it inevitable that the day would come when the proletariat would secure a parliamentary majority and with it the machinery of state.

It is tempting to find in these utterances of Marx and Engels a direct source for the policies of the Comintern and the Soviet government. But it is important to note certain major differences. To begin with, the outlook of original Marxism was internationalist, and it would have been inconceivable for Marx that the policies of international socialism should be dictated by one party or one country. Also, for all the flexibility of the tactics prescribed, the fortunes of the movement were for Marx and Engels rooted in factors of economics. Thus, in discussing imperialism, Marx was far from attributing to it the decisive influence on the development of capitalism that Lenin later did. He foresaw the awakening of India and China. But he considered the overseas rule of the European powers as mainly beneficial, bringing industrialization (which in his terms was almost synonymous with progress and civilization) to backward societies. He would not have accepted the thesis that English capitalism could not withstand the loss of its overseas possessions. In fact, for all of its psychological insights, original Marxism is firmly rooted in the rationalist tradition of the nineteenth century and its economic-determinist underpinnings. Emotional, irrational forces in politics are of importance, yet they cannot supersede the decisive importance of economics. A revolution may succeed in a backward country, but socialism cannot be established until the economic conditions for it are ripe, and no scheme of political organization, no amount of "agitation" can change this fact. In the last instance, the legacy of Marx in international as well as national politics must remain ambivalent. Some parts of it can be claimed by what became after his death the main current of European social democracy, but other elements belong to militant socialism, which finally crystallized in Communism. After the failure of the Paris Commune of 1871 the tone, if not the content, of Marx's statements became less revolutionary and more consistent with the vision of a peaceful evolution to socialism rather than through violence.

The second part of the Marxian inheritance in foreign affairs is found in the history of the Russian Marxists—or, to give the official name of the movement, the Russian Social Democratic Workers' Party, founded in 1898—and particularly the history of its Bolshevik faction between 1903 and 1914. Since there is a direct connection between the Bolsheviks and the Communist Party as it became in 1918,[6] the future policies of the Soviet Union were of course vitally influenced by the experience of the Bolsheviks before they seized power.

The position of the Russian Marxists prior to 1914 did not offer them much leisure or cause to think about international affairs. They were one branch among many in the revolutionary and progressive movement bent on an overthrow of the monarchy or at least its reformation into a constitutional monarchy. Even by their own doctrine the day of the *socialist* revolution in Russia was not imminent. Their doctrine proclaimed that the next revolution in Russia would be a bourgeois-liberal one, and only after a period of further industrial growth would the country become ripe for socialism. At the time of the 1905 Revolution, this time sequence was challenged by the thesis of Trotsky and Parvus who, taking up a term inherited from Marx, formulated the theory of permanent revolution: since the bourgeoisie in Russia was weak and the proletariat though not numerous was the main revolutionary force, the bourgeois-liberal revolution would soon pass into a socialist one. But in the main both the Bolsheviks and the Mensheviks adhered to the orthodox view.

Despite the letter of their doctrine, the two branches of Russian Marxism were in temperament much more revolutionary than any of the other major socialist parties of Europe. Partly this was the product of the specifically Russian condition, where even under the semi-constitutional regime which began in 1906 political parties and activities were persecuted. Partly it was the inheritance of the Russian revolutionary movement of the nineteenth century, with its propensity for violence and its belief that a revolution is an act of will and not the matter of specific social and economic conditions. (The Bolsheviks, under Lenin's influence, imbibed much of the ideology of such organizations as the People's Will, with its terrorist tactics.)

The reliance on organization and conspiracy was a natural consequence of the facts of political life in Russia, but in 1902 Lenin expanded this

[6] Not, however, an identity. There were perhaps 10,000–15,000 Bolsheviks on the eve of the March Revolution in 1917 and about 300,000 by the November one. Then of course even among the leaders of the Communist Party, one found people, notably Trotsky, who had not been Bolsheviks prior to 1917.

into a general principle of twentieth-century Marxism in his *What Is To Be Done?* A socialist party could not be a party in the Western sense of the word; it had to be more like a tightly organized and disciplined order of revolutionaries. Marx's hope that the mere growth of industry and the expansion of the industrial proletariat would create favorable conditions for socialism was reappraised by Lenin. From this primary tenet of Marx's prognosis, he turned increasingly to what we have seen were the secondary elements in Marx's thinking: the exploitation of any and all social elements, rather than just the workers, in the quest for revolution. The socialist party (after 1918 it will be the socialist state) must exploit every social and political discontent. It must learn to subdue its ideological scruples if necessary. Thus, the peasant's discontent with his status and his craving for more land were the most serious threat to the social stability of the empire, but the peasant would turn violently against the Marxists if they urged, as their doctrine would require them to, that individual landholdings be nationalized and merged into state-run farms. Hence, already in 1906, Lenin urged that the appeal to the peasant be couched in terms of his craving for more land, Marxism or no Marxism. This policy, much criticized by ideological purists, was the forerunner of the appeal to peasant self-interest that was to serve the Bolsheviks so well in 1917 and that since then the Communists have used with so much success in the underdeveloped areas of the world, most notably in China.

Of even more fundamental importance for the future development of Soviet foreign policies was the evolution of the Bolshevik ideology-tactic on the problem of nationality. It brings to mind what one Soviet historian said of Lenin, that he never considered an ideological problem or a policy platform apart from its propagandistic aspect. And, to be sure, the ability of Communism to pose as the friend of oppressed nationalism everywhere was to be the key to its most brilliant successes not only during the Civil War in Russia but, especially, since World War II. The elaboration of this policy, which, again, clashed with orthodox Marxism, took place between 1903 and 1912, and its scope was enlarged by Lenin's work on *Imperialism*, written during World War I.

Important though social and political problems were as the causes of revolutionary agitation in Europe, they hardly surpassed the rankling oppression and russification of nationalities within the Russian empire. We spoke before of the Polish problem. In addition, russification policies were directed by the imperial regime against the nationalities of the Caucasus and the Baltic littoral. The existence of a Ukrainian nation was stoutly denied by Tsarist policies, and the Jews numerous in the empire's western provinces were subject to anti-Semitic discriminations unparalleled elsewhere in Europe. And there were other, though less developed, non-Russian nationalisms. The revolutionary and, especially, Marxist movement in Russia was always heavily staffed by non-Russians, notably Jews, Poles, and Letts, who were represented in it out of proportion to their number in the population at large.

Lenin saw that even more effective use could be made of the weapon of nationalism if the Marxists would favor the right of every nationality to independence, if, regardless of the character or leadership of a given national movement, whether upper or middle class, or even clerical, they proclaimed that every national group had the right to separate statehood. There were, as we have seen, excellent precedents for that policy in the writings of Marx himself. But the orthodox position could hardly tolerate that a Marxist party should make an appeal to nationalism one of its main tenets. The full application of this argument would find the Russian Marxists with some strange bedfellows. Polish nationalism was at the time strongest among the Polish upper and middle classes. An independent Poland would most likely be dominated by the landowners and by Catholicism, strong among her peasantry, and the prospects of her eventual socialist transformation would be indefinitely postponed by her separation from Russia. Among some other national groups, especially the Turkic elements and the Armenians, the leaders of nationalist agitation were largely motivated by religious issues. Again, from the strict Marxian viewpoint, their independence would be a step backward, the surrender of a largely primitive population into the hands of semi-feudal and religiously fanatical classes.

Such objectives were voiced most insistently by socialists of non-Russian background, many of them culturally russified and most of them detesting their own upper classes more fervently than they did the Tsarist governors and bureaucracy. But within Bolshevik ranks, Lenin's insistence carried the day. His opponent, Rosa Luxemburg, active in both the German and the Polish Social Democratic parties (the latter had intermittent organizational ties with the Russian socialists) espoused the more orthodox Marxian viewpoint: to the workers, the problem of nationality is a secondary one; what matters is the end of exploitation, whether its perpetrators be Polish or Russian capitalists. Lenin's inherent realism made him see that the appeal of nationalism in the twentieth century often transcended that of class interest, and that socialism struggling for influence (before 1914 he still would not have said power) in a peasant society cannot make its appeal in purely class terms. That national autonomy was in his eyes consistent with the retention of the frontiers of the Russian state and even with a degree of political centralization is indicated by two pre-1914 developments. He rejected the pleas of the Jewish socialist organization— the Bund—that it should have a more or less autonomous organization within the larger framework of the Russian socialist movement. Also, he envisaged that the future socialist state might be multinational, as the treatise on the nationality problem that Stalin wrote under his guidance shortly before World War I indicates: separate nationalities within clearly defined territorial units would be given full autonomy if they so desired; but, presumably, with socialism established and with exploitation both political and economic abolished, these units would prefer to adhere to a federal arrangement. Militant nationalism was thus seen as a disruptive element so long as socialism was not achieved, but in a socialist Russia there would be no reason for the Georgians or Ukrainians to opt out.

From our perspective, Lenin's formulas demonstrate a considerable talent for eating one's cake and having it too or, to put it more baldly, for cynicism. In order to defeat your enemy, you have recourse to the most revolutionary, most disruptive formulas, and yet when in power presumably you will rationalize them out of existence. But before 1914 Lenin and the Bolsheviks could feel with some justification that their policies and pleas were well within the Marxian orthodoxy and that they were simply adjusting Marx's precepts to the spirit of the age and their own society, where emotional factors such as nationalism or the peasants' devotion to the principle of private property were much stronger than Marx, with his Western and rationalist background, had been able to envisage. Neither Lenin nor those closest to him imagined that socialism in Russia was a matter of the near future, still less that it would come in the form of one-party rule.

It is undeniable, however, that the Russian Marxists—and this was hardly less true of the Mensheviks than of the Bolsheviks—felt uncomfortable in the atmosphere of international socialism. In the spectrum of the Second International, both Russian groups were consistently on the left. Much of Western socialism was in their eyes corrupted by the spirit of revisionism and the unwillingness of their German or English colleagues to envisage the coming of socialism as a struggle requiring violent means. Living under a barely reformed autocracy, they could not understand or sympathize with the compromises that Western socialism had made with the bourgeois state, with its occasional tendency to look at parliamentarism as the main means of political struggle, or with the increasing propensity of trade unions in industrialized societies to conceive their task as the securing of economic advantages for the worker, rather than educating him in the spirit of the class struggle. For the Russian Marxists, participation in elections and economic struggle did not mean that socialists should dispense with conspiracy or even violence.

One may refer to another element of pre-1914 political experience that was to prove of great importance to the Bolsheviks once they had become masters of their country and that was to color their psychology in dealing with other countries. Except during the revolutionary period 1905–6, the Bolsheviks were a rather minor element in Russian politics. Their extremism and, at times, their tactics—such as between 1905 and 1907, when they had recourse to expropriations, i.e., armed robberies of state and private funds—brought upon them the disapprobation of their fellow Marxists, not to speak of the liberal elements in Russia. Yet the other branches of the revolutionary and reform movement did not seek to excommunicate the Bolsheviks. Until April 1917 the Mensheviks sought unity with their vitriolic opponents. The climate of what was known as the "liberation movement" in Russia was such that it was difficult, even for the most constitutionally minded liberal, to conceive that there could be an enemy on the left or that any means might be illegitimate in struggling against Tsarism. The inherently undemocratic character of the Bolsheviks' party organization was noted, but its democratic phraseology was accepted in good faith. In fact, it could be argued that the survival of the Bolsheviks as a political force after 1906–7 was in the main due to the tolerance extended to them by socialist and liberal circles both in Russia and abroad. Foreign socialists provided shelter and funds for the Bolshevik leaders within Russia. Liberal lawyers sprang to the defense of accused party members. Non-Bolshevik members of the socialist movement refrained from flaunting too vigorously their undemocratic practices and theories before the Russian workers. Such practices were bound to give some Bolsheviks, especially Lenin, the impression of essential weakness and lack of self-assurance on the part of liberals and other socialists. Marx's teaching about the tenacity with which the bourgeoisie holds on to power and its ruthlessness in pursuing its aims was thus shown to be no longer fully applicable. By the beginning of the twentieth century, the ruling circles in the West were similarly revealed no longer to possess this unremitting resolve and sense of self-preservation. And in Russia especially, liberals and non-Bolshevik socialists seemed very prone to "fall" for humanitarian and democratic slogans and propaganda, even when they were mouthed by a party that was dictatorial in its organization and that was showing, if at that time still unconsciously, a very pronounced authoritarian temper. The lingering effect of these impressions was to be displayed in the Bolsheviks' foreign policies following November 1917. They were to show but little respect for the sense of realism and tenacity of purpose of social democratic regimes and hardly more for those foreign governments and movements that could be called liberal. In world politics, they were to see images of their former domestic protagonists like the Mensheviks and the Kadets; in time, their skepticism as to *any* democratic regime's inner strength or sustained purpose was to color the whole course of Soviet foreign policy.

Lenin's and the Bolsheviks' emendations of the original teachings of Marx touched mainly the psychological substratum of politics. The enormous emphasis placed on propaganda and agitation in the Communists' teaching is sufficient testimony to that fact. Marx had believed that the logic of (economic) facts would by itself educate the working class and bring about socialism. Lenin emphasized preaching and indoctrination. And in a sense these were to become the main weapons of the young Communist state when it was being ravaged by the Civil War, then later when it was a backward and devastated society that yet proclaimed its challenge to every other form of government in Europe, and later still when it had become able to withstand concerted economic, if not military, attack and isolation by the Great Powers. One might argue that some of the psychological habits the Bolsheviks brought with them to the task of ruling their country were, by the same token, to handicap them: extreme suspiciousness of every movement and every government not fully sharing their ideology, an underestimation of the staying power of democracy in the Western countries, and a view of international politics as consisting mainly of the clash of economic and military interests. But the reality of post-1914 world politics was to prove closer to the Bolsheviks' analysis than to that which had been shared by the liberals and more democratically inclined socialists.

It is an obvious truism that World War I changed the tone and content of European politics. But this truism becomes filled with meaning when we observe the change wrought within the Bolshevik Party by the experience of war and the swiftly evolving course of Russian history from July 1914 to November 1917. For all the reservations and qualifications that had been spelled out before, the Bolshevik branch of the Russian socialist movement considered itself part and parcel of European social *democracy* as it existed prior to the shots at Sarajevo. Lenin's impatience with the spirit of the Second International did not lead him to contemplate openly the founding of a rival socialist international. The disagreements with the Mensheviks did not mean that the fissure within Russian socialism was deemed irreparable. The Bolsheviks' *temperamental* dislike of Western parliamentarism did not mean that they anticipated the November pattern —armed seizure of power by their party *alone* and against the opposition of other socialist and revolutionary groups. The official view was still the overthrow of the monarchy (or at least of the remnants of its absolutism), then a period under a bourgeois liberal regime, and only then socialism.

Inherent in all these pre-1914 views, absurdly moderate and misguided as they must have appeared to Lenin and his associates in 1917, were some assumptions about international politics, international socialism, and the situation in Russia, all of which were exposed as hollow by the events of 1914–17.

The strength and stability of the European state system were taken for granted even by its most severe critics. Certainly the apprehension or expectation of a large war was widely shared before 1914, and on several occasions in the preceding decade it did almost materialize. But remnants of nineteenth-century rationalism inhibited most people from envisaging the war's devastating and all-embracing character, its duration, or its casualties, both physical and social. The most extensive war within the memory of the living was the Franco-Prussian War of 1870–71, which, though it had upset the Second Empire and was followed by the Paris Commune, did not undermine the existing social system either in France or in Germany. By the light of the most sophisticated Marxist opinion, it was inconceivable that the ruling classes in Europe—the capitalists in France and England, the ruling houses and bureaucracies in Germany and Russia —would allow competition for territory or national prestige to undermine their economic and political power. A war would be of relatively short duration, it would not be a total war, and though every good socialist had to hope that it would weaken capitalism, he could not even conceive of the destruction of the whole way of life that the war in fact accomplished after four bloody years.[7] Nor did it seem reasonable to expect the fall of dynasties, the disintegration of empires, and the economic ruin of the defeated nations. The victors' self-interest would urge them to impose a lenient peace, for ruinous peace conditions could lead to a state of anarchy in the defeated countries and this anarchy in turn might infect the territory of the victors. But such calculations were belied by the intensity of feeling aroused on both sides, which fed upon the huge casualties and privations imposed upon the civilian populations. As a matter of fact, internal subversion of the enemy became an accepted weapon of the war. By 1916 it was clear that any accommodation between the belligerents in terms of restoring the pre-1914 framework of the European polity was a forlorn hope. The theory of the essential solidarity of the European ruling circles, and of their will and ability to confine any conflict within manageable limits, was exposed as a myth. The international bourgeoisie, the international order, was much weaker and more disunited than the most revolutionary socialist before 1914 had dared to hope.

By the same token, international socialism as embodied in the Second International was exposed as ineffective. Much as it went against the grain of the Russian Marxists to sit in a body that admitted such nonrevolutionary parties as the British Labour Party or the Zionist Poale Zion, they still had considered the International the representative of the

---

[7] The concept of a relatively brief war was inherent in the military planning of all the major powers. Thus, the famous Schlieffen Plan of the German general staff envisaged a lightning blow against the French army which then would allow the Germans to concentrate against the more slowly mobilizing armies of Russia. Implicit in the plan was the conviction that peace could be reached with France after the crushing of her armies and, presumably, that, as against our standards of 1918 and 1945, it would be a lenient peace.

working masses everywhere and as a power on the international scene. As the war clouds had gathered during the decade before 1914, the International was emphatic that the workers everywhere would not allow a protracted international slaughter at the behest of their capitalist masters. It was freely predicted that the two most powerful socialist parties, the German and the French, would use their very considerable influence over organized labor in their countries to proclaim a general strike should their governments plunge into a war. The International's Congress in Stuttgart in 1907 stated, "It is the duty of the working classes and their parliamentary representatives in the countries taking part . . . to do everything to prevent the outbreak of war by whatever means seem to them most effective, which naturally differ with the intensification of the class war and the general political situation." At the behest of the more radically minded delegates, among them Lenin, the Congress added: "Should war break out in spite of all this, it is their duty to intercede for its speedy end, and to strive with all their power to make use of the violent economic and political crisis brought about by the war to rouse the people and thereby to hasten the abolition of capitalist class rule."[8] The same feeling was expressed even more strongly at the Congress in Basel in 1912. The general assumptions behind such sentiments were thus that if the capitalists lost their senses and provoked a European war, the socialists would be strong enough to bring it to a speedy conclusion, or at the least, that if nationalist madness seized the countries of Europe, good socialists —certainly the leaders of the movement, the great parties of Germany and France—would be able to preserve their sense of proportion and their internationalism.

Yet, a few weeks in the summer of 1914 sufficed to shatter those expectations of the socialists' power and resolve to prevent a world war. None of the major socialist parties in Europe opposed the war. The German Social Democratic Party, the acknowledged leader of them all, presented for a true Marxist the most shocking spectacle. Its parliamentary representation voted unanimously for the government motion for war credits.[9] Even more disturbing was the attitude of rank-and-file German socialists, who appeared to share in the nationalistic fervor evoked by the news of the war. Soon, prominent socialist leaders volunteered for war duty, and the party of Marx, Engels, and Liebknecht would, at least during the first two years of the conflict, show loyalty to the Kaiser hardly exceeded by that of the most hidebound Prussian Junkers. Similar developments took

[8] Quoted in James Joll, *The Second International 1889–1914* (New York and London, 1956), p. 139.

[9] Fourteen of the ninety-one socialist deputies voting were actually against the credits, but by party rule they were bound to vote with the majority.

place in France, where some previously militant socialists turned into fervent chauvinists and where the veteran left-wing figure Jules Guesde joined the government, in Belgium, and in England (though a number of prominent British Labour Party leaders stuck to the pacifist traditions of their movement).

The effect of this "betrayal" on the more radical of the Russian socialists can hardly be exaggerated. For Lenin, it meant the final jettisoning of what there was of the social *democrat* in his make-up. His writing from the first days of the war is full of fulminations at the whole world of concepts and strategy of the Second International. Even Marx and Engels are criticized in retrospect for implicitly assuming after 1871 that the road to socialism in most European countries could lead through elections and by parliamentary means. Lenin now called for a return to the frankly revolutionary position of Marxism as it had been prior to 1870, for the abandonment of the very name "socialist" and its replacement by "Communist." Insofar as the Bolsheviks and many other Russian socialists were concerned, the democratic and parliamentary encrustation of socialism had been a fraud and mistake. From now on, the emphasis had to be again on revolution and violence.

The dividing line in the Russian revolutionary camp was thus drawn on the attitude toward the war, rather than on any other issue of ideology or tactics. This was to have an incalculable effect on the course of revolution in 1917. Figures like Plekhanov, who associated themselves with Russia's war effort, were discredited within the revolutionary camp. And the previous hostility toward Lenin of such influential leaders as Martov was dulled because they shared the anti-war position.

Not that this position was clearly ascendant even within Russian socialism. At the beginning of the war, the parliamentary fraction of both the Bolsheviks and the Mensheviks refused to vote for war credits. The Bolshevik deputies in the Duma were soon sent into exile. But many influential Mensheviks were less uncompromising in their opposition; in fact, many rank-and-file Bolsheviks, far from sharing their leader's position, were enlisting under colors.

The war caused Lenin to elaborate for the first time his theory of international relations. Prior to 1914 he had been a *Russian* revolutionary. Now the focus of the revolution was to become international, the fortunes of the socialist movement in Russia were to be subordinated to the greater task of a European or world revolution. The war freed him from previous scruples and hesitations. He proceeded to elaborate a whole network of theory and strategy for international Marxism. From a pupil of Marx and Engels, he became self-consciously their successor. He became completely emancipated from any reverence for the tradition of the Second International and its German leaders like Karl Kautsky. The argument of pro-war socialists like Plekhanov—that Russia was fighting on the side of democracy and civilization against the German threat of militarism and European domination—completely failed to move him. The war became for him no longer a calamity but a stupendous opportunity for an international revolution.

Thus, as the war progressed and the initial elation in the belligerent countries gave way to apprehension as the toll of casualties grew ever larger and no conclusion seemed to be in sight, Lenin's main target became not so much those socialists who still adopted the nationalist position of their governments but the ones who sought a speedy peace. He wrote: "And objectively who profits by the slogan of peace? Certainly not the revolutionary proletariat. Nor the idea of *using* the war to *speed up* the collapse of capitalism."[10] The idea that war could be the main agency to bring down capitalism was something new in Marxian theory. Previously, Marxism had counted on the "inherent contradictions" of capitalism, its inability to run the very economic system it had created, to bring about its downfall. Now, it was capitalism's inability to preserve an international order, to avoid disastrous wars, that afforded the great opportunity. Lenin drew two deductions from that conclusion. First, the task of revolutionary socialism was to wage a constant revolutionary struggle taking advantage of capitalism's propensity for constant wars, an effort to persuade the armed masses to turn their weapons against not the external but the *internal enemy:* their own ruling class. Second, the stages of economic development so crucial to classical Marxism, must be relegated to a position of secondary importance. The war offered *socialists* an opportunity to take over power in countries that were not yet ripe for *socialism*. Hence, a world revolution might well have its starting point in Russia, though that country lagged far behind England or Germany in economic development.

Armed with these assumptions, Lenin proceeded to seek both an instrument and a theory for this new form of revolutionary socialism. The instrument had to be a new International. It could not be like the now hateful Second International—a mere confederation of parties, guided only by a shared outlook and negotiating at occasional congresses a general policy which in any case was not binding upon the constituent groups. He sought, in brief, to achieve on an *international scale* something he had tried ever since 1902 to achieve within Russian socialism: part political party and part militant order, ready to plunge into the revolutionary struggle whenever the central authority decided that it should. The concept of the Third International was not and could not be fully elaborated by Lenin during the war, for the materials and conditions for it were not as yet

[10] *The Lenin Collection,* I (Moscow, 1924), 208.

available. But he strove to create a new spirit to detach from the old social-democratic traditions as many practicing Marxists as possible.

The three wartime conferences of anti-war Marxists held at Berne, Zimmerwald (1915), and Kienthal (1916) failed to respond to Lenin's hopes. The main orientation at all of them was pacifist. At Zimmerwald, Lenin's plea that the imperialist war be turned into a civil one was supported only by eight delegates out of about forty. But in many ways Zimmerwald laid the foundation of the Third International that was to be proclaimed in Moscow in 1919. It marked the emergence of Lenin from his position as leader of a faction of Russian socialists (and one on whom most luminaries of world socialism looked with some distaste) to a position as an international leader—of a miniscule group, to be sure, but one that had a concrete and uncompromising answer to the problems of the day.

As the war progressed, the militancy of Lenin and his followers was bound to bring dividends among foreign socialists. All the elaborate schemes of Marx, with the learned emendations of the Kautskys, Hilferdings, etc., were to seem less important than a theory and plan to bring the inconclusive slaughter to an end and to liquidate the social and political system that had allowed it to happen. In retrospect, much of the credit gained by the Bolsheviks among their fellow socialists, much of the toleration extended by the most orthodox and democratically inclined Marxists to the Bolshevik Revolution which violated all the canons of their creed, is traceable directly to the fact that the war had dulled people's attachment to the niceties and restraints of the doctrine, and put a premium on any revolutionary solution.

The theoretical bulwark of the new position was provided by Lenin's *Imperialism* (1916), in many ways the single most important theoretical treatise for the study of the sources of Soviet foreign policy. The structure of the argument was derived from previous works by J. A. Hobson, an English radical, and Rudolf Hilferding, a German Social Democrat, but the tone and conclusions were new. Lenin now proclaimed that militarism and imperialism were organic characteristics of the most advanced type of capitalism. Thus was Lenin able to dispose of Marx's premise of the essentially peaceful nature of capitalism. Marx was right, he said, but only insofar as early capitalism was concerned. Beginning with the 1870's, capitalism passed beyond its constructive and essentially peaceful phase and entered the stage of monopoly capitalism. The drying out of domestic investment opportunities in the most advanced capitalist countries led those nations to engage in a competition for colonial territories where they could obtain both cheap labor and raw resources. In fact, Lenin proceeded to state, the rise in the living standard of the English, French, or German worker has been purchased by increased exactions from the masses of India, China, etc. The competition of capitalists was bound to turn into political and then military competition from which there was no escape short of the destruction of capitalism as an international system.

The following important conclusions were drawn by Lenin from his argument: 1. The generally peaceful and democratic teachings of Marx and Engels during their last phase (1870's to 1895) were no longer applicable. Mature capitalism became once again exacting and oppressive, much more so than at its earliest stage of development, for now the continuation of the system implied not only the misery of the masses but the enslavement of whole nations and gigantic bloodbaths à la World War I. Militant revolutionary activity once more became the duty of every Marxist. Parliamentarism and peaceful achievement of political power had to be pushed to the second plane.

2. The whole burden of Marxian activity had to be shifted to the international scene. Marx conceived of the collapse of capitalism as proceeding in a succession of *internal* overthrows of existing systems, as the given countries reached a high level of industrialization. Now, the Achilles' heel of capitalism was exposed: its international character, the interdependence of the capitalist countries, their dependence on colonial and backward territories, and so on. The crash of British capitalism was not going to be precipitated by what was happening in Lancashire or Glasgow; rather, the collapse of English rule in India and the colonies was going to unchain a series of events that would turn the English worker into a revolutionary. The weakest link in the chain was not the factory at home, but the possessions overseas.

3. The focus of the revolutionary struggle was thus shifted from advanced industrial nations to semi-industrial or even non-industrialized countries. *Socialism* still could not be achieved in a backward country like Russia, but *socialists* could seize power—a European revolution could be started—more easily in Russia than in England. Implicit in this notion was the assumption that the survival of revolution and the establishment of socialism in less advanced countries was possible only after the flame of revolution had caught on in more advanced nations and with their help. But the starting point was to be in the east. This was the most startling and fundamental revision of classical Marxism, the justification of what the Bolsheviks were to undertake in 1917.

4. Not only the *geographic* but also the *social* focus of revolution shifted. Marx had taught that the only truly revolutionary class was the industrial proletariat. The proletariat was to accomplish the revolution and bring about socialism. Yet in non-industrialized or semi-industrialized countries, the industrial proletariat was obviously nonexistent or still very weak.

Hence, Lenin's *Imperialism* was perfectly correct in appealing to the class interests of the peasant, and the peasant, no matter how poor he was, if he had land at all, was in the classical Marxian terminology not a proletarian at all but a "petty bourgeois." But the tactical consequences of Lenin's rephrasing of the Marxian vision of the world went further. In colonial areas, the good Marxist should feel no compunctions in allying himself with even the middle or upper classes of the oppressed nationality. No matter how reactionary their social views, their *nationalist* opposition to British or French rule, for example, makes them natural allies.

For the moment, Lenin was mainly interested in expanding his pre-1914 tactics of using the nationality problem of the Russian empire as fuel for revolution. Thus, though the influence of Marxism among Ukrainian peasants, say, was almost nil, separatist agitation in the Ukraine would undermine the Tsarist regime or that of its bourgeois successors (as it was to do in 1917) and make the task easier for militant Marxists in Moscow and Petrograd. In this way Lenin combatted the ideological scruples of some Bolsheviks who argued that to foment nationalist unrest among the Tatars of the Volga regions or the Turkic peoples of Central Asia was to play into the hands of the most reactionary elements among them, the *mullas* (the closest equivalent to ministers among the Muslims), whose nationalist stance reflected a desire to preserve their religious influence. No allies were to be scorned in the fight against the Tsarist regime, no social or national element with grievances against the Russian state was to be excluded from the struggle.

But the further implications of his views were to become obvious once his party achieved power. Communist Russia was not to scorn alliance with the nationalist movements of India, Egypt, or Turkey even though the dominant elements among them were often native capitalists or landowners. At times, this collaboration would require acquiescence in the given movement's or government's suppression of its own Communists. But just as the nationality problem was adjudged to be the Achilles' heel of Tsarist Russia, so the colonial problem was seen as the most vulnerable element in the capitalist world order. The thread of tactics implied in *Imperialism* leads through Soviet policy of the 1920's, when it supported such potentates as Kemal Pasha, Chiang Kai-shek, and Amanullah, to Khrushchev's endorsement of "wars of national liberation." Similarly, the tenet that the industrial worker need not be the main instrument of the socialist revolution will find its demonstration in Mao Tse-tung's tactics in the late 1920's

[11] To be sure, this application went beyond Lenin's original injunction. While for Lenin the peasant was a desirable ally and enlisting the peasant on one's side or at least securing his neutralization was a necessary task for the socialist revolutionary, the active force in the revolution was still to be the city proletarian.

and 1930's, when the Chinese Communists based their appeal for power on the aspirations of the peasants and sought to recoup in the countryside what they had lost in the cities of the seaboard.[11] And the current (1965–68) ideological and tactical teachings of the Chinese Communists—when they advocate, in effect, an alliance of the "countryside" (the underdeveloped, mostly rural areas of the world) against the "cities" (the industrialized areas of the world, including the U.S.S.R.!)—is again a descendant of Lenin's teachings as to how imperialism and colonialism can be exploited in the struggle to destroy the established international order.

Thus Lenin's *Imperialism* provided what was soon to become Communism with a framework of reference on international affairs. As we shall see, once he was head of state, Lenin changed or modified many of the arguments in *Imperialism*. But it was and has remained, though of late with diminishing effect, the prism through which Soviet policy-makers have viewed the outside world and one of the basic premises of their foreign policy. And it was the experience of war that made the Bolsheviks learn the lessons enshrined in *Imperialism*.

II

THE PRELUDE: 1914–18

1. *War*

Russia's entrance into the war in August 1914 was greeted with approval if not, indeed, patriotic elation by most of the country's articulate public opinion. The liberals and the moderate left foresaw that Russia's partnership with England and France was bound to have beneficial effects on her internal development, and anti-German feelings were popular among the conservatives. The influence of the opponents of the war—i.e., the Bolsheviks and some other left-wing socialists—was at first insignificant. The wave of strikes that had spread through the country earlier subsided with the declaration of war. Only some isolated individuals, like Witte, the former prime minister, saw the handwriting on the wall: economically backward, with its major social and political problems still unresolved, the empire risked not only a defeat but an internal collapse in the case of a prolonged conflict.

The initial enthusiasm was bound to turn to doubts and then to war-weariness as the Russian armies began, after initial successes, to suffer defeat, as the casualties rose, and as the peasants were diverted from food production, thus aggravating the food shortages and economic crisis. On the eve of the March Revolution, Russian casualties were estimated at a minimum of 5 million, and German and Austrian armies were occupying large stretches of Russia's western territories.

From her Western allies, the empire received considerable loans but little in crucial supplies. Western diplomacy was bent on persuading the Russian high command to launch repeated offensives to relieve German pressure on the French front—thus Russia's advance into East Prussia in 1914, though it ended in military disaster, compelled the Germans to weaken their armies pressing on Paris and probably saved the French capital in the initial phase of the war—but in the nature of things there could be but little collaboration between the Western allies and Russia. As in World War II, but for different reasons, the two war efforts remained uncoordinated. Apart from their insistence on further offensives, the French and especially the British diplomats advised the Tsar to broaden the basis of his government by inviting into it representatives of the public. Such interventions were not viewed favorably by the Tsar and his entourage, with the result that when the crash came the government did not contain a single person with a following in the Duma (Parliament) or the country at large.

The war aims of the Tsarist government were only fuzzily defined. Presumably Russia was to receive eastern Galicia from Austria-Hungary, which would unite within her frontiers the vast majority of the Ukrainian-speaking people. There was some thought of a partition of the Austro-Hungarian empire that would free its Slavic-speaking countries. At the beginning of the war, the Russian commander-in-chief, trying to curry sympathy with the Poles, issued a vaguely worded proclamation that implied a promise of autonomy for Russian Poland and its enlargement by the incorporation of the Polish-speaking parts of Austria and Germany. The only specific pledge the Russian government received from France and Britain was contained in secret agreements of 1915 and 1916 which promised that at the victorious conclusion of the war the empire would be augmented at the expense of Turkey by Constantinople, the Straits, and the surrounding regions. Acquisition of those areas was an age-long aspiration of the Russian emperors, in their self-assumed role as successors to Byzantium. Yet the acquisition of a distant territory peopled by non-Russians could mean very little to the country at large, as distinguished from some nationalistic and intellectual circles. The sufferings of the war were bound to renew and accentuate social stresses and tensions.

To many at home and abroad, the defeats and the palpable mismanagement of the war could only be explained by treason in the highest circles. Russians were particularly insistent about the German-born Empress Alexandra and her entourage, which included the charlatan faith-healer Rasputin. It was believed by many (including Lenin at times), completely incorrectly, that both the Romanovs and Hohenzollerns had a powerful interest in the preservation of the dynastic principle and hence in the conclusion of the war before anarchy should sweep away all established institutions and social distinctions. But the emperor's personal ineptitude and lack of intelligence precluded any such cynicism on his part, just as it did not allow him to entrust the conduct of the war or the government to more capable hands. The murder of Rasputin by a group of conspirators which included members of the imperial family served to discredit still further the monarch himself and the whole system. The collapse of the monarchy was in turn to leave the country without a clearly recognized authority. Food riots in Petrograd in March 1917 turned into a revolution. The army generals and even the conservative politicians refused to lend their support to the emperor, who felt compelled to abdicate. There was a half-hearted attempt to preserve the dynasty, but it also collapsed. The revolutionary regime found itself without a head of state; it was a last improvisation by the parliament, and its name acknowledged the fact: the *Provisional Government*.[1]

The unsettled character of the regime was to prove of great importance insofar as Russia's foreign relations were concerned. The conduct of foreign policy, and most especially of war, more than any other field of governmental activity requires the existence of an indisputable national authority. No people will fight wars for long on behalf of a government that calls itself provisional. Yet the task the Provisional Government set before itself, "the restoration of state and public order," was in fact never accomplished. From March on, Russian society lived in conditions of ever-deepening anarchy. From the perspective of foreign relations, it can be said that this situation did not terminate with the Bolshevik coup in November. It was only with the conclusion of the Treaty of Brest Litovsk in March 1918 which took Russia out of the war that the "restoration of the state" and hence of foreign policy can be said to have begun.

The Provisional Government formed by the Duma consisted of liberals (the Kadet party) and moderate conservatives (the Octobrist party, so called from the imperial manifesto of October 1905 that had established constitutional government in Russia). Its head was Prince Lvov, a widely respected nobleman of liberal tendencies. But the key figures in his cabinet were soon Alexander Kerensky, the Minister of Justice and the only socialist in the government (he was a Socialist Revolutionary, a member of the branch of Russia's radical movement that de-emphasized Marxism and believed in agrarian socialism), and Foreign Minister Paul Miliukov, leader of the Kadets. Unlike the Tsar's cabinet, this was a regime

---

[1] The official communiqué stressed the fact that Nicholas' abdication was followed by anarchy: "The Provisional Committee of the Duma has found itself compelled to take into its hands the restoration of the state and public order." F. A. Golder, ed., *Documents of Russian History* (New York, 1927), p. 281.

of professors, lawyers, and businessmen, people who for a long time had been in the forefront of their country's intellectual and public life. In a *peacetime* Russia, such a government could have gone far to speed the country's evolution toward a fully constitutional and representative regime. But the government's task was set in the midst of a war. Furthermore, it lacked solid backing. Its originating body, the Duma, had been elected in 1912 on the basis of a very unrepresentative franchise. Now, having given birth to the Provisional Government, the Duma virtually faded from the picture.

Side by side with the official government was an unofficial one—the Petrograd Soviet [council] of Workers' and Soldiers' Deputies, an *ad hoc* and chaotically elected body. The Soviet was dominated by Mensheviks and Socialist Revolutionaries, the Bolsheviks playing at first a secondary role. The leaders of the Soviet envisaged their function as that of a watch-dog on behalf of the masses over the activities of the bourgeois government. Their doctrine, in accordance with the views of all branches of Russian socialism before 1914, held that the country was still not ripe for socialism —hence their refusal to participate in the government. In fact, the leaders of the Soviet, while refusing (with the exception of Kerensky) ministerial portfolios, arrogated to themselves a large part of policy-making. On March 14, the Soviet published its momentous Order No. 1, calling on all military units to form their own soviets and to assume much of what had been the officers' disciplinary functions. Soon, even the dual pattern of political power held by both the Provisional Government and the Petrograd Soviet was further diluted when army units, other cities, etc., also formed such soviets, which recognized the primacy of the Petrograd one but were not by any means willing or able to follow it unconditionally.

The March pattern was a perfect prescription for anarchy. It was to give an opportunity for a determined minority to capitalize on economic distress and war-weariness and to make a decisive bid for power. But that was still in the future. For the moment, the Provisional Government announced its intention of prosecuting the war to a victorious end. Both in Russia and abroad, the March Revolution was viewed as strengthening the war effort. Russia now had, it appeared, a truly representative government capable of galvanizing the nation's energies. The soldiers would fight better for a democratic government than they had for the discredited autocracy. This illusion persisted even among the high military officers who had been fed up with the Tsar's indecisiveness and longed for a national government to give a sense of direction and purpose to the war effort. But Order No. 1 went far to disillusion the generals as to the left politicians' comprehension of the military problems. Still, even on the left there was no call for an immediate peace. The Soviet tried to repair the effects of Order No. 1 by issuing additional instructions stressing that the soldiers' soviets should limit themselves to political matters and that in military affairs the officers' authority was to remain undisturbed. But the harm could not, of course, be undone. Order No. 1 became the opening wedge of the "politicization" and hence demoralization of the army.

The Provisional Government could not under these circumstances have a coherent foreign policy. For most of its members, Russia's war aims had not been affected by the overthrow of Tsarism. A full victory over German militarism remained the goal. The Kadet and Octobrist politicians in the cabinet adhered to the territorial aims stipulated in the secret agreement of 1915: Turkey was to be expelled from Europe and Russia was to obtain Constantinople and the Straits; also, though it was not spelled out in the agreement, it was assumed that victory would be followed by the reunification of all Russian-speaking peoples (more concretely, that eastern Galicia would be given to Russia). The liberals and moderate conservatives who comprised the Provisional Government were fervent nationalists who were not going to accept less for democratic and republican Russia than had been promised to the autocratic one.

Their sentiments were shared by the more moderate among the socialists, but among the mass of Mensheviks and Socialist Revolutionaries, the situation was more complicated. Many of them felt that Russia's war had now become a people's war, but by the same token they wanted a peace without annexations or indemnities. The more radical ones stressed the revolutionary aspect of the war, still without any intention of terminating it by a separate peace. Thus, a manifesto of the Soviet dated March 27, the work of its left wing, called upon the nations of the world to "throw out your autocracy, just as the Russian nation has thrown off its Tsar, refuse to serve as the tool of robbery and force in the hands of the kings, landowners, and bankers—with our friendly joint efforts we shall end this terrible war." But at the same time the manifesto declared, "The Russian Revolution will not let itself be conquered by force from the outside."

Even among the Bolsheviks the attitude toward the war was ambiguous. They opposed the Provisional Government, but their own provisional leaders, Kamenev and Stalin, adopted a position not very different from that of the left-wing Mensheviks: the war could not be ended immediately, and as long as German troops faced Russian ones on Russian soil, the duty of every party was to remain behind the war effort. The first five weeks after the March Revolution witnessed almost unanimous support of the defense of the country against the foreign enemies.

With Lenin's arrival in Petrograd from Switzerland on April 16, this consensus was broken. Not that even Lenin dared at first to propose an immediate separate peace with the German and Austrian governments. But the slogans he propagated were designed to make the continuation of the war in fact impossible. He urged, and after considerable controversy had his way, that the Bolshevik Party declare uncompromising opposition to the Provisional Government and its war effort. The slogan "All power to the soviets," which was the main part of his famous April Theses, meant an attempt to upset the closest thing to a centralized government that Russia had and its substitution by a myriad of unconnected and irregularly functioning councils. The slogan "All land to the peasants" meant that large estates would be confiscated and transferred to committees of poor peasants. This in turn would be bound to make the already critical food situation even worse.

On the war, Lenin was careful not to run head-on into the still fervently anti-separate-peace mood of the masses. But he emphasized that this was an imperialist war run for the benefit of bankers and imperialists. Concretely, he proposed that front-line soldiers be allowed to fraternize with the Germans and Austrians. This was bound, of course, to lead to the further demoralization of the army and its ultimate collapse as a fighting force.

The sum of all these requests was a blueprint for deepening the anarchy, and, as I have pointed out, the program ran against many accepted points of the Marxian orthodoxy. (Thus, it was a commonplace of Marxism that Russia was not ready for socialism but only for a bourgeois liberal regime as embodied in the Provisional Government. Also, the distribution of land to the peasants contradicted the socialist belief that small peasant farming was inefficient and undesirable.) But the Bolsheviks found it difficult to oppose the *revolutionary* logic inherent in the April Theses. The fraternization of soldiers could be represented not as a way of destroying the morale of the Russian army and rendering it helpless before the enemy but as a means of spreading the flame of revolution to Germany and Austria, thus speeding the conclusion of a just peace. "All land to the peasants" was a way of currying favor with the vast majority of Russia's population. Nor could one interpret "All power to the soviets" as a demand for a Bolshevik takeover, since the soviets were dominated by Mensheviks and Socialist Revolutionaries.

Had the Provisional Government or the Menshevik–Socialist Revolutionary majority taken immediate steps against Lenin and his party (which after some initial hesitations followed his lead), there is little doubt that they could have counted on wide popular support. In April, the continuation of the war to a victorious end was still considered a duty of the Revolution. Hostile demonstrators in Petrograd denounced Lenin and his followers as German agents and demanded their arrest. But to Russia's temporary leaders, it was inconceivable that the Revolution should be sullied by the suppression of a political party, no matter how radical its program or demagogic its appeal. The anti-Bolshevik socialists could

not conceive of danger from the left; the main task was to ward off the
return of Tsarism or an attempt at a military dictatorship. Given freedom
to propagandize, the Bolsheviks could in turn count on the return of war-
weariness to aid their cause after the interval of patriotic elation that had
greeted the March events.

For the next several months, Russia's foreign policy became mired in
the internal political strife. Russia was not to know any central government.
The constituent assembly promised from the first days of the Revolution
did not convene until after the November coup and then met an ignominious
fate. Apart from the division of political authority between the Provisional
Government and the soviets, the unity of the country began to dissolve.
Claims for autonomy and then independence were advanced in the Ukraine
and Finland. The government was forced to sanction formation of army
units composed of Poles, Ukrainians, etc., and this further debilitated
the armed forces and endowed the separatist movements with private
armies.

The March Revolution coincided with a most precarious period in the
fortunes of the Western Allies. The German submarine campaign was
having a disastrous effect on English shipping and food supplies. Though
the United States entered the war in April, it was felt that the military
effects of American intervention could not become decisive for a long
time. The British and French governments and public were mainly interested in what the Revolution was going to do for Russia's war effort.
Here, after the first exorbitant expectations, it soon became clear that the
Provisional Government was incapable of performing a military miracle.
The extent of Russia's war-weariness was at first but imperfectly understood in the West. The anti-war propaganda and the progressive decomposition of the army were in the Western press blamed on "anarchists" and
"German agents." It was confidently expected that Russia's healthy national instincts would assert themselves, and that such politicians as the
liberal Miliukov, known and liked in the West, could prevail in their
policy of loyalty to the Alliance. The Allied governments hastened to
recognize the new Russian regime and accepted its ambassadors, for the
most part politicians with Kadet backgrounds.[2]

When the complexities of the Russian situation began to be acknowledged
in the West, the Allied governments attempted to supplement the orthodox
ways of diplomacy with what today would be described as propaganda and
public relations. The shaky position of the Provisional Government vis-à-vis
the Petrograd Soviet became known, and hence it was thought useful
to approach Russian socialist circles directly. Delegations of English and
French socialists began to descend on Petrograd in an attempt to persuade

[2] Thus, a noted liberal lawyer and Kadet leader, Maklakov, succeeded the
former Tsarist minister Izvolsky in Paris.

their Russian comrades to postpone their internal bickering and issue manifestoes in favor of a united and resolute war effort. Yet, as we have seen, even before the war the most moderate Russian socialists had been worlds apart from their Western confrères. Now, even the most pro-war Menshevik or Socialist Revolutionary could hardly find a common language with a British Labourite or a French Socialist. It was inconceivable to him that the urgent task of introducing full democracy or social justice should be delayed because of the exigencies of the war. And behind the moderates (known as "defensists") there was the growing body of radical opinion still against a separate peace but demanding that the final settlement be one without annexations or indemnities. This in turn ran against the declared policy of the Western Powers, for whom, to mention one, the recovery of Alsace and Lorraine was a fundamental war aim. The intra-socialist contacts, of which so much was hoped in the West, were thus instrumental in deepening the chasm between the Western and the Russian left, and weakening the latter's position vis-à-vis its own extreme wing.

At one time, it was also thought in Paris and London that things would go better if instead of being represented by professional diplomats England and France should appoint as ambassadors politicians better capable of operating in the new and strange world of soviets. The French Ambassador, Maurice Paléologue, allegedly compromised by his ties with the old court and Petrograd society, was replaced by Joseph Noulens, whose background as a Radical Party politician, it was hoped, would make him more accept-able to the Soviet. (In fact, the French Radicals were, in the eyes of the Russian socialists, the epitome of a bourgeois party.) A similar shift in the case of Great Britain did not materialize because the intended replacement, the Labour member of the War Cabinet, Arthur Henderson, once in Petro-grad realized the fatuity of such a gesture and his own inability to affect the course of events. Britain continued to be represented by Sir George Buchanan, who had been in this post since 1910.[3] For all his great expertise in Russian affairs, Sir George was incapable of influencing the political picture or of conveying to the powers in London the tragic complexities of the Russian situation.

The task, the hopeless task of the Provisional Government in foreign policy was now twofold: to convince the soviets, and with them left-wing public opinion, that it was striving toward a just and democratic peace; and then to convince the Allies that a pronouncement to the same effect would go far to unite Russia behind the war effort. In pursuance of the first task, the government had to appease the Soviet by pressing Allied

[3] Richard H. Ullman, *Anglo-Soviet Relations 1917–1921: Intervention and War* (Princeton, 1961), pp. 8–10.

authorities to facilitate the return to Russia of *all* political exiles—even
the ones with pro-Bolshevik views—some of whom, notably Trotsky, were
to be instrumental in anti-war propaganda and eventually in the overthrow
of the Provisional Government. At the same time, Miliukov tried to reassure
the Allies about Russia's will and capacity to fight and to wrest from
them a declaration that would make easier his relations with the Soviet.

To the latter, however, the Minister of Foreign Affairs remained deeply
suspect. Though the details of the Provisional Government's agreements
with the Western Allies were secret,[4] it was widely and correctly suspected
that they envisaged annexations. Equally correct was the suspicion of the
left parties that the Provisional Government or at least its foreign minister
adhered to the "imperialist" aims of their Tsarist predecessors.

An awkward attempt to refute the charges precipitated the first governmental crisis on May 1. On that day, Miliukov published a note to the
Western Allies that sought on the one hand to remove their apprehensions
about Russia's value as an ally and on the other to stifle the suspicions
of the left. Thus, the note proclaimed:

> Of course the statements of the Provisional Government, which are
> permeated with this new spirit of freed democracy, cannot give the
> least reason to think that the revolution which has taken place has
> brought after it a weakening of the role of Russia in the general Allied
> struggle. Quite on the contrary, the popular aspiration to carry on the
> World War to a decisive victory has only become intensified, as a result
> of everyone's consciousness of the general responsibility.[5]

This pathetic attempt to put a rosy complexion on the ominous reality
brought forth immediate protests and demonstrations on the left. The
declaration contained no specific renunciation of annexations and indemnities, and the phrase "to carry on the World War to a decisive victory"
had a most "imperialist" tone. Miliukov was also unfortunate in his sense
of timing; the note was published on a day that evoked among Russian
socialists a vivid memory of their internationalist creed and their responsibilities to the world proletariat. An attempt by the Kadets to exonerate
Miliukov also had a hollow ring: "Neither the Provisional Government
as a whole nor P. N. Miliukov as an individual carries or can carry on an
acquisitive policy based on the desire for domination over other peoples.
In agreement with the free peoples of the West, they set as the goal of
the War a stable peace based on the self-determination of nations."[6]

[4] They were published after the November Revolution by the Bolsheviks
when they got hold of the archives of the Ministry of Foreign Affairs.
[5] Quoted from William Henry Chamberlin, *The Russian Revolution* (New
York, 1935), I, 444.
[6] Quoted in *ibid.*, 446.

The net result of the whole episode and some accompanying internal difficulties was that Prince Lvov's government was reorganized. Miliukov was dropped and replaced as Foreign Minister by Mikhail Tereshchenko, a young and wealthy industrialist whose name, unlike his predecessor's, meant nothing in the West. The Petrograd Soviet abandoned its self-proclaimed role as observer and watchdog and allowed six of its most prominent members to join it (counting Kerensky, who had been there from the beginning)—including Victor Chernov, the most influential leader of the Socialist Revolutionaries, and Irakli Tseretelli, the most forceful figure among the Menshevik "defensists." The dominating figure after the government reorganization of May 18, 1917, was Kerensky, who took over the Ministry of War and whose name, rather than Prince Lvov's, enjoyed most prestige within the country.

But for all its inclusion of people who at the moment commanded the widest political following (the popularity and political fortunes of the revolutionary politicians changed with dazzling rapidity), the government could no more than its predecessor change the drift of events toward greater and greater social and political disorganization. The patriotic elation of the first weeks of the Revolution had evaporated. The call for peace and bread resounded with increasing frequency. Within the army Bolshevik agitators pursued their morale-destroying activities with impunity. A wave of peasant disorders was sweeping the country. The Bolsheviks, at first the object of popular distrust (their leaders were suspected of being German agents, and Lenin's return trip through enemy territory was held against him), were gaining in influence. So were the anti-war elements among the Socialist Revolutionaries, and the Mensheviks, who, while suspicious of the Bolsheviks, added their voices to those calling for a "people's peace." At the All-Russian Congress of Workers' and Soldiers' Soviets held in June, the Bolsheviks and their close allies the so-called interfraction group (which included Trotsky and was soon to amalgamate officially with Lenin's party) could muster about 130 out of 777 delegates who declared their party allegiance. This was a dazzling accession of strength since the first days of the Revolution, when the Bolsheviks were given seats on the Presidium of the Petrograd Soviet largely out of considerations of courtesy toward a revolutionary party and not because they commanded any sizable following among the workers and soldiers.

In retrospect, the Provisional Government has often been criticized for not taking the only path which could have saved it, and Russian democracy: initiating peace negotiations with Germany and her allies. But such criticism fails to take account of the regime's really impossible predicament. In the first place, Russia's rulers felt—and under the conditions of 1917 it appeared to be a reasonable supposition—that Russia's defection would determine the outcome of the war. The Allies barely held their own on the Western Front, and everything argued that if the Germans augmented their forces there by upward of a hundred divisions, which peace with Russia would release, the struggle would be terminated before the United States, freshly in the war, could fill the gap. The liberals and the moderate "defensist" socialist believed sincerely that the war was being fought for democracy and against the German domination of Europe. Would Russia be able to preserve her freshly won democracy (not to mention her Western provinces) if Germany gained hegemony in Europe?

Another consideration was even more fundamental. While making the conduct of the war increasingly difficult, the Bolsheviks and their unwitting allies, the "internationalist Mensheviks," piously abjured any talk of a separate peace with the "German imperialists." They wanted a peace, but one to be concluded with the German "workers and soldiers." Had the Provisional Government initiated negotiations with imperial German generals and diplomats, this step would have been greeted with not only patriotic but also class indignation, with voices claiming that it meant "selling out to the Kaiser," etc. After all, several months later, when Russia's military and economic position was utterly hopeless and when a more resolute team was ruling the country, it still took a Herculean effort on the part of Lenin and his associates to cajole the *Bolsheviks* into acquiescing in a treaty with the German government.

On the surface at least, the Provisional Government had no option but to continue the war while trying at the same time to disarm the opposition by exacting from its Western allies pledges about a just and democratic peace. As to the latter, one of the key elements was to be a conference on the neutral ground of Sweden between the Allied and German socialists. This conference would have enabled the Mensheviks and Socialist Revolutionaries to ward off charges that they were not doing their most to secure a peoples' peace. But the conference never materialized. After protracted maneuvers, the Western Allied governments felt compelled to deny their socialists passports to go to Stockholm, the more suspicious elements seeing the whole conference as a "German plot." The inability to convene the meeting tended to weaken the standing of Mensheviks and Socialist Revolutionaries among the masses of Russian soldiers and workers and gave further credence to the Bolshevik propaganda that the Western Allies were uninterested in a just and democratic peace and were bent upon prolonging the slaughter for imperialist purposes.

The Provisional Government's attempt to reverse the drift of events, whether in internal or external affairs, was bound to fail because it enjoyed neither the prestige nor the authority to master the situation and to rule in fact as well as name. Between March and November 1917 (and really throughout the Civil War until 1921), a drama was enacted that was to be replayed many times: the presence of a resolute minority bent on achieving power did not make other radical and democratic groups compose their differences or forget their excessive ideological scruples. The Mensheviks and Socialist Revolutionaries lived with their memories of the past, of the Tsarist oppression, and nothing in their experience argued the probability of a dictatorial coup from the left. Those measures of ruthlessness and discipline which were needed to restore internal order and the army's fighting capacity were, in the eyes of the non-Bolshevik left, undemocratic and not to be thought of even in time of war. The true character of Bolshevism was as yet hidden even to its most resolute opponents—and for a very good reason in addition to the essential political naiveté of the democratic left: prior to the November Revolution, and even for some time after it, the Bolsheviks were far from being the disciplined, monolithic, and authoritarian party they were eventually to become. Lenin's resolve to bring about an armed *coup d'état* was to be opposed by some of the party's most important leaders, and his first authoritarian moves after October were also to encounter spirited opposition among his most trusted lieutenants. The most basic and inexcusable defect of the democratic left was thus not its miscalculation about the Bolsheviks, but its failure to realize that an unchecked and ever-deepening anarchy was bound eventually to end up in a dictatorship of one sort or another.

But these reflections anticipate our story. The government as reformed in May appeared, at least on paper, to represent an impressive show of national unity. It should have stilled the cries of "All power to the soviets," for six prominent figures from the Petrograd Soviet were now in the cabinet. But the Bolsheviks continued their agitations, and in June, coincident with the meeting of the Congress of Soviets (at which, as noted above, they were in a minority), they called on the soldiers and people of Petrograd to demonstrate against the government. This was not to be an attempt at a *coup d'état*, but a rehearsal of one and a trial of strength between the Bolsheviks on the one hand and the government and non-Bolshevik left on the other. The March Revolution, after all, also started as a demonstration. However, the non-Bolshevik majority of the Congress summoned enough resolve to ban the demonstration. Members of the soviets were dispatched to the barracks and factories to explain the prohibition and to explain the Bolsheviks' game. At the last moment, the Bolshevik Central Committee called off the demonstration.

This unexpected show of determination on the part of the soviets led Lenin to wonder aloud whether the slogan "All power to the soviets" was still correct. *All* power in the hands of the Menshevik and Socialist Revolutionary majority might mean a suppression of public disorder, the enhancement of which was the Bolsheviks' intermediate aim in their pursuit of power. But the democratic socialists' show of strength was of short duration. They rejected the demands of the more resolute among them that steps be taken to prevent the recurrence of the June threat and that the Bolsheviks' private army, the Red Guards, be dissolved, and persisted in their suicidal delusion that an armed threat to the Revolution could come only from the right.

What was the reorganized Provisional Government doing all this time? In June, largely under the influence of Kerensky, it decided to open an offensive on the Galician front. The front as a whole had been stationary since the March Revolution. The German and Austrian command was expecting a break-up of Russia's armies, and the Germans were shifting some of their troops to France. The Russian decision to attack was taken in the face of expert military opinion which warned against such a move—one general opining that "the Russian army will tumble like a house of cards" —and which held that with the continuing demoralization of the soldiers, the task of holding a front line was formidable enough without undertaking an offensive. But the government was under pressure from the West to relieve the Allies in France. Inactivity, it held, was the greatest enemy of the soldiers' morale. And Kerensky and his entourage were deceived by badly drawn parallels with the French Revolution: now the "freest army in the world" was going to deal a crushing blow to Prussian militarism. In addressing the front-line troops, Kerensky scored great rhetorical success. He was greeted with wild enthusiasm and declarations that the soldiers were ready to die for Russia and the Revolution. But this enthusiasm was short-lived. The offensive itself, which began on July 1, scored some initial impressive successes against the Austrian armies, whose morale was hardly higher than the Russians' and who were at first overwhelmed by their opponents' numerical superiority. But, as in 1915 and 1916, the arrival of German reinforcements changed the picture. The Russians were forced to retreat, and then panic and disorganization seized many units. In some cases, whole regiments refused to go to the firing line or dissolved in wholesale desertion. By the end of the month, the front in the south retreated to Russia's frontiers, and in the north it proved impossible to dislodge the Germans from the Russian territory they occupied. From now on, Russia's still vast armies were clearly revealed as incapable of any offensive action and indeed of containing a serious enemy offensive should one be undertaken. It is against this background that the Provisional Government had to face ever-mounting internal troubles.

With the fate of the July offensive still undecided, the Bolsheviks became involved in another demonstration and attempted coup in Petrograd. The events of July 16 and 17 cannot be described as a premeditated attempt by the Bolsheviks to seize power. They found themselves faced with growing excitement and pressure from their supporters in some Petrograd regiments (which were confronted with the unpleasant prospect of being sent to the front) and factories to lead yet another demonstration, and perhaps more than a demonstration, for "All power to the soviets." After some attempts by Bolshevik spokesmen to discourage the milling soldiers and demonstrators, they realized that abstention might lead the extremist elements to switch their support to outright anarchists. Lenin on July 17 said to his lieutenant Zinoviev: "Maybe we should try it now."[7] Orders went out to the pro-Bolshevik sailors from Kronstadt to arrive, armed, in the capital to carry out a "peaceful demonstration."

There is no doubt that this was to be, though hastily improvised, an attempt at a *coup d'état*. The Bolshevik minority of the Executive Committee of the Soviet elected a group of fifteen that was to take over power after the elimination of the Provisional Government and leaders of the majority in the Soviet. The Kronstadt sailors, 20,000 strong, descended on the capital on July 4 and proceeded, amidst shooting and looting, to the seat of the Soviet in the Tauride Palace. Here they came close to lynching the Minister of Agriculture, Victor Chernov, who had to be rescued by Trotsky. At the same time, the rumor that pro-government military units were being recalled from the front and were approaching the capital caused panic among the mutineers. The pro-Bolshevik soldiers and sailors were in no condition to fight the better disciplined front-line troops. Some other Petrograd regiments, hearing the news, abandoned their previous "neutrality" and sent detachments to protect the Soviet from their turbulent brethren. The attempted uprising fizzled out on the night of July 18. The Kronstadt sailors meekly returned to their base.

The failure of the July coup seemed at first to work wonders with the faltering resolution of the Provisional Government and anti-Bolshevik socialists. The leaders of the uprising were arrested. Bolshevik headquarters and presses were seized. And the government released the information, for some time in its possession, that Lenin and his party had been receiving German money.

These charges have for a long time been dismissed as false by many historians, including anti-Communists. Certainly the circumstances of the accusation, the fact that similar rumors had long been circulated on the extreme right, and the utter implausibility of picturing Lenin as anybody's agent lent strong credence to the countercharges that this was a desperate attempt to smear the leader and party rapidly gaining in popularity. But today there can be but little doubt that the substance of the charges, as distinguished from the details published in July, was true. The evidence is provided by the archives of the German Foreign Ministry secured after

[7] Cited in Adam B. Ulam, *The Bolsheviks* (New York, 1965), p. 345.

World War II and, circumstantially, from Lenin's own letters.[8] They indicate clearly that the Bolshevik center in Stockholm, staffed by such future dignitaries of the Soviet state as Karl Radek and Jacob Fuerstenberg-Hanecki, was in touch with Dr. Alexander Helphand and through him was receiving subsidies from the secret funds of the German Foreign Ministry.[9] Those dealings were conducted under such conditions of secrecy that even most of the Bolshevik leaders were not aware from where their party was getting the very substantial funds used for its very extensive press and propaganda activities, for arming the Red Guards, etc.

It would be at the same time absurd to see Lenin and his group as "German agents." Their temporary objectives—the destruction of Russia's capacity to fight and the overthrow of the Provisional Government—coincided with those of the German high command. But the next item on Lenin's agenda after the seizure of power in Russia was a similar revolution *in Germany*. They considered themselves international revolutionaries bent on the destruction of all the existing regimes in Europe and had no compunctions about getting money for that purpose from any source whatsoever.

But in the immediate backwash of the July debacle, the publication of the charges against Lenin appeared to complete the destruction of the Bolshevik party. Lenin and his closest lieutenant, Zinoviev, were compelled to go into hiding on July 18. Some of the leaders—Kamenev, Lunacharsky, and Alexandra Kollontay—were arrested[10]; the Red Guards were dissolved. Had the regime shown real determination, the Bolsheviks, it is not too much to say, could have been smashed and prevented from becoming again an effective political force for a long time to come. But many of the Party's first-echelon leaders—notably its chief organizer, Sverdlov, and Stalin—were left free. The Party's organizations away from Petrograd were hardly interfered with. The non-Bolshevik socialists' resolution to deal energetically with the instigators of the unrest soon petered out. As even the most reasonable of them claimed, perhaps with some justification, if the Bolsheviks were suppressed completely, soon it would be the turn of

[8] This evidence is reproduced in Z. A. B. Zeman, ed., *Germany and the Revolution in Russia: Documents from the Archives of the German Foreign Ministry* (London, 1958). See also Ulam, *op. cit.*, pp. 326 and 349.

[9] The Russian-born Helphand had been before 1912 active both in German and Russian socialist movements under the name of Parvus, and in 1905 he had authored with Trotsky the theory of "permanent revolution" then rejected by Lenin but in 1917 put to use by the Bolsheviks.

[10] Trotsky, though still officially not a Bolshevik (his "interfraction" group was to join the Party officially only in August), demanded also to be incarcerated and had his wish granted.

the Mensheviks and the Socialist Revolutionaries, hardly less hated in conservative circles and among the army officers. The stories of the "German gold" were indignantly attacked by Lenin's most uncompromising enemies among the moderate socialists. The Ministry of Justice chose not to publish the really compromising evidence they had on Lenin, and some of its officials in fact warned the leader of the Bolsheviks to flee before a warrant was issued for his arrest. No serious attempt was made to apprehend Lenin, though his hideaways—first in Petrograd, then in the country some twenty miles from the capital—were regularly visited by members of his family and Bolshevik officials, and even the most inept police force could have tracked him down. The commission to investigate the charges against the Bolsheviks proceeded at a leisurely pace and never in fact brought out a report. In August, the supposedly suppressed Bolshevik Party held a congress which brought 270 prominent Bolsheviks to Petrograd, but this meeting avoided detection by the authorities. The Party's membership was announced at the congress as being in the vicinity of 240,000, a fivefold increase since April.

The Provisional Government went in the meantime through another crisis. On July 20 Prince Lvov resigned, and the government was now headed in name as well as in fact by Kerensky. The collapse of the July offensive exacerbated the feelings of the Kadets and other moderate elements about their socialist colleagues in the coalition. Abroad, Russia's defeat led to the conclusion that short of a drastic restoration of internal order and discipline in the army, her help to the Western Allies would be negligible. Much was hoped at first from Kerensky's official assumption of leadership. But the government was simply incapable of stemming the tide of anarchy, and the first weeks of Kerensky's premiership brought no improvement. In some circles in the West, just as among the exasperated conservative and moderate groups in Russia, hopes swung to the emergence of a "strong man" who would put down "anarchists and German agents." The most obvious candidate was the new commander-in-chief, General Lavr Kornilov (appointed on July 31 to replace Brusilov, who had commanded the ill-fated offensive).

The involved and in some details still contentious story of Kornilov's attempted coup cannot be discussed in full here. But, to summarize the events, the new commander-in-chief expected the government to take steps to restore discipline in the army. Kerensky did indeed restore the death penalty but implied strongly that it would never be applied. This hopeless pusillanimity made the conservatives all the more frantic in their hopes for a strong man and in their thinly veiled hints to Kornilov to assume the role. A brave man but politically immature, Kornilov lent himself to the intrigue. The final stage of the conspiracy was a veritable tragi-comedy of errors and mutual deception. Kerensky ordered Kornilov to have an army corps ready to march on Petrograd, where he expected a repetition of the July days. This, together with some doubletalk by politicians hanging around his headquarters, convinced Kornilov that the Prime Minister wanted him to become dictator and was willing to serve under him. Kerensky then realized with a start what the general's intentions were and ordered him to lay down his command. Kornilov refused. In a proclamation, he announced his aim of saving Russia from all current ills, including the Provisional Government. The attempted coup was on.

Of particular interest to this study is of course the attitude of the Western Powers toward the Kornilov attempt. As it might be expected, there were many people on the Allied side who sympathized with this attempt to restore order. The British military attaché evidently authorized the British armored-car unit serving with the Russian army to help Kornilov in the march on Petersburg. Sir George Buchanan, with the approval of other Allied ambassadors, offered to mediate between the Provisional Government and the rebel general. This offer was indignantly rejected by Kerensky.

The faltering government might have succumbed to the coup except for the sudden resolution and initiative of the Petrograd Soviet and the Executive Committee of the All-Russian Congress of Soviets. At the news on September 9 that Kornilov's cavalry had been ordered to march on the capital, their Menshevik and Socialist Revolutionary leaders sprang into action. Their previous differences with the Bolsheviks were laid aside. To fight a threat from the right was much more congenial and natural to them than one coming from their fellow socialists. The Soviets' proclamations branded Kornilov as a reactionary who would reintroduce the worst features of Tsarism, suppress the left and liberal political parties, favor the landlords as against the peasants, and destroy Russia's armies in further bloody offensives. Agitators were dispatched to the army units to turn them against the pro-Kornilov officers. Most important was the action of the railwaymen's and communications workers' unions, which refused to pass army trains directed on Petrograd or to transmit messages from the mutinous commanders. Within a few days, the march on the capital disintegrated, practically without a shot. The former commander-in-chief and the leading generals who had sided with him were put under arrest.

The main beneficiaries of the attempted coup were the Bolsheviks. Their imprisoned leaders were released, the Red Guards, their private army, were allowed to come out in the open and to rearm in the wake of the panic attending the news of Kornilov's march. What is most important, the last traces of the discipline and respect for the officers among the soldiers were now finally undermined. The workers' and soldiers' soviets in the major industrial cities turned increasingly toward the Bolsheviks, abandoning their previous following of the Mensheviks (whose influence declined catastrophically) and the Socialist Revolutionaries—who were still potent in the countryside, but more and more divided among themselves and incapable of acting as a united party. The conservatives and the Kadets were exposed by the Kornilov affair both as plotting against the Provisional Government and as utterly ineffective. In mid-September, the Bolsheviks secured a majority in the Petrograd and Moscow soviets.

From the point of view of the Provisional Government and Kerensky personally, the defeat of Kornilov was almost as much of an irretrievable catastrophe as would have been his success. Even those generals and officers who had not followed Kornilov were now fed up with the pusillanimous premier and his government, the personnel of which was being continually changed. If the Provisional Government survived the affair for two months, it was mainly because of the inability of the non-Bolshevik socialists to think of an alternative and because of the Bolsheviks' own hesitations, born of their experiences in July, whether to try yet another coup.

The remaining few weeks of the Provisional Government's existence were filled with hasty improvisations designed to prop up the tottering structure. Thus, elections for Russia's Constituent Assembly were now "definitely" scheduled. While awaiting them, Kerensky's regime sought support in *ad hoc* bodies such as the Democratic Conference, and the provisional parliament, the so-called Council of the Republic, which sat and talked until the eve of the November uprising. All that institutional tinkering could not affect the ever-expanding sea of anarchy: seizure of landlords' estates by peasants and of factories by workers continued; 2 million deserters from the army were now at large.

The Provisional Government in its death throes received but scant sympathy from the Western Allies. The failure of Kornilov's attempt was taken with bad grace in London and Paris. One more appeal was addressed to the Provisional Government urging it to revive the war effort. Its only effect was to produce hurt feelings in Kerensky, who chose to remind the British and French ambassadors that Russia was still a Great Power and its government was not to be lectured in this way.[11] On its part the Provisional Government repeated fatuously its determination to remain in the war till a victorious end.

The great hope of the Provisional Government was centered around the forthcoming conference of the Allied Powers in Paris. As Kerensky was fond of proclaiming, the Russian delegation would insist on a declaration for a just democratic peace with no annexations or indemnities. This was the last desperate attempt to stem the defeatist feelings, to

[11] Robert D. Warth, *The Allies and the Russian Revolution* (Durham, N.C., 1954), p. 140.

persuade the Mensheviks and Socialist Revolutionaries that the government *was* working for a democratic and speedy peace. But the Allied governments demurred against the discussion of war aims at that time. They had been through a series of catastrophic struggles that had exacted huge casualties. Mutinous sentiments had affected a large number of French military units, and it was with difficulty that more serious trouble was avoided. It was felt in the Western capitals that raising the issue of war aims would inevitably strengthen defeatist sentiments and that their armies might follow the example of Russia's. Hence the Western governments warned that only problems connected with a more effective prosecution of the war would be discussed at the forthcoming conference.

The Russian delegation was to include, in addition to the foreign minister and the chief of staff, a representative of the Soviet, Menshevik Skobelev. But in the West the word "Soviet," though it was still not associated with the Bolsheviks, had already acquired an odious significance. It stood for the institution that demoralized the Russian army, plunged society in anarchy, and exposed the Allies to additional sacrifices and mortal peril. It was flatly announced in the West that Skobelev would not be admitted to the deliberations and that only representatives of the Russian government should sit in on the proceedings. This in turn incensed the non-Bolshevik socialists who felt the ground slipping from under their feet. But the November Revolution intervened before any delegation, with or without a representative of the Soviet, could leave for the Allies' councils. The Provisional Government, its fumbling attempts to contain anarchy, to preserve some appearance of a united front with the Western Allies—all that receded into history to become the subject of post mortems of "what might have been," of endless disputes as to whose fault it was, and the like. With the government collapsed the other main actor of the events of March-October 1917, the "revolutionary democracy" of the Petrograd Soviet, led by the Mensheviks and Socialist Revolutionaries. In the hands of the Bolsheviks since September, the Soviet had become an instrument for the overthrow of the regime, sharing this task with the Congress of Soviets, in which the Bolsheviks also by November achieved a majority. In due time, though not until some months after November, the Soviets will become simply tools of the Bolshevik Party; "soviet power," which prior to September was synonymous with domination of the democratic socialists, will come to mean Communist power; and those proud organs of the Revolution once freely elected by the workers and soldiers will simply become an institutional gloss over the dictatorship of a party, then of an oligarchy, and later of one man and his secret police.

The key to the March-November events in Russia lay predominantly in the internal situation and conditions within the Russian army. In retrospect, it appears that nothing Russia's allies could have done would have affected the turn of events. Practically all of the writers concerned with Russia's foreign relations between the two revolutions repeat that there was no understanding in the Western capitals of the true situation, that the Allies' insistence on the prolongation of war contributed to the Provisional Government's fall, and that to the West there was no substantial difference between the Bolsheviks seeking to undermine the Russian democracy and the other socialists who tried, in a confused and inept way to be sure, to preserve it. Superficially this charge is true. To the statesmen as well as public opinion in the West, the troubles in Russia were the work of "nihilists and German agents" and there was the illusion that every patriotic Russian was eager to continue the war to a victorious end. But in fact the Western misconceptions were no more fantastic than those of many people on the spot, of the great majority of the Socialist Revolutionaries and Mensheviks who believed to the very end that the Bolsheviks could not conceivably seize power and even if they did that their regime would last no more than a few days. And the majority of the Bolshevik leaders in their turn were deeply skeptical of the chances of an uprising, even more so of their capacity to cling to power in a completely disorganized country on the verge of a famine. It took all of Lenin's dynamism to drive them to their November undertaking, and even Lenin's boldness was based on a hugely erroneous premise: that a revolution in Russia would soon be followed by similar developments in Germany and then in the other belligerent countries.

Again, the Allies are blamed for not releasing Russia from her obligations. But what Western statesman, his country in a life-and-death struggle, could have pronounced for the release of 130 German divisions from the Eastern Front? They are blamed for not declaring for a peace "without indemnities and annexations," as the anti-Bolshevik left wanted them to do. But again, it is extremely doubtful whether the Russian soldier, granted the atmosphere of the society, could have fought at all even on behalf of the most just and idealistic cause. And as the Treaty of Brest Litovsk was to testify, Germany was not likely to respond to such peace overtures. For all the mounting peace pressures within Germany, her high command was still confident of a decisive victory, and not until the summer of 1918 was this confidence shattered. The Allied statesmen may well be blamed, with the German ones, for prolonging the bloodshed that shattered European civilization. But exactly because of the mounting war-weariness and huge losses, they were afraid—and who can now say whether they were wrong?—of showing signs of weakness that might lead to a situation like that which arose in Russia in 1917.

The discussion of what the Provisional Government might or might not have done lies properly beyond the scope of this book. As suggested above, its hands were tied, most of all in relation to problems of war and peace.

2. *Brest Litovsk*

The end of the Provisional Government came with dazzling rapidity. Only two weeks before its overthrow, Foreign Minister Tereshchenko could speak in rather optimistic terms: "Turning to Russia, the Minister of Foreign Affairs expressed the opinion that notwithstanding all the difficulties we are experiencing, our position objectively still includes enormous resources, both with respect to manpower reserves and food supplies. There is no doubt that we are in better circumstances than other countries with respect to food."[12] But the minister added, more perceptively, that "the principal reason for our difficult position lies not in the material conditions but in the changes in the psychology of the people to which we bear witness."

On November 7, these "changes in the psychology of the people" culminated in the overthrow of the Provisional Government in Petrograd. The overthrow coincided with the meeting of the Second Congress of Soviets in which the Bolsheviks and their allies had a majority.[13] The outright opponents of the Bolsheviks walked out of the Congress in protest against the coup. (This was the occasion on which Trotsky consigned the Mensheviks and the right-wing Socialist Revolutionaries to the famous "rubbish heap of history.") Thus Lenin and his party and their allies were left free to pronounce the Provisional Government deposed, to set up the Council of Commissars, which was to be itself a provisional government "until the meeting of the Constituent Assembly," and to issue the historic declarations on peace and on land.

[12] Speech before the foreign-affairs commission of the Council of the Republic, in Robert Browder and Alexander Kerensky, eds., *The Russian Provisional Government 1917: Documents* (Stanford, Calif., 1961), II, 1133.

[13] Of the 650 delegates who met on the first day of the Congress, the Bolsheviks could muster about 390. By the time the delegates to the Congress dispersed to their homes (transportation facilities in November 1917 were, like everything in Russia, in a chaotic state), the number reached 900. The Bolsheviks' strength reflected their domination of the major cities' soviets, including those of Petrograd and Moscow. The Congress did not represent the countryside, where, as elections to the Constituent Assembly were to show, the Bolsheviks were quite weak. Still, the pro-Bolshevik majority in the Congress of the Workers' and Soldiers' Soviets gave, if not a legal, then a very considerable psychological justification to the Bolsheviks' coup and, conversely, demoralized their opponents among the democratic socialists, who, while disapproving of violence, could not see how they could oppose "the people" as embodied in the Congress.

The *Decree on Peace* accepted unanimously by the Congress on November 8 marks the Bolsheviks' debut in diplomacy; it is in fact the first state paper of Soviet Russia. It embodied two themes subsequently found in Bolshevik diplomacy and propaganda: a general appeal to all governments on behalf of peace, couched in democratic phraseology; and a revolutionary appeal, going over the heads of the governments to the working masses of the warring countries and also, by implication, to the nationalities in the imperial possessions of the Great Powers.

The first element was represented by a forthright plea for peace. "The Government regards as an honest or democratic peace . . . an immediate peace without annexation (i.e., without the seizure of foreign land or the forcible taking over of foreign nationalities) and without indemnities."[14] Along the same line, while listing various conditions of peace the Bolsheviks stated diplomatically: "Along with this the Government states that it does not regard the above-mentioned conditions of peace as ultimative; i.e., it is willing to consider any other conditions of peace, insisting only that these be presented as quickly as possible by one of the fighting countries." An immediate armistice of three months was proposed, again a sensible non-doctrinaire proposal.

But even in the document designed to be persuasive to the governments of the warring powers, the Bolsheviks injected what was to be a continuous theme of their propaganda. Thus:

> The Provisional Workers' and Peasants' Government of Russia also appeals especially to the class-conscious workers of the three leading nations of humanity, and the largest states which are participating in the war, England, France and Germany. The workers of those countries rendered the greatest services to the cause of progress and socialism: the great example of the Chartist Movement in England, a number of revolutions of world significance carried by the French proletariat, finally the heroic struggle against the Exceptional Law in Germany . . . all these examples of proletarian heroism and historic creation serve as a guarantee that the workers of the above-mentioned countries understand the problems which now fall on them.

Further on was a reference to "the cause of freeing the toiling and exploited masses of the population from slavery and exploitation of every kind." This was a new language in world diplomacy.

The declaration underscored the twofold character of the Bolsheviks' aspirations and concerns in the whole realm of foreign relations. One was the immediate need to reach peace, and the certainty (at least in Lenin's mind) that Russia's armies were incapable of carrying on and that unless the Bolsheviks would achieve an armistice very quickly their govern-

[14] Chamberlin, *op. cit.*, I, 472.

ment would meet with the fate of Kerensky's. The elements that brought about the armed coups in Russia's major cities which resulted in Lenin's government were composed mainly of rebellious soldiers and sailors, few of them with any clear-cut pro-Bolshevik sympathies but attracted to the party by its promise of an immediate end to the war. This was, then, what might be called the immediate, short-term aspiration of the Soviet government.

The longer-term aspiration and need found its expression—though as yet fuzzily—in the class-appeal part of the *Decree on Peace*. If in the short run Soviet power had to be preserved by an immediate cessation of hostilities, then in the longer run, the Bolshevik leaders believed equally fervently, peace could be secured only by socialist revolutions in other countries, most importantly in the advanced industrial nations, revolutions which could then extend their helping hand to the Bolsheviks trying to establish socialism in their admittedly backward country. And even peace could not by itself indefinitely preserve the power of the Bolsheviks. In the first place, if the major nations of Europe remained capitalist they would undoubtedly unite against the ideological threat represented by the first socialist country in the world. In the second place, Russia proper was too undeveloped, her working class too small to allow the Bolsheviks to survive in power for long after they had fulfilled the masses' desire for peace.

Before the Revolution, Lenin had urged that simple pacifism was not enough, that the imperialist war had to be turned into a civil one if socialism was to emerge victorious. In these terms, the Bolshevik coup of November could be rationalized only on the premise that the revolutionary stirrings already perceptible in France and Germany could thereby be turned into a full-fledged revolution. This premise has often been criticized by historians for the obvious reason that no such revolution did in fact take place. But under the conditions of 1917 there were reasons—and not only doctrinaire ones—to expect a repetition of the Russian November in the countries of the West. Europe was sickened and weary after three years of inconclusive slaughter. Severe mutinies had shaken the French army. Was it doctrinaire to expect that the French army, having lost more than a million men in dead alone, would come to resemble the Russian one? There had been revolutionary stirrings in the German fleet, an insurrection in Ireland. The unrest among its nationalities was already threatening to break up the Austro-Hungarian empire into fragments. Thus, not only a doctrinaire socialist but a realist politician might have had sound reasons for anticipating a serious revolutionary situation gripping Europe in the wake of the developments in Russia.

Yet it remains equally true that to many Bolsheviks—though not to Lenin, as usual more realistic than most—the European revolution appeared not as a possibility but as a certainty. The appointment of Trotsky as Commissar for Foreign Relations and his behavior in office certainly underscore this fact. The choice of Trotsky, second only to Lenin in prestige among the leaders and the most colorful figure of the revolutionary phase, could be rationalized on the grounds that the new regime did not need diplomatic relations in the old style, but an effective spokesman and propagandist for a world revolution. Trotsky himself had this oversimplified notion of his new duties: "I myself took this job so I would have more time for Party work. All there is to do is to publish the secret treaties. Then I will close the shop."[15] Among the more unsophisticated followers of the Bolshevik cause, it was widely assumed that a world revolution had begun, that Soviet Russia was simply the beginning of the revolutionary chain reaction that in a relatively short time would transform the world. If so, any regard for the niceties of diplomatic procedure was not only inconsistent with the proletarian virtue of the new rulers, but simply useless. The French, British, Italian ambassadors represented regimes that were slated for the rubbish heap of history.

The Bolsheviks' relations with foreign governments in the first weeks following their victory were thus compounded of two incongruous elements. There was the traditional approach to the embassies of the Allied (after November 7 this word should be perhaps put in quotation marks) Powers with the object of persuading them to follow the Soviet initiative as spelled out in the *Decree on Peace*. At the same time, there was what might be described as impudent baiting of the foreign governments, open declarations by the highest Bolshevik officials of their forthcoming doom at the hands of their aroused peoples, and other moves designed to irritate both the baffled ambassadors in Petrograd and their governments. The "treaties" that Trotsky had threatened to reveal as his secret weapon began to be published within two weeks of the Bolshevik coup. Their contents envisaged territorial changes, such as the prospective Russian annexation of Constantinople, that had already been public knowledge both within the country and abroad. Still, their publication was in traditional diplomatic terms a breach of faith with the powers with whom they had been concluded. The introduction to the treaties rubbed in the class character of the new Russian government and the capitalist sins of the Western Powers: "Secret diplomacy is the necessary weapon in the hands of the exploiting minority, which is compelled to exploit the majority

[15] Quoted in *The Proletarian Revolution* (Moscow), No. 10, October 1922, p. 99.

in order to subjugate it to its interests. . . . The Workers' and Peasants' Government abolishes secret diplomacy with its intrigues, codes, and lies. . . . We want a rapid overthrow of the domination of capital."[16] A document of this sort was not likely, to put it mildly, to incline the governments of France and England to recognize the Soviet regime nor to persuade them to enter into negotiations for a general peace. Thus Soviet foreign policy in the first weeks after the Revolution presents a paradoxical picture: on the one hand, there is a clear realization that peace and recognition by other states is a necessary condition for the survival of the Bolshevik regime; on the other hand, no occasion is spared to insult and irritate the outside world.

This seemingly suicidal posture had its explanation in the intoxication of some Bolshevik leaders with their victory, which had come with un-expected ease. During the first few weeks it appeared as if the govern-ments of France, Germany, and Great Britain were in fact no more formidable than the Kadets, Mensheviks, and Socialist Revolutionaries whom the Bolsheviks had overthrown. They also had been first astounded then indignant at Bolshevik threats and abuse, but by the same token the Bolsheviks' self-assurance and impudence had paralyzed their ability to act and delivered the vast state almost painlessly (so it seemed in those first feverish weeks) into Bolshevik hands. This exhilaration clearly went beyond Lenin's own rather cautious revolutionary optimism. Trot-sky (and the very first foreign documents bear the imprint of his personal style) sought to awe the foreign governments by his propaganda and invective, just as before November he had mesmerized the Petrograd Soviet and mass meetings with his oratory. And, as we shall see, Trotsky's faith in propaganda and gesture and the ripeness of revolutionary feel-ing among the enemy was to survive the negotiations in Brest Litovsk and to culminate in the fatuous "neither peace nor war" formula.

Amidst the impassioned dreams of a revolution seizing the German army and then sweeping west, the new rulers had to turn their attention to the prosaic and concrete task of securing an armistice. The *Decree on Peace*, as might have been expected by the more realistic Bolsheviks (first of all, Lenin), did not find any response among Russia's allies. England, France, and the Associated Powers were not going to recognize the Bolshevik regime, which they considered a bunch of adventurers and anarchists, if not outright German agents. Still less were they going to consider sitting at the same table with the usurpers and negotiating for a general peace. In the West, it was widely hoped that the Bolshevik government could not last and that the "healthy elements" in Russian life, mainly the army, would recapture control. The representatives of

---

[16] *Documents on the Foreign Policy of the U.S.S.R.*, I (Moscow, 1957), 3.

the Allies to the Russian high command protested with the acting commander-in-chief of what remained of the armed forces, General Dukhonin,
against any attempt at a separate peace as a violation of a solemn undertaking of the Russian government on September 5, 1914, not to negotiate
with the enemy except in conjunction with its allies. This hopelessly
legalistic step nevertheless aroused great apprehension in Bolshevik
circles: Mogilev (the seat of the high command) might become the residence of a rival regime (indeed, an attempt had been made in that
direction immediately following the events in Petrograd); some army
units might still be persuaded to set out against Lenin's government. This
fear explains the haste with which the Bolshevik regime ordered General
Dukhonin to enter into immediate negotiations with the Germans, and
when Dukhonin refused he was dismissed by telegraph. His replacement
was a Bolshevik ensign, Krylenko.[17] But even before the new commander-
in-chief could reach his headquarters, the government notified all the
army units to enter into armistice negotiations, if need be on their own.
The radio message from Lenin proclaimed: "Soldiers, the fate of peace is
in your hands. . . . Let the units at the front elect immediately the plenipotentiaries for formal negotiations for armistice with the enemy."[18] This
step was sure to destroy what little remained of the discipline and fighting
capacity of the Russian army. The Bolshevik leaders were throwing away
what in any peace negotiation is the strongest bargaining card: the threat
of renewing hostilities if your opponents' terms are unreasonable. But
for the moment they viewed the army, unless utterly demoralized, as a
greater threat to their power and hence to the prospects of a world
revolution than the Germans.

The discordant elements of the Soviet peace offensive began to become
unravelled when on December 2 the Russian delegations reached the
headquarters of the German Eastern Front Command in Brest Litovsk.
The very opening of negotiations with the Germans meant abandoning those
two major promises made by the Bolsheviks before they seized power:
that they would not negotiate separately with the enemy (indeed, accusations to that effect had been rejected by the Bolsheviks as slander); and
that they would seek negotiations with the German people and not with
representatives of the German Emperor. On the first count the Bolsheviks

[17] Thus, the command of a still vast army was entrusted to the man with
the lowest grade of officer. There were officers of high rank, including some
generals, who were known to be sympathetic to the Bolshevik cause, but
Krylenko was a Bolshevik of long standing. And his personal insignificance
offered a guarantee that he could not use the army against the government.
The leaders were very conscious of historical precedents from the French
Revolution and were on their guard against potential Napoleons.

[18] *Documents on the Foreign Policy of the U.S.S.R.*, I, 20.

could claim that their efforts to interest the Western Allies in negotiations had been repulsed. On the second the premise of many Bolshevik leaders up to the very end of the negotiations remained that the very initiation of peace talks would lead to demoralization of the German army and its infection by the virus of revolution.

As it was, the negotiations opened under colorful and—in the history of modern diplomacy—unprecedented circumstances. The Russian delegation had as its ranking personalities Adolf Yoffe, Kamenev, and Gregory Sokolnikov, all three of them Bolsheviks of long standing, chosen as much for their fluency in German and some acquaintance with the outside world as for the fact that they, unlike such Bolshevik stars as Zinoviev and Trotsky, not to mention Lenin, could be spared from Petrograd in those hectic first weeks of the revolutionary rule. The Left Socialist Revolutionaries, then allied with the Bolsheviks, were represented by Mme. Anastasia Bitsenko, a renowned terrorist of the Tsarist period. Since none of the above could qualify as a genuine proletarian, the delegation was complemented by a worker, peasant, sailor, and soldier, all of them more or less at sea as to what was going on. This incongruous team was completed by technical experts, who of course were taken from the ranks of old Tsarist officers. One of them, Admiral V. Altvater, bore a striking resemblance to Emperor Nicholas II.

As against this motley assembly, the German delegation was composed solely of military officers. Its titular head might have indeed epitomized the old aristocratic Europe that had died in 1914: he was Field Marshal Prince Leopold of Bavaria, son-in-law of Emperor Francis Joseph of Austria. In fact, as in the case of most German armies headed by royal personages, actual authority on the German side was exercised by the aged prince's chief of staff, Major General Max Hoffmann, one of the outstanding strategic minds of the German army and a longtime expert on Russia.

The picturesque details of the Brest Litovsk negotiations have often been described in terms of the clash of two worlds—one of the dying old Europe, and the other the new rising revolutionary world represented by the uncouth Soviet delegates.[19] What is of interest to us, however, is the development of Soviet foreign policy, the course of which, as we shall see, was for long to be influenced by the lessons of Brest Litovsk. The Russian proposals as stated by the head of the delegation, Yoffe, envisaged

[19] The most interesting descriptions are by John W. Wheeler-Bennett, *The Forgotten Peace* (New York, 1939), and by one of the technical experts attached to the Soviet delegation, Lt. Col. John (*sic*) H. Fokke, *On the Stage and Behind the Scenes of the Brest Tragicomedy*, in the *Archive of the Russian Revolution* (in Russian), XX (Berlin, 1930).

three main items: (1) an armistice for six months; (2) the evacuation by the Germans of the islands they occupied in the Gulf of Riga, but not of the rest of the Russian territories taken by the Central Powers; and (3) a pledge by the Germans that no troops were to be transferred from the Eastern Front in the course of negotiations. Granted the condition of the Russian army, the proposals were brazen enough, and, as Hoffmann observed, they would have sounded logical coming from a victorious party and not one suing for peace. He in return agreed to an armistice of twenty-eight days' duration, automatically prolonged unless one week's notice was given; rejected absolutely point 2; and on point 3 agreed to guarantee that no units would be shifted to the Western Front or rested except ones that were already being shifted or under orders to move. After Yoffe's trip to Petrograd, the armistice was signed on December 15 along the lines indicated by Hoffmann. An additional and unusual provision was the German agreement that on every sector of the front there be organized special centers where a limited number of Russian soldiers could have discussions with a number of Germans.[20] This was the famous fraternization proposal, the Germans' agreement to which could be hailed by the Soviets as a great victory and the means of sowing revolutionary propaganda amidst the enemy soldiers. And, to be sure, copies of a special German-language Bolshevik newspaper and other propaganda materials soon began to be circulated within the German army.

The German agreement to the fraternization proposals and their pledge not to transfer troops have been seen by some historians as showing incredible naïveté. Yet the non-transfer agreement cost the Germans nothing: because of its phrasing it could always be claimed that the troops being sent westward had been so ordered before the armistice was signed. On the issue of fraternization, Hoffmann was confident—and by and large his confidence was borne out (the collapse of the German army began much later)—that supervised contacts between the Russian agitators and the German soldiers would not do too much harm. It is still true that the German negotiators were unusually solicitous to spare the enemy's face, something for which the German military even in the pre-Hitler era had not been unusually famous. Why? The answer is obvious. Hoffmann and the German general staff were undoubtedly aware how precarious was the Bolsheviks' hold on power. They knew also that the mere initiation of peace talks by the regime, under conditions specifically repudiated by Lenin before the Revolution, was violently opposed in many quarters. A brutal ultimatum might have brought an overthrow of the Bolshevik regime and a renewal of hostilities. That the Russian army could now resist effectively was out of the question, but the vast spaces of Russia

[20] Wheeler-Bennett, *op. cit.*, p. 93.

would devour the German soldiers needed on the Western Front. Also, the Central Powers badly wanted grain and other commodities which a speedy peace could bring them. The Bolsheviks were their best bet for such a peace; their overthrow might be a calamity.

And, indeed, the Bolshevik leaders hastened to make excellent propaganda use of the German concessions. In their speeches, Trotsky and Kamenev proclaimed that the peace negotiations would resemble a trial. The Central Powers would be in the dock, the Russian delegation would play the role of the accuser on behalf of the world proletariat. If the Germans failed to agree to reasonable conditions, the Bolsheviks would refuse to sign and would call for a holy war against imperialism in which the German soldiers would join their Russian brothers. No such bravado was heard in the speeches of the head of the Soviet regime. As he was to demonstrate subsequently, Lenin had few illusions about the outcome of negotiations.

The actual peace negotiations began at Brest Litovsk on December 22. The Russian delegation was again headed by Yoffe. It was now facing the delegations of the four Central Powers, for, in addition to Germany, Austria-Hungary, Bulgaria, and Turkey were also represented. The German mission was headed by Foreign Secretary Baron von Kühlmann, a mercurial Bavarian, keenly aware that peace in the east was almost as urgent for his country as for the Bolsheviks. This awareness was more than shared by the Austrian Minister, Count Czernin, a *grand seigneur* in the pre-1914 Austrian style, whose nervousness reflected his country's dependence on Germany and a consciousness that the multinational empire of the Habsburgs was already showing signs of the impending break-up. The Turks and Bulgarians were there for show. The decisive voice was going to be that of Germany, and even within the German delegation the final word was going to be that not of its titular head but of General Hoffmann, who on one occasion, with scant regard for the constitutional conventions, declared that he represented the German army, the decisive factor in the negotiations. The opening phrases of the conference were taken, however, from the vocabulary of nineteenth-century diplomacy. Prince Leopold welcomed the delegates of "the mighty Soviet republic" with old-world courtesy. Not to be outdone, the Turk Ibrahim Hakki Pasha congratulated the Soviet government for "having had the courage to proclaim humanitarian principles to the whole world."[21]

The harsh realities of the situation soon emerged from behind the courteous diplomatic formulas. Yoffe's proposal—peace without annexations and indemnities—was accepted in principle by the Central Powers on December 25. This created premature joy in the Bolshevik delegation,

[21] *The Peace Negotiations at Brest Litovsk* (Moscow, 1920), I, 3.

who for all their bravado could have hardly believed that Russia would get out of the war without any territorial losses or that the German army would evacuate the occupied territory and withdraw to the pre-war frontiers. But this joy vanished when at the urging of Hoffmann the Central Powers "explained" that since the area occupied by the Germans was not ethnically Russian, their separation from the Russian state could hardly be considered annexation. All that the Germans proposed to do, explained Hoffmann jovially to the abashed Yoffe, was to put in practice the Soviets' own and oft-repeated principle of national self-determination. Hence, Russian Poland and the Baltic areas should be entitled to independence. In modern parlance, the Germans were proposing to carve out satellite states from the body of the former Russian empire. Though the proposals were not nearly so far-reaching as the ones eventually agreed to by the Bolsheviks, when the Ukraine was added to the list of "liberated" states, the news fell like a thunderbolt. One of the delegates, the originator of the Marxist school of Russian historiography, Pokrovsky, broke down and wept. It was the first intimation that deep beneath the internationalist and socialist phraseology of the Bolsheviks lay their unconscious *Russian* nationalism. The first phase of the negotiations was concluded. After a concert and a gala dinner given by the Germans, the conference adjourned until January 9, and the main plenipotentiaries returned to their capitals.

The second round of negotiations which opened in January saw changes in the composition of the Russian delegation. The most striking was the replacement of the fumbling Yoffe as the head of the Russian plenipotentiaries with Trotsky. The Commissar for Foreign Relations still had an unrealistic view as to the eventual outcome of the negotiations, but he was a man of resolve and ability, and even the ex-Tsarist officers attached to the delegation and basically hostile to anything connected with Bolshevism gave in their recollections a grudging praise to the co-maker of the Revolution and the Soviet state. Trotsky brought with him Karl Radek, a brilliant and witty Polish-born Bolshevik. He had rendered the Bolsheviks important services before November in connection with the transfer of German subsidies to them (he was then stationed in Stockholm). Now, even though his Russian was still quite poor, he was a member of the delegation and its expert on Polish affairs. Indeed, he and another Polish Bolshevik, Bobinski, were to claim that they represented the Polish socialist movement. The future of non-Russian territories in the former Russian empire was going to be the crucial issue of the peace, and thus the Bolsheviks were eager to fortify themselves with the alleged representatives of those nationalities—who would assert their nations' desire to live in communion with Soviet Russia. Thus, in Kiev, several Ukrainian parties had just proclaimed an independent Ukrainian republic

(though its future relationship to Russia had not yet been determined),
and the Ukrainian nationalists sent their own delegates to Brest. To
offset this move, Trotsky brought with him his "own" Ukrainians who
were to argue the Bolshevik point of view. And there was also a Latvian
within the Soviet delegation.

Trotsky's arrival changed the whole tone of the proceedings. At the
first session, the Russian delegates who had initially expected to be
snubbed by the representatives of imperialism, had succumbed somewhat
to German sociability and had behaved less than discreetly.[22] Now, to
avoid such unseemly incidents and outpourings of undiplomatic frankness
over refreshments, Trotsky forbade fraternization between the delegations
and ordered the Russians to take their meals alone.

Trotsky proved to be a skillful and dilatory negotiator. His main task
for the moment was to prolong negotiations, for their immediate conclusion either in an unfavorable peace or in a renewal of war was bound
to spell ruin to the Bolshevik power. The Constituent Assembly was about
to meet in Petrograd. The Bolsheviks were in a minority, and they were
in considerable fear as to their ability to suppress the Assembly without
provoking a countercoup. Were they to appear before the Constituent
Assembly with a humiliating peace or with the German army on the march,
they would almost undoubtedly share the fate of Kerensky.

This consideration explains Trotsky's behavior on the Ukrainian question. To the amazement of the German negotiators, he chose at first not
to question the credentials of the Ukrainian nationalists: "Our government
does not accept it as legitimate to question the character and powers of
those nations which evidence their desire to independence." And when
Kühlmann, not trusting his ears, inquired whether the delegation of the
Ukrainian Council (as the self-proclaimed Ukrainian government called
itself) should be considered a fully independent delegation or a part of
the Russian one, Trotsky reached the heights of liberalism on the national
question: "Since the Ukrainian delegation appears here as a completely
independent delegation and since we in our statement have accepted its
participation in the negotiations without limiting it in any way, nobody
here even raises the question of turning the Ukrainian delegation into
a part of the Russian one."[23]

At the same time that he was making these declarations, Trotsky was
repeating somewhat nervously that the whole problem of delimiting the

---

[22] If Fokke is to be believed, Yoffe and Kamenev, on their visit to Warsaw,
supposedly to inspect Russian prisoners of war, let themselves be conducted by
German officers to nightclubs and similar fleshpots.

[23] *The Peace Negotiations at Brest Litovsk*, I, 152.

frontiers between an independent or autonomous Ukraine and Russia was not quite "ripe." The final word about the nature of relations between Russia and the Ukraine was to be said by the Ukrainian nation, which had not yet spoken. The Bolsheviks were in the process of forming their own Soviet Ukrainian government, which in due time was to chase out the Ukrainian Council by armed force. But the time for such a coup had not come. Both Lenin and Trotsky had their attention fixed on the Constituent Assembly, due to meet on January 18. And so for ten days Trotsky conducted his dilatory tactics. Every point raised by his opponents led to a lengthy peroration by Trotsky. The Soviet delegation had no reservations about the right of non-Russian nationalities to secede, but how could the Poles, Letts, Ukrainians, etc., declare their will freely without a referendum taken *after* the German and Austrian armies had evacuated those territories? Though the fate of the Bolshevik regime hung by a thin thread, Trotsky was perceptive enough not to show submissiveness in front of the enemy. General Hoffmann's complaint that the Bolsheviks were trying to demoralize his soldiers was answered loftily: Soviet Russia believed in freedom of press and speech, and the Bolshevik government could not be held responsible for the fact that some people and papers issued on its territory incited the German soldiers to mutiny. He was passionate on behalf of the oppressed nations. The grievances of the Hindus and the Irish were eloquently presented. At a subsequent session, Trotsky took notice of the events in an area that was to attract the world's attention many years later: there was nationalist trouble in Annam, and the French had to replace the emperor of that faraway country.

On the German side the military was getting impatient. It was at this point that General Hoffmann blurted out that he represented the German army, which was growing weary of the Russian evasions—the occasion for a constitutional enquiry on Trotsky's part: was the German army independent of the civil authorities? This led to some embarrassed explanations by Kühlmann.

Trotsky's tactics could not have succeeded except for a division of opinion within the Central Powers. The Austrian government felt that it needed peace and that unless it could obtain grain shipments from the Ukraine, famine and then revolution would break out in Vienna. The civilian representatives on the German side were in disagreement with their military leaders, who were bent on stripping Russia of vast territories under the guise of national self-determination. But the game could not continue indefinitely. Trotsky began to formulate his "neither war nor peace" plan, and the Russians were soon to break off the negotiations, at the same time announcing that they would not conduct any military operations. On January 18 Hoffmann presented the map that spelled out the German claims. According to instructions from Petrograd, Trotsky requested and received a ten-day adjournment of negotiations to consult his government.

On the day of the adjournment, the Constituent Assembly met in its first and only session. As foreseen, the clear majority in the Assembly belonged to the Socialist Revolutionaries. The Bolsheviks had managed to poll about one-fourth of the votes, garnered mostly in the large cities; the countryside belonged to the S.R.'s. The government took elaborate precautions to prevent the Constituent Assembly from asserting its entirely legitimate claim to power. Large blocs of deputies (such as those representing 2 million voters for the Kadets) had been banned in advance as representing counterrevolutionary elements. Petrograd and the place of deliberations of the Assembly itself were filled with armed sailors. Despite the conciliatory tone of the speeches of Socialist Revolutionary leaders like Victor Chernov, who had been elected the president of the Assembly, Lenin gave instructions to the sailors not to allow the sittings to be prolonged, and at 4 o'clock in the morning of January 19 the only freely elected body in Russian history dispersed, never to reconvene. There was hardly any attempt to defend what was on paper the sovereign representative of the Russian people. Those armed units in the capital and environs which showed some disposition to fight were discouraged by the pusillanimous attitude of the Socialist Revolutionary and Menshevik leaders. Once again the Bolshevik gamble succeeded. Their socialist opponents were once more exposed as men without resolution, as "people from the other world," as Lenin contemptuously called them.[24]

Two elements of the dispersal of the Constituent Assembly deserve our attention, as they bear directly on the negotiations in Brest. The armed units employed in clearing the delegates and in policing the capital against the feared repercussions were composed largely of apolitical soldiers and sailors or ones with anarchist affiliations. Their temporary allegiance to the Bolsheviks was based primarily on the Bolsheviks' promise to reach a "democratic peace" and the allegations that their opponents would prolong the war. Insofar as the government had any case in claiming that the Constituent Assembly did not represent the feelings of the majority of the Russian people, it was based on the claim that in voting for Socialist Revolutionaries the peasant masses were for the most part unaware that the party had split and that the Left S.R.'s were now allies of the Bolsheviks and represented in the government. After the signing of the Treaty of Brest Litovsk, the Left S.R.'s were to abandon the government in protest against the peace and clamor for a revolutionary war against the Germans.

[24] Lenin, *Works* (4th ed., Moscow, 1946), XXVI, 392.

Thus it was extremely fortunate for the Bolsheviks that at the time they chased out the Assembly, the outsiders were far from realizing how the negotiations were proceeding and what the future contents of the peace treaty were.[25]

But even within the Bolshevik Party the problem of the peace conditions was to lead to an almost fatal split. Lenin's position that a peace, any peace, no matter how hard, had to be signed, in order to gain a breathing spell for the Soviet power, was opposed by the majority of the Party dignitaries and, insofar as they knew the details, by the mass of rank-and-file members. The conditions as they could now be envisaged amounted to the loss of Russia's most advanced territories and her granary, the Ukraine, and the pushing back of her frontiers to what they had been at the end of the sixteenth century. How could the Bolsheviks survive the revulsion of the feelings were those facts to become known? Not only were an "independent" Ukraine, Kurland, Finland, etc., bound to become German satellites, but the same fate would be inflicted on Russia. The Bolsheviks would not only perish but, in view of all their previous bold talk about "the people's peace," "putting the imperialists in the dock," and so on, go down in disgrace and ridicule. The majority of the Bolshevik leaders cried for the continuation of the war. Bukharin, their spokesman, urged the proclamation of "revolutionary war." Trotsky was more realistic, but even he could not see how the Bolshevik government could subscribe to the ruinous treaty. He now propounded his "neither peace nor war" formula according to which Russia would not sign a treaty but would stop fighting and demobilize. There was at least some hope that the German soldier would refuse to fight were he confronted with an appeal to class solidarity with his Russian brethren who were laying down arms. Lenin's position received some important support from the chief Bolshevik organizer, Jacob Sverdlov, and, after some initial hesitations, from Stalin. The latter spelled out the brutal fact. "The position of Comrade Trotsky represents no policy at all. . . . In October we talked about the sacred revolutionary war because we were promised [Stalin should have said "we promised"] that one word, peace, would bring about a revolution in the West. But that has not come to pass."[26] Lenin pleaded that the army was in full disintegration. It would be incapable of effecting a retreat. To reject the enemy's conditions under either Bukharin's or Trotsky's formula was to fly in the face of reality.

[25] A follower of the events from March 1917 to the end of the Civil War cannot fail to be impressed by the miraculous sequence of good luck the Bolsheviks enjoyed, the amazing number of contingencies where a slightly different twist could have spelled the irretrievable ruin of their cause.

[26] *The Protocols of the Central Committee, August 1917–February 1918* (Moscow, 1929), p. 171.

On January 18 a large gathering of Bolshevik dignitaries was polled on the issue of peace. Bukharin's formula received the majority, 32 votes; Trotsky's "neither peace nor war" position was supported by 16; Lenin's view that a peace treaty must be signed was supported by only 15. After considerable maneuvering, Lenin was able to secure support for the continuation of negotiations. He also concluded a private "treaty" with Trotsky: if the negotiations could not be protracted indefinitely, let Trotsky spring his formula. But if it proved unavailing, he was no longer to oppose Lenin's position. Armed with these instructions, Trotsky left for the negotiations.

When the peace conference opened again on January 30, the Russian position was quite different from what it had been at the adjournment two weeks before. The nightmarish possibility of the Constituent Assembly challenging Bolshevik power had faded away. In the Ukraine, Bolshevik forces had reoccupied most of the territory previously lost to the Ukrainian nationalists. On the other side of the ledger was the fact that Trotsky's impassioned oratory on behalf of oppressed Hindus, Irish, Muslims, etc., had by now lost much of its luster. The Bolsheviks had dispersed the freely elected representatives of the Russian people. In the Ukraine, where the Bolsheviks had received but 10 per cent of the vote to the Constituent Assembly, they were putting down (with the help of mostly Russian military units) the native Ukrainian government, whose legitimacy only a few weeks before Trotsky had so piously refused to question. At the same time, militarily the Bolsheviks' position was still desperate. They could terrorize the Constituent Assembly, evict the feeble Ukrainian nationalists, but it was out of the question that they could face a regular army. This fact was underscored by the Rumanian troops' occupation of Bessarabia, to which the Soviet government could offer no resistance whatsoever.

The Russians decided to brazen out the unenviable situation. There had been some strike activity in Austria-Hungary and Germany, and again the vision of a European revolution began to dance in their heads. The Central Powers' representatives were haughtily told that the real representatives of the Polish and Ukrainian nations were now within the Bolshevik delegation. The impudent Radek infuriated General Hoffmann by informing him that he could also speak on behalf of those German soldiers who came from Prussian Poland. As to the Ukraine, Trotsky proclaimed that the problem was solved. There was only one legitimate government there, the Soviet one. The Ukrainian nationalists' recent proclamation of complete independence of Russia and their subsequent activities were of no interest to the conference. The only territory over which the representatives of the Ukrainian Council could still exercise authority was that of the accommodations assigned to them in Brest Litovsk.

Taunted beyond endurance, the Ukrainian nationalists replied in a
language that was as yet new to diplomacy. What was the Bolshevik
design? asked one of them. It is, as the French saying has it, "Slander,
calumniate, some of it will always stick." Trotsky's argument was a tissue
of lies:

> The Bolshevik regime has proclaimed the principle of self-determination
> only to fight more resolutely against the introduction of this principle
> into life. The government of the Bolsheviks which is chasing out the
> Constituent Assembly, this government which is based upon the bayonets
> of the mercenary soldiers, will never adopt the just principle of self-
> determination because it knows that not only the regions like the
> Ukraine, Don, Caucasus, and others don't recognize it as their govern-
> ment but the Russian nation as well.[27]

This impassioned argument embarrassed Trotsky very deeply. In view
of the recent events in Petrograd, he was in no position to give the lie
to the Ukrainians. "His" Ukrainians were clearly fraudulent as representatives of the Ukrainian nation.[28] The Central Powers now declared that
they recognized the government of Kiev—that is, the Ukrainian nationalists—and on February 8 Germany and Austria signed a separate treaty
with it. German and Austrian troops were soon to chase out the Ukrainian
Bolsheviks and re-establish the authority of the Ukrainian Council, thus
for the time being establishing the separation of this fertile country from
Russia and securing for the Central Powers what they hoped would be
vast quantities of foodstuffs.[29]

The negotiations dragged on for some days. Trotsky was encouraged
by the still continuing difference of opinion between the Germans and the
Austrians, and by the willingness of Kühlmann to allow a face-saving
for the Bolsheviks by releasing some of the German-occupied territory.
But the German high command and its representative, Hoffmann, held
the upper hand. The latter was implacable. When in the commission on
territorial delimitations Pokrovsky quoted statistics to prove that a region
claimed for "independent" Lithuania was predominantly Byelorussian,
Hoffmann answered with military logic: "I trust Mr. Pokrovsky knows
that by using statistics one can prove anything."[30]

[27] *The Peace Negotiations at Brest Litovsk,* I, 152.

[28] One of them was a Russian. The other one had the unfortunate name
Shahray, which in Ukrainian means scoundrel or rogue.

[29] In their eagerness to please the Ukrainians, the Germans and the Austrians
made one tactical error. They granted to the infant republic a former district
of Russian Poland which the Poles felt was theirs on the basis of both history
and population. That incensed the Polish nationalists and destroyed any hopes
the Central Powers had of recruiting a large Polish army to fight on their side.

[30] *The Peace Negotiations at Brest Litovsk,* I, 204.

The negotiations might have continued indefinitely, but Trotsky could have no illusions as to the eventual outcome and he was eager to spring his famous formula for "neither war nor peace." And so on February 10, he read to the dumbfounded enemy delegates a declaration that Russia was proclaiming the end of the war *without* signing a peace. After the embarrassing Ukrainian episode, he had finally recaptured the initiative, and he threw in the teeth of the representatives of the old world the bold defiance of the new:

> We are leaving the war. We notify all the nations and governments of it. . . . We no longer desire to participate in this purely imperialist war, where the requirements of the exploiting class are paid for in human blood. . . . In the expectation . . . of this near moment when the oppressed working class of all nations will, as has happened in Russia, take power in their own hands, we take our army and nation out of the war. . . . The governments of Germany and Austria want to rule nations and lands. Let them do it openly.[31]

In any subsequent conflict in the twentieth century, such a declaration would have been received with amusement. But to people like Czernin and Kühlmann, brought up in the traditions of nineteenth-century diplomacy, it was a most irregular and baffling move. They asked for a clarification, but Trotsky refused to negotiate further. He added a bit wistfully that he was "deeply convinced" that the nations of Germany and Austria-Hungary would not allow their armies to advance. The Russian delegation departed for home.

Trotsky's belief that the Germans would not dare to start an offensive was unfeigned. Most people in the Bolshevik circles shared his optimism. But Lenin was deeply skeptical. A few days later, he was to give a somber appraisal of the German military machine: "Until now our enemies have been miserable and pathetic . . . an idiot Romanov . . . windbag Kerensky . . . a handful of military students and bourgeoisie. Now we have a giant against us."[32] Had Russia dealt only with Austria-Hungary, Trotsky's formula might have succeeded. But the German armies were still capable of exertion. After all, in the spring of 1918 a German offensive was almost to involve the Western Allies in an irretrievable catastrophe. There were people on the German side—mainly in the diplomatic apparatus— who were against a renewal of hostilities; their apprehension springing from the fear that an advance would topple the Bolsheviks and possibly bring back into power anti-German elements. But the German army was eager for an advance and did not anticipate any trouble. On February 16 the Bolshevik authorities were informed that the Germans were going to

[31] *Ibid.*, 207–8.
[32] Lenin, *Works*, XXVII, 43.

resume military activities. On the 18th, the advance began and Hoffmann's most sanguine hopes were surpassed. As Lenin had anticipated, the Russians were incapable even of retreating. Thousands of them surrendered to a handful of Germans. Nobody even thought of mining railway tracks. In the midst of the Russian winter, the German army advanced 150 miles in five days on some sectors—a remarkable pace for infantry even in peacetime and under ideal conditions. A few more days and they would be before Petrograd.

Beginning on February 17, the Bolshevik Central Committee met in continuous session. Lenin's insistence that a peace must be signed was still being resisted. And it was not beyond question whether it was not too late even for that. The ease with which the Germans were advancing was so fantastic that it would have been entirely logical for them to desire to dictate the treaty in Petrograd. On February 18, Lenin received by a bare majority an authorization to ask the Germans for a conclusion of peace. But no immediate answer was forthcoming from Brest, while the German armies were still marching. On the 21st, the Council of Commissars issued an appeal to the population to be ready for a revolutionary war and for the defense of Petrograd. But the language of the appeal reflected panic rather than defiance. It is notable, however, that the phraseology of nationalism began to steal back into the Soviet declarations: "The Socialist Fatherland is in danger." Equally significant was the first systematic attempt to ascertain what help they could obtain from the Western Allies if they had to continue in the war.

The latter move was another milestone in the history of Soviet foreign diplomacy. Only on February 10 had the Soviets voided all foreign debts, a step which strongly affected the French and (to a lesser degree) the British governments and private bondholders of Tsarist loans. This was in accordance with the pledges made long before the Revolution by Russian revolutionaries of all complexions. But the step would have hardly been taken if the Bolsheviks expected that within a few days they might be seeking French and British help. The idea of seeking help even when in mortal danger from French and British plutocrats was distasteful to most Bolsheviks. At the February 22 meeting of the Central Committee, when some very tentative proposals in that direction were discussed, Bukharin (still clamoring for a revolutionary war against Germany) combatted any idea of seeking help from the West. One member exclaimed, "Having seized power we have forgotten about the world revolution!" Lenin struck what was going to be a recurrent motif of Soviet diplomacy: "Please add my vote to those who are in favor of receiving food and weapons from the Anglo-French imperialist robbers." The motion passed. Bukharin burst into tears.

Contacts with various Allied representatives continued up to the final

ratification of the Treaty of Brest Litovsk. Since the Allied Powers had
not recognized the Soviet government, the Bolshevik exchanges with their
ambassadors were infrequent and rather acerbic. (When the Germans
renewed their offensive, the British and French missions left Petrograd
on February 24, soon followed by the Americans. Eventually, most Allied
diplomats got stuck in the dreary Russian provincial hole of Vologda,
though some left for home through Finland.) Actual contact with Soviet
officials had been for some time and would continue to be in the hands not
of the ambassadors or regular members of the Allied diplomatic corps
but of others. On the American side, Raymond Robins, officially representing the Red Cross, kept up a connection with Trotsky. A French
lawyer, Jacques Sadoul (later on to become a Communist), and a former
British consular official, Bruce Lockhart, performed the same functions
for their own governments.[33] Up to the very ratification of the treaty,
these informal representatives of the Allied Powers believed intermittently
that the Bolsheviks, if they could be guaranteed concrete help by the
Allies, were ready to renew the war rather than to sign the peace. The
evidence, though confused, suggests strongly that in this belief they were
led on by Soviet officials, most specifically by Trotsky, with whom most
of their contacts were. On March 5, Trotsky delivered to Robins a list
of questions enquiring what help the United States would be willing and
able to deliver should the war be renewed. As we shall see, by that date
there was no question in Lenin's mind that the peace must be ratified.

The question must be raised as to why the Bolsheviks led the Allied
representatives on, to the extent that they became and remained convinced
that responsibility for Brest Litovsk must rest partly on the Allies' lack of
understanding for and sympathy with the Bolsheviks. Robins especially
believed that as late as March 16, the day of the final debate on ratification
before the Congress of Soviets, Lenin would have opted for a renewal of

---

[33] Those contacts are meticulously listed in George Kennan, *Russia Leaves
the War* (Princeton, 1956), and Warth, *op. cit.* In general, these unofficial
observers tended to be much more sympathetic to the Bolsheviks and more hopeful about the possibility of turning the Soviet government toward the Allies than
their superiors at home. Their optimistic prognosis was based on two premises,
one undoubtedly correct, the other less so. They justifiably saw that the Bolsheviks or at least their leaders were at the moment the only political movement in Russia with the ability and sense of direction to master events and
establish the rudiments of effective government. They were not merely, as many
in London and Paris believed, "German agents" or "Jewish adventurers." By
the same token, they persuaded themselves, especially Robins and Sadoul, that
Lenin and Trotsky were essentially pro-Ally and anti-German. They failed to
realize the deep animosity of the Bolshevik leaders toward *all* capitalist powers,
and that for Lenin at least, Great Britain as the mainstay of the capitalist world
order was enemy number one.

hostilities had there been a favorable response from Washington.[34] In retrospect, many historians have blamed the Soviet Union's hostility to the capitalist world largely on this rebuff received when in a moment of mortal peril it sought help from Washington, London, and Paris.

The Soviet approaches to the Allied regimes—which to Lenin were at least as loathsome as those of imperial Germany or Austria—can be traced to two apprehensions. One was that, even with a treaty with Germany signed, there was nothing to prevent the German army from pushing on to Petrograd and even to Moscow and establishing there a puppet *Russian* regime of their own. In that case, the almost unthinkable step would have to be taken: a Bolshevik government in the Urals or Siberia would have to beg for Allied help and protection. The second and more constant worry continued up to the very end of the war in 1918: it was entirely consistent with their way of thinking for the Bolsheviks to imagine the warring capitalists of the two camps composing their differences and settling down together to the congenial task of carving up Russia's vast territories into colonies and spheres of influence. That it did *not* happen was, at least to Lenin, a real revelation as to the *real* weakness of capitalism, the utter inability of the capitalist states to work together to protect their common interests. Some years later, he talked almost incredulously about this fact: "Weak, torn apart, downtrodden Russia . . . turned out victorious . . . against the rich mighty countries which rule the world. . . . Why? . . . Because among those powers was not a shadow of unity, because all of them worked at cross purposes."[35] It was this lesson that was to be of an overwhelming importance in the evolution of Russian foreign policy. Those words of Lenin are also to be kept in mind whenever Soviet propaganda raises the specter of capitalist encirclement or alleges the West's actions between 1917 and 1921 as grounds for Soviet mistrust and hostility. But, early in 1918, the lesson of the fatal inability of the capitalist powers to compose their differences and to heed their class and national interests was still not firmly implanted in the Soviet mind. Hence their moves and investigations with the Allied representatives to find out whether there was—and if necessary to ward off—any German-Allied settlement at Russia's expense.[36]

[34] Warth, *op. cit.*, p. 240.

[35] *Second Congress of the Communist International* (stenographic report, Moscow, 1920), p. 29.

[36] Was there a possibility of such a settlement at any time? This subject is alluded to by A. J. P. Taylor in *English History 1914–45* (New York and Oxford, 1965), p. 95, who writes that Lord Milner, member of the War Cabinet 1916–18, "continued to advocate a compromise peace at Russia's expense until the conclusion of the armistice." Yet there is no evidence at all that any serious effort at negotiations in this vein was undertaken on either side. Mr. Taylor

The final stage of the Brest Litovsk drama began to unfold on February 23. To Lenin's vast relief, a reply arrived from the Germans. It was an ultimatum: forty-eight hours were given to the Russians to reopen negotiations, which in turn were not to last more than three days. To the Germans', Lenin added his own ultimatum: either the conditions would be met or he would resign from the government. Even so, the vote of the Central Committee was ambiguous: seven for Lenin's motion, four against, four abstaining. Threats were heard, from the Left Socialist Revolutionaries and from Bukharin's followers, of a *coup d'état* against Lenin. Trotsky resigned as Commissar for Foreign Relations but at Lenin's begging promised not to publicize his resignation for a while. No Bolshevik luminary was willing to go to Brest Litovsk and have his name associated with the Carthaginian peace. Finally a delegation was patched up headed by Gregory Sokolnikov and including George Chicherin. They reached Brest on March 1.

On March 3 the treaty was signed that stripped Russia of one-third of her population. The Ukraine, Finland, and her Baltic and Polish territories were wrested away. In the Caucasus, territorial concessions were made to Turkey. Three centuries of Russia's expansion were undone. Sokolnikov insisted that there should be no pretense at negotiations or "agreement." He said with dignity: "The peace about to be concluded is not the result of any agreement by both sides. This peace is dictated to us [by the enemy] with a gun in his hand."[37] But it was dignity in the face of a disaster. Nobody, perhaps not even Lenin, could believe that the Bolshevik power could for long continue after the terms of the peace became known. Should the Bolsheviks survive an internal split, they might fall prey to the nationalist fury of their own people. Should the people acquiesce, the Germans might decide to finish off the job. A few batallions would be all that was needed to occupy Petrograd, precariously close to Finland, where the German army was already assisting Finnish nationalists in ejecting the local Bolsheviks.

---

mentions also in this connection the name of Lord Haldane, a Liberal statesman who had (undeservedly) a reputation of being pro-German. The evidence in our possession would suggest at most that an idea of a peace at Russia's expense may have occurred to some people but certainly there was no organized effort in that direction. Like the charge we shall discuss later on—that appeasement in 1938–39 was designed to provoke a German attack on Russia—the story of the dark designs in 1917 makes the psychological error of crediting modern democracies with the ability of pursuing *consistently* cynical policies. The national hysteria engendered on both sides by the vast losses and the governments' propaganda was so intense that there was simply no possibility of, say, France and Germany coolly coming to an arrangement in the manner of the eighteenth-century monarchs . . . or of the Nazis and the Soviets doing so in 1939.

[37] *The Peace Negotiations at Brest Litovsk*, I, 223.

With the signing of the treaty concluded the most precarious period in the history of the Soviet state. But the peace had been signed and not yet ratified. It was an open question whether Lenin could really force his party to support the treaty. It took the utmost of his oratory and exertions to make the Petrograd Soviet vote for the peace. He brought an array of supporting facts and speakers. Zinoviev explained that the Russian army was in full flight. Its unfortunate commander Krylenko elucidated that properly speaking there was no army. Lenin again used cold logic. If the Soviet government refused to sign and withdrew to the Urals, they would gain two or three weeks. Will the opponents of the peace guarantee that a world revolution will break out in two or three weeks? The Soviet accepted the motion by the vote of 116 to 85 only because the Bolsheviks who disagreed with Lenin felt compelled to vote for the motion out of Party discipline. The Left Socialist Revolutionaries assailed their erstwhile allies with shouts of "Traitors!" "German spies!" "They have sold out the country!"[38]

The main struggle took place at the Seventh Congress of the Bolshevik Party, which assembled on March 6. It was a melancholy affair: only sixty-nine delegates were present; possibly many others who would have voted against the peace were kept out by the machinations of Lenin's faction. Even so, the debate was impassioned, and the Left Bolsheviks, headed by Bukharin, were virulent in their denunciation of the peace and of its proponents. Lenin stated the compelling reasons for signing once again: "Our country is a peasant country, disorganized by war. . . . We have no army, and here we have to exist alongside a robber country armed to the teeth. . . . The [world] revolution will not come as speedily as we expected." Already a few days had been gained, in which the government could shift to Moscow and prepare for the worst possible contingency. Lenin himself said it: he was ready to sign a peace a hundred times as bad. He mentioned the Treaty of Tilsit, when Napoleon not only dismembered Prussia but made her troops fight in his wars: "Beware that history should not bring you to that extreme form of slavery." Some Party members agonized over the treaty provision that the Bolsheviks refrain from conducting propaganda among the German soldiers. To Lenin, this was childishness. Of course true revolutionaries would not keep such pledges. If any breathing space, Lenin continued, was in fact to be granted to the Bolsheviks, it must be utilized in building a real army. "Learn to be disciplined, to introduce severe discipline; otherwise you will be under the German heel, just as you are under it now, just as unavoidably you will continue to be until the nation learns to fight, until it will have created an army which

[38] L. Stupochenko, "The Brest Days," in *The Proletarian Revolution*, No. 4, April 1923.

will not run away, but will be capable of enduring the most extreme hardships." His logic and oratory carried the day. A few days later, this time in Moscow, to which the government was shifted on March 10, the peace treaty was ratified by the Congress of Soviets, legally the highest body of the country, by a vote of 784 to 261. The opposition consisted of the Left Socialist Revolutionaries, and of the handful of Mensheviks and Right S.R.'s still tolerated in that body. The Left Communists, led by Bukharin, abstained. Official ratifications of the treaty were exchanged on March 29, 1918. With the foreign war concluded, the regime could turn its attention to the growing internal strife and civil war, and to the equally ominous problems of restoring at least the rudiments of industrial and agricultural production in what was left of the former Russian empire.

The Treaty of Brest Litovsk became a dead letter following the German defeat in 1918. On November 9, 1918, on the news, this time correct, of a revolution in Germany, Jacob Sverdlov, the official head of the Soviet state, read to the Sixth Congress of the Soviets the decree of the Council of Commissars annulling the Treaty of Brest Litovsk.[39] And it had to be repudiated by the Germans themselves when they signed the armistice agreement with the Allies on November 11 at Compiègne.

Was the Treaty of Brest Litovsk a draconic one, and its severity a contributing cause to the severe handling of the Germans at Versailles? By nineteenth-century standards, it undoubtedly was draconic. Its aim—if not in the opinion of people like Kühlmann, then in that of intermediate German bureaucrats and the high command—was to turn Central-East Europe into a German preserve (perhaps with some nominal partnership with the Austro-Hungarian empire) through a system of satellite states and economic exploitation. It was thus an anticipation of Hitler's *Lebensraum*, even though the most aggressive and brutal German officials of the era were still a different species from those of Hitler. By our recent and deplorable standards, however, the Brest Litovsk Treaty cannot be judged to have been a Carthaginian peace. The Germans did not exact unconditional surrender or install, as they well might have, a puppet government in Petrograd. The vast areas separated from Russia were not ethnically Russian. While nationally conscious Ukrainians, Letts, Lithuanians, and perhaps Poles and Finns would have been willing to live within some federal relationship with Russia, the experience of the first few weeks of the Bolsheviks' rule, and especially the ejection of the Constituent Assembly, made them opt for full independence. On the surface, at least, the treaty did not go against the principle of national determination, even though a quite different consideration was uppermost in the Germans'

[39] Wheeler-Bennett, *op. cit.*, p. 362.

mind. Insofar as the Baltic territories and Poland were concerned, the after-effects of Brest Litovsk lingered on until the Ribbentrop-Molotov Pact in 1939 and World War II made Lithuania, Estonia, and Latvia again parts of the U.S.S.R. and all of Poland a satellite. Thus 1945 saw a neat reversal in the power relations between Germany and Soviet Russia of what they had been in March 1918.

As to the future course of Soviet history, the treaty proved to be a veritable blessing in disguise to the Soviet regime. This view may be deemed extravagant, but the fact is that its terms gave the Bolshevik regime time to sink its roots in Russian soil and to deal with the remnants of internal opposition—mainly the Left S.R.'s and anarchists of various hues—without trying to cope with the militant nationalism of Poles, Finns, Ukrainians etc. When in the late spring of 1918 the Civil War flared up in the south, the Red Army was already in the process of construction, and the Bolsheviks had gained invaluable experience and self-assurance. The most serious consequence of Brest, the loss of the Ukraine, also in a strange way redounded to Soviet benefit. The German and Austro-Hungarian occupation of this fertile area and its excesses went far to discredit Ukrainian nationalism with the people and to split it into warring factions. With the Germans defeated, the reconquest of the Ukraine was facilitated by its condition during its year of "independence."

The nineteenth-century Russian historian S. M. Soloviev deemed providential Russia's defeats by the Poles and Sweden in the last quarter of the sixteenth century: "The withdrawal of the Russian nation into the remote northeast was important because it enabled the Russian state to grow strong far from Western influences."[40] Internally strengthened, Russia could re-enter the West in the eighteenth century as a Great Power. The few months gained by Brest Litovsk may well have performed a similar function for *Soviet* Russia. By the fall of 1918, the Red Army was a reality, quite different from the armed rabble of November 1917, which, as Stalin had said quite truthfully at the time, would break down and run at the first cannon shot.

The Treaty of Brest Litovsk also had profound indirect consequences on the future development and *esprit de corps* of the Bolshevik Party. Lenin's foresight was vindicated by events, and his future position was not that of *a* but *the leader* of his party, standing far above any of the other luminaries. Even after November some Bolsheviks could contemplate a Soviet regime without Lenin. When the tempestuous debates raged about the ratification, views were again expressed that no man was indispensable. But, a few months afterward, he was already recognized as the providential leader of the Party and the state without whom the regime would disinte-

---

[40] S. M. Soloviev, *Collected Works* (St. Petersburg, n.d.), p. 3.

grate. Until his fatal illness in the fall of 1922, he was to be capable by his sheer moral superiority to enforce the most unpopular policy upon his followers. Conversely, Trotsky's star was never to shine so brightly as it did between November and the signing of Brest Litovsk. Then, he had been a co-maker of the Revolution; when people wanted to say "Soviet government" they often said "Lenin and Trotsky." For all his dazzling performance as war minister, Trotsky was never to recapture that standing. Many of his colleagues were to feel that through his vanity, his "neither war nor peace" formula had almost brought disaster upon the Soviet state. He compounded his sins when, with his policy exposed as hollow, he refused to remain as commissar for foreign relations. Some of the threads of the tragic fate that was to overtake this brilliant man are already visible at the time of Brest. Another Soviet luminary, Bukharin, was also never able to erase the memory of his foolish clamoring for a bare-handed "revolutionary war" against the Germans. For all his future Party positions and ideological role, Bukharin was never to be trusted with a government position, was never to be considered seriously for the top position. Conversely, those people with a coarser moral and intellectual fiber who still stuck with Lenin—Zinoviev, Stalin, Sverdlov—gained in the eyes of their leader and of the followers.

In terms of the size of this study, the crowded events of the few months November 1917–March 1918 have been described at disproportionate length. Yet no event in the history of Soviet foreign policy until the outbreak of the dispute with Communist China was so significant, so pregnant with future developments as the crisis over the signing of the Treaty of Brest Litovsk. It marked the end of the age of innocence as far as the Bolsheviks were concerned. They went into the negotiations as world revolutionaries; they emerged as men solicitous mainly about their own state and power. The fundamental steps toward "socialism in one country" and peaceful coexistence had already been taken. November marked the birth of the Bolshevik Revolution. But the signing of the humiliating and costly treaty at Brest Litovsk marked the real beginning of the Soviet state.

III

THE FIRST STEPS: 1918–21

1. *Civil War and Intervention*

The history of the Soviet Union between 1918 and 1921 centered around three developments: the Civil War, foreign intervention, and the attempt to export revolution that finally crystallized in the formation and activities of the Third Communist International. The period is one of a mixture of the old and the new. Russia as yet cannot be classified as a totalitarian country: remnants of the Mensheviks and S.R.'s are semi-tolerated by the regime into 1921; there is sporadically a vigorous opposition to the regime's policies within the Communist Party. Yet, at the same time, terror is occasionally rampant and directed not only against outright enemies of the Soviet regime. The government, in its effort to restore the economy and prosecute the war, has recourse to a variety of drastic and doctrinaire policies that go under the name of War Communism; yet, at the same time, there are already hints of the future toleration of private enterprise which will be called the New Economic Policy. The dream of an immediate and sweeping European revolution does not die down until 1920, but from Brest Litovsk on, the government plays increasingly the traditional game of diplomacy, based on the assumption of a fairly long coexistence of the Soviet state with capitalist powers. The main and rising motif—muting the theme of soviets springing up in Berlin and

Vienna, if not Paris and London—is one of the preservation of the Soviet state from its domestic enemies, from epidemics and famine, and from the frightful destruction and chaos of the economy. At one of the lowest points of his government's fortunes, when the regime was still being ground down by the Treaty of Brest and the Allies' intervention had just begun with the Japanese landing in Vladivostok on April 4, 1918, the new Foreign Relations Commissar, George Chicherin, expressed pathetically the regime's weakness and yet its proud expectations. The invasion was being justified by various Allied sources as being in the real interests of the Russian people, groaning under the Germans and Bolsheviks. Said Chicherin:

> A true friend of the Russian people can have only one task, to help them in their hard work of building a new life on an entirely new basis, the rule of the working masses themselves; i.e., to give the Soviet government every assistance and support in its immeasurably difficult work of reorganizing the entire life of the people. Whoever takes advantage of the difficult transitory period through which we are passing to subjugate vast areas of Russia will sow hatred in the Russian working people who are now his victims but who will repay him in time.[1]

Chicherin's statement echoed the growing tendency of the Bolsheviks to appeal, in their predicament, to national sentiment. To be sure, this appeal was still on behalf of the *new* Russia, the Russia of the working people, but the unalloyed internationalism of the first days after the Revolution was gone. The struggle first to retain as much of Russia's territory as possible, then to recover the Tsarist patrimony was to be conducted in the name of the fatherland, a socialist fatherland but a fatherland nevertheless, not the world revolution, or socialism. At times, as during the Polish invasion of the Ukraine in the spring of 1920, the appeal would be made even more explicitly to Great Russian nationalism.[2] And accompanying propaganda emphasized that the Poles had always been traditional enemies of the Great Russians. To be sure, Lenin would occasionally repeat that a true socialist would not hesitate to sacrifice even the interests of his own people to those of the world proletariat. On at least one occasion after the fall of the German imperial regime in 1918, he was genuinely ready to offer the resources of his still bleeding and enfeebled country to the cause of the German revolution.

[1] Chicherin, in an interview with *Izvestia*, April 24, 1918, quoted in Jane Degras, ed., *Soviet Documents on Foreign Policy*, I: *1917–24* (London and New York, 1951), 75.

[2] Great Russian is a rather awkward translation of the term used in reference to Russians proper, as distinguished from Russians plus Ukrainians and Byelorussians. Thus, at the victory banquet at the Kremlin in 1945, Stalin raised his glass specifically to the Great Russian people.

The basic tactics used by the Bolsheviks in protecting their infant state had to be the exploitation of the differences between various capitalist states. Capitalism, their doctrine taught, was a ruthless and implacable enemy of socialism, hence the capitalists would never cease to try to overthrow the Soviet state. But in Lenin's formulation there was another tenet of Communism: that there are inherent contradictions in capitalism which make the capitalist states compete and hence incapable of true collaboration. Thus the two somewhat contradictory themes of the Soviet theory of foreign policy—on the one hand the perpetual threat of a *joint* capitalist offensive against Communism, on the other the impossibility of capitalists acting rationally (from their point of view), composing their differences, and attacking the common enemy: Soviet Russia. We shall note that while at one time the threat of a concerted capitalist attack dominates the pronouncements and concerns of the Communist leaders, at another such a possibility is contemptuously dismissed.

The classical example of this counterpoint of Soviet thinking on international politics is contained in Lenin's speech to the Central Executive Committee of the Congress of Soviets of May 14, 1918:

> Thanks to those antagonisms, the universal alliance of the imperialists of all countries—an alliance which is natural and essential for the defense of capital, which knows no fatherland . . . is not now the motivating force of [their] policy. Of course, it remains as before the basic economic tendency in the capitalist system. . . . We are in a situation in which the raging waves of imperialist reaction, which appear at any moment about to overwhelm the small island of the Socialist Soviet Republic, time and again break against each other.[3]

Lenin went on to define the two basic antagonisms determining "the international position of our Soviet Republic at the present moment": first, the struggle between Germany and England (assuming that at the moment France and the other allies were in a subsidiary position to Great Britain, as were Austria and Turkey toward Germany); and second the conflict between Japan and America.

It hardly needed great insight in May 1918 to recognize the Anglo-German conflict or to see that Britain was the senior partner in the Franco-British alliance. Similarly, in some Marxist circles World War II was in an oversimplified fashion ascribed to English jealousy over Germany's rapid economic growth and conversely to the German need for more and better situated colonies. And this thinking was in line with the theses of Lenin's *Imperialism*. It required on the other hand some acumen and knowledge of the international situation to perceive the serious if latent American-Japanese conflict as one of the basic factors of international life. The two countries were allies in the war and there had been no

[3] Degras, *op. cit.*, p. 78.

outright hostilities between them. In warding off Japan's designs on her Far Eastern territories and in formulating her Far Eastern policy in general, Soviet Russia was to count heavily on America being an offsetting factor to Japan's power. Soviet historians were subsequently to present the United States as one of the chief interventionist powers during the Civil War, and American attitudes toward Russia, going as far back as Theodore Roosevelt's mediation of the Russo-Japanese conflict, were to be pictured as consistently hostile. Yet during the crucial years 1918–21 and for many years afterward, the American position in the Far East was to be considered of great if indirect benefit to the Soviets. Not long afterward, as we shall see, Lenin was to view with some enthusiasm the prospect of an American-Japanese war. And though this hoped-for development was not to come until 1941, it proved then of the utmost significance in the hour of Russia's supreme peril.

Though he included phrases like "for us the interests of world socialism rank higher than national interests: we are defending the socialist fatherland," Lenin's speech of May 14, 1918, was remarkably nondoctrinaire in its conclusions if not in its tone. Neither Bismarck nor Metternich could have surpassed its realism in appraising the international situation, its rejection of wishful thinking, its implied belief in the irrelevance to world politics of such categories as "justice," "people's welfare," and the like. Even by the standard of Lenin's utterances before the Revolution, his speech showed that great progress had been made in the ability to analyze situations coldbloodedly and without the intrusion of ideology. Politics is a function of power: your success in it depends also on exploiting the enemy's weaknesses, divisions, and illusions. Incidentally, the Bolshevik Revolution itself was credited, not as upon ritual occasions to the heroism of the Russian working class and to the evils of the old regime, but to the sheer incompetence of Tsarism and the flabbiness of the Russian bourgeoisie. It was the continuation of the mighty pedagogical effort begun at Brest Litovsk of educating the Bolshevik rulers not to be carried away by their own propaganda, of teaching them to be more realistic and ruthless. "We must stick to our wartime tactics and exploit conflicts and antagonisms among the imperialists, slowly accumulating strength and maintaining the oasis of Soviet power in the middle of the raging imperialist sea."[4]

Lenin's was to be the decisive voice in Russia's foreign as well as domestic politics. Indeed, in no sphere of policy was his leadership more pronounced and discernible than in foreign affairs. On domestic issues, he was occasionally challenged and, though infrequently, forced to modify his position. In the military sphere, Trotsky played a major role, certainly

[4] *Ibid.*, p. 79.

during the Civil War.[5] But, on foreign issues, nobody, after the experience of December 1917–March 1918, when Lenin as against practically every prominent Bolshevik showed a superior understanding of the realities, felt capable of challenging him. Such important policies as the setting up of the Comintern in 1919, the rigorous form given it in 1920, the general outline of Soviet nationality policy at home and abroad were settled according to Lenin's wishes, even though influential Party leaders were often unconvinced of their soundness.

The official documents of Soviet foreign policy for the month following the ratification of the Treaty of Brest Litovsk have an eloquence of their own. They refer to and represent protests of the Soviet government against the violations of the treaty by imperial Germany.[6] In many cases, German troops failed to withdraw behind the frontier lines as agreed to in the treaty. Detachments of the German army entered the Ukraine and Finland to help the local governments put down Communists. In a flagrant violation of the peace agreement, German and Ukrainian troops occupied the Crimea in April. The impression of the Soviet regime's utmost helplessness is enhanced by the only diplomatic items *not* addressed to Germany during this period. They are protests about the Japanese occupation of Vladivostok and the Rumanian annexation of Bessarabia. For the few months after the Treaty of Brest Litovsk, the Soviet government was incapable of offering serious resistance to any foreign invader. Thus Rumania, herself defeated by Germany, still felt strong enough to encroach upon Russian territory, a situation which would have seemed fantastic before 1917 or after 1921. The writ of the government ran mostly over Central Russia. Flames of civil war were already beginning to spread in the south and Siberia. The Cossack territories and the Caucasus were already dissolving into a number of independent governments either claiming full independence or proclaiming their desire to be autonomous members of a federated Russian state, but not of one dominated by the Bolsheviks. The conclusion of the peace in March 1918, which we see today as the true beginning of the Soviet state and of the consolidation of Bolshevik power, must have appeared in the spring and summer of 1918 as but the first step in the continuing disintegration of the Russian state. Russia's position must have seemed like that of the Turkish or Chinese empire in the beginning of the twentieth century: a certain prey for internal dissolution and foreign imperialists.

In this apparently hopeless situation, the infant regime enjoyed certain advantages that were eventually to assure its survival. We spoke already of the political intelligence and resolution embodied in the leadership

[5] Though not as decisive as he himself and his admirers tended to represent.

[6] See *Documents on the Foreign Policy of the U.S.S.R.*, I (Moscow, 1957), 213–54.

of the Communist Party[7] and especially in its leader. Also, the Great War drew the attention of the world powers away from Russia's prostrate form. Whatever dreams the German high command had of further conquests in Russia or whatever the appetite in other circles for the oil of the Caucasus, etc., the main historical drama was being enacted in France, where the Germans were making their final bid for victory. Of all the major powers, only Japan had the resources and opportunity to concentrate on Russian affairs, and geography prevented Japan from intervening in European Russia. For all the other combatants, the Soviet problem was subsidiary to the main issue of war.[8]

In domestic politics, the very diffusion and heterogeneity of the anti-Bolshevik forces prevented their success in the struggle against Communism. Had the same purpose and a common organization and determination inspired the enemies of the regime in the south of Russia, among the Cossacks, the nations of the Caucasus, and Siberia, as well as in the various dissatisfied elements under direct Bolshevik control, Lenin's government could not have lasted one week after the ratification of the Treaty of Brest Litovsk. As it was, all those movements, parties, and conspiracies working at cross purposes could not dent the Soviet grip over Central Russia, and when more serious challenges confronted Soviet power from the summer of 1918 through 1919, it was no longer a regime without an army or administration.

But it would be unfair to ascribe the Bolshevik survival solely to fortuitous circumstances. As witnessed by the elections to the Constituent Assembly, when it garnered about one-fourth of the votes cast (and this figure will appear more impressive if it is considered that it came mostly from the cities and towns), the government enjoyed considerable popular support. It would be no exaggeration to say that in the first months of its existence the Bolshevik government enjoyed the genuine support of the majority of the working class. The party which had behind it most of the peasants, the Socialist Revolutionaries, was too divided, its leaders (just

[7] Beginning with the Seventh Congress, this was the official name of the Bolshevik Party, thus following Lenin's pledge and desire to symbolize the Bolsheviks' separation from what he considered the decadence of European Social Democracy and the Second International.

[8] This is something which is extremely important and yet difficult to keep in mind. For us *now*, the main event and inheritance of World War I is the creation of the Soviet state and emergence of the world Communist movement. For the Western statesmen, at least until the end of 1918, the importance of Russia lay mainly in its relation to Germany. Even after the end of the war and probably as late as 1941–42, the Russian problem was viewed from Paris and London mainly as it affected *the* problem of European politics—Germany. This has been completely reversed since 1945; the German problem is seen now as subsidiary to and a function of East-West relations.

as before November) too indecisive to offer a challenge. The Left Socialist Revolutionaries collaborated with the Bolsheviks until the signing of the treaty and even after that continued working in various government organs until their attempted coup in July 1918. The Mensheviks were also fatally weakened and split, though they retained some influence in the labor unions (notably the printers' and railwaymen's). Until the events of the summer of 1918, no other socialist party could bring itself to risk a head-on collision with the Bolsheviks. It is thus fair to say that between March and July 1918 the Bolshevik government enjoyed the support or acquiescence of the population in those areas in which it exercised its rather shaky authority.

Those few months mark the real beginning of Soviet *administration.* Between November and March the Bolsheviks' style of government had consisted in issuing proclamations. The tools of government—the army, the police, the diplomatic service, the civil service—in general were simply not in existence, the Provisional Government's institutions having been smashed, the new ones not yet born. Following Brest, Trotsky assumed the direction of military affairs and proceeded to build the Red Army. What remained of the old army was in the main armed rabble. Now, a system of enlistments from among the workers was instituted to provide a nucleus of troops with some ideological motivation and discipline. The key decision was to enlist as many as possible of the old Tsarist officers and to abolish the practice of men electing their own commanders. Gone was the old dream and promise that the Soviet state would dispense with a regular army, with its ranks and discipline, and would rely on a citizens' militia. Of equal significance for the future of the Communist Party was the organization of the secret police. Formally established on December 7, 1917, the *Cheka*[9] soon assumed the powers of a major Soviet agency and enormous importance with the transfer of the government to Moscow on March 10. The sword of the revolution, the agency which was to carry out wholesale terror, the *Cheka* served to tighten the Bolsheviks' grip on the country and to enable them to dispose not only of counterrevolutionaries but of their erstwhile allies the anarchists and Left Socialist Revolutionaries.[10]

A parallel shift from amateurism to strict professionalism marked the development of the Commissariat for Foreign Relations. When a Soviet writer in 1923 described the operations of this agency under Trotsky's leadership, the picture already appeared distant and fantastic.[11] He could already

[9] The abbreviation of the Russian initials of the Extraordinary Commission to Combat Counterrevolution and Sabotage.

[10] See Adam B. Ulam, *The Bolsheviks* (New York, 1965), pp. 419–26.

[11] Ivan Maisky, *Foreign Policy of the Russian Soviet Federated Republic* (Moscow, 1923), pp. 18–26.

find incredible the utmost chaos that then prevailed. The old civil servants and diplomats had fled, and rank-and-file workers and militiamen occupied the ministry's once elegant building. Trotsky was too busy with Party affairs to pay close attention to the commissariat, and actual administration was in the hands of his deputy, one Zalkind. Foreign diplomats who still had occasion to visit the building were put off by the enormous revolver that Zalkind wore on his belt and by the machineguns installed in the corridors. From time to time, the militiamen on duty amused themselves by conducting target practice with their guns and revolvers.

> There were no rules about protocol or order. In the very office of the commissar, mass meetings took place one after another. The collective of the employed [all employees down to and including janitors], having still an unfortunate idea of the constitution of the republic, attempted to arrogate to itself the right to conduct the foreign policy of Russia. [!!!]

This anarchist heaven was drastically transformed in March. Trotsky had resigned in February,[12] and his successor was George Chicherin, who was to head the commissariat until 1930. The reign of Zalkind and the machinegunners was over, and the more traditional ways of diplomacy reasserted themselves.[13]

George Chicherin was pre-eminently qualified to guide the beginning steps of Soviet diplomacy. An aristocrat by birth and one-time employee of the imperial Foreign Ministry, Chicherin experienced in 1904 a spiritual crisis that made him abandon his position and society and turn first to Tolstoyan philosophy and then to socialism. He was at first a Menshevik and, because of his probity and asceticism, enjoyed a high reputation in revolutionary circles. Before 1914 he presided over a special commission of revolutionaries investigating the charges that Bolsheviks had engaged in armed robberies to replenish their resources. The key figure in disposing of the fruits of those expropriations abroad was none other than Chicherin's future deputy and successor, Maxim Litvinov. During the war, Chicherin drew close to Lenin's policies, and, at the last phase of the Brest Litovsk

---

[12] Though in order not to publicize the dissensions within the regime, his resignation was not publicly announced until after the ratification of the Treaty of Brest Litovsk.

[13] One incident of the reign of Zalkind deserves repetition. The Spanish Ambassador, who must have been a very insensitive gentleman, felt that he should not leave the Russian post without receiving, as used to be traditional in the Tsarist times, a decoration from the government to which he had been accredited. He confessed his ambition to Zalkind and begged him to ask his government to award him an order. Zalkind professed to see no point in going through official channels. He pulled out a drawer full of orders stripped from the previous officials of the ministry and asked the Spaniard to help himself to any he wished!

negotiations, he took over the actual leadership of the commissariat. In view of his background and his retiring personality, he was a person of no political influence among the Bolsheviks, and, during his twelve-year occupancy of the office, Chicherin never became a member of the Party's inner circle. By the same token, his linguistic gifts, his long experience in foreign countries, and his gentlemanly bearing made him an ideal "front man" for Soviet diplomacy. Needless to say, the crucial decisions were never made by Chicherin, any more than later they were made by his successor Litvinov. But the style of diplomatic work and the details of the execution of policies as determined by Lenin, the Politburo, or Stalin were worked out by the Foreign Commissar. An indefatigable worker, a discreet counsellor of his masters, and a patient negotiator, Chicherin enjoyed Lenin's respect and managed—for all the future manipulations of the Comintern—to build up the image of respectability for Soviet diplomacy that was to prove of invaluable benefit to his country.

But most of those achievements were to come in the future. In the period under discussion, the bulk of Chicherin's work consisted, as we have seen, in addressing notes of protest to the German government and keeping contacts with the unofficial representatives of the Western Allies still in Moscow. After the signature of Brest Litovsk, the Soviet government was of course officially recognized by Germany and entered into regular (if anything in the period can be called regular) diplomatic relations with her. The other belligerents persisted in their refusal to recognize the Bolsheviks.

The efforts of the Allied governments up to the end of World War I were designed primarily and almost exclusively at reactivating the Eastern Front against Germany. Until November 1918, the Allied intervention in Russia had nothing ideological about it. It was designed simply to relieve the Western Powers' armies in France, which, at the beginning of the German offensive in March 1918, were struggling desperately to contain the most dangerous German advance since the very first weeks of the war. Hence the clutching at straws, like the fantastic plan of bringing the Japanese army over the vast and untraversable expanse of Siberia to engage the Germans west of the Urals. The story propagated by Soviet historians that, from the very beginning, the intervention of the Western Powers was based on their hostility to Communism is thus without foundation. It is sufficiently disproved by an early Soviet verdict on the Allied attitude between Brest Litovsk and the late summer of 1918:

> In contrast to Germany, the powers of the *Entente* exhibited during the first months of its existence relatively little activity toward the Soviet Republic. True, they refused to acknowledge the new regime and exhibited toward it open hostility, but they did not fight it openly. This is explained by the fact that during that period the Western Allies were

too much absorbed in the war and did not have the means or the strength to conduct a very active policy in the East. . . . The Western Powers did not lose the hope of using Russia for war against Germany.[14]

The great external danger for Russia was still represented by Germany. Petrograd and the new capital, Moscow, lay practically defenseless against a potential German advance. Lenin could boast in his speech to the Seventh Party Congress that the Soviets had already violated the Brest Litovsk agreement "thirty or forty times," but the Germans did not on their part exhibit excessive scruples about violating the recent agreement whenever it suited their convenience. German troops chased out the local Bolsheviks in the Ukraine and Finland. In a clear violation of the treaty they helped Ukrainian troops occupy the Crimea and took under their protection Georgia, which had also seceded from Russia. Germans entered into relations with and extended help to other peoples claiming independence from the Soviet state, such as the Don Cossacks. In listing the Germans' various violations of the treaty for the nth time, the Soviet representative in Berlin concluded wearily in a note to the imperial Foreign Office, "All those above-mentioned facts give the lie to the constant assertions of the German Imperial Government that Germany is at peace with Russia and is solemnly observing the Brest treaty."[15]

In the face of this frightful situation, and while the sinews of Soviet strength were still being built up, the course of Soviet foreign policy remained true to Lenin's prescription: wait out the period of the greatest weakness and capitalize on any and all conflicts within the bourgeois world. Hence the avenues of contact with the Western camp were not shut. British occupation in March of the port of Murmansk was quietly assented to.[16] The Allied presence in the distant, almost unreachable regions of northern Russia was potential insurance against the worst possible contingency: a German occupation of Petrograd and Moscow. As seen above, the Soviets were acutely aware of the different motivations and potential conflicts within the Allied camp itself. France was seen as basically the most anti-Bolshevik of the powers. Her very considerable investments and loans to imperial Russia would act against her acquiescence in the perpetuation of the Bolshevik regime. But Britain's attitude was more hopeful, and France was dependent upon her. Japan's interests were recognized as purely annexationist. Russia's hour of trial was but an opportunity to extend Japanese power in China and to occupy the vast areas of eastern Siberia. But here the Soviets counted on the United

[14] Maisky, *op. cit.*, p. 48.

[15] *Documents on the Foreign Policy of the U.S.S.R.*, I, 328.

[16] Murmansk and Archangel had been during 1914–17 two ports of entry for British war supplies and as such protected by a British naval squadron.

States, whose interests would not allow them to permit such a great extension of Japanese power.

It was from America that the Russians expected and in a way received the most encouraging response among the Western Powers. The initial Soviet reaction toward the United States already contained elements that were to persist for the next half century. America was thought to be the least imperialist of the belligerents, her people most sensitive to democratic slogans and arguments. By the same token, American rulers were viewed as the most naïve and least experienced among those of the Great Powers. It was assumed that the United States was least likely to intervene in Russia for any territorial gains, that on the contrary her interest would lie in the preservation of Russia's territorial integrity, especially as against the Japanese.[17]

At the same time, the attitude toward the United States was never tinged by sentimentality or belief in the reality of American professions about democracy. America was the country of classical capitalism, less brutal and exploiting than that of France, untinged by the imperialist mentality of Great Britain or the militarism of Germany, but still based on exploitation and worshipping profit as its only god. Insofar as Lenin was concerned, it was difficult to express sympathy or be tactful when it came to capitalists anywhere. President Wilson's professions of friendship for the Russian people were welcomed, but in less guarded moments Lenin referred to him as "the old hypocrite Wilson." When Raymond Robins, an indefatigable worker for Soviet-American friendship, wrote Lenin a warm note referring to his "prophetic insight and genius-like leadership," Lenin's answer was hardly subtle: "I am convinced that the new democracy is growing up everywhere and will overcome all the difficulties in the imperialist-capitalist systems in the New as well as in the Old World."[18]

In their approaches to the United States, Soviet policy-makers from the beginning used the technique of opening up vistas of a vast and profitable trade that would be America's reward should she adopt a reasonable attitude toward the Bolshevik regime. This approach was to be applied also toward Great Britain, and it has persisted well into our day. With the passage of years and the resurgence of the Russian economy in the 1920's,

[17] Republican America and imperial Russia had enjoyed an almost uninterrupted course of good relations. The main difficulty in Russo-American relations before 1914 lay in the Tsarist government's treatment of Jews, which led to the abrogation of the commercial treaty between the two countries. The March Revolution was greeted in the United States with enthusiasm and with none of the reservations and nostalgia for the imperial regime that modified the approval in London and Paris.

[18] April 30, 1918, in *Documents on the Foreign Policy of the U.S.S.R.*, I, 276.

mutually profitable trade was to become at least theoretically possible. But it is startling to find Lenin in May 1918 sketching out for Robins (for communication to the State Department) a plan for Russian exports to the United States for the current year in the amount of 3 billion rubles. Complete disorganization of the Russian economy, not to mention the unavailability of transport, made such a plan fantastically impractical. Granted the times and conditions, equally fantastic were Lenin's suggestions about the possibility of the United States obtaining concessions on Russian territory to exploit the forests and fisheries of Kamchatka and eastern Siberia, of building electric stations and railroads. "The United States could also participate on a large scale in the exploitation of agricultural areas in order to introduce more contemporary techniques of cultivation, receiving in return a large number of products."[19]

It is difficult to determine to what extent Lenin and his regime were victims of self-delusion: economic realism was slow to penetrate Bolshevik ruling circles. But the proposals were obviously designed to arouse the Americans' interest and cupidity, and the fact that many of the proposed concessions were to lie in those areas of eastern Siberia which were the object of Japan's territorial ambition speaks for itself.

But the main concern of Soviet policy-makers had to be Germany. She remained the only foreign power that could deal a deathblow to the Revolution. For all the German chicaneries, the logical task for Russian diplomacy was to appease the German government and implant the conviction in Berlin that Germany's military interests would best be served by the continuation of the Bolsheviks in power. On May 15 Russo-German negotiations were opened in Berlin for the purpose of concluding a commercial treaty. German economic needs were far from satisfied by her occupation of the Ukraine, and the prospect of large food supplies from Russia was a powerful incentive for continued German toleration of the Bolsheviks.[20]

At the same time, there were influential circles in Germany that viewed this collaboration with distaste and were not unwilling to see the Bolshevik regime fall. The German ambassador in Moscow, Count Mirbach, gradually

---

[19] *Ibid.*, pp. 300–301.

[20] The negotiations were conducted on the Soviet side by Yoffe, now ambassador in Berlin, and Leonid Krasin. The latter was to be for the next few years one of Russia's chief diplomats, intermittently in charge of foreign trade. An old Bolshevik, and at one time second to Lenin in the Party, Krasin had abandoned Lenin after 1908 to devote himself exclusively to his profession, that of an engineer and industrial manager. He rejected Lenin's offer to join the Bolshevik regime after November but later on placed himself at the service of his country. A skilled and urbane negotiator, he was also indispensable in those early days because of his rare economic and industrial expertise, and he deserves much credit for the revival of Russian foreign trade.

shifted to the anti-Bolshevik position. His reports to Berlin emphasized that the regime was likely to disintegrate and that it behooved Germany "to fill the vacuum which will result from its disappearance." He advised a military attack and a replacement of the Bolsheviks by a right-wing combination that would be more satisfactory as Germany's partner or satellite.[21]

A breach in German-Bolshevik relations was also the aim of another party: the Left Socialist Revolutionaries. Still tolerated by the Bolsheviks, though no longer in the government, the Left S.R.'s chafed under the Treaty of Brest Litovsk. On July 6, Ambassador Mirbach was assassinated by two members of that party. This was supposed to be the signal for a general uprising against the Bolsheviks and a renewal of war against the Germans (which the Left S.R.'s hoped to conduct in a partisan fashion and without seeking any help from the other imperialists). But the uprisings both in Moscow and in the provinces were suppressed, and the Bolsheviks were soon more firmly in power than ever before.

The full circumstances of the assassination and the plot must still remain the subject of conjecture. The S.R.'s believed that in killing Mirbach, whom they viewed as the German viceroy of Russia, they would provoke German intervention. It was more reasonable to assume, as proved to be the case, that the assassination would reinforce the German belief that the Bolsheviks were the only element capable of and willing to keep peace. Mirbach's views were known in Bolshevik circles.[22] It is not unlikely that the Bolshevik leadership had some inkling of the S.R. plot and decided to let it take place. The assassination and its sequel enabled it to dispose of the only remaining internal opposition, it eliminated the unfriendly diplomat, and it did not cause a rupture with Germany.[23]

The government's suppression of the several uprisings was its first successful test of strength in the territory under its control. Had the uprisings taken place in January, after the eviction of the Constituent Assembly, they would have encountered widespread popular support. Now, their apparent aim could not but be unpopular: a renewal of war, with all its attendant miseries. As Lenin could say: "We are being provoked to a war with Germany when we cannot and will not fight. . . . But the people will not forgive the Left S.R.'s their attempt to push us into the

---

[21] See Z. A. B. Zeman, ed., *Germany and the Revolution in Russia: Documents From the Archives of the German Foreign Ministry* (London, 1958), pp. 138–39.

[22] Lenin is reported as saying: "Mirbach has continually reported that we are weak and a single blow would suffice." Leon Trotsky, *Lenin* (New York, 1925), p. 156.

[23] The German reaction to the murder was surprisingly feeble. The Soviet government rejected categorically the demand that a German battalion be sent to Moscow to guard the embassy.

war."[24] The Bolsheviks were rid of their last real rivals on the left, and Russia became in fact a one-party state.

Russo-German relations soon improved. A successor to Mirbach arrived in Moscow within three weeks of the assassination. On August 1, he was visited by Chicherin, who discussed with him the possibility of a discreet Soviet-German collaboration in evicting the Allies from Murmansk and Archangel, where fairly sizable landings of Allied troops had just taken place. On August 27, a supplementary agreement to Brest Litovsk was signed with Germany, Austria, Hungary, and Turkey. The conditions of the agreement in their harshness went far beyond the original treaty. Russia pledged to pay Germany 6 billion marks in indemnity, of which 1 billion was to be paid in gold, 1 billion in goods to be delivered through the end of 1920, and the rest in bonds.[25] Further territorial concessions were acknowledged, among them the independence of Georgia. Had the treaty itself not been nullified by Germany's subsequent collapse, Russia proper would have become an economic satellite of Germany, whatever products her ruined economy was able to export being taken by Germany as indemnity. With this treaty, the Soviets were paying ransom for a German promise not to continue carving up Russia and not to sponsor anti-Bolshevik regimes. This was made clear in Chicherin's speech justifying the catastrophic agreement:

> Germany guarantees that Finland will not . . . attack Russia. . . . In view of the fact that fictitious declarations of independence [from the Soviet state] of the frontier regions might make any delimitation of borders fictitious, the Agreement of August 27 marks the obligation of Germany not to support the separation from Russia of new independent units except the ones which are already mentioned in the Agreement.[26]

Though Chicherin tried rather feebly to put some favorable interpretation on the agreements ("We do not recognize the independence of Georgia, but agree to Germany recognizing it. . . . Those agreements represent for us a serious improvement of our position."), he must have recognized their shameful and catastrophic character. There was no reason for Germany to observe the latest agreement any more than she had that of Brest Litovsk. But the Soviet government was now seriously threatened by the Civil War, and there was almost no price the Bolsheviks were not willing to pay for another breathing spell from their most dangerous enemy. The newest agreement continued to be violated by Germany practically up to the day of collapse, as witnessed by a new series

---

[24] Trotsky, *op. cit.*, p. 382.

[25] *Documents on the Foreign Policy of the U.S.S.R.*, I, 446–50.

[26] *Ibid.*, p. 465.

of official complaints lodged by Chicherin and Yoffe. On September 8, the former complained tearfully that Germany's satellite, the Ukraine, has recognized the regime of the Don Cossacks as an independent state and refuses to acknowledge the Don territory as part of the Russian republic.

The appeasement of Germany was dictated by the logic of the situation. Collaboration with Germany meant further carving up of Russia and economic bondage, but from the end of June it became obvious that the Western Allies were directing their activities, even if clumsily, against *Bolshevik* power. This followed from their recognition that the Soviet government would not of its own volition turn against Germany, and if the Eastern Front was to be reactivated some other partner had to be found on Russian soil.

The pattern of Allied intervention as it took shape in the summer of 1918 was of a most variegated character. There were secret negotiations and intrigues by British and French agents in Soviet territory with various anti-Bolshevik groups and conspiracies. There were Allied landings in the north of Russia and Siberia. After the occupation of Archangel on August 1, the Allies sponsored their first outrightly anti-Bolshevik government of "Northern Russia," headed by a venerable relic of Russian populism, N. V. Chaikovsky, thus in effect beginning the search for an official anti-Bolshevik fulcrum on Russian soil, a search that was to continue intermittently and ineffectively until 1921. The token Japanese intervention in Vladivostok in April was succeeded in August by a massive one. "By the Armistice there were more than 70,000 Japanese soldiers in Siberia."[27] They were followed by much smaller contingents of British and American troops.

A special chapter in the history of the intervention and the Civil War belongs to the Czechoslovak Legion. Czech units had been organized in the Tsarist army at the beginning of the war, under the slogan of freeing Bohemia and Slovakia from the Austro-Hungarian yoke. They grew with the enlistment of Czechoslovak prisoners from the Austrian army. After the Bolsheviks' assumption of power, this force, now upward of 40,000 soldiers, was the subject of negotiations with the Allies. It was finally agreed in the winter of 1918 to evacuate the Czechoslovak Legion through Vladivostok to France, where it would fight under French command. It was easily foreseeable that the task of transporting an alien army over more than 6,000 miles of a disorganized country would lead to complications and clashes. And, indeed, beginning with some incidents in May, the Czechoslovaks assumed a hostile attitude toward the Bolshevik authorities. In June, the Czech forces began to seize stretches of the Trans-Siberian Railway and

[27] Richard H. Ullman, *Anglo-Soviet Relations 1917–1921: Intervention and War* (Princeton, 1961), p. 261.

became the mainstay of various anti-Soviet movements from the Volga region into eastern Siberia. Most notably, they helped set up two insurgent authorities: one in Samara, in the Volga area, where some Right Socialist Revolutionaries and other socialist elements proclaimed a free government of Russia in the name of the Constituent Assembly dissolved forcibly the previous January; and one in Omsk, in Siberia. The Volga region was recovered by the Bolsheviks in the late summer of 1918, the new Red Army celebrating its first victories, but the Omsk regime consolidated its power over much of Siberia, and under the leadership of Admiral Kolchak it was to become in 1919 one of the main threats to Soviet power.

The full history of the Civil War even if tersely written would take several volumes of this size. Even its diplomatic aspects cannot be treated at length in a study of this kind. Some general observations may, however, be in order. Allied intervention, to repeat, was not until the end of the war based on any ideological premise or, except in the case of Japan, on territorial ambitions. (Nor was this unceremonious interference in the affairs of a nonbelligerent country confined to Russia. Greece was subjected during World War I to an Allied intervention with no socialist revolution having taken place there.) Legally and morally, the Soviet claim to be the legitimate government of Russia was, at least since their dispersal of the Constituent Assembly, most dubious. While the belief that the Bolsheviks were agents of the Germans was absurd, there can be no doubt that indirectly they were of help to the German cause. The great offensive that shook the Allied armies in France in March and April of 1918 would have hardly been possible without the Brest Litovsk peace. The prospect of the Germans getting foodstuffs and other supplies in the east appeared to negate the whole effect of the Allied blockade of Germany and her allies, and thus promised to prolong the war indefinitely.

The other side of the coin was the puny and dispersed character of the intervention. Granted that the Allies' resources were engaged in a life-and-death struggle in France, the fact remains that such secondary theaters of war as Greece and the Near East were furnished with troops and supplies, a small part of which, if directed to Russia, might well have swung the balance during the crucial spring and summer months of 1918. The first landing in Archangel in August was undertaken with about 1,200 British troops, and thereafter Allied troops there never grew beyond 10,000. Though the Japanese poured tens of thousands of troops into Siberia, they obviously could not affect the fortunes of the war.

The Western expectation that a token troop presence would stir up the "healthy elements" in Russia into vigorous anti-Bolshevik activity was wishful thinking. Just as before November 1917, so now the country was weary of the war and the social forces too disorganized to coalesce in a real alternative to the Bolshevik regime. In every territory held by the Whites (as all the anti-Bolshevik movements and regimes became known) there was to be repeated—for all the differing personalities and circumstances— the main theme of the tragedy of Russian society between February and November 1917: this was the utter incapacity of democratic elements to build a viable government. And the military side of the struggle, the need for discipline, organization, and professionalism remained beyond their comprehension. On the other hand, the professional military men who led the White armies viewed with loathing even the most anti-Bolshevik socialists. Thus attempts to build a wide coalition of anti-Bolshevik forces inevitably broke down, and, as in Siberia under Admiral Kolchak, a military dictatorship was established. A military regime could not in its turn make an effective appeal to the people's hearts and minds. It was bound to be suspected, though often without foundation, of secret longings for pre-1917 Russia of the Tsar and the landlords. As the Civil War progressed, the mass of the population, especially the peasants, turned against the Bolsheviks, but by the same token the Russians were not willing to go back to their pre-1917 society.

As we shall see, however, the failure of the White movements does not have to be traced to "deeper" causes, beloved though they are by moralizing historians. At the crucial points, as in the summer of 1919, when victory appeared to be within their grasp, the Whites failed because of concrete military and diplomatic errors and their inability to act unconventionally in a revolutionary situation. Soviet diplomacy during the Civil War, on the other hand, can hardly be faulted.

At the end of the summer of 1918, eighteen insurgent governments existed in the vast territory of Russia.[28] But by the end of the year the worst threat to Bolshevik rule disappeared. The German war machine collapsed and Germany herself was in the throes of revolution.

Lenin's first reaction to the news of the armistice of November 11 is reported as one of concern. "Now the world capital will start an offensive against us," he is alleged to have said to Chicherin.[29] But this motif, the apprehension that *now* the capitalist world might unite against the Communist state, could not have included all the Bolshevik feelings on the subject. The other aspect was relief at the fall of the enemy. The Bolsheviks feared most the German military machine, "the giant," as Lenin had called it a few months before. And the exaltation at the revolution in Germany was great. A proclamation of the Congress of Soviets of November 8 gave the following analysis: "The Soviet state is in this

[28] Not counting the states carved out of the old empire and now German satellites, like the Ukraine, or the national areas that declared themselves independent, like Finland.

[29] Louis Fischer, *The Soviets in World Affairs* (paperback ed.; New York, 1960), p. 103.

peculiar position: on the one hand we were never so close to an international proletarian revolution as now; on the other we have never been in so dangerous situation as at present."[30] As against the pessimistic part of the analysis, one may set the following passages of the declaration: "The extreme fatigue of the people because of the war has been surmounted. The army is being built and (in large measure) has already been built. A new communist discipline has grown. . . . We can finish building and we will build the socialist fatherland and a victory of the international proletarian revolution."

In analyzing Soviet diplomatic communications for the next few months, one is struck by the note of confidence, so much in contrast to the plaintive and almost helpless tone of the Foreign Commissariat's utterances during the summer. It is not only that the hope of an international revolution once again flares up. Their experience of one year in power could not endow the Bolsheviks with much respect for the Allied ability to act effectively in unison. Against the undoubted hostility of the ruling circles in the West, the Soviets assessed shrewdly the war-weariness of their peoples and the democratic scruples of Western public opinion, which could be played on especially in the case of Britain and the United States. In the case of the German high command, the Bolsheviks had confronted an enemy that had been least subject to such scruples and inhibitions: now that enemy was no more.

2. *The Soviet Regime Prevails*

The considerable propaganda skill that Soviet diplomacy was already displaying was evident in the official announcement: "The Brest treaty and the supplementary agreement have been destroyed by the German and Russian revolutionary workers and soldiers and are no longer binding."[31] It mattered little that the treaty had in fact been destroyed by the Allied armies and that one of the conditions of the armistice obligated Germany to withdraw her occupation forces from Russian territories (with the exception of the Baltic territories). As has been the case with many Soviet analyses of historical events, a misleading interpretation of a past development was to serve as the forecast of the future. A junction of the Russian and German revolutions had for long been a Bolshevik dream. The new provisional regime in Germany was composed of regular Social Democrats and Independent Socialists. While the Bolsheviks had nothing but contempt for the regular socialists, the left wing of the Inde-

[30] *Documents on the Foreign Policy of the U.S.S.R.*, I, 558.
[31] *Ibid.*, p. 568.

pendent Socialists was known to be not unfriendly to them, and anyway events were likely soon to move even more radical elements to the fore. As in Russia in 1917, so in Germany in 1918 workers' and soldiers' soviets were sprouting up all over. But within a few weeks after November 11 the Russian hopes and expectations were dashed. The first disquieting symptom was the refusal of the new German socialist regime to resume regular diplomatic relations with Russia.[32] At the same time the government refused to accept two wagonloads of foodstuffs which, as a gesture of sympathy, the Communist government was offering to send out of Russia, herself on the verge of starvation, to Germany. Chicherin bitterly commented to the German socialists that the Soviet government realized that "the difficult position of Germany in relation to the U.S., which, maybe accompanied by diplomatic pressure, . . . led to the decision of the German Government to try to please President Wilson through that refusal rather than to stand firmly on the basis of the workers' solidarity."[33]

Though the Soviet government continued to woo the German socialists for some weeks, the Bolshevik leaders grew disenchanted in their expectation of a rapid Communist revolution in Germany. The left wing of the Independent Socialist Party did indeed secede and decide to create the German Communist Party. Its founding congress assembled on December 30 in the presence of Radek, as representative of the senior Communist Party. An attempted uprising in which the German Communist Party was involved was suppressed in January 1919 by the socialist government and the Reichswehr, and the two outstanding founders of German Communism, Rosa Luxemburg and Karl Liebknecht, were shot. Thus failed the first attempted repetition on foreign soil of the events of November 1917 in Petrograd. The German majority socialists, whom Lenin had always held to be "renegades" and "Judases," thus lived up to his expectations, and Communism was for the moment checkmated in Germany, its Communist Party banned.[34]

[32] Those relations had been broken in the last days of the imperial regime and Yoffe ordered out of Berlin when Soviet diplomats were discovered carrying on extensive Communist propaganda in Germany. Though some incidents relating to it may have been manufactured by the German police, there is no doubt that Yoffe carried out Communist propaganda. Lenin, in a speech on November 6, publicly acknowledged that the Soviet embassy in Berlin carried on revolutionary activity. Lenin, *Works* (4th ed., Moscow, 1946), XXVIII, 179.

[33] *Documents on the Foreign Policy of the U.S.S.R.*, II (Moscow, 1958), 57.

[34] It is interesting to speculate about the future of the international Communist movement had the original leaders of German Communism, especially Rosa Luxemburg, survived. That indomitable woman had, for all her militancy and revolutionary fervor, often clashed with Lenin. Her estimate of the Bolshevik Revolution and its first year in power was not uncritical. She was especially opposed to the use of indiscriminate terror and to the Bolsheviks'

The flame of Communist revolution that flickered up temptingly in the West was extinguished and with it the last of the Bolshevik hopes for a chain reaction of Communist revolutions throughout Europe. The Communist regimes briefly established in 1919 in Hungary and Bavaria led to some renewal of hope but never to the extent present in November–December 1918. That failure solidified the Communists' enmity to Germany's regular Social Democrats. On January 19, their leaders Scheidemann and Ebert, addressed only a few weeks before as "comrades," were publicly denounced by Lenin as having the blood of Luxemburg and Liebknecht on their hands. The former, in turn, had before their eyes the fate of the Mensheviks and other non-Communist socialists in Russia. The Bolshevik Revolution in *Russia* had been possible because the other radical and socialist parties had felt that they could not really offer resistance to another left movement. But a year of terror and disregard of the most basic democratic tenets had shown even the most militant socialists in Europe who still retained some democratic scruples what they could expect from Communist rule. The majority of German as well as French and British workers were for long to retain an instinctive sympathy for Soviet Russia—the "workers' state"—but they were not willing to see Soviet methods and institutions introduced in their own countries. Hence the final and fateful split in world socialism which has colored so much of recent history, which was bound to make one branch of it until our own day an extension of the Soviet state, and which was to weaken the other branch as a force for democracy and social justice.

1919 was the crucial year not only in regard to the patterns of international Communism. It was decisive in connection with the military and diplomatic dimensions of the Civil War and intervention. It was decisive because in that year the Soviet state inherited the vast majority of the lands of formerly imperial Russia and thus was predestined to resume the status of a Great Power. An important contribution to this feat was the Bolsheviks' ability in the political and diplomatic fields, so much in contrast to the Whites' ineptitude. Economically and administratively, the Bolshevik record was a sorry one: in addition to the devastation and chaos caused by the war, the economy of the Soviet areas suffered by the constant improvisation and unrealistic experimentation. Terror became the main administrative technique, the threat of putting people "against the wall" was assumed to be the only effective way of securing the obedience of the local authorities to Moscow or of securing food for the cities. But this awkwardness, doctrinairism, and fanaticism were lacking when it came

---

departures from Marxist orthodoxy. At least it is arguable that with her alive and at the head of German Communism, the Russians would not have achieved that complete domination of the international movement which was theirs from the beginning of the Comintern.

to the most important political questions. A regime literally surrounded by hostile forces, unrecognized by any foreign power, faced with foreign intervention, displayed an amazing ability to roll with the punch. The expectations of the Communist regime were still unlimited, the hostility to all the other states in the world still undiminished. In March 1919 Lenin said his most often quoted words on Soviet foreign policy: "We live not only in a state but in a system of states, and the existence of the Soviet republic together with imperialist states is in the long run unthinkable."[35] But in the short run there was hardly any concession or promise that the Soviet leaders were not willing to make in order to buy time, to score a point with public opinion in the West, or to weaken the position of a White regime with a foreign state or non-Russian nationality.

Those characteristics of Soviet diplomacy are well displayed in a note Chicherin addressed to the Allied Powers on February 4. The latter, assembled at the Paris Peace Conference, had just invited all the regimes in Russia to attend a conference under Allied sponsorship at Prinkipo, in the Sea of Marmor,[36] to compose their differences if possible or to reach some agreement on delimitation of their authority. Chicherin's note tried to mitigate the Allies' hostility to the Soviet regime and their support of the Whites. Yes, the Soviet government declared its readiness to attend, though it did not recognize any of the rival regimes as possessing any authority and credited their survival solely to the aid they received from the West. To soften the heart of the capitalists, Chicherin declared Russia's readiness to reopen the question of her indebtedness to the Western Powers and compensation for their citizens' property. The Soviet government was declared ready to grant mineral, forest, and other concessions to foreign nationals. Territorial concessions made either outright to the Allied Powers or to the White regimes sponsored by them were not excluded.[37] There was no end of concessions the Soviets were apparently ready to make to the greedy imperialists in the West provided they would leave them with *some* territory. The Russian government, while unable, it was pointed out, to limit the "freedom of the revolutionary press" (i.e., its revolutionary propaganda abroad), stood ready to give pledges of non-interference in other states' internal affairs. In terms implying considerable self-abasement, Chicherin drew Western attention to the Bolsheviks' success in recruiting to their side in the Civil War some previously hostile Mensheviks and Socialist Revolutionaries.

Rather than diplomatic skill, it might be objected, the note reflected

---

[35] *Works*, XXIX, 487.

[36] It was a strange coincidence that it was on Prinkipo island that Trotsky spent his first years as an exile from Stalin's Russia, completing his *History of the Russian Revolution.*

[37] *Documents on the Foreign Policy of the U.S.S.R.*, II, 57–60.

extreme despair, the Soviet government's realization that, unless military operations were arrested one way or another, its days were numbered. Still, it is remarkable that this document of the utmost self-humiliation did not provoke within Bolshevik circles the angry reaction that had greeted Lenin's position on Brest Litovsk. Under similarly desperate circumstances, the *White* governments, as we shall see, were to reject any notion that they could traffic with Russia's sovereignty or territorial integrity. The Soviets were always willing to appease what they considered the territorial and financial greed of the capitalist monster, to recognize their own weakness, and to trade territory for time. It goes without saying that inherent in this Soviet diplomacy of despair was the clear assumption that there was no nonsense about the sanctity of treaties; once power relations were changed, Soviet Russia would claim her own. In any case nothing came of the Prinkipo conference. The White Russian regimes rejected the idea, feeling (as did, for that matter, influential French circles) that there was no point in negotiating with a fast-dying regime.

It is instructive in this connection to note the important psychological advantage enjoyed by the Bolsheviks over their White opponents when it came to diplomatic maneuvering. The latter were for the most part headed by fervent Russian nationalists whose ideological frame of reference was expressed in the term "Russia great and undivided," as the most prominent of the White leaders, General Anton Denikin, was wont to repeat. In their dealings with the Allies, they were bristly and often unyielding, suspecting (quite justifiably) ulterior motives in British or French help. That help they expected to come as a right, as the Allies' moral duty to the Russian people and their former comrades-in-arms, as against the Bolsheviks who almost caused the Allied defeat in the war. The picture drawn by subsequent Soviet historiography of White generals willing to sell Russia to the French and British and of the Soviet regime as the defender of the Russian people and their sovereignty is thus quite misleading. Whatever their other transgressions, and there were many, the main White leaders, Denikin and Kolchak, were constrained in their politics and diplomacy by simple notions of Russian nationalism and an officer's code of honor. It was the Bolsheviks who were ready literally to "sell" parts of Russia, offer concessions, etc. This was not the result of cynicism. They considered themselves as the advance detachment of the world revolution, and to preserve the rule of Communism over *some* territory, as an example to the world, was thought to be of greater importance than to try to cling to all of the territory that had been Russia's at the beginning of the Great War. This ideological frame of reference provided the basis of a cynical, but in the post-war world realistic, view of foreign affairs. The main capitalist powers, or rather their ruling circles, could be moved only by an appeal to their greed, mutual suspicions, or fear of their own peoples. Such time-honored categories as "honor," "sanctity of treaties," and "comrade-ship in arms" were, on the contrary, of very limited viability in a war-weary world. At the same time, the Russian offers to the Western Powers that referred bluntly to their real or alleged territorial and financial ambi-tions were well designed to stir up public opinion in Great Britain and America and create some sympathy for this strange new regime, which did not hide its powerless position behind diplomatic double-talk but appeared to offer no end of concessions in return only for being let alone.

The Allied intervention was certainly vastly increased following the armistice. In December 1918 began the French landings in Odessa and on the Black Sea littoral. British detachments reappeared in the Trans-caucasus. Allied supplies and war missions were furnished to the main White regimes. German troops undid the work of pro-Communist uprisings in the Baltic states. Yet, while the armistice accentuated the extent of the intervention, it also intensified the disagreements among the Allied Powers as to the purpose and methods of intervention and of the ultimate aim to be achieved by it.

The purely ideological element by now played an important part in Western[38] dislike of Bolshevik Russia. But it is important to realize the nature of this fear of Communism. There was little fear as yet of Soviet or Communist *power*, i.e., of the Soviet state's coming to dominate Europe. When Western statesmen expressed fear of Bolshevism or anarchism (and those two terms were used almost interchangeably), they were afraid of the *example* of Russian Communism stirring up social trouble in their own countries and, under the precarious economic conditions of the post-war world, making impossible the return of the pre-1914 pattern of political stability. As a *state*, Soviet Russia lay prostrate, in the throes of war and economic chaos, and few were willing to credit her leaders with the ability to dominate anything. Russia was the locus of an infection sapping the strength of Europe, not a threat herself.

By the same token, some powers felt that they had almost a vested inter-est in the survival of Communism. Tsarist Russia had been a colossus in international politics. A reconstructed nationalist Russia could not fail to make a bid for all her former territories and influence and, cured of her former social ills, could not by her very size but come again to dominate Eastern Europe and East Asia. States like Finland and Poland had little to expect from a united "White" Russia. For all their global ambitions, the Bolsheviks were, on the contrary, impractical and visionary men bound to perpetuate civil war and chaos in their unhappy country. Among the Great Powers, Japan came closest to that position: the Bolshevik Revolution

[38] "Western" is both a bit anachronistic and inaccurate, since the Allied Powers included Japan, but is used here for the sake of brevity.

gave her a free hand in China and in eastern Siberia; a resurgent Russian empire was not unlikely again to become a rival in China if not, indeed, to demand revenge for the defeat in 1905.

France had the most clear-cut case for wishing for the resurgence of a strong non-Communist Russia. Her financial stake in Russia had been the most substantial. But over and above this "capitalist" reason there were cogent political and strategic reasons. French statesmen had to worry about the eventual resurgence of Germany. Russia's absence from the rank of the Great Powers left France in Europe without a potential ally to offset Germany's superior population and resources. The new brood of states did not promise to show enough internal stability or power to replace Russia as an ally.

British policy on Russia was to show several contradictory strains. There were statesmen, like Winston Churchill, who saw Bolshevism as an enemy of Western civilization and urged the necessity of eradicating the threat before it could spread. There were people in the business community who had a stake in Russia free of Communists. White leaders, notably Denikin, were later to record their impression that some Englishmen looked with favor on the prospect of partitioning the vast areas of the former Russian empire. The mineral riches of the Transcaucasus and Central Asia would then inevitably fall within the British sphere of influence, and the centuries-old Russian threat to India would finally disappear.

But such sentiments and motivations could only have a secondary influence on British actions. Dreams of further imperial expansion had already clashed in 1919–20 with the realities: unrest in India and a rebellion in Ireland were sufficient to discourage any further expansion. A multitude of political and economic problems made the Prime Minister, David Lloyd George, tend to take an increasingly pragmatic view of Russian affairs. Britain's interest lay mainly in restoring world trade and hence in insuring some political stability on the Continent. If, for all the external help they received, the White forces were not to prevail, then Britain could not indefinitely maintain her opposition to the Bolsheviks. The influence of the Labour Party was rising, and its leaders were emphatically opposed to using British soldiers and money against a regime which they felt, if undemocratic, still represented the aspirations of the Russian workers.

Over and above this maze of conflicting views, interests, and ambitions, there was one overwhelming fact that nullified any prospect of a really massive foreign intervention in Russia. The nations of Europe had just been through four years of a bloody war. It went against the grain to demand of Englishmen and Frenchmen to go on fighting in a distant country for complex reasons they could not understand. In pre-1914 Europe, foreign policy even in democratic countries had been the preserve of the cabinets, which could commit their countries' resources and men for what they conceived to be reasons of state. But in 1919 that era seemed gone forever. Dissatisfaction and outright mutiny struck French units in the Ukraine and the British in northern Russia. By the end of the summer of 1919 it was clear that any sizable armed intervention in European Russia was attended with danger, and most of the British and French detachments were withdrawn.

One Great Power that was in a position to intervene effectively and on a large scale was, of course, the United States—unscathed by the war, with President Wilson widely acknowledged as the decisive figure at the peace conference. Yet it was precisely America that was most reluctant to undertake intervention while the war with Germany continued, and, once it was over, the pressure of American public opinion was strongest for the proposition that Russian affairs should be settled by the Russians themselves. The Bolshevik leaders appraised the United States—correctly— as the one Great Power whose leaders and people were least hostile to their cause. On March 12, the Soviet government transmitted to Wilson's emissary, Bullitt, for the consideration of the Allied Powers, proposals for armistice. They did not depart essentially from the tenor of Chicherin's proposals of the previous month. An immediate armistice was to take place between the regimes warring on the territories of the former Russian empire, followed by a peace conference to be held in a neutral country. The eventual peace was to be based on each regime's retaining the territory in its possession "until the peoples inhabiting those territories controlled by the de facto government will themselves decide to change their governments." Allied forces on Russian territories were to be withdrawn and the Allied blockade of Soviet Russia terminated. All the rival regimes were to disarm, subject to inspection and control. The proposals ended on a characteristic note: "The Soviet Government wishes especially to receive a semi-official guarantee from the United States and Great Britain that they will do everything possible to make France adhere to the conditions of the Armistice."[39]

The memorandum bore the strong personal imprint of Lenin: it was free from the self-abasement of Chicherin's February note; it was also free of Chicherin's insulting implication that we know we are being held up by a bunch of imperialist robbers. Its proposals reflected Lenin's confidence that without Allied support the rival White regimes would inevitably disintegrate and leave the field to the Bolsheviks. The memorandum was ignored by the powers at the peace conference—Kolchak's advance from Siberia into European Russia seemed to promise a speedy end to the whole Bolshevik problem—but it revealed once again the Soviets' ability

[39] *Documents on the Foreign Policy of the U.S.S.R.*, II, 91–95.

to roll with the punch, to agree to what they considered an unjustified and criminal interference in their own affairs, so as to gain time and to sow more seeds of disunity in the enemy camp. An American historian's verdict has been that, in view of future events, acceptance of the proposals themselves would have been the best way for the Allies to extricate themselves from the Russian mire.[40] One may add that any interruption or lessening of the intensity of the Civil War could have had beneficent results, and not only from the humanitarian point of view. History was to show that the Bolsheviks' greatest problems and crises came *after* the Civil War when they no longer had an excuse for using terror and violating their promises and when their party had not yet hardened into a monolithic and unyielding body. But then the whole history of the Revolution and the Civil War is strewn with wasted opportunities to alleviate the tragedy of the Russian people and of the world.

The fearful year of 1919 saw two moments of apparent mortal danger to the Bolsheviks. One was in the spring when the Siberian armies of Kolchak pushed their way well into European Russia, and the other, much more real, in September, when Denikin's advance actually threatened Moscow while Baltic Whites under Yudenich began a drive that was to reach the outskirts of Petrograd. In retrospect, it is easy to see that Kolchak's venture had no real chances of success, because for all the transient success of his detachments, he had no political or military base. Governmental authority in Siberia lay in a shambles; crisscrossing and conflicting foreign interests—Japanese, British, and French—hampered rather than helped the Whites' efforts. Many of Kolchak's subordinates, such as the notorious Semenov and Kalmykov, were in reality more like bandit chieftains than military commanders. The utmost chaos prevailed in the countryside, with Red and Green (the appellation given to independent, often anarchistic peasant detachments that fought at times with, at times against the Bolshevik guerrilla bands) murdering and pillaging indiscriminately. Kolchak's armies, once faced with by now better trained and better led Red troops, could not escape internal disintegration and military defeat.

The second threat was of a more substantial character. Denikin had the services of able former Tsarist commanders, some nucleus of disciplined troops, and at least some reasonably organized civil authority behind him. Yet he was to meet with a defeat in the fall, and by the beginning of 1920 the White cause in Russia was doomed.

Analyses of the Soviet success in the Civil War have been as varied

[40] George Kennan, *Russia and the West Under Lenin and Stalin* (Boston, 1961). p. 132.

(and as marked by their authors' political outlook) as those of the success of the Bolsheviks in November 1917. There have been often quite justified accusations of the White leaders' corruption, lack of political acumen, and reactionary views. Not until Wrangel's stand in the Crimea in 1920–21— really an epilogue to the war—did the White cause produce a leader who combined military talent with a recognition of the political and economic necessities of the moment. Here we must focus on those elements of diplomatic and related strategy which served the Bolsheviks well and which were absent or deficient in their enemies' camps. We mentioned before the Bolsheviks' lack of sensitivity on the question of territory, which on the contrary seemed to hypnotize their opponents and make them adopt the most uncompromising and foolish stands. The phantom of a quick military victory made the Whites forget or neglect the task of political and social organization of the territory in their grasp. And the art of temporizing, of apparent willingness to compromise, was, as we have seen, completely alien to their mentality. Indeed, Denikin's ultimate failure must be laid to his rigid position on the nationality issue, which made him begrudge not only the claims for independence of the Poles, Ukrainians, and Caucasian nationalities but even claims for simple autonomy advanced by such groups as the Don and Kuban Cossacks. He thus threw away valuable military support. At the time of his advance on Moscow, the Polish army facing the Bolsheviks in the west preserved complete neutrality. A synchronized attack by the Poles could have spelled the utmost disaster for the Red Army. But Denikin was known as an unbudging believer in "Russia great and undivided,"[41] who claimed that the separation of any territory of the former Tsarist empire could be sanctioned only by the Constituent Assembly of free Russia, and he evoked to the Poles their memories of Tsarist imperialism. Similarly, at the time of Kolchak's advance, the Finnish government showed readiness to help with its troops, which would have sealed the fate of Petrograd, provided Kolchak acknowledged uncompromisingly the independence of Finland. But here again, nationalist scruples prevented the "Supreme Ruler" (as Kolchak was called) from acknowledging what was a fact anyway.

Quite apart from the direct and disastrous effects of such nationalist wrongheadedness, it created a most negative impression on public opinion in the West. As Denikin wrote himself: "From Paris we often heard: the help from the Allies is not more extensive because the struggle of the South and East [Denikin's and Kolchak's regimes] is not popular among the European democracies; in order to gain their sympathies it is necessary to say two words: 'Republic and Federation.' Those promises we never

[41] Curiously enough, Denikin was himself half Polish and had been brought up in Russian Poland.

made."[42] This suicidal stubbornness contrasted with the Bolsheviks' apparent openmindedness, with their frank (if acidly expressed) recognition that the Allies and their clients like the Poles, Czechs, etc., could and did interfere in Russia's internal affairs because such were the facts of international life. To offset this interference, the Bolsheviks sought in effect to bribe the foreign powers and, at another level, to appeal to public opinion in the West. The effects of those appeals were not negligible. At the height of the war with Poland in 1920, action committees sprang up in Great Britain, organized for the most part by Labour Party affiliates, to keep the government from a more vigorous support of the Polish cause.

When it came to methods of warfare, there was, as usual in a civil war, little to choose between the two sides. Mass executions of war prisoners, pogroms of innocent civilians, and similar atrocities were common on both sides. Anti-Semitic excesses indulged in by the White troops and tolerated if not indeed encouraged by some subordinate commanders created an especially painful impression in the West. Within the Communist high command, Trotsky himself, hardly a humanitarian, still strove to establish stern discipline and to prevent wholesale executions of the "class enemy."

It is not to be thought that the Communists' political and organizational work was without flaws or that serious dissensions did not split the Bolshevik ranks. Trotsky's attempt to build a professional and disciplined army, staffed in the main by former professional officers who cast their lot with the Soviets, was constantly opposed and undermined by his enemies within the Communist hierarchy, notably Stalin and Voroshilov. Personal quarrels and dissensions were rife. But unlike any White regime, there was among the Bolsheviks one man whose personal and moral authority was unquestioned and whose word usually quieted or smoothed over the most violent personal or political dispute.

Lenin's authority and political skill were most notably employed in devising and preserving the one policy that had the most far-reaching effect on the internal and external fortunes of the Communist regime. The Whites' nationality policy, or rather the lack of it, was a contributing factor to their downfall. The Communists' oft-repeated slogan of national determination, on the other hand, procured them allies in the Civil War and friends abroad. Yet this policy was not adopted and carried through without considerable opposition within Communist ranks. In March 1919, Lenin had to read a lesson on the subject. When Soviet Russia made a treaty granting independence to Finland, he said, there were many Russian Communists who grumbled, though the Finnish regime then was Communist. "Because of such expressions, I then said, 'Scratch some Communists and you will

[42] A. Denikin, *The History of Russia's Time of Troubles* (in Russian) (Berlin, 1925), IV, 245.

find Great Russian chauvinists.'. . . . This example shows that one must not consider the national question from the single viewpoint of state unity. To be sure, this state unity is desirable. But we should struggle for it through propaganda and agitation for a voluntary union."[43] He resolutely refused to accept Bukharin's formula that national self-determination is justified only where the local working class desires it. Always too frank and unsubtle, Bukharin spelled out his naïve Machiavellianism: of course the Communists support the slogan of independence for the "Hottentots, Bushmen, Negroes, Hindus, etc." because their struggles hurt Communism's main enemy—British imperialism; but when it comes closer to home, there is no reason to respect the wish of the Polish or Finnish *bourgeoisie* to have independent states.

Implicit in Lenin's thinking, even if unconsciously, was a version of national self-determination not much different from Bukharin's. But his sense of political realism was as usual translated into an ideological formula: we must acknowledge the right to independence, the right to separate from Russia, of any nationality, even if it were currently led by the most reactionary social elements. The Soviet state, he might have added, was entering the most crucial period of the Civil War. At many subsequent points during 1919, intervention by Poland or Finland would spell disaster. What he did say, however, was clear enough. In the summer of 1917, when the Bolsheviks were fighting for power, Bukharin had also wanted a radical, far-reaching program, and Lenin had said, "We shall conquer power, wait awhile, and then go as far as you want."[44] The implication on the nationality and territorial question was the same: be patient.

The alarms, worries, and pressures from an unbelievable number of directions that were the daily fortune of the Bolshevik regime during those fateful years are well represented by a single dispatch of a Soviet representative abroad to Chicherin on January 26, 1920. From Copenhagen Maxim Litvinov wrote that there were rumors of the British sending an army to the Caucasus to the then independent republics of Georgia and Azerbaijan. In Berlin he heard that the Poles were about to move. Winston Churchill and Marshal Foch were scheming to turn Germany against Soviet Russia. . . .[45] Yet by the end of 1919 the back of the Civil War and Allied intervention had been broken. By the end of 1920, with the evacuation of Wrangel's army from the Crimea, all the major theaters of the war had been cleared. Some territorial and diplomatic adjustments remained to be made in the Far East and in the Caucasus.

[43] *The Eighth Congress of the Russian Communist Party, March 1919* (Moscow, 1933), pp. 107–8.

[44] *Ibid.*, p. 54.

[45] *Documents on the Foreign Policy of the U.S.S.R.*, II, 331.

The heritage of the Civil War and intervention has been variously assessed. Perhaps the least justified of many conclusions is that of Western analysts who saw the intervention as the decisive factor shaping Soviet Russia's subsequent hostility toward the capitalist world and her subsequent distrust in dealing with the non-Communist world. Hostility toward capitalism and toward the main representatives of the Western world—Britain, France, and the United States—had been built into Soviet ideology before the Revolution, and the most scrupulous noninterference by the West in Russian affairs would not have affected this fact. Again, a comparison with an internal political development may be instructive. One group of Mensheviks, headed by Martov, preserved throughout the Civil War the most scrupulous loyalty toward the Bolshevik regime. While opposing its internal policies, they supported the Soviet government in its struggle against the Whites and intervention. Yet, following the war, that party was banned, its leaders either imprisoned or, like Martov, compelled to go abroad. In brief, it did not require the intervention to infuse the Bolsheviks with the conviction that in the long run their ambitions were essentially incompatible with the existence of the capitalist world, and that the capitalist powers were essentially hostile toward Soviet Russia.

It would be fatuous, however, to maintain that the intervention did not have far-reaching effects. It undoubtedly helped to prolong the Civil War, and the latter left a permanent imprint on Soviet society and the Soviet system. Terror by the *Cheka*, the use of force to solve any and all social problems, became the accepted style of political life. It was only partly relaxed during the period following the Civil War, then to resume after 1928 with even greater ferocity under Stalin. At the time of the November Revolution, the Bolsheviks were not by any means a democratic party, yet there were still lingering traces of the humanitarian and democratic traditions of European social democracy within their creed. Had not the Party and the country been exhausted and brutalized by four years of subsequent strife, it is at least possible that this tradition would not have been extinguished. Russia under Communism could have never been a democratic state, but the full and appalling extent of totalitarianism and Stalinism could have been avoided.

In the early months of 1920, the Bolshevik regime stood victorious in its struggle for the main bulk of inheritance of the old empire. Some territorial losses had to be acknowledged. The three tiny Baltic republics—Estonia, Lithuania, and Latvia—were recognized in the course of the year and became the first states to establish regular diplomatic relations with the Russian Soviet Republic. The establishment of relations with Estonia on February 5, 1920, was hailed by Lenin as the opening of a new era in

Soviet diplomacy, and indeed this step had importance out of proportion to Estonia's size and significance. It marked the beginning of "normalcy" and diplomatic coexistence; it opened regular channels of commercial intercourse with the rest of the world.

The Polish war in the spring and summer of 1920 revived briefly the dangers and hopes of the past year. The mirage of European revolution had previously flickered on and off in short-lived Soviet-type regimes in Bavaria and Hungary. (Even in the midst of the Civil War, Lenin was contemplating sending armed help to Bela Kun's Hungarian Communist government, but reverses in the Ukraine and Kun's collapse spared the Soviets this potentially dangerous overextension of effort.) Now, with the Polish war, the mirage of the European revolution once more teased the Bolshevik leaders out of their realistic preoccupation with restoring their state.

Independent Poland was reborn after World War I as the result of the collapse of the three occupying empires: Germany, Russia, and Austria-Hungary. The problem of her frontiers soon became one of the thorniest issues of post-war Europe and at the peace conference. Was she to be confined to her ethnographic limits, or was her territory to take into account the frontiers of the great Polish Lithuanian state which, before its demise in the eighteenth century, had included vast areas settled in the main by Ukrainians and Byelorussians? The determining voice in Polish foreign policy belonged to Joseph Pilsudski, head of state and commander-in-chief of the Polish army. Pilsudski, a former socialist and native of Russian Poland, viewed with apprehension the prospect of a resurrected Russian empire.[46] He leaned to the solution that would emasculate the Russian colossus through the creation of a series of independent states in the Western areas of the former empire—such as the Baltic states, the Ukraine, and Byelorussia, possibly in a loose federal relation with Poland. This would create a safety belt isolating and weakening Russia to the point where she could no longer be a major menace to her neighbors. No White regime was ever likely to discuss or ever to acquiesce in such a solution, which would undo centuries of Russian expansion and throw the state back practically to the frontiers of medieval Muscovy. Thus, at the height of the White successes in 1919, the Polish armies kept their positions in the undeclared war with Soviet Russia, offering not one bit of help to Kolchak or Denikin. Confidential talks took place at the time

---

[46] Prior to 1914 Pilsudski had belonged to the Polish Socialist Party, a party that combined socialism with a strong dose of nationalism, unlike its rival, the Social Democratic Party of Poland and Lithuania, of which Rosa Luxemburg had been the most prominent member and which strenuously opposed Polish independence from the Marxist internationalist point of view. The Social Democratic Party contributed most of the founding members of the Polish Communist Party.

between Pilsudski's emissaries and Soviet agents.[47] In effect Poland remained neutral in the struggle as long as the White forces retained a chance of success.

With the Whites' defeat and reduction to Wrangel's enclave on the Black Sea, the Poles took a decidedly hostile attitude toward the Soviets. The Soviet government would have offered Poland a fairly generous territorial settlement in return for peace, yet there could be no question of its agreeing at this juncture to the independence of the Ukraine—the focal point of Pilsudski's ambitions. Rather disingenuously, the Soviet government tried to draw Warsaw's attention to the dangers it faced in military confrontation with the Soviet republics.[48] Thus Chicherin on February 14, 1920, in a telegram to Litvinov in Copenhagen, indicated the line of propaganda to be taken:

> Rumors are reaching us about the desire of the circles around Ludendorff to unite with us against Poland. We do not want to follow that policy. . . . The Poles are insufficiently aware of the danger of Germany. If against all our peaceful attempts Poland goes against Moscow, she will find herself between two fires; Poland hopes for too much from France, the Ludendorff circle considers that French troops would be incapable of fighting. . . . One should use the press to stress these dangers threatening the Poles.[49]

Actual hostilities began in the spring. The Polish war effort was assisted by the Ukrainian national troops of Ataman Semyon Petliura. At first, the Poles and their Ukrainian allies scored dazzling successes, capturing Kiev early in May.[50] But much as the peasantry of the Ukraine had opposed Bolshevism, Petliura's alliance with the Poles—who until the Revolution had constituted a substantial landowning element in the country—compromised him in their eyes. Ukrainian nationalism had been weakened through three years of internal dissension and constant struggles and depredations in the unhappy country. The Polish army had been improvised hastily, its system of supply and its leadership were in no sense superior to those of the Red troops.

[47] On the negotiations, see Piotr Wandycz, "Secret Soviet-Polish Peace Talks in 1919," *Slavic Review*, September 1965, pp. 425–49.

[48] Theoretically, until the formation of the Soviet Union in 1924 the Ukraine and Byelorussia were independent Soviet republics, yet in fact they were controlled from Moscow.

[49] *Documents on the Foreign Policy of the U.S.S.R.*, II, 370–71.

[50] The military story of the Polish war thus followed the pattern of the Civil War: the attacking side would advance without much difficulty against the enemy usually fleeing before a frontal attack; but then the attacker's lines of supply and communication would become overextended, and an almost equally rapid withdrawal or flight would succeed the initial triumphs.

The Polish war enabled the Soviet regime to capitalize, this time with hardly any compunctions, on *Russian* nationalism. The traditional image of the Pole as the hereditary enemy of Russia was invoked as freely as the class one of landowners greedy once more to enslave the Ukrainian and Byelorussian peasant. Former Tsarist officers flocked to the Soviet armies offering their services in what now had become a national war. Some expressions of this chauvinism became embarrassing. Trotsky felt compelled to reprimand the military journal which contrasted the "perfidious Jesuitism of the Poles" with the "open and honest nature of the Russians."[51] In June the Red Army passed to an offensive, and soon the Polish retreat turned into a rout.

At the end of July, the Soviet army reached Poland's previous frontiers. The problem now arose whether to carry the war into ethnic Poland and whether an attempt should be made to establish there a Soviet regime. As if to show that his prudence and sobriety in foreign affairs were not superhuman, Lenin became an enthusiastic proponent of the latter solution. Once again the flame of revolution promised to spread westward, first to Poland, then perhaps to Germany. The Western Powers now rushed in to save Poland. Foreign Secretary Curzon's note to Russia proposed an immediate armistice along the line formulated according to the ethnographic principle by his advisers in 1919.[52] Chicherin's reply to Lord Curzon bore out the Russians' confidence; it pointed out that neither Great Britain nor the "so-called League of Nations," which Curzon had also invoked, had appealed for an armistice while the Poles were advancing. The Russians' conditions for an armistice, conveyed on August 9, were explicit: within a month the Polish army was to be reduced to 50,000 men; all Polish military supplies beyond the need of that force were to be turned over to the Red Army; the families of all the Polish casualties were to be given free land.[53] Not included in the note to the British government was another and crucial condition addressed to the Poles: a sizable "workers' militia" was to take over "protection of order and the safety of the population in Poland. Conditions and the manner of organization of this militia will be spelled out while settling the details of the peace treaty."[54] The last condition should be considered in connection with the creation by the Red Army of the provisional Polish revolutionary committee. Its head

---

[51] Leon Trotsky, *How the Revolution Armed* (Moscow, 1923), II, Part 2, 153.

[52] E. H. Carr, *The Bolshevik Revolution 1917–1923* (New York, 1953), III, 209. This was the famous Curzon Line which would make its reappearance during World War II.

[53] *Documents on the Foreign Policy of the U.S.S.R.*, III (Moscow, 1959), 100–101.

[54] *Ibid.*, p. 137.

was Julian Marchlewski, the Polish Communist who had negotiated with the Polish government the year before, and it included the Polish-born head of the *Cheka*, Dzerzhinsky, and his deputy Jan Unschlicht. With those conditions fulfilled, the Soviet governments (the fiction of independent Ukraine was still maintained) promised generally to recognize independent Poland and even to grant it some land east of the Curzon Line.

Inherent in this attempt to turn Poland into a Soviet satellite was Lenin's conviction that Polish Communism represented a considerable force and that local uprisings would facilitate the Red Army's task. As to the former, some of his Polish advisers showed greater realism: hostility to the Russians was likely to keep the forces of Polish radicalism in check. A grave psychological error was compounded by the membership of the provisional Communist government of Poland. The very names of Dzerzhinsky and Unschlicht would make even the most radical Polish worker join in the defense of his country.

In August, with the Red Army within reach of Warsaw, the Poles counterattacked. The Soviet troops were dispersed over too wide a front, and it was the Russians' turn to suffer a rout. Analyses of this defeat have always been tinged with politics. Trotsky was to claim that Stalin, as commissar of the Southern Front, delayed the junction with the main forces before Warsaw. The latter's commander, Tukhachevsky, has been accused of political ambitions that made him imprudent in the search for a quick success. Finally, Lenin himself, through his insistence that the Red Army reach the German frontiers as fast as possible, may have contributed to its fatal dispersion. Both sides now gave up their far-reaching ambitions. An armistice was signed in October, and the Treaty of Riga in March 1921 set the Russo-Polish frontier as it was to exist until 1939. Large Byelorussian and Ukrainian areas remained with Poland, but the main body of the Ukraine continued as a Soviet republic.

Lenin's comments on the Polish war continued, even after the armistice, to reflect his nostalgia over what was the last attempt to carry the revolution westward on the bayonets of the Red Army. "If Poland had become Soviet, if the Warsaw workers received the help from Soviet Russia that they expected . . . the Versailles Treaty would have collapsed."[55] Such sentiments were untypically unrealistic. The defeat in the Polish war may well have been providential. The Soviet state in the 1920's was hardly strong enough to absorb and communize 25 million Poles. Conquest of Poland, not to mention an attempt to overrun Germany, would have produced a full-fledged military reaction by the Allies. In retrospect, the defeat was possibly a blessing in disguise for the future of Communism and Soviet Russia.

[55] *Works*, XXXI, 281.

The truce with Poland predetermined the fate of the last enclave of the Whites in Russia. Wrangel's army, defeated and pushed back into the Crimea, was soon afterward (in November) evacuated from Russian soil. The task of regathering the lands of the old empire now proceeded in a more leisurely fashion. The Soviets were willing to bide their time. Thus in the Far East, to facilitate the evacuation of Japanese troops from eastern Siberia, an independent buffer state, the Far Eastern Republic, had been set up.

> From the very beginning the Soviet government regarded the Far Eastern Republic as a temporary creation, having as its aim to put distance between it and Japan and thus to provide a necessary breathing spell. . . . This buffer state indeed avoided a clash between Soviet Russia and Japan at the moment when Russia still did not feel strong enough to rule the Far Eastern territory.[56]

By the end of 1922, the need for such evasions had passed. Japan, especially in view of the position of the United States, was no longer in a position to resume a Siberian adventure, and the Far Eastern Republic was formally annexed to Soviet Russia. The last territory in that part of the world was recovered in 1925 when the Japanese troops evacuated northern Sakhalin.

During the Civil War, the Transcaucasian area was a veritable mosaic of various independent authorities and governments reflecting the fantastically varied national and political complexion of the region. In 1920 they fell one by one into the Soviet lap. The only exception seemed to be Georgia. Here Menshevism had deep roots, and its leaders, like Zhordania and Tseretelli, who had once promised to play an important role in the wider sphere of Russian politics, managed to establish an independent republic that in 1920 was solemnly recognized by the Soviet government. Unlike the case of practically every other anti-Bolshevik regime in the territory of the old empire, there could be no question of the democratic and progressive character of the Georgian regime: it distributed land to the peasants and nationalized transportation and industry.[57] For a few months the tiny republic was the toast of the Western socialists, whose delegations visited Georgia and rendered glowing accounts of its democratic virtues. But as happened with the Mensheviks in Russia proper, those virtues were also to become contributing factors to their eventual fall in Georgia. Under the treaty with the Soviet government, the Georgian authorities amnestied the local Communists and released them from jail. The latter, needless to say, started preparations for an uprising and expected the Red Army's

[56] Maisky, *op. cit.*, p. 178.

[57] Richard Pipes, *The Formation of the Soviet Union* (Cambridge, Mass., 1964), p. 213.

help. In early 1921, when plans for attacking Georgia matured and the Red Army was now free to move, Lenin became once more his cautious self. This conquest could lead to complications with Turkey, and most of all with Great Britain, with whom the Soviets were conducting, at the time, trade negotiations. But pressure from the Bolsheviks primarily concerned with Caucasian affairs, especially Sergo Ordzhonikidze, finally overcame his scruples and apprehensions. Georgia was invaded and taken. The socialist circles in the West fumed and protested, but the only power capable of rendering help to this inheritor of the democratic strain of Russian socialism, Great Britain, did not lift a finger. Georgia became Soviet. Aware of the popular strength of Menshevism, Lenin urged caution and perhaps some combination with Georgian Mensheviks who were willing to serve the Soviet cause. But as events were to show, one did not even have to "scratch" such Georgian-born Bolsheviks as Stalin and Ordzhonikidze to discover All-Russian chauvinists. The usual pattern of centralistic control from Moscow was also applied in Georgia.

Thus what in 1917–18 one would have thought the most improbable sequence of the Bolshevik Revolution had come to pass: the Bolshevik government stood supreme over the vast majority of multinational territories once under the sway of the Tsars. Weak, torn by internal dissensions, the Bolsheviks had been opposed by the world's greatest powers and by considerable elements of their own population. But—and this was the main lesson of the Civil War and intervention—all those efforts proved unavailing for one reason: the opponents of Communism lacked unity and a common sense of purpose.

3. *The Comintern*

The record of Soviet diplomacy between 1918 and 1921 is one of flexibility and reasonableness. Following just the official documents and notes of the Soviet government during that period, one might well conclude that the Soviet leaders learned amazingly well to navigate in the seas of international diplomacy, that the very same men who in November 1917 had planned to "abolish" foreign relations and expected a world revolution within a few weeks, by the end of 1920 accepted the realities of the world situation. Even the Polish incident, an apparent throwback to the earlier millenarian vision, had a more solid justification: beyond the hopes of an uprising of the Polish proletariat and its chain effect on Germany, Lenin and his colleagues counted on the concrete might of the Red Army. Psychologically it was a tremendous distance travelled from November 1917, when it was confidently expected that soviets would soon be set up in Berlin and Vienna, to, say, the spring of 1920, when the Soviet regime settled down patiently to wait a few years for complete Japanese withdrawal from the Russian Far East.

Yet the millenarian dream of Communist victory was not discarded but merely compartmentalized. For all their conciliatory talk and even submissiveness, first toward the Germans, then toward the Allies, there was one thing the Communists refused to promise even at the moment of their greatest weakness: cessation of revolutionary propaganda. Yes, Chicherin would write, they are ready to pledge noninterference in the internal affairs of other countries, but they cannot prohibit "private persons" from issuing appeals to the English or German proletariat. Sometimes, as we have seen, even that fiction would break down and the Commissar for Foreign Relations himself would issue inflammatory revolutionary statements. The belief in the power of propaganda and agitation was inherent in the Bolshevik's makeup. What else, after all, had won Russia for them? From a little, insignificant party of about ten or twenty thousand on the eve of the March Revolution, they had grown by November to a body of 300,000 members and some millions of sympathizers that won power. It is no exaggeration to say that the Bolshevik government would more willingly have parted with an important province than to subject itself to restraint in propaganda and agitation, through which it was confident it could win the world.

But propaganda and agitation were in the Bolshevik scheme of things effective only in conjunction with organization. The thought of a worldwide Communist movement which would unite *parties* professing militant Marxism had been with Lenin since the beginning of the war. He had worked in that direction in exile at the conferences of Zimmerwald and Kienthal, but now, with a Russian base, Communism could reach out to become a world movement. The Third International, or Comintern, was officially inaugurated in March 1919. The Soviet state was still to undergo a very critical period in the Civil War, but just as one year before, when the Germans seemed on the point of taking over Petrograd, Lenin had insisted that the Party be re-named, so now in another deadly emergency he and his companions found time and energy to attend to something connected not directly with their survival but with the future of the world movement. The setting up of the Comintern was prompted by news that the Second International was going to re-establish its organization, shattered by the war. The prospect of the tradition of social democracy being revived and becoming again the predominant tendency in the international workers' movement was alarming enough to hurry up the establishment of a rival International, even though the conditions were inauspicious. In the midst of the Civil War, with communications with the West disrupted, the technical difficulties themselves were overwhelming. The most important Communist movement outside of Russia, that of Germany, was not of the opinion that the time was ripe for setting up a Communist International. Before her assassination in January 1919, Rosa Luxemburg expressed opposition to the idea.

The result was that the First Congress of the Comintern bore a somewhat fraudulent character.[58] About thirty-five delegates purported to represent parties that, with the main exception of the Russian and German ones, existed only on paper or in small groups of the given nationality in Russia. Christian Rakovsky, Bulgarian and former Rumanian citizen, currently the head of the Soviet government in the Ukraine, was because of his background designated to represent the Balkan Revolutionary Federation. Reinstein, a resident of Russia for some years, purported to represent the American Socialist Workers' Party. Of the great number of Poles in the Soviet service, Jan Unschlicht was selected to represent the Polish Communists, his fellow Pole and superior in the *Cheka*, Dzerzhinsky, being presumably too busy. The Russian Communists were represented by a galaxy of stars: Lenin, Trotsky, Bukharin, and Zinoviev. German was the language of the deliberations. Zinoviev was elected head of the Executive Committee of the International; Radek, currently in prison in Germany, its secretary.

Speeches and declarations at the Congress emphasized its unalterable hostility to the orthodox social democratic tradition. The delegates condemned parliamentarism and "bourgeois freedoms" and demanded the establishment of soviets as the only appropriate form of proletarian power everywhere. "Through the soviets the working class, having conquered power, will manage all spheres of economic and cultural life, as is the case at present in Russia."[59] The manifesto of the International, while pointing out the road to revolution in Europe, also paid some attention to the colonial areas. "Colonial slaves of Africa and Asia: The hour of proletarian dictatorship in Europe will also be the hour of your own liberation."[60]

Apart from the regular socialist parties, the main target of the declaration was clearly Great Britain: "Matured by the entire course of events over decades, the war was unleashed through the direct and deliberate provocation of Great Britain."[61] This charge was to reflect the theme of the Comintern for a long time to come: Britain and her empire were the main prop of the world capitalist order; British diplomacy was especially

---

[58] One is reminded of the First Congress of the Russian Social Democratic Party in 1898, when nine delegates with very uncertain credentials proceeded to found the ancestor of the Communist Party.

[59] Jane Degras, ed., *The Communist International, 1919–1943: Documents,* I: 1919–22 (London and New York, 1956), 45.

[60] *Ibid.,* p. 43.

[61] *Ibid.,* p. 39.

wily and perfidious, intent on playing off states against each other; the United States was in turn moving into the British position, "weakening one camp by helping the other, intervening in military operations only so far as to secure for itself all the advantages of the situation."[62] This analysis of the international situation thus went back to Lenin's *Imperialism*. The breakdown and downfall of capitalism, which Marx had proclaimed would be the consequence of *internal* developments in the most advanced industrial countries, was here asserted to be the result of competition among the capitalist states on the world scale plus united revolutionary action by the world proletariat.

Here again, too, was the paradoxical view of the world scene that has persisted in Communist thinking up to our own day: on the one hand the capitalists are said to be heedlessly speeding to their doom through rivalry and wars and through their inability to coordinate their actions to suppress the as yet weak Communist state; on the other hand they are credited with a Machiavellian skill in synchronizing their actions to enslave mankind under the cover of humanitarian and democratic slogans. "Shall all toiling mankind become the bond slaves of a victorious world clique who, under the name of the League of Nations and aided by an 'international' army and 'international' navy, will plunder and strangle in one place and cast crumbs elsewhere, while everywhere shackling the proletariat, with the sole object of maintaining their own rule?"[63]

The circumstances surrounding the creation and early development of the Third International predetermined its evolution into a supporting and subordinate branch of the Soviet state. This was made inevitable by the fact that Communism triumphed only in Russia and the Soviet republics in Hungary and Bavaria in 1919 were of short duration. It was thus natural that loyalty to the "Fatherland of Socialism" would for a foreign Communist take precedence over any other feeling. Yet one should not read the future Stalinist pattern into the beginnings of the Comintern. As late as 1922 the belief in its supranational character was strong enough to make the opposition within the Russian Communist Party address to the Comintern a complaint against their own regime. It took some years before the activities of the Comintern were fully synchronized with those of Soviet foreign policy and before the foreign Communists were to translate affection for Soviet Russia into unquestioning obedience. Until 1925, the leadership of the organization lay in the hands of Zinoviev. A long-time associate of Lenin, Zinoviev had at the same time strained relations with such party notables as Trotsky and Bukharin. He was widely accused of cowardice in 1917 when he had opposed the November

[62] *Ibid.*, p. 40.

[63] *Ibid.*, p. 41.

uprising. An ambitious and unscrupulous man, he was feared rather than respected in the Party, and he obviously hoped to use his prestigious post as head of the Comintern as a stepping-stone to the succession to Lenin. With the latter's incapacitating illness in 1922 there began a covert struggle for the leadership, and until his fall in 1925 Zinoviev had the opportunity, which he misused, to employ the Comintern as a weapon in this struggle.

For the time being, however, his function was that of the executor of policies laid down by Lenin. With the Civil War, the functions of the Comintern's Executive Committee were limited largely to the issuance of flamboyant declarations. The great dangers of 1919–21 were paralleled by great opportunities, and both led to extravagant expectations. The May 1, 1920, declaration of the Comintern proclaimed: "In 1919 the great Communist International was born. In 1920 the great international Soviet Republic will come to birth."[64] By the time the Second Congress assembled in July 1920 the greatest danger to the Soviet state had passsed; the Red Army was approaching Warsaw.

The Second Congress can be considered the real founding and organizing meeting of the Communist International. It was attended by delegates from forty-one countries, and many of them, unlike those at the First Congress, represented real rather than fictitious parties. The theme of help to the Soviet state was the predominant one. An appeal was issued to the workers of Western countries to paralyze their governments' efforts to help "White Poland." The mover of the resolution, the German Communist Paul Levi, who was shortly afterward to part ways with the Party, was carried away by the occasion to the point of paraphrasing Nelson's famous signal at Trafalgar: "Russia expects everybody to do his duty," he exclaimed in English.[65] This would have been a realistic device for the Comintern during the quarter-century of its existence.

If euphoria over the prospects of a European revolution spurred on by the advancing Red Army was to be short-lived, then another aspect of the Congress' work was to prove of a durable and fundamental importance. This was the voting of the famous Twenty-one Conditions of acceptance of foreign parties into the International. Of these, the first twenty are acknowledged to have been written by Lenin and bear his imprint in substance and style. The Conditions require of every party desirous of joining the movement a complete separation from and exclusion from its ranks of all people and groups adhering to the old social democratic traditions. No compromise is possible with other socialist

[64] *Ibid.*, p. 53.

[65] *Second Congress of the Communist International* (stenographic report, Moscow, 1920), p. 41.

movements: "Every party which wishes to belong to the Third International is obligated to unmask not only open social patriotism but also the falseness and hypocrisy of socialist pacifism . . . to admit the necessity of full and absolute break with the policy of the 'center.' "[66] The duty of unconditional support of the Soviet republic is required of every would-be member party, with both legal and illegal means to be used. "It is necessary to have systematic propaganda and agitation in the armed forces and the organization of Communist cells in every military unit. This work the Communists would have to conduct for the most part illegally."[67]

The Conditions are emphatic on the duty of Communists to exploit parliaments wherever they are functioning and at the same time to subordinate their parliamentary representatives to the strictest Party discipline. It is conceded, rather amusingly, that *legal* political work carries with it dangers of demoralization: "The Communist parties of those countries where the Communists conduct their work legally should undertake periodic purges of the membership to purify the party from the petty bourgeois elements which inevitably get stuck to it."[68] Similar imperatives are addressed to the subject of trade unionism, the work for the emancipation of colonies, complete supervision of the party press, etc. In brief, the Twenty-one Conditions made it clear that the Communist movement was an open conspiracy against every government outside that of Soviet Russia, that no constitutional, national, or professional loyalties could stand in the way of a professed Communist.

It is equally clear that this openness was designed to break once and for all with the tradition of the Second International, to shut and bolt the door on any possibility of a reunion of world socialisms. The Communist International, it was emphatically stated, must be infinitely more centralized than the Second International had ever been. All decisions of the Comintern were unconditionally binding on the member parties. (This statement was hardly softened by the admission that the central body was to take cognizance of the conditions under which the given national party operated.) As with the original Bolshevik faction created in 1903, so with the Comintern, Lenin's intention was to create not so

---

[66] *Ibid.*, p. 652.

[67] *Ibid.*, p. 651. This requirement sets in perspective the famous "Zinoviev letter," which was to lead to Russia's diplomatic break with Great Britain in 1924 and which purported to be the order of the Executive Committee of the Comintern to the British Communist Party to conduct subversive propaganda within the armed forces. The letter was in all likelihood a forgery. Yet, as is clear from this Condition, it would have been superfluous in any case, and it is difficult to see how it created the furor it did among both the believers and unbelievers in its authenticity. See below, pp. 157–58.

[68] *Ibid.*, p. 653.

much a political party or a supranational movement, as a centralized, quasi-religious, and quasi-military movement devoted to the revolution and to service of the Soviet state. Future interpreters were to reach for comparisons; international Communism was to be seen as paralleling the Jesuit order, with its vow of obedience, or, more fancifully, the medieval sect of the Assassins, etc. In fact, it was a unique and unparalleled political organization, one that would have startled the most militant socialist before 1917 and that could be understood only against the fantastic background of the world war, the Bolshevik Revolution, and the Civil War.

For all the cosmopolitan training of Lenin and those in his entourage who directed the Comintern, like Zinoviev and Radek, the Twenty-one Conditions reflected a strong belief that foreign Communists should follow the Russian example not only insofar as their ideology and organization were concerned, but also in tactics. Some of the Conditions are almost amusingly irrelevant to conditions in Western countries, lifted out of the history of the Russian revolutionary movement. Article 5 stresses the importance of conducting revolutionary work "through worker revolutionaries who have their ties with the villages." The worker who never lost his ties with his village and who went back to it at the time of distress or unemployment was a common phenomenon in Russia, but Greenwich Village was probably the only one with which most New York workers were acquainted. The straightforward revolutionary and conspiratorial preoccupations of the Twenty-one Conditions were to handicap Western Communists heavily. In 1920–21, most of the workers in Western Europe still looked with some sympathy upon Communism and Soviet Russia, but the contemptuous tone of the Comintern's declaration about such subjects as parliamentarism and trade unionism, above all the strict subjection of local Communist parties to the central authority, was to dissipate much of this initial good will and prevent the main European parties, with the exception of the German one, from developing into mass movements.

Even before the Second Congress, Lenin declared his belief that the Russian road to revolution should be the guide to Communists everywhere. His *Left Communism—Childish Disease of Communism* upbraided foreign Communists who refused to exploit the opportunities inherent in parliamentary institutions, his rejoinder being that the Bolsheviks in 1908 participated (on his insistence) in the elections to the Third Duma and yet did not become a parliamentary party. But the pamphlet had another aim in addition to its ideological one. The British Communists scoffed at the idea of any collaboration with the Labour Party, holding its leaders, as Lenin himself did, to be the most disgusting reformists and opportunists, putting in the shade in this respect such Communist targets as the "renegade" Kautsky and other leaders of German social democracy. Yet the gist of Lenin's advice to the British Communists was to associate themselves with the Labour Party in order to defeat the proponents of intervention in Russia, like Churchill and others. The famous simile used was that the British Communists should support the Labour leaders like "the rope supports a hanging man."

The pamphlet thus had two aspects. One was, for all the dogmatic and unyielding tone of the Twenty-one Conditions, that Communists should everywhere adopt flexible tactics, that left doctrinairism was as inappropriate as reformism. In pursuance of these tactics, the British Communist Party was for years to apply for admission to the Labour Party, with the obvious aim of exploiting its unrivalled influence over the working class. In a straightforward competition for the British workers the Communist Party was bound to lose, hence why not work through more subtle means? But beyond this ideological-tactical advice, the implication was very clear that the policies of foreign Communists should be shaped primarily with a view to helping Soviet Russia and that no ideological scruples were to stand in the way of this aim. The Labour Party, for all its anti-Communism, was strongly against intervention in Russia, and this in 1920 was the decisive factor in determining the Comintern attitude toward that party. The framework of the Twenty-one Conditions was not to bar alliances, shifts, and other flexible arrangements, provided that the given Communist Party always retained its organizational separateness and its allegiance to the Soviet republic.

The organizational strait-jacket of the Comintern was thus bound to alienate some militant socialists in the West; the precept of sudden ideological and tactical shifts wherever so ordained by the Comintern was to prove unbearable to others. The out-and-out revolutionary resolve of the Comintern was also to complicate the task of Communists in countries where the working class has learned to consider as the main duty of *its* party the constant struggle for the improvement of its living conditions. On that subject, the declarations of the early congresses are silent. Indeed, at one of them Lenin reproved a delegate who held that the revolutionary struggle should not lead to the worsening of the living conditions of the worker. The Revolution in Russia, he answered, brought with it untold sufferings for the workers; why then should Communists elsewhere begrudge similar sacrifices for the same ultimate aim?

The sum total of these factors was to condemn Communist parties in highly industrialized countries to be rather insignificant minorities in their national life, and to ensure that—short of very abnormal conditions, like war or the most extreme depression—they could never aspire to be anything else. It is possible to see here simply the inability of the

Russian Communist leaders to understand the psychology of the Western worker,[69] and, as we have seen, there is a great deal of truth in this contention. But there is also another element: Lenin's vision of politics was essentially "catastrophic," i.e., great social convulsions were alone to give the tightly organized and disciplined parties the opportunity to bring about revolutions. No heed was given to the politician's usual aims to win popularity, to convince the majority. In striking contrast to official Soviet foreign policy of the period, with its caution and sobriety, the original concept of the Comintern exuded revolutionary impatience. This concept was bound to undergo a subtle change once the period of the Civil War was over and the capitalist world showed signs of achieving a certain stability. But the lack of prospects of success for foreign Communists in turn increased their dependence, organizational as well as psychological, on Soviet Russia. With no hope of rapid victory in their own country, in their virtual political isolation, they were bound to become more and more identified with and dependent upon the progress of Communism in the country of its origin.

In the very first years, the extent of Russian domination of the Comintern was still irritating enough to bring out some dissonances. At the Second Congress, some delegates objected to the decision to fix the seat of the organization in Moscow. A Dutch Communist urged that the Comintern be transferred elsewhere, as indeed had been planned in 1919. If the seat remained in Russia then one should not pretend that the ruling organs of the Comintern could really be international in spirit; the foreign Communists on its Executive Committee would inevitably lose touch with conditions at home.

But in the immediate post-war situation, still fraught with revolutionary possibilities, the argument that an international revolution required centralization and discipline still carried a great deal of weight. "We cannot change the Communist International into a mere post office, like the Second International," wrote Zinoviev to the German Independent Social Democratic Party, which oscillated between the Second and Third Internationals.[70] He went on to explain the background of the Twenty-one Conditions; the international Communist movement could not afford to be swamped by "opportunists," by those parties and leaders which because of a vague attachment to the idea of revolution wanted to join it: "To a certain extent the Communist International has become the fashion. . . . We open our doors wide to every *mass proletarian* revolutionary organization, but we think it over ten times before opening the doors of the

[69] This is the gist of E. H. Carr's analysis. See *op. cit.*, III, 170–84.

[70] Degras, *op. cit.*, p. 197.

Communist International to newcomers from the camp of the petty bourgeois, bureaucratic, opportunist leaders." This was an attempt to instill in
the international Communist movement the same tortuous tactics, the
ability to have one's cake and eat it too, which had served the Bolsheviks
so well in the political struggle in their own country. By the ordinary
semantics the prescribed Communist tactics were the most opportunistic
of all. What else was the advice to the British Communists to support
the Labour Party and to keep applying for membership in it? In fact, the
Communists wanted to enjoy access to and the use of any mass workers'
movement, at the same time preserving their own freedom of action and
a separate organization. The revolutionary fervor of foreign comrades
was to be doled out or restrained, other socialist parties were to be wooed
or attacked, according to the views of the Comintern's Executive, and
those views corresponded increasingly with the interests of the Soviet state.

But this pattern, which was to become firmly established and accepted,
was still being worked out. The foreign Communist leaders were still not
"trained" adequately to accept without a murmur abrupt and dazzling
changes prescribed from Moscow. The guiding hand of the Comintern
was still not firm enough, and the Soviet leadership itself not as monolithic
as it was to be under Stalin, to assure absolute coordination and compliance. The leadership still could be faltering and indecisive, signals
from the Comintern's Executive might still express the adventurist
feelings of this or that member of its leadership.

This was to be the lesson of the March 1921 action in Germany. With
the general situation in Germany chaotic, riots occurred in the Mansfeld
area which led to intervention by the German army. The Central Committee of the German Communist Party then called for an insurrection
and proclaimed a general strike. It is not clear to what extent the Comintern spurred this action. The top leadership of the Russian Communists
was too busy with the critical situation at home—the Kronstadt mutiny
and the widespread famine—to pay detailed attention to the German
crisis. (Zinoviev was particularly preoccupied, since, as Communist boss
of Petrograd, he had brutally put down some strikes there early in 1921
which contributed to the mutiny of the sailors.) The Comintern's man in
Germany, the Hungarian Bela Kun, was known for his adventurist bent,
and it is not clear to what extent he acted on his own. In any event,
the general strike, opposed by the mass of the German workers, fizzled
out and the Communist uprisings were suppressed. The sequence resulted
in a mass decline in the membership of the German Communist Party
and loud recriminations about the responsibility for the fiasco. Zinoviev's
verdict on the failure was a masterful combination of a platitude with
an understatement: "The leaders of the Communist Party of Germany

made, it is true, only one mistake: they made an incorrect estimate of the situation."[71]

The events of early 1921 marked the passing of an era, both in Russia and in European Communism. Just as the Civil War drew to an end and the NEP succeeded War Communism, so in the life of European Communism the romantic and adventurist period came to an end. In another sphere, however, the revolutionary activity of the Comintern continued along the original lines and was from the beginning more closely dovetailed with "official" Soviet policy. This was the policy in the Orient. It proceeded from the perception of Lenin's *Imperialism* that nationalist movements in the colonial and semi-colonial areas were a potent ally of militant Marxism and that the awakening Orient was the most fertile place for revolutionary agitation. Among the very first diplomatic notes of the Soviet government, after it found its feet upon the conclusion of the Brest Litovsk Treaty, were renunciations of the special position of imperial Russia in Persia and China. The Soviet government hastened to disassociate itself from the standard practices of European powers in the Orient, with their spheres of influence, special privileges for their citizens, etc. We have seen that whenever the phantom of a revolution in the West arose, especially in Germany, all other international concerns of Communism were shoved aside. By the same token, whenever prospects in the West dimmed, new stress was laid on the opportunities in the East. A startling demonstration of this tendency is a secret communication of Trotsky to the Central Committee in August 1919.[72] The paper noted the current reverses in the Civil War and outside the borders of Russia: "The collapse of the Hungarian Republic, our reverses in the Ukraine and the possible loss to us of the Black Sea coast, together with our successes on the Eastern Front, significantly alter our international orientation, bringing into the foreground what yesterday still stood in the middle distance." Trotsky went on to point to what under the circumstances of the moment was assuredly a fantastic dream:

> The road to India may prove at the given moment to be more readily passable and shorter for us than the road to Soviet Hungary. The sort of army which at the moment can be of no great significance in the European scales can upset the unstable balance of Asian relationships of colonial dependence, give a direct push to an uprising on the part of the oppressed masses, and assure the triumph of such a rising in Asia.[73]

[71] *Ibid.*, p. 215.
[72] Jan Meijer, ed., *The Trotsky Papers, 1917–22* (The Hague, 1964), I, 621–27.
[73] *Ibid.*, p. 623.

All this with Denikin's armies moving on Moscow!

Trotsky's vision carries us across the decades to remind us of the Chinese Communists moving a whole revolutionary regime and army thousands of miles and, still more recently, to their theory of the world's "countryside" (the undeveloped rural areas) surrounding the "cities" (the advanced industrial countries), where the revolution either has slackened off or is still quite distant. But Trotsky's view is even more extravagant: the revolution defeated in one continent will move to another to await the recrudescence of the revolutionary situation in Europe. Only at the end of the paper does a note of realism creep in: "In the period immediately ahead preparation of a military thrust against India to aid the Indian revolution can only be of a preliminary, preparatory character."

Trotsky's fantasies apart, the conviction that the Far East offered the most fruitful field for revolution and that the Asian masses could be turned into the most useful allies of the Soviet state matured during the early days of the Soviet regime, and it was to stay with it for a long time. It posed at the outset a very serious ideological and tactical problem: both by the letter of Marxian orthodoxy and as a matter of fact one could hardly expect the establishment of socialism in Egypt or China within a forseeable time. The countries involved had little or no industrial proletariat, they were in the stage of development described by Marxian categories as pre-industrial. But so far as Lenin's thinking on the subject was concerned, no ideological scruples should prevent the Communists from allying themselves with the enemies of their enemies. The logic of his doctrine claimed that one should support a middle-class nationalist movement if it is directed against the imperial power, and one should not scorn even more retrograde social groups—feudal or religious leaders— as long as they worked for the freedom of their countries against Britain or France. Any hesitation on this point or apparent duplicity would strip the Communist doctrine of self-determination of most of its propaganda value. In pursuance of this point, Lenin clashed, as we have seen, with Bukharin, whose Marxian scruples prevented him from taking seriously the claim for independence of the "Bushmen and Hottentots." But the issue went beyond the formulas. There were going to be Communist parties in India, China, etc. Were those Communists to subordinate their aspirations for power and reform to the national struggle and act merely as accomplices of the upper classes?

This issue was to be the subject of many disputes and problems besetting the Comintern and Soviet policy-makers during the next decades. Already at the Second Congress of the Comintern, Lenin clashed on this point with a young Indian Communist, M. N. Roy, who objected to the licensing of any national liberation movement, regardless of its class

character, as a desirable revolutionary ally. In his memoirs, Roy quotes
Lenin: "Expounding . . . his thesis that the movement for the liberation
of the colonial peoples was a revolutionary force, he warned, 'But don't
paint Nationalism red.' "[74]

Lenin's formulation as usual looked toward such an ordering of the
world Communist movement which would serve best the interests of the
Soviet state. It is doubtful that this was tinged with any cynicism. The
formula reflected his clear belief that there could in the nature of things
be no conflict between the two. But to an outsider the picture could not
be clearer: the handful of Communists in India or China was at most of
secondary importance in Soviet calculations. The real anti-imperialist
movements in those countries, which tied down the hands of Britain and
France and would hopefully prevent them from further machinations in
Russia, were embodied in organizations like the Congress Party and the
Kuomintang. To use one example, few contemporary states could be
described with greater justice as being feudal in their social order and
political structure than Afghanistan. The new king of that country,
Amanullah, had just successfully asserted his country's independence
from Great Britain. The Soviet regime hastened to greet that potentate
and to establish diplomatic relations with his regime, which promised to
become a major nuisance to the British in India. In May 1920, the Soviet
representative in Central Asia dispatched a note to the Afghans in which
he hailed "independent Afghanistan, headed by the great and famous Amir
Amanullah," and as a token of Soviet friendship announced that the
Soviet government was presenting Afghanistan with the gift of full equipment for a radio-telegraphic station.[75]

Soviet foreign policy embarked, then, through both the state agencies
and the Comintern, on the course of supporting any and all emancipation
and revolutionary movements designed against the interests of the Great
Powers. In a sense the Amanullahs and Kemals of the 1920's are the
predecessors of the Nassers and Sukarnos of the 1950's and 1960's. But
there are at least two major differences. Soviet Russia in the post–World
War I era was not a super-power capable of giving decisive support to
national liberation movements and new regimes in the former colonial
dependencies. The oriental statesmen and movements could in the earlier
period become more truly partners rather than protegés of Russia. The
second difference lies in the fact that just as in general the pattern of
Soviet foreign policy vis-à-vis the international Communist movement was
not fully worked out, so in the case of the East, Soviet needs still clashed
with the aspirations of local Communists. The almost perfect synchroniza-

[74] M. N. Roy, *Memoirs* (New Delhi, 1964), p. 345.
[75] *Documents on the Foreign Policy of the U.S.S.R.*, II, 550.

tion of Soviet policy with the activities of world Communism was to be established in Asia as elsewhere only at the heyday of Stalinism, and its breakdown, the first sign of which came in 1948, was to be the work of our own day.

Those contradictions were exhibited at the Comintern-sponsored meeting of the peoples of the East in Baku in September 1920. The Baku meeting was a highly colorful if not indeed theatrical affair. The summons to the Congress evoked various themes. One was religious: "Spare no effort to come to Baku in September in as large numbers as possible. Every year you make a pilgrimage across deserts to the Holy Places. Now make your way across desert and mountain and river to meet together to deliberate together how you can free yourselves from the chains of servitude, how you can join in brotherly union and live as free and equal men."[76] Another appealed to the national feelings of the Turks. Thus, Kemal Pasha's struggle against foreign invaders was extolled, but at the same time the Turkish peasants were told, "we know that you are trying to form your own people's and peasants' party which will be able to fight on alone even if the Pashas make peace with the Entente despoilers."[77] The numerous grievances of the Armenians were also noted and appealed to.

The Congress was a hodgepodge of various Asiatic, mostly Near Eastern, nationalities, with quite a few Muslims coming from the Soviet territories. Zinoviev and Radek masterminded the proceedings, calling for a holy war against British imperialism. But the hastily improvised and somewhat fraudulent nature of the meeting had disconcerting effects on its deliberations. Various viewpoints clashed. The budding Communists viewed the outright nationalists with distaste. The most bizarre episode was the appearance of the virtual dictator of wartime Turkey, Enver Pasha. He was currently flirting with Moscow but was known as an enemy of Kemal Pasha, not to mention more progressive elements in Turkey. He could not be actually produced in the hall of the Congress, since many of those present, especially Armenians who had suffered massacres of their fellow nationals in Turkey while he was its ruler, had rather strong feelings on this subject.[78] The Congress was never repeated, its embarrassments and theatrical character must have left a painful impression on the more sober Soviet leaders. Henceforth, Communist work in the East was to be carried on in a more subdued and professional way.

The early activities of the Comintern in the East as well as in Europe

[76] Degras, *op. cit.*, p. 109.
[77] *Ibid.*, p. 108.
[78] Carr, *op. cit.*, III, 265. Enver shortly broke with the Soviets and repaired to Turkestan, where he was eventually killed while conducting guerrilla activities against the Soviet power.

were thus characterized by a number of false starts and unfounded and impatient expectations. Yet from the beginning, the premises of Soviet-Comintern policies in the East and in what is now known generally as the underdeveloped world were sounder than in the case of Europe. The effect of the world war had been to weaken the assurance of the colonial powers and to affect their grip on their colonial possessions. India, China, and the Dutch East Indies were to a much greater degree than before 1914 affected by nationalist stirrings, and their intelligentsia was responsive to the revolutionary appeal. The prestige of European civilization and of what before 1914 was almost synonymous with it, liberalism, was fatally undermined. In brief, France's and Britain's Asian possessions and spheres of influence were, unlike the metropole, fertile grounds for revolutionary propaganda and activity. To be sure, the most potent root of disaffection was in the nationalist aspirations and not yet in economic and social grievances as such. The original beneficiaries of the changed conditions were not the local Communists, but such nationalist leaders as Kemal Atatürk, Reza Shah in Persia, and Chiang Kai-shek. But their successes, while destroying or delaying the chances of Communism, were far from being a total loss for the Soviet Union. The victory of nationalism in Asia was bound to undermine the Western Powers' influence, prestige, and self-assurance. Soviet Russia was not yet strong enough to avoid being at times exploited by rather than exploiting the emergent nationalist leaders. But, quite apart from the indirect benefit to the Russians, the interests of the Communist movement were also bound to profit by the strains and stresses within the old colonial order. The nationalist leaders would not always be capable of dealing with the vast socio-economic problems of their societies. Their rule might be a preliminary phase to the further push of Communism. Thus 1919–21 saw the foundations of policies and tactics that would begin to bear their fruits after a quarter of a century, after another world war irretrievably destroyed the European order in Asia and undermined it elsewhere.

IV

TRANSITION: 1921–33

1. The General Characteristics

1921 marks a watershed in Soviet internal as well as external politics. The end of the Civil War brought the Soviet regime face to face with its most relentless enemy, more dangerous and implacable than Denikin or Kolchak: the frightful economic devastation, in part the product of seven years of war, but in part also the product of economic policies followed since the Revolution. A great famine swept large regions of Russia. The war had obscured the utter collapse of Russia's industry and the catastrophic decline in the standard of living of the class for whose benefit the Revolution and war had presumably been fought. But now, under reasonably peaceful conditions (there were still peasant uprisings and guerrilla activities in the Ukraine and Central Asia), those problems had to be faced. In early 1921 the most distinct danger signal was provided by the rebellion in the great naval base of Kronstadt. The sailors, traditionally the most stalwart followers of the Communists and their main support in 1917, now rose up to demand political freedom for all socialist and anarchist parties, the end of bureaucratic rule, and the alleviation of the economic sufferings of the workers and peasants. The word "rebellion" is perhaps inappropriate; the sailors addressed their demands to the regime, expelled its emissaries, but refused to initiate armed action. But through Lenin's mouth the government denounced the Kronstadt sailors as counterrevolutionaries in alliance with imperialists and White generals. The famous attack across the ice by the Red Army overwhelmed Kronstadt, and the captured mutineers were shot in droves.

The Kronstadt rebellion hastened rather than caused a series of basic reforms which go under the name of the New Economic Policy and which were designed to introduce stability in Russia's economic life and to restore her ravaged agriculture and industry. Their main features were the abandonment of forced requisitions in agriculture and the substitution for them of a tax in kind, the toleration of private ownership in trade and small-scale industry, and the attempt to entice foreign capitalists into Russia in order to acquire their badly needed skills and capital.

The NEP became the general description of the period of Russian history 1921–28. In perspective, it represented but an interlude or breathing spell, in economics between War Communism and forced collectivization, in politics between the Civil War and the full blossoming of Stalin's totalitarianism. But to many people at the time, it seemed like a decisive shift by the Soviet government, the abandonment of doctrinaire and ruinous policies in favor of a common-sense approach. Some proclaimed it as a betrayal of Communism, a capitulation to the peasant and the petty bourgeois. Yet, apart from the common-sense nature of its measures, the NEP was perfectly consistent with Marxism and in line with what Lenin had long sought for the Russian economy. Some anti-Bolshevik emigrés, also mistakenly, saw the NEP as an avowal by the regime that it was abandoning its aim of changing Russia into a socialist society. The NEP coincided with and of course also contributed to the easing of social strains, to the resumption of something like normal peaceful life for the first time since March 1917. By 1928 most of the ravages of the war had been remedied, Russia's economy was restored. But the next phase was to be not further increases in the individual's welfare and an extension of his liberties, but a costly social and economic experiment that was in turn to lead to an abrogation of freedom and to human suffering on a scale unprecedented in modern history.

The reason why the NEP was to be only a breathing spell rather than a definite and lasting turn to a new policy lay mainly in the nature of developments within the Communist Party. Here we can note briefly only the main stages of this development.

By 1921, the Communist Party was the only officially acknowledged party. The remnants of the S.R.'s and the Mensheviks, and some territorial socialist parties, were either dissolved or suppressed—thus no *external* opposition. The internal opposition within the Party centered in 1920–22 around the so-called Workers' Opposition, a group that stuck to the original Bolshevik slogans from the time of the November Revolution and War Communism, and that protested against the rising bureaucracy and economic inequalities. At the Tenth and Eleventh Party Congresses in 1921 and 1922, the Workers' Opposition was outvoted, its leaders removed from all influential positions. The trade unions, which the oppositionists claimed should be independent and in charge of economic life of the country, were in fact subjected to Party control.

The next phase of the political strife opened with Lenin's sickness, which struck him in the spring of 1922 and rendered him a helpless invalid by December of the same year. Gradually the leadership of the state and Party passed to the Zinoviev-Kamenev-Stalin group, which isolated Trotsky. Lenin's attempt to affect this struggle from his sickbed is well known. But by March 1923 he was paralyzed, in January 1924 he was dead, and his warnings about Stalin were to have no effect.[1] Trotsky's attempt to oppose the continuation of the NEP policies by the ruling group was unavailing: in January 1925 he was dismissed as war commissar. There followed his expulsion from the Party and exile. In the meantime, Stalin turned against his former allies Zinoviev and Kamenev.[2] In 1924–25, Stalin solidified his alliance with what was later to become the Right Opposition: Bukharin, Rykov, and Tomsky. Together they prevailed in 1925–26 over Zinoviev and Kamenev and stripped them of their positions of power. Inherent in the Bukharin-Rykov-Tomsky acceptance of Stalin's leadership was the belief that he would continue the policy of moderation—the NEP. But by 1928 its days were numbered. Forced collectivization was ordered and the policy of compulsion applied to the peasant. By 1930, the Right Opposition was in turn destroyed, its leaders humbled and removed from their leading posts. Stalin was now alone at the pinnacle of power, other members of the Politburo his subordinates and no longer partners.

Even this brief recital testifies to what an extent the attention of Communism was turned inward and how the years 1921–33 did not allow the Soviet leaders excessive time or resources to devote to affairs beyond the frontiers of their country. True, contrary to the opinions often expressed then, Russia did not become a "normal state," solicitous only about its internal affairs and its international standing as a *state*. Socialism in one country was not to mean the abandonment of world Communism, still less leaving the foreign Communists to their own devices. Quite the contrary. But it meant the subjugation, this time unequivocal, of the interests of the world movement to those of Soviet Russia. At the end of the period, Communist parties everywhere were to become what the French Socialist

---

[1] See Adam B. Ulam, *The Bolsheviks* (New York, 1965), pp. 515–79.

[2] More correctly, they realized by 1924–25 the growing powers and menace of the Secretary General and tried to curb him.

leader Léon Blum described as "Russian nationalist parties," all other aspects of their ideology being subordinate to their obedience to Moscow. Within Russia the change was one of emphasis. Between 1917 and 1921, the news of a Communist coup in Bavaria or Hungary was greeted with as much if not more enthusiasm as the news of a major victory by the Red Army. During the 1920's, the recognition of the Soviet Union[3] by a foreign power or a new success in industrial production became items of much greater importance and interest than those concerning affairs of Bulgarian or French Communists. And the latter came to be viewed not as events of world revolutionary importance, but as developments ancillary to Soviet power.

At the danger of some oversimplification, it might be said that in November 1917 and for some time afterward the world revolution was a constant expectation; during the Civil War it became a more distant but still sustaining vision, enabling the Bolsheviks to endure privations and reverses; during the 1920's, it was gradually to become something in the nature of an advertising slogan, propounded not cynically but without any of the earlier urgency and enthusiasm. The messianic urge and the millennarian vision had to become weaker simply because the Soviet rulers were becoming absorbed in the task of running their own society and in the process were discovering that many economic and political problems had to be tackled in time-honored ways, regardless of the precepts of Communism. Insensibly, revolution and the achievement of Communism abroad became, rather than ends in themselves, the means toward strengthening the Soviet state, warding off any potential intervention, and even solidifying the position of the ruling group within the Communist Party of Russia.

The twelve-year period 1921–33 thus witnessed the elaboration of a new pattern of Soviet foreign relations. Between the *de facto* recognition by Great Britain on March 16, 1921, when an Anglo-Russian trade pact was signed, and the establishment of diplomatic relations with the United States in November 1933, all the Great Powers and the majority of other states recognized the Soviet government as the legitimate government of the Russian people and entered into trade relations with the Soviet Union. Returning to what used to be known as the community of nations, Soviet Russia was returning on her own conditions. She was not giving up her role as the center of a world-wide revolutionary organization dedicated to propaganda and other activities to overthrow ultimately

---

[3] As the state officially became known through the union of Russia, the Ukraine, Transcaucasia, and Byelorussia—until then all nominally independent Soviet republics—in 1922. The first constitution of the U.S.S.R. was proclaimed in January 1924.

every other form of government. And she did not reverse, despite endless negotiations and tentative agreements about this matter, the repudiation of the national debt of pre-1917 Russia.

While the repudiation of foreign debts by a sovereign state had not been unprecedented in the annals of modern diplomacy, the dual character of Soviet foreign policy, epitomized in the existence and Russian control of the Comintern, was certainly a startling innovation. One has to go back to sixteenth-century Spain, which maintained (at times) normal state relations with England and France while at the same time subsidizing the Catholic parties in both countries in their struggle against their governments, to find even a faint parallel. *Occasional* encouragement of internal subversions within a foreign country was not unknown in pre-1914 Europe, but the scale and nature of the Comintern's activities were again unprecedented. Nineteenth-century United States sheltered Irish revolutionaries, London and Paris were asylums for radicals and opponents of the regimes in Russia, Italy, etc., but in no case was the government of the place of refuge directly and publicly connected with those activities, and in no case was the given revolutionary organization of such a universal character as the Third International. The Soviets' official position—and by sheer endurance and insistence, they managed to impose this fiction upon their diplomatic partners—was that the Comintern was a *private* (sic!) international organization which happened to be situated within the Soviet Union, and the activities of which were in no sense connected with the Soviet government.

In almost every agreement initiating relations with a foreign power, the Soviet government hastened to pledge its noninterference in its internal relations. A classic example was contained in the phraseology of the Anglo-Russian trade agreement:

> The present treaty is conditioned upon the fulfillment of the following: Both sides will refrain from hostile acts or measures against the other party as well as from introducing into its territory any official, direct, or indirect propaganda against the institutions of the British Empire or the Russian Soviet Republic. . . . [The Soviet government pledges that] it will refrain from any attempt or incitement through military, diplomatic, or any other ways of any Asiatic nation to activities hostile to British interests or those of the British Empire . . . and especially in the case of India and Afghanistan.[4]

The verbiage itself is an almost humorously desperate attempt to contain through diplomatic incantations this new and disturbing force in world affairs—Soviet Russian Communism. As such, it was palpably unsuccessful. At the very same moment, Soviet leaders (and not only Zinoviev, who

---

[4] *Documents on the Foreign Policy of the U.S.S.R.*, III (Moscow, 1959), 608.

could with some difficulty be represented as not being part of the Soviet "government," but Lenin himself, Trotsky, and others) were freely offering their advice and instructions to English and Indian Communists and indulging in other activities "hostile to British interests or those of the British Empire." At times, those instructions were almost grotesquely detailed. On August 13, 1921, Lenin wrote to an English Communist, Thomas Bell, about a journal he proposed to set up in South Wales. "You should [at first] be very careful. In the beginning the newspaper should *not be too* revolutionary. If you have three editors, then at least one should *not be a Communist.*"[5] The regime scorned excessive pretense. Chicherin more than once expostulated that his task would be easier if those leaders with unmistakable government connections, primarily Lenin and Trotsky, were to resign from the Executive of the Comintern. But Lenin resolutely refused. Such steps, he wrote Chicherin, would only create the impression in the West of Soviet weakness and would lead to further demands and impositions. By this strange logic the deception was to be limited to official *documents* but not to other official activities.

This surrealistic view of international relations, which has become so familiar since World War II and which now is by no means confined only to the Communist states, was firmly grounded in Soviet premises about the nature of world politics. Treaties and other formulas of peaceful coexistence could not affect the essential incompatibility between the Soviet state and the capitalist world. The very existence of the latter was an anti-Soviet conspiracy, a "capitalist encirclement." The Soviet Union, isolated, still industrially and militarily weak, could not forsake any weapon at her disposal. And by the same token any excessive timidity or apologetic airs about the connections of world Communism with Russia would have been an acknowledgment of that weakness and an invitation to further demands and even armed aggression. Just because Russia of the 1920's was so weak, she could not acknowledge this weakness and give in to the Powers' demands. The situation then in the post-war world constituted a veritable revolution in international relations: one of the main European states maintained trade and diplomatic relations with most other states and had a virtual alliance with one of them (Germany from the Treaty of Rapallo on), while at the same time it directed movements and activities within those countries designed ultimately to overthrow the existing governments.

The Soviet argument, as evolved tirelessly in official statements, especially Chicherin's, was, as we have noted, based on the assertion that the Comintern was a private international organization in no sense taking orders from the regime in Moscow. With more reason Chicherin could

[5] *Works* (4th ed., Moscow, 1946), XXXII, 485.

also point out that while statements hostile to the West might emanate from the territory of the U.S.S.R., official and semi-official persons in Great Britain and France were not backward with condemnations of Soviet Russia, with assertions that Bolshevism was a mortal enemy of Western civilization and as such must be dealt with, sooner or later.[6] If Moscow was the seat of the Comintern, were not the Western capitals filled with White Russian organizations and emigrés who still plotted against the Soviet Union and still sent their agents there?

But perhaps the most persuasive argument for the acceptance of this double standard of diplomatic coexistence was the undeniable fact that in Europe of the 1920's Communism could no longer be considered a serious threat. The NEP coincided with a degree of economic stabilization in the West. The post-war crisis and social disorder abated after 1921; the Communist parties which before had promised to capture most of the working class declined to relative insignificance.[7] Even in the colonial and semi-colonial areas, like India and China, Communism in the 1920's was more of an excrescence on the local nationalist movements than a threat in itself. There was, therefore, a certain note of wistfulness in Chicherin's sarcastic denials that the Communists were behind all the troubles in the world that beset the imperialist powers. A return to the stability, material progress, and Western predominance that characterized the nineteenth-century world was barred by new social and economic forces rather than by a group of conspirators who plotted in Moscow.

From our current perspective, this judgment must be somewhat modified. The great period of containment of Communism, 1921–33,[8] already exhibited some of the causes of its later success. Russia preserved and infinitely strengthened its domination of the foreign Communist parties. The injection of Communism into the anti-colonial and nationalist movement in Asia and elsewhere, while it did not pay any immediate dividends, helped to swerve that movement away from the liberal, parliamentary,

---

[6] The best copy for Soviet purposes in this respect was often provided by the frequent anti-Communist speeches and statements of Mr. Winston Churchill, Chancellor of the Exchequer, 1924–29.

[7] At the French Socialist Party Congress in Tours in 1920, the majority of the delegates voted to affiliate with the Third International. But throughout the 1920's and indeed until World War II, the French Communists remained well behind the Socialists both in respect to votes obtained in parliamentary elections and in their respective influence on organized labor. At the time of the split in 1920, the French Communists had 130,000 members; this number fell to 40,000 by 1930. Val R. Lorwin, *The French Labor Movement* (Cambridge, Mass., 1951), p. 59.

[8] The only accession to the Communist bloc during the period was vast but sparsely populated Outer Mongolia, juridically still part of China but since the middle of the decade a satellite of the U.S.S.R.

and essentially Western direction it had followed prior to 1914. In the European context, the example of a political movement that operated both within and without the accepted rules of the parliamentary game was to prove infectious: in Italy and Germany the Communists were to find apt imitators of their propaganda and agitation techniques. Thus, through its very existence and conscious policy, the Soviet Union helped to unleash the forces that in 1941 threatened it with destruction and that, after the passage of another generation, again confront the state and the movement with an insoluble dilemma.

Essentially, then, the policy of Soviet Russia in the 1920's contained a very basic paradox that has continued down to our own day. On the one hand, the Soviet Union more than any large state required peace and international stability, both political and economic. The amount of war-time destruction, both human and economic, had been greater in Russia than anywhere else. Time was required to heal the wounds. Normal and extensive commercial intercourse with foreign countries was required to bring in badly needed capital and foreign specialists. Foreign Communists might be a valuable ideological asset but foreign engineers, managers, and skilled workers were a vital necessity. Furthermore, by its very ideology the Soviet regime was committed not only to the restoration of Russia's economy but to the development of a highly sophisticated industrial civilization. On that count, there could be no question for a Marxist: socialism meant a high degree of industrialization. The whole world might be conquered for Soviet power, and yet the benefits promised by Marxism upon the achievement of socialism could not be reached without industrialization, without the transformation of a previously backward and largely rural economy into an industrial one. The logic of Marxism went along with the logic of the national interest: backward, even if Communist, Russia could always become prey of a foreign invader. Still more basically, Marxism was a materialist creed. It promised that socialist society, because of its superior social and economic organization, because of the abolition of exploitation, could go on ceaselessly producing more wealth, creating a higher and higher standard of living for its people. All those imperatives spelled out the necessity of peaceful conditions under which Soviet Russia could engage in ever-growing trade with the industrial countries.

The same Marxian logic taught that peaceful and stable conditions in the capitalist world were the best guarantee against foreign intervention. War in Lenin's scheme, as expounded in *Imperialism*, was the result of capitalists trying to remedy the decline of their economy and to solve through aggression and conquest the inherent contradictions of their economic systems. An economic crisis in Great Britain might well push its ruling class toward military adventures at the expense of Russia. One of the classical ways in which capitalists try to distract the attention of the masses from their pitiful living conditions is through the arousal of a nationalist or imperialist hysteria. A long period of economic and political stability and prosperity in the capitalist world was thus by the very premises of Marxism the best safeguard of peace.

On the other hand, general prosperity and stability diminished the prospects of Communism. Lack of international tensions would mean the isolation of the Soviet Union, its inability to play off one capitalist side against another. The world war, though it was a disastrous catastrophe to mankind, still contributed to the disintegration of the Western predominance, to the birth of Soviet Russia, and to the intensification of revolutionary tensions throughout the world. Both during and after the war, Lenin and his party resolutely rejected pacifism as the goal for the socialist movement. The capitalist system bred war, and the abolition of war was neither desirable nor possible as long as capitalism existed. Even after the end of the Civil War and intervention, Soviet commentators and statesmen looked hopefully into the development of new conflicts between Great Powers. In all their analyses it was clear that the conflict between Germany and the victors of World War I, the clash of interests between the United States and Japan in the Pacific, even the conflict between France and Great Britain in which some Soviet writers professed to see the promise of an actual war, were regarded as hopeful developments.[9] Even more fantastically, the shift of economic primacy in the capitalist world from Great Britain to the United States led people as intelligent as Bukharin, Radek, and Trotsky to conjure up the possibility of war between the two Anglo-Saxon powers. All such vast cataclysms were anticipated almost gleefully as favorable to the Soviet interest, as promoting the cause of Communism.

This built-in hostility toward the stabilization of the European and world situation is underlined by the Communist government's attitude toward the League of Nations. From the beginning this organization was viewed as "the robbers' league," its activities decried, its failures eagerly noted. In part this was the reflection of Soviet Russia's exclusion from the Versailles peace conference and of the League's domination by France and Great Britain. But mostly it was the feeling that the League represented an effort to replace the Concert of Europe destroyed by 1914, that its success would mean the lowering of international tensions and the prevention of major wars. As such it would provide a barrier to Communist aspirations. Its main author and the proponent of the new world order,

---

[9] A typical Soviet comment in 1923, when serious differences developed between France and England on the treatment of Germany, held that the situation was parallel to July 1914: "The specter of war wanders throughout Europe, the specter of an Anglo-French war, behind it rises the specter of revolution." M. Panin in *The Red Soil*, November 1923, p. 225.

Woodrow Wilson, the Communists viewed with fear and apprehension. John Maynard Keynes' critique of the Versailles system was eagerly seized upon by Lenin:

> Wilson was the idol of the bourgeoisie and pacifists à la Keynes and of the bunch of heroes of the Second International . . . who prayed for the "Fourteen Points" and wrote "scholarly" books about the bases of Wilson's policy because they hoped that Wilson would save "social peace," would reconcile the exploiters with the exploited, would realize social reforms. . . . Keynes unmasked Wilson . . . as a little fool.[10]

International stability, then, and economic progress spelled danger to Communism. Yet at the same time the Soviet state needed peace and stable economic conditions abroad for its own development. The interplay of these two motifs was visible at the Third Congress of the Comintern, held in June–July 1921. The Congress acknowledged the recession of revolutionary feeling in Europe and the restoration of a precarious stability. Yet, it observed: "Capitalist Europe has finally lost its predominant economic position, that was the foundation of its relatively stable class structure."[11] It threw out the vision of apocalyptic struggles between the capitalists: England "will either be automatically pushed into the background . . . or it will in the near future be forced to engage all the forces it has acquired in the past in a life-and-death struggle with the United States. . . . The hostility between Japan and the United States is now in full swing."[12] And the cataclysmic conclusion: "The destruction by war of capitalist equilibrium throughout the world creates favorable fighting conditions for the forces of social revolution. All the efforts of the Communist International were and are designed to exploit this situation to the full."[13]

Those vast revolutionary vistas were tempered by the acknowledgment that for her own benefit Soviet Russia had to engage in extensive commercial dealings with the capitalist world, which of course could not but also benefit the latter. There was still some grumbling among foreign Communists over this trade and over the pending agreements for concessions in Russia, but the answer given on the Russian side was one that in years to come was to be accepted as a cardinal point of faith: any policy "which is a necessity from the standpoint of Soviet Russia is also a necessity from the standpoint of the world revolution."[14] But here again the limits on coexistence were spelled out: "The conclusion by some capitalist countries

---

[10] *Works*, XXXI, 199.

[11] Jane Degras, ed., *The Communist International, 1919–1943: Documents,* I: *1919–22* (London and New York, 1956), 233.

[12] *Ibid.,* p. 235.

[13] *Ibid.,* p. 238.

[14] *Ibid.,* p. 225.

of treaties of peace and commercial agreements with Soviet Russia does not mean that the world bourgeoisie have abandoned the idea of destroying the Soviet Republic. It is probably no more than a temporary change in the forms and methods of struggle."[15] Behind all this double-talk lay a recognition that the foreign Communist parties should abandon their revolutionary impatience and build up their following, and that Soviet Russia had to turn mainly to peaceful construction.

The latter task was recognized by Lenin in his last years as having first priority on the resources and attention of the country. After his death, the problem of the development of the Soviet Union versus the world revolution received a new twist with the celebrated debate between Stalin and Trotsky, which is usually, and only partly correctly, represented as being a conflict between building socialism in one country on the one hand and striving for the world revolution on the other.

The oversimplified version of this debate, which no amount of elaboration is likely ever to eradicate, pictured Trotsky as being an internationalist, heedless of the economic construction at home but eager to plunge into hazardous revolutionary ventures abroad. Stalin has been portrayed, on the contrary, as a Russian nationalist impatient of the fuss and expense of foreign Communism and intent only upon the industrialization and socialist transformation of his country. Of course, neither man's position was as simple or as clear-cut as that. We are in the presence of one of those disputes that in the strange world of Communist politics and semantics begins with a slight difference of emphasis, becomes exaggerated and sharpened because of the power maneuverings of the two sides, and finally is blown up for propaganda purposes into two apparently hostile ideologies.[16] But it is clear that Stalin did not propose to wind up the Comintern and that Trotsky did not want to mark time in Russia while waiting for revolutionary developments in Germany or China. Due to his background, Trotsky had more feeling and sympathy for foreign Communists. It was the measure of his political ineptitude that he allowed himself to be maneuvered into a position where Stalin's partisans could represent him as a man bent upon mad foreign adventures while neglecting the needs of the Russian economy.

Having once allowed his position to be ludicrously misrepresented, Trotsky sank ever deeper in his predicament. In 1926, at the Fifteenth Communist Party Congress, Trotsky protested that he never doubted

[15] *Ibid.*, p. 236.

[16] One is reminded in this connection of the clash between the consumer-goods and producer-goods factions in 1954–55, which ended with the dismissal of Malenkov, an exponent of the greater stress on consumer goods. The current mutual accusations between the Chinese and Russians, with their epithets of "revisionism" and "dogmatism," partake also of this phenomenon.

the *possibility* of building socialism in Russia but only thought that the task could not be *completed* while the capitalist world surrounded the U.S.S.R. Yet, at the same time, he invoked Lenin's authority in the opposite sense: "To give an integral outline of Lenin's economic and political views conditioned by the international character of the socialist revolution would require a separate work that would cover many subjects, but not the subject of building a self-sufficient socialist society in one country, because Lenin did not know this subject."[17] Such dialectical subtleties were beyond the comprehension of the mass of the Party functionaries, who only saw that Stalin wanted to deal with concrete problems at home rather than postpone their solution until the coming of the Communist millennium. Trotsky's complaint was also that "socialism in one country" spelled the appeasement of the capitalists. "From this there can and must follow (notwithstanding all pompous declarations in the Comintern draft) a collaborationist policy toward the foreign bourgeoisie with the object of averting intervention, as this will guarantee the construction of socialism, that is to say, will solve the main historical question."[18]

Yet it was undeniable that the "collaborationist" policy in the sense in which Trotsky described it had inhered in all the treaties, trade agreements, etc., contracted by Soviet Russia ever since Brest Litovsk, had simply been necessary for the existence of the Soviet state, and, as such, had been accepted by all Communist leaders, Trotsky included. The pattern of Soviet foreign policy as elaborated by the 1920's and represented by "socialism in one country" was, granted Communist premises, a commonsense one. Whenever an unusually promising situation would arise in a foreign country, the Comintern would lend its resources toward a revolutionary push, but day-to-day Soviet policy had to be one of normalization of relations with the capitalist countries. It was an attempt to have one's cake and eat it too, and as such neither a betrayal of the ideology nor a disregard of what could now be called the Soviet national interest.

To be sure, the balancing or equating of the two was bound to be a matter of dispute in each specific situation. How much should Communist propaganda in India be toned down in order not to lose profitable trade with Great Britain? Were German Communist chances of seizing power in 1923 serious enough to warrant strong Soviet support and thus jeopardize the good relations with the German government and the Reichswehr? Was it judicious to propitiate Chiang Kai-shek in 1927 even though this might lead to a catastrophe for the Chinese Communists? In each case, it was not so much a matter of nationalism versus internationalist Commu-

---

[17] Leon Trotsky, *The Third International After Lenin* (New York, 1936), p. 30.

[18] *Ibid.*, p. 61.

nist obligations as simply the analysis of the concrete situation that prompted the given decision. And so long as the direction of both world Communism and Soviet policy was not in the same hands, each failure or missed opportunity would provoke charges of insufficient Communist zeal or, contrariwise, of adventurism and the sacrifice of the interests of the Soviet state to the phantom of revolution.

The real clash between the ideal of the world revolution and "socialism in one country" occurred not at the highest policy-making slope but at the lower levels of administration and execution of policies. There, the Soviet hierarchy was becoming bifurcated: as against those primarily involved in the activities of the Comintern, there were officials responsible for the reconstruction and development of Russia's economy and for the conduct of her diplomatic relations. This division of responsibilities corresponded to some extent to differences in temperament between the two sets of officials. The old-style revolutionary and conspirator would adapt himself with some difficulty to the prosaic tasks of administration at home, to the representation of Soviet commercial interests abroad, and the like. He was more likely to find his place in the Comintern, planning the strategy of foreign Communist parties, or on missions to China or Germany whenever the revolutionary situation there looked promising. Others, on the contrary, considered their service to the Communist state a discharge of their *patriotic* obligation. Many of the latter were former Mensheviks or other people without Communist ties before 1918. Engaged in day-to-day negotiations designed to procure for Russia badly needed trade with foreign countries, they could not but view with some distaste what were from their standpoint the disruptive activities of the professional revolutionaries, which were complicating their own tasks and serving no immediate needs of the Russian people.

The two contrasting types can be best epitomized in the personalities of Leonid Krasin and Karl Radek. For all his pre-1914 background as a conspirator and revolutionary, Krasin after 1918 devoted his energies to serving Soviet Russia's trade and diplomatic interests. Until his death in late 1926, he was intermittently in charge of the Commissariat of Trade and a diplomatic representative in the West. Krasin gained a reputation, but an unfavorable one in some Bolshevik circles, as the protector of the "specialists," the technical and managerial personnel (mostly of bourgeois background) whom he placed in various state agencies and stoutly defended against the envious place-seekers with no technical credentials but of deserving revolutionary and class origin. In foreign policy, Krasin emphasized the great importance of normalizing relations with Great Britain. Russia's trade depended on the establishment of good relations with what was still the leading economic power in Europe, he held. The British needed markets to cope with their post-war unemployment. The British capitalists were less hostile to Soviet Russia than the French ones, who had not forgotten their lost loans and investments in pre-Revolutionary Russia. But for that purpose it was imperative to tone down the anti-British Communist propaganda and especially to respect British sensitivities in Asia. When Lenin was at the helm, Krasin's viewpoint enjoyed his intermittent support. Thus the trade agreement with Great Britain of March 1921 was Krasin's personal achievement.[19] Lenin also sanctioned and supported Krasin's employment of bourgeois specialists and defended them from the attacks of Communist purists and the chicaneries of the secret police.[20] But Lenin the statesman and technocrat alternated with Lenin the world revolutionary. While one Lenin strove mightily for the capitalists' good will and collaboration, the other Lenin in the Comintern directed his attacks at the capitalist camp and its main bulwark, Germany.

Krasin erupted publicly at this Jekyll and Hyde character of Soviet foreign policy when Lenin was on his deathbed. At the Twelfth Party Congress in 1923, he attacked the two main obstacles to Russia's economic recovery: the remnants of an adventurist revolutionary policy which, with Europe now in a period of stability, could not lead to revolution abroad but merely provided pinpricks and irritations that hampered Soviet trade; and, equally senseless, the failure to realize that the Communist Party was now in power and could no longer be run, as in the time of the underground and revolution, by "agitators and journalists." What was needed was professional competence and less oratory and politics. Hardworking managers and engineers who accepted the Soviet system in good faith were being harassed and abused. "What do you think, that you can lead a successful policy by interfering with the recovery of production?"[21] But this viewpoint was still not popular. Krasin was subjected to a withering attack. Radek ridiculed him as a would-be pretender to the leadership and referred bitingly to his contacts and socializing with foreign capitalists and politicians.

Karl Radek himself embodied the type of "agitator and journalist" for

[19] Some months before, Lenin had said: "Our current aim is to obtain a trade treaty with England, to have normal commercial intercourse, to be able to buy as soon as possible the machinery necessary for our broad plan of reconstruction of our economy. . . . Our policy in the Central Committee is to make the maximum concessions to England. If those gentlemen want to obtain some promises, then we state that our government will not conduct any official propaganda, that we do not want to attack any of the British interests in the East." *Documents on the Foreign Policy of the U.S.S.R.*, III, 412–13.

[20] The travails of a technical expert during the early days of the Soviet regime and Krasin's role are well illustrated in Simon Lieberman's *Building Lenin's Russia* (Chicago, 1945).

[21] *The Twelfth Party Congress, April 1923* (stenographic report, Moscow, 1923), p. 113.

whom the revolution was a never-ending adventure and not a matter of trade agreements and production statistics. Radek's field of activity was the Comintern and the Soviet press, in which he was one of the most talented columnists. In 1918–19 his missionary activity led to imprisonment in Germany, and he early diagnosed German nationalism, humiliated by Versailles, as a potential ally for Soviet Russia. Upon his release from jail, he continued receiving not only German Communists, but also substantial industrialists and army officers. Back in Russia, he was an early secretary to the Comintern and, especially, its expert on German and Polish affairs. A chaotic situation in Germany in 1923 once more raised the expectations for a Communist coup. Radek was of course back there to advise the German comrades, but the revolution aborted. In succeeding years, his star paled. He became associated with the Trotskyite opposition, then recanted and resumed his journalistic activity, but never became again a member of the inner group. Like most Communists of his background and generation, Radek became a victim of the great purge.

Thus it is not in the power struggle at the highest level but rather in the types of personalities and attitudes exemplified by Krasin and Radek that one finds coexisting in Soviet policy in the 1920's the strains of both "socialism in one country" and the "world revolution." The tortuous reconciliation of the two rested partly upon a fiction and partly upon the historical perspective inherent in Marxism-Leninism. The fiction was that the right hand, the Commissariat for Foreign Relations and other state agencies, did not know what the left hand, the Comintern, was doing. The historical perspective of the Communists' world outlook held that a revolutionary push and risk-taking by the Soviet state were justified only under especially favorable conditions, such as appeared to beckon enticingly but briefly in Germany in 1923. Under any other conditions, attempts at revolution were to be avoided as adventurism and "putschism," unworthy of a movement that based its tactics on the logic of history and an appraisal of concrete social and economic circumstances.

The underlying fiction was bound to break down even at the level of diplomacy. Chicherin, addressing his notes of protest or sardonically refuting the accusations of capitalist governments, might be and often was ignorant of what the Comintern was up to in Germany or India. But the memoirs of Soviet officials who defected make it clear that, from the earliest days, the Soviet diplomatic and trade delegations contained people whose duties were of a different order than those traditionally exercised by diplomats or consuls. One of a legation's or embassy's secretaries was likely to be charged with Comintern matters and with liaison with local Communists. Still another, especially in capitals that contained Russian or Ukrainian emigrés' anti-Soviet organizations, like Paris or Warsaw, was attached on behalf of the Soviet secret police. Thus, several hierarchies crisscrossed within the foreign representation of the U.S.S.R., and in many cases the head of the given mission was not even apprised of the strange activities indulged in by his supposed subordinates.

The structure of Soviet diplomacy reflected the bizarre politics of the Soviet state. Its official head, Chicherin, was a man of little political weight in the Communist Party, and not until 1925 was he granted the courtesy of membership in the Central Committee. He acknowledged and accepted his almost apolitical position and his role as a technician rather than policy-maker. But during the transitional period of the 1920's, even the former was important if unspectacular when compared to the pyrotechnics of the Comintern or the internal power struggle.[22] His political insignificance secured Chicherin's survival in office during the earlier period of Stalinism. In 1930 he was finally replaced by his long-time deputy, Maxim Litvinov, unlike himself an old Bolshevik. The man who had rendered the Soviet state such a signal service was allowed to live out his years in neglect and poverty, but, unlike so many of his collaborators and subordinates, he died a natural death in 1936.

Around Chicherin there was a small nucleus of Bolsheviks who from the earliest post-Revolutionary days specialized in diplomatic work. Such were Maxim Litvinov, Adolph Yoffe (who was to take his life following Trotsky's disgrace), and Yoffe's fellow delegate at Brest, Lev Karakhan (who after a long career in both the Commissariat and foreign posts was to be a victim of the purges). This core in the 1920's was to become enlarged by many Soviet notables who, having fallen in political disgrace at home, were in effect sent into diplomatic exile. This technique was first used by Lenin with the Workers' Opposition and was then increasingly applied to those who ran afoul of the ruling faction. For many of them, diplomatic service was but an interlude to their frightful end during the great purge. Thus, people of such great importance in the early history of the Soviet state and of Communism as Kamenev, Krestinsky, Sokolnikov, and Rakovsky were employed in diplomatic positions abroad and at home; in the 1930's they were to be among the main actors at the purge trials in Moscow. A rare exception to this pattern was Mme. Alexandra Kollontay, the erstwhile leader of the Workers' Opposition, who survived in the diplomatic service until after World War II. There was an element of almost natural selection about this procedure: people who tended to lose out in politics at home were more often than not Bolsheviks of broader culture

---

[22] Chicherin's role and Soviet official diplomacy are excellently summarized by Theodor H. von Laue: "In the uncertain setting of the 1920's a twilight zone developed, with revolution and diplomacy holding each other in balance. In the end, the relative success of each branch determined to a large extent its standing in regard to the other." Gordon A. Craig and Felix Gilbert, eds., *The Diplomats* (New York, 1952), p. 244.

and cosmopolitan background, hence quite suitable for service abroad. The diplomatic service also became one of the places of refuge for those Mensheviks who had made their peace with the Soviet regime. From their ranks came such luminaries of Soviet diplomacy as Ivan Maisky and Alexander Troyanovsky, ambassadors to Britain and the United States respectively. There were also, especially in the earlier years, foreign Communists who became integrated into the Soviet governmental machinery.

These sources of personnel recruitment largely explain why Soviet diplomacy never developed an *esprit de corps* and why even its most successful members could never aspire to become more than faithful executors of the policies laid down in Moscow (ultimately in the Politburo rather than the Commissariat) and reporters of conditions in the countries to which they had been accredited. Between Lenin's incapacitating illness in 1922 and the tightening of Stalin's grip on all agencies of power in 1927–28, the Comintern, or at least some of its agents, displayed at times a certain independence from the ruling group in Moscow. But with the exception of Krasin, no such examples can be found in the Soviet diplomatic service. By the end of the period in question, the Soviet diplomat had progressed beyond his early low status, when he was considered by the more turbulent Communist spirits as merely a temporary concession to the customs of the rotten bourgeois world and as such expendable.[23] But even then, when it came to formulating the main lines of policy, his role remained a secondary one.

It goes without saying that, as long as he was well, Lenin's was the decisive voice in the formulation of policies. He deferred to Chicherin's detailed knowledge of foreign affairs but left him little discretion. When Chicherin headed the Soviet delegation to the Genoa Conference in 1922 Lenin bombarded him with instructions. He felt, with some justification, that few people could follow his tortuous interplay of establishing good relations with the capitalist states on the one hand and sponsoring revolution abroad on the other. Even in the grip of his mortal illness Lenin prevailed over the hesitations in the Politburo to establish a monopoly in foreign trade. With Lenin's incapacity at the end of 1922, the leadership in foreign policy as in other matters fell to the trio Zinoviev, Kamenev,

---

[23] In the beginning the Soviets refused to adhere to the generally recognized titles. Their envoys abroad were called not "ambassadors" or "ministers" but simply "plenipotentiary" or "political representatives." More than once, Chicherin had to complain to Lenin that the Moscow Party organization, evidently considering his officials as loafers, would "draft" them for Party work. The tragi-comic predicament of Soviet diplomacy was illustrated in a famous *Pravda* cartoon in 1924: Zinoviev crowds the scene delivering a peroration, while in the background Chicherin is seen tearing out his hair in despair at Zinoviev's attacks on foreign governments. Von Laue, in *ibid*.

and Stalin, of whom Zinoviev exercised the most influence in foreign affairs by virtue of his position in the Comintern. The brief and unsuccessful flurry of "adventurist" policy advanced by the Comintern in 1923 was a not small element in weakening Zinoviev's position and beginning Stalin's ascendancy.

Stalin moved in foreign policy at first with his customary wariness and caution. He was not equipped for it by either background or experience. Other Communist leaders—Lenin himself, Zinoviev, Trotsky, Bukharin— had spent years abroad and were at home in French and German. Stalin knew no foreign languages (unless Russian, which he spoke to the end with an accent, be considered as such). He had spent his political life in underground revolutionary work, then in plodding behind-the-scenes administrative labors. He had none of the literary and theoretical polish then considered a prerequisite for a leader of international Communism.[24] For foreign diplomats and Communists alike, Trotsky and Zinoviev were household words, while Stalin was virtually unknown.

The pattern of foreign-policy–Comintern decision-making was thus barely disturbed by the emergence of the new dictator. Zinoviev remained at the head of the Comintern until 1926. He was then replaced by Stalin's ally, Bukharin. Chicherin continued at the head of the *Narkomindel* (the Foreign Commissariat). But before long the new pattern asserted itself, and the hand of the new master was felt.

Control and organization were the key elements in Stalin's philosophy of power. There was no place in the system for a freewheeling diplomat like Krasin or for a foreign Communist Party that was not tightly organized and controlled from Moscow. Soviet diplomats became more firmly controlled than before. The scruples and divisions among foreign Communists were no longer to be controlled by oratory or by the moral prestige of the Moscow leaders but by purges and tight organization. Trotsky's fall had already been followed by the purge of his followers in the diplomatic corps and the Comintern. In 1926–27 came the turn of the followers of Zinoviev and Kamenev, in 1930 those of Bukharin. In 1930, Litvinov was installed in the *Narkomindel*, and, for all the European re-

[24] Stalin's awareness of his limitations and his bitterness about them were pungently expressed more than once. In 1925, he wrote that the "literary" type of Soviet leader was no longer in the front rank, and he gave as an example Anatol Lunacharsky, once a shining light of Bolshevism, now confined to the Commissariat of Education. In an interview with the German publicist Emil Ludwig, he contrasted his own career, that of a man who spent long years in revolutionary work and imprisonment in Russia, with those who had conducted their political work from the cafés of Vienna and Paris. It was a transparent and unfair reference to people like Zinoviev and Trotsky, who for all their years abroad had also suffered imprisonment in Tsarist Russia.

nown that he was to acquire, he was simply a tool of Stalin's. (When he became inconvenient in view of the approaching Nazi-Soviet alliance, he was cast aside in 1939. The legend of Litvinov's pro-Western attitudes made him useful again in 1941 as ambassador to Washington, and he retired in 1946 with the beginning of the cold war. The man who had been a Bolshevik and servant of the Soviet state for upward of forty years was not even given retirement pay, and he died in poverty and obscurity.) The Comintern in 1930 was entrusted to two of the most servile of Stalin's followers, Molotov and Manuilsky. As we shall see, no other agency of the Soviet government was to be purged as thoroughly and pitilessly as the Comintern.

Stalin did not like debates. Congresses both of the Comintern and of the Communist Party of the U.S.S.R.—annual affairs under Lenin—became less and less frequent, and when they did meet, the speeches were in fact recitations on themes proposed by the Secretary General and his closest servants. Several networks of control and espionage intertwined with the *Narkomindel* and the Comintern.[25]

The new dictator considered himself—and to a large extent he was—a pupil of Lenin's in foreign policy. But temperamentally he was averse to those elements of revolutionary romanticism and even adventurism that were not entirely absent in Lenin and were quite pronounced in, say, Zinoviev or Trotsky. Foreign Communism was now *consciously* thought of as an extension of the power of the Soviet Union, eventually as the extension of the power of the dictator. Lenin, at least in the beginning, was ready to make considerable sacrifices of Soviet state interest for the sake of a revolution in Germany. Stalin would have found such a policy inconceivable or, rather, incomprehensible. Lenin never reconciled his desires to have foreign parties be both mass parties and strictly disciplined. Under Stalin, strict discipline and mechanical obedience to the Soviet Union took priority over the number of members or votes cast in elections. It is unreasonable to think that Lenin would have been incapable of concluding a Nazi-Soviet pact, but Stalin's *Realpolitik* was unaccompanied by any lingering ideological compunctions. Lenin would not have raised his glass, as Stalin did, in a toast to the Führer, adding that he knew how much the German people loved him! For the father of Communism, the Germans at Brest Litovsk were imperialist bandits with whom one had to deal. To Stalin, Chiang Kai-shek and Hitler were, as long as they had power, perfectly plausible partners, and there was nothing shamefaced or requiring excuses in being their ally. Stalinism in foreign policy as in other respects was thus Leninism pushed to its logical conclusions, without those remnants

---

[25] As early as 1926, Chicherin acknowledged to a Russian diplomat, a future defector, that his office was bugged.

of social democratic and revolutionary scruples that Lenin never entirely discarded.

Stalin's frank avowal of the Soviet national interest and his exploitation of Russian nationalism belong properly to the years after 1933. Yet already in 1931 he rationalized the need for rapid and painful industrialization by the need for *Russia* to be strong. Old, backward Russia had been beaten repeatedly—by the Poles, by the Japanese, by the West— because she had been poor and weak. He never took up Lenin's motif that the greatest strength of the Soviet Union was the love of millions of proletarians throughout the world. But we are anticipating our story. During the period under discussion, Soviet foreign policy evolved almost imperceptibly according to the pattern laid down in the years of great trials and hopes, 1918–21.

The actual story of Soviet foreign policy during the 1920's must of necessity be concentrated on two theaters, Germany and the Far East. The Near East, the area of great expectations and feverish hopes in the post-Revolutionary era, lapses after 1922 into a secondary role. Soviet activities in Persia and Afghanistan will fail to render direct dividends; they will not become major threats to the British empire but rather a nuisance, the subject of acrimonious diplomatic correspondence between the U.S.S.R. and Great Britain. The virtual Soviet alliance with the resurgent Turkish nationalism of Kemal Pasha, the future Atatürk, helped the latter to preserve Asia Minor and to keep Turkey out of the British sphere of influence. But Kemal turned out to be the rarest type of dictator: bent on internal reforms, eschewing excessive foreign ambitions, he refused to conduct aggressive anti-British activity or to raise the flag of Pan-Islamism. His good will enabled the Soviets to stabilize the Transcaucasus, his Turkish nationalism was discreet enough not to create problems for them in Central Asia, but beyond that, Kemal set the example—unfortunately not followed by future dictators in the "new" nations—of strictly minding his shop and not being a party to the Soviets' larger and disrupting themes.

In other areas of the world, even where there was considerable revolutionary ferment, as in Latin America, the Soviets were not as yet in a position to conduct an active foreign policy. Had the Soviet Union been a world power in the 1920's, the drama of the Mexican Revolution might not have lacked its Castro. But even to the most ambitious activists of the Comintern, Latin America was then far away, a backwater of world politics. In Africa, colonialism appeared firmly ensconced for generations to come.

The West and the Far East, then, had to be the main areas of activity and concern. And here, as it was to be true forty years later, Germany and China were the key points. Even in the nature of the Soviet approach to those two countries we discern certain similarities, to be sure not exact, to our own day. Soviet relations with Germany and Soviet policy on Germany's role in Europe were then handled primarily from the viewpoint of formal Soviet diplomacy, rather than that of its Siamese twin, the Comintern, though the latter appeared intermittently on the scene. The Chinese problem appeared mainly as one for the world Communist movement and its tactics-ideology. In both cases, Soviet policy gravitated toward the weak spots in the world order. Germany was defeated, resentful, burdened with reparations, part of it under foreign occupation. China was in the throes of revolution and anarchy. The condition of both countries precluded the prospects of world stabilization and the re-establishment of a world Concert of Powers or, in Soviet parlance, of the unity of the capitalist world. Great Britain was eager for the reintegration of Germany into the European system; French policy was bent upon preserving Germany in a subordinate status; and the clash of the two victorious powers on this issue appeared at times to the most optimistic Soviet observers to promise a new European war. In the Far East, Japanese ambitions in China were the underlying cause of the American-Japanese conflict, and here again, twenty years prematurely, the Soviets saw an early war between the two Pacific powers.

2. Germany and Europe

An alliance with Germany had been the earliest foreign-policy postulate of the Bolsheviks. From November 1917 until the defeat in the Polish war in 1920, and then again when hopes for it rose briefly in 1921 and 1923, this alliance was envisioned as being ideological as well as diplomatic in character. German workers were to set up their own soviet form of government, and, even if the revolution did not spill further westward, German technical skill and capital were going to rescue Soviet Russia from her wartime devastation and isolation and secure her a rapid economic development.

This first, straightforward, ideological conception was given a new twist after the first of the many disasters that overcame German Communism. In his talks in 1919 with German industrialists and officers, Radek became aware of a tendency that was later baptized "national Bolshevism." In their anguish at the defeat and the burdens and humiliation of Versailles, many essentially right-wing nationalist Germans were turning against the whole realm of liberal concepts and the incubus of pre-1914 capitalism and parliamentarism. In foreign policy, they looked toward an alliance with Soviet Russia and a joint war against the victors of Versailles. Much of the feeling behind "national Bolshevism" was of course later to spill over into National Socialism. But under the conditions of 1919, the foreign-policy ideas of "national Bolshevism" were fantastic, and as such they were denounced by Radek and Lenin himself.[26] A seed of the idea remained, however, and "national Bolshevism" was to beckon enticingly in 1923, and indeed in a strange guise in 1939.[27]

In the more sober post-1921 world, the idea of Russo-German collaboration received still another turn. The Versailles settlement was now a fact, and so was Soviet Russia's survival. Both countries were in fact excluded from the European community of nations and desperately in need of an ally, of an opening out of their isolation. The military conditions of Versailles, if strictly adhered to, would condemn Germany to military impotence not only vis-à-vis the West but even as against Poland. Soviet Russia, while free for the moment from the military threat, was in an equally helpless position economically. Despite lifting of the blockade and events like the Anglo-Russian trade agreement, substantial trade and credits from the West appeared out of reach. The process of diplomatic recognition was going slowly. Extensive trade with the West hinged on Russia's recognition of the Western demands to acknowledge the Tsarist state debts and to provide some compensation for the foreign investments nationalized by the Bolsheviks. Both of those conditions, as Bolshevik spokesmen occasionally exclaimed in exasperation and frankness, were not only against their principles but simply beyond the resources of an utterly devastated country. They were willing to grant huge concessions to foreign capitalists but unwilling and unable to grant the capitalists their pound of flesh: the pre-1917 Russian obligations.

In their duel with the foreign capitalists, Krasin, Chicherin, and their assistants displayed amazing ingenuity. The repudiation of debts by a sovereign state was perfectly valid in the eyes of international law, not to speak of revolutionary morality. Did not foreign intervention violate international law, they asked, and should not Great Britain, France, and the United States pay a huge bill for the devastation of the Civil War? Or, they said, the Tsarist debts *might* be recognized in principle *if* the Western capitalists extended large new credits to Soviet Russia. Attempts were made to breach the solidarity of Western capitalists by granting tentative concessions on especially favorable terms to one group. If eventually an agreement fell through, as it did with the most important of them in

[26] E. H. Carr, *The Bolshevik Revolution, 1917–1923* (New York, 1953), III, 319.

[27] In reporting his experiences at signing the Nazi-Soviet Pact, exultant Ribbentrop gave out that being with Stalin and his gang was reminiscent of a social get-together of old National Socialist comrades. The warfare of the rival Chicago gangs of the Capone era was also occasionally interrupted by friendly socializing.

1921–22, still the capitalists' boycott was broken in principle and a basis was established for dealing with separate groups rather than with a united front. Thus in trade as in diplomacy an attempt was made to play off the rival groups of capitalists against each other.

In a way, commercial boycott loomed for the Soviets as a greater threat than diplomatic isolation. Without considerable help through foreign trade and foreign expertise, the NEP could not work its benevolent effects. Without considerable economic improvement—a rise in productivity and a quick restoration of the economy—the regime confronted dangers as great as those of the Civil War. Peasant mutinies, disaffection of the workers, and the considerable dissidence within the Communist Party in 1921–23 were all by-products of the lag in recovery. The capitalists, by using the economic weapon, could yet achieve what they failed to do through armed intervention.

At one point, Soviet hopes for a major commercial breakthrough centered on the United States. In 1920–21, some contacts with adventurous American capitalists inclined Lenin to believe that under the coming Republican administration the United States was going to abandon her hostile attitude and enter into extensive trade and diplomatic relations.[28] This did not come to pass. American help was of great importance at one crucial point, however. The great famine of 1921–22 was combatted by Hoover's American Relief Organization which through its activities saved many lives in the frightfully stricken Volga region. *At the time*, Soviet officials were unstinting in their praise of American generosity. "Of all the capitalist countries, only America showed us major and real help. . . . The government of the United States showed such great help . . . to the Russian nation in its struggle with hunger that neither the Soviet government nor the masses of workers and peasants will ever forget it," wrote an official journal.[29] But this work of charity was not equivalent to the commercial and diplomatic partnership that the Soviets craved. This partnership, it was clear, could be provided by only one country—Germany.

Commercial and military contacts between the Soviets and German official circles opened in 1921. They included negotiations for German help in rebuilding Russian industry, the creation of mixed companies to carry on air and steamship traffic between the two countries, and agricultural and industrial enterprises to be run by Germany on Soviet soil.[30]

Most important, the German army, which under General Hans von

[28] See Ulam, *op. cit.*, pp. 484–85.

[29] *The Bulletin of the Commissariat for Foreign Relations,* June 1922, p. 19.

[30] Gerald Freund, *Unholy Alliance: Russian–German Relations from the Treaty of Brest Litovsk to the Treaty of Berlin* (London, 1957), pp. 89–90.

Seeckt was carrying on its policies largely independent of the German politicians, started negotiations with the Russians that laid the foundations for that close secret military collaboration between the two sides which was to last for over a decade. The advantages for both sides were apparent: Germany had a superfluity of experts who could instruct the Russians in advanced military techniques and in the development of modern armament industry, especially its chemical, motorized, and aviation branches. The German army in turn could with the help of the Red Army bypass the provisions of Versailles and experiment with new weapons in Russia as well as produce them for its own use.

There had been even before, and there was to be afterward, some desultory talk about even a more binding military alliance: effective joint action against Poland. To Germany, this state, which had divided her from immediate contact with Russia and inherited some lands considered to be German patrimony, was France's policeman on her eastern flank. To Russia, in her weakened condition of the 1920's, Poland still represented a potential military threat; there was still a danger that she might renew her bid for the Ukrainian and Byelorussian territories of the U.S.S.R.

The negotiations and contacts concluded, after several false starts, in the Treaty of Rapallo, the most important formal step in Soviet foreign policy between Brest Litovsk and the Molotov-Ribbentrop agreement of 1939.

The treaty itself was a by-product of the 1922 Genoa Conference of major European powers called for the purpose of reconstructing the economy of Europe, a major means for this purpose being a reintegration of Russia into international trade. The mere fact that the Soviet government was invited to Genoa was seen as a major coup in Moscow: the despised and denounced Bolshevik regime was to sit in with the Powers as an equal. But there was a corresponding fear: Soviet Russia might be presented with a united front of Western capitalists. Some circles in the West envisaged the creation of an international consortium that would exploit Russia under colonial conditions, compelling her in addition to pledge the restoration of the Tsarist obligations. Chicherin's note accepting the invitation struck both *leitmotivs:*

The Russian Government welcomed with profound satisfaction the calling of the Genoa Conference, believing that this action on the part of the Great Powers proved that they had at last understood how useless and harmful the political and economic blockade of Russia has proved to be. . . . But the Russian Government has regretfully to state that the actions of the Great Powers before the conference make it seem probable that some of the nations invited will be faced with decisions already worked out and formulated by a certain group of governments. Instead of a free exchange of views, Russia is threatened with a new form of boycott.[31]

For Germany the conference also represented a re-introduction to the European community. The two governments went to the conference with an understandable intention of exacting the maximum of concessions from the victors of the world war: Germany in reducing the burden of reparations; Russia in opening up trade, credit, and commercial channels. On their way to Genoa the Russians, headed by Chicherin, stopped in Berlin. Here the negotiations almost reached the point of signing a treaty. But within the German government there were still elements, notably its Foreign Minister, Walter Rathenau, who hoped to extract the maximum of concessions in Genoa and were afraid of torpedoing the conference by a previous agreement with Russia.

As such the Genoa Conference came to nothing, like most of those international conferences between the two wars designed to restore the pre-1914 Europe through a revitalization of trade and the world economy. But in the neighboring spa of Rapallo, on April 16, 1922, Germany and Soviet Russia signed a formal treaty initiating normal diplomatic and commercial relations. Both sides maneuvered to the last moment, the Russians trying to scare the Germans into signing by arousing their fear that they were about to make a deal with the Western Powers at Germany's expense. Some of the Germans in turn hoped to use the Russian bogey to soften the hearts of the French and the British. But the logic of their desperate situation finally overcame ideological divisions, and the two pariahs of European politics signed the treaty that shook the Western chanceries.

The provisions of the Treaty of Rapallo appeared hardly world-shaking. Both sides renounced any financial claims from the past and pledged to exchange full diplomatic and consular representation. The German government was to facilitate its citizens' commercial activity in Russia. But the treaty enabled both sides to emerge from isolation with a diplomatic partner to play off against Great Britain and France. The specter of a Western capitalist joint front that would compel Russia to trade only on condition of paying the Tsarist debts and obligations and submitting her economy to a quasi-colonial dependence now disappeared. Had France and England been united in their views on the European questions, had not both of their governments been confronted with numbing economic problems, the Rapallo agreement would not have figured so importantly in the political perspectives of the 1920's. But as it was, it became an act of political emancipation for Germany and the decisive step in the Soviet government's campaign to be treated as a "normal" state that was recog-

[31] Jane Degras, ed., *Soviet Documents on Foreign Policy*, I: *1917–1924* (London and New York, 1951), 293.

nized and traded with on its own conditions. Following the conclusion of the treaty, Chicherin felt emboldened to lay down *Russia's* conditions for participation in the new international organization:

> The Russian Government is even willing to adopt as its point of departure the previous agreements of the Powers regulating international relations, with some necessary modifications, and to take part in the revision of the Covenant of the League of Nations so as to transform it into a real League of Peoples without any domination of some nations by others.[32]

For all their previous convictions about the essential disunity of the capitalist world, the Communists until Rapallo had retained something of a superstitious awe of formal diplomacy, a fear of the guiles of Western (especially British) diplomats.[33] But Genoa and Rapallo demonstrated that they could more than hold their own. The Western countries were often working at cross purposes, and their statesmen were inhibited by political differences and by public opinion at home. The Soviet delegates could on the contrary display the utmost flexibility, profess the great sacrifice their government was displaying in its willingness to deal with governments whose policies were not based on such idealistic and humanitarian principles as its own, assert that the Soviets were in the interests of peace willing to forgive foreign governments for being what they were.[34] Thus Soviet diplomacy managed to achieve what it failed to do at Brest Litovsk: to put the capitalist governments on the "bench of the accused" before world public opinion. It was Chicherin's historical service to the U.S.S.R. that he initiated this style of Soviet diplomacy: without the schoolboy sarcasm characteristic of Zinoviev or Radek, he conveyed to the world that the real question was not whether the capitalist powers would recognize and tolerate Soviet Russia, but whether Soviet Russia would recognize them; not whether his impoverished and devastated country would be helped by others, but whether she would give her consent to the recovery of the world economy.

The Soviet government hastened to assure all and sundry that the Rapallo agreement contained no secret clauses. Strictly speaking, the as-

---

[32] *Ibid.*, p. 300.

[33] As demonstrated, for example, by Lenin's fears that Chicherin might be "taken in" at Genoa.

[34] Chicherin orated in this vein at Genoa: "As Communists we of course cherish no special illusions as to the possibility of really removing the causes from which war and economic crises arise. . . . Nevertheless . . . in the interests of tens of millions of people exposed to privations and sufferings beyond the limit of their endurance . . . we are ready to support every effort calculated to bring an improvement, if only of a palliative nature, into world economy and to remove the threat of new wars." *Ibid.*, p. 301.

sertion was true. But *following* Rapallo, the military contacts and negotiations that had been going on since at least 1921 finally fructified into
a full understanding, even if no written agreement can be definitely
traced.[35] Military bases in Russia were put at the disposal of the Reichswehr for trying out the advanced techniques and weapons prohibited it by
the Versailles Treaty. German industry erected armaments factories in the
Soviet Union the output of which was shared by the two countries.
Finally, the two countries were to exchange their technical military plans
and instructors.[36]

Germany thus laid the foundations for that rapid recovery of her military predominance which could not have been achieved in the few years
separating the accession of Hitler and the outbreak of World War II
without the previous decade of the Reichswehr's training, experimentation,
etc., on Soviet soil. Russia gained the advantages of a sophisticated, up-to-
date, modern armaments industry, something which would have been
beyond her own resources to develop in the 1920's, and of course of
instruction by the German specialists. It is impossible to determine who
got the best of the bargain. On the German side, details of collaboration
were worked out by the Reichswehr, with the official civil authorities of
the Weimar Republic left in the dark. On the Russian side, all the military
decisions had to be dovetailed with the political ones.[37] The German
generals, with the military man's all too frequent disregard of "politics,"
saw in the Russo-German collaboration mainly the means of escaping the
stifling conditions of Versailles. General von Seeckt saw Russia as a
potential ally in a war, in the first instance against Poland. This pro-Russian
orientation of the generals had, needless to say, nothing ideological about
it. They were confident of being able to deal with their own Communists
whenever the occasion arose and were blind to the political danger. Yet
the Reichswehr collaboration with the Russians was to have fateful political
effects. The German generals chafed under the atmosphere of Weimar
parliamentarism, and they were bound to be impressed by the apparent advantage for the armed forces of working under a dictatorial regime where
no parliamentary debates, no troublesome pacifists or humanitarians
complicated the task of the warriors or revealed military secrets. They were
thus conditioned for the acceptance of National Socialism.

On the Soviet side, there was a more realistic appraisal of the political
aspect of the military collaboration. A strong and independent German

[35] Freund, *op. cit.*, pp. 124–25.

[36] Carr, *op. cit.*, III, 436–37.

[37] Much later on, the contacts with the Reichswehr were alleged as one
reason for the liquidation of Russian military personnel during the great purge.
These allegations will be examined below, Chapter V, pp. 239 ff.

military establishment meant, of course, that the German Communists could hardly seize power by a revolutionary coup. But, apart from this unpleasant fact, there were solid advantages—so it seemed in the 1920's—for strengthening Germany and drawing her away from a reconciliation with the Western Powers. The greatest Soviet fear remained, to repeat, a re-establishment of the European order, a united front of the capitalist powers.

The first German ambassador to Moscow, Count Brockdorff-Rantzau, epitomized what became known as the spirit of Rapallo. A stiff German aristocrat who felt ill at ease in a Weimar Germany ruled by socialist politicians and middle-class industrialists, he had at first conceived the *rapprochement* with Russia as the means of forcing the West to alleviate the conditions of Versailles. But soon Brockdorff-Rantzau became an enthusiastic "Easterner," i.e., a proponent of alliance with Russia for its own sake. Like many professional diplomats accredited to Moscow, he failed to perceive the relative insignificance of the *Narkomindel* in the formulation of Soviet policies. He exaggerated the willingness and especially the ability of the Russian diplomats like Chicherin to change the ideological content of Soviet policy. That the various strains of Soviet foreign policy were woven together and that there was no simple and clear-cut division between the diplomats, who thought of foreign policy in traditional terms, and the Comintern, bent on stirring up trouble everywhere in the world, was something that the German ambassador failed to perceive.[38] Brockdorff-Rantzau's personal friendship with Chicherin was a strong factor in his becoming convinced of the "community of fate" between the two nations. The two men shared some characteristics: both misogynists, both ill at ease with the real rulers of their countries, both appearing like ghosts of nineteenth-century diplomats set in an uncongenial twentieth-century environment. But the Russian, though a former Menshevik, was still a Communist whose mental processes could not be fully understood by his German friend.

The difficulties inherent in the Soviet-German partnership became evident in the tempestuous events of 1923. Germany's holding back on the reparations payments under Versailles led in January to the Franco-Belgian occupation of the Ruhr. The German government replied with an artificially stimulated inflation which soon assumed astronomic proportions and plunged the country into an economic and social chaos surpassing the worst days after November 1918. The hotter heads among the German Communists and in the Comintern saw again an opportunity for a German revolution. But in Moscow, the prevailing line was at first one of a very

[38] Gustav Hilger and Alfred Meyer, *The Incompatible Allies* (New York, 1953), pp. 127–28.

demonstrative support of the *German government's* position, extending
all the way to hints that if Polish troops should intervene and occupy
German Silesia, the Red Army would itself intervene against Poland.[39]

In fact, there is no doubt that actual military intervention was far
from the Soviet leaders' mind. The regime was going through a period
of acute political difficulty. With Lenin on his deathbed, it lacked firm
leadership, and the struggle for succession was already in full swing.[40]
Moreover, several groups spawned by the Workers' Opposition were still
demanding an extension of political liberty and curtailment of the Party's
dictatorship. In foreign affairs, Soviet Russia was exposed on other fronts.
Another, this time unusually strong note from the British government—the
so-called Curzon ultimatum—protested Soviet chicaneries and subversive
activities in the Orient and threatened the cancellation of the Anglo-Soviet
trade agreement unless those activities were terminated. The Soviet reaction was characteristic: internal propaganda trumpeted that the British
were preparing a military intervention, but Chicherin and Litvinov's notes
to the British government were quite conciliatory in tone and managed
to alleviate the dispute. That the Soviet leaders really believed that there
was a serious danger of war with Great Britain is most unlikely. But in
a period of great political difficulties and divisions within the ruling party,
magnifying a foreign threat was thought a good way of restoring order
in the ranks. That it was proposed to start a campaign against Poland
under such conditions verges on sheer fantasy.

A further embroilment of Germany against *France* was thought on the
contrary to lie clearly in the Soviet interest. Throughout 1923 Soviet emissaries, notably Radek, commuted between Moscow and Germany. Once
again the gambit of "national Bolshevism," of uniting the extreme right
with the Communists to fight the French jointly, came to the fore.[41]

The sequence of events in Germany in 1923 moved through three main
stages. In the first, the Soviets supported the German government's defiance
of France. This stage merged with the second, in which Moscow began to
encourage the prospects of an alliance between the extreme nationalist
right and the German Communists. The third phase was opened by the
formation in August of the Stresemann government, which, it was clear,

[39] *Ibid.*, p. 120.

[40] Though the leadership was well aware by March 1923 that Lenin's condition was hopeless, official communiqués up until his death in January 1924
spoke optimistically about his recovery and probable return to work.

[41] Its most eloquent expression was Radek's speech eulogizing the German
fascist Leo Schlageter, who had been shot by the French for sabotage. Schlageter subsequently became sanctified by National Socialism. A popular German
play had Schlageter delivering this immortal line: "Whenever I hear the word
'culture,' I release the safety on my gun."

was going to seek a compromise with the French. At this point, and with some serious misgivings, the signal was given in Moscow for a Communist bid to take over power. "In August, it had become apparent that Moscow's policy for Germany was beginning to make a turn, that German Communists until then held back might be spurred on."[42] They were authorized to enter state governments in Saxony and Thuringia in coalition with left-wing socialists, largely to procure arms and the benevolent neutrality of the police in those states. Preparations were set for a general strike and armed action to seize power in the Reich as a whole. But the extent of the Soviet commitment was to be limited. A delegation, headed of course by Radek, was dispatched to advise the German comrades. It included military specialists. The Soviet government also lent its diplomatic support. Its emissaries sought promises from the Baltic countries and Poland that they would not intervene in the German imbroglio and that they would let Russia send matériel and personnel through their territories to the Communist regime in Germany. Poland's acquiescence in a Communist Germany was sought by the promise of cession of East Prussia.[43] These negotiations make clear that even at this relapse into revolutionary adventurism, the Soviet leaders were willing to offer to the German revolution the help of what after 1950 became known as "volunteers" but were not ready for a full-scale military intervention and war.

In any case, the projected Communist coup fizzled out. The German Communists, beset by doubts and divisions, finally called off their coup. An armed attempt to seize power occurred only in Hamburg and was suppressed after two days' fighting. The state governments of Thuringia and Saxony with their Communist members were removed by the Reichswehr without too much opposition. The mass of German workers refused to stir on the Communists' side. Stresemann's government survived and inaugurated its policy of reconciliation with the West. But the most significant preview of things to come in Germany was not in the tortuous story of the German Communists' faltering bid. In November in Munich, Ludendorff and Hitler staged their *putsch*, which was to provide the Nazis with a legend and the Communists with a lesson they largely disregarded: that a period of anarchy and economic chaos is one of opportunity not only for *left-wing* extremism.

The experiences of 1923 were to figure for years in recriminations and purges both in Russia and in the German Communist Party. A somewhat similar and tortuous policy characterized the Comintern's policy in Bulgaria, where the local Communists also came to grief. These events have

[42] Ruth Fischer, *Stalin and German Communism* (Cambridge, Mass., 1948), p. 342.

[43] E. H. Carr, *The Interregnum 1923–24* (New York, 1954), p. 219.

been characterized by one historian as showing the lack of coordination between the Comintern and the Soviet government.[44] But this analysis disregards the fact that the "formal" agencies of the Soviet government also allowed themselves to be carried away by the prospects of a new Communist revolution. The real division was not in terms of separate institutions pursuing different policies, but in the strange duality inherent in the Communist mentality. It was as if a former gambler, who had settled down to a prosaic business existence, suddenly had the vision of again making a fortune. The vision of a Communist Germany crowded out for a moment the advantages of a steady and profitable partnership with the Weimar Republic. To some extent, the lesson of this error was learned in Moscow. "One does not play with war," Lenin had said at the time of the Brest Litovsk debate. And Stalin would not play with insurrections, and there would be no Zinovievs and Radeks to inject their individual preferences and insights into the running of foreign Communism.

The other side of the 1923 picture was a demonstration of a deep and atavistic Communist hostility to parliamentarism and orderly processes of government. When the crisis came, the German fascists appeared as much more desirable allies than the middle-class parties, especially the Social Democrats. The mere fact of social disruption in Germany and possible war in Europe was considered to offer an opportunity for Communism and the Soviet Union. This feeling had its source in the Russian experience: war and the disruption of Russian society had brought Bolshevism to power; the right-wing movements, for all their temporary successes, proved incapable of stemming its tide. A right-wing, anti-democratic reaction in Germany thus was bound to prove but a short interlude before the full triumph of Communism. In 1926, Marshal Pilsudski's coup against the constitutional Polish government was at first acclaimed by the Polish Communists. Soviet Russia's relations with Mussolini's Italy were to be almost cordial. And the same note was struck in the Russians' *initial* analysis of Hitler's overthrow of the Weimar Republic.

The heady atmosphere of 1923 gave way to the return of the Rapallo pattern in 1924. The mutual advantages of commercial and military collaboration between the two governments overcame what would have been the logical consequence of the escapades of the previous year, i.e., a severance of relations. And Stresemann's Germany, as it inched its way toward a reconciliation with the West, needed the Russian card to pressure France and Britain. Thus the essentially polygamous relationship of the Soviet government to Germany—partnership with the government on one side, with the German Communists on the other—had to be discreetly acquiesced in. Not that the relationship was without its constant irritations. Quite apart

[44] *Ibid.*, p. 157.

from policy at the highest level there were incidents at the lower ones which would bring Brockdorff-Rantzau raging to the *Narkomindel* or, conversely, Chicherin expostulating to the German officials. The Communist state had to be a suspicious state: the "vigilance" of its secret police would uncover spies among traveling German students or engineers in the Soviet Union. Arrests and fuss would follow, much as simple logic might indicate that in view of the Russo-German military collaboration the Germans were already in possession of such Soviet military secrets as even the most intrepid spy could not uncover. Or, German Communists might seek the shelter of the Russian diplomatic missions and the German police would violate their immunity. But those incidents, which in the days of stately pre-1914 diplomacy would have brought the countries to the verge of war, were now being recognized as routine occurrences of coexistence with the Soviet Union.

More fundamentally, both sides were hedging their bets. In 1924 Great Britain was led by her first Labour government. Since no socialist movement was viewed by the Soviets with greater contempt than the British one,[45] its victory was assumed to be a good augury for the British Communists, who were bound, so the argument ran, to become the beneficiaries of Labour's ineffectuality and to grow into a mass workers' party.[46] But the immediate dividends were a *de jure* recognition of the Soviet government and the beginning of extensive trade and financial negotiations with Great Britain. The Soviet position in the negotiations was essentially the same one they had pursued on the subject since 1921. They were willing to recognize some of the Tsarist obligations to the British bondholders and investors provided they got in return substantial loans that would cover those obligations as well as provide trade credits. But the long-drawn-out negotiations were interrupted by the collapse of the Labour government. During the election, the "Zinoviev letter" was unveiled, the purported message from the head of the Comintern Executive to British Communist Party officials advising them on their tactics. It was thought particularly outrageous that it prescribed subversive activities in the armed forces. Though the evidence points to the letter being spurious, there was nothing in it that was not required of any Communist Party under the Twenty-one

[45] This feeling predated World War I and was based not only on the Labour Party's moderation but on its disregard of the whole theoretical paraphernalia of Marxism.

[46] The Executive Committee of the Comintern thus expressed this pleasing prospect: "But if as we expect the Labour Government betrays the interests of the proletariat, it will give the proletariat an object lesson on how to be cured of the illusions of capitalist democracy, and so immensely accelerate the movement of the working class towards a revolutionary position." Degras, *The Communist International,* II: *1923–28* (London and New York, 1960), 83.

Conditions of acceptance into the Comintern. Still, this contributed to a "Red scare" and the subsequent defeat of Labour. Baldwin's Conservative government, of course, stopped the negotiations, and Great Britain's relations with the Soviet Union remained strained.

Germany, on her part, was moving toward a reconciliation with the World War I victors. The key step here was the Dawes Plan, the agreement on reparations accepted by the Germans in August 1924. The essence of the Dawes Plan was strikingly similar to what the Soviets had been trying to obtain in their endless negotiations with the French and the British about the Tsarist obligations and credits. Germany acknowledged and began to pay the reparations, but only after securing substantial credits from Western, mainly American, sources.[47] The flow of credits soon worked magic in restoring the German economy. And the European economy as a whole, to the anguish of the Russians, showed signs of being restored, as Germany moved in the direction of a political accommodation with Great Britain and France.

The Soviets' reaction to the Dawes Plan was not unlike their pronouncements on the Marshall Plan a quarter of a century later. The plan was transforming Germany—why, Europe as a whole—into an American colony. It was being "demonstrated" how the economic stabilization of Europe was going to plunge the German proletariat into the worst crisis yet. The Fifth Congress of the Comintern (June-July 1924) concentrated its fire on the Dawes proposals:

> The Experts' report is an attempt by the bourgeoisie of the imperialist powers to solve the problem in common. The report expels Germany from the ranks of independent states and brings it financially and economically under the supervision of the Entente bourgeoisie. The system of reparations payments it envisages is designed to guard the mark against a new collapse and so to guard Europe against the danger of proletarian revolution.[48]

On the diplomatic front, pressure was brought to bear on the German government to stop or alleviate its reorientation toward the West. Chicherin harangued and abused Brockdorff-Rantzau. The latter in turn threatened and cajoled his superiors in Berlin. Soviet diplomacy now evoked the ghost of the Franco-Russian alliance of the end of the nineteenth century, Chicherin travelling amidst much fuss to Paris and stopping demonstratively in Warsaw, the capital of Germany's arch-enemy.

---

[47] This led to the famous and somewhat insane circular flow of reparations and debt payments that continued until the Depression: Germany paid the victors in the war, they in turn paid installments on their debts contracted in the United States and among themselves between 1914 and 1918, and the U.S. lent huge sums to Germany.

[48] Degras, *The Communist International,* II, 115.

But Germany's course was firmly set under Stresemann: without repudiating Rapallo and the Russian connection, which was still the most effective way of pressuring France and Great Britain, she was determined on an accommodation with the West. The Locarno agreement of 1925 was designed to accomplish in the political field what the Dawes Plan had in the economic: a stabilization of the European situation. In it, Germany pledged to observe her frontiers with France and Belgium—a reiteration of Versailles, but this time given without a *diktat*. Great Britain and Italy in turn guaranteed militarily the status quo in the West. Germany was to enter the League of Nations and take a seat on its Council, thus signifying her return as a Great Power. When it came to Germany's eastern frontiers with Poland, they were not included in the Locarno guarantees but were left to the vague protection of Article 16 of the League Covenant, requiring joint action of members against an aggressor. But Article 16 was in turn watered down into virtual meaninglessness by the stipulation of all Locarno powers that reinterpreted action taken against aggression according "to an extent which is compatible with [a state's] military situation and takes its geographical location into account."[49] The exceptions and reinterpretation thus alleviated Russian fears that Germany, under her League of Nations obligations, might become a partner in a coalition against the U.S.S.R. or that Germany's claims on Poland were being abandoned.

Stresemann's success in exacting those concessions opened up the possibility of reaffirming Rapallo. The Treaty of Berlin of April 24, 1926, between the Soviet Union and Germany provided that both sides would stand by their former agreement, which was to remain in force for five years. They pledged neutrality in the case of an attack upon either of them by a third party and abstention from any trade or financial boycott against one of the signatories.

For Russian diplomacy, Locarno—even if softened by the Treaty of Berlin and by the Germans' skill in qualifying their obligations under the League of Nations—represented an undoubted defeat. Germany was no longer a partner in the struggle against the European status quo; she now could and did play the Soviet Union against the West, and her partnership with Russia was no longer the main element but only one of many in her foreign policy. To be sure, economic and military collaboration went on, and in historical perspective their concrete results outweigh the Locarno and Berlin pacts, which in a few years would appear largely irrelevant in the new European setting. So would, for that matter, the Kellogg-Briand Pact on the renunciation of war and the disarmament negotiations, which were to drag on for years and occupy much of the Russian diplomats' time. Those heated diplomats' conferences, those struggles over a proviso, over

[49] Freund, *op. cit.*, pp. 234–35.

the exact wording of this or that communique, over the timing of the Berlin Treaty as against the coming into effect of Locarno—all those petty dramas which occupied the attention of Europe in the 1920's and which generated so much dispute in the chanceries and parliaments appear to us now as ancient as the Congress of Vienna.

The activities of Soviet diplomacy during this period cannot, however, be downgraded. If we compare its achievement with what the Comintern or international Communism managed to do for the extension of Soviet power and influence, we shall appreciate the importance of Chicherin's, Litvinov's, and their colleagues' work. The Comintern sought in vain for a revolutionary opening in a Europe that had settled down. The search for a revolution led to some false starts in Germany in 1923 and in Bulgaria. Some of the experiments smacked of the adventurism of the first post-1917 years—such as the intermittent flirtation with "national Bolshevism" in Germany, or the contacts between the Comintern and the Macedonian revolutionary organization, which operated through terror in Bulgaria and Yugoslavia. Many of these improvisations were abandoned after a short trial. Such was the fate of the Peasant International, set up in 1923 to suck in radical peasant movements mostly in eastern and southeastern Europe, which after a period was allowed to expire and disappeared almost without a trace. The Communist parties in the colonial powers, especially Great Britain, Holland, and France, performed some valuable work in stirring up revolutionary agitation in their countries' possessions, though even on this count they were subjected to some criticism at the Fifth Comintern Congress for their allegedly lukewarm attitude.[50] The record of European Communism was thus not impressive.

If there was an achievement during that period it was of a negative character. Despite the disgrace and purge of the most prestigious leaders of *Russian* Communism, despite the subsequent disgrace of most of the founders and original heads of the European parties, Communism did not split into rival movements, the fall-out of first Trotsky's and then Zinoviev's political defeats being limited to isolated individuals and

[50] In view of current events, it is interesting to quote one sharp criticism: "And what have our Communist parties done—the English, Dutch, Belgian and the parties of other countries whose bourgeoisie owns colonies? What have they done from the time when they had accepted Lenin's theses to educate the working class of their countries in the spirit of real internationalism, in the spirit of solidarity with the working masses of the colonies? All that our parties have done in that respect amounts to nothing. I as a native of the colonies and member of the French Party ought to say regretfully that our French Party has done very, very little for the colonies." *The Fifth Congress of the Communist International* (stenographic report, Moscow, 1925), part I, p. 655. The speaker was Nguyen Ai Quoc, now better known as Ho Chi Minh.

small groups. As explained above, this was largely due to Trotsky's amazing tactical ineptitude and unwillingness to offer resistance until it was much too late. Thus at the Fifth Comintern Congress, Trotsky obediently wrote an eloquent manifesto of the Third International on the tenth anniversary of the world war, while the very same gathering subjected him and his followers to a pitiless censure.[51] And the Congress ordered a more vigorous subordination of foreign Communist parties to Moscow than had been achieved through the Twenty-one Conditions. The Fifth Congress supplemented the ideological strait-jacket with an organizational one. The Executive Committee of the Comintern, resident in Moscow, was now empowered to issue directives binding all parties unconditionally, and to supervise their activities. The decisions of the central organs of the parties, even of their congresses, could now be annulled by the Executive Committee. The latter also received the right to expel foreign Communists and even whole parties from the Comintern. Thus, foreign Communist parties were now bound hand and foot by the hierarchy of the Comintern, which meant of course the ruling faction in Moscow, which in turn was very soon to mean Stalin. This pattern became known as the "bolshevization" of the International. But while "bolshevization" meant that from now on the Comintern was even more than before an obedient tool of Moscow, it meant also a recognition by its membership that the institution had lost vitality and significance.[52]

As against this negative achievement of world Communism, the *Narkomindel*, through its skillful maneuvering, secured the recognition of Russia as once more a Great Power. The German gambit obtained valuable industrial and military advantages. Those seemingly endless and ineffective trade and financial negotiations resulted in a trickle of credits and concessions from the foreign capitalists, which, even if they did not meet the earlier and exorbitant expectations, speeded up the reconstruction of the Russian economy and provided for the importation of experts

[51] "Comrade Trotsky not only has tried to set himself against the rest of the Central Committee but also made accusations bound to lead to confusion in the wide ranks of the proletariat and violent protests in the ranks of the Party. . . . The tendency to separate state organs from the Party's influence was evident in Comrade Trotsky even before the Twelfth Party Congress (1923). . . . We reach the conclusion that in the present 'opposition' we face not only an attempt to revise Bolshevism, not only a clear departure from Leninism, but also an open petty bourgeois deviation. . . . Against this petty bourgeois deviation the whole Party must struggle systematically and vigorously." *Ibid.*, part II, pp. 100–102.

[52] Stalin did not like discussions. Though the statute of the Comintern stated that its congresses were to be held "at least once in two years," after the Fifth Congress in 1924, four years were to elapse until the next one. The Seventh and the last Congress was held in 1935.

and technical skills. Of equal importance was the breach in the hostility of the external world, the implanting among governments and groups abroad of the idea that "one can do business with Russia." Without these foundations, Russia's extensive diplomatic activity in the 1930's, crowned by the German-Soviet pact in 1939, would have been impossible. Had Russia scorned diplomatic coexistence in the 1920's, had her policy in effect been what the Comintern declarations and speeches proclaimed, the real threats of the 1930's—German and Japanese militarism—could not have been deflected for a time or dealt with separately. Skillful diplomacy masked Soviet Russia's weakness during her most vulnerable period and accustomed Western diplomats to include her in their calculations and combinations. The intransigent voices, like those of Churchill in England, were becoming isolated, even among the European right. Astute foreign observers like Brockdorff-Rantzau had come to believe that there were two opposing currents in Soviet policy, that of the *Narkomindel* and that of the Comintern, and that by dealing in a businesslike way with the Soviet government one weakened the influence of the doctrinaires and fanatics.

Along with the official diplomacy, which tried to sway foreign statesmen and bankers, and the Comintern, manipulating world Communism, there was another dimension of Soviet foreign activity. This was the attempt to preserve and build up good will for the U.S.S.R. among progressive and socialist elements in the West, to influence public opinion in the direction of accepting and supporting revolutionary Russia and of thwarting the real or alleged anti-Soviet plots of English and French reactionaries. In a sense, this line of activity clashed more with the line of the Comintern than with the efforts of official Soviet diplomacy. Much of the good will toward Russia and opposition to anything that smacked of an anti-Soviet intrigue was generated by European socialist parties and organized labor in Europe and the United States, and yet those were exactly the Comintern's targets and the objects of its organs' most violent abuse. The language used in the Soviet press about Austen Chamberlain and Charles Evans Hughes, the foreign ministers of Britain and the United States, respectively, was at times quite mild when compared to the abuse poured on Ramsay MacDonald or conservative leaders of American labor like Samuel Gompers or William Green. Stalin, whose first ventures in diplomacy did not display much tact, once put in a nutshell the intermittent Soviet irritation with those progressive circles in the West which, while useful to Russia, pushed their well-intentioned humanitarianism beyond what he felt was the limit of Soviet endurance:

Not long ago a protest was received from the well-known leaders of the English labor movement, Lansbury, Maxton, and Brockway, against the shooting of twenty terrorists and incendiarists from among the Russian princes and nobility. I cannot regard these English labour leaders as enemies of the U.S.S.R. But they are worse than enemies. . . . It is not for nothing that people say: 'God save us from such friends, we can deal with our enemies ourselves.'[53]

But apart from such ill-tempered outbursts, Soviet policy-makers knew most of the time how to placate the leaders of liberal opinion abroad. In 1922, when the Comintern was briefly courting the Second International, the Soviet leaders found it necessary to promise the Western socialists that the great show trial of the Socialist Revolutionary leaders then being staged in Moscow would not end in death sentences and that foreign lawyers and observers would be allowed in the court.[54] Just as the Western diplomats persuaded themselves to believe in the existence of two Soviet Russias—the reasonable one of the *Narkomindel* and the fanatical one of the Comintern—the foreign sympathizers were pushed into a dualism of their own: Soviet Russia was a "workers' state," most of the energies of the government being employed to build a new and better life for the masses; the unreasonable, undemocratic, terror-tinged side of Soviet life was the work of some special organs like the OGPU (this was the new name for the former *Cheka*—the secret police), and its toleration by the government as a whole but a lingering and diminishing reaction to the centuries of Tsarist oppression, to the Civil War and intervention, and to continuing capitalist intrigues. The NEP, its general atmosphere incomparably milder than what had preceded and what was to follow it, made such illusions at least understandable, especially among those distant from Russian conditions.

It was in pursuance of this "third line" of Soviet foreign policy that the regime authorized enterprises like the Anglo-Soviet Trade Union Council in 1925. This was an attempt to find a sympathetic response in one mass workers' organization in the West which as a whole rejected resolutely Communism but professed friendship toward the Soviet Union as a "workers' state." Actually, Soviet labor unions during the NEP enjoyed a modicum of independence. Their leader, Tomsky, one of the

---

[53] Degras, *Soviet Documents on Foreign Policy*, II: *1925–32* (London and New York, 1952), 237.

[54] This demonstrative openmindedness actually backfired. Lenin felt that the Soviet negotiators promised too much. The Western defenders, headed by the Belgian socialist Vandervelde, were appalled to find the charges against the S. R.'s obviously contrived and the court atmosphere one of judicial lynching. Eventually, the main accused were sentenced to death, but the execution of the sentences was suspended provided the S. R. partisans refrained from activity against the Soviet power. None of the sentenced was to live again a free man.

most attractive of the Bolsheviks, played an important role in the formation of the joint council, from which much was hoped as a way of by-
passing the inherently "reformist" Labour Party, which kept rejecting the
pleas of the British Communists for admission.

This premature approach to what in the 1930's was to become known
as a Popular Front backfired and was to be a factor in the worsening of
the Soviet diplomatic position in 1927–28. In 1926, the British general
strike again roused hopes for a revolution in Great Britain. The Russian
trade unions transmitted what was for those days a considerable sum of
money to the British strikers. Cries about Soviet interference and subsidizing of subversive activities now grew louder. An official Soviet note
rejected such imputations, asserted the Soviet unions' full independence
from the government and went on to speak thus of the main enemy of
Russia within the British government: "Churchill has not forgotten the
blockade and intervention. His present activities are designed to renew
a blockade against us. To be sure, one might treat Churchill's statements
as not quite serious, knowing his insincerity, except for the fact that he
is Chancellor of the Exchequer."[55] For the moment, a breach was avoided,
but in May 1927, the Soviet trade mission in London was raided by the
police in search of incriminating documents. Though the harvest was
hardly sensational, the sequence was a breach of diplomatic relations
between the two countries that lasted until 1929.

The rupture came at an inconvenient moment. The Soviet government
set great store by its formal relations with Great Britain as a symbol of
its real acceptance in the international community. Its attitude was tinged
by a note of snobbery. References of the Foreign Office to the Soviet
"mission" or "legation" were indignantly corrected by the *Narkomindel*,
which pointed out that *ever since 1815* Russia had had an *embassy* in
London and not a mere legation.[56] A more substantial loss was that of
considerable credits which had just been negotiated with British bankers.
The rupture occurred in the same year as the discomfitures of the Comintern in China, and the French government's demand that the Soviets recall
their ambassador to Paris, Rakovsky. (As a member of the Trotskyite
opposition, Rakovsky had signed a declaration of repentance and loyalty
to the Party, pledging in the case of war to spare no efforts to induce
foreign soldiers to desert. This was used by anti-Soviet circles in Paris
as a pretext for demanding his recall.)

The accumulation of these and other mishaps (the Soviet envoy in
Warsaw, Voykov, had been assassinated by a White emigré) led in 1927

---

[55] *Documents on the Foreign Policy of the U.S.S.R.*, IX (Moscow, 1964), 328.

[56] The issue was complicated for a few years by George V's reluctance to
receive an ambassador of the regime that had executed his cousin, Nicholas II.

to the resurrection of the ghost of imperialist intervention. Wrote Stalin on July 28: "It is hardly open to doubt that the chief contemporary question is that of the threat of a new imperialist war. It is not a matter of some indefinite and immaterial 'danger' of a new war. It is a matter of a real and material *threat* of a new war in general, and a war against the U.S.S.R. in particular." In his tedious way, Stalin went on to relate various "blows" against the Soviet state, connecting them all with the intrigues of the British Conservatives, who were behind not only the raid on the Soviet mission in London, but also the Soviet mishaps in China and the assassination of Voykov in Warsaw! "These blows should not be regarded as accidental." They were also connected with widespread sabotage against the Soviet Union: "blowing up bridges, setting fire to factories, and terrorizing Soviet ambassadors." It was equally characteristic that Stalin, while trying to fan war hysteria, at the same time held out prospects for peace. "Our task consists in the Soviet government continuing to conduct firmly and steadily a peaceful policy, a policy of peaceful relations, despite the provocative thrusts of our enemies, despite the stings to our prestige."

That responsible Soviet leaders held war to be near is most unlikely. To a student of international politics, the world in 1927 appeared more peaceful than at any time since 1918. Stalin gave away his game in his alarmist article: "Our task consists in strengthening the defensive capacity of our country, raising its national economy, improving industry . . . and getting rid of the indolence which unfortunately is still far from being liquidated." This was, then, an advance rationalization of the forthcoming forced collectivization and industrialization. In another passage, the political motif is even more transparent: "What can we say after all this of our wretched opposition and its new attacks on the party in face of the threat of a new war? What can we say about the same opposition finding it timely when war threatens to strengthen their attacks on the party?"[57]

1927 was the decisive year in Stalin's political destruction (physical destruction was yet to come) of the Trotsky-Zinoviev opposition, the two leaders having finally combined their forces in a last futile attempt to thwart the dictator. To the mass of unsophisticated Party members, the argument that Trotsky and Zinoviev were stirring up trouble while the enemy was at the gates was the most persuasive reason for their ultimate disgrace. Failures of Communism in China, the coming sacrifices of collectivization, the exile of the man who created the Red Army, the expulsion from the Party of Zinoviev and Kamenev, who had been Lenin's closest associates, could all be explained by the desperate foreign

[57] Quotations from Stalin in Degras, *Soviet Documents on Foreign Policy,* II, 233–37.

danger. The "war danger" enabled Stalin also to dispatch secondary leaders of the opposition to foreign posts to get them out of the country at the crucial moment.

Foreign policy, like everything in the Soviet Union, was being integrated into Stalin's totalitarian scheme. Pros and cons of a given policy were from now on to be considered in regard not only to the state interest of the U.S.S.R. and/or world Communism but also to the interest of the despot. In 1928, the military and technical collaboration with Germany was endangered by trumped-up charges against some German engineers accused in the Shakhty trial—one of the first show trials heralding the introduction of the First Five-Year Plan and designed to persuade the Soviet public that dark forces at home and abroad were in collusion, sabotaging the Stalin plan for a "great leap forward." The German engineers were eventually released while some of their Russian co-defendants were sent to death. The German-Soviet collaboration went on; both countries found it too profitable to give up because of such untoward "incidents."

But the introduction of the First Five-Year Plan and all the miseries attendant thereon inevitably lent a new *tone* to Soviet foreign policy. A degree of hysteria, a spy and sabotage mania had to be part of the propaganda campaign designed to explain to the Russian people their vast sufferings.[58] Soviet Russia was to appear like a beleaguered camp; every foreign country, every stirring of opposition to Stalin had to be made part of a concerted plot against the state and its ruler. In exclaiming against the accusations by the British government in connection with the "Zinoviev letter," which kept popping up in the propaganda of this period, Chicherin unwittingly provided a characterization of the Soviet methods of inflating the spy mania and in the conduct of the show trials:

> The British government is pinned to the wall and deliberately evades the disclosure of a truth which is hard for it to bear. It uses methods which were applied of old in the religious courts by the Jesuits who were always ready to advance the most terrible accusations, without any foundations, against those they wished to destroy. The Jesuits demanded that their words alone be believed. But if it is laid down as a premise that one must believe every assertion without proof, and if it is considered possible to decry anybody in any manner, then the possibility of good relations with such Jesuits is excluded from the first.[59]

Whatever one thinks of the historical accuracy of this accusation

---

[58] In a World War II conversation with Churchill, Stalin felt constrained to admit that the human cost of the period of collectivization surpassed even the catastrophic effects of the first phase of the war.

[59] Degras, *Soviet Documents on Foreign Policy*, II, 299.

against the Jesuits,[60] one must admit that he gave an uncanny description of Soviet techniques in the long series of trials beginning with the Shakhty one and leading through the great purge trials of the 1930's. But in one respect Chicherin was inaccurate. He stated that "the possibility of good relations with such Jesuits is excluded from the first." In fact, the network of diplomatic and commercial relations between the Soviet Union and the capitalist countries grew rather than contracted. And during the 1930's some of the Western Powers were to seek not only good relations but an alliance with the "Jesuits."

3. *China and the Far East*

The story of Soviet policy in China, 1921–28, constitutes a companion piece to Russia's exertions, successes, and failures in Western Europe around the focal area of Germany. In both cases, the dates work better than they usually do for a historian, for 1928 is a definite landmark in both areas. In the case of Germany, 1928 is the date of the death of the man who embodied the spirit of Rapallo: Brockdorff-Rantzau. On his deathbed, this strange man wished a cordial message to be transmitted to his protagonist Chicherin. The strange partnership between the two countries went on after his death, but forces were already in motion that were to bring Hitler to power and provide an interlude of hostility before another, even more momentous, and briefer alliance.

In the case of China, 1928 marks the end of the partnership of the Soviets with the Kuomintang, a catastrophe for the Chinese Communists, and their reversal to obscurity and apparent impotence. The two stories are instructive in their similarities, and yet they are different. China, like Germany, was a theater on which were projected formal "Soviet" policy, Comintern policies, and the Soviet leaders' internal intrigues and quests for power. But while in the case of Germany the main plot concerned the relations of the two governments, in the case of China the main weight of activity was thrown into the fairly constant attempt to sway the country in a Communist direction. In the German drama, the stage is occupied by the corpulent figures of such dignitaries as Stresemann, Brockdorff-Rantzau, and General von Seeckt, and only at interludes does it become crowded with the gesticulating figures of German Communists— Ernst Thälmann, Ruth Fischer, Heinrich Brandler, etc. In the Chinese drama, we are given several simultaneous action scenes: in one, Soviet

---

[60] One suspects that the learned Commissar for Foreign Relations confused the Jesuits with the Holy Inquisition, which in the main was in the hands of the Dominican Order.

diplomacy is courting some Chinese warlords; in another, action takes place in relation to the official Chinese government (if in fact China during the period can be asserted to have had a government) in Peking. But the main stage has the Chinese Communists collaborating with, infiltrating, and ultimately fighting the Kuomintang and its (from the Communist point of view) evil spirit Chiang Kai-shek.

Our account of Soviet policies in China in the 1920's must of necessity be brief. Furthermore, in order to set this account within the wider context of Soviet foreign policy in the 1920's, we must keep in mind several factors, disregard of which beclouds the discussion of this extremely involved and contentious story.

The enormous importance of China today, and its conquest by the Communists in the 1940's, leads us naturally to overestimate its importance in the whole spectrum of Soviet policies of the earlier era. Yet, though very important at the time, China was simply one facet of Soviet and Comintern policies in the Orient or in the colonial and semi-colonial world as a whole. Turkey has not become Communist nor is Turkey today a world power. But in the spectrum of Soviet policies in the 1920's, it would be hard to say whether Turkey or China touched on a more important concern. The Turkish Communists were quickly suppressed by the iron hand of Kemal Atatürk. But friendship with Turkey was the key point of Soviet Near Eastern policy, the main means to check the Western Powers' (mainly British) domination of the area. The Soviets considered a treaty in 1925 reaffirming the friendship of the two countries to be an important part of their attempt to avoid isolation in the wake of the Locarno negotiations. Even when it came to the revolutionary potential of the Chinese situation, it was not, except during 1924–27, thought to be equal to that of India, where a revolution, whether a national one or a national one tinged with Communism, would strike more directly at the lifeline of *the* enemy, the British empire.

Another element in the Chinese situation as appraised by the Soviet leaders was the necessarily limited objectives of Chinese Communism. For propaganda purposes, it was not unusual to envisage China as another potential Soviet Union and to compare events in China of the mid-1920's to the Russian Revolution of 1905, thus implying that in a decade or so all of China would be Communist. But the practical objectives had to be much more modest. Chinese Communism could become the revolutionary yeast in a wider nationalist organization like the Kuomintang, or at the most it could become ensconced territorially and militarily in a limited area and thus become one of many movements and governments in China engaged in the apparently endless civil war. Except in the seaboard cities, China lacked the necessary proletarian base for a mass Communist movement. A comparison with Russia of 1917 was tempting but could hardly reveal an exact parallel: for all their oratory, the Soviet leaders well remembered that it was not mainly the proletariat of Petrograd and Moscow which brought about the Bolshevik Revolution, but the soldiers and sailors who saw a Bolshevik victory as the quickest way to end the war. For the workers of Shanghai and Hankow to emulate this feat without an armed force behind them was out of the question.

Supposing that by some miracle the Chinese Communists were to become real contenders for power in all of China, would other foreign powers tolerate this situation? Here again sober reflection in Moscow would point out that in China one confronted not only Western imperialism decadent and in retreat, but also Japanese imperialism. The latter was held in check, just as it had been in Siberia, by the position of the United States. But the prospect of a Communist China could quickly bring Japan and America together and launch Japanese armies into China. And Soviet Far Eastern territories would once again be endangered.

Thus, looking at Chinese conditions through the prism of the 1920's rather than that of the 1940's, one can see that Soviet goals and potentialities were of necessity limited. A strong, nationalistically oriented movement that would deal a decisive blow to Western influence in China, and the laying of foundations for a sound Communist party—those were the aims within the realm of possibility.

That today's student gets a somewhat different impression is due not only to China's current importance. The whole issue of China policy became entangled with the intra-Party struggle in Russia. The years 1926 and 1927 were the years when both the affairs of Chinese Communism and the struggle with the Trotsky-Zinoviev opposition were reaching their climax. There could be no longer any question that the responsibility for Communist foreign policy—including that in China—was ultimately Stalin's. The tragedy of the Chinese Communists thus was blamed on the dictator and became a card in the hands of the internal opposition. In this final act of his performance on the Soviet political stage, Trotsky poured his famous vituperation on Stalin's head. Trotsky's version— that had *his* views on China been adopted rather than Stalin's, the cause of Chinese Communism would have been saved—has found favor with many historians.[61] It is true that by following the tactics laid down by Stalin the Chinese Communists met with disaster. But this leaves open

---

[61] "Unlike Stalin, Trotsky had a superb and almost intuitive grasp of the dynamics of the revolutionary struggle almost everywhere. . . . Trotsky's analyses and warnings about the course of events in China proved strikingly accurate." Harold Isaacs, *The Tragedy of the Chinese Revolution* (Stanford, Calif., 1951), p. 189.

the question how they would have fared had they followed Trotsky's views or the views Trotsky was alleged to have. This question will be touched on below. Trotsky's eloquence in this as in many other respects carried the day with many Western historians even of a non-Trotskyite background. But again, as on the issue of "socialism in one country," if one examines the facts one finds that the difference of views on various phases of the Chinese problem between Stalin and Trotsky was not nearly so sharp as the brilliant maker and historian of the Russian Revolution asserted *post facto*.[62]

Before turning to the actual story, it is important to note the effect of the dispute on the future course of Soviet foreign policy. Trotsky's thesis would have shattered the whole basis of the direction of Soviet external policies. Nobody had dreamed of blaming Lenin for the failure of German Communism in 1919 or 1921 or of Polish Communism in 1920. But the logical consequence of Trotsky's stand on Stalin as the "gravedigger" of the revolution was that a disaster befalling a Communist Party anywhere in the world is directly due to the incompetence of or betrayal by the leader of world Communism and a sufficient cause for his removal. To counteract this thesis, Stalin had to heighten the cult of his infallibility to an extent undreamed of by Lenin. The policy laid down by Moscow was to be always right, and only its local executors might err or betray. Dissent by the local Communists, a claim that they understood their country's conditions better than the Russian comrades, while infrequent enough before 1927, became completely unthinkable from then on. The case of China in the 1920's helped to set the Stalinist mold of world Communism that the victory of the Chinese Communists twenty years later was to shatter definitely and irreparably.

The setting for the involved story of the Soviet thrust into Chinese politics was the disintegration of the Chinese state, which had been proceeding since at least the middle of the nineteenth century and which culminated in the fall of the Manchu monarchy in 1911. A period of anarchy followed, of rival governments and warlords carving out provinces of the vast country, intermittently warring and bargaining with each other and seeking favor with one or the other of the imperial powers whose business interests and concessions encroached upon Chinese territory. As early as 1912, his mind turning to the problems of the Orient, Lenin wrote an article on Dr. Sun Yat-sen, founder of the Kuomintang, whom he hailed as a national revolutionary, even if from the bourgeois democratic point of view, and as a symbol of renascent Asia.

---

[62] One of the best studies of the subject which reaches that conclusion is Conrad Brandt, *Stalin's Failure in China* (Cambridge, Mass., 1958), esp. pp. 154–63.

The bid to the East that followed the Bolshevik Revolution and the failure of Communism to ignite similar revolutions before has already been described.[63] At first the focus of Soviet propaganda and activity had to be in the Near East. China was far away from the focal point of the Civil War in Russia. The practical aim of the Soviet government in the Far East until 1922 had to be not ideological or military, but the recovery of Siberia from partial occupation by Japan. This was accomplished, as we have seen, with the unwitting help of the United States, thus enabling Soviet Russia to plunge into the cauldron of Chinese politics.

Even before, in 1919 and 1920, the *Narkomindel*, over the signature of Deputy Commissar Karakhan, had issued ringing declarations to the Chinese people and governments (similar to those addressed to Persia and Afghanistan) repudiating the unequal treaties forced by the Tsarist government upon China and renouncing all extraterritorial rights, etc. In this initial burst of generosity, the Soviet government pledged to restore to the Chinese people the Chinese Eastern Railway, a branch of the great Trans-Siberian line that ran through Manchuria. At the same time, the Bolshevik Revolution, like any revolutionary stirring in the West, was finding a sympathetic response among Chinese intellectuals and students. A Comintern emissary, Voitinsky, was able to find in 1920 a pro-Communist nucleus in Peking and Shanghai. In 1921, the miniscule Chinese Communist Party, still very much a circle of professors and young intellectuals, held its first congress.

Thus by 1922 the various elements of the Chinese problem were set and ready for Soviet intervention. But because of the peculiarities of China, Soviet efforts there had to be expanded over a wider front than elsewhere. In Europe Soviet foreign policy operated in the two dimensions of the Comintern and the *Narkomindel*. But this symmetry broke down in China, for there was not one Chinese government but several quasi-governments. In addition, there was Sun Yat-sen's revolutionary non-Communist movement, the Kuomintang, which in its aims and objectives resembled Kemal's movement in Turkey but which unlike Kemal's had no military force behind it. To establish good and profitable relations with all those discordant and intermittently warring elements—Chinese Communism, the Kuomintang, the "official" government in Peking, and the warlords—appeared as a formidable task even for Soviet diplomacy *and* the Comintern. And it was complicated by another factor. Now that Soviet Russia had survived the Civil War and held the Japanese at bay, her repudiation of evil Tsarist imperialist practices in China grew much less emphatic. In 1922, she was establishing a protectorate over Outer Mongolia (which, though in fact it had for long been independent, was

[63] See above, pp. 121–25.

held by all the Chinese factions to be part of China), and her earlier pledge of turning over the Chinese Eastern Railway and its right of way to the Chinese people was now being explained away. What is then surprising, with all due apologies to Trotsky, is not so much that the Soviet Union's China policy collapsed in 1927–28, but rather that for the five years the Soviets managed, like a juggler keeping several balls in the air, to keep so many divergent policies going at once.

With the government of the "Chinese Republic" in Peking (whose effective authority extended over some northern provinces of China *minus* Manchuria), the Soviets after several false starts finally signed a treaty on May 31, 1924. The treaty was a diplomatic triumph for Russia: though the Soviets promised to withdraw their troops from Outer Mongolia, the date was unspecified; and though Chinese sovereignty over that country was solemnly acknowledged, the treaty in effect recognized the Soviet protectorate over Mongolia. The Chinese Eastern Railway remained the property of the Soviet government, with some soothing concessions granted to spare Chinese pride. And since the railway itself ran through territory controlled not by the Peking government but by a rival warlord, a gentleman named Chang Tso-lin, the provisions of the treaty were repeated in a special pact made between him and Lev Karakhan, the same ambassador who had negotiated with the government of the "Chinese Republic."[64]

But the most promising horse in the Chinese race was obviously the Kuomintang. This was the organization on which were centered the hopes of nationalistically and progressively minded Chinese everywhere, who dreamed of freeing their country from stultifying traditions, warlordism, and foreign imperialism; of bringing China into the twentieth century. Its founder and moving spirit, Dr. Sun Yat-sen, professed a philosophy not much different from that of other reformers of Asian societies who aspired to modernize and free their countries. It was a mixture of Western ideas, nationalism, and some very moderate doses of socialism, plus what was to become known much later as "one-party democracy." "His hope was to bring about the peaceful and benevolent transformation of Chinese society after first securing power for himself and his followers by purely military means."[65] But for all the popularity of his ideas among the younger generation of intellectuals, durable political power kept eluding him. His ephemeral political successes were scored as a result of a bargain with this or that warlord.

The Bolshevik Revolution was an eye-opener to the Kuomintang, as to many other similarly oriented Asian political movements. What at-

[64] Allen S. Whiting, *Soviet Policies in China* (New York, 1954), pp. 229–31.
[65] Isaacs, *op. cit.*, p. 57.

tracted their admiration and emulation was not the ideological content of Bolshevism, but the example of a small party which, through organizational discipline and superior propaganda techniques, managed to seize power in a backward society and to hold on to it despite the hostility of Western imperialists. It appeared as if the Communists were in possession of some magic political and organizational formulas that until then had eluded the Asian reformers.

Sun's search for a foreign ally had hitherto been unsuccessful. Japan had been the object of his earliest hopes, but Japan behaved in China in the manner of the European imperialists, and during the world war she tried to impose a virtual protectorate over the whole country. The United States had largely thwarted the Japanese designs, but America in the isolationist 1920's was not going to engage actively in sponsoring Chinese revolutionary nationalism.

The marriage of convenience between Communism and the Kuomintang was postponed by Dr. Sun's suspicions of the ideology and his feelings that Marxian socialism was inappropriate for China in her current phase of development. On the Soviet side, despite Lenin's blessing of national liberation movements, the Kuomintang was at first treated warily. Dr. Sun was known to be pro-Western, especially pro-American. The infant Chinese Communist Party might become completely absorbed within the Kuomintang rather than being able to turn it into a tool of Soviet policy. What probably proved the decisive argument from Moscow's point of view was the fact that southern China—which was the focal point of the Kuomintang's political power, with Dr. Sun dominating the so-called Canton government—was the sphere of British influence and extensive business interests. A strongly nationalist movement there, guided by the Communists, was bound to clash with the British.

Comintern emissaries therefore began in 1922 to press the Chinese Communists to enroll in the Kuomintang. In January 1923 came the famous Yoffe-Sun declaration. The Soviet diplomat reassured the Chinese nationalist that Soviet Russia had no desire to export Communism or Russians into China. Chinese Communists were to be admitted into the Kuomintang without giving up their separate party. Soviet help in arms and advisers was to be extended to the cause of Chinese nationalism.

Within the next three years, the power of the Communists within the Kuomintang grew rapidly, while the latter became in turn a well-organized mass movement, its Canton government a contender for power in all of China. Soviet advisers and Comintern missions descended upon southern China. The main Soviet emissary, Michael Borodin, became in fact the chief architect of Kuomintang policies (especially after Dr. Sun's death in March 1925), steering them resolutely in the "anti-imperialist" (i.e., anti-British) direction. In May 1925, the British-led police in the International Settlement in Shanghai fired on a crowd of students demonstrating in support of a strike in a foreign-owned firm. The bloodshed was followed by widespread strikes and a boycott of British goods that spread throughout much of China, including the British colony of Hong Kong. This sequence of events seriously undermined the British position in the area and endowed the Kuomintang government of Canton with a new power and prestige as the generally recognized center of the national revolution.

Communist influence and advice transformed the Kuomintang from what it had been prior to the Yoffe-Sun agreement—a group of intellectuals seeking leverage within this or that warlord group—into a modern, well-organized mass party. Like its Bolshevik prototype, the Kuomintang developed extensive techniques for exploiting all the numerous social ills and grievances that afflicted the unhappy country—the peasants' exploitation by the landlords, the general land hunger, the Chinese workers' struggle to exact a minimum living wage from their foreign employers, the universal resentment against Western imperialism, which was blamed for keeping the country divided and backward. The price exacted for this achievement was the growing Communist power within the Kuomintang, which by 1926 made most of the foreign observers conclude prematurely that it was in fact a "front" for the Communist Party of China. It could not be questioned that much of its machinery, especially in the propaganda and organization departments, was run by the Communists, and that its military forces were being organized by Soviet advisers.

It should be added that, for obvious reasons, China was virtually an unknown quantity to the Soviet leaders. On an issue like Germany, most contemporary Politburo leaders felt with some justification that they were experts: they knew the language, had lived in the country, possessed a detailed knowledge of its social and economic problems. In the case of China—and with all of Russia's other problems, domestic and foreign, pressing upon them—they were absolutely at sea. Hence an obscure Comintern functionary, Borodin (whose original choice for China seems to have been motivated by his perfect command of English and a long stay in the *United States!*), dominated Soviet policies there to an extent that neither Radek nor Zinoviev himself had been allowed to dictate, say, in Germany. Borodin in turn had to grapple with rival groups and personal ambitions within the Kuomintang-Communist *ménage*. Indeed, the jarring elements in the Russia–Kuomintang–Chinese Communist triad were provided by the extremely involved conflicts and rivalries for power within the Canton government. For all their growing influence, the Chinese Communists were far from happy with the arrangements. They suspected that Moscow was growing inordinately fond of the wider organization and relegating them to an auxiliary role.[66] In 1926, the Kuomintang was admitted as a "sympathizing party" to the Comintern. With the typical Soviet penchant for trying to find the strong man in any given situation, Borodin was favoring a Kuomintang general, Chiang Kai-shek, who had had a period of training in the Soviet Union and a strong pro-Russian reputation. There was also a strong left but non-Communist group, and by the same token there was a right-wing grouping, pro-Soviet but apprehensive of the Chinese Communists' gains in the wake of the merger.

In 1926, the fantastically involved Chinese situation was the subject of a study by a special committee of the Politburo presided over by Trotsky. His report of March 26, 1926, preserved in his archives, throws a startling light on the Soviet policy-makers' approach to China and on his subsequent allegations that he had for years disagreed with the official policy (Stalin's) on the issue.[67] Trotsky's report makes clear the subordinate role of China, not to speak of the Chinese Communists, in the Soviet view of the foreign situation. The main premise of the policy he recommended was that, following Locarno, the Soviet Union faced isolation and, perhaps, again a united front of the other powers: *the Soviet Union needs a breathing spell.*[68] And this in turn imposed the need for restraint in the Chinese revolution. Any intemperate attack upon foreign interests in China might lead to the creation of an anti-Soviet coalition. It was especially important not to alienate Japan. Thus, both the Kuomintang and the Chinese Communists should forego any move against the pro-Japanese warlord Chang Tso-lin, who controlled Manchuria. One should reconcile oneself to the fact that "in the foreseeable future Manchuria will remain in the hands of Japan." Until the time when there is one government in China, the Soviet Union should have "loyal [*sic*] relations with the existing regimes in China, the central as well as provincial ones." The main theme of the report—it continues to be one of the main motifs of Soviet foreign policy well beyond December 7, 1941—is the absolute necessity of avoiding a military confrontation with Japan. In pursuance of this necessity, Trotsky (of course he spoke also for the other members of the commission, which included Chicherin and Voroshilov) raised a most bizarre possibility. Would it not be possible to allow Japanese immigrants to settle in the Soviet Far East, provided this

[66] The classical judgment on Communist aims in any political merging or alliance had been delivered by Plekhanov before World War I when he observed that when Lenin sought a merger with another party, it was in the way of a hungry man who wants to "merge" with a piece of bread.

[67] The Trotsky Archive, T870.

[68] This incidentally throws some light on the alleged sharp contrast between Stalin's socialism in one country and Trotsky's revolutionary impatience.

was done "carefully and gradually," so that the Japanese would not ethnically dominate the Siberian maritime provinces?[69]

Trotsky's report also shows that, for Soviet policy-makers (and at the time of writing the report, Trotsky was still one of them, at least in foreign affairs), a basic component of Soviet policy even in China was hostility toward Great Britain. Concessions are offered to Japan so that Japan will not renew her alliance with Great Britain. The report surmises that perhaps even France's interests in the area should be respected, so that she will not throw her weight on the side of Great Britain. The difficulty of persuading Soviet Russia's Chinese allies of the desirability of this Machiavellian policy was shamefacedly recognized: the Chinese nationalists and Communists were to be persuaded that the Soviet recommendations have nothing in common with the old policy of imperialist spheres of influence.

At the time the report was discussed and accepted in the Politburo in Moscow, the political situation in China changed drastically. Chiang Kai-shek, until then thought a pliable tool of Russia, staged a coup in Canton on March 20 that made him the political as well as military master of the situation. Many Communists were arrested and the Soviet advisers confined to their quarters. Chiang followed this consolidation of personal power by compelling the Kuomintang authorities to limit severely the number of Communists in important positions in the party. But, cagily, Chiang avoided a breach with Russia, whose military help he still needed to expand his rule beyond the Canton area. He thus proceeded to reassure Borodin and amazingly enough remained in the good graces of the Comintern, even though the Chinese Communists were now enraged and begged Moscow to allow them greater freedom of action. Chiang then staged his famous Northern Expedition to expand the area controlled by the Kuomintang. Its spectacular success was due in no small measure to Communist help in organizing pro-Kuomintang risings among the peasants and workers. Chiang was once more a hero in Moscow and the apparent chosen instrument of Soviet policy in China. His rough handling of the Chinese Communists was overlooked, in view of his new prominence as the most successful leader of the nationalist and anti-imperialist cause. Soviet advisers were still with him, Comintern delegations descended on his headquarters.

But, in fact, Moscow was once again hedging its bets. When, in October, the Kuomintang armies occupied the three industrial cities on the Yangtze (the triad was known as Wuhan), Borodin persuaded a

---

[69] Undoubtedly to Trotsky's fertile mind this would have been a way not only of appeasing the Japanese government, but of making possible Communist indoctrination of the settlers, with eventual repercussions in Japan proper.

number of Kuomintang leaders to move there, away from Chiang's immediate influence, and to set up their own government. This body in turn declared its independence of Chiang and assumed a much more leftist position. The Left Kuomintang government became known as the Wuhan body and eventually co-opted two Communists as ministers. Thus within the involved Chinese situation the Soviet position was apparently strengthened: the Left Kuomintang was there to exert leverage on Chiang Kai-shek and, should he once again act independently, to act as Moscow's alternative instrument in the Chinese revolution.

The course of events in 1927 in China is of a complexity surpassing that of the previous few years and defying brief description. But it is clear what the Soviet scheme was. Chiang Kai-shek and the Right Kuomintang were to be helped up to the limit of their usefulness or, as Stalin said in a speech to Moscow Party workers in the spring of 1927, "They have to be utilized to the end, squeezed out like a lemon, and then thrown away."[70] Then, presumably, the same unenviable fate would be dealt to the Left Kuomintang. One thing that in the opinion of the ruling group in Moscow could disrupt this desirable sequence of events in China would be undue haste on the part of the Chinese Communists, who might arouse the suspicions of Chiang Kai-shek and the Left Kuomintang by any premature attempt to seize power on their own and by excessive agitation among the peasants and workers. Hence, the Chinese Communists were muzzled and once again told to hold in check their ambitions for power on their own.

Viewed from Moscow, China, it must be repeated, was but part of the world situation as it confronted the Soviet Union and Chinese Communism still a smaller element in it. This was not the product simply of Stalin's cynicism or lack of zeal in propagating the creed. Early in 1927, Trotsky wrote to his recent confederate Zinoviev a letter expounding his views on the international situation. On China, he was again anxious that Chinese revolutionaries of all shades should not complicate *Soviet Russia*'s position by interfering with other countries' spheres of influence. They should work mostly against Great Britain but preserve good relations with France and above all with Japan. To the latter's puppet, Chang Tso-lin, Trotsky would have the Chinese nationalists concede not only Manchuria but much of northern China, which the Kuomintang should not try to conquer. There ought to be, he writes, a "concrete arrangement" with Japan. The immediate enemy is still the British empire, and in contemplating various steps against this main object of Communist hatred, Trotsky's fertile mind ranges over the most bizarre contingencies. Thus it is

[70] Robert C. North, *Moscow and the Chinese Communists* (Stanford, Calif., 1953), p. 96.

an essential element in the anti-British struggle to procure diplomatic recognition by the United States, even if Russia has to promise to pay debts incurred by Kerensky's government (something that the Bolsheviks officially refused even to talk about). If the United States still refused to recognize the Soviet Union, "we should through clever agents stir up anti-American activities in Central and South America, thus to bind the United States' hands in the case of our conflict with England. Agents for those activities should be chosen from trustworthy American and Spanish-speaking comrades."[71]

The complicated structure of Soviet policies in China collapsed in 1927, as perhaps it was bound to in view of their oversubtle character and the personalities and issues involved. It was impossible for Chiang Kai-shek not to perceive the role assigned him by Moscow, and he hastened to strike at them before he could be "squeezed out like a lemon and then thrown away." Having captured Shanghai, largely with the help of the Communists, he proceeded on April 12 to massacre the local Communists and their supporters. This news reached Moscow almost simultaneously with the occurrence of a grotesque incident: the Comintern's Eastern Secretariat had just distributed autographed pictures of Chiang Kai-shek to the main Soviet leaders, including Trotsky, asking them in return to send their own to the Chinese general.[72]

With Chiang Kai-shek now an enemy, the Soviets tried to play their other Kuomintang card, that of the Wuhan government. The Chinese Communists were once again warned not to act on their own but to increase their infiltration and influence within the Left Kuomintang. This policy was strongly assailed by the Trotsky-Zinoviev opposition. Trotsky's position since March 1927 had been that the Chinese Communists should give up their membership in the Kuomintang, though he was still for an alliance with it. "One can have an alliance with the Kuomintang, but an ally has to be watched just like an enemy," he wrote, epitomizing the Soviet philosophy on alliances. He thought the moment ripe for the setting up of soviets in China, provided the manner of election to them was such as not to give "an accidental majority to the reactionary element."

With the news of the Shanghai massacre, Chinese policy became for the moment the main battleground of Soviet politics. Not since the great debate on Brest Litovsk was the difference of views on foreign affairs so much in the forefront of the intra-Party struggle. What was essentially a difference of views on *tactics* became represented, in the heat of partisan-ship and personal hatreds, as an *ideological* conflict: Trotsky and his

[71] The Trotsky Archive, T911.
[72] The Trotsky Archive, T946.

companions believed in the inherent strength and revolutionary zeal of the Chinese proletariat and poor peasants; Stalin, lukewarm to ideological arguments, followed power considerations.

Stalin might have believed, with some justification, that the key to success of Russian foreign policy and its superiority to that of the democracies lay precisely in the ability of the Soviet leadership to formulate its policies secretly, without public discussion and dissension. This totalitarian logic led the Politburo to forbid the Trotsky-Zinoviev opposition to publish their dissent. But even with this muzzling of the increasingly voluble and abusive Trotsky-Zinoviev group, the crash of Soviet expectations in China could not be concealed. The Left Kuomintang disintegrated, the pro-Soviet members of the Wuhan government fled, the remaining ones joined Chiang Kai-shek in an anti-Communist front. *Now*, the Chinese Communists were unleashed by Stalin. A series of armed revolts in the countryside and attempted seizures of the urban centers was directed by them against the Kuomintang forces. But they were suppressed by the middle of 1928, though scattered bands of Communist guerrillas remained in isolated areas. One of them, headed by Mao Tse-tung, was slated for a historic role.

By 1928, Soviet policy in China was in a shambles. The Kuomintang appeared to be the wave of the future, conquering large parts of the country, coming to an accommodation with the most influential northern warlords, thus bidding fair to become the government of united China and recognized as such by most of the foreign powers. Its relations with the Soviet Union were now definitely severed. In vulgar terms, Chiang Kai-shek had beaten the Communists at their own game. This was recognized by the erstwhile Comintern viceroy in China, Borodin, on his departure for Russia and obscurity: "When the next Chinese general comes to Moscow and shouts 'Hail to the world revolution!' better send at once for the OGPU. All that any of them want is rifles."[73]

But if one views the Soviet policies in China from a historical perspective and apart from the emotion-laden Stalin-Trotsky debate, one is constrained to some different conclusions. The initial Soviet aim of weakening the grip of the imperial powers on China was certainly accomplished, through the agency of the Kuomintang. It was the latter's success and its threat to unite effectively all of China that prompted the Japanese military venture in Manchuria in 1931 and later on in the rest of China, tied the hands of Soviet Russia's most feared enemy in the Far East, and eventually brought about the American-Japanese war, an intraimperialist conflict of which Soviet policy-makers had dreamed since

[73] Quoted in Brandt, *op. cit.*, p. 153.

Lenin. This Kuomintang success would have been inconceivable without Soviet help between 1923 and 1926 and without Soviet advisers and military experts.

As for the Chinese Communists, the argument that they could have been successful had they been allowed to make their bid for power earlier is partly answered by the fortunes of the Party for many years after 1928, when it continued to be split into scattered and hunted groups. Their initial participation in the Kuomintang had certainly benefited the latter, since they had brought zeal, discipline, and organizational ability into the larger body. By the same token, their participation was an undoubted and important element in their eventual survival and then in their dazzling triumph after 1945. From a small group of intellectuals professing an esoteric doctrine, they became within a few years a strong movement with roots in the countryside. Membership in the Kuomintang gave them invaluable military and governmental experience, which they could have never acquired just by reading Marxist classics and propaganda among workers in Shanghai or Canton. It is instructive to compare the fortunes of Communism in India, where the Comintern always viewed Gandhi with distaste and allowed only very tangential contacts with the Congress Party.[74] The Communists have always thrived on participation in wider movements and temporary release from the strait-jacket of doctrine, as we shall see again in the case of the resistance movements of World War II.

Those broader perspectives could hardly be perceived in 1928. The Chinese Communists were being hunted down, their leaders, if not executed by the Kuomintang, were continually being purged and reshuffled by Moscow. There, the voice of opposition had finally been stifled. Stalin's view of the debacle was levelheaded, albeit expressed in inelegant terms: Soviet (i.e., his) tactics had been perfectly correct. The help to the Kuomintang had rendered dividends: "We were right, and we were following in Lenin's footsteps, for the struggle of Canton and Ankara dispersed the forces of imperialism, weakened and overturned imperialism, and thereby facilitated the development of the home of the world revolution, the development of the U.S.S.R."[75] So were the later stages of Soviet policies in China. It is simply that the Chinese Revolution "got stuck" at an inconvenient phase.[76] Eventually, the Chinese Revo-

---

[74] To be sure, another and probably more important element in the inability of Indian Communism to get started in the 1920's was that India had an effective government, as against the indescribable chaos of Chinese politics during the period.

[75] Degras, *Soviet Documents on Foreign Policy*, II, 238.

[76] In referring to Turkey he avowed that there the revolution got stuck even earlier: "The Turkish (Kemalist) revolution, for example, is on the contrary

lution was bound to become unstuck and to proceed to a higher stage. And so it would. . . .

The lessons of China conclude the second great formative period of Soviet foreign policy, 1921–28. Between 1917 and 1921, Soviet Russia fought for and won the right to exist as a state. Between 1921 and 1928, she fought for and secured the right to exist as a *new type* of state—one which, while maintaining normal diplomatic and trade relations with the rest of the world, is at the same time the center and directing force of a world revolutionary movement. Furthermore, from a symmetry of those two aspects of Soviet foreign policy, expressed in its Comintern and *Narkomindel* branches, the activities of the Soviet Union abroad often took on an even more complex character. In China, as we noted, at one brief moment the Soviet regime followed four separate yet integrated lines of activity: it maintained diplomatic relations with the official government in Peking; it advised and helped the national movement (Chiang Kai-shek), which was conducting a military campaign that sought to overthrow that regime; it helped and abetted the coalition (Left Kuomintang) that sought to overthrow Chiang Kai-shek; finally, it controlled the Chinese Communists who sought to take over the Left Kuomintang! And, at least for a brief period, it obtained the acquiescence of all the parties concerned to its right to pursue that fourfold policy. The Chinese debacle did not affect the Soviet conviction that the interests of any given Communist movement must be sacrificed in favor of another ally if this policy promises to render greater dividends to the U.S.S.R. Thus, from the position of 1917–18—that Soviet Russia exists to promote the world revolution—the Communist view by 1928 had shifted to the position that the world revolutionary movement exists to defend and promote the interests of the U.S.S.R. Said Stalin, "He is a revolutionary who without reservation, unconditionally, openly . . . is ready to protect and defend the U.S.S.R. . . . He who thinks to defend the world revolutionary movement apart and against the U.S.S.R. is going against the revolution and will certainly slide into the camp of the enemies of the revolution."[77]

There is no question that the containment of Communism in Europe and Asia on the one hand, and the absence of a concrete threat of war on the other, contributed to the decision to embark upon the drastic plan of collectivization and industrialization that Stalin began to implement in

---

still stuck in the first stage of its development, the stage of bourgeois liberation movement, and is not even attempting to pass on to the second stage, the stage of agrarian revolution." *Ibid.*, p. 239.

[77] *Ibid.*, p. 243.

1928. None of the tantalizing possibilities of the early 1920's—a Franco-British war, a clash between the United States and England or between the United States and Japan—had come to pass. Communism both in China and in Germany was definitely stymied. While the decision to collectivize and industrialize was dictated by internal economic factors, its furious pace and the risks taken were undoubtedly related to foreign frustrations and the need to channel a power drive that had been thwarted abroad to vast tasks at home. By the same token, while Stalin repeatedly invoked the threat of foreign intervention and war as the rationale for the First Five-Year Plan, there is little doubt that the regime would not have embarked on a campaign which debilitated Russia economically for several years and brought the peasantry to the verge of a revolt if it had seen a serious threat of imminent war. Implicit even in the very scheme of the First Five-Year Plan was a considerable importation of foreign machinery and influx of foreign technicians. How were those to be obtained, if the very countries from which they were to come were—if one believed the speeches of the Soviet leaders and the "revelations" of the show sabotage trials—about to pounce on the Soviet Union? Nor should one take too seriously the other aspect of Stalin's campaign oratory: his prediction of a vast economic crisis of capitalism, which, when it came with the depression of 1929 and the 1930's, was hailed as a proof of the Communist leader's perspicacity. Predictions of shattering world crises were a perennial feature in Soviet oratory. When one did come, it was eagerly seized by proponents of Stalin's infallibility while the previous ones were forgotten. That is how prophets and economists make their reputation! Circumstantial evidence is very strong that in fact the Soviet leadership in 1928 expected economic stabilization in the capitalist world to continue for some years: the Five-Year Plan required great purchases in the main industrial countries, which in turn had to be financed largely by an increase in Soviet exports to them. A depression would, as it did in fact, make Germany, Britain, and the United States curtail their imports.[78]

The First Five-Year Plan and the onset of the depression mark very fundamental changes in the world situation and in the tone of Soviet policies. With the latter, the change is, again, subtle and not so drastic as presented by some interpreters. Stalin does not "abandon" foreign Communism to concentrate exclusively on internal problems. But the relationship of the Soviet leaders to world Communism undergoes yet another shift. Moscow's analysis of the world situation changes drastically between

---

[78] "The Plan no doubt tended towards a form of economic autarchy. . . . But the immediate result was to strengthen and not to weaken economic ties with the capitalist world." Max Beloff, *The Foreign Policy of Soviet Russia, 1929–1941* (London, 1947), I, 28.

1928 and 1934. The invocation of the threat of war had been since 1921 part of the Communist ritual; the threat of capitalist intervention was at most half believed, though used unrestrainedly for propaganda purposes and as a weapon in the intra-Party struggle. By 1934, this threat was all too tangible and believable, and all the resources of Soviet diplomacy and of world Communism were thrown in to avoid Soviet entanglement or, if worse came to worst, Soviet isolation in a war.

4. *The End of an Era*

Shouting about the imminence of war, inwardly convinced of a lengthy peaceful period ahead, the Soviet Union's leaders embarked in 1927–28 on the execution of a series of momentous policies, the total effect of which was to transform the Soviet Union and the world Communist movement.

Collectivization and industrialization were, perhaps with the exception of similar Chinese efforts in the 1950's and 1960's, the most drastic attempts in modern history to change the social and economic structure of a major country within a brief time. They involved the application of compulsion to the majority of the Russian population, the peasants, in order to transform their conditions of life and work. The price paid was probably millions of human lives lost in famine and through repression; prodigious losses in agriculture; and a general lowering of the standard of living, which some experts estimate at having gone down at the end of the First Five-Year Plan by as much as one-fourth in comparison with 1928.[79]

The Communist Party of the U.S.S.R. was, during the same period, transformed into a fully totalitarian organization. Between 1925 and 1928, Stalin already exercised dictatorial powers, but he was dependent on the support of a group headed by Bukharin, Tomsky, and Rykov, support given him on the assumption that the moderate policies of the NEP would continue. Now his war upon the peasants led to a breach, and the three leaders headed what became known as the Right Opposition. With their defeat by 1930, there was left no nucleus of leadership in the Party and no single man to oppose Stalin during the next quarter of a century. Unlike their predecessors, the Trotsky-Zinoviev group, they lost the struggle because of their ineptitude rather than because of the policies they advocated. Trotsky was admired by many, feared by more, and not very popular with most of the Party membership; Zinoviev was widely loathed. Rykov and especially Tomsky, on the contrary, were people of great popularity with

---

[79] It is a matter of some contention whether the actual extent of forced collectivization was fully intended by Stalin or whether in its course he was compelled because of the peasants' opposition to go beyond the original plan.

the Party masses, and Bukharin was widely credited with being the brains of Stalin's earlier moderate period. That, with this fund of popularity and with the castastrophic results of Stalin's policies, the Right Opposition still went down to defeat can be attributed to its ineptitude and indecision. Bukharin was discharged as the actual head of the Comintern, Rykov as prime minister, Tomsky as the leader of the trade unions. The Left and Right Oppositions were eventually to be reunited in a common fate during the great purge.

The successive purges of the CPSU and of the leaders most closely associated with the Lenin era were to leave an indelible imprint on foreign Communism. Already the purge of the Left Opposition had been pointed out to foreign Communists as a lesson and mandate. The Executive Committee of the Comintern was made to proclaim in January 1928:

> The firmness and boldness with which the C.P.S.U., in the name of party unity, that most important pledge of victory for the revolution, criticized its former leaders [Trotsky, Zinoviev, Kamenev] . . . show all West European communist parties the real advantages which Bolshevik inner party democracy has over that false 'freedom of thought, speech, and fractions,' that freedom for the individual within the party which allegedly exists in social democratic parties and from the survivals of which a few communist parties have still not liberated themselves.[80]

Prior to 1928, foreign Communist parties had been organizationally and financially dependent on the Soviet one.[81] Now they became slavishly subjugated to the ruling machinery of this party and to *the* leader. As long as the Russian leadership had been collective, rather than that of one man, there was room in foreign Communism for a divergence of views that reflected the opinions or patronage of this or that member of the Soviet oligarchy. By 1930, if one wanted to remain a Communist, one had to be a Stalinist.

The disgrace of leaders with international renown—Trotsky, Zinoviev, and Bukharin—did not lead to *mass* defections in foreign Communism or to the foundation of a rival body to the Comintern. Reasons for this are writ large in the whole logic of the development of the international Communist movement. Not until there was a rival power base, i.e., not until there were other Communist states, could a heresy entrench itself successfully and even draw external support. Absence of a power base condemned all the rival Communist sects until 1948 to degenerate into intellectual fads. The most significant of them, Trotskyism, often proved to be a sort

---

[80] Degras, *The Communist International*, II, 421.

[81] E. H. Carr, *Socialism in One Country* (New York, 1964), III, Part 2, 898–913.

of decompression chamber through which people passed before their complete break with Communism and Marxism.

The question of whether and how international Communism and Soviet foreign and domestic policies would have been different had some other man or faction emerged supreme is of a vast complexity and cannot be discussed here. This equation—the interest of the Soviet Union equals the duty of every foreign Communist Party—was firmly established in Lenin's time, and there is no evidence that it would have been disregarded had either Trotsky or Bukharin emerged as the leader of world Communism rather than Stalin. One must take with a grain of salt the assertions of their partisans that had Trotsky and Bukharin prevailed, international Communism would have been *qualitatively* different, the interests of foreign Communism would not have been sacrificed as readily whenever an apparent advantage to the Soviet Union warranted this, and Trotsky would have been more responsive to the revolutionary instincts of the masses, etc.

Yet, by the same token, it is clear that Stalinism represented the extreme in centralization and repression. The old period of excited discussions in the congresses and executive committees of "left," "right," and centrist points of view clashing within each Party was gone forever. All that was required was obedience. Structurally, every Communist Party was now called upon to have its own "Stalin," whose word in intra-Party affairs was to be as definitive as that of Stalin everywhere. From this period date the long reigns of such stalwarts as Togliatti in Italy, Thorez in France, Browder in America, etc. If those men enjoyed the confidence of Moscow, they were granted security of tenure no matter what their errors or transgressions and no matter what the feelings of their subordinates. The German leader Ernst Thälmann was publicly revealed as having covered up an embezzlement of Party funds by his brother-in-law. But Thälmann suited Stalin's purposes: he was a loyal executor of Moscow's policies and had none of the intellectual pretensions and contentiousness of so many German Communist leaders. So Thälmann stayed, and the Comintern attributed his shielding of his relative to a praiseworthy attempt not to furnish ammunition to the class enemies in their slander campaign against German Communism.[82]

When it comes to the differences in appraisals of the world situation as between Stalin and, say, Trotsky, one is again in the realm of conjecture. Such points scored for Trotsky as his earlier recognition of the danger of Hitler—while Stalin and the German Communists under his orders were welcoming the overthrow of the Weimar Republic—cannot be admitted as fair evidence. Trotsky, by that time in exile, was bound to criticize most

[82] Degras, *The Communist International,* II, 550–51.

of Stalin's moves and analyses in the foreign field. Both Trotsky and Stalin were firmly within the Leninist tradition of "catastrophism"—of welcoming any overturn of democratic and stable institutions as a favorable development to Communism and the Soviet Union. Neither of them, nor for that matter any major Soviet leader, can be accused of lingering sentiments for the social democratic tradition, or credited with the recognition prior to 1933 that an overthrow of parliamentary and democratic institutions in any country in the West would present a danger rather than an opportunity for Russia and Communism. The difference in this respect between Stalin and his hapless rivals must be again adjudged one of degree. Trotsky, Bukharin, and Zinoviev were much more in the way of revolutionary speculators, addicted to vast visions of revolutionary convulsions, not free of fantasies like the long-expected and hoped-for one of a clash of the two capitalist giants, the United States and Great Britain. Stalin was a more careful investor, ready to settle for relatively small but steady dividends. It was better to have a small but completely obedient foreign Communist Party than a mass but unreliable one. Why throw away prematurely the ready asset of the Kuomintang for the ephemeral chances of Communism's winning China by itself? Stalin's caution and wariness in foreign affairs was of course the product not only of his own temperament, but of the lessons learned in the decade since the Revolution. Foreign Communists were an expendable commodity; the strength and the prestige of the Soviet Union were not.

All these elements were discernible in the Sixth Congress of the Comintern held in July-September 1928. Bukharin, his star already setting in Soviet politics, was the main rapporteur of the Congress. The old style of work at the congresses—interminable theoretical-tactical discussions and voluminous reports and theses—was still in evidence, a tribute to an era that was passing. But the gist of the conclusions was already Stalinist. Greater emphasis than ever was put on the need for absolute discipline and centralization. "International communist discipline must be expressed in the subordination of local and particular interests of the movement and in the execution without reservation of all decisions made by the leading bodies of the Communist International."[83] The Congress repeated in the most vigorous form the injunction that illegal work and organization were imperative even for those member parties that enjoyed the opportunities for legal existence. In political tactics, Stalinism represented the extreme of the Communist tendency to eat one's cake and have it too. Thus, on trade unionism, it was laid down that "every Communist must belong to a trade union, even to an extremely reactionary one if it has a mass character," while at the same time it was stated somewhat inconsistently

[83] *Ibid.*, p. 525.

and humorlessly that "in contrast to the reformists' attempts to split the unions, communists stand for the unity of the trade unions in each country and throughout the world on the basis of the class struggle and give wholehearted support to the Red International of Labour Unions."[84]

The Congress' most emphatic stand was taken on the issue of socialist parties and what the correct attitude toward them should be. A long section of the resolution gave a detailed and opprobrious characterization to every tendency in Western socialism, every major socialist and radical party. "Subjection to the ideological influence of the bourgeoisie in a cynically commercial form, secular and imperialist in character, is represented by contemporary 'socialist reformism.'" The socialist parties of Austria and Germany were declared "a particularly dangerous enemy of the proletariat, more dangerous than the avowed adherents of predatory social imperialism."

Nor were spared those radical nationalist movements which were at one time thought to be potential allies of Communism. Sun Yat-sen had only a few years back been a revered name in the Soviet Union, the propaganda school for Asian Communists being known as the Sun Yat-sen University.[85] Now, the duty of Chinese Communism was defined as "the elimination of what has remained of the ideology of Sun Yat-sen." On the movement that was inspiring Indians to fight for independence, the Comintern had the following to say: "More and more, Gandhism is becoming an ideology directed against the revolution of the popular masses. Communism must fight against it relentlessly."

For the old device of radicalism—"no enemy on the left"—the Comintern thus substituted a new one: "The main enemy is on the left." The chief practical injunction of the Sixth Congress was thus for the Communists to fight the socialist parties as strenuously as possible and, in the Far East, those nationalist movements which enjoyed the greatest influence in their nations' struggles for independence. Hostility to socialism and to the Second International was, of course, inherent in the very foundation of Communism. But it was never expressed so drastically, never accompanied by such a forthright injunction to fight socialism as the main enemy, as it was in 1928.

Behind this attitude lay ten years of Communism's frustrations in Western Europe. The West European workers looked to the socialist rather than Communist parties as their representatives, whether in parliaments or in the leadership of the trade-union movement. If the West was slated for a lengthy peaceful interlude, as the Soviet leadership believed, though it proclaimed the opposite, there was no point in fruitless revolutionary

[84] *Ibid.*, pp. 523–24.

[85] Just as many years later there was to be a Lumumba University.

endeavors. The most useful work the Communist parties could do was to concentrate their fire on the socialists, "unmask" them, split the union movement, and thus lay the foundations for a capture of the working class whenever a new war or depression offered a chance. According to the new dispensation laid down in Moscow, socialism was also blamed for the survival in the Western Communist parties of lingering democratic and parliamentary superstitions. Any collaboration with the socialist parties was bound to increase susceptibility to ideological infections. Stalinism required that Communist parties everywhere be parties of a truly new kind, with their loyalties due exclusively to Moscow and not to any "workers' solidarity" within their own country.

A similar experience dictated new tactics in the East. The Communists had burned their fingers in their collaboration with the Kuomintang. Now they drew the conclusion.

The Soviet leaders were well aware that Western socialist parties, though opposed to Communism, were the mainstay of that part of public opinion which sought good relations with the Soviet Union. But with no war imminent, it was thought useless to coddle Western opinion. Stalin put it elegantly in 1927 when he exclaimed, "Rather, let them go to hell, all these liberal-pacifist philosophers with their 'sympathy' for the U.S.S.R." When the prospect of a real danger appeared with the coming to power of Hitler, the appeasement of "liberal-pacifist philosophers" in the West became one of the most important tasks of Soviet foreign policy, as did the cultivation of good relations with socialists. But for the time being, destruction of European socialism was the Comintern's primary objective.

The onset of the great depression did not change this basic policy. The depression in fact brought an increase in the Communist parties' militancy. This militancy was not based, as it had been at times between 1921 and 1927, on the Comintern's expectation of the Communists' seizing power within a brief period of time. Rather, it was founded on the conviction of the leaders in Moscow that parties such as the French and German ones should show themselves to be "hard," unafraid to risk casualties in demonstrations and clashes with the police or their leaders' incarceration (as happened in 1930 with the French Communists). The logic applied was that of the lesson of the Bolsheviks' rise to power in Russia. Indeed, one of the subsidiary characteristics of Stalinism, well into 1934, was the belief that the Bolshevik methods and strategies of 1917 could be applied with few variations in Germany and France in the early 1930's. The Bolsheviks had not seized power by collaborating with other socialist and radical groups or by respecting legal norms and proprieties. They succeeded by showing to the proletariat that they were fighters, by seizing upon every social and political grievance, and by adopting the most radical position on practically every issue. Their leaders went to jail and into hiding in July 1917 but within three months they were in power. The great depression was working havoc with Western institutions. Millions of unemployed were discovering how ineffectual parliamentarism and trade unionism were in the struggle to improve their lot. These effects were likened to those of the Great War that disrupted the fabric of society in the advanced countries. The prize was bound to go to the audacious and uncompromising. As to competing right-wing radicals, again the Soviet experience taught that they could not compete with a militant party of the left. The Kornilov episode had been of the briefest duration. Could German militarism or National Socialism be much more durable? There was, to be sure, the contrary lesson of Italy. There the anarchy and industrial unrest in the post-war era had brought the Fascists to power rather than the Communists. But it could be argued that the Italian Communist Party had then been barely organized, and that it was precisely the existence of factionalism and the lingering social democratic traditions among Italian Communists that made them miss their chance.

This unsophisticated use of the "lessons" of 1917 weighed heavily on the fortunes of Communism between 1928 and 1933. The Bolsheviks had been defeatists, i.e., they worked openly for the demoralization and disintegration of the Russian army. They had embraced the slogan of national self-determination and independence for the Poles, Finns, and Ukrainians. Now the same tactics were prescribed for parties working under hugely different conditions. The French Communists were made to embrace the postulates of the Alsatian separatists, and their leaders in some cases had to learn German, in which they addressed Party gatherings in Alsace! In Yugoslavia, the directives imposed by the Comintern upon the Communist Party required it to demand "self-determination until secession" of every constituent nationality. The Party's leadership until 1928 was condemned for its "Great Serbian chauvinism," and their successors were called upon to endorse the most extreme separatist demands, not only of the Croats, but also of Slovenes, Macedonians, and Albanians.[86]

An extreme example of the misapplication of the lessons of the Russian Revolution may be found in the case of the American Communists. The American Communist Party had never been looked upon as a particularly promising pupil of the Comintern. In Communist categories, American capitalism was held to be quite young and vigorous, the American worker most well off and satisfied with his lot. As seen from Trotsky's letter to Zinoviev, quoted above, the American Communist Party was thought useful mainly as a recruiting body for activists to work for the cause in

[86] Adam B. Ulam, *Titoism and the Cominform* (Cambridge, Mass., 1952), pp. 16–19.

Latin America and Asia.[87] (Communist parties in advanced areas had for long been called on to guide Communist activities in their countries' spheres of influence. Thus, the British Party acted as the "elder brother" of Indian and South African Communists, the French Party was charged with a similar task in France's overseas possessions, etc.)

The Sixth Congress of the Comintern turned its attention to the impotence of American Communism. Much of the American Party's failure was ascribed to its inability to recruit Negro members. The Negro problem in general was now for the first time a matter of considerable concern to the Comintern. If propagation of Marxism in Asia was already a departure from the orthodoxy, then advocacy of revolutionary socialism in areas as undeveloped as Africa clearly had no basis in the doctrine.[88] But the Congress severely criticized the failure of South African Communists (practically all of them white) to advance the slogan of an independent native South African republic. In the case of the United States, a similar line of reasoning held that the American Communists neglected the *national* aspect of the Negro question. The term "Black Belt" exercised great fascination on the minds of the Soviet leaders of the Comintern, and it was assumed that this area had a stable majority of Negroes. The protestations of most American Communists that the main focus of the Negro struggle for emancipation was the demand for equal rights, that rural Negroes of the South were migrating increasingly to the urban centers of the North were brushed aside. In October 1928 the Executive of the Comintern laid down: "While continuing and intensifying the struggle under the slogan of full social and political equality for the Negroes . . . the Party must come out openly and unreservedly for the right of Negroes to national self-determination in the southern states, where the Negroes form a majority of the population."[89] This policy was redefined in even more outright separatist terms in 1930, when the Comintern's directive looked clearly to a "national rebellion" in the Southern states to establish a Negro republic in the near future.[90]

The onset of the great depression confirmed the Kremlin's conviction that the policy of attack upon the socialist parties had been and was the correct one. The vast increase in unemployment in the industrial countries, the universal phenomenon of agricultural overproduction, the break-

[87] The Trotsky Archive, T911.

[88] One remembers Bukharin's indiscretion in 1919 that he was for revolutionary propaganda among the "Bushmen and Hottentots" because it struck at British imperialism, but that there was no basis for independent statehood, not to mention socialism, in Africa.

[89] Degras, *The Communist International*, II, 554.

[90] Theodore Draper, *American Communism and Soviet Russia* (New York, 1960), pp. 352–53.

down of the international trade mechanism—all those phenomena spelled out the fulfillment of the Communist prophecies of capitalism's ultimate crisis and its belief that the period of capitalist stabilization (1921–28) was temporary. Said Stalin at the Sixteenth Congress of the CPSU in 1930: "What do these facts testify? That the stabilization of capitalism has ended, that the growth of revolutionary feeling among the masses will grow with new force; that the world economic crisis will in a number of states grow into a political one."[91]

The Communists could and in effect did congratulate themselves on their foresight even before the depression in specifying the socialist parties as enemy number one. With the bankruptcy of capitalism fully evident and irremediable, the main remaining barrier to the conquest of the working masses by the Communists was obviously socialism. As Molotov diagnosed it, "Social fascism with its 'left' wing is the last resource of the bourgeoisie among the workers."[92] "Social fascism" was, needless to say, the name given during the period to social democracy. Thus the policy of precluding any alliance with the socialist parties was continued and re-emphasized. The growing apprehension in certain parties, notably the French one, at the rapid gains made by pro-fascist movements in Europe was held unreasonable by the leaders and analysts in Moscow. The only permissible united front for the Communists during 1928–33 was the "united front from below," i.e., an attempt to seduce the socialist workers from allegiance to their leaders. Again, Molotov, by now the successor of Zinoviev and Bukharin at the helm of the Comintern, spelled it out: "Only on the foundation of basing the work of the Communists upon the sole leadership of the economic struggle of the workers and the struggle against the traitorous social democrats and reformists, only upon this foundation can be developed the Bolshevik tactics of the united proletarian front from below."[93]

The growth of National Socialism in Germany was viewed with equanimity, if not with satisfaction. In the elections to the Reichstag in 1930, the National Socialists from a minor group with twelve deputies became a major political party with more than 100. During the next two years, their influence in German political life grew phenomenally. But from Moscow, this growth of a fascist party was a desirable phenomenon: the German masses were losing their parliamentary and democratic illusions. The National Socialists, it was held, could attract even workers because of the radical character of their program, but soon the masses would realize

[91] *Sixteenth Congress of the Communist Party of the Soviet Union* (stenographic report, Moscow, 1931), p. 22.

[92] *Ibid.*, p. 420.

[93] *Ibid.*, p. 423.

that Hitler was in fact a tool of the bankers and industrialists and would turn to the Communists. The prospect of Hitler's being taken into the government or forming one was far from alarming. He would then be fully "unmasked," and the Communists could only gain. To quote Molotov once more: "The most important task of the [German] party is to fight against submission to trade union legalism, and against any blocs with the social democracy. . . . In Germany we have already made a number of steps in that direction, [but] our organizations ought to continue this course even more insistently."[94]

As is well known, the German Communists did pursue those tactics "more insistently." The net result of their activity between 1930 and 1933 was that they contributed substantially to the paralysis of the Weimar Republic and to Hitler's eventual coming to power. The German socialists' attempts to come to some common understanding with the Communists— to mount a joint front against Hitler—were spurned. Some of those attempts appear to have been made through the Soviet embassy and as late as after Hitler's assumption of power in January 1933. Police and Nazi terror had already been unleashed against the socialists and Communists indiscriminately. But the Party line, as laid down by Stalin and Molotov, held that a brief period of Nazi reaction would solidify the German working class around the Communists. The socialists were by definition a legalistic party unable to survive in the underground; the Communists, on the contrary, were well prepared for such emergencies. What could they and the Soviet Union lose? On April 1, 1933, with Hitler firmly in power and with the socialist and Communist leaders already in concentration camps, the Presidium of the Comintern Executive passed the following resolution: "The Presidium of the Executive of the Comintern, having heard the report of Comrade Heckert on the situation in Germany, declares that the policy carried out by the Executive Committee of the Communist Party of Germany with Comrade Thälmann at its head up to and during the time of the Hitlerite coup was absolutely correct."[95] The official organ of the Comintern on June 15, 1933, ridiculed proposals for a policy that the Soviet Union was to adopt within a year:

Austro-Marxism advises the U.S.S.R. to conclude an alliance with the "great democracies" on an international scale to fight fascism. . . . Social fascism advises the proletariat of the U.S.S.R. to conclude an alliance with "democratic" France and her vassals against German and Italian fascism. This group of social fascists pretends to forget that there is such a thing as French, British, and American imperialism.[96]

[94] *Ibid.*
[95] Quoted in Beloff, *op. cit.*, I, 68.
[96] *The Communist International,* X, No. 11 (June 15, 1933), 367.

Soviet policy toward Hitler and Germany, especially in its opening phases, poses many fascinating questions, most of which cannot be answered, alas, on the basis of any firm evidence.[97] One view would hold Stalin and the Soviets simply blind to the menace and staying power of Hitlerism. Another and far-reaching analysis of the Communists' strange behavior in 1930–33 would, on the contrary, credit Stalin with already having designs that were to crystallize in the Nazi-Soviet Pact of 1939.

On the basis of what we do know, we can say with some assurance first of all that Soviet-Comintern policy in Germany was clearly Stalin's. Its logical basis—the unremitting campaign against "social fascism," against any and every socialist and progressive party—had been predicated in Stalin's statements for years. A German Communist, defending his party's fantastic attitude toward the threat of Hitler, quoted a statement of Stalin's from 1924 "unsurpassed in its exactness and perspicacity of the evolution of Social Democracy towards fascism." The statement contained points of analysis such as: "Fascism is the militant organization of the bourgeoisie, which is based on the active support of Social Democracy. . . . They are not antipodes but twins."[98]

Another Stalinist feature—and this one is probably connected more directly with Stalin's own mentality—was the extreme hostility toward anything that smacked of political toleration, of broad coalitions of the left. By 1930–33, the opposition in Russia had been defeated but not yet physically liquidated. The example of a broad democratic anti-fascist front must have appeared as having certain psychological dangers. If one establishes an alliance with the socialists, why not with Trotsky? The German Communist who quoted so obligingly (and for the period after 1934 embarrassingly) Stalin's insights on "social fascism" then proceeded to make this connection: "Trotsky, the confederate of Hitler, is trying under the guise of a platform of the united front to foist upon the German working class that social fascist tactic of 'lesser evil.' . . . It was he, Trotsky, who carrying out the social orders of Hitler tried to sling mud at the only party which is struggling against fascism."

The perception of Hitler's threat to the Soviet Union grew but slowly during 1933 and 1934. There were several seemingly rational elements

---

[97] The effective elimination of intra-Party opposition in Russia had as its side and deplorable effect a very considerable diminution of our knowledge of the decision-making process in the Soviet Union. We no longer have such priceless evidence as that provided by the Trotsky Archive, which until 1927 gives us a number of Politburo and Central Committee memoranda, correspondence, etc. After 1928, our sources are mainly either official statements or revelations of defectors from the Soviet diplomatic service and the Comintern. Needless to say, both those sources have to be treated with caution.

[98] *The Communist International,* X, No. 10 (May, 1933), 333–34.

in this underestimation of the German dictator. First was the notion that his reign would be extremely short-lived and then succeeded by a time of opportunity for German Communists. (Yet it must be pointed out that there is no evidence that the German Communists in 1933 were being put into a state of preparedness to stage a coup or even to cope with the expected anarchy—unlike 1923 when, as we have seen, detailed plans for strikes and uprisings had been drawn up and military experts were sent from Moscow.) Another was the idea, shared at first by many Western statesmen, that Hitler was a political prisoner of conservative and nationalist politicians in his regime. The Russians also realized full well that there were people in the National Socialist movement who took the "socialist" part of it seriously and grumbled at Hitler's (as it turned out, brief) alliance with the industrialists and landowners. Not until the "night of the long knives" in June 1934, when Hitler simultaneously liquidated his "left opposition" and his conservative guardians, was Moscow finally convinced that he was fully master of Germany.

Still another, and probably the strongest, reason why Moscow viewed the first period of Hitler's ascendancy with equanimity was the conviction that he did not represent an immediate danger to the Soviet Union. The Soviet leaders did their homework more conscientiously than their counterparts in the West. They had read *Mein Kampf* and were aware that anti-Communism was, along with anti-Semitism, a main staple of Nazi propaganda. Still, there was probably some feeling that this represented a kind of campaign oratory designed to secure Hitler financial support from the right and the votes of the middle class. Once in power, Hitler and the German diplomats sought to reassure the Soviet Union. The anti-Communist campaign at home would not interfere with the continuation of good relations with the Soviet Union, the Russians were told. In May 1933 the Treaty of Berlin was officially renewed, and thus, at least on paper, the Rapallo arrangement between Germany and the U.S.S.R. was continued.

In fact, in the initial stages of their relations with Nazi Germany, the Soviets were subjected to diplomatic tactics which they had been the first to elaborate. Ideological differences, they were told, should not interfere with good businesslike relations between the two states. The Soviets on their part were not backward in assuring the German diplomats that Russo-German relations could be pursued along the Rapallo lines and that they were not unduly solicitous about the fate of the German Communists.[99] A cold, unsentimental line could hold Hitler's coming to power to be of potential benefit to the Soviet Union. It would stop the gravitation

[99] Though it is doubtful that Litvinov actually did say, "We don't care if you shoot your German Communists," as reported in Hilger and Meyer, *op. cit.*, p. 252.

of the German parliamentary regime toward the West that had been going on since Locarno. Hitler's professed aim of overturning the Versailles order was also Russia's.

The mystery that the Soviet rulers tried to penetrate during the first year and a half of Hitler's reign concerned not so much his ultimate aims, about which they had no illusions, but his timetable. One could deduce from Hitler's writings and statements that his primary target would be France rather than the U.S.S.R. And the desirability of an *intra-imperialist* war was still high on the list of Communist preferences. It was therefore disturbing that during his first months in power Hitler sought to reassure the West as well as Russia about his peaceful intentions. In a disingenuous and wistful manner, the Comintern sought occasionally to chide Hitler for his appeasement of the West:

Propaganda for a war of vengeance against France was for many years a symbol of faith of German fascism. With such slogans it rallied under its banners millions of the gullible petty bourgeoisie who had been ruined by the Versailles Treaty. And now Goebbels . . . goes into a state of exaltation about Germany's good will toward France, declaring that Germany has no warlike ambitions whatsoever in regard to France.[100]

This "breach of faith" on the part of Hitler had to lead to some sober reflections in Moscow. If Hitler's policy were to be consistently anti-Western, then his staying in power and the consequent catastrophe of German Communism could be rationalized as being not unfavorable to the Soviet Union. If, on the other hand, Hitler were to reach an agreement with the West, the Soviet Union would face her greatest danger since the end of the Civil War. What Soviet propaganda had always noisily proclaimed, but what the Soviet leaders at most half believed, would become a reality: an anti-Soviet coalition of the Great Powers.

The last months of 1933 and the beginning of 1934 mark, then, the agonizing reappraisal of Soviet foreign policy that was due to bring about its most basic shift in tactics since 1921. What was at stake was the abandonment of the whole "catastrophic" premise of Communist policies. The heightening of international tension had until then always been held to be of benefit to the Soviet Union; the elements of political stability like the League of Nations and the economic recovery of Europe, to be disadvantageous to Soviet aims. War, if it should come, was likely to be one between rival imperialist powers and would not expose the Soviet Union to immediate danger but, on the contrary, would present Communism with further chances of expansion. Now, the threat of war, any war, was seen as inimical to Soviet interests. In the case of Hitler's Germany, Soviet Russia was not facing the capitalist ruling class of Great Britain, France,

[100] *The Communist International,* IV, No. 23 (Dec. 1, 1933), 848.

and Weimar Germany, unwilling to take risks, hamstrung by parliaments and public opinion. The new rulers of Germany exhibited ferocious energy in liquidating the remnants of democracy in their country and in rearming. Their diplomacy successfully emulated the Soviet one: a mixture of cajolery and threats before which the Western Powers appeared to be divided and impotent.

The events of 1933 prompted also a general re-evaluation of fascism. Until then, the term had been used freely not only in regard to Mussolini's Italy but as applied to a whole range of political parties and phenomena including, for example, the semi-authoritarian regime of Pilsudski in Poland. As such, fascism failed to alarm the Soviets: it was the final stage of decadent capitalism. After 1928, the use of the term had been extended. Weimar Germany was held to have had a "fascist" regime since 1930, and it was of small moment whether Bruning's "fascism" would be replaced by Hitler's. Now, it was seen, fascism was indeed a dynamic force, and its destruction of democratic and parliamentary institutions was not preparing the ground for Communism but threatening its very existence. The example of Germany was proving infectious. Movements combining social, nationalist, and racist demagoguery were springing up all over Europe. The discrediting of parliamentary institutions and the helplessness of the democracies in the face of the economic crisis were benefiting not the Communists but the extreme right. In France, the evidence of parliamentary and government corruption in the famous Stavisky affair in 1934 was to bring a fascist threat to the Third Republic. The threat of international fascism thus changed from a ritual phrase of Soviet propaganda to a frightening reality. By the same token, parliamentary and democratic institutions, including the long vilified League of Nations, were seen in a new light.

The reassessment of Soviet policies took most of 1933 and 1934. It is clear that this task was proceeding, in true Stalinist style, in secrecy and without foreign Communists being informed of it. As late as March 1934, the French Communists were censored for attempts to form a joint antifascist front with the socialists. A history of the French Communist Party published in 1964 by some Party members (but without the authorization of the leadership) has this wry comment on the trip of its leader Maurice Thorez to Moscow in April 1934: "On his return from the U.S.S.R., having probably [!] benefitted from the counsel of the leadership of the Comintern, Maurice Thorez reverses his previous position of 'unity only from below' and the refusal of agreement with the socialist leaders of their party as such. He will also stop calling the socialist leaders 'social fascists' as he had done prior to his trip."[101]

---

[101] *History of the French Communist Party* (Paris, 1964), p. 166.

The change of signals was to come fairly late in the game. Reasons for the delay are not difficult to divine. There was undoubtedly some fear in Moscow of provoking Hitler unduly by unleashing an all-out campaign against fascism and Germany. There had to be weighed also the danger of precipitating confusion in foreign Communist ranks. For some time now, Trotsky had been calling for an alliance with socialists against the common enemy and blaming Stalin for the catastrophe of German Communism. It was difficult, until the situation left no other recourse, for Moscow in fact to follow Trotsky's analysis. But by the end of 1933, the Soviet policy-makers must have concluded that for the time being any attempt to come to an understanding with Hitler was fruitless. The best proof is offered by the winding up of the military collaboration between Germany and the U.S.S.R. which had been in effect for more than a decade. In the late fall of 1933, German military installations on Soviet soil were closed down at the Red Army's request. German military advisers and observers were politely asked to leave the Soviet Union. This rupture in relations between the two armies occurred in an atmosphere of mutual courtesy, military men on both sides blaming "politics" for the unfortunate interruption of a clandestine collaboration which had benefited both partners.[102] But Germany was now rearming openly and had no need for subterfuges. In view of Hitler's announced intentions, it would have been the height of folly to let German military personnel move freely throughout the Soviet defense establishment. The Russians did not give up some very circumspect probings for a *détente* with Germany, but the days of intimate military collaboration did not return, not even after the Molotov-Ribbentrop pact. Gone forever was the Soviet leaders' dream since the first days of the Bolshevik regime: an alliance of the vast resources and manpower of Russia with the organizing skill and technology of Germany. The actual alliance of the two powers in 1939–41 was to be a mockery of those expectations; within a few weeks of its conclusion, the Soviet leaders were to realize that it had involved them in a mortal danger rather than in a chance to inherit the world.

The historical irony was already evident at the end of 1933. Germany and the Far East, the two hopeful areas for Soviet policy and Communism a few years before, now became areas of acute danger. With official China, Soviet diplomatic relations had been severed since 1928. All the remaining powers now recognized Chiang Kai-shek's government in Nanking as the legitimate regime of the Chinese Republic. In fact, its writ ran only over several provinces; elsewhere, its authority was maintained through very unstable agreements with the local warlords. One of those areas was Manchuria, where, following the Japanese puppet Chang Tso-lin's death,

[102] John Erickson, *The Soviet High Command* (New York, 1962), pp. 343–49.

his son and successor, Chang Hsueh-ling, entered into a working agreement with the Kuomintang.

Having burned their fingers in China, the Soviet leaders spoke of events there with unusual circumspection. Thus Stalin at the Sixteenth Congress spoke with hurt innocence about imperialist slanders on the Comintern's activities in China: "One should consider as completely discredited the lying rumor that the workers of Soviet missions in China are guilty of disturbing 'peace and calm' in China. For a long time there have been no Soviet missions in south and central China. But there are British ones, Japanese, etc. . . . But there are German, English and Japanese military advisers with the warring Chinese generals." As to the situation in the Chinese Communist movement, Stalin was hopeful but professed ignorance as to the details. "The Chinese workers and peasants have already reacted by creating soviets and the Red Army. They say that a soviet government has already been organized there. I think if this is true there is nothing strange about it. There is no question that only soviets can save China."[103] With so many false starts and hopes in the past, and with Trotsky's diatribes still ringing in the ears of Soviet politicians, Stalin's modest noncommittal observations were most judicious.

If the affairs of Chinese Communism were discreetly removed from the main stage, the same could not be done with the over-all Far Eastern situation. On paper, the military-diplomatic situation in the Far East looked ominous for the Soviet Union. Russia's Far Eastern territories were her Achilles' heel, for there she confronted a Great Power, Japan, that could concentrate its entire military effort on this distant and sparsely populated area. And within Manchuria, now under the influence of the hostile Nanking government, the Soviet Union had another vulnerable asset, the Chinese Eastern Railway, which apart from its commercial value constituted a vital link with Vladivostok and the Soviet Maritime Territory.

Japanese designs, both on those Far Eastern possessions and on Manchuria, were public knowledge. The traditional restraint upon the Japanese ambitions had been the fear of a reaction on the part of the Western Powers, especially the United States. But the economic crisis absorbed the energies of the democratic powers and by the same token accentuated the influence of military expansionists in Japan.

[103] *Sixteenth Congress of the Communist Party of the Soviet Union*, pp. 21–22. Obviously Stalin neglected to consult the representative of the Chinese Communist Party who at the *very same Congress* declared, "Soviet power has already been established in the seven provinces of South China, in eighteen districts . . . having the population of 14 million" (*ibid.*, p. 436). The organization of the Chinese Soviet Republic with Mao Tse-tung as president and comprising the soviet-controlled districts is dated from November 7, 1931. See Benjamin I. Schwartz, *Chinese Communism and the Rise of Mao* (Cambridge, Mass., 1951), p. 208.

Yet there was one key element in the situation that offered wide and hopeful scope for Soviet diplomacy. This was the Japanese apprehension at the prospect of a reunification of China under the aegis of Chiang Kai-shek. Japan had a vested interest in a divided and impotent China. The successes of Chiang Kai-shek, modest as they appear from our perspective, were bound to arouse Tokyo's apprehensions. Beginning in 1928, Tokyo's influence in Manchuria declined and that of the Nanking government became paramount. A Japanese military involvement against the Nanking government would therefore serve a double purpose for the Russians: it would considerably minimize the chance of Japan striking at Siberia; and it would tie Chiang Kai-shek's hands in what now became his primary objective—the destruction of the Chinese Communists and the occupation of the areas held by the Chinese soviets. It would render additional dividends in deepening the conflict between Japan and the United States, and the desirability of this conflict and the hope of it turning into an armed clash had been one of the cardinal premises of Soviet foreign policy from the beginning.

In 1929, an incautious action by Chiang Kai-shek's regime gave the Soviet Union an opportunity for a show of force in the Far East. Chinese officials raided Soviet consulates in various parts of Manchuria, seizing documents and detaining Soviet citizens.[104] Later on in the summer of the same year, the Chinese Eastern Railway was in effect seized by the local authorities and its Russian officials chased out.

The official Chinese justification was that the consulates and the management of the railway were spreading Communist propaganda and conducting subversive activities. In addition, the railway with its extraterritorial rights was felt to be a glaring relic of European imperialism and an affront to emergent sovereign China. It was undoubtedly thought that Russia could be persuaded to give up her interest in the railway rather than have a military confrontation. Russia's internal troubles consequent upon collectivization were well known in Nanking and in Manchuria, where there was a sizable White Russian colony.

The Soviet government presented the Chinese authorities with an ultimatum, which being disregarded, Soviet troops began military operations in Manchuria. The Manchurian troops were well suited to the warlords' clashes that had been the pattern in China for twenty years but not to fighting a modern army equipped with tanks and planes. And the central Chinese authorities then had yet another rebellion on their hands. Thus the Soviets scored an easy triumph. An agreement in December 1929 restored the status of the Chinese Eastern Railway as being under joint Russo-Chinese administration.

[104] While no diplomatic relations had been maintained with Chiang Kai-shek, Soviet consulates still functioned in Manchuria and northern China.

The subsequent negotiations dragged on. The Soviet government's request to restore diplomatic relations with China was rejected, but Russia resumed—to be sure, for only a short time—her previous position in Manchuria. The Chinese now realized that insofar as her military strength was concerned, Russia was no "paper tiger," and the proper lessons from the whole incident were undoubtedly drawn in Tokyo. The Soviet Union did not attempt to pursue her military success in Manchuria. Soviet troops were withdrawn. If the Russians had hoped to detach the Manchurian regime once more from Chiang Kai-shek, then this attempt was not pursued very energetically. Soviet hostility to Chiang Kai-shek was now balanced by the consideration that he offered a barrier to Japanese ambitions to dominate China. Militarily, the Chinese could not hope to check the Japanese, any more than in 1929 they were able to prevent the Soviet incursion into Manchuria. But *politically* only Chiang Kai-shek could now provide the focus of national opposition to Japan. To defeat Chinese armies might be easy; to conquer China hopeless.

The Japanese aggression in Manchuria in 1931 is rightly considered to have been a prelude to World War II. Its sequel, the establishment of the Japanese puppet state of Manchukuo, showed the ineffectiveness of the whole system of collective security under the League of Nations. The inability of the Western Powers to react in any effective way, Japan's subsequent withdrawal from the League of Nations—these consequences were bound to deepen the breach between Japan and the United States and Great Britain. The invasion opened an era of unusual danger but also of opportunity for Soviet diplomacy in the Far East. Military adventurism, the Soviet leaders were well aware, created its own momentum. Having swallowed Manchuria, the Japanese armed forces were likely to press their aim to secure hegemony in the Far East. Their next actual target might be the Soviet satellite of Outer Mongolia or even the Soviet Union's Far Eastern territories.

Insofar as the Far Eastern theater was concerned, Soviet policy had to be a mixture of firmness and attempted conciliation with Japan. Firmness consisted in repeated statements by the Soviet leaders that they would fight in defense of their territory and that the armed forces of the U.S.S.R. would protect Outer Mongolia if it were attacked. To underline these statements, the Far Eastern army was significantly strengthened and put in a position where it could maintain military operations without immediate help from European Russia. Its commander was General Blyukher, of legendary exploits in the Civil War and head of the Soviet military mission to China in the 1920's. The Japanese military therefore had to assume that, at best, the conquest of the Soviet Far East would be far from cheap. Parallel with this sensible show of strength, Soviet diplomacy spared no effort to come to an understanding with Japan. Comintern organs might denounce Japan for her rape of Manchuria, but the Soviet government preserved strict neutrality and disavowed any rumors of the U.S.S.R.'s joining in activities to restrain the Japanese aggression. On the contrary, the Soviets offered Japan a nonaggression treaty. As to the Chinese Eastern Railway, the Soviet government now offered to sell it to the Japanese puppet state. In fact, the Soviets pursued, and were to pursue until 1941, a policy of appeasement toward Japan, but unlike the same policy pursued a few years later by the democracies toward Hitler, it was an appeasement without illusions and offered from a position of strength.

This intricate game had yet another element. Were the Nanking government to forego its claims to Manchuria and reach a *modus vivendi* with Japan, the latter again would have her hands free for military expansion in another direction. There were elements in the Chinese Nationalist regime that favored the postponement of a settlement of the Manchurian issue until such time as the government could consolidate its rule over the rest of China and, especially, smash the Communist enclaves within the country. Thus the cultivation of Sino-Japanese hostility and prevention of any "deal" between Chiang Kai-shek and Tokyo became a very vital element in Soviet tactics. While courting the Japanese, the Soviet government was working patiently to re-establish relations with the man who since 1927 had been presented as the arch-enemy of world Communism, Chiang Kai-shek. Late in 1932, diplomatic relations between the Soviet Union and the Nanking government were resumed.

Once again, as between 1923 and 1926, the Soviet government was performing veritable diplomatic acrobatics in the Far East. It was maintaining nominally friendly relations with three partners, each of whom was in a state of hostility with the other two: Japan, Chiang Kai-shek, and the Chinese Communists. The latter, with undoubted Soviet approval if not indeed urging, declared war on the Japanese as early as 1932. Since their main areas of activity lay far away from the Japanese forces in Manchuria and northern China, the point of this declaration was to put Chiang Kai-shek on the spot. He in turn still considered the liquidation of Communists as the first priority, but there was mounting pressure on him to pick up the Japanese challenge rather than to fight his fellow Chinese. In view of the attitude of the Western Powers toward the Japanese invasion, one of high moral indignation but no concrete help, he had to accept a renewal of relations with Russia, which was the only power capable of providing military supplies, etc., should the Japanese proceed to bite off another chunk of China. Tokyo, in its turn, could have few illusions as to the motivations of Soviet policy. But the Japanese felt "misunderstood" by the United States and Great Britain.[105] And above all, the Japanese were in the first phase of that territorial lust that was eventually to push them to disaster. The task of carving up China appeared to be relatively easy; an attack on Outer Mongolia or Soviet territories promised a "real" war. Though the Tokyo government repulsed Russian pleas for a treaty of nonintervention, it took note of the Russian reassurances. The Japanese bombardment and landing of troops in Shanghai in 1932 exacerbated Japanese-Western relations still further, for the great port was still the center of extensive Western commercial interests and the locus of the International Settlement. An actual conflict with the U.S.S.R. promised to confront Japan with incalculable consequences, while those of pursuing the task of dismembering China appeared, however falsely, as quite calculable.

Along with many other countries, Japan in the 1930's experienced a growth in radicalism, partly of the nationalist and partly of the socialist variety. Its spokesmen, found mainly among the younger army officers, focused their resentment on the conservative leaders of their country, the upholders of a policy of cautious expansion and friendly relations with the West. That policy had brought dividends in pushing Japan into the rank of the Great Powers, but its slow pace and the avowed friendship of the ruling elite for what was seen as an effete and plutocratic West did not suit the young hotheads. In the turbulent era of the 1930's, two elements of politics that transcended state boundaries and even national criteria of national interests were a growing hostility toward traditional Western concepts of government and toward all attempts to assure international stability through the ramshackle edifice of the League of Nations, and a desire to throw off the restraints of parliamentarism and conventional diplomacy. In this regard the Japanese militarists were sharing in the mood that possessed the National Socialists in Germany, that was soon to seize the Fascists in Italy, and that appeared less prominently in many other countries. And this mood drove them to be emotionally against Great Britain and the United States much more than against the traditional enemy of their country, Russia. Today, this phenomenon of politics in the 1930's is most often forgotten, but at the time it was tangible enough to make some elements of the Nazi Party

[105] The first line of justification for its actions taken by the Japanese government was that it was restoring the position it had in fact held in Manchuria prior to 1928, disrupted since then by the Manchurian authorities' entering into a relationship with the Nanking government and violating Japanese rights there. Another justification was that it was acting against the "Communist danger," even though the actual consequence of the aggression was, as we have seen, a re-establishment of Russo-Chinese diplomatic relations.

between 1939 and 1941 postulate a plan for a vast alliance of "have-not" but "vigorous" nations, including the Soviet Union, against the declining democratic powers.

Such esoteric considerations could play no role in Moscow's calculations. Insofar as Japan was concerned, the Soviet policy-makers could not be sure that their double policy of firmness and appeasement would deflect Japanese aggression. Some militarists in Japan were eager for a showdown with Russia, which they saw as the main obstacle to their ambitions to dominate China. One could not entirely discount the possibility that the pro-Western orientation of Japanese policy would reassert itself in the form of that old bugaboo of Soviet policy in the Far East, an Anglo-Japanese alliance. Just such an alliance had been terminated in 1922 at the insistence of the United States, and its resurgence might conceivably lead to Japanese pressure not on China but rather on the area where Britain had no special interests, Outer Mongolia or even Siberia.

The historical irony of the situation facing Soviet policy-makers at the end of 1933 consisted in the fact that the fulfillment of many long-standing Soviet hopes in international politics promised not successes but a terrible danger to the Soviet Union. The League of Nations and the Versailles settlement had been the objects of unremitting Soviet propaganda attacks ever since 1919. Now the League had been rendered even more ineffective since Japan and Germany were turning their backs on it. The Versailles settlement was crumbling, with Germany openly rearming and advancing far-reaching claims in other directions. The great crisis of the world economy had come to pass, but its political consequences were seen in the growth and successes of fascist movements rather than Communist ones. The rising level of international tension threatened new wars, but the targets of Japanese and German militarism might become not the other capitalist powers but the Soviet Union. Seldom has an ideology played a comparable trick on its devotees as did Communism in 1933: all the major desiderata of its philosophy of international relations were fulfilled, and their sum total promised disaster to the Soviet Union.

With the end of 1933, Soviet diplomacy starts on a new course. In the next six years, it will probe whether those arrangements and institutions it had denounced and tried to undermine since 1921—the League of Nations, collective security, the Western alliance—will be capable of protecting the Soviet Union from involvement in a war or, if a war should come, of providing her with allies.

The new phase of Soviet foreign policy was spotlighted by Litvinov's statement to the Central Executive Committee of the Supreme Soviet on December 29, 1933. Beginning with truisms—"If it is possible to speak of diplomatic eras, then we are without doubt standing at the junction of two eras"—the Commissar proceeded to statements that sounded rather startling in an official Soviet statement to a *Soviet* audience: "Any state, even the most imperialist, may at one time or another become profoundly pacifist."[106] As against the traditional Communist doctrine that capitalism seeks war to overcome its internal contradictions, Litvinov now sought to educate his audience that "there are also other factors acting against the desire for war, such as, for example, internal disorders, economic weakness, etc."[107]

The main danger spots for the Soviet Union were grimly depicted: "Then followed the revolution which brought a new party to power in Germany, preaching the most extreme anti-Soviet ideas. . . . Japanese policy is now the darkest cloud on the horizon." These developments, said Litvinov pathetically, were entirely unexpected and undeserved by the Soviet Union, which had followed the policy of friendship toward those two powers which now spoke so unkindly and threateningly about Russia: "Enormous advantages, both for Germany and for us, followed from the political and economic relations between us. . . . Excellent good neighbourly relations existed between us and Japan. . . . We had such confidence in Japan . . . that we left our Far Eastern frontier practically undefended." Seldom has a Soviet statesman been so eloquent in defending the sanctity of treaties. The Japanese actions in Manchuria, the Foreign Commissar solemnly declared, have violated the Washington Nine-Power Treaty, the Covenant of the League of Nations, the Kellogg-Briand Pact, and even the 1905 Treaty of Portsmouth between Russia and Japan.

Unlike the tenor of the Soviet statements in the peaceful 1920's, Litvinov's speech exuded none of the "come what may, the Red Army is at its post" boastfulness, none of the traditional assertions that the working class of the imperialist countries would not allow them to defeat the Soviet Union. Speaking to a Soviet audience, with his country still in the midst of a debilitating social experiment, he was frankly and almost humiliatingly insistent on Russia's readiness to do everything in her power in order not to provoke the fascists. "We understand very well the difference between doctrine and policy." This understanding led him to stress that Hitler's persecution of the German Communists need not destroy the prospect of restoring good relations with him: "We as Marxists are the last who can be reproached with allowing sentiment to prevail over policy. The entire world knows that we can and do maintain good relations with capitalist states whatever their regime."[108] The Soviet

[106] Degras, *Soviet Documents on Foreign Policy,* III: *1933–41* (London and New York, 1953), 48.

[107] *Ibid.,* p. 49.

[108] *Ibid.,* p. 56.

Union would not encourage any plans of aggression against Germany.[109] Would not Germany make a similar statement in connection with Russia? And, in a fatuous turn of phrase, very uncharacteristic for a Soviet states- man, Litvinov wanted Germany, i.e., Hitler, to promise not to attack Russia not only now, but also at such time "when Germany will have greater forces to put into effect those aggressive ideas"!!

The same pleading tone in relation to Japan. Litvinov recounted how the U.S.S.R. refrained from joining in any common action against Japan at the time of the Manchurian invasion. "We declined to take part in the international action taken and proposed at that time, firstly because we did not believe in the sincerity and firmness of purpose of the States which did take part, but chiefly because we did not then and we do not now seek an armed conflict with Japan."[110] This was coupled with an appeal to those "intelligent and influential people in Japan" who see how "dubious at best" the results of such a conflict would be for Japan.

Litvinov's speech is memorable in the annals of Soviet diplomacy. The degree of apprehension it exhibits has seldom been matched in any other Soviet political utterance. This apprehension made the Soviet official neglect or forget some time-honored Communist turns of phrase. He spoke of Hitler's taking over power as a "revolution," whereas in Com- munist semantics it was obviously a "counterrevolution"; the outcome of an armed clash between the U.S.S.R. and Japan was classified as "dubious at best" while the ritual phrase used to be a prophecy of over- whelming defeat for anybody who dared to attack the Soviet Union. In fact, insofar as it was possible, the Foreign Commissar was trying to free the minds of his hearers of the stultifying stereotypes and phrases the Soviet leaders themselves had fed their people about the international situation and to make them realize the mortal danger their country was facing. His listeners and the whole country were to be left under no misapprehension that any considerations of Communist solidarity, any traditional phrases and formulas, would stop the Soviet government from seeking peace and security *for Russia*. Litvinov was at some pains to explain why the Soviet government was not successful in lining up with the democratic states against the would-be aggressors, and again his explanation had a strongly apologetic tone:

> We should not forget that we are dealing with capitalist countries whose governments are unstable and change frequently, making it possible for groups and persons to come to power who, because of their class hatred for our state, are sometimes ready to sacrifice the

---

[109] This was obviously in connection with the allegation current at the time that the Polish government had proposed to France a preventive war against Germany before she could rearm.

[110] Degras, *Soviet Documents on Foreign Policy*, III, 58.

national interests of their own state. . . . We shall bear in mind that, should the united efforts of the friends of peace fail, the attack on peace may be directed in the first instance against us.[111]

For all the alleged deviousness and mystification attending Soviet foreign policy, Litvinov laid on the line the principles that would guide it during the next six years, and, had the speech been studied carefully in the Western capitals, there should have been no room for surprise over any subsequent Soviet move, including the Nazi-Soviet pact of 1939. The various priorities and options before the Soviet leaders were fairly clearly outlined. Over and above everything else the Soviet Union would seek noninvolvement in any future war. It would appease Germany and Japan up to the point where this appeasement itself could be interpreted as a sign of weakness and become an incentive for aggression. It would explore, albeit with a degree of skepticism, the possibility that the League of Nations and collective security could function as an impediment to war. Some weeks before Litvinov's speech, Stalin himself said in an interview that the League might act as a brake "retarding or preventing the outbreak of hostilities," in which case the Soviet government would rethink its attitude toward what had been called until shortly before the "league of imperialist robbers."

When it came to intimate collaboration and alliance with the democracies, Litvinov spelled out all too frankly the reasons why the Soviet government had been dubious—and this is perhaps as true in 1968 as it was in 1933—of the advantages of such an alliance. How could one be sure about the firmness of purpose, the stability of policy, on the part of a democratic government? Litvinov chose to express this doubt in quasi-ideological terms: you make a treaty with Great Britain or France, and then another reactionary government comes to power and chooses to make common cause with the fascists. But undoubtedly there was a broader, more functional element in this distrust. The Russians had themselves been to some extent the beneficiaries of a certain gullibility in the public opinion of the West, of a strongly entrenched pacifism and a distrust of their own ruling class among the people of France and Great Britain. Now, ironically, this inherent inability of democratic governments to pursue unsentimental *Realpolitik* was an obstacle to an alliance between the U.S.S.R. and the Western Powers. One could not trust them not "to sacrifice the national interest of their own state," said Litvinov with unconscious irony. The average Englishman or Frenchman saw Hitler's Germany, for all its reprehensible internal characteristics, seeking an equality of status with other countries and trying to throw off the shackles of Versailles. Excessive armaments always led to war, and war never

[111] *Ibid.*, p. 61.

solved anything. Hitler's declarations of peaceful intentions were taken at their face value by many influential circles in the West, just as Chicherin's declarations that the Comintern was a private institution had been. Japanese activities in China were a serious blow to British interests, but when the Chinese Nationalists had attacked British concessions there in 1925 and 1926, with Soviet encouragement, any attempt to use force in their protection was denounced as old-fashioned imperialism. In view of this (now) unhappy "softness" of the democracies, what were the prospects of concluding an effective alliance with them or, if such an alliance were concluded, of their implementing them with resolute policies and sufficient rearmament to scare would-be aggressors? This question would be pondered by the Soviet leaders during the next six years.

There is no reason to embrace any one oversimplified explanation of Soviet policies in the 1930's. One such explanation would see the Russians sincerely converted to collective security and ready to bargain with Hitler only after their would-be allies appeased Hitler at Munich and rejected specific Soviet proposals for military collaboration in 1939. The opposite, equally uncomplicated, view would hold Stalin always prepared to strike a deal with Hitler and awaiting only the appropriate moment. Before examining both hypotheses in the context of events in 1934–39, it is necessary to repeat that neither of them meets the test either of the evidence or of simple logic for 1933. In that year, the leaders of the Soviet Union realized that the main premise of Soviet foreign policy between 1921 and 1931—namely, that any future war would be one among the rival imperialist camps and thus of eventual benefit to the cause of Communism —could no longer meet the new facts of the international situation. As to the policy or combination of policies that would preserve the Soviet Union from the mortal danger of involvement in a major war, the Soviet leaders were (witness Litvinov's speech) quite humanly puzzled.

The problem of peace and war appeared to them in quite a different guise than it did to statesmen in the West. On the one hand, they harbored no pacifist illusions: as long as capitalism existed, war was one of the facts of life, its danger was ever present. On the other hand, the experience of fifteen years of existence of the Soviet state had filled them with some confidence that they could avoid major military entanglements— if a war should come, it would be a war between rival imperialist camps— but the events of 1931 and 1933 shook this confidence. The prospects of a war in 1933 loomed catastrophic. The Soviet regime was battling a revolt, to be sure a passive one, of the majority of the population of its country—the peasants. Would the peasant in uniform fight for the government that expelled his family to a distant region or stripped it of its possessions and forced it into a collective farm? Within the Communist

Party, the opposition whether from the left or the right had been subdued and humiliated, but the Bukharins, Tomskys, Kamenevs, and Zinovievs were still alive, still enjoying the secret support of many Party members. Many military leaders were known to be appalled by the effects of collectivization on Russia's military preparedness. Could the Communist system survive a war, even a war in which Russia would ultimately be victorious? And if the social system by some miracle could survive, it was almost out of the question that the personal regime of the man who had plunged the country into economic chaos, who had gained the mortal hatred of the Bolshevik old guard, would see the end of the conflict. It is in the light of those questions that we can understand not only Soviet external policies between 1933 and 1939 but also much of what went on internally: the cult of Russian nationalism and the ferocious internal purges and spy mania that were to grip the Soviet Union between 1934 and 1939.

V

THE SEARCH FOR PEACE AND
THE COMING OF THE WAR:
1934–39

---

1. *The Search for Peace: 1934–36*

The Soviet Union's vigorous diplomatic activity and extensive series of international and especially nonaggression treaties with her neighbors antedated the crucial year 1933 and the emergence of the Nazi government.[1] The bumper year for nonaggression treaties was 1932, when the U.S.S.R. signed nonaggression pacts with Finland, Estonia, Latvia, Poland, and France.

Those treaties did not mark as yet a definite change of diplomatic course, but they reflected some of the pressures and apprehensions that were to become so much more urgent with the coming to power and continuance in it of Hitler. Excessive faith in the permanence or sanctity of international obligations has never been a characteristic of Soviet policy, but it would be wrong to explain the Soviet passion for treaty-making at that time solely by cynicism or the requirements of propaganda. The

---

[1] Considerable alarm over the future of German-Soviet relations had been felt in Moscow after the formation of the short-lived Papen government in 1932. Franz von Papen was known to be strongly pro-West and against the Russian orientation in German foreign policy.

treaties were designed to lower the level of international tension. They underlined the fact that, preoccupied with great internal dangers, the Soviet government acquiesced in and desired the independence of such former parts of the Russian empire as Finland and Estonia.

The treaty with Poland had a special significance in view of the German danger, already on the horizon. Russian relations with Poland since the Treaty of Riga in 1921 had not been happy. German-Soviet collaboration during the Rapallo period was obviously directed among other things against Poland, even if plans for a joint military action against this country never progressed beyond some informal talks between diplomats and military officers of the two partners. To the Russians as well as to the Germans Poland was, as Molotov was to say in 1939, "an ugly offspring of Versailles," France's watchman in Eastern Europe. The Ukrainian and Byelorussian populations of eastern Poland were bound to be a special worry to Moscow. With a wise and tolerant policy toward those two nationalities, the Polish government could create strong irredentist feelings among the Ukrainians and Byelorussians in the U.S.S.R., especially after the Soviet repression of Ukrainian nationalism which began there in the late 1920's and which coincided with the terrible sufferings of the Ukrainian and Byelorussian peasants during the collectivization drive.[2]

The nonaggression treaty with Poland was signed on July 25, 1932, and subsequent joint actions, the last in 1938, extended its duration to December 31, 1945.[3] It was to share the fate of many such treaties between 1939 and 1945. For a year and a half after its signature, Soviet-Polish relations became more correct than at any previous period, though Poland's rulers, many of them veterans of the revolutionary movement in the Russian empire before 1914, never lost their hostile attitude toward Communism and their realistic view of the Russians' ultimate aims as far as their country was concerned. With the signing of a Polish-German nonaggression treaty in 1934 and the *rapprochement* between the two countries, the Soviet attitude toward Poland again became more reserved. Yet the Polish-Russian pact was far from unimportant in the diplomatic game of the 1930's. It was undoubtedly an element in the Polish rulers' consistent refusals between 1934 and 1938 to pick up Germany's suggestions that

[2] The Polish government for the most part showed itself incapable of such a policy, and militant Ukrainian nationalism was directed against both Poland and the U.S.S.R. and in favor of an independent Ukraine comprising the Soviet republic and the eastern areas of Poland. The Polish Communist Party always acknowledged the Soviet claims east of the so-called Curzon Line, the clandestine Communist groups operating there being known as the Communist parties of Western Ukraine and Western Byelorussia.

[3] Robert M. Slusser and Jan F. Triska, *A Calendar of Soviet Treaties 1917–1957* (Stanford, Calif., 1959), p. 83.

some time in the future the two countries should become partners in a joint enterprise against the U.S.S.R., Poland to be rewarded with part of the Ukraine.[4] Thus the treaty with Poland—and the same is true of the treaties with the Baltic states—made it less likely that those countries would become passageways for German militarism, and it provided added weight to the arguments of those elements in the public life of Russia's eastern neighbors who favored peaceful coexistence with the Soviet Union and distrusted Germany. For formal diplomacy to accomplish that much in an era of growing disregard of international obligations was no mean achievement.

Soviet diplomacy tried subsequently to enlarge the scope of the non-aggression treaties with its neighbors, to create, in fact, an "eastern Locarno" where the independence of the Baltic countries and Poland would be guaranteed by a number of powers including the U.S.S.R., France, and possibly Germany. But this was already 1934; Germany was not going to tie her hands even by means of a treaty; and Poland, after the nonaggression treaty with Germany, was bent on an independent foreign policy. Thus Russia's attempt to create a barrier between herself and the growing might of Hitler by means of a guaranteed buffer zone collapsed, and this in turn led the Soviet policy-makers to envisage a more direct tie to France.

The early phase of the Soviet diplomatic offensive brought one great success, in the form of the establishment of formal relations with the United States in November 1933. This was a development that Soviet leaders had deeply desired from the first days of their regime. Whatever they thought of the United States from the political point of view, the Communists—and this was especially true of Lenin and Stalin—never concealed their admiration for American efficiency and spirit of enterprise. Lenin, a man of the older generation and in some personal characteristics a European *bourgeois* of the pre-1914 vintage, tempered his admiration with some notions of America's "lack of culture," and to him Germany was still the model to be imitated insofar as technical and cultural affairs were concerned. But for Stalin and his entourage, America was obviously the place for learning the most advanced production and scientific techniques, "American efficiency" and "American style of work" being frequent phrases in his pleas for increased industrial production. Formal diplomatic relations with the United States were thought to be sure to

---

[4] It can be argued, in the main correctly, that Poland's refusals to follow up such hints, conveyed mainly during Goering's famous hunting trips to Poland, were based mainly on the realization that such an alliance would transform the country into a satellite of Germany. Yet the temptation would have been greater had the Soviet Union's attitude remained unremittingly hostile.

increase the collaboration of the two countries in commercial and industrial spheres and thus to be a special boon to the Soviet economy entering its Second Five-Year Plan.

But because of the times the political element of the recognition loomed even more important. The United States was the last Great Power to recognize the Soviet Union, which now became a fully acknowledged member of the community of nations. The Soviet leaders had hoped for close relations with the United States also for reasons of high international policy. At one time, they saw in the United States a counterweight to the power they considered their own protagonist and the main obstacle to Communist ambitions—the British empire.[5] But this fantasy about the eventual conflict of the two capitalist giants, which for so long exerted such a fascination on the minds of even the most intelligent and realistic Soviet leaders, was now forgotten and irrelevant. What mattered in the 1930's was another task "assigned" to the United States since the creation of the Communist state, that of counterbalancing Japan. In the post-World War I period, the United States unwittingly performed two major services to the Soviet Union. It was mainly due to American pressure that the British-Japanese alliance was dissolved, and Washington's displeasure was a crucial factor in the Japanese decision to liquidate their occupation of territories of the Soviet Far East. When the Japanese resumed their pushful policies in China in 1931, the United States reacted strongly through Secretary of State Stimson. The common interest of the United States and Russia in checking Japan's expansion in China was a forceful argument in favor of a diplomatic *rapprochement*. The coming to office of the Democratic administration of Franklin D. Roosevelt in 1933 created a favorable atmosphere for another look at Russo-American relations.[6]

[5] Though the Soviets readily recognized that, after World War I, economic primacy in the capitalist world passed irretrievably to the United States, they still considered Great Britain the bulwark of the capitalist world order and their main enemy. Insofar as this judgment reflected an appraisal of the political intelligence of the ruling classes of the two countries, it was perhaps not unduly flattering to the United States.

[6] Initially, as we have seen, the Soviet leaders put great hopes in the Republican Party. This in 1919–21 was due to two reasons: the Democratic Party was for them the party of Wilson, the originator of the League of Nations and the proponent of America's participation in it. The Republicans, through their opposition to the League, carried more favor in Soviet eyes. In the simple Soviet categories of 1920, Republicans were also held to be more representative of big business interests and hence more likely to clash with Japan over China, and, because of their capitalist greed, more interested in trade and concessions in Russia. But the subsequent record of the Republican administration and its refusal to recognize the U.S.S.R. reversed this appraisal of the American political parties.

The first stages of the Russo-American negotiations in 1933 saw the reappearance of the two American figures associated with Lenin's Russia: Colonel Raymond Robins, the informal envoy to the Bolsheviks in 1917–18; and William Bullitt, Wilson's emissary to Lenin in 1919. Both retained warm feelings for Russia, both belonged to that sizable group of men of affairs in the West who believed that had the democracies shown an "understanding" of the Bolshevik regime from the beginning, it would have been more prone to collaborate in preserving peace (though Bullitt's subsequent experience as ambassador was to disillusion him bitterly). After the initial contacts, Litvinov was dispatched to Washington in November 1933.

The two obstacles to recognition on the American side had traditionally been the eternal question of the Tsarist debts and, of course, the Comintern. As to the debts, the Soviet government, with its unvarying attention to the fine points of international diplomacy, held that the details could be entered into only *after* the recognition and establishment of normal diplomatic relations. As to the Comintern, Litvinov in a formal note to Roosevelt expressed assurances which could not, in view of their disregard of the facts, but create trouble in the future course of relations between the two countries. The Soviet government pledged:

> To refrain, and to restrain all persons in government service and all organizations of the Government or under its direct or indirect control ... from any act overt or covert liable in any way whatsoever to injure the tranquility, prosperity, order or security of any part of the United States, its territories or possessions. ... Not to permit the formation or residence on its territory of any organization or group ... which has as its aim the overthrow or the preparation for the overthrow ... of the political or social order of the whole or any part of the United States.[7]

If the demands for such assurances and their acceptance reflected a basic misunderstanding of the nature of Soviet policies on the part of the American leaders, then a parallel misunderstanding on the Soviet side was soon exposed. Ambassador Bullitt's arrival in Moscow was hailed in the Soviet capital as the greatest diplomatic coup since the foundation of the Soviet Union. The new envoy was feted and received with unparalleled cordiality. In an unusual gesture, Stalin, who until then, adhering to the fiction that he was merely a Party official and not a government leader, had refused to meet with foreign diplomats, entertained the American and assured him of his esteem and of the right of personal access to him at any time. Not until the arrival of Ribbentrop in 1939 was Stalin again to exhibit such cordiality toward a foreign envoy.

[7] Jane Degras, ed., *Soviet Documents on Foreign Policy*, III, *1933–41* (London and New York, 1953), 36.

But this cordiality was predicated on the assumption that Roosevelt's administration wanted and was able to pursue a more active policy against Japanese aggression in China. It was not realized in Moscow that the Democratic administration was engrossed in domestic problems arising out of the depression and that the prevailing mood in America was one of isolationism. The American position on Japan's activities in the Far East had been defined by Stimson's doctrine of nonrecognition of the effects of aggression: viz., the United States refused to recognize the Japanese puppet state of Manchukuo. Beyond that, no American administration in the year 1933 could go. Litvinov's first conversations with Bullitt turned on the Japanese threat. Would the United States propose a Far Eastern nonaggression pact to include China, Japan, America, and Russia? This was exactly the kind of "foreign entanglement" that public opinion in the United States would not tolerate. On the American envoy's explaining this fact to Litvinov, the latter pathetically "said that he felt that anything that could be done to make the Japanese believe that the United States was ready to cooperate with Russia, even though there might be no basis for the belief, would be valuable. He asked whether it might not be possible for an American squadron or an individual warship to pay a visit during the spring to Vladivostok or to Leningrad."[8] Bullitt, needless to say, could make no promises.

The course of Russo-American relations during the next few years thus fell far short of Soviet hopes. The Soviet government spared no effort to give out the impression that the Japanese problem was on the Russo-American agenda. The first ambassador to Washington, Troyanovsky, had been envoy in Tokyo. But the fact remained that the America of the New Deal period did not pursue a very active foreign policy. Sympathy toward the U.S.S.R. remained strong among liberals, but concrete results of this sympathy were not found in official policies, and the declarations of good will, etc., toward the Soviet Union failed to appease Russian apprehensions in the Far East. From cordiality the relations of the two powers soon passed into mutual irritation and ill-humored bickering about old debts and the Comintern. Ambassador Bullitt, like many Westerners who had known the Soviet Union during the exuberant days after the Revolution,

---

[8] Bullitt's report in *Papers Relating to the Foreign Relations of the United States: Russia 1933–39* (Washington, 1952), p. 62. The Russian suggestion showed amusingly the growing historical consciousness of the Soviet policy-makers. In the halcyon days of European diplomacy in the nineteenth century, a visit of a naval squadron was understood as a token of friendship, almost an alliance between two powers. Thus the visit of a French naval squadron to Kronstadt in the 1890's was a portentous warning to Germany. The visit of a Russian flotilla to San Francisco during the American Civil War was also an event in the diplomatic maneuvers of the period and a veiled warning to Great Britain, then in strained relations both with the North and with Russia.

could not but become oppressed by the atmosphere of Stalinism. For the Russians, the feeling was that if they could not even get a U.S. squadron to visit a Soviet port, there was not much point in fussing over the United States. The Soviet appraisal of the role of the United States in the 1930's was summarized perceptively in a dispatch of Bullitt's: "Litvinov then expressed his views . . . saying that the truth about the United States was that we desire to remain aloof from all active interest in international affairs. He did not add aloud but implied that therefore really friendly relations with the United States were of small importance to the Soviet Union."[9] The American protest over the Seventh Congress of the Comintern in 1935 in Moscow as violating the Roosevelt-Litvinov agreement was answered rather impatiently with the standard explanation that the Comintern was a body for which the Soviet government bore no responsibility. Relations with the United States thus receded from the plane of primary importance, which they were not to reach again until 1941.

Litvinov's mission to Washington was one of the high points of his diplomatic career. For the next five years, the Soviet Foreign Commissar was to be one of the key figures on the diplomatic horizon. His travels, his impassioned oratory in Geneva, first at the Disarmament Conference, then at the League of Nations, made him a familiar figure in European politics. To large segments of Western public opinion, increasingly fed up with the pusillanimity of their own governments in standing up first to the threats, then to the actual aggression of the fascist powers, Litvinov became the embodiment of the search for peace through collective security. His prominence led many observers to see Litvinov—and this faulty impression still persists in some works on the period—not merely as the spokesman for but as one of the makers of Soviet foreign policies. Yet nothing justifies such an estimate. Never a member of the Politburo or particularly close to Stalin, the Foreign Commissar simply could not in the nature of Soviet politics of the era play the role ascribed to him. He was a faithful executor of decisions laid down by Stalin and the Politburo, and he was incapable of saving the Soviet diplomatic corps from a veritable massacre which befell it in the 1930's. (Among those liquidated were two assistant Commissars for Foreign Affairs who were at one time of much greater stature in the Communist Party than Litvinov: Sokolnikov and Krestinsky.) Like his predecessor, Chicherin, Litvinov had spent a long time before the Revolution in the West. Without Chicherin's encyclopedic knowledge[10] and courtly manners, Litvinov surpassed his predecessor in his ability to establish contact and friendly relations with the statesmen

[9] Bullitt, in *ibid.*, p. 265.

[10] A Soviet diplomat who subsequently defected has recorded a detailed picture of the background of Japanese politics that Chicherin gave him before his departure for Tokyo.

and leaders of public opinion in the democratic countries, and in couching his appeals in terms meaningful and persuasive to the West. His flair and mistaken reputation were probably instrumental in saving him from the fate of countless old Bolsheviks who walked the plank in the purges. Even when dismissed in 1939 his popularity abroad was thought to be of some potential use, and he was sent to Washington as ambassador in the hour of Soviet Russia's mortal danger in 1941.

The struggle for the sympathy of public opinion in the democratic countries occupied a prominent place in Soviet efforts and policies of the 1930's. Facing as they did for the first time since 1921 a real threat of concerted capitalist aggression against them by at least two powers, Japan and Germany, the Soviet leaders had to make sure at least that the rest of the capitalist world would not join or acquiesce in such an aggression. Circumstances for creating a favorable image of the Soviet Union in the democratic countries appeared unfavorable. The terror and sufferings imposed by the Soviet regime upon the majority of its citizens were but dimly realized in the West, the stories of devastation wrought by the collectivization being discounted as inventions of the extreme right and professional haters of the U.S.S.R. But the horrors and the extent of the purges which, beginning with 1934, decimated the Party and the state machinery could not be concealed or discounted. Indeed, the Soviet government itself publicized abroad the great trials where the makers of the Soviet Union confessed to a variety of fantastic crimes, including espionage for Germany and Japan, assassination plots against Stalin and his henchmen, primitive forms of economic sabotage, etc. The subsequent reproach against the French and British governments for their skepticism about military collaboration with the Soviet Union must be weighed against the judicial assassination in 1937 of Russia's top military leaders and the arrest and liquidation between 1937 and 1939 of the *majority* of Soviet officers down to the battalion level, etc.

Against this background, the activities of Litvinov can be seen as instrumental in preserving a link with Western public opinion and in retaining much of the sympathy with which liberal circles there had greeted the creation of the Soviet state. To be sure, the ingenious Foreign Commissar had much help from Hitler, Mussolini, and the Japanese militarists. As against the language of conquests, racism, and threats of violence with which the fascist leaders interlarded their professions of peace, Litvinov and the other Soviet spokesmen maintained a consistently pacific line. The undertones of class war and anti-imperialism, so strong still in the pronouncements of Chicherin and his era, now vanished. A typical statement by the Foreign Commissar spoke only of peace. "The Soviet state is a stranger to chauvinism, nationalism or racial and national prejudice, perceives its stated duty to lie not in conquest, not in expansion. . . . In

the roll call of States which are interested in the preservation and consolidation of peace its reply is always 'Present.' "[11] Litvinov's boss could not
or would not strike the same tone: Stalin spoke to the audiences at home,
and his speeches had to contain the ritual phrases about the economic
crisis of capitalism, the ultimately evil designs of *all* capitalist powers, etc.
But even Stalin's oratory during the period exhibited none of the harshness
and contempt for public opinion in the West that it had shown in the 1920's.

As to the motivation underlying Soviet policies for the period, we can
be sure about its main points, but we lack information as to the details.
As suggested above, the main turning point in Soviet policies was the
conviction reached in 1933–34 that a major war was threatening. On
Bullitt's arrival in the Soviet capital in November 1933, the Soviet leaders
tried to persuade him that an attack by Japan was imminent. But it is
doubtful that the Russian government thought that the war was *that* close.
Soviet policy in the Far East was, as we have seen, a masterful blend of
appeasement, sufficient firmness to impress Japan that a war would be
extremely risky and costly, and encouragement of the Chiang Kai-shek
regime to resist further Japanese encroachments and not to reach a *modus
vivendi* with Japan. The appeasement element was crowned by the sale to
Japan in 1935 of the Russian interest in the Chinese Eastern Railway.
Since officially the sale was to the "independent" government of Manchukuo, it constituted Soviet *de facto* recognition of the Japanese puppet
regime, and as such it aroused the violent protest of the Chinese government. The railroad was sold for a fraction of the sum originally demanded
by the Soviet Union, but it removed a potentially dangerous source of
incidents with Japan, incidents that might blossom into a full-fledged war.
Once again, Japanese militarism could be expected to move in the direction of least resistance: against China.

This policy in the Far East, to which we shall return, gives a good clue
as to over-all Soviet objectives. For the immediate and foreseeable future,
the Soviet aims were not the punishment of aggressors or the preparation
of a grand military alliance against them, but the noninvolvement of the
Soviet Union in war. Not a crusade against fascism, but the sensible
objective of sparing their sorely tried country a military conflict they
secretly realized it could not afford—this was uppermost in the minds of
Stalin and his colleagues. To do them justice, the Soviet leaders during
the period 1934–39 never made a secret of this objective or tried to pretend
that their detestation of fascism was greater than their desire for military
noninvolvement.

The activities of Soviet diplomacy in Europe paralleled those in the
Far East. From the perspective of 1934, the threat was not judged to be

[11] Degras, *op. cit.*, III, 79.

equally pressing: some years would still have to pass before Germany would be rearmed to the point where she could launch an aggression. But what might precipitate a German thrust eastward was the isolation of the Soviet Union. Were the Western Powers to become convinced by Hitler's anti-Communist propaganda, were French politics to turn to the right, if not indeed to fascism, as signs seemed to indicate it might in 1934, the European threat to Russia would be imminent and overwhelming. Hence the first priority for the *Narkomindel* and the Comintern was to prevent the spread of fascism and to avoid the situation arising in the future where a fully rearmed Germany faced the U.S.S.R. alone.

As to the concrete value of the treaty-making in which the Soviets indulged between 1932 and 1935 and of Litvinov's activity in the 1932 Geneva Disarmament Conference, it goes without saying that in Moscow's view, treaties and formal agreements on limitations of armaments could be at most only temporary expedients. Prior to Hitler's rise to power, it was sensible to expect that faced with the Depression democratic powers would make a genuine effort to reduce the burden of armaments. Even so, Litvinov's plea for a complete and total disarmament was a propaganda stance rather than a real proposal. With Hitler's Germany in the game, it became clear that disarmament was a pipedream, that the German proposals and counterproposals were time-gaining devices, and that Hitler was determined to nibble at the provisions of Versailles the way the Japanese were nibbling at China—piece by piece, without provoking a violent reaction at any one point, proclaiming that each infraction was the last, invoking the seemingly irrefutable moral argument that Germany was seeking what was the inherent right of every state. As Litvinov said in the summer of 1934, with a realism that was still missing in London and even Paris, "It has now become quite obvious that the disarmament problem does not lend itself to a solution. The most inveterate optimists . . . do not aspire to more than stabilization of the present level of armaments."[12] As to the value of treaties, the Commissar also spoke with complete bluntness. "To be sure there is the Kellogg pact and the League of Nations Covenant, but since both of these have already been violated with impunity they can no longer satisfy anybody as guarantees of peace."[13]

Litvinov then proceeded to give the Soviet recipe for security:
What other guarantees of security are there—military alliance and the policy of balance of power? Pre-war history has shown that this policy not only does not get rid of war, but on the contrary unleashes it. By a process of elimination we thus arrive at another means . . . pacts of mutual assistance: these should not by any means be regarded as an

[12] *Ibid.*, p. 83.
[13] *Ibid.*, p. 84.

attempt to encircle any country, since every State belonging to a given region may join in these pacts.[14]

This was a clear reference to the "eastern Locarno," the unsuccessful attempt to join Germany, France, the U.S.S.R., and Russia's western neighors in a treaty of nonaggression and mutual guarantees. Yet one suspects that on this point the Foreign Commissar was himself hardly convinced that such a pact could secure the U.S.S.R. from aggression. Soviet rulers held paper guarantees to be of little value. And if the democracies could not be trusted, what faith could be put in a written pledge by Hitler?

But behind such realistic or, if one prefers, cynical views of treaties was a recognition that they were still valuable chips in the diplomatic game. Russia's willingness to pledge the integrity of the countries that were formerly either totally or in part within the Russian empire could not but be contrasted with the German refusal to offer a similar pledge. If one of Hitler's initial policy gambits had been to isolate Soviet Russia and to present himself as the champion of European civilization and the architect of European unity against the Bolshevik danger, then he was being clearly outmaneuvered by the Soviet Union. In December 1934, the U.S.S.R. and France signed a protocol pledging their joint effort to secure the eastern pact. Since this pact was already doomed by Germany's refusal and Poland's hesitations, the next stage had to be their *rapprochement,* if not indeed an alliance. This was clearly underlined in Litvinov's statement on the protocol: "It goes without saying that the agreement now concluded does not in any sense exclude the conclusion of other agreements between the U.S.S.R. and France either now or if, notwithstanding their renewed efforts, the eastern pact should not come into existence. The protocol of 5 December imposes no restriction on bilateral agreements between the U.S.S.R. and France."[15] Litvinov was scrupulous in reiterating the Soviet wish for good relations with Germany. "In particular the U.S.S.R. has never ceased to wish for the best all round relations with Germany. That too, I am sure, is the desire of France in regard to Germany." Nothing could be truer—and more subtle. Germany was put on the spot. Hitler did want to have good relations with France *provided* he could have a free hand in the east. The task of Soviet diplomacy was to make this impossible.

Reading between the lines of Litvinov's statement and in view of future events, it becomes clear that the Soviet objective between 1934 and 1936 was not so much an effective military alliance with France in itself as the prevention of any understanding between France and Germany that could

[14] *Ibid.*

[15] *Ibid.*, p. 98.

push Germany against Russia. This impression is also strongly suggested by an article in *Pravda* of March 31, 1935, which appeared under the signature of Deputy Commissar of War Tukhachevsky. Hitler, wrote the Soviet Marshal (who had been closely connected with the details of the Russo-German military collaboration in the 1920's), was trying to appease France and to lull her to sleep.

It is obvious that Hitler's imperialist plans are directed not only against the Soviet Union. That is merely a convenient screen for his plans in the west (against Belgium and France) and in the south (Posen, Czechoslovakia, *Anschluss* with Austria). Apart from everything else, Germany needs French iron and also needs to expand its naval strength. . . . Thus in order to realize these plans of conquest and revenge, Germany will have by summer of this year an army of at least 849,000, that is, 40 per cent greater than the French army, and nearly as large as that of the U.S.S.R.[16]

The moral of Tukhachevsky's article was crystal clear, and it was intended for foreign, especially French, eyes: if the French think they can appease Hitler by letting him do what he wants in the east, they are mistaken. And, the article suggested, sensibly enough, by themselves the French could not hope to match the German military might. Russia on the other hand could always outbid Germany when it came to the size of the army. To make his argument more vivid, Tukhachevsky exaggerated German military strength *at the time.*

The same nagging worry was evident in the conversations of Soviet leaders with the British minister, Anthony Eden, who came to Moscow in March of 1935. Eden arrived in Russia after a visit to Berlin, where he and the Foreign Secretary, Sir John Simon, had been on one of those pathetic errands British statesmen went on in those years: trying to find out what Hitler *really* wanted. (He had just announced another breach of the Treaty of Versailles: Germany restored military conscription.) Though the Soviets could not but feel slighted by the fact that the senior British minister did not come to Moscow after Berlin, they greeted the junior one[17] with great courtesy.

Litvinov was quick to drop hints. Hitler, he said, "is building on the assumption of continued antagonism between Britain and the Soviet Union. I do not think that Hitler is sincere in disclaiming interest in the west."[18] That an understanding with the U.S.S.R. was in the interests of France and Great Britain, and that as a matter of fact they rather than Russia might be the primary target of Germany's attack was also conveyed by

[16] *Ibid.,* p. 125.
[17] Eden was then Lord Privy Seal.
[18] The Earl of Avon, *The Eden Memoirs,* Vol. I, *Facing the Dictators* (London and New York, 1962), p. 148.

the Foreign Commissar: "The Reichswehr . . . is always ready to make a bargain with the Soviet Union. I have evidence of this from secret sources. The plan of the Reichswehr is always to dispose of France first, rather than to waste valuable time and energy on Russia. . . . Hitler's assurances are not to be believed, not even when he says that he has renounced Alsace-Lorraine."[19]

Eden's reception underlined the frantic Soviet desire to approach the West and to block any Western *rapprochement* with (and to kill any Western illusions about) Hitler. It was most unusual for the Britisher, a junior minister not in the cabinet, to be met at the railway station by the Foreign Commissar rather than a deputy. It was still more unusual to have an audience with Stalin. The latter tried to suggest the danger to the West of any underestimation of the German danger: "Stalin said that German diplomacy was generally clumsy, but maintained that the only way to meet the present situation was by some scheme of pacts. Germany must be made to realize that if she attacked any other nation she would have Europe against her."[20]

On this, as on many other occasions, Stalin's logic was irrefutable and his foresight correct. But, as pointed out above, Soviet policy moves in the 1930's were blocked by the same factor that had been of invaluable assistance in the 1920's, the inability of the democratic governments to act in concert and in disregard of their own public opinion. Eden in 1935 was in no position to pledge the Soviets a British alliance. Great Britain was only now and with the greatest reluctance beginning a modest program of rearmament. Even this program was opposed violently in Parliament and outside by those groups that were most friendly to a *rapprochement* with the Soviet Union, the Labour and Liberal parties. France was in the midst of a deep internal crisis. Her ability to move decisively on the German issue depended on British support. The British public (and general elections were due within a few months) was overwhelmingly in favor of collective security and against any further alliances and entanglements on the Continent. Eden therefore had to inform Litvinov that there was no prospect whatsoever of a British guarantee for the Baltic states, i.e., of actual British participation in an "eastern Locarno."

The Soviet entrance into the League of Nations, which took place in 1934, was designed to emphasize the Soviet Union's role as a *status quo* state and thus to lay grounds for the possibility of more intimate association with the Western Powers, especially Great Britain. Upon her entrance, the U.S.S.R. was given a permanent seat on the Council of the League, a recognition of her status as a Great Power. With their political realism,

[19] *Ibid.*
[20] *Ibid.*, p. 155.

the Russians could not but recognize that the League, crippled from the beginning by the absence of the United States and now abandoned by Japan and Germany, was less capable than ever of assuring the security of its member states. But, as Stalin had said years before, the League could be useful as a brake or delaying device upon aggression. It was not lost upon the Soviet leaders that, as a member, Russia could count on the support of that large segment of Western opinion which saw the organization as the sole means of preventing another world conflagration.

Events were soon to demonstrate that even Stalin's modest estimate of the League's potential usefulness was exaggerated. The Abyssinian crisis into which the League plunged in 1935 showed that the League's effectiveness could be no greater than the determination of its leading members, notably Britain. The U.S.S.R. joined in the sanctions imposed on Italy after her aggression in Abyssinia, undoubtedly in the hope that an effective restraint of aggression would become an important precedent for stopping aggression elsewhere. Britain's leadership in the League's activities and her seeming determination to stop Mussolini revived for a moment the old Russian belief (antedating the Revolution) of the power of the British empire and the guile of its diplomacy. Litvinov showed rare exuberance in his talk with the American ambassador. "He expressed once more the conviction that the British had decided to eliminate Mussolini. . . . Litvinov said that he believed the British would blockade the Suez Canal, if and when necessary. . . . He felt that as soon as the British had finished Mussolini they would finish Hitler."[21] The Foreign Commissar thus showed that the Soviet leaders were not impervious to the illusion and wishful thinking, which affected so many people at that time, that the British lion had shed his apathy and the days of Palmerston and Disraeli were back. The subsequent collapse of the League's sanctions and Italy's conquest of Abyssinia showed the hollowness of such expectations. The League's ineffectual intervention was if anything to heighten the danger of war, for it pushed Italy closer to Germany and once more demonstrated the incapacity of the democracies to carry through a resolute policy.

This lesson was only too well learned in Tokyo and Berlin. Stalin's lapidary summary of the international situation reflected the Soviet impression. As against the two main focal points of tension, Germany and the Far East, "the Italo-Abyssinian war is merely an episode. . . . It is possible, however, that the emphasis may shift to Europe. . . . Even when he wants to talk of peace, Hitler cannot avoid uttering threats. That is symptomatic."[22] There was more behind this curt statement than an

[21] Bullitt to the State Department, November 9, 1935, in *Papers Relating to the Foreign Relations of the United States: Russia 1933–39*, p. 264.

[22] From an interview given by Stalin to an American journalist, quoted in Degras, *op. cit.*, III, 168.

insight into the German dictator's mentality that was sadly missing in London and Washington. Hitler wanted not merely more territory and bloodless victories. He wanted war. Soviet Russia needed peace. An alliance even with the most powerful states was for Stalin but the *second* best recourse if it did not protect the Soviet Union from a military entanglement. When the European war became a certainty, Stalin was to make a supreme, and foreseeable, effort to deflect the aggressor from the boundaries of the Soviet Union.

The avoidance of war thus had priority in the minds of the Soviet leaders over the securing of strong allies in the case of war. If a powerful coalition could be mounted to discourage a would-be aggressor, then well and good. If such a coalition could show its value *only* in a war, then the ominous lesson of 1914–17 stood to warn Stalin and his associates. The League of Nations was demonstrating its incapacity to be even a brake upon aggression. The great hopes put in the United States in 1933—that she would bring her enormous power into the balance and would safeguard the Soviet Union at least from the Japanese threat—were shown by 1935 to have been unfounded.

Nor could the Franco-Russian treaty of mutual assistance, signed on May 2, 1935, be expected to fulfill the Soviet requirements for security. The treaty pledged each country to come to the other's aid "in the case of an unprovoked attack on the part of a European state." The French, largely to assuage British apprehensions, insisted on tying the provisions of the treaty to the Covenant of the League and the Locarno agreement. Thus, the fact of aggression was to be recognized as such by the Council of the League under Article 16 of the Covenant. To be sure, if the Council failed to find the fact of aggression unanimously, the obligation of the other state to give "aid and assistance" to the injured state still held, but at least some interval could be envisaged in, say, the action of France, if Russia were attacked, and the obligation could not be called automatic.

There were other, more serious limitations in the treaty. In the first place, it did not provide for French assistance to the U.S.S.R. in the case of an attack by Japan. In the second place, and even more important, Russia had no common boundary with Germany: short of an adherence by Poland to the treaty (and Poland in 1935 was thought by the U.S.S.R. to be a potential accomplice of Germany in case of an aggression against the U.S.S.R.), how could Russia render effective help to France in case of a German attack upon her? One might then superficially conclude that the whole advantage of the treaty accrued to the U.S.S.R.: a German-Polish attack on the U.S.S.R. called for French action; in the case of a German attack upon France, with Poland's and the Baltic states' neutrality, the U.S.S.R. had a perfect excuse for nonintervention. But even this interpretation misses the meaning of the pact from the Russian point of view. The securing of an ally *in case of war* was not the Soviet objective in signing the Franco-Soviet alliance.

This seeming paradox is best explained by contrasting the provisions of the Franco-Soviet agreement of 1935 with the alliance signed by the two countries in the bygone Tsarist era in 1891–92. The earlier alliance had specific military provisions laying down the number of troops to be used by each partner in the case of a German attack upon the other. Both countries agreed on close collaboration between their general staffs. And in those days there could be no misunderstanding as to the automatic applications of the provisions of the treaty: there was no League of Nations, and pre-1914 Russia had of course an extensive common frontier with Germany. In contrast, the 1935 agreement left the whole problem of military collaboration in the air, though some exchange of military missions took place. Not until the summer of 1939 was an attempt made to implement the military side of the agreement, and by then the whole European situation had drastically changed.

Without a military convention, the Franco-Soviet agreement of May 1935 was at most a preliminary to an alliance rather than an alliance in itself. That no real talks on the details of military collaboration were to take place for four years was of course symptomatic of both sides' reluctance to enter into any detailed and binding obligations. On the French side, this reluctance was due to the French general staff's doubts about the value of the Russian army, doubts that could not but grow with the increasing extent of the purge in Russia and its decimation of the officer corps. Any talks would have had to touch on the sensitive subject of the role of Poland in the alliance and Poland's well-known refusal even to contemplate the passage of Soviet troops through her territory. That the treaty itself was far from being a binding alliance was inferred by the third party most interested in it. Writing to his Foreign Ministry, the German ambassador in Moscow, Count Werner von der Schulenburg, stated that the pact's "extremely cautious and elaborate language does not give the impression of two partners wishing to bind themselves to one another at all costs. On the contrary, one could if one were so minded infer from the very text of the Treaty and the attached Protocol that France at least has left herself a good many loopholes."[23] Schulenburg concluded his dispatch, "The policy of free hand, of uncommittedness which has up till now seemed desirable as an aim of Soviet foreign policy would appear to have been temporarily abandoned with the signature of the Pact of May 2, 1935."[24]

[23] *Documents on German Foreign Policy, 1918–45*, Series C, IV (Washington, 1959), 129.

[24] *Ibid.*, p. 130.

The German ambassador's impression that the treaty benefited mostly France and that the Soviets had given up their freedom of action in foreign affairs brings to mind Stalin's remark about the clumsiness of German diplomacy. Schulenburg failed to see the meaning and importance of the treaty from the Soviet point of view. This importance is illuminated by a dispatch from another German ambassador, the one in London, relating to his superiors the conversation with the new British Foreign Secretary, Sir Samuel Hoare. Speaking to him on June 13, 1935, Sir Samuel remarked that "Germany was constantly accused here of intending to gain a free hand in the East against Russia."[25] The German envoy could but feebly protest and adduce the Führer's peaceful intentions toward the whole world.

The importance of the treaty lay precisely in the fact that it blocked, insofar as any written agreement could block, the first phase of the German attempt to gain a free hand against the U.S.S.R. Stalin was under no illusions that the essentially right-wing government that signed the agreement was motivated by tenderness toward the U.S.S.R. or that it would cease its efforts to relax the tension between France and Hitler (especially in view of the British pressures toward that end). But the possibility of Western support for Russia could no longer be excluded from German calculations. If Hitler's whole anti-Communist stance was an attempt to isolate the U.S.S.R. diplomatically and make sure that Germany could deal with her at her leisure, then the Franco-Soviet agreement was a resounding defeat for that policy and propaganda. In the nature of things and given the conditions of 1935, it forced Hitler to look to less risky adventures.

As to the implementation of the treaty through a military convention, nothing suggests that the Russians at the time were any more eager than the French to enter into binding and detailed agreements. There is also no scintilla of evidence that the destruction of Hitler through a preventive war was even suggested on the Soviet side. One can only speculate as to how the eventual resolution of the Hitler menace appeared to the Soviet leaders. They were by now convinced of the durability of the Hitler regime. They could not share the illusions, widespread in the West, that somehow the Nazis could be domesticated and that once the German grievances were met Hitler would settle into peaceful coexistence. Like the prudent politicians they were (at least in the foreign sphere), they worked for one thing at a time. For the moment, the worst danger of all, that of concerted capitalist action against the Soviet Union, had passed. The danger of war, once Hitler was rearmed, remained.

The treaty with France was soon followed by a similar mutual-assistance treaty with Czechoslovakia. Signed on May 16, it included the provision

25 *Ibid.*, p. 205.

that help to the attacked country would be forthcoming only if France, which had a long-standing treaty with Czechoslovakia, would come too. Thus the treaty did not obligate the U.S.S.R. to unilateral help to Czechoslovakia but only in conjunction with France. It therefore did not significantly extend Russia's commitments beyond those already assumed in the treaty with France. And Czechoslovakia did not have a common frontier with the U.S.S.R. But the treaty could only enhance the growing reputation of the Soviet Union as the stanch defender of collective security. To Hitler, the Czech treaty could well demonstrate that his anti-Soviet policies, instead of winning him any dividends, were only blocking his designs in other directions. Was the Soviet policy designed in fact to build up in German eyes the value of an understanding with the U.S.S.R.? If so, the evidence in that direction remains scant. It rests largely on one curious episode. In the summer of 1935, commercial negotiations were taking place between the two countries. The German Minister of Economic Affairs, Dr. Hjalmar Schacht, minuted for the Foreign Ministry an intriguing incident with the head of the Soviet delegation, Kandelaki:

> [Kandelaki] began by saying that he had been in Moscow where he had spoken to Stalin, Molotov and Rosengoltz[26] and that these persons had taken note of and approved the substance of our previous conversations about the possibility of further large-scale credits and commercial transactions with Russia. . . . I observed that Mr. Kandelaki had told me this some weeks earlier, whereupon, after some embarrassment, Mr. Kandelaki expressed the hope that it might also be possible to improve German-Russian political relations.[27]

Schacht refused to bite and referred his Soviet interlocuter to the normal diplomatic channels. Soviet diplomats pursued this subject with German officials throughout the year, and in December 1935 the counsellor of the Soviet embassy suggested "privately" the idea of a bilateral nonaggression treaty between Germany and Soviet Russia.[28]

The Kandelaki episode has served for some as proof that the U.S.S.R. was ready in 1935 for the kind of "deal" with Hitler which subsequently took place in 1939 and the mechanics of which also evolved out of innocent-sounding trade and commercial negotiations. That the Soviet diplomats should have expressed the hope for a Soviet-German *détente* was not surprising. That was their job, and they were largely repeating what Stalin and Litvinov were saying publicly. But that a trade official should broach the idea of a *rapprochement* of the two countries may perhaps suggest that the Soviets were probing for a far-reaching political understanding going beyond a mere nonaggression treaty. But on the basis of the available

[26] Rosengoltz, subsequently liquidated, was then Commissar of Trade.
[27] *Documents on German Foreign Policy, 1918–45*, Series C, IV, 453.
[28] *Ibid.*, p. 933.

evidence the notion that in 1935 the U.S.S.R. was ready for an *alliance* with Germany on the pattern of the Molotov-Ribbentrop pact cannot be accepted. The Russian statesmen were after all not entirely immune to the illusions that ruled Europe's minds in 1935: the democracies were sluggish, but they represented tremendous power, dwarfing Germany's. Litvinov's feeling that the British were about to finish off Mussolini had been already recorded (and he repeated to Schulenburg the gist of his conversation with Bullitt on the subject). The French army was still the best in the world. To engage *in 1935* on any far-reaching designs to carve up Poland and the Baltic states would have been entirely out of tune with the prudence that characterized Soviet foreign policy. Even the most dazzling prospects of territorial or ideological expansion could not compensate the Soviet Union for the risk—and let us repeat that this risk was felt to be as much internal as external—of an actual involvement in war.

The various motivations and cautions of Soviet foreign policy become clearer if one studies the activity of the Comintern. The year 1935, the year of alliances, is of course also the year of the official proclamation of the Popular Front, of this seemingly drastic reversal of the hostility toward socialist and progressive parties that had been such a prominent feature of international Communism's policies. Again, much of the genesis and the meaning of the Popular Front policy has been misunderstood. In its essence, the policy paralleled the shift in *official* Soviet foreign policy: from an uncompromising struggle against the "social fascists," etc., the Communist parties passed to a wooing of the socialists and other democratic elements and to attempts to mount a joint front against fascism. Yet it is mistaken to see the policy of the Popular Front as being in any sense comparable to the policies adopted by the Communists in World War II, i.e., *after the German attack on the U.S.S.R.*, when Communists everywhere proceeded to associate themselves fully and without reservation with the struggle of their countries against the Axis. The policy of collaboration with democratic forces and of association with the nationalist slogans during the Popular Front phase was much more limited and reserved. We shall not be mistaken if we ascribe to the Popular Front tactics the aim of *containing* the spread of fascism rather than of *destroying* its focal points in Germany and Italy.

This characteristic comes out most strongly if we examine the attitude of the Communist Party in the vanguard of the movement, the French one, on the subject of national defense. In May 1935, following the Franco-Soviet pact, the French Foreign Minister, Pierre Laval, visited Moscow. For internal political reasons, the Frenchman sought a declaration by the highest authority of Communism that the defense policy of his government was understood and supported in Moscow. Stalin, forgetting his usual plea that he was not an official of the government, felt compelled to oblige.

Thus the famous formula that created much stir in Europe at the time, since it involved a right-wing politician invoking Soviet interference in the internal politics of his country: "It is precisely for the sake of maintaining peace that these States are obliged above all not to weaken in any way their means of national defense. On this point, in particular, Comrade Stalin expressed complete understanding and approval of the national defense policy pursued by France with the object of maintaining its armed forces at a level consistent with its security requirements."[29]

The policy of the Popular Front had been pursued by the French Communists for about a year. Yet their attitude toward the vital problem of French rearmament remained at best ambiguous. Without continuing its pre-1934 noisy anti-militarist and defeatist campaign, the Party did not come out for a vigorous defense effort. Stalin's statement, while in fact admonishing the French Communists to bury their militant anti-defense position, hardly breathed an air of urgency about increasing the pace of French armaments. Nor did the French Communists subsequently display the nationalist zeal they were to show after June 1941. Speaking at the Seventh Comintern Congress, their leader, Maurice Thorez, still displayed reservations on the subject of supporting his country's defense effort and did not pledge his party's support in any war effort except one in conjunction with the Soviet Union: "We Communists who do not judge war in the fashion of the bourgeois reformist or pacifist parties take a stand on war as Marxists, declare that in case of aggression against the Soviet Union we shall know how to rally all our forces and defend the Soviet Union in every way." That the defense of the Soviet Union demanded in 1935 *drastic* improvement in the French military effort was in fact denied by Thorez when he said in the same speech: "We continue to fight in the name of the working class of France against the enslavement of the people, and against the return to the two-year term of military service."[30]

It goes without saying that the policy of the French Communist Party was attuned to the wishes of Moscow. If the Party embraced France's defense needs in this very qualified way, it could only mean that the U.S.S.R. was not unduly solicitous about an increase in the French military potential. In view of the reintroduction of compulsory military service in Germany, it was being pointed out at the time that France, with her much smaller population, could match the German threat only by lengthening her soldiers' term of service. Yet this was one point on which Thorez specified his party's opposition. It might be thought that Moscow's and consequently the French Communists' reserve could be attributed to the fact

---

[29] From the official Soviet communiqué in Degras, *op. cit.*, III, 132.

[30] *Seventh Congress of the Communist International* (in English) (Moscow, 1939), p. 224.

that the French government of the moment was right-wing and, in addition, was being dilatory about ratifying the Franco-Soviet pact (it did not come into force until March 1936). Yet even after the coming to power of the Popular Front government in June 1936, one looks in vain for that single-minded devotion to the defense of the country, that rejection for the moment of every and any social and political postulate which could interfere with defense and national unity, which was to characterize the French Communists in Russia's hour of peril.

The conclusion is inescapable, then, that the original aim of the Popular Front tactics insofar as the Soviet leadership was concerned was defensive in nature. It was not to provide the Western countries with the resolution and the material means to fight Hitler. It was to make sure that they would not fall prey to fascism themselves and/or become allies of Hitler in a bloc against the U.S.S.R. The distinction may appear pedantic, but it is an important one in judging the perspectives of Soviet foreign policy in 1935. Once the threat of Hitler's attack was countered by an alliance with France, once fascism was barred from further expansion, the Soviet Union had no interest in restoring the hegemony of France in Europe, certainly no desire to see the French and British empires fully rearmed and infused with new resolution and confidence in their foreign policies. As late as 1939, Stalin was confident of the British and French ability to stave off the German might for some years in a stalemate war. In 1935, provided fascism was stopped and the U.S.S.R. secured by an alliance with the still greatest military power in Europe, the threat of war did not appear pressing enough to cause the Communists to make a present of national unity and military power to the French and British imperialists.

This thesis is reinforced by an analysis of the proceedings and resolutions of the Seventh and last Congress of the Comintern, held in Moscow in July-August 1935. The Congress has often been considered as the high point of the policy of the Popular Front (which it was), and also as a resounding call for joint action of Communists and the democracies, a proclamation of a sacred war to the finish upon fascism. This latter interpretation is not borne out by the proceedings of the Seventh Congress. Its mere convocation was bound to rub the wrong way those circles in the West which the Soviet government was attempting to persuade of its abandonment of world revolutionary aims.[31] Superficially, there was no

---

[31] A dispatch from Bullitt to the State Department relating a conversation with Litvinov, or more properly his torturing of the Foreign Commissar, is not without a humorous interest: "I replied that in addition to my concern over the present international situation I was gravely concerned with regard to the impending meeting of the Third International. Litvinov said: 'What, is there to be one?' I answered, yes, on the twentieth of this month. Livinov replied with a broad grin: 'You know more about the Third International than

urgent need to call a Congress. None had been held, in defiance of the statutes, for six years. Soviet viewpoints and directives could be and were conveyed to the individual parties without the cumbersome spectacle of the mass assembly.

The Congress was called for two reasons. One was to enthrone the policy of the Popular Front, the other was to prevent the policy of the Popular Front from running away with Communism. The latter danger was not negligible in the eyes of the suspicious men of the Kremlin. The newly found enthusiasm for collective security and the struggle against fascism was leading some Communist parties into strange associations with right-wing socialists, even with Trotskyites; the anti-Hitler attitude among certain Communist circles was assuming a degree of militancy that was beyond the current posture of Soviet policy. Hence the Congress, which was to establish and publicize the correct formula.

The Congress, to digress, could not perform this difficult task with complete success. For all their discipline and their boundless devotion to Stalin and the U.S.S.R., the foreign Communist leaders could not always penetrate and follow the Comintern's oversubtle and often contradictory directions, and they were not, even at the highest point of Stalinism, entirely immune to pressures from their rank and file.

The struggle against fascism was the *leitmotiv* of the Congress, and the casual observer could conclude that international Communism issued a life-and-death challenge to Hitler. Ernst Thälmann, the leader of the German Party, then languishing in a Nazi concentration camp, was elected honorary president of the world assembly of Communism. George Dimitrov, who not long before had taunted the Nazi dignitaries at the Reichstag Fire trial, was the dominant figure and was elected Secretary General of the Comintern. Most speeches breathed defiance and contempt for Hitler, the Fascists, and the Japanese militarists. But underneath the patina of rhetoric, the policy directives failed to recommend implementation of this militancy. The resolutions of the Congress had in fact a curiously old-fashioned tone. The old chestnuts once more were in evidence: "The main contradiction in the camp of the imperialists is the Anglo-American antagonism," proclaimed the unanimous voice of world Communism.[32] The authority granted to the French Communists to support the defense

---

I do. The other day when I was talking with Stalin I said I had heard there was to be a meeting of the Third International on the tenth of this month. Stalin replied, "Is there?" He knew about it no more than I do.' I answered, 'You will have to tell that one to somebody else. You cannot expect me to believe that Stalin knows nothing about the Third International.' Litvinov replied: 'No, I assure you.'" *Papers Relating to the Foreign Relations of the United States: Russia 1933–39*, p. 221–22.

[32] *Seventh Congress of the Communist International*, p. 588.

effort of their country was not extended to other Communist parties in nonfascist states. On the contrary, the resolution stated, "The Communist Parties of all capitalist countries must fight against military expenditures [war budgets] . . . against militarization measures taken by capitalist governments, especially the militarization of the youth."[33] This clause was but partly weakened by the proviso that approved Communist participation in the defense of the independence of a "weak state" attacked by "one or more big imperialist powers." The Communist Party of China was also authorized to "extend the front of the struggle for national liberation and to draw into it all the national forces that are ready to repulse the robber campaign of the Japanese." The Congress feebly intimated that the extreme measures of fighting the military laws in the capitalist countries, such as "refusal to appear for military service . . . so-called boycott of mobilization . . . sabotage in war plants," were not allowed. The sum total of such concessions fell far short of a clarion call to oppose Hitler and fascism by all and any means. On the contrary, there is an unmistakable caution against the Communists' rendering too much help to the European democracies in their effort, slow and feeble as it was, to bring their armaments up to the level of preparedness where they could meet the potential German challenge.

This is most striking when we compare the instructions to the Chinese Communists with those addressed to the clandestine German Party. The Chinese are instructed to fight the Japanese by any and all means, though in fact 1935 was the year when the Japanese were not pushing their aggression in China and the Chinese Communists were fighting hard to avoid annihilation at the hand of Chiang Kai-shek's forces. What were the German Communists urged to do? As the representative of the German Party said, "Work inside the fascist mass organizations must become our principal method."[34] The German Communists were urged to enter such organizations as the Nazi Labor Front (delicacy undoubtedly prevented mentioning the Storm Troopers), there to work for higher wages and other similar postulates. This policy was characterized by Dimitrov as the policy of the Trojan Horse, but the Greeks did not get into the belly of the horse just to stay there and argue about securing better accommodations. In October of the same year, speaking to the German Central Committee meeting in Brussels, Togliatti, as the representative of the Comintern, urged the German Communists to adopt the following slogans: "For the complete annulment of the Versailles Treaty. For the unification of all Germans, not through war but on a voluntary basis and by international agreement. For the abolition of the Polish Corridor."[35]

[33] *Ibid.*, p. 592.
[34] *Ibid.*, p. 240.
[35] *The Communist International*, XIII, No. 13 (March, 1936), 42.

It might be pointed out that these directives were combined with other slogans of a more inflammatory character calling for the overthrow of the Nazi regime and that, in view of Communism's being in shambles in Germany, the policy of lying low and exploiting the nationalist mood of the masses was a realistic and prudent one. But the over-all analysis of the policy imposed upon German Communism suggests strongly that the overthrow of Hitler in 1935–36 was *not* seen as a life-and-death necessity for the Soviet Union. On the contrary, collaboration with Germany was thought to be still possible and desirable. One of the slogans the German Communists were to propagate was "Re-establish agreement with the U.S.S.R."[36]

The Popular Front tactics thus fitted in with what in the light of all available information were the conclusions reached in Moscow about the international situation in mid-1935. The initial alarm and sense of isolation experienced in 1934 at the successes of fascism, at the prospects of fascism taking over France, and thus at the U.S.S.R. becoming an object of joint capitalist aggression, had by now abated. The alliance with France, it was felt, secured the Soviet Union from an immediate danger of the outbreak of a new imperialist war "which daily threatens humanity." But this motif had been heard even during the most peaceful days of the 1920's. What was characteristic was the qualification: "The acuteness of the imperialist contradictions renders the formation of an anti-Soviet bloc difficult at the present moment."[37] For the moment, the danger of war *in Europe* receded insofar as the Soviet Union was concerned. There seemed to be no reason to worry unduly about the state of French armaments. Though the policy of the balance of power had always been denounced by the Communists, in fact it had been one of the aims of Soviet policy in Europe. The resolutions of the Comintern expressed the apprehension, reasonable in view of the events of the next three years, that, thwarted in his attempt to mount a great coalition against the Soviet Union, Hitler might turn against some weaker opponent. Hence permission was extended for the Communists in a "weak country" to join in the defense of its independence. The German government was currently threatening Lithuania, which possessed the German-speaking area of Memel. Hitler's ambitions about Austria were, of course, common knowledge.

Insofar as other areas of the world were concerned, the Soviet Union had no direct interest in Abyssinia, currently threatened by Italy. Anyway, as we have seen, the Russians were firmly convinced that the British—for their own imperialist reasons, needless to say—were going to finish off Mussolini. But in the Soviets' lingering awe of the British empire, there

[36] *Ibid.*, p. 43.
[37] *Seventh Congress of the Communist International,* p. 589.

was certainly no desire to see its power grow, and the British Communists remained opposed to rearmament. In a speech in the House of Commons, its sole Communist member declared: "You cannot ever hope to combat the war spirit that has remained in Germany by building up armaments. . . . We say, not a penny for armaments."[38] The Anglo-German Naval Agreement of June 1935, in which the British acquiesced in the German violation of the armament clauses of the Versailles Treaty—and without a prior concurrence of France—must have aroused the deepest Soviet suspicions.[39] Hitler, blocked in France, might still strike a bargain with the British Conservatives.

The area of deepest concern in 1935 was again the Far East. The attempt to have the United States play a role there that France had assumed in Europe, i.e., of a formal ally discouraging the potential aggressor, had failed. Russia's sale of the Chinese Eastern Railway had lowered the tension with Japan but had not removed it. The most perplexing element was the apparent *modus vivendi* arrived at between the Nationalist Chinese government and the Japanese. Following the loss of Manchuria, Chiang Kai-shek adopted a policy which not unfairly might be likened to that taken by Lenin after Brest Litovsk: he acquiesced in a territorial loss in order to consolidate his power over the rest of the country rather than to persist in a militarily hopeless war. If this historical parallel occurred to the Soviet leaders, it did not make them appreciate the policy of China's leader. Peace with Japan enabled Chiang to concentrate on fighting the Chinese Communists. His offensive in 1934 forced them to embark on the famous Long March, abandoning Kwangsi Province to Nationalist troops. Their new area in northwest China might come under attack by superior forces and Soviet China would become obliterated. Even more alarming was the possibility that without a further involvement in China, the Japanese militarists might direct their aggression against the Soviet Union or her satellite Mongolia.

To put it bluntly, the renewal of hostilities between China and Japan was clearly in the Soviet interest. At the Comintern Congress, while the speeches of all other Communist representatives breathed a genuine desire for peace and nobody as much as mentioned the possibility or desirability of a preventive war against Hitler, the Chinese delegate asserted "the earnest desire of the Chinese people to take up arms against the Japanese oppressors."[40] This desire led him to express the eagerness of the Communists to join with the Kuomintang provided the latter would stop its acquiescence in the Japanese conquests. The previous dilatoriness of the

[38] *The Communist International*, XIII, No. 1, 70.
[39] The agreement granted the Germans the right to build up to 35 per cent of the British strength in all categories and up to parity in submarines.
[40] *Seventh Congress of the Communist International*, p. 291.

Chinese Party in working for a coalition with the Nationalists was subjected to self-criticism. It would be absurd to believe that this desire of the Chinese Communists to renew fighting between China and Japan, much as it was probably an expression of their nationalism and self-interest, did not correspond exactly to Soviet wishes.

2. *Toward the War: 1936–39*

Much of the apparent equilibrium reached in Europe with the signing of the Franco-Soviet alliance and the entrance of the U.S.S.R. into the League of Nations lay in ruins by the middle of 1936. The League of Nations proved to be not even a "brake on aggression," as Stalin had put it. Abyssinia had been conquered; sanctions against Italy were to be lifted; Mussolini, far from committing suicide, as Litvinov with some relish had expected him to do, was very much alive. Italy was for the next five years to be taken seriously as a Great Power. The Abyssinian affair had alienated her from Great Britain with which, until 1934, her relations had been of the best. She would no longer stand as a guarantor of Austria's independence. Mussolini would no longer view Hitler as a parvenu imitator but as a partner in profitable blackmail and, eventually, as a model for emulation.

The most fundamental change was caused by the entrance of German army units into the Rhineland on March 7, 1936. Demilitarized under Versailles and under the German pledges at Locarno, the Rhineland had lain open to French troops in the event of war and had thus made practical the French guarantees to Poland and Czechoslovakia. Given the military technology of the time or (which amounts to the same thing) the currently held military dogmas, German remilitarization of the area would make those guarantees of very limited value. Germany now would fortify her western frontier, and Poland or Czechoslovakia could be overrun while France and Germany would settle down to prolonged position warfare behind their fortifications, as was actually to be the case during the "phony war" of 1939–40. Remilitarization of the Rhineland thus at one stroke abolished France's ascendancy on the Continent and deprived her of the possibility of pursuing an independent foreign policy. It was clear in 1936 that in two or three years France would be incapable of bringing effective aid to an eastern ally attacked by Germany; and, if attacked herself, under the very best of circumstances she could stave off the attack only with British help. Nobody in 1936 could or did foresee the fatal weakness of the French army in 1940 or the lethargy and disorganization of its leadership, but the situation of 1939, i.e., France's eastern ally (Poland) being overrun while her army was contained by the German defenses, *was* foreseeable. The value of an alliance does not lie in the promise of *eventual* victory; it must rest on the assumption of additional security, a reasonable guarantee that while the war is being fought the territory of the given state will not be occupied by the enemy. That assumption could no longer be entertained by France's eastern allies following the remilitarization of the Rhineland. The usual platitude is in this case dramatically correct: March 7, 1936, was the turning point in the history of Europe between the two wars.

The French failure to act decisively in answer to Hitler's coup can be discussed here but briefly and only insofar as it bore on the Soviet position. The story in its main outline is well known: the French generals would not move without a mobilization, and with general elections forthcoming shortly the French government would not authorize one. The British reaction to the violation of the whole Locarno system on which peace had been based in Europe was epitomized by the fatuous headline of an editorial in *The Times*, "A chance to rebuild": Hitler had only done what any self-respecting government would seek to do—to exercise full sovereignty in its own territory.

Hitler accompanied his thrust with an olive branch and with an extensive apology which alleged that the Franco-Soviet alliance (which the Chamber of Deputies had just ratified on February 28) constituted a violation of Locarno, thus rendering Germany free of her obligations. In his speech, Hitler expanded on his favorite theme: the French pact opened the door to Soviet interference in all of Europe. Soviet Russia was not merely a state but an exponent of world revolution. Hitler's bluff worked, but if the objective of his diplomacy at the time was to isolate the Soviet Union, then the march on the Rhineland had the opposite effect: now directly threatened, France would cling to her Soviet alliance, hoping that if the worst came Russian manpower would relieve the threat to Paris as it had in 1914.

The Soviet reaction to Hitler's move had to be one of concern. *Militarily*, the value of the alliance with France was sharply decreased if Hitler could get away with it. But *diplomatically*, as the means of preventing Hitler's attack on the U.S.S.R., the value of the treaty was if anything enhanced. This was subtly suggested by Molotov in an interview with a French newspaperman: "The remilitarization of the Rhineland undoubtedly accentuates the danger to the countries east of Germany. . . . However, the entry of German troops into the Rhineland . . . is in the first place a threat to Germany's western neighbors, France and Belgium. We understand the disquiet which this action has aroused in those countries."[41] For their own protection, the French would have to cling to the alliance rather than to listen to Hitler's siren call.

[41] Degras, *op. cit.*, III, 182.

Litvinov, in a speech to the Council of the League, which had assembled in London to consider the Rhineland question, took a line that could not be faulted: Germany had violated her obligations; unless the League took some action it would become a laughing stock, or even "harmful because it may lull the vigilance of the nations and give rise to illusions."[42] Litvinov expressed the readiness of his government to join in any and all actions that the Council might undertake on the motion of the signatories to the violated Locarno agreement. His speech warned Britain and France not to agree to the new treaties Hitler proposed, having just torn up the old ones.[43] They might delude themselves that Hitler merely wanted a free hand in the east, but "his attacks on the Soviet Union may, so far, serve merely as a screen for aggression which is being prepared against other States."[44] The same motif, the same apprehension more openly expressed, appeared in Ambassador Maisky's speech of March 19: "I know that there are people who think that war can be localized. These people think that given definite agreements war may break out in (shall we say?) the east or southeast of Europe but can pass by without affecting the countries of Western Europe. . . . This is the greatest of delusions. . . . Peace is indivisible."[45]

If from the perspective of 1939 and the Nazi-Soviet pact such warnings appear Machiavellian, in the context of 1936 they were quite natural. An even more authoritative spokesman for Soviet policy, Molotov, reaffirmed at the same time that the road to improved Soviet-German relations was not entirely blocked. Again, this was entirely aboveboard and expressed nothing to which the French could take exception. But it is interesting that Molotov chose to express this view in a very coy fashion. In the interview quoted above, he said, "There is a tendency among certain sections of the Soviet public toward an attitude of thoroughgoing irreconcilability to the present rulers of Germany, particularly because of the ever-repeated hostile speeches of German leaders against the Soviet Union. But the chief tendency, and the one determining the Soviet Government's policy, thinks an improvement in Soviet-German relations possible."[46] This, one might think, was a very transparent and awkward bait. Who could ignore that "those sections of the Soviet public" which might be even remotely suspected of being opposed to the "chief tendency" of Soviet policy were being liquidated right and left? But, in fact, it was a shrewd thrust designed to appeal to that childish passion for intrigue which was incongruously

---

[42] *Ibid.*, p. 171.

[43] The German proposals were for a twenty-five year pact of nonaggression with France and Belgium, to be guaranteed by Britain and Italy.

[44] Degras, *op. cit.*, III, 177.

[45] *Ibid.*, p. 179.

[46] *Ibid.*, p. 184.

part of the Nazi make-up. Somebody in Berlin might prick up his ears: maybe the opprobrious tone held about Germany and Hitler was the work of "Jews" like Litvinov and the "fanatical Communists" of the Comintern? Stalin, a "Russian nationalist," was still seeking ways to come to an understanding with Germany. The somewhat unnecessary air of mystification that accompanied Soviet approaches to Germany in the years before the war, inquiries by obscure trade officials when the regular diplomats might have done equally well—all this was calculated to exploit that quirk of the Nazi psychology. The barely suggested hint that Stalin was trying to overcome the intrigues of his diplomats was perhaps also likely to appeal to a certain trade-union feeling of a fellow dictator: Hitler was having troubles with his own diplomats and generals, who for all their servility could not always understand his sublime schemes and inspirations.[47]

For the moment, Molotov's hint was but an apparent digression which must have passed unnoticed in the West. The formal gist of Molotov's remark was similar in substance though milder in tone to Litvinov's statement: yes, the Soviet Union would welcome collaboration even with Hitler's Germany provided the latter would abide by international agreements and, say, rejoin the League of Nations. The U.S.S.R. would stand by France if attacked, according to the terms of the Franco-Soviet alliance. "Help would be given in accordance with the Treaty and with the political situation as a whole." The latter phrase referred unmistakably to the fact that the U.S.S.R. had no common frontier with Germany. In March 1936 the offer of Soviet help to France if attacked was cold comfort. A French military move into the Rhineland could not conceivably be described as defense against German aggression. Was the U.S.S.R. ready to support her French ally if, in answer to the German violation of the Locarno agreements, the French started military action against Germany and became involved in a protracted military conflict? That question remained carefully unanswered.

Nothing, then, would suggest that in March 1936 the Soviets desired the destruction of Hitler or prodded the French to take the military action that, in the opinion of many observers, would have made Hitler back down over the Rhineland and possibly led to his overthrow. The Polish government, though currently engaged in a flirtation with Germany, declared its willingness to assist France should the French army march. The Soviet government limited itself to the declaration that it would support sanctions if they were ordained by the League Council and desired by the Locarno powers. But it was common knowledge that neither Britain nor Italy would support sanctions. The League Council decided gravely that

[47] We shall see how with Roosevelt at Yalta Stalin was to play the role of a fellow politician in trouble: were he to desist from the Russian claims on Poland, his Ukrainian and Byelorussian subjects would be angry!

Germany did in fact violate a treaty. Versailles was dead; the last occasion to stop Hitler cheaply passed, never to return.[48]

There can be no doubt that the Russians deemed the destruction of the Versailles system and the practical collapse of what had been left of the idea of collective security a threat to the Soviet Union. That the outlines of the future Nazi-Soviet pact were already in 1936 firmly in Stalin's mind is, however, a piece of fantasy. The most logical explanation of Soviet policy in 1936–37 is the simplest one: confronted with a terrible danger, the Soviets felt a desperate need to keep all the options open, hoping that one of them would enable the U.S.S.R. to postpone or avoid an actual entanglement in war. It still ran against the grain for the Soviet leaders to believe that in the case of war against Germany they would get effective help, as distinguished from diplomatic maneuvers, paper alliances, etc., from the West. An overthrow of Hitler in 1936 might have been a mixed blessing. His successors might be the conservatives and militarists, and while those in the past had shown themselves favorably inclined toward the Rapallo policy, now thwarted in the West, they might turn their expansionist tendencies eastward, without Hitler's pyrotechnics but with a greater acquiescence from France and Britain. Too deep an involvement in an anti-Hitler campaign might lead the Soviet Union to the position where, abandoned by the West, she would face alone the onslaught of German militarism. One finds it difficult to sympathize with Stalin and his confederates under any circumstances. But the strain of the 1936–39 international situation must have been even harder on them than on the Western statesmen. They could have few illusions as to the possibility of a permanent appeasement of Hitler or the lasting value of any treaty or formal engagement. Deep suspicion of any and every capitalist government was ingrained in their nature. Every possible solution appeared to contain a trap, every move on the international chessboard was attended by dangers. One remembers Trotsky's dictum that an ally has to be watched like an enemy.

The strivings for an agreement with Germany, never entirely abandoned, brought no concrete results in 1936 and 1937. On the contrary, Hitler's tone grew more strident and menacing. The Führer would soliloquize about the benefits that would accrue to Germany if she could have

---

[48] The case that the French intervention could not have solved anything *in the long run* is argued brilliantly but perversely by a British historian: "The French army could march into Germany, it could exact promises of good behavior from the Germans; and then it would go away. The situation would remain the same as before, or, if anything, worse—the Germans more resentful and restless than ever." A. J. P. Taylor, *The Origins of the Second World War* (London and New York, 1962), p. 101. To this one may rejoin, with Lord Keynes: "In the long run, we will all be dead."

the fertile plains of the Ukraine at her disposal. There was some feeling that Hitler's bark was worse than his bite, but the Soviets could not be sure.[49] The signing of an Anti-Comintern Pact between Japan and Germany on November 25, 1936, appeared to confirm the worst Soviet apprehensions. The pact was actually empty of any practical content and filled only with high-sounding phrases about the dangers of international Communism and the two countries' resolve to concert their actions to combat them. Both Germany and Japan were embarking on the diplomatic game in which each partner intended the other to contain the U.S.S.R. so that he could scoop up easier conquests, the game that was to bring both disaster to Hitler and the Japanese militarists and triumphs to the U.S.S.R. and world Communism. But this outcome could not be foretold, and the Soviet sense of danger must have been heightened.

The Franco-Soviet pact remained, though not implemented by a military convention, the most solid guarantee against a German attack. But apart from the Soviets' traditional distrust, political circumstances in France made the real value of the pact increasingly dubious in their eyes. The remilitarization of the Rhineland made the treaty more important than ever for the French. But the victory of the Popular Front, the growth in Communist votes and influence in the election, and the wave of sit-in strikes and social reforms that followed (mild by our current standards, revolutionary to the French *bourgeoisie* of the period) alarmed a large segment of the French public.[50] The Civil War in Spain increased the polarization of French political life. The alliance with France and the Popular Front government had removed the Soviet fear that France might become an accomplice of Hitler's—the original reason for the treaty—but even a less suspicious regime might well in the fall of 1936 have doubted the efficacy of the alliance in preventing Hitler from embarking on an eastern adventure.

The great purge of the 1930's, which reached its climax in the public trials of the alleged right-wing and left-wing conspirators between 1936 and 1938 and in the execution of the leading military figures in 1937, was undoubtedly a very important factor in estimates of Russia's current

[49] To pursue this metaphor, Litvinov retold in one of his speeches the story of the man who was frightened by a barking dog; on being assured that barking dogs do not bite, he replied that he realized that, but did the dog?

[50] The French Communist Party played an ambiguous role in the strikes and waves of socialist disorder that gripped France following the elections in May. To be sure, the Communists must have been afraid to put too much of a brake on the spontaneous strike action for fear of losing some of their influence. But, following the German attack on Russia in 1941, any strike, any hint that even the most justified aspirations of the workers in an Allied country might come before increased production was branded by local Communists as direct help to Hitler.

strength made both by her potential friends and by her enemies. Several aspects of the purge and trials are related to the international situation. While the main reasons for them are to be sought in Russia's internal politics and Stalin's own psychology, the scenario of the trials and the crimes attributed to the accused (to which, of course, they confessed) bore the imprint of the desperately dangerous international situation. The accused, followers whether of Trotsky or of others, were made to confess to a fantastic variety of treasonous designs not only against Stalin and the Party but against their state and nation. Several of them were identified as outright agents of foreign intelligence services. The states that allegedly employed these veteran Bolsheviks were primarily Japan and Germany, but some of the accused were linked to Great Britain and Poland. France and the United States were exempt from the corruptors of the Bolshevik élite, an amusing testimony in the first case to Bolshevik delicacy on account of the alliance, and in the second to their dismissal of the United States as a "serious" state insofar as foreign relations were concerned. Who would think seriously that the Americans could manage a respectable intelligence service!

The charges, often appalling in their absurdity and crudity, still reflected Stalin's historical sense and consequent apprehensions. Russia's defeats in World War I had enabled initially tiny political movements first to complete the demoralization of the armed forces and then to seize power. Now an attack upon the Soviet Union would undoubtedly bring, at least at first, catastrophic defeats. Hence any potential and conceivable focus of opposition within the Party and the army had to be extirpated, any future criticism of the regime had to be branded outright treason. Nobody would be left in any position of influence who would be inclined to say: "Would we be in this position if Trotsky or Bukharin were running things?"

The scenario, or the act of accusation, paradoxically included the Soviet leaders' own estimate as to how their country might be overcome and their regime destroyed. A group of traitors in high Party and state positions would seize the government by a violent coup. They would assure themselves of foreign support by ceding to their imperialist employers huge areas of the Soviet Union. The territories mentioned in this connection included invariably the Ukraine, sometime Byelorussia, and the Soviet Far East. One is struck by the fact that the charges are similar to what the *enemies* of the Bolsheviks claimed was the role of Lenin and his partisans at the time of Brest Litovsk. They also had been "German agents" repaying their debts to the foreign masters by cession of vast areas of the empire. But beyond that ironic parallel the trials and charges presented the enemies of the Soviet Union—one might think gratuitously—with a reminder of the Achilles' heel of the regime: its nationality problem. In 1937, no more than in 1917 or 1812, could Russia be conquered militarily in the usual sense of the word. But, as in 1918, the country could be stripped of its outlying territories, peopled largely by non-Russians, the granary and mineral resources of the Ukraine and the Caucasus could be detached, and the rest of Russia could be left to vegetate as a very inferior state. Leaving apart the question whether Stalin and his associates believed in those tales, why should a regime advertise the fantastic extent of this treachery at home and the most effective way of undermining the regime?[51] Dismissing all subtle and oversubtle explanations, one must see in this nightmarish sequence a huge public-relations blunder, a reflection of the fact that for all its guile and perspicacity, the Soviet regime had its blind or, more exactly speaking, paranoid side.

Many Soviet citizens undoubtedly believed the truth of the charges and confessions; the foreign Communists and fellow travellers also, with few exceptions, swallowed the stories of Trotsky being a German agent and of the highest officials of the state and Party plotting to assassinate Stalin, Voroshilov, Molotov, and other worthies.[52] But among foreign statesmen and on foreign general staffs, whether friendly or hostile, the impression produced by the purges was disastrous. The credit accumulated by Litvinov's diplomacy and by Russia's industrialization was largely dissipated. The hesitations, then the unwillingness, of the British and French to collaborate more closely with Russia during this period is usually ascribed to ideological scruples and the fear of Communism, but at least equally potent was the conviction that a country whose internal affairs were exhibiting such fantastic perturbations could not be of much value as an ally or much of a threat as an enemy. Typical of the views of "well-informed foreigners" was the following given in a lecture by the German ambassador in Moscow, Count von der Schulenburg, before the German War Academy in 1937: "There is no doubt that the wave of murder and persecution that is still unspent has gravely shaken the organism of the Soviet state and

[51] It can be argued that the purge of the size of the one between 1936 and 1938 could not be concealed. But certainly very few people abroad realized the extent of the sufferings imposed by the great collectivization of 1929–32. Also, the publicity given to the three great purge trials (of Zinoviev, etc., in August 1936; of the "Trotskyite Anti-Soviet Center" in January 1937; of Bukharin, Rykov, et al., in 1938) and to the execution of leading military figures in June 1937 was intentional, the proceedings of the trials being translated and circulated abroad.

[52] To be along with Stalin on the list of the intended victims of the Trotskyites was at the time a mark of high standing. When one such list did *not* include Molotov rumors began to circulate immediately that the Prime Minister was being purged.

is weakening the political prestige of the Soviet Union. . . . Today the
Soviet Union is politically and economically heading for a depression."[53]
Schulenburg, being a cautious diplomat, qualified his diagnosis by stating
that one could not write off Russia as a major international factor in the
future. But for the present, the implication was clear, the regime was too
much absorbed by its internal problems to play a decisive role in international affairs. The first year of Hitler's major aggression, 1938, saw
this confidential report by the German chargé d'affaires in Paris:

> During the past year serious doubts have arisen in respect to the firm-
> ness of the Soviet regime, the strength of the Red Army, and the good
> faith of the Soviet government. The execution of generals whom the
> French General Staff regarded as good officers and the numerous trials
> of former leading Bolsheviks demonstrated to the French public
> opinion the precariousness of a regime in which prominent persons,
> as asserted by the regime itself, had for years been engaged in sabotage
> and treason. . . . Under such circumstances the question was frequently
> asked whether in view of the present military and political situation,
> the Soviet Union was a useful and reliable ally.[54]

With such reports reaching the German Foreign Office, it was easy for
Hitler, as against the objections of his nervous diplomats and generals, to
discount Russia's might and to embark on the first phase of his conquests.
At the famous conference of November 5, 1937, recorded in the Hossbach
Memorandum, Hitler in the presence of his commanders-in-chief laid down
his ominous intentions concerning Austria and Czechoslovakia. What
primarily worried the Führer, and even more his generals, was what the
French army might do should the French choose to intervene (which he
did not believe they would). Russia in contrast was dismissed almost
contemptuously. "Military intervention by Russia must be countered by
the swiftness of our operations; however, whether such an intervention
was a practical contingency at all, was in view of Japan's attitude more
than doubtful."[55] Thus the French army, which was to crumble like a
house of cards in 1940, was seen as a great danger, the huge Russian army
was dismissed. If worse came to worst, it could be neutralized by the
threat of Japanese action.

That such an estimate could be made by Hitler and not vigorously
questioned by the military men in his presence (one of whom, Blomberg,
had been involved in the military collaboration with the Russians in the
1920's) was directly due to the impression produced by the purges.[56] If

[53] *Documents on German Foreign Policy, 1918–45*, Series D, I (Washington,
1949), 900.

[54] *Ibid.*, p. 1071.

[55] *Ibid.*, p. 36.

[56] We shall discuss why and to what extent the German estimate of the
Russian potential changed by 1939. See below, pp. 272–79.

the accusations produced in the trials were true, then the whole political and military machine of the Soviet state was permeated by treason. If they were but invention (and the Germans had good reason to know that insofar as they related to treasonous activities with themselves, they were fictitious), what could one think of the stability and resolution of the regime that indulged in such phantasmagoric procedures?

Most fundamentally of all, the purges affected the Soviet regime's estimate of its *own* vulnerability. If the initial motivation was a rational if cruel decision to destroy any *latent* opposition that might raise its head in the case of war, then the vicious circle of terror could not but end in persuading the regime that it was in fact in the presence of a widespread, all-pervasive network of treason and subversion. In the parlance of modern social science, the extent of terror became dysfunctional from the point of view of the leaders. Or, in plain English, the leaders became convinced that their country was much weaker and more vulnerable in time of war than was to prove to be the case. The Soviet leaders' public pronouncements continued to exude confidence and faith in the Soviet defense forces. Probing operations by the Japanese in the Far East were to be met with spirited counteraction. But as the events of 1939–41 were to show conclusively, the necessity of avoiding involvement in a major war dominated the thinking of the policy-makers to an even greater extent than prior to 1936.

The inherent caution of Soviet policies was well illustrated by the Russian attitude toward the Civil War in Spain. The war—a traumatic experience for liberals and progressives throughout the world, a real milestone in the Western left's attitude toward fascism[57]—was not allowed to deflect Soviet policy from its main course. Both Italy and Germany stressed from the beginning their ideological commitment to the rebel cause, and, having signed the fatuous nonintervention agreement proposed by England and France, publicized their help to the insurgent Nationalists. The Soviet attitude on the contrary was one of discretion. The U.S.S.R. signed the nonintervention pact, though Soviet spokesmen denounced the lack of force in a nonintervention agreement which, without inhibiting Germany and Italy, put restraints on help to the legitimate government of the Spanish Republic.

[57] It is not too much to say that the Civil War brought the socialists and liberals in the West from an attitude of *passive* dislike of the regimes of Italy and Germany into militant opposition to them. Prior to July 1936, the attitude of British socialists and progressives, for example, toward Hitler was tempered by their pacifist inclinations and the feeling that Germany had legitimate grievances. Nobody was more opposed to a forcible intervention against Hitler's remilitarization of the Rhineland than the Labour Party. The Spanish Civil War was the source of the feeling that led to the stand the British left took in 1939.

Still, the war in Spain was a major complication for Soviet international policies. Though the insurrection started on July 28, it was not until October 4 that Stalin in a telegram to the Secretary General of the Spanish Communist Party expressed support for the cause of the Spanish Republic. Despite all the *Realpolitik* of the U.S.S.R., it was clearly inconceivable to withhold public support in a struggle that ranged the left against the right throughout the world, or to lend substance to the consistent propaganda of the Trotskyites who alleged Stalin's betrayal of the Communist cause. Yet the complete identification of Communism with the cause of Spain was almost as undesirable as a victory of fascism. For the Soviet Union was still in the midst of an effort to secure an alliance and friendship with Britain and France, to appear as a proponent of peace and democracy rather than exporter of revolution. A letter sent to the Spanish Prime Minister, Largo Caballero, in December 1936, over the signatures of Stalin, Voroshilov, and Molotov, was almost pathetic in urging the Spanish Republicans to eschew social radicalism, to enlist the middle class on their side, and to spare no effort "to prevent the enemies of Spain from presenting it as a Communist Republic." Much against their natural inclinations, the Spanish Communists were ordered to restrain their anarchist and left socialist allies from pursuing too radical policies. The polarization of political feeling in Britain and France, the fact that under the impact of Spain many anti-German elements in those countries were re-examining their general attitude toward fascism, was obviously a source of profound concern in Moscow.

Hence the Soviet government was at pains to channel all its help, insofar as manpower was concerned, through the Comintern. Italy and Germany sent sizable contingents of their regular troops and air forces to fight on Franco's side. As against these "volunteers," the Communists provided the International Brigades, recruited all over the world but not in Russia. It was a fantastic incongruity that while Thälmann and Abraham Lincoln battalions were fighting on the Republican side, no outfit in the International Brigades bore the names of Lenin or Stalin. The U.S.S.R. did not spare military and technical advisers; munitions as well as medical supplies were provided. But no Soviet army units were committed to a head-on collision with the German and Italian forces fighting quite openly on the insurgents' side.

With the war moving to its bloodiest phase in 1937, another worry entered the Soviet mind. Among the fantastic profusion of Spanish radical parties, one bearing the initials POUM had a fairly clear Trotskyite coloring. It was not out of the range of possibility that the POUM and the anarchists, especially strong in Catalonia, might coalesce to create a semi-Trotskyite regional regime, thus creating even if temporarily a political focus for the heresy. Hence the systematic campaign of assassination conducted by agents of the Soviet secret police and the Spanish Communists against Trotskyites and declared anti-Communists among the anarchists, a campaign that led to incidents of civil war *within* the Republican camp.[58] The purge in turn spread to the Communists themselves, and in view of the Stalinist atmosphere, it is not surprising that most of the Soviet officials connected with the aid to Spain fell victims to the purge. Many foreign Communists engaged in the struggle were in years to come to suffer for their participation in the Civil War, and an amazing number of the victims of the post–World War II purges in the Communist countries were veterans of what at the time had been presented as an epic struggle of Communism against fascism.

The Spanish Civil War thus helps to expose various threads of Soviet policies, internal and external, of the time. It shows first the essentially defensive character of Soviet foreign policy: nothing was further from the Soviet government's intentions than a satellite Spain. The conquest of a backward nation would have been more than offset by the almost inevitable consequent hostility of France and Britain. Insofar as any advice from Moscow could be effective under the conditions of civil war and mutual slaughter, this advice was on the side of moderation in social and economic policy, extending in the case of Stalin's letter to such proposals as guaranteeing foreign citizens' property in Spain, the use of parliamentary methods, etc. It is equally exaggerated on the other hand to credit Stalin with the desire to sabotage the Spanish Republic. Victory by Franco could not be desired by Moscow, and to the extent this could be avoided through Soviet war matériel and advisers and instructors, the U.S.S.R. did help within the bounds of prudence. It was perhaps realized in Moscow (as it was in Berlin, though evidently not in Rome) that Franco's victory would bring to fascism increased prestige but not necessarily military or political advantages.[59] The history of Spain offered abundant warning that Spaniards no matter what their ideological complexion do not readily become tools of foreign powers.

Another moral of the Spanish story was how unfeigned was Moscow's fear of Trotskyism and how seriously was viewed the possibility that the detested creed might obtain a foothold in a European country. The struggle against the real or alleged Trotskyites in Spain came close to

[58] Many of the clashes between the anarchists and the Communists were due to the former being naturally averse to discipline and insisting on what was to the Communists an untimely radicalism.

[59] In his November 1937 conference, Hitler, who had already had a discouraging time trying to persuade the Nationalists to turn over various mineral properties to Germany, said rather perceptively that the continuation of the Civil War would be more to Germany's advantage than a speedy victory by the right.

overshadowing the struggle against the Nationalists. The Executive Committee of the Comintern in its proclamation on the Civil War spoke unashamedly: "Since the Trotskyists in the interest of fascism are carrying on subversive work in the rear of the republican troops, the presidium approves the policy of the party aimed at the complete and final destruction of Trotskyism in Spain as essential to the victory over fascism."[60] The struggle against Trotskyism destroyed much of the prestige the Soviet Union and Communism were acquiring in liberal circles as the only effective helpers of the Spanish Republic. But just as the Soviet regime equated the interest of world Communism with that of the U.S.S.R., so it equated the interest of the ruling group with that of its country. By that logic, Trotsky was as dangerous as Hitler. A hunted exile with small groups of supporters dispersed all over the world was viewed as a grave danger. Superfluous to say, not a shred of evidence has ever been uncovered linking any of the Trotskyites to German or Italian agents. But Stalin and his colleagues were haunted by history. Barely twenty years before, another exile had returned to Russia to lead a handful of supporters, and within six months they were in power.

Ironically enough, the Spanish Civil War shows again how both the strengths and weaknesses of Soviet policy helped the cause of Russian diplomacy. Though the fearful danger of Communism was forever on the lips of German, Japanese, and Italian spokesmen, though the Berlin-Rome Axis was now supplemented by the Anti-Comintern Pact—all in the name of defense of Western civilization against the Soviet danger—the limited Soviet performance in Spain could not but reassure the policy planners in the Axis capitals and in Tokyo. And the obvious irrationality of the hunt for the Trotskyites, the willingness of the regime to lacerate its own wounds, presented yet another reassurance of its weakness and ineffectiveness. We know that in the early days of his regime, Hitler was gravely concerned over the industrialization of Russia and over the possibility of what it might do within a decade to the Soviet Union's military potential. But his conferences in 1937 and 1938 reflected a new preoccupation: the pace of French and especially British rearmament would by 1943–45 make an adventurous policy by the Axis extremely risky and would strip Germany of her initial advantage in modernizing her armed forces. Russia could wait. To the German general staff, the Russian problem now must have appeared reminiscent of World War I. Then, the German armies, whenever they confronted Russia, scored easy victories, but the drain on German manpower and resources and the vast distances involved robbed them of the chance to score a decisive victory in the west.

[60] Jane Degras, ed., *The Communist International, 1919–1943: Documents,* III (London and New York, 1965), 398.

Even the occupation of the Ukraine following Brest Litovsk had eaten up the troops which, had they been available in France during the great spring offensive of 1918, might have tilted the balance. Over and above Stalin's diplomatic moves and Hitler's "intuitions," a strange fatality pushed events toward the crucial turns of 1939 and 1941.

The same paradoxical view of Russia's strengths and weaknesses which now influenced the policies of Germany appears to have inspired Japan's military leaders. Russia was too strong (strength, to repeat, meant in this connection vast distances and unlimited manpower) to be attacked, too weak to be considered a major obstacle to the aggressor's aims. To be sure, there were major differences in the picture in the Far East. The Japanese, without launching a war, were continuously probing Soviet resolve and preparedness through a series of border "incidents" that were to grow at times into sizable military operations. Consequently the Soviet line toward Japan was much harder. It would have been fatal to give the slightest indication of weakness, the merest glimmer of a painless victory.

In a situation replete with ironies, perhaps the most vivid one was that the Anti-Comintern Pact, bad as it was for the Soviet leaders' nerves, actually decreased the chances of the Japanese *or* the Germans attacking the U.S.S.R. Each partner assumed complacently that the threat of the other would be sufficient to keep Russia from interfering in projects dear to its heart—Hitler's in central Europe, those of the Japanese in China. A secret addendum to the treaty specified that should one of the signatories become the object "of an unprovoked attack or threat of attack" by the U.S.S.R., the other would take "no measures which would tend to ease the situation of the Union of Soviet Socialist Republics" and that neither of them would sign a treaty with Russia without the other's consent.[61] This tortuous language (who in 1936 could believe that the U.S.S.R. could make an "unprovoked attack" on Japan or Germany?) already contained a hint of mutual bad faith. And to be sure there was to be no honor among thieves. Germany was to conclude a "political agreement" with the U.S.S.R. in 1939, and the Japanese reciprocated prettily in 1941. But those big betrayals were, practically from the time of signing the pact, anticipated by smaller ones. The renewal of the Sino-Japanese war in 1937 provoked understandable anguish in Berlin: Japan was supposed to stand guard over Russia rather than plunge deeper into the bottomless morass of China. The Japanese on their part were grieved by the continued presence of German military advisers to Chiang Kai-shek and German military supplies going to China. Where was the solemn resolve of the two powers to save the world from the evils and dangers of Com-

[61] *Documents on German Foreign Policy, 1918–45*, Series D, I, 734.

munism? In a wire to the embassy in Tokyo, the German State Secretary explained humorlessly, "We have given the Japanese clearly to understand that they cannot invoke the Anti-Comintern Pact in their action in China, since the Pact does not have for its object the combatting of Bolshevism on the territory of a third state."[62]

Yet the threat of an attack by Japan could not be discounted by the Kremlin. And in 1937 this threat was obviously more imminent than that of a German attack. In Europe, Hitler had to destroy Poland or turn her into a satellite before mounting an offensive against Russia. In the Far East, Russia shared a common frontier with the would-be aggressor. The Soviets were well aware that some Japanese put the solution of the Soviet problem first on the list of priorities. In Europe there were prospective allies against Germany, and by the same token there was room for diplomatic maneuver vis-à-vis Hitler. The great hopes that the Soviet Union had put in the United States as a would-be ally or bargaining point vis-à-vis Japan were by 1937 almost entirely given up. Stalin never made Hitler's fatal mistake of contemptuously dismissing America entirely as a factor on the international scene. (After Bullitt, whose dislike of the Soviet Union had reached fantastic proportions, had departed the scene, Stalin received his successor, Joseph Davies. No such favor was granted even to the representative of Russia's official ally, France.) But for the time being it was realistically recognized that isolationism precluded any active role for the U.S. And France and Britain had by now become almost negligible as factors in the Far East.

Bleak though the situation was in the Far East, at the end of 1936 it had threatened to become even bleaker. Chiang Kai-shek still pursued what has been described here as his Brest Litovsk policy. Internal consolidation and especially the destruction of the Communist areas in northwestern China were to precede any attempt at rescuing Chinese territory from the Japanese invader. The Communists' proposals for a joint front against the Japanese, pressed since the Seventh Congress of the Comintern, were being rebuffed. On the contrary, direct negotiations were proceeding between the Nanking government and Tokyo, and German military advisers with Chiang were needless to say pressing him, under instructions from Berlin, to stabilize the informal truce with the Japanese. Any firm agreement between the Chinese and Japanese governments would have been a disaster to the Chinese Communists and a grave danger to the U.S.S.R.

It is against this background that the famous "Sian Incident" took place. Chiang Kai-shek was planning another campaign against the Chinese Communists. The troops to be used for this purpose were to be commanded by a former boss of Manchuria, Chang Hsueh-ling, one of the

[62] *Ibid.*, p. 742.

warlords currently in precarious alliance with Chiang Kai-shek. Whether it was the Manchurian background of the commander and his entourage or the Communist intrigues or both, he refused to fight his fellow Chinese. Chiang Kai-shek flew to Chang's base in December 1936 and was there promptly imprisoned. Negotiations followed with the participation of the Communist emissary Chou En-lai. Eventually Chiang was released, but only after he pledged to cease the fratricidal war and to take a strong anti-Japanese line. There followed further negotiations as to details of collaboration between the CCP and the Kuomintang for the achievement of a united front against Japan. These negotiations envisaged the subordination of the Red Army to Chiang Kai-shek's command and at least a formal dissolution of the Chinese Soviet Republic.

The mere fact of the negotiations and of Chiang Kai-shek's abandonment of his *modus vivendi* with Tokyo was an obvious incitement to the Japanese. On July 7 they struck. The attack, which within a short time brought most of the maritime and outlying areas under Japanese occupation, speeded up the collaboration between Chiang Kai-shek and the Communists. The latter, on September 22, 1937, declared their repudiation of the revolutionary program and their subordination to the government of the Chinese Republic. Thus the Sino-Japanese conflict resumed its violent phase which was to continue through World War II.

The renewal of hostilities between Japan and China was an undoubted triumph for Soviet policy. That some elements in the Chinese Communist Party balked at the collaboration with Chiang Kai-shek is possible, but the story that this collaboration was imposed by Moscow upon an unwilling Mao Tse-tung is most unlikely. The war saved the Communists from another and probably disastrous campaign by Chiang. Their subordination to the central government was to remain mainly on paper. The Japanese occupation was likely to and did in fact extend mainly to areas that had constituted Chiang's basis of support. Thus the Kuomintang was prevented from carrying on its Brest Litovsk policy, based on the assumption that the main task before it was that of consolidating power. With the insight which they did not lack when it came to policies of *other* totalitarian states, the Germans represented to their Japanese allies that their policies in China were bound to benefit the cause they were ostensibly fighting, i.e., Communism. And such was eventually the case.

Japan's involvement in China made a major move by her against the U.S.S.R. most unlikely. To be sure, World War II was to show that the Japanese were more than capable of operating militarily in other theaters besides China. The threat to the U.S.S.R. could not be discounted entirely until December 7, 1941. But in 1937 the best informed military opinion (i.e., German military circles) held that Japan's involvement in China would preclude full-scale hostilities with a major power. Japanese naval superiority, a vital factor though a temporary one in her successes in World War II, could not have been of much help in a campaign in Siberia. At any rate, following July 7, 1937, the Kremlin could breathe more freely.

The change in Soviet attitude toward Japan was instantaneous. In June 1937 there had been an unusually sharp border incident and an armed Russo-Japanese clash involving two islets in the Amur River. The Soviets withdrew from the area and acquiesced in their occupation by the Japanese. But once it became evident that the Japanese were involved in extensive operations in China, the Soviet attitude immediately became sharper. In August, the Chinese government and the U.S.S.R. signed a treaty of nonaggression and friendship. Soviet munitions, credits, and military instructors began again to flow to Kuomintang China. The extent of help was nicely balanced. Chiang had to be reassured that he was not entirely alone in his struggle and that the U.S.S.R. had abandoned for the moment any intention of expanding Communism in his country. Yet the help was not to be on a scale that would lead the Japanese army to reassess its list of priorities. The policy toward China was thoroughly unsentimental. There was no question of relinquishing the Soviet protectorate over Outer Mongolia. Another outlying Chinese province, Sinkiang, had for some time been in effect under an informal Soviet-Chinese condominium. The Soviet tone toward the Japanese in time grew harsher. In a speech on January 17, 1938, Zhdanov, then a man close to Stalin, criticized the *Narkomindel* for its toleration of "the insolent, hooligan, and provocative sallies of the agents of Japan and Manchukuo." Once more for the edification of foreign observers the Soviets tried to impart the lesson that there were conflicting ideas among their policy-makers: let Tokyo pay heed to the patient and persevering voice of Litvinov and the Foreign Commissariat, for there are people in the highest circles who would be ready to go much further in anti-Japanese measures.[63]

By 1938 the situation in the Far East still required the utmost watchfulness, but the danger of war which had appeared so imminent in 1933 and 1936 had passed. Europe once more occupied the main stage.

In February 1938 Hitler had his own purge of generals. He was, to his subsequent regret, incapable of acting as thoroughly as Stalin: dismissals rather than executions were his means. But by assuming the supreme command of the armed forces, Hitler went far in taking over

---

[63] It is no part of the argument that there were no differences of views among the Soviet leaders as to the direction and strategy of their foreign policies, to maintain which would be absurd. But everything we know about Stalinism entitles us to say categorically that none of this debate went on in public.

the control of one institution that had retained some measure of independence in Germany. The German generals in the years to come would still play with the idea of a *coup d'état*, but at each decisive point they would draw back. Anyway, from February 1938 the professional officers' objections could no longer play a *decisive* role in restraining Hitler's moves. The German high command's position was still strong enough in 1939 to be an important factor in Germany's agreement with Russia, but for all their professional caution and their loathing of Hitler, the German generals from now on influenced only details of his aggressive plans and were impotent to prevent or postpone them.

Yet another species of purge was going on at precisely the same time. Neville Chamberlain, now determined to put his philosophy of appeasement of dictators to a test, made the situation untenable for Anthony Eden, who resigned as Foreign Secretary.

Both events attracted intense interest in Moscow. From their previous contacts with the German generals, the Russians must have been well aware that the generals had been a restraining influence on Hitler, and above all many of them had been proponents of Soviet-German collaboration.[64] Chamberlain's assumption of actual direction of British foreign policy must have been greeted with mixed feelings. As the then ambassador to London, Ivan Maisky, makes clear in his memoirs (in general unreliable but credible enough on this point), insofar as foreign affairs were concerned Chamberlain produced the impression of innocence bordering on idiocy.[65] He was not likely to see through Hitler. But by the same token Chamberlain was clearly not a man to lead Britain into an anti-Soviet, German-led crusade. Maisky's memoirs, for all the ritual phrases about Chamberlain following his "class interests," well underline the fact that the prevailing impression he gave the Russians was one of sheer incompetence.

With the occupation of Austria in March 1938, Hitler passed to the second stage of his program, from the violations of Germany's treaty obligations to active aggression against neighboring states, this time still in the name of the ethnic principle of uniting all Germans in the Greater Reich. Austria's independence had been doomed since Mussolini had disinterested himself in her fate and submitted to Hitler's leadership. But

[64] Not for any sentimental reasons, as is sometimes alleged, but simply because the avoidance of a two-front war had come close to being dogma for them. Stalin's purges modified this opinion, but only in the sense described above, i.e., the Red Army was discounted as an offensive force. An involvement in the vast spaces of Russia still gave nightmares to the German general staff.

[65] One may still doubt that Churchill, whose acquaintance Maisky much cultivated despite Churchill's notorious anti-Soviet past, made the following remark in his presence: "Neville is a moron. He thinks one can ride a tiger." Ivan Maisky, *Memoirs of a Soviet Ambassador* (Moscow, 1966), II, 432.

the speed with which Hitler now began to execute his aggression time-table must have caught the Soviets by surprise. The *Anschluss* coincided with the last days of the purge trial of such notables as Bukharin, Rykov, and Krestinsky. No such trials were again to take place, though the purge continued for some time and was to destroy some members of the Polit-buro and some of the most prominent remaining Red Army leaders (notably Marshals Blyukher and Yegorov). With war no longer merely a possibility within a few years but an imminent danger, it must have been finally realized in Moscow that a *publicized* purge was creating a fatal impression abroad: Russia's importance either as an ally or as an enemy was being discounted. And, to be sure, with the Czechoslovak crisis ripening, Count Ernst von Weizsäcker, State Secretary for Foreign Affairs, one of the more level-headed men on the German side and fearful of Hitler's policies, said as much. In a confidential letter to a fellow German diplomat on May 30 he wrote: "Russia hardly exists in our calculations today. As long as Stalin makes himself as useful as now, we need not particularly worry about him as regards military policy."[66]

The Czechoslovak crisis was a direct outcome of the *Anschluss*. It be-came clear that Czechoslovakia, an outpost of France in central Europe, was next on Hitler's timetable and that the issue of the Sudeten Germans was being raised first to dismember her, then to destroy her.

The sequence of events that led to Munich cannot be considered here at length. Our interest lies mainly in the policies and attitudes of the Soviet Union. Munich is not only a historical event. It is still a hotly contested issue. As such, much of the discussion turns on the effect that France's and Britain's capitulation to Hitler had on the subsequent course of Soviet policy and what the U.S.S.R. would have done had the Western Powers stood by Czechoslovakia. The first problem, as we shall see, is largely spurious. As to the second, we lack definitive information that would entitle us to a categorical statement that the Soviet Union would or would not have intervened with her full forces on behalf of embattled Czechoslovakia and her Western allies. But on the basis of what we do know, there is no need to assume that the question posed itself so cate-gorically to the Soviet leaders. There was a whole gradation of steps possible for the Soviet Union in "fulfilling all [her] obligations under the Soviet-Czech Treaty," as her spokesmen pledged she would throughout the crisis, especially since she had no common frontier with either Germany or Czechoslovakia. Thus it is unnecessary to assume that Russia was ready to "betray" France and Czechoslovakia in case of war or, conversely, that every available Soviet soldier was to be thrown into the fight if Germany attacked.

[66] *Documents on German Foreign Policy, 1918–45*, Series D, I, 864.

The official Soviet reaction to the Austrian events came on March 17. A statement by Litvinov stressed the grave dangers lying in the future and the readiness of the Soviet government to consult with the states concerned as to the means of avoiding them. "It may be too late tomorrow, but today the time for it is not yet gone if all the states and the Great Powers in particular take a firm and unambiguous stand."[67] Litvinov specified Czechoslovakia as the area threatened. He took note also of the danger on the Polish-Lithuanian frontier.[68] Litvinov's initiative was courteously rejected by Lord Halifax. His Majesty's Government felt the undesirability of dividing Europe into two camps and of holding a conference that would pinpoint Germany as a would-be aggressor.

The Soviet move of March 17 is supremely important. First, the Western reaction to it must have convinced the Soviet policy-makers that chances were more than even that the Western Powers would give in. France had not reacted to a direct threat when Germany, then much weaker, had remilitarized the Rhineland. Was she now to respond at a much greater risk for the sake of an ally? Chamberlain's delusions about Hitler were well known.

The second important fact about the Soviet statement is that it meant exactly what it said. This was no call for a crusade against Hitler, for overthrowing him, or for wresting Austria from his grasp. The aim of the projected conference was to devise means "of checking the further development of aggression and of eliminating the increased danger of a new world massacre." The note reflected the Soviet belief, which was then shared by many in the West, that a firm enough guarantee of Czechoslovakia by the three Great Powers would make Hitler back down.[69] Hitler was still a masterful bluffer: a war could be avoided by a show of strength and resolution.

[67] Degras, *Soviet Documents on Foreign Policy*, III, 277.

[68] Following a border incident the Polish government addressed an ultimatum to Lithuania demanding an *establishment* of diplomatic relations (they had not existed in the past because of Lithuania's claims on Vilna). There was a suspicion (unjustified) that the Polish demands went further than that, and a feeling (justified) that the semi-authoritarian government of Poland was flexing its muscles at the expense of a small neighbor. Lithuania agreed to have normal relations, and thus passed the bizarre and unique incident in the annals of diplomacy, where the threat of war was used to procure an exchange of diplomatic representatives.

[69] We now know that this belief was erroneous. Hitler was determined to have his way come what may. What is possible, but barely so, is that a firm stand by Britain, France, and Russia, or even the first two, would have emboldened his generals to overthrow him rather than to plunge into a world war. Whether the latter was a real possibility is discussed in John Wheeler-Bennett, *The Nemesis of Power* (London and New York, 1953), pp. 404–424.

The deepening crisis over Czechoslovakia lasted through the spring and summer of 1938. For the Soviets, another and grave event accompanied the rising war fever in Europe. Beginning in July 1938, serious fighting developed between Russian and Japanese military units. This was no "frontier incident"; tens of thousands of troops, planes, and artillery were involved. Though the hostilities were arrested in August, the Russians having essentially won their point, the episode was taken in Moscow as an instance of Japan's pressuring of the Soviets so as to tie their hands in the developing European crisis. The Russians' spirited action must have given the Japanese general staff some second thoughts about the allegedly debilitating effect of the purges on the Soviet military establishment. But in Berlin, as the German documents of the period show, either the possibility of Russian intervention in the forthcoming conflict was being entirely discounted, or it was thought that at most the Russians would intervene through aerial attacks and by supplying Czechoslovakia. Such was also the gist of advice reaching Berlin from Count von der Schulenburg in Moscow.

The position of the Soviet Union was defined both in terms of formal treaty obligations and in terms of geography. Soviet help to Czechoslovakia was required only in case France intervened militarily on behalf of her ally. The nature of this possible help was in turn conditioned by geography, and indeed the story of Soviet policy in those months should be studied with a map in hand.

The Soviet armies could intervene in one of three ways in case of a conflict. They could cross Latvia and Lithuania to get at German East Prussia. They could cross Rumania to join the Czech army. Or they could march the width of Poland to strike at Germany. The first possibility was so absurd from the military point of view that it was not even a subject of discussion during the feverish summer months of 1938. The second one, though discussed, was almost equally so. Soviet troops would have been required to move across the wretched Rumanian roads and railways to the mountainous regions of eastern Slovakia, far from the presumed theater of military operations in Bohemia and Moravia. Under the circumstances, a division might be sent as a gesture, but no military man in his senses would dream of sending an army.

The only way in which Soviet troops could be deployed *en masse*, in the sense of creating a second front as understood and feared by the German generals and even by Hitler in his more sober moments, was through Poland. The Polish government would not acquiesce in the Soviet passage, even if it were ready to help Czechoslovakia, something which was very far from being the case. As the Sudeten crisis ripened, the Polish government as a matter of fact began to advance its own territorial claims on Czechoslovakia. (They concerned mainly the small area of Teschen.)

Thus Poland, officially an ally of France, was with a tragic lack of fore-sight pressing the dissolution of Czechoslovakia. In the West, it was often assumed that Poland would range herself on the side of Germany in a conflict. The Russians knew the Poles better: it was not complicity with Hitler but the megalomania of Polish ruling circles that prompted them to a course of action so injurious to their own interests and even more to their reputation.

In any case, the road through Poland remained barred. The Russian troops would have to fight their way through. Russian military opinion, unlike that of the French general staff, did not consider the Polish military potential as very formidable. But Soviet diplomats had a perfect reason for remaining vague in answers to inquiries from Paris as to how the U.S.S.R. meant to implement her pledges in case of an armed conflict. As the French ambassador in Moscow wrote: "[Litvinov,] not counting in any case on a favorable response of Poland, has eliminated the idea of forcing [passage through her] apart from a decision by the League of Nations. 'We would appear as aggressors and that is something we cannot do.' "[70] The Commissar was not consistent in this delicacy of feeling. At times he did inquire what France would do in the hypothetical case of Poland, having invaded Czechoslovakia, being in turn attacked by the Soviet Union.[71]

Czechoslovakia occupied an important but not absolutely vital place in Soviet calculations in case of a general European conflict involving the U.S.S.R. But from the beginning of the crisis, if one thing was precluded it was the possibility of the U.S.S.R. rendering help to Czechoslovakia in case France reneged on *her* obligations. This point was underlined by the Russians even in unofficial propaganda publications. Thus in May 1938, when it was falsely believed that Hitler backed down after a partial mobilization ordered by the Czech government, the press published a variety of sensational statements. One of them, published by the Czech Communist journal and by the organ of the German Communist Party (printed in Prague), bore the sensational headline "3,000 Soviet Bombers over Berlin the Day the First German Soldiers Cross the Czechoslovakian Frontier"—this from an alleged broadcast by the "Moscow Comintern radio station." This absurd communiqué was strongly denounced in the journal of the Communist International[72] as false and a provocation. One cannot doubt that the Soviet leaders were eager to have Britain and France stand fast by Czechoslovakia. Thus, though Soviet intelligence must have known that the story of Hitler's intended move and then back-

[70] Robert Coulondre, *From Stalin to Hitler: Memoirs of Two Embassies, 1936–39* (Paris, 1950), p. 156.

[71] *Ibid.*, p. 152.

[72] *The Communist International*, XV, No. 6 (June, 1938), 575.

down was false, the story continued to be circulated in the Soviet and Communist press.

Schulenburg from Moscow kept reassuring Berlin that the Soviet Union would not intervene with *her army* on behalf of Czechoslovakia. The German ambassador, a diplomat of the old school, was fearful of Hitler's warlike designs, hence his testimony is all the more valuable. He quoted approvingly the remark of his French colleague: "You know as well as I do for whom we are working if we come to blows." Schulenburg's attempts to draw out Litvinov as to the exact form Soviet help to Czechoslovakia would take were, needless to say, fruitless. The Commissar chose to beguile him by philosophical asides: "If the old democratic Germany had still existed, the Czechoslovak question would have assumed quite a different aspect for the Soviet Union. The Soviets had always been in favor of the right of self-determination of peoples."[73]

The notorious editorial in *The Times* of September 7 advising Czechoslovakia to cede the Sudetenland, and Chamberlain's first "pilgrimage," as Maisky puts it, to Hitler on September 15 must have confirmed the Soviet leaders in what they probably had suspected since the rejection of their March 17 proposal: Britain and France would back down over Czechoslovakia. On September 19 came the joint British-French pressure on the Czechs to consent to a dismemberment of their country. The Czechs refused, though in terms implying that they would be amenable to further pressure. The Czech government's request to the Soviets to elucidate their position brought a reaffirmation of the Soviet position. The Commissar for Foreign Relations wired to the Soviet minister in Prague to tell Benes that "the U.S.S.R. will, in accordance with the treaty, render immediate and effective aid to Czechoslovakia *if France remains loyal to it and also renders aid.*"[74] As to Benes' query as to what the U.S.S.R. would do if Germany attacked (and if presumably France stood aside), the U.S.S.R. expressed her readiness to act under Articles 16 and 17 of the League Covenant if the Council of the League applied those articles. At the meeting of the League on September 21, Litvinov again stated: "We intend to fulfill our obligations under the pact, and together with France to afford assistance to Czechoslovakia *by the ways open to us.*"[75] Litvinov proposed staff talks with France. On the same day the Czechoslovak cabinet caved in to the combined British-French pressure and agreed in principle to cession of the Sudetenland.

The danger of war reappeared with Hitler's brutal rejection of Chamber-

[73] *Documents on German Foreign Policy, 1918–45*, Series D, II (Washington, 1950), 630.

[74] My italics. From *Documents and Materials Relating to the Eve of the Second World War*, I (Moscow, 1949), 204.

[75] My italics. From Degras, *Soviet Documents on Foreign Policy*, III, 303.

lain's offer on September 22 and his demand for an immediate German military occupation of the Czechoslovak districts. Having conceded the substance of the German proposals, the French and British countenanced a war over the means and timing of putting them into effect. For all the faintheartedness of the British and French officials, it is possible that a world war would have broken out had Hitler crossed the Czechoslovak frontier between September 23 and 28. It is unlikely that this lesson, which was apparently lost on Hitler and his colleagues, as events of 1939 were to show, was ignored in Moscow.

On September 23, the Soviet government warned Poland that should the Polish troops that were concentrated on the Polish-Czech border enter Czechoslovakia, the U.S.S.R. would renounce the Polish-Soviet nonaggression pact of 1932. This was the most forcible Soviet intervention during the Czechoslovak crisis, and it came, one should note, *after* the Soviets had become aware of the initial capitulation of Chamberlain and the Czech government. The Polish government considered the Soviet note as a purely propagandistic gesture, and so perhaps it was, though that government's record of foresight at the time of the Munich crisis is not very good, to put it mildly.

The final act of the Czechoslovak drama took place without Soviet participation. The Soviet public reaction was naturally scathing. The September 29 Munich conference was proclaimed by the Soviets to be not only a shameful betrayal of Czechoslovakia, but also an attempt to exclude Russia from European affairs.

The Western Powers' behavior in the Munich crisis is almost universally credited with changing the course of Soviet foreign policy. The Soviet leaders, so runs the argument, abandoned any remaining illusions about collective security. Their ingrained suspicion about the West now extended to the conviction that Britain and France had left Hitler a free hand against Russia. Hence a direct line leads from Munich to Stalin's eventual decision to sign a pact with Hitler. Yet that thesis cannot be defended either in terms of logic or on the basis of the available evidence.

In the first place, the Soviet government had no illusions to lose. Unless one assumes that the men in the Kremlin had ceased to be Communists, it is difficult to see how they could have believed in the Western Powers' disinterested solicitude for small countries or in their special friendship for the Soviet Union. The policy of collective security so indefatigably followed by Litvinov between 1934 and 1938 could not be considered a total loss, even in view of Munich. It had been designed to prevent the possibility of *all* the capitalist powers joining in a crusade against the U.S.S.R., of France and Britain *actively* joining with Germany. As such, it had been a success: there was no fascist government in Paris, of which there had appeared to be a chance in 1934. For all Chamberlain's real and alleged feelings of hostility toward the U.S.S.R., there was not the slightest chance that he would have been willing or able to lead Britain into an alliance with Germany.

There were two lessons of Munich, however. The obvious one of the Western Powers' backing down could not be excluded; it was indeed possible that Hitler's next aggression in eastern or central Europe would be acquiesced in by London and Paris. But the other one was that Europe had come very close to war and that there were powerful currents of public opinion in Paris and, especially, London which would not tolerate a repetition of this humiliating capitulation to the dictators. How to balance and utilize these two lessons became the first practical task of Soviet diplomacy following Munich.

On October 4, the French ambassador in Moscow called on the Deputy Commissar for Foreign Affairs, Potemkin, to discharge the unenviable task of notifying him of the official French reasons for the capitulation. The French ambassador's dramatic recital has been quoted by practically every historian dealing with the period: "Silence had fallen. Then, driven by emotion, though a Slav and a diplomat [Potemkin] tells me all on his mind. 'My poor friend, what have you done? As for us, I don't see any other conclusion than a fourth partition of Poland.' "[76]

This was taken by Coulondre as a clear indication of Soviet determination to seek an accommodation with Germany. The French ambassador did not pause to consider that Soviet diplomats were not given to spontaneous outbursts during which they revealed state secrets.[77] In the second place, without possessing occult powers it would have been impossible for Potemkin, or Stalin, to figure out the exact circumstances that were to lead to the partition of Poland in 1939. On October 4 no one could be sure that Hitler would turn against Poland next, or that if he did Britain and France would guarantee Poland against Germany, or that under those circumstances Hitler would be amenable to a bargain with the Russians. The tentative Soviet approaches to Germany in 1935 and 1936 had been spurned. Even when there was a prospect of war over Czechoslovakia, Hitler discounted the possibility of a Russian intervention. When the fateful indiscretion of Potemkin's took place, relations between Poland and Germany were outwardly at their friendliest, and many in fact believed that the two countries had a secret arrangement about a joint action against the U.S.S.R.

In fact, rumors of a German-Soviet "deal" that circulated in the fall

[76] Coulondre, op. cit., p. 165.

[77] Especially in 1938. Several Soviet diplomats, including three former holders of Potemkin's office, fell victims of the purge in the very same year. Potemkin would have bitten off his tongue rather than say something he had not been authorized to be indiscreet about.

of 1938 were largely inspired by Soviet sources and for obvious reasons. Munich undoubtedly lowered the Kremlin's opinion of the British and French regimes. It must have strengthened the suspicion, never absent, that at least some official persons in London and Paris would not be unhappy to see Hitler's further aggression directed eastward. But, unlike Hitler, Stalin did not shape his foreign policies according to whether he got mad at this or that country or regime. A resumption of at least the appearance of collaboration with the West was a vital necessity for the Soviet Union *even and especially if she sought* an agreement with Germany. Hitler was not going to bargain with Stalin out of ideological sympathy, but only if the latter had some cards in his hands. And the strongest card of all would be the possibility of a binding military alliance between the U.S.S.R. and the Western Powers.

Nothing until March 1939 indicated that such an alliance was anywhere near. The Franco-Soviet treaty remained in force but still without any implementing military clauses. In December 1938 Ribbentrop visited Paris and there signed with the French Foreign Minister, Georges Bonnet, a vague declaration of mutual peaceful intentions between Germany and France. The visit was bound to raise the Russians' suspicions to a new height. Among the Western statesmen, Bonnet was the principal object of Soviet attacks and suspicions. But the Franco-Soviet pact remained in force, and at no point did the U.S.S.R. raise the question of renouncing it.[78]

In fact, more than before and after, Soviet diplomacy *between* October and March displayed masterful coolness and strength of nerves. The Russians realized that their previous eagerness on behalf of collective security had, in conjunction with the purges, persuaded foreign powers of Russia's weakness. Now they tried hard to create an impression of Russian aloofness and self-confidence. "Anyone who wants to be convinced of the strength and power of our forces is welcome to try," said Molotov in a speech on November 6, 1938. The same theme was suggested almost casually by Litvinov and other Soviet diplomats in their talks with Western diplomats: yes, the Western Powers were in for a hard time from Hitler; as for the U.S.S.R., she was not particularly interested. Eager inquiries as to whether the Soviets were not nervous over the German designs on the Ukraine were passed off almost jocularly: Hitler would attack only countries unwilling or unable to defend themselves; the U.S.S.R. had nothing to fear. The Soviet taunts and studied indifference did not fail to produce the expected effect in Western official circles: Russia once more was included in the calculations in London and Paris.

[78] Such a step would have been logical had the U.S.S.R. wanted at that time to woo Germany, in view of the demonstrated worthlessness of the French guarantee to Czechoslovakia.

In November 1938, the Soviet government took a step, apparently unimportant, but pregnant with consequences. Sometime after Munich, the Polish ambassador dropped in on Potemkin and casually observed to the Deputy Commissar that perhaps their governments might take some steps to improve their relations. Potemkin did not choose to repeat this "impulsive" revelation to the French ambassador. He found the idea interesting. The Pole was after a few days summoned to Litvinov who also casually inquired what his government had in mind. The outcome of such casual conversations was the communiqué issued by the Polish and Soviet governments on November 26, 1938, stating that both governments would continue to base their relations on the Polish-Soviet Nonaggression Pact of 1932, valid until 1945, and pledging friendly solution of all the outstanding problems between them.[79]

That the Polish government, which had adopted such an arrogant attitude toward the U.S.S.R. only a few weeks before during the Czechoslovak crisis, was now interested in talks could only mean one thing. But much as they would have enjoyed it, neither Litvinov nor Potemkin chose to read the Polish ambassador a lesson and send him contemptuously away. The stiffening of the Polish attitude toward Germany and a public avowal of it was at the time a vital step in the Soviet game. (It was Litvinov who proposed the declaration reaffirming the nonaggression treaty.)

We now know, and the Soviets must have deduced (if indeed they did not know from their special sources), that following Munich the German diplomats, at first casually but then with increasing insistence and brutality, had been suggesting that the time had come for a "definite solution" of all the outstanding differences between Poland and the Reich. Hitler proposed to incorporate the Free City of Danzig into Germany and to have an extraterritorial road linking East Prussia with the rest of Germany. Having made those proposals, Hitler fell into raptures at his own moderation, and his incomprehension grew as to why these *concessions by Germany* were being refused by ungrateful Poland. The Polish Foreign Minister, Beck, for whom they meant a catastrophic bankruptcy of his foreign policy, which was based on the fatuous assumption that Germany's previous pledges could be trusted, kept the facts of the German pressure secret both from the Polish public and from Poland's allies. They were not to become public knowledge until April 1939.[80]

---

[79] *Official Documents Concerning Polish-German and Polish-Soviet Relations* (London: Polish Ministry of Foreign Affairs, 1940), pp. 181–82.

[80] The incredible obtuseness of Western diplomacy, which could be considered comical except that it was a prelude to a catastrophe, was demonstrated by the fact that as late as April 1, 1939, British official circles did not deduce that Poland was being drastically pressured by Germany. Thus Lord Halifax could take as genuine the Polish ambassador's statement that "the Ger-

The Soviet government had little sympathy for the Polish regime or indeed for Poland as it emerged after World War I. Poland had been first part of France's *cordon sanitaire* around the Soviet Union. Later on Poland appeared to flirt with Hitler's Germany. Throughout, the country had been an obstacle and threat to Russia's aims. The Soviet leaders, however, knew Poland and the Polish mentality. Unlike some people in the West, they probably never made the mistake of considering the Polish government as a simple accomplice of Hitler's or as likely to offer Poland as a passageway for German armies. But in 1939 the prospect of Poland becoming a German satellite or being conquered by Germany had to be viewed as a mortal danger to the Soviet Union. Were Poland to agree to Hitler's "moderate" proposals, she would enter on the fatal path Czechoslovakia had taken. Were she to resist and fight Germany, she would be conquered.[81] Either way, Germany would effectively become a neighbor to the Soviet Union. Such neighborhood, devoutly wished for by the Soviet leaders in the years following the Revolution, was now thought of in a quite different light. In view of what was to happen within a few months, it may seem paradoxical but is nevertheless true that it became a vital objective for Soviet foreign policy that Poland should resist the German demands and, if attacked, should find allies in the West. The joint Polish-Soviet communiqué was a small but significant contribution in that direction.

The Polish government had additional reasons for second thoughts after the Czechoslovak drama. What remained of Czechoslovakia was in an obvious state of dissolution, and all its parts were within a few weeks of Munich satellites of Germany. The central government felt compelled to grant substantial autonomy to Slovakia, and part of the irredentist movement there, financed by Berlin, was clamoring for full "independence," i.e., a direct rather than indirect status as Germany's satellite. The prospect of German troops along a still longer stretch of Poland's frontier was already bad enough. But what was even worse

---

man Government had put forward no definite complaints or demands as regards either the Corridor or Danzig"—this despite the fact that in the very same conversation the Polish ambassador committed a most transparent slip by saying that negotiations between Poland and Germany would be impossible "on the basis of the claims which *some papers* had attributed to Germany" (my italics). *Documents on British Foreign Policy, 1919–1939*, 3d Series (London, 1951), IV, 575. Thus His Majesty's Government knew less than the press as to what had been happening in Polish-German relations for the past few months.

[81] As will be shown below, the Russians did not think (as did military men in the West) that Poland could offer prolonged military resistance. But they did not expect that the military disproportion between Germany and Poland was as great as was to be shown in 1939.

was the emergence within post-Munich Czechoslovakia of an autonomous Carpatho-Ukraine also clamoring to be "independent." When further surgery was performed by Germany on the rump of Czechoslovakia in November,[82] most of this backward area, inhabited by a few hundred thousand Ukrainians, remained an autonomous part of the decomposing Czechoslovak state. Needless to say, with discreet German encouragement, this miniscule state became the center of nationalist Ukrainian propaganda directed to brethren in eastern Poland and in the Soviet Ukraine.

Indeed, the backward mountainous region became for a few months the focal point of east European politics. Poland's pleas in Berlin for a joint Polish-Hungarian frontier were being answered playfully by the question as to why such a frontier was thought to be necessary, and the Hungarians were sternly warned that a violation of the territorial integrity of Czechoslovakia and the right of self-determination of the Carpatho-Ukrainians could not be tolerated by the Führer. The Soviet Union did not choose to confess its nervousness over the Carpatho-Ukraine. In a speech to the Eighteenth Congress of the CPSU on March 10, 1939, Stalin, while ridiculing the whole notion that a country of 30 million (the Soviet Ukraine) could be annexed by a region of 700,000 (Carpatho-Ukraine), still devoted an unusually lengthy passage to this apparently ridiculous proposition of a "merger of an elephant with a gnat." Litvinov, in conversation with Western diplomats, likewise ridiculed the notion. His information was that Hitler would turn next against Poland, if not indeed the West. And, indeed, the whole winter was spent by the Western cabinets waiting nervously to see where Hitler would strike next. At one time, London became almost convinced that Germany was about to invade the Netherlands or Switzerland, and even the possibility of an aerial strike against London was mentioned. No one has ever traced satisfactorily the source of those rumors.

It is against this background that Stalin addressed the Eighteenth Party Congress. The survivors of the great purge were treated to a confident assessment of the international situation.[83] Only a "lunatic" would dream of detaching the Ukraine from the Soviet Union. In fact, Stalin accused the Western press of spreading such rumors "in order to poison the atmosphere and provoke a conflict with Germany for which there are no visible reasons." Stalin insinuated further that "one might think that they gave the Germans regions of Czechoslovakia for a pledge to begin war

[82] This was the so-called Vienna award, where Ribbentrop and Count Ciano, the Italian Foreign Minister, "arbitrated" the claims of Hungary to parts of Slovakia.

[83] *Eighteenth Congress of the Communist Party of the Soviet Union* (Moscow, 1939), pp. 4–15.

against the Soviet Union and the Germans now refuse to honor their pledge." The tone was distinctly unfriendly toward the West: taunts, insinuations, and, against this, a reassertion of Soviet indifference since the Soviet Union was strong and confident of its ability to take on all aggressors.

Stalin himself and his colleagues obviously could not believe this confident assessment. The stories of German designs on the Ukraine, far from being invented by the Western press, had been publicly stated in the great purge trials, and on charges of treasonous collusion with Germany the highest Party, diplomatic, and military officials had been sentenced and sent before a firing squad within the past three years. In fact, Stalin's main and equally transparent purpose was to undo the fatal impression created abroad by the purges. What are all those lies, he asked, about the "weakness of the Soviet army," the "decomposition of the Soviet air force," the "unrest in the Soviet Union"? Wasn't the purpose of all those lies to suggest to the Germans: "You just start a war with the Bolsheviks, everything will go easy"?[84] That even at the height of terror it must have been represented to the dictator that he was destroying the efficiency of the armed forces is obvious also from a speech by Marshal Voroshilov: "One might ignore the insinuations of the *fascist* scribblers about the weakness of the Red Army, etc., if the *fascist* aggressors were not drawing concrete conclusions from them."[85] Voroshilov asked his audience to believe that the purge of "scoundrels and traitors: Tukhachevskys, Yegorovs, Orlovs, and their like" could only strengthen the armed forces.[86] In apparent disregard of military security, Voroshilov went on to quote actual figures demonstrating the growth of the major branches of the Soviet armed forces.

Stalin's performance at the Congress was later on interpreted as a clear-cut indication that the Soviet Union was already seeking a bargain with Germany. His words that the Soviet Union would not be involved in a conflict "to pull somebody else's chestnuts out of the fire" have been quoted to that effect time and time again since September 1939. Yet in fact his statement was in line with every aspect of Soviet policy after Munich: through taunts, expressions of self-confidence, and insinuations of an as yet nonexistent *rapprochement* with Germany, it was intended to draw out the Western Powers. "We don't need you, but you may

[84] Stalin's salient points, the record notes, were often interrupted by "cheers" and "laughter." Nobody laughed at this one.

[85] *Eighteenth Congress of the Communist Party of the Soviet Union*, p. 196. My italics.

[86] This was the first official intimation that Marshal Yegorov and Admiral Orlov had shared the fate of Tukhachevsky.

need us; if so, better hurry up" is the most sensible translation of what Stalin was saying.

On March 10 nothing indicated that a bargain with Hitler was a real possibility. Stalin had nothing to sell. For all his dark hints, it was obvious that he did not believe in any stories of Hitler's forthcoming attack in the West. In fact the Soviet leaders had a flattering opinion of Western strength. "Peaceful, democratic states," said Stalin, lapsing into very strange language for a Communist, "are without doubt stronger than the fascist ones both militarily and economically." Soviet military intelligence must have been in a deplorable state (not surprising, considering the wholesale liquidation of its personnel), for Voroshilov gave comparative figures for the air strength of various states in 1938 which indicated that the French air force was not much inferior to Germany's and which credited Poland with more than 1,000 combat planes.[87] Under these circumstances the prospects of Germany attacking in the West and requiring Soviet neutrality were not very great.

The Eighteenth Party Congress was still sitting when the international situation underwent a drastic change. What was left of Czechoslovakia was swallowed up. Bohemia and Moravia became a Reich Protectorate, Slovakia got its "independence" and was immediately occupied by German troops. After some hesitation, Berlin allowed the Hungarians to annex the Carpatho-Ukraine and thus liquidate the focal point of Ukrainian irredentism. That this was done as a gesture toward the Russians, as *the Germans* were to claim when negotiating toward the Molotov-Ribbentrop pact, is unlikely. The main reason appeared to be Hitler's conviction that after such a magnificent gesture by Germany, the Poles would surely not hedge over trifles like Danzig. The Poles were likely to be unhappy over the German troops in Slovakia, which Polish diplomacy with its megalomania had begun to imagine to be in the Polish sphere of influence. Let them have their Polish-Hungarian frontier!

The latest aggression by Hitler was met by a Soviet note to Germany which denounced in the strongest terms the rape of Czechoslovakia and refused to acknowledge its legality. For all the "disappearance" of the Carpatho-Ukraine, the fact was that Hitler was moving eastward closer to the U.S.S.R. A Ukrainian Communist official in a speech at the Congress on March 19 did not seek to ridicule the threat of Germany: "Let those base hypocrites, the German fascists, this scum of mankind, realize that Soviet Ukraine is strong and powerful. . . . Every attempt of the enemy

[87] *Eighteenth Congress of the Communist Party of the Soviet Union*, p. 189. At the time she was attacked in September 1939, Poland had barely 200 combat planes, and they were obsolete. The French never acquired an up-to-date modern air force. The British began mass production of modern fighter planes only in 1939.

to cross the frontier . . . will be met by lightning and devastating destruction on his own territory."[88]

On March 17, Chamberlain gave vent in a public speech to the indignation that seized him, along with the British public, at this most flagrant breach of faith yet on the part of Germany. From then on, just as diligently as he had pursued appeasement in the past—but, alas, equally unintelligently—the Prime Minister was to pursue the policy of mounting a united front against further German aggression. The immediate threat in those hectic March days appeared to be directed against Rumania. To give an effective guarantee to Rumania, it was necessary to obtain the concurrence of her neighbors: the U.S.S.R. and Poland. Drawing in Poland at this stage was believed to be one way of assuring Soviet concurrence: the Polish clash with the Russians at the time of Munich was vividly remembered; and the British ministers thought that by bringing in Poland, still believed to be close to Germany, they would increase the chances of Russia's associating herself with the rebuilding of collective security in Eastern Europe.

The Russians "played it cool." On March 22 an official communiqué denied rumors that "the Soviet Government recently offered its aid to Poland and Rumania in the event of their becoming victims of aggression."[89] The Soviet government, in answer to a British inquiry as to its intentions in the case of an aggression against Rumania, once again proposed the holding of a conference, this time of Britain, France, Rumania, Poland, Turkey, and the U.S.S.R., to investigate the situation.

Linking Poland with Rumania as threatened nations was an improvisation on the Russians' part. There were indeed rumors that Poland was being threatened, but officially the Poles kept denying, though more and more feebly, to the British and French that any German threat had been issued over Danzig or anything else. In any event, the Soviet proposal for consultation was vetoed by Poland and Rumania. Foreign Minister Beck was striving for guarantees from Britain and France and tried still to keep them in the dark as to the seriousness of the situation. He thought that bringing in Russia would incense Hitler still further. And Rumania too feared Russian guarantees almost as much as German aggression—a fact of which the Russians were aware and by which they were not too displeased!

The pace of the crisis quickened. On March 23 Hitler exacted the region of Memel from Lithuania. Some conservative elements in Germany, fearful of Hitler's next move, decided to inform the British government as to what was going on between Poland and Germany and thus to press

[88] *Ibid.*, p. 597.

[89] Degras, *Soviet Documents on Foreign Policy*, III, 324.

it to take a firm stand to avoid Hitler's sudden move in that direction. A British newspaperman was briefed, and he brought the news to London on March 29.[90] Though the British ministers still were being lulled by Polish reassurances, they decided now to issue a *unilateral* guarantee to Poland. Beck, needless to say, jumped at the proposal. Without the British guarantee, the eventually inevitable revelation of the menacing German pressure would have meant his being hounded out of office once his country realized the ominous turn of events.[91]

The British formula, drafted by Chamberlain himself, pledged the British and French governments to "lend . . . all support in their power" if the Polish government felt compelled to resist aggression. Before Chamberlain's historic declaration to that effect in the House of Commons on March 31, Lord Halifax invited Ambassador Maisky to acquaint him with it.

Halifax's minute on the conversation reflects considerable obtuseness on the part of the noble lord. The Soviet ambassador did not bat an eye at a declaration that meant a historic and fateful reversal of British foreign policy. "His first comment was that the phrase 'lend the Polish government all support in their power' might be a phrase greatly minimized by those who . . . would profess doubts as to the genuine character of British intentions."[92] Halifax asked Maisky whether the Soviet government would agree to the Prime Minister saying that the Soviet government approved of the declaration. Maisky was noncommittal, but not too much so. He, of course, could not speak without consulting his government, but, as Stalin had said, the U.S.S.R. was ready to help all "those who fought for their independence." The Poles, the ambassador thought, might not be very happy about too strong a Soviet endorsement. "Although they thought it groundless, they understood the fear of the Poles, which was that if Russian troops come into Poland, Polish conditions were such that the contacts that would be made would probably produce disturbing effects on Polish society." But Maisky believed that the Prime Minister might say *on his own authority* (!) that the Soviet government understood and appreciated the principles on which the British government acted. And so it was stated the same afternoon in the House of Commons by Mr. Chamberlain.

[90] Wheeler-Bennett, *op. cit.*, pp. 436–37.

[91] This pressure was applied most brutally in an interview between Ribbentrop and the Polish ambassador on March 26, and Beck's own with the German on March 28. At the latter, the German said, "You want to negotiate at the point of the bayonet." Beck: "That is your own method." *Official Documents Concerning Polish-German and Polish-Soviet Relations*, p. 69.

[92] *Documents on British Foreign Policy, 1919–1939*, 3d Series, IV, 557.

With incredible blindness Halifax did not observe Maisky's concern that the declaration be made as strong as possible. (It was already much stronger than any declaration made by the British during the Czechoslovak crisis.) Nor did he notice Maisky's concern that the pledge to Poland should not be jeopardized by a refusal to permit Chamberlain to speak of the Soviet government's understanding and sympathizing with it. On issues much smaller than this, the Soviet ambassador had previously asked for an opportunity to consult with his government. To a man more perceptive than Lord Halifax, it would have been clear that Maisky must have been briefed for precisely such an occasion and that beneath his nonchalant and amiable behavior there was an obvious anxiety that the declaration be made and that it not be delayed by one day, one hour.[93]

It is not too much to say that the British declaration of March 31 made possible the whole train of events leading to the Molotov-Ribbentrop pact of August 23, 1939, and thus was indirectly responsible for the most momentous development of Soviet foreign policy since Brest Litovsk. On its face, the British government's pledge guaranteed Poland; in fact, *its timing and circumstances* provided a guarantee to the U.S.S.R. and doomed the Polish state.

Prior to the declaration, the power most vitally interested in the preservation of Polish independence was the Soviet Union. Were Germany to attack Poland and were the Western Powers to stand aside, it would have been a staggering blow to their prestige and an incitement to Hitler to proceed elsewhere, but to the U.S.S.R., it would have been a mortal danger. Without allies the U.S.S.R. would now stand face to face with German power. In eastern Poland, Germany could create "independent" Ukrainian and Byelorussian states exerting strong attraction on the contiguous Soviet areas. Following the Polish conquest, Hitler might still decide to turn westward, but in view of his anti-Communism and the universal conviction of Russia's internal and military weakness, the U.S.S.R. would most likely be next on his timetable of aggression. The British-French guarantee completely changed this dismal perspective: even were Hitler to conquer Poland, he would now be embroiled in a war with Britain and France. They in turn would *need* the U.S.S.R. as an ally, and for all his contempt for Soviet power Hitler might wish to avoid

[93] Maisky's own account in his memoirs speaks for itself. The conversation is alleged to have taken place with Chamberlain. But Maisky "remembers" every word. To "Chamberlain's" proposal to be allowed to associate the Soviet government with it, Maisky replied, "No, whatever the content of your declaration, I cannot give you on my own responsibility such an authorization." Maisky, *op. cit.*, II, 458.

fighting on two fronts. A few words spoken by Mr. Chamberlain transformed the U.S.S.R. from being in a hopeless diplomatic situation to being the arbiter of Europe's fate.

Needless to say, on March 31 the situation could not be defined so categorically. Britain, and with her France (now completely in Britain's tow diplomatically), might relapse into appeasement and break the pledge to Poland. Hitler, with his irrational hatred of the U.S.S.R., might embark on a war with the West and still scorn a deal with Russia. But the probabilities looked the other way. There was now room for maneuver, and the frightful anxiety which the Soviet leaders had suffered since Munich must have abated.

That the Soviet government may well have contemplated taking an initiative in proposing guarantees to Poland, had not the British by their declaration removed the need to do so, is strongly suggested by the action it took on March 28 in regard to Latvia and Estonia. Those two small Baltic states were told by Litvinov in the most emphatic language that the Soviet government would not tolerate any "abatement or restriction of [their] independence and self-determination . . . permitting in it political, economic or other domination of a third state . . . granting to the latter any exceptional rights and privileges," and this no matter "what kind of agreements were signed, voluntary or concluded under outside pressure."[94] In plain language, the Soviet government declared its readiness to go to war with Germany were Germany to establish bases or send troops to the Baltic states. Yet a German occupation of Latvia and Estonia would have presented Russia with only a fraction of the political and military danger of a similar situation in Poland.

Once the British declaration was made, the Soviet government's official reaction was one of surprise and absolute denial that the U.S.S.R. had taken any position on it. The British ambassador in Moscow wired this unpleasant discovery to his minister: "M. Litvinov made it quite clear that His Majesty's action is misunderstood and not at all appreciated." The Commissar claimed that Maisky was misunderstood, that the U.S.S.R. had never expressed "sympathy and understanding" for the pledge for Poland. The British ambassador pleaded: "Surely in the Soviet Union where we were always attacked for alleged capitulations a welcome should be accorded to a momentous change of front." Litvinov was not mollified. "We could pursue our own policy: the Soviet Government would stand aside."[95] But for all his professed indifference as to the British policies and guarantees, the Commissar was fishing and probing. "He expressed

[94] Degras, *Soviet Documents on Foreign Policy*, III, 325.
[95] *Documents on British Foreign Policy, 1919–1939*, 3d Series, IV, 574–75.

doubts whether we would regard an attack on Danzig or the Corridor as threatening Poland's independence."

The last remark underlines how, for all its undoubted guile, for all of its firmly held objective of keeping war from Russian soil as long as possible, the intricate Soviet diplomatic game was attended with risks and uncertainties at every step. Poland might be induced by the pressure of the British and French appeasers to make a first small but fatal concession to Hitler. She might have to fight alone. In either case, the two objectives of Soviet foreign policy—first, if at all possible to avoid a war fought on Soviet soil, and second, if it came to that, to be sure of having the Western Powers as allies—would not be served. Hence it became a vital necessity for the Soviets to have the British commit themselves as unequivocally as possible to the defense of Poland and to extend their guarantees to other areas of importance for the U.S.S.R. On April 6 the British pledge, now accompanied by a reciprocal pledge by Poland, was announced in London. On April 13 Chamberlain gave unilateral guarantees against aggression to Rumania and Greece. At each step the Russians probed for the exact nature and extent of the British commitment. Were Polish-British military talks in prospect? asked Maisky of Halifax on April 6. And Litvinov in effect demanded of the British ambassador, "How do we know that Great Britain will declare war in case of aggression?"[96]

There must remain a strong conjecture that following Chamberlain's declaration on Poland on March 31 and its reaffirmation on April 6, the Soviet government expected to be approached by Germany. No such step took place. The reason may be found in a dispatch to his ministry by the German counsellor in Moscow, who wrote with an insight subsequently missing among German policy-makers: "The Soviets wish to join the Concert of Europe and desire also a development which would preferably bring about war between Germany, France, and Britain, while they can, to begin with, preserve freedom of action and further their own interests."[97] The Germans were not biting, and the British for the moment appeared to have acquiesced in Litvinov's statement to them of April 1: they could pursue their own policy; "the Soviet government would stand aside." Hence, in an apparent reversal of the last sentiment, Maisky called on Halifax on April 14 to inform him: "On instructions from his Government that in view of the interest shown by His Majesty's Government in the fate of Greece and Rumania the Soviet Government were prepared to take part

[96] *Ibid.*, V, 224.

[97] *Documents on German Foreign Policy, 1918–45*, Series D, VI (Washington, 1956), 139.

in giving assistance to Rumania."[98] Thus within two weeks the Russians seemingly changed their position: from a complete aloofness they now wanted to be engaged in negotiations with the West and, as we shall see, as publicly as possible and on as wide a variety of issues as possible, as the means of erecting a barrier to German aggression.

The British government responded: it was under attack from the Opposition and Mr. Churchill for ignoring the Soviet Union in its plans. Such attacks were readily reproduced in the Soviet press and quoted in Litvinov's and Maisky's conversations with the English diplomats. Hence, Halifax invited the Russians to elucidate their position. On April 18 Litvinov handed the British ambassador the Soviet proposals: the three powers were to guarantee militarily all the "Eastern European states situated between the Baltic and Black Seas and bordering on the U.S.S.R." They were to hold military conversations as to the details of such help. They would pledge themselves not to conclude any separate peace following the outbreak of war. The English were "to explain that assistance recently promised to Poland concerns exclusively aggression on the part of Germany."[99] Britain could not readily comply with these conditions. Under them, Britain and France would be compelled to come to Russia's aid in the case she fought Germany over Latvia, but Russia would not be equally bound in case of an attack on Holland or Belgium. Knowing the British mentality, it was clear that the negotiations would be long and drawn-out and that at the same time, given the political pressure at home, the British and French governments would not break them off. Once a political agreement was reached, military conversations would have to take place, and the Russian pledge would not be given until and unless a military convention was agreed on down to the last detail.

The subsequent charge of bad faith against the Russians is inaccurate or, rather, irrelevant. For the U.S.S.R., the negotiations with the Western Powers were meant both as a bait to Germany and as reassurance. This is the probable sequence of priorities in the Soviets' mind. If war came, the first priority was that it not be fought on Soviet territory. The Western Powers could not guarantee that. Over and above the Polish objections, which the Soviets anticipated, to having Soviet troops on Polish soil, the experience of World War I clearly taught that even with the best intentions the West would be unable to prevent a considerable penetration of Soviet territory and the consequent political catastrophe to the Soviet regime. Were the capitalists of the West eager to save the Soviet system, something which Stalin was unlikely to be convinced of, to put it mildly, they still could not dictate German military strategy. And in view of the Maginot Line and the reputed strength and *defensive* intentions of the French army,

[98] *Documents on British Foreign Policy, 1919–1939*, 3d Series, V, 209.
[99] *Ibid.*, pp. 228–29.

Germany's logical first blow would be eastward. This had to be the prime consideration in Stalin's mind, or, for that matter, the mind of any other Russian statesman in his place. It is unlikely that even the prospect of a long and exhausting war between the capitalist states (except insofar as it would prevent or long delay Hitler's eventual move against Russia) or of the territorial loot to be gathered by Russia under an agreement with Hitler approached the importance or urgency of this first consideration.[100]

About the same time that the negotiations with the British were begun, an approach was made to Germany. On April 17, the Russian ambassador in Berlin, Alexei Merekalov, called upon Secretary of State Weizsäcker. This was his first call on an important German official since he had assumed his post one year before.[101] "The Russian asked me frankly what I thought of German-Russian relations. . . . There exists for Russia no reason why she should not live with us on a normal footing. And from normal the relations might become better and better."[102] Having dropped this hint Merekalov vanishes from the scene. Future contacts in Berlin were made by officials of a lower rank, the Soviet counsellor Astakhov and members of the Soviet trade mission. These negotiations went on in some secrecy,[103] in contrast to the ones with Britain and France which, of course, were accorded full publicity.

In the diplomatic game that went on well into August 1939, each of the three parties had its own primary and secondary objectives. The British hoped to exact solid Russian guarantees that would dissuade Hitler from attacking Poland and, if he did attack, to make the U.S.S.R. an ally in war. Hitler hoped until the very last that signing a treaty with Russia would persuade the Western Powers to leave Poland to her fate. Or rather to himself. If he could not have that, then he needed Russian benevolent neutrality: Goering and his generals balked at a war with the West, and the generals might rebel at the prospect of fighting both the West and the

---

[100] The French diplomat Coulondre, in his talks with his German colleagues, used to suggest that a war between their countries would benefit only Stalin. When it appeared that the Soviet Union would participate in it, he amended his warning by saying that *Trotsky* might be the eventual victor. Who can tell whether a variation on the last idea, extravagant as it turned out to be, did not occur to Stalin? Hitler used to say in those summer months that Stalin was as much afraid of his generals, should he win the war, as of defeat.

[101] The circumstances of Soviet diplomacy are well illustrated by the fact that between 1937 and 1941 the U.S.S.R. accredited four ambassadors to Berlin and for much of that time they were away from their posts.

[102] R. J. Sontag and J. S. Beddie, eds., *Nazi-Soviet Relations: 1939–1941: Documents from the Archives of the German Foreign Office* (Washington, 1948), p. 2.

[103] Not absolute secrecy; for obvious reasons German officials were dropping hints of their existence to Western diplomats.

U.S.S.R. Stalin wanted most of all a situation where Russia would have a free hand while Germany would be locked in a war with the West. Barring that, he needed military help from Britain and France. Of all the parties concerned, only Stalin got his first wish, but already in September 1939, he was to realize that he had bought considerably more than he bargained for. Hitler got his second wish, the Western Powers neither.

Merekalov's interview was not followed, as the Soviets had probably hoped it would be, by German inquiries and approaches. The situation grew more ominous. On April 28 Hitler renounced the Polish-German nonaggression treaty and the Anglo-German naval treaty. On May 3 Litvinov was replaced as Foreign Commissar by Molotov. The official statement that Soviet foreign policies would remain unaffected by the change was only too true. But for some time the Soviets had built up the legend that Litvinov was a proponent of collective security and had half-insinuated that Stalin, a "realist," did not quite see eye to eye with him. Thus the change was a "come on" both to the Western Powers and to Germany.

It worked. The Western Powers were shocked into speeding up the hitherto agonizingly slow negotiations with the Russians. The Germans, though still wary, were yet pleased that a Jew was no longer directing Soviet foreign policy. On May 5, Astakhov, in a conversation with a German trade official, casually mentioned Litvinov's dismissal "and tried without asking direct questions to learn whether this event would cause a change in [the Germans'] position toward the Soviet Union."[104] But a serious approach to the Soviet Union did not take place until May 30. On that date Weizsäcker wired the German embassy in Moscow. "Contrary to the policy previously planned we have now decided to undertake definite negotiations with the Soviet Union."[105] The German State Secretary invited Astakhov for a comprehensive conversation.

This decision on the part of Germany was clearly influenced by two factors. The negotiations between the U.S.S.R. and the West were picking up; and on May 23, following the signing of a military alliance with Italy, Hitler instructed his generals that he intended to smash Poland even if it involved war with Britain and France.[106] Hitler on that occasion raved and ranted in a wilder fashion than usual: if need be he would smash Britain in a few lightning strokes; the war might last fifteen years. On Russia he was quite incoherent. The U.S.S.R. might intervene in the war, or, he implied as he had one year before, Japanese pressure might keep

[104] Sontag and Beddie, op. cit., p. 3.
[105] Ibid., p. 15.
[106] Documents on German Foreign Policy, 1918–45, Series D, VI, 574–80.

the Russians fully occupied. (In fact, fighting between the Russians and the Japanese started once more in the Far East.) But to the military mind it was inconceivable to begin a war on the basis of such "ifs." Hence Hitler had to mollify the generals with prospects of an agreement with Russia. He himself abhorred the necessity of such a step, and several times in the next few weeks when the conversations were to take a decisive turn they were interrupted on express orders of the Führer. It is only because Ribbentrop virtually convinced him that a pact with the Russians would make the West abandon Poland, and that he would thus be able in effect to doublecross Stalin, that Hitler gave in.

The bait was finally swallowed on July 27, 1939, when Julius Schnurre, in charge of commercial negotiations with the Russians, invited Astakhov and the Russian trade delegate Babarin for dinner in a Berlin restaurant. Here he laid down the German suggestions, which bore Ribbentrop's unmistakable imprint—there was some nonsense about the similarity of the Bolshevik and Nazi *Weltanschauung*, which must have made Stalin smile when it was reported to him. But hints were clearly formulated as to the future points of agreement and the definition of spheres of interest of the two powers. Astakhov kept questioning closely on the Ukraine. Schnurre was encouraging on this point as well as on the Baltic countries and Rumania. The Soviet diplomat "would report it to Moscow, and he hoped it would have visible results in subsequent developments there."[107]

The "visible results" were that "Molotov abandoned his usual reserve," in Schulenburg's words, but also that the Russians *now* appeared in no hurry to come to an agreement. There were preliminary problems to be solved between the two countries. The legacy of the past distrusts was so great, the Russians kept explaining, that it might be best first to sign a commercial agreement, then *gradually* to arrive at a political one. Ribbentrop was burning with impatience, which he thought he was concealing from the Russians. It was August now. The British-French military mission was about to arrive in Moscow. Most of all, autumn rains would soon turn the Polish roads into quagmires and military operations against Poland could not be postponed much longer.

What were the Russians waiting for? Even Ribbentrop perceived dimly that they were waiting to be absolutely sure that a war would break out following the signature of the Russo-German agreement. They saw through Ribbentrop's game. If another Munich were to take place, the German-Soviet treaty would immediately become a meaningless piece of paper—or worse. Germany in one way or another would become a neighbor of the U.S.S.R. and the Western Powers, having been deceived, would not be likely to interfere if Hitler's next venture were in the Ukraine or the Baltic

[107] Sontag and Beddie, *op. cit.*, p. 35.

area. Quite possibly the Russians would have liked to have the war break out while they were still negotiating with both sides.

Now driven to distraction, Ribbentrop wired to his ambassador on August 18 that he must immediately be invited to Moscow to conclude the treaty, that otherwise the whole deal might be off: "The Führer considers it necessary that we be not taken by surprise by the outbreak of a German-Polish conflict. . . . He therefore considers a previous clarification necessary if only to be able to consider Russian interests in case of such a conflict, *which would of course be difficult without such a clarification.*"[108]

Molotov at first would not budge. Ribbentrop's trip would be welcome, but it would require preparation; "it was not possible even approximately to fix the time of the journey," he said on August 19 to Schulenburg.[109] But half an hour later Molotov recalled the ambassador to the Kremlin: the Soviet government were ready to receive Ribbentrop on August 26 or 27. He also handed Schulenburg the proposed draft of the nonaggression treaty. In that half hour Stalin evidently decided not to push the game with Hitler too far.

The latter was frantic to use some August weather for the destruction of Poland. There came the first test of nerves between the two dictators. Hitler's personal message to Stalin reached Moscow on the night of August 21. Ribbentrop *must* be received in Moscow on August 23 *at the latest*. He would not be able to stay more than two days. This could mean only one thing: Germany planned to start hostilities on the 26th, and such indeed was the case.[110]

The two hours that Stalin took to agree to what was virtually an ultimatum must have been occupied by one agonizing problem: was the West to be trusted to declare war on behalf of Poland? In a message to Hitler, Stalin agreed that Ribbentrop should arrive in Moscow on August 23.

The story of the Western negotiations with the Russians between April 18 and August 21 has often been told and needs no repetition in detail. The Western statesmen have been blamed, and justly, for the dilatory and half-hearted character of the negotiations. Indeed, Messrs. Daladier and Chamberlain appeared almost determined to provide future Soviet historians and propagandists with abundant material to justify the charge

---

[108] *Ibid.*, p. 62. My italics.

[109] In the same conversation Molotov displayed a sense of humor that escaped the German. As to the text of the proposed nonaggression treaty, he mentioned the treaties the Soviet government had concluded with Poland, Latvia, and Estonia. Any one of them could serve as a model for the Russo-German one!

[110] The atmosphere of confidence that already prevailed between the two allies is well illustrated by Ribbentrop's instructions that Hitler's message be delivered to Molotov on a piece of paper *without the letterhead* of the German embassy.

of the West's bad faith. They took their time; they dispatched a second-echelon Foreign Office man to Moscow instead of a cabinet member; when their joint military mission finally departed in August, it travelled to Moscow by a slow boat instead of a plane. But it can be said that none of those facts vitally influenced the final outcome of the negotiations, i.e., their failure. The Russians, it is true, always answered promptly, but at each crucial turn of the talks they raised new demands which were guaranteed at least to lead to long deliberations in the West and to the kind of commitments they knew the Western Powers could not immediately agree to.

The final issue on which the negotiations allegedly broke down was the Soviet demand that the Red Army be allowed to operate on and through Polish territory against Germany. This was something, as Maisky had told Halifax on March 31, the Soviets knew the Poles would not agree to. Had the Poles by any chance been willing to concede to it under Western pressure, the Soviets would undoubtedly have demanded that Russian troops be allowed to enter Poland in peacetime. Had *that* by any stretch of the imagination been agreed on, the Russians had another condition that clearly belonged in the realm of political and military fantasy: the British and French fleets were to enter the Baltic and to occupy Finnish, Latvian, and Estonian ports.[111] Even in World War I, the Baltic had remained a German lake, and to demand that the British fleet operate in that narrow sea in the airplane age "with the object of defending the independence of the Baltic states" could not have been meant seriously. The Baltic states would not have agreed and at least one of them, Finland, would have fought.

There was one and only one argument that could have swayed Stalin to accept an alliance with Britain and France. This would have been a declaration that the West would *not* defend Poland *unless* the U.S.S.R. joined in her defense. But both morally and intellectually Chamberlain and Halifax were incapable of such Machiavellian diplomacy, and even had they been capable of it, public opinion in Britain would have forced their resignation when news of such an agreement had been leaked.

Were the negotiations with the West then conducted entirely for the purpose of deception? No. The Russians were not sure until August 21 that they would sign with Germany. Hence they wanted to have the most precise information of what the West would and could do for them in case the German gambit failed and they found themselves in war. Some of the information they got was clearly mendacious. Thus the French stated

---

[111] Voroshilov's statement on August 15. *Documents on British Foreign Policy, 1919–1939*, 3d Series, VII, 576–77. And it was not made clear whether this was to take place before or after war began!

that the Maginot Line extended *all the way to the sea*.[112] But this lie probably had the opposite effect to that intended: it implied that the French army in case of war would sit snugly behind its fortifications. Hence Russia made *numerical* demands which, unlike the demands about passage through Poland and in the Baltic, were serious and intended to become operative in case of war: the British and French should pledge that 70 per cent of their forces would be committed to an offensive against Germany if the latter struck in the east; the Soviets would pledge a similar proportion of their army if the blow were delivered in the west.[113] (Incidentally, the conversations reveal what was to become apparent in 1940 and 1941: neither the French nor the Russian army was ready for modern war. The Russians were to learn from the Polish and French campaigns, but in 1939 they still thought that cavalry was an important offensive weapon. The Soviet military confrontation with Germany in 1941 was to be disastrous enough; in 1939 it would have been a catastrophe.)

On August 21 Voroshilov adjourned the military conversations. He did not break them off even now, when Stalin was wiring Hitler to send Ribbentrop, but asked a longer postponement because the Soviet participants were needed at the Red Army's fall maneuvers(!). Not until August 25, when the Nazi-Soviet Pact had been announced and Britain reiterated her determination to stand by Poland if attacked, did Voroshilov break off the negotiations and send the Anglo-French mission home.

The Nonaggression Pact entered into by Germany and the Soviet Union on the night of August 23 was indeed very much like any other pact of this kind except for one detail: the usual provision allowing one of the signatories to opt out if the other one commits aggression against a third party was missing. A Secret Additional Protocol provided that in case of a "territorial and political rearrangement" taking place in Poland the two signatories' "spheres of interest" would run roughly through the middle of the country. Russia would thus receive the Ukrainian and Byelorussian territories *but also a sizable portion of ethnic Poland* in the province of Lublin and part of Warsaw province. The possibility of preserving some rump of the Polish state was to be decided by Germany and Russia after the "rearrangement" took place. A similar "rearrangement" was envisaged in the Baltic area, and here Russia was to have a free hand in Estonia, Latvia, and Finland, Germany in Lithuania. The U.S.S.R. declared its "interest" in Rumania's Bessarabia.

On almost every point Ribbentrop conceded to Soviet demands. He was burning with eagerness to produce the great coup. The social hour that followed the signing was amiable. Stalin drank to Hitler's health; he

---

[112] *Ibid.*, p. 567.

[113] Voroshilov thought in terms of the Franco-Russian pact of 1892, when the numerical proportions of the two armies were similarly defined.

knew, he said, that the German nation "loves its Führer." Ribbentrop drank to Stalin's. But there were already dissonances. The Foreign Minister vented his hatred and contempt of the British and implied they would never fight. Stalin gave his opinion: England "would wage war craftily and stubbornly." He could not enjoy Ribbentrop's attempted injection of humor: a joke was making the rounds in Berlin that Stalin would yet join the Anti-Comintern Pact. But he had a joke of his own: "the Germans desired peace." Ribbentrop bit, and reassured Stalin that for all their love of peace the German people *would* fight Poland. Stalin gave his "word of honor" that the Soviet Union would not betray Germany.

On August 25, Hitler and his "Bismarck," as he now dubbed Ribbentrop, had their first shock. Far from capitulating at the news of the Nonaggression Pact, Britain reaffirmed her obligations to Poland and signed a formal alliance. Momentarily, Hitler faltered. The marching orders to the German army for August 26 were canceled. The Nazi-Soviet Pact had not worked the way the Germans had thought it would. But even when the German armies did cross into Poland on September 1 and for two days afterward, the Germans half-believed that the Western Powers would dishonor their pledge. Stalin's estimate of the British mentality and his gamble on it proved more correct than Ribbentrop's.

At the other end of the Soviet Union, the Nazi-Soviet Pact had a soothing effect on the attitude of Japan. The treaty at first was greeted in Tokyo as a betrayal of the Anti-Comintern Pact and led in August to the collapse of the cabinet. But by the middle of September the fighting that had gone on between the Russian and Japanese troops in the Far East stopped, and on September 15 a formal agreement between the two countries specified conditions for the conclusion of hostilities and for negotiations to settle the frontier problems between Manchuria and Mongolia.[114] This *détente* in Soviet-Japanese relations was a direct result of Tokyo's disenchantment with Germany. With the latter abandoning its pressure on the Soviet Union in order to pursue its interests elsewhere, there was every reason for Japan to do likewise.

The agreement and the steps leading to it represent the quintessence of Stalin's diplomacy. It is clear that he himself made crucial decisions at every step and, as we shall see, even took a hand in drafting notes. Not even Molotov, the second man in the Soviet Union, was trusted to decide on his own when Ribbentrop should be invited to Moscow. Any judgment on the moral aspect of the Nazi-Soviet Pact would be superfluous. But what is of interest to us is to consider whether Stalin left himself any escape should the events of the next few weeks take a different turn. The

[114] Degras, *Soviet Documents on Foreign Policy*, III, 373.

Soviet government took special pains not to burn all its bridges with the West. Insofar as the world knew, the Nazi-Soviet Nonaggression Pact was literally just that. Voroshilov in his final words to the British-French mission blamed the failure of the talks on Poland. But two days later in an interview he held out the prospects of Poland receiving war materials and other supplies from the U.S.S.R.—in line with Potemkin's statement of May 10 that in case of an armed conflict with Germany, the U.S.S.R. would adopt a "benevolent attitude" toward Poland.

Most interesting in this connection is one clause in the secret protocol that was to be discarded in a few weeks: the one that assigned to the U.S.S.R.'s "sphere of interest" a sizable slice of purely Polish territory. Were the unexpected to happen and the French armies to pour into Germany following Poland's defeat, Stalin could have had his Lublin Polish government then and there, instead of in 1944. Whether such in fact was his intention is impossible to say, but it would have been entirely in line with his diplomacy before and afterward. He could have posed as the savior of the Polish nation, and, as the hour of Germany's defeat neared, he could have poured his troops across the Vistula, the projected frontier under the August 23 protocol between his domain and Hitler's.

Within three days of the signing of the Nonaggression Pact, mutual hints of bad faith were already being aired. Berlin was inquiring of its embassy to ascertain the truth of rumors that Russian troops were being withdrawn from the Polish frontier (thus enabling Poland to concentrate all her forces against Germany).[115] Another piquant detail: the two new allies obviously required close military liaison, but the post of military attaché in Berlin remained vacant until September;[116] it was obviously difficult to find a Soviet officer who could be counted on to hold his tongue and be absolutely loyal. The German pressure in all these respects did not reflect an excessive faith in Stalin's "word of honor." The Russians had to be pressured into speeding up the Supreme Soviet's formal ratification of the Nazi-Soviet Pact. After Molotov's expostulations that the Supreme Soviet first had to do some other business and he did not know how long it would take, the pact was finally ratified on August 31. The Germans were beginning to be brusque and pre-emptory in their demands. They were no longer suitors for Soviet friendship, as they had been between July and August 23. And they could not but draw conclusions

[115] *Documents on German Foreign Policy, 1918–45*, Series D, VII (Washington, 1956), 362.

[116] The Russian personnel in the Berlin embassy was to be continually reshuffled during the next two years, no ranking diplomat being allowed to stay in Germany for any appreciable length of time. Most of them were clearly recruited from the secret police.

as to the inner strength of a regime where no military officer, no diplomat was fully trusted by the dictator.

Molotov's speech on the ratification of the treaty bore the impress of the German pressures of the last week. It contained sneering references to the "ruling classes of Britain and France" who would like to involve the U.S.S.R. in a war with Germany. Yet he reasserted the absolute neutrality of the Soviet Union in the coming conflict and assaulted those "who read into the pact more than is written in it." But speaking on August 31, and even for propaganda purposes, Molotov could not make himself express a pious wish that the Nazi-Soviet Pact would prevent any war from breaking out. And within the next three days, the first part of the Soviet leaders' calculations was proved correct: Germany attacked, and on September 3, France and Britain declared war on Germany.

VI

COEXISTENCE
WITH GERMANY: 1939-41

World War II was to prove practically all previous military forecasts and analyses to have been wrong. It is therefore not surprising that the first rude shock received by the Russians was in an area where their intricate calculations had been based on "expert" military advice.

Poland's military potential had been held in considerable respect by the professionals. Even the German general staff estimated that it would take several weeks for the mass of the German forces to destroy the Polish army and that fighting might go on considerably longer. The French believed, as the French commander-in-chief testifies, that the Poles would hold out on their own until the spring of 1940. The Soviet view must have been in between those two estimates. Furthermore, while everybody assumed a largely defensive posture by the West in the beginning, it had to be expected that the French army would at least make a demonstration in force to relieve the pressure on her Polish ally.[1]

The actuality surpassed the rosiest German hopes. Nothing except for some skirmishes took place in the West. Within a few *days* the Polish

---

[1] The secret Polish-French military convention agreed to in May 1939 called for the French to begin full-scale military operations *sixteen days* after the beginning of the hostilities.

By the end of the third week in September, the Soviets were both re-assured and resigned. The reassurance was due to the conviction that Hitler meant to keep his end of the bargain. The resignation was the product of a final realization of Germany's tremendous power. Therefore one could not continue playing games with Hitler, leaving room for a suspicion on his part that one was not firmly and unhesitatingly on his side. With the same diligence with which he had planned before for every conceivable contingency, Stalin now went about removing every possible point of future friction with his terrible ally.

The previously envisaged Polish rump state obviously had to go. Before the demonstration of German might and the West's inactivity, such a state, partly within the Soviet sphere of influence, would have been a useful card to hold in reserve for the day when Germany's fortunes began to decline. Now the whole idea seemed like a trap. Germany was going to approach the West with peace proposals on the ground that there was nothing left to fight about, and the survival of an "independent Poland" of sorts could prove a strong argument to the former appeasers.

The idea of retaining millions of Poles within the Soviet domain also looked quite different on September 21 than it had on August 23. The slightest attempt to organize them into a Communist state or autonomous part of the U.S.S.R. might arouse the Führer's wrath. Hence the Polish ethnic territory had to be turned over to Germany. This was elucidated by Stalin to Schulenburg on September 25 with a frank enough explanation: "In the final settlement of the Polish question anything that in the future might create friction between Germany and the Soviet Union must be avoided."[7] In return for the provinces of Lublin and Warsaw, Stalin wanted Germany to yield him Lithuania, reserved under the protocol of August 23 to the Germans.

The Germans were in a position to drive a hard bargain. But the Russians were helped by an unexpected element: the vanity of the Reich's Foreign Minister. The Russian treaty was the culminating point of Ribbentrop's diplomatic career and the continuance of good relations between the two totalitarian powers his most fervent wish. He had already balked at the German high command's attempts to modify the original protocol, i.e., to take some territory that had been promised Stalin. He was now eager to return to the scene of his triumph.[8]

[7] Sontag and Beddie, *op. cit.*, pp. 102–3.

[8] It was of course Molotov's turn to go to Berlin, but as seen before Stalin had no confidence in anybody except himself conducting the negotiations. And Ribbentrop agreed only too readily to return to Moscow: the Führer might be struck by an irresistible revulsion on actually meeting a Communist, the generals and others might interfere if the negotiations were to take place in Berlin. In Moscow he would be on his own.

The agreements signed by Ribbentrop and Molotov on September 28 mark on the Russian side the real beginning of the alliance of the two powers that was to endure until June 1941. This time there were no loopholes left for future evasions or double-dealing. The Soviet Union would extract all of the loot yielded in agreements with Germany but would observe faithfully (with one exception, to be noted below) all the conditions of the alliance. Thus it will be possible for Molotov to say to the German ambassador on that day in June 1941: "What have we done to deserve this?"

The negotiations lasted into the small hours of September 28, and then from 3:00 P.M. until 5 in the morning of September 29. When Ribbentrop took an hour off to attend the ballet, his sixty-year-old host utilized the interlude to talk with the Latvians. (The Baltic states were already being invited to negotiate the first stage of their absorption by the U.S.S.R.) The new secret protocol confirmed the exchange of Lithuania for the Polish provinces. But, even so, it was provided that when the U.S.S.R. "shall take special measures on Lithuanian territory to protect its interests," Germany would get the southwestern slice of the country.[9] Otherwise the secret protocol of August 23 was confirmed. Both countries pledged themselves to suppress any Polish agitation in their respective territories and to synchronize police measures for that purpose. The principle of mutual voluntary exchange of nationals of the two countries was also agreed upon.[10]

The fact of alliance of the two powers was established in a public declaration claiming that now that the collapse of Poland was a fact, "it would serve the true interests of all peoples to put an end to the state of war existing at present between Germany on the one side and England and France on the other. . . . Should, however, the efforts of the two governments remain fruitless, this would demonstrate the fact that England and France are responsible for the continuation of the war." Both powers pledged, in case of the continuation of the war, to "engage in mutual consultations in regard to necessary measures."[11] This was the price the Soviet Union had to pay for Hitler to keep his end of the bargain. From the Soviet point of view, the re-establishment of peace would have been a catastrophe, and it must have been a considerable relief to the Kremlin when they learned in October of Chamberlain's and Daladier's rejection of the German peace offers. But the joint communiqué was a definite repudiation of any alleged Soviet neutrality; it held out, as a matter of fact, the prospect of the U.S.S.R. joining Germany if the Western Powers

[9] The only significance of that territory was strategic, i.e., in case of war between the U.S.S.R. and Germany.

[10] Many German Communists in Russian jails, some of them of Jewish descent, were surrendered to the Gestapo.

[11] Sontag and Beddie, op. cit., p. 108.

did not come to their senses and conclude a peace with Germany.[12]

For the Soviet Union this was a profound humiliation: in the summer she had been the arbiter of the fate of Europe; now she appeared to be merely Germany's most important satellite. Even Italy at this time exhibited more independence vis-à-vis Germany. Other aspects of the agreements emphasized this degrading dependence: the U.S.S.R. was to provide Germany with vast quantities of raw materials. She was to act as Germany's agent, purchasing supplies from third countries, thus trying to evade the blockade. The terms of trade were not equal. "Soviet deliveries [of grain, iron ore, and oil] of the first six months are to be compensated by us within twelve months"[13] with industrial products and war matériel. (Needless to say, most of the German goods, especially the war matériel, proved to be obsolete.) A Soviet naval base near Murmansk was turned over to Germany for the use of her submarines.

The most conspicuous demonstration of the altered relationship of the two totalitarian states was the abrupt change of attitude on the part of the foreign Communist parties. The first Nazi-Soviet Pact had been a shock for them but did not lead to a repudiation of their anti-German positions. The French Communists pledged their support of their government's declaration of war on Germany. The Communist group in the Chamber of Deputies voted for war credits. Communist leaders, with their Party's approval, answered the call to colors. That no instructions could have reached the French Party between August 23 and as late as September 19, when a Communist leader pledged solidarity with the rest of the French nation in the struggle against Hitlerism, is most doubtful. It was only at *the end of September* that the French Communists along with other Communist parties drastically changed their policy and demanded peace with Germany. Their leaders deserted from the army, and the Party, now officially banned, entered upon a defeatist campaign. As in other things, so in the case of the Comintern, Moscow decided that a double game was too dangerous. Hitler could not be convinced of Moscow's commitment to his cause while foreign Communists remained the most vocal and energetic advocates of resistance to Germany. The Comintern therefore had to work for a solution that its Russian masters most dreaded: a re-establishment of peace between Hitler and the West.[14]

[12] Sometime later, Ribbentrop wanted permission to quote Stalin practically to the effect that the Soviet Union would join Germany in case of an armed showdown with the West. Stalin insisted on and obtained a version of "his" remarks that was less threatening to the West.

[13] Sontag and Beddie, *op. cit.*, p. 132.

[14] The relative degrees of fear inspired in Moscow by Germany and Japan respectively can be indicated by the fact that the Comintern propaganda continued to assail Japan and urge a united front against her in China.

We may never know the exact balance of fears and calculations that inspired the Kremlin in its new policy. The interpretation put upon it at the time—that Stalin genuinely associated himself with Hitler in his plans for conquests—is obviously absurd. He could have had no doubts about Germany's long-range plans. The policy formally proclaimed on September 28 had to be the product of fear. This fear was political as well as military: Russia, despite her military and industrial inferiority, might withstand a German attack, but, as postulated here before, the Soviet regime and certainly Stalin's personal power would not survive the inevitable initial reverses. If the policy of August 23 could find ample justification in the tradition of Soviet foreign policy going back to Lenin's times, then the turn of events epitomized by September 28 was a definite break with that tradition. Russia was becoming an accomplice of one protagonist— and to her the vastly more dangerous one—in the imperialist war. Under such conditions how long would Hitler refrain from reclaiming the ancient centers of German settlement in the Baltic and from using the ready-made weapon of Ukrainian nationalism? Even the greatest optimist among the Soviet leaders could not have seriously believed that once Great Britain and France had acquiesced in Hitler's conquest of Poland they could be persuaded or cajoled into resuming an alliance with Russia. In its infancy, the weak and civil-war-torn Soviet state had never helped German imperialism to the extent that Stalin's Russia was to do between 1939 and 1941.

Apart from the long-run danger, the policy of collaboration with Germany involved certain immediate risks. The Western Powers might again take Stalin at his word and consider the U.S.S.R. as an actual enemy in the war. We now know that, incredibly enough in view of what was to happen in 1940, the French and British general staffs considered armed action against Russia. An Allied expeditionary corps was on the point of being dispatched to aid Finland during her war with Russia. And in March 1940, it was seriously proposed to bomb the oil fields and refineries of Baku. These proposals were in line with the general imbecility that characterized the Allies' military planning during the "phony war," and fortunately they were never put into effect. The Finnish war ended before the expeditionary corps could be dispatched. The German attacks in April and May 1940 made the Allies forget the Baku oil fields in a hurry. But either action would have unloosed a train of events that might have changed the course of history.

For all the incalculable risks involved both to their country and to their personal fortunes, the Soviet leaders put on a brave appearance in their role as Germany's allies. Stalin's and Molotov's cordiality at the reception of Ribbentrop in September made the latter feel, he declared, as if he were at a Nazi social gathering. The tone of the Soviet press toward Great Britain and France became more and more scathing, toward Germany and even National Socialism more friendly. The average Soviet citizen had no reason to suspect the real feelings or fears of his masters. Stalin's wisdom (and it was emphasized in public speeches and statements that the new policy was specifically Stalin's, inaugurated by him in his speech at the Eighteenth Party Congress) had kept Russia from being embroiled in the imperialist war. And when Germany struck in June 1941 the architect of the fatal alliance did not or could not bring himself to address his people. Only after *twelve days* was Stalin able to broadcast to the peoples of the U.S.S.R. and to try to explain to them the policy that at the time was engulfing them in disaster.

For the time being, the Russians took steps to cash in their rewards for the Nazi-Soviet Pact. The secret protocol of August 23, as subsequently amended, clearly left the three small Baltic states and Finland to the mercy of the U.S.S.R. It was envisaged that Latvia, Lithuania, and Estonia would eventually be absorbed by Russia. The case of Finland, it was assumed on the German side, was to be somewhat different, though it was not clear how. The first installment for the three Baltic states was the Soviet demand for military bases and the quartering of the Russian troops on their territories. Warned by Germany to accede to those demands, the three small states had no option but to agree, though fully aware what the Soviet bases portended for their independence. Lithuania on this occasion was given the equivalent of the "condemned man's breakfast." Out of her Polish loot the U.S.S.R. ceded to Lithuania the city and province of Vilna, a gesture eloquent of the firm belief about the country's eventual and full absorption into Russia.[15]

The Baltic agreements were completed in October and offered a poignant commentary on the Russo-German alliance. Against whom did the U.S.S.R. need military and naval bases in the small Baltic countries?

The haste to implement the territorial changes envisaged under the Molotov-Ribbentrop pact was evident in other Soviet moves during this fateful fall of 1939. Logically the next Soviet objective should have been the recovery of Bessarabia from Rumania. But unlike the case of the Baltic area and eastern Poland, the German agreement about Soviet action on Bessarabia was *not* phrased in clear-cut language: "Attention is called by

---

[15] At the time the cession was made, the U.S.S.R. suggested that Germany should now claim her southwestern strip of Lithuania, as agreed on September 28. The Germans, as the Russians probably knew they would, objected to this transaction at that time: it would make them appear as robbers of Lithuanian territory at a time when Russia was generously giving of her own to Lithuanians. There was some delicacy of feeling, after all, in Berlin.

the Soviet side to its interest in Bessarabia. The German side declares its complete disinterestedness in these areas."[16] Rumania, though not highly regarded as a military power, was not an Estonia. Furthermore, Germany could not have tolerated Russia's *complete* absorption of this mineral-rich country. And, at the time, Italy (still not in the war and consequently still enjoying the reputation of a Great Power) evidenced an interest in Rumania. But there was some thought in Moscow of trying to repeat the Baltic gambit with Rumania and Bulgaria. An article in *The Communist International* in December 1939 suggested that Rumania should sign a mutual-assistance pact with the U.S.S.R. on the Baltic pattern. But for the moment a move in the direction of the Balkans was evidently judged to be too risky. The Bessarabian issue was postponed.[17]

The involved situation created for Soviet diplomacy by the alliance with and fear of Germany was demonstrated by the long negotiations that ensued in September and October with Turkey. This country, Soviet Russia's first ally, had been growing close to Britain and France. The Turkish Foreign Minister arrived in Moscow on September 26 and was not to depart until October 17, and then without any agreement having been reached. The length and fruitlessness of his visit reflected the predicament of his Soviet hosts. They were eager for an agreement with Turkey to safeguard their southern flank and the entrance to the Black Sea. At the same time, they were being pressured by the Germans to prevent Turkey from committing herself militarily to the West. Hence Molotov put forth the demand that Turkey should refuse to allow Britain and France passage of the Straits and should not under any circumstances agree to go to war against Germany. Secretly, needless to say, the Soviets were far from being displeased by the anti-German posture of the Turks. On October 19 a formal alliance between Turkey and the Western Powers was signed in which Turkey pledged assistance in the case of war breaking out in the Mediterranean. But Turkey stipulated its neutrality in the case of any conflict that might involve her in war against the U.S.S.R. The treaty, of course, never became operative. When Italy entered the war in 1940, the position of the West appeared hopeless, and even later on the Turks refused a confrontation with Germany, then in complete occupation of the Balkans. But the treaty marked an effective end to that special relationship between Turkey and

---

[16] Sontag and Beddie, *op. cit.*, p. 78.

[17] Another factor in the Soviet restraint over Rumania was of course the joint British-French guarantee granted this country in the spring of 1939. Following the collapse of Poland, the Western Powers informed the Rumanian government that the guarantee could not become operative unless under special circumstances. But until the spring of 1940, the Soviets could not be sure that a move against Rumania would not involve them in a war with the Allies, the contingency feared by them most, next to an attack by Germany.

the U.S.S.R. which had persisted since the early days after World War I, when the two countries felt weak and isolated. In the future the more traditional policy of Turkey would take its place: the historical distrust of Russia as the power bent on the domination of the Straits and the Balkans.

The territorial expansion that partnership with Germany made possible for the U.S.S.R. was exploited immediately and in a manner suggesting that the new areas were expected at some time to become a battlefront. Western Byelorussia and the western Ukraine were speedily united with the corresponding Soviet republics, thus becoming integral parts of the U.S.S.R. There were still Ukrainian-speaking areas left in Rumania (Bessarabia and parts of northern Bukovina) and in Hungary (the old Carpatho-Ukraine), but the vast majority of Ukrainians and all the Byelorussians were now within the U.S.S.R. When the enemy would strike, there would be no sizable detachments of Ukrainians accompanying him into Soviet territory and subverting the 30 million Soviet Ukrainians. In the newly acquired areas, mass deportations in the usual Stalinist style removed any conceivable anti-Soviet elements. It goes without saying that the Polish officials, landlords, etc., were either imprisoned or sent to distant areas of the U.S.S.R. But the deportations in 1939 and, especially, in the summer of 1940 fell heavily also upon elements which under no circumstances could be expected to become pro-German: the Polish and Jewish intelligentsia and professional people. Especially severe measures were applied to Ukrainian nationalists.

The attempt to bolster up the defensive posture of the Soviet Union had to include an arrangement with Finland. This country, in the hands of or in alliance with an enemy of the U.S.S.R., could present a much greater danger than any of the three small Baltic countries. The 1939 Finnish frontier ran within twenty miles of Leningrad. The Finnish government then was known to be anti-Soviet. In April 1939, when negotiations between Britain and the U.S.S.R. had touched on the famous guarantee for the Baltic states, the Finnish Foreign Minister let it be known in London "that they would resent an offer of Soviet help. . . . He added . . . Soviet Russia was more in need of help than the Finns were."[18] Germany was known to be interested in Finland, and it was only the extreme urgency of the negotiations in August that had made the Germans abandon Finland to the Soviet sphere of interest—with the obvious hope that she would not be treated as peremptorily at Latvia or Lithuania.

[18] *Documents on British Foreign Policy, 1919–1939*, 3d Series (London, 1951), V, 253.

The negotiations with the Finns which began in October did in fact develop differently from those with Finland's small Baltic sisters. The Russians demanded that the frontier on the Karelian Isthmus be moved away from Leningrad and that they be permitted to lease naval bases on Finnish territory. They proposed a territorial *quid pro quo* by granting Finland in return for her concessions a large though desolate area of Soviet Karelia. These proposals were not in themselves unreasonable, but the example of the Baltic states prevented the Finns from acquiescing in them. An exchange of territory was accepted as possible, but bases on Finnish soil were rightly held as the first step in a Soviet attempt to recover what had been Russia's before 1917—i.e., all of Finland. The Soviet leadership's usual caution gave way to irritation at the way this country of less than 4 million people was resisting its demands. Armed action began at the end of November. By that time, it was evidently decided to deal with the Finnish problem in a wholesale fashion. Thus on December 1 the Soviet Union recognized and signed a treaty with the "Government of the Democratic Republic of Finland," i.e., with a few Finnish Communists long resident in the Soviet Union, headed by a veteran official of the Comintern, Otto Kuusinen.[19]

If this treaty was a reflection of the hope that the Finnish campaign would be brief and glorious, then the Soviets were in for a cruel disappointment. The Winter War began with a series of reverses. For all their vast numerical and technical superiority, the Soviet armies were repulsed in their repeated assaults upon the Mannerheim Line of fortifications guarding Finnish territory.

The political repercussions of these first, militarily calamitous months of warfare with Finland were not long in coming. The least important was the expulsion of the U.S.S.R. from the institution almost everybody had forgotten about. On December 14, the League of Nations solemnly expelled Russia for her aggression against Finland. But what the Soviet authorities could not disregard or ridicule was the wave of indignation against Russia that swept through many countries. Most notable was the reaction in the United States, where there was considerable public sentiment for Finland, both as a small country fighting aggression by a vast empire, and as the only European nation that had not defaulted on its debt to the United States. Though Molotov was characteristically scathing concerning the American protests on behalf of Finland, it is quite likely that they made an impact in Moscow. Good relations with the United States and concern for American reactions to Soviet moves constituted a corner-

[19] Jane Degras, ed., *Soviet Documents on Foreign Policy*, III: *1933–41* (London and New York, 1953), 410.

stone of Stalin's foreign policy. It is possible that the memory of this American interest and indignation helped to save Finland's independence at the end of World War II, when so many of Russia's neighbors were to become her satellites.

But even more than the reaction of the United States, then barely awakening from the isolationist phase, the Soviet government had to fear the tangible measures of support for Finland contemplated in the West. Plans for a Franco-British expeditionary corps to help the Finns have already been mentioned. Had the Finnish war not ended in March 1940 this force was to have been sent to Finland in conjunction with an operation the Allies were mounting to occupy points in northern Norway. According to Churchill's account, the French were to send 50,000 "volunteers" and 100 bombers, the British a proportionate force.[20] As it was, some real volunteers from the Scandinavian countries came to help the Finns, and a considerable flow of supplies came in from other countries, including warplanes sent by Germany's ally Italy.

Considering that the war lasted a little over three months and that it was carried out against a small and weak nation, the Soviet casualties were huge. By Molotov's own admission, they were in excess of 200,000, with about 50,000 killed. But the course of the war brought even greater dangers and grave side effects. From the Soviet viewpoint, the official German attitude was impeccable: the Finns were told to seek the best accommodation they could find with the Russians. And Hitler and Ribbentrop tried to soothe the newly aroused anti-Communist fervor of the Italians, going as far as to excuse the Russians' lamentable military performance. But for the Germans, the Finnish affair was, beneath the surface, both an embarrassment and a temptation. It was embarrassing from the material point of view: it interfered with the supply of badly needed minerals from Finland. An added element was an unspoken reflection that a "Nordic" nation, a natural ally of Germany in the Baltic, was being sacrificed to the Moloch of Bolshevism. But beyond such sentimental considerations there was the lesson once again of Russia's military weakness and the temptation to press harder on her deeply compromised and isolated regime. Typical of the attitude of certain Germans was a letter from the German Minister in Finland written in January 1940 to Weizsäcker:

> In view of this experience the ideas on Bolshevist Russia must be thoroughly revised. . . . Actually the Red Army has such shortcomings that it cannot even dispose of a small country and the Comintern does

[20] Winston L. S. Churchill, *The Gathering Storm* (London and Boston, 1948), p. 573.

not even gain ground in a population that is more than 40 per cent socialist. . . . In these circumstances it might now be possible to adopt an entirely different tone toward the gentlemen in the Kremlin from that of August and September.[21]

In the suspicious atmosphere of the Kremlin, it had to be considered once again whether Germany might not be tempted to try to purchase a peace with Britain and France by a common endeavor against Russia or whether, without going that far, she might not be secretly pleased by the Allies' military intervention on behalf of Finland. Beneath the cordial veneer serious dissonances were developing between the two totalitarian powers in their economic relations. The Russians were eager for the latest German industrial methods and armament models; the Germans, of course, were far from eager to provide them. It is characteristic that Stalin himself participated in technical trade negotiations with subordinate German officials: only his personal insistence could make a dent in the high-handed German treatment of the Russians' economic requests. At times the all-powerful dictator had to endure rebuffs by inferior German officials.[22] The Russian military and purchasing mission in Germany was told abruptly not to pry into military and technical secrets. The Russians at the time were particularly eager to learn in the field of naval technology, but, as Stalin said plaintively, "Germany did not wish to deliver the few periscopes" or storage batteries needed for submarines. It is hard to decide what is more remarkable in this connection: Stalin's mastery of technical details and attention to business, so different from Hitler's endless philosophic-strategic rantings, or his apparent willingness to subject himself to humiliation at the hands of Ambassador Ritter or Counsellor Hilger of the German embassy.

But Russia was still protected, most of all by Hitler's determination to wreak vengeance on the British and the French and by his Foreign Minister's continuing strong passion for the Russians. Ribbentrop managed to convince Hitler that Stalin had become a Russian nationalist pure and simple and had forsaken world Communism. Ribbentrop's love of the Russians, or rather of his diplomatic success with them, knew no bounds. He explained to the skeptical Mussolini that Russia "was not only in the process of becoming a normal national state but had even progressed quite far in that direction."[23] Even on a point that always made Hitler and his gang see red, Ribbentrop exuded fantastic self-deception:

[21] *Documents on German Foreign Policy, 1918–45*, Series D, VIII (Washington, 1956), 651.

[22] "Ambassador Ritter rejected the view of M. Stalin as unworkable in practice and contrary to the Agreement of September 28, 1939. M. Stalin then proposed to come back to that point later on." *Ibid.*, p. 594.

[23] *Ibid.*, p. 886.

there were no more Jews in high circles in Moscow. When the name of Kaganovich was brought up, Ribbentrop assured the Duce that this member of the Politburo "looked more like a Georgian"(!).

But even the Foreign Minister's solicitude had its ominous undertones. It must have amazed Count von der Schulenburg, a diplomat of the old school, to be told to seek an interview with Molotov or Stalin in order that Ribbentrop might "lease" an estate in Russian territory where he might hunt stags and incidentally meet Soviet statesmen. Schulenburg was also told to procure (this time on his own) some caviar, allegedly for the "badly wounded who can take no other nourishment."[24] Stalin and Molotov, inaccessible at the time to Western ambassadors, thundering about and pouring ridicule on Roosevelts and Chamberlains, were thus assumed to be quite ready to cater to the personal needs of the German minister.

Equally characteristic but even more shameful is the implication of another request to the Russians. The following, from a dispatch from Ribbentrop to Schulenburg, speaks for itself: "We plan to send Herr Nikolaus Rost, a man born in Russia and familiar with conditions there . . . as a courier to Moscow. . . . He is to prepare an investigation of whether it is possible to bring influence to bear on the French Section of the Third International and whether Soviet information files on French Communists could be inspected."[25] This request was met by the Soviet Foreign Commissariat not with indignation but with embarrassed hints that the matter be pursued through other channels. It is unknown whether Herr Rost met with better luck from another Soviet agency. In any case, the French Communists on their own or rather under the Comintern's instructions were already carrying on a vigorous defeatist campaign, which in the opinion of many observers was to contribute to the French collapse some months later. But the mere fact of the Germans' request and that on communicating it their ambassador was not shown the door throws a glaring light on the nature of the relations between the two powers.

The Finnish war, unless concluded in a hurry, promised to reach proportions of a catastrophe. The Anglo-French plans for intervention were hardly a secret. And the Soviets might also have learned that Mussolini was at the same time egging his German colleague on to a drastic change of front, if not indeed an outright attack on the U.S.S.R. In a letter to the Führer of January 3, 1940, he wrote: "The day when

<hr/>

[24] *Ibid.*, p. 324. Ribbentrop's passion for real estate had already caused at least one possessor of a fine villa in Austria to be sent to a concentration camp.

[25] Dispatch of January 3, 1940, *ibid.*, p. 597.

we shall have demolished Bolshevism we shall have kept faith with our two Revolutions."[26] Mussolini's eagerness for an adventure always reflected his belief in the proposed opponent's weakness. Russia's military reputation that winter was at its nadir.

It is then not surprising that, in March, the U.S.S.R. concluded a peace agreement with Finland. Some time before, the Russian troops had finally breached the Mannerheim Line and could be now expected to overrun the country and to foist the Communist government upon it. But the international situation grew threatening. The Kuusinen "government" was told to disband, and on March 12 the Soviet Union concluded the peace with the real Finnish government. Conditions were also more lenient than could have been expected. They adhered in the main to the Soviet proposals of the preceding fall: the frontier was moved away from Leningrad, the Isthmus of Karelia as well as some other border territory going to Russia. The Soviets obtained military and naval bases on Finnish soil. Molotov's review of the treaty in a speech on March 29 reflected the Soviets' ill-humor at this moderate treatment of an enemy who had exacted such a bloody price from the Red Army, and a clear implication that the Soviet government acted under the apprehension that the war might be enlarged. The latter was also the conclusion reached by Schulenburg, who wired to Ribbentrop that the Soviet government broke off the war and abandoned its Communist "government" of Finland out of fear that it might become embroiled in a war with the West.[27]

For all that the Kremlin knew, such a war might have suited the Germans. Or worse still, the Germans might listen to the Italian and other voices calling on them to cease their confrontation with the West and to become once more the defenders of Europe against Bolshevism, which after the Finnish war promised to be both popular and easy. The nagging uncertainties of the situation were reflected in the Soviets' increased worries in their dealings with the Germans. Difficulties developed over Soviet supplies to Germany. Ribbentrop's pleas that Stalin or at least Molotov visit Berlin (in his then infatuation, the German foreign minister firmly believed that a meeting of the two dictators would be the beginning of a life-long friendship) were met with refusals.[28]

The German invasion of Denmark and Norway in April was greeted in Moscow with obvious relief, noted even by the usually not very perceptive Schulenburg. "Our Scandinavian operations must have relieved

---

[26] Ibid., p. 608.

[27] Sontag and Beddie, op. cit., p. 136.

[28] Schulenburg realized how fatuous it was to expect Stalin to go to Berlin and that even Molotov, as he wrote, "has strong inhibitions against appearing in strange surroundings."

the Soviet Government enormously."[29] He then surmised that the Soviets' main fear had been that the British and French might occupy Norway and Sweden.[30] A more perceptive observer would have seen the other reason for this relief. Germany was getting deeper into the war; the chances of her reaching an accommodation with Britain and France were vanishing. But the relief was, as in the past, succeeded by new apprehensions. Though on being informed of the invasion (at the time it was already taking place), Molotov wished "Germany complete success in her defensive measures," the German conquest of Denmark and Norway was far from welcome. The hapless Foreign Commissar soon asked for reassurances (how much could they be worth in view of the past record?) that Germany had no designs on Finland or Sweden. The abject condition of Soviet diplomacy is reflected in the fact that Molotov found himself pleading rather than warning; he "hoped that the inclusion of Sweden in [German] operations would not take place if this could at all be avoided."[31]

The methodical German way of doing things was not abandoned even under Hitler. The news of the Scandinavian invasions was communicated as per instructions on April 9 by the ambassador requesting an interview with "Herr Molotov at 7:00 A.M. German summer time." One can then imagine Molotov's feelings when on May 10 "at 7:00 A.M. German summer time" Count von der Schulenburg requested to see him again. At news of the German attack in the West and the invasion of Belgium and Holland, Molotov expressed no surprise. "He understood that Germany had to protect herself against Anglo-French attack. He had no doubt of our success."[32]

With the German attack on the Low Countries and France, the whole rationale of Soviet policy since September 1939 was put to the test. If the war developed into a prolonged stalemate à la World War I, this policy would be vindicated. If a rapid decision were forthcoming, the policy would be revealed as a fatal gamble.

The latter was to be the case. Within two weeks the Anglo-French armies in the north were either destroyed or beginning to be evacuated. Unlike World War I, no "miracle" then followed, either on the Marne or on the Somme, on which the French tried to establish a new line of defense. By the middle of June, it was obvious that no military resistance was possible in metropolitan France. On June 23, the armistice agreement between Germany and France was signed. Outside the British Isles, only

[29] Sontag and Beddie, *op. cit.*, p. 139.
[30] In reporting this, Schulenburg expressed his belief that the Soviets were always well informed about the plans and strategies of the Western Allies.
[31] Sontag and Beddie, *op. cit.*, p. 140.
[32] Schulenburg to the German Foreign Office, in *ibid.*, p. 142.

the most inveterate optimist could believe that with practically no army, with all of Europe at Hitler's feet, Great Britain would be able or willing to resist.

As seen before, especially in Stalin's speech at the Eighteenth Party Congress, the Soviets had an exaggerated opinion of the Western Powers' strength.[33] The September 1939 German victory in Poland (and France's inaction at the time) must have given that conviction a serious blow; the events in Scandinavia another. Whether the Soviets shared the opinion of most of the world outside of Britain that she could not continue resistance alone is not clear. The power and influence of the British empire had in the past been held by the Bolsheviks in almost superstitious awe. For all the experience with Chamberlain and Halifax, the British were still supposed to be "crafty," as Stalin had assured Ribbentrop on the night of August 23, 1939. Wasn't British Intelligence supposed to be involved in every major case of espionage and sabotage in the Soviet Union? This view of the British—derived, alas, more from the spy stories of E. Philips Oppenheim and Somerset Maugham than from reality—may have helped to convince Russia that Britain's defeat was not as yet inevitable. And behind the British was the United States, beginning to supply Great Britain with weapons. But whatever those calculations and future contingencies, every sober analysis of the situation following France's capitulation had to recognize as a fact Hitler's absolute domination of the Continent. Against Hitler and his allies, only the Red Army remained as a factor. Italy declared war on June 10, an excellent indication that Mussolini considered the war as good as won.

The only clue to the Soviets' feelings about Germany's rapid and unexpected successes is contained in a German Foreign Ministry dispatch to Schulenburg of June 14, which asked him to make a *démarche* with Molotov concerning an alleged statement by the Soviet minister in Stockholm (Mme. Kollontay) to the Belgian minister there to the effect that all European powers should place themselves in opposition to Germany.[34] Schulenburg wisely chose not to interview the Russians on the subject. (Any inquiry would have probably led to the discovery of the Germans' informer in the Soviet legation in Stockholm.) On June 23, an official Soviet communiqué denied rumors of Soviet troop concentration on Russia's western border and reasserted the "good neighborly relations" between the U.S.S.R. and Germany.

A rather coarse Russian proverb describes the utmost of a tight situation in life as such in which one can neither relieve himself nor sigh over

---

[33] It will be remembered that he declared that the democratic powers were economically and militarily much stronger than the totalitarian ones.

[34] Sontag and Beddie, *op. cit.*, p. 147.

the need to do so. This was close to the Soviet situation at the end of June. The Soviet leaders had to put on a brave appearance. Molotov congratulated Schulenburg on June 18 on the "splendid success" of the German arms. Attempts of Churchill's government to establish some friendlier basis with the Soviets were repulsed. Upon its formation in May the National Government in Britain dispatched Sir Stafford Cripps as ambassador to Moscow. The choice was typical of the still lingering misunderstanding of Russian policies in the West. Sir Stafford, a high-minded puritanical socialist who had been excluded from the Labour Party for advocating close collaboration with the Communists, was thought to be peculiarly suited for thawing out British-Soviet relations. In fact, a man of his type and ideas was least appropriate to deal with the Communists, and his experience in Russia was not to be a happy one. Cripps brought a message from Churchill "to Monsieur Stalin" (Stalin still had no official position) but its cautious probing was coldly ignored, and the message received no reply. In the interview with Cripps, Stalin was "formal and frigid"[35]: the Soviet Union was not worried about the German successes or sorry that the old balance of power in Europe had been destroyed. Molotov communicated to Schulenburg the gist of this reply to Cripps.

In fact, the Russians were going through an agonizing reappraisal—to use an anachronistic term—of their policies. The attempt to put the country's industry on a wartime basis is indicated by a decree of June 26, 1940, instituting a seven-day work week and restoring an eight-hour working day. A severe strengthening of labor discipline was also decreed.[36]

The German victories also led to the speeding up of the Soviet timetable for cashing in on the territorial gains under the secret agreements of August and September 1939. From military occupation of the Baltic states, the Soviets moved to annexation. On June 15–16 a thorough occupation of Lithuania, Latvia, and Estonia was undertaken. The course of events was then swift: "coalition governments," deportations of active non-Communist elements, new elections, and, in August, the admission of the three small Baltic countries as integral members of the Soviet Union. This step, though clearly in line with the previous Nazi-Soviet agreements, was bound to be viewed somewhat wryly by German diplomats. (Germany also was losing some important agricultural supplies she had been getting from those countries.) Russia was clearly cashing in on German obligations

[35] Winston L. S. Churchill, *Their Finest Hour* (London and Boston, 1949), p. 136.

[36] *Resolutions of the Eighteenth All Union Conference of the Communist Party of the Soviet Union* (Moscow, 1941), p. 11.

before the Third Reich, having concluded peace in the West, could renege on them. That the move was inspired by a distrust and fear of Germany was obvious. Yet complete Soviet inactivity and subservience to their terrible partner would, given the Nazis' mentality, have increased the German temptation to strike eastward. Thus, beginning with the summer of 1940 the Soviets faced an insoluble dilemma in dealing with Germany: too conciliatory a tone would increase the Germans' itch to strike; too independent a policy could inspire the Führer to one of his rages where he would remember his hatred of Bolshevism and forget his and Ribbentrop's recent discovery that the Bolsheviks had become "Muscovite nationalists."[37]

Increased tension between the two allies, granted their premises and the situation in the summer of 1940, was thus unavoidable. If the Baltic states for all their economic ties with Germany had but a marginal importance for Germany, the same could not be said of the next target of Soviet expansion—the Balkans, in particular Rumania. Rumanian oil was vitally important to the German war effort. Complete absorption of Rumania by the U.S.S.R. was clearly unacceptable. Consequently when in June the Soviet government began to pressure Rumania, German-Soviet relations underwent their greatest crisis since August 1939, and though outwardly this crisis was to be smoothed over it was a vital element in Hitler's beginning in July 1940 to contemplate a concrete plan of attack upon the U.S.S.R.

It is characteristic of German diplomacy that in his haste to conclude an agreement with Russia in August 1939 that would free his hands in Poland, Hitler evidently did not realize the extent of the concessions his foreign minister granted the Russians. Hence on June 24, 1940, Ribbentrop had to remind Hitler that he had then stated that "Germany was politically disinterested in 'these areas' i.e., in the southeast of Europe."[38] The Foreign Minister evidently felt under some pressure, for he declared in the very same memorandum that "the Führer authorized

---

[37] This is not a whimsical way of describing the situation. Following his triumphs in France, achieved in the face of his professional military advisers' earlier doubts and apprehensions, decisions on matters of war and peace depended literally on Hitler's impulsive "intuitions." The extent of Soviet knowledge of German military designs and plans must remain a matter of conjecture. In Japan, Soviet Intelligence penetrated the highest circles of the policy-makers. See F. W. Deakin and G. R. Storry, *The Case of Richard Sorge* (New York, 1966). As we have seen above, Schulenburg was certain that in the Western capitals the Soviets had excellent sources of information. As to the situation in Germany, 1939–41, we simply do not know how far Soviet espionage had been able to penetrate the Nazi agencies responsible for the conduct of the war.

[38] Sontag and Beddie, *op. cit.*, p. 158.

me to declare German disinterestedness in the territories of southeastern Europe, even if necessary as far as . . . Constantinople and the Straits." But that had been in 1939, and now with the Continent at his feet the Führer was bound to have second thoughts.

The Soviet demands on Rumania in addition contained a surprise. If not Hitler then Ribbentrop at least was prepared for the Russians at some point to claim Bessarabia. This country, lying between the rivers Prut and Dniester, with a population of 3 million, had been a part of the Russian empire but following the Revolution was seized by Rumania. Its population was mixed: Rumanian, Ukrainian, and Jewish, with some German settlers. Soviet Russia had never abandoned its claim to the territory which in fact had been seized by force by the Rumanians in 1918, but now in June 1940 Russia put in an additional claim for the Rumanian province of Bukovina. The latter, though largely Ukrainian in population, had never been a part of Russia. It had not even been mentioned in the hasty bargaining of August and September 1939.

The Germans, though acquiescing in the Soviet demands for Bessarabia, now tried to dissuade the Soviets from further claims upon Bukovina. But Schulenburg ran into Molotov's typical stubbornness: "Molotov countered by saying that Bukovina is the last missing part of a unified Ukraine and that for this reason the Soviet Government must attach importance to solving this question."[39] And Rumania could be the logical path into the Soviet Ukraine in case of war. Hence even the mounting danger of a clash with Hitler was not going to stop the Soviets from trying to secure their flank there.

The Germans on their part were put in the unpleasant situation of pressuring the Rumanians to acquiesce in the Soviet demands. By June 28 Rumania acquiesced in her heavy territorial loss. The Italian Foreign Minister, Count Ciano, observed ungraciously (and incautiously, in view of Italy's subsequent record in this respect), that the Rumanians' behavior was in line with their reputation for military bravery. Both Bessarabia and northern Bukovina were occupied promptly.

Molotov's statement reflected the real apprehension behind much of Soviet foreign policy of the last few years: in any possible war the Ukraine was the Achilles' heel of the Soviet Union; any move to detach this fertile and rich part of the U.S.S.R. would be facilitated by the existence of sizable pockets of Ukrainians outside the U.S.S.R. Rumania occupied a vital strategic position on the Black Sea, the sea bordering on the non-Russian parts of the Soviet state: the Ukraine, the Caucasus. As everything since Stalin's speech at the Eighteenth Party Congress had

---

[39] *Ibid.*, p. 159. Molotov forgot for the moment about the Carpatho-Ukraine, then part of Hungary, and so did Schulenburg.

indicated, the Ukrainian issue was felt to be the critical element in any internal danger within the integral parts of the Soviet Union.

If the Soviet leaders expected that the rest of Rumania would now fall into their sphere of influence, they were in for a cruel disappointment. The authoritarian regime of King Carol had been for some time under considerable internal pressure from the pro-German fascist organization, the Iron Guard. Now the king, soon to be expelled anyway, saw the only hope of saving his throne and his country in complete submission to Hitler. The Rumanian government, having petitioned Germany for protection, soon had an occasion to discover what this protection meant. Rumanian ministers were summoned in July to the august presence of the Führer and Ribbentrop. There they were given one of those long historical-philosophical lectures in which Hitler delighted.[40] What was even worse was Hitler's intimation that the unfortunate country was expected to make new territorial sacrifices to its greedy neighbors Hungary and Bulgaria.[41] Also Hitler expressed displeasure concerning King Carol, unacceptable to the Germans both because of his Anglophile sympathies and his Jewish mistress. After Rumania had complied with his wishes in those respects, the Führer was going to guarantee her independence, i.e., take her over.

The fear that Russia might anticipate Germany and move into Rumania led Hitler to order on August 26 preparations for German troops to move into Rumania.[42] On August 30 the Rumanian Foreign Minister was summoned to Vienna and there Ribbentrop, with some nominal assistance from Ciano, proceeded to "arbitrate" the quarrel between Hungary and her neighbor. Rumania had to cede a large portion of Transylvania to Hungary and southern Dobruja to Bulgaria forthwith. After the Rumanian Foreign Minister recovered from a fainting fit, he announced his country's acceptance. The ungrateful Hungarians, who wanted even more territory, were bullied into agreeing. Germany and Italy simultaneously guaranteed "the integrity and inviolability" of what remained of Rumania.[43] Russia's

[40] *Documents on German Foreign Policy, 1918–45*, Series D, X (Washington, 1957), 307–16.

[41] Hungary's constant importuning of Germany to "restore" the territories she lost after 1918 provides some humorous interludes in the somber diplomatic story of the years 1938–40. Having gotten a slice of the old Czechoslovakia, the Hungarian leaders pestered the Germans to get more, and though Hitler was getting heartily sick of the Hungarians, they—simply by threatening to create trouble in the Balkans at inconvenient periods—largely got their way. At one time a Hungarian minister intimated to Ribbentrop that his country expected to get a slice of pre-1938 Austria, i.e., of the current Greater Reich. The German, who could not believe his ears, advised the Hungarian to retire and reflect on what he had just said.

[42] *Documents on German Foreign Policy, 1918–45*, Series D, X, 549.

[43] *Ibid.*, p. 584.

further expansion into the Balkans was definitely checkmated. Rumania soon would receive protection from the *Wehrmacht*.

The Rumanian story led to a stiffening of Soviet-German relations even on the official side. Molotov repeated several times to Schulenburg that the German action in guaranteeing the stump of Rumania "was not entirely in good faith" and constituted a breach of the original agreement between the two powers, which required consultations between them in matters of mutual interest. On September 21 the Russian grievances were embodied in an official memorandum handed to Schulenburg.[44] The Soviets were sorely trying the Führer's famous temper.

What led to the stiffening of the Soviet attitude at the moment of Germany's greatest power and seeming omnipotence on the Continent? The decision must have been reached that excessive subservience to Germany, toleration of flagrant disregard of Russia's "rights" (Rumania was supposed to be in her sphere of interest), would increase the chances of Hitler's attacking. Germany now began to encroach in another sphere supposedly reserved to her ally: negotiations between the Reich and Finland became suspiciously intimate, German armed forces were granted right of passage through Finnish territory. Moreover, Britain's rejection of Hitler's peace proposals on July 19 and the successful struggle of the RAF against German air attacks must have buoyed up the Soviet leaders.

The internal situation in the U.S.S.R. during the summer of 1940 must remain a subject of conjecture. Certainly every attempt was made to minimize for the Soviet newspaper reader the importance of the German successes in the West. At the most decisive moments of the fighting in May and June 1940, a reader of *Pravda* would find on its front pages a smiling picture of Stalin attending the theater or a State Agricultural Exhibition. Soviet political cartoons exuded hostility to Britain. But a significant straw in the wind was the restoration of the grades of "general" and "admiral" in May, part of an obvious attempt to solidify the loyalty of the officer corps to the Party and its leader. Several important generals were co-opted into the Central Committee. Was there any fear in Stalin's mind that in view of the still fresh effects and memories of the purges, and in view of the terrible danger that his policy of *rapprochement* with Germany had brought the U.S.S.R., further subservience to Hitler might threaten his own position? We can only pose the question.

Certainly Molotov's speech to the Supreme Soviet of August 1, 1940, tried to point out, albeit in an extremely cautious way, that Russia was not indissolubly tied to Germany. Attempts "by the British and Anglophile press" to sow discord between the Reich and the U.S.S.R. were rebuffed. But, Molotov said: "The end of the war is not yet in sight. . . . The war

[44] Sontag and Beddie, *op. cit.*, pp. 191–94.

between Germany and Italy on one side, and Britain assisted by the United States on the other, will become more intense."[45] He dwelt gleefully on the great accession of strength to the Soviet Union due to the "voluntary accession" of the Baltic states and Bessarabia, and tried to strike a balance between continuing appeasement of Germany and as yet cautious and vague hints that this appeasement was not unlimited. The speech ended with a reaffirmation that the utmost watchfulness was needed as against any enemy. If this is remembered, said Molotov, "no events will catch us unawares, and we will achieve new and even more glorious successes for the Soviet Union."[46]

In fact, even before, in late July, Hitler reached a tentative decision to attack the U.S.S.R. in 1941. General Halder's diary notes that on July 31, at a conference of his military chiefs, the Führer announced his intention to start military operations in May and to "smash" Russia in five months.[47] The reasons then given were that the invasion of England might have to be postponed and Britain relied on an eventual war between Germany and the U.S.S.R. By the end of August the operations division of the German high command made a tentative plan of attack. In November and December the actual plans were rehearsed by the general staff. Hitler signed the actual directive for "Operation Barbarossa" on December 18, 1940.[48]

The reasons that impelled Hitler to order the attack on Russia before concluding war with England have often been discussed and cannot be dwelt on here at length. That the accommodation with the U.S.S.R. was always felt by him to be a temporary one there can be no doubt. Insofar as his unbalanced personality admitted of any long-range political scheme, it was the co-domination of the world by Germany and the British empire. On the more involved psychological side his "love-hate" complex about England urged him to postpone the destruction of that Germanic state until and unless the hateful Bolsheviks were first disposed of. His enjoyment of actual military operations, first in Poland and then in France, urged Hitler to have another satisfying land war, where the German armies would move swiftly and mercilessly through the enemy. On a more rational basis, the whole nexus of irritations concerning the Baltic states, Finland, and finally Rumania probably decided Hitler to take the plunge. There were people in his entourage who were appalled by the prospect. The generals submitted technical objections, but after the Führer's intui-

---

[45] Degras, *op. cit.*, III, 462–63.

[46] *Ibid.*, p. 469.

[47] *Documents on German Foreign Policy, 1918–45*, Series D, X, 373.

[48] *The Second World War, 1939–1945* (Moscow: Ministry of Defense, 1958), pp. 130–31.

tion had so often been justified they hardly dared object too strenuously. (The attempts of Hitler's civilian advisers to avoid or postpone the confrontation with Russia are related below.)

Soviet suspicions of Germany were naturally increased by the signing on September 27 of the Tripartite Treaty between the two Axis powers and Japan. Russia was notified of the pact on the eve of its signature. Though the treaty specifically mentioned that the contracting powers' relations with Russia were not to be affected, and though Schulenburg explained soothingly that its main aim was to scare the United States and dissuade her from intervening on the British side, the Russians were understandably unhappy. The clauses of the treaty were in the pompous language of the totalitarian powers' diplomacy. Japan recognized the "leadership of Germany and Italy in the establishment of a new order in Europe." The two European powers reciprocated in recognizing Japan's in Greater East Asia. Military, etc., help was to be forthcoming in the case of any one of the three being attacked by a power not currently engaged in the existing conflicts.[49]

Molotov's tone in his discussions with the German ambassador now became strident: he asked petulantly to see the secret clauses of the Tripartite Treaty. He complained about German troop movements into Rumania and Finland. This behavior inspired Ribbentrop with the idea that the Foreign Commissar was becoming anti-German and was in a way sabotaging Stalin's policy toward the Reich. Hence, with a clear disregard for protocol, he addressed a personal letter *to Stalin* explaining German policies of the last months and once more pressing for the dispatch of Molotov to Berlin for intimate conversations on the future of the Russo-German collaboration.[50] As against Ribbentrop's lengthy epistle Stalin's reply was couched in a few paragraphs: Molotov would come.

The visit of the Chairman of the Council of Commissars and Foreign Commissar to the land of the Nazis was an event in itself. Previously in the Stalin era, no Soviet politician of the first rank (as distinguished from officials of the Foreign Commissariat, like Litvinov) had been

[49] *Documents on German Foreign Policy*, Series D, XI (Washington, 1961), 204–5.

[50] Ribbentrop's notion about Molotov was on the face of it absurd. Yet there are some rather curious sidelights on the direction of Soviet policies of the period. Stalin, previously readily available to the German diplomats, ceased being so with the German offensives in the West. Schulenburg himself felt that he could not request an audience with Stalin and against his minister's implicit instructions handed to Molotov his letter to Stalin.

allowed to go abroad.[51] A special detachment of the security police, headed by its deputy commissar Merkulov, watched over Molotov. The new ambassador to Germany, Paul Dekanozov, was also in the party.[52] It was only with the greatest difficulty that the Russians were persuaded to change into the German train at the border (which was necessary because of the difference in railway gauges between Russia and the rest of Europe), and needless to say they immediately started looking for hidden listening devices.[53]

The conversations in Berlin began on November 12 and lasted two days. Molotov conferred at length with Hitler and with Ribbentrop.[54] Hitler's lengthy discourses were to the effect that the U.S.S.R. should join the Tripartite Pact. The loquacious Führer tried to dazzle his guest by the prospect of Russia's participation in a distribution of the "bankrupt British Empire": certainly the "natural" tendency of the U.S.S.R. was to move in the direction of the Indian Ocean. The fabulous treasures of the Orient did not seem to enchant Molotov, who tried to turn the talk to Finland and Rumania and what exactly the Germans were up to there. At times the conversation became strained, with Molotov interrupting Hitler—something the latter had not been accustomed to in recent years. Thus, he questioned the Führer's opinion that German moves in Finland were designed to protect that country from Britain(!). And how, wondered the Commissar, could it be said that the German soldiers in Rumania were there really to guard against British landings in Greece?

The ineptness of German diplomacy and Hitler's megalomaniacal lack of patience with the country whose policies had enabled him to score his fabulous victories emerge clearly from the record of the conversations. It would have been obvious to a person much less suspicious than Molotov that the Germans wanted Russia to become entangled in some anti-British adventures in the direction of India and Persia while Germany

[51] In the 1920's such figures as Trotsky, Bukharin, Rykov, etc., went frequently for the "cure" on vacations to Germany.

[52] Dekanozov too came from the security apparatus. In 1953 he was shot along with his boss and countryman, Beria. At the time, however, he was a rising star in Soviet politics, known to be in Stalin's confidence. Dekanozov was the third Soviet ambassador since 1939. His predecessor had not known German and in his conversations with Nazi officials was attended by *Stalin's own interpreter*.

[53] The story of the visit is related by Valentin Berezhkov, then attaché in the Soviet embassy, in the Soviet magazine *Novyi Mir* (*New World*), July 1965, pp. 143–55.

[54] One of the latter conversations took place in an air-raid shelter during a British raid on Berlin. Ribbentrop repeated on that occasion that Britain had lost the war. If so, said Molotov, why are they in an air-raid shelter and whose bombs are falling? *Ibid.*, p. 154.

was solidifying her hold on the Balkans, reclaiming Finland for her sphere of interest, and pointing a dagger at the Soviet Union's vulnerable spot, the Ukraine, through her occupation of Rumania. The proposed treaty between the Tripartite Powers and the U.S.S.R. was one of those pompous and largely meaningless declarations in which Hitler delighted, but its actual effect for the U.S.S.R. would have meant complete estrangement from the United States and a possibility of war with Britain.

On Molotov's return to Moscow, Soviet policy again underwent a subtle change. On November 26, 1940, Molotov talked to Schulenburg in the presence of Dekanozov. He now expressed a willingness to sign the proposed Four-Power Pact but attached several conditions. The most important ones were Russia obtaining bases in Bulgaria and the withdrawal of German troops from Finland.[55] Both conditions had been previously rejected by the Führer, despite Molotov's assurance (less than credible in view of what had happened in the Baltic countries) that Russia would respect Bulgaria's independence. But Molotov's willingness to adhere to the pact at all marked a considerable change from his skeptical attitude in Berlin. Stalin, it appears, was still eager to appease the Axis; whether and how far Molotov had tried to change his master's opinion is, of course, unknown.

The Soviet counterproposals never received a formal answer from Berlin. One might have thought that withdrawing German troops from Finland (which most likely would have been followed by another Soviet attack upon that country) and allowing Stalin to move into Bulgaria would have been an ideal cover-up for German preparations to attack the U.S.S.R., but German policy operated by fits and starts. In August-September 1939 Hitler did not bother to check what was being promised in his name to Stalin; in November-December the mere idea of further concessions to Russia infuriated him.

Soviet policies, in the face of the Germans' almost contemptuous silence, were to remain, as we shall see, an amazing mixture of occasional defiance and utter blindness to what by March 1941 was rumored in all the capitals of the world: Hitler's approaching attack on the U.S.S.R. Fairly solid clues and deductions based on the logic of events can guide us in relation to Soviet motivations before, but what went on between November 1940 and June 1941 must in the absence of any further evidence remain most puzzling. Pronouncements by the Soviet armed forces and an occasional speech by Stalin warned against a possible surprise attack and urged constant vigilance. Yet when the attack did come the frontiers were poorly defended and no systematic plan of defense against Germany seems to have existed. The Germans' shifts of huge numbers of troops to their

---

[55] Sontag and Beddie, *op. cit.*, pp. 258–59.

eastern frontiers could not have escaped the notice of even the most inept intelligence service. Overflights of Soviet territory by German aircraft became a frequent occurrence beginning in March 1941, and Soviet protests about them were virtually ignored. Yet no comprehensive preparations against attack were allowed, no diplomatic moves for possible alliances in case of war were undertaken. Warnings by the British ambassador were rudely spurned. Did Stalin believe that any countermeasures would in themselves precipitate a German attack? Did he fear that any attempt to warn the Soviet people about the forthcoming struggle would create such a revulsion against the main author of the pro-German policy that his hold on power might be threatened? Or did he humanly enough oscillate between hope that somehow the blow might still be averted or postponed, and sporadic measures of preparedness? The fact remains that *in September 1939* the Soviet war forces had been put on war footing and partial mobilization had been ordered. Nothing resembling that order of preparedness was in existence on June 22, 1941, when the enemy did strike.[56]

The course of events leading to the fateful move on June 22 can now be briefly summarized. On February 27 Schulenburg was told to call on Molotov to inform him of what, in view of the Soviet position on the issue, was a direct challenge to his government: Bulgaria was going to accede to the Tripartite Pact, and German troops were moving into Bulgaria. The reasons given for the troop movement were, for a change, genuine enough. Germany had to rescue her ally Italy, currently being trounced ingloriously by little Greece—hence the need for a *place d'armes* in Bulgaria. But over and above this consideration was the Führer's determination not to have Bulgaria fall to Russia and to keep Russia from the Straits.

The declaration was received frigidly by Molotov, and both privately and publicly the Soviet government signified its displeasure.[57] Schulenburg, a strong advocate of continued peaceful relations with Russia and not privy to Hitler's intentions, became at the same time alarmed at the rumors of an impending clash. Mrs. Laurence A. Steinhardt, wife of the American Ambassador, met him at a party and begged him to tell her if a war was coming. If so, she wanted to leave immediately. He reassured her, needless to say, but the fact that he transmitted to his superiors this tale of silly and undiplomatic behavior meant that he himself needed reassurance. It was not forthcoming.[58]

March brought a further airing of German-Soviet differences. On

[56] On the chaos in Soviet military preparations in the spring of 1941, see John Erickson, *The Soviet High Command* (New York, 1962), pp. 567–73.

[57] *Documents on German Foreign Policy, 1918–45*, Series D, XII (Washington, 1962), 195.

[58] *Ibid.*, p. 285.

March 25, the Soviet government publicly reiterated its benevolent attitude toward Turkey and its determination to preserve complete neutrality in the case Turkey became involved in a war with a third state. This sounded like a go-ahead sign to Turkey to pursue an independent policy vis-à-vis Germany and an assurance that Russia would not pull the gambit she had used in Poland in 1939 if Germany moved against Turkey. A more direct defiance of Germany's Balkan schemes was soon forthcoming.

On March 25 Yugoslavia followed Bulgaria in declaring its adherence to the Tripartite Pact, i.e., she entered Germany's New Order. But the Yugoslav government that signed the pact was within two days overthrown, along with Prince Regent Paul. The group of Serbian officers who assumed power under the nominal rule of King Peter expressed the wish to continue good relations with Germany, but Hitler considered their act as a gross personal affront. Hence, unmindful of the risks involved, he decided to invade Yugoslavia as well as Greece—thereby postponing "Operation Barbarossa," the invasion of Russia.

During the week that intervened between the installation of the new regime in Belgrade and the unleashing of the *Blitzkrieg* upon it, the Soviets adopted an attitude of extreme friendliness toward Yugoslavia. What possessed them to take this step, a blatant provocation of Hitler? Undoubtedly, the hope of forestalling another German coup à la Bulgaria, possibly of dissuading the Germans from attacking Yugoslavia. There might have been some hope that if attacked Yugoslavia and Greece would hold out for several weeks or even months. At any rate, the new regime was courted vigorously, and the Russians dropped hints of a military alliance. On April 4, Molotov informed Schulenburg of an impending treaty of friendship and nonaggression with Yugoslavia. The German ambassador tried in vain to dissuade him from this undertaking. On the night of April 5, the treaty was signed, pledging the U.S.S.R., among other things, to a policy of friendship toward Yugoslavia in case she was attacked by a third country.[59] The next day the news was announced in the Soviet press, accompanied by a photograph showing Stalin smiling broadly in the company of the Yugoslav ambassador. The same day Germany struck, and within a few days the Yugoslav and Greek armies were defeated and the two countries occupied.

This smashing German victory was a reminder to the Russians of the awesome might of the German war machine. The difficult, mountainous terrain of Yugoslavia and Greece might have suggested to the Soviet experts (especially in view of the Greek performance against Italy) that those countries might have put up a considerable struggle against an army dependent on motorized transport. But within one week the German

[59] Degras, *op. cit.*, III, 485.

conquest was complete. The lesson urged the Soviet leaders to a last-ditch attempt to appease Hitler. On May 9, Soviet recognition was withdrawn from the Belgian and Norwegian governments in exile, and the same step was taken in regard to Yugoslavia, thus flagrantly violating the treaty with the Royal Yugoslav Government which was barely one month old. Ambassadors of the three countries were ordered out of the U.S.S.R.

In the few weeks of peace remaining, the Soviet government was able to score one great diplomatic triumph, and it was to have incalculable consequences. This was the signature, on April 13, of the Soviet-Japanese Neutrality Pact. The treaty was a result of Foreign Minister Matsuoka's trip to the European capitals. In lengthy conversations in Berlin, the Japanese statesman was given veiled hints of German designs on the U.S.S.R. But Hitler and Ribbentrop were also most eager for Japan to strike against the British in Asia. In his lust for adventure and conviction of omnipotence, Hitler had by now lost the gift that in the past had been instrumental in helping him score fantastic successes: the ability to concentrate on one thing at a time. Hence he did not press the Japanese on the need to move against Russia and, on his own initiative, gave Matsuoka an assurance of Germany's immediate assistance if Japan found herself at war with the United States.[60] The vain and garrulous Japanese minister thus returned to Moscow with no imperative warning against signing a treaty with Russia. Here he was subjected to the most sedulous flattery by the Russians, with Stalin himself toasting Matsuoka as a fellow Asian. The points of Russo-Japanese disagreement in the negotiations touched mostly on Sakhalin, the southern part of which was owned by Japan, which also ran oil and coal concessions in the northern, Russian-held part. The original Japanese proposal that the Russians sell northern Sakhalin was abruptly rejected. (He must be joking, Molotov told him when Matsuoka broached the subject.) The Russian counterproposal for the Japanese to give up their concessions was for the moment put aside. Both sides were eager for a treaty of neutrality that would enable Japan to concentrate on her plans of conquest and Russia on her danger.

Just such a treaty was announced on April 13. It provided for neutrality as between the two parties in the case of an aggression by a third party, as well as for nonaggression. The duration was set for five years, and there was to be automatic renewal unless one party renounced the treaty before the expiration of the term. Both powers pledged also to respect the inviolability of their satellites, Manchukuo and Outer Mongolia, a step that provoked a protest by the nominal suzerain of both, the Republic of China.[61]

[60] *Documents on German Foreign Policy, 1918–45,* Series D, XII, 456.
[61] The text in Degras, *op. cit.,* III, 486–87.

On the departure of Matsuoka, Stalin indulged in a most unusual gesture: he went to the railway station to bid the minister goodbye. Among those gathered there was Ambassador Schulenburg. On seeing him, Stalin threw his arm around his shoulder and said, "We must remain friends and you must now do everything to that end."[62] He then repeated the gesture and words with the acting German military attaché.

Nothing, it seems, could be more transparent than this courting of the representatives of two states that had been, and one of which was soon to be again, a mortal enemy of the U.S.S.R. But appeals to the vanity of statesmen are surprisingly often effective—witness the charm cast on Ribbentrop by his earlier Soviet receptions. Matsuoka, himself strongly pro-German, had his head momentarily turned by Stalin's flattering attentions, and he promised to persuade his government to give up the concessions in northern Sakhalin, something the Japanese government did not do until the final disaster was staring it in the face. The courting of Schulenburg was useless: the German ambassador was a firm believer in the continuance of good relations with Russia, but neither he nor anyone else could by now sway Hitler.

The treaty with Japan was a great coup for Stalin's diplomacy. Nobody, least of all he, could have believed that the treaty would preclude the Japanese from striking whenever they thought it to their advantage to do so. But the treaty was an indication that a party within Japanese ruling circles desired relief of tension with Russia, hoping to free Japan's hands to work against the British empire and to exert new pressure on the Chinese. There was undoubtedly also an incentive for the Japanese to take belated revenge on their German allies for their treaty with the Russians in 1939. Most of all, from the Soviet point of view, the treaty allayed the fear felt in some Soviet circles over Hitler's continuous successes and the recent failures of Russian diplomacy in the Balkans. It "proved" that avoidance of war with Germany was not hopeless; otherwise, would Germany have allowed Japan to sign the treaty with Russia?

In fact, the chances of avoiding war were by now nil. Schulenburg returned from an interview with Hitler on April 28 convinced that the Führer was preparing for war. He was not told that in so many words, for Hitler by now did not trust his discretion.[63] The ambassador's minute of May 7 to Weizsäcker exuded despair over the chances of avoiding a conflict, the outcome of which, he was sure, would be disastrous to the Reich.[64] As usual, Schulenburg was rather badly informed about what

---

[62] *Documents on German Foreign Policy, 1918–45*, Series D, XII, 537.

[63] Schulenburg was eventually to be involved in the anti-Hitler plot in 1944 and to pay for it with his life.

[64] *Documents on German Foreign Policy, 1918–45*, Series D, XII, 734–35.

was going on in the Soviet Union and even more amazingly ignorant of the psychology of the people among whom he had served for so long. He was sure, he wrote, that in case of war the Soviet government would evacuate Moscow and Leningrad and proclaim them open cities. But such a step would have been out of keeping with the whole Russian national tradition and psychology.

On May 6 Stalin assumed the chairmanship of the Council of Commissars, Molotov reverting to his former position as deputy chairman and retaining his foreign portfolio. The step created a sensation, since it was the first time since he became dictator that Stalin chose to take a governmental post. The reason for his decision must remain obscure. He had always displayed knowledge of and took a hand in the most minute governmental decisions, and it would be ridiculous to think that his power was in any way augmented by his new position. It is probable that his decision was motivated by two other considerations. The Germans thought—and the Soviets with their special means of information were undoubtedly aware of it[65]—that Stalin represented the "peace party" within the Soviet government. If anything could reassure Hitler on that point, this new assumption of the chairmanship could have been it. In the second place, Stalin's assumption of the actual headship of the government could, given the psychology of a totalitarian society, have a soothing effect on the Soviet citizen. The "boss" himself took over the reins, everything was guaranteed to come out well.

On June 14 the famous communiqué of the Soviet press agency was published denying "rumors spread by forces hostile to the Soviet Union and Germany, forces interested in the further expansion and spreading of the war," that a conflict between the two powers was imminent. It called absurd the notion that the transfers of German troops were connected with any plans of invasion of the U.S.S.R. The rumors were largely attributed to the British.[66] The text of the communiqué was handed, prior to its publication, to the German ambassador. What possessed Stalin, in view of hundreds of intelligence reports which by now must have been coming to him about the German preparations, to issue a statement bound to lull the vigilance of the army and the people is difficult to say. Was it a last desperate attempt to allay Hitler's suspicions and stay his hand?[67] Was

[65] Schulenburg employed Soviet citizens both in his embassy and in his home. They were of German descent, hence he rather naïvely believed they were reliable. The German embassy in Tokyo was penetrated by the Soviet intelligence network.

[66] Degras. *op. cit.*, III, 489.

[67] How seriously the Germans believed their own subsequent stories that the Russians had been massing troops on the border is difficult to say. The Soviets were in a "damned if you do, damned if you don't" situation. At times for obvious reasons they themselves spread rumors of powerful con-

it to convince his own people that if the Germans struck it would not be the fault of the machinations of his own regime but an undeserved and perfidious aggression? Quite in line with the psychology of a totalitarian regime, after June 22 Soviet propaganda stressed the fact that the Soviet regime was not guilty of any aggressive measures that might have provoked Hitler.

If the Russians took no serious account of real warnings, they did become alarmed over a really silly episode. On May 10 Rudolf Hess, Hitler's deputy for Nazi Party affairs, flew to England with the fantastic idea of persuading the British to make peace with Germany. Writing twenty years after the war and in a Soviet magazine known for its open-mindedness, a Soviet diplomat can still maintain that the mission was on behalf of the German government and that there were men in the British government eager for a joint British-German crusade against Russia.[68] One can then imagine the panic that the news brought in 1941. On May 15, the enterprising German ambassador in Turkey, Papen, intercepted the Turkish ambassador's dispatch from Moscow which pictured Stalin as willing to go to any lengths to appease Germany: "Stalin is about to become a blind tool of Germany."[69]

What would have happened had the Germans advanced new demands in May is open to conjecture. There are limits even to the most absolute dictator's powers, and it is unlikely that Stalin could have acceded, even if he wanted to, to really demeaning conditions (e.g., cession of Soviet territory) and yet remained at the helm. But everything indicates that he was otherwise willing to go quite far. But nobody on the German side was now willing to put him to a test. The meticulous Germans were already

---

centrations of their troops on the western frontier. The Soviet ambassador in Sweden, Mme. Kollontay, leaked out news that never had the Soviets had such powerful troops on the border. (*Documents on German Foreign Policy, 1918–45*, Series D, XII, 832.) But such a considerable concentration could not have been concealed and presumably would have provoked the Germans. In fact, as the official Soviet war history reveals, the entire 2,000-kilometer frontier was covered by forty infantry and two cavalry divisions, most of them *not* on the alert when the blow fell. (*The History of the Great Patriotic War* [Moscow: Ministry of National Defense, 1961], II, 14.) It was too much if a defense in depth was intended, much too little to defend the frontiers against the more than 170 German divisions that struck on June 22.

[68] Berezhkov, *ibid.*, pp. 162–63. Hess, it is well known, unbalanced and irked by his removal from participation in important war decisions, flew entirely on his own initiative. He had fallen under the influence of some people in the circle of the German geopolitician Karl Haushofer, and from them he got the idea that the Duke of Hamilton, then Steward of the Household to the King, could persuade the British government to make common cause with Germany.

[69] *Documents on German Foreign Policy, 1918–45*, Series D, XII, 876.

drawing up plans for occupation regimes for most of European Russia. In true Nazi style, quarrels were already erupting as to which Nazi bigwig was to control which area and whether the SS, the Foreign Ministry, or Hitler's specialist on Russian affairs (Rosenberg) was to have supervision of the whole. The Ukraine, the Baltic states, and Byelorussia were to become protectorates of the Reich. "Muscovy" was also to be occupied. An overanxious official regretted that nothing had yet been planned about the German personnel for the government of Asiatic Russia.[70]

On June 21, the Soviet government instructed its ambassador in Berlin to make yet another protest about constant violation of Soviet airspace by German planes. Ambassador Dekanozov could not be received by the Foreign Minister and left the protest with his deputy. The note pointed out that previous protests, the last one on April 18, had not been answered. Since then, 180 violations had taken place, some overflights being more than 100 miles into Soviet airspace. The same day, Molotov repeated the protest to the German ambassador in Moscow and begged him to explain what had brought on the deterioration in relations between the two powers.

During the night (i.e., on June 22, about 3 A.M. Berlin time, 5 A.M. in Moscow), Dekanozov was summoned to Ribbentrop and Schulenburg made his last call on Molotov. The Germans handed notes to the Russians listing alleged Soviet treacheries and threats that compelled the Führer to take "preventive steps." These meant 190 German and satellite divisions pushing into the Soviet Union and warplanes destroying Soviet planes on the ground and bombing cities. Two details of those interviews are worth noting. Molotov, expostulating with Schulenburg, said, "Surely we have not deserved that."[71] Ribbentrop, during his talk with Dekanozov, was obviously highly intoxicated and kept repeating in an uncertain voice that he had not wished this war.[72] On their return to the embassy, Dekanozov and his staff turned on the Moscow radio. The invasion had been going on by then for more than two hours, but the radio began with its 6 A.M. calisthenics lesson, followed by the children's program. The news, when it came, consisted of the usual recitals of achievements of Soviet industrial workers, etc. Only at 12 noon did Molotov read the official announcement of the German invasion of the U.S.S.R. His speech again emphasized that the attack was unprovoked: "Until the very last moment the German Government had made no complaints to the Soviet Government."[73] Molotov sought to draw a distinction between "the bloodthirsty

---

[70] *Ibid.*, pp. 960–62.

[71] Gustav Hilger and Alfred Meyer, *The Incompatible Allies* (New York, 1953), p. 336.

[72] Berezhkov, *op. cit.*, p. 168.

[73] Degras, *op. cit.*, III, 491.

clique of Germany's fascist rulers" and the German people, a distinction Soviet propaganda was to mute for the next three years. The attack was "a perfidy unparalleled in the history of civilized nations."

Ivan Maisky, ambassador in London, who heard the speech on the radio, records his first impression: "Why Molotov? Why not Stalin?" The same question must have been repeated by millions of Soviet citizens who, as Maisky also notes, had been taught about "Stalin's gift of foresight and the infallibility of his moves."

VII

THE DIPLOMACY OF
THE GRAND ALLIANCE: 1941–45

1. *The Time of Danger*

Speaking in the Kremlin on May 24, 1945, Stalin for once came close to describing what must have been his innermost sentiments on that fateful day in June 1941:

> Our government has made many mistakes. We had some desperate moments in 1941–42 when our army was in retreat, forced to abandon our native villages and cities . . . abandoning them because there was no other way out. Some other nation might well have said to its rulers: You have not fulfilled our expectations, go away, we shall set up another government, which will conclude peace with Germany and will secure us quiet.[1]

And he drank to the *Russian* nation, the leading nation of the U.S.S.R., for its understanding and support during those cruel days—support which, he implied, had come as something of a surprise to its masters.

As mentioned before, once the specter of war arose with the coming to power of Hitler in 1933, the Soviet regime had been acutely aware of the threefold danger involved in any conflict that might take place on

---

[1] J. V. Stalin, *The Great Patriotic War of the Soviet Union* (5th ed., Moscow, 1950), p. 352.

Soviet soil. There was the obvious one of military defeat at the hands of an industrially and technologically more advanced country. In addition to the usual hazards of war, the Soviet regime recognized that a prolonged war on Russian soil, even if the Soviet Union were eventually victorious, could bring with it a breakdown of the Communist system—just as the three years of World War I spelled disaster for the Tsarist regime, even though at its downfall in 1917 the front line had been stabilized and the Germans were in occupation of a much smaller part of the Russian empire than they were to hold between 1941 and the end of 1943. If the Communist system could survive the war and if the multinational structure of the U.S.S.R. would hold together, there was still another danger: would Stalin's personal regime, which had treated its people so cruelly, withstand the test of war? Or would "the nation" say, "You have not fulfilled our expectations, go away"? It is this threefold problem which is important to remember in assessing Soviet military strategy and diplomacy through the first eighteen months of the war. Only with the triumph at Stalingrad was the regime assured that the war would be brought eventually to a victorious conclusion and that Stalin, far from being displaced, had become the symbol of the national resolution to destroy the invader.

These considerations explain why Russia's great weapon, space, was allowed to figure but little in Soviet military doctrine. A temporary loss of territory might not affect the final outcome of the war, but it could spell disaster to Stalin. On the evening of June 22, despite the total surprise of the German attack and the complete chaos prevailing in the army, the Soviet high command directed its forces "to enter upon attack in the main directions with the aim of destroying the attacking enemy formations and *to shift military operations to enemy territory*."[2] This was utter folly from the military point of view and could only have been dictated by the most desperate political considerations. The results were disastrous, as were also the continuous refusals of the high command (i.e., Stalin) throughout the summer and fall of 1941 to sanction timely withdrawals, thus making the Soviet forces incur vast, often fruitless, casualties.

Stalin's failure to address his people between June 22 and July 3 has been attributed to various causes. Khrushchev claimed that the despot for once lost his nerve and could not immediately recover in the face of the immense disaster. The indiscreet Maisky fills in on his boss's behavior: "Then [June 22] I did not know that from the moment of attack by Germany Stalin locked himself in his study, would not see anybody, and did not take any part in state decisions."[3] But it is at least reasonable

---

[2] My italics. *History of the Great Patriotic War of the Soviet Union*, II, (Moscow, 1961), 30.

[3] Ivan Maisky, in *Novyi Mir (New World)*, December 1964, p. 163.

to assume that the dictator waited to assess the internal as well as the external situation before making his appeal and report. Had the first days of the war been less disastrous, it is conceivable that Stalin might have been replaced by the marshals, but the overwhelming threat and the speed of the German advance called for unity and not for a settling of the old scores. If there had been such a possibility, it must have been overcome by June 30 when the State Defense Committee was set up to assume the supreme leadership of the Party and the state. It was headed by Stalin and included Malenkov and Beria, neither of them then a Politburo member but both especially close to the leader. And the supreme command, initially entrusted to Marshal Timoshenko, was in July also assumed personally by Stalin, Timoshenko being assigned to a field command.

Stalin's famous radio address of July 3 has been described in countless Soviet novels and stories dealing with the war. It has been credited, even during Khrushchev's anti-Stalin campaign, with having had an important effect in raising the people's morale. But Ambassador Maisky, who listened to it in London, records a different impression: "It came out badly. Stalin spoke in a dull and colorless voice often stopping and breathing heavily. . . . He seemed ailing and at the end of his strength. The speech could not have led to an upsurge of enthusiasm among his listeners."[4] The address for the first time revealed the extent of the German advance. It was couched in almost pleading tones: "Brothers, sisters . . . I speak to you, my friends. . . ."[5] Much of the burden of Stalin's argument was a justification of his decision to sign the treaty of nonaggression with "such monsters and cannibals as Hitler and Ribbentrop." The treaty had won for the Soviet Union a breathing-spell of a year and a half. "Our war for the freedom of our Fatherland will become one with the war of the nations of Europe and America for their independence and democratic freedoms."[6] He acclaimed the "historic declaration" of Churchill about forthcoming British help to the Soviet Union and noted a similar declaration by the government of the United States. And he called rather disingenuously on his people to unite not only around the Red Army but also around "the Party of Lenin and Stalin."

Churchill's "historic declaration," delivered on the very day of the invasion, must have come as a pleasant surprise to the Soviets. The arch-instigator of intervention during the Civil War, the arch-enemy of Communism declared without any prior conditions or hedging: "We shall

---

[4] *Ibid.*, p. 165. This attack on the official legend was probably the main factor in the severe criticism of Maisky at the Twenty-third Party Congress.

[5] Stalin, *op. cit.*, p. 15.

[6] *Ibid.*, p. 29.

give whatever help we can to Russia and the Russian people. We shall appeal to all our friends and allies in every part of the world to take the same course and pursue it, as we shall, steadfastly to the end."[7] This should have stilled any suspicion of the British, but that suspicion was built into the Soviet mentality. A generation of Soviet leaders had been taught and had come at least partly to believe that the British empire was the mortal enemy of Communism and (this justifiably) the bulwark of the world order Communism had set out to overthrow. Even during the most crucial days ahead, Stalin could not refrain from referring to the Hess "mission" in terms that implied the British were not telling the whole truth about it.[8] If during the war the Russians could never bring themselves to exhibit toward the British the same degree of trust and amiability they were to show (to be sure, not always) toward the Americans, this was to be not only the product of deliberation and of shrewd appraisal of changing power relationships, but an almost instinctive response, bred into them by their ideology.

Churchill's speech received coverage in the Soviet press, but no message was forthcoming from Stalin. If at first he was stricken by panic, Stalin must subsequently have been feverishly busy. Even so, it is simply incomprehensible that he could not have addressed a few words of appreciation and greetings to his ally after June 30, when evidently he was back at the helm. On July 7 Churchill sent another message, addressed with old-world courtesy to "Monsieur Stalin." A Soviet military mission got to London on July 8. Only on July 18 did the Soviet dictator reply.

His letter contained, as Churchill was to note, the sole effort to excuse the Nazi-Soviet Pact that the Allies were to hear from the man who had concluded it. The Germans' position, wrote Stalin, would be even more favorable had not an additional distance been put between them and the centers of the U.S.S.R. in 1939. But the gist of Stalin's letter consisted of the first of what were to become innumerable requests for an *immediate* second front to be established in France to relieve German pressure in the east. Stalin also suggested a front in the "north," i.e., in Finland and Norway, where the British would be required to furnish naval and air support while the Russians would send an army unit to collaborate with a Norwegian force shipped from Britain. The latter suggestion was related to the Soviet fear about Leningrad, now in danger from the Finns and their German allies. Churchill had to give an answer which in 1941 and

[7] Winston L. S. Churchill, *The Grand Alliance* (London and Boston, 1950), p. 372.

[8] When, during a conversation with him, Churchill became indignant on the subject, Stalin remarked amiably that *his* secret service did not tell him everything, so how could the Prime Minister be so sure?

for some time afterward was only too true, that given the present state of British armaments and manpower any invasion remained in the realm of fantasy. The Russians never accepted this excuse as having been made in good faith. In addition to their desperate situation and the never quite abated suspicion of their British allies, their bitterness was undoubtedly caused, as Churchill noted, by their incomprehension of the vast complexities and demands of an amphibious operation required for an invasion. On the British side, there was the natural feeling, to which Churchill was to give vent, that in view of the Soviet attitude toward the British prior to June 22, Soviet importunities (and later on insinuations) were to put it mildly undeserved. Much later on, when the invasions of France became feasible from the military viewpoint, Churchill's opposition to it was motivated by the desire to avoid a blood bath on the scale that the British armies had undergone in World War I. Understandable though this attitude was, it could not find much sympathy in Moscow.

The formal alliance was patched up in a brief treaty signed by Molotov and Cripps on July 13, 1941. It did not seek to deal with any political questions; there was no time or inclination for that. Both powers pledged mutual help; under no conditions would they separately negotiate or conclude a peace with the enemy.

By the middle of July, the Soviet government must have felt that the immediate danger had been staved off and that the worst had not come to pass. The Soviet armies, while retreating, had not in most cases disintegrated. No widespread popular uprisings had taken place. Stalin's supreme authority had been reasserted. Britain and the United States, far from applauding the German attack, had hastened with promises of help. At the end of the month, Stalin expressed confidence to President Roosevelt's emissary, Harry Hopkins, that "the line during the winter months would be in front of Moscow, Kiev, and Leningrad, probably not more than 100 kilometers away from where it is now."[9] Yet the most painful and costly defeats for the Soviets were to come during August and September, the main one being the encirclement and capture of Kiev, where, if Khrushchev is to be believed, Stalin's refusal to sanction a timely withdrawal was responsible for the heaviest Soviet casualties in a single battle during the first year of the war.

A detailed or even a general history of the war cannot be dealt with here. Yet it is important for an assessment of Soviet foreign policy to note certain effects of the military situation at least during the first two years of the war.

The illusory lessening of German pressure gave way in August-Septem-

[9] Robert E. Sherwood, *Roosevelt and Hopkins* (New York, 1950), p. 339.

ber to a renewed offensive that belied the Russian hopes.[10] Stalin's messages
to Churchill reached a degree of frankness never subsequently approxi-
mated: "The relative stabilization of the front which we succeeded in
achieving about three weeks ago has broken down. . . . Without . . . help
the Soviet Union will either suffer defeat or be weakened to such an
extent that it will lose for a long period any capacity to render assistance
to its allies."[11] A message of September 4 specified as the help needed
a "second front in the present year somewhere in the Balkans or France,
capable of drawing away from the Eastern Front thirty to forty divisions."
Churchill's explanation as to the impossibility of such a step drew from
Stalin an agonized response: "It seems to me that Great Britain could
without risk [*sic!*] land in Archangel twenty-five or thirty divisions, or
transport them across Iran to the southern regions of the U.S.S.R."[12]

Churchill's comment was that "it seemed hopeless to argue with a man
thinking in terms of utter unreality." But the Prime Minister failed to
grasp the full import of Stalin's request. It was normal for Stalin to ask
for a second front in the west, only a bit less than normal to ask for one
in the Balkans (which from 1943 on the Russians were to consider largely
as their preserve). But that a sizable British force should be established
on Soviet soil was a request that could have been motivated only by a
feeling of urgency bordering on despair. Later on, when their military
situation improved, the Russians would balk at Allied *observers* with their
armies; a single base on Soviet soil for American shuttle-bombing of
Germany became the subject of long discussions and was soon abandoned;
a proposal for an Anglo-American air force to defend the Caucasus was
entertained by Stalin when the situation again became grave in the
summer of 1942 but vetoed by him in December when the fortunes of
war had turned definitely in the Soviet favor. That a regime so deeply
suspicious of any contact with the West, so intent on preserving its people
from any exposure to foreigners should beg for a force of three or four
hundred thousand British soldiers to fight on its soil—and in a region
that it had traditionally suspected the British of having designs on—is
convincing proof that at least between September and December 1941 all

[10] They had probably been based on an exaggerated idea about the number
of German casualties. Though official figures were undoubtedly blown up for
propaganda purposes—e.g., Stalin's statement in November that the enemy
had already lost 4.5 million men (a figure surpassing the *total* of the German
forces on the Eastern Front)—they reflected also the Soviet commanders'
swollen estimates, which under conditions then prevailing could not be
checked.

[11] Churchill, *op. cit.*, p. 455.

[12] *Ibid.*, p. 462.

other aspects of the war were pushed aside, and only one, the imperative need of stopping the Germans, remained. This would not occur again.

The fact that for two weeks in July the war situation could be considered more hopefully affected one crucial—as it turned out—aspect of the Soviet Union's relations with the Allies. This was Poland.

Under the Molotov-Ribbentrop agreement, the U.S.S.R., as we have seen, had occupied a large part of pre-1939 Poland. This part subsequently was annexed to the Soviet republics of the Ukraine and Byelorussia. The demise of the Polish state was accepted by the Soviet government, which, needless to say, maintained no diplomatic relations with the Polish government-in-exile in London. An end to this state of affairs became a matter of urgency to Britain, because of the obviously abnormal situation in which her two allies were vis-à-vis each other; to the Soviet Union, because the Polish issue was the strongest element in the anti-Soviet feelings lingering in Britain and America; and to the Polish government, because upward of 1.5 million Poles evacuated from eastern Poland after the Soviet entry were still in Soviet camps and jails including, *it was hoped,* thousands of Polish officers and tens of thousands of soldiers captured by the Russians in September 1939. Negotiations, which began on July 5 in London, were bitter. The Poles naturally enough wanted a guarantee that their pre-1939 eastern frontiers would be restored after an Allied victory. The Russians stubbornly talked about the restoration of "ethnic Poland," i.e., a Poland shorn of the areas annexed by the U.S.S.R. How much the temporary brightening of the military situation in July contributed to Russian inflexibility it is difficult to say. It is likely that, had British pressure been brought to bear not upon the Poles but upon the other party, the negotiations would have taken a different turn. As Churchill puts it delicately: "We had the invidious responsibility of recommending General Sikorski to rely on Soviet good faith in the future settlement of Russian-Polish relations, and not to insist on any written guarantees for the future."[13] Yet one must observe that whatever written guarantees Russia might have given in the hour of her peril, it is inconceivable that Stalin would have accepted *in victory* a large Ukrainian region remaining outside of the U.S.S.R. Ambassador Maisky, conscious of the British pressure on his behalf, proved to be a stubborn negotiator. General Sikorski, head of the Polish government, had to acquiesce finally in the noncommittal formula by which both governments recognized the Nazi-Soviet agreement of 1939 on Poland as nonexistent and resumed diplomatic relations. The Polish leader was moved by the desperate need to resume contact with the mass of the Polish deportees in the Soviet Union and to extend some measure of protection to them. His decision to sign a treaty (it was ini-

13 *Ibid.,* p. 391.

tialled on July 30) without any Soviet commitment about the frontiers led to a crisis in his government. In the House of Commons, Foreign Secretary Eden asserted that His Majesty's Government did not accept the Soviet annexations of 1939, but the effect of this declaration was undone by his simultaneous declaration that they did not guarantee the Polish frontiers of September 1, 1939. As stated above, whatever was signed on July 30 would not, perhaps, have proved decisive in 1945. But Britain's readiness to appease her Soviet ally at the expense of another one was to set a precedent and to constitute a lesson.[14]

The course of Soviet-Polish relations until the new breach between the two governments in 1943 may be briefly noted. Simultaneously with the July 30 Soviet-Polish agreement, the Presidium of the Supreme Soviet amnestied Polish prisoners and deportees, and Polish army units began to be formed on Soviet soil. The high point of the Soviet-Polish reconciliation was reached in the first days of December, when General Sikorski visited Stalin. The Soviet dictator again implied that he was willing to discuss the territorial issue and that he had in mind a Polish-Soviet frontier that would be a compromise between the one established by the Treaty of Riga and the Molotov-Ribbentrop line. Sikorski felt, however, that any concession of the pre-1939 Polish territory was out of the question, and the subject was dropped.[15]

Within a few days, the great Soviet victory before Moscow drastically improved the military picture, and the Soviet attitude toward the Polish government hardened. Persons from former eastern Poland who were of Ukrainian, Byelorussian, or Jewish origin were declared to be Soviet citizens and beyond the reach of the Polish authorities. 1942 witnessed rising tension and repeated statements by the Soviet government that it would not yield on its annexation of 1939. The Polish embassy in the U.S.S.R. and the relief work among the Poles was subject to interference by the secret police; prominent Polish personages would disappear.[16]

[14] That the Soviet government would, if pressed by the British, have been agreeable to a compromise solution on the territorial issue is strongly suggested by an editorial in *Pravda* on August 4. Gently upbraiding General Sikorski for repeating the Polish claim to the pre-1939 frontier, it remarked that the Soviet government, in referring to the nullity of the Nazi-Soviet Pact of 1939, "underlined that territorial changes are not permanent" and that the problem of the Polish-Soviet frontier is one for the future. The editorial referred with obvious satisfaction to the British refusal to guarantee the Poles their pre-war frontier.

[15] Jan Ciechanowski (Poland's ambassador to the United States during the war), *Defeat in Victory* (New York, 1947), pp. 78–79.

[16] The most notorious case concerned two Jewish socialists, Polish citizens, Henryk Erlich and Victor Alter, who vanished in December 1941. Only in December 1942 did Ambassador Litvinov in Washington reveal that those

The Polish military units formed on Soviet soil were, after heated debate, evacuated to Iran and then to the Middle East and the West. The Soviet authorities sponsored a Union of Polish Patriots, a largely Communist-guided organization of Poles in the U.S.S.R., which presumably could and eventually did become the nucleus of a rival Polish government. Thus did relations between the two countries that were suffering most cruelly from Hitler go from bad to worse. And the Polish problem was to cast an increasingly dark shadow over the Grand Alliance, becoming the source of those dissonances, recriminations, and, finally, diplomatic crises that ripened into the cold war.

In the fall of 1941, many of the future dilemmas of Soviet foreign policy could already be discerned. The Soviet Union was an ally of the power traditionally held to be the arch-enemy of the Soviet system and Communism. It was in partnership—and on December 7 this became a full alliance—with the United States, the new center and bulwark of world capitalism. The travails of the Grand Alliance, and the apprehensions, doubts, and illusions of the British and American statesmen, are a matter of public record. But the wartime calculations and apprehensions of the *Soviet* leaders must be drawn mostly by inference. For Britain, June 22, 1941, meant that she was no longer fighting alone, and December 7 of the same year was to offer the probability of victory. For all of Churchill's worries about the future of the empire, the Soviet and American involvement removed the most pressing concern. British and American statesmen could plot the course of the war, confident that victory was assured, even if distant, and that the future of their countries' democratic institutions was secure. For all their political ambitions, their own perpetuation in power could not be for Churchill or Roosevelt as primary and intense a consideration as for a totalitarian leader. But the war Stalin was fighting was a threefold one. As well as being a national war, it was a war for the preservation of the Communist system and of his own totalitarian powers.

That these three aspects could not be separated even at the moment of the greatest military danger is evident from certain crucial decisions announced soon after the beginning of the hostilities. The institution of political commissars with every unit of the army was restored, some of the most important Party leaders being assigned to the military fronts.[17] Some of the great commanders during the war were men who had suffered imprisonment and torture during the purges (e.g., Marshal Rokossovsky and Army General Gorbatov). All of them had seen comrades and friends executed or disgraced. Now they were leading their troops into

---

two Jewish veterans of the Russian and Polish revolutionary movement had been shot on charges of pro-German activities.

[17] Notably Zhdanov, in besieged Leningrad, and Khrushchev, with the Southern Direction, as the over-all Ukrainian front was at first known.

a mortal struggle "for the country and for Stalin," but whether their loyalty to the latter would endure when the greatest danger had passed was far from certain.

The huge police network, shortly before split into two commissariats, was now reunited into one, headed by Lavrenti Beria, one of the original members of the State Defense Committee. The U.S.S.R.'s vast propaganda resources emphasized from the very first announcement of invasion, when Stalin was still allegedly locked in his office and refusing to see anybody, that he was guiding the destinies of his people and exercising control over the most minute aspects of the struggle. Stalin, this time somber and unsmiling, was in every picture of international significance: with Molotov and Cripps signing the Anglo-Soviet alliance, with Harry Hopkins on the occasion of Hopkins' visit to Moscow. He was not only Chairman of the Council of Commissars and of the State Defense Committee but also Minister of War and supreme commander. Thus, whatever might have been the feelings of his commanders and of the common people on June 22, there could be hardly any question a month later that the destiny of the country and of Russia's alliances was bound up, at least until the moment of victory, with that of Stalin. The confusion and disorder that seized the army and the country at the moment of invasion would without him turn into utter chaos and an irretrievable national catastrophe.

A map of Soviet fears—or, one should perhaps say, Stalin's fears—as to what might happen in the case of war had been revealed during the great purge trials of 1936–38. Prior to August 23, 1939, it had been considered almost axiomatic that Germany and Japan would synchronize their attacks against Russia. The Japanese-Soviet nonaggression treaty could not be taken as an ironclad guarantee against such a development; there was no reason for the Soviets to attach exaggerated importance to such treaties in view of their own and the Axis Powers' past records. Indeed, on July 1, Ribbentrop wired to Matsuoka that "the impending collapse of Russia's main military power and thereby presumably of the Bolshevik regime itself offers the Japanese the unique opportunity. . . . The need is for the Japanese Army to seize Vladivostok. . . . The goal of these operations should be to have the Japanese Army in its march to the west meet the German troops advancing to the east halfway even before the cold season sets in."[18] (The Foreign Minister's strategic concepts must have brought some interesting comments from the Japanese armed forces. Even Hitler's "Operation Barbarossa" envisaged German military occupation only up to the Archangel-Astrakhan line. The Japanese army

[18] *Documents on German Foreign Policy, 1918–45*, Series D, XIII (Washington, 1964), 62.

would have had to undertake a rather long march to meet their Axis partner "before the cold season sets in"—to be more specific, one of about 6,000 miles in four months!) There were officials in Japan, most notably Matsuoka, who were untroubled by such a trifle as the non-aggression pact, and who shared the desire to attack the Soviet Union in the rear.[19] But the prevailing military view favored expansion southward, while the Germans were taking care of the U.S.S.R. anyway. A determined German effort would probably have brought Japan into the war. But, fortunately for its opponents, never was the mixture of pride, ineptitude, and ignorance so characteristic of German policy as in 1941. To the urging of his advisers that he pressure the Japanese to attack, the Führer (and this was in September when the Russians had already shown themselves much tougher than expected) said no: "He is concerned that this would be interpreted as a sign of weakness (as if we had need of Japan)."[20] Matsuoka resigned, and the imperial conference in September decided to turn the Japanese expansion southward.[21]

It is often asserted that the Soviets were reassured about Japanese intentions through espionage reports they were receiving from many sources, mainly from their network in Tokyo, headed by a *confidant* of the German ambassador there, a veteran Soviet spy, Richard Sorge.[22] Yet, though Sorge's reports appear to have been very accurate and though his services to the Soviet Union were later acknowledged (in 1964) by the government of the U.S.S.R.,[23] it is difficult to see how the Soviets could have been completely reassured about the Japanese designs until December 7, 1941, and perhaps not even then. There had been considerable dispute and uncertainty within Japanese ruling circles as to the direction in which they should strike, whether to attack the United States as well or only the British empire and the Dutch East Indies, etc. The Russians had disregarded hundreds of intelligence reports about the forthcoming German attack—and indeed in studying World War II one is often struck by the fatuity of much of espionage activity, except for that at the technical level (breaking of codes, information about new weapons, etc.); that they shifted many of their Siberian troops to the European theater was simply a reflection of their desperate situation. But even so, considerable military forces remained on guard in the Far East. Pearl Harbor freed the Kremlin from a major part of their worry over Japan, and then Hitler, com-

[19] Toshikazu Kase, *Journey to the Missouri* (New Haven, 1950), p. 48.

[20] *Documents on German Foreign Policy, 1918–45*, Series D, XIII, 466.

[21] Kase, *op. cit.*, p. 46.

[22] See F. W. Deakin and G. R. Storry, *The Case of Richard Sorge* (New York, 1966).

[23] The acknowledgement included a posthumous order, naming a street in Moscow after him, etc. *Ibid.*, p. 350.

pounding the folly of the Japanese, declared war on the United States.

Probably more than the Japanese threat, questions about the loyalty of the population of his western territories must have preyed on Stalin's mind. As the German armies moved through the Ukraine, the Baltic regions, and Byelorussia, they were conquering regions that had been most cruelly hit by the forcible collectivization of 1930–33, famine and Stalin's russification policies. In the areas acquired in 1939 and 1940, the brutal methods of the Soviet occupation were still a very fresh memory. Had the Germans been capable of humane and moderate treatment of the conquered populations, the effect of their occupation would become a danger to the Soviet system even after the invader was chased back. The Ukrainian problem had been, as we saw above, one of the most persistent worries of the Soviet leaders in the 1930's, and this worry, one of the main keys to their foreign policy. What would have been the fortunes of the war, or even of the U.S.S.R. after the eventual defeat of Germany, had Hitler in 1941 or 1942 proclaimed the independence of the Ukraine, Byelorussia, and the Baltic states, and had he appealed to the Russian people in the name of the true spirit of the Revolution of 1917, as against Stalinism? Granting the character of the Nazis, this was as likely as the prospect of Stalin instituting a two-party system at the end of the war. The German authorities were incapable even of a modicum of common sense which would have assured them the acquiescence and passive support of the population of the conquered territories. At the time when repeated successes still had not destroyed his political realism and when German diplomacy was still cunning and wary, Hitler in 1934 had said that his army might conquer in Russia an area larger than Germany and still eventually lose the war. The implication was clear. Russia could be conquered only through politics supplementing military successes. But Germany's plans for the conquered territories envisaged only subjugation and exploitation. Their very administration became a welter of intrigue and infighting between rival groups of Nazi gangsters. The nominal overlord, Rosenberg, by birth a Baltic German, was an obscurantist held in contempt by the tougher breed of his party comrades.[24] It is well known that Hitler's explicit orders were that Moscow and Leningrad were not to be taken by the German armies even if they should offer to surrender but to be

---

[24] A memorandum of the Nazi conference on the rule of the occupied territories may be briefly quoted: "Rosenberg states he intends also to employ Captain von Petersdorff because of his special merits: general consternation. . . . The Führer and the Reichsmarshall both insist that without doubt Petersdorff is insane." On the problem of pacification, the Führer offered this ingenious and humane directive: "Naturally this giant area would have to be pacified. The best solution was to shoot anybody who looked askance." *Documents on German Foreign Policy, 1918–45*, Series D, XIII, 154.

razed to the ground.[25] The surviving inhabitants were to be made to shift for themselves. On this, the best commentary is offered by another incident recorded in the German archives. Ribbentrop was entertaining one of the satellite leaders, Mr. Tuka of Slovakia. The latter stated "that being a teacher of international law he had to note that German policy in recent years had brought about a new epoch in international law, and was striving finally to establish a true legal order." Ribbentrop was most touched by this handsome compliment.[26]

There were a few far-sighted people in the German military and civil hierarchies who realized not only the criminality but the utter folly of the Nazi plans and behavior in the occupied areas, but by and large they were heeded but little and only when utter military disaster faced the Reich. In the Nazis' philosophy, the Slavs were generally considered as *untermenschen*—subhuman—an epithet perhaps applicable to the people who coined it, and their policies toward them were barbarous in the extreme, sufficient after a while to dim the memories of the cruelties of the Stalinist regime. That there was considerable apathy about the coming of the Nazi invaders and, at first, not negligible collaboration with the Germans can be attributed to some extent to the general phenomenon of inertness of the people ground down for a generation under another totalitarianism,[27] and to the fact that the full horrors of the Nazi regime took some time to sink in. That there had been considerable collaboration or at least acquiescence in the German rule in the Ukraine and Byelorussia was acknowledged by implication by Stalin's toast when he drank at the victory banquet to the *Russian* people. (To be sure, Russians were the most numerous element in the U.S.S.R. and the Red Army, but not as fully exposed to the ravages of occupation as the Ukrainians and Byelorussians.) Several national regions were, following their reoccupation by the Russian army, disbanded as autonomous units of the U.S.S.R., their surviving population dispersed among other areas as a punishment for their alleged widespread collaboration with the invader. Among them were the Volga Germans, the Tartar region of Crimea, and the Chechen-Ingush. On the latter two, it is pertinent to observe that the German treatment of the non-Slavic, especially Muslim and Turkic, groups was mild as compared to that meted out to Russians and Ukrainians.

This digression concerning German occupation policies is necessary to illustrate another aspect of Soviet internal problems during the war and their projection into the future that must have influenced Stalin's foreign policy. He could not be sure how much Hitler's policies were going to help

[25] *Ibid.*, p. 623.

[26] *Ibid.*, p. 824.

[27] This point is made by George Fischer, *Soviet Opposition to Stalin* (Cambridge, Mass., 1952).

him to reconquer his country and to reimpose his iron rule. His personal regime might not survive the effects of a long war. In 1914, patriotic elation had greeted the war with Germany, but two-and-a-half years later no general would raise his hand to save the tottering Tsarist government. Or the regime could survive and military victory would come, and yet large areas of the Soviet Union would still be in a state of rebellion against Communist rule and/or Russian domination. Hence many features of the Soviet intercourse with the Allies which gave the impression of pathological suspicion are explained by those considerations. The continuous demands for a second front, even when the Germans could no longer win in the east, were prompted by the urgent necessity of reconquering Soviet territories as soon as possible and before any form of anti-Soviet organization could take root there. That and the natural desire, natural even in a regime that was most cruel toward its own citizens, to rescue its countrymen from foreign occupation motivated the harsh, demanding, at times insulting tone that Stalin adopted in his communications with Roosevelt and, especially, with Churchill.

The insistence on the U.S.S.R.'s retaining territory acquired in the period 1939–41 found its source in the Soviets' realization that at the end of the war, at best, the country would find itself exhausted and the regime vulnerable. The two capitalist powers might well relapse into a position of hostility. A Ukrainian enclave *outside* the Soviet Union's territorial limits might once again prove a source of danger and might indeed appeal to the people of the U.S.S.R.'s second most important republic. At the end of the war, the Soviets were to snatch even the Carpathian Ukraine from their Czechoslovak allies. (Thus the "gnat," as Stalin described it in March 1939, was united to the "elephant.") And, as we know, some anti-Soviet partisan activity in the Ukraine did go on until 1947.

These premises of Soviet diplomacy were reflected in its methods. To allow extensive Western military missions into Russia, to have British and American observers at the front, would mean exposing Soviet vulnerabilities and problems. During the first few months of the war, the Russians were well aware that the "best informed" Western sources expected a speedy Soviet collapse. They suspected, not entirely without reason, that to some in the West the prospect of Germany and Russia bleeding each other to death was not displeasing. Plans for a future European settlement were watched by them with apprehension. (Thus the tentative arrangements made during 1942 for a future federal arrangement in eastern Europe which would begin with a union between Poland and Czechoslovakia were brought to an end through determined Soviet pressure upon President Benes' Czechoslovak government-in-exile.) The apprehension that the Western Powers would consider making a separate peace with the Germans could not have survived the first contacts with the British and American statesmen and the realization of the state of public opinion in Britain and, after December 7, 1941, in the United States; occasional charges to this effect were undoubtedly designed to feed propaganda fuel to the idea of the second front. But nobody who sat in the Kremlin through the war and watched unfold the fantastic industrial and military potential of the United States could have failed to be apprehensive about the post-war settlement, or could have failed to realize that only the utmost diligence and skill would prevent the Anglo-Saxon powers from dominating the post-war world and, in so doing, from presenting a danger to the Soviet Union, where the vast task of economic and political reconstruction would have only begun.

No mention has been made here of the role of Communist ideology in the assessment of Soviet war aims and fears, but whatever the intricate balance of ideology and the national interest in the mind of the leaders, the interests of international Communism could not occupy their attention, at least not until their own survival was assured. The victory at Stalingrad in early 1943 provided considerable assurance in that respect, and, as we shall see, Soviet war diplomacy was to undergo some important changes in the spring of 1943. June 22, 1941, marked a drastic reversal of course on the part of all Communist parties. The struggle with the German occupying power became the first, in fact the overwhelming, priority of good Communists in Europe; the British and American parties shifted from defeatism to a violently pro-war course. Ideology took a definitely second place to resistance, and service to the "Fatherland of Socialism" and to their own countries happily blended for the duration.

Such, then, was the background against which Soviet diplomacy was to operate during the war. Modern technology made it possible for much of the burden of actual negotiations to fall upon the leaders of the Allied countries: Churchill, Stalin, and Roosevelt settled the great issues either through personal get-togethers, in messages, or via their men of confidence: Eden, Beaverbrook, Molotov, Hopkins, and Harriman. The role of diplomats, unless they happened to be in the preceding category, like Harriman, became strictly secondary. As during the alliance with Germany, so now the conduct of Soviet foreign relations reflected the fact that there was only one person in the Soviet Union who could make on-the-spot decisions, and he, of course, could not leave the U.S.S.R., his only trips abroad (to Teheran and Potsdam) being to places where there were Soviet troops. The role of the Soviet ambassadors in London and Washington was principally that of reporters of the events and moods in the Allied countries and of whippers-up of public opinion in favor of a second front. The Washington post became of overwhelming importance from that point of view, and consequently it was filled in the fall of 1941 by one Soviet diplomat who enjoyed unique prestige in the West, Maxim Litvinov. The former commissar had fairly recently been disgraced by the public announcement of his dismissal from the Central Committee of the Party in February 1941, but now he was recalled, for both he and Maisky in London possessed great expertise about and personal ties in the West, something of which the newer generation of diplomats and secret policemen, brought into the *Narkomindel* with Molotov, was utterly bereft. When both Maisky and Litvinov were recalled in Moscow in 1943, it was a sign that good will in the West was no longer thought to be of desperate importance and that for the tough negotiations ahead Stalin preferred people who were entirely products of his own system.

Both diplomats, men of perspicacity and charm, faced at first an unenviable task. Maisky recalls a scene in November 1941 when Churchill's message to Stalin had suggested that two distinguished British military leaders visit Moscow for consultations with the Soviets. Stalin's answer was insulting: if Generals Wavell and Paget were empowered to sign an agreement about a forthcoming invasion of the Continent, well and good. If not, neither he nor his generals could spare the time just to talk with them.[28] Maisky recalls his apprehensions about delivering this wounding message to Churchill, who had so unhesitatingly, despite bitter experience, cast his country's destiny on the Soviet side. He went to see the Prime Minister after ensuring that Eden would also be present to soothe the old warrior's wrath. "The Prime Minister's face became purple, he clenched his fist." There followed a verbal explosion, and Maisky had to beg Churchill to calm himself.[29] There were to be many such scenes.

The overwhelming need for unity against the enemy was, however, to prevail over such clashes. If the Americans and the British were not ready to send their troops, they were eager and able to provide vast material help. On October 1, the Beaverbrook-Harriman mission signed in Moscow an agreement stipulating huge war supplies to be assigned to the U.S.S.R. "These included 400 planes a month, 500 tanks . . . scout cars and trucks . . . aluminum, tin, lead, oil," etc.[30] The story of Allied aid to the Soviets during the war is yet another subject which cannot be considered here at length. Suffice it to note that in one of the rare public acknowledgments of material help on June 11, 1944, the Soviets listed supplies hitherto received from *the United States alone* as including "6,340 aircraft, and in addition 2,442 aircraft received from the U.S.A. on account of British obligations . . . 3,734 tanks . . . 206,771 lorries. . . . Food deliveries

[28] Maisky, *op. cit.*, p. 175. Churchill dates the message and subsequent scene in September. *Op. cit.*, p. 457.

[29] Maisky, *ibid.*, p. 176.

[30] Herbert Feis, *Churchill, Roosevelt, Stalin* (Princeton, N.J., 1957), p. 16.

amounted to 2,199,000 tons."[31] It is quite true that the Western material help could not have affected the outcome of the first and most important Soviet victory, before Moscow, in December 1941. It is also true that the most extensive material help cannot be equated with the huge losses in men the Soviets were to suffer. But the Western aid—and it is sufficient to note that it surpassed in quantity, not to mention quality, the *total* equipment in the critical categories possessed by the French army in 1940 —was undoubtedly to be a vital factor in the Red Army's victories from the winter of 1942–43 until the end of the war.

Other aspects of cooperation in war soon imposed themselves upon this at first incongruous alliance. In August, Soviet and British troops in a co-ordinated drive occupied Iran in order to end the German intrigues there, but principally to provide a secure supply line to the U.S.S.R. The occupation pattern followed a venerable precedent: an Anglo-Russian convention of 1907 had proclaimed northern Persia a Russian "sphere of influence," the southern part a British one. Now the British were in control in the south, the Russians in the north, and the capital, Teheran, was under joint protection of the two powers.

The Persian operation was practically unique in the completely harmonious synchronization of British and Russian actions. The diplomatic propriety of the latter could not be faulted. The Soviets had expressed the willingness to move into Persia only if the British moved in simultaneously.

A thorny point in the Anglo-Soviet collaboration was removed with the British declaration of war on Germany's allies, which occurred on December 6 and concerned Finland, Rumania, and Hungary. There had been some resistance in London to this step, especially in connection with Finland. It was felt that it was useful to keep up some channels of communication with this small country, which, unlike Rumania and perhaps Hungary, was not an out-and-out satellite of Germany's and whose armed forces provided but little help to the Germans once they reached the Finnish frontiers of 1939. To the Russians, Britain's full concurrence was, however, of great importance. It was obviously a dangerous precedent to allow a country to pursue war against the Soviet Union and yet be at peace with her allies.

The Japanese attack on Pearl Harbor and then the equally incredible folly of Hitler and Mussolini in declaring war on the United States even in the face of Japan's continued abstention from the war against the U.S.S.R. drastically transformed the whole picture. The problem of defeating the Axis Powers shifted from "how" to "when." A Marxist had to appraise a nation's power in terms of its industrial potential, and Stalin's

[31] *Soviet Foreign Policy During the Patriotic War: Documents and Materials* (London, 1945), II, 87.

opinion of American power was not likely to be affected by such inanities as Hitler's contempt for the "uncultured" North Americans.[32] Japan's dazzling initial successes could not affect the main question: how in the long run could a nation with an annual production of 7 million tons of steel (Japan) defeat one that produced 75 million (the United States)?

But the assurance of an Allied victory was, again, not the same thing as a guarantee of the survival of the Soviet system. The American entrance into the war might make the British more inclined to postpone a second front in Europe. An immediate technical problem was the probable diversion of war supplies to America's own needs. (Few in 1941 realized that the tremendous productive power of the United States would suffice to arm both the Americans and their allies.) But the most important apprehension must have been one concerning American intentions and long-run plans. American indignation over the Russian invasion of Finland was a fresh memory. So was the United States' categorical refusal to recognize the annexation of the Baltic countries and eastern Poland. The United States was viewed as being less likely to indulge in Machiavellian anti-Soviet machinations than Tory leaders of the British empire, but the United States had 5 million citizens of Polish origin. The Soviet Union's diplomatic relations with America since 1933 had not been entirely happy: the celebrated American naïveté in foreign affairs was unfortunately matched by the rather literal frame of mind of many American politicians —the difficulty that had led to so much unpleasantness between Litvinov and Bullitt. It was not forgotten in Moscow that after June 22, some American public figures, including the then senator from Missouri, expressed delight at the prospect of two totalitarian powers hacking away at each other.[33] The Atlantic Charter, elaborated by Churchill and Roosevelt at their August meeting, was greeted with some suspicion. The provisions that all peoples have the right to choose the form of government under which they live and that territorial changes have to be made in accordance with the "freely expressed wishes of the peoples concerned" were capable of many and, possibly, from the Soviet point of view, uncomfortable interpretations. The Soviet accession to the Charter, conveyed by Maisky on September 24, was couched in a cumbersome and qualified way.[34]

In view of the situation that prevailed later on in the war, it is interesting to note that Stalin desired a quick commitment by Britain to Soviet war aims prior to any discussion with the Americans. To Eden, who arrived in

[32] Hitler once confided to Mussolini that he himself could never contemplate living in America, where everything was subordinated to the craze for money and there was no feeling for the finer things in life, such as music!

[33] During the cold war, Mr. Truman's statement to this effect was frequently quoted in Soviet publications.

[34] Feis, *op. cit.*, pp. 23–24.

Moscow on December 15, he handed a very extensive set of Soviet proposals to be embodied in a *secret* protocol to the proposed Anglo-Soviet treaty of friendship. In brief, the Soviet Union wanted British agreement to its 1941 frontiers. In return, Stalin was willing to support any British demands for bases in France, the Low Countries, Norway, and Denmark. This proposal, unpleasantly reminiscent of the Ribbentrop-Molotov agreement, was produced by Stalin without any prior consultation with Ambassador Maisky, who accompanied Eden to Moscow. Maisky said *in 1964* that, had he known of Stalin's intentions, he would have pointed out to him that the British could not conceivably agree, especially since Secretary of State Cordell Hull had specifically warned Eden against any sanctioning of the Soviet annexations of 1939 and 1940.[35] There were some other interesting suggestions: East Prussia was to go to Poland; the Rhineland and Bavaria were to be detached from Germany. Eden, needless to say, refused to accept these proposals, despite continuing pressure from the Soviets. He was buttressed in his refusal by Churchill, who wired characteristically that he should not be scared by the Russians' refusal to sign a treaty: "The Russians have got to go on fighting for their lives anyway and are dependent upon us for very large supplies which we have most painfully gathered, and which we shall faithfully deliver."[36] Eden's conversations ended with a friendly but not very specific communiqué.

The balance of Soviet fears and hopes in the year of ordeal 1941 may be indicated from some passages from Stalin's speeches. On the anniversary of the Revolution, November 6, 1941, in threatened Moscow, Stalin spoke in terms that indicated considerable doubts still lingering in his mind about the domestic front. Otherwise, with the German breach of faith, with rapine and cruelty potent facts, why read these lessons to the Soviet people: "Can the Hitlerites be considered *nationalists?* No, they cannot. . . . As long as the Hitlerites were occupied in reuniting German lands, the Rhineland, Austria, etc., they could with justification be considered nationalists. But after they captured foreign territories and enslaved European nations . . . the Hitlerite party ceased being nationalist . . . became imperialist."[37] A superfluous lesson, one might think, and a strange compliment to the earlier activities of Hitler and his gang, implying among other things that the "reunification" of Austria and the Sudetenland were justified. "Can the Hitlerites be considered socialists? No, they cannot. . . . To cover up their reactionary character the Hitlerites attack the Anglo-American regime as a plutocratic one. But in the United States and England there exist democratic freedoms, trade unions, labor parties and parliament,

[35] Maisky, *op. cit.*, p. 182. The reader may well feel that Maisky overestimated both his power and courage as of 1941.

[36] Churchill, *op. cit.*, p. 630.

[37] Stalin, *op. cit.*, p. 49.

and in Germany all those institutions have been extirpated." Stalin went on to compare Nazi Germany to Tsarist Russia, an undeserved insult, one might think, to the latter.

One interesting aspect of these passages is that they show that the regime was obviously at pains to undo the effects of its own propaganda of 1939–41. Another is the clear differentiation they make between the evils of *latter-day* Hitlerism and the German nation: "Only Hitlerite morons do not understand that not only the other nations of Europe in the rear of the German armies but the German nation itself is a veritable volcano ready to erupt and bury the Hitlerite adventurers."[38] On February 23, 1942, Stalin was to say in the same vein: "The experience of history shows that Hitlers come and go but the German nation, the German state, remains."[39] In November of the same year, when Soviet propaganda at the lower levels was already violently anti-German as well as anti-Hitler, Stalin still drew categorical distinctions: "It is just as impossible to destroy Germany as it is to destroy Russia. . . . It is not our aim to destroy every organized military force in Germany . . . because it is just as impossible in connection with Germany as with Russia, and undesirable from the point of view of the victor. But to destroy the Hitlerite army, that one can and must."[40] The consistent pattern of such public statements of Stalin's throughout the first and critical eighteen months of war has its own eloquence. Soviet policy-makers had not given up the hope that some circles in Germany, conceivably the anti-Nazi military groups, might overthrow Hitler and attempt to conclude peace. For such a peace, Stalin implied in 1941, Hitler's initial acquisitions, e.g., Austria, might be acquiesced in.

This *public* attitude of Stalin's clashed, of course, with what he implied to Eden about the possibility of partitioning Germany. The differentiation between "honest" German nationalism and Nazism was an astute propaganda posture, but was there more behind it? It is quite likely that there were two elements in this line. In the first place, until the winter of 1942–43, the military situation was so critical that every conceivable option had to be kept open. In the second place, the Soviets, for all the conviction of their leaders that Britain and America were with them to the end in the struggle *against Hitler*, could not bring themselves to believe that an accommodation between the Western Powers and another German regime was out of the question. If so, this subtle and hardly discernible distinction between Nazism and "German nationalism" could have its uses.

The complicated machinery of the Grand Alliance groaned and creaked

[38] *Ibid.*, p. 59.
[39] *Ibid.*, p. 84.
[40] *Ibid.*, pp. 136–37.

but held together through 1942. It was not to be expected that the three great allies would find the synchronization of their policies, not to mention their military plans, an easy task. Ostensibly, the British and the Americans were working out their joint policy and military moves and then discussing them with the Russians. Thus, a combined war council composed of the American chiefs of staff and representatives of the British ones was set up in Washington, but Soviet war plans were made by their own high command and were announced, if at all, only in the most general terms to the Anglo-American planners. In retrospect, Soviet historians of World War II have reproached the "Anglo-Saxons" for the exclusion of the Russians from their war council, but in fact it was inconceivable and in fact never demanded by the Russians that they should sit in on a joint Allied council, which then could exercise some control over the Soviet armed forces. It was inconceivable in the nature of things that Stalin would allow information about Soviet military potential, plans, etc., to be given to the Western military leaders, or that any of the first rank of the Soviet military commanders would be allowed a prolonged stay in a Western capital and intimacy with their Anglo-American counterparts. Thus there was to be the Russian war and the Anglo-American war, and their diplomacies and strategies were to be separate though discussed in general terms at the summit meetings of the three leaders and, more frequently, in their messages and through their emissaries.

The great Soviet fear had to be that Britain and America would adopt a joint position concerning Russian demands and aspirations. If so, 1942 soon exhibited a number of dissonances between the two Western powers. The demand for the second front in 1942 was received with some sympathy in the United States but encountered a resolute opposition by Churchill and the British chiefs of staff. Though the latter had some excellent technical points in their favor, and though Churchill's other and perhaps more fundamental reasons were connected with memories of the British losses in World War I and with the importance to the empire of concentrating the British military effort in North Africa and the Near East, the refusal to invade Europe had to be viewed by Moscow with bitterness and suspicion. In what was, in a way, a more remarkable military achievement than their previous victories, the German armies prevented the defeats at Moscow and Rostov from turning into a rout and yielded but relatively little ground to the Soviet winter offensive. The coming spring and summer were obviously to be a time of renewed ordeal to the Soviet army, of renewed danger to the Soviet regime.

British unwillingness to create the second front in 1942 had an immediate consequence: Churchill's proposal to appease the Russians and, presumably, to raise their morale for the coming period of renewed German offensives by granting them their territorial desires. He wrote to

Roosevelt on March 7: "The increasing gravity of the war has led me to feel that the principles of the Atlantic Charter should not be construed so as to deny Russia the frontiers she occupied when Germany attacked her."[41] While the Russians may not have learned of this secret message at the time, they could not have overlooked that a similar point of view was expressed in *The Times'* editorial *of the same date* and by several members of both Houses of Parliament.[42] For the time being, Roosevelt and the State Department balked at this step, but the British initiative was a significant straw in the wind, a preview of the subsequent dissonances between Britain and the United States and, as a matter of fact, within the governments of each country as to the best way of dealing with the "Russian problem."

Molotov's visit to Britain and the United States in the spring of 1942 undoubtedly yielded a valuable lesson to the Soviet policy-makers as to how, despite all their intimacy, joint war councils, etc., the British and American statesmen lived in different worlds. Roosevelt was eager that Molotov should come first to the United States—a reflection, undoubtedly, of the growing fear in his entourage that the Soviets and the British might strike some territorial deal and confront the United States with a *fait accompli* the American public would find hard to stomach. Roosevelt's fear was undoubtedly Stalin's hope, and Molotov was ordered first to London.

Both in Britain and the United States, the hosts had to notice the strange precautions observed by Molotov: he slept with a revolver by his side, the arrangement of sheets had to be such that he could be out of his bed in an instant, etc. It could not be appreciated that since he was travelling by air, Molotov was not accompanied by a hundred or so security people, as he was on his trip to Berlin in 1940, and that the years of purges and terror made the Soviet leaders justifiably fearful when not guarded by swarms of their secret policemen.

On the more substantial points of the visit, the British rejected the Soviet proposal to recognize the frontiers of June 22, 1941, despite Molotov's insistence. Only after three sessions spent in wrangling did Stalin authorize his minister to sign an alliance with Britain that made no mention of the frontier issue. The treaty signed on May 26 appeared, then, quite momentous. It repeated the previous pledge that both sides would fight Germany until the final victory and would not sign a separate treaty with her. But a new provision included a twenty-year alliance, and pledges to render each other help in case of a new German war, not to participate in any coalition or treaty directed against one of them, and

[41] Winston L. S. Churchill, *The Hinge of Fate* (London and Boston, 1950), p. 327.

[42] V. L. Israelian, *The Anti-Hitler Coalition* (Moscow, 1964), p. 138.

not to interfere in internal affairs of third states.[43] In his memoirs of the war published in 1950, Churchill does not even mention the details of the treaty; it was already then ancient history. But eight years before, it had appeared as a momentous development: the Soviet Union signing an alliance with its arch-enemy, the British empire.

In the United States, Molotov's main task was to pressure for the second front in 1942. More than in London or on any previous occasion, Molotov felt constrained in his conversations with Roosevelt to depict the possibility of a *complete* military collapse by the Russians unless the Western Allies were to invade Europe.[44] The very qualified approval of the second front *in principle* by the American military men could not have made the Russians very happy. But Roosevelt agreed to a formula that sounded like a promise: "In the course of the conversations, full understanding was reached with regard to the urgent tasks of creating a second front in Europe in 1942."[45]

More important in the long run was the insight Molotov reached about American thinking on the post-war world. The President's frankly voiced anticolonial feelings and his readiness to dispose of what were other countries' possessions were undoubtedly to leave a lasting impression: "There were, all over the world, many islands and colonial possessions which ought, for our own safety, to be taken away from weak nations."[46] It turned out that in Roosevelt's thinking, Britain was not excluded from the "weak nations," for Britain's Asian possessions were also to be "internationalized" until they could achieve independence. Molotov listened with interest; through his mind must have gone the prophecies of Soviet writers and theoreticians of the past who had predicted that an eventual clash between the two main imperialist powers would occur and the United States would eventually strip Britain of her empire. And more than three years later, in his speech at the United Nations, one of Molotov's main themes was a violent attack upon the colonial powers and colonialism.

On his trip home Molotov stopped in London, and here again he exacted something which looked like an official commitment to a "second front in Europe in 1942."

There was to be no such front, and the situation in Russia was almost as critical as in November 1941 when in August Churchill alighted in Moscow to meet "the great Revolutionary chief and profound Russian statesman and warrior with whom for the next three years I was to be in intimate, rigorous, but always exciting, and at times even genial associa-

---

[43] *Soviet Foreign Policy During The Patriotic War: Documents and Materials*, I, 158–60.

[44] Sherwood, *op. cit.*, p. 562.

[45] Feis, *op. cit.*, p. 67.

[46] Sherwood, *op. cit.*, p. 572.

tion."[47] The story of that visit is one of the most famous of Churchill's narratives. The British statesman had the unpleasant duty of telling Stalin that instead of invading Europe in the summer, the Allies were in the fall to land in French North Africa. What happened then is the most dramatic part of Churchill's story. The Soviet dictator seemed to be appeased and inquired with interest into the details of the proposed landings. Great was Churchill's surprise and bitterness when, the next evening (August 13), Stalin returned to attack and accused the British soldiers of cowardice and fear of the Germans.[48] Churchill, shocked by this change in mood, contemplated leaving Moscow without further discussions. In a dispatch to the Cabinet, he revealed once again the darkness in which the Western statesmen groped about politics in Russia: he attributed Stalin's sudden change and abusiveness to "his council of Commissars [who] did not take the news I brought as well as he did."[49] We now know precisely what was on Stalin's mind that day. The very day before he received Churchill at 11 P.M., he presided over a meeting of the high command that considered the desperate situation on the approaches to Stalingrad. Dispositions were made for the last-ditch defense; new plans were devised; new commanders named.[50] Not the "Council of Commissars," but the utmost danger, verging on hopelessness, of the military situation must have been behind Stalin's outburst. It tells much of his self-control that during the next few days he was capable of exhibiting friendliness and even geniality, that during a dinner he was to taunt his faithful Molotov, for the Prime Minister's amusement, as a gangster and was to confide how the terrible ordeal of collectivization had surpassed even the current sufferings of the Russian people.[51] It was in a friendly atmosphere that Churchill departed for the threatened Middle East and then home.

In the fall and early winter of 1942, the situation in all Allied theaters of operation underwent a drastic improvement; though the decisiveness of the German defeat at Stalingrad could not be tested until the summer of 1943, it appeared unlikely, after the beginning of 1943, that the Germans would ever be able to resume their great offensives on the 1941 or 1942 scales. Even without a second front in France in 1943, German resources would be strained in North Africa and Italy, and the massive bombing of Germany had already begun in the spring of 1942. As Stalin said in his order of February 23, "There has begun a massive expulsion of the enemy from the Soviet land." The tone of his public references to

[47] Churchill, *The Hinge of Fate*, p. 477.
[48] *Ibid.*, p. 486.
[49] *Ibid.*, p. 489.
[50] Marshal A. I. Yeremenko, *Stalingrad Notes of the Front Commander* (Moscow, 1961), p. 87.
[51] Churchill, *The Hinge of Fate*, p. 498.

the Western Allies had hardened. "Since there is no second front in Europe the Red Army bears the whole burden of the war."[52] But that the attention of the dictator was already turning to the post-war world was best illustrated by one of his concluding slogans: "Long live the Bolshevik Party, the inspirer and organizer of the victories of the Red Army." There had been but little mention of the Communist Party in Stalin's speeches or messages after July 3, 1941. Now, the political and ideological motif was to return and to recur with increasing frequency.

Thus, the winter of 1943 marked the end of one period and the beginning of another for the Soviet Union. The war was to take on an increasingly political character, or, rather, the Soviets' solicitude about their political aims was to become, now that the military disaster had been averted, much more explicit.

2. *From Alliance to Cold War*

The Casablanca conference of Roosevelt and Churchill in January 1943 coincided with the concluding stages of the Stalingrad battle. Stalin therefore had excellent reasons for refusing to attend. Our only—alas, not very reliable—guide into the inner workings of Soviet diplomacy of those years, Ambassador Maisky, criticizes Stalin for not meeting with the two Western leaders. His absence, he writes, hurt Soviet interests, i.e., the second front was again postponed.[53] But it is difficult to see how, apart from his obvious dislike of going abroad, Stalin could have attended, at this very crucial point of the war on the Eastern Front. It is characteristic on the other hand that the Russians were quite content to have the conference have a purely Anglo-American character and did not propose sending Molotov or some other representative. They were evidently unwilling at this stage of the war to commit themselves to any long-range plans for post-war Europe or to sanction publicly the rather tortuous Allied policies in French North Africa.[54] There was no need for the Soviets to get into the involved wrangling about de Gaulle versus other French elements, etc., at this point. But the absence of the Russians at

[52] Stalin, *op. cit.*, p. 161. This was after El Alamein, after the invasion of North Africa, and in the period of the 1,000-plane raids of the RAF.

[53] Ivan Maisky, in *Novyi Mir (New World)* August 1965, p. 177.

[54] Following the Allied landing in November there was great indignation in some circles in the West about the use of Admiral Darlan and other Vichy types in pacifying North Africa. Stalin's communication to Roosevelt on this subject bore the no-nonsense character of one who had supped with Ribbentrop. He assured Roosevelt and Churchill that "Eisenhower's policy with regard to Darlan, Boisson, Giraud, and others is perfectly correct." Churchill, *The Hinge of Fate*, p. 667.

the Casablanca conference undoubtedly contributed to the Anglo-American decision to concentrate on Mediterranean operations for the balance of the year, which effectively precluded an invasion of France. Stalin's reaction was predictable: "Fully realizing the importance of Sicily, I must, however, point out that it cannot replace the second front in France."[55] The Russians did not view operations in Africa, in Sicily, or even on the Italian mainland as a "real" second front. In March 1943, when Stalin sent this message, he still could not be sure that the Germans might not at least stabilize their front in the east, and his language, while no longer frantic, was still harsh: "The uncertainty of your statements concerning the contemplated Anglo-American offensive across the Channel arouses grave anxiety in me about which I cannot be silent." He was equally indignant about the suspension of the Allied convoys to the northern Russian ports, which took place in March, because of the severe losses suffered on account of German planes, submarines, and surface vessels. It would have been quite natural for the Soviets to conclude that after Stalingrad the Western Allies felt that the Russian collapse was now unlikely and that there was no pressing reason for them to help the Soviets *advance*.

Soviet apprehensions must also have been aroused by the rumors that began to circulate around that time and that were to persist for long about the possibility of a separate peace between the Western Allies and Germany. The slogan of "unconditional surrender," which Roosevelt proclaimed at Casablanca in regard to Germany and with which Churchill, not without serious apprehensions, associated himself, could not entirely dispel Soviet fears. Public opinion in Britain and the United States was by this time in a strongly pro-Soviet mood, the heroism and successes of the Soviet armies having erased the original incongruity of joining with one totalitarian system to fight another. Certainly in Britain, at least, the slightest attempt to negotiate a separate treaty would have brought a political crisis. Prominent public figures, e.g., Wendell Willkie in the United States, were publicly seconding Soviet pleas for a second front *now*.[56]

But distrust of the capitalist West was of course second nature to the Soviets, just as, it is fair to say, a hard view of Soviet intentions was to Churchill and his ilk in the West. Churchill's visit to Turkey following the Casablanca conference was one of those moves that was bound to be viewed with suspicion in Moscow. Turkey was in a unique position of being bound (perhaps not the correct term) by treaties of friendship

[55] *Ibid.*, p. 750.

[56] Ambassador Maisky, with slight regard for diplomatic propriety, was publicly criticizing the government to which he was accredited for its dilatoriness in invading the Continent.

with Germany, the U.S.S.R., *and* Britain. The Turkish leaders, though pupils of Atatürk, who had made friendship with the U.S.S.R. a cardinal point of his policy, were by now most apprehensive of the future role of the Soviet Union. Hitler's invasion of Russia brought some discreet rejoicing in Ankara; the recent German reverses, consternation. Churchill's attempt to bring Turkey to adopt a more actively anti-German posture did not meet with success. He declared to the Turkish leaders (not with much conviction, one should think) that after the war there should be a strong international organization to secure peace and security. "I added that I was not afraid of Communism."[57] He was more convincing when he stated: "I would not be a friend of Russia if she imitated Germany. If she did so, we should arrange the best possible combination against her." Churchill's thoughts now turned to a post-war Europe being organized into a number of confederations, e.g., a Balkan one, a Danubian bloc, etc., in short, to the task of preventing small East European countries from falling under Russia's sway.

Stalin was curious to know what, pray, Churchill was doing with the Turks. Churchill informed him about the main lines of his conversations but discreetly omitted his meditations on the post-war confederations and their uses. It was natural enough, though undiplomatic, for Stalin to wire back: "I have no objection to your making a statement that I was kept informed on the Anglo-Turkish meeting, though I cannot say that the information was very full."[58] Churchill desired to have Turkey in the war to speed up the collapse of Hitler, but it did not take a very subtle or overly suspicious mind to see that another strong reason was to have other than Soviet armies liberate southeastern Europe from the Germans.

The maneuvers concerning Turkey represented the kind of jostling for post-war advantages that is a feature of every, even the most solidly knit, coalition of Great Powers. But the Polish issue, which now cast an increasingly large shadow on relations among the three great allies, was a more fundamental challenge: it involved a moral as well as a power-politics dilemma. The Polish story contained already in wartime the main ingredients that were to go into the tragedy of post-war international politics.

As the Soviet military defeats changed into victories, relations between Moscow[59] and the Polish government-in-exile went from bad to worse. The Russians stressed in their communiqués and utterances that they considered their acquisitions at the expense of Poland in 1939 now to be

[57] Churchill, *The Hinge of Fate*, p. 710.

[58] *Ibid.*, p. 715.

[59] Actually, at the moment of the greatest danger, in the early winter of 1941–42, most of the governmental agencies were shifted to Kuibyshev, but Stalin and the State Defense Committee stayed in Moscow.

integral parts of the U.S.S.R., and that there could be no question that those territories would return to the U.S.S.R. after the final victory. The Polish army formed on Soviet soil had been evacuated to Iran. The Polish embassy in the U.S.S.R. found itself, at the beginning of 1943, prevented from exercising its functions, especially that of collecting and evacuating those Polish citizens who after the Soviet invasion in 1939 had been imprisoned or resettled in Russia. And the sounds of the Stalingrad battle had hardly died down when the Soviet press began to attack the Polish government in London for being a bunch of reactionaries greedy to reassert their mastery over Ukrainians and Byelorussians. Unmistakably, the Soviet government began also to sponsor "its own" Poles. The Union of Polish Patriots formed before March 1943 now emerged into public view, with its own newspaper. The leadership of the organization was clearly in Communist hands, its chairman being Wanda Wasilewska, who during the war turned from left-wing socialist to Communist and who was currently the wife of the Ukrainian writer Korneychuk, recently elevated to Assistant Commissar for Foreign Affairs.[60] The non-Communist members did not include any political figure of importance in pre-war Poland. The organization eschewed any Communist, indeed any radical, propaganda or statements. Its platform was merely insistence on good post-war relations with the U.S.S.R. As a token of this determination, the "Moscow Poles," as they became known, began to organize Polish military formations which, unlike the troops under the control of the "London Poles," would fight on the Eastern Front alongside the Red Army and presumably would enter Poland when the German invaders were pushed back.

Confronted with this warning and threat, the Polish government-in-exile could only pressure London and Washington to take an unyielding attitude toward the Soviet claims. It pointed out the indubitable facts that it was the legal government of Poland, that, unlike the regime which collapsed in 1939, it was democratic in the sense that it represented Poland's major political parties and as such enjoyed the support of the Polish underground and its clandestine military organization, the Home Army.[61]

The Polish government-in-exile was in an almost hopeless predicament:

[60] Mme. Wasilewska, herself a novelist, had accepted Soviet citizenship in 1939 and had been elected to the Supreme Soviet. Her political role ended with the setting up of the Soviet-sponsored Polish provisional government in 1944.

[61] After the German invasion of Russia the Polish Communist Party was reconstituted and organized its own clandestine organization, the Polish Workers' Party, and its own military force. But it never was accepted as part of the "official" underground, and its influence and anti-German activities remained almost insignificant in comparison to those of the London-sponsored organizations.

all of the legal and most of the moral right was on its side, yet as compared with its Soviet protagonist it was militarily impotent, a fatal combination. An astute political sense and an insight into Anglo-American politics and psychology might have saved the situation, but those were the qualities that were largely wanting among the London Poles. Their own government was riven by dissension and clashing views as to how to deal with the cruel dilemma. Some banked on an unavoidable clash between the democracies and the Soviets following the war. Some had an exaggerated view of Poland's post-war role in world politics. Some thought more realistically about the need for Poland, a small power, to establish some *modus vivendi* with the U.S.S.R., to save at least her independence and perhaps some of the territory torn away by Russia. But all of the leading political figures exuded bitterness that Poland, the most cruelly tried country of all, should now be a very secondary consideration to America and Britain, and most of them failed to perceive that even conservative politicians in the West were eager for a post-war arrangement with Russia, and that strident Polish complaints, precisely because they were unanswerable, were bound to provoke the kind of irritation and contempt that is often the product of bad conscience. Such, at least, was to be Churchill's reaction. To the growing body of public opinion in the West, not just to those who were left of center, Poland had become a nuisance and a major threat to what by 1943 had become the main goal of the war: a solid understanding among the three Great Powers, which alone could guarantee a peaceful world. As against this aim, what importance would an American or British voter attach to obscure frontier problems in Eastern Europe or even to the personalities and ideological complexion of the post-war Polish regime? The feats of the Polish resistance and the subsequent exploits of the Polish Corps in the Italian campaign were of necessity dwarfed by the massive operations of the Soviet armies. The unpleasant part played by Polish foreign policy at the time of Munich was now increasingly made a reproach against the current Polish regime, even though it was composed of people who had then been in opposition to Colonel Beck and his policies. But the main factor was that in the Western governments' post-war plans, Poland played a very insignificant role. Churchill's thinking was in terms of spheres of influence and of the preservation of the British empire. He hoped to keep *south*eastern Europe largely out of the Russian sphere of influence; he was bound to assume that Poland, whatever her frontiers and her internal politics, would have to heed her neighbor. The American policy-makers hoped to engage Russia in a world security organization; they were also eager that, following Germany's defeat, Russia would enter the war against Japan, which otherwise—or so it seemed in 1943–44—threatened to be a long-drawn-out and costly conflict.

All those facts appeared to make the task of both Soviet policy-makers and Soviet propaganda in the West relatively easy. But by the same token the Polish issue required caution. An attempt to ride roughshod over the Polish claims would envenom public opinion in the West, especially in the United States, where there were millions of voters of Polish descent. It would hurt the newly emerging image of the U.S.S.R. Though Western statesmen, looking at the feats of the Russian army, had no doubt of the Soviet Union's overwhelming position on the Continent, Stalin and his colleagues had a realistic view of the perplexing internal and external problems to be faced by the Soviet Union following the war. A drastic breach with the West in the concluding phase of the war might have incalculable consequences. Thus a great deal of effort and concern was to go into the Soviets' Polish policy. Apart from the issue of the frontiers, on which, for reasons spelled out above, the Soviets would not have yielded except partially and only under extreme pressure, the Polish policy of the Kremlin remained flexible until well after the end of the war rather than committed to any specific blueprint.

The actual breach of relations between Moscow and the Polish government-in-exile occurred in April 1943. Its direct cause was the Germans' discovery, in the Katyn Forest near Smolensk, of the corpses of thousands of Polish officers who had been captured by the Russians in 1939 and kept in prisoner-of-war camps. The German allegation was that they had been murdered by Soviet authorities in May 1940. The Polish government requested the International Red Cross to investigate. Churchill's reaction to this step is recorded in his memoirs. He said even to Sikorski, "If they are dead, nothing you can do will bring them back."[62] The Soviet reaction was an indignant denial, an assertion that the murders had been committed by the Germans when they captured the area in July 1941, and a rupture of relations with the London Poles, a rupture that proved to be final.

A careful weighing of the evidence[63] leads to an almost unavoidable conclusion that the murders had been committed by Soviet security forces in the spring of 1940. The one irrefutable element is the disappearance of some 15,000 Polish regular and reserve officers who had been in the Soviet camps until April 1940 and of whom thereafter one could find no trace, until some of them were found in the mass graves in Katyn. When the Polish army was being formed in the U.S.S.R., Polish authorities had kept requesting those officers and had been met with evasive answers by Soviet officials from Stalin downward—in fact, with protestations that no one knew where they were. Yet granted their death in 1940, an element of

[62] Churchill, *The Hinge of Fate*, p. 759.
[63] E.g., J. K. Zawodny, *Death in the Forest* (South Bend, Ind., 1962).

mystery remains as to the Soviet motives. The thousands of Polish officers represented valuable human material in the case of an eventual conflict with Germany. Many of them were, in addition, professional men, doctors, engineers, etc., whose skills could have been used in the U.S.S.R. While Soviet security forces have never been known to suffer from humanitarian inhibitions, the Katyn action was thus uncharacteristic of Soviet practices on such occasions. The most likely conjecture is that the Germans had learned of this stockpiling of Polish officers by the Soviets (there was obviously contact between the Gestapo and the NKVD during the period of the Soviet-Nazi collaboration), and their importunities led the Soviet officials to sanction the frightful step. The spring of 1940, *before* the German attack in the West was, as we have seen, the period of the greatest Soviet nervousness about German intentions, and the greatest eagerness not to provoke Hitler.

That Sikorski's request was a diplomatic blunder, however, has been asserted by some of the most anti-Soviet members of his regime. Without any previous communication with Moscow, he thereby placed a ready-made weapon in the hands of the Soviet authorities, which had for some time sought a pretext for such a breach and could now accuse the London group of following the German slander and attempt to destroy Allied unity. He was gripped by an understandable emotion, but it was equally understandable that in the middle of the war the British and American people could not bring themselves to believe, and could not afford to believe, that the government which had been directing a heroic defense of its soil had been capable of such atrocities. Churchill's obviously and deeply embarrassed account of the incident quotes a statement he made to Maisky, who brought him Stalin's indignant message about the Poles: "We have got to beat Hitler and this is no time for quarrels and charges."[64]

The hideous story had the ironic consequence of freeing the Soviets of the incubus of their relations with the Polish government. From then on, Moscow insisted—and London and Washington could give no counter-argument, unless they wanted to associate themselves with the terrible charges—that the Polish government, if it wanted to resume relations with Russia, had to be "friendly," i.e., repudiate its accusations and grant the Soviet demands about the frontiers. Seldom has a crime been translated into a comparable diplomatic and propaganda victory.

In May, the Soviet government announced officially that it sanctioned the formation of Polish military units under the sponsorship of the Union of Polish Patriots. It was clear at the moment, however, that the Moscow Poles were still an expendable commodity and that the Soviet aim re-

[64] Churchill, *The Hinge of Fate*, p. 761. Maisky in his memoirs preserves complete silence about the Katyn issue.

mained, in view both of the sensitivities of its allies and of the future conditions in liberated Poland, to supersede or combine them with some Polish political grouping that might enjoy greater political support in the country.

When between 1945 and 1948 Soviet policies sponsored the progressive "satellization" of several east and southeast European states, and when similar pressures were exerted in the areas that ultimately avoided that fate (e.g., Greece), many Western observers were drawn to postulate the existence of a definite blueprint that was being applied to sovietize Europe. It is fairly clear that no such blueprint existed, that in fact Soviet policies responded to the specific circumstances and to the wider repercussions of Soviet thrusts in this or that area. But it is also clear that the spring of 1943 marked the beginning of a more political phase of the war, and of an assessment of post-war opportunities for the Communist movement. The crucial period from the German invasion to Stalingrad had been marked by a stress on defeating Hitler and the rejection, insofar as the Communist parties outside the U.S.S.R. were involved, of any ideological, indeed any political, postulates. It was the period when an American Communist wrote, "There are no economic classes in America. There is only one class, the American people."[65] People who argued that the war against Hitler should not take absolute precedence over economic or political reforms were branded as fascists or Trotskyites. In the resistance movements in Europe, the Communists were the most outspoken exponents of the national and anti-Hitler points of view. That this reaction was largely spontaneous and did not require messages or instructions from Moscow, there can be no doubt. But where the ideological element still intruded, Moscow was quick to express a disapproval. Thus, in March 1942, the Partisan movement in Yugoslavia received a reprimand for stressing the Communist character of its leadership. The movement was headed by the Secretary General of the Yugoslav Communist Party, Josif Broz (Tito). He sought to separate himself from the pro-royalist Serbian resistance movement of General Mikhailovich. But Moscow's reaction was characteristic: "Is it really so that besides the Communists and their followers there are no other Yugoslav patriots with whom you could fight against the enemy?"[66] The Yugoslav Brigade formed and equipped in Russia to fight alongside the Red Army wore a royal emblem until 1944. Though

[65] Jane Degras, ed., *The Communist International, 1919–43: Documents,* III (London and New York, 1965), 472.

[66] Adam B. Ulam, *Titoism and the Cominform* (Cambridge, Mass., 1952), p. 74.

a British mission had been at Tito's headquarters since 1942, an official Soviet mission was not to arrive until February 1944.

The reappraisal of the role of the Communist parties was combined with a seemingly paradoxical step, the dissolution of the Comintern, solemnly announced on May 15, 1943.[67] The resolution spoke about the Comintern having outlived its usefulness and the time having come for greater independence of the constituent units. Stalin, in an interview, spelled out not too subtly the significance of the act: an end would be put to the slanders that the Communist parties took their orders from outside and worked on behalf not of their own working class but of Moscow. Also, the Communists of various countries could now, more than before, collaborate in a wide national front against Hitler and build a better world.[68]

The real reason for dissolving the Comintern was somewhat different from those announced: that the spirit of obedience to Moscow and the machinery of enforcing it were now built into every major Communist party, and there was no need for outward forms of unity. The era of purely national struggle by the Communist parties was coming to an end; they were supposed to maneuver for post-war positions of strength, and this release from Moscow's centralized direction was designed to strengthen their hand and clear their reputations. In retrospect, the main motives in the decision to dissolve the Comintern seem transparent and can be ranged under the heading *deception*.

There are two other aspects of the dissolution. At the time, it marked Moscow's very serious concern with the problems involved in bargaining about the post-war world with its allies, its expectation of very considerable resistance to the sovietization of future satellites, and perhaps the necessity for compromise in the struggle to do so. The license issued to foreign Communists to become nationalists was not without certain obvious dangers: it might (and did in some cases) carry them beyond the point where they could be recalled to the simple, unquestioning loyalty of the pre-1939 years.

And in another historical sense, the decision to liquidate the Comintern was not without its deeper unwitting irony. For with the post-war expansion of Communism, with the erection of Communist regimes outside the U.S.S.R., tensions and fissures would develop which within a decade of the dissolution would endow it with meaning: the monolithic, centralized Communist movement would be a thing of the past. In another decade,

[67] In fact, the procedure was that the Presidium of the Executive Committee of the Comintern proposed the dissolution on May 15, and on June 8 it announced that having received approval from the constituent sections, it now officially dissolved the Comintern.

[68] Degras, *op. cit.*, p. 476.

Soviet policy-makers would try and fail to recreate what the Comintern had been supposed to be: an organ to guide and synchronize the policies of autonomous parties. The Third International had been established in 1919, when the Soviet regime in Russia was hanging by a thread but in Europe prospects for a revolution appeared bright. Now, a generation later, the Soviet Union was on its way to her greatest victory and a position as one of the world's two super-powers. The international Communist movement no longer had to cast its protective mantle around the world's first socialist state; the Soviet Union's successes abroad were to be reflections of its great power.

The problems of the post-war world thus cast their shadows on inter-Allied relations in 1943. We do not know how those problems looked from Moscow and how those two aspects of Soviet foreign policy, coexistence and expansion, were envisaged in the post-war setting. We can be sure that foreign policy was viewed, as it had been since the beginning of the Stalin era if not before, through the prism of internal needs and problems, principally that of maintaining the dictator's rule unchanged. Peace was going to find much of the U.S.S.R. laid waste, the wounds of the forced collectivization, which had barely begun to heal when the war started, reopened and intensified. In the West, fear of Russia's power and post-war designs was beginning to be felt acutely, especially by people like Churchill. It is clear, in retrospect, that the Russian military performance and the colossal power of the Red Army blinded many to the very serious economic and political problems that the Soviet regime was to face on the morrow of the victory and that were likely to dampen any overambitious schemes of expansion. There was a perhaps more valid reason for Soviet statesmen to be apprehensive of the post-war role of the United States. The war had awakened America's tremendous industrial and military potential. Unlike Russia's, this potential would hardly be strained at the end of the war.[69] Was America to revert to isolationism? Was she, as appeared much more likely in view of her expanded production and the needs for markets, to assume a vastly more active role in international affairs? The traditional Communist view that the United States was bound to despoil Britain and France in one way or another of their empires appeared to be supported by the dissonances that arose between Roosevelt and Churchill on the colonial and especially the Indian issue and that could not be concealed within the Anglo-American circle. But the great power of the United States could also be employed on the Continent of Europe, and there it might clash with the interests of the U.S.S.R. Such steps as the dissolution of the Comintern and Russia's

[69] Bearing always in mind that it was envisaged in 1943 that the Japanese war might take two or three years beyond the capitulation of Germany.

readiness to participate in a post-war international security organization find their partial explanation in the Soviets' appreciation of the need to propitiate American public opinion and policy-makers.

The mystery which to the Western mind surrounded the mechanics of Soviet policy-making was perhaps no greater than the puzzlement of the Soviet leaders over the strange practices and opinions of their American allies. It was easier to perceive the main lines of British policy: Churchill's by now almost despairing solicitude over the preservation of the British empire, and the traditional British aim of restoring some balance of power in Europe. But in 1943, it was already clear that the determining voice in the West would belong to the United States, and that the post-war world would be a bipolar one, dominated by the Soviet Union on the one hand and what Europeans called the Anglo-Saxon powers on the other. It was this fact which led in 1943 to rumors that Stalin, who had never learned German when it was thought to be a necessary equipment for a Marxist leader, was now taking lessons in English.[70]

The shape of the post-war world as well as the interrelationship of the Great Powers was going to be largely determined by the character of their collaboration and the agreements they made during the concluding phases of the war. Two great issues dominated the picture. One was, of course, the future of Germany. The other was dominant not only because of its intrinsic importance but also because it was to set the pattern for the Soviet attitude toward other countries in eastern and southeastern Europe: the fate of Poland. Both issues occupied much of the diplomatic exchanges and summit negotiations in 1943.

On August 14, 1943, Churchill wrote to his Foreign Secretary: "The displacement of Ribbentrop by von Papen would be a milestone of importance and would probably lead to further disintegration in the Nazi machine. There is no need for us to discourage this process by continually uttering the slogan 'Unconditional Surrender.' "[71] If known to the Soviets, this dispatch would have enhanced their suspicion, never entirely absent, that their allies, while they would not negotiate with Hitler, could not be trusted to resist this temptation in connection with another German regime. The Russians were doubtless aware through their own intelligence system of the existence of the underground German conspiracy that was to culminate

---

[70] Churchill developed at this time considerable interest in Basic English, which extended to appointing a cabinet committee to study the means of propagating it. In one of his minutes on the subject there is this tantalizing entry: "The matter has become of great importance as Premier Stalin is also interested." Winston L. S. Churchill, *Closing the Ring* (London and Boston, 1951), p. 666. No record exists of Stalin mastering the 850 words of Basic English, or indeed any English words at all. Perhaps the unexpected emergence of Communist China diverted him to another language.

[71] *Ibid.,* p. 663.

in the anti-Hitler plot of July 20, 1944, and of the conspirators' attempts to contact the British and American governments. Rumors of secret Soviet negotiations with the Germans were possibly circulated by the Soviets themselves, as an attempt to warn off their allies from pursuing any devious paths. A more public countermove to any potential accommodation between the West and anti-Hitler Germans was the setting up in Russia on July 12, 1943, of the Free German Committee. Composed partly of German Communists, partly of officers and soldiers captured in the war, this committee issued an anti-Hitler manifesto and a call for his overthrow by the German nation. As was the case with all such "free" committees set up in wartime Russia, its program was couched in nonideological terms, and the national colors displayed in its first proclamation and thereafter in its journal, *Free Germany*, were those of imperial Germany. The Committee's actual importance was to lie in its propaganda activities among the German prisoners of war. If there were any plans for using it as a nucleus for the future regime in Soviet-occupied Germany, they were never to materialize. But, at the time it was set up, it represented a reinsurance against any future contingencies. Britain and America would not be able to monopolize the nationalist and conservative elements of the German anti-Hitler movement.

That such suspicions should have existed on the Soviet side is not too surprising. Yet, ironically enough, it is clear in retrospect that of the three great allies only the Soviet Union was in a position if she so desired to deal leniently with post-Hitler Germany. Public opinion in the democracies was too strongly anti-German for their leaders to envisage anything but meting out the most severe treatment to defeated Germany; the concept of the "other Germany" was in abeyance; schemes for partitioning Germany were frequently entertained by Western statesmen. The Soviet attitude toward such proposals was cautious. They were willing to leave to their allies the initiative on those matters.[72] This position reflected, perhaps, a greater historical sophistication of people bred in Marxism: a great nation could not be indefinitely partitioned; once the wartime passions abated in Britain and America, their peoples would not tolerate the expense and trouble of policing Germany or Germanys — witness events after 1918 — or so it must have seemed in 1943. But in addition, it was a sound policy not to commit oneself to a rigid scheme with the war still far from won. That Hitlers came and went while Germany remained was not only a clever propaganda statement but also the reflection

---

[72] Secretary of State Hull records in his memoirs: "Molotov added that his Government was somewhat behind in its study of the postwar treatment of Germany. . . . To the United States and to me in particular belonged the honor of setting forth the first definite expression of an attitude toward Germany." *The Memoirs of Cordell Hull* (New York, 1948), II, 1287.

of a more realistic view of history than that contained in Churchill's notion of detaching Bavaria or, later, in American plans for "pastoralizing" Germany under the Morgenthau plan.

The problems connected with the second front and with the future configuration of power in eastern Europe took precedence in the Soviets' attention over any elaborate schemes for post-war international organizations and over eloquent declarations of intent for the post-war world. Thus, at the conference of foreign ministers in Moscow in October 1943, the Russians pressed to obtain the most definite pledge yet for an invasion of France by the spring of 1944 and for the resumption by the British of supply convoys to Soviet ports. Satisfied on those two points, Molotov made but little trouble over the Declaration of the Four Powers that was to spell out their policies and aims. This declaration, deeply desired by the American government, laid down in sonorous and vague terms the general purposes pursued by the Great Powers in their fight against the Axis.[73] Secretary Hull's old-fashioned liberalism and legalistic concerns were very much in evidence at the conference, and he must have struck the Soviet officials as a being from a different world.[74] (His legal training notwithstanding, Hull proposed on one occasion a summary execution of the Axis leaders after the victory, and this suggestion did not meet with any Soviet objection. As the old statesman fondly recalled, "Molotov and his entire delegation broke into loud exclamations of approval.")

The new style of diplomacy, which came into its own during World War II, made the position of even a foreign minister of a Great Power little more than that of an errand boy while the burden of policy-making on important issues was shifted to the heads of governments. Hence the Moscow conference could do little but to lay the groundwork for the meeting where the important decisions were to be made: the Teheran conference of the three supreme leaders. The meeting-place was predetermined by Stalin's absolute refusal to go to any other spot in the Middle East: he could not and would not go to a place that was not under control of the Soviet armed forces, and no pleadings by Roosevelt would make him shift to Cairo or Baghdad. (The Soviets also refused to send a first-

[73] The association of China with the declaration was resisted by the Russians, as it had been previously by Churchill. This simply reflected the view that Chiang Kai-shek's government was not in the same class as the Big Three and also, to some extent, an unwillingness to take a position publicly hostile toward Japan. The Russians yielded only after realizing the importance attached by America and Roosevelt personally to classifying China as a Great Power.

[74] He told Molotov, "One of our difficulties had come from the efforts to promote Communism in the United States from abroad and also from the question of freedom of religion in the Soviet Union. Happily, steps have been taken in recent months to improve this situation." Hull, *op. cit.*, II, 1288.

rate political figure to Cairo, where Roosevelt and Churchill were to meet Chiang Kai-shek, again an indication of Soviet unwillingness to take an anti-Japanese posture before the time was ripe.)

Unlike the Moscow conference, with its largely platitudinous and vague declarations, the Teheran meeting was momentous in its consequences. As a diplomatic historian observes, "Matters that are generally thought to have been decided at Yalta in February 1945 were foreshadowed at Teheran."[75] Teheran gave Stalin an occasion to observe at first hand the growing fissure between the British and American positions on the post-war settlement, it basically settled the fate of Poland, and it adumbrated the arrangements for Germany and the Soviet conditions for entering the war against Japan.

Stalin's personal diplomacy has been grudgingly admired by such first-hand observers as Churchill and de Gaulle. A veteran polemicist whose debating skill has been unreasonably disparaged (he had, after all, scored debating victories when power was not yet fully in his hands over such opponents as Trotsky and Zinoviev), he impressed also by his blunt simplicity and certain geniality, astounding to Western statesmen who were awed by his sinister reputation. The despotic temperament would seldom be in evidence as when he shook with fury at the rather innocuous observation that he was known in the West as Uncle Joe. Thus the foreign leaders were able to see him as what they wished him to be: Churchill, as a hard-boiled national chieftain capable of bargaining in old-fashioned terms of spheres of influence; Roosevelt, as a fellow politician not unmindful of his electorate; Ribbentrop, as a sort of Muscovite tsar with no trace of Communism in his make-up. There was no diffuseness, no empty oratory and gestures, as was the case with Hitler. He had a feeling for historical occasions and a sense of dignity that could not but impress outsiders.[76]

On the most pressing issues Stalin could be intractable. Thus, his insistence helped finally to nail down the date of the Allied invasion of France and defeated Churchill's last-minute attempts to schedule additional operations in the Mediterranean which might have diverted or delayed *the* second front. Stalin prompted and badgered his colleagues on the issue, but his remarks had an undoubted logic about them: how could they say the invasion was definitely scheduled if its commander-in-

---

[75] Feis, *op. cit.*, p. 255.

[76] He *almost* captured Churchill's heart when at Teheran the latter handed him the Sword of Honor given by the King to the people of Stalingrad in memory of their heroism. Stalin "raised it in a most impressive gesture to his lips and kissed the blade." Lord Moran notes Churchill's reaction: "This afternoon this hard-boiled Asiatic thawed and seemed to feel the emotions of ordinary people." Lord Moran, *Churchill: Taken From the Diaries of Lord Moran* (London and Boston, 1966), p. 136.

chief had not yet been selected? Would additional German strength in France make them again postpone the invasion?

On matters that were of secondary importance to him, Stalin knew how to bargain so as to give the other party the impression of the Soviet Union making great and fundamental concessions. He disputed vigorously with Roosevelt over the shape of the future world organization, something the Americans set a great deal of store by, but which to the Russians, with their ingrained conviction that international politics is simply a reflection of the Great Powers' interests, was at that juncture of little consequence. But in the end Stalin communicated to the President that he had come over to his point of view. It is difficult to say how much the future course of Soviet politics was affected by Roosevelt's rather incautious statements. In discussing the problems of enforcing peace after the war, he stressed that America could not be relied upon to send troops to Europe again and "that England and the Soviet Union would have to handle the land armies in the event of any future threat to peace."[77] The American statesman let Stalin in on his worries. He stressed the presence within the American electorate of a strong Polish element and the problems it created in regard to the settlement of the Polish issue. Stalin was understanding: "some propaganda work should be done among those people."[78]

On the crucial German issue the three leaders did not come to any definite decision. But on Poland, Stalin, having outwitted his partners, made them put forward proposals which they subsequently could not withdraw, and these determined the fate of that country and of Eastern Europe.

By November 1943, when the Teheran conference took place, the Western statesmen were laboring, it is not too much to say, under a certain feeling of guilt and inferiority toward their Soviet allies. The Soviet armies had defeated the German war machine, their own armies were mired in Italy in a theater of war which could not compare in scope or casualties to the huge Russian front. Was Churchill's initiative on the Polish issue influenced by the thought that it might propitiate Stalin and make him tolerate a delay or change in the invasion of France? Was it influenced by Roosevelt's reluctance to take the initiative because of the Polish vote? In any case, the Prime Minister turned to Stalin: "I suggested that we

[77] Feis, op. cit., p. 270.

[78] Sherwood, op. cit., p. 796. Some time later Professor Oskar Lange, a distinguished economist from the University of Chicago, and Father Orlemanski, an obscure parish priest, both of Polish extraction, were invited to Russia amidst a blare of publicity and received by Stalin, who assured them of his benevolent intentions toward Poland.

should discuss the Polish question. He agreed and invited me to begin."[79] A paradoxical situation ensued. Churchill specified all the main points of the future frontier settlement. Stalin merely agreed, at times raising pious objections about the need to preserve independent Poland, etc. "We agreed to look at the problem. Stalin asked whether it would be without Polish participation. I said 'Yes' and when this was all informally agreed between ourselves we could go to the Poles later."[80] Churchill proposed moving Poland westward, i.e., granting the Soviet Union's territorial desires and compensating Poland at the expense of Germany, her western frontier going as far perhaps as the Oder River. Stalin offered no objection. What he may well have expected to be the most contentious issue at the conference was thus settled without his taking initiative on the subject. Prior to Teheran even the Soviet-sponsored Poles had not proposed such extensive future annexations from Germany. It had been assumed that Poland would receive East Prussia, Danzig, and some parts of German Silesia. But now Churchill and Eden outlined what *were* to be the *Soviet* demands on behalf of post-war Poland. The nature of the post-war Polish regime was not discussed, but even Churchill's shamefaced account of the exchange, one which must have cost him dearly to put into print, makes it clear that the British let Stalin understand then that he could pretty much have his way in that respect too.

The resolution of the Polish problem was bound to predetermine much of the German one. For one thing, from the Russian point of view, it effectively barred any "deal" by a post-Hitler regime with the Western Allies: no German group would voluntarily surrender large areas of ethnic Germany. And after the victory the millions of German refugees from the territories granted to Poland would throw the rest of Germany into economic chaos for decades. It was not to turn out that way, but certainly in 1943 the chances of it happening looked overwhelming. The Polish government, of whatever political complexion, would be in a state of complete dependence on the U.S.S.R.—who else would protect it from German territorial vindications? (This premise certainly remains true today.)

The lighthearted manner in which the Western statesmen conceded points of such tremendous importance contrasts with Stalin's caution. Though he was enormously pleased (and probably surprised) at thus being offered on a silver platter what the most powerful rulers of Russia in the past had not dared to dream of, he did not commit himself completely to moving Poland to the Oder line. Perhaps the Russians would

[79] Churchill, *Closing the Ring*, p. 361.
[80] *Ibid.*, p. 362.

still find it useful to play the card of German nationalism! But on a subsequent occasion at the conference, when Poland was discussed in some detail, the Soviets were naturally more specific in their ideas on the subject. "Soviet Russia adhered to the frontiers of 1939, for they appeared to be ethnically the right ones."[81] Given the green light before, Stalin was now violently abusive about the Polish government-in-exile, about which he had not said a word during Churchill's original exposé of the Polish solution: "The Polish Government and their friends in Poland were in contact with the Germans. They killed the partisans."[82] There was evidently no objection to this slanderous statement from either the President or the Prime Minister.

Apart from any concrete issues, the Soviet leaders (Stalin was accompanied by Molotov and Voroshilov) could not have emerged from the conference with an exaggerated respect for their allies' unity or tenacity of purpose when it came to issues other than the defeat of Japan and Germany. The difference of outlook between Churchill and Roosevelt was again much in evidence. The democratic leaders were eager to please their Soviet colleague. To conquer Stalin's legendary distrust, Roosevelt indulged in teasing the Prime Minister. Stalin's "joke" that fifty thousand German officers must be shot summarily at the end of the war was taken up in a spirit of levity by the President and led to Churchill stalking out of the room, only to be reassured by Stalin in "a very captivating manner" that it was all said in fun! But no account of the conference can fail to reveal Churchill's obvious apprehension about the post-war role of Britain and her empire, and Roosevelt's fear that the American people would be tempted back into isolationism unless they saw absolute harmony prevailing among the Big Three. In contrast, the vast problems and worries that the Soviet leader must have felt remained unrevealed. In addition, the Teheran conference took place at a point in time of the greatest psychological advantage to the U.S.S.R. over her allies. Stalin might admit in conversation that without American production the war could not be won, but the British and American statesmen were looking forward with some apprehension to the forthcoming landings in France. Their fears of casualties on the scale of World War I were combined with the realization that the Soviet army had already suffered losses of that order. It is this fact which explains much about the ineptitude of Western diplomacy concerning Poland, and also Churchill's apparently gratuitous remark that after the war the U.S.S.R. should be granted warm-water ports.[83] This amounted to an invitation for Russia to pressure Turkey for

[81] *Ibid.*, p. 395.

[82] *Ibid.*, p. 394.

[83] *Ibid.*, p. 381. Churchill's moment of generosity came almost immediately after Stalin's long and sharp disquisition as to how he would find it difficult to

special rights and bases in the Dardanelles, for it is difficult to see where else those ports with "access to the broad waters," as Churchill put it, could be found.

The results of the Teheran conference became immediately perceptible in the much bolder political line the Soviet Union took in regard to political problems in Eastern Europe. On December 12, 1943, the Soviet government signed a treaty of friendship and alliance with the Czechoslovak government-in-exile, President Benes having gone for that purpose to Moscow. Earlier, the British Foreign Office had discouraged the Czechs from signing an agreement of this kind. Now, after Teheran, the Czechs felt that they had to make an accommodation with Moscow before the Soviet troops reached the Czech frontiers in pursuit of the Germans. The U.S.S.R. recognized the pre-Munich Czech borders, which implied, of course, the return of Teshen as well as the Sudetenland; it was intimated to Benes, though not stated publicly at the time, that the U.S.S.R. might demand some "rectifications" in northeastern Czechoslovakia when the Soviet army entered the country. These "rectifications" turned out to consist of the Carpatho-Ukraine. Benes promised to grant the Communists some ministerial posts in the post-war government. Thus finally was buried the idea of a Polish-Czech federation or even a joint policy that would enable the two countries to enjoy a modicum of independence in foreign policy. The treaty was a clear indication that small East European states had to seek an accommodation with Moscow and could not expect Western support in any intransigence toward the U.S.S.R. It was a sign too that the Soviets expected those governments to be purged of "nondemocratic" elements, i.e., to be acceptable to them in their personnel and to allot at least a share of power to the local Communists. Within two months, the Soviets were to dispatch an official mission to the Yugoslav Partisans. The future pattern of things in Eastern Europe was becoming predictable.

Poland, like Banquo's ghost, was to sit in on all remaining summit meetings and increasingly to poison the political and diplomatic atmosphere of the Grand Alliance. That it should have been so must have led first to puzzlement and then to deep irritation in Moscow. In Teheran, on their own initiative, the Western Powers had conceded all the essential points of the Polish issue. What was the subsequent wrangling about unless it meant the United States and Britain were concocting some devious scheme or going back on their word? A critique of Anglo-American diplomacy does not belong in this book, but it is impossible not to observe that it had one fatal flaw in dealing with the U.S.S.R.: the West's objectives were always stated in lofty and idealistic terms; then in actual negotiations the Soviets on occasion were told that these principles need

---

prevent "bad feeling in the Red Army" unless there were an invasion by the spring of 1944.

not always be taken seriously. Having then seemingly sealed a bargain, the Anglo-American statesmen would revert to wrangling and moral admonitions. The problem remained, over and above the question of Soviet objectives and ruthless methods, one of communication: at times it must have been as difficult for Stalin to understand what his allies really wanted as it was for Churchill and Roosevelt to understand the alleged enigmas and puzzles of Soviet policy. At Teheran, the Western statesmen vigorously interceded on behalf of Finland, and the subsequent relatively lenient Soviet treatment of Finland and the fact that she neither was absorbed into the U.S.S.R. nor became a satellite may be traced largely to that intercession. Their attitude on Poland, as we have seen, was quite different. One year later, the Anglo-American armies were rolling toward Germany and the Western statesmen's feeling of inferiority in face of the Russian military feats and sacrifices was no longer as strong as it had been at Teheran. But by then the Polish issue had been largely determined.

On January 11, 1944, an official Soviet communiqué spelled out with decisiveness for the first time that the western frontiers of the U.S.S.R. were to be those of the Curzon Line, as the Soviets for obvious reasons chose to call the frontier agreed on in the Molotov-Ribbentrop pact.[84] It fell to Churchill now to ask the Polish government to agree to this amputation of their country. This government was headed, since the death in July 1943 of General Sikorski, by Stanislas Mikolajczyk, a leader of the Peasant Party, who did not enjoy either among his colleagues or among the foreign statesmen anything like the prestige of his predecessor. The pressures now exerted upon the unfortunate politician became ferocious. He was pressed brutally by Churchill to accede publicly to the Soviet demands. Some of his colleagues were goaded into increasingly anti-Soviet attitudes and statements, which Moscow then offered as tangible proof that it could not deal with the Polish government or recognize it again, short of its drastic reorganization. The Poles deserved at least a clear-cut warning that their position on frontiers was hopeless. But no such warning could be given, for Roosevelt, with an election coming up in 1944, preferred to leave the distasteful business to Churchill, and the American officials were intimating to the Poles that their position was not quite as categorical as that of the British government. The West's attempts to soften the Soviet resolve were met with contemptuous reminders of Teheran; Stalin said to Ambassador Harriman, "Again the Poles, is that the most important question?"[85] The focus of the dispute now clearly

[84] At Teheran Eden expostulated that the line proposed by Lord Curzon in 1920 did not run south through Galicia and that what the Soviets proposed was the line commemorating Ribbentrop and Molotov. "Call it what you will," answered Stalin.

[85] Feis., *op. cit.*, p. 298.

shifted to the character of the future Polish government, an issue the Soviet Union had not even raised with her allies prior to Teheran. But since Churchill and Roosevelt had not reacted to Stalin's insulting characterization of the Polish government and its underground, the Soviets had no reason to suppose that firm pressure would not bring the desired results.

If the Soviet leaders were puzzled about the vagaries of the West's moves wherever moral issues intersected *Realpolitik*, it did not require unusual insight or special intelligence sources to perceive the fissure between Britain and the United States when it came to certain fundamental strategic and political considerations. The wide disparity of views between the two powers, or rather between their leaders, when it came to the postwar fate of colonies had been noted before. That the American "line" toward post-war Germany was harder than the British one was also perceptible by 1944. The Americans saw security and peace in Europe as dependent on the creation of an effective international organization. Churchill, like every British statesman since the seventeenth century, had to think in terms of the balance of power. To subjugate Germany completely, to destroy her industrial potential, as some officials in the American government wanted, would have meant complete Soviet domination of the Continent, whatever the formula for the future United Nations. Again, the British recognized that strategic decisions during the final phase of the war were to affect the shape of the post-war world. If all of Central and Eastern Europe was not to be sovietized, Anglo-American troops had to get there. Hence, having accepted the cross-Channel invasion, Churchill still wanted a maximum effort in Italy to open the road to Vienna and the heart of Europe. The Americans, in a "let's get it over with" spirit, were for concentrating the Western effort in France.

On all those issues, the Soviet government was thus presented with considerable room for maneuver and for leaving the initiative on some of the most troublesome points to others. America could be associated with the most draconian proposals on Germany. To Churchill could be left the "cynical" initiative on spheres of influence (the mere term suggesting to the Americans something infinitely sinful and redolent of the wicked practices of Old World diplomacy). Naturally, the Soviets found themselves closer to the American position on most issues, and efforts to accommodate the Americans on some of the "stickiest" points were forthcoming during 1944. Thus, in June, Soviet bases were provided for the American air force, thus enabling U.S. fliers to engage in shuttle-bombing of Germany. This step, running against the Russians' inborn repugnance at allowing military bases on its territory to a foreign, even if allied, power, testified to the Russians' desire to please the Americans.

If the Polish problem and all that it portended could be extracted from the picture, the state of the Grand Alliance in the spring of 1944 was fairly satisfactory. Soviet gambits for a closer relation with de Gaulle or the maneuver to get diplomatic representation with the Italian government, now under Anglo-American control, though they both displeased the West, were the kind of jostling for position that goes on in the most cordial alliances. The chicaneries and suspicions that surrounded English and American officials in the U.S.S.R., which were duly recorded by them after the war alongside the interludes of Slavic hospitality and cordiality, were the inevitable product of a totalitarian system that suspected and supervised its own high officials with as much if not more assiduity. The Allied landing in France on June 6 dispelled much of the Russian bitterness at carrying an unequal burden of the war, a bitterness that was not confined to Soviet officialdom. Later Soviet interpretations of the Allied landing stressed that it was hastened by the fear of the Soviet armies appearing on the English Channel, or, as Khrushchev was to express it in 1959, "Our allies hastened to open the second front in order not to let the nations of Western Europe defeat the Germans themselves with the help of the Red Army."[86] But, at the time, Stalin hailed the achievement, and the Soviet press resounded with its praise. The idea that the Soviet leaders were always preoccupied with cold calculations and were incapable of generous recognition of their allies' achievements is sufficiently refuted by Stalin's praise not only in messages to his Western colleagues but in a statement published in the Soviet press on June 13, 1944, and read by millions of Russians. It pointed out that the Anglo-Americans had succeeded where Napoleon and Hitler had failed: "One must admit that military history does not know a similar enterprise, so broadly conceived, on so huge a scale, so masterfully executed." For once, as Churchill notes in his memoirs, "harmony was complete."[87] In July both Churchill and Roosevelt received special photographs of the Soviet leader, with suitable inscriptions—a gesture reminiscent of the pre-1914 practice, when heads of state, among them the Tsar of All the Russias, would bestow such pictures on foreign statesmen as marks of their special favor. A more tangible measure of Soviet good will was the opening of the great summer offensive, to synchronize with the Allies' attack in Normandy.

Soon the Polish trouble was to erupt again. In a message to Stalin of June 19, Roosevelt had found it necessary to inform him that *he* had found it necessary to receive Premier Mikolajczyk, and hastened to inform Stalin that "the visit was not connected with any attempt on my part to interfere with the matter of discords which exist between the Polish gov-

---

[86] Nikita S. Khrushchev, *The World Without Armaments—World Without War* (Moscow, 1960), I, 165.

[87] Winston L. S. Churchill, *Triumph and Tragedy* (London and Boston, 1953), p. 9.

ernment-in-exile and the Soviet government."[88] He was at pains to excuse himself for inviting the unfortunate Pole, and asked Stalin to receive him in Moscow. The President's apologetic tone, and Ambassador Harriman's assurance that Roosevelt *had* to see Mikolajczyk mainly on account of the approaching presidential elections made it easy for Stalin to escalate the Soviet demands. He would be glad to see Mikolajczyk, he wired Roosevelt on June 24, but the basis of any Soviet recognition of the Polish government would have to be its reorganization to include "Polish politicians in the U.S. and the U.S.S.R. and especially Polish democratic leaders who are in Poland," as well as recognition of the Curzon Line. This was another turn of the screw. Previously the Russians' price was the *elimination* of certain members of the London regime, but now the burden of their demands shifted to a wholesale reorganization of the Polish regime in which pro-Soviet elements would have a dominant voice. The reference to the Polish politicians in the U.S. and the U.S.S.R. obviously referred to such figures as Professor Lange[89] and in the U.S.S.R. to the Union of Polish Patriots. As to the democratic leaders in Poland, Stalin had in mind a recently organized underground council, the so-called National Council of Communist and left-wing elements which was operating in opposition to the "official" Resistance Council that recognized the government in London.

As the Soviet armies now poured into ethnic Poland, the government took another step. On July 21, in Soviet-occupied territories, the Committee of National Liberation was founded, the personnel of which was composed of members of the Union of Polish Patriots and the National Council. To this pro-Soviet body, headed by a Communist, Boleslaw Bierut, the Soviets turned over the civil administration of conquered Polish regions. On July 27, Stalin entertained the leaders of the Committee of National Liberation at a gala banquet in the Kremlin. At this very moment Mikolajczyk was finally on his way from London to see Stalin. What he had to expect in Moscow had been clearly outlined by Stalin in a message to Churchill: the Soviet armies as they entered Poland found there only the elements that had coalesced in the Polish Committee of National Liberation. "The so-called underground organization headed by the Polish government in London turned out to be ephemeral entities with no real influence."[90] He would be willing to see Mikolajczyk, but why shouldn't

---

[88] *The Correspondence Between the Chairman of the Council of Ministers of the U.S.S.R. and the Prime Ministers of Britain and the Presidents of the U.S. During the Great Patriotic War* (Moscow, 1957), II, 145.

[89] See note 78 above, p. 352. The other visitor to Stalin from the United States, Father Orlemonski, was by now confined by his bishop to a monastery.

[90] *Correspondence Between the Chairman of the Council of Ministers of the U.S.S.R. . . .*, II, 151.

the Polish statesman turn rather to the Polish Committee, which was not prejudiced against him? Thus the premier of the legitimate Polish government was to seek audience with this hastily constructed Soviet creation.

In Moscow, Mikolajczyk was received at length by Stalin and Molotov (the official communiqué described him merely as a "representative of the Polish emigré government") who advised him to seek his luck with those being described as the "Moscow Poles," who in turn intimated that they might take him into *their* government but only if he hurried up about it and left his undemocratic colleagues in London. For all their haste in constructing the Polish Committee and suppressing the agencies of the legitimate Polish government, the Soviets realized the need, both for internal Polish reasons and for their relations with the Allies, of associating with their satellite regime a Polish politician who enjoyed genuine support in his country and whose presence would soothe the conscience of the Western statesmen. As yet Mikolajczyk did not fall completely for the bait, but he returned to London with the impression that Stalin did not desire to sovietize Poland.[91] Mikolajczyk was to press this point of view upon his colleagues in the Polish government, many of whom adopted a contrary and, as it turned out, more realistic attitude.

The pattern of development in the Polish issue undoubtedly affected Soviet policies in regard to the countries that after 1945 found themselves in the position of being Soviet satellites. As the Polish problem unfolded between Teheran and Yalta, the Soviets could with a great deal of logic conclude that their allies' views on the future of, say, Bulgaria or Rumania were going to be shaped by the form rather than the substance of their political organization. Public opinion in the West would be appeased by those countries being ruled by a coalition of parties, even if from the beginning real power lay in the hands of the coalition's Communist members and if some elections took place. Such an arrangement in turn would render inoperative any attempt at delimiting spheres of influence such as Churchill sought to achieve with Stalin. Spheres of influence in the nineteenth century sense, and in Churchill's view, meant that a given country within a Great Power's sphere of influence would, in its foreign and defense policy, pay heed to the desires of that Great Power. But the decisive influence of Communists in the Rumanian, Polish, etc., governments was to mean much more, for it implied a gradual abrogation of civil liberties, specific social and economic policies, and, at the end, in fact if not in form, a one-party state. In justification of this procedure, the Soviet government could claim that the unfolding of its policies toward Poland never met vigorous opposition from London or Washing-

[91] Edward Rozek, *Allied Wartime Diplomacy: A Pattern in Poland* (New York, 1958), p. 238.

ton and that on occasion, as in Roosevelt's dispatch to Stalin of June 19, 1944, the West appeared practically to invite the U.S.S.R. to raise her demands. The Russians could also claim that when it came to the Anglo-American dispositions within *their* spheres, they never caused much trouble. They had acquiesced in the deal with Darlan, they did not object to the use of monarchical and conservative elements in Italy after the fall of Mussolini, while on both occasions the more purist liberals in Britain and America complained strenuously. The pleas of the unfortunate Polish government-in-exile were always being answered by Churchill and Roosevelt with the assertion that Britain and America did not propose to go to war with Russia on behalf of Poland. But skillful and persistent diplomacy can perform much without the slightest hint of recourse to war.

For all the successful development of the Polish issue, the Soviets proceeded warily. On August 9, Stalin wired Roosevelt his impression of Mikolajczyk. He added that he "had information that the Polish Committee of National Liberation in Lublin decided to invite Professor Lange to join it as member in charge of foreign relations."[92] It is not too bold to assume that the idea for this came from the Russians, since Lange had not been connected with Polish politics for years and was in fact an American citizen. But he was a distinguished economist and not a Communist, and on both counts likely to improve the reputation abroad of the rather motley group that constituted the Moscow Poles. Furthermore, he was a university professor, and Stalin could be excused for not knowing that in the United States this status did not carry the same high prestige as on the Continent!

The drama of Poland was at this point highlighted by one of its most tragic incidents: the uprising of the Polish underground in Warsaw. This uprising had been ordered by the Polish government-in-exile in face of vigorous opposition from several of its members. The latter realized that unless the rising were succored by the Red Army it would have no long-run chance of success against the Germans, who disposed of heavy weapons. And while it was true that the Red Army was approaching the Vistula, to order the underground and the population of Warsaw to undergo new sufferings meant to gamble on (1) the crossing of the Vistula being in the Soviet high command's plans at the time, and (2) if so, the Soviet government not holding its army back, which it might do for political reasons, thus allowing the destruction of the underground force loyal to the London government, since the underground's success would be a dramatic demonstration that the Polish people were not behind the Soviet-sponsored Lublin Committee. The first hypothesis was fairly

[92] *Correspondence Between the Chairman of the Council of Ministers of the U.S.S.R. . . . ,* II, 153.

reasonable; after scoring tremendous successes in their summer offensive, the Soviet troops were approaching the eastern bank of the Vistula.
But the second one was not. To be sure, the Moscow-based Union of Polish
Patriots on July 29 had broadcast to Warsaw an appeal to rise. But in
view of the Soviet Union's past policy, how likely was it that it would consent to crown with success an undertaking of the *London* Poles and accept a
fait accompli that would discredit their own Polish regime?[93]

The uprising started on August 1. The ability of the Polish underground
to mobilize considerable forces that engaged several German divisions obviously caught the Russians by surprise. Stalin's first reaction to Churchill's
plea that he order help for the Polish city minimized the whole affair. On
August 5 he wired Churchill: "I think the information given you by the
Poles full of exaggerations and untrustworthy."[94] How could the Poles with
no tanks, artillery, etc., fight off several choice German divisions? His
disbelief probably reflected a conviction that the whole business would be
over in a matter of days. But as the fight continued (it was to last for eight
weeks), the Russians' attitude wavered. Some supplies were dropped to
the beleaguered Poles. But they persisted in viewing the Warsaw uprising
as a "reckless venture" and refused to allow British and American planes,
which would otherwise have to fly from distant bases in Italy to drop
supplies to the Poles, to land on Soviet-held territory. On August 22, the
Soviet tone stiffened, and Stalin's answer to yet another appeal by Churchill and Roosevelt was grating in its brutality: "Sooner or later the truth
about the group of criminals who have unleashed the Warsaw adventure
in order to seize power will become known to everybody."[95] The Soviet
Union would have nothing to do with it.[96]

The unequal struggle went on. In September, when the prospects for the
uprising's success were gone, the Soviets softened their stand. Much of the
good will the Soviet Union had previously earned in the West was being
undone by the repercussions of Warsaw. So some Soviet supplies were

[93] Soviet historians and generals have strenuously denied that the Red
Army encouraged the uprising or was at the moment capable of crossing the
river in force and rescuing Warsaw. Unlike the story of the Katyn murders,
which is barely referred to in post-war Soviet historiography, the Polish allegations about the Warsaw uprising are often and angrily rebutted.

[94] *Correspondence Between the Chairman of the Council of Ministers of the
U.S.S.R. . . . ,* I, 252.

[95] *Ibid.,* p. 258.

[96] On August 19 the State Department had urged Ambassador Harriman
not to press the Russians too hard, since this might jeopardize the continuance
of the American bases in Russia for the shuttle-bombing of Germany. (See
Feis, *op. cit.,* p. 386.) It must remain an open question whether this message
was intercepted by the Russians and whether it affected the tenor of Stalin's
August 22 note.

dropped for the Poles, and American and British planes bringing munitions, etc., were finally allowed to land on Soviet territory. Nevertheless, Marshal Rokossovsky's army, though within a short distance of the city, remained inactive. A Polish unit attached to it tried to cross the river but was repulsed.[97] Early in October, the remnants of the Warsaw resistance surrendered to the Germans. The city was utterly destroyed.

Whatever the validity of Soviet technical excuses and the foolhardiness of the Polish enterprise, the fact remains that the very considerable help that could have been rendered to the Poles *without* crossing the Vistula was not given. The Germans' destruction of the underground army and of the city broke the back of the Polish resistance, and it implanted in many even anti-Soviet Poles the conviction that in view of the Western Powers' attitude, the problem was no longer that of Polish independence but of the *biological* survival of the Polish nation. And the latter could be secured only by submission to the Soviet Union. For the next twelve years, the memory of Warsaw was to ward off any major popular resistance to the progressive Soviet satellization of Poland.

The outline of the Soviet sphere of influence was becoming clear in the summer and fall of 1944. It was being hammered out by the Soviet armies as they surged through Rumania and into Hungary and imposed a capitulation on Finland. The latter signed an armistice on September 19. The terms were lenient, adhering in the main to the territorial provisions of 1940. Most important of all was that alone of Germany's eastern satellites Finland escaped occupation by Soviet troops. Thus Finland entered the Soviet sphere of influence, but in the classical nineteenth-century sense of the phrase, i.e., her foreign relations were to depend on her powerful neighbor's wishes but her internal affairs were to remain the concern of the Finns, with the understanding that personalities and parties repugnant to the Soviets would be barred from political influence. How far this Finnish pattern could have been applied to the other East European countries, had Anglo-American pressure been exerted on their behalf to prevent them from passing into the Russian sphere in the *twentieth*-century style, is one of those tantalizing questions we can only speculate about.

There can be little doubt that Soviet military strategy in the summer of 1944 was heavily attuned to the post-war political needs and aspirations of the Soviet Union. Thus, a heavy and costly military effort was expanded in the Balkans, though a purely military logic would have dictated a determined push toward Germany proper through the shortest route—Poland. The pressure on Rumania could be justified in view of the great importance of Rumanian oil to the German war effort. The Rumanian capitu-

[97] Its commander, General Berling, paid for this gesture. In Communist-dominated Poland he was shuffled aside to a secondary position.

lation and declaration of war on Germany, which came in August, did not stop the Red Army from occupying the whole country. Bulgaria, which had never declared war on Russia, in September contacted the British and Americans to sue for peace. This step led the Russians to declare war on the small Balkan country on September 6 and to occupy it before the Bulgarians could make any arrangements with the West. Especially costly was the struggle of the Red Army in Hungary. The foolishness of the Germans in keeping large forces in a secondary theater with the war approaching their own frontiers is hardly more remarkable than the Russian resolve to fight for Budapest as if it were Stalingrad or Berlin. But the Russians were staking out a post-war sphere of influence and were willing to pay heavily for it.

The problem of the arrangement of post-war Europe was uppermost in Churchill's mind when he reached Moscow on October 9, 1944. But much of the hoped-for effect of his visit was undercut by a message from Roosevelt to Stalin stating that the United States could not be bound by any decision reached by the two men and that "in the current world war there is literally not a single problem, military or political, in which the United States are not interested."[98] Stalin's answer was in character: he, Stalin, had supposed that Churchill was coming empowered to negotiate on behalf of Roosevelt as well, especially after their recent conference in Quebec. Now he was puzzled as to why the Prime Minister was coming at all.[99] Once more Roosevelt's advisers had made him advertise the fact that the United States and Britain did not see eye to eye on many issues. The main factor here was the perennial American antipathy to any talk of spheres of influence.[100]

But this is precisely what Churchill wanted: an agreement on spheres of influence. In his first session with Stalin he thrust under the latter's nose a list with some very strange calculations. Rumania was to be 90 per cent under Russian predominance and 10 per cent under British; the reverse situation was to prevail in Greece. Yugoslavia and Hungary were to be shared 50-50. Bulgaria was to be 75 per cent Russian and 25 per cent British.[101] Stalin looked at the list and "made a large tick upon it" with his blue pencil. The Prime Minister—the percentage plan was not one of the happier inspirations of his glorious career—was then seized with remorse: should they not burn the compromising document disposing cynically of millions of human beings? "No, you keep it," said Stalin.

Churchill's "plan" was not so much cynical as childish: what could it

[98] *Correspondence Between the Chairman of the Ministers of the U.S.S.R. . . .*, II, 161.
[99] *Ibid.*, p. 162.
[100] Feis, *op. cit.*, p. 442.
[101] Churchill, *Triumph and Tragedy*, p. 227.

mean that Bulgaria was to be one-quarter in the British sphere of interest and three-quarters in the Russian? The formal arrangement in the case of Hitler's satellites capitulating envisaged an Allied control commission in which the Big Three were to participate. Yet the dominant fact in the case of Bulgaria or Hungary was the presence of the Soviet army, and that meant that the Western Allies were to be left eventually with not so much as 1 per cent! The only concrete result of this sinful or ridiculous (depending on one's viewpoint) proposal was the Soviet agreement to leave the British a free hand in Greece and for the moment not to support the Greek Communists.

The other issues on Churchill's agenda in Moscow concerned, needless to say, Poland, and eventual Soviet participation in the war against Japan. On Poland no progress was made in reaching an agreement. Mikolajczyk and some of his colleagues were once again brought to Moscow and subjected to hectoring not only by Stalin but by Churchill as well. The Prime Minister was frantic. Much as he came to loathe the Lublin Poles,[102] he had to browbeat Mikolajczyk into accepting the Soviet territorial demands. The London Poles were now told that in fact the whole issue had been decided at Teheran. Churchill shouted at Mikolajczyk: "You are callous people who want to wreck Europe. I shall leave you to your own troubles."[103] The Polish premier withstood this bullying while in Moscow, but upon his return to London he was to advocate accommodation with the Russians. On being attacked by a majority of his cabinet, Mikolajczyk was to resign in November 1944. The subsequent (London) Polish government was virtually ignored by the British and the Americans.

Apart from the Polish problem, the atmosphere of the Moscow talks was in Churchill's opinion quite cordial: "We got closer to our Soviet allies than ever before—or since."[104] Stalin extended promises that the U.S.S.R. would enter the war against Japan within three months of the conclusion of the German one, and he implied that they expected to be rewarded for this help. In sketching the proposed Soviet moves against the Japanese, the Russian military men also implied that their thrust would be not only into Manchuria but also into parts of northern China. Thus the focus of strategic-political considerations gradually became enlarged to include the problems of the Far East, where, as well as in Eastern Europe, the Soviets expected to have a sphere of influence.

The few months separating the Moscow meeting from the Yalta conference were the high point of Anglo-Soviet relations during the war. The tone of Stalin's personal messages to Churchill was impressively cordial.

[102] This was so for both personal and political reasons.
[103] Rozek, op. cit., p. 283.
[104] Churchill, Triumph and Tragedy, p. 242.

On more substantive issues the Russians hastened to demonstrate their loyalty. Thus both prior to and during de Gaulle's visit to Moscow in December, Stalin kept Churchill informed of the gist of negotiations. De Gaulle, still somewhat snubbed by the Americans, was eager to get Russia's concurrence to the restoration of France as a Great Power. On December 2, Stalin asked Churchill for advice: de Gaulle would like a bilateral alliance with the U.S.S.R., and is also likely to demand that France should annex the Rhineland. What does Churchill think?[105] As a matter of fact Stalin suggested at one point a three-country pact between Britain, the U.S.S.R., and France, but he agreed to a Franco-Soviet one when assured that neither the U.S. nor Britain objected to it.[106]

Soviet cordiality toward the Allies and especially the British reflected the fact that with the invasion of France the Russians' darkest suspicions had been dissipated and the vigorous Anglo-American military effort was indeed highly appreciated. But an additional reason might well have been that for the time being Churchill was seconding the Soviets' efforts to browbeat the London Poles into capitulating to their demands, while the Americans were preserving a hands-off attitude. That attitude, as Roosevelt kept reassuring Stalin (the bulk of their correspondence concerned Poland), was due to political reasons—first the elections, and, after Roosevelt's re-election, the obvious desire to have a decent interlude elapse before disappointing the expectations of the Polish American voters. But this must have created a feeling of profound irritation in Moscow: how could one deal with the Americans and their strange political system? The dictator tried to appeal to Roosevelt's democratic conviction:

I think it would be natural, just, and useful for our common task if the Allied governments as the first step should send representatives to the Polish National Committee and then would recognize it as the legal government of Poland. If not, I am afraid that the Polish nation will lose faith in the Allies. I think we cannot tolerate that the Polish nation could say that we sacrificed Polish interests for a small bunch of Polish emigrés in London.[107]

Roosevelt's answer, asking Stalin to postpone the recognition, was met by

[105] *Correspondence Between the Chairman of the Council of Ministers of the U.S.S.R. . . . ,* I, 282. An identical message went to Roosevelt.

[106] An interesting sidelight to de Gaulle's visit was the strong Soviet pressure, which de Gaulle resisted, to have France recognize the Lublin Committee as the legitimate government of Poland—a proof that despite all that had gone on before, Stalin still was not fully confident that *his* solution to the Polish issue would prevail and hence needed additional arguments before the next meeting of the Big Three.

[107] *Correspondence Between the Chairman of the Council of Ministers of the U.S.S.R. . . . ,* II, 179.

a rather disingenuous reply: the Presidium of the Supreme Soviet had decided to recognize the Lublin Committee if it should proclaim itself the government of Poland; hence he, Stalin, was "powerless" to satisfy his friend's desire.

A strange turn of events made the Western Allies at this point once again experience some of the feeling of guilt they had had when the Red Army was bearing the brunt of the land fighting in the war. A German counter-offensive in the Ardennes caught the Americans by surprise. There was a momentary fear of a serious military debacle, and Churchill and Roosevelt found themselves pleading for the Russians to unleash their offensive in the east. Churchill's wire to Stalin amply revealed his anxiety. "I do not consider the situation in the West bad, but it is obvious that Eisenhower cannot accomplish his tasks without knowing your plans."[108] The Russians duly opened their offensive in January. Rundstedt's thrust by that time was clearly revealed as a diversion rather than a major offensive, of which the Germans were no longer capable. But the Russians could now imply that they saved the Allies from a major defeat.

Such was the prelude to Yalta. The conference itself took place in February 1945 and was the occasion of the last appearance of Franklin Roosevelt in the councils of the Grand Alliance. Some years later, the decisions of the conference were to become the subject of vigorous dispute in American politics. Allegations were made that Poland and China had been "sold down the river." Sinister implications were read into the fact that Alger Hiss was a member of the American delegation. But those charges were to reflect the unfortunate American penchant for oversimplification. The crucial decisions concerning Poland had been taken at Teheran; it would have taken a most determined and *united* American-British effort to arrest or affect the drift of events and to save something of Poland's independence. Decisions on China taken at Yalta were in themselves certainly not the main factor contributing to that country's future conquest by the Communists. It might be claimed that had American military officers and statesmen been endowed with prophetic gifts, they could have foreseen that Japan would capitulate in the wake of two atomic-bomb attacks on her cities. But of course they could not know that. Nor could they be absolutely sure, despite specific assurances from the Manhattan Project, that the atomic bomb would prove to be the frightful weapon it was to be.[109] In this uncertainty, American policy-makers had to contemplate an invasion of the Japanese mainland and American casualties on a huge scale, since

[108] *Ibid.*, I, 292.
[109] This assurance was conveyed by General Groves to Chief of Staff (General Marshall) on December 30, 1944. See *Foreign Relations of the United States: The Conferences at Malta and Yalta 1945* (referred to from now on as *Yalta Papers*) (Washington, 1955), p. 383.

it was widely held that the Japanese "do not surrender." In February 1945 there was therefore every incentive to bring the Russians into the war, thus to cut down the anticipated toll of American lives.[110]

The essential fact about the Yalta conference is that with victory by now certain and foreseeable in the near future insofar as Germany was concerned, it represented a perfectly natural process of bargaining among three great allies as to their influence in shaping the post-war world. One great interest they shared—and this was as genuine and obvious a desire for Stalin as it was for Churchill and Roosevelt—was to avoid for a long time to come a new world war. Beyond that, however, their views sharply diverged. The weakest of them, Great Britain, needed a new balance of power in Europe. Hence it was natural for Churchill to tend to be most lenient on Germany and to be most eager for France to resume the status of a Great Power. Most of all the British wanted a continued involvement of the United States in the affairs of the Continent. Without this, the pattern the British had opposed since the seventeenth century would become a reality more pronounced even than it had been in the heyday of Napoleon: one power would dominate Europe.

The Russians sought their security in exactly the opposite way: the interests of the Soviet Union, her ability to rebuild her shattered economy and to avoid any threat to her western regions (where Ukrainian nationalist partisans would continue sporadically to fight well into 1947) required complete Russian dominance of Eastern Europe and preponderance on the Continent. Foreign observers might well be impressed by the revelation of Russia's tremendous military power, but her rulers had to keep in mind the vulnerability of the *Soviet* system.[111]

American aims and hopes for the post-war world are harder to assess in a capsule-like form. Her tremendous industrial power finally fully awakened, her immense military resources still hardly strained, the United States did not feel the sense of insecurity experienced by her two more sorely tried allies. But the American government was haunted by the memories of isolationism and economic depression. To prevent both, it put its greatest faith in the construction of a new international organization that would decrease the American people's dislike for long-range international entanglements. To secure an effective international organization, it was thought imperative to overcome Soviet suspicions of the two Anglo-

[110] Why was it thought necessary to invade Japan rather than, with the Japanese navy utterly destroyed, to settle down to blockade and bombing to force surrender? This is a problem for a study of *American* foreign policy. But in the simplest terms it reflected the unfortunate American penchant to "get it over with."

[111] How far Russia's aims meshed with the wider prospects of expansion of Communism will be considered in the next chapter.

Saxon powers "ganging up" on them. The most troublesome issues—
Poland, control of Germany, etc.—were assumed to be capable of solution
through the agency of the United Nations. To secure wholehearted Soviet
participation in this new league of nations was worth, it was thought, considerable sacrifices and concessions. As happens not infrequently in the
making of American foreign policy, different branches of the administration had different ideas about the possibility and means of securing the
Russians' good will. Some of the military and State Department officials,
especially those who had experienced the tedious and frustrating business
of negotiating with the intermediate level of Soviet officialdom, favored
"tough" negotiating techniques. General John Deane, head of the American
mission in Russia, emphasized in his dispatches the need of securing a
quid pro quo in the case of any concession to the Kremlin. At the other
end of the spectrum were officials who believed in making large and
generous gestures toward the Russian ally. There had been some intimations from Russia that she would like long-term credits from the United
States for the purposes of reconstruction. The amount mentioned was $6
billion for thirty years, at an interest rate of 2.25 per cent. Secretary of the
Treasury Morgenthau proposed a $10-billion credit at 2 per cent.[112] The
whole problem was only barely alluded to at Yalta and then became quickly
anachronistic.

The personal setting of the Yalta discussions was of some importance.
Once again, as at Teheran, the President tried to reassure the Russians
that there was no collusion between the British and Americans. In his first
talk with Stalin, he specifically referred to Stalin's gesture that had earned
Churchill's fury at the previous conference: "He hoped that Marshal
Stalin would again propose a toast to the execution of fifty thousand
officers of the German Army."[113] Roosevelt then felt compelled to assert
that "the British were a peculiar people and wished to have their cake and
eat it too"—this in connection with the British desire to restore French
military power.[114] Such deliberate indiscretions were unlikely to incline
the Soviet leaders to yield when presented with apparent British-American
unity on an issue like Poland, and unlikely to decrease Soviet suspicions.

The crucial American statement at the conference, one that was probably
decisive in hardening Soviet intransigence on many substantive issues,
was made by Roosevelt at the plenary session on February 5:

> The President replied that he did not believe that American troops would
> stay in Europe much more than two years. . . . He could obtain support
> in Congress and throughout the country for any reasonable measures

[112] Feis, *op. cit.*, p. 646.
[113] *Yalta Papers*, p. 571.
[114] *Ibid.*, p. 572.

designed to safeguard the future peace, but he did not believe that this would extend to the maintenance of an appreciable American force in Europe.[115]

This represented an honest assessment of the realities of American politics: "more than two years" after the capitulation of Germany would be some time in 1947; the next presidential election would be approaching, and in view of past experience there would be a clamor to "bring the boys back." But this incautious revelation provided every incentive for the Soviet leaders to be stubborn: American patience and perseverance on such issues as Germany, Poland, etc., was bound to run out. Why make major concessions to the Anglo-American viewpoint, if in two years the American military presence in Europe would disappear? This well may have set in motion the fateful train of events which in the end were responsible for the presence of American troops in Europe a quarter of a century after Yalta.

On the other hand, one must not exaggerate the advantages of Soviet diplomacy or assume that, in contrast to their allies, the Russians always knew what they wanted and how to obtain it. There are intimations that on the crucial problem of the future of Germany, the Soviets were not quite sure what they wanted: a Germany definitely divided into several states, or one German state diminished only by the loss of Pomerania and Silesia (to Poland) and East Prussia (to Poland and Russia). It is certainly a gross misrepresentation by post-war Soviet historians to present the U.S.S.R. at Teheran and Yalta as a staunch defender of German unity.[116] Ambassador Harriman had wired Washington that Maisky (now in charge of post-war planning in the Soviet Foreign Ministry) talked about dismembering Germany into three or four units.[117] This was raised again by Stalin at Yalta, when he proposed that if his two partners were for dismemberment this should be stated in the eventual document of German surrender. But Stalin did not press this point with the same tenacity he displayed on issues where the Soviet mind was definitely made up.

For reasons that are not difficult to divine, the party most opposed to the dismemberment of Germany was Britain. The same reasons made Churchill fight strenuously against exacting excessive reparations from defeated Germany and against any attempt to reduce Germany's industrial production permanently. The final formula, with British reservations,

[115] *Ibid.*, p. 617.

[116] While the "ruling circles" of Britain and the U.S. wanted dismemberment, at Yalta "the question of the dismemberment of Germany was taken off the agenda on the initiative of the Soviet Government." Israelian, *op. cit.*, p. 480.

[117] *Yalta Papers*, p. 176.

envisaged as the basis of the future decision a sum of $20 billion of reparations to be exacted in industrial goods, 50 per cent of it going to Russia.[118] The Soviets also made plain that they would like to have 2 or 3 million Germans as forced labor to help rebuild the country they had so cruelly ravaged.

The decision on Germany that was to have supreme importance in the long run was the confirmation of a previous plan to have conquered Germany divided into zones of occupation by the Great Powers, with greater Berlin also being occupied in this manner. British insistence was largely responsible for one important modification: France was to receive a zone of her own and was to be admitted to the Allied Control Council. The peculiar fact that the West's zones in Berlin were to be deep in the Russian occupation zone and thus like a hostage in the Soviet hands does not appear to have struck the attention of the two Western statesmen.

Another major point on the agenda concerned Soviet conditions for joining the war against Japan. Insofar as the Soviet demands for annexing Sakhalin and the Kurile Islands were concerned, the Americans raised no objections.[119] But Roosevelt felt some compunction in granting Stalin what in terms of international law was clearly the domain of another ally, China. Thus, Stalin advanced demands on Port Arthur and Dairen and for the Manchurian Railway. He appealed to President Roosevelt as a fellow politician: how could the Soviet people support the war against Japan, a "country with which they had no great trouble," unless they got something for it? Then "it would be much easier to explain the decision to the Supreme Soviet."[120] Roosevelt tried to take the edge off the argument by once again exploiting the absent British. He hoped that after the war Hong Kong would be given back to China and become an internationalized free port. Why could not the same be done with Dairen? Or even Indochina and perhaps Burma, added the American statesman. In the end Roosevelt was made to promise that he would take up these thorny Soviet demands with Chiang Kai-shek, it being understood that gentle pressure would be exerted on the Chinese leader to meet the gist of them.[121] The status quo, i.e., virtual Soviet possession of Outer Mongolia, was also to be included in the future Soviet-Chinese treaty.

The problem of an effective international organization to replace the practically defunct League of Nations occupied the center of the American plans. This indicated perhaps a feeling of guilt: had the United States adhered to the League of Nations, of which President Wilson had been

[118] *Ibid.,* p. 979.
[119] When it came to Far Eastern questions, the British discreetly let the Americans carry on the bulk of negotiations.
[120] *Yalta Papers,* p. 769.
[121] *Ibid.,* pp. 895–96.

the main initiator, the dreadful catastrophe of World War II might not have taken place. And, as said before, the American policy-makers were firmly convinced that only under such auspices would their people sanction American involvement in international affairs. The Dumbarton Oaks conference, which had taken place between August 21 and October 7, 1944, had been meant to reconcile the views of the Big Three on the organization and procedures in that body, which, unlike the ill-fated League of Nations, was supposed to secure world peace through law.

The basic Soviet attitude on the issue was entirely realistic, unsinister, and aboveboard. If the Big Three could work together, then peace could be preserved. If not, no formulas, organizations, etc., could guarantee it. If the Soviet Union was asked to enter an organization in which at least ideologically she would be isolated, then she required solid guarantees that her sovereignty and interests would be guaranteed. The element of Soviet guile, but in this case pardonable guile, entered into the negotiations when the Russians confronted what amounted to a frantic American preoccupation with procedures in this proposed organization. If the United States was so intent on organizing the United Nations according to a certain pattern, it was pardonable to exact in return concessions on what the U.S.S.R. considered to be its *vital* interests. Nor was the Soviet policy so unsubtle as to bargain directly. But a long-standing Soviet objection to this or that point or procedure would suddenly be lifted in a manner such that the Americans would feel in turn embarrassed not to be more understanding about the Soviet desires concerning, say, Poland.

Two very important issues were left in contention after the Dumbarton Oaks conference. The first concerned the voting procedure in the Security Council, and here the famous veto reared its head. It had finally been agreed that unanimous agreement of all permanent members of the Security Council (the Big Three supplemented, later on, by China and France) would be required before the Council could determine a threat to peace or take any measure of enforcement. This part of the Dumbarton Oaks decision had already saddened the more confirmed internationalists in the West—people who believed in simply majority rule and who believed that the Great Powers should have no special privileges. But the Soviets intended to have the permanent members' veto go even further. They did not want even procedural questions in the Council to be decided by a simple majority, nor did they agree that a permanent member who was a party to the dispute before the Council should be unable to veto discussion of it. Those were, as it turned out and as the Russians probably perceived, even then issues of secondary importance at most. But the Soviets put on a brave show of intransigency up to and through the first phase of Yalta.

The other bone of contention was the Soviet demand that *all* sixteen of the Soviet republics be represented in the General Assembly. Many of them, Stalin had informed Roosevelt, were of larger size and population than several other prospective members of the U.N. Besides, the Supreme Soviet had passed some time before—and this was undoubtedly done with a view to such a contingency—a constitutional amendment enabling the republics to have their own foreign and defense ministries. Now not even the most naïve or pro-Russian American official could swallow the notion that the Ukraine or the Karelo-Finnish Republic had or was likely to have a foreign policy independent of Moscow. But the Soviet Union had a shadow of an argument. Britain was going to be surrounded by her dominions and India, then in fact a British dependency. The United States would have a group of docile (as they were in 1945) followers among the Latin American states. Russia was going to be all alone! Again, in view of the fact that the Assembly was not going to have very extensive powers, the whole problem of whether the U.S.S.R. was going to have one or seventeen votes was hardly of major importance. Yet much of the American preparation for the Yalta conference was spent in drafting and redrafting memoranda on those secondary issues. Some cantankerous senators were likely to balk at giving the Soviet Union plural representation. Others might demand forty-eight or forty-nine votes for the U.S.

There was relief at Yalta, therefore, when the Russians after some brisk bargaining were to show themselves amazingly conciliatory on these two United Nations questions. On November 7 Molotov suddenly declared that the Soviet government adhered to the American view on voting in the Security Council. Roosevelt was overjoyed. "He felt that this was a great step forward which would be welcomed by all peoples of the world."[122] The Soviets also adopted an attitude of openmindedness on the membership question. They no longer insisted on all *sixteen* republics being represented. Three would do. Here Stalin wanted Ukraine, Byelorussia, and Lithuania as additional members. Why those three? Well, they had suffered most during the war and their people wanted to be represented in the U.N. He, Stalin, would have difficulty in explaining to them why, after their sufferings, they did not receive equality with countries like Turkey or Ecuador that had contributed little or nothing to the common effort.[123] Was there a deeper scheme behind the Soviets' brazen demands? Was there some thought that before long Bulgaria or even Poland would find themselves associated in the U.S.S.R. and yet keep their personality

---

[122] *Ibid.*, p. 713.

[123] The peculiarity of the Soviet argument which escaped notice was that if the Soviet republics were in fact autonomous units, the one with prime claim to enter the U. N. would have been by far the biggest one, the *Russian* Soviet Socialist Republic. Yet the 100 million or so Russians were evidently not as pressing or ambitious in their demands as 2 million Lithuanians!

for foreign affairs? It is more likely that the whole demand was precisely to enable the Soviets to make another "concession" at an appropriate moment. But surprisingly easily, the U.S. and Britain agreed. The Ukraine and Byelorussia were to join the U.S.S.R. in the United Nations. Lithuania was dropped. Though it was not stated at the conference, her case was really too embarrassing: the U.S. government never recognized the absorption of Lithuania in the U.S.S.R. (it has not done so up to this moment). The final solution was estimated a great victory for the American viewpoint, especially as Stalin in a personal note to Roosevelt promised to support the U.S. in the case the Senate would insist on parity with the U.S.S.R.[124]

One can understand how, against this background, at the last session of the conference Harry Hopkins could send a note to the President which began, "The Russians have given in so much at the conference that I don't think we should let them down."[125] Hopkins' note concerned the issue of reparations, but it epitomized the Americans' feeling on the whole range of contentious issues.

Among them the outstanding one was Poland. "The Polish question was a dishevelled presence in every conference hour."[126] It would be of little profit here to go into the tangled problems of Rumania, Yugoslavia, etc., also discussed at the conference. It was clear that if the Western Powers could prevent or limit Soviet hegemony in Poland, then there was hope for similar arrangements in other east and southeast European countries that were then or were going to be occupied by Soviet troops. (Yugoslavia's case was somewhat different; she alone had a strong native Communist movement that did not need Soviet bayonets to set the process of communizing the country in motion.) But if Poland was to become a Soviet satellite, then no arrangements about Allied Control Commissions, no solemn pledges about free elections could save Bulgaria, Rumania, Hungary, and Czechoslovakia from a similar fate.

Yet, as we have seen, the Western Powers in effect had surrendered most of their bargaining points about Poland long before Yalta. The Curzon Line had implicitly been accepted at Teheran. Since then, both Britain and the United States had accepted a further desideratum of Russia's: that she had the right to have a government in Poland that was not objectionable to her. Now, at Yalta, the West was confronted with another turn of the screw: Stalin's demand that—if one goes through the verbiage on the subject, this is what the Soviet position amounted to—the Polish

[124] Roosevelt never revealed which two American states would become U.N. members in that event, a tantalizing problem which would have opened all sorts of possibilities for internal American politics!

[125] Sherwood, *op. cit.*, p. 860.

[126] Feis, *op. cit.*, p. 521.

government was to be of Soviet making. How could the Soviet position be shaken or affected, in view of the fact that the gist of Soviet demands had already been conceded and that Soviet armies were occupying Poland?

To do so would have required the utmost tenacity and clarity of purpose on the Anglo-American side. Yet even from a technical point of view the Western statesmen and their suites were poorly equipped to deal with the Polish problem. There was no expert on Poland among them.[127] On the Soviet side, Stalin and Molotov did not need an expert. Stalin in particular appears to have been excellently briefed. He knew such data as the extent of literacy in pre-war Poland. He was as usual a skillful and versatile negotiator, and his opposite numbers could not even refute his most daring misstatements of fact.[128] He, Stalin, could thus pose as a defender of the Polish people against the schemes of a handful of reactionary emigrés. Stalin's verbal fencing was masterly. He would not press the Yugoslavs because "Tito is a proud man . . . and might resent advice."[129] (He might have had occasion to reflect on this three years later!) Churchill's somewhat sheepish explanations about the British actions in Greece, where they were suppressing a Communist uprising, brought out the democrat in Stalin: "Marshal Stalin said that the Greeks had not yet become used to discussion and therefore were cutting each other's throats."[130]

The decision to confirm the Curzon Line passed almost without dissension, after a rather feeble attempt by Roosevelt to preserve the city of Lvov for Poland. The issue then arose as to the territorial compensation post-war Poland would receive for her losses in the east. Churchill's interest in "moving Poland westward," as he himself had proposed at Teheran, had cooled off considerably. In addition to everything else, the Polish problem was complicated by a curious geographic coincidence. There had been talk before of a "Oder-Neisse line," but now the Western statesmen discovered that there were two rivers Neisse! It made a considerable difference in territory and population whether new Poland was to expand to the

[127] Names of Polish political figures are frequently misspelled in the notes of the American diplomats at Yalta.

[128] Thus Stalin said that "his" Poles had stayed in Poland during the German occupation while the London government was composed of people who had fled and consequently enjoyed no support at home. In fact, since Mikolajczyk's resignation, the London government was headed by the veteran socialist leader Tomasz Arciszewski, who until shortly before had been active in the underground resistance and then had been smuggled out of occupied Poland. But no one was able to contradict Stalin on the point and on the subsequent thrust: "It is necessary to bear in mind the psychology of people under occupation. Their sympathies are with those who stayed and not with those who left the country." *Yalta Papers*, p. 779.

[129] *Ibid.*, p. 781.

[130] *Ibid.*, p. 782.

western Neisse, as the Russians plainly wanted, or be limited to the eastern one, as the British and Americans pleaded. The final communiqué, while definitely recording the agreement on the Curzon Line, stated merely that "Poland must receive substantial accessions of territory in the north and west,"[131] the details to be worked out by the peace conference. The accession of territories up to the Oder–western Neisse line would bring to Poland lands that had been ethnically German for at least three centuries and would mean—has, in fact, meant—the displacement of 6 or 7 million Germans. Thus, in addition to everything else, the new Poland would have to rely on the U.S.S.R. for protection against a resurgent Germany, not likely to forget or forgive the loss of Silesia and Pomerania as well as East Prussia.

But even that aspect of the Polish problem paled in comparison with the cardinal one: was Poland to have a government of her own or one of Soviet choosing? The Soviets insisted that their partners recognize the "Lublin Provisional Government" and abandon the London Poles. Roosevelt and Churchill viewed the latter without enthusiasm, but they were aware that the former was considered by the mass of Poles as a Soviet creation. Beirut, its head, had been before the war an obscure official of the Comintern little known even among Polish Communists. Its prime minister was Osobka-Morawski, a minor socialist official before 1939 who had thrown in his lot with the Soviets but who was soon to reveal himself as too independent and to be discharged. The rest of the regime was composed of people of similar background: Communists, political opportunists, and a few who saw no other choice for Poland but to submit to her powerful neighbor. It was clear that after some interval this motley crew would be purged and become in name as well as in fact Communist. But no amount of argument could swerve the Soviet determination that the Provisional (Lublin–Warsaw) Government be made the basis of the future, officially recognized regime. Yes, the Russians were willing that some "democratic" politicians be invited to join their puppets. But they would have to be in a minority and in inferior positions. There was some thought that Beirut and Osobka-Morawski might be brought to Yalta, but Stalin announced that for the moment the Soviet authorities could not locate them. The final agreement, as stated in the communiqué, granted the substance of Soviet demands. The Provisional Government was to be reorganized but form the basis of the future Polish regime. Molotov and the British and American ambassadors in Moscow were to function as a commission to preside over this reconstruction and to consult with the Provisional Government and "other democratic leaders from Poland and

[131] *Ibid.*, p. 974.

"anti-fascist" parties would be allowed to compete. Stalin thought the elections might be held within a month.

It is clear that the Russians agreed to those two points in the hope that they were needed to appease some sectors of public opinion in the West and that, in fact, Churchill and Roosevelt, having conceded the substance of the Soviet demands, would not fuss about details. That subsequently American and British representatives would insist on really seeing a large number of representative Poles, that they would expostulate with Molotov when he insisted that the only "democratic Poles" were those the Warsaw government, i.e., he himself, certified as such, must have appeared as another attempt by the West to go back on the bargain struck at Yalta.

Within two months of the conference the Soviets proceeded with a number of *faits accomplis* in Eastern Europe. Deputy Foreign Minister Andrei Vyshinsky, in an unusually brutal way, compelled the King of Rumania to appoint a Communist-dominated government, even though the previous Rumanian regime could not have been more desirous to fulfill Soviet wishes—it simply was not Communist enough. The long and elaborate compromise arranged in Yugoslavia between the royalist regime and Tito was now in effect being scuttled by the latter. Similar developments were taking place in Bulgaria and Hungary. In Czechoslovakia, President Benes, after his trip in March to Moscow, felt compelled to incorporate several Communists in his regime and to entrust the premiership to Zdenek Fierlinger, who, while not a Communist, had become during his tenure as ambassador in Russia a thorough fellow traveller. This last development was due not so much to any direct pressure upon Benes as to his perception as to what was in the offing and an attempt to prevent something worse. This was characteristic: just as after Munich, there now was a tendency to mollify the victor, to anticipate his wishes, and thus to save some shreds of independence. Both the British formulas about spheres of influence and the American-inspired Declaration on Liberated Europe accepted at Yalta, with its sonorous phrases like "the right of all peoples to choose the form of government under which they live," were turning out to have been mere scraps of paper.

The Western statesmen groped for reasons for this "change" in Soviet policies. Secretary of State Stettinius returned to an explanation of some years' standing: "It was the opinion of some of the State Department group who were on President Roosevelt's staff at the Conference that Marshal Stalin had difficulties with the Politburo when he returned to Moscow, for having been too friendly and for having made too many concessions to the two capitalist nations."[2] In view of such insights, Churchill's pleas for a tougher stand vis-à-vis the Soviet encroachment were waved

[2] Edward Stettinius, Jr., *Roosevelt and the Russians* (New York, 1949), p. 309.

aside by the American policy-makers. Only on the Polish issue did the Americans appear to share the British obduracy and to demand, to the growing fury of Stalin and Molotov, more access to "democratic Poles." The American-British demands to send their observers to Poland were rebuffed on the grounds that this would wound the national pride of the Poles, i.e., of the Warsaw government.

This Polish problem complicated the return of the British and American prisoners of war liberated by the Red Army from camps situated in Polish territory. They were detained by Soviet authorities, and the Western missions in Russia were denied access to them. While the main reason for these delays was undoubtedly the unavoidable red tape and confusion always present in wartime, it is clear that the Soviets were also apprehensive about any stories the ex-prisoners might carry west concerning the behavior of the Red Army in Poland. For all the devastation of the country, resistance to the Soviet-imposed regime was proving harder than the Russians had expected—hence their unwillingness to have Allied observers there or to hold elections, as had been promised at Yalta. The same consideration led the Soviet authorities to undertake a step that could not but create a most painful impression, even among pro-Soviet elements in the West. Through intermediaries, the Red Army extended an invitation to the leaders of the Polish underground to reveal themselves and to discuss measures to prevent conflicts between the Polish resistance faithful to the London government and the Russians. Having been assured of immunity, the Poles did so, and sixteen of their leaders were invited to the headquarters of Marshal Zhukov, Russia's most famous commander in World War II. Here, at the end of March, the Poles "disappeared." Only in May did the Soviet government announce that the sixteen leaders were being held on charges of sabotaging the Red Army and would go on trial in Moscow.

The Polish problem darkened the last weeks of President Roosevelt's life. His correspondence with Stalin grew acrimonious. To pressure the Americans who still refused to recognize Stalin's Polish government or invite it to the founding meeting of the United Nations in San Francisco, Stalin announced that Molotov would not attend—his presence was urgently required at a suddenly called meeting of the Supreme Soviet![3] Thus the Soviet delegation at this meeting on which the Americans placed so many hopes would be headed by the ambassador in Washington, Andrey Gromyko, then a young and insignificant functionary. The im-

[3] *Correspondence Between the Chairman of the Council of Ministers of the U.S.S.R. and the Presidents of the United States and Prime Ministers of Great Britain at the Time of the Great Patriotic War, 1941–45* (Moscow, 1957), II, 198.

plication was clear that if the Americans remained obdurate the Soviet Union might stay out of the U.N.

The Soviet leaders now experienced a recurrence of a suspicion that had lain dormant since the Allied invasion of Normandy: might not the Western Allies still make a separate deal with Germany? This concern was occasioned by an initiative taken by some German military officers to negotiate the surrender of the German armies in northern Italy and by subsequent secret negotiations in Switzerland. The Russians were notified of the German approaches, but the Allied commanders refused to have a Soviet officer participate in contacts with the German emissary. A series of accusatory messages from Stalin culminated with this incredible outburst on April 3, 1945: "And thus the situation arises that at this moment the Germans have stopped fighting against England and America while they continue the war against Russia—an ally of England and the United States."[4]

Once more one sees the incongruity of Soviet foreign policy as practiced under Stalin: cool deliberation and masterly diplomacy would at times yield to unreasoning suspicion that threatened all the achievements of the former. Stalin's own intelligence services could have assured him that the Germans had not stopped fighting in the West; if the allies were trying to doublecross him, why would they reveal the original German approach? Roosevelt's dignified and indignant reply brought Stalin as close to an apology as he was capable of: he did not question the good faith of the Allies, but why do they engage in dealings that can be so interpreted by the enemy? And why are Germans still stubbornly resisting the Russians when they yield so easily to the Anglo-Americans?

The incident of the Swiss negotiations was barely put in its proper perspective when on April 12 President Roosevelt died. His guidance of American diplomacy had borne such a personal mark that his disappearance must have deeply perturbed the Soviet policy-makers. The meeting of the Supreme Soviet was hastily forgotten and Molotov was dispatched to the San Francisco Conference, in reality to take stock of the new president and the new situation.

It is an "iffy" question, as President Roosevelt himself used to say, to what extent his death on the eve of victory affected the subsequent course of Russian policies. As bureaucrats set in their ways and as men given to occasional bouts of morbid suspiciousness, the Soviet leaders preferred to deal with people whom they thought they knew and whose reactions they could gauge. Stalin was probably quite sincere when he told Churchill at Potsdam that he hoped the Conservatives would win the elections and

[4] *Ibid.*, p. 204.

he could continue his collaboration with him and Eden. Beyond that, everything must be a conjecture.

The concluding phases of the war against Germany have often been described, and it has often been claimed that a different disposition of the Western Allies' armies would have vitally affected the future political dispositions in Eastern and Central Europe. Had the Allies only pushed forward beyond their allotted zone in Germany, rather than awaiting the Russian armies, had they only reached Berlin and Prague first rather than letting those prizes go to the Russians—then the subsequent course of events would have been different. The gist of Churchill's opinion in the last phase of the war was precisely that such political-military measures were necessary, in order to have some assets in hand when bargaining with the Soviets about keeping their engagements in that area of Europe. But from the American point of view, Soviet good will was of paramount value, especially in view of the desire to wind up war in the Pacific, where Soviet assistance was still felt to be vital. Whether harsh bargaining at *this* point would have affected the final outcome is again quite doubtful. And whether public opinion in the West, eager to "get it over with," would have tolerated such a confrontation is even more so.

But on the Soviet side, the possibility of such a confrontation led to increasing suspicions and feverish haste to stake out claims in Europe no matter what the cost. The suspiciousness was reflected in another outburst in April that Stalin's chief of staff had been misinformed by American intelligence officers: they had told him to expect a German counteroffensive in northern Poland; it actually came in Hungary. Stalin was later to express to General Eisenhower, then in Moscow, his personal regrets for his rudeness on this occasion.[5] A more serious consequence of this frenzied uncertainty and impatience was the unnecessary waste of Russian lives. Heavy casualties attended the Soviet conquest of Hungary, which the Soviets could have achieved cheaply had they waited a few weeks rather than pursuing an offensive. The final struggle for Berlin was also accompanied by heavy losses; a few days' wait and those losses—heavier, probably, than those incurred by the Allies in the West in any single battle—could have been avoided.

The Anglo-American rejection in April of intimations from Himmler that Germany might capitulate in the west while continuing to fight in the east went far to still *for the moment* Soviet suspicions. Stalin's wire to Churchill is of human interest as well: "Knowing you, I had full confidence that you would not act differently [in rejecting Himmler's proposals]."[6] Though this was a diplomatic phrase, perhaps even a Stalin is

[5] Dwight D. Eisenhower, *Crusade in Europe* (New York, 1948), p. 464.
[6] *Correspondence Between the Chairman of the Council of Ministers of the U.S.S.R.* . . . , I, 339.

occasionally grateful to find loyalty and trust in a political protagonist!

Such interludes could not affect the basic and deepening conflict between the West and the U.S.S.R. As befitted a true tragedy, this conflict was based, beyond all the diplomatic maneuvers and posturings, on the two sides' different concepts of international affairs, which in turn reflected differences not so much in ideology as in the political psychology of the leaders on both sides. The best illustration of this is an exasperated message sent from Stalin to Churchill on—surprise!—the Polish problem, dated April 24: "You, it is clear, do not agree that the Soviet Union has the right to demand for Poland a regime that would be friendly toward the U.S.S.R."[7] Here Stalin pointed out that the Soviet Union did not object to any arrangements the *British* might make in regard to Belgium and Greece, "since [the Soviet regime] understands the great importance of Belgium and Greece for the security of Great Britain." There was simply no way of establishing communication on this subject between Churchill and Stalin and the Americans. Neither the rough-and-ready version of Marxian ideology in which the Soviet leaders believed nor their engross-ment in the type of politics with which they had lived allowed them to admit the differences between the "sphere of influence" the British claimed in Greece and their own actions and goals in Poland. And, to repeat, in the case of Poland (unlike that of Finland), the Western Powers had countenanced the substance of Soviet domination as far back as Teheran. Why were they now making difficulties about details?

On April 25 the founding conference of the United Nations opened in San Francisco. In May, the war in Europe came to an end with the capitulation of Germany. But the basic conflict continued. Poland was not represented at San Francisco, and Molotov admitted finally to his British and American colleagues that Russian authorities were holding the sixteen Polish resistance leaders who had disappeared.[8] The currently worsening state of Russo-American relations was reflected in the Russians' once again raising difficulties about voting procedures in the Security Council and objecting to Argentina joining the U.N. The new President of the United States was the same Senator Harry S. Truman who was, undoubtedly, remembered by some in the U.S.S.R. as the man who was quoted as saying, at the news of the German invasion of Russia, that it would be a good thing for the two countries to finish each other off. His first days in office must have created the impression that he was closer to Churchill's view on Russia than his predecessor had been. Stalin as much as said that when he wired: "One must characterize as unusual the circumstances under which two governments—the United States and Britain—having

[7] *Ibid.*, p. 335.

[8] The story has it that when asked what was going to happen to them Molotov replied, "The guilty ones will be tried."

previously agreed about Poland . . . put the representatives of the U.S.S.R. in an insufferable position, attempting to dictate their demands to the Soviet Union."[9] President Truman's suspension of Lend Lease on May 8, though it was subsequently modified and though it applied equally to Britain, was interpreted in Moscow as a means of pressuring the U.S.S.R.

In fact, Truman, inexperienced in foreign affairs and not having been privy to Roosevelt's policy-making, was simply feeling his way and was being swayed by conflicting counsels. At the very first, he was inclined to take a "tough" line with the Russians. An occasion for a show of strength was soon furnished by the behavior of Tito, who, having now achieved mastery in his own country, was revealing himself, to Churchill's chagrin, as very much a Communist and one bent upon expansion of his own. His forces advanced into the Italian province of Venezia Giulia and invaded Trieste, which the Yugoslavs claimed. The mercurial Yugoslav leader also displayed keen appetite for some territory in Austria and Hungary. The Allied commander in Italy to whom authority in Trieste and environs belonged, Field Marshal Alexander, expostulated with Tito but to no avail. Churchill now contemplated with some satisfaction the prospect of Allied forces thrashing Tito's; this would in turn have an educational effect on the Russians. The implications of his wire to Truman were clear: "I trust that a standstill order can be given on the movement of the American armies and Air Force from Europe. . . . Even if this standstill order should become known it would do nothing but good."[10] But the President, having at first supported him, became more restrained in tone. Eventually Tito sulkingly retreated from Trieste and agreed with Alexander on a demarcation line between the Yugoslav and Anglo-American forces.

It became known three years later, during the outburst of the Stalin-Tito controversy, that the whole incident created profound irritation in Moscow. Stalin was in the midst of his maneuvers over Poland; he was not going to face a confrontation with the West over a miserable Adriatic port. The Yugoslavs, in turn, could not understand why the all-powerful Soviet Union would not risk a war on behalf of her Yugoslav co-believers. It was a first intimation to the Russians of how their erstwhile docile agents, once they became masters in their own countries, could be transformed into troublesome allies.

The redeployment of American forces toward the Pacific threat was not stopped. And Truman was prevailed on to seek a *détente* with Stalin.

---

[9] *Correspondence Between the Chairman of the Council of Ministers of the U.S.S.R. . . .* , II, 218.

[10] Winston L. S. Churchill, *Triumph and Tragedy* (London and Boston, 1953), p. 556.

Hence, in late May, Harry Hopkins was dispatched to Moscow. Former Ambassador Joseph E. Davies was sent at the same time to London, mainly to persuade Churchill not to object to the President meeting Stalin separately before the projected meeting of the Big Three; Stalin would thus be disabused of his notion that the United States and Britain were ganging up on him.[11] Both the person of the emissary and the purport of his mission brought Churchill close to an apoplectic attack, and it is with a great deal of effort that he composed a message saying that he could under no circumstances countenance a separate meeting between Truman and Stalin.

Effectively, however, Hopkins' mission dealt a decisive blow to Churchill's belated efforts to put curbs on Soviet expansion in Eastern Europe. In his conversation with Stalin, Hopkins stressed the need for a Soviet-American understanding and did not object when Stalin blamed all the trouble on Britain: "Great Britain wanted to revive the system of *cordon sanitaire* on the Soviet borders."[12] Stalin carefully listed the Soviet grievances: the sudden suspension of Lend Lease, admission of Argentina to the United Nations, etc. On Poland, he let the Americans take the initiative. Hopkins stressed repeatedly that Poland "was not important in itself" but as a problem in American-Soviet relations. Stalin repeated his proposal: let four or five portfolios in the Polish government of twenty ministers be taken by people not currently associated with the Warsaw group. He reassured Hopkins on freedom of speech, etc. Of course democratic freedoms would be fully respected, but they could not extend to "fascist parties." Also in wartime one had to limit those freedoms somewhat. Hopkins did not object; his knowledge of Polish affairs was well-nigh nonexistent. "He recognized such names as Mikolajczyk or Lange, but as names of other men came up he had no direct knowledge of their political background or the precise extent of their reliability."[13] He was also a very sick man. He tried to make Stalin release the sixteen underground leaders, but Stalin represented that he had knowledge of their crimes that the West did not possess, could not interfere with the judicial procedure, but appeared to think that the sentences when finally passed would not be

[11] Davies gained fame as the author of *Mission to Moscow*, in which book the Russia of the purges in the 1930's was presented in a light no Soviet official could object to. This book was subsequently made into a movie and duly reached Moscow where it was presented in a private showing in the Kremlin. "The big Russian bosses laughed themselves nearly sick but agreed that the film was friendly and useful in debunking the Red bogey idea, still according to Davies very strong in the U.S.A." Alexander Werth, *Russia at War: 1941–45* (New York, 1965), p. 617.

[12] Robert E. Sherwood, *Roosevelt and Hopkins* (New York, 1950), p. 890.

[13] *Ibid.*, p. 908.

too severe. Hopkins' acquiescence in these matters led the Russians to a concession of their own: they dropped their objection to the American plan for the voting procedure in the Security Council. The Polish issue was thus in effect settled according to Soviet wishes: the Warsaw government would soon be recognized by Britain and the United States as the legal government of Poland. It would be joined by Mikolajczyk and a few other Polish politicians from London, but they were to be given no important positions. At the last session, Stalin said "that he wished to thank Mr. Hopkins for his great assistance in moving forward the Polish question."[14] On July 5, the Americans and the British withdrew their recognition from the Polish government-in-exile and recognized the one in Warsaw.[15]

Thus was consummated a plan for which the Soviets had worked relentlessly but in which they had been helped by the ineptitude and divisions of the London Poles, by Churchill's feeling of guilt at the time of Teheran because of the achievements of the Russian army, and by the Americans' ignorance and the exaggerated importance they gave to procedural questions in the United Nations. Diplomatically the Soviet achievement, for all the assets in their hand, must be ranked as a masterpiece. But if the true goal of statesmanship at the end of a costly war, even for a regime like the Soviet one, must be a reduction of tension and a degree of international stability, then the price subsequently paid for this achievement was disproportionately high.

Issues other than Poland occupied a secondary place during the Stalin-Hopkins conversations (though to the American the problem of voting in the Security Council appeared of paramount importance). But Stalin expressed strong opinions on the Japanese question. The Soviet Union was going to enter the war in the Pacific once China agreed to the stipulations concerning her that had been made at Yalta. The date of the Soviet attack was specified as some time in August. Stalin felt that despite peace feelers put out by the Japanese, the Americans should insist on unconditional surrender. Like Germany, Japan was to be occupied by Allied forces. "The Marshal expects that Russia will share in the actual occupation of Japan and wants an agreement with the British and us as to occupation zones."[16] But Stalin did not press his views on this subject. He knew that American interest in the Far East was direct and intense. He reassured his American listener that the Soviets looked to Chiang Kai-shek as the leader of China and did not propose to sovietize that country.

[14] *Ibid.*, p. 910.

[15] The announcement was scheduled to be made on July 4, but the ambassador of the London regime in Washington begged not to have it come on the day commemorating American independence.

[16] Sherwood, *op. cit.*, p. 904.

The preoccupation of the United States with China, Roosevelt's insistence on treating it *then* as a major power must have impressed Stalin as much as it baffled Churchill. It is unlikely that he could have envisaged or wished for the full extent of the Chinese Communists' success in the next five years. But any realistic view of the Chinese situation in 1945, not to mention special sources of information the Soviets must have possessed there, would have indicated the great odds against which the Nationalist Chinese regime would have to struggle merely to recoup the situation as before the war with Japan, not to mention to achieve a unified China.

The conference at Potsdam was to unite leaders of the Big Three for the last time. It took place near the ruined capital of conquered Germany, and it began on July 16, 1945, the same day that in New Mexico the Americans exploded the first atomic bomb. The news of the development of this new weapon buoyed up Churchill's spirits. The British statesman, depressed by the rebuff from the Americans, whom he wanted to be tougher in bargaining with the Russians, beset by secret doubts about the British general elections, which had just concluded,[17] saw in the bomb a valuable asset to use in bargaining against the Russian armies—which, to the Anglo-American statesmen, appeared limitless and capable of sweeping to the Channel should they withdraw their own armed presence from Europe. The news about the existence of this frightful weapon was communicated by Truman to Stalin with studied nonchalance. To the great relief of the Western statesmen, the Soviet dictator expressed pleasure at the news and did not seem at all inquisitive; they had had a vision of Stalin demanding immediate access to the weapon and a dispatch of an army of Soviet scientists to Los Alamos! They therefore concluded what they were eager to believe—that the Soviets were entirely ignorant of the nuclear developments. We now know from Soviet sources that research on nuclear weapons had begun in the U.S.S.R. in June 1942. Though at first conducted on a modest scale, it gathered momentum by the beginning of 1945. It is thus unlikely—apart from intelligence reports that the Russians had been receiving about the American efforts—that Stalin could have been completely ignorant of the matter as late as July 1945.

The full implications of the new weapon could not, of course, have been grasped by Stalin, any more than they were clearly appreciated even by the American military establishment and the statesmen who had watched the development of the bomb. Thus, Soviet assistance in the final phase of the war against Japan was still thought to be of great importance. Yet the Soviets, for all their previous commitment to enter

[17] Those doubts were justified. Before the conference ended, the new Prime Minister, Clement Attlee, took his place at the head of the British delegation.

the Pacific war, had escalated their hostility toward the Japanese but warily. On March 30, 1944, they had exacted what had been promised them informally in 1941 at the time of the Soviet-Japanese nonaggression treaty: a new convention between the two countries surrendered Japan's oil and coal concessions in northern Sakhalin. On April 5, 1945, the Russians, as they were legally empowered to do under the 1941 agreement, gave notice of termination of the neutrality pact within one year.

For some time, Japanese efforts to get the Soviets to mediate between them and the Western Allies had been rebuffed by Russia. At Potsdam, Stalin acquainted his partners with the Japanese approaches. But the American course on Japan had been set, and on this more than any other issue the British had to go along. A document issued in the name of the United States, Great Britain, and China, dated July 26, called on the rulers of Japan to surrender unconditionally and face Allied occupation. This Potsdam ultimatum was rejected. The first atom bomb was dropped on Japan on August 6. The Soviet entrance into the war was not, as is often believed, precipitated by this news. For some time they had specified August 8 as the target date on which the Soviet Far Eastern armies were to sweep into Manchuria.

But the business at Potsdam touched mainly on Europe. The Soviet pattern of domination of Eastern Europe had already clearly emerged. In Bulgaria, Rumania, and Yugoslavia, non-Communist partners in the coalition governments were being either squeezed out or reduced to complete subservience. The function of the British and American members of the control commissions in former enemy countries, or of diplomatic missions in the Allied ones in Eastern Europe, was reduced to that of submitting fruitless protests to their Soviet colleagues or to the governments. At the same time, there already began the process of economic exploitation that was to be such a prominent feature of Soviet domination of the satellites until Stalin's death and that was to arouse the vigorous protests of even the local Communists. There was the rough-and-ready method of simply looting industrial equipment and transferring it to Russia, but in addition the Soviet government was exacting trade treaties on an unequal basis, claiming shares in industrial and utility state monopolies in Rumania, Bulgaria, Yugoslavia, etc. The utmost docility toward the Soviet Union was no guarantee against the new exactions. Thus, the Czech government, reorganized in March to include Communists, found itself in June presented with the demand for cession of the Carpatho-Ukraine. It complied without even seeking an intervention of the West. Now the fondest dreams of the Tsars, "gatherers of the Russian lands," had been surpassed. The Carpatho-Ukraine, never a part of the historic Russian state, was "reunited" with the Soviet Ukraine.

Soviet policies in the Russian sphere of occupation reflected several motivations and drives, not always well coordinated. Even the most thoroughly totalitarian system must have been baffled by the variety and complexity of problems. If the satellite countries were to be fitted into the Soviet economic sphere, then it made little sense to indulge in indiscriminate looting: equipment that could produce goods for an enterprise partly owned by the Soviets in, say, Rumania would often reach its destination in Russia as so much junk. But a totalitarian system does not always escape having its various agencies working at cross purposes. People responsible for the recovery of Russian industry were not likely to listen to the arguments of the Ministry of Trade. And the behavior of Soviet troops in the occupied countries did not make the task of the local Communists easier. Milovan Djilas, then very much a fanatic believer in Stalin, referred scathingly to the rapine and destruction wrought by Soviet troops in friendly Yugoslavia and had to go to Russia to apologize personally to Stalin.

But on the main lines of Soviet control in these countries, the Russians were not going to compromise. Whenever the issue was raised, the Soviets cited the example of Greece. When Churchill in turn would go back to his "bargain" with Stalin and present the case of Yugoslavia, where the British had barely 1 per cent of influence rather than the 50 per cent stipulated in October 1944, Stalin played the role of a democrat: Why, Yugoslavia had its own government and the Russians very often themselves did not know what Tito was going to do.[18] While his chief fenced, faithful Molotov wielded hammer and chisel: why were the British suppressing democracy in Greece and supporting the fascists? By the time Eden finished his indignant denial (complicated by the fact that liberals in his own country and, especially, in the United States were making identical charges), the Anglo-American case about Bulgaria or Rumania appeared weaker than before.

The Western Allies' previous commitments and "near commitments" continued to haunt them. At Teheran, Churchill had volunteered the opinion that Russia was entitled to a port or base with better access to the main sea routes than her existing facilities. This remark *then* could have meant only a hint about a Soviet base in the Straits acquired at the expense of Turkey. Now, as in 1939, Soviet pressure was being applied on that country, including a claim for the restitution of those districts Turkey had detached from Transcaucasia following the Revolution and the Treaty of Brest Litovsk. Lenin's Russia and Kemal's Turkey had then agreed to have the districts retained by the latter. But now the Soviet press called for their return to Soviet Armenia, and repeated that the powerful

---

[18] Churchill, *op. cit.*, p. 636. How dangerous is continuous deception! By repeating it so often the Soviet dictator soon convinced himself of the truth of his allegation, and that was to lead to his momentous blunder in 1948!

U.S.S.R. of 1945 was bent on redressing the concessions made by the weak Soviet Russia of 1921. Russia also wanted a revision of the Montreux Convention about the Straits, which in itself would have been a perfectly natural demand on the part of a Black Sea power desiring freedom of movement from that sea. But the crux of the demands was the proposal that she be granted a military and naval base in the Straits. This was again a striking sign of the historical continuities of Russian foreign policies. How many Tsars dreamed of a Russian base on the Bosphorus, indeed of Constantinople itself! But this consideration failed to move the heirs of Ataturk, who refused even to talk of territorial concessions or a Soviet base.

At Potsdam, Churchill and Truman expressed sympathy with the Soviet demand for a revision on the Straits but felt bound to reject the two other demands. The Soviet pleadings were countered by Truman's incursion into history: wars, he had learned as an amateur historian, have always started in disputes over water routes; hence, all such waterways should be put under international supervision. While some professional American diplomats viewed with secret amusement their president's emergence as a philosopher of international affairs, Stalin was visibly displeased by this distraction, though an alert response would have been to inquire about the Panama Canal, which most likely would have restrained Truman's passion for internationalizing any and all waterways. The "but won't you give me something?" gambit of Soviet diplomacy found amusing expression in Stalin's last (as it turned out) exchange of toasts with Churchill. With his flair for great historic occasions, the British leader filled their glasses with more than the usual portion of brandy and gave his awesome partner a look that was supposed to elicit a statement of world-shaking importance. Instead, "after a pause, Stalin said, 'If you find it impossible to give us a fortified position in the Marmora, could we not have a base at Dedegeatch?' "[19] Perhaps the Georgian's Russian soul would have melted had Churchill said, "What is a base between friends?" and the cold war would never have erupted. But Churchill would not. Nor would Truman. In two years the continued Soviet pressure on Turkey would be a principal reason for the Truman Doctrine.

The Potsdam conference was not supposed to produce a peace settlement. The trouble with the settlement at Versailles, it was held justly, was that it had been produced too hastily, with the wounds and rancor of World War I still present in the victors' mind. The trouble with the Potsdam arrangements was to be largely the opposite. They are witness to the truth that nothing endures like the provisional. The final drafting

[19] *Ibid.*, p. 669.

of the peace treaties was delegated to the Council of Foreign Ministers of the Big Five, which would be ready to work out agreements with the former satellites of Germany for submission to the United Nations. The final peace treaty with Germany was to be signed with the government of Germany, when such a body was finally constituted—which, with huge optimism, was assumed would occur in four or five years. The Yalta scheme of the control of Germany by the victorious powers through their respective zones was confirmed. France was to receive an occupation zone of her own. The Control Council of the four Allied commanders-in-chief was to act as the supreme body for all of Germany and to coordinate policies for the four zones. "For the time being, no Central German Government shall be established."[20]

These arrangements were accepted by the Soviet Union without fundamental objections. It occasioned some surprise, especially among the Americans, that the Russians had abandoned their previous notions about dismembering Germany. But, as emphasized before, they never had been fully committed to the idea of partitioning Germany. If Stalin at one time wanted to specify dismemberment in any instrument of surrender by Germany, it was probably with the notion that such a stipulation would prevent any *post-Hitler* regime from surrendering and would make it fight to the bitter end, i.e., until Germany was occupied. If Germany was to be occupied under a zonal arrangement, she was in fact going to be dismembered anyway, and her reunification could take place only with Soviet approval. The zone assigned to Russia was the largely agricultural east, while the more industrially developed areas were left to the West. But apart from an attempt to have the industrial Ruhr under the Four Powers rather than as part of the British zone, the Soviets acquiesced in the arrangement as the only practical one. They might have reflected also that their grasp on the surplus-food-producing area was, for the moment, of greater importance than the West's control of the industrial areas, with much of its productive capacity in ruins. Besides, some of what remained of German industry was to be dismantled for reparations. And it must have appeared then that western Germany, burdened by millions of refugees from the Russian-occupied east, would for years be a huge economic liability for its masters.

Reparations to be exacted from Germany had been the subject of a violent dispute at Yalta, where Churchill's fear of Britain being linked to the "corpse" of a pastoralized Germany clashed with the undeniable Soviet case for demanding huge reparations from the country that had inflicted such devastation on the Soviet economy. At Potsdam, the Soviets

[20] From the official communiqué of the conference, quoted in Herbert Feis, *Between War and Peace: The Potsdam Conference* (Princeton, 1960), p. 342.

were induced to drop their insistence first on the figure of $20 billion, then on any fixed sum. On the issue on which the Soviet claims were strongest and most justified, they were to show themselves most tractable, though not without some hard bargaining. The final formula provided that each power would exact reparations from its own zone. In addition, the U.S.S.R. was to get 15 per cent of the industrial equipment removed from the western zones in exchange for raw materials they would furnish, and 10 per cent without any counter-deliveries.

Soviet reasonableness on the issue of reparations was not unconnected with the fact that Secretary of State Byrnes announced that to the American delegation, the issue of reparations was linked to the issue of Germany's frontiers, i.e., that the Americans would be willing to agree to Soviet proposals on the German-Polish frontier provided the Russians would be reasonable on reparations. Though Stalin heatedly refused to heed this linkage, it is clear that the Russians recognized the skill of the move, worthy of a veteran Southern politician, and gave way on what for them was the less important issue.[21]

Soviet insistence on Poland's receiving a larger slice of Germany than either the British or Americans were at first willing to concede must today appear as one of the ironies of post-war history. Had they acquiesced in their allies' views that the Oder and eastern Neisse rivers be the frontier, Communist East Germany would be today a much more feasible state, their own bid as protectors of German nationalism more convincing. Poland, on the contrary, has won a measure of independence from Russia since 1956 and may conceivably become again a problem for Soviet foreign policy. But the arrangements on which the Soviets insisted so strenuously in 1945 and for which they were willing to pay fairly substantially reveals another point: there was obviously no certainty in the Soviet mind in 1945 that Germany would not be reunited within a few years and free of all foreign military occupations. They thus contemplated without regret territorial diminution of Germany even though this diminution was at the expense of their own zone. One must not exaggerate the extent to which the Soviets, unlike their Western protagonists, were able to plan in long-range terms or to divine the future.

The Western Allies, however, could not foresee the post-war economic miracle of western Germany or the fact that 10 million German refugees from the east and the Sudetenland could be absorbed into its economy. The amputation of Silesia and of much of Germany's food-producing areas was to throw their own zones into complete economic chaos, and Germany, even if eventually reunited, was never going to be able, it seemed, to stand on her feet economically.

[21] *Ibid.*, p. 265.

Much of Churchill's original enthusiasm for moving Poland westward evaporated when it became clear that this Poland would be Communist-dominated. He clashed repeatedly with Stalin, demanding that the Polish frontier adhere to the Oder–eastern Neisse line. This would leave Germany the cities of Breslau and the port of Stettin, and important mining and agrarian areas. Stalin bargained furiously: there were practically no Germans in that area anyway; they had all fled; and the Poles transplanted from the areas ceded to Russia were filling the void. He, Stalin, could reassure Churchill that most of the coal to heat Berlin came from Saxony and not Silesia. The Polish leaders were invited to attend, and, not surprisingly, they agreed with Stalin. Bierut and Mikolajczyk, though fellow members of what was humorously called the Provisional Government of National Unity, were already deadly enemies, but on the territorial issue they saw eye to eye. Churchill assures us in his memoirs that had he won the election he would have let the conference break rather than agree on the proposed Polish-German frontier. But one may be allowed to doubt his statement: the Americans were getting tired of the wrangling and eager to wrap up the conference. The agreement in *substance* followed Russia's wishes. The "final determination" of Poland's western frontier was left to the peace conference, but in the meantime (and a long meantime it has turned out to be) the German territories claimed by Poland were left under Polish administration.

Such were the main features of the final assembly of the Big Three leaders. Soviet desires were stymied on a number of issues: Turkey, the demand for diplomatic rupture of Britain and the United States with Franco's Spain, a plea for Soviet trusteeship of part of Italy's colonial empire. But on the main issues, the Soviets could have firm grounds for satisfaction. Writes a Soviet author: "One must admit that on the whole the decisions of the conference represented a victory for democratic principles of postwar reconstruction of the world. Decisions on Poland, Germany . . . peace negotiations placed solid foundations for a durable and lengthy peace."[22] But the same author notes the rising discord: the American delegation already bore the imprint of partisans of a "hard line" with the U.S.S.R. Truman, though by and large he repulsed the intrigues of the British (since he needed the U.S.S.R. for the war with Japan) was already basically unfriendly toward Russia. The appearance of the British Labour government was not a good sign: "Bevin's position on certain issues was so openly anti-Soviet that even the Americans were somewhat taken aback."[23] And the Soviet author quotes wryly Truman's comment

[22] V. L. Israelian, *Diplomatic History of the Great Patriotic War* (Moscow, 1959), p. 336.

[23] *Ibid.*, p. 338.

in a letter to his family that he wished never again to have another conference with the Soviet leaders, but alas there would have to be further Potsdams.

But there were to be no more summit meetings in Stalin's time. Once the common struggle was over, relations soon cooled off to the point where the atmosphere of Teheran, Yalta, or Potsdam became unimaginable. And quite apart from the drawing apart of the Big Three, the leaders of the West could not, under peacetime conditions, enjoy the authority of their predecessors or the power they had had to make commitments not communicated to Parliament or Congress. This inevitable "democratization" of foreign-policy-making in the West was in itself a contributing factor, to be sure a minor one, in the development of the cold-war atmosphere. Much as Stalin played up to Roosevelt's democratic rhetoric, the Soviet leaders could not and would not understand their Western colleagues' preoccupation with public opinion. The American people should learn to obey their rulers, said Vyshinsky at Yalta to Charles Bohlen.[24] Even more than Churchill, Stalin could not understand the American position that small nations were repositories of democratic virtues and idealism in foreign affairs that were sadly missing in the Great Powers (except for the United States). In recent years, the Soviets had painfully and awkwardly staked their claim to the formal trappings of a great power: commissariats were renamed ministries and their diplomats were put in uniform. Gone were the days when Trotskys and Zalkinds made fun of diplomatic procedures, when the very terms "diplomacy" and "ambassador" were eschewed as counterrevolutionary. Under these circumstances, ready to revert to the elegant days of diplomacy in the era of Metternich and Talleyrand, the Soviets found it jarring to encounter Truman's Wilsonian rhetoric and the populistic arguments of the British Labourites, whom they had always loathed anyway.[25]

But immediate developments during and after Potsdam touched on more momentous affairs. On August 6 came Hiroshima. On August 8 the Japanese ambassador paid a visit to Molotov with yet another plea to have the Russians transmit peace proposals to the Anglo-Americans. Molotov informed his visitor that this was a happy coincidence; he had something to tell him: as of August 9, the U.S.S.R. would be in a state of war with the Japanese empire.

[24] The future ambassador replied that Mr. Vyshinsky should tell that to the American people. Vyshinsky, of sinister fame as the brutal prosecutor in the purge trials, then offered to try his powers of persuasion in the United States.

[25] Bevin's vaunting of his own working-class background was to irritate Molotov who, for all his revolutionary past, was very much a bourgeois in his background and demeanor. Snobbery is not a negligible factor, even in international relations, even in this century.

This time, Soviet historians have a legitimate grievance against the statements often repeated in the West that Soviet entry into the Pacific war was prompted, if not indeed caused by, the dropping of the atomic bomb. August had been the month specified for some time for this step, and the 8th had been specifically mentioned as the target date. Soviet preparations for the campaign had been thorough: 1.6 million soldiers had been assembled for the lightning strike into Manchuria and northern China. Soviet superiority in numbers and equipment was overwhelming. Official Soviet statistics specify Soviet superiority over the enemy as 2 to 1 in men and planes and 5 to 1 in tanks.[26] But those statistics do not tell the whole story. Only a bit more than half of the enemy troops were Japanese; the rest were puppet Manchurian ones of little fighting value. The Soviet troops were helped by those of Outer Mongolia. Units of the Chinese Communist armies opened their own offensive on August 10 "with the aim of rendering help to the Soviet armed forces entering China, and to be in position to accept capitulation of the Japanese armies and those of the Manchukuo."[27]

A look at the map of the operations and their story in the official Soviet military history makes it clear that the aim of the operation was the speediest possible occupation of Manchuria and northern Korea and a linkage with the forces of the Chinese Communists. Thus, though most of the Japanese forces were in the east of the theater of operations facing the Soviet frontier, the major Soviet thrust was through Outer Mongolia into northeast China and Manuchuria. Militarily, this might have been justified by the "hit them where they ain't" principle, but it also linked Soviet forces with the Chinese Communists and barred any attempt by Chinese Nationalist troops to move into Manchuria from the west while the Soviets would be entering from the east.[28] In their hurry to occupy Manchuria and the other targets, the Soviets did not spare their men and resources. It made little sense to attack southern Sakhalin, which was away from the main theater of operations and assigned for return to the U.S.S.R. anyway. But, typically, operations against Sakhalin were undertaken at the same time as the mainland attack, and the casualties were not light. The announcement of the Japanese capitulation on August 14 did not stop the Soviet offensives. It is true that some Japanese units were still fighting, but obviously the decision had been reached, and it would have spared Soviet as well as Japanese lives to withhold further

[26] *History of the Great Patriotic War of the Soviet Union*, V (Moscow, 1963), 551.

[27] *Ibid.*, p. 590.

[28] Officially the Soviet high command prohibited Chinese Communist units to move into Manchuria proper at the time of the offensive, but of course they were in a position to do so later.

offensive action and await the local Japanese commanders' surrender. But the order of the high command required offensive actions along the whole front. Soviet sources make a specific reproach to the American command that *after* the Japanese announcement of capitulation it refused to land troops in Korea and attack the Japanese there: "The American command preferred to land troops in Korea only after the end of all fighting without incurring any risk and with purely imperialist aims."[29] Rather than wait a few days, thousands of Russian lives were expended.

This was dictated by political considerations. Unlike what is often believed in the West, the post-war memoirs of the Russian generals make it abundantly clear that they, no more than most professional military officers, were not eager to expend their soldiers' lives needlessly. But while the atom bombs did not *make* the Russians declare war, they imparted to Stalin a sense of urgency and a fear that a "premature" Japanese capitulation might rob Russia of some of the expected gains. On August 15, in his General Order No. 1 General MacArthur specified the Allied commanders to whom the given Japanese armies should surrender. The ones in Sakhalin, Manchuria, and Korea north of the 38th Parallel were to surrender to the Russians. In a dispatch to Truman, Stalin pleaded for more: the Japanese forces in the Kuriles should also surrender to the Russians. (This proposal was in line with the decision arrived at in Yalta that the Kurile Islands should go to the Soviet Union.) The main thrust of Stalin's communication was that Soviet forces should participate in the occupation of Japan proper. Half of the northernmost island of Hokkaido should be occupied by the Soviets. If, in his earlier pleadings with the Americans, the Russian leader invoked the pressures of the Supreme Soviet, this time it was Soviet public opinion that was called for help: "Russian public opinion would be seriously insulted if the Russian armies were not to receive an occupation zone in some part of Japan proper. I earnestly hope that my modest wishes as expounded here will meet no opposition."[30] Truman's answer was not designed to appease Soviet public opinion. He rejected the plea for an occupation zone. As to the Kuriles, he agreed that the Soviets should occupy them but asked for an American base there. This in turn brought an eruption of Stalin's bitterness: "We have not expected such an answer from you"; only a defeated state granted such bases.[31] The Kurile incident was eventually smoothed over: Truman explained that the Americans only wanted landing rights; the Kurile Islands were not *yet* Soviet territory. Stalin's reply on August 30 was all sweetness and light: it was all a misunderstanding; he would be glad to grant the

---

[29] *History of the Great Patriotic War of the Soviet Union*, V, 586.

[30] *Correspondence Between the Chairman of the Council of Ministers of the U.S.S.R. . . .* , II, 264.

[31] *Ibid.*, p. 265.

landing rights on *Soviet* airfields in the Kuriles, but should not the Russians in return be granted such rights in the Aleutians?

The Soviet intervention in the Japanese war has been consistently represented in the Soviet sources as the decisive blow that made the Japanese sue for peace. In more recent treatments of the subject, it is also unabashedly claimed that the success of the Chinese Communists was made possible by the timely Russian seizure of Manchuria. For all the intervening occupation of Manchuria by Chiang Kai-shek's forces, the ultimate victory of the Communists is ascribed to the stacks of Japanese arms surrendered to them by the Russians. "The success of [the Chinese Communists'] forces was also secured by the fact that they in their struggle against the reactionary Kuomintang forces could use the arms and supplies of the former Japanese and puppet armies crushed by the forces of the Soviet Union. This had an enormous importance for the victories of the national liberation forces."[32]

Both in his announcement of the beginning of the operations against Japan and in his victory statement on September 2 (the day of the official Japanese capitulation), Stalin stressed the old scores Russia had to settle with Japan. He recalled the Russo-Japanese War of 1904–5, begun by a "faith-breaking" Japanese attack without any prior declaration of war on the Russian fleet, the Japanese intervention after the Revolution, the undeclared frontier war of 1937–39. They of the old generation, declared Stalin, have waited too long for this day of reckoning. This was hardly sound history; in 1905, Joseph Djugashvili, like the rest of the Russian social democrats and revolutionaries, undoubtedly had welcomed Tsarist Russia's defeat as a spur to revolution. But the disappearance of Japan as a Great Power lifted another long-standing anxiety for the Soviet Union. As we have seen, in the 1920's, while spurring revolutionary activity everywhere else in China, the Russians were careful not to interfere in the Japanese sphere of interests in Manchuria. In the early 1930's they expected with dread a full-fledged Japanese attack. Only Japanese involvement in the Chinese war of 1937 relieved part of their anxieties, and December 7, 1941, the rest. Now the situation in the Far East was drastically transformed.

But the Russians had also been extremely nervous about the United States fulfilling her earlier pledges for a post-war rearrangement in the Far East. Stalin's intemperate telegram about the base in the Kuriles showed how this nervousness affected the usually subtle and restrained Soviet diplomacy. The fact that the Americans, following their occupation of Japan, did not proceed to a wholesale liquidation of the Japanese general staff and the armed forces was another source of suspicion. Were

[32] *History of the Great Patriotic War of the Soviet Union*, V, 600.

they thinking of recreating the Japanese armed forces, and if so to fight against whom? That this was not a propaganda point is demonstrated by our rare glimpse into an "internal" Soviet document. On September 22, 1945, the high command informed the Commander-in-Chief Far East, Marshal Vasilevsky, that MacArthur "repeats the same mistake that was committed in 1918 in relation to Germany,"[33] i.e., leaving Japan's leading military officers at large.

The preservation of the monarchy in Japan, even though it was to be stripped of its quasi-divine character and emasculated politically, also aroused Soviet displeasure. But in Japan, unlike Eastern Europe, the Soviets encountered American resolution to play a dominant part. Repeated Soviet efforts to get an occupation zone were thwarted: the furthest the Americans would go was to grant that a detachment of Soviet troops could serve under MacArthur's command, and this was something the Soviets were not eager to accept. The masterful American commander was also not a man to tolerate Soviet interference with his own quasi-imperial rule. After much Soviet insistence and harassment, an Allied Council was set up, composed of the representatives of the Big Four, to supplement the eleven-power Far Eastern Commission in Washington. But MacArthur made it clear that he considered the council to be a purely advisory body. The wranglings on the Commission led at times to the recall of the Soviet representatives, but reading between the lines of the official Soviet accounts of post-war Japan, one can see that the Soviets were not too displeased with MacArthur's trusteeship. Japan was thoroughly disarmed. The Communist Party of Japan was accorded opportunity for political activity. And the Allied Council, for all the limitations put on its activity, was no mere rubber stamp. In view of the role of the Allied Control Commissions in Bulgaria or Hungary, the Soviets could hardly have expected more.

And thus the Grand Alliance triumphed over the Axis Powers and by the very completeness of its victory made sure that it could not endure. Looking from the historical perspective of more than twenty years, it is clear that few developments in modern times bear such an air of inevitability as the melancholy turn of events we describe as the cold war. Reviewing Britain's Irish policy in the 1830's, Lord Melbourne exploded that what all the wise men had promised did not come to pass and what all the damned fools said must happen had taken place. And so with East-West relations. What sober statesmen had envisaged as the solid framework for world peace, what economists and historians had deduced as the

[33] *Ibid.*, p. 601.

lessons of the past, lay in ruins within two years of the victory. What simple people argued out of ignorance or anti-Soviet bias had come true.

Reasons for these developments have been sought, depending on the authors' political persuasion or bias, either in sins of commission and omission on the part of the West, which in view of the configuration of real power means after 1945 America, or contrariwise in the Soviet quest for world domination. None of those conjectures can be entirely proved or disproved by the evidence available to us today. But it is clear that the main reasons for the conflict must be sought in the character of the state systems that then dominated the world.

It is sometimes argued that the change in American foreign policy after Roosevelt was bound to maximize Soviet suspicions. But, with the war concluded, it was impossible for large segments of Western public opinion to remain unconcerned at what was happening in Soviet-dominated Europe and this could not but affect the policies of the American and British governments. Then, in turn, it was impossible for the Soviets to abandon their suspicious about the intentions of the Western Powers. Not the most intensive credits, not even the turning over to the Russians of sample atomic bombs could have appeased them or basically affected their policies. Suspicion was built into the Soviet system; it was inherent in the character of its ruler. In Alexander Solzhenitsyn's *One Day in the Life of Ivan Denisovich* there is an incident (based on a true story) which relates to a Russian naval commander, an inmate of a Soviet forced labor camp. This man, a loyal Communist, was imprisoned for the sole reason that during the war he accepted a present from a British naval officer. Suspiciousness of that dimension could not have been prevented or modified by the most strenuous Western efforts at displaying good will and cooperation. Soviet suspicion fell heavily on a most loyal vassal who desired a modicum of internal autonomy: Tito's Yugoslavia. Stalin, although he had been accorded, as he himself acknowledged, unexpected support by his people in an hour of trial, proceeded after the victory to subject them to most cruel restraints and privations. New purges shook the highest echelons of the oligarchy, and even those closest to Stalin, people like Molotov and Mikoyan, had their wives and children exiled and imprisoned. How, then, could such a man and such a system indulge in the usual give and take of a concert of powers or the United Nations?

The other side of the argument—that "tougher policies" by the West would have produced a better result, preserved more countries from Communism, and compelled the Russians to "play ball"—has its own element of unrealism. It is predicated on the assumption that after a lengthy war in which their own governments' propaganda contributed to an unrealistic popular picture of the U.S.S.R., the American and British peoples would have tolerated a drastic about-face and the type of confrontation which only the experience of the next four years made them accept in the form of NATO and rearmament. Apart from any moral or technological considerations, the nature of the democratic countries did not permit them in 1945 to contemplate the use or even threat of the atom bomb against their ally. Churchill's plan to recoup by a tougher stand in the spring of 1945 much of what had been conceded at Teheran and Yalta was likewise almost a psychological impossibility. At the Congress of Vienna, Britain and Austria, by combining with their erstwhile enemy France, were able to exact concessions from their quite recent allies Russia and Prussia. But that was in an era when monarchs and cabinets made foreign policy, happily oblivious to such matters as public opinion.

But our concern is not primarily with what Western policy might have been but with the development of Soviet foreign relations. Here, while Soviet policy could not have been *essentially* different after 1945, the problem remains as to the reasons for its abrupt shift in line and method at that time. Why, in their satellites, did the Soviets ruthlessly and speedily crush all effective opposition, rather than follow the Finnish model? Prudence would seem to have argued that a cautious approach, leaving Poland or Hungary internal autonomy after securing their subordination in matters concerning foreign policy and defense, was preferable to a policy that so grated on Western sensitivities and that made inconceivable that technical and financial aid from America which was so badly needed by the ruined Russian economy. If, as is often argued, the Soviets were fearful of America's aggressive intentions and nuclear weapons, why maximize the danger by brutal and uncompromising policies rather than disarming suspicions through a more subtle and conciliatory diplomacy?

The basic explanation must be sought in the same consideration that dictated the course of events leading to the Nazi-Soviet Pact. Then, it was Stalin's conviction that any war fought on Soviet soil, however victorious, in the end would spell disaster to the regime and to his own personal power. Now the same internal policy dictated isolation from and hostility toward the West. The artillery salvos celebrating the victories over Germany and Japan were barely silenced and the inhabitants of Moscow were recovering their hearing[34] when the rulers must have turned from their exultation to the depressing condition of their country. The western part of the U.S.S.R. lay in ruins. For all the industrial development of the central and Siberian regions, total production had fallen by almost one-half. Soviet losses in the war have variously been estimated at between 15 and 20 million lives. When the war had started, Soviet agriculture was barely recovering from the ravages of collectivization; now that recovery

[34] Victory over Germany was celebrated with thirty salvos by one thousand pieces of artillery!

had been undone. While the world was impressed by Russia's military achievements, her rulers must have been aware of the weakness of the economic base behind the imposing military strength. In view of the gigantic increase in America's industrial production, the U.S.S.R. had to strain her own human and material resources just to stay in the race, not to mention "to catch up and overcome." Thus, when it came to labor discipline and the work week, Russia could not afford to slacken the wartime effort. The recovery of the pre-war standard of living, low though it had been, was now postponed; and, though the fighting had stopped, people had to be pressed toward further sacrifices.

The patriotic wartime exhilaration gave way to a suspicious scrutiny of the behavior of people in the regions once occupied by the Germans. Several autonomous regions and republics had already been disbanded, their surviving population dispersed throughout the U.S.S.R. But now this scrutiny became generalized and was applied to the vast categories of population exposed, through no fault of their own, to contact with the enemy: former war prisoners, the millions used as forced labor in Germany, the populations of the Ukraine and Byelorussia. It is impossible to estimate how many of these found themselves in forced labor camps, but the number was not inconsiderable. Against this background it becomes clear why the regime felt it could not afford relaxation or liberalization, why on the contrary the outside world had to be presented in a hostile light and the atmosphere of urgency and vigilance inculcated. Years later, when many wounds of the war had healed, when the standard of living was much higher, a very limited contact with the West and relaxation of security regulations were to bring a ferment among certain elements of the population—students, intellectuals—even some isolated instances of strikes. What would have been the result of intense intercourse with the West in the *immediate* post-war years, considering both the general devastation and the people's aroused and betrayed expectation of a freer and more abundant life once the war was over?

In the old days of Muscovy, in the sixteenth and seventeenth centuries, the Tsar's government was careful to ban travel and residence of foreigners from the West, and even insisted on keeping foreign ambassadors in strict seclusion. The strangers might report back to their monarchs about Russia's backwardness and weakness. They might stir up discontent among the nobles by presenting to them a picture of freedom and prosperity in other countries, enticing some of them to revolt or to flee to a neighboring country. The same conditions and the same mentality appear to have been recreated in Russia between 1946 and 1953. Not even during the purge period of 1934–39 had there been such a frantic attempt to isolate Russian life from any foreign influences and contacts. As in the West, the regime had to undo the effects of its own wartime propaganda:

Americans and British became potential enemies, any information conveyed to a foreigner a betrayal of an official secret. The few Americans and Englishmen who in the course of the war became married to Russian women found it impossible in most cases to get their wives out of the country. Only Stalin's death brought an end to this chicanery, the inhumanity of which is less striking than its incredible pettiness. Books and plays abounded urging the population to be vigilant against foreign enemies, depicting the ways in which appeals to the internationality of science and culture were used to lull the vigilance of the Soviet people and exploit their innate generosity for the benefit of the foreign enemy.

The same motif was apparent in the vast campaign that became associated with the name of Andrei Zhdanov and which was undertaken to purify Soviet cultural life of foreign and hostile accretions. The heirs of Marx and Engels denounced "cosmopolitanism," which they found manifested in practically every acknowledgment of foreign achievement or contribution to the fund of Russian national culture. Soviet non-Russian literatures and arts were scrutinized for the slightest evidence of something that could be construed as derogatory to "the leading nation of the Soviet Union," to its historical mission of having emancipated and decisively influenced the cultures of all other nations, from the Ukrainian to the Chuvash. Even famous figures of Russian literature and arts were being denounced and silenced for their "innovationism," latent cosmopolitanism, and lack of roots in the Great Russian culture. The world had not witnessed—and was not to see again, until twenty years later and in another Communist state—such an exhibition of violent cultural chauvinism and obscurantism, such an attempt to seal off a vast country against any and all foreign influences. A traditional appurtenance of xenophobia, anti-Semitism, now came out in the open, and was expressed in a mounting stream of less and less veiled official policies and utterances until the last days of Stalin's life.

On the morrow of Russia's greatest victory and her emergence as one of the world's two super-powers, the regime seemed to be panic-stricken not by a foreign invader, but by what a few writers, scholars, musicians, etc., might do to the Soviet people's internal cohesion and sense of purpose. It is hard to see how this attitude could be combined with any policy of even perfunctory friendliness with the West, participation in such enterprises as the Marshall Plan, or any other form of international collaboration. This peculiar isolationism surpassed anything in that line in the 1920's, when the Soviet state was desperately weak and *ideologically* more hostile to capitalism; it was more frantic and pathological than at the time of the great purge and the growing German menace.

The aura of secrecy and isolationism is also responsible for the fact that we know less about what went on in the Soviet Union during this period of the cold war than during any other period of Soviet history. Hence it is impossible to define precisely the motivations and factors that went into those somber decisions and policies. Even Khrushchev's indiscretions were productive of very little information on the period in question. He preferred to discourse about the time of the great purge rather than about the post-war era. Were there indeed pressures and internal dangers that justified this repression or isolation? We know of sporadic partisan activity in the Ukraine that went on until 1947. We know that the regime was apprehensive about the effect of having exposed millions of Soviet soldiers to conditions outside the borders of the U.S.S.R., even though the countries they saw were devastated by war.

It is equally uncertain how the internal repression and consequent heightening of international tension reflected the inner politics of the Soviet oligarchy. At the end of the war, Stalin was 66. It is unlikely that he would be capable of that kind of detailed attention to the most important affairs of the Party, state, and economy which had been such an important feature of his personal power. Milovan Djilas, who had seen him in 1945 and then two-and-a-half years later, on the eve of the Soviet-Yugoslav break, was struck by his transformation and how much he had aged. A suspicious despot, Stalin must have been aware that the struggle over his succession had in effect begun. With the war over, the most prestigious Soviet marshals were quietly removed from the public eye. The most prominent of them, Zhukov, after a short term as Soviet commander in Germany, found himself in the obscurity of a provincial command. Within the highest Kremlin circles, the end of the war brought Andrei Zhdanov into renewed prominence in domestic politics, where he apparently replaced Malenkov as the heir-apparent. Zhdanov's death in 1948 was followed in turn by a purge of his former supporters, culminating in the still mysterious "Leningrad affair" in 1949, when the whole leadership of the Party and government organs in this city, long a bailiwick of Zhdanov's, was liquidated, as was Nikolai Voznesensky, member of the Politburo and Russia's chief economic planner.

These internal convulsions, and the need to strain all resources in order first to rebuild and then push Russia's economy forward, suggest very forcibly that a decisive factor in the shift of Soviet foreign policy following the war was the internal one. That Russian policy toward the West immediately following the war was not affected by any fears of the West's aggressive intentions is convincingly demonstrated by the pace of Soviet demobilization. Speaking before the Supreme Soviet on January 14, 1960, Khrushchev gave the following statistics: on the eve of the war with Germany Soviet forces comprised 4,207,000 men. At the end of the war, they had reached a total of 11,365,000. "As a result of demobilization carried out immediately after the war, by 1948 the numerical strength of the U.S.S.R. Armed Forces had been reduced to 2,874,000 men."[35] Considering the Soviet garrisons in eastern Germany, in the satellite countries, and elsewhere, the latter figure is not extraordinary. It hardly suggests any fear of an imminent attack or of "atomic blackmail." Only Stalin's death and his successors' fear that the West would profit by the consequent disorganization within the Soviet Union and unrest within the Soviet satellites brought a doubling of the Soviet armed forces.[36]

Khrushchev's figures, and there is no reason to doubt their veracity, thus throw a vivid light on the Soviet appraisal of the world situation following the end of the war with Germany and Japan and the beginning of the cold war. The legend of massive Soviet armies ready to march to the English Channel still persists among many Western writers, both among those who believe that such a move was contemplated in answer to an expected atomic attack upon the U.S.S.R., and those who credit the Soviets with the ambition to conquer the rest of Europe.[37] Khrushchev's figures tell a different story: the Soviet armies were substantially increased as against their number in the mid-1930's, but they now had to perform police duties over vast areas of Eastern Europe, in the countries where passive acceptance of Moscow-imposed regimes could not be taken for granted. Furthermore, even without figures, it is simply a challenge to common sense to envisage the Soviet Union between 1945 and 1950 as either desirous or apprehensive of a major war. The country was launched on a vast program of economic reconstruction. Nobody who has followed the course of British and American politics at that time could in turn remain under the fantastic misapprehension that those countries were preparing an anti-Soviet crusade or a preventive war. The simplest and most banal explanation is not necessarily wrong; the Soviet Union was bent upon expanding her sphere of power and influence but without incurring the risk of war.

[35] *Pravda*, January 15, 1960.

[36] In a typical effort to conceal the real significance of the figures, Khrushchev blamed the increase of the Soviet armed forces on "the formation of the aggressive NATO bloc" and "blackmail with the atomic bomb at a time when we did not yet have it." But the figure of 5,763,000 men for the armed forces is given by him for the year 1955, while NATO was formed in 1949 and the American monopoly of nuclear weapons came to an end in the same year. Thus the implication is clear that the great increase came not because of the atom bomb, nor even with NATO and the Korean War, but following Stalin's death in March 1953. Otherwise why is not the higher figure specified as having been reached in 1950 or 1951 rather than 1955?

[37] "By 1948 the Soviet Union was the strongest power on the Continent. . . . The Anglo-American armies had been weakened by demobilization while the Russian forces were maintained at almost wartime level." Max Charles, *Berlin Blockade* (London, 1959), p. 20.

The end of World War II left Russia the only Great Power on the Continent. France's status as such was clearly an honorific one, and in fact the Fourth Republic—emerging from defeat and occupation, soon engulfed in new internal squabbles and colonial wars—had neither the capacity nor the desire to play a balancing role. Even Britain, as became increasingly clear with each succeeding year, could no longer provide a countervailing force. Soviet Russia, her own huge internal problems shielded from the outside world, appeared in contrast as an invincible colossus. A recent parvenu among the states, believed not only by foreigners but also by her own rulers to be incapable of withstanding a war fought on her own territory, Russia was now clearly one of the two superpowers. Consequent upon this fact was the determination of Russia's leaders to enjoy all the prerogatives of that position, quite apart from any ideological considerations. This simple nationalistic credo was enunciated by Molotov in a speech of February 6, 1946, before the voters of his electoral district: "The Soviet Union achieved victory first in the West, then in the East, something of which pre-Soviet Russia had been incapable. . . . The U.S.S.R. now is one of the mightiest countries of the world. One cannot decide now any serious problems of international relations without the U.S.S.R. or without listening to the voice of our Fatherland."[38] And the faithful servant made clear whose voice in fact it was. "Comrade Stalin's participation is considered the best guarantee of the solution of the most intricate international problems."

In that address, Molotov echoed the theme of his remarks at the foreign ministers' conference in London in September 1945. That body had been charged with the preparation of peace treaties with Italy and the secondary Axis Powers. To the stupefaction of the British and American representatives, Molotov demanded that Russia be given trusteeship over the former Italian colony of Tripolitania. Though the Soviets had given notice of their ambitions in that respect before, they had not been taken seriously. Molotov was explicit: "The Soviet Union should take the place that is due it and therefore should have bases in the Mediterranean for its merchant fleet."[39] Recently the U.S.S.R. had acquired bases in Dairen and Port Arthur in the Far East; hence, said Molotov with his curious logic, it should have some in the Mediterranean. Soviet expansion in one place was given as the reason for acquiring bases and territories in another. And the "voice of our Fatherland" had to be listened to in yet another country. Molotov was insistent that Japan should not remain a preserve of the United States but that an Allied Control Council should be established there to curb the proconsular reign of General MacArthur. There

[38] V. M. Molotov, *Problems of Foreign Policy* (Moscow, 1948), p. 24.
[39] James F. Byrnes, *Speaking Frankly* (New York, 1947), p. 96.

was a crude logic to his position: the British empire had bases every-where; now that Russia was a Great Power, she wanted the same preroga-tives. And the same type of logic applied to his rejection of Secretary Byrnes' complaints about the Soviet subjugation of Rumania and Bulgaria, where anti-Communists were being eliminated from the governments and persecuted. Those countries had, in effect, been accorded to the Soviet Union in her sphere of influence. The Anglo-Americans had conceded Soviet dominance in an Allied country: Poland. Why were they now "going back" on their concession of Bulgaria and Rumania? Every pre-vious concession made by the West was tenaciously clung to and used as an argument for a new one. Stettinius had once said to Molotov that Russia was "eligible" for a trusteeship. Now the Americans were going back on their word. Secretary Byrnes' attempts to correct his predecessor's slip and to discourse on the meaning of the word "eligible" had little effect on the tenacious Soviet leader.

Molotov's final demand, which led to the conference breaking up with-out any tangible result, was that China and France be excluded from the deliberations on the treaties. Truman's attempts to appeal to Stalin on this issue proved unavailing. The conference adjourned even without the customary official communiqué.

Both in substance and procedure, this was typical of the future course of such negotiations. Apart from Molotov's irritation at France's and China's invariable support of the American position (how odd this sounds in 1968!), his final stand reflected the Soviet feeling, incomprehensible to the Americans, that international issues have to be settled by bargaining, and bargaining between the Great Powers, which in 1945 still meant the Big Three. The American position, compounded of idealism and legalism, grandiloquent in its stress on the rights of small states, simply did not fit the accepted categories of Soviet thinking on international affairs. Why did the United States insist on dragging in first France and China, then a multitude of smaller states, on something which should be the business of those states which won the war? Why should those countries which contributed so little to the defeat of the Axis be entitled to judge the Soviet Union's claims and policies? As is often the case, incomprehension led to suspicion.

The sequel to the London failure was a meeting of the foreign ministers, this time only of the Big Three, which took place in Moscow in December. Both the meeting place and the membership represented a concession to the U.S.S.R. Though in Secretary Byrnes' book, the chapter on the con-ference is entitled "Moscow Ends an Impasse," the main gains of the meeting were procedural rather than substantive. "The proposal for a peace conference rejected at London, had been accepted at Moscow, with

the participating states selected in accordance with the American list."[40]
The Russians made similar procedural concessions about Rumania and
Bulgaria, concessions which, however, were not to interfere with the
rapidity of the process with which those countries were being turned into
Soviet satellites. On the American side a similar formal concession about
constituting an Allied Control Council for Japan was not destined to
interfere seriously with General MacArthur's rule there. Likewise, on
China, where Molotov vigorously objected to American troops helping
Chiang Kai-shek, and on Iran, where in turn Byrnes and Bevin assailed
the Russians' intentions of staying beyond the agreed time limit and
sponsoring a separatist movement in Azerbaijan, no real progress was
achieved, if by progress is meant a reconciliation of the two sides' objectives rather than a soothing communiqué. There were flashes of the old,
if somewhat spurious, wartime intimacy. Stalin, who took part in the
negotiations, was as usual congenial and argumentative as against his
foreign minister's dourness and obduracy. The Russian troops, he said
with a straight face, had to stay in Persian Azerbaijan because of the
potential danger of sabotage to the Soviet oil fields in Baku. It was an
argument reminiscent of his evocation of the restraints put upon him by
the Supreme Soviet: the pitiful Iranian army might attack the U.S.S.R.
by sending saboteurs to Baku! He sternly admonished his second in command when Molotov, with his quaint humor, enquired at a dinner whether
Conant, who accompanied Byrnes (some discussion of the atomic problem
was also on the agenda), did not have an atom bomb in his pocket. There
was no reason for Molotov to joke about the achievements of American
science, Stalin said.

But such lighter touches could not conceal the reality of the two super-
powers drifting apart. A personal letter from Truman to the dictator spoke
pleadingly and pathetically about the need for the U.S. and the U.S.S.R.
to continue their collaboration: "I am convinced that the general interest
of our two countries in maintaining peace stands above any specific differences between us."[41] But Secretary Byrnes put his finger on one basic
trouble in Russo-American relations in the post-war world when, writing
in 1947, he contrasted "our desire . . . to build collective security" with
the "Soviet preference for the simpler task of dividing the world into two
spheres of influence."[42] Yet the lesson of history, and fairly recent history
as well, has always been that collective security, in the absence of an
agreement between the Great Powers, is a mirage. The American policy-

[40] *Ibid.*, p. 122.

[41] *Correspondence Between the Chairman of the Council of Ministers of the
U.S.S.R. . . . ,* II, 276.

[42] Byrnes, *op. cit.*, p. 105.

makers who in 1945 congratulated themselves on avoiding the division of the world into spheres of influence by erecting the United Nations were thus to experience a cruel disillusionment: they had at Teheran, Yalta, and Potsdam conceded the substance of the Soviet demands for a sphere of influence in return for Soviet agreement to the constitution of the United Nations, which, however, could function as an effective supranational organ *only* with Soviet concurrence. Those dearly-fought-for American schemes for voting procedures in the Security Council, for the basis of membership in the United Nations, etc., were to turn out to be of minimal importance in the disheartening atmosphere of post-war international politics. Against them, the gains the Soviets had elicited, often in return for their "concessions," were to prove concrete and durable. The passage of time was to show, to be sure, that in a deeper historical sense the diplomatic victories the Russians achieved during the last two years were somewhat illusory: national security in the nuclear age cannot be purchased by acquiring real estate. The spread of Communism to other countries was to erode its monolithic unity to the point where, even before Stalin's death, the interests of world Communism and those of the Soviet state could no longer be considered as identical. But in the immediate context of the year of victory, those considerations could hardly impress themselves on the rulers of the Soviet Union, who were to return to their traditional policy of expansion, tempered by the need for coexistence, and who in a vastly different world could still take as their device the words of the Russian statesman of the eighteenth century: "That which stops growing begins to rot."

2. *America and Russia: The Cold War*

Beginning with 1945 the United States had to become the main concern of Russian foreign policy. Prior to 1939 America's role in world affairs and American politics engaged the attention of the Russian leadership mainly insofar as the United States could stand as a counterweight to Japan in the Far East. Now America's role and potential moves in every corner of the world became of vital interest. The two main concerns of Soviet policy from 1945 on had to be the management of affairs in what has become the Communist bloc of states, and the United States.

This is vividly illustrated even in 1945 by the published correspondence between Stalin and the heads of the American and British governments. With V-E Day and then with Churchill's replacement in power by the Labour government, Stalin's correspondence with its head, Attlee, becomes increasingly slim and perfunctory. To the British Prime Minister's message announcing his assumption of power Stalin replies without a word of congratulation. On the crucial issues arising out of Japan's capitulation and occupation problems there, Stalin corresponds exclusively with President Truman, something which for all of America's predominant role in the Japanese war would hardly have been conceivable had Churchill remained in power. And for all of Bevin's volubility and dynamism, the foreign ministers' meetings now became the scene of diplomatic duels between Molotov and the American Secretary of State with the British representative playing a secondary role. The British empire, historically the protagonist of Soviet Russia, the bulwark of world order such as it existed even between the two world wars, was to play an increasingly reduced role in world affairs. Insofar as world politics is concerned, the scene was to be—throughout the remainder of Stalin's life, and even afterward, though to a diminished degree because of the rise of Communist China as an independent and major power and the increased role, if not power, of what became known as the Third World—a duel between the United States and the Soviet Union. The pretense of the continuation of the wartime alliance was to dissolve, certainly by 1947. After the announcement of the Truman Doctrine and the Marshall Plan the two super-powers settled down to what might be called competitive coexistence punctuated by sharp crises over Berlin, Korea, and other areas. Their realms of interests, hence of conflict between them, became the whole world. A peculiar irony of history decreed that the two states which before World War II had stood more or less apart from the main currents of world politics, the United States by choice, the U.S.S.R. until 1933 through the ostracism of other Great Powers, the two states that ever since the birth of the United States had had no conflicting interests and even at times (as during the American Civil War, or after the Japanese aggression in China) had been linked by sympathy if not formal alliance should now find their policies intertwined all over the globe, their viewpoints clashing on almost every international issue, whether inherited from the war or thrown up by the turbulent flow of post-war developments.

From the available Soviet sources it is difficult to deduce any guidelines on Russian policy and attitudes toward the United States. The period of late Stalinism (1945–53) is one of great paucity of documents bearing on decision-making in the U.S.S.R. We have neither materials like the Trotsky Archive, with their airing of actual views within the leadership during the early and mid-1920's, nor documents like the diplomatic exchanges between the U.S.S.R. and Nazi Germany for 1939–41, which throw at least some light on Stalin's and Molotov's activities and ways of thinking. For the period under consideration we have analyses of international relations as contained in the reports of Zhdanov and Malenkov at the foundation meeting of the Cominform, we have Stalin's analysis of the still existing "contradictions within the imperialist camp" as contained in his *Economic Problems of Socialism in the U.S.S.R.*, etc., but in the main these are designed in varying degrees for public consumption and do not entitle us to say with assurance that the same things were being said within the Politburo or in the privacy of Stalin's office. We are largely reduced to conjectures.

It is unlikely that their wartime experience with American diplomacy left the Russians with an excessive respect for it. Statements like Roosevelt's at Yalta that American troops would not be stationed in Europe beyond two years after the end of hostilities must have greatly tempted the Russians to probe American tenacity and endurance in their unprecedented engagement on the Continent. An exchange of views among Soviet economists which took place after the war concluded in an officially sponsored verdict that another depression was in the offing for the United States. This view (and an official reprimand for the dean of Soviet economists, Varga, who believed that such a depression could be postponed for a long time) was hardly surprising, since variants of similar opinions were widely held by a majority of *American* economists. And so it was easy to believe that the Americans, faced with increasing frustrations in Europe and with the inability to resolve the intractable problems of Germany and other facets of the international situation, would be drawn back into isolation. Throughout this period, including the prolonged blockade of Berlin, Soviet diplomacy often seemed to have operated on the assumption that, confronted with protracted and apparently fruitless negotiations, Americans would simply "give up" out of sheer exhaustion, out of the inability of a democratic nation to keep attention and energies focused on a subject so peripheral to the interests of a vast majority of its citizens. This, after all, has been the lesson of American involvement in Eastern Europe: by 1948, for all the previous American protests about the violations of wartime agreements, squabbles about the Allied Control Commissions, peace treaties, and the like, the American government acquiesced in virtual Soviet domination and Communist control of the whole area without so much as withholding diplomatic recognition from those countries which now could be described as satellites of the U.S.S.R. A similar calculation must have entered in the Soviet sanctioning, if not indeed ordering, of the attack by the North Koreans upon South Korea: America after all had by 1950 acquiesced in China's becoming Communist; having accepted a shift of power of such colossal historic consequences, would the Americans throw their arms and resources in opposition to a relatively insignificant territorial acquisition by the Communists?

The last example illustrates again that apart from the clash of ideologies and interests, the main difficulty with American-Soviet relations has been that for the most part the policies of the two countries moved at different levels and reflected different understandings of the realities of international life. In the same way, each country "betrayed" the other's expectations of its prospective role in international affairs. Disillusioned America did not lapse into isolationism, leaving the U.S.S.R. a free hand in those areas of the world where Russia counted on safe and profitable expansion. In turn such American statesmen as Roosevelt and Hopkins had assumed during the war that Russia's previous policies were rooted in various complexes inherited first from the period of the Civil War and intervention, second from the long era of nonrecognition or overt hostility by the Western Powers; that, once shown understanding, afforded guarantees of her security, and accorded her rightful place as a Great Power, the Soviet Union would lose those neurotic complexes and would lend her hand to the construction of a stable international order built upon the United Nations. These mutual delusions were naturally exposed in the course of the post-war years. They were then bound to give way to excessive mutual recriminations and the conviction, at least as expressed in public pronouncements on both sides, that it was the very nature of the opponent's social and political system and ideology that was the source of all the troubles in the world, rather than a clash of interests between the two states.

Though the full impact of the change becomes evident only during the period covered by the succeeding chapters, it is useful to note that already by 1945 it should have been obvious that the configurations of power and international practices which had constituted a world order before 1914 and the remnants of which had lingered until 1939 was irretrievably gone, and that unless a new order was constituted the world was going to experience an ever-deepening state of anarchy, punctuated by dangerous crises. The United Nations was conceived in a more ambitious spirit than the old League of Nations, but it should have been clear from the beginning that it had much less chance of succeeding than the old organization. The League of Nations, despite important omissions in its initial membership, consisted of states with similar political and social systems, and its dominant members, Britain and France, for all their initial disagreements on the German question, were in basic agreement on the major political and economic problems of the day, and it was only the febrile imagination of the Communists that could envisage the two super-powers of the day going to war with each other. During the first decade of the League's existence even the other two major members, Japan and Italy, were content to be status-quo powers. For all their conflicting views on Germany or Eastern Europe it would not have occurred to the French government to help the Irish Nationalists in their struggle against the British, or to Britain to sponsor the Moroccan rebels fighting the French. The only challenge to the whole system of international relations came then from the Soviet Union, then weak and undeveloped.

The United Nations, notes a Soviet author, "was founded on the basis of collaboration of states of two systems. It was destined to comprise both capitalist and socialist states."[43] To its American proponents it embodied the hope for a lasting peace. Certainly even the more cynical among them saw the U.N. as an organization of major importance, and the more optimistic as a surrogate for a world state. But to the Russians from the beginning the U.N. was at best a facade covering the domination of the world by the super-powers. Even writing in 1960, the same Soviet author feels bound to quote Stalin on the subject, for his words express in the pithiest form the Soviet concept of the international organization: "Can one trust that the role of the United Nations will be sufficiently effective? ... [It] will be effective if the Great Powers that carried on their shoulders the main burden of war against Hitlerite Germany will act afterward in a spirit of unity and collaboration. It will not be effective if this necessary condition is absent."[44] This position represented, and it still represents, the maximum extent of support the Soviet Union was willing to render to the United Nations. It meant from the beginning a cruel disillusionment for those who imagined that the United Nations could act as a supranational arbiter of peace, or even more fantastically that it could alleviate or avoid a conflict between the two super-powers.

Quite apart from the content of Soviet policy during the period under discussion, it is clear that in view of its origin and history no Soviet regime, even one most peacefully and amicably disposed toward the West, could abandon this position on the U.N. The Soviet Union was then and was going to be for a long time in a minority in both the Security Council and the General Assembly. She was not going to entrust any vital decisions affecting her to an organization where the United States and Britain could always secure a majority. The mere fact that a large part of public opinion, if not most statesmen, in the West could not understand this simple fact of international relations was in turn bound to deepen Soviet suspicions and increase their resentment. Thus it is paradoxical but true to say that the existence of the U.N. and the unrealistic hopes placed in it by the United States during the initial period of postwar coexistence with the U.S.S.R. increased the tension and reduced the possibilities for a meaningful dialogue between the two super-powers. This, one must hasten to add, was bound to change once the United Nations came to include a multitude of new African and Asian states and the Soviet side was no longer condemned to be in a minority on most issues. Also, the U.N. became a useful instrument in muffling some minor disputes between the two super-powers, enabling them to disengage

[43] S. B. Krylov, *The History of the Founding of the United Nations* (Moscow, 1960), p. 7.

[44] *Ibid.*, p. 7.

from a direct confrontation on issues that were not absolutely vital to either. But on the major issues of international politics, on questions of war and peace, the agreement of the two super-powers—and this is as true in 1968 as it was in 1945—remains both indispensable and decisive. Nothing, not even the most elaborate and perfectly constructed international organization, even in a world in which most of the present unhappy conflicts have been eliminated, can take its place.

The other side of the coin—the Russians' increasingly skillful use of the United Nations first as a tribune for propaganda, then, with the rise of the Third World, as an arena for exploiting the underdeveloped nations' grievances against the United States and her allies—belongs to a further period. But on this count also the expectations and hopes of many in the West have been betrayed. Realism in politics may not always be the highest value. In their own way, the Soviets had been guilty of pursuing a chimerical goal (something which Yugoslavia and especially Communist China later amply demonstrated) when they searched for security and expanded power by promoting Communist regimes in other countries. But their initial appraisal of the U.N. contained elements of realism, while in the West, the vision of a world organization resolving major problems of world politics and allowing its individual members to turn their attention to crucial domestic issues provided a distraction from the unpalatable facts of the post-1945 world.

The Soviet position on the United Nations soon became entangled with an issue of supreme importance in the immediate post-war world, that of international control of atomic energy. No subject lends itself to so much speculation or is capable of evoking so much moral, strategic, and historical argument as that of the opportunities and motivations of American foreign policy during the brief period of American monopoly of the atom bomb, 1945–49. A future historian may well conclude that this monopoly of the weapon created a mentality akin to that engendered in the French by the Maginot Line before 1939: it encouraged a false sense of security, distracted attention from the urgency of solving certain basic political and social problems. Had the French been without this wretched line of fortifications in 1936, they might have felt the necessity of making Hitler pull back his troops from the Rhineland. Had the mirage of a long monopoly on atomic weapons not exercised its baleful fascination over the minds of American policy-makers, it is possible they would have tackled in a more urgent spirit the need to set up that balance of power without which in this sinful world of ours any world order is but a snare and delusion. As it was, the North Atlantic Treaty Organization was set up when the American monopoly was a thing of the past. The two years that intervened between the end of the war and the announcement of the Marshall Plan also left their fateful imprint on the world. It is largely because of that delay that Britain entered upon the process of liquidation of her imperial obligations in a manner and at a pace which was to lead within fifteen years to the complete collapse of the European empires, leaving in their wake countless areas of instability and danger to world peace.

As noted before, America's possession of nuclear weapons, insofar as we can judge from any evidence in hand, did not produce among the Soviet leadership either panic or undue apprehension that American policy-makers would employ it in the furtherance of their political aims. Stalin's comment at Potsdam, that he was glad that the Americans had the frightful weapon and hoped they would use it, represented a matter-of-fact acknowledgment of the new weapon's existence. Only much later on did Soviet politicians or publicists attribute the Americans' use of the bomb on Hiroshima and Nagasaki to a sinister attempt to blackmail the U.S.S.R. and rob her of her fruits of victory. The period of American monopoly of the bomb was the period of the greatest Soviet pushfulness in foreign policy, of the rapid satellization of Eastern Europe, and of the Communist conquest of China. It was also the period of an extensive demobilization of the Soviet armed forces. None of those factors, it is necessary to repeat, suggests apprehension of an imminent war or the readiness of the Soviet army to sweep over Europe to the English Channel in answer to an atomic attack. American policy-makers, who in the anxious days of the Berlin blockade were to ponder seriously such a possibility, ignored the enormous industrial power of their own country as evidenced during World War II and as contrasted with the still unreconstructed state of the Russian economy; Russia's formidable task of policing her satellites where, with the possible exception of Czechoslovakia, the Communist regimes depended in the last recourse upon Soviet bayonets; and many factors of a similar nature which, quite apart from the atom bomb, made any military clash with the United States simply inconceivable to a man as realistic and cautious as Stalin. The Soviet ability to conjure up millions of troops for an *offensive* war beguiled Western statesmen, yet the fact is that at the end of World War II the total number of men under arms in the U.S. forces surpassed that of the Soviet Union.[45]

In fact the ominous apprehensions aroused in the West by Stalin's policy of isolation and expansion between 1945 and 1950 underlines, granted the premises of the totalitarian regime, the psychological insight contained in that policy. A Russia adhering to the Marshall Plan, "behaving" in the United Nations, pursuing a more liberal policy in her East European sphere of influence, would have been much less an object of fear, much

[45] The Russian figure as given by Khrushchev was 11,360,000; for the United States the figure was 12,300,000 as quoted in the U.S. Department of State's *Documents on Disarmament: 1945–1959,* I (Washington, 1960), 682.

more susceptible to pressure and outright challenges than the mysterious and threatening colossus seemingly ready to unleash countless hordes upon a defenseless Europe. In his first audience with Stalin in April 1946, Ambassador Walter Bedell Smith asked as his first question: "What does the Soviet Union want and how far is Russia going to go?" This question, from the ambassador of the then incomparably greatest power in the world, addressed to a dictator engrossed in rebuilding the shattered economy of his country and in reimposing full totalitarian rigor upon it, has an eloquence of its own.[46] So does Stalin's answer: "We are not going much further."

This background makes it understandable why American efforts to bridge the widening gulf between the two countries through the agency of the United Nations were bound to be fruitless. The cornerstone of the American policy to expand the functions and importance of that body was to entrust it with far-reaching functions concerning the problem of disarmament. But here again the American monopoly of the atomic bomb played a perversely ironic role, frustrating American intentions and undercutting the United Nations' potential role on the disarmament question. Had the dread weapon not existed, it is possible that America's demobilization in the wake of the war would not have been so rapid or so thorough. Her retention of a large standing army and a stress on production of conventional weapons would in turn have put pressure on the Soviet Union to increase her military effectiveness and arms production proportionately (notwithstanding her confidence that war was not imminent). And at the time the Soviet Union was desperately anxious to devote as much manpower and resources as possible to rebuilding and expanding her heavy industry. There would have been, then, a considerable incentive for the Russians to engage in serious negotiations about disarmament.[47] Here again—and perhaps unavoidably, in view of the nature of democratic regimes—a military advantage could not be translated into a political one, and the existence of the international organization proved to be a barrier to that type of realistic bargaining which could have changed the course of Soviet foreign policy.

The American proposals for international control of atomic energy were embodied in the Baruch Plan, envisaging the establishment of an International Atomic Development Authority "to which should be entrusted all phases of the development and use of atomic energy, starting

---

[46] Walter Bedell Smith, *My Three Years in Moscow* (New York, 1950), p. 50.

[47] It could be argued that the original construction of atomic facilities and the bomb must have absorbed considerable resources between 1945 and 1949. But under the existing conditions of the Russian economy, the cost was probably but a fraction of what would have been required to maintain, say, an additional million men under arms.

with the raw material and including . . . ownership of all atomic energy activities . . . power to control, inspect and license all other atomic activities . . . research and development responsibilities. . . ."[48] The International Authority would thus acquire a virtual monopoly on all forms of production of atomic energy. It would be endowed with the power to impose sanctions on any state violating the agreement: "The matter of punishment lies at the very heart of our present security problem." Sanctions on a violator of the agreement or of the Authority's rules would be imposed by a majority vote, and thus the right of veto reserved to each of the five Great Powers (permanent members of the Security Council) on other types of violations of international agreements would be removed on this crucial issue. Once the Authority were established and effectively functioning, the United States would be willing to dispose of her stock of bombs and to cease manufacturing them.

To this proposal Gromyko, the Soviet delegate to the U.N. Atomic Energy Commission, offered a counterplan envisaging an international convention that simply prohibited the production or use of atomic weapons and required the destruction of existing ones. As to inspection, penalties, and the abolition of the veto, he stated forthrightly: "Attempts to undermine the principles, as established by the Charter, of the activity of the Security Council, including unanimity of the [permanent] members of the Security Council in deciding questions of substance, are incompatible with the interests of the United Nations. . . . Such attempts must be rejected."[49]

Such was the Soviet position at the first meeting of the U.N. Atomic Energy Commission in June 1946. There would be little point in following the tortuous course of the disarmament negotiations—the variants of the original proposals, the discussions before the Assembly, Commission, Security Council, and the like. From the beginning it should have been clear that several aspects of the American position ran counter to the most strongly held convictions of the Soviet rulers. Even if atomic energy had been entirely devoid of military significance, it still would have been impossible for the Soviets to agree to an international agency prying and probing into their economy, maintaining or sending inspectors into the U.S.S.R., etc. Again, the abolition of the veto on *any* issue deemed vital to the Soviet Union would, in their view, put their country at the mercy of an agency in which she was bound to be in a minority. To give the Soviets their due, one may note that in 1946, three years before the first Russian atomic tests, it would have been in their interests to temporize, to feign agreement on the principle of atomic disarmament, and to delay

[48] *Documents on Disarmament: 1945–1959*, I, 10–11.
[49] *Ibid.*, p. 24.

the final convention in the usual diplomatic way for as long as possible. But though there are traces of such a technique being used in subsequent proposals, the Soviets refused to budge on the principal issue, that of abandoning the veto on punitive decisions by the International Authority.

Knowing the nature of the Soviet regime and its view of the outside world, it should have been equally clear that Russia would devote all her efforts to the acquisition of the atomic bomb and the means of delivery. The American monopoly of the weapon was to endure not for decades, as some American statesmen and scientists fondly imagined, but for about four years. It is hard to say how much Soviet espionage and the help rendered to Soviet nuclear research by foreign scientists sympathetic to Communism contributed to shortening the interval. But as long as the American monopoly endured, the Soviets pursued the psychologically sound propaganda line of minimizing the importance of the new weapon. Certainly their behavior up to 1949 shows, on the surface, but little apprehension that the United States, challenged and thwarted on a number of issues, might resolve to employ the new weapon or at least threaten to do so. Whether this confidence was based on a general appraisal of American foreign policy or on special information derived through espionage, and whether some more nervous persons in the Kremlin advocated a more accommodating policy—these are questions that given our present state of knowledge are unanswerable. Clearly by 1949 there was a perceptible change in Soviet foreign policy. For the period under discussion, however, if the Soviet leaders had any fears they did a masterful job of concealing them. While more and more often attributing hostile intentions to "certain circles" in the West, exploiting such obvious openings as Churchill's "Iron Curtain" speech, they publicly exuded cool confidence that the Soviet Union could take care of herself. To be sure, public display of confidence in the face of real danger had been a long-standing tradition: in the mid-1930's, confronted with danger from both Hitler and Japan, Molotov invited anybody who doubted the Red Army's might to try invading Russia. But then Soviet policy was very much on the defensive, while between 1946 and 1949 it cannot be described as other than expansionist. The task of Soviet foreign policy in the 1930's had been to discourage attack upon the country through a mixture of sheer bravado and diplomatic maneuverings. In 1946 the task was to expand Soviet power and influence without setting in motion a sequence of events that would lead to a confrontation with the greatest power in the world.

In the diplomatic duel with the United States, the Soviet Union had the great advantage that America's rise to world power was recent, and the State Department's scope of attention, not to mention the American electorate's, still limited. To a society that had only a few years before abandoned a very conscious isolationist attitude, that still tended to regard

World War II as an interruption of "normalcy" rather than the beginning of a new era conferring enormous powers and terrifying responsibilities upon the United States, it appeared hardly credible that America's influence had to be thrown into the balance to save a small Balkan country from Communist takeover, that the State Department should haggle over the composition of the government in Bucharest or Warsaw, that the activities of Kurdish tribesmen in Iran should be a matter of concern and watchfulness to American policy-makers (and, hence, to American citizens), or that a just retribution for Germany's and Japan's crimes and follies must be tempered by the realities of world politics and Soviet Russia's aims. Such universal awareness of the shifting factors of world politics had been characteristic of the Old World empires, but they were now in retreat. From its very earliest days the Soviet regime had been conditioned to attention and activity on a world scale, and now after the war it was finally in a position to put its thirty years' training to concrete and often profitable use. It had lived and thrived in an atmosphere of world crisis— much as the greatest of them, in 1939–42, almost brought it to an end. During the first fifteen years of the Soviet state, the very terms "international stability" and "reconciliation of international contradictions" had aroused in Soviet publicists the same alarm and disappointment that "world depression" or "threat of war" now created among statesmen in the West.

Thus it was to take both the government and the people of the United States several years to absorb the fact that international crisis was a normal and constant condition, that as such it could not be conjured away by the United Nations but had to be faced in its multifarious aspects. It was perhaps unavoidable that this education in the facts of international life, and the sense of mounting frustration at the inability to resolve international problems through any means familiar within the American historical experience, was to lead to internal strains and stresses. These in turn were in due time to change dramatically the Americans' stereotyped image of the Soviet Union and Communism, the new one being quite the opposite of the one that had emerged in the wartime collaboration but equally oversimplified, both in its nature and in its practical applications.

The formula "friends in peace, enemies in war," which served the Republic since its foundation as the guideline in foreign affairs, could no longer contain the phenomenon of a recent ally and partner in the United (it already sounded ironic) Nations clashing with the United States on practically every major issue and exuding general and public hostility and suspicion. To fit this new and, to the Americans, unprecedented situation, new terms and concepts were devised. Such was the "cold war," coined by Walter Lippmann. The search for an over-all explanation of Soviet behavior led a distinguished diplomat and student of Soviet affairs to postulate an essentially ideological explanation of Soviet expansionism and to see a ray of hope in the eventual attrition of that ideology: "The palsied decrepitude of the capitalist world is the keystone of Communist philosophy. Even the failure of the United States to experience the early economic depression which the ravens of Red Square have been predicting with such complacent confidence since hostilities ceased would have deep and important repercussions throughout the Communist world." And Mr. Kennan continued in his article (which was to make another new term, "containment," a household word): "For no mystical Messianic movement —and particularly not that of the Kremlin—can face frustration indefinitely without eventually adjusting itself in one way or another to the logic of that state of affairs."[50]

But when this subtle and sophisticated view was expressed in 1947 it was still far from being a firmly held judgment of the American public. In their own search for the sources of *American* conduct, the Soviets could well be encouraged by some developments in American politics to believe that the patience and endurance of a democracy would be strained beyond the tolerance point first by the burden of watchfulness over developments all over the world and then by the financial burden of bolstering up Europe's economy. And indeed if by 1949 the Soviets had to conclude that American isolationism was a thing of the past, in view of developments both in Europe and in internal American politics, it could also be seen by then that the policy of containment could not fulfill the original hopes placed in it by the American policy-makers. Soviet rule became entrenched in Eastern Europe. Between 1947 and 1949 China came under the power of Communists. It is equally true that these developments cannot, as of today, be presented simply as failures of American policy or as Soviet successes.

The prosaic fact must remain that neither the "mystical Messianism" of Soviet goals nor the counterthrust of American "containment" can explain in full any major points of agreement or disagreement between the two Great Powers. Before 1946 the Soviet Union had had two periods of close collaboration with other major powers: during the Soviet-Nazi alliance in 1939–41, and during the wartime alliance with Britain and the United States.[51] The reasons for the latter were obvious. As for the former, it was based on an agreement for respective spheres of influence of the two partners. The idea of spheres of influence would have been repugnant to American policy-makers after 1946, and whether it would

[50] George F. Kennan, "The Sources of Soviet Conduct," *Foreign Affairs,* July 1947; reprinted in *American Diplomacy 1900–1950* (Chicago, 1951), p. 123.

[51] The Rapallo period of collaboration with Germany cannot be put in the same class.

have been accepted or adhered to by the Soviet leaders is something we don't know. It is clear, however, that the absence of such an arrangement deprived both the West and the U.S.S.R. of any conceivable "handle" in settling the many political and territorial issues left in the wake of the war.

In fact, Soviet armies and diplomacy had hammered out such a sphere in eastern and central Europe before the end of the war. But even in the face of this indisputable fact, which no realist could hope to reverse short of a most drastic challenge to the Soviet Union, the character and the means of Soviet control in that area could still remain a matter of debate and bargaining. Soviet influence varied from country to country. Finland, which might have been the one country to fare worst and to be absorbed most directly into her vast neighbor, was allowed complete control over her internal politics, and for all the subsequent moments of stress and danger, she remained within the Soviet sphere of influence in the classical nineteenth-century way. While her freedom in foreign and defense matters was severely circumscribed, no determined attempt was made to impose a Communist regime, and even a subsequent ejection of the Communists from a coalition government failed to bring a Soviet reaction. What lay behind this relative leniency toward the country that had most directly opposed Soviet aims? One must see in it a mixture of conscious policy and, from the Finnish point of view, sheer luck. Also, the Soviet leaders no doubt remembered the emotional reaction in the United States to the Soviet attack on Finland in 1939 and thought it prudent not to excite the unpredictable American public too much. Compared with the importance of firmly securing Poland or Rumania, Finland must have appeared to them, as Molotov put it crudely to a Yugoslav visitor, a "peanut."[52] Later, after 1948, the troubles within the Communist bloc and the increasing strains of the general world situation again made a diversion against Finland too risky in proportion to the possible gains.

In Poland, Hungary, Rumania, and Bulgaria the process of satellization was virtually completed by the end of 1947, in the sense that by then the local Communists with the help of some Russian supervisors were firmly in control of the governmental machinery. That the Finnish pattern was not followed in those countries may be traced to a variety of reasons. One was, paradoxically, the weakness of the native Communists. Unless they were speedily hoisted into power and established as the wave of the future, the danger always existed that the numbing effects of the war and the Russian occupation might wear off and a firm anti-Communist constellation might arise which, once in control, would require direct Soviet military action. What would have been the effect of a Hungarian situation of 1956 occurring in 1947 or 1948? The other reason lay, alas, in the nature of

[52] Milovan Djilas, *Conversations with Stalin* (New York, 1962), p. 155.

the Western reactions to the Communist takeovers. They were not strong or determined enough to secure a Finnish solution, but to the Russians they were irritating enough to increase their suspicions of the non-Communist politicians on whose behalf the West intervened. This, then, was the tragic predicament in which politicians like Petkov in Bulgaria or Mikolajczyk in Poland found themselves and which was to lead them to death or exile. The coalition governments that included some Communists gave way either to outright Communist rule or to coalitions which were so only in name, the effective levers of power being exercised by faithful followers of Russia and Communism.

Of the countries of Eastern Europe, one that for some time appeared likely to enjoy a modicum of autonomy and political freedom was Czechoslovakia, one reason being its relatively advanced state of economic development and another being the considerable popular following enjoyed by the Czechoslovak Communist Party, which in the May 1946 elections (which were genuine ones) obtained close to 40 per cent of the vote. Russia, despite the depradations of the Red Army and the separation of the Carpatho-Ukraine, was still to many Czechs (if fewer Slovaks) the country that had stood loyally by her ally while the Western Powers abandoned Czechoslovakia at Munich. In view of the strength of the Communist Party and its leading role in the government, there was therefore less incentive to secure power by strong-arm means or to abrogate civil liberties. The reality of Czechoslovakia's being within the Soviet sphere of influence even if still a functioning democracy was brought home to the Czechoslovak government in 1947 when the Soviets made it abandon its previously stated intention of participating in the Marshall Plan. But it is most likely that any post-war Czech government, even one with no Communist members, would have followed a policy of deference to the U.S.S.R. in foreign affairs. Had the Communist-led but not-quite-satellite regime managed to survive for a few months, it is possible that Czechoslovakia might have followed the Finnish rather than the Bulgarian pattern. For with the eruption of the Soviet-Yugoslav dispute in the summer of 1948, Soviet suspicions turned against their own Communist followers in Eastern Europe, and a docile part-Communist regime might well have been safer than a Communist one infected with Titoism. But a strange fatality ordered that a showdown between the Communist and non-Communist elements in the Czech government come in February 1948, when Soviet designs against Tito were a secret known by but a few, and when nobody could be sure that the Russians would not resort to armed intervention when challenged by a satellite.

In the beginning of 1948 the Communist Minister of the Interior intensified his policy of staffing the Czechoslovak police forces with Communist henchmen. In a challenge to this policy twelve non-Communist ministers resigned from the cabinet on February 20. President Benes had the option to dissolve the government and order new elections, while neutralizing through the army the activity of Communist action committees and armed workers' militia. But in addition to the threat of civil war, Soviet pressure was applied through the mission of the Deputy Minister of Foreign Affairs, Valerian Zorin, the same diplomat who fifteen years later was to represent Russia in the United Nations at the time of the Cuban missile crisis. For a second time Benes had to bow to foreign pressure and sign away his country's independence. On February 25 he accepted a Communist-designed government, and a few months later the Communist premier, Klement Gottwald, succeeded to the presidency of the republic. Thus the Communist takeover of Czechoslovakia was consummated. There were the usual obituaries of the Czech democracy in the Western press but little recognition of the fact of how much the death had been preordained by Western policies since Teheran.

In the catalogue of the Soviet satellites, the position of Yugoslavia was again of a special nature.[53] Here the strength rather than the weakness of the local Communist movement was to confront the Soviet leaders with an excruciating dilemma. It has already been recorded how the intransigence of the Yugoslav Communists over Trieste, their tendency to provoke a premature conflict with the West through excessive Communist zeal, was a source of displeasure to Moscow. The incompleteness of Soviet control of Yugoslavia was thus based on the very thoroughness of the local Communists' takeover and their confidence that they could retain power without the actual or threatened presence of the Soviet army. This confidence—and Tito's belief that unlike Communists in other countries he had won power largely through his own resources—at first did not clash with loyalty to the Soviet Union. But pride in their own achievement was to endow the Yugoslavs with considerable expansionist ambitions. Little Albania was between 1945 and 1948 their virtual subsatellite, a pro-Yugoslav faction occupying the most strategic positions of power and Yugoslavia's total absorption of the country awaiting only the final Soviet approval. But even wider vistas—of primacy in the Balkans as a whole—dazzled the rulers of Yugoslavia. The Yugoslav Communists' state of mind between 1945 and 1948 was in many ways not unlike the Chinese Communists' in the 1950's and 1960's: Communism was believed to be the wave of the future; Russian hesitation and caution about provoking the West were not understood and were resented. In 1946 the Yugoslavs shot down two American planes that wandered near or over Yugoslav territory, and it required a strong American protest and evident Russian

[53] A more detailed treatment of the Yugoslav case is reserved for the next section. See below, pp. 461–66.

pressure before Belgrade's government provided compensation and de-
sisted from its defiant behavior.

In all these developments in Eastern Europe, the United States could
play no significant role. The resources of the West were exhausted in
diplomatic protests and in stretching out the negotiations for peace treaties
for those states in the area that had been in the enemy camp. In 1947,
with the signing of peace treaties with Finland, Bulgaria, Rumania, and
Hungary (as well as with Italy), the United States (together with France
and Britain) conceded the *fait accompli* of Soviet domination. World
War II had begun as an attempt by the West to prevent Germany's goals
of domination of eastern Europe and consequent destruction of the
European balance of power. Within two years of the war's end, those aims
had been achieved by the U.S.S.R.

The price Russia paid for this achievement was a hardening of public
opinion in the West against her and the beginning of those elaborate
measures which were to find their fruition in the Marshall Plan and the
NATO Alliance. But the latter was essentially a *belated* defensive arrangement designed to prevent further expansion by the U.S.S.R. rather than
to reverse or modify its character in eastern and central Europe. Even
the Marshall Plan, so vast, original, and beneficial in its scope, was also
belated insofar as its political effects were concerned. The two years that
passed between the end of the war and the announcement of the Marshall
Plan in June 1947 allowed for a serious deterioration of the British
economy, and this in turn undermined Britain's world-wide position and
opened gaps in the Western security system that could not be filled even
when Britain's economic situation improved. In the rest of western
Europe, the Plan, through restoring the economy, was to make its countries
less susceptible to the virus of Communism. While the eventual success
of the Plan surpassed the wildest expectations of its authors, it is not un-
gracious to say that in essence it was a long-run remedy for a situation
that also called for immediate political steps.

The rhythm of international politics between 1945 and 1950 was feverish, beset with vast opportunities but also with great dangers for both
sides. That timing was of supreme importance was obviously realized
by the Soviet leadership. A pushful policy in eastern Europe carried
risks, but Soviet gains had to be foreclosed before Western policy became
more determined and anti-Soviet. The Berlin blockade was imposed when
it still seemed opportune to render a shattering blow to the Western prestige in Germany, before a viable West Germany (presumably with its own
armed forces) could be created.

The same sense of urgency could not be duplicated among the democracies. The doctrine of "containment," which crystallized the sophisticated
American philosophy of opposition to Soviet expansionism was, after all,

a doctrine of historical patience: in the long run, Russia's attitudes will change, once she is denied *further* acquisitions and the capitalist world demonstrates its political and economic viability. But in the short run? The only significant voice in the West that felt the task of "containment" to be urgent and not to be delegated to the slowly working forces of history was Churchill's. On March 5, 1946, in a speech at Fulton, Missouri, before an audience including President Truman, he sought to shock the Western public into this sense of urgency about Soviet expansion. His speech counselled strength and watchfulness in the face of the threat. Stalin professed to hear a voice calling for armed intervention against the U.S.S.R. and chose to remind his erstwhile partner in arms how a previous intervention, warmly endorsed by Churchill, had fared against Russia, then incomparably weaker. But, as we have seen, it was a different idea that had agitated Churchill since the last months of the war. Peace in the real sense of the word and not mere coexistence could still be established if the West would make a fundamental stand against Soviet expansion. Impressed by this show of strength, the U.S.S.R. would behave as an *old-style* imperial power demanding security and domination within her agreed sphere of influence, but not always pushing and trying to expand it whenever or wherever a tempting opportunity or political vacuum occurred. Churchill was gripped by fearful anxiety: time was being lost. Britain's imperial commitments would have to be largely dismantled and the resulting vacuum would offer new opportunities and temptations to the Russians. And they, said the old warrior to Secretary Forrestal, will "try every door in the house, enter all the rooms which are not locked, and when they come to one that is barred, if they are unsuccessful in breaking through it, they will withdraw and invite you to dine genially that same evening."[54]

Churchill's drastic view of the situation was still far from widely shared in the West. The reaction in the United States to his Fulton speech was reserved: voices complained about British imperialism and insisted that Britain and the United States should not "gang up" on Russia. In Britain *The Times*, rising to its best tradition of the Munich era, gently reproved the wartime leader: instead of talking about things that divided the West and Communism, one should seek common ground; they had much to learn from each other. And so they did, but perhaps not on the matters *The Times* wanted them to—"Communism in the working of political institutions and in the establishment of individual rights, Western democracy in the development of economic and social planning."[55] Once a faithful sounding board of Mr. Chamberlain, *The Times*' editorials now

[54] Walter Millis, ed., *The Forrestal Diaries* (New York, 1951), p. 145.

[55] *The Times* (London), March 6, 1946.

expressed faithfully the still prevailing view of the majority of the Labour government, for whom, despite Bevin's increasing disenchantment and irritation, the Soviets were fellow, if somewhat aberrant, socialists.

The Western reaction to Churchill's speech, especially in view of his recent electoral discomfiture, was thus not of the kind to alarm Moscow. But the speech must have sounded a warning to the Russians that unabated pressure on their part carried with it the danger of stirring up the United States to the point where the views expressed in it would gain wider acceptance. Between 1946 and 1953, the problem before the Soviet policymakers was to balance expansion with those gestures of accommodation and moderation which would prevent the international atmosphere from overheating. It is thus no accident that after the Fulton speech the Soviets chose to retreat on an issue which, though presumably more remote from the American public mind than Eastern Europe, was agitating the State Department: Soviet expansion in Iran.

The reasons for the United States' concern about the territorial integrity of Iran might have appeared puzzling at this juncture in view of her acquiescence, say, in Soviet domination of *all* of Poland, the country which, apart from any legal and moral obligations incurred on its behalf by the United States, had special ties with millions of American citizens. But Poland was an "old" issue of which both the United States government and American public opinion had grown weary. Iran was a "new" one on which Truman's administration felt that its hands had not been tied by previous deals and negotiations under Roosevelt. There were two other elements in the Iranian situation as it shaped up in the spring of 1946 that engaged attention: the American legalistic mentality was roused by the Soviets' obvious violation of the Three Power agreement to withdraw troops by a scheduled date; and in Iran as a whole there was a government that called for foreign intercession against the Soviet usurpation. Such a legalistic approach was undoubtedly a revelation to the Soviet policymakers: Iran had appeared as a safe area for expansion; there had been ample historical precedent for a Russian sphere of interest there, going back to Tsarist times. The United States' economic stake in Iran, unlike that of Britain, was as yet negligible. And there were hardly very many voters of Iranian origin in the United States! But Iran, just as in a much more serious way Korea some years later, was to illustrate the incalculable ways of the United States in foreign affairs.

The agreement signed at Teheran during the first Big Three conference had pledged the signatories to observe the independence of their host country and withdraw their troops from Iran following a suitable interval after the end of the war. But already during the war's last stages Soviet activity indicated that the Russians had long-run plans for expanding their influence there after the end of hostilities. The Tudeh Party, virtually

Communist in leadership, was created under the sponsorship of Soviet occupation authorities. Most of all, the Russians gave added impetus to separatist movements in Azerbaijan, where, many years before, after World War I, a Communist-sponsored republic had briefly existed. And to be sure, December 1945 saw the establishment under the benevolent gaze of the Soviet military authorities of the Autonomous Republic of Azerbaijan, headed by Jaafar Pishevari, who had played a leading role in the earlier Communist experiment in the province. In the same month, in the Kurdish part of the province, the Kurdish People's Republic was set up, similarly oriented and inspired. Attempts of the Teheran government to reassert its authority in the north were stopped by Russian troops.

We have already seen how at the Moscow foreign ministers' conference the issue of Iran was raised by Bevin and Byrnes, and how Stalin in one of his least satisfactory diplomatic performances tried to impress Byrnes with the danger the Baku oil fields were exposed to and how consequently the Soviets to their regret might have to keep troops in Iran longer than they had agreed. But the American reaction was hardly a strong protest, and in the absence of such a response Bevin proposed a time-consuming and in the past ineffective device of a three-power commission to "investigate" the conditions in Iran.[56] The United States withdrew her remaining troops on January 1, 1946, Britain was pledged to do so on the scheduled deadline, March 2. But the Russians did not give the slightest indication of following suit. The stakes appeared to be greater than just Azerbaijan. Britain, an age-long antagonist of Russia in Iran, was now withdrawing from the contest. (One cannot imagine Churchill withdrawing British troops before the Russians did theirs.) In January the Iranian government became headed by a man reputed to be friendly to the Russians. He began to purge his administration of officials with pro-British sympathies. The new premier, Quavam, then left for Moscow where, during his stay of nearly a month, he listened to Soviet intimations as to how the crisis might be solved. The Soviets insisted on an "autonomous" status for Aberbaijan but offered the generous concession that "its [Azerbaijan's] correspondence with the central government would be in Persian" rather than in Azerbaijani (a version of Turkish)! They no longer wanted an oil concession in northern Iran but would be satisfied with a "joint company" of the type being now installed in their European satellites, 51 per cent of the shares being owned by the U.S.S.R. and 49 by Iran.[57] The Premier temporized and negotiated with proverbial oriental finesse, but on their part the Soviets would not evacuate their troops until he accepted their

[56] George Lenczowski, *Russia and the West in Iran* (New York, 1949), p. 294.
[57] *Ibid.*, p. 296.

demands, which would constitute the first step in transforming at least northern Iran into a Soviet dependency.

The March crisis thrust the Iranian issue into a glaring light. From the Soviet point of view the trouble with the situation was that the outburst of Western interest and indignation was occurring not over a *fait accompli*, as was to be the case in February 1948 in Czechoslovakia, but over a situation that was still fluid and unresolved. British and American protests over the Soviet retention of troops were delivered on March 4 and 8 respectively. On March 5 came Churchill's Fulton speech. Iran presented her complaint to the Security Council. Secretary Byrnes headed the American delegation to that body and supported the Iranian cause, despite the usual Soviet procedural complaints and counterarguments about the West's misdeeds elsewhere. It was a classical case of what the language of diplomacy calls "complications" arising out of what had promised to be a simple exercise of Great Power politics. The American involvement might prove to have ominous consequences extending far beyond the Middle East. One day after the convening of the Security Council, on March 26, Gromyko pledged the evacuation of Soviet troops within six weeks. The Council, on Byrnes's request, prudently decided to defer proceedings on the issue until the scheduled date of evacuation.

On April 4 an agreement between Iran and the U.S.S.R. repeated the Soviet pledge to withdraw troops. An Iranian-Soviet oil company was to be formed, the proposal for it to be ratified by Iran's parliament. The Soviets professed to see Azerbaijan as an internal Iranian matter. This agreement represented a partial Soviet victory, but within a few months it became clear that events were to frustrate Soviet hopes. In December, after a tangled series of political developments, the government decided to liquidate the two separatist regimes in the north, which were put down by the Iranian army and their leaders put to death. Members of the Tudeh Party were ejected from the cabinet, the party for the time being was suppressed. Later on, as a Soviet author indignantly records: "Under the pressure of the imperialist forces of the U.S.A., the external policy of Iran took on an anti-Soviet character. . . . To please the American and English 'protectors,' parliament on October 22, 1947, refused to ratify the agreement about the Soviet-Iranian Company for exploitation of oil in northern Iran."[58] The same author notes melancholically the diminution or rather virtual disappearance of commercial intercourse between Iran and the Soviet Union: from constituting 24 per cent of total Iranian foreign trade in 1945–46, trade with Russia fell in 1947–48 to less than 1 per cent.

[58] A. G. Mileykovsky, ed., *International Relations After the Second World War, I* (Moscow, 1962), 259.

Such is the history of the setback in Soviet policy suffered in an area where both the proximity of the Soviet Union and her historic involvement in the society's social and economic weakness (it could, with much greater truth than in most other areas so designated by Soviet propaganda, be described as monarcho-feudal) seemed to favor Russian expansion. The circumstances attending that setback were instructive. The main factor was undoubtedly the involvement of the American government to the point where, while no drastic confrontation between the United States and Russia threatened, the Soviets became convinced that their interests in more important areas would be challenged if they remained obdurate about Iran. America's involvement was in turn facilitated by the fact that Britain's influence in that country, while definitely on the wane, was still quite considerable.[59] When it appeared that Quavam's vacillating government was swinging over to the Soviet side, the British were able to pressure it through their friends and clients in southern Iran, for long their traditional sphere of influence.

The case of Iran, while it demonstrated the meaning of containment before the doctrine was actually enunciated, also demonstrated that doctrine's pitfalls. The United States' task in Iran was facilitated by the fact that another power was still involved in the area and brought its resources and experience in on the side of the United States to counter the Soviet thrust. Within a few years the complete collapse of British and French imperial positions was to leave to the United States the invidious task of rushing into the breach alone. This task in turn would be complicated by the discovery that the "Soviet threat" consisted not so much in direct or indirect Soviet pressure on this or that country as in (1) the absence of an agreement between the Great Powers and (2) the political and economic fragility of many former colonial and semicolonial societies, which freed from the tutelage of the imperial powers would become, alas, not virtuous democracies striving for economic improvement, but areas of perturbation and competition between the two super-powers. At the end of 1947 the State Department could not confine Iran to a file marked "Saved from the Soviet Union," much as this would have been the popular understanding of America's diplomatic exertions and help extended to that country. Within three years another political and economic crisis was to threaten Iran's vulnerable links with what in the official American phraseology had become known as the "free world."

The full implications of the demise of the imperial powers were to become clear during the next few years, and we are still living with them. But for the Soviet leaders even before 1950 the picture must have looked

[59] It was virtually to disappear with the events that occurred between the removal of the British military presence in India in 1947 and the nationalization of the Anglo-Iranian Oil Company in 1951.

somewhat familiar. In the 1920's the infant Soviet state carried on a vigorous anti-Western campaign from China to Turkey, using the resources of diplomacy, of nascent indigenous Communist movements, and of local nationalism. At that time, the power of the Soviet state had proved ludicrously inadequate, the position of the established imperial systems still strong enough to meet the challenge. Now, in the late 1940's, Russia was in a position to retrace her steps, but this time from a position of strength and prestige acquired in World War II and against Western Powers that no longer had the resources and even less the will to defend their imperial spheres of influence.

To the Western world this Soviet dynamism smacked of monstrous aggressiveness. Soviet motivations appeared incomprehensible. "There are no experts on the Soviet Union. There are only varying degrees of ignorance," quoted Ambassador Smith lamely.[60] Was the Soviet Union after world domination? Was her drive a symptom of "insecurity"? It is useful to consider how various aspects of Soviet expansion in those years must have appeared to the Kremlin.

None of Russia's post-war moves can in all fairness be described as bolts from the blue. In most cases they had ample precedent in age-long aspirations of Russian foreign policy. And in many cases Stalin and his associates must have felt that they had stated their post-war ambitions and aims to their Western associates during the course of the war and that their allies' reaction had then been, whether at the governmental or public-opinion level, of the kind to encourage them to pursue those aims. Eastern Europe and northern Persia have already been mentioned in that connection. But the sequence of events that led to the Truman Doctrine can be used to illustrate yet another case where, to use Churchill's metaphor, the Soviets had reasonable grounds to believe that the door to the room was unlocked, and where they had some success in prying it open only to find it banged in their faces.

In their attempt to gain a foothold in the eastern Mediterranean, the Soviets continued what has been one of the oldest traditions of Russian foreign policy. Ever since Catherine the Great the vision of a base in the Straits, the idea of breaking out of the Black Sea, has dazzled Russian statesmen. During the war Stalin tacitly accepted Churchill's insistence that Greece should remain within the British sphere and, in view of the British statesman's obduracy, dropped his demand for bases in Turkey. But the Soviets could not have been unmindful that the British anti-Communist intervention in Greece in 1944 received a bad press in the United States and among some Labour Party circles in Britain. Most of all, full American influence was not *then* thrown behind Britain in her

[60] Smith, *op. cit.*, p. 55.

efforts to keep those countries out of the Soviet sphere. For the Russians, there could be at least a reasonable presumption that, with the fall of Churchill, intensified Soviet pressure on Turkey and Greece could not fail to bring fruit. Greece was now surrounded by Communist-dominated states, and in the summer of 1946 the Communist guerrilla movement renewed its operations there on a large scale. It could count on bases and sanctuaries in Yugoslavia, Albania, and Bulgaria. The usually disorderly state of Greek politics enhanced the danger that the little country would share the fate of her neighbors. "What little stability and order could be found in Greece was due primarily to the presence there of forty thousand British troops and to the counsel and support given the Greek government by the British."[61] But, though American gestures of support for the British position now were forthcoming, it did not seem likely that the U.S. would fully support a government fighting Communism in a *civil war*. After all, in China, where the stakes were vastly greater and the American interest was of long standing, the U.S. government was sponsoring an attempt to weld a coalition between the Nationalists and the Communists. Who, then, among the American experts in the U.S.S.R., could have predicted that it would be little Greece, her link with the United States mostly that of tourism, that would provide the occasion for the American President to appear in the halls of Congress and proclaim that "it must be the policy of the United States to support free peoples who are resisting attempted subjugation by armed minorities or by outside pressures."[62] Given the fact that Greece was not the first or the most important of the countries in that situation, one may well conjecture that Truman's statement was the source of some bewilderment and apprehension in the Kremlin.

Britain in her imperial decline had also to shoulder the burden of financial help to Turkey. Again, by their own lights the Soviets might well have felt that their demands on Turkey were, in view *of previous Western concessions* to their viewpoint, both moderate and justified. After the war, Russia claimed the territory that had been her own between 1878 and Brest Litovsk: the districts of Ardahan and Kars. A parallel concession by Rumania (Bessarabia) occasioned not a word of protest from Britain or the United States. To be sure, Rumania had been an enemy state, but Turkey's attitude toward the U.S.S.R. during the first and successful phase of the German invasion could hardly have been described as friendly. Russia wanted a base in the Straits. This again could be "justified" (Soviet memory in such things was nothing short of phenomenal) by those hints made by none other than Churchill at

[61] Harry S. Truman, *Memoirs* (New York, 1958), II: *Years of Trial and Hope*, 98.

[62] *Ibid.*, p. 106.

Teheran that Russia should have an opportunity to find an egress from her landlocked seas and have a suitable port. The Soviet campaign against Turkey between 1945 and 1947, conducted both through diplomatic pressure and through shrill propaganda accompanied by the massing of Soviet troops on the Turkish frontier, was based on the justifiable assumption that the burden of helping the Turks to modernize their army, like that of keeping troops in Greece, would eventually prove beyond the means of Britain's Treasury and the patience of her Labour government.

The traditionalist bent of Stalin's foreign policy was not an unimportant element in the Greco-Turkish entanglement. Just as Russia instituted elaborate diplomatic uniforms when other countries were abandoning them in favor of bourgeois tails and cutaways, so did she now propose to play, in addition to the role of the "Fatherland of Socialism," the role of an old-fashioned imperial power with old-fashioned spheres of influence around her borders, client states, etc. In the past the decline of one imperial power led to another one wresting away its territories or spheres of influence in an undeveloped area. Stalin could thus have a reasonable expectation that Britain's withdrawal from the eastern Mediterranean would be followed as a matter of course by the rise of Soviet influence there. But this "natural" course of Soviet expansion was to be suddenly and, to the Kremlin, unexpectedly blocked by the United States—the power which until a few years ago had limited her international involvement to the Western Hemisphere—at a point when the Soviet commitment had already been made.[63] The post-war world appeared full of beckoning opportunities for Soviet expansion, but once a Soviet move was made the President of the United States would suddenly bar the road and in effect exclaim, "Halt! Such things are not done anymore. Now we have the United Nations."

The British intimations in February 1947 that they were no longer capable of supporting Greece and Turkey were followed by the United States' assumption of that task. On March 12, 1947, addressing a joint session of the Congress, the President proclaimed what became known as the Truman Doctrine. The U.S.S.R. was not mentioned in the President's speech, but the implication was only too obvious: America has stepped in to block Soviet expansion—whether direct, as in the case of Turkey, or indirect, through the indigenous Communist movement, as in Greece. Faced with the necessity of explaining the new policy to the American

---

[63] Later, in talking to Djilas in 1948, Stalin was to be pessimistic in appraising the chances of the Greek Communists: "The United States is directly engaged there—the strongest state in the world." Djilas, *op. cit.*, p. 182. Characteristically, it was argued that this *direct* involvement of the United States explained the difference between the situations in Greece and in China, where the Communists were in the process of scoring their historic victory.

people, Truman had to resort to high rhetoric: the Communist way of life, he instructed, was "based upon the will of a minority forcibly imposed upon the majority. It relies upon terror and oppression, a controlled press and radio, fixed elections, and the suppression of personal freedoms."[64] The speech could not have unduly ruffled the Soviet leaders' feelings. In the years since 1945, their own language in reference to the United States and Britain had hardly been more complimentary. But it was a startling departure from wartime oratory. Truman could not go into the hopeless complexities of the world crisis; instead, that crisis was dramatized as a contest between two ways of life, the Communist one spreading in "the evil soil of poverty and strife," and the democratic one "based upon the will of the majority . . . free elections . . . guarantees of individual liberty . . . freedom of speech." But where in this dichotomy did Chiang Kai-shek's China, the current Persian government, or, in fact, most of the areas of contention belong? Just as during the war alliance with Stalin's Russia had been justified by presenting that country as a virtual democracy, so now the policy of containing Soviet expansion was presented as a struggle between light and darkness. In both instances the departure from political realism was to have a debilitating effect on American foreign policy.

The Truman Doctrine was succeeded by another foreign-policy initiative by the United States—the Marshall Plan. It is doubtful that this grandiose scheme of economic help and reconstruction would have been put into effect except for the now acutely felt threat of Russia and Communism. Massive economic help was now proposed to revivify Europe economically and, most of all, by so doing to avoid the danger that Communism, which emerged from the war very strong especially in Italy and France, would entrench itself in the governments of the West European nations or, worse, assume power on its own. The danger was felt to be especially acute in Italy, where the Communists had the support of a majority of the socialists and where many felt that the elections scheduled for 1948 might bring them an outright majority. But Secretary Marshall's initial proposal for the European Recovery Program was addressed not only to non-Communist countries; it called upon *all* the European states to assess their needs, the possibility of economic collaboration, and the required American help. The chance of the U.S.S.R. and her satellites participating and receiving help from America was thus officially envisaged, even though Truman and his advisers must have realized that it was dubious whether the Congress would approve a plan subsidizing

[64] Truman, *op. cit.*, p. 106.

the Communist states as well as their intended victims, especially in view of the ringing oratory of the Truman Doctrine.

There must, therefore, have been some private groans in Washington when Molotov accepted the invitation to attend an exploratory meeting in Paris with British and French delegates and when, accompanied by a bevy of economic experts, he alighted there on June 27, 1947. But Soviet behavior over the Marshall Plan was to provide a useful antidote to the belief in Russian diplomacy's consistent efficiency and subtlety or the idea that on important issues it was free of ideological inhibitions and limitations. There were undoubtedly voices in the Kremlin urging Soviet participation in the European Recovery Program. How could Russia lose by such a step? Her adherence to the plan might cause the Congress to shelve or at least severely limit the program.[65] In this case, West European recovery would be impeded, Britain's economic situation would grow desperate, and Russia would certainly gain. Or, the Marshall Plan might be voted through intact and Russia's economy would receive much needed foreign help. There were, to be sure, possible disadvantages. The posture of isolation from the West would have to be modified; something approaching the wartime atmosphere of collaboration would have to be reinstituted. And the Americans had made clear that this was not a give-away program: Russia's economic needs, plans, and prospects would have to be elucidated, the unwelcome possibility of prying American officials and Congressional delegations had to be faced. But it was two years since the war's end, and neither Soviet society nor its totalitarian system was going to collapse because of this exposure.

Molotov's first speech at the Paris meeting reflected these conflicting feelings in the bosom of the Soviet regime. The Soviet Foreign Minister welcomed the American initiative, though not very graciously. He admitted that the task of recovery would be facilitated by American help. At the same time he could not refrain from attributing the American offer to something else than sheer generosity: "It is also known that the United States in its turn is interested to use its credit facilities to enlarge its foreign markets, especially in view of the approaching crisis."[66] But on the whole Molotov seemed to augur Soviet participation. He warned that the Marshall Plan should not intrude on the sovereignty of the participating states, yet he did not object to the widest possible scope for it, including the participation of Germany. And he envisaged the formation of appropriate organs of European cooperation and consultation. Truman's comment that Molotov intended to sabotage the plan from the beginning and

---

[65] As it was, the Marshall Plan was in for hard going at the hands of the Congress, which had a Republican, i.e., anti-Administration, majority.

[66] Molotov, op. cit., p. 467.

that the Russians wanted merely to have Bevin and Foreign Minister Bidault ask the United States for a dollars-and-cents figure of the total aid that Europe might expect[67] is thus wide of the mark. As of June 28, the Soviets leaned toward collaboration. For a man of Molotov's habits, his statement was in fact surprisingly constructive, a testimony to his personal belief in the desirability of the Soviets' joining in.

But on July 2 he felt compelled to break off the negotiations and announce Soviet nonparticipation in the Marshall Plan. He did this with obvious embarrassment, and his alleged reasons were voiced in a strained way. The Marshall Plan, he said, would infringe on the European states' sovereignty. "In any case, the possibility of obtaining American credits is tied in with obedience toward the proposed organization and its steering committee."[68] One country might be told to produce more coal and less machinery, another country *vice versa*, etc. Yet Molotov had not advanced these arguments in his first statement, and anyway having once joined the recovery program the U.S.S.R. could always refuse to abide by this or that American request. The arguments were obviously spurious and did not carry the ring of inner conviction. The Foreign Minister dragged in issues not directly connected to the problem at hand: "Nothing is being done to set up an all-German government, which could better than anybody else take stock of the needs of the German people." His confusion was so great that he forgot to repeat or enlarge on his previous statement (which subsequently became a refrain in Soviet propaganda) that the Marshall Plan was an attempt by the United States to capture foreign markets and avoid a new depression.

There was only one man in the Soviet Union capable of overruling Molotov, and it is reasonable to assume that it was Stalin's personal decision which thus cut short the prospect of renewed East-West collaboration and vital aid to the Soviet economy. It is probable that the despot, while still retaining much of his political and diplomatic cunning, was already subject to those fears and delusions which were to lead within a year to rupture with Yugoslavia, renewed internal purges, and the persecution of the Soviet Jewish community. Not long after the Paris meeting, the appalled Djilas was witness to a scene when the ageing dictator exclaimed that the Benelux Customs Union did not include the Netherlands, and none of those present, including Molotov, dared contradict him: "Stalin looked at Molotov, at Zorin, at the rest. I had the desire to explain to him that the syllable *ne* in the name of Benelux came from the Netherlands . . . but since everyone kept still I did too."[69]

[67] Truman, *op. cit.*, p. 116.

[68] Molotov, *op. cit.*, p. 474.

[69] Djilas, *op. cit.*, p. 181.

Under such circumstances the rejection of the Marshall Plan was hardly surprising.

Soviet pressure was soon exerted on Czechoslovakia to withdraw her acceptance of an invitation to a subsequent larger meeting of European states interested in the Marshall Plan. Thus were the Communist states cut off from the massive economic aid which in the next few years was to help bring Western Europe to new heights of economic prosperity and which was to demonstrate that modified capitalism—a combination of private enterprise with the welfare state—possessed an amazing vitality and power to lift up living standards far beyond the most optimistic hopes of an observer who in 1945 had contemplated the shattered economy of Western Europe.

The future effects of the Marshall Plan on the fortunes of Soviet foreign policy and of Communism may be briefly noted at this point. The success of the European Recovery Program did not "stop" Communism in Western Europe, but, it might be reasonable to argue, it helped to contain it. The Communist parties of France and Italy, while they are no longer as formidable as they were in 1947–48, are still powerful organizations enjoying the support of a large proportion of the electorate, still not to be dismissed lightly as claimants for power. Their lessened militancy and greater independence from Moscow are the result less of the great rise in the Western workers' well-being than of general changes in the anatomy of world Communism. A historian writing today is constrained to admit that the economic success of the Marshall Plan and of the European economic integration built on its foundations was not paralleled by a political one. Europe's fantastic economic recovery and growth did not arrest the spectacular decline in world power and influence of Britain and France.[70] The idea of a politically integrated Europe which would establish a new super-power and thus transform world politics appeared on the threshold of realization in the late 1950's and early 1960's but is today as far from realization as ever. Indeed, a pessimistic observer might conclude that the Marshall Plan's very degree of economic success was to prove politically deleterious. The sense of danger and urgency that drew the Western states together was to become dissipated a decade later. A belief that *all* political problems are susceptible of solution through economic means and that the pursuit of economic growth is the main if not indeed the only legitimate goal of the modern state became entrenched in the democratic electorates, and this was to contribute to the fact that Western Europe, more prosperous than ever before, became less significant mil-

[70] The combination of economic prosperity and decline as a world power is rather unprecedented. In the cases of Rome and Spain, for example, severe economic crises preceded their collapse as imperial powers.

itarily and politically in the world than at any time since the seventeenth century. But this view may well be reversed by a historian delivering his judgment from a longer historical perspective.

The initiation and then the success of the European Recovery Program also had a *direct* influence on Soviet policies. Once Soviet opposition to participation had crystallized, Soviet propaganda had to picture the Marshall Plan as designed exclusively for the benefit of American capitalists and their European servants and as being of no real benefit to the nations of the West. Writing many years after Stalin's death, an official Soviet source still presents this analysis: "Under 'the restoration of the economy and the restoration of economic vitality in the whole world,' the imperialist circles of the United States openly understood the return to a situation where the world [capitalist] economic system would recover hegemony, and the socialist area would first be pushed back to its frontiers of 1939 and then fully liquidated."[71] This is a revealing commentary on what Stalin must have felt at the time was the original aim of the Marshall Plan: not only to salvage Western Europe, but through an infusion of American aid to enable Great Britain and France to resume their places as Great Powers and restore the pre-1939 world system. This restored prosperity in the West would in turn exert irresistible attraction on the not yet fully secured Soviet satellites. Hadn't Poland and Czechoslovakia been ready to join the Marshall Plan until pressured against it by the U.S.S.R.? The defection of Russia's satellites would then present a challenge to the survival of the Communist system in the U.S.S.R. Thus into the Americans' "containment" policy the morbidly suspicious Kremlin mind soon read the implications of what became known some years later as the "rollback" scheme. The creation of the Comintern in 1947 and the faster tempo at which Russia imposed controls on her satellites were thus undoubtedly affected by the United States' great plan of economic assistance.

Recognition of the fact that economic aid was an increasingly important part of modern diplomacy ran against the grain of Stalin's foreign policy. The post-war trade agreements between the U.S.S.R. and her satellites represented unabashed exploitation of the latter by means ranging from terms of trade weighted heavily in favor of Russia to the even more blatant device of the joint stock companies. But for propaganda purposes the Soviets felt constrained to set up their own equivalent of the European Recovery Program. This was the Council of Mutual Economic Assistance (Comecon), established in January 1949 and including the U.S.S.R. and the other Communist countries of Eastern Europe, except Yugoslavia, then already in sharp conflict with Moscow. The Council's charter aped the

[71] Mileykovsky, *op. cit.*, 374.

provisions of the Western scheme. Comecon proposed to coordinate the economies of its members, exchange experience, loans, etc. In fact, the concept of economic aid remained as alien to Stalin's Russia as, say, the notion of a two-party system. Until 1953, Comecon was simply a new piece of machinery for milking the satellites. It is sufficient to recall such fantastic cases of Soviet penury as the Russians' demand of repayment from the Yugoslavs of the money advanced them in 1944 (not a great amount at that) and then considered by both sides as a free gift to fellow Communists, and their insistence that the Yugoslavs pay for the costs of educating their citizens in the U.S.S.R., this "education" consisting in 1947–48 of training Yugoslav officials and military officers to be Soviet agents and to work against their own leadership![72] Even Stalin's successors, hardly models of charity, had to acknowledge publicly the exploitative nature of these dealings with Russia's satellites and to renounce the worst features of her "economic collaboration," such as the notorious joint stock companies. It was only during the Khrushchev era that the concept of economic aid as part of international politics became assimilated into Soviet political thought and the U.S.S.R. began to compete with the United States in this respect.

The beginning of the Marshall Plan constitutes a watershed in the cold war. We are justified in seeing the beginnings of the cold war in post-Yalta developments, when, with the victory now virtually secure, the Allies began to diverge on a number of issues, when an increasing number of skirmishes occurred over Poland, German reparations, the nature of governments in Eastern Europe, etc. These skirmishes were terminated or smoothed over by foreign ministers' conferences or other forms of diplomatic accommodation, but the basic problem, the inability of the United States and the U.S.S.R. to communicate meaningfully in the absence of a common enemy, remained. With the Marshall Plan the cold war assumes the character of position warfare. Both sides become frozen in mutual unfriendliness. It was no longer a question of this or that political difference or of a contested territory; it was the totality of foreign policies of each side that became the object of attack by the other.

The Soviet version of this "total cold war" was epitomized in a statement of an official Soviet publication referring to the Vandenberg Resolution, passed by the U.S. Senate on June 11, 1948: "The new course of American foreign policy meant a return to the old anti-Soviet course, designed to unloose war and forcibly to institute world domination by Britain and the United States."[73] The resolution, the statement went on,

---

[72] Robert M. Slusser and Jan F. Triska, *A Calendar of Soviet Treaties 1917–1957* (Stanford, Calif., 1959), p. 256.

[73] Mileykovsky, *op. cit.*, 376.

was breaking a tradition going back to George Washington, the tradition prohibiting alliances except in times of war. Now, bewailed the Soviet author, "the formation of an American–West European alliance was proposed in peacetime and at a time when in fact nobody threatened the security of either the United States or Western Europe." An American author has summarized the Western version of the new phase of the conflict: "In the conclusion of World War II Russia, almost by force of circumstances, had begun a rapid and already far-reaching expansion over Europe toward its Atlantic rim. The United States, which had intended to withdraw from Europe, had been alarmed by this expansion and had come back into Europe to stop it from going any farther."[74]

Both formulations overdramatize the other side's intentions and capabilities. The figures for the Soviet armed forces given above certainly do not suggest that the U.S.S.R. was planning or able to march to the Atlantic. The sequence of U.S. foreign-policy moves beginning with the Marshall Plan and ending with the creation of the North Atlantic Treaty Organization likewise cannot be considered as a preliminary to an outright aggression against the U.S.S.R. A sober analysis of the effectives at the disposal of the Atlantic Alliance would have precluded any military man from arriving at such a judgment. But while the Soviet leaders obviously did not expect an American attack—and if in fact there are indications that Stalin's successors were to consider him overconfident in this respect— the dictator and his clique expected mounting pressure on the Soviet Union, economic and psychological in its character, to make her surrender some of her wartime gains. Once again, paradoxical though it sounds, one of the main reasons for the aggressive Soviet posture between 1945 and 1950 was the awareness of her leaders of her weakness and vulnerability. In view of such apparently reckless steps as the blockade of Berlin, it may sound perverse to speak of the essential caution of Stalin's foreign policy. But an illustration of this caution that escaped contemporary observers was the case of Yugoslavia. Tito's defection in 1948 was a major political defeat for the U.S.S.R., his continuation in power a personal challenge to Stalin. Yet despite the provocation, despite the fact that it was unlikely that the West would intervene in this intra-Communist dispute on behalf of a regime that was well into 1950 as hostile to the United States as the Soviet one, the Russian, Hungarian, and Bulgarian armies did not march on Yugoslavia. The blockade of Berlin could be lifted momentarily at the first sign that it might lead to a shooting war. The entrance of Soviet troops into Yugoslavia might have set in motion

[74] Louis J. Halle, *The Cold War as History* (London, 1967; New York, 1968), p. 137.

an incalculable sequence of events in the satellites, events which in turn
would have found a response in the West. By studying the Berlin blockade
versus Yugoslavia we come to appreciate the essential points of Stalin's
foreign policy. The dictator's irrational quirks, so pronounced during his
last phase, did not preclude a degree of calculation and caution when it
came to foreign affairs.

The "aggressiveness" of the Marshall Plan and of the Atlantic Alliance
was in the Soviet mind connected with the persistence and enhancement
of the American presence in Europe. President Roosevelt had stated at
Yalta that American troops would not stay in Europe more than two years
after the conclusion of the war. Why then was his successor breaking
this "promise"? Why was the United States departing from a pattern of
her foreign policy that had prevailed since the Founding Fathers? In the
strange psychology of Soviet totalitarianism there has always lurked a
moralistic-traditionalist motif. People and governments are supposed to act
according to their pledges and traditional characteristics. Thus the German
attack on the Soviet Union has seldom been referred to without a preceding
clause about "faith breaking" or "perfidious" behavior, as if it were a
matter of surprise that Hitler should break his word. Now the departure
of the Americans from their isolationist ways produced first indignation,
then incredulity, and finally the darkest suspicion.

This paradoxical alternation of moods was of course of long standing
in Soviet foreign policy. The capitalist West has always been pictured
as either devilishly devious or incredibly naïve. The British empire in the
1920's was considered to be a moribund organization, with the Comintern
brazenly conducting anti-British activity in its far-flung regions. But at
times, as in 1927, the Soviet leaders were on the point of convincing
themselves that such unlikely persons as Baldwin and Sir Austen Chamberlain were about to launch a new intervention in Russia. Thus, despite
the American commitment in the Marshall Plan, the Soviets were ready
the very next year to probe the solidity of the American intent to stay in
Europe. Secretary Forrestal noted on April 23, 1948:

> Mr. Lovett spoke of meetings which he and Bohlen have had recently
> with Panyushkin [then Soviet Ambassador to the United States] and
> members of the Embassy staff. These conversations have taken the
> form of apparent probing by the Russians as to our real position vis-
> à-vis the Russians. They asked, for example, at the first meeting between
> him and Bohlen and Llewellyn Thompson whether America really in-
> tended to stay in Europe.[75]

It would be unwise to consider the Berlin blockade, which ensued shortly

[75] Millis, *op. cit.*, p. 424.

after the meeting referred to by Forrestal, as merely an attempt to test American determination, but such probing was clearly a part of the total picture.

We are thus brought back to Germany as the main battlefront of this second phase of the cold war which began with the Marshall Plan and was to endure until 1950. It would be of little profit to recount the formal aspects of Soviet-American diplomacy on the subject of Germany between 1945 and 1948; the foreign ministers' conferences became lengthy wrangles, and the prospect of concluding a German peace treaty became ever more distant. It is difficult to trace Soviet intentions about Germany during those years, but what evidence we have suggests forcibly that the Soviet policy-makers were themselves in a considerable quandary as to what their policy should be.

The Western Allies' agreement at Potsdam to persevere in the concept of total occupation of Germany by the victorious powers, in exacting reparations, and in a drastic reduction of the country's industrial potential removed the earliest and greatest Soviet apprehension: that Britain and the United States would employ German nationalism in an outright challenge to the Soviet Union. Those Soviet-sponsored German organizations which could have been employed to compete in an appeal to German nationalism, like the National Committee for Free Germany, were disbanded in 1945. Nothing in that year suggested the West's intention or ability to rebuild the German military machine as a threat to Russia. The initial American attitude toward Germany emphasized the punitive and preventative character of the occupation. Even to the Russians' suspicious mind, it must have seemed inconceivable, if the Americans intended to use the Germans against Russia, that they would have imposed such measures as the famous prohibition against American personnel fraternizing with the natives, that the original directives about the German economy should have prescribed drastically reduced levels of industrial production, etc. One voice on the Western side which would have objected to such measures, Churchill's, was missing in the Allied councils. Occupied by the Four Powers, devastated, her population practically at the subsistence level, Germany could hardly threaten the Soviet Union, and her Western zones seemed more a liability to than an appendage of the United States and Britain.

Under these circumstances the initial post-war Soviet policies toward Germany, both within the Soviet occupation zone and on the German problem as a whole were far from consistent. The prevailing theme was that of exploitation, of getting as much in reparations as possible. The Russian looting and dismantling of German industrial equipment reached proportions that often alarmed the Russian administration responsible for political affairs in the Soviet zone. And as for those political affairs, Soviet directives were subject to abrupt changes. A member of the first Communist team dispatched to Germany after the occupation offers this testimony:

> The creation of independent Communist and Socialist Parties was in direct contradiction with the directives which we had received in Moscow in March and April 1945. . . . At that time we had been told that political activity on the part of the German people could only be developed initially in the context of a large-scale comprehensive anti-fascist movement. . . . Now, on the contrary, what was being talked of was the foundation of political parties. Earlier, again, it had been said that land reform could not be undertaken before the beginning of 1946. Now we were to carry out the land reform immediately after the foundation of the Party in the summer of 1945.[76]

Here again is a useful corrective to the idea that the Soviets always operated from a master plan prepared well in advance and providing for every contingency.

The prospect of installing Communism in *all* of Germany must have dazzled those who remembered Lenin's hopes on that count. But even in their own occupation zone the Soviets proceeded warily at first, with an eye to Western reactions. The political picture there soon began to resemble that of the satellite states: in addition to the Communist Party there was the socialist one, slated to merge with the Communists after a suitable interval (which it did in 1946 under the name of the Socialist Unity Party). There were also two docile nonsocialist parties designed to soak up support for the regime among what remained of the German middle class and those with a religious orientation in politics. This outwardly multiparty facade was, in the Russian zone of Germany as in the satellites, found preferable to a formally one-party state since it was hoped it would minimize tension and enlist professional and administrative talent, rare in Communist ranks at that time. The usefulness of the device proved so great that the auxiliary parties were forbidden to perform the act of political self-immolation and dissolve—the logical move for them when the reality of the situation became apparent.

The multi-party organization was designed also to create the appropriate impression in the western zones. But here Communism after its immediate post-war resurgence remained weak. The socialists resolutely refused to merge or to cooperate with the Communists.

How far were the Soviets determined to make a bid for all of Germany? Djilas recalls the "statements by Stalin and the Soviet leaders made before the Bulgars and the Yugoslavs in the spring of 1946 that all of Germany

---

[76] Wolfgang Leonhard, *Child of the Revolution* (Chicago, 1958), p. 413.

must be ours, that is, Soviet Communist."[77] But the Soviet leaders were seldom in the habit of revealing their innermost thoughts and plans to foreign Communists. From the perspective of 1946–47 the prospects of a Communist Germany were at best distant. First there would have to be increasing economic chaos and poverty in the western zones, industrial depression, and the burden of millions of refugees. The financial burden of maintaining West Germany would have to become too heavy for the Western Powers, especially Britain. And Americans would perhaps have to pull out, as they had "promised," in which case it would only be a question of time before the British and the French would also abandon their too heavy commitment and leave the way open for Communist penetration.

In studying Soviet policies between 1945 and 1950 one receives the strong impression that the idea of a united Germany, even a Germany in which Communism played a considerable role or actually achieved power, never received wholehearted acceptance. It clashed with the apprehension that a united Germany of whatever political complexion would in some vague way constitute a menace to the Soviet Union. After 1948 and the defection of Yugoslavia, this unspoken apprehension must have been magnified. Even the Berlin squeeze of 1948–49 does not entitle us to believe that the Soviets were at that time hoping for an outright sovietization of all Germany. It *was* designed to push the West out of Berlin and to hasten the American exodus from the rest of Germany; this would hopefully begin an attrition of Western influence in what was to become the Federal Republic of Germany, which might then become a larger Finland. On Germany more than any other major problem of the post-war world the Soviets oscillated in their hopes and fears. Djilas quotes Stalin as saying *in 1948*, "The West will make Western Germany their own, and we shall turn Eastern Germany into our own state." Yet within a few months the Soviets were to apply pressure on Berlin and convince many in the West that all Germany was at stake.

The Yalta and Potsdam agreements prescribed that while Germany was to be divided into occupation zones, it was to be treated as a single political and, especially, economic unit, with the four Allied commanders synchronizing their policies, acting as a four-headed supreme power for the defeated country. This, to lapse into vernacular, would have taken some doing, even if the Four Powers had been bound by closest friendship and shared the same political and economic systems and ideologies. As it was, it must be considered a tribute to the lingering tradition of the wartime comradeship in arms that the original occupation pattern endured, even if in a faltering way, for almost three years.

[77] Djilas, *op. cit.*, p. 153.

"Our first break with Soviet policy in Germany came over reparations," writes General Lucius Clay, who for four years shouldered the main burden of representing the United States in the councils of the occupation regime.[78] Since the Russians refused to make an accounting of their exactions in their own zone, the Western commanders decided that they could not continue to deliver industrial equipment, etc., from their zones to the Soviets. In the spring of 1946 the Western deliveries were stopped, and the Potsdam provision that Germany was to be treated as a single economic unit became a dead letter. The stage was thus set for the progressive erosion of Allied unity in administering Germany and for the consequent rise of two Germanies. The Allied Control Council, no longer an organ of coordination, became a scene of wrangling, reproducing on German issues the larger areas of contention between the two super-powers. A typical report of its activities speaks for itself:

> On demilitarization the Western Powers cited the large number of prisoners of war held in Soviet Russia. . . . The Soviet representatives charged the Western Powers with failure to destroy war plants and to deliver reparations. On denazification they made a general charge of failure to denazify . . . failure to agree on a decentralization program. . . . The Western Powers charged them with building up a large concentration of economic power through their seizure and incorporation under Soviet ownership of plants and enterprises in their zone.[79]

Even if the chasm separating the West from the Russians had not been widening, the latter would have argued that their wartime sacrifices entitled them to exact as much as possible from the German economy. The Westerners, especially Americans, came equally naturally to feel that they were being called on to subsidize Russia's recovery at the same time that strict adherence to the Potsdam document would prevent West Germany's recovery and retain her economy as a huge liability to its conquerors. The American point of view saw German economic recovery as necessarily based mainly on the resuscitation of free enterprise, the virtues of which were unlikely to be appreciated by the Soviets. Conflict was thus built into the ramshackle edifice of Allied control. Had some common purpose animated the two sides as it had during the war, the differences of ideology and approach might have been overcome. Had Germany been of secondary importance, like Austria, they might have been smoothed over. But Germany was and is the pivot of European politics, and the growing dissonances between the two super-powers in other areas, Poland or Czechoslovakia, say, were to reverberate loudly in this center of Europe. Furthermore, Germany was one area where the contending sides could

[78] Lucius D. Clay, *Decision in Germany* (New York, 1950), p. 120.
[79] *Ibid.*, p. 145.

"get at" each other without recourse to military hostilities. The United States and Britain could do little about the progressive satellization of Poland, but they could limit or suspend deliveries of industrial equipment to Russia from the western zones of Germany. And the Soviets had tempting but dangerous opportunities in Berlin. Deep in the eastern zone, its British, American, and French sectors lay at the mercy of the Soviet occupation forces, which by disrupting supplies and communications could at any moment create a major crisis or, less dramatically, could by occasional interference irritate and pressure the Western Powers. The occupied status of Germany in general and that of Berlin in particular were an ideal blueprint for trouble: somebody with common sense and a feeling for history should have remembered in the concluding stages of the war that in German history Berlin had never had the symbolic meaning of, say, a Paris or Rome, and that it would have been a reasonable arrangement to leave it entirely in the Russian sphere in return for an appropriate quid pro quo to the western zones. But nobody did; the idea of an extraterritorial corridor to Berlin had been briefly considered and then dropped. The West's rights of access to Berlin were explicitly spelled out in a number of documents to which the Soviets subscribed, but beginning with 1946 various wartime arrangements about Germany began to be disregarded on both sides, and had the Soviets been fanatical observers of legality and of the maxim *pacta sunt servanda* they could have found a multitude of pretexts for their squeeze play. Thus Berlin was designed to become the number-one trouble spot of post-war Europe and a source of profit to innumerable writers of spy stories and films.

General Clay in his account of the years 1945–46 points out that friendly relations existed between the Western and Soviet personnel in Germany. This cannot, of course, be attributed exclusively to the personal amiability of the successive Soviet commanders, Marshals Zhukov and Sokolovsky. For all the deepening fissures, the worst Soviet apprehensions about the West rapidly remilitarizing "its" Germany and turning it against the U.S.S.R. were not materializing. Various steps taken by the Western Powers in 1946, such as the stopping of reparations from the western zones and the combining of the British and American sectors, while they evoked strong Soviet protests were not received with the verbal violence and countermeasures aroused in subsequent years. The explanation for this relative amiability must be found in the over-all caution and uncertainty of direction that characterized Soviet policy on the German issue during those years. Russia was feeling her way carefully.

Apart from the basic issues involved, the very nature of the Soviet-American discourse after the war precluded any progress on Germany. There was no attempt at discreet negotiations and bargaining. Both sides declared their positions in the full glare of publicity, usually at the countless foreign ministers' conferences, whose participants, unlike the heads of their governments, could only follow instructions rather than engage in give-and-take. Any initiative by one side automatically aroused the suspicion of the other. When opportunities for agreement miraculously appeared, one side or the other would eventually pull back, suspecting a trap. The American policy-makers felt that they had burned their fingers on secret diplomacy during the war, and they were not going to revert to it now. For their part, the Soviets were incapable in public negotiations of going beyond their usual rhetoric. Thus, had there even been concrete possibilities of an arrangement of the German problem between 1945 and 1947 they were bound to remain unexplored.

These characteristics come out most vividly in the accounts of the foreign ministers' meeting in Moscow in March–April 1947. Molotov's oratory on this occasion was uncharacteristically circumspect, devoid of the usual charges that the West was turning Germany into a haven for fascism and militarism and that the Western Allies held aggressive intentions against the U.S.S.R. Now the Soviets might well have felt that there was still a chance of preventing the West from consolidating the western zones of Germany and embarking on a more resolutely anti-Soviet course. But the conciliatory *tone* of Molotov's speech was not matched by any concrete proposals. Thus the Soviet foreign minister proposed the formation of a central government for Germany, but what could this mean? wondered the representatives of Britain, the United States, and France. Were the Soviets going to rig the elections in their zone, while enjoying the freedom of propaganda for Communism in the western zones? Were they going to outbid the Western Powers in courting German nationalism and thus turn a central German regime in their direction? The Soviets proposed termination of the occupation of Germany "when the Allied Powers will consider that the basic aims of the occupation of Germany have been satisfied."[80] But again, those basic aims were defined with infuriating vagueness as "the securing of German demilitarization" and "firm re-establishment of the democratic system." The only points of precision in Molotov's proposals were his recurrent requests that the Soviet reparation demands, i.e., the original $10 billion, be fulfilled and that the Ruhr industrial basin be placed under Four Power supervision. To the Western Powers, quite understandably, these proposals implied that Russia wanted them to make concrete concessions—undoing the first steps taken to unify the western zones, resumption of reparations to the U.S.S.R., and permission for Soviet interference in the Ruhr—in return for some vague and hence redefinable and revocable promises about Soviet intentions in Germany as a whole. Yet it would have been impossible for Molotov

[80] Molotov, *op. cit.*, p. 450.

to say in a public speech: "If you Anglo-Americans give up your attempt to build a separate West German state and eventually to rearm it, we shall give up the idea of building a Communist state either in eastern or in all Germany and will let the German people find their own destiny." It is of course impossible to assert that such indeed had been the Soviet government's intention or that, had such a pledge been formulated, it would have been adhered to. But diplomacy consists in sensitivity to a favorable moment for settlement of a dispute, and statesmanship in the ability to transform a fragile agreement into reality through appropriate political and economic measures as well as military vigilance. Neither of these arts could flourish under the conditions of the Soviet-America discourse after the war. The American version of the failure of the Moscow conference underlines this fact. It was expressed by General Marshall: "Agreement was made impossible at Moscow because . . . the Soviet Union insisted upon proposals which would have established in Germany a centralized government adapted to the seizure of absolute control of a country . . . [which] would be mortgaged to turn over a large part of its production as reparations principally to the Soviet Union."[81] Ambassador Walter Bedell Smith appends his own comment: "In the Kremlin it must have been fully appreciated that at long last Soviet objectives in Germany were clearly understood by the Western powers and now were impossible of attainment by diplomatic manoeuvre."[82]

On the basis of what we know (admittedly not very much) it is still difficult to endorse such categorical judgments. "Soviet objectives in Germany" were, one submits, not as clear-cut and all-encompassing as the exasperated American officials assumed them to be. To be sure, the U.S.S.R. had an abiding interest in preventing the consolidation of the three western zones into one effective political and economic organism, because such a state could *then* become a potential danger, perhaps even a military danger, to the U.S.S.R. Yet at the same time they objected to a proposal which would have most effectively crippled the future West German state: the French plea that the Rhineland and Ruhr be made a separate entity. "To adopt such a policy means to turn the German nation into an irreconcilable enemy and push it into the arms of the German revanchists and militarists," said Molotov.[83] Were the Soviets, then, shamelessly courting German nationalism and setting up to revive the Rapallo spirit? If so, how can one explain Molotov's insistence that the status of German territories occupied by Poland had been definitely settled at Potsdam and there could not even be a question of territorial modification? Try as you may, you cannot develop a consistently Machiavellian version of

[81] As quoted in Smith, *op. cit.*, p. 227.
[82] *Ibid.*, p. 229.
[83] Molotov, *op. cit.*, p. 434.

Soviet policy toward Germany at this particular point in 1947. It is reasonable to conjecture that the Russians knew that a major reorientation of American policy was in the offing (the Truman Doctrine had just been announced) and they were being pulled to and fro by conflicting fears and hopes. In the instance of the Moscow conference, to prevent West Germany being rapidly rebuilt and rearmed, they were willing to renounce for the immediate future the idea of building their own Communist Germany. Stalin's words to General Marshall would also bear out this interpretation: "It is wrong to give so tragic an interpretation to our present disagreements. . . . When people have exhausted themselves in dispute, they recognize the necessity for compromise."[84] But in the eyes of Generals Marshall, Clay, and Smith, and for the American public, there now existed a huge "credibility gap" insofar as Soviet proclamations and actions were concerned.

The next phase of the German problem was crucially affected by the new phase of American foreign policy opened by the Marshall Plan. It might be asked again why the European Recovery Program should so quickly have become for the Soviet policy-makers the central link in an American policy to isolate and push back the Soviet Union. It was no longer simply an attempt by American big business to avoid depression at home and to seize control of the West European economy, as the first and relatively "innocent" version presented by Molotov at the Paris conference had it. The Program's apparent altruism, its "unsordid" character, now enhanced Soviet suspicions to a nightmarish extent. Since when do capitalists divest themselves of billions of dollars just to save another country's economy? Granted the lesson of Lend Lease and granted the internal conditions in the United States, the Soviet rulers in the beginning of 1948 evidently arrived at the conclusion that the ultimate meaning of the ERP went beyond an attempt to save Western Europe from Communism or to seduce the Russian satellites by the example of a higher standard of living. The eventual aims were clearly military. While unwilling to expand her own armies, and still deliberating whether to pull her forces out of Europe, the United States was clearly bent upon recreating the military potential of Western Europe, with the view to eventually employing it to restore the balance of power and wrest from the U.S.S.R. her wartime gains. The real purpose of the Marshall Plan was to create large standing armies that could threaten Russia while the Americans would back them up, if necessary, with their naval strength and their atomic-armed Strategic Air Command.

This tortuous analysis, the Kremlin experts must have felt, made all the pieces fall in place. It explained the apparent generosity of the Ameri-

---

[84] Smith, *op. cit.*, p. 221.

can capitalists: it was cheaper to purchase British, French, German, etc., soldiers than to equip American ones. It explained why the Americans were not building a large standing army: the danger to the Soviet Union was still not imminent; the West European economy had to be built up and *then* turned to military uses.

This interpretation resolved the two seemingly contradictory Soviet views of American foreign policy; one that the Americans were loath to risk a military confrontation with the U.S.S.R. and were unwilling to prolong their military presence in Europe, and the other that they were determined not only to arrest Soviet expansion but also to arrive at a state of affairs where, in the words quoted above, "the socialist area would first be pushed back to its frontiers of 1939 and then fully liquidated." The formula of containment took on a much more sinister meaning: "the doctrine of 'containment' foresaw such a build-up of 'the position of strength in the free world' (this phrase was authored by Secretary of State Acheson) as would allow a series of successful local wars against socialist states at the same time that one would be prepared for a major war."[85]

This version of the Marshall Plan and "containment" ascribes to American policy a strategy which the Soviets were to adopt themselves in their formula of "coexistence"—i.e., avoiding a major nuclear conflict and at the same time justifying and inciting wars of "national liberation" —a not untypical projection. The real aim of the Marshall Plan was, they thought, to arm Western Europe to the point where American satellites would be capable of taking on the Soviet ones. The burden of an agonizing decision would then be placed on the U.S.S.R.: should she let the "frontiers of socialism" be pushed back, or should she intervene militarily and risk American nuclear intervention? Thus in Europe the Soviet Union believed she would be faced with the kind of predicaments that the United States was in fact to find herself facing in Korea and Vietnam, and at a time when her economic reconstruction was still incomplete and her nuclear armament still nonexistent or definitely inferior.

Were the Soviets really capable of such fantastic misconstructions of their opponents' intentions? We saw how on September 10, 1939, Stalin was half convinced that German troops would not stop at the line agreed upon by Molotov and Ribbentrop but would march to and perhaps beyond the frontiers of the Soviet Union. Was the construction put upon American policy in the summer of 1947 much more extravagant than the belief held in the West between 1945 and 1949 that the U.S.S.R. was about to unloose her armed hordes across Europe to the English Channel?

The interpretation reached in the Kremlin between April and July 1947

[85] Mileykovsky, *op. cit.*, 364.

about the meaning of the new directions in American foreign policy led
to what the Soviets undoubtedly considered measures of self-defense. The
formation of the international Communist Information Bureau (Cominform) in 1947 was caused primarily by certain internal needs of the
Communist bloc, but the Soviet spokesmen Zhdanov and Malenkov utilized
its initial meeting in September to dramatize the division of the world
into two camps, an imperialist one led by the United States, the other that
of socialism and peace. The action most relevant to the general European
situation taken at this founding meeting was the pressure put on the
representatives of the French and Italian Communist parties to subordinate all their other activities to a struggle against the Marshall Plan. Both
parties had preserved until then the general national and nondoctrinal
attitude they had developed during the war, a policy that had brought
them solid dividends in electoral strength. While no longer in the government, the two parties still could hope that coming parliamentary elections
would strengthen their position still further and perhaps with the assistance
of left-wing socialists lead to the achievement of power through perfectly
legal means. The new line laid down at the Cominform meeting made such
prospects unlikely. They were now supposed to "struggle," through strikes
and riots, against the measures that unmistakably brought relief to the
economies of their countries and a rise in the standard of living of their
working class. Writes a former Italian Communist, a participant in the
founding meeting: "Togliatti was personally in favor of accepting American economic aid. . . . Afterward [after the meeting] . . . he took a position contrary to his convictions. . . . He made a speech . . . asserting that
American economic aid was bound to hurt the Italian economy."[86]

What especially infuriated the French and Italians was the savage
criticism, mainly from the Yugoslavs but inspired by the Russians, that
they had virtually capitulated to bourgeois legalism, that after the war
they had meekly disarmed their own resistance forces and thus enabled
the bourgeoisie to resume power. Yet all their actions in 1944–46 were in
line with, if not indeed at the explicit instructions of, the Soviet leadership.
The brutal lesson taught to the French and Italian Communists was, again,
that they must subordinate their own aims and ambitions to what at any
given moment was the priority goal of Soviet foreign policy. And in
September 1947 this first priority was the failure of the Marshall Plan
in Western Europe. The retrospective criticism of the French and Italian
Communists' legalism did *not* carry with it the injunction that they should
now try to seize power through illegal means. Such a policy would have
been too drastic a provocation of the United States and Britain and hence
too dangerous. On the other hand, the paralysis of the French and Italian

[86] Eugenio Reale, *With Jacques Duclos at the Bench of the Accused* (in
French) (Paris, 1964), p. 23.

economies would have precluded the build-up of those countries as military outposts of the West and as threats to the Soviet Union. Thus neither a legalistic pose nor full insurgency was allowed to the hapless French and Italian Communists—convincing proof that their activities were to be tailored to suit Soviet aims. In subsequent years, the Communist parties of Western Europe were to proclaim loudly—and, one would think, unnecessarily—that they would sabotage any military efforts of their governments against the U.S.S.R. and the socialist camp. This policy if anything hastened the *rapprochement* among West European countries and the eventual formation of the Atlantic Alliance.

The period 1947–49 thus marks a complete (as distinguished from the previous partial) lack of communication between the two super-powers. Both the United States and Russia became convinced of the other's essentially aggressive design. On the Soviet side the danger was still viewed as indirect and not imminent. In the West the conviction grew that the strikes and violence perpetrated by the Comunist parties were but an initial phase in an attempted Communist seizure of power in France and Italy. The "peace movement" launched by Soviet propaganda at the same time, which was to intensify in 1948–49 and reach its climax with the Stockholm Appeal in 1950 to ban the atom bomb signed allegedly by 500 million people, is still held by many Western writers to have been a transparent and crude attempt to hide essentially aggressive Soviet aims. But it undoubtedly reflected very genuine Soviet apprehensions. As to its crudity, this heavy-handed Soviet effort must be understood, as so many moves in Soviet diplomacy, in terms of historical precedents. In 1920, at the time of the Soviet-Polish war and with the Civil War still going on in the south of Russia, the prospects of a renewal of British intervention were foreclosed, or so at least the Soviet historians came to believe, by the pressure on Lloyd George's government brought by action committees set up by the British Labour Party. Now, again, the pressure of the "masses" was supposed to paralyze the evil designs of their governments toward the Soviet Union. To a Westerner, it is almost incomprehensible that the Marshall Plan should have unloosed such a sequence of fears, as complex as they were unreal, in Stalin's Russia. But to the contemporary Soviet historian, who now lives in an atmosphere much less affected by paranoid suspicion, the world in those years "faced the catastrophe of war, and only major shifts of power in favor of socialism, the active foreign policy of the U.S.S.R., and the resolute struggle of nations in favor of peace managed to avoid that catastrophe."[87]

We stressed that in 1947–49 the Russians still believed this danger to be an indirect and distant one. It was the future, revivified Europe that

[87] Mileykovsky, *op. cit.*, 377.

would act as America's instrument in forcing the rollback of the Soviet sphere of influence. The contribution of the Marshall Plan in enabling Western Europe to play this role would not be immediately effective. From the Soviet point of view, the real danger signal would be the unification and economic rehabilitation of the western zones of Germany, for this would inevitably augur their remilitarization. When in the spring of 1948 the three Western zones were finally united—the French abandoning their previous objections to such a scheme—and when they adopted a currency reform that was to prove decisive in healing the economy, the Soviets felt that a determined effort had to be made to prevent the establishment of what was to become the Federal Republic.

In the spring of 1948, Soviet views of America were nicely balanced between hopes and apprehensions. The "aggressive" American designs against the U.S.S.R. were believed still to be indirect, i.e., expressed through the agency of America's European satellites. Direct involvement by the United States, or a preventive war, was believed to run against the grain of American tradition, and much as it might appeal to some isolated officials and military figures it would not be approved by the vast majority of the American people or their elected representatives. Furthermore, 1948 was an election year in the United States. Henry Wallace's Progressive Party was about to begin its campaign, largely on the platform that the deterioration of relations with Russia was unnecessary and dangerous and that a return should be made to the traditions of the Roosevelt-Stalin partnership. Not even the most optimistic American expert in the Kremlin could believe that Wallace had a chance of being elected, but the Russians had reasonable cause to believe (as had most American experts and politicians) that the challenge from the left could well cost Truman the election. The President had good reason, then, not to act rashly in foreign affairs, to propitiate the peace sentiment, and to demonstrate that he was carrying out his predecessor's tradition. Truman's efforts in that direction are still of some embarrassment to his biographers. At one point in his campaign he opined that Marshal Stalin was personally a man of good will but, alas, a prisoner of the Politburo. Somewhat inconsistently he planned on the even of the election to score a coup by sending the Chief Justice of the United States to Moscow to confer with the "prisoner of the Politburo" and to restore the good relations fouled up by those two categories of villain in the eyes of American liberals: the "striped-pants diplomats" and the "hard-line Communists."[88]

The Soviets were correct to deduce that under such circumstances the

---

[88] Secretary Marshall's threat to resign led Truman to abandon this idea. Truman's explanation of his hopes deserves to be quoted: "If we could only get Stalin to unburden himself to someone on our side he felt he could trust fully, I thought we could get somewhere." Truman, *op. cit.*, II, 215.

American government was not likely to answer a Berlin blockade with an ultimatum or military demonstration. It was probably known through intelligence channels that many American and, especially, British military figures considered the Allies' position in Berlin untenable if subjected to Russian pressure and thought the three Western Powers' military effectives did not permit them even to think of a land war. Still, everything considered, the blockade was an exercise in what later became known as brinkmanship and, as such, must have been viewed with apprehension by some Soviet leaders. The Soviets still did not possess an atom bomb; an unexpectedly tough American stand would lead to a humiliating Soviet backdown. But the possible gains were enticing. The West might have to leave Berlin, in which case the West Germans were not likely to become obedient tools in the hands of American policy-makers. Or, more probably, the setting up of the West German state might be deferred or even abandoned, and then the damage to American prestige would be almost as great.

The actual story of the diplomatic side of the blockade will be given here in a most summary way. It was preceded by careful probing operations: demands by the Russians to examine passengers and freight on the Western military trains, and similar pinpricks and chicaneries. The Soviet representatives on the Allied Control Council and on the Berlin *Kommandatura* began to behave with that ferocious scowling and rudeness which to their American counterparts, with their national predilection for all-around cheerfulness and the memories of the Russians' quite different behavior over vodka and whisky, suggested that the Soviets were about to launch something desperate and not count the consequences. A man as level-headed as General Clay, inclined (subsequently) to call the Russian bluff, could wire Washington on March 5, 1948, that war "may come with dramatic suddenness."[89]

In May, alarmed by this behavior and concerned lest the Soviet government misinterpret the developments of the presidential election year, the American government instructed its ambassador to communicate with Molotov. Ambassador Smith read to the Russian statesman what amounted to a lesson on American politics—the bipartisan nature of American foreign policy, plus the generally benevolent and nonaggressive nature of American policies.[90] Ambassador Smith's *démarche*—like the later idea of sending Chief Justice Vinson to Stalin—aimed at reassuring the Russians about American intentions on the one hand, and impressing them with the firmness of the American resolve to contain Communist expansion on the other. But it is difficult to see how this could have succeeded; in

[89] As quoted in W. Philipps Davison, *The Berlin Blockade* (Princeton, 1958), p. 73.

[90] Smith, *op. cit.*, pp. 159–64.

all likelihood it deepened Soviet suspicions and doubts on both counts. The statement was couched in generalities; it offered no opening for the kind of secret bargaining that had been the preferred method of Soviet diplomacy. At the same time, the American request that the Molotov-Smith conversations be kept confidential suggested to the Kremlin that the Department of State was afraid that the American allies might draw the wrong conclusions from the bilateral conversation. With some relish Moscow released a statement about the conversations having taken place, and it remained to Secretary Marshall to explain lamely that the United States "had no intention of entering into bilateral negotiations with the Soviet Government on matters relating to the interests of other governments."[91] The Royal Institute of International Affairs' comment well summarizes the Russians' motives for indiscretion: "Western Europe discovering what was afoot, became hurt, because it had not been told, and alarmed, lest the Americans, always suspected of diplomatic ingenuousness and instability, should have switched to a new policy involving two-Power agreements to be concluded behind everybody else's backs."[92]

The blockade of Berlin, which began on June 24 with the cutting off of passenger and freight traffic to West Berlin, can be studied as a classic exercise of strategic-political pressure. The choice of the location was masterful: without massive supplies from the Western zones, Berlin could not be fed or provisioned with fuel. The Allies would have to leave or bow to the Soviet demands. The timing was equally dexterous. The election campaign was heating up in the United States; Britain was on the threshold of a serious economic crisis. The original Soviet explanations of the blockade were diffuse enough to allow retreat if the United States took drastic countersteps: sometimes it was alleged that the reason was the West German currency reform; sometimes the suspension of traffic was blamed on technical difficulties; other Soviet voices alleged the more basic reason of the Allies' repudiation of the Yalta and Potsdam agreements and their preparations for the West German state. It fell to a Soviet historian many years later to provide more original reasons for the blockade: "Those measures were taken in order to prevent bandit-like looting of Berlin's economy, precious cultures [sic], raw materials, and other treasures, and also to prevent the illegal infiltration of Berlin by speculators and agitators coming from the Western zone."[93]

[91] *Ibid.*, p. 166.

[92] *Survey of International Affairs, 1947–48* (London, 1952), p. 56. This volume carries the following most appropriate *envoi* from T. S. Eliot's *Cocktail Party:*
"They make noises and think they are talking to each other;
They make faces and think they understand each other;
And I'm sure they don't."

[93] Mileykovsky, *op. cit.*, p. 473.

The American commander, General Clay, and his political advisers favored calling the Soviet bluff and a demonstrative armed forcing of the railway blockade. But their voices did not prevail. What did take place was something that probably nobody had expected as a means of resolution of the crisis: the Anglo-American airlift managed to provide West Berlin with bare essentials for well nigh a year. Diplomatic attempts to solve the crisis proved unavailing. In August, the three Western ambassadors in Moscow had two conferences with Stalin. The despot chose to play a conciliatory and amiable role: no, the Soviets did not mean to push the West from Berlin; "we are still allies"; the trouble was in the West's attempt to set up its own German state. At times he seemed agreeable to the idea of lifting the blockade, but then the Western envoys would discover, in discussing the details with Molotov, that the old Soviet objectives and demands were being reiterated. The minimum Soviet demands embraced Soviet currency control in all of Berlin and such a statement on the question of the West German government as would, the Western Powers believed, lead the West Germans to suspect that their state was simply a bargaining point between the U.S. and the U.S.S.R. With the failure of direct negotiations, the issue was shifted to the foreign ministers' conference, that graveyard of international disputes, with the predictable result.

Only in May 1949, following confidential negotiations between American and Soviet representatives, was the blockade of Berlin lifted. The maximum Soviet aims had obviously not been achieved. The West German state was coming into being. On April 4, 1949, the North Atlantic Treaty was signed in Washington. Soviet hopes of an American weariness and disengagement over European affairs had not materialized; if anything the Berlin blockade had produced the opposite effect. To prolong the blockade meant needlessly prolonging the strain and danger.[94] But from the Soviet point of view the blockade was not a total loss: the West secured from them no new pledges on the access to Berlin. The demonstration of America's tenacity in standing by her rights was balanced by a demonstration of her unwillingness to risk a direct confrontation with the U.S.S.R. Even the *indirect* American response was not very forceful. A group of atomic bombers was flown to Britain, but there was no spectacular rise in America's military effectives in Europe. Since politicians in all cultures are adept at rationalizing their lack of success, it is quite possible that the Soviets persuaded themselves that the blockade had forced the Americans to drop their devious schemes of indirect aggression

[94] There are signs that the Russians were ready to give it up after the airlift proved effective even during winter conditions, but they stuck it out a few more months in the expectation that they might still get "something" for it.

and to revert to a defensive posture; even with their monopoly of atomic weapons, the Americans had not dared to risk a showdown.

1949 marked the end of one phase in Soviet-American relations. Both sides set up their "own" German states. The Soviet leaders could not close their eyes to one fact: the Soviet position in Germany became morally and psychologically much weaker as the result of the blockade and its failure; setting up the German Democratic Republic was an oblique acknowledgment that there was no point in trying to woo German nationalism or revive visions of a new Rapallo. The division of Germany became the symbol of the unsteady stalemate in Europe. The illusion of quadripartite control, of any lingering unity of purpose among the victors of World War II, finally disappeared. Both sides took steps to fortify their own positions: on the Western side, the cumbersome machinery and structure of NATO was erected; in the Soviet satellites purges and further consolidation of Soviet influence were designed to eliminate what remained, in fact or in the imagination of the Russian security personnel, of links to the Western world.

The study of the origins of the cold war will always be a fruitful field for those who mix their history with moralistic considerations, who over and beyond the facts seek an answer to "Who was guilty?" or "Who started it?" Then there are those who view this subject not ideologically but as a sequence of missed opportunities, of misunderstood signals. Had the Russians but seized upon the offer to join the Marshall Plan. . . . Had the West taken up Molotov's initiatives in the spring of 1947. . . .

The period is replete with historic ironies. America's monopoly of nuclear weapons lasted until the fall of 1949, and her economic preponderance in the world was never again to be as great. Yet for all this, the vision of Soviet armies sweeping to the English Channel panicked some American policy-makers. For their part, the Soviets appear to have been less alarmed by and responsive to American possession of the atom bomb, than by the implications of that most nonaggressive initiative of U.S. policy —the Marshall Plan. Perhaps the real responsibility for the cold war must be shared by the Founding Fathers and Lenin, who in creating their respective societies did not account for the roles they were called upon to play in that strange post-war world.

IX

THE END OF AN ERA

Had he lived until 1945, Lenin would have had the satisfaction of observing how many of his hopes for the post–World War I world were realized in the wake of World War II. Instead of ephemeral Communist regimes in Bavaria and Hungary, a galaxy of Communist-dominated states was rising in eastern and southeastern Europe. The British and French empires had been fatally weakened and were soon to distintegrate. In the Far East the main obstacle to the traditional aspirations of both Russia and Communism—Japan—lay prostrate. The Communist movement of China would make its bid for power and within four years succeed beyond the fondest expectations of the fathers of Communism. The Soviet Union was no longer the weak and underdeveloped country of the 1920's. To be sure, her splendid military victories obscured the extent of wartime devastation, and her post-war isolation from the Western world had to be enforced partly to conceal that devastation and the drastic new sacrifices imposed upon the people for the sake of rapid industrial recovery. But to the outside world Russia was one of the two main victors, one of the two super-powers, and her survival and triumphs were taken as proof of the viability of Communism and as exoneration from the charges which the era of the great purges and the Nazi-Soviet Pact had produced among the more fastidious fellow-travellers before 1941.

From the post-Revolutionary generation of Bolsheviks, such fantastic opportunities would have evoked a most activist foreign policy. As head of a state beset by civil war on several fronts, Lenin in 1918–19 contemplated sending Soviet troops to help the revolutions in Germany and Hungary, and, in the face of famine conditions over much of Russia, he offered food shipments to Germany. But after a generation in power, such idealistic and altruistic concepts were no longer compelling. Unlike Lenin, Stalin had no faith that Communist expansion was self-generating. It had to be shaped everywhere according to the interests and strength of the U.S.S.R. Above all, he and his assistants were conscious of the real weakness (albeit concealed from the rest of the world) of the U.S.S.R., of the risks of provoking the United States in the areas where she had indicated she had vital interests. And the full extent of Britain's weakness and her readiness to abandon her imperial responsibilities were not to become clear for some years. The prestige of the U.S.S.R. and of Stalin was so great that no non-Soviet Communist would have dared to raise his voice against the "Fatherland of Socialism" and its leader for not pursuing some of the most enticing prospects for the expansion of Communism. Yet we know that some of them chafed at the restraints—certain of the Greek Communist leaders, for example. There were those among the French Communists like André Marty who felt that the great prestige accumulated by the Party during the Resistance should be cashed in by a revolutionary action following the war.[1] But Stalin knew that it would be a direct and intolerable challenge to the Anglo-Americans to make this bid, and officials of the French Party still had high hopes of clinging to and expanding their influence in the government through constitutional means. We have already mentioned how the all-powerful Soviet Union's reluctance to risk war to get Trieste chagrined Tito and the Yugoslav Communists. An area as susceptible to Communist penetration as Latin America was consistently underplayed after the war (as it had been, for that matter, in the old Comintern days, when for quite different reasons the U.S.S.R. did not choose to ruffle the North American giant). In another area where the Americans displayed great sensitivity, China, the Soviets professed often and loudly their lack of interest in the local Communists. Why, they were not real Communists at all, Stalin and Molotov would at times assure their American visitors.[2]

In brief, the Soviet leaders sensibly enough concentrated on the area deemed of direct importance to the Soviet Union: eastern and southeastern Europe. They avoided any appearance of a many-sided frontal attack on the Old World's positions that would increase American suspicions and countermeasures. The policy was not without its inconsistencies. The

[1] Marty was to be ejected from the Communist Party in 1952, when the sins of his premature militancy of 1944–45 were revealed.

[2] How genuine those statements were will be considered below, pp. 470–74.

American Communists had gone so far in their wartime nationalist position that their leaders had virtually dissolved the Party and spoke glowingly about collaboration with progressive capitalists. This near self-immolation went too far in the closing months of the war, and they were nudged gently but firmly into a more realistic position, the shift involving the discarding of their overcommitted leader Earl Browder.

Again, this whole picture does not allow us to imagine a blueprint of action deposited in the Kremlin vaults marked "to be used once victory is secured" and imposed on world Communism step by step. The war had created fluid conditions in many Communist parties. Many leaders got into the habit of acting independently when, as before Stalingrad, the Soviets had more pressing duties than issuing detailed instructions to various foreign parties. For others, nationalism was no longer a pose but had become a habit and genuine belief. The dissolution of the Comintern was a gesture to appease the West, yet undoubtedly it was welcomed by many Communists who for all their veneration of Russia and Marshal Stalin longed, as most politicians do, for some independence and ability to operate on their own. There was certainly enough hesitation in Moscow to encourage such fissiparous tendencies well into 1947. Furthermore, the leaders of world Communism were only human: they could not be expected to deal simultaneously and efficiently with a baffling array of opportunities and dangers throughout the world, to assess scrupulously the claims to leadership of William Z. Foster vs. Earl Browder, the relative merits of the French Communists' nationalist position as against the demand for independence pressed by the Vietnamese Party, the Yugoslavs' imperialist claims in the Balkans as they affected the infant Albanian Communist organization, etc.

During the first phase of their conflict with Moscow, the Yugoslav Communists allowed themselves a playful fantasy which today appears to have been endowed with elements of prophecy. It was unfortunate, held the Yugoslavs, that following the war a major country like France did not fall under Communist domination. Once in power, the French Communists' servile attitude toward Moscow would inevitably have been transformed into stout defiance. Stalinism would thus be challenged not only by a small Balkan country (their own) but by a leading Western Power, and the nature of international Communism would be changed. Few today might endorse this historical dream as enthusiastically as a harassed official of the State Department: a Communist France would have clung tenaciously to her empire, sparing America her troubles and dilemmas in Vietnam and North Africa. The need to pursue the "French road to socialism" would have brought Thorez and his successors into violent conflict with Moscow, and they would then have been unable to be as unpleasant and abrasive to the Americans as General de Gaulle. Yet a price would be paid: Picasso would have had to paint glaring canvasses in the "socialist realist" manner; Mlles. Sagan and de Beauvoir would not have been able to write their books; French cuisine would have suffered. . . . Anyway, at the same time the Yugoslavs put high hopes in the Chinese Communists. When wishes materialize, they often do so in a most unexpected form. . . .

The paradoxical insight contained in this Titoist analysis does, however, fit the paradox of politics after World War II: countries have been saved by their recent enemies, states and empires have been pulled down by their alliances. And the fantastic success of Communism in spreading both as an ideology and as a power system has spelled its disintegration as a monolithic system.

Prior to 1948 such forebodings probably did not enter the mind of the Soviet leaders. The weak and isolated Soviet Russia of the 1920's and 1930's had dominated the Communist movement, and the liquidation or defection of people as famous as Trotsky and Bukharin could not shake this domination. It appeared incredible that even the most prestigious foreign Communist could defy the Soviet Union and Stalin or, if he did so, that he would not be repudiated by his own followers. But problems of coordination and synchronization of Communist policies were obviously pressing. To deal with foreign Communists in control of their own states was obviously not the same thing as dealing with them when they were small and often persecuted minorities.

The need for a *formal* framework uniting at least some Communist parties was then felt strongly in Moscow by the summer of 1947. It was underlined by the unsynchronized reactions of European parties to the Marshall Plan, and by Moscow's desire to enforce its commands through the means of an agency where several Communist parties would be associated on a formal basis of equality. It would have been awkward to revive the Comintern barely four years after its dissolution. Furthermore, an all-inclusive organization appeared at the time to be inconvenient. There would be a great hue and cry in the United States if the American Communists were once again to be found within the framework of an International. And, for different reasons, it was equally undesirable to have the Asian Communist parties, especially the Chinese one, in the same organization with those of the European satellites. The French Communists had displayed ambivalent feelings concerning the Vietnamese struggle for independence, and a confrontation with their ideological brethren from Vietnam or Algeria might well lead to trouble. So the new organization was to unite the parties of the U.S.S.R., her European satellites (with the exception of Albania), France, and Italy. The omission of Albania was understandable insofar as she was dominated by Yugoslavia and slated, if Russia (which was developing increasing doubts on the subject) would sanction it, to be absorbed by Marshal Tito's enterprise.

The new organization was launched in an atmosphere of rather naïvely contrived mystification. Thus it was announced that representatives of the nine Communist parties met in September "near Warsaw" at the initiative of the Polish Communist Party, whereas actually the meeting was in Silesia, some distance from Warsaw, and the initiative did not come from the Polish Party, whose chief, Gomulka, was dubious about the whole business. Adding to this unnecessary air of conspiracy there was an equally awkward attempt to conceal the purpose and character of the organization. It was, if you please, but an innocent enterprise designed to enable the nine fraternal parties to exchange information, to compare their experiences, to learn from each other by mutual and frank discussion. Presumably, the Bulgarian Communists would tell their Rumanian colleagues that they did not pay enough attention to propaganda. "But you Bulgarians neglect agitation," the Rumanians would retort. Hence the name Communist Information Bureau, to confound the slanderers who maintained that Communists were directed from Moscow. The seat of the organization was to be in Belgrade. Its journal was to bear the name "For a Lasting Peace, For a People's Democracy," the title designed by Stalin himself, a fact which silenced the objections of some delegates who felt that while it expressed noble sentiments it departed from the usual brisk nomenclature of Communist journals: *Truth, Unity, The People's Voice*, etc.

Apart from such puerilities, the business of the conference was serious. Zhdanov delivered his "two camps" analysis of the world situation: a warning that collaboration between the U.S.S.R. and the West was now definitely a thing of the past and that those present should draw the clear conclusions from this fact. The attack on the French and Italian Communists meant the end of their hopes of sharing or acquiring governmental power through constitutional means; at the same time, as it was noted above, they were *not* given the license for full-scale revolutionary action. They were simply to disrupt and destroy any prospects for success of the European Recovery Plan. The Yugoslavs joined in this attack with special gusto. They were still in a state of arrogant euphoria, basking in the—alas, erroneous—impression that they were the favorites of Moscow and the future masters of the Balkans. The fury of the Frenchman Duclos and the Italian Longo was thus understandable: they were accustomed to bowing to the Russians, but not to those Balkan barbarians! One year later they had occasion for revenge.

There was, to be sure, an "exchange of information." If Zhdanov issued instructions on the international situation, Malenkov described the measures being taken in Russia to purify the atmosphere of cosmopolitanism and the Soviet policies in culture and science where "idealistic" and "cosmopolitan" influences were being erased in favor of Lysenko, *et al.* The implication was clear: Russian standards as to what was proper in the arts, literature, and science were to be applied in other Communist parties as well. This was something new, even by the standards of pre-1939 Communist uniformity. Picasso might be a loyal member of the French Communist Party, an invaluable asset of the "struggle for peace," but woe to the French Communist who would now state publicly his preference for Picasso's painting as against those glaringly "realistic" canvasses so much *en vogue* in the "Fatherland of Socialism."

The Cominform was thus launched on its brief and uneventful life. It became clear that it was not to function as a general staff of world Communism, for such an institution already existed in the machinery of the Central Committee of the Communist Party of the U.S.S.R. The Soviet personnel assigned to the Cominform's headquarters in Belgrade were a dreary mixture of second-rate political propagandists and secret service men, some allegedly combining the two vocations. The Cominform journal with its insufferable name carried dreary exegeses of Communist propaganda, surpassing in dullness even domestic Soviet efforts in this line.

In fact, it is something of a mystery what exactly the Cominform was supposed to accomplish. The caliber of the people assigned to it certainly does not allow us to assume that it was endowed with any policy functions or even with any initiative concerning the more important propaganda moves. It lacked entirely the heady atmosphere of the Comintern during its first years. The most reasonable conjecture must be that the Cominform was to serve to cover up the increasingly centralized direction of foreign Communism now assumed by the Soviet Union and especially as the means through which she could rap the knuckles of a dissident member Party—the rebuke or discipline coming ostensibly not from the Kremlin but from the collective body. If so, the device was amazingly transparent, but excessive subtlety is not always characteristic of Soviet endeavors.

Within one year the Soviet-Yugoslav dispute and the failure of the Cominform to resolve it deprived the organization of any real reason for existence. It lingered on for a few years longer in the now more hospitable location of Bucharest, but it was clearly a fifth wheel. Finally, with Khrushchev in power, the Soviet Union resolved to erase Stalin's blunder, and the Cominform, a standing monument to that blunder, was allowed to die an inglorious death.

The Soviet-Yugoslav crisis that erupted in March and became known to the world in June 1948 shook the "people's democracies" (as the European satellites of Russia were known) and was a portent of incalculable importance for the future of Communism. Few phases of Soviet foreign policy are equally well documented, and none offers a better example of how this usually subtle and devious policy was occasionally capable of the most monumental blunders, how Stalin and his associates, capable on occasion of outwitting statesmen as formidable as Churchill, were at other times, through childish arrogance combined perhaps with senile suspiciousness, drawn into the most unnecessary crises and defeats. Unlike Russia's dispute with China, an almost inescapable clash between two huge states, there was nothing inevitable about the quarrel with Yugoslavia.

Tito and his group were content to remain faithful servitors of the Soviet Union. They had excessive pride in their own achievement: at the founding meeting of the Cominform, Kardelj, Tito's right-hand man, had the bad taste to emphasize that their victory, unlike the Communist victories in the other "people's democracies," did not depend on Soviet help, that they began their uprising against the Germans *before* Germany's attack on the U.S.S.R.—a statement that was as tactless as it was inaccurate. The Yugoslavs had their own expansionist plans, but at times the Soviets looked indulgently on these ambitions. It was "inconvenient," said Stalin, that some Albanian Communists would commit suicide for fear of being disgraced for their anti-Yugoslav views, but "we agree to Yugoslavia swallowing Albania."[3] Tito had still greater digestive ambitions: Bulgaria too was to be united with Yugoslavia; despite the fact that Bulgaria was not "little" Albania, despite the prominence of the Bulgarian Communists, there was little doubt which would be the boss of this new federation. And the help the Yugoslavs extended to the Greek Communists carried with it the implication that the latter, if successful in their civil war, would contribute Greek Macedonia to Tito's federation. Even greater territorial ambitions passed through the mind of the masterful Yugoslav leader. But if these plans were beginning to be bothersome to Russia, and if Tito's provocative attitude toward the West at times went beyond what the Russians might have wished, still they had it within their power to bring Tito down a peg and to smooth over the situation without a full-blown crisis and their first defeat in intra-Communist relations.

What perturbed the Russians most, it is clear, was the extent of Tito's hold on his party and state. Not only was he the leader of the Yugoslav Communist Party; with all the prestige of his wartime achievement, he was idolized by his closest associates in a way that was unique in Communist parties, whose leaders for the most part were creatures of Moscow (as Tito had been when he was made Secretary General in 1937) and

[3] Milovan Djilas, *Conversations With Stalin* (New York, 1962), p. 143. The fastidious Yugoslav Communist was shocked by the crudity of the expression.

whose subordinates watched anxiously for signs of Moscow's displeasure. In Yugoslavia, Russia's attempts to subvert the Party and to recruit disgruntled Yugoslav Communists into her services were bringing meager results.[4] Tito was a Communist of old standing and one with great personal loyalty to Stalin, but he was at the same time a man of cunning with a strong instinct for self-preservation. He had spent some time in Moscow during the period of the great purge and did not need to be taught about what happens to those whom Moscow discards.

In their pique, the Russians—or, if we are to believe the post-1953 revelations, Stalin and Molotov personally—in January 1948 vetoed plans for a Balkan federation. The Yugoslavs responded with countermeasures against the handful of Party and army leaders who were known to be in the direct service of Moscow. (One of them, Andrija Hebrang, according to the official story, hanged himself in jail. His more fortunate partner in treason, Sreten Zhujovich, who furnished the Soviet ambassador with information as to what went on at Central Committee meetings, later on recanted, was released from jail, and published the story of the Soviet intrigue and subversion.[5]) In March there began a correspondence between the central committees of the Soviet and Yugoslav parties, which, when published later on, was an eye-opener as to the atmosphere prevailing in intra-Communist circles.[6] The Soviet letters, signed by Stalin and Molotov, are appalling in their crudeness and brutality. There is hardly any pretense of addressing fellow Communists, still less the rulers of a supposedly independent state. They are written in a tone of a superior addressing his servants. The Soviet grievances range from unself-conscious impudence —how dare the Yugoslavs object to the Russians subverting their Party and state, recruiting agents in Yugoslav institutions, etc.?—to paranoid insinuations—the Soviets informed Tito that such-and-such Yugoslav officials were British agents (no proof is given nor had any been, evidently), yet they have not been fired or punished!

Then the Soviet correspondents, almost as an afterthought, hit on the ideological deviations. Yugoslavs are not collectivizing agriculture fast enough. (At the time the charge was made the Yugoslavs had gone further in collectivization than any other "people's democracy" and prior to this time the Russians had objected that they were collectivizing too fast.) At the same time, the solicitous Russians alleged, to cover up their

---

[4] For the background of the dispute see Adam B. Ulam, *Titoism and the Cominform* (Cambridge, Mass., 1952), pp. 69–95.

[5] *Ibid.*, pp. 112–13.

[6] Most of it was translated in Royal Institute of International Affairs, *The Soviet-Yugoslav Dispute: Text of the Published Correspondence* (London, 1948).

"Bukharinite" agrarian policies Tito and his associates were overly hasty in nationalizing medium and small industry—thus combining ultra-left and ultra-right policies.

The third line of accusations would be humorous if it did not reveal a tragic lack of introspection on the part of the Russian leaders. The Communist Party of Yugoslavia is run, if you please, undemocratically. The most important matters are settled within the closed circle of the Politburo—in fact by the dictator and three or four of his associates. Even the Central Committee of the Yugoslav Party is not informed of the more important issues—like, for example, Soviet dissatisfaction with the way things are run.

In their replies, the Yugoslavs chose to adopt a conciliatory rather than indignant tone. They expressed genuine shock and chagrin at the charges and the hope (which was not to die for some time) that Stalin and his associates had been misinformed by their subordinates and by circles hostile to Tito. Yet at the same time the Yugoslav rejoinder was written with dignity and a restrained sense of grievance at the injustice and absurdity of many of the charges. Much as they loved the Soviet Union, explained Tito and his comrades, they could not love their country less. Thus a nationalist theme was fused onto what began as a power struggle.

The conflict was brought into the open with a Cominform communiqué issued at its meeting in Bucharest on June 28. This message castigated Tito and his associates for their nationalist deviations and their policy of "discrediting the Soviet Union." The "healthy elements" of the Communist Party of Yugoslavia were called upon to replace their unworthy leaders.

If Stalin expected that the last injunction would be speedily realized, he was in for one of the most unpleasant surprises of his life. Most of the Yugoslav Communists united around their leadership. Those who did so less than enthusiastically were dealt with by the secret police. The Fifth Congress of the Yugoslav Communist Party (the first one since 1928!) was held in July, and it approved the policy of the leadership. The latter possibly sincerely still took the line that the conflict was not irrevocable, that Comrade Stalin would come to understand the baselessness of the Russian charges.

The first major international repercussion of the Soviet-Yugoslav split was the virtual collapse of the Greek Communist movement. Its leadership had been intimately connected with Tito; Yugoslavia was its main sanctuary and base of supplies. Now the compromised leaders were purged by Moscow, and when in 1949 the Yugoslavs stopped aiding the Greek partisans, they became unable to withstand the offensive of government troops. We have the Yugoslavs' rather dubious testimony that Stalin had always viewed the Greek rebellion with dislike. In any case, it now became a very secondary affair in comparison with the necessity of suppressing another rebellion, that of Yugoslavia. Within a year it became clear that no *internal* force was going to upset Tito and his group. And in turn their attitude hardened: from specific complaints, they moved to a general attack on Soviet imperialism and a general critique of Stalinism as a monstrous perversion of the ideas of Communism. This position was to gain Tito some sympathy among circles in Yugoslavia that previously had had no use for him and his regime. In 1950, he cautiously began to liberalize his policies, and within a few years this led to the abandonment of the most doctrinaire and economically disastrous measures such as collectivization.

A history of Titoism does not belong in this study. It is sufficient to say here that the Yugoslavs soon felt the need to endow their schism with an ideology, to introduce features in their regime designed to demonstrate that theirs was a "pure" Leninist Communism as distinguished from its perversion under Stalin. Yet for all their considerable—and at times genuinely inspired—measures in that direction, they, no more than Stalin's successors in Russia, could change the basic reality of a one-party state and the attendant repression and denial of freedom. The Yugoslav regime grew more enlightened and less doctrinaire, it eliminated unnecessary and pathological repression. Yet it had recourse to police measures whenever its basic dictatorial structure and premises were challenged.

Yugoslavia could hardly become a rival of the U.S.S.R. But given the psychopathology of Stalinism the survival of a Communist regime that had defied Moscow was bound to have violent repercussions. "Tito and his clique" soon were denounced as counterrevolutionaries, then as agents of American imperialism.[7] Frontier accidents on the borders of Yugoslavia and the satellites became a common occurrence. Bulgaria advanced her claims to Yugoslav Macedonia. In Albania the pro-Yugoslav elements of the Communist Party were liquidated, and this small country became again a direct satellite of Moscow.

The ferocity of the propaganda assault on Yugoslavia would have made it reasonable to expect military action. The country was open to invasion from several directions, and the split with the U.S.S.R. did not at first make Yugoslavia popular in the West. Certainly had a Russian attack come in 1948 it is most unlikely that the West would have been forthcoming with any help, and the same can probably be said about 1949. But by 1950, with NATO constituted, with Yugoslavia's relations with

---

[7] Nobody, not even American capitalists and military men, were depicted with the ferocity which the Soviet press showed toward Tito between 1949 and 1953. A favorite motif in Soviet cartoons of the time was Tito as a dog being led on a leash by an appropriately villainous American capitalist.

the West on a friendlier basis, and finally with the eruption of the Korean War, a precipitous move against the schismatic Communists would have been too risky. It is probably right to say that until 1950 Russia expected internal convulsions in Yugoslavia to enable her to get rid of Tito and that after 1950 outright military intervention was judged too dangerous. Once again, the Stalinist paranoid behavior was paralleled by caution when the wider international implications were considered.

This paranoia became evident in Soviet policies in the satellites. The reverberations of Titoism were to cost many East European Communists their lives and many others their freedom. The cautious tempo of sovietization in the satellites was jettisoned. Violent measures were adopted to assimilate the political and economic pattern of the "people's democracies" to that of the Soviet Union. Thus a drastic tempo of collectivization was imposed, even though in some countries until a few months earlier the Communists had pledged, evidently sincerely, that the peasants' property would not be interfered with for a long time. The mere postulation of "separate ways to socialism"—a commonplace with the Communist leaders between 1945 and 1948—now became a crime.

A sober analysis of the situation in the satellites would have revealed that none of them was capable of following the example of Yugoslavia. Some still had Russian troops stationed in their territory. No other Communist leader in Eastern Europe enjoyed the kind of domination over the Party, army, and state machinery that was Tito's. The very weakness of the Communist parties in those countries acted against the possibility of a successful challenge of Moscow. The whole rationale of the Polish Communists' domination of their country was based on the assumption that any challenge to it would be suppressed by *Soviet* troops. How, then, could the Polish Communists, no matter what their grievances against Russia, even dream of following Yugoslavia's example? But such rational considerations seldom swayed the Russians during Stalin's era, once the underlying suspiciousness was aroused, not to say permitted to blossom into hysteria and spy mania. The Soviets' conspiratorial methods and mentality led them on the slightest provocation to see plots and far-flung conspiracies against them. And after all, the Soviet Union herself was between 1949 and 1953 in the throes of another purge, which, had Stalin survived for a year or two, would most likely have assumed the horrendous proportions of the ones in 1936–38. "A defection within Communist ranks, no matter how personal or apolitical may be its background, sends a tremor throughout the whole system. Pressure is exerted at every level of the Party and government, and those having personal ties with the accused, or even a similar background, become automatically suspect and liable to political destruction."[8]

[8] Ulam, *op. cit.*, p. 145.

The purge of the Communist parties of Europe between 1948 and 1953 affected in the first place the leaders and officials who had aroused the displeasure or suspicion of the Russians. Gomulka, the Secretary General of the Communist Party of Poland, had been dubious about the foundation of the Cominform. Through inexperience rather than a deliberate posture (he had emerged from the Communist underground in wartime Poland and never had a prolonged training in Moscow), he failed to follow every twist and turn of Soviet policies. As late as June 1948 he wondered aloud whether Tito should not be negotiated with rather than peremptorily condemned. Now a series of disasters descended on the head of this loyal but unsophisticated Communist. He was fired as Secretary General. Within a year he was to be stripped of his governmental position. Imprisoned in 1951, he escaped a worse fate and lived to see a dramatic reversal in his fortunes only because of the timely demise of the "genius-like leader" of world Communism in 1953. Traicho Kostov, in Bulgaria, had protested in an incautious moment against Soviet exploitation of his country. Now in December 1949, after a series of demotions, he was brought finally before the court and this erstwhile factual ruler of Bulgaria was executed as a Titoist and Western spy. In fact, Kostov had been known as a bitter enemy of Tito and as hostile to Bulgaria's union with Yugoslavia.[9]

Now the pattern was set: massive purges affected each of the satellites. Some of the most prominent Communist leaders were arrayed in court where, like their Russian counterparts in the 1930's, they promptly confessed to an amazing and improbable variety of crimes: Titoism, collusion with the Germans during the war, with American and British intelligence personnel after it, etc. A charge of increasing popularity was one of having been recruited for American intelligence through the agency of international Zionism. Charges of complicity between Zionism and Titoism were raised as early as 1949 in the trial of the former Hungarian minister of the interior, Rajk, and later in the trial of Rudolf Slansky (himself a Jew) in Czechoslovakia. From then on the accusation of a Zionist-imperialist conspiracy were repeated in purge trials throughout the satellites, and the anti-Semitic motif was also a strong element in the Soviet Union during Stalin's last years, one of the victims being a former deputy minister of foreign affairs, Solomon Lozovsky, as well as other prominent Jewish writers and public figures.

As is characteristic of such operations, the purges transcended any conscious or even half-rational purpose of weeding out the anti-Russian

---

[9] The Yugoslav Communists' emancipation from the mentality of Stalinism was, at the time, still so incomplete that Kostov's initial disgrace and then arrest were greeted with gloating, Tito himself accusing the Bulgarian leader of having been an *agent-provocateur*.

or even potentially intransigent elements. In many cases, intra-Party or personal scores were being settled, the satellite leader having Moscow's ear managing to dispose of his rival by branding him a Titoist or Western spy. Rajk in Hungary was obviously a potential rival of the Party boss Rakosi; Slansky in Czechoslovakia was too influential to please President Klement Gottwald. Similar clashes took place at lower levels of authority and then spread, again as in Russia, to the supporters, friends, and relatives of the victims. Stalin's death arrested the process before it reached the extent of the great purge of the 1930's. In 1956 and after, the chief victims were posthumously exonerated, and the revelations attending this "rehabilitation" were instrumental in touching off the unrest in the satellites culminating in the Hungarian revolt.

The purges were viewed from Moscow not only as a weeding out of traitors and waverers, but also as a necessary prophylactic step in view of the polarization of international politics. They not only affected the ruling class, but spread to all levels of society. Any link with the non-Communist past was severed. The repression of religious bodies, especially of the Catholic Church, attained new intensity. (An intermediate aim in those years was to break the connections between the various East European branches of the Catholic Church and Rome, to create in fact national churches that would be as docile toward the Communist governments as the Orthodox Church was in Russia.)

Soviet policies in the satellites between 1949 and 1953 (as a matter of fact the momentum of the purges went on for a year or so after Stalin's death, and in some countries, like Poland, 1954 was the year of the most intense repression) seemingly put an end to any hope that there could be a half-way house between national independence and Communist domination. The Soviet aim was such a political and social transformation of the "people's democracies" that there would be no possibility of "separate roads to socialism," not to mention Titoism, being raised again in them. In 1950 this aim appeared to be close to realization: a feeling of despondency and hopelessness pervaded the satellites, their Communist parties were completely cowed and submissive. But it did not require much insight to see that a sharp international conflict, or an internal perturbation in Russia, would reveal the weakness of the Soviet grip on those countries.

Most of all, the Yugoslav-Russian conflict showed the fatal flaw in the whole international concept of Communism, the inherent self-contradiction of its expansionist and missionary goal.

An ideology which in its essence is nothing but a worship of power by its very victories must endanger the power system which propagates it. Because Tito and his group were devout Stalinists, they could not part voluntarily with their rule, even when threatened with the hostility of the very people they had worshipped. And in their rebellion they demonstrated that, for the rulers of Russia, the Communist fanaticism of their foreign colleagues is a poor substitute for a purely mechanical system of controlling the Communist parties abroad. The latter, and especially those in power, present the rulers of Russia with a veritable dilemma. A strong Communist regime is not unlikely to develop the virus of Titoism, which is nothing but Stalinism transplanted to a foreign soil.[10]

These words were written in 1951, when it could not be foreseen how in two years Stalin's death would drastically transform the whole problem, how his successors would strive to supplant the purely administrative and police controls of foreign Communism with a new ideological meaning, and how in this effort they would find themselves on the brink of disaster in East Germany, Poland, and Hungary.

The Yugoslav story loomed large in international politics between 1948 and 1954, and we shall return to its impact on Soviet policy after 1950. In the late 1950's and 1960's the Titoist controversy came to be overshadowed by a much more basic and important intra-Communist split. Yet it would be unwise to minimize it. The Yugoslav Party, of all Communist parties, had the best reasons and opportunity to be friendly to and understanding of the West: they had received generous help and recognition during the war from none other than Churchill, at a time when Moscow could provide little and its advice for Tito was to conceal the Communist character of his movement until the proper time. Yet during the first two years after the war no branch of international Communism was as defiant toward the West, as militant and ready with provocation— whether on the issue of Trieste or by shooting American planes that strayed over Yugoslav territory. Then, within two years of their clash with Stalin, the Yugoslav Communists were to find themselves in perfect comity with the United States and Britain, recipients of Western aid, and shortly afterward allies of *monarchist* Greece. None of those phases and transformations was purely tactical or purely cynical: to a large extent they corresponded to the psychological evolution of the rulers of Yugoslavia.

"I shall shake my little finger and there will be no more Tito," Khrushchev reported Stalin as saying at the outset of the dispute. This statement is of dubious veracity; it belongs with such assertions of the voluble First Secretary about his predecessor as that he had studied military situations on a globe, etc. But there must have been people in the Soviet officialdom who felt that the Soviets were overreacting to the Yugoslavs' impudence, that diplomacy rather than pressure and subversion was the proper way to deal with the problem. Still, there was a degree of reason in Stalin's

[10] Ulam, *op. cit.*, p. 231.

madness: there was no point in the expansion of Communism if the regimes of the new Communist states had to be dealt with on a basis of
equality. As long as he lived the tyrant could have the satisfaction of
knowing that his anti-Yugoslav policy "worked," i.e., the alleged deviation
was localized. The Soviet grip on the satellites was tightened. As in the
case of Trotskyism in the 1930's, so Titoism gained but a handful of adherents outside the Soviet bloc, its reverberations in such parties as the
French and Italian ones were insignificant. The present official Soviet
view is that while Stalin's original anathema was a mistake, so was
Khrushchev's overly eager attempt after 1955 to domesticate Titoism and
to drag Yugoslavia back into the Soviet camp. Reading between the lines
of the current Soviet commentaries about the dispute, understandably
brief and restrained, one gets a strong impression of nostalgia for the
Stalinist pattern of domination of international Communism and the feeling that somehow in 1948 the charm was broken and things have never
been the same.

Had Communist expansion in the post-war years been confined to
Eastern Europe, perhaps that transformation of world Communism would
not have been so extreme and significant. The quantitative weight of the
Soviet Union in relation to any single satellite or even compared with them
all would have assured Soviet domination, if not in the Stalinist manner
then in the modified form for which Khrushchev was striving after 1957–
58. But the Communist conquest of China was to dwarf the implications
of the Tito affair.

In Western historiography the victory of the Chinese Communists has
produced a greater polarization of views and a greater emotional intensity
with which those views are expressed than any other event in modern
history. There is hardly any common ground between those who view the
victory of the Chinese Communists as "inevitable"—a product of the grim
forces of history, the result of their opponents' corruption and the consequent indignation of the Chinese peasant against Chiang's government—
and those who view it as the result of Western, especially American, ineptitude and naïveté, if not indeed of a conspiracy which, having spread
to various agencies of the U.S. government, hampered and then paralyzed
the timely help that could have saved Chiang Kai-shek and kept China in
the "free world." And the subject has inevitably become entangled in
domestic political disputes in the United States.

The situation is further complicated by the enormous importance of the
Chinese issue to the Soviet Union. Khrushchev chose to be indiscreet and
occasionally truthful about various aspects of Stalin's foreign policy. Yet
on the despot's attitude toward Chinese Communism and its triumph he

kept almost silent. On their own part, the Chinese Communists, engaged in ever more violent quarrels with Stalin's successors, needless to say have not chosen to depart from the official version of the dead leader as a "great Marxist-Leninist" whose successors have betrayed him through their "revisionism" and unseemly accusations. Thus we are largely in the dark as to what must be the fascinating story of Stalin's expectations of and relations with the Chinese between 1945 and 1953, his reactions to their triumph, and whether he realized that China was not a small East European country but a threatening colossus that would not preserve the attitude toward the Soviet Union of a Bulgaria or Rumania.

The turn of events since 1960 has rendered superficial plausibility to the view of some historians that the relations between the Russians and the Chinese Communists had *always* been strained, that Stalin from the beginning distrusted Mao and disapproved of his tactics of securing the revolution by reliance on peasants rather than workers, etc. Yet there are few facts to justify this projection of the dispute back to the distant days of the 1920's or 1930's. No *public* criticism of Moscow by the Chinese Communists dating back to those days can be substantiated. Like every other Communist Party, so the Chinese acquiesced in the belief that their interests had to be subordinated to those of the "Fatherland of Socialism." If there was emotional resentment of the memories of the late 1920's, of Moscow's demand in the 1930's that they collaborate with Chiang Kai-shek, or of the Soviet-Japanese nonaggression pact of 1941, then they had to be suppressed and rationalized, just as had been those, say, of the German Communists after the Molotov-Ribbentrop pact. If Moscow disapproved of Mao, then again this fact is not documented. At the Seventh Congress of the Comintern in 1935 the mention of Mao's name was greeted with an ovation, a sign that officially he was acknowledged as being in the same category as Thorez or Thälmann, a faithful follower of the Soviet Union and Stalin. It is a bit naïve to attribute Moscow displeasure to Mao's basing his movement on peasants rather than workers: such ideological-tactical niceties never disturbed the Kremlin in Stalin's era; from his followers Stalin expected obedience and success, and the socio-economic basis of any Communist movement, provided it satisfied those criteria, was of secondary importance. Once a power clash occurred the old ideological reservations would be remembered and indeed magnified, just as on the other side those occasions when the interests of one's party had to be sacrificed because of Soviet orders and interests would be remembered and bitterly recalled—witness the Yugoslav case.

To be sure, Mao's position had differed from that of other stalwarts insofar as his party did control some territory and did possess an armed force of its own. Like any astute Communist leader—Tito between 1942 and 1945, say—Mao could combine loyalty to the Soviet Union with a shrewd policy of eliminating his own potential rivals. That the Soviet Union did grant important aid to the Chinese Communists in their struggle first to survive and then to gain power is confirmed by the unimpeachable testimony of Chou En-lai. With the Soviet-Chinese dispute already reaching an acute stage and prior to his walking out of the Twenty-second Congress of the CPSU, Chou chose to acknowledge this aid. Thus the argument that there had been substantive differences in the relationship of the Chinese Communists to Moscow from that of any other Communist Party cannot be documented. All the available evidence points the other way.

There was, to be sure, a very strong incentive both for Moscow and for the Chinese Communists to stress that the latter were "different," perhaps not Communists at all, but essentially "agrarian reformers" with tenuous links at best with the U.S.S.R. Reports along this line, which began to emerge in the early 1930's and were propagated sometimes by impartial observers but sometimes by partial ones (among the latter was the famous Dean of Canterbury, Dr. Hewlett Johnson, a devoted friend of Communism and the U.S.S.R.) had their rationale in obvious exigencies of Soviet foreign policy. At least from the late 1920's the avowed Soviet aim was to get American support in the Far East to stave off the Japanese menace, and the chances of acquiring this support would not be increased by an open avowal of a link between Moscow and the CCP. And after 1931 another priority of Soviet policy was to prevent any *rapprochement* between Chiang Kai-shek's Nationalist government and the Japanese. While the Chinese Nationalists were likely to be skeptical about the Chinese Communists' independence from Moscow, they could perhaps appreciate the oriental punctilio expressed by such disavowals.

With the end of the war approaching, the Soviet position in the Far East began to pass from one of danger to one of opportunity. It was natural that the summer of 1943, following Stalingrad and the definite turn for the better in the fortunes of the war, should see public Soviet criticism of the Chinese Nationalist regime and extensive references to the Chinese Communists.[11] (For some years before that, the Chinese Communists had been virtually unmentioned and much praise had been given to Chiang Kai-shek for his anti-Japanese stand.)

At the same time the Chinese Communists continued to maintain the united anti-Japanese front stipulated by their agreement with Chiang Kai-shek in 1937 and recognized his authority as the national leader. But strains in this unnatural alliance were there from the beginning, and since 1941 there had been occasional armed clashes between the Communists

[11] Charles B. McLane, *Soviet Policy and the Chinese Communists, 1931–1946* (New York, 1958), p. 167.

and Nationalists. With the defeat of Japan now virtually certain, both sides were obviously preparing for the possibility of a renewal of the civil war.

On the surface Soviet deference toward Chiang's regime continued unabated well beyond the victory in Asia. In private Stalin no less than Churchill took a skeptical view of the American position that China was a Great Power either actually or potentially. The Russians had realistic reasons to treat skeptically this infatuation of Roosevelt and his advisers with China, and their efforts to enhance Chiang's prestige, etc.[12] They had every reason to know how Chiang's position had been built up through arrangements with local warlords, to know of the weakness and corruption of his governmental machinery and the virtual absence of military effort on his part against the Japanese. It is unlikely that they realized the full weakness of his position or that in four years he would lose all of mainland China to his rivals. They were apt to judge by precedents and history, and for all his weakness Chiang had come close to rendering the Communists a death blow between 1934 and 1936. The probable Soviet assumption—that Chiang was too strong to be entirely eliminated but too weak to weld China into a united and powerful country—argued for the desirability of continued friendly relations with his regime. He was not powerful enough to replace Japan as a threat to the U.S.S.R., he would be amenable to Soviet pressures and renewed penetration of various areas of traditional interest to Russia. In one border province, Sinkiang, the Soviets acquiesced in Chiang's liquidation of the predominant Russian interest in 1943. But in the course of 1944 and 1945 they made it clear that they would not tolerate similar efforts in Outer Mongolia. Her neighbor, little Tannu Tuva, like Mongolia officially a part of China but in fact for decades a dependency of Russia, was in 1944 officially annexed to the U.S.S.R., probably a warning of what would happen should Chiang dare raise the issue of Outer Mongolia.

We do not know what role the Chinese Communists played in these calculations. But it is clear that they were to serve as insurance against American domination of China. That the Communists could conquer all of China was unlikely; that they would continue to control large areas in northern China was probable. Thus, whether in open conflict with Chiang

---

[12] Reasons for this infatuation are complex. Their roots are to be found in the connection through American missionary and philanthropic work, etc. But in addition there was a definite feeling that while there was a degree of sinfulness about America's main allies, Britain being "imperialist" and Russia Communist, Chiang's China represented a newly born and struggling democracy. Harry Hopkins, in a memorandum on foreign affairs written not long before his death, referred to China becoming before long most important to America's foreign policy (true!) and the United States' most likely partner in carrying democracy throughout the world (alas!).

or in some coalition arrangement with him, they would remain an effective brake upon too great an accession of power to China and upon American predominance. The only fly in the ointment was the possibility that after the war the Americans might render such massive help to Chiang as to enable him to do what he had been unable to do with the assistance of German military advisers before 1936, i.e., liquidate the Chinese Communists and establish an effective government that would resist Soviet claims in Manchuria, Mongolia, etc. Hence as one studies Soviet diplomacy on China vis-à-vis American policy in the last phase of the war, one is struck by the fact that its main motif was to convince the Americans that Chinese Communists were not Communists at all and that the United States should take the initiative in attempting to reconcile them with Chiang Kai-shek in a real coalition, as distinguished from the uneasy coexistence they had maintained during the war, and to live happily ever after.

Thus in September 1944 Ambassador Patrick Hurley, President Roosevelt's special representative to Chiang, stopped in Moscow on his way to China, then reeling under a lightning Japanese offensive. Here he heard from Molotov that the so-called Chinese Communists "were related to Communism in no way at all. It was merely a way of expressing dissatisfaction with their economic condition and they would forget this inclination when their economic condition improved."[13] This was a breathtaking lie, so much more amazing than similar Soviet statements about Tito, the Lublin Committee, etc., insofar as it could be refuted by the slightest acquaintance with the speeches of Mao, references to Chinese Communists in the Comintern press, etc. But General Hurley, a rock-ribbed Republican, fell for it. Later on he was to assert that Mao's faction was no more Communist than Oklahoma Republicans(!).

The interesting point about Molotov's statement is that he did not seek to disabuse the Americans about Chiang. There was growing disenchantment in Washington about the Nationalists—the fact that they were being trounced easily by the Japanese, that, as the choleric American commander in China General Joseph Stilwell had emphasized, Chiang, rather than fighting, was waiting for the Americans to win the war for him, etc. But Molotov did not choose to denigrate Chiang, and he hoped that the Americans would continue their efforts: "Molotov said in conclusion that the Soviets would be glad if the United States aided the Chinese in unifying their country, improving their military and economic conditions." In April 1945 Hurley, this time in a discussion with Stalin, heard that whatever the weakness of his government Chiang himself was "selfless"

[13] *U. S. Relations with China, with Special Reference to the Period 1944–1949* (Washington, 1949), p. 72. To be referred to hereafter as the *China Paper*.

and a "patriot." Hurley on his part briefed Stalin on the Chinese Communists, who according to him were interested mainly in "creating a free, democratic and united government in China."[14] Stalin agreed. George Kennan, then chargé d'affaires in Moscow, sent back to Washington a commentary on this amiable conversation in which he poured cold water on Hurley's optimism and gave a realistic picture of Russia's aims in China, which included "acquiring sufficient control in all areas of north China . . . to prevent other foreign powers from repeating the Japanese incursion."[15]

The Soviet aims in those involved maneuvers in 1944–45 was clearly to prevent things in China from coming to a boil. Their solicitude that the Americans should play the leading role in trying to arrange for some sort of a coalition was designed to disarm the Americans' suspicions and to prevent the outbreak of a full-scale civil war. Such a war *at the time* could not but harm Soviet interests: Chiang might trounce the Communists, or if he began to lose the Americans might aid him, change their view about the need for Japan's unconditional surrender, etc. Moscow's disavowal of any responsibility for and interest in the Chinese Communists was a master stroke. The whole responsibility for settling the Chinese mess was generously delegated to the Americans: they were to pester the Nationalists to mend their ways and at the same time implore the Communists to arrive at a *modus vivendi* with Chiang. Thus the Americans could not say: "We shall take care of our Chinese, you of yours, and here is what has to be done." It was reminiscent of the manner in which the Russians delegated to Churchill the job of browbeating the Yugoslav monarchists into a suicidal "compromise" with Tito, and of forcing Mikolajczyk to make a similar arrangement with the Lublin Poles.

The Treaty of Friendship and Alliance between the Republic of China and the U.S.S.R., which was signed on August 14, 1945, constituted a partial payment for Russia's entrance into the war against Japan as stipulated at Yalta. Despite the earlier fears in Washington, it did not require undue pressure to make Chiang's government agree to the main features of the treaty, although they had been formulated without its knowledge. The treaty contained provisions painful to Chinese national pride, such as the acquiescence in the loss of Outer Mongolia,[16] Soviet sharing of the port facilities of Dairen, and their acquisition of Port Arthur as a naval base. But the most important provision was the one that stipulated that

---

[14] *Ibid.*, p. 95.

[15] *Ibid.*, p. 97.

[16] For the purpose of face-saving, a formal plebiscite was to resolve the question of Mongolia's independence. Nobody could doubt its outcome, but when the results were in it was still remarkable that the vote in favor of "independence" was 100 per cent!

the Soviets would again share the ownership of the Manchurian Railway, for the Japanese had built the line into a many-sided business and industrial enterprise, and ownership of it would give the Soviet Union a powerful voice in the economy and hence politics of Manchuria.

The Chinese leaders undoubtedly thought that these concessions were more than compensated for by the Soviet pledges not to deal with or help any Chinese faction except the official government of the republic and speedily to withdraw Soviet troops from Manchuria after the end of military operations against Japan. The treaty was to run for thirty years.

Unless one adopts a super-Machiavellian interpretation of Soviet policies, the mere fact of signing the treaty is convincing demonstration that, at the time, the government of the U.S.S.R. expected Chiang Kai-shek and the Kuomintang to remain the main factor in the politics of China for a long time to come. The Soviets could have bargained harder; their armies were, after all, overrunning Manchuria. Sinkiang, which in the 1930's was in a fair way of becoming another Outer Mongolia, they evidently abandoned. To be sure, the Russians could and soon would put their own interpretation on the treaty. But on the surface it was a clear sign that Moscow thought the Chinese Communists were expendable. Those elements in China which were wavering could be impressed by this Soviet affirmation that Chiang's was and would remain *the* government of the republic. Had the Chinese Communists been anything but a disciplined party accustomed to accept Moscow's word as final, they would have cried out in bitterness at this new betrayal. They did not.

The next phase of Soviet policies in China was attuned to two factors. The first was the degree of political and military effectiveness of the Nationalist government. The Russians had reasons to think and hope that it would not be too effective, yet they evidently believed that it could maintain itself in most of mainland China. A closely related and probably more important consideration was the extent of the American commitment in China. The course of events that had brought the United States into the Pacific war was essentially determined by America's opposition to the domination of China by any foreign power. Now the United States made it clear that she would not allow any Soviet share in the military occupation of Japan. Would then the United States, having barred the Soviet army in the barren region of northern Japan, acquiesce in the Communist conquest of China or even let her most important industrial region, Manchuria, fall under Soviet or Communist domination?

One naturally hopeful view of the problem was expressed by Mao Tse-tung in a speech to the Communist cadres on August 13, 1945. It was an obvious attempt to lift the Communists' morale after the Russo-Chinese pact and the demonstration of America's might in dropping the two atomic bombs. It contained an oblique admission that the Chinese Communists would try their luck but could not expect any great Soviet help: "Relying on the forces we ourselves organize, we can defeat all Chinese and foreign reactionaries."[17] Chiang relied on American imperialism. "But U.S. imperialism while outwardly strong is inwardly weak." This presumably was a polite way of saying that American policy-makers had neither the intelligence nor the endurance to achieve their goals in China. And, added Mao, the day will come when the United States will abandon Chiang.

This analysis represented one variant of a theme then current in Moscow, but it is likely that it was being countered by more pessimistic speculations. It is probable that the Chinese Communists were told, in effect, "You are on your own, but don't do anything drastic to provoke the Americans. We may help you, but not obtrusively, for we must not run into too great dangers and complications with the Americans." There were still several strings to the Soviet bow. One was to work through direct arrangement with Chiang, whose autocratic nature was chafing under the American advisers' pressure to initiate democratic reforms. Another was to assist discreetly the American efforts to work out a compromise between Chiang and the Communists and to listen with understanding to the American tales of the difficulties they were encountering in making the willful Generalissimo mend his ways and rid his regime of corruption and police methods. Soviet diplomacy intermittently played upon all these themes, and for all of them the Chinese Communists were a valuable asset and, it appeared at the time, an uncomplaining instrument.

The Soviets' caution and careful probing methods were evident in their occupation of Manchuria. It has already been pointed out how the whole plan of campaign against the Japanese forces was dictated by the need to occupy as much as possible in the shortest possible time, and to achieve this goal the Soviets did not hesitate to incur large casualties that could have been avoided by a few days' wait. Manchuria was, then, to be a valuable pawn in the Far Eastern game. But the use of this pawn depended on the American and Nationalist moves. Chinese Communist armed units were not allowed to enter Manchuria, but could the Soviet commanders object to Communist "civilians" entering the region, helping themselves to Japanese arms, and "becoming" soldiers? On the other hand, Chiang's attempts to have his troops beat the Communists to various strategic areas in Manchuria encountered continuous "technical" objections by the local Soviet commanders. The Communists could then build their power base in the strategic province. Until their final withdrawal in May 1946, the Soviets pursued an involved game. At times they heeded the Nationalists' requests and even helped them to occupy some main centers. At other times they obstructed their efforts. Only in very recent years were the Soviets ready to lift the veil of secrecy from the help they rendered to Mao's forces in Manchuria. Thus a Soviet publication quotes Mao Tse-tung as

[17] Quoted in Tang Tsou, *America's Failure in China* (Chicago, 1963), p. 304.

writing on November 19, 1945, to his representative there: "Due to the support of our Elder Brother (the U.S.S.R.) and the growth of our party in Manchuria, the armies of Chiang could not move into the area and could not take over power there." Before the Soviet entrance the armed Communist forces there numbered 10,000; by November 1945 they grew to 215,000, the Russians equipping them with captured Japanese arms.[18] Then occasionally they hinted to Chiang that the Manchurian problem could be solved overnight if only Chiang got rid of the American troops in China. Feelers were extended to the Nationalists about having most of Manchurian industry run by joint Russo-Chinese companies on the pattern prevalent in Russia's European satellites. In the meantime the Soviets thoroughly looted Manchuria's industrial equipment. By 1946 when they moved out, the area's industry lay in ruins and most of the country was under Communist control. Thus the Nationalists had to reconquer Manchuria. This effort, at first successful, involved their best troops. Chiang thus dissipated his greatest asset and, when the tide in Manchuria turned against him, his over-all military situation became catastrophic. Manchuria was a trap.

Such an outcome could not be foreseen in 1945 or early 1946. Moscow's aims at that time, insofar as they could be divined, were limited. They included first the withdrawal of the fairly substantial American forces that had been landed in China following the Japanese capitulation to assist Chiang to accept the surrender of the Japanese garrisons; second, the securing of a sizable Chinese Communist area, possibly including Manchuria. This second goal, if achieved, would put the Soviet Union in a very comfortable position, but as the Kremlin must have reflected since 1950, both Chiang Kai-shek and the Americans let the Soviet Union down!

That the Americans would not show the same obduracy in China that they were currently displaying in Japan had become clear toward the end of 1945. At the Moscow conference of foreign ministers in December 1945, Stalin and Molotov put very persistent pressure on Byrnes to give an American commitment to withdraw troops from China, intimating that they would be ready to withdraw Soviet troops at the same time. It did not occur to Byrnes to point out that formally at least the situation of the American and Soviet contingents was quite different. The Americans were there at the invitation of the Chinese government, the Soviets had pledged to withdraw once the operations against the Japanese were completed. But a joint communiqué stated the "desirability of the withdrawal of Soviet and American forces at the earliest practicable moment consistent with the discharge of their obligations and responsibilities."[19] Molotov at the time was very insistent about fixing a date for the mutual withdrawal of the troops, but Stalin as usual proved more subtle. He

[18] A. M. Dubinsky, "The Liberating Mission of the U.S.S.R. in the Far East." *Problems of History*, no. 8, Moscow, October 1965, p. 61.

[19] James F. Byrnes, *Speaking Frankly* (New York, 1947), p. 228.

was really concerned for Chiang(!). "If the Chinese people become convinced Chiang was depending on foreign troops, Stalin remarked, Chiang would lose his influence." Byrnes did not catch on. At the time he was interested in obtaining Soviet cooperation in a multitude of bothersome problems ranging from the peace treaty with Bulgaria to the withdrawal of Soviet troops from Iran, and the mere readiness of the Russians to withdraw their troops from anywhere appeared too good to be true. Writing in 1947, he had this insight: "The one safe generalization that can be made about China is that it stands on the threshold of great change."[19a] Though this may seem banal, it was a better prophecy than that expressed by Molotov—"The Chinese never wish to do any fighting but prefer that others do it for them"—or by Stalin—"All Chinese are boasters who exaggerate the forces of their opponents as well as their own." It was not only the American who failed to foresee the near and somber future.

An added element was the obvious disenchantment of American policy-makers and the American public with the Chiang Kai-shek regime. Part of this was due undoubtedly to left-wing propaganda within the United States, but in the main to a closer exposure to the Chinese leader and his circle. The image of a Chinese George Washington could not be maintained, and Chiang in turn could not understand the American advisers' demands that he institute instant democracy. As in the case of future similar American involvements with Asian potentates, the original enthusiasm soon turned into a bitter realization that he was not a "democrat," and then into recriminations and accusations that took no account of local conditions or the burden of history. His reliance on America was itself to become a factor in Chiang's fall. His position prior to 1937 had been built up through a system of alliances with various local leaders and through a keen sense of timing. Now in 1945 and 1946 such caution appeared ludicrous. Behind him stood the greatest power in the world. Americans airlifted his armies into areas that had been out of Nationalist rule for more than a decade. No attempt was made to secure the good will of the local population, and the extortions and oppression of Nationalist officials imported from other provinces soon made the newly acquired areas a fertile field for Communist propaganda and infiltration. The more perceptive American officials felt that Chiang was overextending himself: he should first try to consolidate his power in areas adjoining his war-time holdings. But the Generalissimo felt he could scorn such advice. He had outwitted both the Russians and the native Communists in the late 1920's; now he had in addition the priceless asset of American support. Whatever schoolmasterish objections the Americans had he could always, he felt, silence them by threatening to turn to the U.S.S.R. He forgot that the latter was no longer the weak state she had once been and that the Chinese Communists had consolidated the areas under their control and trained their forces. Before 1937 they had been barely a match for the

[19a] *Ibid.*, p. 226.

Nationalist troops, but eight years of training and indoctrination had changed this picture.

The American attempts to effect a conciliation and compromise between Chiang and the Communists were flawed by some basic misconceptions. Generals Hurley, who threw up the task in disgust by the end of 1945, and Marshall, who did the same by 1947, sought a "democratic and united China." The first part of this aim was humanly unattainable. As to the second, China could become united only with the victory of one or the other faction. On paper the idea of a coalition government looked feasible. France and Italy, at the time, had such governments, with Communists in them yet not in a dominant position. But the main among many differences was that the French Communists did not have armed forces in control of, say, Burgundy and Champagne. Judging from their experiences of 1926 and 1927, the Chinese Communists could have a graphic idea of what fate was likely to befall them should they eventually enter a coalition with Chiang and dissolve their armed forces. With equal logic, Chiang could feel that he could not tolerate the Communist Party having an army of its own controlling large areas. A few American officials had the realistic idea that the only solution lay in a "two China" arrangement—acquiescence in a Communist state in the northeast under the veneer of some formal framework of Chinese unity. Such a solution could conceivably have obtained Soviet support, and in 1946 it probably would have been accepted, though grudgingly, by the Chinese Communists themselves. But any such suggestion evoked in the minds of most American policymakers the wicked Old World formulas of "spheres of influence" and as such would have been condemned by both the left and the right in the United States.

The task of arbitration was all the more incongruous in that as it proceeded America's bargaining power steadily diminished: by the middle of 1946 America's armed forces in China had been reduced to a few thousand. An arbitrator can be successful under one of two conditions: that he is genuinely neutral in the dispute, or that he can force the solution through threatening to throw his strength into the balance. The official American position was that of being "neutral against" the Communists. And it became increasingly clear that while money and equipment were being furnished to Chiang, no American troops would be allowed to help him in the civil war and large numbers of officers and noncoms would not be sent to stiffen his armies.

But our main problem is not the travails of American policies in China, but the relationship of the Chinese Communists to Moscow. Judging from indirect evidence, as unfortunately we must, it is probable that the Chinese Communists' willingness to continue negotiations with Chiang throughout 1945 and 1946 and to lend at least a superficial appearance of reality to the search for coalition government through American mediation was the result mainly of stern Soviet admonitions. It is equally likely that those admonitions evoked among the Chinese something bordering on incomprehension. Like Communists everywhere, they had been brought up on, and sustained in adversity by, belief in the power of the Soviet Union. Now with this power visibly demonstrated in the war, it was hard for them, just as it was for Tito on the issue of Trieste, to believe that the Russians should advise them to temporize and be cautious. *Before* the Russians made this claim, Mao himself was to declare that it was not the American atom bomb but the Soviet intervention that had decided the Japanese war. Why, then, were the Russians so careful not to offend the Americans? The Chinese Communists could clearly see that for the Soviet Union, American mediation efforts were a convenient cushion against the charge that she was trying to seize the vast country through their agency. General Marshall recalled in 1949 that while the Russians were still maintaining that the Chinese were not real Communists, Chou En-lai in his conversations with him never made any bones about the fact that they were devout Marxists and a Communist China was their ultimate aim. But like most of the world, the Chinese Communists did not realize the bewildering and complex problems faced by the U.S.S.R. after the war and her imperative need for peace. They felt that she should sternly warn off the United States about supporting Chiang and could not quite understand the involved game she was playing. As to Chiang, they evidently thought that his regime was in its death throes and that beating him would be fairly easy.

The above suggests, unlike other interpretations, that it was not within Mao's power to take a course of action completely independent of Moscow. This was 1946. An official condemnation by Stalin would have catastrophic results for the Chinese Communists. The Yugoslav Communists, fully masters in their own house, when asked by Moscow to put their heads in a noose, did not dare attack the Soviet Union until more than a year later, despite being subject to the most scurrilous vituperation. How then could the Chinese Communists in the middle of the civil war dare to question Comrade Stalin on the over-all management of world Communism? At the same time, Soviet caution and apprehensions about possible American moves probably laid the basis for the CCP's future bitterness and suspicion of the U.S.S.R.

The year 1946 was consumed in intermittent civil war and at the same time in negotiations with the Nationalists under the aegis of General Marshall. The Communists refrained from breaking these off, at the same time that their criticisms of the Americans and their role in China were increasing. While Chou En-lai pursued the conversations with Marshall the dominant voice in Chinese Communism, Mao Tse-tung's, was more and more disparaging of America's strength and resolve. America was a "paper tiger." This comforting analysis was undoubtedly for the benefit of Moscow, as well as for those Chinese Communists who were overly impressed by Moscow's warnings about the need for caution and restraint. Early in 1947 the chief of information of the Chinese Communist Party published an analysis of the world situation which tried to dispel various "pessimistic" views (where those views were expressed was not specified) that overestimated America's strength, and most of all gave the idea that the United States might in the near future attack Soviet Russia: "The American imperialists cannot attack the Soviet Union before they have succeeded in suppressing and putting under their control the American people and all capitalist colonial and semi-colonial countries."[20] The implication was clear: the progress of Communism in China was not a provocation of the United States and hence a threat to the U.S.S.R., but, on the contrary, the victories of Communism in China were a means to defend the U.S.S.R., a guarantee of peace. America's hands would soon be tied by an economic crisis "which will arrive this year or next" and which "cannot but be turbulent in its nature." Another comforting thought: while currently under American control, such capitalist countries as Britain and France would inevitably turn against their American masters —"so-called capitalist encirclement, therefore, does not exist."[21]

The article is very interesting insofar as its main theme is to dispel the fear not of what America might do to China, but of a possible attack by the United States, in rancor at her reverses in China and other national liberation wars, upon the U.S.S.R. "The contradiction between the United States and the Soviet Union, though it is one of the basic contradictions, is not an imminent one, nor a dominant one in the present political situation."[22] The author carefully refrains from saying that in the case of war between the two super-powers the U.S.S.R. would win. No, such a conflict is at present simply unimaginable. But he implies very strongly that if the imperialists are allowed to check the progress of Communism in underdeveloped areas, *then* they might be emboldened to strike at *the* Communist power. His article was addressed purportedly to the doubters and fainthearted among "Communists, some left-wing critics, some middle-of-the-road critics."[23] But it also sounds like a brief presented by Chinese Communists in Moscow in their plea that they be allowed to open an all-out effort against Chiang, an action they believed would not endanger the Soviet Union.

In a conversation held with the Yugoslav Communists early in 1948,

[20] Quoted in *China Paper*, p. 713.
[21] *Ibid.*, p. 716.
[22] *Ibid.*, p. 714.
[23] *Ibid.*, p. 710.

Djilas reports that Stalin said: "When the war with Japan ended, we invited the Chinese comrades to reach an agreement as to how a *modus vivendi* with Chiang Kai-shek might be found. They agreed with us in word, but in deed they did it their own way when they got home: they mustered their forces and struck. It has been shown that they were right, not we."[24] The same statement is quoted, somewhat differently, by Vladimir Dedijer, in whose account Stalin refers specifically to his advice in 1945 that the Chinese Communists should dissolve their army and mentions the presence of Chinese Communists in Moscow at that time.[25]

If the Yugoslavs' recollections are correct—and the second version, which has Stalin recommending that the Chinese Communists disband their armies there and then, is at least open to doubt[26]—we get strong corroboration of the thesis that Mao was dependent on Moscow. The Chinese are "invited" to Moscow. Here they have to promise to continue negotiations with Chiang Kai-shek. For reasons that are obscure (he was talking with people he had already decided to eliminate as leaders of *their* party), Stalin declares to the Yugoslavs that the Chinese went back on the word they had given in Moscow.[27] But in fact they *did* continue negotiations with Chiang and these were not broken definitely until January 1947. In February 1948 with the Yugoslavs, Stalin could still be smug about his advice and Mao's alleged insubordination; 1947 had been a good year for the Chinese Communists but they were evidently some distance from conquering all of Manchuria and northern China. When that happened at the end of 1948, it was still incredible that they would conquer the rest of the mainland in a matter of months. After all, the population of south China ran into hundreds of millions. The Americans were quite fed up with Chiang, but would they really let *all* of China go Communist?

The years 1946 and 1947 were thus of great educational value to the Chinese Communists. To the Chinese, those years taught them that the Soviet Union, no longer a beleaguered country but a victor in the war,

[24] Djilas, *op. cit.*, p. 182. An added piquancy is provided by the fact that this story is recounted in connection with Stalin's statement that the Greek Communist uprising had to be wound up because the "United States, the most powerful state in the world," would not tolerate its success; but in the Far East "relations are different."

[25] Vladimir Dedijer, *Tito* (New York and London, 1953), p. 322.

[26] Why should the Soviets turn over captured Japanese arms to the Communists if they wanted them to disband their armies?

[27] Stalin's indiscretions in February 1948 may have been intentional. He was then convinced that the Yugoslav government was seeded with British intelligence agents; the story of how he wanted the Greek rebellion to end and how the Chinese Communists chose to fight on their own would undoubtedly reach London and Washington. Such naïve Machiavellianism was quite in his style.

balked at giving full support to fellow Communists, measured her commitment in China according to probable American reactions and their possible effect on the U.S.S.R., and, most of all, neither expected nor apparently wished for dramatic Communist successes in colonial and underdeveloped areas. Lastly, she overestimated America's potential strength and resolve. Whether at this point the Chinese could admit even to themselves the horrible truth that the Soviet Union had no particular reason to wish for a *full* victory of Communism in a country of several hundred million people is something that is impossible to determine. Certainly for many years afterward they did not dare to voice such thoughts publicly or, as long as Stalin lived, to challenge publicly his authority and his direction of world Communism. Their line, insofar as we can determine it, was then and was to be for some years to say to Moscow: "You do not know how strong you are and how weak your enemies. You can afford to take greater risks." This prodding was quite consistent with the acknowledgement of, indeed with the insistence on, Russia's primacy in world Communism. The Soviets, engrossed in the enormous problems of socialist construction in their own country, could be excused for not realizing the enormous revolutionary potentialities in the post-war world. The United States was floundering in China. In their revolutionary enthusiasm and optimism, the Chinese Communists could not attribute this faltering American policy just to the ineptitude and confusion of American policy-makers. It evidently reflected a growing contradiction within American society. As early as July 1945, with the American Communists' ejection of Earl Browder and repudiation of his policies, Mao took it upon himself to address a congratulatory message to his successor, "Comrade Foster," and the Central Committee of the American Communist Party, in terms suggesting that he believed the latter played an important part in the politics and even foreign policy of the United States.[28] From the Soviet point of view, this must have appeared as a fantastic piece of imprudence: at the time, Stalin and Molotov were profuse in their assurances as to how Chinese Communists were not really Communists at all. To the Russians' warnings, Mao and his lieutenants could retort that they also knew the Americans and did not find them so frightening!

On the Soviet side the suspicion that they were raising a Frankenstein probably did not occur until Mao, then master of all of mainland China, arrived in Moscow in late 1949 and began those lengthy negotiations which were to conclude in the Soviet agreement to surrender Soviet rights and bases in China the possession of which for more than half a century had been an objective of Russian foreign policy. Until then, the first priority of Soviet policy in China was to avoid the danger of confronta-

<hr/>

[28] Stuart R. Schram, *The Political Thought of Mao Tse-tung* (New York, 1963), p. 292.

tion with the United States over China. When that danger grew distant with the withdrawal of most of the American troops in 1946 and in view of the obvious trends of American public opinion, a tempting opportunity beckoned: the erection of a Communist state in north China which of course would be a dependable satellite of Moscow. Chiang has recalled that in May 1946 he was twice invited to visit Moscow, and that at that time the Russians were painting a tempting picture of a Russo-Chinese collaboration under which Chiang would repudiate his pro-American stand, in return for which the Soviets would help him preserve his dominance. What lends credence to this story, which is not corroborated in any other source, is that Chiang does not picture Stalin as willing to throw the Chinese Communists to the wolves but simply as assuming that they would play a secondary role in a coalition government: "He suggested that the Kuomintang and the Chinese Communists would 'compete in peace.' "[29] In any case, in June and July 1946 the Soviet press adopted a sharper tone toward the Nationalists, and it is likely that at this point the Soviets accepted the Chinese Communists' contention that the civil war must be stepped up and any idea of coalition with Chiang abandoned.

The Nationalists reached the highest point in their military fortunes in the spring of 1947. The civil war was now in full swing. But in May-June the Chinese Communists scored large-scale military successes. At the same time, rampaging inflation and the ascendancy within the Kuomintang of its right-wing elements contributed to widespread and mounting popular dissatisfaction with Chiang's regime. General Wedemeyer, dispatched by President Truman to China in July, reported that the Nationalists' position was grave and would require extensive American help, both military (he did not recommend that American troops be employed—only "advisers") and economic. Manchuria, he felt, was as good as lost, though Chiang unwisely still held on to its main urban centers.

How did these developments fit in with Soviet policy and with the (probable) Soviet analysis of the situation? The spring of 1947 was the period of sharpening Soviet-American conflict, of the announcement of the Truman Doctrine and the Marshall Plan. Moscow's fear was still not one of a direct American-Soviet clash in Europe. The American policy-makers, it was thought, were building up satellites that would exert pressure on the edges of the Soviet sphere, on Soviet satellites, without any direct military risk to the United States. This analysis fitted in with the Chinese view that militant Communist policies in Asia did not threaten the U.S.S.R. with war but, on the contrary, were the most efficient way of postponing

[29] Chiang Kai-shek, *Soviet Russia in China* (New York, 1957), p. 151. Chiang claims he rejected this invitation because it would have meant abandoning the American camp. In fact, at the time his military prospects appeared promising.

or avoiding war between the two super-powers. Granted those assumptions, there was no reason for Moscow to put any brake on the Chinese Communists' advance or to seek an accommodation between them and Chiang. They were fighting Russia's battle against an American puppet. Their victory (which the Russians believed would have to be a partial one) would also be a reinsurance against a remilitarized Japan, which was thought to be part of the American scheme of "containment."

But the Soviets' essential caution is evident in the omission of China from the list of those invited to become founding members of the Cominform. In September 1947 it was still thought unwise to advertise the international links of the Chinese Communists. Comments on China in the Soviet press throughout 1947 and 1948 remained restrained, though criticism of the Kuomintang grew in intensity, the attack shifting from the reactionary circles *within* the Kuomintang to the Kuomintang as a whole.

One aspect of Russo-Chinese Communist relations about which we are completely in the dark is the extent of Soviet influence within the Chinese Party. We know from the Soviet-Yugoslav dispute that the Russians liked to have their own men, both as informants and as potential rivals to the leaders, within every Communist Party, no matter how loyal its leadership. In the case of Yugoslavia Soviet methods used to recruit such elements were incredibly crude. Presumably, had Stalin and his lieutenants had a sense of proportion, they would have been more subtle in China. After Japan's defeat, many Chinese Communists long domiciled in Moscow (among them a former leader of the Party) returned to their homeland. Here some of them, including the former Secretary General, Li Lisan, were given Party jobs of secondary importance. Some years later, after the Communists' victory, the head of the Manchurian government and member of the Politburo of the CCP, Kao Kang, was to be disgraced and commit suicide. But the story, if there is one, remains to be told.

The year of decision in China was 1948. The Nationalists' position in Manchuria and northern China now became untenable, and the Communists, shifting their tactics, engaged in a series of pitched battles in which they were almost invariably victorious. The situation then came to justify Mao's triumphant prediction of December 1947 that nothing, including American advisers and matériel, could save Chiang. By the end of 1948 it thus looked probable for the first time that the Chinese Communists would not only dominate Manchuria and northern China, but in fact completely eliminate the Nationalists.

The Soviet attitude on the Chinese Communists' progress continued to be one of extreme caution. It might have been thought that recognition—or a step toward it—of the Chinese Communists as the *de facto* rulers of northern China would have been a great stimulus to their effort.

Yet nothing even approaching this was undertaken for another year. It also might have been thought that the Chinese Communists, now definitely committed against Chiang, would have proclaimed their government as the legitimate one of China. But there was no point to such a move until Soviet recognition was sure to be immediately forthcoming, and this was not guaranteed until the Chinese Communists had definitely conquered all of mainland China.[30]

It is clear that the Chinese Communists must have wished for an earlier proclamation and for an earlier Soviet recognition, which would have signified Soviet commitment and faith in their ultimate victory and warned off the United States from helping Chiang and, perhaps, from securing the survival of the Nationalist regime in part of China. But precisely the last consideration would furnish Russia with a convenient excuse about the danger of a premature proclamation. American reluctance to help Chiang extensively still depended, they could argue, on the distinction made between the Chinese Communists and Moscow. If the two were shown in real collusion, then America's aid to the Nationalists might be increased and American troops might even reappear in China to guard the still unconquered southern areas. That Mao largely discounted such prospects is demonstrated by the increasingly vituperative and scornful tone which the Chinese Communists adopted toward America. At the time, the Russians' objections may have appeared as endowed with some validity. In retrospect they are undoubtedly seen as proof of Soviet duplicity and Soviet unwillingness to have all of China become Communist.

Soviet caution on China in 1948 contrasts with the Russian moves in Europe, where the Berlin blockade raised the specter of an outright clash with the United States. Yet one can find an explanation for this contrast in the Russians' prognoses of America's intentions in different parts of the world. The American interest in the Far East was assumed to be tenacious and of long standing: witness her uncompromising stand on the occupation of Japan. In Europe, it was believed that the United States would tire of keeping troops in Germany and would pursue her anti-Soviet intrigues through the agency of other countries and "economic help." But in China would not the United States even at the last moment bolster the Chinese Nationalists militarily, or proceed frantically to rearm Japan (a worse possibility from the Soviet point of view)?

It could be argued that Soviet policies in 1948 were most inconsistent. Here you have the Soviet Union seemingly risking war over Berlin yet observing great caution over China. For a variety of essentially trivial reasons or fictitious assumptions, Stalin moves to destroy the leadership

[30] In contrast, the U.S.S.R. and China recognized Ho Chi Minh's government in 1950, when Vietnam was still in the midst of the war between the Vietminh and the French.

of the Yugoslav Communist Party, yet nothing apparently is done about the increasingly independent and confident Mao, who if successful will control not a piddling little country but a colossus of several hundred million people. But from the Kremlin it must have been America's policies that looked baffling. Here was America pursuing what was assumed to be a deep and devious game under the guise of the European Recovery Program, pouring billions of dollars into her European satellites but being niggardly in helping Chiang. American advisers in a regular military mission were directing the operations of Greek government forces against Communist rebels and were reorganizing the Turkish army. Yet in China Chiang's pleas that the same type of help and commitment be extended to the Nationalists were being rejected. The official reasons for these differing policies must have seemed equally baffling. Chiang's policies, the Americans said, were dictatorial, his regime was sunk in corruption. Yet it could hardly be claimed that the Greek or Turkish regimes corresponded to the precepts of Thomas Jefferson or John Stuart Mill! It was claimed that the Chinese Communists represented a genuinely domestic movement while in the case of Greece and Turkey the pressure was applied from the outside. But if so, why were the Americans opposed to the French and Italian Communists and pouring in billions of dollars to prevent them from attaining power? Certainly the votes cast for those parties showed that they had widespread popular support. Stalin in the past had shrewdly appraised and exploited the weaknesses of the democratic outlook and rhetoric, but had the Soviet rulers really been capable of believing that American policies could be *consistently unsinister*, that they represented merely the faltering response to a world crisis by a society traditionally devoted to peaceful pursuits, they would not have been Marxist-Leninists.

The undoubted Soviet bafflement at this juncture redounded to the Chinese Communists' benefit. The whole world picture in 1948 supported their thesis that American imperialism was a danger, but not an imminent danger, that could be fought by aggressive rather than conciliatory policies. Some of the rationalizations that began to be made in the United States were probably also current in Moscow—even if united, China would confront insoluble problems; it would be decades, if ever, before she could stand on her own feet or become an industrial and military power, etc.

The Russians' willingness to follow the Chinese analysis is also revealed in the proliferation of Communist-sponsored "national liberation" movements in Asia in 1947 and 1948. The Indochinese struggle was in full swing. An abortive Communist coup took place in Indonesia. Guerrilla activities blossomed in the Philippines, Malaya, and in 1948 even in Hyderabad, in India. There is no reason to attribute them to some specific plan or plot laid in Moscow, but it is equally clear that they would not have occurred on such a widespread scale without the appropriate body in Moscow saying, in effect, "go ahead and try it" to those Communists who felt so inclined. It could not escape Soviet attention that these ventures appeared to present a minimal risk to the U.S.S.R. as compared with the slightest Soviet initiative in Europe or the Near East.

And thus the Chinese Communists proceeded to their historic victory. Allegedly their decision to press on with positional battles rather than through primarily guerrilla activities was reached in the summer of 1948 against Russian advice. In early 1949 all of north China was theirs; in the spring there began their triumphant sweep across the Yangtze.

The proximity of success often brings with it increased apprehension. Communist armies were rolling across south China virtually unopposed, but huge provinces were still in the hands of the Nationalists or secured to Mao only through the defection of the local Nationalist governor. Something might still happen, and this something was thought to be connected with the Soviet Union. The government of the U.S.S.R. was not ready to help the crumbling Nationalist regime—the belated efforts of some circles within the Kuomintang to seek Soviet mediation or help were spurned as late as January 1949—but there were disquieting symptoms. The Russians were negotiating with the Nationalist governor of Sinkiang as late as May. When the Communists occupied Nanking in April most of the ambassadors, including the American one, remained in the former capital, but the Soviet ambassador followed the fleeing Nationalist regime to Canton.

It is therefore no coincidence that in the spring of 1949 the Chinese Communists chose repeatedly to assert their solidarity with the Soviet Union in international affairs. Previously such statements had usually been linked to an attack on the United States' support of Chiang Kai-shek and his "reactionary clique," but now they stressed support for the U.S.S.R. on a global scale. On April 3 the Chinese Communists, like the Communist parties in Western Europe, issued a declaration condemning the North Atlantic Treaty and affirmed their loyalty to their "ally, the Soviet Union."[31] Such a declaration involved a gratuitous risk: a violent debate was raging in the United States over the impending "loss of China," and even at this moment American power might be thrown in the balance to keep part of it outside the Communist sphere. But Mao at this time was evidently more apprehensive of what Moscow might think than of what Washington could do. On July 1 came his own emphatic assertion that "we must lean to one side. . . . Not only in China but throughout the world, one must lean either to imperialism or to socialism.[32]

[31] Schram, *op. cit.*, p. 505.
[32] *Ibid.*, p. 506.

Even more characteristically, the Chinese Communists joined in the violent denunciations of Tito and his party that were emanating from the Soviet bloc. The Yugoslavs still pinned great hopes on the Chinese Communists and reported their victories with enthusiasm. (The implication was that the Soviets were in for a rude jolt, that it was not only a small Balkan country but an oriental giant that would challenge the domination of Stalin.) But these compliments were not appreciated in Peking, where the Communists now established their capital.

In July, with their regime still not officially proclaimed (i.e., with Moscow still not ready to recognize it), the Chinese Communists had to approve or acquiesce in what was undoubtedly a painful episode. A delegation of the Manchurian region headed by the local Communist boss Kao Kang went to Moscow and there concluded a trade agreement between Manchuria and the U.S.S.R. Since *all* of China was to be within a few months under Communist domination, and a general trade agreement would have to be concluded then, this action suggested an ostentatious declaration by Russia of her interest in Manchuria. That Peking approved this was an equally ostentatious profession of docility.[33]

On August 5, 1949, the State Department published its famous White Paper on China. Though the gist of the documents and opinions in the paper must have been known to Communists in Moscow and Peking either from the acrimonious political debate raging over China in the United States ever since 1946 or through their intelligence sources, its effect on the future course of events in the Far East was considerable and, from the American point of view, deplorable. Released for internal political reasons, it bared the anatomy of American foreign policy in Asia in a way that was most embarrassing for a friend, and most hopeful for an opponent. Presumably to appease domestic opponents of the State Department, the paper represented the Chinese Communists as, Secretary Acheson put it, "having foresworn their Chinese heritage . . . a party [working] in the interests of a foreign imperialism."[34] To propitiate those who criticized the Nationalists, the paper painted a detailed picture of their corruption and inefficiency, revealed how various elements in the Kuomintang sought American assistance to remove Chiang, and, contrariwise, stigmatized the right wing of the Kuomintang for clinging desperately to power, even at the price of sabotaging the anti-Communist effort.

At the time the report was issued, there was conceivably an infinitesi-

---

[33] After Kao Kang's suicide in 1954, it was declared that he had tried to turn Manchuria into his private preserve, still later on that he had represented "reactionary forces at home and abroad." Klaus Mehnert, *Peking and Moscow* (New York, 1963), p. 252.

[34] *China Paper*, p. xvi.

mally small chance of the Nationalists' holding out in an area of resistance
to the Communists on the mainland. Conceivably, there was an equally
small chance of the Chinese Communists coming to modify their view of
America as *the* enemy. But both of those possibilities were effectively laid
to rest for decades to come by the White Paper. That the most powerful
state in the world could fail in achieving its policy objectives in an area
and situation as involved as China could perhaps be understood and
rationalized, but not so the fact that the United States professed to have
no policy at all there and awaited the action of the proverbial forces of
history to save her the bother of developing one. "Ultimately the profound civilization and the democratic individualism of China will reassert
themselves and she will throw off the foreign yoke," wrote the Secretary
of State in transmitting the White Paper.

It would be hard to maintain and impossible to prove that the White
Paper had any major influence on Moscow's policy toward the Chinese
Communists. It is unlikely that Acheson's assertion about the servility
of the Chinese Communists to Russia dispelled the doubts that must have
existed on the subject in the Kremlin. But the effect of the paper was to
reinforce the thesis propounded by the Chinese Communists that American imperialism was "outwardly strong but inwardly weak," that America's great economic and (potential) military strength could not be effectively employed in Asia, at least apart from Japan, because of the inherent contradictions and confusions of American policy. The official
reaction in Moscow to the White Paper was one of amusement and
superiority, perhaps paralleling the reactions in the West when the correspondence between the Yugoslav and Soviet central committees became
public. An impartial observer could bewail the condition of a world where
the leaders of one super-power were subject to occasional paranoid seizures
and senseless suspicions, while the leaders of the other thought it necessary to spell out painfully for the whole world to see all the premises,
illusions, and errors of their policy. Mao Tse-tung himself saw fit to cele-
brate the appearance of the White Paper by devoting to it a series of
articles which included a somewhat snobbish remark that it demonstrated
the immaturity of American imperialists, "the newly arrived upstart and
neurotic."[35] The British imperialists, or even some "smaller imperialist
countries" would have never done anything so childish and transparent.
But, as usual with the Communists, Mao refuses to equate American
naïveté with innocence. The American reactionaries had not revealed *all*
their tricks. They would continue their counterrevolutionary efforts in
China. But they had revealed their duplicity. "What a loss of face! What
a loss of face!" exclaimed Mao,[36] who must have felt that the White Paper

[35] *Selected Works of Mao Tse-tung* (in English) (Peking, 1961), IV, 442.
[36] *Ibid.*, p. 430.

was a vindication of his tactics against doubters and the fainthearted, and not only in China. "And so the White Paper has become the material for the education of the Chinese people."[37]

A casual reader of the Soviet press in the summer of 1949 might have been excused for not realizing the full importance of the events taking place in China. The news about the successes of the Chinese "national liberation army" continued to be brief and factual. In fact, until August the activities of the Greek Communists, then on the verge of defeat, were given more space. And the coverage of both events in the daily press was dwarfed by the daily columns of abuse poured on Tito and his regime, the lengthy reports of trials and liquidations of alleged Titoists in the "people's democracies." This fantastic lack of proportion cannot be accidental; it reflected a conscious effort to minimize the importance of events in China, an effort that in turn could be traced if not to the displeasure then to the instinctive dislike that Stalin and his group felt for another Communist movement and another leader moving into the spotlight hitherto reserved exclusively for themselves. This was the year of the seventieth anniversary of the birth of the "genius leader" of world Communism, and even the reports of the villainies of Tito and the predictions of the dire fate in store for him and his clique were quantitatively insignificant when compared with the mass of birthday greetings, articles, stories, etc., eulogizing Stalin on a scale unprecedented in history and not to be matched again until, almost twenty years after, his Chinese counterpart was to sanction a personality cult of similar proportions.

On October 3 the Chinese Communists "made the front page" of *Pravda* for the first time with the story of the official proclamation of the People's Republic of China on the preceding day. On the same day, Chou En-lai having informed the Soviet consul general in Peking of the fact, the U.S.S.R. extended her diplomatic recognition, withdrawing at the same time her recognition from the Kuomintang regime in Canton. The former Soviet ambassador to the Nationalist regime, recalled only in May, was now assigned to Peking. All these circumstances, not very significant in themselves, were still undoubtedly painful to a people as sensitive to considerations of prestige as the Chinese. They seemed to minimize the historical importance of their victory, they appeared to impart an oblique warning not to put on any airs or assume that they were in any special category among the Communist states.

When on December 16, 1949, Mao Tse-tung himself disembarked from a train at the Yaroslav Railway Station in Moscow, he was greeted by a

[37] *Ibid.,* p. 442.

number of Soviet dignitaries, headed by Molotov. With his historical memories, he may have reflected that it was not so long ago (eight years) that Stalin himself had gone to the station to say goodbye to the Japanese foreign minister. Now, the head of Communist China was greeted with no greater fanfare than that which would have been extended to the chief of state of, say, Bulgaria. The official communiqué spoke of Stalin "receiving" the Chinese leader—again, a grating expression implying unequal status (during the war Stalin used to "meet with" or "receive visits" from Churchill and Roosevelt). In his brief address at the station, Mao paid special tribute to the Soviet Union as the country which after the October Revolution was first to annul unequal treaties with China. Thus began the negotiations that concluded only on February 14 and that evidently required the presence of Mao throughout, for he was not to leave Moscow until February 17.

This was an unusually long period for a head of state and government to stay abroad, especially on the morrow of victory and with a multitude of problems at home calling for his personal attention. It is not surprising that rumors arose about Mao being detained in Moscow against his will. Even stranger things were going on in Russia and within the world Communist movement during Stalin's last years.[38] Mao chose to make the long trip to and from Moscow by train, again a very uncharacteristic behavior in a very busy man. (Seven years later, in the more easy-going period of Khrushchev's ascendancy, he was to go by plane.) But whatever the tantalizing possibilities, the most probable explanation is that his two months' stay in Moscow witnessed some very hard bargaining, and that the man who until the very last moment of struggle showed every intention of dispelling Soviet suspicions and earning Stalin's good will now was proving to be a hard bargainer. The past pattern of negotiations between the U.S.S.R. and the satellites was not that involved; representatives of the latter had agreements thrust under their noses and were told to sign. Those like Kostov who raised objections soon had reason to regret their obduracy.

On January 21 Chou En-lai, the Chinese prime minister and minister in charge of foreign relations, joined the negotiations. Other participants included the representative of the Manchurian Communist regime and a special representative from Sinkiang, the presence of both signifying Soviet special interests in those areas. The publicity attending the presence of the representatives of the border areas, the implication that they were negotiating in a semi-autonomous manner, and the fact that both delegates remained for some time in Moscow after the main Chinese negoti-

---

[38] Djilas, during his visit one year before, was haunted by the fear of an "accident" befalling him. Similar apprehensions led Tito to refuse an invitation to Moscow in the spring of 1948 to "talk things over."

ators left again could not be very pleasing to the Chinese. These embarrassing circumstances were gleefully commented upon in the United States, where Secretary Acheson, kibitzing from afar, affirmed that Manchuria and Sinkiang were being turned into Soviet dependencies.

The treaty signed on February 14, 1950, replacing the 1945 agreement with the Kuomintang, went far, apparently, to confound such capitalist critics and skeptics. A preamble spelled out the reasons for the new agreement in terms pleasing to Chinese *amour propre:* "A new People's Government was formed which has united all of China . . . proved its ability to defend the state independence and territorial integrity of China, the national honour and dignity of the Chinese people."[39] So much for Acheson!

It provided for mutual assistance against aggression by Japan or "any other state which should unite with Japan, directly or indirectly, in acts of aggression."[40] This reflected the Soviet fear of *indirect* aggression by the United States, for in Asia the only possible instrument of such an aggression was Japan. But for Communist China the agreement was far from providing an automatic pledge of help by the U.S.S.R. Presumably an aggression could be launched from Formosa with American assistance, and nothing in the treaty obligated the U.S.S.R. to help in such a contingency.

The real gain from the Chinese side was the Soviet agreement to transfer the Manchurian Railway with all its property to the Chinese government, the transfer to take place upon the conclusion of a peace treaty with Japan but in any case not later than 1952. It was clear from the current configuration of world politics that a peace treaty with Japan would not be signed by 1952, at least no peace treaty to which both the U.S.S.R. and the United States would agree. The Soviet reluctance to promise to abandon the Railway—i.e., her position in Manchuria—before 1952 reflected, it is not too much to say, last-minute doubts that *something* still might happen to Communist China and hence there was no reason to be in a hurry in turning over the Railway. Similar provisions were agreed on in connection with the Soviet-held base of Port Arthur; by 1952 at the latest it was to go to China and Soviet troops were to be evacuated. The question of Dairen, where the U.S.S.R. had acquired rights also under the 1945 agreement, was to be discussed after the conclusion of the peace treaty with Japan, but its administration was to be vested in Chinese hands. It was hard for Stalin's Russia to part with anything she acquired. And in the case of the agreement with Mao, the U.S.S.R. was pledging to abandon rights and possessions which had been Russia's even before the

[39] *Documents on International Affairs, 1949–1950* (London, 1953), p. 543.
[40] *Ibid.,* p. 542.

Revolution and which the defeat of Japan had appeared to secure for decades to come.

Stalin was not only tenacious but incredibly stingy. That an agreement on Soviet credits to China was published at the same time as the main treaties must have been due to the fact that Mao had said on his arrival that he was going to negotiate for loans and it would have been embarrassing for him to go back without some credit arrangement. But in fact the amount agreed upon was under the circumstances but a pittance: $300-million worth of credits spread over five years at 1 per cent interest. Considering the amount of industrial equipment the Soviets had looted in Manchuria and considering the vast needs of the Chinese economy, this loan was embarrassingly small and could not be compared with the billions the Americans had given Chiang. Even the European satellites had received (at least on paper) credits greater than that now extended to the most populous country in the world.

That the treaty also provided for the Soviet military presence in China and help in the mopping-up operations against the Kuomintang forces on the mainland was first revealed in a recent Soviet publication. "Soviet aviation units took part in the final stage of the war, being sent there in accordance with the Sino-Soviet treaty of February 14, 1950. Soviet aviators soon stopped Kuomintang raids on Shanghai, providing a reliable air shield for this multimillion city."[41]

The treaty marked also the acquiescence of Peking in the new status of Outer Mongolia. In March and April followed a series of commercial agreements about joint companies for the exploitation of Sinkiang, air communications between the U.S.S.R. and China, and a general trade agreement between the two countries.

Such, then, was the first formal agreement and alliance between the two Communist giants. On February 15 *Pravda* carried a photograph of the officials at the formal signing of the treaty—Stalin, Mao, and most of the members of the Soviet Politburo. In previous pictures of this sort, or when shown greeting foreign diplomats, Stalin invariably affected a broad smile, those around him also displaying the appropriate mood. On this occasion, the photographer forgot to tell the assembled dignitaries to smile. Stalin's head is bowed, his expression is almost wistful. Mao, on his left, looks rigidly into the distance. The others have unsmiling somber expressions. Though this could not have been the intended effect, the whole picture conveys a feeling of strain and apprehension on an occasion which to any true Marxist-Leninist should have been one of jubilation. There were those on the Russian side who perhaps sensed that an era of world Communism—the era of complete Soviet domination— had come to an end and that things would never be the same again.

[41] V. I. Glunin, A. M. Grigoriev, and others, *The Recent History of China, 1917–1970* (Moscow, 1972), p. 246.

X

CHANGING DIRECTIONS:
1950–56

1. *Stalin Departs*

Three events of 1949 marked the passing of an era: the final victory of Chinese Communism, the detonation by the Soviet Union of her first nuclear bomb, and the formation of NATO. The first event we have already dealt with. Soviet acquisition of nuclear weapons had always been foreseen, but few in the West expected that it would come only four years after Hiroshima and that America's monopoly would prove so short-lived.[1] But while the first Soviet experiments did not mean that the U.S.S.R. was even close to matching the American nuclear arsenal, the acknowl-

---

[1] The Soviets, it is reasonable to assume, benefited by knowledge acquired through espionage and also through information procured from "open" American sources relating to the technology of nuclear weapons. It is beyond the scope of this study and the competence of its author even to conjecture how far those sources accounted for the speed with which the Russians produced their first atomic bomb. One may be skeptical, however, of the two extreme points of view—i.e., that information procured through espionage did not speed up the development of the bomb, and that without "stealing" the information and help of such scientific spies and defectors as Klaus Fuchs and Bruno Ponte Corvo the Soviets would not have reached their goal for decades.

edgment that the American monopoly was a thing of the past had a profound psychological effect on the American people. The feeling of security
that the American public, if not their policy-makers, had enjoyed was
gone. This feeling of outrage and surprise was probably one of the factors
that contributed to the hysteria underlying what became known as the
McCarthy era. Both China and the bomb had been "stolen." How deep
the disenchantment was over the Russians' acquisition of the bomb is
indicated by a rather incredible incident: on leaving office in 1953, President Truman indicated doubt as to whether the Russians *really* had the
bomb.

The juxtaposition of the formation of NATO with the Soviet acquisition
of the bomb has its own somewhat ironic significance. NATO in its conception was attuned to the pre-nuclear phase of Soviet foreign policy.
The formation of a united, allied command and a joint army was to lay
at rest the fear that had agitated American and British statesmen between 1945 and 1949—of Russia's armies sweeping rapidly through Western Europe, with the United States having as her only recourse to bomb
the U.S.S.R. proper and having no early opportunity of retrieving Soviet
territorial gains. But now the countervailing power of NATO would soon
be considerably affected, if not neutralized, by the Soviet nuclear arsenal.
The fatal weakness of the West's position prior to 1949 had been seen
by its policy-makers to lie in the cruel alternatives confronting it in the
case of Soviet "semi-aggression," e.g., Czechoslovakia in February 1948:
either to give in and acquiesce in a *fait accompli,* or to start a nuclear
war. (To be sure, in the case of the Berlin blockade, which also could
qualify as semi-aggression, a third way was found, but the example was
hardly encouraging. Had a fully organized NATO force been in existence
in the summer of 1948, the American chiefs of staff would probably not
have objected to testing the blockade by sending through an armored
train.) NATO was designed primarily to deter aggression, but its secondary purpose was presumably to provide the West with a land force that
would deter semi-aggression of the type described above without necessarily involving the threat of full-scale nuclear war.[2] With the Soviet acquisition of the nuclear bomb, this secondary if unstated premise became
immediately inoperative.

Thus in retrospect one may venture to say that the era of the American
monopoly of the atom bomb passed without any special advantage accruing to the United States on its account. If the United States had not
had it, the Soviets *still* would not have marched their armies across Western Europe. And they *still* arranged Eastern Europe according to their

[2] One may well speculate as to whether the Russians would have used their
armies to put down the East German uprising of June 1953 or the Hungarian
Revolution of 1956 if they had not had atomic weapons.

liking. The mystery and awe attaching to Soviet power and intentions between 1945 and 1949 counteracted any material and technological advantages, including the atom-bomb monopoly, the West then possessed. It is only when some of this apprehension disappeared, as a consequence of the confusion and conflicts following Stalin's death, that internal convulsions shook the Soviet empire in Eastern Europe. But by then the Soviet Union was no longer in the position of decided economic and technological inferiority she had been before 1949, and the West could not or dared not cash in on its improved political situation. Thus, much as one hates to admit it, Stalin's policy of isolationism and apparent aggressiveness proved at least partly effective. It obscured Russia's real weakness during that period: her economic devastation, the enormous tasks she faced in imposing Communist regimes on Eastern Europe against the wishes of the majority of its populations, etc. It imposed a defensive mentality on American policy-makers. And the best illustration of this was the avowed purpose of NATO: to enable the West to negotiate with the U.S.S.R. from a position of strength. *Yet never again, no matter how many divisions NATO would have in Europe, would the position of the West vis-à-vis Russia be as strong as it had been before 1950.*

Such must be our judgment from the perspective of almost two decades. But at the time, from the point of view of the Kremlin, 1949 marked the opening of a most dangerous period for the Soviet Union. On April 4 the North Atlantic Alliance was signed in Washington by representatives of twelve countries headed by the United States, Britain, and France. It would be some time until the cumbersome machinery of the Alliance and of the American financial help for it under the Mutual Assistance Act signed by Truman on October 6, 1949, would become effective. But on paper it promised to be a most powerful alliance, uniting the vast resources and population of the United States with those of European countries whose combined populations reached 150 million. The two major setbacks in American policy during 1949—the Communist victory in China and the loss of the monopoly of the atomic weapons—were likely to accentuate the danger. Time, the Russians undoubtedly reasoned, was growing short for any attempt to push back their sphere of influence. In a few years they would acquire an atomic arsenal, and Communist rule in China, a vast country on its way to becoming a major industrial and military power, would become solidified. If the Americans wanted to prevent their position from growing worse they would have to act fast. The year 1948 marked, as we know, the end of reductions in Soviet armed forces. From 1949 they grew to the point where in 1955 they would be twice as large as they had been in 1948. A Soviet author comments: "In the beginning of 1950, with the erection of the military-political mechanism of NATO and with the development of its strategic doctrine, there was completed the first stage in the policy of consolidation of aggressive military blocs begun by the United States and other imperialist states soon after World War II."[3] In the opinion of Moscow, NATO posed a definite threat to the Soviet empire.

Yet as to the imminence and character of this threat there were undoubtedly conflicting opinions. Though for propaganda purposes it was convenient to credit American ruling circles with the intention of launching an aggressive war against the U.S.S.R., no Soviet military expert studying the strategic doctrine and resources of NATO could have endorsed such a conclusion. In 1951, when the complicated network of commands, councils, etc., was finally set up, the commander of NATO forces, General Eisenhower, could dispose of barely eight divisions. Even with the expected reinforcements it was calculated that in the case of a full-scale Russian assault NATO could at best fight a holding action for only two or three months. No officer of the Soviet general staff in possession of his senses could have reported to his superiors that the purpose of this motley assembly of American, French, British, etc., troops was an invasion of the Soviet Union or that its purpose was anything but defensive. Under the political and economic conditions of Western Europe in 1950, the mounting of a really effective armed answer to the Soviet land threat would have required a feverish effort to remilitarize West Germany, and that was still in the future. The most optimistic projections for 1952 envisaged fifty NATO divisions by the end of 1953. Hitler had launched his invasion with 170 divisions.

There was still the threat of the atom bomb. 1950–51 was the period of the building and acquisition of American air bases "stretching from the Atlantic almost to the Persian Gulf,"[4] from which American aircraft could reach Russia's interior and most of her industrial centers. But the idea of preventive war by atomic attack on the U.S.S.R., though it was occasionally broached by some people in the United States, was never seriously contemplated in official circles. Stalin's policy between 1945 and 1949 rested on a very realistic assumption, as it turned out, that a democracy would not use its monopoly of the frightful weapon even as a means of intimidation. There must have been people in Russia who felt less confident on this score, and special nervousness must have been experienced in the wake of the first Soviet atomic explosion in September 1949 and the consequent shock to American public opinion. But thereafter every passing month made the possibility of preventive atomic war more remote. Whatever isolated voices in the United States advocated such a step, they certainly never approached the implicit or even explicit threats

[3] A.G. Mileykovsky,ed., *International Affairs After the Second World War*, I (Moscow, 1962), 629.
[4] *Survey of International Affairs, 1951* (London, 1954), p. 26.

uttered by Khrushchev in his vaunting of Soviet missiles and atomic weapons between 1956 and 1962.

In what sense, then, was NATO and the whole posture of the West a threat sufficient to prompt a speedy build-up of Soviet armed forces? Undoubtedly it was viewed as the intensification of the danger already perceived by the Soviets in the Marshall Plan. The United States would enable and help her satellites to put pressure on or attack the Soviet ones, while American atomic superiority would inhibit the Soviet army from coming to the latter's aid. Before the Soviet policy-makers there arose the vision of such contingencies as were to take place in the June 1953 uprising in East Germany and the Hungarian revolt of 1956. During the latter the Soviets were momentarily to hesitate about the use of their troops. What would their position have been if the Hungarian affair had occurred in 1950 or 1951, Nagy's revolutionary government had requested Western help, and the United States had given Russia to understand that Soviet intervention would be considered a hostile act? Or suppose that a Titoist satellite government requested Western military help in putting down the resistance of pro-Russian elements in its own country? The resources of NATO would be sufficient to help, say, a rebellious regime in Czechoslovakia. The Soviet Union might be confronted with a series of "wars of national liberation" in Eastern Europe.

It might be objected that nobody analyzing the world situation with an unbiased mind could have conceivably arrived at such a fanciful picture or could have credited the Western democracies with either the adventurousness or the resolve to devise and execute such intricate plans. Political opposition was still strong within the United States to far-reaching commitments in Europe. In Britain, a left-wing group within the Labour Party opposed Bevin's policies of association with the United States in an anti-Soviet front. The Fourth Republic was in the throes of almost continuous political crisis, with one-fourth of its electorate voting steadily for the Communists, the Indochinese war tying down the best units of the French army, stirrings in North Africa promising new and even more involved and costly colonial wars. Surely this whole picture went far in conveying the impression that NATO was in fact what it professed to be—a patchwork alliance having not even remotely aggressive intentions and designed simply to enable the West to hold on to what it had, to enable it to have better bargaining power in a future contingency similar to the Berlin blockade. How could people like Stalin and Molotov, who had so astutely capitalized on the democracies' weaknesses, on the irresolution and naïveté of their leaders, now credit those very same people with the most intricate schemes of subversion and aggression?

But even though such a construction of the West's intentions verges on madness, it was very much in the tradition of Soviet thinking on international politics. An incident like Yugoslavia's defection threw the apparently rational leaders of the U.S.S.R. into a veritable hysteria. Imperialist spies and Titoist traitors were discovered in the most unlikely places, in persons whose whole career had been one of slavish devotion to Communism and Stalin. Under such circumstances a cool and calculating foreign policy could be incongruously combined with the most fantastic interpretations put upon actions and intentions of other states.

That much of the paradox of Soviet foreign policy between 1949 and 1953 can be traced to Stalin's personal views and predilections will be seen from the actions of his successors. In foreign as well as domestic policies he evidently labored under an increasing sense of his own infallibility, a confidence that he could gauge exactly the threat from abroad and counter it without incurring the risk of all-out war. Many of his aides must have felt that the very atmosphere of isolation and hostility with which he surrounded the Soviet Union, not to say the aggressive *tone* of his policies, enhanced the danger of an all-out confrontation with the United States without at the same time procuring any visible benefits for the U.S.S.R., and must have seen the fantastic campaign against Tito and Yugoslavia as being not so much in the interest of the country as an attempt of an old man to assuage his wounded vanity. To the last Stalin evidently remained confident that he could raise the level of hostility to and provocation of the West without plunging into war. In his *Economic Problems of Socialism in the U.S.S.R.*, written in 1952, he argued that conflicts within the imperialist bloc remained greater than those between the bloc as a whole and the U.S.S.R. This was demonstrated, he argued, by World War II, when "the capitalist countries' struggle for markets and the desire to crush their competitors turned out in actuality to be stronger than the contradictions between the camp of capitalism and the camp of socialism." He went on to argue that "the inevitability of wars among the capitalist countries remains."[5] Thus Stalin credited Soviet— i.e., his own—diplomacy with the ability to divert the threat of war from the Soviet Union and yet to exploit the existence of contradictions within the capitalist camp. He was arguing, Stalin wrote, against those who held that "after the second World War, wars among the capitalist countries have ceased to be inevitable" and who pointed out that the United States was now so dominant in the capitalist camp that no other country or combination of countries would dare to challenge her. But, points out Stalin with the insistence of an old man who sticks to what he has learned a long time before, Germany and Japan used to be powerful nations and

[5] Leo Gruliow, ed., *Current Soviet Policies*, I (New York, 1953), 8.

"to think that these countries will not attempt to rise to their feet again, smash the U.S. 'regime' and break away on a path of independent development is to believe in miracles."[6] And naturally Britain and France will also have to rebel against America "and enter into conflict with the U.S.A. in order to assure themselves an independent position and of course high profits."

This sounds like an echo of the argument Stalin used to soothe the fears of subordinates who tried to point out that the aggressive tone and the pushful character of Soviet foreign policy presented great dangers. No, said Stalin, for all their agitation about Russia the capitalists are more likely to fall out among themselves. Look what happened after World War I and in 1939 and 1941! Both history and personal experience led him to minimize the chances of the capitalist countries uniting effectively to block Soviet expansion. He was even in his last days too intelligent a man to match Hitler's recklessness and repeat after the German: "I have seen your democratic statesmen and they are nothing but worms." And for all his "brinkmanship" in the Berlin blockade and in Korea, he never approached Khrushchev's adventurousness in the early 1960's. But his lieutenants must have felt that in view of the fact that the U.S.S.R. had acquired atomic weapons only recently and her missile system was still to be developed, the risks were excessive.

It is not clear how far this division of opinion was responsible for the changes in the Soviet government which took place in 1949 and which included Vyshinsky superseding Molotov at the Foreign Ministry. The over-all design, which included the relegation of such important figures as Molotov, Bulganin, Beria, and Mikoyan to nondepartmental duties, seemed to be connected with the struggle for succession and Stalin's decision to reduce the influence of—and, if we are to believe Khrushchev's later information, eventually to liquidate—his closest associates. Vyshinsky's appointment certainly marked no major change in foreign policy. The opprobrious prosecutor of the purge trials was a man of no standing within the Party and thus more acceptable than Molotov to the current favorite and intended successor, Malenkov. But the history of Soviet domestic politics in the years preceding Stalin's death is still obscure, as is its relationship to foreign policy.

The new premises on which Soviet policy began to operate in 1949–50 contained a reversal of the earlier expectation of an early American pullout from Europe. The U.S. commitment to stay in Germany and to defend Western Europe was now seen as a cornerstone of American for-

[6] *Ibid.*, p. 7.

eign policy. The Atlantic Alliance was the visible expression of this policy and the means through which the United States meant to push back the Soviet sphere of influence.

In this setting the Soviet policy-makers still did not conclude that a war with the United States was either imminent or inevitable. The Americans, in their opinion, wanted, as Churchill had said of the U.S.S.R., "not war but the fruits of war." Furthermore, though the earlier expectations (before 1948) of American impatience with European entanglements had now evaporated, it was still believed possible to pressure American public opinion to the point where American guidance of NATO would be stripped of its potential aggressiveness and the organization itself rendered largely ineffectual. Those early hopes had been laid to rest with the poor showing of Wallace's Progressive Party in the 1948 elections. But if America by and large could not be convinced of the peace-loving virtues of the Soviet Union, public opinion and Congress might still weary of the troubles and expense of the European alliances, and become skeptical of the feasibility of France and Italy as effective allies, with their large Communist electorates and Communist-dominated unions. Thus the declaration of the West European Communists that the working classes of their countries would refuse to fight against Russia was designed for listeners not only in Europe. The "peace movement," which in 1949 and 1950 became a gigantic propaganda enterprise and to which the European Communist parties were told to devote a major share of their activity, offers another testimony about the Soviet conviction that American policy was not set on a direct confrontation with the U.S.S.R. No such campaign was mounted at the height of the German danger in 1936–38: Hitler and the Japanese were not likely to be inhibited by millions of signatures on any peace appeal. The Stockholm Appeal to abolish atomic weapons was yet another testimony of Russia's enduring optimism that all-out war could be avoided. If the government of the United States was susceptible to such pressures, it was obviously neither ready nor determined to start a preventive war. If it *was* determined, then obviously the whole peace movement would not have been worth all that effort and hullaballoo.

For all of its huge oversimplifications and the obsolete phraseology in which it was couched, Stalin's thesis that contradictions within the imperialist camp prevented it from mounting a resolute anti-Soviet drive contained a grain of truth. A non-Communist writer would translate "contradictions" as differences of opinion and interests attending the elaboration of an alliance between democratic states. They certainly did not amount to the danger of a new intra-imperialist war, as Stalin fondly expected. But those dissonances affected one vital aspect of the Atlantic Alliance, causing it to be regarded by the Kremlin as a serious but not as yet grave or imminent threat to the Soviet position. This was of course the issue of rearming West Germany.[7]

To the Soviet Union, West German rearmament was the main danger to her post-war positions, and the prevention of such a contingency was a principal aim of her foreign policy. In retrospect it is not too much to say that a rearmed West Germany was considered a greater danger than the American monopoly or superiority in atomic weapons. One does not have to go into the psychological and historical reasons for this feeling. But the Kremlin clearly believed that any anti-Soviet alliance, to be really effective, had to include a revivified and rearmed West Germany. Without it, NATO was bound to remain a cumbersome agglomeration of a few American, French, and British divisions, some stray Belgian, Norwegian, etc., brigades. This still aroused Soviet apprehensions and led to increased Soviet preparedness and substantial growth in the Soviet armed forces. But without a German army the type of political-military pressure that the Soviets most feared and that would be able, they thought, to provoke and exploit a revolt in their satellites, could not become an imminent danger. It was a rearmed West Germany that could become the really effective cats-paw of American imperialism.

We have seen how the Soviets pursued a number of strategems to avoid this danger. The great risks involved in the Berlin blockade were undertaken largely in the hope of dissuading the West from setting up a unified West German state. By the spring of 1949 that attempt was proved futile, and the blockade was discontinued. The still earlier hopes that West Germany would find itself in a hopeless economic mess in the wake of the war and the influx of millions of refugees were also exposed as groundless. The currency reform of 1948 set Germany on the road to recovery; by 1950 West Germany was already a major industrial power and the German economic miracle was on its way. The hopes of political dissension also failed to materialize. The Federal Republic set up in 1949, unlike its Weimar predecessor, showed every sign of political stability; its two major parties, the Christian Democrats and the Social Democrats, were

[7] One might object that this critique of Stalin's views is unfair. Some "internal contradictions within the imperialist camp" did develop after all, most notably on the issue of colonial policies between Britain and France on one side and the United States on the other. The disagreement which was demonstrated in the Suez affair of 1956 was to have extremely important consequences in the post-war world. And de Gaulle's policies since 1962 might also be seen as a vindication of Stalin's foresight. But these developments occurred for different reasons and in a quite different form than Stalin postulated in 1952. They do not constitute a vindication of his prophetic power any more than those who between 1944 and 1949 claimed that the Chinese Communists were "different" can claim a justification for their views in the current developments in China.

united in an anti-Soviet posture. The psychological effects of the Berlin blockade went far to minimize any possible pro-Soviet feeling in West Germany, whether of the Communist or of the "Rapallo spirit" variety. Konrad Adenauer's government followed the path of full collaboration with the Western Powers; at the same time the Chancellor began his skillful game of exacting maximum sovereign powers for his regime. Adenauer was also a warm believer in European military and economic integration as the only way of restoring Europe from the disasters of the two world wars and, in the immediate future, as the most effective barrier to Soviet expansion. Thus his regime and its relationship to the West, especially to the United States, was bound to arouse the worst Soviet apprehensions.

That under these circumstances West Germany did not immediately adhere to the North Atlantic Treaty was due, to use Stalin's language, to "internal contradictions within the imperialist camp." One of its members, France, was not ready, four years after the collapse of Hitler, to agree that there should again be a German armed force of large proportions. And until 1947 France had persisted in her proposals to have the Ruhr industrial complex internationalized and the Rhineland detached from Germany; even after that, the problem of the Saar was a stumbling block to France's recognition and collaboration with the West German state. The memories of the Nazi period, the realization that West Germany would surpass France as an industrial power—all those factors fed French reluctance to admit West Germany to a partnership in the Atlantic Alliance. The opening years of the 1950's saw the beginning of the Franco-German reconciliation that eventually blossomed into a partnership. But French opposition was largely responsible for the fact that West Germany's entrance into NATO was postponed for five years. These years were spent in the search for a formula by which West Germany could contribute to the alliance and yet under which there would be no separate *West German* armed force. This was the celebrated and fatuous attempt to construct a European army. Only after the collapse of the European Defense Community in 1954 did France agree to the inclusion of West Germany in NATO and was an effort mounted to build a modern German armed force.

The fact that West Germany did not participate in NATO in the beginning, that five years—a long time in the nuclear age—were to pass before it was admitted as a full member, had a profound effect on the Soviets' appraisal of the importance and potential threat represented by NATO. We shall note again that only *after* Germany entered NATO was a formal counterorganization (the Warsaw Pact) created. The Soviets did not consider NATO, especially without West Germany, as a direct menace to the U.S.S.R.—this is clear even in the propaganda-oriented formulation of official Soviet publications. The United States led in the organization of

NATO because, "basing its policy on such a military organization, it sought to secure the success of its policy from a position of strength in relation to the Soviet Union and other socialist countries, cheap victories in 'local wars,' at the same time preparing for a global thermonuclear war."[8] Despite the sacramental phrase about nuclear war, it is clear that the Russians conceived the primary purpose of NATO to be that of being a bargaining asset in negotiations with the U.S.S.R. and a secondary one to support "wars of national liberation." As to the first, a Western analyst has no reason to quarrel with the Soviet assessment; as to the second, he might point out that it was another instance of the Soviets attributing to their protaganists some of their own mentality and methods. But either way, NATO was thought crippled without the inclusion of West Germany. When that was finally secured under the Paris agreements in October 1954, four years had passed during which the U.S.S.R. had developed her nuclear arsenal and acquired a hydrogen bomb, and during which the value of NATO as a bargaining asset had obviously declined. A Western author puts this point succinctly, though in a somewhat exaggerated form:

> The four years . . . during which negotiations with the Russians had to be abjured because of their possible effect on the European Defense Community were precisely the years in which the negotiating strength of the parties involved changed most radically. The delay postponed the arming of Germany beyond the point at which the prospective German army was a negotiable asset to the West.[9]

This is too strong. The West German army was to remain a negotiable asset beyond 1954, and a West Germany armed with nuclear weapons was to remain a very negotiable asset indeed into the 1960's. But it is probably true that the Russians feared a remilitarized West Germany most acutely between 1950 and 1954 and that to avoid this contingency they would have been willing to pay a fairly high price.

As to what this price would have been, it is difficult to say. It is tempting to postulate that the West could have secured a united, non-Communist—if neutralized—Germany. The wartime experiences left the American statesmen with an almost superstitious fear about negotiating directly with the Russians. And by 1950 there was a substantial body of public opinion in America that believed such negotiations with Communists would lead to a "sell-out," "being tricked," etc. The West, it was held, had finally taken the right course of building up its strength. Once completed, this process would finally make the Russians "behave." (What this was supposed to mean was never specified.) Yet the idea of new summit talks found a convert in a man whom not even Senator McCarthy could identify as be-

[8] A. Lavrishchev and D. Tomashevsky, eds., *International Relations After the Second World War*, II, (Moscow, 1963), 357.

[9] Coral Bell, *Negotiation From Strength* (London, 1962), p. 62.

ing soft on Communism. In March 1950 Churchill said, "I cannot help coming back to this idea of another talk with Soviet Russia upon the highest level. The idea appeals to me of a supreme effort to bridge the gulf between the two worlds so that each can live their life, if not in friendship, at least without the hatreds of war."[10] But Churchill was not in power. Britain's position had drastically declined since the war, and in American eyes the idea of negotiations was seen, a bit justifiably, as a reflection of British weakness.

While the difficulties and weaknesses of decision-making on the Western side are easily seen and those on the Soviet side are largely hidden, it would be a mistake to conclude that the Russians at this point were free of indecision or of the burden of their past policies, ready and able to present East Germany as a peace offering. The German Democratic Republic was created by the Russians in 1949, and its existence was now a fact of European politics. The idea of sacrificing this German Communist regime was not likely to stir up violent emotions in the bosom of a Soviet statesman. Russians were not sentimental, as Litvinov had aptly put it as far back as 1935, explaining why the Soviet Union sought peace with Hitler despite all the things he was doing to German Communists. But such a renunciation could not remain without an effect on what might be called the credibility of the Soviet position in the satellites. From the outside this position looked in 1950 impregnable. The Communist parties in those countries had been thoroughly purged, the populations cowed through terror and new social and economic policies imposed since Tito's defection. But the Soviets knew that any display of weakness—and Soviet abandonment of any Communist regime would be interpreted as such—could have repercussions throughout the satellite bloc. Titoism had been contained, but a demonstration that the Soviet Union could be pushed out of an area she had acquired in World War II would have a demoralizing effect on the Communist leaders and a dangerous one on the populations of Eastern Europe. The year 1956 was to show what could happen if the idea gained ground that defiance of the Soviet Union was not necessarily a hopeless and suicidal proposition.

Thus in 1949–50, on the German problem, the Soviet Union, having tried other stratagems, was seemingly confronted with an invidious choice between two policies, both attendant with grave dangers. She could stick to the status quo of 1949, the existence of two Germanies, and then she confronted the specter of hundreds of thousands (if not millions) of German soldiers taking their place within the Western establishment. Or she could seek an accommodation with the West, but then the minimal Western demand would be a united Germany, and conceding this might set off a chain reaction throughout the satellite bloc.

[10] Quoted in *ibid.*, p. 20.

That the second alternative was not, however, excluded is suggested by several developments in 1949–50. They centered on Poland, then rightly thought to be the most vulnerable dependency of the U.S.S.R. In 1949 the Polish Ministry of Defense and the command of Poland's armed forces was entrusted to Marshal Rokossovsky, who though of Polish descent had spent his whole career in the Red Army. For all the previous seeding of the Polish (and other satellite) armies with Communists and even Soviet citizens, this was a most drastic step, testifying to Soviet eagerness to secure the fullest and most direct control over the Polish armed forces. In June 1950, Walter Ulbricht, on behalf of the German Democratic Republic, signed an agreement with the Polish regime recognizing the Oder-Neisse line as the permanent frontier between Germany and Poland. That a Soviet-controlled East German regime should renounce the lands occupied by Poland since 1945 was hardly surprising, but the timing was. Less than a year had passed since the German Democratic Republic had been set up. It was alleged to represent the genuine will of the people of the eastern zone and a nucleus for the future democratic all-German state. This pre-emptory renunciation of lands that had been German for centuries was not likely to enhance its standing either among its own people or in the western zones. If the German Communist regime was forced to make this sacrifice, it meant that it was held to be of smaller importance than Poland, that the possibility of throwing it to the wolves—i.e., dissolving it within a unified Germany—was not being excluded. Over Poland, the U.S.S.R. now acquired an additional means of pressure and a way to guarantee her staying within the Soviet sphere. Who would protect Poland against future territorial claims by a unified Germany? Even the most anti-Communist Pole could not fail to admit that without Soviet support Poland's western territories could not be protected against a reunified Germany. This very obvious favoring of the Polish Communists over the German ones could only mean that in 1950 Moscow considered the latter expendable, while Poland was regarded as the kingpin of the Soviet position in Eastern Europe.

The specter of a rearmed Germany was brought closer by the September decision of the Western Powers to revise the Occupation Statute, and by the North Atlantic Council simultaneously issuing a statement implying that a West German force would be included in the NATO network. These steps were countered by a meeting in Prague of the foreign ministers of the U.S.S.R. and her satellites. There, the Communists denounced the Western actions but then proposed a solution of the German problem.

One would think that in 1950 the Soviet Union did not have to explain her policies to the satellites, still less seek their approval. Only two days before the Prague meeting, the Soviet government alone had protested the Western actions of September and evidently decided on its own response.

But on the German issue, appearances were thought to be of great importance to the diplomatic game. The foreign minister of the Soviet Union went to the capital of one of the earliest victims of Nazi aggression to take counsel with his colleagues from the socialist camp, among whom was the minister of the German Democratic Republic. There was an air of urgency about the whole venture. The Albanian foreign minister evidently could not be found in a hurry, so obligingly Vyshinsky brought along the Albanian minister in Moscow, so that even the voice of that most miniscule satellite could be raised against the remilitarization of Germany. Was this haste and improvisation connected with events in the Far East, where the Chinese Communists were about to strike in Korea? It was reasonable for the Russians to expect that once the massive Chinese strike became known, any inhibitions about rearming Germany would be dropped and the building of the West German army would proceed at a frantic pace.

The Prague proposals repeated the Soviet demand that the four occupying powers pledge to forbid the remilitarization of Germany and "sincerely [to] carry out the Potsdam Agreement to ensure conditions for the creation of a unified, peace-loving democratic state."[11] More specifically, the Prague proposals submitted that a peace treaty be concluded without delay and that occupation forces be withdrawn from Germany within one year of its signing. An all-German Constituent Council was to be composed, with equal representation of East and West Germany, to prepare a new constitution for the whole country and advise on the preparation of the peace treaty. "Under certain conditions the German people could be directly asked to give their opinion on this proposal."[12]

As was to be expected, the Soviet government on November 3 submitted that the Prague proposals be placed on the agenda of a meeting of the foreign ministers' council of the Big Four to be called forthwith, and be discussed there in conjunction with the statement of the foreign ministers of the three Western Powers on September 19. This last interesting item lends substance to the belief that the Prague proposals were not formulated *entirely* for propaganda purposes. The linking of the two sets of proposals was on the face of it illogical: the September 19 communiqué of the United States and her two associates looked forward to Germany contributing to the defense of the West; the Prague declaration was emphatic about "the prevention of the revival of the German war potential." Thus the proposed meeting of the Big Four was to discuss two sets of proposals and reconcile two plans, one looking to a remilitarization of West Germany (to use the Soviet expression), the other to solid guarantees that Germany would remain disarmed! This apparent absurdity is resolvable only on the assumption that the Soviet note was a clumsy hint that the

[11] *Documents on International Affairs, 1949–1950* (London, 1953), p. 167.
[12] *Ibid.*, p. 168.

Soviets were ready to trade some concessions for the West's abandonment of its intention to rearm Germany. Otherwise, why not simply denounce the September 19 proposals and say they were unacceptable to the U.S.S.R., which would never tolerate a rearmed West Germany. Yet the language of the Soviet declaration is studiously moderate: "The Soviet Government considers that the questions concerned in the communiqué of the Ministers of Foreign Affairs of the United States, Great Britain and France of September 19 and also in the Prague declaration possess the greatest significance for the cause of assuring international peace and security and touch fundamental national interests of the peoples of Europe."[13]

That the Soviet diplomatic gambit was so clumsy, and the reference to a possible bargain so obscure, was due to the Soviet policy-makers' long-standing conviction that nothing is as fatal as to impart a feeling of weakness or to spell out too clearly one's real fears and apprehensions. That one should create the impression of negotiating from a "position of strength" was a maxim of Soviet foreign policy long before the phrase became fashionable in the United States. In the 1930's when this possibility inwardly panicked the Soviet leaders, Molotov in public speeches used to declare that anybody who doubted the might of the Red Army was welcome to try to invade the U.S.S.R.

But if the Russians were alarmed at the prospect of a reborn Wehrmacht, American policy-makers were no less alarmed at the idea of negotiating with the Soviets. The Korean War was going on. The whole record of a decade of negotiations with the Communists was currently an explosive political issue. It would be a decade before an American President said, "We must never fear to negotiate." The tragi-comic situation into which world affairs had been plunged due to Soviet oversubtlety on the one hand and American feeling of inferiority when it came to negotiations with the Communists on the other was epitomized in Secretary Acheson's reaction: "We will always hope for and welcome tangible proof that Soviet intentions have changed. The Prague statement gives us no such proof."[14] Thus, near the end of his days, Stalin was called upon to perform a rite he had so often inflicted on others: confession and recantation. And Acheson did not realize that in 1950 he could have been negotiating from a "position of strength," while a few short years would erode that position.

To say that negotiations could have been fruitful is not to say that they would have been successful. The American concept of diplomacy—before a negotiation succeeds both sides must demonstrate that they are "sincere"—clashed with the Soviet one, in which negotiations are a means of assessing your opponent's intentions and strengths and, if necessary, of arriving at a bargain. The Prague proposals had several built-in devices

[13] *Ibid.*, p. 170.
[14] *Ibid.*

for evasion and procrastination. There was, as Western observers were quick to point out, a special "catch" in the provision about the Constituent Council composed in equal numbers of the representatives of East and West Germany. Why should East Germany, whose population was not much more than one-third of that in the West, be equally represented? More important, the eastern representatives were in fact bound to be the nominees of the Soviets and subject to their orders. They could prolong the discussion until Doomsday unless Soviet *desiderata* were accepted. And the foreign ministers' conference of the Big Four had met many times before and the German peace treaty was as far from being agreed upon as ever. Perhaps the Soviet initiative was designed to shelve, or avoid, the issue of rearming Germany while at the same time not committing the Soviet Union to anything.

The last point was well taken. Yet there was nothing to prevent the Western Powers from pursuing West German rearmament and at the same time probing Soviet intentions and discovering the price Russia would be willing to pay for assuagement of her apprehensions. But precisely here, the counterargument would run, lay the danger of negotiating with the Russians at all. Any conference, any glimpse of a solution to Europe's most vexing problem, would raise false hopes in the West, weaken the all too recent resolve of the democracies and especially of the American people to spare neither money nor men to stop the Communist threat.

The situation in September-October 1950 epitomizes the whole impasse that East-West diplomacy had reached within five years of the end of the war. By her truculence and apparent readiness to risk war, the Soviet Union had successfully masked her weakness and made it possible to consolidate her grip on eastern and southeastern Europe, something a more amenable Russia, openly bent on avoiding war, might not have been able to get away with. To put it more plainly, if in oversimplified form, if the Western statesmen had not been scared that Russia at a moment's notice would launch her armies on a sweep to the Atlantic, they would not have reacted so supinely to Russia's satellization of Poland, Rumania, etc., and certainly would not have acquiesced in the February 1948 events in Czechoslovakia or in the cutting of their rail and road links to Berlin in 1948–49. But precisely because of the weakness of the West's earlier responses, the belated effort by the United States and her partners to set a barrier against Soviet expansion had to be interpreted by the U.S.S.R. as an aggressive step. The Russians knew that they would not and could not move against the West. What, then, was the purpose of NATO, if not to push them from the positions they had secured in Eastern Europe between 1944 and 1948? Contrariwise, the Western statesmen, at least in 1949, and 1950, knew that they would not and could not reverse the *faits accomplis* in Poland and Rumania, etc. Why, then, did the Russians try to sabotage

NATO unless they wanted a disarmed and weak Western Europe as their prey?

In this new situation, the U.S.S.R. was willing to pay a price to prevent the rearming of Germany, the key issue. But because of her previous diplomatic record, there was no meaningful way to indicate convincingly to the West that she *now* wanted to negotiate seriously about Germany, that she *now* was seriously disquieted about the West's intentions. The U.S.S.R. could not say in so many words: "When we said before that you imperialists are preparing war, it was propaganda. But now we are almost ready to believe it, so can't we sit down and really negotiate?" Such an approach, at least by the Russians' own standards, would have meant an open invitation for the West to exploit Soviet weaknesses. The Western price for not rearming Germany might rise. And the whole threatening posture of Soviet diplomacy might be seen as bluff and bluster.

To Soviet diplomacy was thus entrusted an impossible task: to negotiate on and to prevent Germany's rearmament without at the same time conveying how much Russia feared this contingency and how much she would be willing to pay to avoid it. But from this impossible task Soviet diplomacy was largely rescued by two developments on the Western side: first, the general Western reluctance to negotiate with the Russians; and second, the snail's pace at which negotiations were proceeding about the extent and form in which German rearmament should take place. Acheson's original reluctance to discuss the Prague proposals was mitigated by conversations with the European allies, and what emerged was the usual unfortunate compromise: the West agreed to negotiate about negotiating. As Bevin phrased it, the Western governments were willing to talk with the Russians, but "they could only undertake this after careful preparation and in circumstances which provided a real opportunity for them to contribute effectively to a solution of fundamental world problems."[15] This cautious language of old-time diplomacy was ill suited to the circumstances of 1950. From the point of view of the United States the "fundamental world problem" was the existence of the U.S.S.R., and from that of Russia it was the existence and power of America, and these could not be solved or wished away.

After further sparrings, a meeting of foreign ministers' deputies convened in Paris on March 5, 1951, to discuss the agenda for the Big Four foreign ministers' conference. But the Soviet Union's original willingness to broaden the proposed discussions beyond the German issue soon vanished. The reason was obvious.

The principal, and possibly the sole, cause of that [Soviet] initiative was the American determination to rearm Western Germany. This de-

[15] *Ibid.*, pp. 171–72.

termination was made plain in September 1950. But a few months later, even as early as the meeting of the North Atlantic Council in December of that year, it was becoming evident that for all practical purposes German rearmament was not going to be quickly effected.[16]

There was thus no reason for the Russians to bare their soul or, to put it more prosaically, to intimate the possibility of concessions on German unity. Gromyko, the Soviet delegate at the Paris meeting, was obdurate: he insisted that the foreign ministers' conference have as the main item on its agenda the issues of the North Atlantic Treaty Organization and American bases abroad. The United States could hardly be enchanted by the prospect of a conference whose main business would be to listen to Soviet denunciations of American policies and to witness Soviet probing for weak spots in the Western Alliance. On June 21 the conference collapsed.

The sequence of events between September 1950 and June 1951 brings out once again the characteristic features of Soviet diplomacy of Stalin's era. A concrete danger, German rearmament, brings an instant reaction— willingness to negotiate—and intimations, though not very clear ones, that these negotiations are to be in earnest, i.e., that they might involve genuine Soviet concessions. But as the danger recedes Soviet tactics become dilatory, propaganda rather than a settlement becomes the Soviet objective. The months between September and June enabled the Soviets to perceive and appreciate the fissures in the Western camp: the French were still alarmed at the prospect of a German army and in its place proposed the obviously impractical and ill fated scheme of the "European army," in which the West German quota would be carefully limited and West German units would not be larger than batallion size. The British government believed in conferences as a means of allaying international tension and of relieving the British public, increasingly fearful of the effects of American rashness and impatience. The American government went into the whole conference business with profound distaste and many apprehensions: in addition to the political reverberations at home, the whole painfully elaborated scheme of NATO had just been launched, finally. What would happen to NATO, to the American commitment to Europe, if the Russians showed signs of becoming reasonable *before* NATO was finally established, before its table of organization, commands, committees, etc., were finally elaborated? Against this elephantine gait of Western diplomacy, Soviet foreign policy appears nimble, designed to keep its opponents off balance. The Paris conference had barely collapsed, the State Department scribes were barely ready with their position papers and documented recitals of Communist bad faith and abuse of negotiations, when the Soviets were ready with yet another "peace initiative." On June 23, the Soviet repre-

[16] *Survey of International Affairs, 1951*, p. 138.

sentative at the United Nations broadcast a speech suggesting that the time had come to have discussions on a possible armistice in Korea. The timing was not coincidental. As the long-drawn-out period of truce negotiations in Korea was to demonstrate, the Russians were not yet convinced that the time had come to wind up the Korean venture. But it was thought unwise to let the international situation reach the boiling point. Baffled and frustrated, the Americans might ride roughshod over their allies' scruples and reservations, insist on the immediate creation of a West German army. Having slammed the door in Paris on any international *détente*, the Soviets within two days were willing to leave it ajar.

It is a hugely oversimplified view of Soviet foreign policy to say that the Soviet drive for expansion that was checked in Europe was intensified in Asia with the Korean War. But there is no question that events and opportunities in Asia were viewed from the Kremlin in conjunction with developments in Europe. In both places the crucial element in Soviet tactics was the appraisal of American intentions and capabilities. The loss of prestige suffered during World War II by the colonial powers because of the Japanese victories, the intimations that the United States would not strain herself to help to re-establish the French and British empires,[17] and finally the obvious weakness of the British, French, and Dutch in the wake of the war—all these augured well for the Communists' chances to exploit the nationalist tendencies of the colonial peoples. It is, then, all the more remarkable that despite all these developments, and despite the Communist interest and activity in Asia going back to the beginnings of the movement, Asia except for China and Japan was not a primary concern of Soviet foreign policy between 1945 and 1948. The reasons for this are complex. They have to do, for example, with Communists remaining in the French government well into 1947 and consequently taking a rather ambiguous attitude toward Indochina, with the Soviets' long-standing dislike of the Congress Party in India and hence their apparent lack of interest in the transfer of power in that subcontinent in 1947, etc. But the main reason lies in the Soviet Union's concentration on those areas of Communist expansion that were of *direct* interest to her—Europe and the Far East. By 1948 the Soviets seem to have determined on a shift in this attitude: Western imperialism in Asia had proved much weaker than their most optimistic analyses could have prophesied. Above all the successes of the Chinese Communists found an echo in guerrilla activities in Malaya, in the intensification of the war in Indochina and in the at-

[17] E.g., President Roosevelt's musings about an international mandate after the war for Indochina, his prodding the British to make a gift of Hong Kong to Chiang, etc.

tempted Communist coup in Indonesia. While none of those activities can be traced to a specific directive from Moscow, they must have received Soviet approval.

By 1949 the nexus between events in Asia and the European situation became of even greater interest to the U.S.S.R. Two of NATO's principal members were bogged down in colonial wars in Asia. The British involvement in Malaya and the French in Indochina were tying down military power and resources that might otherwise be devoted to NATO. The French involvement in Indochina was especially serious: it increasingly absorbed regular French army units, since conscripts were not being sent overseas, especially the officer corps. The resulting weakness of the French army in Europe had a double effect on NATO: it would be unable in the foreseeable future to dispose of a sizable French contingent; and, paradoxically, because of this fact French politicians were strengthened in their doubts and temporizing over West German participation in the organization, fearing the prospect of a European army where the German contingent would be dominant. Thus inevitably Asian affairs forced themselves on the attention of Soviet policy-makers to the point where the complexities of the Philippine guerrilla movement, or Ho Chi Minh's balancing act between nationalism and Communism would become a matter of concern not for some subordinate official of the Central Committee but for the very top of the Soviet hierarchy.

The summit talks between Stalin and Mao Tse-tung that took place between December 1949 and February 1950 undoubtedly covered the whole range of Communist prospects and tactics in Asia. The first apparent fruit of the discussions was the two Communist super-powers' recognition of Ho Chi Minh's government: Peking announcing its recognition on January 18 and Moscow on January 30. On its face, the step was a drastic departure from usual Soviet practice. After all, the Chinese Communists were recognized as *the* government of China only after there could be no doubt of the completeness of their victory. The Greek Communist government (i.e., the insurgents of 1946–49), despite vociferous Soviet support, had never been accorded official recognition. Indochina had been a colony of France, and France had recently acknowledged the regime of the former emperor Bao Dai as an independent state and member of the French Union. With the civil war still raging, it was far from sure whether Ho Chi Minh's regime would prevail or whether in fact it would not arrive at some sort of compromise with the French-sponsored Vietnamese government. Soviet haste in recognizing it was, then, most uncharacteristic. Furthermore, at a time when there was still a deep division within the French public as to the desirability of NATO, such a step must have appeared as a needless taunt to France and a discouragement to the French neutralists.

Was the January 1950 action, then (in which, again uncharacteristically, Peking took the initiative and Moscow followed), one of the first steps by the Chinese to force the Russians to adopt a more militant posture in Asia? Prior to these events Ho Chi Minh talked moderation, hinted at the possibility of remaining under certain conditions in the French Union. Now his recognition by the Communist bloc effectively barred the prospects of a coalition-type solution in Indochina. It had not been entirely within the realm of fantasy to suppose that the Soviet Union might have recognized the French-sponsored Vietnam regime or bargained for such a recognition and an alleviation of the war in Indochina in return for France diluting her allegiance to NATO. Now such a possibility was excluded.[18]

Since we have not been vouchsafed a record of the Stalin-Mao talks, it is, of course, impossible to go beyond conjecture concerning in what detail the two leaders discussed future plans, including Korean affairs. That the Chinese Communists at that time could have forced the Soviet Union to make a major shift in her foreign policy—or would have dared to try it with Stalin at the helm—is most unlikely. But as the record shows, they could and did prod the Soviets into a more militant pose. Stalin could be a good listener. The Chinese themselves had a most impressive record in making him attend to them. One can imagine respectful hints conveyed in Communist semantics. The imperialist bloc is still strong and determined on its policy in Europe; in Asia, on the contrary, the imperialists are confused and irresolute, witness the American White Paper on China. By keeping relentless pressure on them in Asia one could frustrate their aggressive plans in Europe. One can also visualize Stalin warning, in his indirect way, that one should not underestimate the Americans, then asking his Chinese guests for an opinion—would the people of South Korea indefinitely support the rule of the American puppet Syngman Rhee or were they ripe for revolt? And how determined were the Americans to keep their grip on Japan? Would not the increasing amount of trouble in that country, combined with the recent events on the Asian mainland, persuade them to terminate their occupation?

Both Stalin and Mao must have recognized that whatever their differences of opinion they had to create the impression of solidarity. Acheson and his fellow American policy-makers have been much criticized in retrospect for voicing publicly in 1949 and 1950 the hope that Communist China would diverge from the Kremlin and that a species of Titoism would eventually flourish in Peking. But in all fairness it must be remem-

---

[18] Tito's Yugoslavia, still entertaining great hopes about "the light from the East" and of Stalinism finding its downfall in Asia, hastened to recognize Ho. The initiative came from the latter, even though Vietminh organs continued to denounce Titoism in the usual Communist style of the period.

bered that the same hope was being even more vigorously expressed by
the greatest current experts on Titoism—namely, the Yugoslav Communists themselves. What was being overlooked in this wishful thinking was
the fact that Communist Yugoslavia had turned to the West in *despair*
and only *after* it became clear that her liquidation was Stalin's aim. That
rumors about Chinese susceptibility to Titoism were current in the beginning of 1950 was probably helpful to Mao in his negotiations. He had
been dropping hints in his speeches and writings that there were *still*
people in his party who were not fully convinced of the Americans' evil
intentions and of the Soviets' true international spirit. It thus behooved
the Russians, he implied, to lay such base rumors to rest by being helpful
to the Chinese, giving up their special privileges in China, etc. Even before the negotiations were concluded, the Soviets were willing to oblige
their Chinese partners in one respect: the Soviet Union refused to participate in United Nations agencies as long as the Nationalists had not
been expelled and Peking seated as the legitimate government of China.
The absence of Soviet representatives was of course to have fateful consequences when the Security Council convened in June 1950 to consider
the invasion of South Korea. On the face of it, the Soviet action of January
1950 was not so much petulant as superfluous: within a few months, it
was assumed, the forces of Chiang Kai-shek would be chased out of their
remaining bastions in Hainan and Formosa. But to the Soviets this undoubtedly appeared as a "cheap" way of showing concern for their Chinese comrades' prestige.

Whatever indignities or disappointments they suffered at the hands of
the Russians, the Chinese then and there had a clear interest in maintaining and accentuating the tension between the United States and the
U.S.S.R. This tension raised the value of China as an ally, made Soviet
economic and military aid more likely, Soviet divisive maneuvers within
the Communist Party of China, or an attempt to detach Manchuria or
Sinkiang, less likely. Their own power in mainland China had not yet
been consolidated. Any accommodation between the United States and
the U.S.S.R. would give the latter time and leisure to re-examine her
China policy, to take steps to hang on to her special position, perhaps
even to bolster it, in Manchuria and Sinkiang. And furthermore the history
of the last twenty years demonstrated that Mao and his group had a
genuine revulsion toward the capitalist world and a genuine fear that the
Soviets might lapse into "revisionist" practices. Apart from their own national and personal interests, the Chinese had felt it their ideological duty
to spur the Russians on to greater enthusiasm and greater efforts on behalf of world Communism.

As to the role of the Chinese in deciding on the events as they unfolded
in June 1950 in Korea, we are entirely in the dark. North Korea had been

a Soviet bailiwick ever since its occupation in 1945 by the Soviet army sweeping from Manchuria; the top posts in the regime had gone to Korean Communists who had been trained in the Soviet Union or whose ties had been predominantly with the U.S.S.R. rather than with China. The first Chinese ambassador to North Korea did not arrive until August 1950. The method chosen in attacking South Korea, an outright military attack across the frontier line, diverged from the "Chinese" pattern of "wars of liberation," where widespread guerrilla activities and the virtual paralysis of the enemy authority were to precede operations by regular massed armies. (This was the pattern which in November 1949 was advocated by Mao's then second in command, Liu Shao-chi, as a model for all revolutionary movements in Asia and other colonial and semi-colonial areas.) Eager as the Chinese were for Communist revolutionary expansion everywhere, minimal as the chances of an American response to the invasion of South Korea were undoubtedly held, it is still unlikely that they could have wished for this invasion to take place at the time and in the form it was to assume. In June 1950 they still had as their first priority the completion of the conquest of China, i.e., the conquest of Tibet and, especially, of Formosa. Any drastic development in the Far East just *might* conceivably make the Americans change their officially avowed policy of not interfering in the case of a Communist attack on Formosa.

Everything then would point to the conclusion that the Korean affair was undertaken at Soviet initiative. That the North Koreans would have attacked on their own is inconceivable. That the Chinese wished a development of that nature to take place in June 1950, when preparations were maturing for an invasion of Formosa, is unlikely.

The question now arises, what did the Soviets hope to accomplish in ordering or allowing the North Koreans to invade the Republic of Korea? The divided status of Korea dated from the Cairo conference of 1943, which promised this country independence, and from a subsequent decision on the occupation zones—Russian in the north, American in the south. The Soviet troops withdrew on January 1, 1949, the Americans a few months later, but both left in their wake separate regimes, each of which claimed to represent the genuine will of the entire Korean nation. The Korean National Democratic Republic presented the usual appearance of a Soviet satellite. In the south, President Syngman Rhee's regime disturbed its American protectors by its illiberal and dictatorial ways. Border warfare and guerrilla activities in the south had been going on for some time prior to June 25, 1950, when a full-scale invasion threatened in rapid order to turn the whole country into a Soviet dependency.

The most widely accepted explanation of Soviet motivations is still the most logical one: looking at the situation from the Kremlin vantage point, there was no reason to suppose that there was any appreciable chance of an American intervention. It promised to be an easy tidying-up operation: the badly equipped and trained South Korean troops were no match for the North Koreans. The Americans had not intervened to save Chiang Kai-shek's toe-hold on the mainland of China. That, having thus allowed Communism the Asian *pièce de resistance*, they would now overreact to this swallowing of what was at most an *hors d'oeuvre* must have appeared most unlikely. Where was the logical difference in, say, the Chinese Communists crossing the Yangtze and taking south China and the crossing of the 38th Parallel by the North Koreans? There were no Soviet troops or indeed advisers with the advancing North Koreans. As in the Chinese case, it could be classified as a civil war—and such indeed the Soviets dubbed it from the beginning.[19] Authoritative American spokesmen had more than once specified—Secretary Acheson's speech on January 12, 1950 is the clearest case in point—that South Korea was not within the sphere of American vital interests or defense commitments in the Pacific (as distinguished from Japan and the Philippines). Under these circumstances it would have been fantastic to allow for the possibility of the United States pouring men and treasure into Korea during the next few years on a scale which, if applied in China, would have probably enabled Chiang to preserve power in at least a sizable part of the mainland.

This, then, is the explanation which in the absence of any hard evidence we must accept as the most logical one. If it was a case of miscalculating the American response, the action was more excusable and at all appearances less risky for the Soviet Union than setting up the Berlin blockade. But the question still remains why it was undertaken in the first place. While the Russians might be able to discount American armed help to South Korea, it could not be assumed that yet another Communist conquest would increase the popularity of the U.S.S.R. in America or pass without effect on the American defense effort. In that sense the Korean adventure represented a risk, one which must have been assessed against some expected advantages going beyond the mere conquest of more territory.

The inference is very strong that the Communist absorption of South Korea was designed to transform the whole Pacific situation, especially in regard to Japan. Late in 1949 the Soviets had redoubled their campaign against General MacArthur's occupation regime. The Japanese Communists were at the same time vigorously pushed to engage in more militant and disruptive tactics. The fall of yet another Pacific area into Communist hands would intensify pressures on the American occupation

---

[19] Official Soviet sources have invariably claimed that it was the South Korean government that started the war by invading the north, in which case it is remarkable that within a few hours North Korean troops were ten to fifteen miles within southern territory.

forces and would lead many Japanese to conclude that Communism was indeed the wave of the future, at least in Asia. The Americans could react in one of two ways: they might decide to cut their losses and give up their plans of rebuilding Japan as a military power.[20] In that case the Americans might agree to a Japanese peace treaty on conditions agreeable to the U.S.S.R., i.e., to a demilitarized Japan and withdrawal of their forces. Once that occurred, prospects for a Communist takeover of Japan, it was believed, would be bright indeed. Between a Communist China and Communist Japan, the U.S.S.R. could exercise balance-of-power politics indefinitely and could maintain unquestioned hegemony in the Far East. Or the United States might react in the opposite way and cling to Japan at all costs. This would presumably lead to America's increasing her forces in Japan and commitments in the neighboring areas. In that case the Americans would have to re-examine and reduce their commitments in Europe. The enhanced American presence in Japan and the Pacific would undoubtedly increase the Chinese Communists' dependence on the U.S.S.R. We do not know whether the Soviet-Chinese alliance of February 1950 had secret military clauses. But it is reasonable to suppose that a provision was made for a joint (i.e., Soviet) over-all command of the forces in the event of an apparent threat from Japan. We know that the Korean War was the occasion of the Chinese agreeing to the Soviets' postponement of the evacuation of Port Arthur. Moscow must have expected that an expanded American presence in Japan would inevitably lead to virtual Soviet military control of Manchuria. And what such control would mean, especially in the case of the area crucial to China's industrial development, does not have to be spelled out.

The Korean venture could thus be rationalized as promising great advantages to the Soviet Union with minimal risks. Yet there must have been voices urging caution. The decisions taken within a short time after Stalin's death by his successors reflect a feeling that in his last years the old despot had forsaken his customary prudence. To be sure, by then they had the Korean experience behind them.

That the Chinese Communists acquiesced in the scheme must be attributed to their unequal position in 1950 vis-à-vis the U.S.S.R. The Russians could well point out that the prospective invasion fitted in with the Chinese concept of militant Communist tactics and of the United States as a "paper tiger." Presumably the Chinese could have rejoined that their concept of militancy implied the avoidance of a head-on collision with the main imperialist power, and that the concept of the U.S. as a "paper

[20] The Soviets believed firmly in American intentions to that effect. Visits of various American high personages to Tokyo in the spring of 1950 were thus interpreted. In particular, a sinister motivation was attributed to the visit of John Foster Dulles to Korea and Tokyo a few days before the Korean invasion.

tiger" was meant to present America not as weak but as irresolute and incapable of utilizing her strength. It was in situations as unclear and confused as in the civil wars in China and Indochina that the Americans were reduced to ineffective scheming. An outright military invasion of what was in fact an American protectorate might produce a different response. But, to repeat, in 1950 the Chinese could argue with and prod the Russians, but they could not disagree with clear-cut directives laid down by the master.

The United States' vigorous reaction to the Korean invasion caught the Russians by surprise. The Security Council from which the Soviet delegate had been absent from January met the very same day and called upon the North Koreans to withdraw. On June 27, in view of their refusal and continued advance, the Council condemned them as aggressors and ordered its members to help South Korea. The same day President Truman ordered American naval and air units to help the invaded country. At the same time the U.S. Seventh Fleet was ordered to quarantine Formosa, thus barring a Communist invasion of the island as well as Chiang's return to the mainland (at the moment a very remote possibility). On June 30 American ground units were also ordered into action, and thus the American commitment to defend South Korea under the auspices of the United Nations became a full one.

The Soviets' public reaction testified to their bewilderment. If the fiction of the action being a *South* Korean invasion was to be maintained, the Soviet government should immediately have addressed notes of protest to the United States and the United Nations. But no such notes were delivered; instead, the U.S.S.R. on June 27 was the recipient of an American note asking the Soviet government rather disingenuously to disavow its "responsibility for this unprovoked and unwarranted act" and to use its influence with the North Korean authorities to withdraw their forces. In a reply of June 29 the Soviets were delighted to disavow their responsibility but indicated that *their* information was that it was South Korea which attacked and not vice versa. This Soviet retort was mild: it did not contain any of the usual ominous warnings about the consequences of U.S. actions or possible spreading of the conflict. Instead it spoke only of the "impermissibility of interference of foreign Powers in the internal affairs of Korea."[21]

The American note of June 27 (to emphasize still further that it was not an ultimatum, it was officially designated as an *aide-memoire,* a note of record in loose translation) had relieved the Russians from any immediate concern about a possible confrontation with the United States. It reflected widespread concern lest Truman's action should precipitate World

---

[21] *Documents on International Affairs, 1949–1950,* p. 635.

War III; the great fear in the United States was about possible Russian reactions. But, to use a phrase employed during a later crisis, this was *not* an "eyeball to eyeball" situation. There was then no reason for the Russians to "blink" or, in the immediate context, to do anything.

From the Soviet point of view, another encouraging element in a generally embarrassing situation was that Truman's actions included provisions that were bound to incense the Chinese. The latter, whose responsibility for the actions in Korea was at most secondary, were dealt a stunning blow about Formosa. And, for good measure, in the same message the President ordered the strengthening of American aid to the Philippines and a dispatch of a military mission to Indochina. The intricacies of American domestic politics that made Truman present this package could not be appreciated in Peking, where there was undoubtedly deep bitterness at the fact that they were being punished for this action by the Soviets and their satellite. Mao's statement of June 29 that Asian affairs ought to be left to Asian nations may have had wider connotations.[22] But whatever their private feelings about Russia, the Chinese had to store their bitterness against them for some future time. For the moment it was the United States that had insulted and was apparently threatening their state.

The Soviet government elaborated its response to the new situation with some leisure. This task evidently took about a week. Between June 27 and July 3 the news from Korea was tucked on the back pages of the Soviet press, and nothing suggested to the Soviet reader that a major world crisis had just been unleashed or that a threat of war confronted the U.S.S.R. On the contrary, Comrade Stalin had just committed to print his monumental thesis on linguistics, and tributes to it from various philologists, etc., dwarfed the news from the Far East. An *almost* equal amount of space was devoted to a learned discussion of the theories of the late academician Pavlov. If the Soviet citizen might become alarmed that, while his leaders pursued such learned and peaceful pursuits, the Americans would get away with their imperialist schemes, he was undoubtedly comforted by the news of literally hundreds of millions of people throughout the world signing the Stockholm Appeal demanding the banning of the atom bomb, and the commentaries pointing out that in view of this mighty upsurge of world public opinion no government, not even the American government, would dare to unleash an atomic war. Preoccupied as they were with linguistics and physiology, the rulers of Russia kept a vigilant watch over even minor transgressions of the American warmongers. On July 2 the Soviet government solemnly protested the action of the American air force in dropping the Colorado beetle over the territory

[22] *Pravda,* June 30, 1950.

of the German Democratic Republic, where this imperialist bug would consume a large portion of the flourishing socialist potato crop.

On July 3 the indignation of the Soviet people finally exploded. On that day, mass meetings throughout the Soviet Union demanded "hands off Korea" and condemned the American aggressors. The next day the Soviet Foreign Ministry published a lengthy statement on United States intervention in Korea. It was obviously the product of considerable staff work and historical research. The American action, it said, had long been premeditated. The final touches were put on by Dulles who a few days before the aggression inspected South Korean troops on the 38th Parallel.[23] The decision of the Security Council was illegal in the absence of the Soviet and legitimate Chinese representatives. The Secretary General of the United Nations, Mr. Trygve Lie, had played an "unseemly role." Why, having repulsed the "invasion," should the North Koreans now find themselves deep in South Korea? Here a felicitous historical analogy occurred to the Soviet diplomats. Remember the American Civil War? There the reactionary South also attacked the progressive North! Did the progressive northern forces content themselves with repulsing the attack of the "slave-owners of the South?" No. They "transferred military operations to the territory of the Southern states, routed the troops of the planters and slave owners, who did not enjoy the support of the people . . . and created the conditions for establishing national unity."[24] The note dwelt with some satisfaction on the American action on Formosa, an "outright aggression against China." It prophesied that the United States meant to take over not only South but also North Korea.

There were other historical digressions—how during the Russian Civil War the American interventionists "shot Russian workers and peasants," etc. But it ended on a rather anticlimactic point: the Security Council should demand an immediate American withdrawal from Korea. There was no threat, even an indirect one, of Soviet action: "The Soviet government invariably adheres to a policy of strengthening peace the world over and to its traditional policy of noninterference in the domestic affairs of other states."

The relaxed tone of the Soviet note reflected, it is fair to say, two elements in the situation: first and above all, the lack of any imminent threat to the Soviet Union and recognition of the obvious concern of the Amer-

---

[23] The "proof" was triumphantly displayed several days later in the form of a photograph from an English newspaper. It shows Dulles on this very parallel accompanied by an American major and a South Korean military officer. And what is Dulles doing? Why, looking at a map. And, as the caption explains, he is studying the area through which the South Koreans would launch their attack on the 25th.

[24] *Documents on International Affairs, 1949–1950*, p. 653.

ican policy-makers not to provoke Russia. In the second place, the North Koreans were scoring military successes. That the hastily organized and scattered American units would be able to prevent the invaders from conquering the peninsula must have appeared unlikely. And, judging from the American mood and actions, the United States was likely to "take out" this new defeat on Communist China. If there was at any time some thought of ordering the North Koreans to stop after having repelled the "invasion," the gambit was evidently abandoned by July 3.

Soviet composure also reflected confidence that Moscow could control the actions of the Chinese Communists. Following the events of June, Peking violently denounced the United States, but mainly concerning the American action off Formosa. Throughout July the Chinese showed no signs of either giving or promising help to the North Koreans.[25] Had they been primarily involved in planning the Korean action, it would have been logical for them to render help in July if that would spell (as it might well have) the end of the U.S. toehold on the peninsula.

By the middle of the month Soviet policy shifted. It was becoming more probable that the U.S. would not be chased out of Korea and that her military build-up there could result in an eventual setback for the Communists. In addition, other members of the U.N. were hastening to support the United States. This solidarity and the prospect of a dramatic reversal in the fortunes of war would create a bad precedent. Prime Minister Nehru's initiative of mid-July called for the Security Council to take speedy steps to terminate the conflict. The Council should admit, the Indian statesman proposed, a representative of Communist China and Russia should return for the talks. Stalin's answer to Nehru represented a considerable shift from the position of July 4: he granted the desirability of the Security Council's solving the conflict "with the obligatory participation of the five Great Powers, including the People's Government of China," and added a suggestion that the Council should hear "representatives of the Korean people."[26] Not a word about American aggression or about the need for the immediate withdrawal of U.S. troops. Nor was it a clear-cut demand for seating Communist China in the Security Council. She was to participate in the solution of the conflict—which again left a latitude for varying interpretations.

Nehru's initiative had no immediate results because the United States would not at this juncture admit Communist China to a seat in the Security Council or even explore the possibility of negotiating with her. Undaunted,

[25] Allen S. Whiting, *China Crosses the Yalu* (New York, 1960), pp. 54–62.

[26] This phrase was assumed to mean *only* the North Koreans. Yet the phrase was studiously ambiguous. Had Stalin meant to exclude South Koreans he would have used the usual Communist semantics: the "real representatives of the Korean people."

the U.S.S.R. now proclaimed her intention to end her boycott of the Security Council. On August 1, Ambassador Malik took his seat, and by coincidence this was the month for the U.S.S.R. to assume the rotating chairmanship of the Council.

The Soviet return was rightly taken by world public opinion as a confession that her original decision to boycott the United Nations until Communist China were accorded a seat had been a blunder. And it meant that the U.S.S.R. would now try to weaken the virtual unanimity of the United Nations on the Korean question. In his activity in the Council, Malik began to hint at the need for negotiations. His formula, as officially proposed on August 4, went back to Stalin's of July 15, but it was now spelled out that the representatives of both Korean regimes would be invited and that Peking would be asked to participate *without* necessarily being admitted to the United Nations.

American diplomacy during the Korean conflict is still the subject of violent controversy. And the lessons of Korea were to influence the course of American foreign policy well into our own day. The many points of that controversy cannot be discussed here. In the absence of an equally revealing debate and self-criticism on the Soviet side, it is impossible to determine the validity of various criticisms about the political aspect of the Korean conflict. What were the Soviets' calculations once they reached the conclusion that the Americans would not be pushed out of Korea and that they inevitably would move north again? Were there Soviet MacArthurs proclaiming that this was the moment to try to involve the United States in a war with China, the war that could bog down American forces for decades and that would prevent China from ever challenging the primacy of the Soviet Union? Were there other voices warning that the Soviet Union could not remain uninvolved in a conflict of that kind? What was, finally, the position of the Chinese Communists, who, great as their faith in world Communism was, could not fail to appreciate that they were being asked after twenty years of civil war and with their power still unconsolidated to meet a powerful enemy and possibly to become the target of atomic attack? None of these intriguing questions can be answered on the basis of our current knowledge.

One thing remains clear, and that is the extreme reluctance of the Soviets to become involved militarily in any phase of the Korean conflict. The epithet "peace-loving," bestowed on herself by Stalin's Russia, was certainly well merited from that point of view. The course of events in 1950 was ironic. Here was the Soviet Union which had licensed or ordered its Communist satellite to attack. Once the latter began to be defeated and was faced with destruction it would have been logical for the U.S.S.R. to warn the United States against pursuing the struggle into the territory of North Korea. And if those threats proved unavailing, then at least a contingent of Soviet "volunteers" should have joined the Chinese "volunteers" in repulsing this attack upon a fellow member of the socialist camp. North Korea borders, after all, not only on China but also on the Soviet Maritime Province. The precedent of a Communist state going down to defeat and being obliterated would, after all, be dangerous not only to China but to the Soviet satellites in Europe. It is almost unimaginable that something in the nature of this argument would not have been intimated by the Chinese to their Russian colleagues when their strategy was being elaborated in August and September and their decision was made to throw the Chinese People's Volunteers into Korea. Why should the weaker partner assume the greater risk? Was it not somewhat shameful that the great Soviet Union should call on poor China to retrieve her own original blunder?

But Stalin's Russia was not easily susceptible to embarrassment or to being shamed into action against her better judgment. There were cogent reasons for the Chinese to assume the burden. The great power of the U.S.S.R. would be held in reserve and would prevent the imperialists from unleashing a full-scale war against China. Finally, Stalin and his associates could piously declare that it was up to the Chinese to determine their actions. If they felt that the destruction of their Communist neighbor did not represent a threat to their newly acquired mastery of the mainland, it was their business. But who could tell what the American imperialists, emboldened by this new experience of erasing a Communist state, might do next?

Several events in August added poignancy to the dilemma faced by Peking. In August, after General MacArthur's visit to Formosa, he and Chiang Kai-shek issued a joint communiqué which contained the phrase: "The foundations were thus laid for a joint defense of Formosa and for Sino-American military cooperation."[27] On August 17 the American delegate to the Security Council stated that the U.N. (i.e., the American) objective was not merely to drive the Communists back to where they came from but also to unify the whole of the peninsula in a democratic state, i.e., to erase the North Korean state. On August 20 Chou En-lai in a telegram to the Security Council placed his government squarely behind Malik's proposals of August 4: Peking was thus willing to go to the Security Council without the prior ejection of Nationalist China. This would indicate that the general line of Sino-Soviet policy on Korea had been elaborated some time before and a tentative decision to throw in the Chinese army if necessary had been reached. On August 22 Ambassador Malik warned that "any continuation of the Korean war will lead inevitably to a widening of the conflict."

[27] *Documents on International Affairs, 1949–1950*, p. 658.

Thus within two months of the beginning of the Korean War the U.S.S.R. managed to improvise a new policy, shift the burden of American resentment and hostility onto Communist China, and in turn persuade or pressure Peking to hold itself in readiness to pull its chestnuts out of the fire. That there were grave dangers involved there was no doubt. There were voices in the United States calling for a preventive war against Russia. The fact that in August President Truman dismissed the air force general who was imprudent enough to make such a statement, and that the secretary of the navy who implied that much was promptly rebuked could not remove the apprehension which must have been felt in Russia. Presumably the Soviets had special sources of information about American plans; two subsequent British defectors, diplomats with special liaison functions with the United States, Maclean and Burgess, are often mentioned in this connection. But as the American reaction to Korea showed, one simply could not trust any forecasts about possible American behavior when that nation was faced with an entirely new situation. It would have been a bold man who precluded the possibility that, if faced with a disaster in Korea as the result of Chinese intervention, the Americans would have recourse to atomic weapons. Or that in a moment of deep frustration the American public would not demand measures against the *main* Communist power. One unfavorable result of the Korean conflict was already evident: the American rearmament effort, which had not been greatly stimulated by the events of 1948 and 1949, was now being pursued at a rapid pace. This in turn led to an upward revision in the Soviet defense budget.

In other words, there could be no absolute certainty that the tensions created by the Korean conflict would not bring grave consequences for Russia. Yet even after the initial miscalculation in June, and after about a week's delay in formulating her response, the Soviet Union was to appear to depart from her usual prudent and calculating diplomatic pattern. Even the Berlin gamble had not involved such risks. There the "technical difficulties" could be removed overnight and the blockade terminated if the United States attempted a show of force. But here, once the Chinese armies were set against the United States nobody could guarantee, especially if the United States had to evacuate Korea, that an overwhelming shift in American public opinion would not call for "getting it over" with Communist aggression.

The other tantalizing question is the extent of the Soviet commitment to their Chinese allies. If, as was at least quite possible, the United States would react to a massive Chinese intervention by shifting the war to China either through atomic attack or by unleashing, as the phrase later went, Chiang Kai-shek, what were the Russians likely to do? Most likely nothing. Had they tried to relieve the pressure on their allies and dissuade the Americans from a possible overcommitment in Asia, the most logical move would have been to increase pressure in Europe. In fact, as we have seen, they were doing the opposite. In November 1950 the Soviet Foreign Ministry proposed a Four Power conference to discuss the German problem and couched its proposals in what was for them and at the time fairly conciliatory terms. To the Chinese Communists was thus left the dangerous task of "containing" the American imperialists.

As the fortunes of war changed dramatically, after the Inchon landing and the offensive of the U.N. forces in the second half of September, it became increasingly clear that the complete defeat and conquest of North Korea would be only a matter of weeks. The Chinese warnings that they would intervene if forces crossed the 38th Parallel and pushed toward the Chinese border became quite explicit. The frequency and urgency of these warnings[28] suggests most forcibly that the Chinese aimed to avoid an armed clash with the United States then and there. Otherwise why broadcast your intentions, deprive yourself of the element of surprise, and enable the Americans to plan more fully for the contingency of full-scale attack by the Chinese armies? Even after the Chinese acknowledgment of the presence of their volunteers and the first armed clashes, their units broke off action on November 7 and counterattacked *en masse* and with dire results for the U.N. forces only on November 26. This course of events does not lend itself to the hypothesis of the Chinese eagerly seizing the opportunity to expose the American "paper tiger" and luring U.S. troops deep into North Korea. It suggests, on the contrary, a considerable reluctance to enter upon a head-on collision with the United States and some awareness, at least, of the great risks involved.

The Chinese warnings were being conveyed mostly through India, a circumstance which was bound to decrease their credibility in American eyes. The Chinese, it could be and was held, were trying to bluff, playing on the natural nervousness of their Asian neighbors and trying to exploit the growing apprehension within the British Commonwealth about the United States becoming more and more involved in Asia. Logically those warnings ought to have been conveyed by the senior Communist power, but in that case the U.S.S.R. could be held *directly* responsible for the Chinese actions, the responsibility that the Russians modestly refused to assume. That it was not simply Chinese pride which made them abjure the Soviet intermediary for those warnings is strongly suggested by the fact that when the time came for suggesting armistice negotiations in June 1951 it was Ambassador Malik who was to announce that such negotiations might be in order. But in October and November the Russians played it cool as a bystander, friendly and interested in the Chinese and

---

[28] E.g., the one conveyed by Chou En-lai to the Indian ambassador, whom he summoned at midnight, October 2. Whiting, *op. cit.*, p. 108.

North Korean actions to be sure, but seemingly not involved in the decisions being taken in Peking. In the Security Council on October 2 Vyshinsky introduced a resolution that on the face of it had no chance of being accepted by the United States. It called for an immediate cease-fire—thus apparently it would stop the U.N. forces from surging deep into North Korea. Its other provisions called for immediate U.S. withdrawal and eventual all-Korean elections to be observed by the U.N. commission but with Communist Chinese participation. A few weeks later, after the U.S. defeat in the north, such a resolution would have perhaps been acceptable, but in the current American mood, as the Russians must have known, it was not.

How did the Russians "get away" with thus steering the Chinese into a dangerous conflict and trying to retrieve what was their own blunder? The detailed answer must await future revelations as to the communications that passed between Moscow and Peking in those months. But the main factor was undoubtedly the Soviet Union's dominant position in world Communism. However bitterly the Chinese Communists must have viewed the idea of venturing into a dangerous undertaking without a public commitment by the U.S.S.R. that she would come to their help if the venture ended in disaster, they still could give no vent to their feelings. An authoritative Peking journal, in analyzing the possible effect of the Chinese intrusion into Korea, spelled out two alternatives—either an American defeat and withdrawal from Korea, or the United States "will continue to increase reinforcements, ceaselessly expending men and material, becoming mired ever deeper and more helplessly." She would thus be weakened in other parts of the world, and gradually her allies and her own public would tire of the war, and this in turn would frustrate the plans of American imperialism elsewhere.[29] The analysis then indicated how far the Chinese were ready to subordinate their actions to the interests of the socialist camp, i.e., of the Soviet Union. To be sure, at the very highest level this readiness must have been combined with the realization of how unfair was the share of the burden assigned to the Chinese. But in 1950 this realization had to be subordinated to other considerations. A complete U.N. victory in Korea would have been a palpable demonstration of how easy it was to push back and undo the victories of Asian Communism. Even a less suspicious and fanatically anti-Western group than the rulers of Communist China could not have believed that such a lesson would be lost on the American policy-makers. And if China had to react to the American advance to her borders, could she afford at the same time the slightest hint of dissonances with the U.S.S.R.? The very uncertainty in which the outside world lived about the nature of relations between the two Communist powers was an element of strength

29 *Ibid.,* p. 140.

in China's international position, a possible shield against an all-out American attack on the mainland. And thus on November 26 the Chinese People's Volunteers fell upon the American and South Korean units moving up toward the Yalu River and the Manchurian border and inflicted upon them a defeat that sent them fleeing back to the 38th Parallel.

The Chinese armies that entered Korea were equipped with the weapons they had used during the civil war.[30] That they were not furnished with up-to-date Soviet weapons throws another curious light upon Sino-Soviet relations of the period. The North Korean troops which attacked in June *were* equipped with modern Soviet-manufactured arms. By October and November, the Chinese Communists had been in control of China for more than a year, and several months had passed since the signing of their alliance with Russia. Yet this alliance evidently did not contain provisions for a re-equipment of the Chinese army with Soviet weapons.[31] It was only in the course of the Korean War that the Chinese acquired Soviet weapons, and as we know they did not come free. They had to pay Russia for the arms used to fight what was essentially Russia's war.

Should Chiang's and American forces have landed on the Chinese mainland, Stalin's main concern would have been to secure Manchuria as a satellite. This comes out vividly from a recent and tantalizing Soviet revelation: "At the request of the Chinese Communist regime special Soviet air units were sent to *Manchuria* to protect the industrial centers of north-eastern provinces of China from American air raids."[31a] No such units were sent to the most vulnerable part of the mainland, in the south opposite Formosa.

With the Chinese intervention in November and then with the virtual stabilization of the front in Korea in the spring of 1951 the Korean "crisis" was over as far as the U.S.S.R. was concerned. The great danger that existed between May and November, that of a "roll-back" of the Soviet sphere of interest and of annihilation of a Soviet satellite, had been avoided. The reverberations of the crisis fell primarily on China. The deadlock in the war between 1951 and 1953 could be viewed by the Kremlin with some equanimity. The Soviet armed forces had the opportunity to test at second hand the effectiveness of their weapons against those of the United States. The Soviet atomic arsenal was growing.

There were, of course, major setbacks for Soviet interests occasioned by the Korean miscalculation. The most obvious one concerned Japan. Far from weakening the American position there or compelling the United States to abandon her bases, the attack on Korea led to the perpetuation of the American presence in Japan. In September 1951 the United States rushed through the peace treaty with Japan at the San Francisco confer-

---

[30] *Ibid.*, p. 124.

[31] An additional inference is that the Chinese intervention in Korea was not envisaged at the time the alliance was signed in February.

[31a] Glunin, Grigoriev, and others, *op. cit.*, p. 259. My italics.

ence. To the considerable surprise and some uneasiness of the State Department the U.S.S.R. chose to attend the conference, though there was no chance of her demands being met. Furthermore, Communist China was not invited, and the Soviet presence could not have been pleasant to Peking. But the Soviets counted on the possibility of last-minute defections among America's allies, some of whom were disturbed over the relative leniency of the settlement with Japan. Having failed in his maneuvers Deputy Foreign Minister Gromyko refused to sign the treaty. The treaty was followed by a security pact between the United States and Japan, conferring on the former the right to maintain bases and armed forces. These forces could also be used at the demand of the Japanese government to suppress any internal riots instigated by an outside power. The two treaties represented a defeat for Soviet diplomacy, the end of any hopes that a Communist Japan might soon arise to counterbalance Communist China.

Still, from the over-all diplomatic point of view, the Korean venture could not be counted a complete loss. The original solidarity of the United Nations after the events of June 1950 gave way in 1951 to growing apprehensions about American rashness and overcommitment in the Far East. These apprehensions were not laid to rest by the dismissal of General MacArthur and American acquiescence in the localized character of the war. As time went on what was originally a heartening (from the American point of view) or threatening (from the Russian) example of the non-Communist nations of the world rising to meet Communist aggression with force and making the aggressor pay for his misdeeds became a less edifying (to the Americans) and more encouraging (to the Soviets) picture of the democracies squabbling about the nature of their commitments and the extent of their contributions to the war, unable to define their ultimate aim, and increasingly distrustful of the American leadership. The "lesson of Korea" was no longer clear, any more than that of the Berlin blockade. On the one hand, the United States showed the resolution to commit her armed forces to fight the Communist aggressor. On the other hand, the Communists' beloved "internal contradictions within the imperialist camp" were obviously in evidence, and it was not the U.S.S.R. that became the target of the reprisals, even the diplomatic ones. In fact, the American diplomats, while steadily denouncing the Chinese Communists as being practically in a condition of colonial dependency upon the U.S.S.R. and as acting at the express orders of the Kremlin, were almost cavalier in their regard for Soviet susceptibilities. Thus Japan in her peace treaty was expressly made to renounce southern Sakhalin and the Kurile Islands, an act of unreciprocated courtesy toward the U.S.S.R. which might at least have been postponed until such time as the U.S.S.R. would deign to sign a peace treaty.

But the most momentous aftermath of the Korean adventure was undoubtedly seen in its long-range effects on Sino-Soviet relations. The war contributed to that psychological emancipation of the Chinese Communists which otherwise might have taken a long time and a different form. Communist China entered the conflict as a satellite, albeit the most important one, of the U.S.S.R.; she was to emerge as a partner. The regime could and did mobilize the resources of Chinese nationalism behind it. Its ability to inflict first a defeat then a stalemate upon the U.S. armies illustrated dramatically the emergence of a new world power. Mao and his comrades undoubtedly now saw the cautions and duplicities of Soviet foreign policy in a clearer perspective and in contrast to the forthright Chinese resolve to meet the imperialists in armed struggle.

The feats of the Chinese People's Volunteers in Korea were reported but warily in the Soviet press and without any unusual emphasis or fanfare over the setbacks suffered by the "imperialist aggressors." For the most part, credit for the defeat of the United Nations forces was attributed equally to the North Korean armies and to the Chinese ones, in that order. In an official account of the Chinese intervention, the Chinese successes are rather ungraciously though realistically qualified by the reminder that they were possible only because of the self-imposed restraints of the United States.

> In the failure of the American plans to expand aggression the decisive role was played by the Soviet-Chinese alliance. This was more than once admitted by American public figures who lamented especially the fact that the alliance was the main restraint upon the "free use" of American naval and air forces against China. The allies of the United States warned the Americans that any step which might compel the U.S.S.R. to fulfill her military obligations under the treaty with China would be a major mistake.[32]

But the authors do not propose to spell out the steps the U.S.S.R. would have taken had the United States extended the war to China.

For all the Soviet restraint in discussing the Chinese feats of arms, for all the suspicions one must entertain concerning Stalin's schemes about Chinese Communism, it is evident that China's performance produced a deep impression in Moscow. "All the Chinese are liars," Stalin had said to Secretary Byrnes in 1946, one Soviet statement to Americans on the subject of China that has an air of sincerity. Now, undoubtedly, there was a reappraisal of the potentialities inherent in the fact that the world's most populous nation had become Communist. "The great People's Republic of China" was singled out in recitals of the membership of the socialist camp. Its performance in the war enabled Mao and his associates to exact more in the way of industrial aid from the Russians. The economic empire of the Chinese Eastern Railway in Manchuria passed over to Peking at the

---

[32] Lavrishchev and Tomashevsky, *op. cit.*, p. 424.

end of 1952. Thus the pattern of relationships between the two powers was shifting from Soviet domination to interdependence. To be sure, nothing approaching equality could be granted to the Chinese Communists, certainly not while Stalin was alive. The history of the Korean War suggests strongly that the crucial decisions concerning first the beginning of negotiations in 1951, then the conclusion of the armistice of 1953 were made by Russia, and for reasons reflecting Soviet rather than Chinese interests.

The continuation of hostilities in the Far East was undoubtedly viewed in Moscow with mixed feelings. On the one hand, it was desirable insofar as it would tie down American armed forces and resources in Korea and, by the same token, detract from the strength of NATO. Another favorable element was that as long as the war continued the Chinese Communists were increasingly dependent on the U.S.S.R. But both of these "positive" aspects had their corresponding dangers. The Americans were capable, if exasperated about the war, of having recourse to at least partial mobilization, which would provide them with enough manpower to strengthen their forces in Europe as well as intensify their efforts in Korea. Most dangerous of all, they might—they were showing signs of doing so—overcome the reluctance of the Europeans and go full speed ahead in arming Germany. The Chinese angle was also not without dangers. Already the Chinese had exacted modern army and air-force equipment for their task in Korea, and their price might go up. The war gave Peking an opportunity to solidify its hold on the mainland of China and to eliminate or reduce in significance those elements which had joined the Communists for opportunistic reasons. If the Russians had entertained hopes of cutting down Mao's predominance and setting up other foci of power within Chinese Communism, then the war obviously had to postpone them. In brief, the cold war could not be allowed to heat up beyond a certain safe degree and the shooting war in Korea could not be allowed to get out of hand. The great hopes put by the Soviets in dissonances within the Western alliance acting to hamper American military and diplomatic efforts were only partially realized. The vast propaganda efforts carried through the "peace movement" and the Stockholm Appeal also fell short of the expected effect.

Malik's initiative on June 23, 1951, laid foundations for the truce negotiations that were to absorb two years while sporadic but bloody fighting continued. It is no coincidence that his speech—in which, for the first time, the Soviets suggested that an armistice could be arranged in Korea *without* the settlement of outstanding political issues or the withdrawal of American troops—came only two days after the collapse of the Paris talks on Germany. No doubt the Russians felt it was unwise to exasperate the United States, not to leave the door to peace ajar. The proposals and subsequent truce negotiations omitted those items which were of the greatest interest to the Chinese Communists: the problem of Formosa and that of the representation of China in the U.N. This was an obvious concession to American intractability on the subject but could not have been pleasant to the Chinese.

The fact that the negotiations which began in July 1951 were to last two years can also be taken as an indication that it was Russia which decided that a complete cessation of hostilities in Korea, and the release of a portion of the American forces for service in Europe, was not in her interest. It could not have escaped Russian notice how the continuation of the Korean War fed the flames of discontent among certain American politicians with the performance and policies of America's allies, and how in that sense the United States' ability to concentrate on European issues and the build-up of NATO was handicapped by the Korean entanglement. To be sure, some of the substantive demands on the American side were extremely hard for the Communists to acquiesce in.[33]

By the summer of 1951, then, the Korean situation was by Soviet lights stabilized, i.e., the U.S.S.R. had cut her losses consequent on the original miscalculation but was still drawing some secondary benefits from the deadlock. Barring drastic and unexpected events, there was no reason to hurry with the negotiations. Europe moved to the forefront again.

In the West, the Korean War led to some alarm that, in the ensuing confusion, the U.S.S.R. would create a *fait accompli* in Europe. But this view seriously misjudged Soviet intentions and capabilities of the moment. Yet it is not entirely inconceivable that without the surprising and vigorous American reaction in Korea Stalin would have moved in those areas where Soviet expansion did not *appear* to present the threat of a large-scale war, i.e., in Yugoslavia and Finland. Certainly Marshall Tito's regime throughout 1950–52 believed that it was on the verge of becoming a victim of aggression and that the military preparations of its neighbors, Soviet satellites, indicated the imminence of a Balkan Korea. In 1951–52 the Yugoslavs' ardor for the Chinese Communists, who had reciprocated their warm sentiments with vilification and a refusal to establish diplomatic relations, slackened appreciably. Also, Yugoslavia indicated that she would deign to receive both military equipment and help in case of war from the West. Much as his hand must have itched to destroy the little Balkan satrap that had dared to defy him, Stalin must have realized that, as Secretary Acheson had expressed it in a public speech referring to Yugoslavia, an-

[33] Primarily the famous proviso about the voluntary repatriation of enemy soldiers. As with Soviet soldiers in World War II, the mere fact of being in captivity was often assumed to offer a putative proof of cowardice or treason. And the whole principle of voluntary repatriation was in Communist eyes an exceedingly bad one, endowed with all sorts of unfortunate implications.

other aggression would strain the over-all fabric of peace. Business had to come before pleasure.

The main item of this business was the danger of a rearmed West Germany. The creaking machinery of NATO made some progress under the stimulus of events in the Far East, but it was still far from producing a sizable army. It was in the beginning of 1952 that signs first appeared that some flesh was going to be put on the skeleton of West European defense and that West Germany would assume a considerable share in the undertaking. By the end of February, drafts of both an agreement between West Germany and the three occupying powers and a treaty setting up the European Defense Community were ready. The Bonn government was to be granted sovereignty and West German soldiers and airmen would take their place in the joint armed force. It was at this point that Moscow opened its diplomatic offensive aimed at preventing what was in effect though not in name a separate peace treaty between West Germany and the Western Big Three and the foundations for West Germany's rearmament.

The Soviet Union's note of March 10 once again proposed Big Four negotiations leading to a peace treaty with and unification of Germany, and the withdrawal of occupation troops. Her proposals, however, went beyond the Prague draft of 1950 insofar as this time she expressed readiness to have a unified Germany rearm, provided the new state would be pledged to neutrality.[34] The Russians went far in courting public opinion in West Germany, for in addition to their concession on rearmament they proposed that civil and political rights be restored to "all former members of the German army . . . all former Nazis . . ." except those serving sentences for crimes. On the face of it, the Soviet note granted a number of important concessions, and had it been presented in 1947 or 1948, it is fair to say, the West would have eagerly seized upon it as a basis for negotiations. But in 1952 it was bound, at least in Washington, to create consternation and the feeling that the Russians were not "playing fair." Here American diplomacy has finally put together a plan for the defense of Europe and the construction of a sizable army—in the process overcoming American neo-isolationism, British apprehensions, French suspicions, and German touchiness—only to find the wretched Russians with yet another beguiling plan, again hinting obscurely that under certain conditions they just might throw their East German regime to the wolves.

---

[34] The relevant passages of the note are: "Germany will be permitted to have its own national armed forces (land, air and sea) which are necessary for the defense of the country," and Germany obligates itself not to enter into any kind of coalition or military alliance directed against "any power which took part with its armed forces against Germany." *Documents on International Affairs, 1952* (London, 1955), p. 88.

Before the sorely tried officials of the State Deparment there arose another endless vista of negotiations, with the Soviets squabbling about procedures, while the painfully and precariously erected edifice of the European Defense Community would be subject to second thoughts by the French and Germans. Next to an all-out war, the prospect of negotiating with the Communists inspired the most fear in the bosom of American diplomats. And with the past record of such negotiations and with the current example of the Korean parley, one has to sympathize with Acheson's predicament. The American reply of March 25 seized on all the contentious points of the Soviet note, such as the insistence that Germany's frontiers would have to be those "agreed upon" in Potsdam—i.e., that she would have to renounce territories assigned there to Poland. What endowed the American note with a faint air of hypocrisy was its pious surprise that the Soviets should propose to grant Germany the right to have an army while at the same time prohibiting her from entering into an alliance: "The United States Government considers that such provisions would be a step backwards and might jeopardize the emergence in Europe of a new era in which international relations would be based on cooperation and not rivalry and distrust."[35] Moscow must have felt that something of the Soviet style of argumentation had slipped into the language of American diplomacy!

The Soviet proposals of March 10 remain one of the most contentious and puzzling documents in post-war Soviet foreign policy. Were the Russians really in earnest? Were they ready to concede a unified, rearmed, albeit neutral Germany? The crucial test would have been their readiness to permit free elections in East Germany, for no realistic observer could expect that the Communists would win in such a test. The United States was, this time, on firm ground in proposing that a United Nations commission should supervise the elections. The Soviets retorted that the task of the supervision should be entrusted to the four occupying powers. But whatever the formula and regardless of irregularities of elections in the eastern zone, the Russians could not have hoped for an over-all Communist victory in all of Germany, with the Communist vote in the much more populous western zone having always been well below 10 per cent. Any all-German government formed as a result of elections would assuredly be a non-Communist one.

Were the Russians really ready to give up *their* Germany in return for the promise of neutrality by the reunited country? This would have meant that the Soviets had suddenly developed a striking belief in the sanctity of international agreements. What could prevent a unified Germany, once

[35] *Ibid.*, p. 90.

rearmed and free of occupation troops, entering into an alliance with the West, treaty or no treaty?[36]

It is impossible to determine the exact proportions of propaganda vs. a serious bargaining offer in the Soviet proposals. From what we know about Stalin's foreign policy, we must conclude that only an extremely urgent danger would have made him surrender a Soviet territorial conquest, which East Germany was in fact. By the same token the vision of a million or so German soldiers readied before the Soviet Union had acquired a sizable atomic arsenal would have answered the definition of such an urgent danger. It is impossible to say with certainty that in 1952 the West could have traded West German rearmament for a Soviet surrender of East Germany.[37] But the fear of a German army backed by the United States and on the borders of the Soviet empire was a real fear felt by the Soviet policy-makers, unlike the fear, partly the product of genuine apprehension but also a bogey for propaganda purposes, of the evil machinations of American capitalists.[38] And to conjure away his real fears Stalin was ready to pay highly.

Nothing came out of the Soviet diplomatic initiative of March 10 except an exchange of long and rather discourteous notes. In refusing to launch into what undoubtedly would have been long and exasperating negotiations, the Americans overlooked the truth that patience and a sense of timing are major ingredients of the art of diplomacy.

Time was running out on Stalin's management of foreign policy, the one sphere of his rule where to the end, and despite his declining years, he exercised direct control. Thus his only intervention at the Nineteenth Party Congress in October 1952 was a brief address in which again he alluded to the theme of inherent contradiction within the imperialist camp and stressed the role of the Communist parties in the Western countries leading national opposition to American domination. In December the old

[36] There was of course a catch in the Soviets agreeing to German rearmament. Germany was to have forces "necessary for the defense of the country," i.e., presumably their size was to be stipulated in the treaty.

[37] This is strongly suggested in one of the best treatments of the whole subject, in Bell, op. cit., p. 99. "The point being made here is simply that, suspending judgment for the moment as to whether this bargain was desirable from the point of Western power interests, this appears the point at which the best terms ought theoretically to have been obtainable."

[38] The Soviet writings of the times make it clear that the Russians believed that in any European defense arrangement the "German revanchists," though formally in a subordinate position, would be able to manipulate their American and West European allies.

despot, in answer to a journalist's query, held himself ready to meet with President-elect Eisenhower. It is interesting to speculate on the results— indeed on the atmosphere—of a meeting in which Stalin would have encountered Dulles. But that was not to be. In the midst of what were apparently the preparations for a new and vast purge, which would have claimed most of his successors, the "genius leader of all mankind" expired in March 1953.

With Stalin ended the era when a decision by one man could change abruptly the whole course of foreign policy of the Soviet Union and world Communism. His successors neither collectively nor singly would ever again have that power. Increasingly, though still enjoying a flexibility for maneuver inconceivable to democratic statesmen, they would become slaves of the past and susceptible to domestic and intra-Communist bloc pressures. With Stalin's death, it is also now clear, effective unity of the Communist bloc also passed. When within a short time of the despot's death it was thought desirable to bolster Malenkov's image by a fake picture of him with Stalin and Mao Tse-tung, it was symbolic both of the lack of self-assurance which Stalin's heir felt and of the already vast changes occurring in world Communism.[39] These changes had of course been implicit in the emergence of Communist China, but they were now part of current politics.

Paradoxically then, even though he was such a fervent Soviet—indeed Russian—nationalist, Stalin embodied the last hope of Communist internationalism. Even the absolute subordination of foreign Communism to the interests—or, rather, commands—of Stalin's Russia could be rationalized as the necessary preliminary to the establishment of a supranational Communist world order, which however cruel and destructive its beginnings would eventually abolish war. Paradoxically also, even though he embodied and was responsible for Soviet Russia's expansionism and hostility toward the West, with Stalin disappeared for some time the prospect of any fundamental and lengthy *détente* with the United States. His successors would strive to reduce tension, would use friendlier language toward the capitalist world, but they would not be capable, because of their weaker position both internally and within the Communist bloc, of the kind of major concession or abrupt shift in policy that was in Stalin's power. Whether or not it was among his intentions, it was entirely conceivable for Stalin to sacrifice a major conquest like East Germany without the slightest effect on his position at home or within the Communist bloc. His successors would have to measure their foreign-policy moves against their possible effect on the leadership of the U.S.S.R. and world Communism.

[39] The picture was a composograph of a photograph taken at the signing of the Sino-Soviet treaty on February 14, 1950, when the three gentlemen in question were seen with a number of other Soviet and Chinese dignitaries.

To be sure, the great luck that attended Stalin on many occasions was evident at the time of his death.[40] He died surrounded by an aura of omnipotence, but another purge, which was then on the way, might well have shaken the foundations of his state and Party. And in foreign affairs even Stalin could not have preserved for long the type of subordination of other Communist parties, especially China's, which he preferred. The clash of the two Communist giants might have come much sooner and might have had incalculable consequences. He was fortunate to die at a time when the inherent conflict between the interests of the Soviet state and those of world Communism was already apparent but when its full extent and effects could not yet be gauged.

For the West, Stalin died either too late or too early. Had he died immediately after World War II, his successors might have launched on a course of internal reforms and improvements of the Soviet citizen's life, which as it was had to wait until 1953. Consequently their foreign policy would have been more conciliatory and less pushful. In the face of the industrial and technological superiority of the United States, they could not have displayed the same self-assurance and defiance that for several years masked Russia's real debility and persuaded the Western Powers that they were much weaker *vis-à-vis* the U.S.S.R. than in fact they were. Had he lived a few more years, the clash with China might well have come sooner and in more violent form than it did under Khrushchev. Such was the vastly ambiguous heritage of an era of tyranny which in its cruelty and personal concentration of power stands without precedent in modern history.

2. The Transition: 1953–56

Winston Churchill in a speech delivered in 1949 drew an analogy between the Russian threat of that time and the one posed by the Mongols in the thirteenth century. This scourge from Asia was almost ready to burst upon the heartland of medieval Christendom, having conquered and plundered Russia and Poland, when "the Great Khan died." The frightening hordes turned back in their tracks, their commanders eager to participate in what was the thirteenth-century equivalent of a Politburo meeting on the subject of succession. And thus Europe was spared. . . .

Churchill's rather indelicate speculation on the possible effects of his

[40] One thinks in this connection of the events of June 1941 when, shocked by the German invasion, Stalin was unable to attend to affairs of state for a week. Had the German advance been less rapid and the need of showing the unity and determination of the leadership been less desperate, his subordinates might well have gotten rid of the man they so hated and feared.

erstwhile partner's demise underlies the importance attached abroad to Stalin's personal leadership and the conviction that without him the U.S.S.R. might become less of a menace.[41]

Certainly the events following Stalin's death on March 5, 1953, suggest that at least temporarily the whole governmental apparatus of the U.S.S.R. was thrown into disarray. What took place on the morrow of the death was a veritable *coup d'état,* in which the enlarged Presidium of the Central Committee, established only five months earlier at the Nineteenth Party Congress, was reduced to roughly its old size. The people ejected were mostly the newcomers, the people who stayed were Stalin's old oligarchs, many of them undoubtedly slated for liquidation had their boss survived for awhile. At the top was the triumvirate of Malenkov, Beria, and Molotov. Malenkov, Stalin's putative successor, took the post of prime minister but in the bargaining that took place was evidently forced to abandon his place on the Party Secretariat. Beria reclaimed control of the organs of state security which had gradually been wrested from his hand during Stalin's last years. Molotov resumed the Ministry of Foreign Affairs which he had surrendered in 1949. Coming up from behind, to use the language of racing, was Nikita Khrushchev, who after Malenkov's resignation was the Party's senior secretary though not yet designated as such. The new team began its rule in an atmosphere of diffidence and mutual suspicion. The first communiqué spoke frankly about the need of "prevention of any kind of disorder and panic." It sought to bolster its position by drawing upon every conceivable form of support. Malenkov's supporters faked the picture of their hero with Stalin and Mao as if to suggest that this alleged intimacy *à trois* meant that Malenkov had the blessing of the deceased tyrant and the support of the leader of the most populous Communist country.

Emerging from the obscurity of a provincial garrison was Marshal Zhukov, brought in as a deputy minister of war to suggest that the army, as personified by its most prestigious World War II commander, was also behind the new team. At a time of confusion even the position of titular head of the Soviet state was thought important. Thus its holder, Shvernik, was dropped and replaced by another faded star, popular because of his military background, but not likely to compete for leadership because of his age, Marshal Kliment Voroshilov.

All those steps suggest, it is not too much to say, the new rulers' fears of considerable disorders if not indeed of popular revolt. They had a realistic view, it must be assumed, of the real conditions in Russia and in

[41] The parallel could not, however, be a particularly comforting one. While the Mongols were not to threaten Central Europe again after the middle of the thirteenth century, their rule in Russia and in parts of Asia was to endure for centuries.

the Communist bloc. That the whole bizarre structure had been able to continue functioning despite the sufferings and deprivations of millions, and despite the uncertainty about their own status and indeed lives under which the highest officials of the U.S.S.R. and the satellites had to carry on must have appeared to the successors as somehow peculiar to the late despot and his special magic or luck. For all the strictures of Marxism-Leninism and for all the paraphernalia of modern totalitarianism the situation must have appeared reminiscent of that which in Russian history followed the deaths of Ivan III, Ivan IV, and Peter the Great, when the demise of the tyrant would open the door to a struggle among various factions in the state and even to an era of anarchy that would threaten all the achievements and conquests of the previous reign.[42]

Thus the loss of "Comrade Stalin, whom we have all loved so much and who will live in our hearts forever"[43] had to be followed immediately by a rapid if prudent course of de-Stalinization. The extent and form of this de-Stalinization was probably a matter of some dispute in the ruling group, but they all must have acknowledged that in Stalin's absence neither foreign nor domestic policy could be conducted according to Stalin's methods.

The regime was well aware also of the necessity of sustaining the impression of unity and strength. To betray its weaknesses and vulnerabilities, the deadly enmities which divided the ruling group, would have been an open invitation to its protagonists. A different type of succession had just taken place in the United States when the Republican administration took office. Its Secretary of State, John Foster Dulles, long a *bête noir* of Soviet publicists but by the same token treated by them with a respect not accorded to his Democratic predecessors, had announced what on paper appeared as a very vigorous foreign policy: not "containment" but "roll-back" and "liberation" were going to be the device of America's efforts in Europe. Eisenhower had also "unleashed" Chiang Kai-shek, i.e., he had withdrawn the injunction against possible attacks from Formosa on the mainland. Time was to show how little substance there was in all these gestures and slogans, but the Soviet leaders had to take them seriously. In a way, through one of those ironies with which the history of

---

[42] Parallels to such figures of the past were not absent from Stalin's own mind. He sponsored the glorification of Peter the Great and even of Ivan the Terrible. In discussing the latter with an actor who was going to impersonate the royal psychopath in a movie, Stalin, while noting with approval Ivan's positive achievements, also expressed some criticism: how unnecessary it was for Ivan to have bouts of religious contrition following his bloody purges! And speaking of the latter, Ivan really did not do a thorough job: he left alive several princely families which in succeeding reigns brought the Russian state in the beginning of the seventeenth century close to disintegration through their competition for power.

[43] Excerpt from the funeral oration by Molotov.

the Soviet Union is replete, all those bold pronouncements might have done a favor to the Communist rulers. We know that on the morrow of Stalin's death the center of Moscow and the Kremlin were ringed by security troops. A violent struggle, perchance a civil war, might have erupted then and there. But the international situation urged a compromise and a patching up of differences. Said Beria significantly: "The enemies of the Soviet state calculate that the heavy loss we have borne will lead to disorder and confusion in our ranks. But their expectations are in vain: bitter disillusionment awaits them."[44]

Beria's subsequent words that the Party was "united and unshakable" were belied almost immediately by his own actions. Presumably not satisfied with his No. 2 position, the artful master of the secret police must have decided that what was good for one Georgian should not be denied to another, and he made his bid for supreme power. He operated on two fronts, strengthening his control over the secret police on the one hand and courting popularity on the other. Regional chiefs of police who had been installed during Beria's decline in Stalin's last years were now promptly replaced by Beria's men. The dreaded chief of police himself, subsequently to be credited with being Stalin's evil genius and of displaying professional devotion to the point of choking a Party secretary with his own hands, assumed also the role of protector of liberties and restorer of socialist legality. His ministry promptly found out that the famous "doctors' plot," an evident prelude to a new purge before Stalin's death, was a fabrication, and the Kremlin doctors who had survived the investigation were returned to their practice, though one may wonder with what feelings the Soviet bigwigs would now submit to their ministrations. Soviet citizens were constantly reminded of their rights, and of how Comrade Beria's ministry was setting out to protect them. Much was also made of the rights of the non-Russian nationalities, a startling reversal of the heavy russification pressures of the Stalin era.

These activities of Beria were not viewed with favor by his colleagues. When on an evening in July the Presidium of the Central Committee decided to take time from its labors to attend an opera, it was observed by those who scan such lists for Kremlinological purposes that Beria's name was not among the high-ranking music lovers. And to be sure on July 10 an official announcement unmasked Beria as an enemy of the people, foreign agent, and would-be restorer of capitalism. Though de-Stalinization had already begun, the act of accusation followed the best Stalinist precedents. Thus from his adolescence, it was asserted, Beria had been an agent of foreign intelligence and a counterrevolutionary. In December Beria and several high-ranking associates were tried by a special court and

[44] Gruliow, *op. cit.*, p. 261.

received the usual verdict. Beria's fall was followed by the curtailment of the security forces. From now on they were strictly controlled by the Party and, while still of enormous importance in Soviet politics and society, would never achieve again the position they had had under Beria.[45]

Beria's actual role in foreign policy remains unknown. The irrepressible Khrushchev was later on to allege that he carried a major share of responsibility for the Soviet-Yugoslav break, but like many of Khrushchev's tales this one must be taken with more than a grain of salt. The same holds for the stories that following the East German disturbances in June 1953 Beria advocated the abandonment of East Germany and far-reaching concessions to the West. Had the loathed security chief succeeded in seizing supreme power it is very likely that Soviet foreign policy under his regime would have been one of retrenchment, since so much of his attention would have had to go into liquidating internal opposition.

But quite apart from any real or alleged initiatives of Beria's, it is evident that the new leadership as a team believed in the need of improving at least the tone of relations between the U.S.S.R. and the outside world. The tyrant's foreign policies had created an air of tension which, apart from being a source of danger to Russia, was largely unnecessary. The policy toward Tito had not brought down the Yugoslav regime, but it was having unfortunate effects on various left-wing elements elsewhere that might otherwise sympathize with the U.S.S.R. Relations with Turkey, to use another example, had been frozen ever since 1945 in a posture of hostility that again was unproductive and even dangerous. By now there was no chance of extracting Soviet territorial goals from Turkey without starting a major war, while a hostile Turkey was a pivot of anti-Soviet orientation in the Balkans and the Near East and, in the case of international conflict, a factor contributing to the vulnerability of the Soviet Union's southern flank. Like new managers taking over an enterprise run for a long time by one man set in his habits and distrustful of new ideas and opportunities, the post-Stalin leaders must have felt that new methods were needed and new and profitable ventures could be introduced. Stalin talked a great deal about the growing contradictions within the imperialist camp but never really set out to exploit them. His experience in the 1920's when various oriental potentates like Kemal, Chiang, and others in effect tricked the Communists made him wary and contemptuous of the new independent regimes in Asia such as India and Indonesia. Yet here, in this Third World, was to be found the Achilles' heel of the West: to treat Nehru and Sukarno as mere tools of imperialism, as they had been described in

---

[45] Thus one of Beria's accomplices executed with him was Dekanozov, who in the early 1940's as we have seen was first ambassador to Berlin and then deputy foreign commissar, a small demonstration of how extensive were the ramifications of the police empire.

the Soviet press practically up to Stalin's death, was to pass up brilliant opportunities to embarrass and outflank Western diplomacy.

Another aspect of Stalin's foreign policy that called for re-examination and revision was the pattern of relations within the Communist bloc. In a fluid and dangerous situation, it was imperative to maintain an impression of absolute solidarity between the U.S.S.R. and China. "Let all the imperialist aggressors and warmongers tremble in the face of our great friendship," wrote Mao Tse-tung in a eulogy to Stalin printed in *Pravda* within days of his death. If Stalin had had some ideas about influencing the personnel of leadership of the Chinese Communist Party, all such notions now had to be dropped. Chinese support had to be invoked to bolster morale at home—witness the Stalin-Malenkov-Mao "photograph"—and to discourage any Western attempt to profit by what might become Russia's new Time of Troubles.[46]

Somewhat similar considerations dictated changes in methods of Russian domination of the satellites. To continue to rely primarily on terror and police methods, to continue exploiting those countries for the benefit of Russia's economy meant to court the chance of a popular explosion with which the local Communist parties, weakened and demoralized by the purges and factional hostilities of the last four years, might not be able to cope. Soviet military assistance would then be required to suppress the revolts. A preview of such revolts was vividly demonstrated in the events of June 1953 in East Berlin and other East German cities. Driven to despair by increased work norms and poverty, sensing a degree of confusion and uncertainty among their masters following Stalin's death, the workers rose in a spontaneous revolt, a classical type of proletarian rising so often eulogized in Communist propaganda. Soviet armor had to be brought in to put down what threatened to become a revolution. This was but a sample of what might conceivably flare up in any satellite, spread to others, and then—who knows?—find echoes in Soviet Russia. Prudence demanded immediate steps to raise the standards of living in the satellites as well as in the U.S.S.R. The morale and effectiveness of the Communist parties in the satellites had to be raised by giving them greater autonomy and greater opportunity to gain if not popularity then acceptance by their own peoples. The local Stalins had to be removed or curbed.

All this suggests the complexity of the problems with which Stalin's successors had to grapple. They worked feverishly, while watching each other with suspicion and loathing, and in fear of their own people, whose capacity for suffering and endurance of tyranny could not be taken for

[46] The Time of Troubles is the name given to the period in Russian history around the end of the sixteenth and beginning of the seventeenth centuries when the extinction of the old dynasty was followed by internal anarchy and foreign intervention.

granted now that the man who had contrived the whole fantastic system was gone.

There were, to be sure, some elements of comfort in the over-all situation. Soviet nuclear armament was now sufficiently advanced to offer an effective deterrent. In August the Soviets would explode a hydrogen bomb. To the military strategists these achievements were still unconvincing in view of Russia's marked inferiority to America in the means of delivering nuclear weapons, but insofar as the psychological meaning of the weapons was concerned Russia's achievement and the publicity attending them were to endow her rulers with an element of security in an otherwise dangerous and confusing situation.

On the main front of world diplomacy—East-West relations—the Soviets could also draw comfort from the Western statesmen's apparent bafflement over the implications of Stalin's disappearance. Now that the "Great Khan" had died, Churchill was eager to meet and assess his successors. This initiative, contained in a speech of May 11, met with some resistance in Washington, where the new administration did not wish its stern and businesslike attitude toward Russia compromised by the tittle-tattle of a Big Four meeting. The Prime Minister's subsequent stroke and incapacity soon made the prospect of a summit meeting unlikely. A summit meeting in the spring of 1953 could have been rather embarrassing to the Russians. The main lines of post-Stalin foreign policy had obviously not yet been worked out, and it is likely that there was some contention over them among the top leaders. Under the conditions of mutual confidence which prevailed among them, it is unlikely that any of the three top leaders would have gone abroad by himself. Even in the more relaxed Khrushchev era, the leader's absence from his desk in the Kremlin was to be attended by some risks. A summit meeting then would have been attended by the congenial trio of Malenkov-Molotov-Beria. But this was not to be. In their predicament the Soviet leaders must have been encouraged by the continuing dissonances between the Western Powers. The European Defense Community was still the subject of negotiations and wrangling, the West German army was still on paper. The stern admonitions and warnings that emanated from Washington and mostly from the mouth of Mr. Dulles could thus be largely discounted. Though they retained respect for Dulles to the end, the Soviet leaders must occasionally have reflected on an old Russian proverb: "A bellowing cow gives little milk."

Toward the United States Stalin's successors appear to have developed a more flexible attitude. On one hand they stood in much less awe of American might; after all, in industry and nuclear weapons the Russian position was rapidly improving. The prospect of a West German army did not look nearly so frightening as it had in 1949 or 1952. On the other hand, they had at least initially much less confidence in being able to out-

wit the United States diplomatically, of being able to string out a dangerous situation like the Korean conflict without incurring grave risks. The decision to liquidate the Korean War was evidently taken shortly after the
great event of March. Not long after his return from the funeral festivities
in Moscow, Chou En-lai broadcast his willingness to break the deadlock
over the prisoner-of-war issue. The ensuing delay was caused mainly by the
intransigence of the South Koreans, but in July an armistice restored an
uneasy peace to the Korean peninsula. The American administration's
eagerness to conclude peace in Korea must have been spoken more convincingly than all the tough talk emanating from Washington. The Americans did not attempt to take advantage of the period of transition and confusion in the Soviet Union to press for a more favorable resolution of the
Korean problem, or to test the vaunted Sino-Soviet solidarity. There was a
note of genuine relief in Malenkov's reference to the armistice: "In the
East, the bloodshed which has carried off so many human lives and which
harboured a threat of the most serious international complications has
been stopped."[47]

With Beria and Korea out of the way, Malenkov could give a fairly confident appraisal of the world situation. On August 8 he listed the steps
taken by the Soviet government to lessen world tensions. The Soviet government had relinquished its territorial claims in Turkey. It extended a
hand of friendship to Turkey and Iran. It re-established diplomatic relations with Israel.[48] Ambassadors had been exchanged with Yugoslavia and
Greece. Malenkov spoke flatteringly of India, held out a prospect of friendship to Japan once she freed herself from her American tutelage. British
public opinion was praised. The French were warned of the danger of
German militarism and about joining the European Defense Community.

Of the United States Malenkov spoke more in sorrow than in anger.
What do the Americans plan to achieve by pursuing the "cold war," by
those elaborate schemes of psychological warfare, etc.? Above all the
United States has become the center of world-wide subversive activities;
"certain American circles have gone so far as to elevate subversive activity
against the lawful governments of sovereign countries to the level of government policy,"[49] he pointed out indignantly. Or perhaps the Americans
believe their own stories of how weak the U.S.S.R. is or how divided her
leadership? Well, they should get rid of such ideas. Incidents such as the
unmasking of Beria as "a double-dyed agent of imperialism" testify only
to the growing strength and unity of the U.S.S.R.

[47] *Documents on International Affairs, 1953*, p. 24.
[48] They had been broken after the "doctors' plot" discovery in December,
1952, and the allegations that the doctors, most of them Jewish, were enlisted
by some Zionist organizations for anti-Soviet activities.
[49] *Documents on International Affairs, 1953*, p. 28.

Compared to the ominous hints and barely veiled threats that so often characterized the statements of the Soviet spokesmen in Stalin's lifetime, Malenkov's speech breathed peace and relaxation. There was little of the "if anybody thinks we are weak let them try us" motif. There was on the contrary a "look, let us be sensible and talk things over" flavor. In many respects, especially in the passages concerning Turkey and Yugoslavia, the speech was a virtual disavowal of Stalin's foreign policy. An insider also might have felt that in emphasizing continuously that the U.S.S.R. was *not* weak and her leadership was *not* divided, Malenkov protested too much. The theme of how disastrous a new world war would be to *everybody* clashed with the previous Soviet theme that, terrible as a new war would be, it would signal the end of capitalism and the world-wide triumph of Communism.

For all the pat phrases about "unshakable unity," etc., Malenkov's speech displayed some nervousness. To some extent this must have reflected the still uncertain situation at the top. Beria was gone, but the struggle for supremacy continued. In September Malenkov's position was weakened by the formal designation of Khrushchev as First Secretary. And it was Khrushchev who, at the plenum of the Central Committee, delivered the main speech dealing with the agricultural situation. The speech was a severe if veiled condemnation of previous policies and an acknowledgment of the rather desperate situation in that vital sphere of the national economy. The regime obviously placed its first priority on internal reforms. Though its alleged champion Beria was gone, the leaders continued to stress "socialist legality." Forced-labor camps were being emptied, and countless victims of Stalinist terror and repression were coming back to normal life. The new government was pledged to improve the standard of living. The defense budget was slightly decreased.[50] Against these developments, it is clear why the Russian passion for a summit meeting or even any comprehensive review of the East-West problems had somewhat abated. When, prodded by her allies, the United States now advanced the proposal for a foreign ministers' meeting to discuss the German and Austrian issues, it was the U.S.S.R. that played a delaying game. The Soviet counterproposals spoke of the need for a prior renunciation of the European Defense Community by the West and urged the convocation of a meeting of the Big Five—i.e., inclusive of Communist China. Finally the Soviets agreed to a Big Four foreign ministers' meeting in Berlin in January 1954. All those gambits suggest that there was considerable uncertainty in Moscow during the waning months of 1953 as to the general lines of Soviet foreign policy, and a desire to probe the

---

[50] Though as mentioned before there is a strong presumption that the armed forces were actually increased after Stalin's death.

intentions and capabilities of the new American administration before tipping the Soviet hand.

On one front of foreign relations the new Soviet team displayed feverish haste. This concerned relations within the socialist camp, and Soviet actions there suggest an awareness of weaknesses and dangers in Russia's position that were but dimly perceived in the West. The Soviet leadership impressed upon their subordinates in the satellites that the new order of things precluded combining in the same person the highest state and Party positions, that collective leadership, currently the style in Russia, should also become the rule in the satellites. This reduction in status for the local Stalins was dictated not so much by solicitude for democratic principles as by the danger of too much power being concentrated in one person or clique and of the consequent opportunities for Titoism. The June events in Germany had demonstrated the danger of excessive repression and economic exploitation, and signals went out from the Kremlin for a new consideration for the consumer and for a reduction in the status and power of the secret police. The Soviet Union, for her part, undertook to curtail her ruthless economic exploitation of the satellites. A significant indication was provided when she reduced her exactions from East Germany and agreed to forego further reparations after 1953. And as the prisons and forced-labor camps began to surrender their inmates in the U.S.S.R., a similar process began to take place in the satellites.

The new course—or the "thaw," as it was christened in the U.S.S.R.— involved undoubted political and psychological risks. It was based on the assumption that Soviet domination could be preserved without that detailed supervision of politics in the satellites which had been the rule under Stalin. And it contained the hope that the Communist regimes in the satellites could now exist without recourse to the extremes of terror, that their leaders, given some autonomy, would remain loyal to Moscow and would not demand more substantive freedoms. That such concessions were granted by people schooled in Stalin's school, not given to parting easily with the appurtenances and advantages of absolute power and economic exploitation, is an eloquent testimony of how critically urgent they considered the situation to be and how dangerous they considered the alternative of continuing in the old ways.

An even more significant shift took place in the tone of Soviet-Chinese relations. Here there could no longer be any question of the Russians imposing their ideas as to how to run a Communist state. As a matter of fact, if one surveys the course of Russo-Chinese relations from the morrow of Stalin's death to about 1958, one gets a definite impression of the Soviets courting their Chinese partners and somewhat nervously according them status and concessions unimaginable during the old tyrant's lifetime. A symptom of the change was the assignment of V. V. Kuznetsov as am-

bassador to Peking. His appointment was announced within four days of
Stalin's death, and he replaced a career diplomat who had been in China
but one month. Kuznetsov had for years been close to the top of the Soviet hierarchy and was currently deputy minister of foreign affairs.[51]
Obviously the delicate problem of liaison with China required a more prestigious person than a career diplomat.

A more substantive proof of the Soviet desire to please China was forthcoming in agreements on trade and economic assistance signed on March
26. A Chinese trade and industrial delegation had been in Moscow cooling its heels for several months. Stalin's death appears to have speeded
up the conclusion of negotiations: under the new arrangements the Soviets
were to provide assistance to China's industrialization by sending technical
experts and training Chinese personnel, as well as with material help. To
be sure, the Russians were still not giving anything free to China. This
was brought into relief in 1953 when the Soviets did make a free grant of
1 billion rubles to North Korea. But for the next several years they were
going to make a considerable contribution to China's emergence as a
major industrial and hence military power, something which could not
have come easily to the sober and apprehensive men in the Kremlin.[52]

Undoubtedly, there was still no question of equality of status between
China and the U.S.S.R. or of the former influencing decisively the policy
or defiance on Mao's part, at a time when the system was shedding its
much more than a nuisance, were they not propitiated. Open disapproval
or defiance on Mao's part, at a time when the system was shedding its
Stalinist skin, when the leaders were maneuvering against each other,
when millions of people were returning from the camps, could have shaken
the entire regime. But the Chinese had at least as much interest as the
Russians in maintaining the fiction of the monolithic unity of the Communist bloc. They needed Russian help and protection. They had no reason
to mourn the passing of Stalin who, had he lived, would undoubtedly
have held on to the Soviet Union's special privileges in China and whose

[51] Kuznetsov had been chairman of the Soviet trade unions. At one time he
appeared to have been slated for an even higher position. He had been one of
twenty-five members of the Presidium elected at the Nineteenth Party Congress
but lost this position in the reshuffle after Stalin's death.

[52] As to the actual credits extended to China, Soviet sources are extremely
reticent in divulging the actual figures. An official Soviet publication in 1963
lists just two loans to China, one in 1950 and the other in 1954 for a total of
about $430 million. (See Lavrishchev and Tomashevsky, *op. cit.*, p. 50.) Some
other Soviet sources hint at a figure of $2 billion in loans for the period of
1950–60. But in 1963, when these figures were released, and for that matter
before, it would not have been wildly popular with the Soviet public to spell
out how much the U.S.S.R. helped to make China an industrial and military
power.

fertile mind had probably been preparing surprises for Mao and his group. But this was their chance to exact some advantages, and, as events of the next five years were to show, they were not going to be reticent in seizing them.

By the end of 1953 the Soviet rulers had every reason to congratulate themselves on having steered the U.S.S.R. successfully through the first and most perilous period of the transition. With the background of vast human misery and oppression, with the almost unbearable international tensions which had existed on March 5, 1953, this had been no mean achievement. In domestic politics the regime for all of its reforms and "liberalism" had certainly not sacrificed any of the *substance* of totalitarian power. In foreign policy a general relaxation and the end of the Korean War had been obtained without making any concessions to the West. The main reasons for apprehension lay in the still unsettled pattern of relations with the satellites, and especially in the increasing dilemma of China's position within the Communist camp. But for the moment, even those problems were contained. Stalin's successors must have felt that they had done a good job. Furthermore, as the year ended, with one exception they were alive, the likelihood of which must have appeared at least problematical prior to the death of their "dear leader and comrade-in-arms."

This successful weathering of the problem of succession, usually the Achilles' heel of a totalitarian system, can be attributed to several factors. Some of them have already been mentioned. In addition, the Western Alliance was going through a "succession crisis" of its own. The new administration in Washington, for all its ringing phrases and formulas about foreign policy, had difficulties having its main themes accepted either at home or abroad. Dulles' rhetoric was designed perhaps to propitiate domestic right-wing critics and to obscure the similarity of his approach to Acheson's. But the talk of "massive retaliation," of the art of "going to the brink" of war, etc., while it may or may not have impressed the Communists (and the conjecture must be that it did to a degree) certainly panicked America's allies. Most of all, they were perturbed by the United States' increasing entanglement in Asia. For their own part, Britain and France had the agonizing problem of whether to liquidate or hold on to their imperial possessions and obligations, a problem that was to sap much of the vitality and resolution of the policy of these erstwhile Great Powers. Under such conditions there was little opportunity for the type of concentrated, probing diplomatic pressures and maneuverings that would put the Russians on the defensive or extract real concessions from them.

Traditionally, Soviet policy-makers have always responded readily either to a danger or to an opportunity for aggrandizement. But in the situation as it crystallized late in 1953 and early in 1954 the one threat the West could evoke—a West German armed force within or without a European army—was receding in importance both in view of the lack of ratification of the European Defense Community pacts, and also because of an added element of Soviet strength: the acquisition by Russia of the hydrogen bomb and the means of delivery of nuclear weapons. In modern international politics the element of timing has assumed supreme importance. For reasons spelled out before, the Soviets considered a German army a grave danger as long as they did not possess an effective nuclear counter-deterrent. With the development of their hydrogen bomb and long-range bomber, the threat of a remilitarized Germany was less urgent and no longer would require considerable Soviet concessions to ward it off.

This attitude became evident at the Berlin meeting of the foreign ministers of the Big Four. If the Soviet note of March 1952 at least left the door open to the possibility of sacrificing the East German regime for the sake of securing a neutralized Germany, this time the Soviet statement on Germany definitely precluded it. The provisional German government was to be set up by the existing East and West German regimes, or if this was to prove too difficult the existing governments were to be maintained "for a certain period of time." All-German elections under the 1952 stipulations were to have been conducted under the supervision of the occupying powers; now they were to be conducted by the "provisional German government," i.e., with the participation of the East German satellite. In the unlikely contingency that the Western ministers would agree to these proposals, the Soviets obviously had in mind some special gimmicks to counteract the numerical superiority of West Germany, for their proposal stipulated that the elections be carried out under conditions "of genuine freedom which would preclude pressure upon voters by big monopolies,"[53] and that the interim government should take measures to provide for "conditions necessary for holding democratic elections." It required an excessive amount of optimism to see in these conditions any readiness to abandon the East German regime unless the Soviets were guaranteed an all-German government in which Communists and fellow travelers would play an important part. With the revolt of 1953 a recent memory, the Soviets must have been especially careful not to leave the impression of being ready to jettison their East German puppets. As a matter of fact even the carefully phrased Soviet proposals involved a risk. A resourceful and self-assured protagonist might have seized upon them and probed into such of their features as the declared readiness to withdraw Soviet armed forces prior to the elections ("with the exception of limited contingents left to perform protective functions"). The West's categorical refusal even

---

[53] *Documents on International Affairs, 1954* (London, 1957), p. 75.

to discuss the Soviet proposals was probably greeted with a private sigh of relief by the Russians, and even more so by their East German agents, who must have contemplated with a sinking heart the prospect of confronting their own people without the reassuring presence of Russian tanks and guns.

The Berlin conference spawned another one: the conferees agreed that a meeting should take place in Geneva to confer on Indochina and Korea and that for this occasion Communist China should join the Big Four.[54] In retrospect it is at least probable that the Soviet decision to have a conference in Geneva at this time was due to Chinese pressure. Peking was eager to assume a direct role in the concert of powers. It is also not unlikely that the Chinese wished for international tension in the Far East to subside. The Indochinese war carried with it the danger of an American intervention to bolster up the faltering French military effort. The Chinese hailed the Korean armistice as a great victory, but their campaign must have impressed them with the necessity of at least a breathing spell for an intensive industrial development before their country could be ready for another military confrontation with the United States. Yet a speedy end to the Indochinese war could not have been viewed with equal enthusiasm by the Russians. The war was one of the main reasons for the successive French governments balking at West German rearmament, and its unpopularity also served to strengthen the position of the French Communist Party. But the Russians were at a point where they felt they had to go at least half-way to meet their Chinese allies' demands.

As could easily have been foreseen, the Geneva conference brought no settlement in the sense of reunification of Korea.

The Indochinese "settlement," which was to prove of such grave consequences, was precipitated by the fall of Laniel's government in France and the installment of one headed by Pierre Mendès-France. The new Premier made it clear that he proposed to obtain a compromise peace within one month or resign. The mood in his country was strongly for peace. Recent French military reverses made it clear that the French position in Indochina was becoming untenable, and short of an American intervention more defeats on the scale of Dienbienphu were in the offing. The complexities of the Vietnam situation at the Geneva conference need not detain us. To us, of main importance is the obvious interest of Communist China in securing peace at that point, and the deference shown by Molotov for the Chinese position.

The eventual agreement must have been viewed with mixed feelings by

[54] Those U.N. members which sent contingents to Korea, as well as the two Korean regimes, were also to attend the Korean phase of the meeting; the three Indochina states and a Vietminh delegation were to attend the Indochinese phase.

the other concerned parties. To the French it meant the lifting of a heavy burden and the possibility of turning their attention to already trouble-some North Africa,[55] but it was a definite loss of their Far Eastern em-pire (it was obvious that South Vietnam would not cling to its French connection after this admission of defeat) and the first step in the series of events that within a few years were to strip France of most of her over-seas possessions. To the Vietminh the settlement gave a state of their own, but on the other hand Ho and his associates could confidently have ex-pected that continued fighting would in a short time secure all of Vietnam. To the Russians a *temporary* disappearance of the Indochinese issue meant the removal of a lever of pressure on France. Had they possessed complete freedom of action on Indochina it is quite likely that they could have bar-gained for a settlement against France's pledge not to permit a rearmed Germany, whether within or outside the European Defense Community. (As it was, belief that the Mendès government would veto the EDC was inherent in the Soviet acceptance of the Geneva agreement.)

For China, on the contrary, the settlement represented an unqualified diplomatic success. Continued fighting would have meant the probability of American bases and soldiers on China's frontiers. Now there would be a Communist buffer state, and the very incompleteness of Ho Chi Minh's success would make him more dependent on China than would otherwise be the case. Had he been able to conquer all of Vietnam Ho would natu-rally have looked to the U.S.S.R. for protection against his powerful neigh-bor. That a Korean-type solution for Indochina was at the time most at-tractive to the Chinese Communists was almost disarmingly revealed by Chou En-lai in his speech at the conference: "The delegation of the Peo-ple's Republic of China stated at the beginning of this Conference that since the Korean war had stopped the Indochinese war should likewise be stopped."[56] Logically it was difficult to see parallels between the two wars in different countries and which had vastly different origins and fortunes. But to the Chinese they represented two similar conflicts on the periphery of their own country, conflicts that threatened them with U.S. attack, jeopardized the development of their economy, and delayed the prospect of emancipation from humiliating (and expensive) Soviet military aid. It is therefore not surprising that Chou almost showed enthusiasm in ad-vocating a solution that to his Vietnamese colleagues must have been only half a loaf, and that postponed the prospect of a Communist take-over of Cambodia and Laos for an indefinite period of time.

[55] The burden, though heavy, was not overwhelming. Financially, the United States had carried for some time most of the expense of the French operations in Indochina, and the French casualties there were on a smaller scale than those of the Americans in the 1960's.

[56] *Documents on International Affairs, 1954,* p. 131.

While the end of the Indochinese war must have been greeted privately in Washington with relief, the official American attitude was one of peevish disapproval of the Geneva conference. Dulles' pique was especially aroused by Communist China, "fanatically hostile to us and demonstrably aggressive and treacherous," strutting on the world stage and assuming the posture of a Great Power. He had previously, during a debate in the United Nations, recalled America's traditional benevolence toward the Chinese people, how in many American communities at the turn of the century a special collection would take place under the auspices of the local church and how dresses, goodies, etc., thus collected would be dispatched to a missionary in China for distribution to his congregation. The Geneva accord evoked another string of reminiscences: how his grandfather had negotiated the Sino-Japanese treaty of the 1890's, how he himself had labored on securing peace in the Pacific area, crossing the ocean twelve times. And now Chou En-lai, oblivious of such obligations, was covering the United States and her Secretary of State with abuse.

This chagrin was blinding American policy-makers to the already visible strains in the Russo-Chinese alliance. Molotov, whose private feelings about his Chinese colleague were probably not much kindlier than Dulles', still had to treat Chou with ostentatious deference and on the basis of equality—a new experience for a Soviet statesman dealing with an official of a "fraternal socialist country." Following the conference Chou toured Eastern Europe in a rather grandiose manner—a practice that, when indulged in by Tito between 1945 and 1947, had led to some somber reflections in Moscow. The Chinese Prime Minister's travels then brought him to India and Burma, and in both countries joint statements were issued emphasizing their friendship with the Chinese People's Republic and having unmistakable "Asia for the Asians" undertones. This was also a novelty—a Communist country initiating a line of foreign policy on its own and not in association with the U.S.S.R. It is impossible to say whether these tours were the means also of pressuring the Russians into extending their aid and abandoning their remaining bases and privileges in China.

In September a Russian delegation headed by Khrushchev and Bulganin arrived in China. Its personnel indicated, incidentally, that though the official announcement of it would not be forthcoming for some months, Malenkov had in fact been downgraded and that the No. 1 position in the U.S.S.R. was held by the First Secretary. Also in Khrushchev's entourage were Mikoyan, Shvernik, and Shepilov, the last being groomed for the foreign ministry, Molotov's star having also set. The personnel of the delegation and the fact that the negotiations were taking place in Peking instead of Moscow were vivid proof of the new status assumed by Communist China and of the continuing Soviet effort to propitiate her. The time had passed when Mao could be summoned to Moscow and await Stalin's pleasure. Now the top leaders of the U.S.S.R. came to him.

The negotiations included a wide range of topics. It was a foregone conclusion that special Russian privileges in China would have to go, and so they did. The base of Port Arthur was to be evacuated by the Soviets and turned over to the Chinese. The joint Sino-Soviet companies for the exploitation of minerals in Sinkiang and for civil aviation were to be dissolved and their assets turned over to China. "This decision . . . will contribute to a further strengthening of economic cooperation on the basis of equality, mutual aid and a respect for mutual interests."[57]

Those were significant steps: the end of the last foreign concessions and privileges on the mainland of China. The Soviet withdrawal from Port Arthur, though foreseen in the agreement of 1950 and reaffirmed in 1952, had first been stipulated to come only after the conclusion of a peace treaty with Japan. Now it would come by the end of May 1955. The base itself had by now only symbolic and political rather than military importance. But the Chinese did not want Russian soldiers on their soil.[58]

On the economic side, the Soviet reluctance to give away anything for free was still in evidence. A new and rather modest loan was granted. But the Soviet assets in the joint companies were to be compensated by Chinese exports to the U.S.S.R. Soviet economic, scientific, and technological help was greatly extended, and in the next few years thousands of Chinese students would be instructed in the U.S.S.R. and Russian experts and equipment would pour in to build up Chinese heavy industry. Still, the Chinese would have to pay for all this help. Russian niggardliness may have been a strong factor in establishing that personal enmity between Khrushchev and Mao which would become of such importance during the coming decade. For their own part, though not in a most gracious manner, the Russians were contributing to the military and industrial development of China which would in a few years accentuate their dilemma in dealing with the Asian giant. The agreement on scientific collaboration included Soviet help in China's nuclear research (in three years the Soviets would specifically pledge to furnish China with a sample atom bomb). Those were far-reaching and fateful commitments.

That they were being made at all reflected two factors. There was still considerable turmoil within the Soviet leadership and considerable tensions in the country at large. As usual those strains were skillfully concealed or minimized, yet they dictated the policy of prudence in external relations. The extent of both the "thaw" and "de-Stalinization" were the

[57] *Ibid.*, p. 325.
[58] In 1955 the Soviets were to renounce their rights to a naval-military base in Finland, a step which might well have been calculated to offset the psychological effect of their not so voluntary renunciation of Port Arthur.

subject of rigorous debate within the highest circles. If Beria had made his gambit and lost as the advocate of "socialist legality" and the enemy of russification, then evidently some other circles (identified with Malenkov) were making their move as proponents of a greater abundance of consumer goods and of slowing down investments in heavy industry. In turn this was seized on by opponents of Stalin's former favorite as an un-Marxist abandonment of the primacy of heavy industry and likely to lead to the weakening of Russia's defense potential. How close the charges and countercharges were to the actual position of the conflicting parties is difficult to decide. But Malenkov, closest to Stalin between 1948 and 1953 and probably his intended successor, fell victim mainly of personal jealousies and the apprehensions of his colleagues. He had shown himself inept in allowing the Party machinery to be snatched from his hands. He was removed in February 1955 but retained in the Presidium and in a ministerial position. The notion of collective leadership was still strong enough, however, not to allow Khrushchev the headship of government as well as of the Party. The new Prime Minister, Bulganin, for all his one-time membership in the secret police, presented a reassuring and dignified appearance and manner. He looked in fact like a Tsarist governor or general, and like many of the former was inordinately addicted to vodka. This was perhaps part of the reason why he proved ineffective as a foil to Khrushchev, though the latter was also not averse to strong drink.

The enhanced role of the army was epitomized by the succession as defense minister of Marshal Zhukov, the most renowned soldier of World War II. To accord such political eminence to a professional soldier must not have come easily to the Communist bosses, but they evidently still felt the need to tap every source of popularity and represent themselves as a government of national union. A younger, more ambitious and energetic man in Zhukov's position could have become a considerable danger to the Party, divided within itself and uneasily trying to maneuver between the aroused expectations of the people and the need to retain its totalitarian grip. But Napoleon was in his early thirties when he snatched power; Marshal Zhukov was going on sixty. Two years later, having performed another service to Khrushchev in consolidating his hold on the Party, the Marshal was abruptly dismissed as a "would-be Bonaparte"—one thing the gallant soldier was not.

This background makes it more understandable why the regime was eager for the Communist bloc to appear united, with no ideological or tactical dispute marring the picture of harmony. A *public* dispute with China would severely shake that image. De-Stalinization was still being pursued discreetly without an open attack on the dead leader. Many in the highest circles felt that a dramatic disclosure of Stalin's crimes would prove too great a shock and danger. The current crop of leaders had been without exception among Stalin's closest collaborators. They would in the future try to attenuate their responsibility or try to shift it to just some of them, but they could not be sure at this point—nor were they to be certain in 1956—that a great wave of indignation and shock would not shake the foundations of the whole system that had tolerated and abetted such crimes and cruelty. And to acknowledge publicly at this period the fact that Communism, this time in its international extension, had spawned another Frankenstein's monster, that Communist China presented a greater potential danger to the Russian national interest than capitalism, would be to court disaster.

There was another consideration that might have helped the Soviet leaders to rationalize their help in arming and developing the future rival of the U.S.S.R. Extensive Soviet help might still prove a lever of control over China, could strengthen the position of those Chinese Communists who looked to Moscow for help. It is especially within the Chinese armed forces that the Soviets hoped to develop a clientele of their own, and the means to offset any hostile policies of Mao and his group. The Chinese complaints of 1963 were to be quite explicit on this point: the Russians had expected to secure control of the Chinese army under the guise of arrangements for joint defense, etc. Similar hopes might well have explained the readiness to have thousands of Chinese students and specialists receive advanced training in the Soviet Union. But if so the Russians underestimate the wariness of a fellow totalitarian regime and the national pride of the Chinese. As early as 1956, when relations were still harmonious on the surface, a prominent Chinese Communist leader committed suicide under circumstances that left no doubt he had been disgraced for his pro-Soviet leanings. And in 1959 and 1960 summary dismissals were the lot of high officers and Party leaders, including the minister of defense, suspected of excessive fondness for the "Fatherland of Socialism." The self-imposed discipline and isolation of the Chinese students studying in Russia and the "people's democracies" were to become notorious, and afforded little opportunity for seductive contacts and fatherly explanations of how Comrade Mao and his ilk had in their own day performed valiant services, but times had changed and required new men and new ideas. . . . It is not easy to subvert people who have been trained in subversion.

The depressing prospects in China did not crowd out other problems and preoccupations. The defeat of the European Defense Community in the French National Assembly on August 30 meant but a temporary setback to the threat of a rearmed West Germany. Under the Paris agreement of October 1954 West Germany was admitted to full membership in NATO. Germany as well as Italy joined the Western European Union, which was to place its armed forces under NATO command. As against the abortive European Defense Community, the new plan envisaged national armies rather than a single integrated European army.

The rearmament of West Germany (or rather an agreement on it) had been six years in gestation. It would still be some time before an actual West German army would exist. In the meantime the U.S.S.R. had acquired a nuclear stockpile and was on the threshold of developing an intercontinental ballistic missile. Either as a bargaining card or a factor of real military strength, a rearmed West Germany was not nearly so formidable in 1955 as it would have been in 1949 or 1950. Furthermore, while the original plan of an integrated European army would have been technically cumbersome, in the early 1950's it would have provided a powerful impetus to a real European union, leading perhaps to a supranational state. In forthcoming years there would be a considerable degree of *economic* integration, but prosperity and the more amiable *tone* of Soviet foreign policy was to remove the sense of *political* urgency, and Western Europe—because it is still essentially divided—was to be unable to translate its great economic strength into equivalent political power.

All these considerations may have been present in the Soviet leaders' minds, but the mere fact that there would again be a Germany army and that West Germany would be a member of the Western military alliance was still a threat. The actual proportions of propaganda and genuine fear present in the Soviet agitation and activity about German rearmament are difficult to assess, but it would be wrong to discount or minimize the latter. A half-million-strong West German army, as envisaged under the Paris agreement, could not become a mortal threat to the Soviet Union, but Soviet apprehensions were as always of a long-run variety. In 1954–55 it appeared probable that West Germany would be able to dominate its European partners, that the revanchist spirit, as the Soviet notes put it, would reassert itself in the Bonn republic, and that not only East Germany but the western provinces of Poland would become its objectives. NATO, for all of its constitutional arrangements designed to prevent such a development, might yet become an instrument of Germany's recapturing her old domination in Europe.

It is amusing to note that the Italian enlistment in NATO provoked practically no Soviet protests—hardly a tribute to Italy's record as a military power. On the other hand, a veritable barrage of Soviet diplomatic notes continued to attempt first to prevent West Germany's accession to NATO and then to undo it. At one time, and rather humorously, the Soviets proposed their own joining of the Western defense organization. At other times, as in the note of October 23 with the German entrance into NATO imminent, the Soviet government held out the alluring prospect of *discussing* the Western proposals for all-German elections, as well as the

Austrian peace treaty and atomic disarmament, if only West German remilitarization were to be abandoned. But the Western Powers which had dawdled over German rearmament for six years were not buying. There was some temptation in France and among the British and German socialists to explore the Soviet intentions, which in all likelihood would have meant yet another interminable conference, but the West European governments were under the threat of Dulles' "agonizing reappraisal." As was to become clear in 1955 and for reasons spelled out above, there was no chance at this juncture that the Soviets would sacrifice "their" Germany for the sake of keeping West Germany disarmed. By the end of the 1954–55 period the renewed Soviet passion for conferences on the German issue stemmed from a desire to avoid or postpone the rearmament but without any readiness to pay for this achievement in hard currency.

The Moscow conference on European security which convened in November 1954 was thus attended only by the Communist-bloc countries (with China sending an observer). Except for a chorus of indignation about West German rearmament and NATO the conference could hardly produce any spectacular results. That China was brought even in an observer capacity to what had been a jealously guarded Soviet preserve— the family of East European satellites—was again a symptom of the times. This Chinese association was to help to produce within the next two years some startling—and, from the Soviet point of view, hardly desirable—developments in their East European enclave.

The rather feeble bombshell produced at the Moscow conference was a threat that materialized next year in the form of the Warsaw Pact, a defensive alliance of the European Communist states (including East Germany), a counter-NATO should the remilitarization of West Germany become a fact. Even the Kremlin could hardly expect the West to blanch at this announcement. Treaty or no treaty, the satellites' military establishments were at the disposal of the Russians, and it was preposterous to imagine that the elaborate military machinery of a joint command set up in 1955 made any real difference. As a matter of fact, the strengthening and re-equipment of the satellite armies had some rather unpleasant consequences for Russia. This came close to being demonstrated in October 1956 in Poland. When the dramatic events in the Polish Communist Party aroused Soviet apprehensions and when some Russian military units in the country began a move toward Warsaw, the Polish army, though still officially under the command of Soviet Marshal Rokossovsky, was obviously on the point of counteraction. How lucky it was for the Soviets that the Hungarian army in November 1956 was not larger and better equipped.

But the Warsaw Pact when it came into being in 1955 was not merely a propaganda move. It gave the Soviets a convenient basis for continuing to station their troops in some of the satellites. Furthermore, on the German issue (as against practically every other one) the Soviets enjoyed a wide degree of popular support in countries like Poland and Czechoslovakia, and the threat of German rearmament and German territorial vindications was a useful lever of Soviet control.

The year 1955 was one of treaties, trips, and transition. In the year and a half since the death of Stalin, the regime had obviously acquired a degree of stability and self-confidence. A symptom of this precarious—as events were to show—degree of normalcy was the civilized way in which the change of leadership was transacted. Malenkov's demotion was followed not by bloodcurdling accusations, a secret trial, and liquidation, but by the assignment of Stalin's pudgy ex-favorite to a ministerial post and his continued presence in the highest councils. Economically and culturally the intercourse with non-Communist countries grew. The Soviet system was shedding some of the pathological traits it had evidenced in the Stalin era, and some of the near panic it had exhibited on the dictator's death. The tone of Soviet politics was now being dictated increasingly by Khrushchev. Still not the unchallenged leader (his bid for supreme power came with his dramatic denunciation of Stalin in 1956), the ebullient First Secretary was clearly the first among equals. In foreign policy he also moved to the front; though Molotov retained official guidance of the foreign ministry, more and more often he was excluded from conferences and diplomatic trips, and his opinion on such important matters as the degree of reconciliation with Yugoslavia was evidently disregarded. But even the dour-faced Foreign Minister—the "iron behind," as Lenin had once dubbed him—responded to the spirit of the times. He appeared at the tenth anniversary of the founding of the United Nations wearing a straw hat and actually smiling. It was a far cry from the days when he travelled surrounded by numerous guards and when he insisted (in Blair House!) on sleeping with a revolver on the night table.

Travel in foreign lands had indeed become popular with the Soviet leaders. Men in their late middle age who had been confined to their desks and rarely allowed out of the country by their suspicious boss, they obviously longed for a glimpse of the "rotten West" and the "backward Orient." With Khrushchev, a homegrown Communist if ever there was one, foreign travel became a veritable obsession.

But there were cogent state reasons for some of these peregrinations. The new leaders were propagating a new image of Communism in capitalist and uncommitted lands, and their presence was needed to solve the vexing problems in the satellites, where de-Stalinization was having perturbing effects on the Communist parties—some of them going too far, from the Kremlin's point of view, while in others leaders like Rakosi in Hungary tried stubbornly to hang on to the old Stalinist ways. In the fall of 1955 the now inseparable duo of Khrushchev and Bulganin descended on the Orient and toured India, Burma, and Afghanistan. This tour emphasized the new importance of Asian affairs in over-all Soviet policy. Communist China, currently also in a coexistential mood, had made strong efforts to become leader of all Asia, indeed of all underdeveloped nations. The Bandung Conference of the preceding spring found Chou En-lai charming his fellow delegates from Asia and Africa by the moderation and breadth of his views and his forcible renunciation of any idea of exporting revolution. China, he had declared, was ready to talk with the United States about a peaceful solution of the Formosa question, why she was not even averse to talking with the Nationalist Chinese about a peaceful and decorous way of taking them over! His own delegation, Chou declared for the benefit of the Indonesians and Arab Muslims, contained a devout Mohammedan, visible proof of how the Chinese Communists respected everybody's beliefs. Such ideological catholicity and openness of mind, coming from the Chinese and combined with the now quite transparent appeal to the non-European world to coalesce into a bloc (Soviet Russia, though an Asian power, had not been invited to Bandung), could not have been warmly greeted in Moscow. Though on the surface the policies of the two Communist super-powers were synchronized and the Russians hastened with approval of the Chinese initiatives, they could not take kindly to their exclusion from the new club of "developing nations," as the American social scientists were to call them.

The stay in India was the high point of the Khrushchev-Bulganin tour of the Orient. The Soviets spared no effort in flattering their hosts. Unlike the Chinese they were in a position to promise badly needed economic and technical aid. Similar promises and largesse, though on a smaller scale, were dispensed in Burma and Afghanistan. This Soviet economic help to non-Communist nations, though now only on a small scale, was to become an important instrument of Soviet foreign policy. It undermined the image of the United States as the only benefactor of underdeveloped countries, and it soothed the conscience of the new nations, which had been feeling guilty because of receiving help only from the materialistic West. Nehru's India was then at the height of her self-congratulatory phase. Courted by the Chinese, Americans, and Russians, widely acclaimed for their spiritual superiority which precluded them from taking sides in the world conflict, the Indians could now find a justification of their neutralism in this descent of the top Soviet leaders. It was visible proof that virtue paid off and that one could have the best of both worlds—unlike Pakistan, which had joined one of Dulles' treaty organizations and was now being punished by not being included in the Khrushchev-Bulganin itinerary. Khrushchev's inherent boorishness was still being kept under restraint.[59] He submitted to being garlanded with flowers by young girls, suffered through official receptions, where in deference to the Congress Party's ban on alcohol orange juice was substituted, and only occasionally uttered tactless remarks about wicked British and American imperialism, which had not as yet abandoned its evil designs on the Indian people. While his hosts could not but contrast his manners with the mandarin graces of Chou, the ebullient Soviet leader could dispense economic help and his Chinese counterpart only Asian solidarity. Soviet-Indian friendship was to endure, while as for China and India. . . .

The most startling trip of all in 1955, however, took place in Europe. It would not have been surprising if visitors to the Lenin-Stalin Mausoleum on May 26 had observed one of its illustrious tenants stirring wrathfully, for on that day his two current successors were paying court to Marshal Tito in Belgrade. In the presence of the unsmiling Yugoslav leader the head of the Soviet delegation which had invited itself to his country topped this brazenness by blaming all the past troubles between the two socialist states on "Beria, Abbakumov,[60] and other exposed enemies of the people . . . the contemptible agents of imperialism who had fraudulently wormed their way into the ranks of our Party." Since the language employed about Beria and Abbakumov was identical with that which his guests had employed about Tito himself until March 5, 1953, the Marshal could be expected and did in fact reply rather coldly to Khrushchev's "let us be friends and forget about the past" gambit. Though a sense of delicacy and proneness to embarrassment had never been among their strong characteristics, the Soviet leaders found themselves under visible strain in the course of their visit. This may explain such attempts at relief as Khrushchev stopping a tour of the Serbian countryside to indulge in a wrestling match with Mikoyan. And the strain finally told at an official party where the First Secretary, overcome by emotion and drink, passed out and had to be carried away by members of his suite.

Such comical interludes notwithstanding, the Belgrade visit, startling in its brazenness—to think of something comparable one has to imagine Dulles alighting in Peking or Colonel Nasser in Tel Aviv—was both a

[59] In a later trip, while being treated to an exhibition of famous Indonesian handicrafts, he could not contain himself and exploded: all this was nonsense and a symptom of backwardness. Where were the factories? To be sure, by that time the U.S.S.R. had poured a lot of money into Indonesia, the visible products of which were a handsome athletic stadium and a high style of living for Sukarno, while even the Indonesian Communists ungratefully looked to Peking for inspiration rather than to Moscow.

[60] One of the heads of the Soviet secret police under Stalin, shot in 1957.

calculated and fruitful move. Especially since her 1954 alliance with Greece and Turkey, Yugoslavia had become a bulwark of the Western position in the Balkans. Tito's continued estrangement from the U.S.S.R. was costing the Russians dearly among the uncommitted nations and those left-wing but non-Communist circles that otherwise would be attracted by the new Soviet posture in foreign relations. Contemptible as Tito undoubtedly found his guests' lies and false excuses, his regime was at this point in need of some *rapprochement* with orthodox Communism. The split with the U.S.S.R. had produced, after the initial nationalist elation, a feeling of ideological vacuum that was sapping the foundations of his totalitarian rule. There was restlessness in the Communist Party of Yugoslavia, as epitomized in the Djilas affair, claims for greater freedom and even for the abandonment of the one-party system. A renewed link with the "camp of socialism" would thus be most convenient, and that was the reason why the rather comic proceedings culminated in an official statement of both governments pledging a renewal of friendship and collaboration, promising to abide by the principle of noninterference in internal affairs, etc. The Russians were to prove powerful wooers. The erstwhile "agent of imperialists and Zionists" was to become during the next year their trusted adviser, whose opinion as to how to run things in the satellites was sought and appreciated. It was given out that Molotov, who had *not* been on the historic trip, was still clinging to the old Stalinist prejudices about Yugoslavia but that his voice now counted for little in policy-making.

Tito fell in with his new role. Publicly as well as privately he dispensed advice as to how de-Stalinization should be carried out in Hungary, Bulgaria, etc., and how unwise it was to leave in power those people who had slandered him and the Yugoslav Communists. His language about some of the rulers of Eastern Europe was understandably violent. "These men have their hands soaked in blood, have staged trials, given false information, sentenced innocent people to death."[61]

Such sentiments were not appreciated by the Soviet satraps in the satellites. It could be, and was, pointed out that such utterances and indeed Russia's fawning on Tito were having a demoralizing effect on the Soviet empire as a whole. The unrepentant sinner was given a place of honor while the Rakosis, Bieruts, *et al.* who had faithfully groveled before Stalin were discredited before their own parties and peoples. There were undoubtedly members of the Presidium of the CPSU who were unhappy about the whole business. But the dynamic First Secretary felt that in the renewed liaison with Tito he had found a key to the new image of Communism: a vigorous creed, not ashamed to confess its past errors, and

[61] *Documents on International Affairs, 1955* (London, 1958), p. 271.

compatible with national sovereignty and the dignity of non-Soviet members of the socialist camp.

One year after the Belgrade visit Tito and his wife were invited to Russia. By that time Stalin had been denounced and Molotov removed as foreign minister. Tito could enjoy the satisfaction of having triumphed over the most powerful dictator of modern times and of having been instrumental in starting one of the most monumental developments of post-war history: the evolution of international communism, once a monolithic Soviet-controlled movement, in the direction of polycentrism. The latter fact explains why at the time (1955–56), strange as it seems in view of their earlier and later attitudes, the Chinese Communists applauded Tito. He was a welcome symbol of the relaxed Soviet control over other Communist countries. His example would force the Russians to make further exertions on behalf of international Communism and to abandon the idea of merely using it for their own interests. Tito's tour of the U.S.S.R. was a triumphant procession. His friendship with Khrushchev seemed now based on mutual political benefits. His re-entry into the Communist family confounded the Djilases at home, while Khrushchev used the personable Yugoslav to demonstrate how a Communist regime did not have to be based on repression and suspicion—while those relics from the past, Molotov and Kaganovich, were arguing and harping on the dangers of the new course. But then, alas, shadows overlay the new friendship; Russo-Yugoslav relations were never to recapture the rapture of this summer of 1956.

To many observers the year 1955 appeared the most hopeful of the post-war era insofar as the relaxation of international tensions and prospects for an East-West settlement were concerned. The Soviet leaders were on their best behavior, the "five principles of peaceful coexistence" and noninterference in other countries' internal affairs being their constant refrain. And, beyond words, Soviet Russia was ready to offer tangible concessions—evacuating territories and war bases, a phenomenon almost unimaginable in the Stalin era. The evacuation of a naval base in Finland was not very costly in itself; even in 1945 the base was obsolete and useless in view of modern military technology and Russia's position in Eastern Europe. But it was tangible proof of Russia's abandonment for the time being of any idea of enlisting Finland among the satellites, the possibility of which had been raised sharply several times between 1945 and 1952.

A much more important and hopeful step was the signing of the Austrian peace treaty on May 15, 1955. This lucky little country had two great strokes of good fortune following World War II. First, it was decided on sound historical but dubious psychological grounds that Austria had been a liberated rather than an enemy territory.[62] In the second place, though divided into four zones of occupation, no Communist regime had been foisted on any part of the country. Until 1953 the Russians had stoutly insisted that an Austrian peace treaty had to await the solution of the German problem, but they now relented. The treaty provided for the termination of occupation and complete withdrawal of foreign troops. To be sure, the Russians had to be paid off: Austrian goods were to compensate them for the properties they had seized as German-owned and which they now turned over to the Austrians. Austria was to preserve absolute neutrality.

Austria's good luck was partly the product of the country's military and industrial insignificance. But the Russians' readiness to withdraw their troops and to agree to a treaty also reflected their belief that the example of Austria would have an educative effect on the Germans: once you agree to forswear foreign alliances you get rid of foreign troops and can settle down to enjoy opera, beer, and tourists. But the case of Germany was hugely more complicated. West Germany was now a partner in NATO, East Germany was a Communist state. By 1955 both East and West had left themselves rather limited room for maneuver over Germany. Had the Russians inclined to do so, had they been offered the disbanding of NATO as a price for it, it is still doubtful that they could have afforded to disband the East German regime. As 1956 was to demonstrate, there was already enough explosive material in the satellites to keep the Russians from risking such a step. For their own part, the Western policymakers looked on Russian concessions as a justification of their own "tough" position and of West German rearmament. Such insinuations, coming especially from Washington, were indignantly denied by the Russians and obviously imposed certain limits on their willingness to be "reasonable." Interspersed with their conciliatory gestures and statements were such warnings as the abrogation of the alliances with Britain and France contracted during World War II, etc. Nobody in 1955 could think that those alliances possessed the slightest significance. But the abrogations served as a reminder that Soviet policy could always be drastically reversed and that despite the Austrian treaty Russia was not acquiescing in German rearmament. The situation then possessed certain elements of humor as well as drama. The Western democracies thought, but were not sure, that they had achieved a "position of strength"—that elusive goal sought for ever since 1949. But even if they had, what were they to do with it? Soviet policy statements breathed amiability interspersed with

[62] Nazism, it appears, had as much genuine support in the country that gave birth to its author as in Germany. Not a scintilla of resistance movement or any serious trouble was encountered there after 1938.

warnings, but in concrete issues this amiability could not be translated into concrete policies, for any major concessions to the West, as distinguished from peripheral ones (over Austria and Finland), were deemed too dangerous.

Soviet policies in 1955 reflected a variety of factors. In the first place, the Soviets were temporizing while awaiting a "position of strength" of their own. They were confident that their breakthrough in the development of long-range missiles would soon enable them to speak more resolutely with friend and foe alike. A nuclear reactor for China, a peace treaty with Austria for the West appeared small enough concessions to gain time, while they recovered from the backwash of Stalinism and gained economic and military strength that would enable them to become if need be tough and businesslike vis-à-vis both China and the West.

Furthermore, the obvious hesitations and inconsistencies of Soviet policies reflected the still unstable position within the Soviet leadership. It is impossible to say what a man with Khrushchev's instincts and Stalin's powers would have done in foreign or domestic policies, but such combinations are not often granted in history. The First Secretary was still limited in his freedom of movement—and he remained so even after his spectacular victory in 1957. In 1955 the old guard of Molotov, Malenkov, and Kaganovich was still in an influential position and capable of restraining the pace of de-Stalinization. When it came to foreign policies, they must have grumbled—certainly Molotov did—about the dangers of too cordial a *rapprochement* with Tito and the risks of giving the West a feeling that its "tough" policies were paying off. Neither then nor in the future was Khrushchev's position as the leader of his country and of world Communism to be strong enough to enable him to effect really fundamental changes either in the Soviet system or in foreign policy.

The Geneva conference of the heads of the Big Four underlined the new form of impasse in East-West relations, largely because the atmosphere of superficial friendship and amiability had succeeded the aura of suspicions and menaces, and the chances of a war seemed distant. There was no need for either side to envisage substantive concessions.

The Soviet delegation was headed by Khrushchev, Bulganin, Molotov, and Zhukov. The last one was brought, it seems, with General Eisenhower in mind. The two old warriors might exchange reminiscent chit-chat about the war, thus enhancing the cordiality of the occasion. A private interview did take place between the two leaders—a significant change from Stalin's days, when a Russian general was not likely to converse at length with a foreigner without the soothing presence of a political supervisor. But nothing momentous ensued[63] from the tête-à-tête. Khrushchev,

---

[63] General Eisenhower found Zhukov more reticent and unsure of himself than ten years before. But since Eisenhower also believes that in 1945 Zhukov

who let Bulganin play the role of leader of the delegation, spent his time observing the capitalist statesmen, a species he had not previously encountered. He was on his best behavior, but some years later in a burst of bitterness after the U-2 episode, he was to recall ungraciously how on any important question the President would turn to an aide, usually Dulles, for information and opinion.

The Soviet position on Germany precluded any meaningful discussion of the problem. The Russians offered to disband the Warsaw Treaty Organization in return for a dissolution of NATO and "withdrawal of foreign troops from the territories of European countries." This meant that a discussion of German reunification would have to await the dissolution of the Western alliance and the withdrawal of American troops from Europe. The Soviets must have known that those proposals would be unacceptable to the United States, as was a variant envisaging a general European security pact which in two or three years would supersede both NATO and Warsaw and in which East and West Germany would participate. The actual effect of any even tentative agreement to entertain the Soviet proposals would have been to stop the rearmament of West Germany, and this was something the Western Powers, certainly Washington, was not going to accept.

The conference was to prove no more fruitful on the issue of disarmament than on Germany. The Soviet proposals envisaged a limit on the armed forces of the Great Powers (1.5 million for the U.S., the U.S.S.R., and China) and a gradual reduction and eventual elimination of nuclear weapons. (In the Soviet proposals for the gradual abandonment of nuclear weapons, there was an interesting reflection of what must have been the Chinese position at the time. One of the first steps in the implementation of the program would be "that the states *possessing* atomic and hydrogen weapons undertake to stop the tests of these weapons."[64] Thus it was carefully implied that the proposed convention would not in itself bar new states from acquiring nuclear weapons.[65]) These Soviet proposals— indeed, the whole issue of disarmament—were then and for years to come to bog down on the issues of inspection and control. The American position as stated by President Eisenhower in Geneva was that "disarmament agreements without adequate reciprocal inspection increase the dangers of war and do not brighten the prospects of peace."[66] The Soviet retort was

was "a great personal friend of Stalin's" and second to him in power in the Soviet government, one may respectfully question his powers of observation when it comes to Soviet affairs. Dwight D. Eisenhower, *Mandate For Change 1953–1956* (New York, 1963), pp. 524–25.

[64] My italics. Quoted from *Documents on International Affairs, 1955*, p. 38.

[65] At the time the only atomic powers were the United States, the U.S.S.R., and Great Britain.

[66] *Documents on International Affairs, 1955*, p. 39.

that an extensive system of inspection of atomic production and research, so intimately connected with the whole of a given country's military and industrial establishment, would be an intolerable intrusion on sovereignty and could not be tolerated. Both positions had unassailable logic behind them. Furthermore, the sad fact was that had all the practical difficulties somehow been ironed out it was still unlikely that the conditions of confidence prevailing between the U.S. and the U.S.S.R. would have allowed a genuine and synchronized measure of nuclear disarmament—as against an agreement on a peripheral issue like the ban on testing nuclear weapons. The whole rationale of the discussions on nuclear disarmament, one must conclude, was based on the tacit assumption that the technical difficulties in establishing an effective system of inspection and sanctions would prove insuperable. To break away from this vicious circle would have required a drastic change in the whole tone of relations between the two super-powers, and such a change even in the relaxed atmosphere of the mid-1950's looked as unlikely as it had under Stalin.

One American contribution to this atmosphere was to have rather ironical consequences. This was Eisenhower's famous "open skies" proposal. The two countries were to exchange blueprints of their military establishments and provide each other with facilities for aerial photography. The vision of a host of American planes snooping over the territory of the U.S.S.R. did not strike a responsive chord with the Russians. They had too much delicacy to explain that the proposed arrangement would not really be fair: an assiduous reader of American newspapers and magazines could arrive at a fairly accurate notion of the American defense establishment, location of bases, etc., while as for the U.S.S.R. the task was more complicated. Eisenhower's proposals, the fruit of the attention now being paid in Washington to the psychological aspect of the cold war, must have appeared to the Soviets as an answer to the Stockholm Appeal gambit of their own. Little did they suspect that the ingenuous Americans, undaunted by their refusal, would go into the "open skies" business on their own and that within a few years U-2 planes would cruise over the Soviet Union collecting all sorts of interesting information.

Other "touchy" subjects made their appearance at the conference only to be shoved firmly aside by one or the other of the major conferees. The President delicately raised the issue of world Communism and of the East European satellites. With equal delicacy, but also with firmness, Marshal Bulganin pointed out that the Four Powers had no mandate to interfere in the affairs of Poland, Rumania, etc., where the existing governments had been set up by the people concerned and were nobody else's business. World Communism? They were gathered to discuss international affairs, not the activities of political parties. He for his part wanted only to mention the fact that Formosa and the Chinese seat in the United Nations belonged by right to the People's Republic of China, which would not be loath to settle these aggravating questions by direct talks with the United States.

The Soviet position adhered to what might be described as imprecise friendliness. The old virulent style of Soviet oratory, references to "imperialists," the "ruling circles in the U.S.," "the instigators of World War III," were missing. The dignified Soviet leader stressed his country's desire for expanded cultural and commercial contacts with the West, praised neutralism as a positive force in international relations, and affirmed Soviet readiness to establish diplomatic relations with the Bonn republic.[67]

The last two points emphasized the new flexibility of Soviet foreign policy and brought into relief the moralistic-legalistic rigidity of American policy as enunciated by Dulles. The newly found virtues of neutralism contrasted with the "who is not with us is against us" stance of the Stalin period. Bulganin's praise took shameless liberties with history. "Experience teaches us that some states which have pursued a neutral policy in time of war ensured security for their peoples and have played a positive role. That is shown by the experience of the Second World War."[68] This had *not* been the experience of such states as Belgium, Norway, and Denmark, and the Soviets conveniently chose to forget what they themselves had said during the war about the neutrality of Turkey and Sweden. But the Soviet attitude could be and was favorably compared with America's eagerness to push various states into SEATO's and CENTO's, those treaty arrangements which, experience was to show, were of such dubious value.

The same lesson applied to the diplomatic recognition of the regime that had consistently been characterized by the Soviets as one of "Hitlerite generals and big-business revanchists." If the Soviets could have relations with both West and East Germany, why, pray, could not the Americans adopt a parallel policy on China? Those were the questions being asked in Asia and also among left-wing circles in Europe. The fact was that the rigid character of Stalin's policies left to Russia's new masters great scope

[67] A formal agreement on establishing diplomatic relations with West Germany was reached during Chancellor Adenauer's visit to Moscow in September. As against previous West German expectations, the conversations brought little else in practical results apart from the Soviet pledge to repatriate German prisoners still in the U.S.S.R. The Soviets' now clear adherence to the "two Germanies" position was underlined by the arrival, soon after Adenauer's departure, of an East German delegation and the conclusion of a treaty between the U.S.S.R. and the German Democratic Republic in which the latter was granted full sovereignty, at least on paper, including the right to conduct its own foreign relations.

[68] *Documents on International Affairs, 1955*, p. 26.

to be flexible and liberal without sacrificing anything of substance. The virtues of American policy, being of long standing, were bound to appear tiresome and irritating, while the newly found liberality of the Soviets seemed exciting and appealing. It was thus being demonstrated how in this world as well, much as it clashes with a logical approach to justice, a repentant sinner enjoys an undue advantage over one who has dully and unimaginatively followed the straight and narrow path.

The July conference of heads of state was followed in the fall by a conference of the foreign ministers of the Big Four, equally full of amiability and reasonableness, equally devoid of any progress on the fundamental issues of Germany and disarmament. The pattern of "summitry" departed considerably from what Churchill, no longer at the head of the British government, had expected in urging such meetings. They were not, and could not be in view of the changes that had occurred since the war, intimate and secret bargaining sessions between three or four leaders who could unconditionally commit their countries and drastically change the course of international affairs. The Geneva meetings inevitably became exercises in public relations, the leaders addressing not so much each other as world public opinion and trying in an ostensibly friendly manner to undermine the policies of each other. From the Soviet point of view "the Geneva spirit" marked the great success of post-Stalin policies, a general relaxation of tensions, a grudging acquiescence by the United States in Soviet gains in Eastern Europe, a new image of the U.S.S.R. in the Third World, a strong impetus toward neutralism in those left-wing European circles which had been alienated by Russia's isolation and menacing tone under Stalin. This relaxation enabled the U.S.S.R. to turn to pressing domestic tasks and to begin reducing her armed forces. In the next two years the Soviets would be able to release more than 2 million young men badly needed in their farms and factories.

Was this policy stance "sincere"? This question has been fully explored, and we might simply add that the Soviet leaders' ideology was extremely helpful in allowing them to justify to themselves as well as to their followers those drastic shifts and improvisations which led their opponents, flustered and furious, to protest Russian "insincerity," attempts to "lull the free world to sleep," etc. To such accusations the answer was and is invariably that the "objective historical circumstances have changed" and indeed are always changing, and with them the appropriate policies. In less dialectical terms one may say that the Soviet posture at the end of 1955 reflected the belief that *both* the dangers to the Soviet system and the opportunities for expansion of Communist-Soviet power were now greatly diminished. Hence a policy of *détente* was logically indicated, since it neither incurred undue risks to the U.S.S.R. and her satellites nor meant passing up any spectacular opportunities.

Within a year both these assumptions were to prove inaccurate. The de-Stalinization process was neither as easy nor as safe as had been expected. Great convulsions were to shake the Soviet empire and Soviet society. This was to enable some within the Soviet hierarchy to urge that *rapprochement* with the West and cordiality toward Tito had indeed gone too far. Nor was the expectation of the relative stability of the Western system to be justified. The decline of Britain and France had already been obvious to the Soviet statesmen: at Geneva the heads of those two governments really played the role of onlookers, the dialogue being mainly between the U.S.S.R. and the United States. And for all his good manners Bulganin could not help implying to Sir Anthony Eden and M. Faure that they now represented second-rate powers. But the full extent of the collapse of the imperial systems and of the consequent dilemmas of the West was not to become completely clear until 1956, and with it was to come the irresistible temptation to exploit the predicament and disarray of the opponents. Thus both new dangers and new opportunities were to alter the course of post-Stalin foreign policy. For all the dramatic denunciation of him, the dead despot would have an opportunity for a sardonic smile over his successors' predicament: it was not so easy after all to erase Stalinism from the Soviet system.

XI

THE PERILS OF KHRUSHCHEV

1. *Toward the Grand Design*

With his historic denunciation of Stalin at the Twentieth Party Congress in 1956, Nikita Khrushchev opened a new era in Soviet politics. From being first among equals in the hierarchy, he now became the focal point of the government and, as time went on, the possessor of a modest cult of personality of his own. But his career at the top was precarious. It was shaken by events during the fall of 1956, and in the winter of 1956–57 it appeared that he might be superseded. He recovered his balance in the spring, and then what amounted to a palace revolution in June 1957 actually unseated him, the verdict of the Presidium being reversed within a few hours, however, by the hastily convoked Central Committee. But even after that Nikita Sergeievich could not enjoy a peaceful rule. Problems domestic and foreign crowded upon each other. To resolve them, or rather to remove their urgency, the dynamic First Secretary resorted to dazzling improvisations: Soviet agriculture, for example, was to be rescued by cultivating vast new "virgin lands": when in a few years they became exhausted and uneconomic, Khrushchev was ready with a new "solution," a great increase of investment in the chemicals industry to increase the supply of artificial fertilizer. In foreign policy, dire threats of Soviet nuclear and missile power alternated with what seemed like offers to conclude an alliance with the United States. China was propitiated by Soviet aid toward the development of her nuclear weapons, but within two years of this dangerous concession all scientific assistance to China stopped. A pushful foreign policy designed to change the status of Berlin involved the Soviet Union in her most dangerous confrontation yet with the West. To offset pressures at home and abroad Khrushchev would tantalize the world with successive installments of the story of Stalin's Awful and Unbelievable Crimes. And the same juggler's ability served him well, for a time, in the struggle for power. The intra-Party opposition was confounded with the help of the army. Then, having performed his task and seemingly on the threshold of power himself, Marshal Zhukov was ignominiously dismissed.

By 1962, the First Secretary was running out of improvisations. There are grounds for believing that the Cuban missile crisis irretrievably undermined his position. His last two years in power were spent in peevish disputes with China and with Russia's intellectuals, in devising what his successors were to describe as "harebrained schemes." On an October day in 1964 Nikita Sergeievich was engaged in one of his more agreeable occupations: from his Crimean villa he was conversing with his orbiting cosmonauts—he would meet them in appropriate ceremonies after their descent and arrival in Moscow. But now he had to ring off because Anastas Mikoyan was impatient to snatch the receiver from his hand. And with this message to outer space, exited Nikita Khrushchev. His colleagues were to install a less colorful but seemingly safer and more stable team of leaders, but they in turn were unable to avoid the perplexing dilemmas that made Khrushchev's tenure of office so tempestuous.

For Khrushchev's troubles reflected not only his dynamic personality but the inherent problems—or, to use a Marxist term, contradictions—within post-Stalin Russia and post-Stalin Communism. Even a greater man might not have succeeded where Nikita Sergeievich failed. The regime first of all had to find what might be called the proper level of de-Stalinization, at which it could expose and remove the horrendous abuses of the past but in a way that would not threaten the foundations of the one-party state. It also struggled valiantly to find the proper level of coexistence: a pattern of relations with the United States that would minimize the risk of a nuclear war at the same time that it permitted the expansion of Communism, since a standstill in the latter case, apart from its foreign-relations implications, could not but have disturbing effects within the U.S.S.R. And it had to establish a new pattern of relations in the Communist camp: the satellites could not be run by Stalin's methods, yet what were the desirable limits of their autonomy?

Possibly those formidable tasks could have been solved, at least temporarily, but for the presence of one vast disturbing factor: Communist

China. In the Soviet leaders' moves, whether on the domestic front or in foreign affairs, one detects their awareness of a disturbing shadow at their elbow, their anxiety at what the Chinese reaction might be, their irritation that freedom of movement and the unanimous applause of the Communist world at whatever decision they make are no longer theirs. And as the Khrushchev era draws to an end the dispute becomes both public and acrimonious. It challenges Russia in a way that is unparalleled in the history of Soviet foreign policy, for there is no precedent for it and no formula that can contain the awesome consequences of Communism's greatest success since the October Revolution.

The denunciation of Stalin at the Twentieth Party Congress was a calculated risk undertaken by the Soviet regime, its leaders aware that it might trigger off a momentous reaction. What were their reasons? There was, in the first place, a natural feeling that the other shoe had to be dropped, that the emotional tension created by three years of de-Stalinizing without specifying the root cause and main author of the past oppressions, could in itself become dangerous and undermine the people's faith in the regime. Those past crimes could not indefinitely be blamed on "Beria, Abbakumov, and other enemies of the people who wormed their way into the Party." It was a gamble, but it might reasonably be expected that by telling the truth about the past—well, part of it anyway—the Party could gain credit (especially among the youth) and reactivate ideologically its rank and file. Three years had now passed since Stalin's death, the regime appeared stable, foreign tensions relaxed; now presumably was the logical moment to say what could not have been said in March 1953.

That political calculations were also involved there can be no doubt. Though he had been a high official of Stalin's regime, Nikita Khrushchev had never been as prominent as Molotov, Kaganovich, or Malenkov, who still sat in the Party's highest councils and still blocked him on many issues. They undoubtedly pleaded for the continuation of a quiet nondramatic de-Stalinization; Khrushchev thought rightly that by this bold initiative he would increase his pre-eminence and gain the support of those who dreaded the return of the bad old days.

The foreign implications of this dethronement of the dead idol also had to be considered. *Later on,* the Chinese Communists were to assert that they had objected to the denigration of Stalin as being an unfair and one-sided strategy that was bound to injure the image of world Communism. Yet the evidence points out that *in 1956* they were not unhappy at having Soviet Communism baring its scars. They had little reason to feel sentimental about Stalin. He had disparaged their revolution, treated them in a niggardly fashion, and, were he alive, both the amount of Soviet help they were getting and their currently independent position would have been inconceivable. Most of all they perceived that this self-criticism would weaken the position of their Soviet colleagues in the Communist world, certainly psychologically, and would make them more eager to have their concurrence and support—and to pay for it. In that expectation, the Chinese were certainly justified. The next two years were the period of the Russians' most assiduous wooing of them, invoking their help in solving the troublesome situation in Eastern Europe and coming out forthrightly with the promise of helping them develop nuclear weapons. An article by Mao, written shortly after the Twentieth Party Congress, echoed the main points of Khrushchev's secret speech and, though somewhat more restrained in tone, indicated no reservations from it. And Mao mentioned as one of Stalin's main errors his treatment of Tito and Yugoslavia. The Chinese regime's attachment to Stalin and its touching solicitude for his reputation were to come only later, when the Soviets reneged on their promise to help China, when the full import of the revelations could be perceived, and when the issue became a convenient pretext for denouncing Khrushchev.

Khrushchev's secret speech[1] sought to soften the blow by attributing to Stalin considerable merits in leading the country through collectivization and defeat of the "people's enemies,"—Trotskyites, Zinovievites, Bukharinites, etc.—before 1934. Only after 1934 does the cult of personality purportedly develop its full, evil characteristics. Now Stalin licenses wild terror and authorizes the liquidation of faithful Communists. He loses his nerve at the beginning of the war, ignores the Party and its organs, demands the glorification of himself in every possible way. And on the eve of his death, he is plotting yet another purge in which his remaining "faithful comrades in arms," including Khrushchev, are slated to be victims. In some of his future performances, Khrushchev was to expand considerably on Stalin's crimes, and at the Twenty-second Party Congress in 1961 he carried his denigration back to the period before 1934. The terrible stories he told later suffered also from the speaker's propensity to tell fibs: few of the audience could have believed the tale that during the war Stalin followed the actions of the Red Army on a *globe*.

For all the qualifications and improbabilities in the speech, its effect was evidently devastating. Many of the delegates are reliably reported to have broken down and cried. At subsequent meetings of Party cells throughout the country when the text of the speech was read, similar shock gripped the audiences. The older generation could find in the speech little that they did not know or suspect, even if they did not fully admit this to themselves, but to the young, brought up from kindergarten days with

[1] It has never been published in the U.S.S.R., but of course its text, delivered before thousands of people and communicated to other Communist parties, became generally known.

the radiant image of Stalin in the forefront of all their studies and activities, the revelations could not but constitute a devastating shock.

Khrushchev's indictment of Stalin touched mainly on the late tyrant's domestic policies. For understandable reasons, it has never been Soviet practice to publicize dissent on foreign policy. Hence the rather obscure reference: "During Stalin's leadership our peaceful relations with other nations were often threatened, because one-man decisions could cause, and often did cause, great complications."[2] This statement hardly helps a historian of Soviet foreign policy. What were those "great complications" caused by Stalin's unilateral decisions? Possibly the effects of the blockade of Berlin was one of them. But Khrushchev did not tell.

He was more explicit on Stalin's sins against fellow Communists. Both at the Twentieth Congress and later he went into some detail about this. "I shall shake my little finger and there will be no more Tito," Stalin is alleged to have said. (This was undoubtedly the way Stalin *felt* about Tito, but he is unlikely to have *used* such vivid language.) Toward Communist China, the First Secretary was to suggest later, Stalin had advanced demands of a "colonial nature." Compared with the wealth of details Khrushchev and his collaborators were to reveal about Stalin's internal crimes and senseless domestic actions—or about *his own* authorship of passages in the official Soviet military history hailing Stalin as the greatest strategist of all time—their restraint concerning the tyrant's activities in the foreign sphere is both striking and instructive. (Stalin was, however, accused of having caused the deterioration of Soviet-Turkish relations through his territorial demands on Turkey following World War II.)

Everything considered, the *domestic* consequences of Khrushchev's secret speech did not prove so overwhelming within the Soviet system as some leaders must have feared it would. This was, after all, only another case—to be sure, the most dramatic and far-reaching one—of denigrating a man who had once been a revolutionary hero. After Trotsky, Bukharin, etc., etc., Stalin. The problem of de-Stalinization and its permissible limits remained—and still is—a live issue in Soviet politics and literature; Khrushchev himself was to vary the image of Stalin according to what he considered the needs of the hour, and his successors have prudently attempted to soft-pedal the whole issue. But the immediate shock was contained. No angry crowds stormed the Kremlin demanding the end of the system that had produced such a monster. No one tore up his Party card in revulsion. Most Russians, with the exception of that always troublesome element the intelligentsia, were inclined to count their present blessings and assurances about the future.

<hr>

[2] Quoted in Bertram D. Wolfe, *Khrushchev and Stalin's Ghost* (New York, 1957), p. 236.

But in other Communist nations, China excluded, the effect was shattering. Their leaders were virtually cast adrift. How far and in what direction were they to de-Stalinize? The more adventurous leaders in the "people's democracies" were bound to think of the example of Tito; the more timid ones (a great majority), of how they could contain their ambitious colleagues, not to mention their people, without firm Soviet support. Ghosts from the very recent past arose to challenge the Communist first secretaries, prime ministers, and presidents. The Soviet Union was launching a campaign to rehabilitate some of the victims of the cult of personality. Presumably the same process was to be repeated in the satellites. But they had not had the long period of indoctrination and subordination that Russia had; a confession that people like Rajk, Slansky, Gomulka, and countless others had been tortured, imprisoned, or executed on forged evidence was likely to be greeted not merely by passive indignation, as had been the case in Russia, but by active forms of protest against the current masters. And more than personalities were involved. Communism in the U.S.S.R. had successfully merged with Russian nationalism. But in the satellites the explosive force of nationalism was ready to be set off by sparks of discontent. The last phase of Stalinism there had been marked by the Party's intensified struggle against remaining autonomous areas in society—against the Catholic Church, for example—and by the stepped-up pace of collectivization. All these measures of repression had gone far to create a maximum of discontent but had not been in force long enough to extinguish the people's hopes of reversing them.

One form of security for the Communist regimes was provided by Soviet armed units stationed in the "people's democracies," now by virtue of the Warsaw Pact alliance. The allegiance of the national armies themselves, albeit staffed by former Soviet officers and tightly controlled by security and Party organs, could not be taken for granted. In fact, as events in Poland and Hungary were to show, those armies were a potential danger to the Communist, certainly to the Stalinist, masters of their countries, and a possibility of a clash with Soviet troops could not be excluded.

Caught thus in a cruel dilemma, without any clear-cut directives from the Soviet Union, whose rulers were too divided among themselves to offer clear guidance, the satellite rulers temporized and improvised, trying to adjust their policies to the constantly shifting winds from Moscow. Some of them, like Rakosi in Hungary, clung tenaciously to power, authorizing more lenient policies for a time, yielding part of their power to more reformist Communists, like Nagy, only to stage a comeback when the moment seemed opportune. In the fashion which the Twentieth Congress had rendered obsolete, Rakosi and his counterpart in Bulgaria, Chervenkov, blamed the enormities of the past on police chiefs and security organs. But this was to avail them but little; the bitter personal hatreds, previously repressed by the iron hand of Moscow, now split the central committees and spilled out among the Party rank and file. More consistent than most, the Czechoslovak Party leaders kept quiet about de-Stalinization, hoping, no doubt, that the present aberration in Moscow would pass and that *they* would not be required to rehabilitate the quite sizable number of their comrades who had been liquidated as "Zionist and imperialist agents."

In one case, at least, the shock of the secret speech seems to have proved too much. In the aftermath of the Twentieth Congress, Stalin's faithful henchman in Poland, Boleslav Bierut, succumbed to a heart attack while still in Moscow. The confusion in the Polish Party was such that Khrushchev himself flew to Warsaw to supervise the election of a first secretary. Here he astounded the Polish Central Committee by warning them against having too many Jews in leading positions. "You have too many Abramoviches around," he is reputed to have said, thus revealing himself to share at least some of his late boss' prejudices.[3] This remark changed the Polish Committee's inclination to entrust the leadership of the Party to one Zambrovski, whose parentage was similar to that of Trotsky, Zinoviev, Kamenev, and many other *past* leaders of the movement dedicated to racial and national equality. In his place Edward Ochab, of impeccable Stalinist and Aryan credentials, was elected. But in a few months he was to prove a cruel disappointment to his Soviet benefactor.

Outside the Communist-ruled countries, the reverberations of the Twentieth Congress among the faithful, while serious, did not have the same shattering effect. Not having been in power, the Communist movements had after all not had the chance to practice Stalinism or to liquidate their most prominent heroes. Their reactions ran the whole gamut— from visible embarrassment at (and attempts to suppress the consequences of) this devastating critique of their past policies and beliefs, to relief and hope that now they would be able to shape their own policies and tactics without waiting for the word from Moscow. The French Communist leaders clung tenaciously to the first position, influenced undoubtedly by their special Gallic sensitivity to appearing ridiculous and inconsistent. The Italian Communist leader Togliatti, for many years a faithful and uncomplaining servant of the Comintern, epitomized the latter attitude. Communism, he said, using a term that was to achieve much currency, had now to become polycentric; it had to be attuned more to the needs and policies of individual countries than to the directives emanating from

[3] As in many of Khrushchev's outbursts, his example was not only indelicate but ill informed. Abramovich is a name borne by many Poles and Byelorussians of non-Jewish origin, and anyway there was no Abramovich in the leadership.

one center. The wily Italian thus demonstrated how easy it was for a thoroughgoing and cynical Stalinist to adjust to the new line while more independent or simple-minded Communists were lost in doubt or confusion. In Italy, where the Communists were still in uneasy alliance with the majority socialists, a Party line stressing different roads to socialism, gently upbraiding the Soviet comrades for not having revealed enough about the past scandals, was also likely to be politically more rewarding than it might be in other Western countries. Togliatti now made an astounding discovery. "The search for an Italian road to socialism has been our constant preoccupation."[4] When attacked later on by the Soviet comrades for going too far in criticizing the U.S.S.R., the Italian leader executed a graceful retreat. He was to alternate in these shifts until his death and even beyond: on his death, he was accorded the honor, rare for a foreign Communist, of having a sizable Soviet city (Rostov on the Don) renamed Togliatti; it was *afterward* discovered that he had left behind an ideological testament severely criticizing Russia's management of the world Communist movement.[5]

Thus the denunciation of Stalin did not immediately or significantly weaken the Communist movement outside the Communist countries. Needless to say, the effect on individual foreign Communists, even more so on sympathizers, may have been shattering. But, as could be expected, horror at the past was soon balanced by hopes for the future. Actual defections and protests were to be more numerous after the suppression of the Hungarian revolt. The strength of Communism in most Western countries and attraction to it in the underdeveloped world were and are based on certain psychological needs among the elites (especially the intellectual one) and on objective social and economic factors among the people at large. Once the Communist parties recovered from the initial shock, they were able to continue capitalizing on those factors. That they were able to do so, especially notwithstanding Western Europe's unprecedented economic prosperity, was due very largely to the *political* weakness of the Western system, of which events in 1956 were to offer a dramatic demonstration. Indeed, those events were to obscure and eventually to obliterate the huge vulnerability of the Soviet system.

[4] Quoted in Leo Labedz, ed., *Revisionism* (London and New York, 1962), p. 326.

[5] One of the minor but perplexing by-products of the liquidation of the cult of personality was the problem of erasing its physical remnants: place names, statues, etc. In the U.S.S.R., they came to grips with it only after the Twenty-second Congress in 1961, when various Stalingrads, Stalinos, Stalinabads, etc., were rebaptized or reverted to their previous names. In the satellites, most of such name-shifting occurred unobtrusively after 1956. Thus, in Poland Stalinogrod, a sizable industrial center, became known again by its pre-1953 name, Katowice (literally translated, Hangman's Place).

The year 1956 was thus truly a watershed in post-war international politics. At the risk of oversimplification, one can picture both opposing systems—the Soviet and the Western—struck by tremors and threatened by dangers in their most vulnerable sectors: the Western world in its relations with former and present spheres of influence and colonial possessions, the Soviet system in its relations with other Communist states. But while in the case of Britain and France the decline from Great Power status now became irretrievable and the conflict (or at least alienation) between the West and the underdeveloped world continued to grow, the Communist camp was able to recover its balance by the end of the year and was able to exhibit at least surface unity during the next five years. The tragedy of post-1956 international relations consists largely in Russia's need to offset the fissiparous tendencies in her own camp by more vigorous exploitation of the growing chaos and political turbulence, itself largely a result of the decline of the Western empires, in the underdeveloped world. Soviet weaknesses as well as strengths dictated pushful foreign policies. Not only was the Suez affair to obscure much of the meaning of the eruption and suppression of the Hungarian Revolution, but in general Soviet policy-makers were to become more and more eager to seek compensation for their weakening hold on the Communist bloc in the Near East, Cuba, etc.

This counterpoint of Soviet policies became evident in the summer of 1956. It was a period of hurried trips and consultations by Soviet leaders throughout the bloc and of return visits by satellite leaders and foreign statesmen. The most notable visitor to Moscow was Marshal Tito. In the spring of 1948 he had been invited to the Soviet Union but had refused, feeling with some justification that under the circumstances he might not be able to leave again the "Fatherland of Socialism." Now he returned in triumph to the land where he had been converted to Communism,[6] where he had visited as a head of state and was subjected to Stalin's flattery and scrutiny, and where for five years he had been vilified more than any international statesman. In contrast, he was now feted and glorified more than any other visitor to the U.S.S.R. since the war. His reception was at once more cordial and more festive than that accorded to any Chinese Communist leader, including Mao—something which was certainly not overlooked in Peking. If in the previous year in Belgrade the two *states* had agreed to extensive political and economic contacts, this time Tito's visit marked the re-establishment of cordial relations between the two Communist parties. A friendly communiqué stressed the permissibility of each Communist country seeking its own way to socialism. Tito's advice was sought on the best means of allaying ferment in the satellites. Not

[6] During World War I, as an Austrian prisoner of war.

surprisingly, he stressed Yugoslavia as an example to be followed; ideological solidarity rather than centralized direction was the best way to preserve unity in the bloc. He also argued that the Communist parties, especially in Hungary and Bulgaria, were still seeded with unrepentant Stalinists who, incidentally, had slandered him in the past and who could not now be expected to abide honestly by the new course or gain the confidence of their peoples.

Throughout the rest of the summer Khrushchev clung to Tito like a drowning man to a straw. He was to visit him in return, bring him back to Russia in September, delegate to him the task of explaining to the Hungarian leaders how one could be a good Communist and yet popular, and in general treat him with deference and seek his advice in a manner both unprecedented and never matched afterward with any foreign Communist.

In retrospect these tactics appear, as indeed they did at the time to some of Khrushchev's colleagues, as disingenuous. But it must be remembered that Khrushchev was fighting both to save his political life and to avoid a blow-up in Eastern Europe—which in the last resort would have to be suppressed by Soviet armies; and could one be absolutely sure that the reverberations of a Polish or Czech uprising would not find an echo in "de-Stalinized" Russia? There were grim historical reminders: the Polish insurrection of 1863 was instrumental in the intensification of the revolutionary struggle within Russia, and some Russian officers paid with their lives for refusing to fight the Poles. Tito was known to be popular among rank-and-file Communists in the satellites, much as many leaders disliked him. He offered, it was hoped, convincing proof of how one could have a solid one-party Communist regime and yet eschew oppressive social and economic measures (collectivization in Yugoslavia had now been discontinued) and enjoy national freedom. Thus the positive effect of his adhesion could with some justification be thought to have soothing effects and to allow the U.S.S.R. and the satellites to pass over the worst period of the transition.

This ferment, however, continued to grow. It found its most violent expression, needless to say, among the youth and intelligentsia, followed at a safe distance by Party functionaries, but it eventually spread to the people at large. In June, in the major Polish city of Poznan, an industrial strike turned into a national revolt, with the offices of the secret police and local Party organs being attacked and sacked. The Polish government had to have recourse to the use of armed forces, who extinguished the uprising, but the reaction of the soldiers was most alarming.

A meeting of the Polish Central Committee in July, following the riots, was attended by Bulganin and Marshal Zhukov (the latter's attendance was significant). The leading figures of Polish Communism were still divided on the possible remedies. It was obvious that the regime could not rely on the armed forces indefinitely and that another Poznan would possibly be the beginning of a country-wide uprising. The rulers decided to bring back into the Party's central organs Gomulka, the former Secretary General of the Party, who had been expelled and imprisoned for alleged Titoism and who had acquired as a consequence wide national popularity. But to the hardboiled conservative faction this would be but a ruse to exploit Gomulka's popularity while denying him any real power, and they would continue in the good old ways. This faction (known from the place of its meetings as the Natolin group) also had the ingenious idea of exploiting anti-Semitism to distract the public: previous excesses and errors could be blamed on Jews in the Party and security apparatus.[7] Another group viewed the situation more pessimistically and realistically: unless real reforms and changes in personnel were forthcoming, the regime would be unable to prevent a revolt within the Party and the country at large. Hence policies toward the Catholic Church had to be softened, forcible collectivization discontinued, etc. And there was only one Communist who enjoyed widespread popularity and could soothe the nation's dangerous mood: Gomulka. He had to be brought back not in a secondary capacity but as *the* leader of the Party.[8] These would-be proponents of radical reforms were for their part unable to preclude the possibility of Soviet intervention should Gomulka, who had the reputation of being a "national Communist," be returned to power. For all their own chumminess with Tito, the Russians were not overenthusiastic about Communists who had been purged for real or alleged "national Communism" being restored to the top position, although they felt that such people should be rehabilitated (if still alive), restored to the Party, and given an honorable job—say, as director of the National Library or something of the kind. This must have been the message Bulganin and Zhukov left with their Polish comrades. The latter in turn began tortuous negotiations with Gomulka (who was present at the post-Poznan meeting of the Central Committee) as to under what conditions and in what capacity he would share their burden. As most men would under the circumstances, he wanted his old job.

Similar travails were experienced in other satellite regimes. The leaders of the smallest of the "people's democracies," Albania, had a special reason to worry about the Soviet-Yugoslav reconciliation: their own tiny country might become, as it almost had before 1948, the means to seal the new

---

[7] Zbigniew Brzezinski, *The Soviet Bloc* (Cambridge, Mass., 1967), 249–50.

[8] The lines of division did not run necessarily between Stalinists and anti-Stalinists. As in Russia, some of the most prominent Stalinists were now among the "liberals," and they supported Gomulka.

alliance, the Russians allowing Yugoslavia to swallow its neighbor. In Hungary, the embodiment of local Stalinism, Rakosi, was finally pushed out of the leadership of the Party, but his successor, Erno Gerö, was almost equally unpopular. Unlike Poland, prominent Communists had earlier not only been imprisoned but sent to the gallows, and their rehabilitation in 1956 raised the excitement against the current leaders of the Party, who had been in fact their executioners, to fever pitch. The ferment was stimulated by various student and intellectual clubs, which suddenly mushroomed all over the landscape and which gave the people— denied for more than a decade any means to express political opposition —the opportunity to vent their long-suppressed rage and express the need not for a slow and tepid reform but for a drastic change in the conditions of their politics and their daily lives.

The indecisiveness of Soviet leadership in the face of this mounting wave of discontent reflected not only deep divisions but also apprehension about the global implications of any move it made. The Chinese reaction to developments in Eastern Europe was enigmatic. Though Mao's "Let a hundred flowers bloom" speech was not to be delivered for another six months, a certain liberalization of policies, especially in the cultural sphere, was already visible. And, as we have seen, strains and stresses in the Soviet empire, embarrassment and disunity within its leadership, were advantageous to the Chinese. When First Secretary Ochab visited Peking at the head of a Polish delegation to the Chinese Communist Party Congress, he is said to have received discreet encouragement to follow more independent policies vis-à-vis the U.S.S.R. Russia's embarrassments were thus China's opportunity, enabling the Chinese Communists to extract more aid from their penurious Soviet colleagues and to gain more prestige in the Communist world.

The possible reactions in the West also had to be assessed. In November, all of Dulles' rhetoric about "roll-back" and "liberation" was to be exposed as hollow. But in August or September one could not be sure. The Soviet policy-makers' nightmare ever since 1947—an uprising in one or more of the satellites and then aid in one form or another from the West—could not be entirely discounted. Even if one disregarded Dulles' pronouncements on the subject and correctly assessed the pacific and lethargic nature of American foreign policy during the Eisenhower administration, one could not discount the possibility of a violent emotional eruption on the part of the American public should it be exposed to the spectacle of Soviet troops suppressing a national uprising in Poland or Hungary. The predicament of Soviet policy-makers was thus a real one and, quite apart from any internal divisions, and any recriminations about what had led to it, dictated prudence and a closing of the ranks.

While the Soviet system was undergoing these strains and stresses, the Western alliance was thrown into an equally severe crisis. For, while the Soviet leaders were preoccupied—some of them, like Mikoyan, were practically commuting between Moscow and the satellite capitals that summer —this did not make them lose sight of the opportunities opening for Soviet policy in the troubled Near East and North Africa. And here it is necessary to go back.

Prior to 1948, Soviet influence in the Near East was practically nil. From at least the end of the eighteenth century, an entry into the Mediterranean has been a deeply cherished aim of Russian policy, but the effort was always concentrated on trying to get bases and/or influence in Turkey. But apart from Turkey, the Near East had been traditionally the sphere of French and especially British influence. The impact of the Bolshevik Revolution was smaller here than in practically any other underdeveloped area. The reasons for this are involved. The British and French influence between the two world wars was strong, for one thing. For another, Arab nationalism never developed firm ties with or reliance upon either Russia or Communism. Thus, the Soviet courtship or occasional penetration of Turkey, Afghanistan, or Persia was not matched in the rest of the Muslim world.

World War II changed this picture. Soviet Russia's power and prestige were now immensely greater than before; much of Britain's and France's powers had been eroded. Even so, Arab nationalism, whatever the local focus, did not appear likely to seek support in the U.S.S.R. In the Arab world, the religious underpinning of nationalism was still important. News of Stalin's treatment of the sizable Muslim community in Russia, of the forcible secularization of the Turkic peoples of Central Asia, and the barbarous treatment of the Crimean Tartars during the war trickled down to the Arab elites and did not make them overenthusiastic about seeking Soviet support in their struggle against the waning imperialisms of the West.

Here the issue of Palestine was to alter the picture drastically. The Zionist struggle against the British was viewed with discreet but genuine sympathy in the Soviet Union. This was ironic—in view of both the long-standing Communist opposition to Zionism and the anti-Semitic trends evident at the time (1946–48) in Stalin's entourage. But the Soviets were not being sentimental. They saw clearly, as did some helpless British and American diplomats, that with the British forced out of Palestine Britain's power and prestige in the Near East would come closer to complete collapse. A Jewish state in the midst of the Arab world would be a continuous cause of conflict between the West and the Arabs and would offer Russia some interesting opportunities in an area from which she had been completely excluded. Thus, undoubtedly with Soviet authorization, Czechoslovakia furnished the Jewish underground with arms for their struggle against the British Mandate. When the state of Israel was proclaimed, the U.S.S.R. hastened to become, on May 26, 1948, the first power to recognize Israel *de jure* (though the United States preceded her with *de facto* recognition).

Once Israel was established, Soviet friendship predictably cooled off while sympathy toward the Arabs became more pronounced. Not merely Machiavellian calculations were responsible for this shift. As we know from his daughter's memoirs, Stalin's anti-Semitism was not simply a matter of political choice but toward the end of his life became a veritable obsession. The foundation of Israel found a response among Soviet Jewry, and, when the new country's foreign minister, Mrs. Golda Meir, came to Moscow in 1948 she was the focus of a tumultuous demonstration during her visit to a synagogue. Any attachment of a group of Soviet citizens to a foreign country, even be it on purely sentimental grounds, was especially during the last years of Stalin equated with treason. The "Zionist spy network" now became recognized as yet another agency of the imperialists and was accused of complicity in the bizarre affair of the Kremlin doctors.[9] Diplomatic relations with Israel were broken off shortly before Stalin's death, to be restored in July 1953 as part of the post-Stalin *détente*.

After 1953 the quagmire of Near Eastern politics began to attract more Soviet attention. The Arab world was seething. France was moving toward granting independence to Morocco and Tunisia and, beginning in 1954, found herself with a major rebellion in Algeria. The center of Arab nationalism was more than ever before Cairo, where after the overthrow of the monarchy in 1952 an ambitious group of officers set as their goal not only modernization of their country but also the extirpation of all vestiges of foreign imperialism. Its leader, Nasser, soon established himself as the most aggressive proponent of Pan-Arab unity. The Soviet attitude toward Nasser had undergone several shifts. The original coup was not viewed with much sympathy, since the insurgent officers' group dealt harshly with Egypt's Communists. When it appeared in 1954, on the conclusion of the Anglo-Egyptian treaty and the withdrawal of British troops, that Nasser would now live amicably with the West, official Soviet comments pictured him as a virtual puppet of Dulles. A confederation of Arab states maintaining friendly relations with the West was certainly not fervently desired in Moscow.

We mentioned before how at the Bandung Conference Chou En-lai touched the hearts of the Arab conferees by his avowal that his delegation included a pious Chinese Muslim. Contacts were certainly estab-

[9] See above, p. 467.

lished then between Colonel Nasser and the suave Chinese Foreign Minister, and these led in turn to cultural and economic intercourse between the two countries.[10] The Egyptian leader's once uncompromising opposition to Communism as yet another form of imperialism perceptibly weakened. But the Soviet Union was not backward in friendship with this most dynamic Arab state. In July 1955 Shepilov, editor of *Pravda* and already being groomed to succeed Molotov, visited Cairo at the head of a delegation. Cultural and economic contacts were now expanded. And it so happened that some Soviet Muslims suddenly desired to visit Mecca, and Cairo was of course the logical stopping point for the pious pilgrims. . . . In the fall of the same year Nasser announced that Egypt had contracted for deliveries of arms from Czechoslovakia for which she was to pay with cotton. A pattern of dependence on the Soviet bloc was thus evolving, even though Nasser called the whole transaction a purely commercial one.

The mutual courtship could not yet be described as an alliance. With her memories of Kemal Atatürk and Chiang in the 1920's, Russia was wary of full commitment on behalf of a nationalist leader who might drop her once his main aims were achieved. From another point of view, the outbreak of a real war between Israel and, say, Egypt (as distinguished from frontier raids and hostilities, which went on incessantly) was certainly not a Soviet aim. Faced with great problems at home and in the Communist bloc, the Soviet leadership did not desire such a dangerous conflagration. Rather, it desired a steady diminution of British and French influence (a drastic decline would bring in the Americans), the removal of obviously pro-Western governments like Iraq's and Jordan's and the dissolution of Western-inspired defense arrangements such as the Baghdad Pact, which was designed to keep Soviet influence from the Near and Middle East.

The main events of the Near Eastern crisis of 1956 are well known. A fantastic compounding of errors by the Western Powers, lack of policy coordination between the United States and her two main European allies, finally the most inept kind of Machiavellian tactics attempted by France and Britain—these resulted in a colossal defeat for the West as a whole during the Suez affair. And the repercussions went beyond the Near East. The British withdrawal from their imperial obligations, once an orderly retreat, became a headlong rush. Any chances of a compromise settlement of the Algerian issue were probably lost in the wake of the demonstration of French duplicity and then impotence in the Suez crisis. Thus both the Fourth Republic and what remained of the French empire were doomed.

[10] Walter Laqueur, *The Soviet Union and the Middle East* (New York, 1959), p. 218.

Nasser's nationalization of the Suez Company took place in July 1956. It was precipitated by an abrupt withdrawal by the United States and Britain of a tentative offer to finance the Aswan Dam.[11] The crisis over Suez deepened during the summer. From the beginning there was at least a strong possibility that Britain and France would intervene militarily —the British because the Conservative government (or, rather, most of its members) felt that the whole issue of the country's survival as a Great Power was at stake, the French because Cairo was the focal point of material support and propaganda on behalf of the Algerian rebels. This possibility of Anglo-French intervention was very much on the mind of the Soviet leaders. Bulganin addressed a series of private warnings to the prime ministers of Britain and France. They were moderate in tone and, probably truthfully, protested that the Soviet government had had no prior knowledge of nor provided the impetus for the Egyptian seizure of the canal.[12] Soviet prudence, plus traditional Soviet parsimony, which was being abandoned but slowly and painfully, was also responsible for the fact that the Russians did not rush in with offers to finance the Aswan Dam. Vague hints to this effect had been dropped in 1955 and 1956, but the actual Soviet commitment toward financing the project was not to take place for two years.

This was the background against which the concerted Anglo-French-Israeli action against Nasser was planned. The United States was not consulted or informed. The oversubtle plan bore the mark of Gallic ingenuity (indeed, the details seem to have been worked out by the French): Israel was to attack; Britain and France were to come in as mediators and demand that both sides pull away from the canal, which would be occupied by "neutral" Anglo-French forces. Since Nasser was bound to refuse this military evacuation of Egyptian territory, the Anglo-French forces would occupy the canal zone. The question of the ownership of the canal could then be reopened. Anyway, Nasser's government would fall, it was hoped, and the cause of Arab militant nationalism be dealt a decisive blow. And it was expected that the United States would be too preoccupied by forthcoming presidential elections to stay the hands of her unruly allies. The U.S.S.R. had troubles aplenty in Eastern Europe.

On paper this exercise in Machiavellianism appeared perfect; in fact, the whole scenario might have been concocted by the Russians as a vivid

---

[11] It could be easily surmised that once the last British soldier left Egyptian soil, Nasser would nationalize the canal sooner or later, and as a matter of fact he was to confess that the U.S. action made him simply advance the timetable. Still, no plans had been made on the Western side for such a contingency, eloquent testimony to the general disarray of British foreign policy of the period.

[12] Laqueur, *op. cit.*, p. 237.

demonstration of how wicked and inept Western imperialism could be.

Israel attacked on October 29. The Anglo-French ultimatum followed the next day. As events were to show, Israel was quite equal to the task of handling the Egyptian army by herself (with some help in the form of French air equipment and technicians), and the Anglo-French intervention was not only wicked but unnecessary. On the expiration of the ultimatum, British aircraft began bombing Egyptian territory and dropping leaflets urging the people to oust Nasser. Contrary to expectations, American disapproval of this chain of events was instantaneous and vigorous. The inherent moralistic strain of American foreign policy, so often frustrated in dealing with the Communists, this time found an effective outlet in chastising America's luckless allies. Eisenhower addressed the British and French prime ministers in terms belying his usual mildness and restraint. The Security Council was mobilized to demand an immediate cease-fire, and the Soviets had the satisfaction of seeing Britain and France exercising their vetoes and "challenging world public opinion," on which wicked practice it had previously been assumed they had an exclusive monopoly.

To the imbecility of the original conception, the British and the French now added an excruciating slowness of execution. British and French landings in Egypt began on November 5. This reflected the weakening British resolve, despite the frantic French urgings that the whole thing be gotten over with. On the 6th, after pressure from Eisenhower, this time brutal, and when faced with a split in his own cabinet, Prime Minister Eden announced the scuttling of the ill-fated operation.

The whole affair was a godsend to the Soviet Union. At the time, it tended to lessen the worldwide reaction to her military intervention in Hungary. But apart from this fortunate coincidence the Suez affair dealt a decisive blow to lingering Anglo-French power and prestige in the Near East and seriously damaged it elsewhere. The closing of the Suez Canal, the blowing up of the Western-owned oil installations, these were only some of the most immediate repercussions. After it became clear that the United States disapproved of the whole business and highly likely that the American pressure would make the British and French desist, the Soviet Union could at small risk but with great profit proffer help to the victim of the aggression. On November 5 Premier Bulganin addressed stark warnings to Israel, France, and Britain, contemptuously reminding the latter two that they were now second-rate powers and that Russia could deal with them as they were dealing with Egypt. Russia was determined to crush the aggressors, and they should know that she now possessed intercontinental ballistic missiles capable of carrying nuclear weapons. To President Eisenhower Bulganin also wrote a public letter but in a different vein: should not the two super-powers pool their military resources under United Nations aegis to put down the aggression? The Soviet statesman was also worried about what would happen to the United Nations should this armed interference in the affairs of an independent state go unchecked and unpunished. (He was *not* referring to Soviet actions in Hungary at the time.) [13]

Predictably, the Bulganin initiative for a joint Soviet-American move in the Mediterranean did not meet with a warm reception in Washington. Much as her allies had misbehaved, the United States became alarmed about Soviet threats against them. It became known subsequently that an alert was ordered for the Strategic Air Command. Whether this was instrumental in the next Soviet move is not known, but in the next few days, with the armistice in the canal zone already a fact, the Soviet government continued to issue threats—but of a different kind. The U.S.S.R. was ready to send volunteers to help Egypt, and thousands of Soviet citizens, veterans of World War II, were in fact volunteering to help the heroic Egyptian people. Why it was necessary to send volunteers when Russia had offered to apply her full military resources to the task of punishing the aggressors and, besides, when the armistice was already in force, was never explained. Such questions are seldom asked in a moment of high tension and great emotion. In the eyes of the Arabs, the Russians stood ready to spill blood on their behalf while the Americans merely indicated disapproval of the Anglo-French actions and pressed for some resolutions in the U.N.

The coincidence in time between the Suez crisis and the Soviet "time of troubles" with her satellites was to lead to many speculations about their interconnection. There was, needless to say, no *direct* connection. The Anglo-French plan was undoubtedly influenced by awareness of the difficulties the U.S.S.R. was experiencing in Eastern Europe. And Soviet apprehension about the possible repercussions of the Hungarian suppression might well have been lessened by awareness of the divisions and preoccupations within the Western alliance consequent upon the Egyptian venture. But in neither case was the situation on the other side the decisive factor. There can also be no equation in the effects of the two crises. It would be a hollow moralism to assert that both the West and the Soviet Union were equally or nearly equally discredited through their actions in 1956. The brutal fact is that following a series of grave mistakes the U.S.S.R. retrieved most of her previous position within the Communist bloc and achieved her aims. The West did not. To be sure, the Polish and Hungarian crises were to have serious consequences for Russia, and a new pattern of relations between the U.S.S.R. and the "people's democracies" was to emerge after a period of stress and dis-

[13] *Survey of International Affairs, 1956–1958* (London, 1962), p. 66.

equilibrium. This new pattern marked a serious advance on that which prevailed under Stalin, yet it did not mean, as it appeared at several times in 1956 that it might, the satellites' full independence of the Soviet Union, extending even to foreign-policy and defense matters, with ideology and a certain community of interests being the only links—in other words, the pattern of relations which had by now been established between Yugoslavia and Russia.

The first stage in the drama was a *dénouement* in the long-lingering drama in the Polish Communist Party. By October the state of feelings in the country at large and within the Party indicated that unless decisive steps were taken a major explosion—perhaps civil war and Soviet military intervention—could not be avoided. The idea of exploiting Gomulka's prestige without entrusting him with leadership had to be abandoned, for he repeatedly stressed that he would not return to the central Party organs without assuming the number-one position. Gomulka's demands also included the removal from the Politburo of the adherents of the Natolin faction and Marshal Rokossovsky, the Soviet general who since 1949 had been the Polish minister of defense.

Those were stiff demands, and the last one especially raised the specter of Soviet military intervention. But most of the Polish Party leaders, some of the staunchest former Stalinists included, became convinced that the risk had to be taken. Considerations of a personal nature also influenced such former pillars of Stalinism as Ochab and Alexander Zawadzki, the titular head of state. In other "people's democracies," notably Hungary and Bulgaria, men like themselves were being offered up as sacrificial lambs to the popular wrath while less prominent exponents of the old course were allowed to succeed to the top positions. A switch might still keep them in important jobs while endowing them with popularity. Thus Ochab and Zawadzki became selfless advocates of Gomulka's return to the headship of the Party and government. The only hope for their opponents, the Natolin faction, remained Russian intervention, which would turn the scales, put Gomulka and his followers back in jail, and inaugurate a neo-Stalinism (which would, to be sure, exhibit certain concessions in agricultural and religious policies to allay the discontent of the people).

Why did the Russians allow the Polish situation to rise to the boiling point before they took a firm stand or at least indicated what their position was on such crucial issues as Rokossovsky's dismissal? The only explanation lies in the deep cleavages that currently split the Soviet leadership. The Soviet government for the moment could not speak with one voice. And there was no machinery for an "impartial" solution of the Polish problem. The Cominform, long moribund, had been dissolved in April as a further peace offering to Tito.

While the Polish crisis was ripening, the Soviet press was unstinting in its criticism of the new trends. What provoked its greatest anger were the expressions of dissent coming from some Polish Communist intellectuals who called for "openness in state life, decentralization, democratization and sovereignty."[14] *Pravda,* commenting on these demands, remarked ominously that the working masses in Poland demanded "that the rampant revisionists and capitulators who are using the Polish press for their own filthy purposes be curbed."[15] But it was precisely the knowledge that the "broad working masses" were behind Gomulka which stayed the Soviet hand. Soviet military intervention might spark a real war. While the Soviet armies were thinly spread throughout the satellites, there could be no doubt about the *eventual* outcome of a Soviet intervention, but in the meantime what would be the repercussions in the West, in China? And even within the U.S.S.R.?

The Polish Central Committee assembled on October 19 to install Gomulka as First Secretary and to comply with his other demands.[16] At news of this, the Soviets were stirred to action. Khrushchev, Kaganovich, Mikoyan, and Molotov took a plane for Warsaw—a delegation evidently representing both factions of the Soviet Presidium: one tending toward military action, the other one not having yet lost the hope of talking the Polish comrades out of their dangerous course. At the same time Soviet military units began moving north from Silesia and east from East Germany. The Polish army, still under Marshal Rokossovsky, also began maneuvers that brought some large units closer to Warsaw. The possibility of an outright clash could not be excluded, since the security forces now under Gomulka's partisans were assuming defense positions and in many factories workers were calling for arms for what might become a new battle of Warsaw. It was touch and go.

The primary managers of the Polish proceedings, erstwhile Stalinists turned partisans of Gomulka, showed admirable cold blood. Their leader, Ochab, proposed to and got from the Central Committee a one-day adjournment for the Politburo to discuss the situation with the Russian delegation. But the latter was to be confronted with a *fait accompli*: Gomulka was co-opted into the top body and would lead the discussions. Even so, it was difficult to persuade some hotheads that the Central Committee should adjourn. The Soviet comrades should, they thought, be

[14] Paul E. Zinner, ed., *National Communism and Popular Revolt in Eastern Europe* (New York, 1956), p. 259.

[15] *Ibid.*

[16] The proceedings of the meeting—somewhat edited, one must assume—are covered in a special issue of the Party's organ, *Nowe Drogi* (New Paths), No. 10, November 1956.

told politely that the Central Committee has to get on with its business and would later have a friendly discussion with them.[17] Perhaps not surprisingly, this point of view was argued most vehemently by two lady members of the Central Committee.

One would give much to have a transcript of the discussions between the Poles and the Russians. One unauthorized version has it that at seeing Gomulka Khrushchev exclaimed, "What is this agent of Wall Street and the Zionists doing here?"—which would go to show how difficult it is to lose certain habits of speech. But the Poles must have convinced the Russians that there was no alternative. The discussion, as was later freely admitted, was tempestuous. The Soviet delegation faced a united front of all the leading Polish Communists, the Natolin faction having been reduced to people with no current following either in the Party or in the country at large. Equally important must have been their impression, subsequently confirmed, that Gomulka was both a loyal Communist and a man who would not lead Poland out of the Soviet bloc. A reassuring joint communiqué was issued. The Soviet delegation flew back to Moscow where some of their comrades were possibly surprised to see them back: it would have been an ingenious way of getting rid of both Khrushchev and the hardened Stalinists, but it would have set a bad precedent. . . .

Having weathered the storm, the Polish Central Committee formally elected Gomulka First Secretary and restored his partners in disgrace to positions of honor and power. Marshal Rokossovsky explained that the movements of his army were in the nature of routine maneuvers. As to the Soviet troops, they were in fact moving toward major Polish cities, but they stopped and withdrew when he communicated with his old comrade Marshal Konev. If the official transcript of the Central Committee meeting is to be believed, Rokossovsky's explanations were greeted with tactful silence. Some Natolin followers still tried to fish in the troubled waters: should not Rokossovsky be retained? What would be the effect of his dismissal on the Soviet comrades? But he failed of re-election to the Politburo, which was now organized according to Gomulka's demands. He subsequently went on leave as minister of defense, then resigned, and returned to the U.S.S.R. His exact role in the October events is still unclear. Some Poles chose to believe that Rokossovsky's national feelings prevailed over loyalty to his adopted country and that he helped to stay the Soviet hand. But since he subsequently held an important Russian command and then went into honorable retirement there, it is hard to believe such romantic tales. Most likely he simply reported to his Soviet superiors the state of feelings among his soldiers, and these were not encouraging for any Russian military coup.

[17] *Ibid.*, p. 15.

On the Polish side there was evidently a genuine attempt to convince the Russians that, while claiming autonomy, Poland would stick loyally with the U.S.S.R. as far as foreign policy and defense arrangements were concerned. The agreement of October 19, 1956, was still a tentative one and subject to review in Moscow. A more elaborate understanding was reached on November 18, when a Polish delegation headed by Gomulka visited Russia. By then the Polish Party had weathered the Hungarian crisis, and the Soviets were, by their lights, quite liberal in rewarding Polish loyalty. Both countries agreed on the "similarity of goals" in their foreign policies. Soviet troops would continue to be stationed in Poland under Warsaw Pact arrangements, but their movements and uses had to be agreed to by the Polish government. Some Polish debts to the U.S.S.R. were cancelled, and, in a further recognition of the brutal economic exploitation of Poland under Stalin, the U.S.S.R. extended long-term credits. Thousands of Polish citizens detained in the U.S.S.R. were to be released and returned to their country. In return, Poland agreed to give back probably the only item she had received from Russia under Stalin free of charge: Marshal Rokossovsky.

The Polish agreement was to serve as a pattern for similar treaties with other "people's democracies." They too included compensation through long-term Soviet loans and, sometimes, cancellation of the outstanding debts incurred during the earlier economic exploitation of the satellites. Stationing of Soviet troops was likewise linked to the Warsaw Treaty, thus removing the stigma of military occupation and likening the arrangements to NATO's. It would be a gross exaggeration, of course, to assert that the Soviet Union's watchfulness over and interference in the internal affairs of her Communist allies was over. But this interference was now to take the form of discreet hints and advice. The Polish solution freed the U.S.S.R. from what had become, even under Stalin, an intolerable burden—supervising every small detail of the satellites' internal policies, deciding in every intra-Party dispute whether Comrade X was to be dismissed and sent to the gallows. The substance of Soviet influence was retained while the manner of its exercise became more tolerable both to the parties and to the people. In theory at least, foundations were laid for a genuine Communist commonwealth of nations. The dangers inherent in the Polish solution were, of course, to become apparent immediately in the Hungarian events and, after an interval (and less dramatically), in the Rumanian developments of the mid-1960's and the Czechoslovak ones of 1968. But for several years the arrangement hastily improvised in those hectic days of October and November was to serve the Soviet Union well. Not surprisingly, Khrushchev came to regard his acceptance of Gomulka as one of the greatest successes of his foreign policy. And since all politicians in all systems are sometimes subject to self-delusion he almost came to believe that he, Khrushchev, was the main architect of the "Polish October," the man who had raised from disgrace to power this priceless man who combined Polish patriotism with impeccable Communist beliefs and behavior.

In Poland, to digress, the enthusiasm and hopes raised in October could not, of course, be maintained. In time Gomulka had to crack down on those very intellectuals and students who had had so much to do with his elevation to power. And some of his most zealous opponents in the Natolin faction were to become his most valuable subordinates, while many of those who had shared first in his disgrace and then in the triumph of his return were to return to the obscurity of minor state and Party roles. From exhilaration at his return, the attitude of the majority of his countrymen turned after a few years to resignation; Gomulka was universally recognized as honest and selfless, but he was narrow-minded and pedantic in his outlook—similar, in fact, in his personality to those working-class Communists who had surrounded Lenin in the early days of the Soviet Union. Who could have foretold that by the mid-1960's there would be more intellectual autonomy in Hungary, greater independence from the U.S.S.R. in Rumania, than in Gomulka's Poland? Or that in 1968 the juxtaposition of events in Poland and Czechoslovakia was to be still more startling?

Russia's acceptance of the Polish solution also must have been influenced by the Hungarian developments, which showed the Khrushchev regime how fortunate it was to have in Poland a man who could contain popular discontent and who would not allow a revolt *within* a Communist Party to turn into a revolt *against* Communism. In a way, the Polish events precipitated the Hungarian uprising. In another way, the lesson of Hungary possibly saved the fruits of the Polish October.

There were important differences between the two crises. Military intervention in Hungary, a country of 9 million people, did not carry the same risk as would have the struggle in Poland, with 25 million. And, while it would be difficult to judge the relative degrees of the anti-Russian and anti-Communist feelings in both countries, one can say that, hard as Hungary's fate had been during the war, it did not reach the level of frightfulness suffered by Poland, where the most hotheaded anti-Communist felt the need of some restraint lest his country suffer a new bloodbath when it had barely begun to recover from the last one. Finally, the Polish Communist leadership, largely inherited from the Stalin era, synchronized its reactions with Gomulka's demands. The main difference between the Hungarian and the Polish Octobers lay, then, in the former's lack of that careful preparation which enabled the Polish Communists to confront the Russians with a *fait accompli* and master the ferment in their country before it got out of hand.

The news of the October crisis in Poland and of its resolution, at least temporarily, in favor of the Polish "national Communists" was bound to raise the temperature of would-be reformers and revolutionaries in Hungary. It was a novel experience to have a powerful Soviet delegation fly to a satellite capital only to yield there to leaders installed against Soviet wishes, and to see an overt Russian military threat being defied. Since the Hungarian Communist Party was of all the satellite parties the one in by far the greatest disarray, it was evident that the lightning would strike next in Budapest.

Poland now had at the head of its Party a man who was, for the moment, a national hero. In Hungary, the Communists were still led by the hateful Gerö, blamed almost equally with Rakosi (now safely in retirement in the U.S.S.R.) for the crimes and tribulations of the past. Russian attempts to bolster their unfortunate satrap by conveying him to Belgrade to be photographed with Tito, etc., failed utterly to endear him either to his comrades or to the people. The closest thing to a Hungarian Gomulka was Imre Nagy, who had been premier for a while after 1953 but then had been outmaneuvered and stripped of power by the envious Rakosi. He was now hastily restored to the Party and its central organs. But by October 22–23 the whole totalitarian structure was crumbling. Gerö's speech on the 23rd blaming fascists and imperialist agents for the troubles sparked the actual revolt. Mobs stormed the secret-police headquarters, some of the hated oppressors being seized and lynched. Hastily Nagy was installed as prime minister, and the government, if one can still use this term, requested the help of Soviet military units to suppress the uprising. (It is still not clear to what degree Nagy himself was responsible for this request.) Soviet military strength currently in Hungary was scarcely sufficient to suppress what was now a full-scale revolt. The Russians fought indecisively—which reflected either ferment among the soldiers or, more likely, confusion among their commanders and lack of directives and time to explain to their men why and against whom they were fighting. On October 25 Mikoyan and Suslov flew to Budapest (the Soviet team was to visit Hungary twice more during the coming week) and advised Gerö and some of his henchmen to get out of the country in a hurry. Janos Kadar was installed as First Secretary of the Hungarian Party, but, for the moment, this party was in a state of disintegration, as was recognized even in the official announcement.[18]

[18] The transient popularity enjoyed by some of the Communist leaders was based largely on accidents of their past career rather than on any genuine appraisal of their policies or personalities. Everything in Nagy's record indicated that he had been a docile, Moscow-trained Communist. His popularity sprang from the fact that he had happened to be Prime Minister at a time when it suited the Party *and* the Russians to have a liberal course in Hungary. Kadar had been minister of the interior at the time of the most severe repression following Rajk's trial but then himself fell afoul of Rakosi and was im-

The main highlights of the Hungarian Revolution may be briefly summarized. The Nagy-Kadar team could not stem the rising tide of revolution. While appeals for moderation and a stop to the fighting were issued in their names, revolutionary committees, workers' councils, etc., sprang up all over the country. The new government, announced on October 27, included a number of prominent non-Communists. Among the Communist members was George Lukacs, an elderly intellectual and literary critic whose disquisitions on dialectical materialism had long enjoyed considerable vogue among connoisseurs of Marxism in the West. But neither the broadened base nor the inclusion of Marxian savants could endow the government with real power or stem the revolutionary tide. Nagy felt himself compelled to issue increasingly imprudent statements and concessions. Having secured on October 28 a cease-fire and withdrawal of Soviet troops from Budapest, on October 30 and 31 he announced that Hungary would definitely cease to be a one-party state and that she would leave the Warsaw Pact and become neutral.

On November 1 Soviet reinforcements began pouring into Hungary. The U.S.S.R. stoutly denied any intent to use force. But in the meantime Kadar was evidently spirited away and persuaded or compelled by the Russians to lend his name to Soviet intervention and suppression. On November 4 all dissimulation was abandoned. A recording of a speech by Kadar was broadcast, announcing the formation of the Hungarian Revolutionary Worker-Peasant Government, headed by himself. Nagy was denounced for having succumbed to counterrevolutionaries. The important part of the speech was the request to the "Soviet Army Command to help our nation smash the sinister forces of reaction and restore order and calm in the country."[19] The same day, Soviet forces began a massive attack on Budapest and other cities. They were met with spirited resistance, but the poorly armed workers' militia and the few Hungarian military units could be no match for Soviet tanks and heavy guns. Within a few days Kadar's "government"[20] or, rather, the Soviet army was in control. Massive strikes and other forms of resistance continued through the bleak winter of 1956–57 while close to 200,000 refugees escaped across the Austrian frontier to the West.

---

prisoned. Both men, it is fair to say, were probably more liberally inclined as well as inherently nicer human beings (which was not difficult) than Rakosi or Gerö. But Nagy was to show incapacity to master the situation and Kadar was to yield to Russian pressure and become an instrument of the suppression of the Hungarian revolt.

[19] Quoted in Melvin J. Lasky, ed., The Hungarian Revolution (New York, 1957), p. 237.

[20] Such was the haste in forming it and such was the lack of candidates for members that several important ministerial positions were not filled for some time.

The development of the Soviet attitude toward the Hungarian Revolution and the actual timing of the decision to intervene militarily cannot be traced with full assurance. Soviet attitudes and utterances during the first phase of the revolution, which ended on October 28, were restrained. The previous military intervention was recognized as a mistake. On October 29, both Minister of Foreign Affairs Shepilov and Marshal Zhukov released soothing statements implying support of the Nagy government and confidence in its ability to master the situation.[21] On October 30 the Soviet government issued an official declaration on the nature of relations within the socialist camp which contained the usual phrases about "full equality, respect for the member nations' territorial integrity . . . sovereignty and noninterference in the domestic affairs of one another."[22] But as to the possibility of a member state withdrawing from the Warsaw Pact and demanding the withdrawal of the others' troops from her territory, this could be done only on the basis of an agreement of all the signatories of the pact. In plain English this meant sovereignty or no sovereignty Soviet troops could be withdrawn only with Soviet permission. Was the decision to intervene taken, then, because of Nagy's declaration that Hungary was withdrawing from the Warsaw Pact and his demand that Soviet troops leave? This seems unlikely for the simple reason that a military operation of this magnitude, involving many Soviet divisions, could not have been mounted in three days. The Soviet blow had to be, and was, devastating and overpowering, with the issue not left in doubt within twenty-four hours of the attack on Budapest on November 4. It appears likely that contingency plans must have been formulated as early as October 23 and 24 and that, when the Soviet declaration on "friendship and cooperation" among socialist states was issued on the 30th, Soviets units, some coming from as far as the central Ukraine, were already on the move. Could anything have stayed the Soviet hand? It is probable that had Nagy proved amenable to and capable of preserving order the Russians would still have occupied Hungary but would have allowed him to stay at the head of the government provided it were purified of the recently co-opted "reactionaries."

The Soviet decision represented a considerable gamble. What would have happened had similar revolutions simultaneously exploded in other satellites? What if the West had adopted a threatening attitude? As to the first contingency, it became clear that between October 28 and 31 the Communist parties in Eastern Europe, including Marshal Tito's, became deeply disquieted by the evolution of events in Hungary. It was one thing for local Communists to assert their independence of Russia, but

[21] Lasky, *op. cit.*, p. 133.

[22] Cited in Brzezinski, *op. cit.*, p. 230.

quite another for a Communist Party to be virtually swept away in a national uprising. That the Polish events had preceded the Hungarian ones was from the Soviet point of view a great piece of luck.

So, of course, in view of the second contingency, was the Suez crisis. Very early in the Hungarian affair it became clear that the West would confine its protests to solemn declarations in the United Nations and appeals to "world public opinion." But any action in the Security Council could be and was vetoed, any resolutions of the Assembly could be ignored. That many Communists in the West, especially intellectuals, were outraged by the Hungarian events, some of them tearing up their Party cards, was to the Soviets hardly a catastrophe. The reactions in the neutral bloc were also negative—intellectuals friendly to Communism, like Sartre, issued eloquent condemnations and appeals—but again the Soviet experience was that waves of moral indignation among their sympathizers were ephemeral. Time would pass and the majority of them would return to the more congenial task of criticizing their own societies and the United States. And so it was. To be sure, many in the West were to be alienated permanently, but as against them were those who consciously or unconsciously had been disquieted by Khrushchev's secret speech and who now saw welcome proof that Soviet Communism had not lost its toughness and decisiveness. In the eyes of the Russians, at least of the government, the protests and sermons were—and it is difficult to deny this argument some crude logic—hypocritical. Why had this moral indignation of the Western Left been missing at the time of the worst excesses of Stalinism? Now that Soviet concessions had produced revolt and the U.S.S.R. *had* to intervene, the delicate moral sensitivity of their friends erupted in angry manifestos! That on the other hand there was deep concern and indignation even in Russia among students and intellectuals, and that some Soviet soldiers in Hungary did not relish their task and said so also appears probable. But this was an additional reason to suppress the Hungarian eruption quickly and decisively.

It is idle to speculate whether a different posture taken by the West could have forestalled the Soviet intervention. It was not in the nature of American politics to adopt the vaguely ominous tone that Bulganin adopted over the Anglo-French move in Suez, nor could Dulles or Eisenhower talk about dispatching American volunteers to Hungary. Indeed, the first concern of the State Department was to make clear that the United States would act only through the United Nations, i.e., not act at all. Even within the debilitating context of American politics in an election year, there was probably some scope for imaginative policies that could have, if not prevented, then moderated Soviet actions—threats of diplomatic and commercial reprisals, *immediate* dispatch of a U.N. mission to Budapest, and the like. They were not enacted.

Thus any Soviet apprehensions about possible unfavorable consequences had to be focused mostly on the reactions within other countries of the socialist camp. The Chinese hastened with expressions of support. In January 1957 Chou En-lai, visiting Moscow, Warsaw, and Budapest, gave the strongest possible support to Soviet foreign policy and hailed the U.S.S.R. as the head of the socialist camp. In view of the still bitter feelings that animated the rank and file of the Polish Communists, not to speak of the Hungarians, and also in view of the fact that to the East European countries China was still a possible counterfoil to total Soviet domination, Chou's help was of the highest importance to the Kremlin. Chou's position meant the end of the last lingering hopes that any outside power or agency could provide a shield against the U.S.S.R. or that anything going beyond the Polish solution would be tolerated by Russia.

The events of 1956 were bound to affect the Soviet leaders' opinions about one old and one recent friend. As to the former, favorable references to Stalin found their place in official Soviet utterances as early as November. And at a gala reception at the Chinese embassy in January 1957 Khrushchev himself mentioned how the late Joseph Vissarionovich had taught Communists how to deal with their enemies. As to the second, the recent passion for Tito had in contrast cooled off. In a sober reappraisal of the October events, Titoism was no longer seen as a reliable antidote to nationalism but as a virus that might induce it. The Yugoslav leader gave grudging approval to the Soviet intervention but combined it with some schoolmasterish remarks to the effect that the whole thing would not have happened had his views and example been followed. The Soviet and Chinese tone about Yugoslavia grew harsher. Some satellite Communist leaders for whom the implication of a Soviet-Yugoslav détente had been quite ominous—notably those in East Germany and Albania—now began to refer to the Yugoslav Communists in terms almost reminiscent of the pre-1953 style.

But the new shift in Soviet foreign policy was neither abrupt nor complete. There was to be no return to Stalinism, no new break with Tito. To supplement her force exhibited in Hungary, the U.S.S.R. now proceeded to base her relations with the satellites, especially in the economic sphere, on a more equitable foundation. As seen in the case of the Polish agreement, Russia extended loans and technical help to the "people's democracies" and provided other compensations for her previous and lengthy economic exploitations. The tactful Chinese intercession on the Soviet side was rewarded by the most extensive Soviet help thus far rendered on economic and technical matters, including nuclear armament of China. According to a later Chinese version, an agreement of October 1957 included a Soviet pledge to deliver to China a sample atom bomb. In many ways the main beneficiaries of the 1956 unrest were the Chinese.

The new policy as it crystallized in 1957, in relation both to internal politics of the U.S.S.R. and to policies concerning the satellites, called for a "centralist" position avoiding both "dogmatism" and "revisionism." What those hideous semantic classifications meant was simply that a "people's democracy" could not become another Yugoslavia, nor, on the other hand, could it be administered in the Stalinist manner. Some elements of the Yugoslav position were now viewed with increasing suspicion. There was, first and foremost, Tito's completely independent foreign policies, which, of course, could not be tolerated in the case of, say, Hungary or Poland. Less important but also disquieting were such Yugoslav practices as the workers' councils sharing in the management of industrial enterprises—which the leaders of the "Fatherland of Socialism" believed was not conducive to social cohesion and discipline. In brief, Yugoslavia was acting like an independent country collaborating with the U.S.S.R. when it suited her rulers, but not feeling any obligation or restraint on her internal or external policies due to her *ideological* link with Moscow.

This ideological link fitted in with and was supplemented by one of self-interest. The latter led Tito to approve, as we have seen, the military intervention in Hungary. And he reacted but mildly to what under the usual international code of behavior was a most brutal and to the Yugoslavs most insulting breach of diplomatic amenities: Nagy and his associates had taken refuge in the Yugoslav embassy but, after a solemn pledge by Kadar that they would not be arrested, were persuaded to leave their asylum, whereupon they were promptly arrested by the Russians. For a year and a half they were kept in prison in Rumania. On June 16, 1958, it was announced in Moscow and Budapest that Nagy and his three closest associates had been condemned to death and executed. The sentence fitted the current Soviet mood about "revisionism." It was meant as a warning against any possible repetition of the Hungarian October. Yet in effect it was a needless piece of barbarity, for by 1958 new forms of opposition were springing up, and soon tiny Albania was to challenge the U.S.S.R. more basically and drastically than it would have been within the power of the luckless Hungarians to do.

Much as they might secretly have wished for a similar end for their Yugoslav friend, the Soviet leaders found themselves unable to solve the problem of Tito with equal neatness. In fact, since 1955 Yugoslavia had not been entirely in or entirely out of the Soviet camp. The Soviet inability to cut the Gordian knot of Titoism has always reflected a complex of issues much greater than Yugoslavia alone. How could one define the nature of relationships in the socialist camp in a way that would preclude the repetition of the events of 1956 and yet secure Soviet domination? How could one avoid the need for constant watchfulness and

occasional military intervention and yet make sure that the foreign policies
of the satellites would be synchronized and their internal policies at least
not too discordant? With their long-standing predilection for having
their cake and eating it too, the Russians have simply refused to acknowledge that this problem is insoluble and that no formula exists that can
make a country feel and be independent and yet do at any given moment
what the rulers of another country require it to do.

A valiant attempt to square the circle was undertaken during the four-
tieth anniversary of the Bolshevik Revolution. This celebration brought
all the leaders of the ruling Communist parties, including Mao, to Moscow. (On his arrival the Chinese statesman was greeted by the top Soviet
hierarchs—in marked contrast to his previous visit, when Stalin did not
deign to welcome him.) But the in-and-out prodigal son, Marshal Tito,
decided this time to absent himself. It had been known that the Chinese
and Russians would insist on a declaration condemning revisionism and
that some attempt would be made to resurrect an international Communist
organization à la Cominform, and neither of these ideas appealed to the
Yugoslavs. Their representatives refused to sign the declaration of the
ruling Communist parties, thus casting a pall over what was to be a festival
of Communist unity. The declaration itself was much weaker than the
Russians and, especially, the Chinese had wished. It condemned revisionism, to be sure, but acknowledged that "dogmatism and sectarianism"
(read: the old Stalinist ways) could also be a danger to a Communist
Party—each had to decide which aberration was more dangerous for itself. Instead of a new international Communist structure, a journal was
founded to discuss the problems of world Communism. (When it finally
appeared in 1958 in Prague it became obvious that it was not going to
serve as a substitute for the Cominform.) That such a weighty conclave
produced such modest results was due largely to the reluctance of some
of the Communist leaders, notably the Poles, to resurrect anything smack-
ing of the old Stalinist institutions or to license a new attack on Tito under
the cover of a vigorous denunciation of revisionism.

The declaration also stressed the leading role of the Soviet Union.
Strangely enough, in view of what was to take place later, it was the
Chinese who were the most vigorous proponents of the formula expressing
this Soviet primacy. Only subsequently did the Russians realize that their
Chinese friends wanted them to lead in the sense that an officer leads his
platoon into battle and then finds himself first under fire. The Chinese
Communists were now bitter about Tito's variety of Communism, which
they viewed as a rather sedate, unadventurous version of the ideology,
and they considered that the Yugoslav leaders wanted and occasionally
succeeded in having the best of both the Communist and the Western
worlds. What if the same type of mentality spread to the U.S.S.R. and her

rulers? They might find an accommodation with the United States and refuse to help China acquire Formosa. Less Communist militancy in Moscow—and such tendencies were already plainly visible—would mean that
the supply of goods, armaments, and experts to China would dry out.
Hence, the Chinese strove mightily not to let the Russians lapse into a
dangerous amiability toward the West or catastrophic leniency toward
those who practiced their Communism in an easy-going way.

For their own part, the Chinese concluded their "hundred flowers"
phase by the middle of 1957 and were about to embark on the "great
leap forward." Dissent and revisionism were to be extirpated. All the
nation's energies had to be poured into an attempt to make China a mighty
industrial and military power within the shortest possible time. This
policy was again undoubtedly connected to a realistic appraisal of the
Soviet position and its probable evolution. Sooner or later the Russians
would tire of maintaining high-risk policies versus the United States. And
how long would they continue to purchase Chinese approval of their
policies with arms and equipment, when many of them secretly viewed
China as the Soviet Union's eventual and most dangerous rival?

From the Soviet point of view too, the whole revisionism-Yugoslavia-
China complex of issues was full of unhappy possibilities and hopeless
conundrums. But Khrushchev as usual was a master of improvisation
and of short-run solutions which, while leaving the basic issues unsolved,
postponed an immediate and acute crisis. In the short run the cheapest
way to appease the Chinese and keep order within the Soviet empire was
to denounce the Yugoslavs.

An occasion for this was provided by the publication in March 1958
of the theses for the approaching congress of the Communist Party of
Yugoslavia. The program contained nothing new; it simply spelled out
those ideological premises of Yugoslav policies which had been practiced
when the Soviet-Yugoslav reconciliation was at its warmest in 1956 and
to which the Russians had not then taken exception. Thus the program
spoke of Yugoslavia's attempt to maintain good relations with both the
West and the Soviet bloc, of following her own road to socialism through
institutions like the workers' councils, etc. But what had been accepted
in 1956 became, in the wake of the Hungarian Revolution and given
China's aroused ideological vigilance, a tactless exhibition of revisionism
and opportunism. As a matter of fact, the Yugoslavs moderated their program in a pro-Soviet direction in answer to pleas from the Hungarians
and Poles, for whom continued Soviet-Yugoslav friendship meant a greater
scope for independent policies. But when the Yugoslav Party congress
met in April, it was boycotted by representatives of the ruling Communist parties (their ambassadors attended) and a new campaign of anti-
Tito vilification began, the harshest insults coming from China and Al-

bania. The old accusations of 1948, wrote a Peking daily, were essentially
correct: the Yugoslavs have sold out to the imperialists. The Yugoslavs
held their ground. Why, pray tell, was Khrushchev critical of their getting money from the West, when the U.S.S.R. itself was not averse to receiving credits from the same source?

For all the ominous hints and vile language from Moscow, the Russians' heart was not really in the dispute. Some Soviet credits to Yugoslavia were cancelled, ceremonial state visits were likewise demonstratively
abandoned. But no new break took place. With Peking and Albania, a
break was now definite, and the Yugoslavs correctly diagnosed the whole
trouble as having its source in the new posture of the Chinese and in the
Chinese hatred and fear of the whole principle of coexistence between
Communism and the West, of which Yugoslavia was the most vivid symbol
as well as the most successful beneficiary. Within a year, Russo-Chinese
relations went from bad to worse and gradually a new warmth stole into
the contacts between Moscow and Belgrade. In the meantime, an innocent
and powerless man was to suffer for those quarrels and intrigues among
the mighty; for no other reason than to emphasize the struggle against
revisionism, Imre Nagy and his associates were judicially murdered.

We must now go back to the effect of Hungarian politics on Russia's
internal politics. Khrushchev was by no means the sole author of the
policies toward the satellites that had reaped such a dangerous harvest
in 1956, but any failures or near failures in Soviet foreign policy threatened him—something which, as we have seen, was unimaginable under
Stalin. That Khrushchev was in fact slated for removal, and that, in the
typically prudent tradition of Soviet politics, this step was postponed so
that it could not be linked to any specific policy, is strongly suggested
by events in the winter of 1956–57. At a December meeting of the Central
Committee, the First Secretary did not give an address—ample warning
to those in the know that his authority was on the skids. Even more
significantly, the Central Committee entrusted the responsibility for supervision of the economy to the State Economic Commission headed by
Presidium member M. Pervukhin. An alert Kremlinologist should have
concluded that indeed Nikita Sergeievich was on his way out and that
after a decorous passage of time somebody else, possibly Pervukhin himself, would succeed him. But his opponents underestimated Khrushchev's
tenacity and his gift for improvisation. In February he presented to the
Central Committee a new plan for reorganizing the nation's economy.
Its main proposal was to decentralize economic administration and establish a system of regional economic councils. This, incidentally, would confer additional powers on the local Party secretaries, the dominant ele-

ment in the Central Committee, who in turn could be counted on to support Nikita Sergeievich, who had enhanced their status as against the ministerial bureaucrats in Moscow. In May Khrushchev's proposals were put into effect, and the administrative "revolution" of the previous December was undone. Outmaneuvered in the Central Committee, the anti-Khrushchev majority in the Presidium struck in June 1957.

Readers of the *Pravda* issue of June 19, 1957, could congratulate themselves and the Soviet Union on the unshakable unity of the government. There on the first page was a large photograph of Comrades Khrushchev and Bulganin being met at the railway station on their return from a state visit to Finland with flowers and embraces from their fellow members of the Presidium. Any unworthy suspicions about a split among the rulers could be set aside: Malenkov and Molotov beamed at Khrushchev, in company of his comrade-in-arms Bulganin, whose dignified appearance bespoke loyalty and sincerity. However, immediately following this touching event, as *Pravda* did not reveal, the Presidium repaired to the Kremlin, where a majority (including Bulganin) informed the First Secretary that he was fired. What happened then has been released in installments, the fullest version provided by Khrushchev himself at the Twenty-second Congress in October-November 1961. To the consternation of the majority Khrushchev refused to resign, a flaunting of precedent that left his opponents aghast and confused. In the meantime some of Khrushchev's partisans got wind of the intrigue and Central Committee members present in Moscow began to beat on the door of the Presidium demanding to be let in. The First Secretary, supported by three out of eleven members of the Presidium, announced that as he had been elected by the whole Central Committee he could be fired only by the same body.[23] According to the colorful version presented at the Twenty-second Party Congress, Bulganin's bodyguards at first sought to keep the zealous advocates of Party democracy from the deliberations of their elders, and when the former grew unruly the fatherly Voroshilov was delegated to appease and mollify them.[24] But another soldier, Zhukov, turned the scales in Khrushchev's favor. Army planes were dispatched to bring Central Committee members from all over the country. They descended on Moscow, three hundred strong, most of them determined to protect their friend and benefactor from the vile intrigues of the Stalinists. The tables were turned: Molotov, Malenkov, and Kaganovich

[23] Though technically correct, this version overlooked the fact that personnel changes following Stalin's death were made within the smaller body and then merely *ratified* by the larger one.

[24] He appeared now as a broken old man, said Khrushchev of Voroshilov in 1961, but you should have seen him then: he was full of zest as if leading a cavalry charge!

were ejected from their posts. With them went Shepilov, lately foreign minister, then Party secretary, "who had jumped over to their side."[25] The remaining purge took place gradually: Bulganin continued to work and travel with Khrushchev for some months. In March 1958 he was fired and replaced and in November identified as a member of the "anti-Party group." Pervukhin and Saburov, another economic administrator, were at first demoted and then also identified as members of the same group. They all remained alive and free—in startling contrast to the practice under Stalin—and were given subordinate jobs to keep them busy and out of mischief. Even the sixty-seven-year-old Molotov, who might have been ripe for retirement, was disposed of in this way: the man who was once second only to Stalin was sent to spend his declining years as ambassador to Mongolia. For a while it appeared that Marshal Zhukov, rewarded with full membership in the Presidium, might be the coming man. A national hero and untainted by any complicity in Stalin's crimes, he well might have expected to become the top man in the regime. But this thought must have occurred to others. In October, on his return from a visit to the Balkans, the Marshal was informed that he had been removed from his Party positions and as minister of defense. There is no gratitude in politics, and travel in foreign lands (or, as Khrushchev was to discover in 1964, even to the Crimea) is always attendant with dangers.

This tale—reminiscent in some strange ways of those incidents in Russian politics in the seventeenth century when the boyars were scheming against the Tsar in the Kremlin while outside the crowds milled around, aroused by the rumors of intrigue against their father and protector—is not without importance to an assessment of Soviet foreign policy during the remainder of the Khrushchev era and even beyond. For all his victory in 1957 and his subsequent assumption of the chairmanship of the Council of Ministers, his position remained precarious. Foreign-policy decisions often had to be made on the spur of the moment for reasons of internal politics or politics within the bloc, Khrushchev still feeling the need to stay one jump ahead of his domestic and Chinese critics. Hence the feverish character of external and internal policies even during the period of his greatest ascendancy in 1957–62. Those policies were to include gambles that in riskiness surpassed even the Berlin blockade, as well as sporadic gestures of friendliness toward the United States unimaginable under Stalin (except for the period of the

---

[25] This phrase was evidently something in the nature of a private joke among the oligarchs, for each time it was used at the Twenty-second Congress it produced gales of laughter. Shepilov, it was also revealed, had the endearing habit of keeping a little black book in which were recorded various misdeeds and indiscretions of his colleagues.

wartime alliance). Thus between 1957 and 1962 Khrushchev's regime pursued two apparently contradictory policies: one of militant Communist expansionism designed to weaken the West's position or to push it out of Berlin, the Middle East, Africa, and even Latin America; and the other a strenuous search for accommodation (or more) with the United States.

The search for foreign successes reflected both the ambition of the leaders and the need to present Communist ideology as the "wave of the future" still. To the average Soviet citizen the heyday of the ideology was long past. In his everyday life he expected his rulers to improve his material well-being and to extend his freedoms. In this sense Soviet society was becoming increasingly secularized: the bracing Communist slogans still rang in the newspaper columns and official speeches, but they were met with indifference by the mass of citizens, for whom they represented neither a menace nor the promise of a brighter future, but merely ritualistic language inherited from the past. Soviet patriotism, a justifiable pride in the technological and economic achievements of their country, replaced Communist ideology as the main factor of social cohesion. But the prospect of a complete erosion of ideology was—and is— viewed by the regime with apprehension. If the ideology is to become decorative and meaningless in terms of concrete problems of Soviet life, where in the last resort will be the rationale for the totalitarian system, for the assumed omnipotence and omniscience of the highest councils of the Communist Party? The focus for "proving" Marxism-Leninism— and by the same token of preserving something of the old ideological élan and sense of mission, without which the most efficient totalitarian regime runs the danger of internal disintegration—thus lay increasingly outside the U.S.S.R., in the successes of Communism and defeats for the West in foreign lands.

Yet this policy of militant expansionism was bound to multiply the chances of a confrontation with the main Western Power and, in the case of miscalculation, of bringing about the unimaginable catastrophe of nuclear war. Hence, inconsistently but understandably, Khrushchev combined menacing and expansionist policies with the search for a *détente* with the United States. The most characteristic expression of this ambivalence came at the Twenty-second Party Congress, held in 1961 after the most extensive Soviet nuclear tests so far. Dire threats were uttered against the United States by the First Secretary himself and by his defense minister, Malinovsky, yet from the same rostrum Foreign Minister Gromyko uttered what sounded very like a plea for an outright alliance between the two super-powers.

How did Khrushchev reconcile these two divergent strains of Soviet policy in his own mind? At one time the uninhibited Nikita Sergeievich made a felicitous comparison. In capitalist countries, he observed, it is not uncommon for a young man to marry a rich, elderly woman; they then live in perfect amity, he (while presumably impatient) kind and deferential to his wife; she obligingly sinking into decrepitude as time goes by. This, then, was his formula for coexistence, and need we ask who corresponded in his mind to the flourishing young man and who to the old woman?[26]

One can recognize in the First Secretary's formulation of the concept of coexistence a certain delicacy: it is not desirable that the old woman— the United States—should expire quickly; a gradual decline rather than abrupt demise is in order. The same generosity was evident in his oft-quoted, off-the-cuff statement during his American trip: "Your grandchildren will live under Communism." With China providing a disturbing example of what happens when a large country becomes Communist, Khrushchev was perhaps not entirely selfless in relegating this development in the United States to the distant future, a problem to be dealt with by a successor rather than himself.

Khrushchev's predicament was not merely humorous. It embodied the tragic dilemma of the Soviet rulers—a dilemma that did not disappear with his fall from power. He and his circle were genuinely interested in expanding their subjects' material well-being, in enlarging their freedom and their cultural horizons, in passing into history as the emancipators of the Soviet people from the horrors of Stalinism, as the restorers of humanistic and humanitarian Communism. By the same token they were pursued by the fear that excessive concessions and unbridled freedom would bring the whole system crashing down. It was not a new dilemma in Russian history. To a progressive nobleman urging him to crown his reforms with a constitution, Alexander II had replied with great earnestness that he would sign the most far-reaching constitution at this very moment were he not convinced that the resulting anarchy would ruin the empire and create great human misery. Thus the First Secretary could at one time authorize the publication of such shattering indictments of Soviet life under Stalin as Solzhenitsyn's *One Day in the Life of Ivan Denisovich* and at other times break out with abuse and menaces at the sight of a modern painting, at the appearance of a book or article free from ideological bias. Where would full freedom in the arts and literature lead?

One aspect of this need to find a formula combining greater freedom with safeguards for preserving the ideological and social cohesion of the Soviet people has been illustrated by the issue of contacts with the West.

[26] There is an uncomfortable fact Khrushchev overlooked: as against statistical probabilities an amazing number of rich old women survive their younger husbands.

By 1956, extreme isolationism was abandoned; foreign travel and cultural and scientific exchanges with the West were encouraged, if closely measured and carefully watched. The results were predictable: quite a few Soviet writers and journalists broke away from the hitherto stereotyped picture of the West; curiosity about Western arts, fashions, and ways of thinking were enhanced among the Soviet intelligentsia and youth; new appetites were aroused, new horizons revealed. To the progressive elements in the hierarchy, sometimes to Khrushchev himself, the whole process was despite its obvious dangers healthy and necessary. The Soviet system should be no longer afraid of competition and comparisons. Just as Soviet athletes who entered international competitions more than held their own, so Soviet writers, scientists, and artists could be trusted to profit by the lessons of the West without losing pride in their own country. But to the reactionary elements in the bureaucracy, notably the secret police and the apparatus of the Communist youth organization, foreign visitors, foreign travel by Soviet citizens, foreign films, etc., tended to complicate their tasks and arouse apprehensions. Foreign art and films carried with them the moral decline and indiscipline of the West. The foreign student was a potential corruptor of Soviet youth if not indeed a spy. The broadening aspects of foreign travel could and did include new discoveries and a revulsion against the stereotypes of Soviet propaganda and a craving for greater freedom at home. Said a typical bureaucrat: "individual immature writers, artists and composers—from among the youth as a rule—suffer from such illnesses as pseudo-innovationism and formalism in art. True, they are a paltry few, *but if an illness is not nipped in the bud, it can become dangerous.*"[27] Khrushchev himself was to speak violently against the reportage of his trips to America and Italy by the talented writer Victor Nekrasov, who, while writing from an impeccably Communist point of view, strove "to report only what he saw and to see nothing through the eyes of prejudice."[28] That, and his critical discussion of some aspects of cultural censorship at home, made Nekrasov a target for official wrath. The details of the struggle waged by the Party against the new and independent tendencies in literature—from the condemnation of Pasternak to the more recent trials and reprimands—do not belong in this study. Yet the problem, while not of the weight of, say, the German question or nuclear proliferation, illustrates a fundamental dilemma in Soviet foreign relations. The regime obviously has a stake in preserving a degree of tension vis-à-vis the West, and this in turn complicates the problem of coexistence.

[27] Party Secretary P. N. Demichev at the Twenty-second Congress, quoted in *Pravda*, October 20, 1961. My italics.

[28] Priscilla Johnson, *Khrushchev and the Arts* (Cambridge, Mass., 1965), p. 53.

The problem of coexistence in the most literal sense of the word requires the prevention of nuclear war. This in turn leads logically to the search for a formula for the abolition or—in view of the impossibility of such a step—the reduction of nuclear armaments. The Soviet position on this subject has already been indicated: for all the interminable discussions about disarmament since 1945, it was clear that the Russians would aim at getting nuclear weapons and the means of delivering them. Having achieved this aim and having presumably accumulated a sizable nuclear stockpile, they equally predictably began to indulge in what they had accused the United States of using—namely, "nuclear diplomacy." We have seen how Soviet notes to Britain and France at the time of the Suez affair contained unmistakable references to the Soviet possession of nuclear weapons and missiles capable of delivering them—then in Europe and by 1957 presumably anywhere in the world. The same motif appeared in the official Soviet notes and pronouncements in connection with the Middle Eastern crises of 1957 and 1958. The achievements of Soviet space science in 1957–58 (having concentrated earlier than the United States on guided missiles, the U.S.S.R. was able to gain an edge on America in this respect) added weight to the Soviet warnings. In October 1957 the first artificial satellite was put in orbit. From then on Russian successes in the space race were to beguile the world, irritate the American government and scientific community, and cost the American taxpayer dearly. For all the ritualistic and hollow verbiage about the purely scientific nature of the space race, its military significance was unmistakable. And the whole complex of fears aroused by nuclear weapons could, needless to say, be exploited much more fully by a totalitarian government than a democratic one. The latter can seldom threaten a foreign power without scaring its own citizens. In contrast the Soviet government could hector, cajole, and threaten foreign powers while at the same time piously denying any attempt to use the frightful weapons that it kept repeating it had in such abundance.

The favorite target of such tactics was Great Britain. There, a large part of public opinion grew extremely nervous in view of the country's vulnerability and her function as a base for American forces. The Soviet hints were, to put it mildly, unsubtle. Bulganin's note[29] to Macmillan in December 1957 is a typical communication of this kind:

> How can such NATO measures as, for instance, the round-the-clock flights over the British Isles by British-based American bombers carrying atom and hydrogen bombs help to reassure people, to improve the situation? . . . I say frankly that we find it difficult to understand what, in taking part in such a policy, guides the government of such a country as Great Britain, which is not only in an extremely vulnerable position

[29] Despite Bulganin's signature, the style is unmistakably Khrushchev's.

by force of its geographical situation but which according to the admission of its official representatives has no effective means of defense against the effects of modern weapons. Nor can there, it is true, be any such defense.[30]

Khrushchev's position on nuclear weapons and disarmament reflected a rather typical ambivalence: the awareness of the terrible perils of the arms race was incongruously combined with confidence that the U.S.S.R. could outscare and outwit the West; the eagerness to reduce the outlay on the nuclear and space races and to devote larger resources to other segments of the Soviet economy like agriculture which badly needed it was combined with a desire to score technological and military "firsts" that would confound the United States and add prestige to the Soviet Union and glory to Khrushchev's reign.

To those fears and ambitions were added secondary but nevertheless real fears about the proliferation of nuclear weapons. China was, with Soviet help, on the way to having her own nuclear weapons. In the late 1950's, there was for a Soviet statesman a more imminent danger: that of West Germany acquiring atomic weapons in one way or another. As one studies the Soviet attitudes one gets the strong impression that America's possession of nuclear weapons was *not* a source of urgent concern to the Russian leaders. Whether it was the experience of her failure to exploit diplomatically the period of her monopoly (what would Stalin have done had the U.S.S.R. been the sole power with the atom bomb?) or a touching belief in the essential peacefulness of American democracy, the Russians seem to have assumed between 1953 and 1962 that, short of a catastrophic miscalculation or a cataclysmic accident, an American nuclear attack was out of the question. Dulles' occasional incantations about massive retaliation or the occasional musings of some retired American air force officers were eagerly seized on and exploited by Soviet propaganda, but they did not appear to make the inhabitants of the Kremlin[31] lose any sleep. The acquisition by the West Germans of even a token nuclear force was (and remains), on the contrary, a contingency that produced unfeigned, acute anxiety. With even a few nuclear weapons a militarist group in West Germany could blackmail the Soviet satellites or even the U.S.S.R. itself. The effectiveness of the bomb as a *political* weapon, the Soviets came to realize very quickly, was not necessarily dependent on the size of the stockpile but on a government's ruthlessness and *apparent* disregard of the consequences of using it.

One might think that it would have been an effective gambit to threaten that in case of the nuclear arming of West Germany the U.S.S.R. would

---

[30] *Documents on International Affairs, 1957* (London, 1960), p. 39.

[31] A figure of speech by this time: in the wake of de-Stalinization the living quarters of the Soviet rulers were moved out of the historic enclosure.

provide similar arms to the German Democratic Republic. But nothing of the kind! The fact is that the prospect of nuclear arms in the hands of a Communist state, albeit their own satellite, was and is a most unwelcome one. It has already been explained in what tortuous ways the Chinese extracted Soviet help in atomic technology. By 1959 the Soviet leaders had gone back on their promises. At least the Chinese Communists bitterly asserted this in 1963.[32] And it is clear that by the 1960's the original decision was the most bitterly regretted Soviet policy since World War II. A similar mistake was not going to be made even in relation to a smaller Communist state. There was more than an element of truth in the Chinese accusation that "the real aim of the Soviet leaders is to find a compromise with the United States in order to seek momentary ease and to maintain a monopoly of nuclear weapons and to lord it over the socialist camp."[33]

Still, the Chinese statement oversimplified the situation as it related both to the Soviet leaders' motivations and to their freedom of maneuver. How exactly could they "find a compromise" with the United States when it came to nuclear matters? Mutual renunciation of the manufacture and possession of nuclear weapons was, and alas remains, out of the question. Beyond the technical problems of inspection and sanctions for the violation of an agreement, the stark fact is that in the conditions of international politics of the 1950's (as well as the 1960's) such a momentous development was inconceivable. When it came to less ambitious proposals, each side was bound to view an initiative made by the other with deep suspicion: was it designed really to minimize the possibility of a nuclear holocaust, or was it a clever move made to secure an undue advantage in the political-technological competition? Such were the suspicions encountered by the Rapacki proposal, formally initiated by Poland's foreign minister but having the full support of the U.S.S.R. First enunciated in October 1957 and repeated in February 1958, it looked forward to a very modest agreement on the creation of a "denuclearized zone in Central Europe." This zone would comprise "Poland, Czechoslovakia, the German Democratic Republic and the German Federal Republic. In this territory nuclear weapons would be neither manufactured nor stockpiled, the equipment and installations designed for their servicing would

---

[32] "As far back as June 20, 1959, when there was not yet the slightest sign of a treaty on stopping nuclear tests, the Soviet government unilaterally tore up the agreement on new technology for national defense concluded between China and the Soviet Union on October 15, 1957, and refused to provide China with a sample of an atomic bomb and technical data concerning its manufacture." Quoted in William E. Griffith, *The Sino-Soviet Rift* (Cambridge, Mass., 1964), p. 351.

[33] *Ibid.*, p. 348.

not be located there, the use of nuclear weapons against the territory . . . would be prohibited."[34] This, American spokesmen exclaimed immediately, would redound solely to Russia's benefit: it would effectively prohibit the United States from ever furnishing atomic weapons to Bonn, it would undercut the American advantage in having developed tactical nuclear weapons without offsetting the current Soviet superiority in longer-range atomic missiles.

The inevitable sequence to the Rapacki Plan, i.e., its rejection by the West, demonstrated how in disarmament diplomacy all the advantages belonged to the Soviet side, at least outwardly. The U.S.S.R. could speak publicly with one voice, no matter how passionate the prior discussion behind the closed door of the Presidium. It could improvise the most far-reaching proposals and then reap the propaganda harvest of a rejection or an "if" or "but" by the West. It could threaten and soothe at the same time. Thus Khrushchev in the same statement could say: "I shall not be revealing our military secrets if I tell you that we now have all the rockets we need: long-range rockets, rockets of intermediate range and close-range rockets"; and, "I have said all this not to intimidate anyone or exert political pressure."[35] In the West, on the contrary, there were always some voices who would seize on the latest Soviet proposals and then reproach their governments for not taking the golden opportunity to banish the nuclear nightmare forever. There were also bound to be other voices, equally useful to Soviet propaganda, calling for the governments to have no truck with *any* Soviet proposals and not to slacken in the accumulation of an arsenal of destruction.

It would have been a very perceptive observer who would have seen at the time that all those triumphs of Soviet diplomacy, whatever the West's sins of commission or omission, were essentially hollow. However many times the U.S.S.R. "scored" against the United States in world public opinion, her tactics did not contribute to what was clearly in her interest: a prompt ban on nuclear proliferation. If there ever was a period when the nuclear armament of Communist China could have been prevented or limited, that time was clearly passing in the late 1950's. By pursuing a double aim of outwitting the United States and appeasing China, the U.S.S.R. was bound to succeed in neither.

A possible goal in nuclear disarmament remained, a measure of immediate and obvious mutual interest to the two super-powers and one which could be self-enforcing: namely, the suspension of testing of atomic and hydrogen weapons. Here the Soviet Union seized the initiative with the announcement on March 31, 1958, that she was voluntarily suspending

[34] *Documents on International Affairs, 1957*, p. 157.
[35] *Ibid.*, p. 161.

all such tests. The United States and Great Britain were then about to launch a series of tests, which did take place. On October 31 the United States and Britain in turn proclaimed their willingness to suspend testing, and they continued the suspension despite new Soviet tests in November. (The massive Soviet tests in 1961 and the agreement between the Big Three in 1963 prohibiting tests in the atmosphere, under water, and in outer space will be dealt with later on. By that time the situation had drastically changed: Russia had irretrievably lost her power to influence China's nuclear policy, the United States that of France.) The original Soviet decision of March 1958 might well have reflected the intention of tying down China's hands, but who could blame the American and British leaders for not seeing it in that light? Oversubtlety can carry its own penalties, with statesmen as well as with private individuals.

Beginning in 1957–58, Soviet foreign policy was increasingly dominated by the triangular relation between the United States, China, and the U.S.S.R. To put it in plain language, the Soviets found themselves under pressure to reassert the policies of coexistence so as to minimize the chances of nuclear conflict, and at the same time forced to conduct expansionist policies so as to prevent an open break with China. Not that the latter policies can be explained purely in terms of Chinese pressures, for as we have seen they also relate to ideological dilemmas within the U.S.S.R. Also, not insignificantly, the disarray of Western policies, especially concerning non-European areas, created an almost irresistible temptation for the U.S.S.R. to try to score points. The dazzling succession of opportunities presented in the Middle East and later on in Africa undoubtedly would have tempted the Soviet policy-makers even had there been no Communist China.

Having contributed to the defeat and humiliation of their Western partners in the Suez affair, the American policy-makers made two unpleasant discoveries: first, the almost total collapse of the French and British positions contributed to create what is known as a power vacuum in the Middle East; second, among the Arab nationalists the credit for foiling the Western imperialists' wicked designs was attributed to Soviet threats rather than to American virtue. Reflection on these unwelcome conclusions led to the Eisenhower Doctrine promulgated in January 1957 in the form of a Congressional resolution authorizing the United States to render economic and military help to countries in the area that asked for it and also envisaging American military aid "to secure and protect the territorial integrity and political independence of such nations, requesting such aid, against overt armed aggression from any nation controlled by International Communism."[36] This ponderous declaration offered an obvious target for Soviet propaganda. With injured innocence the Soviet government could point out, "It is well known that the Soviet Union, as distinct from the United States, does not have and does not seek to have any military bases or concessions in the Middle East with the object of extracting profits." This masterful thrust would make many an Arab leader swallow the other less self-evident assertions of the Soviet note: "the Soviet Union never sought to worsen the relations of . . . [the Arab] countries with the United States. . . . [She] does not strive to gain any privileges in that area since all this is incompatible with the principles of Soviet foreign policy."[37] Especially in view of the United States' ties with Israel, militant Arab nationalism was not going to be drawn into relying on American help. Arab states and rulers that sought the assistance of the United States would become targets of intensified campaigns calling them betrayers of Arab nationalism. The situation became complicated by virtue of the opposition of a sizable portion of Western public opinion to aiding any country whose politics did not combine Jeffersonian democracy with the practice of liberalism à la John Stuart Mill. And on this score countries like Saudi Arabia or Jordan did not present an encouraging picture. American support for such countries was thus bound to be provided in an uncertain and somewhat guilt-ridden way, irritating to the recipients as well as to their opponents. In contrast, the U.S.S.R. could help Egypt or Syria with but scant regard for the fortunes of the local Communists, who in the eyes of Moscow were expendable if Soviet interests warranted chumminess with the current rulers. A sober Soviet diplomat might well regret the *excessive* American incapacity in international affairs: it irresistibly tempted his own rulers to intervene in more and more areas of the world where the U.S.S.R. had no direct interests, where she might score easy and spectacular successes but where in the *long run* she would become dangerously and inextricably involved.

This in brief has been the story of Soviet policy in the Middle East. Already in 1957 a new crisis gave Moscow an opportunity to repeat its tactics over Suez, this time in regard to the United States. A pro-Soviet tendency asserted itself in the Syrian government and army. There were rumors of a possible Syrian move (Syria's defense minister turned up in Moscow in July to negotiate for Soviet help) against her pro-Western neighbors. This in turn produced stories that the Turkish army was concentrating on the Syrian borders. American arms shipments to Jordan and Lebanon and a dispatch of an American diplomat on a fact-finding mission added to the tension. Dulles expressed the hope that the sinister

[36] *Ibid.*, p. 238.
[37] *Ibid.*, p. 246.

hand of "international Communists would not push Syria into any acts of aggression against her neighbors." Moscow inevitably saw the sinister hand of American imperialists and equally loudly warned them not to push Turkey into aggression against Syria. Having recently been bested in an anti-Khrushchev intrigue and being justifiably worried about his future, Prime Minister Bulganin turned undoubtedly with relief to the congenial task of threatening Turkey. He knew, he wrote his Turkish opposite number, that "the recent visit of American envoy Henderson to the Middle East was obviously brought about by a desire to organize military intervention from outside in Syria's international affairs . . . so as to satisfy the big American monopolies and in accordance with the interests of the major colonial powers."[38] He warned Turkey about the consequences of participating in such wicked plots. And, to under-line the Soviet warnings, it was publicly announced that Marshal Rokos-sovsky was now at the head of the Caucasian military district, the recently unemployed Soviet warrior thus being entrusted with the com-mand of the army against Turkey if. . . . The Turkish Prime Minister replied in a level-headed way, pointing out the curious fact that the U.S.S.R. had complained about a Turkish threat against Syria, even though the latter had not yet lodged a formal protest about any such thing![39] The ominous threats on both sides were to continue for a few weeks. On October 30 the crisis was abruptly terminated: Khrushchev appeared, beaming and friendly, at a reception in the Turkish embassy in Moscow. He had recently got rid of his potential rival Zhukov, the timing of whose dismissal gives one added reason for skepticism about the alleged seriousness with which Moscow had viewed the events in the Middle East.

The crisis of 1957 offered a seductive example of how in the Middle East more than in any other area of the world the Soviet Union could outscore the United States at relatively little expense and with little risk. She did not even have to initiate anything or risk direct confrontation with the Western Powers. She could wait for the next turbulent develop-ment in Arab nationalism, the almost equally inevitable American reac-tion against it, and then issue warnings and threats that did not have to be acted on but that earned her even higher repute in the Arab world and brought even greater discredit to the United States and her friends. A wiser statesman than Khrushchev might have pondered that in interna-tional politics nothing comes so easily, that eventually the U.S.S.R. would be drawn both into danger and heavy expense in that sector of the world. But for a politician like Khrushchev, with his gambling instincts and his

---

[38] *Ibid.*, p. 336.

[39] This embarrassing omission was promptly remedied: Syria sent an of-ficial note to Ankara three days after the poignant hint.

constant need for improvisations, the prospect was quite irresistible.

The year 1958 brought welcome crises in pro-Western Lebanon and Jordan. Colonel Nasser, who had recently become head of the United Arab Republic, a short-lived merger of Egypt and Syria, was believed to be at the root of the trouble. Influencing him, diplomats in Washington saw the inevitable "international Communism," especially in view of Nasser's visit to Moscow in May and the cordial communiqué issued then on his talks with the Soviet leaders. The next development was a *coup d'état* in July against the monarchy and pro-Western regime in Iraq, which installed a new regime under General Kassim. To prevent such disturbances from spreading and to prevent the loss of their remaining clients in the Middle East, the Western Powers acted with speed. The Americans landed Marines in Lebanon, the British parachutists in Jordan.

These steps gave Khrushchev, in an official communication to Macmillan and Eisenhower, another opportunity to remind the West that the Soviet Union had "atom and hydrogen bombs, aircraft and navy plus ballistic missiles of all kinds including intercontinental ones."[40] A similar repetitiousness characterized other parts of the document. "The powers which have started the aggression are playing with fire. It is always easier to kindle the fire than to put it out."[41] Hectoring and bullying the British had become almost a psychological necessity for Soviet statesmen—a pathetic testimony to the awe and envy in which the mighty British empire had once been held by the Russians. Did the British not remember the consequences of their recent aggression against Egypt? asked the ever helpful and tactful First Secretary.

But the new element in the Soviet notes on the Middle East crisis was Khrushchev's proposal for an immediate summit meeting of the heads of the governments of the Big Four *plus* India. The Soviet government proposed to have this meeting in Geneva but was willing to have it anywhere else if the interested parties (this meant in effect the United States, since the British passion for a summit meeting already knew no bounds and qualifications) so desired.

From the point of view of Russia's relations with China, this initiative was an incredible blunder. It was bad enough to propose a summit meeting without China, to imply that Khrushchev would agree to go to the United States, and then to agree (as he did subsequently) to a summit meeting within the context of the Security Council where the head of the Soviet government would sit in the same body as Chiang Kai-shek's ambassador. But on top of all this the Soviet leader proposed to bring in as one of the Big Five *another Asian power*, to enthrone it in fact as a

---

[40] *Documents on International Affairs, 1958* (London, 1962), p. 301.
[41] *Ibid.*, p. 302.

Great Power. What was behind this move is still difficult to determine. Presumably Khrushchev intended the summit meeting to deal only with a peaceful solution of the Middle Eastern situation. But it is not inconceivable that he hoped for some dramatic resolution of wider problems. The role envisaged for India is also far from clear. Rather belatedly Khrushchev sought to diminish the slight to Communist China by saying that India's participation in the meeting would be beneficial as against the participation of that permanent member of the Security Council "who does not in fact represent anybody" (Nationalist China). The American dislike of a summit meeting, and the consequent protracted correspondence on the subject, was to save Khrushchev *some* of the embarrassment on the issue; a quick American acceptance of his original idea would have put him in an impossible situation.

Still, the reaction from China must have been prompt and drastic. For it was certainly most incongruous for the top Soviet leader—who had just asserted that the world was in daily danger of a conflagration: "Time is precious, as the guns are already beginning to fire," exclaimed Khrushchev on July 22—to leave his country for a capital not involved in the crisis. "There is not a minute to be lost," he had asserted, but on July 31 he left for a four-day visit to Peking.

Whatever happened in Peking, it somehow removed his enthusiasm for a summit meeting. On August 5, in a new note, the versatile First Secretary claimed that the Anglo-American position made such a meeting impossible. He now demanded an emergency meeting of the General Assembly to discuss the situation in the Middle East. How could anybody ever suppose that he would have agreed to go to the Security Council "when most of its members are states which belong to the aggressive blocs and when the great Chinese People's Republic is not represented in it?[42] It remained for Macmillan to express polite astonishment: "I . . . regret that in your letter of August 5 you have withdrawn your agreement, very clearly set in your letter of July 23, to a Special Session of the Security Council to be attended by Heads of Government."[43]

The Middle Eastern crisis cooled off only to be succeeded by a Far Eastern one. It is unlikely that it was a coincidence that within three weeks of Khrushchev's visit, Communist China should choose to open heavy artillery bombardment of the Matsu and Quemoy islands. Though some authorities in Washington regarded with irritation Chiang's holding on to those coastal islands and placing on them a sizable proportion of his armed forces, Eisenhower and Dulles felt constrained to reiterate the American pledge to Chiang to stand by him if the Communist Chinese

[42] *Ibid.*, p. 318.
[43] *Ibid.*, p. 321.

actually invaded the tiny islands. With some unhappiness, one should think, the Soviet government felt compelled in its turn to advise the United States (through a letter from Khrushchev to Eisenhower) that "an attack on the Chinese People's Republic, which is a great friend, ally and neighbor of our country, is an attack on the Soviet Union."[44] The extraction of this statement was undoubtedly one of Communist China's main .objectives in her intense shelling of the islands.

As. to the actual Soviet communications to Peking on this subject, we are naturally left in the dark. It would serve China badly even at the height of her quarrel with Russia to reveal how qualified and uncertain were the Soviet offers of help.[45] (There is one tantalizing revelation in an official Chinese statement of 1963: "In 1958 the leadership of the CPSU put forward unreasonable demands designed to put China under Soviet military control. These unreasonable demands were rightly and firmly rejected by the Chinese government.")[46] But it is clear that the Soviet government was not going to let the Chinese or anybody else precipitate a war in which she would have to be involved. As to the actual form of the Soviet demands, Moscow would have insisted, at least, on a Warsaw Pact arrangement, i.e., over-all Soviet command in the Far East and the agreement of both parties on any defensive or aggressive measures.

The situation in the Formosa Straits was allowed to simmer down in November 1958. The year of crises and alarms, one might justifiably have expected, was finally over. To believe so was to underestimate both Khrushchev and the predicament of Soviet foreign policy. The First Secretary and other Soviet statesmen had begun in 1958 to make guarded criticisms of Chinese policies, and their apprehensions were aroused by the "great leap forward." An extremely ambitious plan featuring agrarian communes, and an attempt to overcome China's industrial backwardness quickly by the most fantastic and unrealistic improvisations, it was viewed with consternation as likely to involve the Chinese in an economic catastrophe (it did) and to produce new claims for Soviet aid and credits. It was also, and rightly, viewed as a symptom of China's impatience with Soviet tutelage and of the desire to become a great industrial and military power in a hurry. The Russians could view the Chinese claim

---

[44] *Ibid.*, p. 1871.

[45] Though the Chinese were to say, as we shall see, that the Soviet guarantee was given after the nuclear threat had passed.

[46] Quoted in Griffith, *op. cit.* p. 399. A recent Soviet source puts this interpretation on the Quemoy-Matsu crisis: "In August–September, trying to give a push to the 'Great Leap Forward' by creating tension close to China, Mao and his partisans without consulting the U.S.S.R. . . . entered upon a *provocation*, the shelling of islands in the Formosa straits. . . . They played with the idea of a 'local war' with the U.S., and the U.S.S.R. was to be drawn into it at a certain stage." (Glunin, Grigoriev, and others, *op. cit.*, p. 319.)

that they were leaping over the phase of socialism right into Communism with amusement, except it contained a covert criticism of Soviet society for being insufficiently militant ideologically, and a threat that China would try to compete with her within the Communist world by exporting her "purer" version of Communism and revolution. The earlier Soviet aid to China could be rationalized on the ground that China would not become a real problem and competitor for a generation or two; in 1958 this began to look like an overoptimistic conclusion.

Paradoxical as it must appear, the growing trouble with China was to precipitate the Khrushchev regime into another crisis with the West. The most basic issue in Europe, that of Germany, had to be solved. And the greatest Soviet fear—of West Germany acquiring atomic weapons—had to be removed before the "unshakable unity" of the socialist camp was exposed as something less than that. There were also sound secondary reasons for what became the "Berlin crisis": the perennial need of Khrushchev and the Soviet regime to score successes in foreign policy; the need to close off West Berlin, a gaping wound in the flank of the German Democratic Republic, the main gate through which hundreds of thousands of East Germans sought their way to the freedom and prosperity of the West. And the timing of the Berlin crisis leaves no doubt as to the wider context in which the Soviets made their move, nor, even more forcibly, does the fact that the Soviet note to the Western Powers of November 27 which opened the crisis was followed on December 21 by an official Chinese statement from Peking endorsing it. The Soviets were going to squeeze the last ounce of benefit from their fast-waning alliance with China. The latter complied for her own reasons, welcoming any new confrontation between the United States and the U.S.S.R.

The Soviet note was of an unusual length,[47] but the gist was simple. Thirteen years had passed since the war, but the situation in Germany was still abnormal. The U.S.S.R. recognized that, lamentably, two German states had come into existence instead of one. But the Western Powers must also recognize this fact. One remaining abnormality was the status of West Berlin and its continuing occupation. It should be terminated. The U.S.S.R. was quite willing to have West Berlin be a free demilitarized city. It proposed *for the next six months* to make no alteration in Western access to the city. But if no agreement was forthcoming in that period of time then the Soviet Union would turn East Berlin over to the East Germans and sign with them an agreement renouncing any vestiges of her occupation powers. It would thus be up to East Germany to negotiate with the three Western Powers as to their rights of access to West Berlin, and East Germany would have full right to ban the Western Powers' communications across its territory. Any attack on East Germany would,

---

[47] *Documents on International Affairs, 1958*, pp. 146–64.

of course, be regarded by all the signatories of the Warsaw Pact as an attack upon them.

On the face of it, the Soviet note was but another in a long series of threats and pressures exerted upon the West. But this time there was also the air of an ultimatum: recognize East Germany within six months or get out of Berlin, the Western Powers were told. If they refused to do either, they faced the probability of East Germany barring their access to Berlin, and any attempt to break this new blockade (and the implication was clear that it would also extend to air traffic) would mean war with the U.S.S.R. To anybody familiar with the dominant voice in Western diplomacy, that of the ailing Dulles, it was obvious what the *immediate* Western reaction would be: this was but another Soviet exercise in blackmail. To be sure, the American attitude later softened, largely in answer to British pleas to explore what the Soviets had in mind, but that the United States would agree to recognize East Germany or clear out of Berlin was inconceivable.

What, in fact, *were* the Russian motives? To us *now*, it is clear that the main Soviet objective was to secure an agreement that would make it impossible for West Germany to obtain nuclear weapons. This was indicated in the Soviet note, which said that "the best way to solve the Berlin question . . . would mean the withdrawal of the Federal German Republic from NATO, with the simultaneous withdrawal of the German Democratic Republic from the Warsaw Treaty Organization. . . . Neither of the two German states would have any armed forces in excess of those needed to maintain law and order at home and to guard their frontier." The Soviets thought that pressure on Berlin was the most efficacious way of obtaining what they really wanted, the neutralization of Germany, and one suspects that for the moment they would have settled for a firm pledge that West Germany would be barred from being a nuclear force.

But Khrushchev might have pondered the tale of the little boy who used to alarm his elders by exclaiming that he was drowning, eventually lost his "credibility," and was allowed to drown. He had threatened with rockets and bombs over Suez, over the landings in Lebanon and Jordan, and now over Berlin. How could one tell in which case he considered the issue to be one of national security for the U.S.S.R. and in which he was bluffing? Even for a person without Dulles' rigorous moralistic and legalistic attitude, it would have been impossible to tell that on the German issue the Russians were deeply in earnest and not just eager to score another triumph. Not being mind-readers and not having an agent in the highest Kremlin circles, the Western statesmen were likewise unable then to deduce that in setting a time limit, the Soviet leaders were influenced by the widening split with China: in a year or two this increasingly violent controversy might become public knowledge, in which case their bargaining powers vis-à-vis the United States would be seriously reduced.

In addition to this complicated design of Soviet fears and hopes, one receives the impression of clashing tendencies within the Khrushchev regime which did not allow him a completely free hand either in foreign or in domestic affairs. The special Twenty-first Party Congress summoned with great fanfare for January 1959, apart from confirming the new seven-year economic plan, failed to make any dramatic decisions, and one suspects that some of the original plans for the Congress had to be cancelled because of a division among the leaders.[48] And there were interesting undertones in the foreign-policy part of Khrushchev's speech at the Congress. First of all, he put stronger emphasis than ever before on the absolute inadmissibility of war in the nuclear age and made warm references to the United States and the need for an East-West *détente*. But the crucial sentence—it is one of the few that is underlined in the official text—was: *"One can and must construct in the Far East and the whole Pacific Ocean area a zone of peace and, first of all, a zone free of atomic weapons."*[49] This supremely important passage, the most open expression thus far of the Soviet hope that somehow Communist China might be prevented from ever acquiring atomic weapons, was overlooked in the West, in contrast to Khrushchev's threats and taunts[50] about West Germany.

In view of this proposal, and Khrushchev's fervent affirmation of the Soviet desire for peaceful coexistence and an end to the cold war, how did the Soviets manage to get (for the last time!) a cordial endorsement of their policies from Chou En-lai (present at the Congress) and, in a special message, from Mao himself, who stressed once more the "unshakable unity of the socialist camp"? The explanation is provided by a Russo-Chinese announcement of February 9, 1959, of the most extensive Soviet economic and technological aid thus far to Communist China —5 billion rubles' worth of Soviet services and goods, mostly in heavy industry, to be provided during the next seven years. In addition, Chinese experts were to be trained in the U.S.S.R. and more Soviet technicians were to be sent to China. The "unshakable unity of the socialist camp" was becoming increasingly expensive.

[48] Thus Khrushchev probably contemplated the further attacks on the Stalinist old guard which he was not to deliver until the Twenty-second Party Congress.

[49] *The (Extraordinary) Twenty-first Congress of the Communist Party of the Soviet Union* (stenographic report, Moscow, 1959), p. 78.

[50] A typical Khrushchevism: Chancellor Adenauer is a believing Christian; he should consequently worry about his soul, for surely for his policies he will go straight to hell!

This agreement with China, plus what he undoubtedly considered as Western obtuseness, largely accounts for Khrushchev's erratic and irritable behavior during the months between the Twenty-first Congress and his trip to the United States in September 1959. He needed a success in Germany because he undoubtedly felt this would strengthen his position at home and within the Communist camp. It might, he probably felt, still enable him to impose the Soviet viewpoint and Soviet caution on the Chinese Communists, then in the midst of serious economic troubles. Yet the West was refusing his (by his lights) perfectly reasonable proposals on Germany while remaining oblivious to the real danger: China's eventual emancipation from Soviet influence and her acquisition of nuclear weapons.

Secondary irritations were provided by developments in the Middle East. There the U.S.S.R. was being drawn into increasingly expensive commitments. In 1958 she undertook to finance the enormous Aswan Dam enterprise, but President Nasser exhibited scant gratitude. Alarmed by the close Soviet ties with and Communist influences in the new government in Iraq, he now began to denounce Communism as an enemy of Arab nationalism and was rather severe on the Communists in the United Arab Republic. Impatiently Khrushchev characterized Nasser as "a hot-headed young man" and insisted that Iraq was pursuing more progressive policies than he. But, alas, even in Iraq Soviet hopes were to be disappointed, and General Kassim's flirtation with the Communists and, in fact, his reign were not to last long.

The First Secretary's bad humor erupted during Prime Minister Macmillan's visit to Moscow in February 1959. Britain was known to be the Western nation most eager for a summit meeting, British public opinion most ready to accept some form of a compromise solution on Germany. But in view of the American and French reservations, all that Macmillan could propose was yet another foreign ministers' meeting of the Big Four. To Khrushchev, who hoped for a breakthrough on the German question and who had hopes that a summit meeting would take up a larger agenda, this was insufferable, and he was rude to his British guest.[51] But before Macmillan departed, he grudgingly agreed to a foreign ministers' conference and indicated that his deadline on Berlin need not be taken too literally.

The conference of foreign ministers of Britain, the United States, France, and the U.S.S.R. which met in Geneva followed the melancholy

[51] The foreign ministers could never settle anything since they did not have the power that only heads of governments possessed, said Khrushchev. In a colorful illustration of this, he explained that were he to ask his foreign minister to take off his trousers and sit on a block of ice Gromyko would have to comply.

pattern of such previous meetings: it was long (two sessions, May 11–June 20 and July 13–August 20) and inconclusive. The British were eager for a compromise. The French, with General de Gaulle now in power, were already suspicious of anything which might smack of a deal between the "Anglo-Saxons" and the Russians. The United States' position (Dulles was now out of the picture) was more amenable to the British viewpoint, but, by the same token, she was not, in view of Chancellor Adenauer's warnings,[52] going to agree to anything which smacked of recognition of East Germany. The Soviet position on the "two Germanies" was unyielding, but Gromyko was flexible on the time limit, indicating that negotiations could take a year or a year and a half before the U.S.S.R. would feel compelled to act unilaterally on a peace treaty with East Germany. The Soviets, in brief, wanted a summit meeting and were not going to agree to a binding solution anywhere else.

In fact we now know that the attention of the Soviet leaders during those summer months was centered on events elsewhere. A violent secret dispute was taking place between the leaders of the Soviet and Chinese Communist parties. The later Chinese version of this dispute is quite pat, as we have seen, consisting in an allegation that in June 1959 the Soviet government went back on its 1957 agreement to provide China with atomic "know-how" and a "sample" atom bomb. The Soviet answer to this charge, made in 1963, implies very strongly that the Soviet government had wanted in 1959 to be empowered to pledge that China would refrain from the production of nuclear weapon if for her part the United States would make a similar pledge about West Germany.[53] And this was in fact to be Khrushchev's ace argument at the forthcoming summit conference: accept my proposal for two neutralized Germanies, and we shall guarantee that China will not produce nuclear weapons. It is not difficult to reconstruct Khrushchev's argument to the Chinese: Why, especially in view of the deplorable state of your economy, do you sink your resources into this expensive business of making atom bombs? The U.S.S.R. has made it clear that she would consider any nuclear attack upon China as an attack upon herself? But this argument evidently found no favor with Mao. Was it convincing to some other Chinese leaders? A very important

[52] The old man decided to take back his offer to resign, feeling that because of Dulles' disappearance, he, though eighty-three, was still needed to put some iron into the Western resolve.

[53] "The authors of the [Chinese] statement hint that the Soviet Union could, if it wanted to, present nuclear weapons to China with one hand, and with the other could struggle against the United States giving nuclear weapons to Western Germany. . . . Indeed, what would have happened if the Soviet Union had on the one hand, started arming its allies with atom bombs, and on the other, had poured forth declarations against similar actions on the part of the United States . . . ?" Quoted in Griffith, op. cit., p. 434.

meeting of the Central Committee of the CCP took place in Lushan in July and August 1959, at which much of the anti-Mao opposition was evidently crushed.[54] Marshal Peng Teh-huai, Minister of Defense, and some other high officials were dismissed. Had they been in favor of accepting the Soviet proposals? Or, as was hinted later (in 1966 and 1967), were they at the prompting of the Russians even attempting to remove Mao and his group? We have no way of knowing. We simply know that a new and decisive turn was taken at that time in Sino-Soviet relations and that from then on neither Khrushchev nor any Soviet leader was able to speak for China.

Awareness of this fact soured what otherwise would have been the crowning point of Khrushchev's career, his visit to the bastion of capitalism. Freed from Dulles' tutelage, President Eisenhower was eager to have the mercurial Soviet statesman visit the United States, despite the misgivings of personages as diverse as Adenauer and Cardinal Spellman: Chairman Khrushchev, as the official American term had it, thus referring to the *less* important of his two jobs, would be able to see for himself the peaceful, friendly ways of the Americans, he would be able to disabuse himself of the Marxian stereotypes about capitalism, etc.[55]

For his part, Khrushchev considered the invitation a personal triumph. He was the first head of the Russian government to visit the United States: the Tsars wouldn't, and his incomparably more powerful predecessor couldn't. Apart from his love of travel, there was the undoubted fact that the trip would raise his standing at home (if not in Peking): in the nuclear age even social amenities between the heads of the two super-powers took on the appearance of political acts and tended to be reassuring. In the rather amusing account of the visit compiled by his journalist son-in-law Alexei Adzhubei, this theme is somewhat pompously spelled out: "The head of the Soviet government, accepting the invitation, went overseas not as a private person . . . but as head of the government of one great power to meet the head of another. . . . Behind him there stood the 200 million people of the first socialist country in the world and more than that the whole socialist camp with its billion people."[56]

As to the substantive results of the visit, Khrushchev could be under few illusions. The late Mr. Dulles, despite or perhaps because of his inflexibility, enjoyed a certain respect in Soviet official circles, as, one would think, a kind of American Molotov. But the Russians, as Khrushchev's

---

[54] But not all, as we have been given to understand by Peking since 1965.

[55] To be sure, Eisenhower's account of the visit, given in his memoirs, is less than enthusiastic, but some of this coolness reflects the falling out between the two leaders in the wake of the U-2 episode in 1960.

[56] Alexei Adzhubei et al., *Face to Face with America—The Story of the Voyage of N. S. Khrushchev to the United States* (Moscow, 1959), p. 429.

actions were to indicate in 1960, despite their undoubted esteem for his human qualities did not consider President Eisenhower to possess a firm grasp on the realities of the world situation or to be capable of initiating a new bold line of policy. Most important of all, Khrushchev's freedom of operation was by now severely limited by his quarrel with China. Peking was seething with rage, first at the very fact of the visit, and secondly at the official Soviet communiqué issued on September 9 on the occasion of the flare-up between Chinese and Indian troops on the Himalayan border, which urged both countries to be reasonable, refused to support the Chinese side, and, to Peking in its current frame of mind, lent substance to the worst suspicions about the purport of Khrushchev's visit to America.

Thus Khrushchev was unable to bargain for an atom-free zone in Asia against a similar one in Germany. The most that he could now expect from the visit was an American agreement to have a summit meeting, and a careful exploration of the possibility of drawing the United States away from her unyielding position on Germany.

As an exercise in public relations, the visit, which began on September 15 and went on two weeks, was an imposing affair. Nikita Sergeievich traveled with a suite that would have been thought excessive for a Tsar; one can understand the presence of the foreign minister, members of Khrushchev's family, and a bevy of Soviet newspapermen, but there were also physicists, medical authorities, and, most surprising of all, Khrushchev's (and Stalin's) favorite author, Sholokhov.[57] Theatricalities filled the American and Soviet press: Khrushchev sparring with newspapermen, indignant about the refusal (for security reasons) to let him visit Disneyland, shocked by the levity of a Hollywood movie, extolling his favorite crop, corn, on a visit to an Iowa farm, everywhere proclaiming the virtues of coexistence. In the Soviet versions, each appearance was a personal triumph: "simple Americans" came to realize how Communism and its great leader had been misrepresented to them, malicious interviewers were confounded by calm and incisive replies, everybody agreed that never had such an impressive foreign statesman visited the United States. With the Americans, the greatest hit was Mme. Khrushchev, whose dignity and affability made up for the often boorish behavior of her husband.

The latter brought to the United States, in addition to his suite, an enormous chip on his shoulder. Any Russian was liable to be irritated

[57] This once distinguished writer, now heavily addicted to alcohol and hated by the younger generation of Soviet intellectuals for his fawning ways toward whomever was in power, was lost in the crush. The few newspapermen who noticed him insisted on asking about Pasternak and received boorish answers.

by Eisenhower's well-meaning but insensitive hints about American affluence, but Nikita Sergeievich reacted to them with absurdities: no, the average citizen of the U.S.S.R. did not long for a house of his own, he preferred an apartment; he abhorred the notion of a private automobile, being quite satisfied with public transportation. The Soviet leader could not help openly taunting Vice President Nixon, with whom he had had a run-in before, at an American exhibition in Moscow. It had been stipulated that Khrushchev was to be treated like a head of state, but he lacked both the awesome dignity of Stalin and the suppleness of a lesser official like Mikoyan, and the occasional impetuousness and boorishness he revealed in America was to be a factor in his eventual downfall.

In his account of the visit, Eisenhower has the following passage, which unwittingly explains perhaps some of his guest's irritation:

> Referring to Red China, Khrushchev said that he had some personal viewpoints about our attitude towards that nation. He asked if I would like to discuss the subject. I answered that I thought there was little use to do so, for the simple reason that Red China had put herself beyond the pale so far as the United States was concerned. . . . He took my refusal in good part and implied that he had been specifically asked to bring up the subject with me, by whom, he did not say. He did add, however, that allegations of differences between the Soviets and Red China . . . were ridiculous by their very nature. He and Mao Tse-tung were good friends; the two nations, he said, would always stand together in any international dispute.[58]

The President's refusal to discuss what was, after all, the most important international problem facing the two countries, Berlin or no Berlin, could be taken as a sign either of American obtuseness or of extreme cleverness (having gotten wind of the dispute, the Americans did not propose to tip their hand). Alas, there is no doubt which it was. Later on, Khrushchev was to credit himself with additional delicacy on this occasion. In the intimate atmosphere of Camp David, the President's retreat, he had felt like asking Eisenhower why he was allowing U-2 flights over the U.S.S.R., but it would have been too embarrassing.

Whatever Khrushchev's real reasons for not mentioning this subject and for not opening his heart about his troubles with China, it is likely that he had concluded that neither jarring questions nor excessive frankness would be conducive to the aim uppermost in his mind: a summit conference. To this end, Khrushchev modified his position on the Berlin-Germany settlement and accepted that, while negotiations could not be prolonged indefinitely, there should be no fixed time limit on them. In

---

[58] Dwight D. Eisenhower, *Waging Peace, 1956–1961* (New York, 1965), p. 445. It is remarkable that Eisenhower printed this passage, written as it was when the Sino-Soviet dispute was in the open, without comment.

other words, the element of ultimatum was removed from the Soviet position, and with this difficulty out of the way President Eisenhower agreed to a summit meeting later on in the year. In 1960, he was supposed to return Khrushchev's visit and become the first head of the American government to visit Russia. These two agreements lent an air of cordiality to the final phase of the Soviet-American talks; "the spirit of Camp David," as it became known, seemed to promise some form of settlement of the German issue, a decisive East-West *détente*, and perhaps even more.

Soon practical difficulties were to interfere with the time-table of the *rapprochement*. In two Western capitals, Bonn and Paris, the spirit of Camp David was viewed with suspicion. To Adenauer, the American-British position was not firm enough; a Big Four meeting might result in at least partial capitulation by the West on the question of recognition of East Germany. For his part, General de Gaulle was already apprehensive of a possible "deal" between the United States and the U.S.S.R. by which the two super-powers would establish a dual hegemony in the world. It was largely in answer to his objections that the summit meeting was postponed until the next May. By that time, Eisenhower's ability to enter into a binding agreement with the U.S.S.R. would be restricted in view of the approaching presidential elections, and French pride could be appeased by Khrushchev coming to visit France *before* the summit meeting. Most of all, de Gaulle counted on something happening before the summit meeting that would prevent the United States and the U.S.S.R. from reaching a comprehensive agreement, that would preclude France's playing the role for which she was so eager—of a Great Power dominating Western Europe. And, to be sure, "something" did happen.

For the Soviets the delay was an inconvenience. Time was running out; the Soviets could not long prevent disclosure of their disagreements with China and, thus, a weakening of their bargaining position. And Khrushchev needed visible successes to bolster up his position at home. On his return to Moscow, he was given (or, properly speaking, gave himself) a triumphant reception, on which occasion he hailed Eisenhower as a constructive statesman and confirmed his invitation to Russia. (He must have known how uncertain was the current direction of American policy, how West German objections and French pressures were likely to strengthen the case against reaching an agreement with the Soviets— hence the quite open flattery of the American President.) But almost immediately he had to go on a less congenial trip to Peking.

General de Gaulle's objections to a summit conference were undoubtedly dwarfed by the Chinese Communists'. Four years later, this is what they had to say: "Back from the Camp David talks, [Khrushchev] went so far as to try to sell China the U. S. plot of the 'two Chinas' and, at the state banquet celebrating the Tenth Anniversary of the Founding of the People's Republic of China, he read China a lecture against 'testing by force the stability of the capitalist system.' "[59] As usual the Chinese interpretation is probably too drastic. Khrushchev must have attempted to appease the rising Chinese anger by pointing out that a Soviet success in Germany could not but strengthen the position of the socialist camp as a whole, that Russia would then be able to press more energetically on behalf of Chinese interests in Formosa, etc. In the speech in question, he took great pains to soothe the Chinese fears of Soviet appeasement. What entreaties or even threats Khrushchev employed we do not know. But for the moment he succeeded in preventing an open break and in preserving the veneer of that great friendship with Mao Tse-tung about which he had so fervently assured Eisenhower. On their part, the Chinese leaders were most likely to count, as did de Gaulle, on a development that would wreck the prospects of Soviet-American *rapprochement*. Until the summit meeting was actually to materialize and bear fruit, they would hold their fire.

The evidence presented above suggests very strongly that the diplomatic maneuvers executed by Khrushchev in 1958–59 were part of a grand design through which he hoped to effect at least a partial solution of the German problem as well as to prevent or considerably delay the Chinese acquisition of atomic weapons. Some tantalizing questions still remain. What would have happened had there been a more perceptive appraisal in Washington of Soviet problems and aspirations? What if a summit conference had taken place in December 1959? There were voices in the West (among them, paradoxically, General de Gaulle's) that recognized the multitude of Russia's problems, principally that concerning China.[60] But while viewing the Sino-Soviet problem in apocalyptic long-range terms, the West ignored how intense the conflict already was, and that a *united* and *prompt* initiative might affect it. But it is doubtful that, even had Khrushchev unburdened himself to Eisenhower, the lackadaisical course of American policy would have changed. Bold improvisations were not in its style. It is equally doubtful that, China's precarious economic

[59] Quoted in Griffith, *op. cit.*, p. 400.

[60] At his press conference in November 1959, General de Gaulle phrased it in his usual elegant rhetoric: Russia was facing a China "numberless and wretchedly poor, indestructible and ambitious, building by dint of violent effort a power which cannot be kept within limits and looking around her at the expanses over which she must one day spread." *Documents on International Affairs, 1959* (London, 1963), p. 462.

position (undoubtedly a factor in his calculations) notwithstanding, Khrushchev could have subordinated Chinese foreign policy to Soviet interests. Still, on the Western side no attempt was made to explore this whole problem.

There can be no question that this grand design represented also a very personal commitment on Khrushchev's part. He was going to pass into history as a man who secured a long-term *détente* in the cold war, a lengthy period of peace for the development of his people's economy and well-being.

A book published after his visit to the United States contains sample tributes from "simple Soviet men":

> Peacefully and confidently can live the Soviet people . . . seeing how the party and government and our own Nikita Sergeievich live and breathe at one with the nation. . . . I hear that since Lenin there has not been in our government a man whom the people have loved and respected so much . . . and trusted with the custody of their future . . . as now. . . . It is well that you, Nikita Sergeievich, took your family with you. . . . Nina Petrovna [Mrs. Khrushchev] is an ideal example of the Russian woman.[61]

Such "spontaneous" homages to the man who had allegedly abolished the "cult of personality" undoubtedly made some of his colleagues wince, but by the same token they indicate that Khrushchev had a personal stake in the success of the summit meeting and in receiving Eisenhower in Russia. It is unlikely that his rage was entirely an act when those plans came crashing down the next spring.

2. *Confrontations with the United States and with China: 1960–64*

In the course of 1960, two elements in Khrushchev's juggling act came crashing to the ground. The Soviet Union's now intense conflict with China became public knowledge, first in the Communist world and then in the West. Coincidental with this, but not unconnected, came the collapse of the summit meeting and of any hope of solving the German issue through negotiations. The remaining years of Khrushchev's rule were to bring dangerous confrontations with the United States over Berlin and Cuba and then an amelioration in Soviet-American relations with the relief felt over the peaceful resolution of the Cuban missile crisis. But the latter in turn contributed to the intensification of Russia's quarrel with China and then public disclosure of its main points.

[61] Adzhubei *et al., op. cit.,* pp. 594–95.

We do not know to what degree Khrushchev's failures and dangerous gambles in foreign policy contributed to his fall. His successors chose publicly to emphasize his "hare-brained schemes" and lack of manners in domestic politics, and to overlook similar derelictions in foreign affairs. But the latter were probably also considered when the Presidium reached a consensus, sometime in 1964, that Nikita Sergeievich was too unpredictable and too arbitrary to be tolerated as head of the regime. He had ceased to be respected and trusted and was not feared enough—a fatal combination for the head of a totalitarian regime.

Why had not those defects been fatal to him before? Because, one would think, the content if not the style of Khrushchev's policies expressed faithfully the aspirations of the ruling oligarchy: cautious liberalization at home which would not harm the power of the Party hierarchy; coexistence abroad which would not prevent the spread of Communism and Soviet influence. But eventually these tasks grew too difficult even for a man with Khrushchev's juggling ability. His irritability grew accordingly. He had to go.

In the spring of 1960 the Soviet grand design lay all but shattered, and it was inconceivable that the results of any summit conference could make it feasible in the future. The Chinese attitude on the subject must have been made clear to Khrushchev on his visit to Peking in 1959, but just to make sure that the Russians labored under no illusions, the Peking leaders fired their heaviest salvo thus far as the conference approached. On April 16, 1960, *Red Flag*, a Peking journal, published "Long Live Leninism!," an article whose authorship was subsequently attributed to Mao himself. The article did not attack Khrushchev and the Soviets in so many words, but opprobrious references to Yugoslav Communists and assorted revisionists were transparent enough. The involved semantics and esoteric allusions amounted to a public warning: if you Russians push *détente* with the West one step further, we shall denounce you by name as being as vile as the Yugoslav revisionists. As for any schemes for limiting the spread of nuclear armaments at their expense, the Chinese were not buying. They were not afraid of an atomic war:

We consistently oppose the launching of criminal wars by imperialism. . . . But should the imperialists impose such sacrifices on the peoples of various countries, we believe that, just as the experience of the Russian revolution and the Chinese revolution shows, those sacrifices would be repaid on the debris of a dead imperialism. The victorious people would create very swiftly a civilization thousands of times higher than the capitalist system and a truly beautiful system for themselves.[62]

The last sentence, as was to become clear some years later, left the Soviet

[62] *Documents on International Affairs, 1960* (London, 1964), p. 200.

leaders breathless. They overlooked the fact (proof of how lacking they were in introspection) that it came close to what Khrushchev himself had said on several occasions; now the Chinese were saying that socialism would survive a nuclear war—why, it would flourish better than before! It was one thing, though, for the Soviets to frighten the capitalists with such supposed equanimity about an atomic holocaust. But for Chinese Communists to express such sentiments seriously for the benefit of fellow-Communists!

Even more eloquent than all the dialectical flourishes of Mao's article was its intent to provide an ideological underpinning—and from the hand of the highest Chinese authority—to an earlier statement made by the Chinese observer at the conference of the Warsaw Treaty powers in Moscow on February 4. The conference had been summoned as part of a strategy of putting psychological pressure on the West before the summit conference—i.e., to warn it against giving atomic weapons to West Germany (thus Ulbricht made noises about asking the Soviet Union for "modern rocket weapons")—but what the Chinese delegate said was designed not to scare the West but to warn his Communist colleagues: "The Chinese Government has to declare to the world that any international disarmament agreement and all other international agreements which are arrived at without the formal participation of the Chinese People's Republic and the signature of its delegate cannot, of course, have any binding force on China."[63] As if to mock his hapless Soviet listeners, the Chinese delegate added, "The Chinese Communist Party and the Chinese people have always taken the safeguarding of the unity of the socialist camp headed by the Soviet Union as their international duty."[64]

One-half of the grand design was thus completely lost. Khrushchev would go to the summit without any possibility of producing a dramatic proposal to prohibit nuclear weapons in the Pacific area in return for a similar prohibition in Germany.[65] What was left was the increasingly dim prospect of securing one-sided concessions from the West. There was little that the Soviet government could offer in exchange. The time had past when the East German state could be considered expendable. The threat of arming East Germany with nuclear weapons was likely to petrify the Poles and the Czechs, if not indeed the Russians themselves. After a while, it was wisely decided to discard this gambit as a bargaining weapon.

---

[63] *Ibid.*, p. 185.

[64] *Ibid.*, p. 188.

[65] Once the summit meeting collapsed and relations between the U.S. and the U.S.S.R. became more strained that ever during a new Berlin crisis, Chou En-lai could in *September* declare blandly: "The Chinese government has repeatedly proposed that the countries in Asia and around the Pacific, including the United States, conclude a peace pact of mutual nonaggression to make this region free of nuclear weapons." *Ibid.*, p. 487.

What, then, was left? Khrushchev's hopes were obviously based on Eisenhower's incautious admission at Camp David that the situation in Berlin was "abnormal" and on the well-known British eagerness to secure a Berlin agreement that would relieve the anxiety about a possible clash there.

For their part, the responsible American officials approached the prospect of the summit conference in the spirit of a young girl being asked out for the evening by a well-known seducer, previous encounters with whom had led to scandalous propositions rather than honorable declarations. Whether there was some nervousness in the State Department as to what the President might say while in a private meeting with Khrushchev, with Macmillan whispering his entreaties, or whether they wanted to warn the American public against excessive hopes, Secretary of State Christian Herter and Under Secretary C. Douglas Dillon proceeded to adopt an unyielding attitude in public speeches. The latter, in a speech of April 20, spoke in terms calculated to raise the temperature of the already sorely tried Khrushchev: "Is the Soviet Union prepared to remove its forces from East Germany and the Eastern European countries on which they are imposed? Is it willing to grant self-determination to the East Germans and the peoples of the Soviet-dominated states in Eastern Europe . . . abandon the fiction of a separate North Korea . . . ?"[66] The answer to all those questions was obviously no, or, rather, if Khrushchev had chosen to be painfully frank, he could have explained that it was not within his power to do these things, that, alas, they confused his powers with Stalin's. In Baku on April 25, the Soviet leader wondered plaintively:

> Why then did Dillon have to make a statement so obviously out of tune with the tenor of relations between the U.S.S.R. and the United States since my conversations with President Eisenhower at Camp David? Perhaps this is no more than a manifestation of the pugnacity of a diplomat who has taken into his head that some pressure on the other side before the talks might make it more compliant. . . . Some people apparently hope to reduce this meeting to an ineffectual exchange of opinion and pleasant—it may be—talks.[67]

Khrushchev repeated that concrete progress must be made at the summit meeting on two issues: disarmament and a peace treaty with Germany. Otherwise, and he was now more emphatic than before, the U.S.S.R. would go ahead with her own treaty with East Germany; and then—on this also he was more emphatic than before—the West would lose its rights of access to West Berlin by "land, water, and air."

This speech did not mark, as has sometimes been asserted, Khrushchev's abandonment of hopes for the summit. It marked his growing pessimism—justified, in view of Herter's and Dillon's speeches—that the Soviets would

---

[66] *Ibid.*, p. 8.
[67] *Ibid.*, p. 12.

not get their way, and an escalation of his psychological pressure on the West. (It was interesting that he distinguished between Eisenhower and the State Department, implying that the latter was not in line with the President's conciliatory position.)

The celebrated U-2 incident began on May 1 with the downing of an American spy plane deep within the territory of the U.S.S.R. and the imprisonment of its pilot. (Such flights had been taking place since 1956. While the Russians had had no reason to be enchanted with the Americans flying over their territory and were undoubtedly irritated by their inability to bring the high-altitude planes down, it is reasonable to assume that they had accepted the flights as an unpleasant fact of international life.) On May 5, in a dramatic speech to the Supreme Soviet, Khrushchev announced the downing of the plane but chose to withhold the fact that the pilot, with his photographic equipment, had been captured. After the State Department issued a feeble communiqué about the pilot having probably lost consciousness and the automatic pilot bringing the "weather research plane" down into the heart of the U.S.S.R., Khrushchev with some delight revealed that the Soviets were holding the American flier and the evidence proving the real purpose of the flight. Caught red-handed, the State Department chose on May 7 and 9 to reveal the full extent of previous American penetrations of Soviet air space, to defend and justify this record, and to associate the President with the decision to employ this form of spying. This was to compound the original error of answering the first Soviet announcement: it was unprecedented in diplomatic history for a government to admit responsibility for spying publicly, and incredible that a head of state should be drawn into this admission.

Khrushchev's actions are still difficult to analyze. But it is entirely conceivable that his statements of May 5 and 7 were prompted by the belief that discomfiture would make the Americans more pliable, that something might be rescued from the summit meeting after all. But Eisenhower's incredible assumption of the responsibility for the flights made his anger, feigned in the beginning, very real. We do not know whether there had been any voices in the Soviet leadership who had expressed skepticism about Khrushchev's summit tactics, or his invitation to Eisenhower, or his apparent belief that the President could shake off the objections of Adenauer and the State Department and strike a bargain over Germany. But Khrushchev had committed himself when he presented Eisenhower to the Soviet people as a man of "wise statesmanship . . . courage and will power." Now he was made to look ridiculous, if not to the Russian people, who were accustomed and somewhat indifferent to drastic shifts in official evaluations of foreign statesmen, then to his colleagues. And it was not difficult to imagine the reaction in Peking! Khrushchev's subsequent course of action suggests considerable personal vindictiveness toward the President and an attempt to embarrass his party in the approaching presidential elections.

In Paris, where he arrived on May 14, Khrushchev continued his theatricalities: unless Eisenhower apologized, promised to discontinue the flights, and punished those responsible for them, the Soviet government would walk out of the conference. Since the President obviously could not apologize (he did indicate that the overflights would be stopped), especially in view of Khrushchev's insulting tone, the summit conference was aborted. Khrushchev rubbed salt into the wound by suggesting that a new gathering take place in six or eight months—i.e., after the new president was installed—and he withdrew his invitation to Eisenhower to visit Russia.

After some further antics at a press conference, Khrushchev flew to Berlin. The world held its breath, expecting a treaty to be signed between the U.S.S.R. and East Germany and an immediate challenge to Western rights in Berlin. In fact, Khrushchev simply repeated his suggestion for another, later summit meeting and recommended that in the meantime neither side take unilateral action on Germany. The immediate fears of a cataclysmic clash—sufficiently great for the Secretary of Defense to order a world-wide alert of American forces—were for the moment appeased.

There were naturally many conjectures in the West about the reasons for the break-up of the summit conference. Was Khrushchev's anger real, or was it simulated in order to provide a pretext for breaking up a meeting at which the Soviets were unlikely to secure any gains? This question has already been discussed. Were his hands in some sense tied by "pro-Chinese members of the Presidium," as the phrase went? This is a most unlikely conjecture. Khrushchev most probably had come under more severe internal criticism for his original promise in 1957 to help China with nuclear development than for his subsequent backing down on that agreement. With their intense nationalist orientation, who among the Soviet leaders would seek a road to power by endorsing the Chinese viewpoint, against Russian interests? In 1961 Molotov was accused by implication of connections with Peking, but this was simply a modern variant of such accusations as those in the 1930's that Trotsky and Bukharin worked for British Intelligence. Khrushchev was undoubtedly on the spot simply because his schemes had not worked and he was getting into more and more trouble with the West and with the Chinese.

The violence of Khrushchev's public attacks on Eisenhower[68] may re-

[68] Eisenhower rather immodestly convinced himself that the reason for the failure of the summit meeting was Khrushchev's fear of the possible consequences of his visit to Russia: "And if a visit by the United States Vice President had raised misgivings and questions in the minds of his people,

flect the fact that he could not as yet indulge in public criticism of another world figure who crossed him much more seriously and stood even more firmly in the way of Soviet designs. Khrushchev's now terrible fury against China still had to be confined to closed-door Party meetings (from which, to be sure, some customarily indiscreet Italian Communists would leak the news to bourgeois sources). A great user of Russian proverbs, the First Secretary might well have pondered an American one: "Sticks and stones may break my bones, but words will never hurt me." Even Stalin had found it difficult to gain the upper hand in verbal duel with another Communist (Tito). The rising wrath against and abuse of his Chinese co-religionists were to bring Khrushchev little profit during his remaining four years in power. His vituperation was echoed in the utterances of most foreign Communist leaders, still tied to Russia by the bonds of self-interest and now appalled by China's apparent nonchalance about atomic war, but it did not budge the Chinese from their position. They rightly calculated that for external and internal reasons the Soviets would not dare to make a clean break. What would be the consequences if the Soviet leaders clearly enunciated that the Soviet national interest was no longer identical with the spread of Communism, that proletarian solidarity was a myth, that China was a greater danger than West Berlin or the intrigues of the imperialists? What rationale would remain for the rule of the Communist Party in Russia, for the propaganda fed to the Soviet citizen from childhood to the grave? What had it availed the Mensheviks and other enemies of the Bolsheviks to "unmask" the Bolsheviks as un-Marxist adventurers and anarchists? There was a triumphant note in the Chinese taunting of the Russians: *you* have made us what we are, and now you cannot undo it; you are more powerful than we, but we are the wave of the future; your accusations and pleas only prove that you are faint-hearted revisionists, but you will never have enough courage to do what you secretly desire— combine with the capitalists against us! And there has been a kind of mad logic in this position.

A little more than a month after his collision with the West, Khrushchev had another furious clash, this time with the East. He chose to attend the Third Congress of the Communist Party of Rumania, which opened in Bucharest on June 20, 1960, in order to intimidate personally the Chinese delegation, headed by Peng Chen, member of the CCP Politburo. (He may have thought that Peng Chen, who was not one of the four or five most important leaders of the Chinese Party, would not dare to talk back to the still acknowledged head of the world Communist movement.) In 1963 Peking described Khrushchev's behavior at the meeting thus:

It is a plain lie for . . . the Central Committee of the CPSU to describe

what would be the consequences of a visit by the United States President?" *Waging Peace*, p. 559.

that meeting as "comradely assistance" to the Chinese Communist Party. . . . Khrushchev took the lead in organizing a great converging onslaught on the Chinese Communist Party. . . . He vilified the [members of the] Chinese Communist Party as "madmen," "wanting to unleash war" . . . "pure nationalists" . . . "dogmatic," "Left adventurists."[69]

The Russians circulated among the assembled Communist leaders a lengthy diatribe against the Chinese. And the Chinese delegation reciprocated by making public a Russian letter to the Chinese Central Committee full of intemperate abuse.[70] Khrushchev now broke loose with a personal attack on Mao—did not Mao have recourse to Stalin-like persecutions? Marshal Peng Teh-huai had been disgraced and sent to a forced labor camp[71]— and with accusations that the Chinese were hampering Soviet defense arrangements on the Manchurian border, etc. The most obtuse foreign Communists must have realized that they were in the presence of a funda- mental split in the Communist movement. The Chinese Communists were not doomed to linger on as mere sectarians, as the Trotskyites had been, nor did they represent the heresy of a small Communist state and Party, like Yugoslavia; their huge country posed a basic challenge.

Each side tried to convince the other and in the process managed largely to convince itself that their differences sprang not from what in plain language must be called competition between two imperialist systems, but from their ideologies. "Revisionism," "left-wing sectarianism," "under- estimate of imperialism"—these were to become the currency of the dis- pute, together with ample quotations from Lenin and reminders of how each side had changed from its original position. Infinitely more powerful, supported by a great majority of other Communist parties, the Russians found themselves on the defensive from the beginning. Until recently the sole possessors of the radical and revolutionary Communist rhetoric, they dared not meet the Chinese charges with a firm admission that, Lenin or no Lenin, much of the ideological ballast of Communism had become irrelevant in the nuclear age. Fully conscious of the dangers inherent in China's militant definition of Communism, the Soviet Union found herself compelled to pursue dynamic rocket-rattling foreign policies as if to prove— to the Chinese, to other Communists, and to herself—that she had not become what she essentially was, that is, "revisionist."

Throughout the summer and fall of 1960, when the attention of the world was focused on the deepening crisis between the U.S.S.R. and the

[69] Griffith, *op. cit.*, p. 401.

[70] Edward Crankshaw, *The New Cold War: Moscow v. Peking* (Baltimore, Md., 1963), p. 106.

[71] Five years later, during the Chinese "cultural revolution," both Pengs—the Maoist one of Bucharest and the former defense minister—were identified as revisionists and enemies of Chairman Mao.

West, the real preoccupation of the Soviet leadership was the temporary patching up of the Sino-Soviet split. The head of the Soviet regime was as usual hectoring and bullying the West: let them keep their hands off the Congo; let President Eisenhower, before he undertakes anything against Castro's Cuba (now increasingly friendly with the Russians), remember that Russia has rockets and nuclear weapons. In September, at the United Nations General Assembly, where he went to court the newly independent states of Asia and Africa, he surpassed his usual antics, shouting to people from the balcony of the Russian consulate in New York and banging his shoe during a solemn session of the Assembly. But this performance, it is fair to say, was due only in part to his natural boorishness. Khrushchev was working under intolerable strain. In addition to the open challenge from China and clear hints of further splits within the Communist world (while threatening the United States, the Soviet Union was impotent to compel tiny Albania to remain obedient), domestic problems were calling for drastic readjustments: the rate of industrial expansion was falling; the virgin-lands plan, which Khrushchev had once thought would solve the troubles of Soviet agriculture, was now shown to be a failure. It was not surprising that Khrushchev, now sixty-six, was showing signs of wear and tear.[72]

The attempt to patch up the difficulties with China was, as the Soviet leadership probably realized, unlikely to succeed. On the other hand, there was every incentive to present a united front, at least to the outside world. This, then, explains the laborious negotiations begun in the summer and continued in the early fall which culminated in a conference in Moscow of eighty-one Communist parties. As late as 1965 the official Soviet source had the following to say about this meeting and the lengthy declaration made at it: "The Marxist-Leninist parties unanimously stated in the declaration of 1960 that the unbreakable law of relations among socialist countries consists in the observation . . . of socialist internationalism . . . of full equality . . . and comradely help."[73] But a more informative version was offered by the Central Committee of the Chinese Party in 1963:

> It is true that, both before and during the meeting, the leadership of the CPSU engineered converging assaults on the Chinese Communist Party by a number of representatives of fraternal parties, and relying on a so-called majority attempted to bring delegations of the Chinese and other Marxist-Leninist parties to their knees and to compel them to accept

[72] He travelled to the United States by boat. It might be asked why he was not replaced at this point. But his dismissal would have been taken both as a sign of capitulation to the Chinese and as an acknowledgment of the failure of Soviet policy on Germany.

[73] D. E. Melnikov, ed., *International Relations After the Second World War*, III (Moscow, 1965), 129.

its revisionist line and views. However, the attempts to impose things on others met with failure.[74]

The reader will be spared a detailed analysis of the 1960 declaration, a lengthy and ponderous statement of principles which in its crucial passages was ambiguous enough to warrant each side's claim that its views prevailed. Thus the statement on coexistence with the capitalist states could be interpreted in the Soviet way (hard but necessary in the atomic age or the Chinese (possible but unlikely, given the nature of imperialism). The rather vituperative passage about Yugoslavia and revisionism was undoubtedly a concession to the Chinese viewpoint, but the Soviets almost immediately made clear that they did not take this passage too seriously and proposed to treat Yugoslavia as a fellow, though somewhat aberrant, socialist country.

The subsequent quarrel as to who won the day in Moscow and who then broke the agreement reveals the incongruous childishness in which the eminently practical—nay, at times cynical—leaders of world Communism occasionally indulged. The important point about the Moscow meeting was not the painfully patched up declaration but the violent quarrel which erupted between Khrushchev and the leader of the Chinese delegation, the Secretary General of the CCP, Teng Hsiao-ping. The latter, this time before a wider audience than in Bucharest and in a more violent tone than Peng Chen's, took Khrushchev personally to task for libelling China and Mao, for being soft on capitalism, for favoring India in her dispute with China, etc.[75] That, having made that statement, the Chinese did not walk out was probably due to two factors. In the first place, few among the delegations were in sympathy with them, an overwhelming majority of the eighty-one pressing for at least an outward show of unity. Secondly, and more importantly, there was the Soviet economic squeeze. During the summer the Soviet Union had recalled all her industrial, technical, and scientific experts and advisers from China. (Some of them, the Chinese were to complain, took back with them the blueprints of the industrial plants whose building they were supervising or aiding.) If *any* trade or aid was to be forthcoming from Russia, the Chinese had to pay the price of at least outward agreement.

During the next year the two protagonists were able to vent their anger through a convenient third party, Albania. Long suffering under the Soviet *rapprochement* with Yugoslavia, fearful that the Russians would seal that understanding by making Tito a present of their country, the Albanian Communists finally found a more stable source of support. Enver Hoxha, the leader of the Albanian Party, emboldened by the Chinese attack, let go

[74] Quoted in Griffith, *op. cit.*, p. 404.
[75] Teng also was to be "unmasked" as an alleged "enemy of Mao" during the cultural revolution.

with an assault on Khrushchev that surpassed anything the Chinese had yet said, and he combined it with an emotional eulogy to Stalin, a wise Marxist-Leninist statesman slandered by the current leadership of the CPSU. Relieved to be provided with a less dangerous target than the ominous Chinese, Khrushchev's followers scolded the impudent Albanian for his "disgusting, shameful gangsterish attack,"[76] and the Chinese in turn defended Comrade Hoxha's "Marxist-Leninist position." Quite a family gathering! Thus was born the incongruous Chinese-Albanian alliance. It was reminiscent, in a way, of the far-off days of the nineteenth century when Tsarist Russia maintained cordial relations with the miniscule principality of Montenegro and an ambitious Montenegrin statesman had exclaimed, "We and the Russians are 150 million strong!" But the Crown Prince of Montenegro became the model for the hero of "The Merry Widow," and it is unlikely that a musical comedy will be written about Mao and Hoxha.

Why, it might be asked, were the Russians so eager to secure the Chinese signature on the declaration of the eighty-one parties at Moscow? At this precise moment the Soviets were escalating their pressure on the West, and even a mere appearance of unity with China was an important asset in obtaining concessions on Berlin and Germany. To be sure, stories of the scandalous goings-on would leak out, but officially the U.S.S.R. and China would stand shoulder to shoulder: the United States would then have less reason to interpret Moscow's threats as bluff. One-half of Khrushchev's grand design was lost, but perhaps the other half—obtaining the West's recognition of East Germany and its prohibition of atomic weapons for Bonn, or at least forcing it out of Berlin—might still be secured. And, in turn, these successes in Europe might persuade the Chinese to be more compliant. Strangely enough, the whole problem of Western rights in Berlin, which Khrushchev had originally raised in order to pry out of the United States and her allies the recognition of East Germany and/or the barring of nuclear weapons for West Germany, became increasingly the object of dispute in and of itself. We have seen that in the 1940's Churchill said that the Russians, finding a door shut, would try to pry it open; finding it bolted, would attempt to get through the window. Now, unable to do either, unable to obtain what they wanted (or, more properly, to prevent what they feared) in Germany by making a deal over China's nuclear development, the Russians tried a circuitous route. The route to Berlin was to lead through Havana.

But before discussing the momentous Berlin and Cuban confrontations, it is necessary to go back to the summer of 1960. Russia's increasing difficulties within the Communist bloc alone might well have inhibited Soviet foreign policy. But the West, through sins of commission and

---

[76] Quoted from Gomulka's speech, in Crankshaw, *op. cit.*, p. 133.

omission, continued to present the U.S.S.R. (as it had since 1945) with dazzling temptations and opportunities.

The problems of colonialism and decolonization have always been productive of peculiar masochistic and guilt-ridden responses in American public opinion. And so have been the cases of association with right-wing, dictatorial, or semi-dictatorial regimes that are clients or allies of the United States. A handful of State Department officials might murmur in private that one should not go borrowing trouble; that there were enough troubles and danger spots in the world already without adding dozens of African nations bound to lapse into anarchy upon the complete severance of ties with their former imperial masters; that a dictatorship like Batista's in Cuba, detestable though it was, did not pose a direct threat to American interests, that it could not be as long-lasting or oppressive to its own people as a left-wing one. But such worldly-wise—or, if one prefers, cynical—sentiments ran against a deeply held moralistic and democratic strain in the American tradition. Until World War II this latter theme in American foreign policy found expression mainly in verbal condemnations of the wicked ways of the Old World. But with the assumption by the United States of world-wide responsibilities, it became an active force both in the acceleration of the process of decolonization and in the dangerous direction that it took.

That the colonial systems of the European powers could for long have been preserved is, of course, most unlikely. It would also be incorrect to assume that American policies have been *primarily* responsible for their break-up. But American public opinion and even American policy-makers showed little comprehension of the complexities involved in bringing the colonial territories to statehood, little sympathy for the tasks and dilemmas of the colonial powers in trying to bring about this transition in an orderly way. The United States' competition with the U.S.S.R. enhanced rather than diminished the passionate anti-imperialist feelings in the American democracy, and the fullest possible national emancipation of every hitherto dependent territory was held to be the best prophylactic against Communism. This was an excellent general principle but, like most general principles, subject to exceptions and qualifications.

The "winds of change"—to use Macmillan's phrase—began to blow in 1960 with great force in Africa. The American predicament on this issue and the Soviet Union's superior maneuverability are well epitomized in the dialogue between Khrushchev and Kennedy which took place in Vienna in 1961:

Kennedy pointed out that the United States had in fact backed liberation movements in Africa and hoped that the number of independent

African states would increase. Khrushchev replied with scorn that American policy was uneven, its voice timid. It might endorse anticolonialism for tactical reasons but its heart was with the colonialists. Why not adopt the Soviet policy of tolerance and noninterference?[77]

Many years before, in 1919, Bukharin argued with passion that Communism inscribed among its postulates the liberation of all, even the most primitive, countries, "even the Hottentots and Bushmen," not because it believed that these countries would be able to become modern states, not to mention socialist ones, but for the purpose of embarrassing and weakening the main imperialist powers. In 1960 such frankness was out of fashion, but the Communist leaders most likely shared Bukharin's sentiments. In 1960 Belgium precipitately granted independence to the Congo, having done little to prepare its people for self-government. The resulting chaos and confusion led to the intervention of a United Nations force personally sponsored and supervised by Secretary General Dag Hammarskjöld. The subsequent tangled course of events provided the Russians with an opportunity to contrast their own anticolonialism with that of the West, and to assail the United Nations and its Secretary General, an untiring advocate of the cause of small nations, as tools of imperialism. "Here are the facts," said an official Soviet government statement of September 9, 1960:

> The imperialist powers . . . are pursuing a policy of fomenting civil war in the Congo Republic. . . . NATO countries and in the first place the United States . . . are openly attempting to discredit the legitimate government of the Congo Republic headed by Prime Minister Lumumba. . . . There has been formed a coalition of colonialists which aims to suppress the young African state—the Congo Republic—by the hands of African soldiers from Tunisia, Morocco, Ethiopia, and Ghana.[78]

The Soviets' direct stake in the Congo was small. It suited Soviet purposes to support first Patrice Lumumba and, after his murder, the group around Antoine Gizenga simply because they appeared to be more anti-Western than their rivals. But though the Soviet moves at first met with resistance from the majority of the then independent African states, the Russians' position on African liberation movements was bound to enjoy advantages over that of the United States. The U.S.S.R. could hardly be called an ally of the main imperialist powers. She could afford to be and was both more realistic and more demagogic than the United States: it did not evince surprise and pain from her that most of the new African states did not immediately embark upon a two-party democracy or that most of their leaders were not exclusively concerned with peaceful internal development and the improvement of their peoples' economic well-being.

[77] Arthur M. Schlesinger, Jr., *A Thousand Days: John F. Kennedy in the White House* (Boston, 1965), p. 364.
[78] *Documents on International Affairs, 1960,* pp. 294–98.

The example of the Soviet Union—supposedly a backward rural country that managed to industrialize herself in a hurry—held great attraction for the African intelligentsia. The U.S.S.R., unlike the West, did not proffer schoolmasterish advice—don't persecute the opposition, don't waste your resources on armaments, etc.—but, rather, she encouraged this exuberant behavior with a sort of avuncular indulgence; and consequently such ambitious rulers as Kwame Nkrumah and Sekou Touré soon found themselves closer to the Soviet bloc than to the generous but tiresome West.

To be sure, Soviet motivations and aims in Africa were often transparent and their methods clumsy. And despite the economic and technical aid she offered, Russia was to suffer spectacular setbacks in a number of cases: Touré became disenchanted, Nkrumah was overthrown. American Kremlinologists eagerly catalogued these setbacks as Soviet "defeats" in Africa and Western gains. But such verdicts are shallow and premature. The Soviet Union's main objective in Africa has not been the establishment of Communist regimes in this or that nation, but a deepening estrangement of African politicians and intelligentsia from the West and the prevention of any orderly pattern of political development, so as to keep this vast continent a source of division, conflict, and danger to the West. And on this count Soviet expectations have not been disappointed.[79]

The Congo crisis, combined with his insatiable appetite for travel, led Khrushchev to make another, this time uninvited, appearance in the United States. (Technically speaking, he was going not to that country whose President he had publicly insulted but to the international territory of the United Nations in order to make official recommendations about the reorganization of that international body.) He called upon other heads of governments to make the trip to New York, an invitation which was hastily followed by the heads of satellite governments, by such neutralist leaders as Nehru, Nasser, and Nkrumah, and finally and quite unwillingly, by President Eisenhower (whose main comforting thought during the waning months of his presidency must have been that he would not have to deal

[79] Following Lumumba's murder in 1961, the Soviets opened a university in Moscow bearing his name, intended especially to cater to African students. Despite special efforts to win over the future elite of Africa with large scholarships, etc., the exposure of the Africans to Soviet life has not always justified the official hopes. Many of the students who came to Lumumba University had had experience of a freer and more affluent life in the West, and instances of overt racial prejudice on the part of the Russians have not been infrequent. On the theory that young men often rebel against their environment, it would perhaps have been wiser for the Russians to count on *indirect* indoctrination, to which African students are subjected in Western universities through the exposure to the seamier side of Western life and through contacts with rebellious young Americans, Frenchmen, and Englishmen.

again with Khrushchev). Only General de Gaulle refused to attend a session of what he called "that thing the United Nations."

Quite likely, Khrushchev's private opinion of the institution was not different. But in provoking this descent of notables upon the United States (which was bound to complicate the life of the New York City police, embarrass the protocol division of the State Department, and infuriate his "old friend" Eisenhower), he was playing up to the expanding Afro-Asian bloc and attempting to secure its support. With the new nations joining the United Nations in droves, the days of American ascendancy there were over, and the Russians for the first time were becoming interested in the propaganda and other possible uses of the body—for which, as long as they had been hopelessly out-voted in it, they had had nothing but contempt. Still, this issue alone was hardly promising enough to warrant such threaticalities, or to explain the absence from the U.S.S.R. of her chief leader for a not inconsiderable period. It must be conjectured that both politically and personally Khrushchev was eager for a diversion. He was undoubtedly glad to be away from Moscow, where wrangling had already begun between the Russians and Chinese about the forthcoming conference of the eighty-one parties. Going to New York would obscure the fact that his Chinese and German policies were at an impasse, keep him in the limelight, and give him a chance personally to appraise Castro, who was also coming. (The Americans would have been hard put to decide which guest, the Cuban or the Russian, they disliked more.)

Predictably, the momentous meeting, which united (only in a fashion, since Eisenhower made certain that he would avoid a tête-à-tête with any Communist leader except Tito) more heads of governments than any other occasion in modern history, produced absolutely nothing. Khrushchev's expected bombshell turned out to be a dud: it was a proposal that the Secretary General's office be made into a commission of three men, one representing the Western, one the neutral, and one the Soviet bloc. This proposal failed to gain any real support among the Afro-Asian group to which it was supposed to appeal. Most of its members appreciated the United Nations as being in fact a pressure group on their collective behalf and a platform from which they could denounce in ringing tones the past and present evil deeds of their former masters. Secretary General Hammarskjöld was recognized by most of them not as an accomplice of the United States but on the contrary as a zealous (from the viewpoint of such countries as France, overzealous) advocate of the rights of the emergent nations. Khrushchev's other proposal—to transfer U.N. headquarters to Switzerland, Austria, or, if they should so desire, the Soviet Union—was plainly ignored. And in enunciating it Nikita Sergeievich showed lamentable ignorance of human psychology. What young representative, especially of a new nation, would exchange the exhilarating diversions of New York for the, alas, now provincial atmosphere of Vienna, or for Geneva, with its two night clubs? And as for Moscow. . . .

Embittered by the failure of his proposals and irritated by the restrictions placed upon his and some of his fellow Communists' movements (allegedly for security reasons),[80] Khrushchev responded with his most boorish behavior. Shouting and laughing during other delegates' speeches, the high point came during Macmillan's speech when he removed his shoe and banged it on his desk. Though other Communist dignitaries supported him in his outbreaks, he must have reinforced the feeling among some of his colleagues that Nikita Sergeievich was getting old and perhaps needed a rest. Still, those colleagues understood better than Western newspapermen the frustrations expressed in such behavior. From New York Khrushchev was returning home not to a triumphant reception but to another round of quarreling behind the closed doors of the international Communist meeting. And he was returning without any tangible victory that would enable him to chastise or temper the increasingly insolent Chinese.

The results of the New York expedition could not have been unexpected to the Russians. They could not have hoped for a meeting between their leader and Eisenhower; furthermore, in view of the latter's term coming to an end, such a meeting would have been pointless. Nor could the two meetings between Khrushchev and Macmillan produce any tangible results. The Prime Minister might convince himself and British public opinion—smarting under England's now frankly secondary role in world affairs and apprehensive about the leadership of the West being in the hands of the unsophisticated Americans—that he kept the "door open" for further negotiations. But Khrushchev was not interested in shutting it. He was waiting for the new American administration before he made his next move.

For the next two years, American-Soviet relations centered on the issues of Cuba and Berlin. It must, in the present state of our knowledge, remain entirely conjectural that, in the mind of Russian policy-makers, the two problems were connected, that by using Cuba they intended to gain vital concessions from the Americans on Berlin and Germany. But, as will be seen, there is strong *circumstantial* evidence that the Cuban crisis of 1962 was conected with the impasse in which the Soviets found themselves over Berlin, and that the gamble in Cuba, which bears all the traces of having been conceived by Khrushchev's fertile mind, was to bring them solid dividends in Berlin.

Prior to Castro's take-over of Cuba and his tempestuous flirtation and

[80] He, Kadar, Castro, and, ironically enough, the Prime Minister of Albania were confined to Manhattan.

then liaison with Moscow, Soviet policies in Latin America had been characterized by caution and self-restraint. The reasons for this are to be found only partially in the weakness of Latin America's Communist parties, the lack of an industrial proletariat, etc. For there is no doubt that the masters of world Communism would have viewed any ambitious Communist venture in Latin America with disfavor. Before 1933 recognition by, and after 1933 good relations with, the United States were considered by the Russians to be of infinitely greater importance than Communist successes in Mexico or Chile. The Americans had learned to tolerate their own miniscule Communist Party as a fact of life, but a Communist state in the Western Hemisphere would inflame the most sensitive nerve in the American body politic. Therefore, even in the most hopeful revolutionary situations, such as in Mexico in the 1930's, the Russians gave the local Communists no encouragement to strike out for power on their own. And the activities of Latin American Communists were but discreetly and infrequently reported in the Soviet and Comintern press.

This prudent policy was followed even after World War II, despite the greatly changed configuration of power and despite the cold war. The Soviets could not fail to take notice of such great assets for revolutionary activity as the rising tide of anti-American feeling among Latin America's intelligentsia and students, the vast social and economic problems of the continent, and the increasing importance of American capital (with the virtual elimination of its former rival the British financial interests), etc. Perón's regime in Argentina, with its anti-American orientation and populistic character, was undoubtedly viewed as a hopeful development. It was simply a question of timing that its ideological affinities were with fascism rather than with Communism. Had Peronism come to power in the 1950's it might quite conceivably have resembled Castroism. There is a note almost of nostalgia in the official Soviet appraisal of Perón:

> Perón's regime, especially during its first period, expressed to a large extent the national feelings of various elements of the population and especially of the bourgeoisie. . . . At intra-American meetings representatives of Argentina often opposed the designs of the United States to dominate completely the Latin American countries. . . . Perón and his followers had promised to defend national sovereignty from foreign interference.[81]

A sort of Latin American Nasser. But Stalin, unlike his successor, did not believe in overcommitment.

As late as 1954 in Guatemala, the overthrow of a regime that was thought to have pro-Communist leanings, which was accomplished largely

[81] A. G. Mileykovsky, ed., *International Affairs After the Second World War*, I (Moscow, 1962), 291.

with the help of the Central Intelligence Agency, brought but a feeble reaction from Moscow.

By 1959 such prudent behavior was no longer in fashion. The U.S.S.R. had made a successful bid for influence in the Middle East; she was not content to concede another sphere where Communism might skillfully exploit the local grievances and accumulated resentments of more than a century's domination by the "colossus of the North." Twisting the British lion's tail used to be a favorite game of the Comintern in the 1920's, but now this lion was old, and it appeared to be more exhilarating, possibly more profitable, to pursue a similar policy in regard to the United States. And, at a point where the Soviet regime appeared to be stymied on Germany, fate—or, to use a Marxist term, the forces of history—presented it with a rather unexpected opening: Cuba.

Since the American approach to the problem of Communism has traditionally been dominated either by a form of demonology or by a sense of guilt, American post-mortems of Castro's assumption of power are usually characterized by one of two rather barren themes: conspiracy (from the beginning, or from very early in the game, the young revolutionary was a Communist, a Moscow agent cleverly concealing his identity); or, "it is all our fault" (the young idealist, revolted by the American business domination and exploitation of his country, repulsed by the unfeeling Eisenhower administration, had no one else to turn to but the U.S.S.R.). The facts confound both stereotypes. *Fidelismo* was in the beginning a *sui generis* revolutionary movement of neither the leftist nor rightist variety. It started in 1953 as a madcap (and unsuccessful) revolutionary assault on an army barracks by a handful of young people. Following his trial, sentence, and release, Castro tried "invading" Cuba from Mexico late in 1956, and he successfully established a base in the Sierra Maestra, again with a mere handful of followers.[82] The main purpose of both ventures was to overthrow the increasingly oppressive Batista dictatorship; otherwise, it was very much a revolutionary movement in search of an ideology. Batista himself had begun his career as a leader of popular revolt. But after 1952, when he seized power unconstitutionally, he had become a dictator in the more traditional Latin American mold, ruling increasingly through police-state methods. He encountered growing opposition from various segments of the population, including some business interests.

To orthodox Communists the Castro movement was bound to appear as a juvenile exercise in revolution and not of great interest. Deeply ingrained in the Communist ideology is a dislike of *putschism*, a distaste for the idea that a small group of people can, through exhibitionist heroics, affect decisively the course of history and seize power in an armed coup without

[82] Theodore Draper, *Castro's Revolution: Myths and Realities* (New York, 1962), p. 11.

the social and economic conditions being ripe for it; the Communist Party of Cuba had vegetated for a long time in a typical Communist Latin American manner without showing signs of excessive ambition. At one time it had collaborated with Batista, who in 1943 appointed Communists to his cabinet.

In 1958 the Cuban Communists made secret contact with Castro, still in the mountains avoiding capture or destruction by Batista's forces. At that moment, he was far from heading a victorious guerrilla movement in the Chinese style; until the end of 1958 his forces did not surpass a few hundred men.[83] But Batista's days were obviously numbered; abroad and at home Castro was becoming known as the *symbol* of resistance to the tyrant. (In March the United States suspended arms shipments to Batista.) Under such circumstances a closer acquaintance and collaboration with the man who represented the wave of the future was clearly in order. Whether this *rapprochement* was suggested or authorized by Moscow is not known, but it would not have been surprising; for some time the Soviet line had been one of alliances with nationalist leaders—Sukarno in Indonesia, Nasser in Egypt, the FLN in Algeria. It was not yet clear into what category Castro might fall: would he, like Sukarno, tolerate and use Communists in his regime; would he, like Nasser (for all his pro-Soviet leanings) deal harshly with native Communists; or would he merely restore the pre-1952 democratic and constitutional liberties? The results of the investigations must have been favorable, since from mid-1958 on the Communists collaborated with Castro.

The rest of the story is well known. Confronted by widespread opposition and an imminent revolt, Batista fled without being overthrown in the technical sense of the word. The victorious opposition, including the most diverse elements—from Communists to dignitaries of the Catholic Church—invited the hero of the mountains to come ordain a new democratic Cuba. At the time of his triumph Castro still had fewer than 2,000 armed followers. Thus in no sense was the Cuban Revolution a triumph of a guerrilla movement turning into a mighty revolutionary army, as in China. It was a case of divergent social and political forces uniting to entrust their destinies to a man who had impressed them by his courage and whom most of them expected to exercise his leadership to re-establish a constitutional regime.

Quite apart from the real or alleged political sympathies of Castro or his closest lieutenants, such as his brother Raúl and "Ché" Guevara, such expectations from a man barely thirty years old and of no clearly defined political past were clearly the height of naïveté. And it was unreasonable to believe that, like a Greek hero of antiquity, Castro would be content to restore the liberties of his people and return to a humble station in life,

[83] In April 1958, by his admission, he had only 180 men. *Ibid.*, p. 41.

or that he would settle down as a constitutional head of state to be replaced at some future turn in Cuba's turbulent politics.

There were, on the other hand, cogent reasons for a dynamic young man with a sense of special mission to draw close to the Communists. In the first place, they provided a ready administrative cadre for needed social and economic reforms; the non-Communist intellectuals who surrounded Castro were like the proverbial Russian intelligentsia before the 1917 Revolution: "They could talk about everything, they could not do anything." In the second place, the Communists could dazzle the ambitious leader with the prospect of becoming a new Bolívar, an example for and leader of a continent-wide movement that would rid Latin America of Yankee imperialism. As against such prospects, all the Americans could offer was perhaps a loan and a lot of virtuous advice about holding elections, not executing former Batista officials *en masse* in an atmosphere of a Roman carnival, etc. Dictatorial regimes in the traditional Latin American style were becoming unfashionable and vulnerable to internal intrigues and American disapproval (witness Perón and Batista himself). In trying to compete for the allegiance of young dictators and revolutionary movements, the United States, quite apart from any deeper social and economic difficulties, found herself in the predicament of an older person gravely admonishing a youth to forsake drinking and wenching.

Within a few months of Castro's triumphant enthronement in January 1959, the drift of events became unmistakable, and his disillusioned non-Communist followers began fleeing to the United States, followed in increasing numbers by the dispossessed Cuban middle class. The official United States attitude throughout the next two years was to pass through the predictable phases of disenchantment with Castro, warnings about him, and, finally, scheming against him. What form the latter was likely to take could be surmised from the Guatemalan precedent. If the United States had felt compelled to sponsor and covertly assist the overthrow of a faintly pro-Communist regime in a distant banana republic (though close to the Panama Canal Guatemala was farther away and less strategically located than Cuba), was she likely to tolerate one that was rapidly and blatantly becoming not only leftist but pro-Soviet in a country ninety miles from U.S. shores? Rumors of developments that were eventually to result in an invasion at the Bay of Pigs were rampant even before March 17, 1960, when President Eisenhower in fact authorized the Central Intelligence Agency to form an anti-Castro coalition among the Cuban exiles and to prepare a force capable of guerrilla activities against his regime.[84]

The problem of whether and how far to embrace Castro's regime must have caused considerable debate in Moscow. Even in the free-wheeling era of Khrushchev it was undoubtedly debatable whether to extend support to

[84] Schlesinger, *op. cit.*, p. 226.

a regime headed by a political adventurer who was unlikely to be entirely reliable and subject to control. Some of the old-line Cuban Communists must have sulked at the prospect of being put, after many years of faithful service to the cause, in secondary positions to men who were, so to speak, "instant" Marxists, and must have objected to treating Castro not as the Kerensky but as the Lenin of the Cuban Revolution. The argument that they must do so in all probability hinged on the possible effect this would have on relations with the United States.

The extent of Soviet temptations (and reservations) on the subject of Castro is revealed by the fact of Anastas Mikoyan's visit to Cuba in February 1960. The Vice Chairman of the Council of Ministers brought with him Soviet promises to purchase a sizable amount of sugar for the next four years, a $100-million loan, and offers of technical assistance in the construction of industrial plants. In view of these boons, the statement made at the time about renewing diplomatic relations between the U.S.S.R. and Cuba[85] was exceedingly odd: the two countries agreed "to consider at an opportune moment the question of resuming diplomatic relations on terms of complete equality and independence."[86] Why not resume them then and there? They were in fact to be resumed only on May 8, 1960, seven days after the U-2 was shot down in the U.S.S.R.

This joint Cuban-Soviet statement was also unusually restrained inasmuch as it omitted the usual imprecations against imperialism, not to mention anything that could be taken as a criticism, threat, or warning to the United States. Instead there was some soothing language about the United Nations and "coexistence, cooperation, and friendship of all peoples of the world." And the key to the moderation of the statement (which must have disappointed Castro and his more fiery lieutenants) is found in the last sentence, where both parties piously place "well-justified hopes on the coming summit conference appreciably reducing international tensions, which today could hamper the prospects of freedom, prosperity and peace on earth."[87]

The collapse of the summit conference must have been as welcome in Havana as in Peking. The temptation for the Russians to embrace Castro closely and without reservations was now well-nigh irresistible. Vice President Nixon's opinion, given in the spring of 1959, that Castro was a "captive" of the Communists was both premature and one-sided; by the summer of 1960 it would have been equally true to say that Khrushchev became a captive of Castro. On July 9 Khrushchev exploded in a public speech: "I should like to draw attention to the fact that the United States is obviously planning perfidious and criminal steps against the Cuban

---

[85] They had been severed in 1952 by Batista.

[86] *Documents on International Affairs, 1960*, p. 534.

[87] *Ibid.*, p. 535.

people."[88] He now offered to buy from Cuba the sugar the United States was about to stop purchasing. Rocket-rattling, by now become an obsession with the Soviet leader, continued: "It should be borne in mind that the United States is now not at such an inaccessible distance from the Soviet Union. . . . Figuratively speaking, if need be Soviet artillerymen can support the Cuban people with their rocket fire, should the aggressive forces in the Pentagon dare to start intervention against Cuba."[89] Subsequently he informed the Americans that the Monroe Doctrine was a thing of the past.

In the autumn, Guevara made a trip to the Communist countries. Not content with stopping in Moscow, where he declared the solidarity of the Cuban Revolution with the declaration of the eighty-one parties, he saw fit to go on to Peking, where he spent two weeks. Guevara was never to be a Russian favorite after that. Since China could at this point give Cuba nothing either in terms of protection from the United States or in substantial economic help, Guevara's pilgrimage to Peking is good proof of the lack of sophistication that still prevailed in Castro's circle about intra-Communist relations.

The Cuban problem was to be the key issue in Soviet-American relations during the first two years of the Kennedy administration. Cuba was the occasion of Kennedy losing his balance, so to speak, in April 1961, with almost catastrophic results, and in turn the second Cuban crisis, of October 1962, of which we still don't know the full background, restored American foreign-policy-makers' balance and self-confidence. It is curious how these small countries—Cuba, Albania, Israel, Vietnam—provide the world with the most momentous crises, and how they have obscured and complicated the two major issues calling for the attention of the rival super-powers: Germany and China.

The new American administration was viewed by Moscow with mixed feelings. Khrushchev might well have flattered himself that he had helped to elect Kennedy by not allowing the Eisenhower administration credit for a successful summit conference and a relaxation of international tensions. And he greeted the new president courteously; some American pilots interned in Russia were released for the occasion. On the other hand, Kennedy's age and background were bound to irritate a Communist of Khrushchev's generation. And Khrushchev revealed his feelings (conscious or unconscious) when in a speech on internal Russian problems he interjected the irrelevant remark that he had not become the head of the Soviet regime by virtue of his papa's being a rich man. A strange psychological quirk has always made Communists prefer that the capitalists they deal with run true to type. Intellectuals and liberal capitalists make them intermittently nervous and contemptuous.

[88] *Ibid.*, p. 563.
[89] *Ibid.*, p. 564.

Though at the time of the break-up of the summit meeting Khrushchev had suggested that another one would be necessary in six or eight months, he did not appear very eager for it when the time was up. Kennedy, on the contrary, unlike his predecessor, was anxious to meet with and assess his opposite number. On February 22, 1961, Ambassador Llewellyn Thompson was dispatched in pursuit of Khrushchev, then on a tour of Siberia, with a letter suggesting a meeting in late spring in Vienna or Stockholm. On being handed the message on March 9 the Soviet leader was pleased, but he did not reply officially until May 12.[90] Here again Khrushchev displayed that fatal overcleverness in his diplomacy which frustrated his quite statesmanlike concepts. As long as the West had been reluctant to have a summit meeting, he had been an ardent suitor; as soon as he was pursued himself, his ardor cooled. Now he was waiting for the new administration to tip its hand on Cuba and on Laos. He must have been pleasantly aware of the nervousness created in Washington by his threats and boastings.[91] (The Americans were fortunately overlooking or ignoring that this reckless and apparently triumphant leader was incapable of imposing his will on Albania.) In the spring the Soviets would accomplish the first manned space shot, and the West's apprehensions would be increased.

The ill-fated Cuban venture that ended in April in the disaster of the Bay of Pigs undoubtedly increased Soviet self-confidence. It is most unlikely that Soviet Intelligence could have remained ignorant of the preparations carried on by the CIA for an invasion of Cuba: stories about mysterious doings in Guatemala, etc., had been appearing in the American press for some months. And on April 12 President Kennedy somewhat disingenuously hinted at both the nature and the limitations of the forthcoming venture. Said the President in a press conference: "There will not be under any conditions an intervention in Cuba by *United States armed forces*. This government will do everything . . . to make sure that there are no Americans involved in any actions *inside* Cuba." The recent indictment of a follower of Batista should indicate "the feelings of this country towards those who wish to re-establish *that kind* of an administration inside Cuba."[92] It is therefore at least remarkable that at no point did the Soviet government seek to warn the Kennedy administration either publicly or privately against sponsoring the Cuban enterprise. Such a

[90] Schlesinger, *op. cit.*, p. 343.

[91] A member of Kennedy's entourage has portrayed Washington's reaction: "Moscow had its own euphoria in January 1961 and the Khrushchev speech [of January 6] gave it truculent expression. The Soviet leader undoubtedly felt then and for the rest of the year, as he could never feel again, that Communism was riding the crest of history." *Ibid.*, p. 302.

[92] *Documents on International Affairs, 1961* (London, 1965), p. 18. My italics.

warning had been made in July 1960 when there was no reason to assume that an invasion was imminent; it was not repeated when solid evidence revealed that it was.

On April 17, with the invasion launched, the U.S.S.R. was prompt with a protest and a warning. But the two Soviet statements of April 18—one a message from Khrushchev to Kennedy, the other a general statement by the Soviet government—were quite circumspect in saying what steps the Soviets might take. There was talk about nuclear rockets, etc.: "We will extend to the Cuban people and its government all the necessary aid for the repulse of the armed attack on Cuba."[93] And the government statement called for the United Nations to take steps: "The Soviet government reserves the right, if armed intervention in the affairs of the Cuban people is not stopped, to take all measures with other countries to render the necessary assistance to the Republic of Cuba."[94] But it was only on April 22, with the invasion definitely defeated and the United States definitely committed to not following it up with any further action, that Khrushchev transmitted another, this time startlingly insulting, message to Kennedy.[95] In tone it managed to surpass the Soviet leader's utterances on the U-2 incident—not an easy thing: "aggressive bandit acts cannot save your system,"[96] etc. In view of this raving, how could Kennedy take at face value the eminently sensible statement: "We wish to build up our relations with the United States in such a manner that the Soviet Union and the United States, as the two most powerful states in the world, would stop saberrattling and bringing forward their military or economic advantage."

This "other," sensible Khrushchev may have been in evidence during the next few weeks, however, for they saw considerable de-escalation of the conflict in Laos, that picturesque Asian land that had threatened to become a major center of dispute between East and West. Neutralized under the Geneva Agreement of 1954, it had been the scene of a CIA intrigue that had helped to push out the neutralist government and thus "secure" its 2 million inhabitants "for freedom." Not for long, however, since soon the local Communists went on the attack, with the help of supplies flown from Russia. In March and April 1961, a sizable American intervention was seriously contemplated. Mercifully, however, a ceasefire was arranged in May, and the dispute was referred to the Geneva conference powers which, meeting again in Geneva, finally agreed on reinstating the neutralist Premier Souvanna Phouma at the head of a coalition government. Whether Soviet restraint in this issue was en-

[93] Ibid., p. 20.

[94] Ibid., p. 22.

[95] To be sure, Kennedy's message to him on the 18th hardly adhered to nineteenth-century standards of diplomatic intercourse.

[96] Documents on International Affairs, 1961, p. 33.

couraged by the relative unimportance of Laos, or by the fear of defying the United States still more after her Cuban humiliation, this problem in Southeast Asia appeared for the moment adjourned. Only very assiduous followers of the news could realize at the time how serious was the situation in South Vietnam and how extensive the American commitment in that country was becoming. The vicious circle continued: Soviet successes and pressures in the areas where America was most vulnerable— Cuba and Berlin—goaded the administration to display resolution in areas where as yet the issue had not been put sharply, notably Laos and South Vietnam. In addition, there was the usual American inability to do, or to propose to do, anything in moderation: to the incantations of massive retaliation, there succeeded a passionate interest in and desire to master the arts of "brushfire wars" and "counterinsurgency."

On May 12, to Kennedy's surprise and delight, Khrushchev answered his message of February and agreed to meet in Vienna. In retrospect, it is at least questionable that Kennedy should have agreed to a meeting so shortly after the Bay of Pigs humiliation and within three weeks of receiving the most insulting message that the Chairman of the Council of Ministers of the U.S.S.R. had ever sent to a President of the United States. But perhaps a critic of American policy cannot have it both ways: if he reproves Truman and Eisenhower for being reluctant about such meetings, he should not be harsh on Kennedy for his eagerness. Still, the timing was awkward.

The available evidence about the June 1961 meeting between the two leaders leaves little doubt that Khrushchev's intention was to frighten the young American President. One suspects that for some psychological reason of his own he went beyond his original intention in this respect. Kennedy's "let us be reasonable and discuss things in a businesslike manner" approach aroused passionate ideological diatribes. And when the President started to explain America's attitude toward social and political change, Khrushchev became sarcastic and offensive. There seemed to be no chance for Kennedy to achieve any kind of communication with the ranting Russian. Undoubtedly Kennedy had received all sorts of sophisticated advice from his Soviet experts—the trouble with his predecessors was that they did not appreciate Russian idiosyncracies, the Truman-Acheson approach had been too unrealistic, the Dulles line too inflexible, etc. Now, helplessly, he tried to talk first about the balance of power ("the Russians are realistic"), then about the American sympathy for change and decolonialization ("they believe we want to preserve the status quo"). Nothing worked.

On the most important concrete issue, Khrushchev turned the screw a bit tighter. If there was no German treaty forthcoming, he said, he would sign with East Germany in December. West Berlin would be a free city, but —and this was a small addition to the earlier Soviet position—if the West wanted to keep its troops there so would the Russians. Agreement on access would have to be negotiated with the East Germans.[97] On a nuclear test ban, the Americans would have to accept Russian conditions. The office of the U.N. Secretary General would have to be transformed into a commission of three. On matters that were to become public knowledge within a few months, Khrushchev lied, assuring Kennedy that Russia would not be the first to resume nuclear testing, and implying that Russia's relations with the Chinese were of the best (if he were in Mao's place he would have attacked Formosa a long time ago[98]). Attempts at small talk were unavailing: a reference to Walter Reuther brought a genial observation that the Bolsheviks had hanged people like him during the Revolution.

In retrospect much of this seems funny, especially if one remembers that at the time Khrushchev was in very much the same position vis-à-vis the Chinese that Kennedy was vis-à-vis him: pleading anxiously that they cannot *really* mean what they are saying, that they would not *really* risk nuclear war over a doctrinal point, etc. But, for the moment, President Kennedy could only conclude that the Russians meant to force the West out of Berlin and risk a nuclear holocaust.

Indeed, the Berlin issue was far from a laughing matter in the summer of 1961. The war of nerves was relentlessly kept up by Moscow, with a profusion of threats, menacing "off-the-record" remarks by Soviet diplomats,[99] and the like. Some classes of American reservists were recalled to active duty and defense estimates were increased; the Russians reciprocated with similar measures. On August 13 the East German authorities took radical measures to bar the egress of their citizens to the West: the Berlin Wall and similar barriers along the East German frontier effectively stopped further escapes of East Germans, of whom 3 million had already fled, many of them at the most productive age and in the most skilled professions.

The Berlin Wall could have been taken as an indication, and indeed it turned out to be one, of the Soviet Union's possible retreat from her intention of signing a treaty with East Germany and posing the Berlin question in the *most* menacing way. But the West—with its councils divided, the fear of all-out war now rampant—had to acquiesce in this gross violation of the Potsdam agreements. This in turn led to further Soviet threats and pressures: attempts to interfere with Western air communications with Berlin, actual confrontations between Western and Soviet tank units in Berlin which, though accidental, could easily have flared up.

[97] Schlesinger, *op. cit.*, p. 371.

[98] *Ibid.*, p. 364.

[99] Such as the observation made by the Soviet ambassador in Washington, Menshikov, that the treaty with East Germany had in effect been signed but that the American people would never fight over Berlin.

At the end of August, the Soviet Union announced her resumption of atmospheric nuclear tests; they continued for two months and culminated in the explosion of the most potent nuclear devices yet tested by any power. There can be no doubt that the intent to frighten the West still further was instrumental in the decision to resume the tests and that preparations for them must have been undertaken months before—certainly by June, when Khrushchev was assuring Kennedy that the Soviet Union would not be the first to break the unwritten ban on testing. The Soviet announcement on the resumption of tests made it painfully clear that any conflict, however insignificant, could grow into a universal nuclear war if the nuclear powers were drawn into it. The clarification of this thesis was for the benefit of those American planners who were anxiously debating whether and how a show of force with conventional arms could be employed to call a Soviet bluff over Berlin.[100]

Soviet tactics in the summer of 1961 and indeed throughout 1962 raise a very important and interesting question. Possibly Khrushchev believed that there was enough fear in Britain, and divided counsel and apprehension in Washington, for his tactics to work: the West would be forced out of Berlin. But to a man of his undoubted intelligence, the question must have remained, what next? The American public would not endure humiliation endlessly. There was a gleam of hope that the Americans might pack up and leave Europe—in Vienna Khrushchev returned to the theme that had been in Soviet policy-makers' minds for over fifteen years: Roosevelt's comment at Yalta that American forces would not stay in Europe for more than two years after the war—but one American defeat after another in the nuclear age was bound to lead to the result he most dreaded. Then why?

The only reasonable explanation appears to be that Khrushchev felt that a militant posture toward the West and a success in Germany would enable him to resume some degree of control over China's foreign policy and to reduce the Chinese incentive to acquire nuclear weapons. We do not know what the concrete premises were for his believing such a thing— perhaps there were none. But politicians in desperate straits resort to desperate measures. It could not wholly have escaped notice among the Soviet leaders that there was a strange paradox in their country proclaiming her readiness to risk nuclear war over Berlin, while at the same time a beggarly Communist Party in a tiny country defied the mighty U.S.S.R., threw out the Soviet navy, and executed pro-Soviet officers and Party officials without their being able to do anything about it.

[100] The Soviets seem to have been well aware of each stage of the American contingency plans and discussions in this crisis. This does not necessarily mean that they had special intelligence sources; Washington's agonizing dilemmas and plans seldom remained secret for long.

These contradictions were visible at the Twenty-second Congress of the CPSU, which assembled on October 17. The fearful world expected news of an imminent signature of a peace treaty with East Germany and a challenge on Berlin, but the ordeal of anxiety and hope was prolonged. Said Khrushchev: "We shall not then insist on having a peace treaty definitely by December 31, 1961. The main thing is to decide the issue, to liquidate the remnants of the war, to sign a peace treaty with Germany. That is the most important and essential problem."[101] For a time, the policy of pressure was relaxed. Khrushchev's language was still opprobrious (the West, previously referred to as "the capitalist nations," was now almost invariably described as the "imperialist" ones), his tone threatening (as in his relating of the latest and biggest Soviet atomic tests[102]). But there was a hint of moderation in the language about Germany and a strange though muted reference to what had been his design three years before. "We place great importance on the problem of arranging atom-free zones, in the first place in Europe and in *the Far East*."[103] It seems hardly credible that at this late date he still thought it possible to prevent or restrict Chinese nuclear armaments. Unlike his pronouncement of 1959, this one was not emphasized or underlined in the official protocol of the Congress.[104]

If Khrushchev was restrained by his standards in his references to the United States, then his foreign minister Gromyko adopted a tone of warmth that exceeded anything heard since the brief interlude of the "spirit of Camp David," if not, indeed, since World War II. Gromyko—speaking *after* Chou En-lai, who denounced the United States as the "worst enemy of peace" and the Kennedy administration as the "wiliest and most adventurist yet"—maintained that the Vienna meeting was one of the momentous events of modern times. "How happy [I] was to have participated in it! . . . One had to see with one's own eyes what happened in Vienna, in order to carry for the rest of one's life the memories of this event in which one was fortunate to participate."[105] Gromyko then launched into what on its face sounded like a plea for a Soviet-American alliance. "Our country places special importance on the character of the relations

---

[101] *Twenty-second Congress of the Communist Party of the Soviet Union* (Moscow, 1962), I, 45.

[102] They could try a hundred-megaton bomb, he said, but he had been told such a bomb would break windows in Moscow.

[103] *Twenty-second Congress of the Communist Party of the Soviet Union*, I, 46. My italics.

[104] To repeat the January 1959 pronouncement: *"One can and must create in the Far East and in the whole Pacific basin a zone of peace and first of all an atom-free zone."*

[105] *Twenty-second Congress of the Communist Party of the Soviet Union*, II, 337. President Kennedy would have agreed, for a different reason.

between the two giants—the Soviet Union and the United States. If those two countries united their efforts in the cause of peace, who would dare and who would be in a position to threaten peace? Nobody. There is no such power in the world."[106] This truth, Gromyko assured the delegates, was plainly recognized in the United States; a man in the street in New York would tell you without hesitation that peace will be secure if only Khrushchev and Kennedy could reach an agreement. And there were warm words about the President.

Such honeyed words could bring little comfort to Washington, for the Americans had their own memories of Vienna and were aware that Khrushchev's threat over Berlin was not discarded but merely suspended. Gromyko's remarks were more than balanced by the threats of Marshal Malinovsky, who "joked" that Soviet long-range missiles were more accurate than medium-range ones, etc. Yet Gromyko's words, coming as they did from a man in a conspicuous position but relatively low in the Party hierarchy, had undoubtedly been carefully authorized by the top leadership. Some of his statements contained a clear challenge to Peking: thus Gromyko called "wise and sober" the statement of Secretary of State Rusk that "problems of world security depend equally upon the Soviet Union and the United States as the two largest countries in the world."[107] And he called on the leaders of the two nations to "harvest the fruits of the great victory" of World War II. Quite a contrast to Chou's assessment!

There were probably at least two reasons for the amazingly conciliatory tone of Gromyko's speech. The first was the need to quiet the apprehensions of his listeners. Passages in Khrushchev's speech and all of Malinovsky's may well have created a somewhat panicky feeling among the delegates to the Congress and the foreign guests, who were not privy to the tortuous designs of their leaders—a fear that nuclear war with the United States was in the offing. Now the delegates could go back to their factories, farms, and offices reassured that their regime would do nothing foolhardy. In the second place the speech was obviously designed to be read in Washington as saying: don't let de Gaulle and Adenauer persuade you into adopting an absurd "let us be firm on Berlin" posture. A bit of give and take (more on the give side!) will enable you to enter a real partnership with the U.S.S.R., to open up the vista of peaceful settlement on a large number of issues. Why let the minor problem of Berlin, of recognition of the facts of life in East Germany, stand in the way of such a development?

If so, Gromyko's speech completely failed of its intended effect. The passages implying the possibility of the United States and the U.S.S.R. jointly solving the world's problems were probably read with a great deal of interest in Peking and Paris, but they were virtually ignored elsewhere.

[106] *Ibid.*, II, 343.
[107] *Ibid.*, II, 344.

How could it be otherwise, in view of the still ominous tone of major Soviet pronouncements, of the almost daily threats and provocations about Berlin, even after Khrushchev's extension of the time limit on the German settlement. Was the Gromyko speech, then, merely a smoke screen to soften Washington's stand without offering anything in return? It is important to draw attention to one interesting characteristic of Soviet diplomacy: whenever it seeks a large-scale accommodation with another Great Power, it operates initially through rather vague hints leaving it to the other side to spell out details and mutual concessions. In the sequence of events leading to the Molotov-Ribbentrop pact, desperate though the Soviet government was for an agreement, it was the Germans who had to initiate the concrete proposals and insist on the timetable. Even after Stalin, Soviet statesmen showed an almost pathological fear of baring their real anxieties in the field of foreign policy, of hinting at any internal or external vulnerabilities. Up to a point this wiliness, born of suspicion, nourished by the weakness and isolation of the Soviet state during the first decades of its existence, served the Russians well. But in the nuclear age, with its rapidly changing and hazardous course of international events, it was a dangerous legacy.

Of this truth the Twenty-second Congress offered a startling example. As we have seen, Khrushchev, in his conversations with the American leaders, had tried valiantly to preserve the fiction of the "unshakable unity of the socialist camp." By his lights, a free admission of the U.S.S.R.'s desperate difficulties with China would weaken her bargaining position on Germany; it might even encourage the Americans to fish in troubled waters and pursue a more conciliatory line toward Peking. (If he thought that, he underestimated, alas, the rigidity of American foreign policy.) But complete adherence to this fiction was by October 1961 impossible. There was no Albanian delegation at the Twenty-second Congress, and this absence was clearly ordained by the Chinese. To ignore or gloss over its defiance would mean an unheard-of loss of face for the First Secretary. He thus launched upon a violent (if confused) attack on the leaders of the Albanian Communist Party, giving as the main reason their disapproval of Soviet attacks on the cult of personality and Stalin.[108] And in his concluding remarks, he elaborated with a personal attack on Hoxha and Shehu and their barbarous ways of dealing with intra-Party opponents.

To begin with, Khrushchev rather naïvely had not mentioned the Chinese-Albanian tie-up. (Many in the same room undoubtedly still remembered his remarks at the Twenty-first Congress, two and a half years before, when he had said that revisionists [Yugoslavs] spread absurd rumors about "alleged differences between the Communist Party of the Soviet Union and that of China. . . . Those are illusionary hopes destined

[108] *Ibid.*, I, 108.

to utter collapse. . . . We are fully in agreement with the fraternal Chinese Party."[109] Just as you cannot see your ears, so you will not see such differences, Nikita Sergeievich said then.) But for their own reasons the Chinese were not going to let Khrushchev get away with this. For the first time in decades, a Party congress heard open criticism of its highest leader, an unmistakable attack upon official policy. Said Chou: "Open and one-sided attack upon any fraternal party does not contribute to solidarity, does not resolve the problem. To expose openly a dispute among fraternal parties and fraternal countries for enemies to see cannot be considered as a serious Marxist-Leninist approach."[110] Then, while the Congress was still in session, and having deposited a wreath on Stalin's tomb inscribed "to the memory of a great Marxist-Leninist," Chou ostentatiously returned to Peking. Here, equally ostentatiously, the entire leadership of the Chinese Party (including Mao himself) greeted him at the airport—this to dissipate any lingering doubts that his attack might not have been authorized.

Restrained though the challenge was, it was real. Chou's words could be read by millions of Soviet newspaper readers. Few could believe that the real issue was Albania. The challenge had to be accepted. In his concluding remarks at the Congress, Khrushchev repeated his attack on the Albanians, and added sarcastically that if the Chinese cared so much for the unity of the bloc they should persuade the Albanians of the errors of their ways. Whether the enemy was watching or not, the Communist Party of the U.S.S.R. was not going to let foreigners interfere with its internal politics. The "great Marxist-Leninist" J. V. Stalin was now abruptly removed from the place of honor next to Lenin, his mummy reburied in the Kremlin wall with a host of lesser lights. Who knows? There might have been voices suggesting that it be sent with the Chinese guests to Peking!

The Congress, which was supposed to center on the triumphant note of the new Party program announcing the entrance of the Soviet Union into the Communist phase of development by 1980, thus developed a sour note. Ever experts at diversion, the Soviet leaders now intensified the attack upon Stalin and upon the hapless anti-Party bloc of 1957. This was flogging a dead horse, but now that Chinese objections to de-Stalinization were in the open, they went undoubtedly beyond their original intentions. The dead dictator was no longer a man who, after useful service to the cause, began in 1934 to commit errors. He was now depicted as a ruthless and paranoid tyrant from the beginning of his leadership. Khrushchev implied Stalin's complicity in the murder of Kirov. His associates Malenkov,

---

[109] *Twenty-first Congress of the Communist Party of the Soviet Union*, p. 109.

[110] *Twenty-second Congress of the Communist Party of the Soviet Union*, I, 326.

Molotov, and Kaganovich were portrayed as criminals and murderers. Grisly details of their crimes, shocking stories of their intrigues even after Stalin's death, were now revealed for the whole nation to read and hear. This undoubtedly went beyond what many of the Soviet leaders thought prudent, but Khrushchev realized how popular was denunciation of the past, and how it would obscure and turn attention away from his failures in foreign policy.

Superficially, the Congress marked the highest point as yet in the ascendancy of Nikita Khrushchev; other leaders eulogized him in terms almost reminiscent of the "cult of personality" (none more so than his eventual successor Leonid Brezhnev). But there were barely perceptible fissures in the highest leadership. Though several speakers called for the ejection of Molotov, Malenkov, and Kaganovich from the Party, if not indeed for their trial, no announcement to this effect was made at the Congress.[111] Khrushchev stressed that his speeches and proposals did not merely express his personal sentiments but were in pursuance of decisions taken by the Presidium and Central Committee. "Not one major undertaking, not one official pronouncement is the product of a personal preference but of consideration and decision by the collective [leadership].[112] This was becoming modesty, to be sure, but it must also have reflected a desire to liquidate rumors that certain decisions reflected Khrushchev's own preferences and aroused dissent within the leadership. Yet the very stress on this point surely aroused suspicions among the more knowledgeable delegates. After the Congress was over, measures that could logically have been expected were not taken (an exemplary punishment of Molotov et al.), there were vague hints in the press of a faction that believed in still more vigorous liquidation of the consequences of Stalinism—and all these facts strongly support the view that the "unshakable unity of the leadership" was somewhat in the way of the "unshakable unity of the socialist camp." One suggestion of Khrushchev's was certainly his own and certainly unworkable. The Party, he said, should build a monument to all the victims of the cult of personality, on which would be inscribed all their names. How could you build a monument large enough?

The conclusion that Khrushchev's personal position was vulnerable was soon reached in Peking and Tirana. On November 4 Enver Hoxha, at a meeting of the Albanian Communist Party, violently abused the First Secretary: "blackmailer" and "slanderer" were some of the milder epithets

---

[111] Molotov was a special target of attacks. It was implied that in some way he was involved with the Chinese ("he was fishing in troubled waters" was the euphemism). That the by now aged and thoroughly discredited Molotov was in a position to indulge in an international intrigue was more than doubtful, but it made a good story.

[112] *Twenty-second Congress of the Communist Party of the Soviet Union,* II, 591.

this leader of the Lilliputian state applied to the head of the regime of one of the world's two super-powers. For all the personal incentive that Hoxha had in thus paying Khrushchev back in kind, the main tenor of his remarks must have been established in Peking. What precisely was to be accomplished by this piling up of invective is difficult to decide. Knowing the deep national pride of the Russians, nobody could imagine that the Presidium of the Communist Party of the Soviet Union would remove its leader in answer to a vituperative attack by an Albanian. The Sino-Albanian attacks may have in fact prolonged Khrushchev's tenure of office. But, as usual, there was a degree of system in the apparent Chinese madness. The Sino-Soviet split was now in the open, but few as yet could gauge its depth or permanence. Through the convenient Albanian intermediary, the Chinese could pressure the Soviets without at the same time barring the road to reconciliation. Yet to obtain the latter the Russians would have to make concessions—whether material ones to China, or indirect ones in the form of assuming a more militant posture vis-à-vis the West. The Soviet leadership was thus caught in a vicious circle: in order to obtain concessions from the West, it thought it had to preserve *some* appearance of unity in the Communist bloc; in order to obtain China's agreement to go along with the game, it had to be militant, which jeopardized any prospect of reaching a peaceful resolution of the issues it considered most urgent. It was in order to break out of this vicious circle that the U.S.S.R. in 1962 devised a most ingenious plan, which brought the world even closer to nuclear war.

As one observes the course of Soviet foreign policy throughout 1962, one cannot but conclude that the priorities in the minds of the Soviet leaders were as follows: (1) to prevent China from acquiring nuclear weapons, or somehow to limit and control Chinese nuclear armament; (2) to prevent West Germany from acquiring such weapons, which in turn led to (3) the signing of a German peace treaty which would perpetuate the division of Germany and secure a limit on West Germany's war potential.

As to Point 1, it would seem fantastic, as we have seen, that at this late date the Soviet leaders were still hopeful of persuading the Chinese or denying them something they were absolute determined to obtain. Even in 1958, such hopes were probably forlorn. But as against all that had happened since and as against plain logic, there were still some developments that could keep alive the hope of Chinese compliance, especially in the minds of people who desperately wanted to believe in it. In the first place, China was then enduring a severe economic crisis, the backwash of the "great leap forward," with famine sweeping large parts of the country. In addition the Chinese, in contrast to their openly insolent and defiant tone in 1963, were in 1962 (at least until the Cuban missile crisis) clever enough not to dash Soviet hopes completely or to cut off their channels of communication. *Perhaps* a dazzling Soviet success in the international arena, a demonstration of continuing Soviet dynamism in foreign policy, might persuade the Chinese comrades to trust their nuclear defense to the Russians and to abandon their excessively costly and strategically futile efforts to become a nuclear power?

These hopes may appear as the epitome of naïveté, especially in people as hard-boiled as members of the Presidium of the Communist Party of the Soviet Union. Yet the actual arguments they used with the Chinese, as revealed by official documents, are almost embarrassing in their disingenuousness. As late as the summer of 1963 they were to argue plaintively:

> China is as yet unprepared to produce nuclear weapons in quantity. Even if the People's Republic of China were to produce two or three bombs, this would not solve the question for it either, but would bring about a great exhaustion of China's economy. . . . That is why the most reasonable policy for the People's Republic of China in present conditions . . . would be to devote its efforts to the development of the national economy . . . devoting them to improving the well-being of the Chinese people.[113]

The message was plain: Why do you need atomic weapons? We are protecting you anyway, and we will unselfishly go on producing nuclear weapons to thwart the imperialists; you had better concentrate on producing rice and soybeans! Such arguments must have been greeted with a mixture of fury and amusement, but evidently until the fateful days of October 1962 the Chinese, while stoutly resisting the Soviet leaders' cajoling, left them hoping that *something* might make them change their minds.

Public controversy between the Chinese and the Soviets was stilled, then, in the first months of 1962—largely on the initiative of other Communist parties, for whom the dispute was of course a source of embarrassment and danger. But this also suited Chinese needs and Soviet hopes. A new Sino-Soviet trade agreement, of modest dimensions, was signed. Even the polemic between the Soviet Union and Albania grew less acrimonious, although Albania was thrown out of the Warsaw Pact and Comecon; the Soviets were not going to let the Chinese lead them by the nose. And they were not going to let the Chinese dictate their policy toward Yugoslavia either. Yugoslavia *per se* was not of an overwhelming importance to them, even though Tito was an important confidential adviser and guide to such neutralist leaders as Nasser and Sukarno. But a *rapprochement* with Yugoslavia was a useful reminder to the Chinese not to press the Russians too much; after all, Yugoslavia could liquidate Albania overnight. In April Gromyko visited Belgrade.

[113] Griffith, *op. cit.*, p. 363.

In the West, the Sino-Soviet dispute was needless to say completely over-shadowed by the German problem. The Berlin crisis continued with inci-dents, notes, and harrassment, the Soviets never letting the bothersome issue disappear from the front pages for long. Khrushchev, incorrigibly, con-tinued to titillate and terrify the West with his musings. There were several ways to gore the ox, he implied. He might still sign a separate treaty with East Germany; or there might be just enough accidents in the air ap-proaches to Berlin to persuade people that it was not a safe place to travel to, enough difficulties on the land routes to dissuade people from investing in such a vulnerable location; how sad, then, that West Berlin would become impoverished and depopulated.

Had the Russians been solely interested in Berlin *as such*, it is clear that they could have continued such nervewracking tactics indefinitely, and it is far from certain that they would not have succeeded in securing some change of status for West Berlin. There was considerable division of opinion in the Western alliance—ranging from Olympian disdain on the part of General de Gaulle to Britain's noticeable nervousness. In Washing-ton the young President was subjected to conflicting advice and countless position papers trying to establish what the Russians were really after, how one could stand firm on Berlin and yet minimize the chances of a nuclear war, etc. In fact, for the Soviet policy-makers Berlin was but a promising tool for prying out of the West a more fundamental concession on the German question: an iron-bound guarantee against West Germany getting nuclear weapons.

Soviet fears on this count have never been properly understood in the West, and hence no attempt has really been made either to assuage Soviet susceptibilities on this score or to use the possibility of giving nuclear weapons to Bonn as a bargaining asset. This is so partly because of certain inherent trends in American diplomacy and in the nature of the Western alliance, but also partly because of the difficulty of assessing Soviet thinking on the relationship of nuclear weapons to politics. The Soviets cannot *really* be alarmed by the prospect of Bonn having a few tactical nuclear weapons, ran the prevailing view in the West. Given their own vast superiority in such weapons and rockets, and given the smallness of West Germany, the Russians ought to realize that nuclear weapons in the hands of West Germany could only be purely defensive. Hence, if they really make a fuss about this, it must be for other and devious purposes. But to the Soviets, who would not give one atom bomb to the Poles or Hungarians, the problem necessarily appeared in a different light. What if a nuclear-armed Bonn threatened East Germany? Would the U.S.S.R. have to launch a pre-emptive attack, thus risking American retaliation? Would she have to launch a suicidal attack on the United States? As to the possibility of a "small" nuclear war, the U.S.S.R. had to think in political terms: against a *small* nuclear power she would undoubtedly emerge victorious; but could a *Communist regime* survive such a war? What would be the consequences of even one nuclear missile falling on Moscow and destroying the top leadership of the Party and state? That the Russians were genuinely afraid of West Germany possessing atomic weapons was acknowledged somewhat contemptuously by the Communist Chinese in their polemic in 1963. The German issue, then, by 1962 had merged with the problem of "nuclear proliferation."

The Soviets had learned to live with the inescapable—if not exactly comfortable—facts that the United States was a nuclear power and so, in a much smaller way, was Britain. They also realized, if never stated, that, short of some "madmen in Washington" getting their hands on the trigger, the United States would not use her nuclear weapons except under extreme provocation. Therefore the Soviet position on nuclear disarmament had long been that in view of the existence of the two hostile systems such disarmament was, to put it succinctly, impractical, and indeed Soviet participation in the endless international talks on the subject was mainly for propaganda purposes. With the acquisition of a nuclear arsenal of their own, the Soviet leaders evidently concluded that since their nerves were stronger than those of the democracies the continuing nuclear race would redound to their advantage—witness Khrushchev's rocket-rattling. Soviet quantitative inferiority in this race was not considered to vitiate this point. The agitation aroused in the United States during the presidential campaign of 1960 by the issue of the alleged missile gap, the alarm caused in 1961 by the civil-defense (shelter) proposals of the new administration, could be adduced as additional proof of the correctness of this analysis: the capitalists are much more frightened of nuclear war than we *seem* to be.

Once nuclear proliferation became imminent, this Soviet equanimity was shaken, and Soviet interest in nuclear disarmament became real. Soviet spokesmen continued to pay lip service to the idea of complete nuclear disarmament, prohibition of nuclear warfare, eventual destruction of existing nuclear weapons, etc., but the practical difficulties were rightly judged insuperable. The more modest steps, such as a test ban, were evidently thought of little consequence: in 1958 it suited the Soviets to initiate a moratorium on atmospheric tests, but in 1961, when political and possibly technical reasons urged them to resume testing, they did so without compunction. Humanly enough, they were undoubtedly concerned about atmospheric pollution, which reached new heights after the massive tests in 1961 and 1962. But the main incentive to explore what they had previously rejected contemptuously was the welcome prospect of preventing other countries, especially China and West Germany, from acquiring the dreaded weapons. In 1963, after the signing of a partial test ban treaty between the U.S.S.R., the United States, and Great Britain, the Chinese publicly attacked the Russians and their motives in signing the pact. To be sure, the charges were highly colored and exaggerated—viz., the allegation that the Soviet leaders were betraying the interests of their own people and no longer cared whether Bonn acquired nuclear arms or not—but the main Chinese point was that the Russians' primary objective was to find some means of preventing China from acquiring the weapons. If we add "and West Germany," we are close to the truth.

How could a test ban signed only by the three nuclear powers accomplish this objective? On the face of it, the treaty would just be an agreement not to test nuclear weapons; it would not ban their further manufacture or, if the powers should so decide, their endowing other states with the armaments. But the treaty could be—and was—open to ratification by other states, which in signing it would *practically* forsake their right to produce atom and hydrogen bombs (an *untested* weapon is not a reliable one). Furthermore, it is clear that the Soviets were hopeful that the treaty would and could be expanded into a rigorous nonproliferation agreement banning the nuclear powers from sharing their weapons and know-how with third parties, and imposing upon the latter an obligation not to develop nuclear weapons of their own.

The following Chinese statement contained in the Russo-Chinese exchange of 1963 deserves very careful reading:

> On August 25, 1962, two days before the United States and Britain put forward their draft treaty on the partial halting of nuclear tests, the Soviet Government notified China that U.S. Secretary Rusk had proposed an agreement stipulating that, firstly, the nuclear powers should undertake to refrain from transferring nuclear weapons and technical information concerning their manufacture to non-nuclear countries, and that, *secondly, the countries not in possession of nuclear weapons should undertake to refrain from manufacturing them,* from seeking them from nuclear powers or from accepting technical information concerning their manufacture. *The Soviet Government gave an affirmative reply to this proposal of Rusk's.* The Chinese Government sent three memoranda to the Soviet Government on September 3, 1962, *October 20, 1962,* and June 6, 1963, stating that it was a matter for the Soviet Government whether it committed itself to the United States to refrain from transferring nuclear weapons and technical information concerning their manufacture to China; but that *the Chinese Government hoped the Soviet Government would not infringe on China's sovereign rights and act for China* in assuming an obligation to refrain from manufacturing nuclear weapons. We solemnly stated that we would not tolerate the conclusion, in disregard of China's opposition, of any sort of treaty between the Soviet Government and the United States which aimed at depriving the Chinese people of their right to take steps to resist the nuclear threats of U.S. imperialism, and that *we would issue statements to make our position known.*[114]

[114] *Ibid.,* p. 351, my italics.

It is impossible to exaggerate the importance of this statement. Of immediate relevance here is the light it throws on the Cuban missile crisis, which was ripening and then occurred during the very period when the exchange of notes was taking place between Moscow and Peking (August 25, September 3, October 20).

Is the Chinese statement true, or is it a product of their paranoia about the United States and Khrushchev ganging up on them? The *facts* alleged in it have not been denied in the Soviet rejoinders. Yet we know that in 1962 no agreement between Russia and America on a nuclear test ban was reached. Disarmament talks in Geneva dragged out inconclusively throughout the year. The *apparent* issues preventing agreement were those of inspection and of verification—the Americans holding out for several annual inspections of nuclear sites, the Soviets for none or very few, etc. At the *end of August*, the Russians turned down the latest of the Anglo-American proposals: either for a complete test ban or for one on atmospheric tests alone. The vagaries of the Soviet position—at one time close to agreement, at another resolutely opposed to it—were blamed in Washington on the same factors besetting the American side: the opposition of some military and scientific advisors who were unwilling to relinquish the right to test their toys.

The mystery deepens when we consider that there is no record on the American side of Secretary Rusk making proposals of the kind described in the Chinese statement and certainly none of the Soviet government agreeing to them. That the Russians at the time would or could have stopped China from gaining nuclear armaments must have been held in Washington as an unachievable dream; any Soviet hint to that effect would have been trumpeted very loudly. What, then, is the truth?

Secretary Rusk and Gromyko were in Geneva in late July 1962 for the signing of the final agreement on Laos. There they engaged also in talks on nuclear disarmament, with the usual inconclusive results. The disarmament talks recessed on September 7. The wider issues of disarmament and of the test ban were to be discussed at the meeting of the U.N. General Assembly in late fall. Now, it is quite likely that in an informal discussion Rusk mentioned the subject of nuclear proliferation and that Gromyko responded, confining himself to his usual noncommittal grunts. Hardly a proposal, hardly "an affirmative reply" by the Soviet government!

As we have seen, the evidence is clear that the Soviet government hoped *somehow* in the summer of 1962 to prevail over China's determination to become a nuclear power. It is less certain, but highly probable, that the alleged "Rusk proposal" was in fact manufactured in the Kremlin. Despite China's first (and presumably violent) reaction on September 3 to "Rusk's proposal," Moscow must have persisted with it, for another Chinese protest had to be dispatched on October 20. By this time, the nature of the "somehow" was becoming clearer.

The Soviet Union's decision to install missiles capable of carrying atomic warheads in Cuba must have been taken sometime around the beginning of July 1962. Around the same time Raúl Castro, Fidel's brother and Cuban Minister of Defense, was in Moscow. It is improbable that he was told *exactly* what kind of missiles the Soviets would install and *quite* improbable that he was told for what purpose; the Cuban leaders—notably Fidel—were always running on at the mouth, and they were probably simply told that the Russians would supply some defensive missiles, the details of which they need not worry about. The Cubans' understandable concern as to what was happening in their own country was no doubt responsible for the dispatch of Guevara to Moscow at the end of August; from the *Russian* viewpoint, there was every reason not to draw attention thus to the strange doings in the Caribbean island. On that occasion an official Soviet communiqué acknowledged that to protect Cuba from "aggressive imperialist" threats, the Soviet government would send armaments and technical specialists to train Cuban servicemen.[115] On September 4, in view of the increasing agitation in the United States over the volume of Soviet shipments to Cuba, President Kennedy issued a statement that American intelligence sources had learned that the Russians were setting up in Cuba "anti-aircraft defense missiles with a slant range of twenty-five miles," radar, etc., and that they were sending military technicians to Cuba (3,500, Kennedy estimated, were already there). The President stressed that as far as was known, no Soviet bases or "offensive ground-to-ground missiles" had been or were being installed. "Were it to be otherwise the gravest issues would arise."[116] (The same day, Ambassador Dobrynin conveyed through the Attorney General a most unusual message to the President: Khrushchev pledged that he would not stir up any international incidents before the American congressional elections in early November!) An official Soviet release one week later fell in with Kennedy's statement. All the shipments to Cuba were purely defensive. Why should the U.S.S.R. need a missile base near the United States? If need be, "the Soviet Union has the capability from its own territory to render assistance to any peace loving state, and not only Cuba."[117]

As an American overflight of October 14 was to reveal and further investigations to confirm, the Soviet Union was in fact constructing twenty-four launching pads for medium-range missiles (500–1,000 miles) and

---

[115] Henry M. Pachter, *Collision Course* (New York, 1963), p. 175, quoting a *Tass* communiqué of September 2.

[116] *Ibid.*, p. 176.

[117] *Ibid.*, p. 177.

sixteen for intermediate-range ones (1,000–2,000 miles).[118] There has been considerable dispute about the technical details, but not about the indubitable fact that if they had been completed, a large part of the United States would have found itself within the range of atomic attack from Cuba.

Now, the question of timing is important in analyzing the Soviet reasons for all these things. The dispatch of equipment and specialists must have begun months before, possibly before July, but the fateful step of erecting missile sites and emplacing the missiles could not have begun much more than one month before the United States' discovery of them, i.e., in early September (before that time American overflights revealed only anti-aircraft missiles). The CIA had quite reasonably assumed that the Russians would not proceed to build long-range missile sites until "an operational network of SAM's (anti-aircraft missiles) would make their detection from the air difficult."[119] The conclusion must be that the planning and preparations for the installing of the long-range missiles had been going on for some time, but that the actual decision to install them was taken only in the early days of September and then in a great hurry, forsaking the usual precautions of elaborate camouflage and erection of an extensive anti-aircraft missile network.

Two events of early September may be connected with the Soviet decision hurriedly to put into effect the plans prepared for so long but not yet executed (possibly because of last-minute hesitations and realizations of the vast risks involved): (1) the receipt of the Chinese note of September 3; (2) Khrushchev's decision to attend in person the meeting of the United Nations in late November. Not content with his message of September 4, Khrushchev had his ambassador meet with one of the President's closest advisers, Theodore Sorensen, on September 6. Ambassador Dobrynin, seemingly unnecessarily, repeated that the Russians would do nothing "before the American Congressional elections that could complicate the international situation or aggravate the tension in the relations between our two countries."[120] But *after* that, the Soviets insisted, the problems of a German peace treaty and Berlin must be finally solved, and Khrushchev would, most likely, come at that time to the United States to address the United Nations.

There is therefore a very strong presumption that for some time the Soviet leaders had been toying with the idea of installing nuclear missiles in Cuba and, around the beginning of September, were seized with an irresistible desire to solve the most gruelling dilemmas of Soviet foreign policy

---

[118] Schlesinger, *op. cit.*, p. 796.

[119] Theodore C. Sorensen, *Kennedy* (New York, 1965), p. 673. And the President's Special Assistant adds, "Why the Soviets failed to coordinate their timing is still inexplicable."

[120] *Ibid.*, p. 667.

with this one bold stroke. Once in Cuba, the missiles would become negotiable, their removal conditional upon the United States' meeting Soviet conditions on the German peace treaty and other pressing international issues. Appearing in New York in November, Khrushchev would present to the world a dramatic package deal resolving the world's most momentous problems: the German peace treaty, containing an absolute prohibition against nuclear weapons for Bonn; and a similar proposal in reference to the Far East, where the Soviets would demand a nuclear-free zone in the Pacific and, under this guise, extract a pledge from China not to manufacture atomic weapons. This second part was of course the weakest point of the Soviet scheme. It was unlikely that the Chinese Communists would agree to any limitations on their freedom to manufacture and test nuclear weapons, and evidently they at least implied this in their note of September 3. But the Russians could hope that by their dramatic coup they would create an atmosphere in which the Chinese would have to reconsider. In addition, part of the price the Americans would pay for the removal of the Soviet missiles in Cuba could well be the withdrawal of their protection from Formosa. This would add an almost irresistible incentive for the Chinese at least to postpone their atomic ambitions.

No other explanation fits the tangled story of the Cuban missile crisis or accounts for the risks undertaken by the Soviets at that precise moment. Granted the stakes involved, the risks were not too unreasonable. That the whole operation was undertaken just to force the West out of Berlin is clearly unreasonable. What would it avail the U.S.S.R. to have Berlin become a free city, if the United States equipped West Germany with nuclear weapons? That the operation was undertaken simply to protect Cuba, as Khrushchev was to "explain" later, is as fantastic as it is mendacious, and the best commentary on this explanation is provided by a party not overly friendly to the United States. Said the Chinese Communists in 1963, repeating their taunts of the preceding year: "Before the Soviet Union sent nuclear weapons into Cuba there did not exist a crisis of the United States using nuclear weapons in the Caribbean Sea and of a nuclear war breaking out. If it should be said that such a crisis did arise it was a result of the rash action of the Soviet leaders."[121]

As for the risks involved, the Russians displayed touching faith in the peacefulness of the American government and people. If, as Soviet propaganda has held, there was a hotheaded faction in Washington eager to loose a nuclear war on the world, held in check only by the combined strength and peaceloving policies of the U.S.S.R., then it was reasonable to fear that with Washington's first inklings as to what the Russians were doing, there would be an atomic attack not upon Cuba but upon the source of all

[121] From an official statement of the Chinese government, September 1, 1963, quoted in Griffith, *op. cit.*, p. 383.

trouble, the U.S.S.R. proper (especially since, as both sides knew, the United States enjoyed a considerable edge in intercontinental ballistic missiles). Yet evidently this contingency was not considered likely, for special emergency measures were announced only after the crisis was in the open; perhaps something would have leaked out if special precautions on civil defense, etc., had been taken in September and early October. Of course there was bound to be a wild wave of excitement and indignation in the United States at the revelation that sixty-four atomic missiles were pointed at the United States from Cuba, but since Khrushchev thought that *he* would make this revelation, he also believed its effect would immediately be countered by his simultaneous generous and far-reaching proposals, for accession to which he would remove the deadly weapons. Warming to his task and to his appearance in the United States, Khrushchev must have thought that in the long run the Americans themselves would be grateful: his gambit would resolve the German problem, remove or delay China's acquisition of atomic weapons, and lay the foundations for far-reaching measures of disarmament. If the Russians were guilty of deception, was it not true that the Americans had really started the game by placing nuclear missiles in places like Turkey, closer to the boundaries of Russia than Cuba was to the United States? The Soviet move was a necessary one to dramatize to the American people the dangerous game their own government was playing and to break the impasse in which the obduracy of de Gaulle and Adenauer had placed America, against the best interests of the American people themselves.

It could be argued, against this construction, that if the ultimate Soviet objectives were so reasonable they could have been reached through negotiations. The Soviets could have intimated that a reasonable American stand on a German peace treaty would induce them to pressure the Chinese, etc., etc. But the inherent flaw of Soviet diplomacy is exactly its unwillingness to divulge its own dilemmas and weaknesses. Any revelation of how serious the Chinese problem was could, the Russians thought, make the Americans harden rather than weaken their position on Germany and on disarmament. One year later, at the signing of the partial test ban treaty and with the Sino-Soviet dispute now in full swing, Khrushchev still refused to talk about China to Harriman. "China was another socialist country, Khrushchev said, and he did not propose to discuss it with a capitalist."[122] And by the fall of 1962 it was probably realized that it was useless to try to *persuade* China to change her intentions concerning a nuclear role. The last hope was to stage a dramatic coup—at one blow achieving aims that had eluded Stalin: a German peace treaty and the removal of American protection from Formosa—that would illuminate the power and dynamism of the Soviet Union and create an atmosphere in

[122] Schlesinger, *op. cit.*, p. 908.

which no Communist country, not even China, would dare object to her proposals. If the Chinese raised objections, the U.S.S.R. would stand justified before the whole socialist bloc in maintaining that she had done all she could to help Peking restore her sovereignty over Formosa; if the Chinese did not like the conditions, they could henceforth deal with the United States by themselves.

The great difficulty was the possibility of a premature revelation of the missile build-up. Extreme secrecy was therefore essential on the Soviet side. Evidently no satellite leaders were told of the scheme. (The Chinese statement on this subject was most explicit: "Without consulting anybody you willfully embarked on a reckless course and irresponsibly played with the lives of millions upon millions of people."[123] Certainly had the Chinese known, they would not have started their frontier war with India at the same time.) Still, as the Russians must have realized, the odds were strong that the news would leak out. The Cubans had to be told that *some* kind of missiles were being installed, and, being the people they were, they were bound to talk, as indeed some of them did. Furthermore, with refugees streaming out of Cuba and with American overflights, the chances of the CIA being left in the dark until a moment in late November when Nikita Khrushchev, broadly beaming, rose in the United Nations, were indeed very slim. But here the Soviets counted—and gravely miscalculated—on the vagaries of American politics and the supposed weakness of President Kennedy, who they believed would not want to rock the boat before the Congressional elections. With naïve Machiavellianism the Soviet leader kept telling the President to go ahead and concentrate on the elections without worrying whether his pal Khrushchev would do anything untoward. It was not inconceivable that he misjudged the character of the man to the point where he believed that even were the administration apprised of the facts it would still suppress them rather than face the dreadful choice between acquiescence or war on the eve of the elections. To an oversubtle mind, the President's statement of September 4 (made in the face of widespread rumors and Republican charges) that the weapons being installed in Cuba were purely defensive would lend credence to this theory. Some of the devices used by the Soviets to lull the administration were amateurish in the extreme, and they do not indicate a high regard for American intelligence: a Soviet diplomat friendly with New Frontiersmen would drop indiscreet hints as to what Khrushchev and Mikoyan had been telling him about how placing long-range missiles in Cuba was the farthest thing from their minds, and so on. Expectation in Washington of a forthcoming crisis centered mainly around West Berlin. And it was in connection with this perennial problem that the President obtained an authorization from Congress to call up the reservists. A Congressional resolution in September

---

[123] Griffith, *op. cit.*, p. 384.

asserting the American determination to prevent Cuba from becoming a military base directed against the United States was not taken seriously in Moscow.

The Cuban crisis developed swiftly, as far as Washington was concerned. Evidence of Soviet surface-to-surface missiles in Cuba was presented to President Kennedy on October 16. His announcement of a blockade of Cuba—"quarantine" was the euphemism used—was made simultaneous with the release of this information on October 22. Thus Soviet intelligence sources had no opportunity to alert their government about the dramatic turn of events. On October 18, the President held a long-scheduled meeting with Foreign Minister Gromyko, who had been at the United Nations and was about to return home.[124] The President did not tip his hand. Gromyko concentrated on Berlin and the German peace treaty, problems which, he stressed, must be solved promptly after the elections on November 6. Otherwise the U.S.S.R. would be compelled to sign a treaty with East Germany. "It was his personal view and the view of Premier Khrushchev that if the Berlin problem were only resolved then there would be no other questions, except possibly disarmament."[125] He raised "obliquely" the possibility of a meeting between Khrushchev and Kennedy later on in the year. On Cuba Gromyko was insistent that Soviet activity there was not connected with any offensive intentions against the United States. But the United States should watch her step: Why were the Americans agitated? How could Cuba become a danger? The Soviet minister could not resist the temptation of being a bit threatening. "This was not the nineteenth century, it was not 1812, and the calling of 150,000 reserves had no military significance. Modern weapons had changed all that."[126] And so the conversation went. Its gist was no different from the conversation between Khrushchev and Ambassador Foy Kohler two days before in Moscow.

Readers of *Pravda* during those October days could not have suspected that a momentous crisis was in the offing. On October 21, the paper printed Yevtushenko's poem "On Stalin's Heirs"—"Oh double triple the guard, that Stalin should not rise again"—with its references to Stalinists still in positions of influence. In licensing its publication Nikita Sergeievich probably contemplated with pleasure how his forthcoming triumph would enable him to dispose of his remaining opponents. On October 23 *Pravda* carried for the first time disquieting news from the United States: military and naval activity in the Caribbean. The ruling circles in the United States were playing with fire! On October 24 the bombshell of Kennedy's speech given in the evening of the 22nd was finally out. Russian readers were

[124] The story of the conference, from an officially inspired account, is given in Pachter, *op. cit.*, pp. 188–92.

[125] *Ibid.*, p. 190.

[126] *Loc. cit.*

given only the gist of the Americans' "piratical" intentions in instituting a blockade of Cuba, of the American decision to search for and turn back all shipments of offensive weapons to Cuba. But for the Soviet *leaders*, the most impressive part of the President's statement was that passage in which he declared that any nuclear missile launched from Cuba would lead to a full retaliation by the United States directed also upon the U.S.S.R. Almost as important was the clear implication that unless the missiles were quickly removed the United States would take steps against Cuba—invasion, air strike, or both.

The official Soviet response, judging by the report of actions taken on October 23, was one of alarm and some bewilderment but not of panic. An official statement hinted that the "technical weapons" provided to Cuba for her defense could not be removed. It then must have aroused the deepest anxiety among Soviet citizens, perhaps unmatched since June 1941, when the government announced that it was taking steps to prevent the country "from being caught by surprise" and enabling her to be in a condition "to give a worthy answer to the aggressor." The Ministry of Defense proclaimed an alert for the rocket, air, and submarine branches of the armed forces and cancelled all leaves. An alert was ordered for Warsaw Pact forces. Still, there was a gleam of hope for the Soviet citizens on that gloomy day: Khrushchev and members of the Presidium chose to attend a gala performance of *Boris Godunov*. Jerome Hines, an American, sang the title role exceptionally well, stressed the official communiqué, and was personally congratulated by the First Secretary and his colleagues. Probably never in history was the singing of one man so much comfort to so many people. If the Soviet rulers went to the theater to enjoy an American's singing, was it conceivable that nuclear missiles could be launched against the United States?[127] On October 24 Khrushchev found time to have a lengthy talk with a visiting American businessman, a fact duly recorded in the press, and he sent a hopeful letter to Bertrand Russell, the elderly philosopher, who had begged him to save mankind.

As if the situation were not sufficiently involved and dangerous, at precisely this time the Chinese decided to teach the Indians a lesson and launched on October 20 a large-scale offensive on two sectors of their disputed frontier in the Himalayas. The cause of the attack was the continuous border flare-ups between the two countries, but its intensity was perhaps due to the Chinese irritation over the increasingly friendly relations between Russia and India and with their suspicions that the former might be thinking of building up the latter as a counterweight to them in Asia. Some time before, the Soviets had contracted to provide India with their

---

[127] One of the minor characters in the opera happens to be named Khrushchev, a nobleman who in the wave of anarchy then enveloping Russia is seized by peasants and beaten.

latest jet engines. Now, within a month, the Chinese were to trounce the Indians decisively, explode the myth of India's potential as a Great Power, and show that they could have occupied at will large parts of Assam if not indeed Bengal. During and following the Cuban crisis, the U.S.S.R. could confine herself to advising both sides to be reasonable, and the Indians to accepting China's rather humiliating conditions for a cease-fire.

The basic Soviet decisions were evidently made on October 23. The U.S.S.R. was not as yet bowing to the blockade; a probe was under way to find out what could be saved from the venture; a hastily mounted propaganda campaign stressed the danger to *Cuba*. "Wisdom should prevail," ran the *Pravda* headline on October 26—this in reference to Secretary General Thant's proposal that the blockade be postponed while Soviet shipments were stopped. In Cuba, work on the missile launches proceeded at a frantic pace in evident preparation for the "cooling off" period proposed by U Thant. Khrushchev's private letters to Kennedy on October 23 and 24 evidently[128] reflected this hope of being able, through the U.N. and "world public opinion," to induce the United States to accept the status quo and abandon her tough attitude. On October 25, however, it was decided that the game was up: the U.S.S.R. would yield. This is the gist of the letter President Kennedy received on October 26 from the Soviet leader (also never published), described by Sorensen as "long, meandering, full of polemic, but in essence appearing to contain the germ of a reasonable settlement: inasmuch as his missiles were there only to defend against invasion, he would withdraw the missiles under U.N. inspection if the U.S. agreed not to invade."[129] There must have been a strong temptation in Moscow to save something from the ghastly miscalculation—perhaps a blockade of Berlin with a simultaneous appeal for an immediate summit meeting—but it undoubtedly was quickly dismissed.

In Moscow, October 27 was a day of obvious relief, judging from the press headlines: the usual Soviet stuff about new production records and achievements, exhibitions, and Party gatherings. But in Washington it was a day of extreme anxiety, for another, this time public, letter from Khrushchev was received, and it proposed a swap of the U.S. missile bases in Turkey for the ones in Cuba. The relationship of this letter to the one received on October 26 has never been clarified. But, simultaneous with the dispatch of the first letter or right after it, the Russians must have taken notice of the suggestions in the Western press that the by now obsolete missile sites in Italy and Turkey be swapped, as a face-saving concession to the Russians. On October 28 Khrushchev's second letter was printed in full in *Pravda*, accompanied by a drawing showing the locations of American bases all over the world.

[128] Their text has not been released.
[129] Sorensen, *op. cit.*, p. 712.

By October 28, as we know, the crisis, or at least its major aspect, had been resolved. Kennedy had accepted Khrushchev's suggestion in his earlier letter of October 26; Khrushchev in turn abandoned the idea of getting a dime where he had hoped originally for a jackpot—the Turkish bases were forgotten. The President's message of October 27 was printed in full in *Pravda* on October 29, and with it Khrushchev's answer: "The motives which led us to give Cuba weapons are no longer valid." The missiles would be removed, the launching pads dismantled. "We have lived through the most difficult week since World War II," said *Pravda*'s columnist and Khrushchev's confidant, Yuri Zhukov.

Public attention all over the world was drawn naturally to the details of the Soviet withdrawal, about which there was most of all enormous relief. But to the Soviet leaders, the Cuban fizzle represented much more than was realized in the West; it was the collapse of the most comprehensive and far-reaching policy design effected in the Soviet Union since the end of World War II; and it was now necessary to pick up the pieces and rethink the whole problem. To Khrushchev personally, it was a disaster from which he was never to recover. It is unimportant in this connection whether he himself thought up the plan[130] or somebody else. He was the boss, and in retrospect the Cuban gambit was considered as a prime example of his "hare-brained schemes."

There were, first of all, minor if perplexing difficulties with the alleged cause and object of the whole operation: Castro. The irascible Cuban leader finally understood what the Soviets had been doing on his island and, perhaps, why. His initial reaction was that he would not submit to any inspection made to ascertain whether the missiles had been removed; then that the United States would have to meet some fantastic demands of his. Privately he was alleged to have said that, if he could have, he would have beaten up his Soviet benefactor. Mikoyan was dispatched to try his Armenian wiles on the insubordinate Cuban, and for weeks he had to plead with and cajole Castro, not returning even to the bedside of his dying wife.

From the moment the whole story of the Soviet missiles in Cuba became public, Khrushchev had had to stress, just as much for the benefit of his people as for the Americans', that the weapons were and would always be strictly in the hands of Soviet military men.[131] That somebody like Castro might have his hand on the button of a nuclear device was enough to send shivers down the spine of any Soviet officer. But in addition the

[130] Any more, say, than whether it was Stalin who had thought up the details of collectivization.

[131] This reinforces the presumption that they were put in Cuba only to be removed after a bargain; not even a considerable Soviet military force in Cuba could *absolutely* guarantee the safety of the devices.

Russians had given Cuba planes capable of carrying nuclear bombs; they were, Khrushchev later said—probably truthfully, for a change—in a speech of December 12, obsolete and to be used for defensive purposes only (i.e., *without* atomic bombs). But the Americans insisted on their removal, and the Soviets wearily agreed by November 20 to force Castro to give up the planes—which, unlike the missiles, were supposed to have remained his own. All in all, most embarrassing.

But there were more serious repercussions. The most dangerous moment was hardly over when one by one the satellite leaders descended on Moscow in a series of one-day visits. They had undoubtedly been shaken and now were curious as to what had been going on and why the "Fatherland of Socialism" had not kept its friends informed as to the dangerous games its leaders were playing. In Peking, the resolution of the missile crisis had been greeted with sheer delight. When the crisis was on and war threatened, the Chinese had duly supported the Russians with flamboyant declarations, but now that it was over, even their indignation took back seat to amusement at the discomfiture of Khrushchev and his fellow revisionists. Why was it necessary to put the missiles in Cuba? To defend Cuba? Sheer adventurism! Once you put them there, why did you have to pull them out? Sheer capitulationism! You accuse us of being reckless, but for a political gamble you endanger the whole of mankind! On November 7, the anniversary of the Russian Revolution, Mao and the other Chinese leaders were conspicuous by their absence from the celebrations at the Soviet embassy in Peking. At the festive gathering in the Kremlin, the official guest list indicated that in their predicament the Soviet leaders were not neglecting any possible source of help and comfort: for the first time in a long while, the Metropolitan of Moscow and members of the higher clergy were among those invited and present.

To be sure, there were countervailing factors and elements of comfort in the collapse of the Cuban operation. To his people, as well as to such people abroad as Bertrand Russell, Khrushchev may well have appeared as the man who saved the peace and avoided the catastrophe of nuclear war. The sense of having been so close to danger made the likelihood greater—alas, for a short time only—of the United States and Russia pressing forward to settle the most urgent issues. The Soviet leader's letter to Kennedy of October 28 mentioned such possibilities as a *détente* between NATO and the Warsaw Treaty countries, a prohibition on atomic and thermonuclear weapons, etc.

But as the danger receded, the Soviet leadership had to take realistic stock of the damage done and of the future prospects. Any hope of constraining China's nuclear armament was now wholly lost. The other part of the original design, the securing of a German peace treaty, also had to be abandoned. This was no time to start dangerous new games over Berlin. Even such a relatively minor gambit of Soviet foreign policy as the proposal to turn the Secretaryship General of the United Nations into a three-man commission was abandoned. For the time being, the gambling instincts of Soviet policy-makers were drained away.

On December 12 Khrushchev addressed the Supreme Soviet and gave for the first time a comprehensive version of the Cuban missile affair. The speech was not notable for its candor: it was the Cuban government that during the past summer had requested the missiles, said Khrushchev, and Russia put them there for the "defense of Cuba," making sure that they were under the control of Soviet military officers. On October 27, he said, the Soviet government had received information that unless a settlement was made within two or three days Cuba would be attacked; once having received a pledge from Kennedy that Cuba would not be attacked, the U.S.S.R. had no reason to keep the missiles there. Khrushchev was more honest in answering his own question: who won? "Prudence, peace, and the world's security have won." He painted a realistic picture of the horrors that had been averted: Russia could have survived a nuclear war, but tens of millions of people would have died. As to the taunts about "capitulationism," Khrushchev in his turn became sarcastic: the Albanians "and those who support them" chide Russia for her withdrawal, and they call themselves Marxist-Leninists! Does anybody call the Chinese cowardly because they tolerate foreign occupation of Hong Kong and Macao? Or take the Chinese withdrawal to a cease-fire line after their Indian campaign: *some* might say this was done because China was afraid of the United States and Britain; but Khrushchev thinks it was wise moderation.[132] And, in further defiance of Peking, he stressed Russia's warm relations with Yugoslavia (whose leader was in the audience).

Though Khrushchev continued to insist that the problem of West Berlin must be solved and a German peace treaty signed, he stated these requirements without giving any time limits or making any bombastic threats. One passage in his speech gives a clue that his internal position was now more vulnerable: the Party will continue to denounce Stalin's errors, he said, but acknowledges his "historical merits." It was a sober speech, in which relief and a degree of zest were balanced by awareness that there were no quick solutions to the most perplexing problems facing Russia in her relations with the outside world.

---

[132] Some time later, the Chinese Communists, never at a loss for the last word, answered that Khrushchev did not mention *all* the remnants of colonialism tolerated *for the time being* by the Chinese: how about the territories wrested from China by *Russia* from the seventeenth to the nineteenth century?

The events following the Cuban crisis did not justify the fervent hopes expressed at the end of those anxious October days that an important milestone in U.S.-Soviet relations had been reached, marking the beginning of an era of real coexistence. This was so because of many factors, but mainly because of China. The missile crisis marked the collapse of the last attempt by the U.S.S.R. to *control* in any meaningful way the foreign policy of the other Communist giant. Attempts at a *détente* with China were made again in the spring of 1963 and following Khrushchev's ouster. And, in a sense, even the ever more violent dispute between the two countries does not rule out the possibility of such an attempt being made again or even being, for a time, successful. The harsh words exchanged so often between the U.S.S.R. and Yugoslavia have not prevented the two nations from drawing together at other times. But it is precisely this example that is instructive. *Never* after 1948 was the U.S.S.R. to regain full control of Yugoslavia's foreign policy—and this despite the vast disproportion of power between them. An agreement between China and the U.S.S.R. will never restore the relationship (which was ceasing to exist even before Stalin's death) that had been based on Soviet domination.

This change in the basic relationship with China was to inhibit Soviet foreign policy in other areas. Not primarily, as is sometimes argued, because the Soviet leaders were so afraid of being denounced by the Chinese as fainthearted that they had to be especially pushful; not because they had to be sure that the New Zealand, North Korean, and other Pacific Communist parties would not line up against them. When the interests of the Soviet state are at stake, a united chorus of all the Communist parties of the world against them would not make them budge. But, as we have seen, the Soviet leadership considered the fiction of unity of purpose in the world Communist movement to be of importance for the survival of the Soviet Communist regime. Hence the problem of either containing China within the Communist camp or somehow expelling her has absorbed the Soviet policy-makers to the point where other issues have become secondary. Were the Kremlin to confess what it undoubtedly feels—that the major threat to the security of the Soviet Union is China and not the United States—it is not what foreign Communist notables would say but the Soviet citizens' reactions that would be of concern.

This unhappy dilemma thus curbed the Soviets' freedom of movement in making foreign policy. As we have seen, it was fondly hoped on the American side that the resolution of the Cuban missile crisis would be followed by Soviet willingness to meet at a summit conference or, at least, to make far-reaching proposals on disarmament.[133] But in fact his passion for summit meetings temporarily abandoned Khrushchev. On disarmament,

---

[133] On December 19 Khrushchev wrote to Kennedy: "The time has now come to put an end once and for all to nuclear tests." Schlesinger, *op. cit.*, p. 895.

the hopeful prospects failed to materialize, and discussions settled down once again to the problems of on-site inspections, etc.; much of the previous Soviet zest for such an agreement was now lacking. And indeed, at least half of the original Soviet motivation was gone, for the Chinese would never agree now to stop their nuclear-weapons development. There was a very faint hope that *maybe* a test ban agreement would somehow shame the Chinese into a form of compliance, but common sense told the Soviet leaders that this was wishful thinking. Was it then worth signing an agreement with the United States and Britain and bringing down upon themselves the inevitable violent outpouring of Chinese abuse? A test ban agreement might have an inhibiting value in regard to West Germany, but the Americans for all their talk were apparently not going to give Bonn nuclear weapons after all. Still, there were cogent secondary reasons to have an arrangement that might slacken the pace of the armaments race. The Soviet economy was in difficulties throughout 1962 and 1963, and a reduction in the defense budget was highly desirable.

One form of nuclear proliferation that the Russians viewed with concern was the proposal for a multilateral nuclear force in NATO (the MLF), with which Washington planners hoped to appease the French and German ambitions for nuclear weapons without at the same time adding new members to the "nuclear club." Anything involving German participation in the disposition of atomic weapons, however "internationalized" the decision-making, aroused the Russians' deepest fears.

All these considerations entered into the series of negotiations that led to the agreement of July 25, 1963, in which the United States, the Soviet Union, and Great Britain agreed not to test nuclear weapons in the atmosphere, in outer space, or under water. The unsolved problem of how inspections would be made made it impossible to extend the ban to underground testing. The Russians would agree to no more than three on-site inspections per year, any presence of foreign observers on Russian territory going against their grain, and the Americans insisted on more. The dilemma was solved by exempting underground testing from the treaty and by abandoning the whole issue of inspection, since atmospheric explosions were detectable without it in any case.

Negotiations over the test ban treaty in Moscow overlapped with Russo-Chinese discussions held, allegedly, to explore the possibility of the two nations resolving their disagreements.[134] There is probably a reason for this coincidence. The likelihood of reaching an agreement with the West, the Russians may well have thought, would make the Chinese more amenable. But the most that could be hoped for was a papering over of the continuing disagreements and a moratorium on mutual public abuse. Since

[134] The Sino-Soviet talks were July 5–20; the U.S.-U.S.S.R.-British ones, July 15–25.

at least March, Peking and Moscow had made accommodating noises to each other. The Chinese expressed interest in having Khrushchev visit them; the Soviets in return extolled the beauties of Russia in spring and summer—wouldn't Comrade Mao take this occasion to travel in the U.S.S.R. and acquaint himself with the people? Both leaders spurned the invitations. (If, as was to be alleged in Peking in 1966, Mao was at this time engaged in a desperate struggle to preserve his hold on the Party against the faction headed by Liu Shao-chi, Soviet solicitations for a lengthy visit may well have been motivated by reasons other than the desire to show him the beauties of their vast country.) But the main reasons for the refusals were the question of prestige and the strong personal aversion that Khrushchev and Mao held for each other. The conversations were therefore conducted without the participation of the top men— the Chinese delegation being headed by Teng Hsiao-ping, the Soviet one by Suslov—and were adjourned without any tangible result on July 20. Five days later the test ban treaty was initialled, and Khrushchev entertained Harriman and Lord Hailsham with ostentatious cordiality.

The theatricalities of hostility both before and after the break-up of the negotiations[135] somewhat obscure the fact that the Soviet leadership had been careful not to burn all their verbal bridges to China. Ambassador Harriman's hint that the test ban treaty should be supplemented by one forbidding the transfer of nuclear weapons from one country to another was, undoubtedly sorrowfully, rejected by Khrushchev. The Chinese were going to raise a storm, he knew, over the test ban; to include a non-proliferation provision would drive them to frenzy and to making the kind of revelations he feared. But even after the failure of the Sino-Soviet talks and in virtual certainty that new public displays of controversy would issue from Peking, Khrushchev refused to discuss China with Harriman. The American diplomat kept probing: "Suppose we can get France to sign the treaty. Can you deliver China?" Khrushchev replied cryptically, "That is your problem." Harriman tried again. "Suppose their rockets are targeted against you?"[136] The usually voluble Soviet leader was silent. Not only was the problem insoluble, but he was now probably under some constraint from his Russian colleagues. It would be fantastic to suppose that a "pro-Chinese faction" existed in the Presidium, but many of its members probably wished that the dispute would cease to be publicized and that Nikita Sergeievich would stop aggravating the already difficult situation by his constant popping off.

But Khrushchev's unusual discretion did not improve the matter. Neither

---

[135] Such as the Russians' expulsion of some Chinese diplomats and students who had circulated the Chinese letter of June 14, 1963, in Russia, and Chou En-lai's personal welcome of these men on their return to Peking.

[136] Schlesinger, *op. cit.*, p. 908.

China nor France was to sign the treaty. That West Germany did sign was a gain.[137] There was scant consolation in the fact that about one hundred other countries did sign, since a vast majority of them could not produce a jet engine, much less a nuclear bomb. On the American side the treaty was hailed as a major breakthrough in the cold war.[138] But in Moscow it could arouse neither elation nor deep apprehension. The major objective of all the Soviet maneuvering on nuclear disarmament during the past five years was still out of reach.

Khrushchev's delicacy about China—his desire to propitiate her by not attaching explicit nonproliferation provisions to the treaty—availed Russia but little. What the Chinese had had to say about their Soviet comrades before the treaty were now surpassed with a cascade of abuse unequalled in the intra-Communist epistolary tradition since the memorable correspondence between Yugoslavia and the U.S.S.R. in 1948. Much of the correspondence, which has already been cited, bears on relations between the two parties and countries since 1956. In all fairness, it must be admitted that in the exchange the Chinese come out better. For all their recklessness and alleged madness, the correspondence reveals the Mao circle as shrewd analysts when it comes to foreign-policy matters (It is thus reminiscent of Stalin's foreign policy in the 1930's, which was usually based on quite rational considerations, at the same time that elements in internal politics must be traced to some clearly pathological aberrations.) The Chinese pitilessly dissect the selfish and nationalistic motivations hidden beneath the Soviets' language of international solidarity and devotion to the socialist camp. The Russians, they point out, were always ready with offers of help *after* an emergency, as in the 1958 statement of support for China over the crisis in the Formosa Straits. Equally shrewd (and insolent) is their appreciation of the Soviet government's predicament in the face of the Frankenstein monster it helped to create. "The Soviet Government . . . is insolent enough to say that we are able to criticize them only because China enjoys the protection of Soviet nuclear weapons. Well, then, leaders of the Soviet Union, please continue to protect us awhile with your nuclear weapons. We shall continue to criticize you, and we hope you will have the courage to argue the matter out with us."[139]

To be sure (again the parallel with Stalinism is striking), this shrewdness occasionally shades into obsessiveness; a realistic view of international

---

[137] An ingenious procedure enabled the U.S., U.S.S.R., and Britain to eschew the ticklish problem of recognition: other countries could signify their adhesion to the treaty by signing with *any one* of the three main signatories— East Germany signing in Moscow, Bonn in Washington.

[138] That is, by the administration. Some of its opponents considered it a devilish ruse invented by the Russians to outwit the United States.

[139] Chinese statement of September 1, 1963, quoted in Griffith, *op. cit.*, p. 371.

politics leads at times to pathological suspiciousness. Already in 1963 (and how this theme will be magnified by 1965–67!), the Soviet leaders are not merely pursuing their own power interests but actively *plotting* against China with the connivance of the United States, and the Yugoslav Communists are not merely revisionists but agents of imperialism. Khrushchev cannot take a vacation in Yugoslavia without some deep ulterior motive.

On their part the Soviets all too readily show their fear of the Chinese. The *leitmotiv* of the main part of the correspondence is, "Why do you need nuclear weapons? We are protecting you anyhow." Goaded to fury by Chinese taunts on this count, the Russians go to great lengths to prove the irresponsible Chinese nonchalance on nuclear war, citing Mao's famous words about 300 million Chinese surviving the holocaust, "asides" made by Chinese officials that if "small nations" such as Czechoslovakia and Italy disappeared entirely, well, it would be in the interests of the socialist camp as a whole! But here the Chinese could retort, as they *almost do*, that such statements were intended to unnerve the *capitalists*; had not Khrushchev indulged in pretty much the same game? The Chinese argument in essence is: it pays to be tough when talking with the capitalists and to be unyielding in one's principles; this does not mean that one should not be prudent in action and flexible on concrete problems.

In what sense, then, is the Sino-Soviet dispute ideological? Communist habits of thought do not allow major disagreements on policies to be merely accidental or products of differing national interests. Thus both sides have groped for deeper explanations for their dispute, but the basic one is that Russia is now highly industrialized, while China is not but has 600 million people.[140] The Chinese view Russia's intermittent attempts to reach accommodation with the United States as expressing not only personal cowardice and treason on Khrushchev's part, but also an un-Marxist and un-Leninist revisionism on the part of the Soviet elite. From this point of view, the root of the trouble goes to the original denunciation of Stalin, which the Chinese believe—quite logically, from their point of view— lowered the prestige of Communism in the international arena and opened the door to the evolution of Soviet society and policies on the pattern of Yugoslavia. The fact that Stalin would have been much harder on them than his successors, and that in all likelihood he would not have confined himself to *verbal* attack, is conveniently overlooked.

The Russians, on their side, have seen in the Chinese grievances an equal departure from the Marxist-Leninist orthodoxy. What was the Chinese experiment with communes, their stress on personal asceticism, and their encouragement of adventurist revolutionary attempts but left-wing dogmatism and sectarianism? China's unwillingness to subordinate her policies

[140] Chinese statistics, not entirely above suspicion, in 1967 moved this figure up to 700 million.

to those of the Soviet Union was both evidence for and the substance of a many-sided heresy.

This proneness of practical, often cynical men to rationalize a quarrel in terms of ideology has not been without its uses. It has enabled both sides to eschew the agonizing question: does Communism, or any other universalist ideology, make sense in today's world? It has enabled both sides to keep alive hopes of reconciliation. Nothing can change the *facts*—that Russia is a generation or two ahead of China in industrialization and military power and that there are many more Chinese than Russians. But it is always possible to hope to bridge an *ideological* gap: "Khrushchev's clique" might be removed, and then the Soviet Union would acknowledge the correctness of the Chinese interpretation; or the Chinese "might come to their senses" and realize that it was they who had departed from the 1957 and 1960 declarations. Here it might be interjected that the trouble with international politics since 1914 has been precisely this tendency of statesmen to universalize their aims and to couch their objectives in ideological semantics. And on this count the West, with its slogans of "making the world safe for democracy," "preserving the free world," etc., should display more understanding for the dilemmas of the Maos and the Khrushchevs.

The public eruption of the Sino-Soviet dispute naturally had serious effects throughout the Communist world. To some parties, especially those most vulnerable to the threats of the "capitalist" world (Cuba and North Vietnam), the dispute was and is a grave embarrassment, if not an outright danger. Other parties lined up on one side or the other, depending on their proximity to or dependence on the giants. It is not surprising that the East Germans followed Moscow or that the North Korean and Japanese parties at least initially drew toward Peking. Elsewhere, the temperaments and prospects of local Communist leaders have influenced their allegiance. A miniscule Communist Party, such as New Zealand's, has no earthly prospect of coming to power in a peaceful world, and its leaders respond favorably to Peking's militancy. The Albanians have their own reasons. And in all Communist parties and movements, there are adventurous spirits yearning for action, chafing under pro-Moscow Party bureaucracy, and drawn to the exciting new variety of Chinese Communism.

The Soviets have accused the Chinese, with some justice, of giving a racist tinge to their variety of Communism. Certainly Peking's "splitting activities," to use the Soviet expression, have been most noticeable in Asia, Africa, and Latin America. And especially in the last few years Peking has in some ways been trying to portray Soviet Communism as "the rich man's Communism"—cautious, sedate, working in an informal (or perhaps even formal!) alliance with imperialism; as against which Peking extends the helping hand to the *real* wretched and underprivileged of the

world (or at least to the parties purporting to represent them, which have
nothing to lose but Soviet subsidies and invitations to Moscow). But the
long reach of Chinese propaganda extends even to the Communists in
"overdeveloped" countries. Why, said a choleric statement of the CPSU
in 1963, "The leadership of the [CCP] is organizing and supporting various
anti-Party groups of renegades who are coming out against the Communist
parties in the United States, Italy, Belgium. . . . In the United States support
is being given to the subversive [sic] activities of the left opportunist
'Hammer and Steel' group."[141]

Another aspect of the Sino-Soviet dispute revealed by the publication
of the 1963 correspondence is the matter of disorders and sporadic troubles
along their common border. The Chinese allege that in the spring of 1962,
"the leaders of the CPSU used their organs and personnel in Sinkiang
China to carry out large-scale subversive acts in the Ili region and enticed
and coerced tens of thousands of Chinese citizens into going to the Soviet
Union."[142] How a few consular officials could coerce "tens of thousands" of
people is left unexplained, but what occurred, evidently, was a mass flight
of Sinkiang Kazakhs to the U.S.S.R. On their part, the Soviets alleged more
than 5,000 border violations by the Chinese in 1962 alone. The implications of this aspect of the dispute are quite obvious.

The best comment on the 1963 outbursts between Russia and China is unwittingly provided by a quotation from Lenin given in a Chinese statement:
"Abuse in politics often covers up the utter lack of ideological content,
the helplessness and the impotence, the annoying impotence of the
abuser."[143] Neither side could budge the other. In a different world, even
a few of the grievances aired would have led to war. To paraphrase a
saying, if one has such "fraternal parties" one does not need bourgeois
imperialists. But both parties had to go on making sounds and gestures
about possible accommodation, exchanging (increasingly cool) greetings
on their respective national and Communist holidays, and expressing
"unshakable confidence" that in due time the dissonances would be overcome.

However, as long as the Gordian knot of Sino-Soviet disputes remains
uncut, Soviet freedom of operations in foreign affairs is severely restricted.
The Soviet Union must compete with the United States and at the same
time with China for the allegiance of Communist parties and national
liberation movements all over the world. She must try to coexist with the
United States (in the sense of avoiding a nuclear war) and at the same
time with China (in terms of avoiding a definite breach). A Stalin might
have been able to cut this Gordian knot by formally renouncing the Sino-

141 Griffith, op. cit., p. 320.
142 Ibid., p. 410.
143 Ibid., p. 423.

THE PERILS OF KHRUSHCHEV

Soviet alliance and securing an official condemnation of China from the majority of the Communist parties of the world thus casting the Chinese Communists and their allies out of the Soviet-controlled Communist bloc. But these options were not within Khrushchev's power.

The predictable effect of the Sino-Soviet conflict was that it made a *partial* American-Soviet *détente* more possible but a far-reaching one impossible. The test ban agreement was accompanied and followed by a series of measures, hardly momentous in themselves, indicating the Soviet leaders' continuing interest in lowering the level of tension with America: the "hot line" established in the summer of 1963 permitting instantaneous communication between the Kremlin and the White House; in October, the Soviet Union's adherence to the U.N. resolution asking all states to refrain from orbiting nuclear devices in outer space.

The Soviets would have liked to accompany the test ban treaty with a nonaggression pact between the Warsaw Pact powers and NATO. This proposal was never enacted owing to the United States' fears of possible difficulties with West Germany and the all too actual ones with France. The latter, or more properly General de Gaulle, refused to sign the test ban treaty. Though they severely criticized France's decision to acquire atomic weapons, the Soviet leaders refused to view it with the seriousness they attached to this possibility in the case of West Germany and especially China. Khrushchev chose to joke about it: "De Gaulle has said that he wanted his own 'nuclear umbrella,' but to construct a nuclear umbrella is not such a simple thing. One may end up both without one's pants *and* without the umbrella."[144] Like practically everything else he was saying at the time, this was supposed to be read and pondered in Peking. But within three years, de Gaulle, who had acquired a modest atomic force while keeping his trousers, was to be a cordial friend of Khrushchev's successors.

A nonaggression treaty would have meant the West's implicit recognition of East Germany and of Poland's territorial gains under the Potsdam decision. Though the Russians do not take such treaties terribly seriously, it would have strengthened their case against the Chinese indictment that they were appeasing the United States without getting anything in return. As it was, Khrushchev had to give a warning on the eve of signing the test ban treaty: "This of course does not mean, comrades, that one should let oneself be prey to illusions, that the dawn of new relations between us and the United States has already risen. No."[145] Would further concrete measures of *détente* with the United States have strengthened Khrushchev's personal position? Quite likely. Without making Nikita Sergeievich into a

[144] *Plenum of the Central Committee of the CPSU, June 18–21, 1963* (Moscow, 1964), p. 267.
[145] *Ibid.*, p. 266.

warm friend of America, it is clear that following the Cuba fiasco he was readier than most of his colleagues to improve Russia's relations with the United States. And he was badly in need of tangible successes and a vindication of his position.

Between July 1963 and his ouster, Khrushchev's position as leader of international Communism was to be gravely compromised by domestic setbacks and difficulties. He could have survived the reverberations of the Cuban crisis and the worsening relations with China if his domestic plans and policies were succeeding. But 1962 and 1963 were years of considerable economic difficulties and shortages. The contrast between Khrushchev's boasts and the reality was shatteringly revealed following his ouster. Said a member of the Presidium: "We heard the slogans [that we must] catch up and overcome in the near future the United States in per-capita production of meat and milk. We heard slogans about fulfilling the Seven-Year Plan in three and four years, [slogans] that we live well now and tomorrow we shall live even better. But what did we have in fact?—Bread lines!"[146] In his attempt to overcome the difficulties, Khrushchev had recourse to various administrative improvisations, which disturbed his hitherto faithful bureaucratic followers. His temper grew short. A few minutes' conversation with Khrushchev, a ruffled bureaucrat was to lament, and an important Party official was fired or transferred. (The speaker did not reflect how much more serious the results of an interview with Stalin had often been.)

The dilemmas and dangers involved in a simultaneous *rapprochement* with the United States and conflict with China were vividly illustrated in a Central Committee meeting held shortly before the signing of the test ban treaty to discuss the ideological tasks of the Party. The theme of the report delivered at the Plenum by a secretary of the Central Committee, Ilichev,[147] was the absolute impermissibility of confusing the (desirable) principle of peaceful coexistence among states of differing social systems with the (subversive) notion of coexistence of ideologies. "To call for the peaceful coexistence of Communist and bourgeois ideas is to act as scouts of the enemies of socialism, to sell out the basic interests of workers, to work in the interests of our enemies, who want to exploit even cultural ties between nations for subversive purposes."[148] Ilichev went on to reveal the leadership's fears about ideological erosion in the Soviet Union and, especially, about the yearnings for a greater freedom expressed by the intellectuals and students. Khrushchev himself, in the concluding speech,

[146] *Plenum of the Central Committee of the CPSU, March 24–26, 1965* (Moscow, 1965), p. 36.

[147] A close collaborator of Khrushchev's, one of the few top officials to fall with him.

[148] *Plenum of the Central Committee of the CPSU, June 18–21, 1963*, p. 23.

acknowledged a petition from a number of Party members calling for greater freedom. ("Straightened out" by the leaders, those comrades then withdrew their petition.[149]) The whole tenor of the meeting testified to the Party's very serious concern with the potential dangers of this intellectual unrest. The outstanding sinners mentioned in this context were people like the writer and journalist Victor Nekrasov, who liked what he had seen in the United States and Italy too much; the abstractionist sculptor Neizvestny (the sight of whose works threw Khrushchev into a veritable tantrum); the young poet Andrei Voznesensky, who had given an incautious interview to bourgeois journalists; "unvigilant" movie producers and magazine editors, etc.

The proceedings of the Plenum, though they contained no secrets and could hardly be a revelation to even a casual reader of the Soviet press, were not published as a whole until one year later—and this underlines its connection with international politics.[150] In the international context of mid-1963, the call for ideological vigilance was bound to be confusing: was a loyal Soviet citizen to feel closer to his co-religionists in China, who poured vile abuse upon his leaders, than to the Americans, with whom a friendly agreement has just been reached? Didn't perhaps those comrades who argued for greater intellectual and artistic freedom allege the Chinese danger as a reason for their position? How could one deprecate a degree of ideological coexistence with the bourgeois world, when ideological unity with the largest *Communist* state was clearly a sham?

These bewildering questions must have been asked repeatedly in the Presidium of the Central Committee. Since there was no easy way of answering them, Soviet policy went by fits and starts until the ouster of Khrushchev in October 1964. At one point the leadership pressed for another conference of Communist parties, where presumably the Chinese and their allies would be condemned and isolated, if not indeed expelled from the international movement. At other times it proposed an end to the public polemic and a further exploration of the possibilities of reconciliation. But the image of Communism as a united movement was visibly crumbling. Among many parties still loyal to Moscow the idea of a conference met with little enthusiasm: it was bound to advertise the internal dissensions, perhaps cause an irreversible split. In the Communist states this might well lead to a repetition of the events of 1956, perhaps on a larger scale. In non-Communist states the influence of the orthodox (Soviet-type) Communist Party might also weaken, fickle intellectuals and adventurous youths being drawn to the Chinese "Marxist-Leninist" parties, or

[149] *Ibid.*, p. 263.

[150] Such a delay often reflects official uncertainty as to how much of the proceedings should be published. It is thus entirely possible that some of the most interesting passages have been censored.

many people might simply abandon a divided movement that no longer promised to be the wave of the future.[151] The vision of high officials of the Communist Party of the Soviet Union haggling with their counterparts in the New Zealand and Danish parties, imploring the Italians, being snubbed by the Rumanians, would have brought a smile to Stalin's face. He had said, "You will be lost without me."

China's "subversive" activities were not limited to world Communism. That profitable sideline exploited by the Soviets since World War II, the national liberation movements, now became the locus of keen competition between the two Communist super-powers. Superficially, all the advantages here might appear to be on the Soviet side: the Soviet Union had power and resources dwarfing those of China; she could provide economic help that China could not match. But the Soviet Union had to move more cautiously and sedately, while China could proffer reckless advice and encouragement to the ambitious heads of the new states. In the under-developed world the Soviet Union found herself competing with China under disadvantages somewhat similar to those the United States experi-enced in competing with her. For figures like Sukarno or Nkrumah, Soviet policies were beginning to sound as "square" as the tedious American insistence that the best course was to concentrate on economic development. The billion or so dollars expended by the Soviet Union on helping Indo-nesia were an almost complete waste; the mercurial Sukarno drew closer to Peking, and the Indonesian Communist Party cautiously but distinctly ranged itself on the Chinese side.

The Chinese moves were made in a deliberately provocative manner, Soviet Communism being pictured as not only the "rich man's" but the "white man's" Communism. Mao himself authored the theory of the "three spheres"—that of imperialism (the United States and her allies), that of the Soviet Union, and that of most of the rest of the world (Asia, Africa, and Latin America) where presumably China was destined to lead. In December 1963 Chou En-lai toured Africa propagating the Chinese brand of revolution; Soviet representatives were reduced to undignified haggling and protests over China's demand that they be excluded from the conference of Afro-Asian states.

It might be thought that Soviet sensitivity over the Chinese tactics was excessive, if not ridiculous. The notion of the Third World being united in any meaningful way is sufficiently refuted if one remembers that its constituent parts are usually found in the most acute conflict with each

---

[151] The phenomenon of the New Left, impatient of the old organizational forms and doctrines, clearly reflects the deep split in international Communism. The slogan "better red than dead," which could perhaps have a rational justi-fication in the days when Communism was a monolithic movement, has also lost most of its appeal for the same reason.

other rather than with the former colonial powers: India vs. Pakistan, Somalia vs. Kenya, Algeria vs. Morocco—this melancholy enumeration can be carried further. The idea that one could capitalize on the revolutionary potential of African nationalism also flies in the face of the fantastically unstable nature of politics in that continent (of which the fate of Nigeria provides the most vivid illustration—the very state which, it had been assumed, had the most solid chances for stable economic and political progress). But this Soviet sensitivity revealed an awareness that their old monopoly in exploiting strains and stresses of decolonization and underdevelopment was at an end. At the very moment when the West's weaknesses and confusions presented Soviet Communism with the opportunities it had dreamed of since its very foundation, the anti-imperialist game could no longer be played with the old zest and self-assurance.

The Chinese challenge was the specific subject discussed at a special session of the Central Committee of the CPSU, held on February 14–15, 1964. Published two months later, the proceedings constitute the first *public* report of the Central Committee's deliberations devoted to the Chinese problem. Moreover, since the Plenum of the Central Committee was held in the presence of a large number (hundreds if not thousands) of Party and government officials,[152] the gist of the discussion and the seriousness with which the leadership viewed the problem could not but become known immediately to every Party and government official.

The main part of this Plenum was taken up by a very lengthy report given by Suslov. Two aspects of the report and the subsequent discussion deserve special attention. The first is the violence of the personal attacks on Mao Tse-tung. He was unabashedly portrayed as another Stalin desirous of establishing personal dictatorship over the entire Communist movement. "The leadership of the [CCP] is trying to propagate the cult of personality of Mao . . . so [that he], like Stalin in his time, would tower god-like over all the Marxist-Leninist parties and would decide all questions of their policy and activity according to his whim.[153] But what was once tragedy repeats itself in history only as farce, said Suslov with bitter sarcasm. The Communist Party of the Soviet Union has finished with the cult of personality once and for all. Yet in China, said another speaker, silly verses written by Mao in a free moment are presented as a historic event in the nation's life!

[152] Their presence was purportedly connected with the first part of the Central Committee's session, devoted to agricultural problems, but the fact that they stayed on for the "Chinese" part could not be accidental. The Chinese later alleged that the final session was attended by 6,000 people.

[153] *Plenum of the Central Committee of the CPSU, February 10–25, 1964* (Moscow, 1964), p. 546.

The nature of these attacks leaves no doubt that if there was any hope of re-establishing some *modus vivendi* with China, the Soviet leadership had definitely abandoned it as long as Mao was at the helm. This in turn leads to the possibility that the Russians knew of the dissensions within the Chinese Party that came to light with the cultural revolution and were encouraging and abetting the efforts to remove Mao. Knowing the man, they could not think that he could ever forgive or forget these scathing attacks and ridicule.

The second striking aspect of the debate was the great stress—excessive, one would think—on the devotion and attachment of the Soviet leadership, Party, and nation to Khrushchev:

> Our nation knows well and trusts without reservation its leaders, and it knows well and has boundless confidence in Nikita Sergeievich Khrushchev, a passionate revolutionary, outstanding continuator of Lenin's tradition, indefatigable fighter for peace and Communism. . . . We the Soviet people credit our successes to the untiring efforts of Nikita Sergeievich for the benefit of our nation, for the welfare of all toilers in the world. . . . He expresses the deepest thoughts and dreams of the Soviet people.[154]

Letting the cat out of the bag, Suslov perorated, "the Chinese leaders, and not only they, should get it through their thick skulls that our Central Committee, headed by this faithful Leninist Nikita Sergeievich Khrushchev, is more than ever united and monolithic."[155]

Eight months to the day after this statement was made, the Central Committee fired the "universally acknowledged leader of our Party and nation." If to the Soviet leaders Mao's person became the primary obstacle to renewed negotiations with the Chinese Communists, the Chinese felt the same way about Khrushchev.

Substantively, Suslov's report added but little to the known sins and derelictions of the Chinese as they had already been catalogued. Their leaders were once more accused of "adventurism in foreign policy, attempts to preserve the atmosphere of the 'cold war,' sectarianism, putschism."[156] It was ominously pointed out how closely their ideas paralleled Trotsky's, how leaders of the Trotskyite Fourth International applauded and helped Peking's activities. But above and beyond the tortuous ideological formulations and parallels, Suslov had to acknowledge the underlying *national* hostility: "Strange as it may seem, the education of the Chinese nation in the spirit of hostility to the U.S.S.R. and the Community Party of the Soviet Union has become practically the main concern of the Central

[154] *Ibid.*, pp. 572, 578, 551.

[155] *Ibid.*, p. 551.

[156] *Ibid.*, p. 470.

Committee of the Chinese Communist Party."[157] And, in a seeming refutation of his presentation of the Chinese leaders as fanatics, Suslov admitted that in *deed* as distinguished from word they were fairly realistic. And he delivered an unwitting commentary on the inflexibility of American foreign policy:

> With a stubbornness worthy of a better cause, the Chinese leaders attempt to prevent the improvement of Soviet-American relations, representing this as "plotting with the imperialists." At the same time the Chinese government makes feverish attempts to improve relations with Britain, France, Japan, West Germany, and Italy. It is quite clear that they would not refuse to improve relations with the United States *but as yet* do not see favorable circumstances for such an endeavor.[158]

As against the Chinese fear of Soviet-American collusion, the Russians were already nurturing a modest nightmare of their own: what if the Chinese and Americans ganged up against *them*?

"Where do we go from here?" the lesser participants at the Plenum must have wondered as they dispersed to their ministries, offices, and kolkhozes. Short of a complete breach of relations, if not indeed war, there appeared to be no way out. However, in the *short* run the trouble hinged on the personalities of the top leaders. If they could be got out of the way, perhaps a temporary solution might be found or at least the dispute might proceed under conditions of greater decorum. And it could not have escaped the attention of people sensitive to such details that for all the avowals of love for and solidarity with Nikita Sergeievich, only one other full member of the Presidium chose to repeat Suslov's endearing remarks about the First Secretary.

The split within the Soviet leadership must have been very acute. The "usual" crises of the year in the Congo and Cyprus evoked the usual Soviet responses. In the Congo, the Russians provided arms for the rebels against the central Congolese government, and official protests were lodged about American help to the latter. Since the rebels were strongly supported by the Chinese and since the whole movement was of a most primitive tribal variety, this Soviet response was based on the traditional need to react adversely to any "imperialist" initiative rather than any great hopes and solicitude for the rebels. In Cyprus the Soviet Union was simply happy to collect the dividends of the quarrel between two allies of Washington— Greece and Turkey. The latter, once the stanchest ally of the United States in the Mediterranean, now became friendlier to the Soviet Union, as a result of what the Turks considered to be American indifference to their grievances in Cyprus and even though the Soviets continued to supply and support Archbishop Makarios' regime.

---

[157] *Ibid.*, p. 471.
[158] *Ibid.*, p. 495, my italics.

Such small successes—as well as the visible disintegration of NATO consequent upon General de Gaulle's increasingly anti-American stance and the customary impasse of American foreign policy in a presidential election year—could not really make the Soviet leaders rejoice, beset as they were by aggravating internal problems and baffled as they were by *the* problem in foreign policy. Both the attempt to set up a Communist-parties conference and half-hearted attempts at some sort of *détente* with China continued through the spring and summer. Were it not a matter affecting the lives and fortunes of hundreds of millions of people, this phase of Sino-Soviet relations could provide rich material for a comedy. Letters bristling with invective—to choose a mild example, "you are telling a whopping lie"—would conclude "with fraternal greetings" by the given Central Committee. Attempts to mediate were undertaken by such unlikely go-betweens as the Rumanians. A few years back a frown by a minor Soviet official had the power to bring down the entire Central Committee of the Rumanian Party. Now its representatives argued with the Russians, were consulted by the Chinese, and successfully strove to establish a degree of independence in foreign and economic policies. Any "expert" who would have predicted such developments a few years before would have been stripped of his Kremlinologist's epaulets, if not consigned to a lunatic asylum.

Further shocks were in store. In August Palmiro Togliatti, long a faithful follower of Stalin and then of his successors, succumbed to a heart attack while vacationing in Russia. A sizable Russian town was renamed in his honor (the Soviets not having learned the lesson of how troublesome such practices had been in the past), but it soon came out that Togliatti had left behind him a memorandum critical of Soviet internal *and* external policies. He criticized Soviet leadership for not taking more resolute steps to liquidate the backwash of Stalinism and for not allowing more cultural and even political diversity. On foreign policy he warned against any attempt to deal drastically with the Chinese. His "testament," as it became known, was not the product of any sympathy for the Chinese position, but simply of his realization that a permanent split would injure Communism everywhere. Hasty attempts were made to prevent the publication of this embarrassing document, but Togliatti's successors were obstinate. That a man with his record would write such a memorandum was palpable proof of how low had fallen the prestige of the Soviet leadership in the Communist world; now at the height of her industrial and military power, the Soviet Union was incapable of even approximating that absolute control of the movement which the weak and backward Russia had had in the 1920's and 1930's.

Nothing, however, could have prepared the Kremlin for the shock it received in August when the Japanese press published a report of an interview given by Mao to a group of Japanese socialists. Diplomatic efforts were made to have the interview declared spurious, but they were unavailing. On September 2 *Pravda* published a summary of its text, together with a full page (one-fourth of the issue) devoted to a commentary on Mao's startling pronouncements.

Mao classified the U.S.S.R. as an imperialist state. In Europe, she had "appropriated" part of Rumania, taken East Germany for Poland after taking eastern Poland for herself, in both cases chasing out "local inhabitants." "The Russians took everything they could." But Mao was only warming up. How about the territories taken from China in the nineteenth century? And Mongolia, which he, Mao, had reclaimed for China in 1954, when Khrushchev and Bulganin were in Peking? On these issues the Chinese leader graciously conceded: he was willing to wait. But the Kurile Islands should be returned to Japan forthwith. The Soviet Union had more territory than she needed for her population, in comparison to Japan, say, crowded on her little islands. (Other interesting parts of Mao's interview praised Japan as a great nation, the proof being the Japanese conquests in World War II!)

The average Soviet reader must have rubbed his eyes in disbelief. What Mao said about the Soviet Union surpassed the most ambitious statements of the late Dulles about the need to "roll back" the Soviet sphere. The "German revanchists," as reported in the Soviet press, at their worst would have been incapable of the insolence and provocation contained in every sentence of Mao's interview. He proposed an eventual partition of the U.S.S.R.! He claimed for China enormous territories of more than 1.5 million square kilometers, inhabited by millions of Soviet citizens! In the past a claim for a few miles of Soviet territory brought forth declarations from the Soviet government about readiness to strike with missiles, "the mighty Red Army," etc. Now, for all its length, the editorial on Mao was noticeably weak in tone, plaintive rather than threatening. Khrushchev, currently in Prague, made noises about Mao's theories of *Lebensraum*, compared him to Hitler, etc. But the provocation was so huge that any *verbal* response had to be anticlimactic. The Chinese Chairman had had his revenge: *now* let them laugh at his poems.

Time was growing short for Khrushchev. There were obscure signs that his colleagues were reaching the end of their patience. At a reception for the President of Indonesia on September 29, Mikoyan, as head of state, was put ahead of Khrushchev on the list of Soviet leaders. On October 2 the Presidium of the Central Committee and the Council of Ministers held their joint meeting in the presence of many other officials and activists: this fashion of holding Central Committee meetings had long enraged the members of the oligarchy, since the mass of uninitiated Party members, for whom any criticism of the First Secretary would have sounded like treason, prevented them from voicing their objections and reservations. Now Khrushchev evidently proposed to use the same technique in respect to the Presidium. We do not know whether this was the last straw, or whether Khrushchev had other "hare-brained" proposals that his colleagues could not stomach. In a few days he took off for a vacation in the Crimea. The press was full of the doings of the Soviet cosmonauts: a three-man team was orbiting the earth. The Central Committee members began to assemble for their triumphant reception, to which Nikita Sergeievich was scheduled to fly from Sochi.

On October 14 Osvaldo Dorticos, President of Cuba, arrived in Moscow. He well might have wondered at the sparsity of the dignitaries greeting him—only a few Presidium members—and possibly also at their preoccupied air. To Mikoyan, Dorticos divulged the purpose of his trip in a little speech: he came principally to exchange his "impressions and views with dear Comrade Khrushchev." Alas, this was not to be. On the same day the Central Committee "acceded to the plea" of N. S. Khrushchev that on account of his advanced age and ailing health he be released from his numerous state and Party duties. So ran the announcement on October 16. Brezhnev and Kosygin were to succeed him, and the man who had dominated the Soviet Union for ten years, and who had shaken the world with his threats and designs, became overnight an obscure emeritus.

XII

IN THE SHADOW OF VIETNAM

Caution was the main characteristic of the new team which took over the reins of power from Nikita Khrushchev. In retrospect, during the almost ten years that separate us from the virtual coup d'état of October 1964, the Soviet Union has been ruled by an oligarchy. The collective leadership which succeeded Stalin in 1953 had been an unstable one. Khrushchev when he forged to the front was clearly not an absolute dictator, but he was certainly more than just first among equals. Foreign policy especially bore the mark of his ebullient personality: he was a subtle and, as has been seen, sometimes an oversubtle manipulator and improviser.

The two people who inherited his main offices were in contrast cautious bureaucrats who were selected by their fellow oligarchs—members of the Presidium—because of the expectation that they were "safe," unlikely to rock the boat, an expectation which they more than fulfilled. Leonid Brezhnev had worked his way through the Party apparatus during the Stalin era. A Central Committee secretary in 1952, he was dropped a notch following the despot's death and then worked his way up again. Titular head of state for a while, he returned to the secretariat in 1963 and was obviously the prime mover in the coup that toppled his predecessor as First Secretary. His tenure of the office has, as of this writing, been unsensational. He has been careful both to act and to give the impression of acting on behalf of the Presidium-Politburo (it regained its old name in 1966). It is safe to assume that he has been its most influential member, but on crucial policy decisions

695

he has had to rely on a majority consensus. His influence has been discernible especially on domestic and intra-Communist-bloc policies. One detects Brezhnev's hand in the regime's cautious back-tracking from the liberalizing tendencies of the Khrushchev era and in the restoration of some of the features of Stalinism, such as the more vigorous repression of dissent in cultural life. The General Secretary (it was symbolic that Brezhnev chose to resume this title in 1966) forged to the forefront in over-all foreign policy matters only in recent years, playing the leading part in the negotiations with the Americans during the Nixon visit in May 1972.

Alexei Kosygin fits even better the stereotype of a cautious bureaucrat. A beneficiary of the great purges, he advanced in the late 1930's, first from an industrial manager to minister, then within a year to Prime Minister of the Russian Federated Republic. A member of the Politburo during Stalin's last years, he then suffered a partial eclipse and did not return to the highest body until 1960. Now he inherited Khrushchev's job as Chairman of the Council of Ministers of the U.S.S.R. His primary responsibilities have been in the spheres of economic planning and relations with non-Communist states. A careful, tactful politician, no one could present a greater contrast to the uninhibited style of Khrushchev with his incongruous mixture of cajoleries and threats vis-à-vis the West.

Two other veterans of the Stalin era, Mikhail Suslov and Nikolai Podgorny, have also been prominent in shaping Soviet foreign policy during the past decade. Suslov, a Party secretary since 1947, has been the principal figure in liaison with foreign Communist parties. Podgorny, who took over in 1965 as titular head of state, has been used on a number of confidential foreign missions, such as assuaging the Arabs' bitter feelings over what they considered the lack of adequate Soviet support in their disastrous 1967 conflict with Israel.

The new leaders stressed, not entirely truthfully, that the regime did not intend to depart from earlier decisions and the spirit of the Twentieth and Twenty-second Congresses and that the bad old (Stalin's!) days would not return.

The same caution and prudence characterized the first statements made by the new team on foreign relations. The Brezhnev-Kosygin regime adopted the "we are not mad at anyone" theme. It would have been both dangerous and inaccurate to give the impression that Khrushchev had been sacrificed to the Chinese.[1] There was a frequent reassertion that peaceful coexistence

[1] Khrushchev's inability to prevent the conflict with China from becoming so intense and well publicized was undoubtedly a contributory factor in his fall. Yet it was not nearly as important as his derelictions on the domestic front—what was deemed a too drastic de-Stalinization—and such, to quote his successors' uncharitable characterization, "hare-brained schemes" as the one which led to the Cuban missile crisis.

remained the guiding principle of Soviet foreign policy. The press soon commented favorably on President Johnson's victory in the American elections.

To be sure, Khrushchev's downfall was received in Peking with delight. Never the ones to abide by the rather absurd bourgeois principle of not kicking a man when he is down, the Chinese openly exulted over the fall of the "arch-schemer" and described it as a great victory for the true Marxist-Leninists. There was another reason for rejoicing among Mao's cohorts: China had just exploded its first nuclear device; what the Russians had for so many years striven to prevent had become a fact.

In 1964 there was what was to prove to be a short-lived *détente* in Sino-Soviet relations. On the anniversary of the November Revolution, a high-ranking Chinese delegation headed by Chou En-lai arrived in Moscow.[2] The visit was not an unqualified success; discussions between Chou and the Soviet leadership failed to produce any tangible results. The Soviets postponed the conference of twenty-six Communist parties originally scheduled for December 15 but refused to give it up entirely. But for the time being the tone of the dispute became more subdued, and professions of "unshakable unity" against the imperialist bloc found their way again into the press of the two countries.

Did the Soviet leaders hope that with Khrushchev out the Chinese Communists would return the compliment and get rid of Mao? We now know, and the Soviets might have known then, that the Great Helmsman was experiencing great difficulties with his top-ranking aides, whom he would soon purge through the Cultural Revolution. Yet even at this high point, since 1960, of *ostensible* good feelings between the two Communist regimes, Chou went out of his way to indicate the remaining difficulties and dissonances. He and his fellow delegates demonstratively refused to join in the applause for the Yugoslav representatives at the celebrations. And even more eloquently, the Chinese Prime Minister once more deposited a floral wreath at Stalin's tomb.

The Sino-Soviet *détente* might have lasted longer but for a new turn of events in Vietnam, which began with the massive American intervention in the civil war in that little Asian country in 1965. That this American intervention against a Communist-sponsored insurrection should have led to a drastic worsening of relations between the two main Communist powers has been just one of the paradoxes resulting from what is now universally recognized as a most unfortunate decision by the U.S. Government.

Concerning the American involvement, a future historian may well echo Lord Palmerston's dictum about the involved Schleswig-Holstein problem

[2] The initiative for the visit came from China. See Chou in *Peking Review*, January 1, 1965, p. 19.

of his day: there had been only three people who understood the back-ground—one had died, one had gone mad, and one, he himself, had for-gotten. And so, despite the profusion of books, articles, recriminations, attempted rationalizations of the American involvement, etc., only a bold and incautious analyst would formulate his opinion on the subject without reservations or qualifications.

We have seen that the Soviet Union's policy in Southeast Asia since 1950 has been dictated largely by her relations with China. Thus the U.S.S.R., prompted by a *prior* Chinese recognition of Ho Chi Minh, recognized in January 1950 the Viet Minh regime. The 1954 Geneva accord, which parti-tioned the unhappy land, suited the interests of *both* Communist super-powers: the Russians counted on the subsequent repudiation of the EDC by the Mendès-France government; the Chinese *at that time* were chary of a further war in Indochina that was likely to bring massive American inter-vention. They had a very recent experience of being pushed by the Kremlin into a confrontation with the United States and did not relish the prospect of repeating it at that moment. Many Western sources claim that Ho was the aggrieved party, that after Dienbienphu he had reason to believe that all of Vietnam would be his. This seems a bit strong. The Geneva agreement gave the Viet Communists an opportunity to organize their own state in peace and then in good time to resume the struggle to capture the South.

With the French now out of Indochina, the United States hastened to throw its protection behind the nationalist regime of Diem. Vietnam joined the unhappy group of divided nations: a Communist regime ruling the North, one dependent on the American support, the South. Between 1954 and 1960 this situation appeared, illusorily, stable. Southeast Asia in gen-eral and Vietnam in particular were at the time of secondary importance to the Soviet Union, which, in 1957, proposed that *both* Vietnamese states be admitted to the United Nations.

With the Sino-Soviet conflict in the open in 1960 the situation was drastically transformed: China now felt it in its interest to encourage wars of national liberation, for they decreased the chances of any accommoda-tion between the United States and the U.S.S.R. It cannot be an accident that it was in September 1960 that the Third Congress of the Communist Party in North Vietnam stressed the importance of freeing the South from "American imperialism"[3] and that in December, in a secret location in the south, the National Front for the Liberation of South Vietnam was created. If Peking hoped to provoke even an indirect American-Soviet confronta-tion, Vietnam must have appeared a promising place. The U.S. stake in the country was by now considerable and the downfall of the Diem regime and the country's absorption by the North would involve a considerable loss of

---

[3] Jean Lacouture, *Vietnam Between Two Truces* (Paris, 1966), p. 71.

face and American credibility as the protector of non-Communist regimes n Asia. The Soviet Union would then be put on the spot in any conflict between the resurgent guerrillas (assisted by the North) and the American protégé (and perhaps the Americans themselves) in the South.

While Hanoi undoubtedly had the decisive voice in initiating a new phase of the civil war, it is improbable that Ho would have ventured on this risky course *against* resolute advice to the contrary by *both* Peking and Moscow. But the Chinese now had a stake in renewed insurgency. And after May 1960 (the U-2 episode), the Soviets—Khrushchev's design for an accommodation with the U.S. stymied—would not be unhappy to see the U.S. being harassed in yet another part of the world, though the Kremlin undoubtedly urged caution upon Hanoi. The Soviet Union had to keep its hand in the affairs of Indochina and not let the Communist movements in the area lapse exclusively into the Chinese sphere. Hence, as we have seen, Soviet activity in the renewed civil war in Laos in 1960–61.

But the Soviets had every reason to avoid their own overcommitment in Indochina. Khrushchev, as we have seen, was after bigger game. At his meeting with Kennedy in the spring of 1961 he brushed aside the whole issue of Laos as unimportant. The subsequent solution of neutral Laos represented what the Soviets at the time aimed for. What emerged was a fragile neutralist regime with pro-Communist forces still occupying part of the area, thus enabling North Vietnam to send through Laos men and supplies for guerrilla activities in the South.

With the escalation of the Sino-Soviet conflict in 1963 the situation received a new twist. The North Vietnamese leaders had every reason to listen to Peking's insinuations that the Russians, as part of their *détente* with the United States, were giving up their support for wars of national liberation. Naturally Hanoi drew closer to China, and in 1963–64 it took Peking's side in the dispute with Moscow. It refused to sign the nuclear test ban treaty. The Chinese version of the Soviets' "betrayal"—"When the struggle of the Vietnamese and the Laotian people grew acute [the Soviets'] policy on the question of Indochina was one of 'disengagement'. . . when the U.S. imperialists engineered the Boc Bo Gulf incident,[4] Khrushchev went so far as to concoct the slander that the incident was provoked by China."[5]

Whatever the exaggeration in the Chinese version, it is true that in 1963–64 the Soviets became alarmed by the developments in Vietnam. The tempo of guerrilla activities in the South was quickening, and so was the American involvement. The number of American military "advisers" grew. President

[4] Known to the Americans as the Tonkin Gulf incident. On August 5, 1964, the U.S. forces conducted air strikes against North Vietnamese units in retaliation for alleged attacks on American destroyers in the Tonkin Gulf by North Vietnamese torpedo boats.

[5] *Peking Review*, November 12, 1965, p. 15.

Diem and his family were overthrown on November 1, 1963. The official American sources denied Washington's previous knowledge of or complicity in the military coup, but the Soviets, and with good reason, found it hard to believe. Rumors had been rife that the murdered Vietnamese leader, caught between the increasing American pressures to enact democratic reforms and the increasing activity by the Vietcong, had been contemplating some modus vivendi with the North.[6] Some time later, in an interview with an American journalist, Mao referred to the murdered nationalist leader: "Both Ho Chi Minh and [Mao Tse-tung] thought that Ngo Dinh Diem was not so bad. They had expected the Americans to maintain him for several more years. But impatient American generals became disgusted with Diem and got rid of him."[7]

Whatever construction one puts on Mao's words, it reflects an assessment common to Moscow and Peking that the Americans (and contrariwise to Mao, not so much "generals" as American politicians) were impatient. Confronted with an involved situation, they were likely to overact.

In addition to impatience, America's disastrous overinvolvement in Vietnam was prompted by Washington's rather oversimplified analysis of the situation in the Communist world. Following the settlement of the Cuban crisis of 1962 and the Soviet Union's agreement to the nuclear test ban, Soviet Russia was seen by the planners of American foreign policy as no longer bent upon dynamic expansion of Communism. China, it was felt, now represented the main threat. And so, before Peking acquired a stock of nuclear weapons, one had to demonstrate for the benefit of Mao and Co. that wars of national liberation "do not pay." And what better place for the lesson than Vietnam!

This was then the setting of the preliminary stage of the Vietnam tragedy which was unfolding late in 1964. Both Washington and Peking were eager to use the unhappy land as the testing ground for their policies. The North Vietnamese leaders by now realized that following their Chinese friends' advice might get them in very serious trouble with the United States and that they would need more than just sympathetic cheers from Peking. In August the Secretary General of the Communist Party of North Vietnam traveled to Moscow. There he heard some counsel of caution and probably Khrushchev's "slander" that the Gulf of Tonkin incidents were the product of Chinese provocation. The Russians may well have surmised, or indeed

[6] During the months of August and September 1963, Ho Chi Minh approached President Ngo Dinh Diem of South Vietnam with requests that the latter should demand the departure of U.S. military personnel and should declare South Vietnam a neutral state. In return Ho was prepared to offer very generous terms, including the cessation of Vietcong attacks. P. J. Honey, *Communism in North Vietnam* (Cambridge, Mass., 1963), p. 197.

[7] Edgar Snow in the *New Republic*, February 27, 1965, p. 18.

learned through their intelligence channels, that following the presidential elections the Americans would step up their activity in Vietnam and conveyed this information to the North Vietnamese. At the same time there took place the still obscure initiative from Hanoi, transmitted through the Secretary General of the United Nations, for *pourparlers* with the United States, an initiative which Washington rejected.

This was the situation which the Brezhnev-Kosygin team inherited. In January 1965 (the Chinese obligingly inform us) the Soviet Government transmitted to North Vietnam American proposals that it stop supporting the Vietcong. The Soviets for their part asserted their willingness to provide material aid to Hanoi and announced that Kosygin was going there in February.

The Soviet Premier was going there to offer both help and advice. It is not difficult to divine what was the gist of the latter: the Vietcong was clearly winning the war in the South; it would be unwise for the North Vietnamese to push the issue too strongly or violently. They could cash in their gains at a conference table—some arrangement on the Laotian pattern of a coalition and a neutralist regime could be achieved—and then within a few years the South would lapse peacefully into the Communist camp. But as Kosygin was negotiating in Hanoi, the Americans staged their first bombing raid on North Vietnam.

The American bombings were at first presented as a reprisal for the Vietcong raid on the American base at Pleiku that took place on February 5. Yet, as we now know, the decision to bomb had been arrived at some time before, in the summer of 1964, as the means of pressing North Vietnam to discontinue its support and direction of the guerrilla movement in the South. Though anticipated by the Soviets, the bombings, as the Chinese had hoped, did put the Russians on the spot. Vietnam now became the testing ground not only for the Americans' theories on how to cope with wars of liberation but also for the Soviet readiness and ability to protect a Communist regime from the superior power of the United States. Without the bombing and the other dramatic developments, which were to rivet the world's attention to Vietnam, the Soviet Union might well have continued its effort to find a discreet diplomatic solution to the crisis. But the bombing of the North was in the eyes of the Communist world a challenge, not to North Vietnam or even China, but to the senior Communist power.

It was this last mentioned fact which was totally and fatally disregarded in the previous calculations by the American policy-makers. The Soviet Union was no longer, as it had been during the Stalin era, in a position to ride roughshod over the interests and sentiments of another Communist state or movement. The Soviet failure to react sharply to the bombings would have eroded its credibility as the protector of Communist movements and states, would have "proved" the Chinese thesis that Russia was not a fit leader of world Communism. It was at least naïve on Washington's part to expect Russia to react to the U.S. actions with indifference, if not indeed secret approval on the grounds that Vietnamese Communists had ranged themselves on China's side.

By the same token the Soviet reactions were bound both to disappoint and to infuriate Peking. The Chinese expected Moscow to enter on a sharp collision course with the United States, possibly by challenging the Western position once again in Berlin. But in Washington's parlance the Soviets adopted a "measured response." The Soviet regime proposed to adopt a tough but subtle course of action designed to frustrate American aims at the same time that it would minimize the chances of a catastrophic confrontation with the United States.

Its main ingredients were: (1) strengthening of North Vietnam's defenses through supply of war matériel; (2) an attempt to bring the issue to the negotiating table, possibly through the reconvening of a Geneva conference; (3) an effort to scare the Americans out of further escalation with tough talk, including threats of sending "volunteers" to North Vietnam; and (4) establishing some procedures with other Communist countries, principally China, for jointly aiding Vietnam.

It soon became clear that this whole plan of action was repugnant to China. Any idea of dealing with the crisis through negotiation was viewed in Peking as a betrayal. On his way to and from Hanoi, Kosygin stopped in Peking, being accorded on the second occasion an audience with Mao. And his hosts were to give this version: "When Kosygin . . . passed through Peking on his visit to Vietnam in February 1965 and exchanged views with Chinese leaders, he stressed the need to help the United States 'find a way out of Vietnam.' This was firmly rebutted by the Chinese leaders."[8]

The Chinese opposition centered on Item 2 of the Soviet plan. Since they hoped for an aggravation of relations between the Soviet Union and the United States, any negotiated settlement of Vietnam ran counter to their interests. This position, in which Mao's regime was to persist until 1972, also colored its position on Item 1. Massive Soviet help and the introduction of Russian military specialists to North Vietnam would obviously increase Soviet leverage in Hanoi. And so, seemingly paradoxically, the Chinese Communists put difficulties in the way of the U.S.S.R.'s supplying of the North with matériel and expert help. Early in 1965 the Soviet Union asked China to allow passage for 4,000 Red Army troops and requested air bases on Chinese soil to expedite the transit of war matériel, and both requests were allegedly refused.[9] Then, though

[8] *Peking Review*, November 12, 1965, p. 15.

[9] William E. Griffith, ed., *Sino-Soviet Relations, 1964–1965* (Cambridge, Mass.: MIT Press, 1967), p. 73.

shipment of Soviet war matériel through China was allowed, it was still interfered with, and the Chinese contemptuously declared that the U.S.S.R. was sending obsolete weapons and in insufficient quantity. These startling actions were explained by Peking in language that speaks for itself: "If we were to take united action on the question of Vietnam with the new leaders of the CPSU who are pursuing the Khrushchev revisionist line, wouldn't we be helping them to deceive the people of the world? Wouldn't we be helping them to bring the question of Vietnam within the orbit of Soviet-U.S. collaboration?"[10] And more explicitly: the Russians "in giving a certain amount of aid" to North Vietnam are trying "to keep the situation under their control, to gain a say on the North Vietnam question, and to strike a bargain with U.S. imperialism on it."[11]

Peking's motivations were transparent. The Soviet Union was supposed to help Hanoi through pressuring the United States elsewhere, say in Germany. As for Vietnam, this was China's bailiwick, and the extent and type of help furnished to the North and the guerrillas in the South was to be decided by Peking. In brief, as had been the case since 1960, the Chinese demanded virtual control of the international Communist movement and hence of Soviet foreign policy. And when these demands were not met, Sino-Soviet relations took a turn for the worse.

The meeting of Communist parties held in Moscow between March 1 and March 5, 1965, was thus bound to end in a failure. Of the twenty-six parties invited only eighteen sent delegates. North Vietnam and Rumania were conspicuous by their absence. In view of the abstentions and the Vietnam crisis, the latter persuasive, even to the most pro-Soviet parties, that this was not the moment to publicize and aggravate Communist disunity, the meeting could not lead to any concrete decisions. Yet the very fact that it took place increased Peking's fury. It "will remain forever infamous," wrote the Chinese press.

On March 4, 1965, the Soviet authorities organized a "spontaneous" demonstration at the American Embassy in Moscow to protest the latest bombings. But then the demonstration did in fact become spontaneous, for the Chinese students who were in its forefront broke through the protective police cordon and manhandled Soviet militiamen. Citizens of Moscow were thus treated to the unusual spectacle of representatives of the Soviet state being beaten up by foreigners. In the Kremlin's eyes this was the last straw, and it brought an end, at least temporarily, to the cultural exchange between the two Communist powers. The Chinese students were expelled, to receive a heroes' welcome on their arrival home.

The post-Khrushchev reconciliation was thus in shambles. For the next

[10] *Peking Review*, November 12, 1965, p. 17.
[11] *Ibid.*, p. 16.

four years Sino-Soviet relations were to stabilize at the level of mutual hostility and public recriminations. We still don't know, and perhaps never will, how close the two Communist giants came to an actual confrontation; whether the sporadic border fighting in Asia was at any point close to turning into a sizable military conflict on the order of the Soviet-Japanese clashes in 1938 and 1939 or worse.

It is easy, however, from the perspective of the 1970's to reach two conclusions. First, the patching up of relations following the Khrushchev ouster would not have lasted in any case, even without the immediate clash over policies to be pursued in answer to America's intervention in Vietnam.

Second, while Vietnam was the immediate cause of the new crisis between China and the Soviet Union, by the same token America's continued and massive involvement in Southeast Asia kept the Sino-Soviet conflict from becoming even sharper than it did. For, until the moment the United States pulled its troops out of Southeast Asia and when it became clear that, whether and whenever the U.S. would disentangle itself from the Vietnam conflict, its original aim to "teach the Communists a lesson" had failed, the American involvement undercut both the ability and the incentive of Russia and China to seek an accommodation with the United States. And without such an accommodation neither side could risk a *very drastic* escalation of hostility with the other Communist power.

The U.S. massive blunder had thus the ludicrous effect of unwittingly and in different ways aiding *both* China's and Russia's diplomatic position. The Chinese might trumpet loudly about Russia's selling out North Vietnam, about the revisionists' and imperialists' readiness to join in an attack on China. But rationally they recognized that, for the time being at least, Vietnam was a barrier to an understanding between Moscow and Washington, and in the absence of such an understanding the Soviet Union was not likely to attack China. Mao and his clique launched in mid-1966 the Cultural Revolution, which split the Party and state apparatus and brought China to the verge of civil war, but they could do so with some confidence that the indirect Soviet-American confrontation over North Vietnam would keep the Soviets, who were obviously itching to do so, from intervening in the Chinese crisis.

To the Soviet Union the U.S. policy was helpful in a different way. True, during the first phase of the American bombardment and the buildup of U.S. forces in the South, Russia's prestige became tarnished. At the Twenty-third Party Congress, in March 1966, some foreign Communists (notably representatives of North Vietnam and Cuba) implied strong criticism of the U.S.S.R. for not taking greater risks to bring this dangerous precedent to an end. But when it became clear that American bombs were not bringing Hanoi to its knees, when the domestic and foreign consequences of

America's inclusive war became apparent, Soviet actions vis-à-vis Vietnam, that is, large-scale material and diplomatic support, were bound to impress world Communist opinion as just the right blend of firmness and moderation. What at first looked like faintheartedness appeared then as prudence. And when cultural revolution shook both China and the United States, the restraint of the Soviet leaders stood out, again to borrow from Pentagonese, as a masterpiece of "measured response."

Thus as we shall see the catastrophic overcommitment in Vietnam drastically depreciated America's diplomatic assets. In 1964 Washington enjoyed tremendous political advantages and even greater opportunities. The outstanding fact of world politics was the Sino-Soviet conflict, which, though papered over with Khrushchev's dismissal, was bound to flare up again. Within one year this conflict, though again acute, became overshadowed by America's even deeper commitment, as well as its helplessness to conclude the Vietnamese involvement. And by 1971–72, in order to extricate itself from that predicament, the United States, far from having taught China and Russia any lessons, would in fact be obliged to try to appease both Communist powers with the kind of concessions that the original intervention in Vietnam was designed to avoid. The defeat of Communist insurrection in South Vietnam was pursued by the American policy-makers mainly with the aim of arresting the growth of Communist China's influence in Asia. And by going on an official visit to China in 1972, the President of the United States was to recognize that country's status as at least a future superpower. And, as we shall discuss, the impetus for the U.S. concessions in 1972 on the German question, concessions that would have been inconceivable a decade before, was to be motivated by America's reduced bargaining power (again largely because of the Vietnam imbroglio) vis-à-vis the Soviet Union.

The discomfitures of the U.S. policies in the 1960's obscured, but could not detract from, the palpable fact that the Soviet Union was suffering from disappointments and setbacks in its foreign policy. The developments since Khrushchev's fall bear further witness to the fissiparous tendencies within the Communist world. Soviet attempts to arrest the erosion of unity, to restore even a semblance of solidarity (and the Kremlin does not even try any more to reassert its *absolute* direction) of the movement have proved unavailing. The coup of Prague in 1968 was to demonstrate that the Soviet Union set definite limits on the autonomy of its *European* Communist partners and the extent of internal liberalization it would allow in members of its Eastern bloc. But changes since 1953 have made outright Soviet control of the satellites impracticable. And the Sino-Soviet conflict made it possible for one of them, Albania, to skip the leash entirely and for another, Rumania, to achieve considerable autonomy in foreign and economic policies.

The case of the latter has been very instructive. Rumania has demonstrated how a Communist regime sure of itself (that is, confident that it did not need Soviet military support to keep it in power and sufficiently monolithic not to fear internal dissidence) could disagree on important economic and foreign policy matters with the U.S.S.R., which would have been unthinkable before 1953 and unlikely before 1960. The paradox has been all the greater because Rumania did not purchase this autonomy vis-à-vis one Communist giant by a slavish adherence to the policies of the other, as in the case of Albania. Its policies toward the West had been *more* flexible and friendly than those of the Soviet Union. China's support and continuance of cordial relations with Rumania thus reflected the Peking view that defiance of Moscow by a Communist regime offsets many of its possible ideological and foreign-policy aberrations. Because Rumania is in Europe, its increasing commercial and diplomatic contacts with the West were not seen as dangerous, as they would have been in the case of an *Asian* Communist regime or movement.[12]

With the post-Stalin developments and especially with the lesson of China in their minds, the Soviet leaders have had second thoughts about the desirability of new, especially of large, nations' joining the socialist camp. India is a case in point. Under Khrushchev the Soviet Union developed friendly relations with India's Congress party regime. His successors expanded the support of and cordial relations with New Delhi. Implicit in those policies has been a clear preference for a *non*-Communist India and very real fear lest the vulnerable fabric of the Congress rule disintegrate under the vexing problems that beset one of the world's most populous and poorest nations. The Communist Party of India has in recent years split into several factions. The "official" pro-Soviet Communist Party has been the object of Chinese vituperation, second in its intensity only to the attacks on the Communist Party of the Soviet Union.

As early as 1965 the Indian policies of the Brezhnev-Kosygin regime brought Peking's wrath:

> The new leaders of the CPSU have taken over and expanded the enterprises of the firm of Kennedy, Nehru, and Khrushchev which Khrushchev worked hard to establish. They have carried further their alliance against China with the Indian reactionaries who are controlled by the U.S. imperialists. During Shastri's visit to the Soviet Union they granted India aid to the tune of U.S. $900 million in one year, which is more

[12] The Chinese Communists' denunciations of Yugoslavia (toned down in recent years) have reflected the fact that Khrushchev and his successors identified themselves with the policy of reconciliation with Tito's regime. Peking has seen the progressive *embourgeoisement* of Yugoslav society and its regime's maneuverings between the East and West as a possible and dangerous precedent for similar developments in the Soviet Union.

than all the loans Khrushchev extended to India in nine years. They
have speeded up their plans for military aid to India.[13]

For all the shrill exaggeration of the Peking charge, it contained a per-
spicacious insight as true in the 1970's as it was then: the new Soviet
leaders have persisted in the attempt to balance off China with India. Hence
their lack of enthusiasm for the prospect of Communism's coming to power
in the subcontinent. How long would Indian Communism remain pro-
Soviet if it, or even its currently pro-Russian faction, came to power in
New Delhi? Would it not gravitate toward a fellow *Asian* Communist
power? Would it, as had China in the 1950's, demand Soviet help on a
scale Moscow could not or would not grant? For some time now, the
Soviet leadership has shown little inclination for such fateful experimentation with history. Better a friendly, non-Communist regime, which can
serve Moscow's interests, if not in direct confrontation with Peking, then
with Peking's allies, such as Pakistan.

The Soviet Union's policies on the convoluted problems of Communism
in Asia were evidenced in the Russian reactions to the two major events
of 1965 on that continent. One was the eruption of the India-Pakistan
military conflict in August; the other was the bloody suppression of the
Indonesian Communist Party, which followed its unsuccessful coup on
September 30.

The India-Pakistan flare-up threatened to turn into a full-fledged war.
At that time such a war was adjudged by the Kremlin as not in the Soviet
interest. "The Soviet Government called upon India and Pakistan to start
negotiations to settle the conflict peacefully. It proposed its mediation if
both sides would find it useful."[14] The same Soviet source, after ritual-
istically blaming the "aggressive circles of Western countries" for inciting
the conflict, then becomes explicit about China's role: "The government
of the People's Republic of China in its notes of September 16, 19, and 21
accused India of provoking border incidents with China and concentrated
its armies on the Indian border, thus threatening to invade her territory."[15] A Tass communiqué of September 15 conveyed an oblique warning to Peking. On September 22 the hostilities were stopped; the leaders
of the two warring countries, Lal Shastri and Ayub Khan, accepted Premier Kosygin's offer to mediate their differences.

The meeting between the heads of the two governments took place on
Soviet soil, in Tashkent, from January 4 to January 10, 1966, in Kosygin's
soothing presence. The resultant declaration pledged both sides to refrain

[13] *Peking Review*, November 12, 1965, p. 14.
[14] J. A. Kirilin, ed., *History of International Relations and Foreign Policy of
the U.S.S.R.* (Moscow, 1967), III, 434.
[15] *Ibid.*

from using force in their dispute and to return their military units to the lines they occupied before the August imbroglio. This settlement postponed a further India-Pakistan clash for five years, and then it would take place under conditions much more favorable to India. For the Soviet Union, it was an undoubted diplomatic success. It prevented China from intervening, thus depreciating its standing as *the* Asian power. In India and Pakistan the failure of Britain and the United States to support one side unqualifiedly led to increased resentment of the West while, illogically but not surprisingly, *Russia's* neutrality enhanced its standing in both countries. Once again it was shown how long-standing virtues lose their glitter in a contest with newly acquired ones: The United States' constant urgings for moderation and peaceful solution to the dispute were felt, especially in India, to insult and derogate the country's national dignity; the recent Soviet shift to this attitude was hailed as indicating genuine interest in peace and real feelings of friendship. To many Asians it must have appeared that friendly relations with Russia provided better protection against the Chinese colossus than alliance with the United States.

The consequences of the attempted coup d'état in Indonesia were the most serious setback suffered by Communism in Asia since the Korean War. The strongest and most influential Communist Party in any Asian non-Communist state was practically erased. (The victims of anti-Communist terror have been estimated from 100,000 up.) Had anti-Communist repression on this scale occurred in any country allied with the United repression on this scale occurred in any country allied with the United States or struck a Communist Party *not* close to Peking, the Soviet Government and the press would have reacted with righteous indignation; mass meetings throughout the country would have called for punishment for the "fascist executioners and tools of American imperialism"; official Soviet Government notes would have bristled with threats. But the actual Soviet reactions were mild. An official account speaks for itself:

> In Indonesia important events took place that exerted great influence on the situation in Southeast Asia. On September 30 there was an unsuccessful attempt at a coup d'état. There began in the country mass terror against Communist and left organizations. Power passed into the hands of military leaders. The president issued a decree dissolving the Communist Party of Indonesia.[16]

Unusual language to describe the bloodiest suppression of Communism since World War II—"coup d'état," where one would have expected "people's uprising"; "military leaders," where traditionally a Soviet source would speak of "fascist and reactionary circles."

---

[16] *Ibid.*, p. 432.

Of late, Indonesia has been a sore disappointment to the Kremlin. In the 1950's no "neutralist" leader with the possible exception of Nasser was courted by the Russians as assiduously as President Sukarno of Indonesia. Though navigating skillfully in world politics (he had enchanted American statesmen and the American public on his first visit to the United States), Sukarno ultimately responded by leaning more and more toward the Communist bloc. The latter encouraged his expansionist policies. He, through threats, secured Dutch New Guinea, though its inhabitants were ethnically as distinct from the Indonesians as from the Dutch. The ambitious leader then plunged his country into a "confrontation" with newly created Malaysia, demanding in the first instance that it cede North Borneo, though most likely his ambitions extended to all of the former British possessions. Indonesia's harassment and intermittent guerrilla infiltration of Malaysia required considerable British help to the new state and indeed threatened at one time a major conflict. Soviet diplomacy seconded Sukarno's demands, echoed his description of Malaysia as a bastion of "neocolonialism," and provided Indonesia with economic help and military supplies.

Sukarno's foreign adventures were paralleled by his increasing reliance on the Indonesian Communist Party, its members and sympathizers penetrating the entire state apparatus. As with another leader of a new nation, Nkrumah, so with Sukarno: personal indolence and a taste for luxury, combined with a craving for power and inordinate ambition, pushed him toward the Communists rather than toward the Western powers, with their tiresome precepts of moderation in foreign policy and sermons about the need for peaceful economic development. He was feted and praised in Moscow and Peking, and Indonesia's policy became increasingly anti-Western to the puzzlement of Washington, which recalled its previous favors to the personable dictator. As late as 1964 the U.S. policy-makers sought to appease Sukarno and attempted to mediate his feud with Malaysia. And yet in no "neutralist" country was an anti-American demonstration so speedily organized and the U.S. Information Agency office and library so frequently burned as in Sukarno's land.

This evolution of Sukarno was at first highly esteemed in Moscow, and indeed at one time it earned him the Lenin Peace Prize. But then trouble stole into the Moscow-Djakarta relations. First, there was (and remains) a certain ascetic strain in the psychology of the Soviet leaders, combined with an understandable aversion to wasting their money. Except for the military weapons with which Indonesia was carrying out, and not very effectively at that, its "confrontation" with Malaysia and Britain, its leaders could show little or no productive return on the billion or more dollars the Soviet Union had sunk into the country. We have already seen how Khrushchev undiplomatically exploded on his visit to Indonesia. He was entertained with a profusion of dances and exhibitions of native arts and crafts but, alas, no tours of industrial plants and complexes for which, presumably, the hard-earned money of Soviet citizens was poured into the country. Perhaps this boorish behavior, so reminiscent of the schoolmaster-ish ways of Western statesmen, led the fickle Sukarno into, from Moscow's point of view, a much more serious transgression: he drew increasingly close to China. In January 1965, against Soviet advice, Indonesia pulled out of the United Nations. This development plus the pro-Peking stance of the PKI and the existence of a sizable Chinese community in Indonesia, comprising much of its merchant class, made the future evolution of this potentially very rich land of 100 million people the source of very con-siderable anxiety in Moscow.

The abortive coup of September 30 was an attempt by Sukarno, assisted by some elements in the Communist Party, to remove the last obstacle to his and the Communists' full rule—the well-entrenched and cohesive leadership of the armed forces. The failure of the coup and the subsequent relegation of Sukarno to a figurehead position—he became a virtual pris-oner of the generals—was greeted in Moscow with relief and in Peking with anguish. Had the coup succeeded, Indonesia would have become a complete satellite of Communist China. The U.S.S.R. concealed but faintly its satisfaction over the turn of events. Following the liquidation of tens of thousands of real and alleged Communists, the Soviet Government did not even go through the motions of temporary suspension of diplomatic relations with Djakarta. After the issue was no longer in doubt, there were some crocodile tears and an unconvincing show of indignation. Brezhnev, *in March 1966,* demanded "an end to the criminal murder of Communists —the heroic fighters for national independence of Indonesia and for the interests of the workers."[17] But even this belated slap on the wrist was offset by simultaneous and rather smug comments about the foolishness of Sukarno and the Indonesian Communists in lending themselves to Chinese designs and official expression of solicitude about maintaining good relations with the new masters of Indonesia.The old revulsion about the "neocolonialist" nature of Malaysia disappeared, and Indonesia's end-ing of the confrontation was warmly approved as marking the end of Sukarno's "adventurist" policy. An official spelled out the new line of Soviet policy: "The U.S.S.R. has commercial relations with Singapore and Malaysia and . . . an agreement has been reached about establishing dip-lomatic relations with the latter."[18]

Soviet reactions to the India-Pakistan clash of 1965 and to the disaster

---

[17] *Twenty-third Congress of the Communist Party of the Soviet Union* (Mos-cow, 1966), I, 31.

[18] Kirilin, *op. cit.,* III, 432.

that befell the Indonesian Communists were thus dictated almost entirely by the Sino-Soviet conflict and the fear that any further expansion of Communism in Asia would redound to China's advantage and would be contrary to Russia's interests. By 1965 the Soviets had in their own way developed a philosophy of "containment" of Asian Communism.

It is in Asia, then, that the inherent contradictions of world Communism, in a way much more complex than those of world capitalism as postulated by Lenin, can be best observed. The Soviet Union as a state, the Soviet people as a nation, must view every accretion in the power and influence of Communist China as a threat. But, paradoxically, the rulers of the U.S.S.R. cannot disentangle themselves completely from their ideology and pursue policies that are solely in Russia's national interest. To some extent the Soviet Union's help must be extended to revolutionary movements throughout the world; it must continue to play the old game even in view of the probability that some other power will walk away with the chips. The Kremlin could be cynical over the Indonesian Communists' fate, yet it cannot *permanently* assume the posture of indifference over what is happening to Communism in Southeast Asia or any other part of the world. When and if it assumes such a posture, we shall have to speak of *Russian* and no longer *Soviet* foreign policy. Ever since the death of Stalin the Soviet Union's rulers have been not only exploiters but also, to an extent, prisoners of their ideology.

Thus, throughout the 1960's and even at times when the relations between the two countries threatened war, the Soviet Union supported Communist China's right to occupy the Chinese seat in the United Nations and denounced the claims of Chiang's regime as fraudulent. But much more important has been the support and material help extended by the U.S.S.R. to North Vietnam. In pure power-politics terms, a complete and speedy failure of Hanoi to conquer the South would have been a blow to China and hence of indirect benefit to Russia. The Chinese recipe for wars of national liberation would have lost its attraction. With the success of American policies in Southeast Asia, an outright clash between the United States and China would have become a distinct possibility; certainly Washington would not have tried to appease China, the policy it entered upon in 1970–71 because of the frustration in Vietnam. In fact, with what might be described as naïve cynicism, President Johnson's administration did in fact expect, if not actual Soviet help over Vietnam, then Moscow's indifference to the American campaign against Communism in Indochina. But such a policy, while it might have been possible under Stalin, who did not have to hesitate when the Soviet Union's interests or his own whim urged the sacrifice of a foreign Communist movement, has not been open to his successors. They do not enjoy his absolute power over the world Communist movement, nor is their grip on their own society as firm as was his. And so it is only *intermittently* that they can afford to disregard the interests and opinions of their fellow religionists abroad.

These dilemmas of the current phase of Soviet Communism were vividly demonstrated at the Twenty-third Congress of the CPSU, which assembled on March 29, 1966. It could be seen how the collective leadership no longer disposed of that plenitude of power and that freedom of action which at one time were one man's. There had been rumors before the Congress that the new rulers would order at least partial rehabilitation of Stalin. It is interesting that at this juncture something resembling public opinion became, for the first time in many years, of some importance in Soviet politics. A group of Soviet intellectuals, disturbed over the prospects for and actual signs of a new "freeze" in Soviet life (such as the trial and conviction of the writers Sinyavsky and Daniel for their nonconformist writings and their circulation of their books abroad), addressed a private letter to the Presidium imploring it not to whitewash the dead tyrant and not to jeopardize the social and intellectual gains made since 1956. This gesture, and one suspects also the mainly divided counsels on this issue within the Presidium itself, stymied for the time being the attempt to restore Stalin to full respectability. And by the same token the reversal of Khrushchev's "liberal" domestic policies was not as drastic as expected.

The new leaders gave, however, clear signs of their determination to stabilize Stalin's stature at a safe distance from both its divine image of pre-1953 and that of an unbalanced criminal as projected by Khrushchev during the last years of his power. The highest Party organs were symbolically returned to the nomenclature they bore under Stalin: the First Secretary once more became General Secretary; the Presidium once more the Politburo. There was an ample warning that the regime would no longer tolerate the overly candid novelists, the indiscreet memoir writers, the film producers depicting unflattering aspects of the Soviet past. The oligarchs were quite explicit about their determination to put in their places, which in some cases would turn out to be forced labor camps, all those who worried "about what they will say about us abroad" rather than following the Party's directives. Nikolai Podgorny had a word for foreign advocates and prophets of liberalization of Soviet society: "How silly are the assertions made abroad about the supposed capitalist transformation taking place in the Soviet economy, about some 'liberalization' of socialist society which is developing, if you please, in the direction of convergence with the 'democracy' of the so-called 'free world.' "[19] These were "slanderous fabrications" without a shadow of truth, said the Presi-

---

[19] *Twenty-third Congress*, I, 235.

dent of the Soviet Union. And this for the benefit of not only some Western scholars but the main purveyors of such "slanders" from Peking.

While the regime spelled out its aim to tighten, though gradually and without reverting to Stalin-like terror, the political reins, it proposed at the same time to offer concessions to the Soviet citizen in his capacity as the consumer: for the first time in the history of Soviet planning, the scheduled increase in consumers' goods under the Five-Year Plan for 1966–70 was to be proportionately higher than that of producers' goods. Special care was to be devoted to agriculture, where, the leaders implied, in large measure correctly, the result of Khrushchev's "hare-brained schemes" had been particularly harmful. Along with color television, more cars were to be provided to Soviet citizens (who, Khrushchev had assured, in their socialist probity preferred better public transportation to the evils consequent upon mass individual ownership of automobiles).

These were, then, policies formulated by cautious, conservative-minded men. Through the use of the stick and the carrot, they sought security for their continued rule. They proposed to put an end to what they deemed to have been both scandalous and dangerous license, especially on the part of intellectuals. At the same time the Soviet citizen was to be compensated for his political and intellectual deprivations by the vision of a better material future. Such people were not, and are not, likely to depart from what they consider the safe course in foreign policy, to seek a basic improvement, or to risk a drastic deterioration in their relations with the West; to discard entirely the militant element in Communist ideology or to subordinate to it the interests of their state.

The language of the leaders on East-West relations was neither as blustering and threatening as Khrushchev's at his worst nor as promising and cordial as he had been in his most "coexistential" moments. They would avoid dangerous confrontations, as over Berlin. The Soviets would continue their long-range aim of neutralizing West Germany, but they would seek to achieve it through patient diplomacy, through profiting from Western Europe's growing disenchantment with the United States—on account of Vietnam and America's internal turmoil—rather than through threats and ultimatums.

The same pose of patience and firmness in the face of provocations was adopted by the regime vis-à-vis the Chinese. The Chinese Communist Party was invited along with others to send its delegates to the Congress. To this polite invitation the Peking leaders replied that the Central Committee of the CPSU must surely be joking. Why, just before the Congress it had distributed a report charging that China meant to propel the Soviet Union into war with America and that it was "encroaching on Soviet territory." How could the "dear Comrades" (of the salutation), otherwise known as "lackeys of imperialism" (in the body of the letter), expect true Marxist-Leninists to attend this sham performance? Someday, the Chinese asserted, the true revolutionaries who constituted "90 per cent" of the CPSU would remove their revisionist leaders, but until that day the Central Committee of the CCP remains "with fraternal greetings—" In their boycott the Chinese were joined by the Albanians, the Japanese Communists, some minor Asian parties, and, oddly enough, the New Zealanders. But Soviet help to North Vietnam reduced the number of Asian parties that otherwise might have been absent. Delegates of North Vietnam and North Korea and of the National Liberation Front of South Vietnam came to the Congress. Thus even before the Cultural Revolution the CPSU succeeded in reducing the influence of China among Asian Communist countries and the attraction of what it had branded as "dogmatism and left-wing sectarianism of Peking everywhere else."

The Soviet leadership's need to restore some appearance of unity in world Communism weakened by the same token its freedom of action in foreign policy. Gone were the days when it could appear that the relationship between Moscow and the foreign parties was strictly one-way: its to command, theirs to obey. Now, even those foreign Communists ready to acknowledge Soviet primacy would occasionally criticize Soviet foreign and even domestic policies. The Yugoslav Union of Communists was treated at the Congress as a full-fledged member of the Communist family for the first time since 1948, its delegation "greeted warmly" in Brezhnev's opening remarks, as against just being "greeted" as were non-ruling Communist parties. Its chief representative, Minister of the Interior Alexander Rankovic, chose somewhat patronizingly to read a lesson to his hosts: in *his* country, he said, economic and social reforms had led to the development "of the workers' economic and social self-government," an unmistakable hint that the Soviet Union had a long way to go in this respect. Ironically enough, shortly after his return to Belgrade, Rankovic was removed and accused of hampering Tito's efforts at further democratization.

And so the Twenty-third Congress witnessed the novelty of foreign Communists' presuming to hint to the Russians what was wrong with *their* Communism. The Yugoslavs' boldness was not an isolated case. The Italian Luigi Longo chose to state that the Italian Party struggled "for the defense of cultural freedom, for the development and renovation of education and science."[20] This was a but thinly veiled criticism of the Soviet regime's persecution of nonconformist writers. The Rumanian Ceausescu reminded his hosts and the Congress that the safeguarding of peace required the observance "of national sovereignty and independence, equality, noninterference in internal affairs, mutual benefits [in interstate relationships], of

[20] *Ibid.*, I, 315.

the sacred right of every nation to decide for itself its own fate and to choose in accordance with its interests the nature of its political, economic, and social development."[21] These words referred clearly to the Soviets' past efforts to get the Rumanian Communists to choose a more pliable leader and, in general, to abandon their independent line in foreign policy. And on that, Ceausescu was unrepentant: his government, he said, was "developing cooperation with all countries regardless of their social systems."

On the most excruciating dilemma of world Communism 'the Soviets had to confess their helplessness. The official post-Khrushchev view was expressed by Brezhnev: the Communist Party of the Soviet Union watched the developments in China with sadness but without rancor. It desired friendship with the Chinese people and their Communist Party. But it is not *Russian* Communists who will abandon their ideological position as a price for unity. There was unconscious humor in Brezhnev's sad reflection: "Life has shown that departures from Marxism-Leninism, whether of the left or right variety, become especially dangerous when they are combined with symptoms of nationalism, great-power chauvinism, and striving for world hegemony."[22]

Some of the visitors did not profess to view the Chinese problem with such philosophical detachment. Hungary's Kadar implied that the obstreperous Party should be declared outside the pale: "There is no such thing as Communism which is anti-Soviet, and never will be." In a number of countries the pro-Chinese elements were setting up rival Communist bodies. "Splitters from afar," bewailed the Peruvian representative, had set up such a body, "which has few members, but rich protectors." Similar tales were heard from other Latin American countries and from Australia. Some of the Latin American delegates announced their unhappiness not only over the Chinese intrigues but also over those of another intruder: Castro. The brash self-proclaimed newcomer to Communism had been advocating guerrilla activities, urging rejection of such "square" notions as the need to build a mass base for the Party. Argentina's Victorio Codavilla, a veteran of the Comintern, expressed what might be called the conservative Communist approach to Castro: "We reject the anti-Leninist views of certain bourgeois ideologists who attempt to reject or minimize the role of the Party." It was well known that many in the Soviet hierarchy were unhappy over Castro's disruptive activities and his all too transparent ambition to be the Latin American Lenin.

World Communism was obviously in its greatest disarray since at least the mid-1920's. Appeals to unity and promises of yet another conference

---

[21] *Ibid.*, I, 288.
[22] *Ibid.*, I, 31.

of the "fraternal parties" to try to solve the insoluble, the Sino-Soviet split, could not obscure this fact. But this disunity and the consequent Soviet discomfiture were tempered by two facts. In the first place, the enormous power of the Soviet Union made it impossible for most foreign Communists to contemplate seriously a breach with the Fatherland of Socialism. The Italian Communists might publicly sulk about the *extent* of intellectual repression in the U.S.S.R., but this was largely for the benefit of the non-Communist left in their own country, whom they were wooing. The Rumanians, for all of their assertions of the right to their own economic and foreign policy, were far from wishing or daring a definite breach with Moscow. Soviet power was for the ruling Communist parties a guarantee of their own—for the nonruling ones, the main ingredient in their hopes of achieving their own one day. Where would they all be should the Soviet Union decline as a world power or should it *publicly* profess its disinterest in world Communism? And so these were family squabbles—the leadership of the host country no longer presenting the frightening father image of the Stalin period—rather than intimations of an outright rebellion.

In the second place, it was Vietnam that lessened the existing dissonances and obscured the lack of unity of purpose. True, some of the visitors felt that the Soviet Union was doing far from enough in countering the American imperialists. Le Duan, Secretary General of the North Vietnamese Communists, hinted at the need for more Soviet aid and a more militant posture vis-à-vis the United States. "The only correct line at present is unity of all revolutionary forces in order to frustrate the aggressive political course of the imperialists headed by the United States to force them to retreat step by step, to wrest from them one position after another."[23] A Cuban delegate was more explicit: "For the victory over imperialism in Vietnam, it is necessary to put an end, using all the available means *and taking the necessary risks,* to that criminal aggression which is the bombing of Democratic Republic of Vietnam."[24]

But to the majority of other parties, not to mention the domestic contingent, moral and material help, short of a dangerous confrontation with the United States, constituted precisely the right course. The Cuban's speech was listened to in silence, without any applause, and it is reported that its more explicit criticisms of the Soviet restraint were greeted by scattered boos. Not only the Russians but foreign visitors in the audience as well felt it out of place that a representative of a regime that owed its survival to the U.S.S.R. should demand new commitment and further risks from the Soviet people. Because a Communist dictator in the Caribbean

[23] *Ibid.,* I, 222
[24] *Ibid.,* I, 322 (my italics).

felt thwarted and restless, his island not big enough for his ambitions, was peaceful construction at home to be jeopardized, were the interests of the whole movement to be threatened and the world exposed to the danger of a nuclear war? And the same went for the Chinese. Brezhnev's final formulation must have appealed not only to his Soviet listeners: "We . . . had the opportunity to hear the speeches of our comrades-in-arms, our foreign friends. . . . Hearing them, we were reassured that our class brothers around the world realize that the main help to their revolutionary strug-gle and our main contribution to it lies in the successful construction of Communism in our own country."[25] Support and material help for em-battled Communist movements abroad—yes; unduly militant policies risk-ing a nuclear clash—no. This was the formula that Russia's new leaders proposed to follow. The taste for dramatic improvisations that would drastically change the appearance of world politics on the order of Soviet designs between 1958 and 1962 had gone out with Khrushchev.

Early in 1964 the international scene appeared on the eve of some very basic changes: there were prospects for a far-reaching *détente* be-tween the U.S.S.R. and the West, a very real likelihood for an escalation of the Sino-Soviet conflict. The removal of Khrushchev and, even more so, the intensification of the American commitment in Vietnam led instead to a continued impasse both in Soviet-Western and in Sino-Soviet relations. By becoming bogged down in Vietnam, the United States, apart from everything else, thus passed up major opportunities for improving the diplomatic and political position of the West vis-à-vis the Communist world.

Vietnam, in the first place, inhibited the Soviet leaders from new initia-tives and possible concessions toward the West. Then it became clear that the ever growing American commitment—large-scale military intervention came in the wake of air raids—was far from producing the expected results: the United States had denied the South to the Communists but was ever farther from terminating the conflict. It was thus tempting and natural for Moscow to proclaim American failures and discomfitures as *Soviet* successes. The Soviet Union did not have to do much to impress both foreign Communists and its own people that it was more than holding its own in the competition with West. American casualties in the indecisive fighting in a small Asian country were growing, while no Soviet soldiers were being killed on foreign soil. The war was costing the United States on the order of $30 billion annually, not to mention the incalculable harm it was causing to American society and American prestige abroad. The Soviet help to North Vietnam was below $1 billion annually: Soviet pres-tige grew while that of the United States declined. For the run-of-the-mill

25 *Ibid.*, II, 295.

bureaucrats who took over from Khrushchev, the U.S. predicament must have soon appeared as a heaven-sent answer to many of their own problems. The world's attention was focused on Southeast Asia and on the reverberations of the war within the United States rather than on the parlous condition of Soviet and world Communism. Domestically, Khrushchev's heirs found it easier to undo his sporadic and quite modest concessions to liberalism and to reimpose some of the controls and spirit of Stalin's era. Diplomatically, the Soviets were cashing in heavily on Washington's prodigious miscalculations. Exasperated by the unending predicament, Johnson's administration clung rather pathetically to its original premise that it was combating in Vietnam *Chinese* Communism, hence it was incumbent upon the Russians to understand the American actions— why, even to help the United States out of the mess. Moscow was naturally not above encouraging this touching belief by occasionally using a more restrained tone about the United States and by showing interest in American peace initiatives. To give Washington's illusions their due, the Soviets did have a vital interest in the Vietnam situation's not overheating. But once it became obvious that the Americans would neither master the situation nor resort to drastic measures that would really put the U.S.S.R. on the spot, such as using nuclear weapons or invading the North, there was every reason for Moscow just to sit back and enjoy the situation.

To be sure, there was, from the Russian point of view, a fly in this ointment. America's folly was helping not only Moscow but also Peking. At first there might have been some expectation, possibly hope, in the Kremlin that America's massive involvement would bring about a clash, perhaps a full-scale war, between China and the United States.[26] But very soon it became clear that (1) the United States did not plan a direct confrontation with China (whatever some U.S. Air Force generals might secretly desire, neither the government nor public opinion was ready for an extension of hostilities) and (2) on their part, for all their intemperate language, the Chinese leaders were too prudent to provoke such a clash. Chou En-lai, in an interview with a Pakistani journalist, was careful to specify that "China will not take the initiative to provoke a war with the

[26] It is largely forgotten how in the beginning it was widely feared in Washington that Peking would not take the bombing of its Communist neighbor and then the introduction of large numbers of American troops in Southeast Asia without reacting in the manner of its intervention in the Korean War. There were also intimations that *then* the United States would not observe its self-imposed restraint of the previous conflict, that is, the United States might strike aerial blows at China. There were no longer any sanctuaries, Secretary Rusk said pointedly at one juncture in 1965, meaning presumably that Chinese "volunteers" or Chinese planes over North Vietnam would bring U.S. retaliation against China proper. To the Kremlin this must have meant the not unpleasing possibility of the U.S. Air Force "taking out" the Chinese nuclear facilities.

United States." He then went on to refer to those diplomatic contacts between Washington and Peking which had been taking place since 1955 on the neutral and "revisionist" soil of Poland: "China has been making efforts in demanding through negotiation that the United States withdraw all its armed forces from Taiwan province and the Taiwan Straits, and she has held talks with the United States for more than ten years, first in Geneva and then in Warsaw."[27] To the oversuspicious Soviet mind, this sounded dangerously close to a hint that China might offer itself as the one to help the United States out of the Vietnam mess, but only if the price was right.

Each of the Communist powers viewed the Vietnam conflict as placing special obligations *on the other* to confront and risk a war with the United States. Each was conscious of the possible benefits that might accrue to it should the United States, frustrated in its policies, seek an outside intercession to bring the Vietnam nightmare under control. But such coldblooded calculations alternated with phantasmagoric fears. The Soviets, as early as February 1964, referred publicly to the possibility of Peking's making a deal with the United States at their expense. On May 28, 1966, the voluble Foreign Minister Chen Yi mentioned a parallel Chinese nightmare: the Soviets and the Americans might join hands hands in an attack upon China.

Amidst the welter of these suspicions, near possibilities, and outright fantasies, one fact stood as indisputable: whatever the possibility of an *eventual* collusion between Moscow and Washington, the Vietnam conflict made an immediate and extensive Soviet-American accommodation impracticable. And so this must have been one of the decisive factors in Mao's decision to launch the Cultural Revolution, which between mid-1966 and 1969 plunged China into virtual anarchy. For the time being he felt he had little to fear from the United States or the Soviet Union locked in a conflict over Vietnam.

The exact motivation of the campaign, whether it was planned in its full extent or whether, as seems likely, it got out of hand beyond the original intentions of the Great Helmsman, there are questions that still remain in dispute. But obviously one element in the campaign was Mao's conviction that he had to overcome his own oligarchy, which, while promoting his worship, sought to turn the seventy-three-year-old chairman into a figurehead. In decimating the Party and state hierarchy, Mao was following Stalin's example between 1934 and 1939. (To be sure, it *appears* that, unlike the previous purge, this one did not involve wholesale executions but mainly dismissals and imprisonments.) Instead of Stalin's use of secret police, Mao's group employed fanatical youths, the Red Guards,

[27] *Peking Review*, May 13, 1966, p. 5.

who invaded ministries and other institutions, beat and humiliated senior officials and "revisionist" Party leaders, professors, artists, and others of the hitherto China "establishment," as well as foreign diplomats. This was, in fact, an anarchist revolution, but on behalf of the highest leader and his currently nominated deputy and successor, Lin Piao. Some other oligarchs were cruelly treated: in July, President Liu Shao-chi had been No. 2 man in the country; one month later he was denounced; his very name was now omitted, he being referred to in the colorful English of the Peking Review as "China's Khrushchev" or "No. 1 capitalist-roader." Several others close to the top, such as the Party's General Secretary Teng Hsiao-ping and Peking's former mayor Peng Chen, also fell from their heights. In many places the local Party and state organs ceased to function, and it was the army, *then* assumed to be loyal to its leader Lin Piao, that preserved some semblance of authority.

Apart from promoting the cult and power of Mao (though Lin Piao's recent fate suggests that his reasons for sponsoring the revolution might have been different from those of the Chairman), the upheaval was carried out in the name of egalitarianism and of extirpating the noxious bourgeois and bureaucratic excrescences that allegedly had sprouted up in China. As one might expect from a *cultural* revolution, cultural life came to a virtual standstill, schools and universities being shut down, professors and eminent scientists and artists compelled to go to the countryside to imbibe the salutary influence of physical labor. Not only the hordes of young vandals, but senior leaders like Lin and Chou En-lai (his own position in jeopardy at one point) would appear in public carrying the little red book of Chairman Mao's sayings. He himself, while seen at various receptions and demonstrations, the only one *not* required to wave the little red book, preserved silence.[28]

The Soviet public reaction to the Cultural Revolution was a mixture of apprehension and amusement. Such a monumental outburst of irrationality in a country that was developing a nuclear stockpile was certainly a source of worry. There were some unpleasant parallels with Stalinism at its most horribly grotesque. Yet at the same time, the Soviet newspapers reported in a deadpan fashion the story of Mao's famous swim in the Yangtse on July 16—when, according to the calculations provided by the Chinese sources, the septuagenarian leader surpassed several world swimming records—the table-tennis players who attributed their success to the study of Mao's thought, and similar absurd incidents. There were more substantial grounds for Moscow's amusement: many foreign Communists previously drawn to China now recoiled at this baffling tragicomedy.

[28] The reason for his silence might have been similar to the statement in an American children's book about John XXIII: "Since the Pope is infallible, he must be very careful about what he says."

At the highest level of the Soviet Government, there was probably some appreciation of the real reasons for the developments in China. The purged leaders were almost invariably accused of being "revisionists," that is, pro-Soviet, but such accusations need not have been more valid than those leveled at victims of Stalin's purges in 1936–39, that they were German and Japanese agents. Yet it is quite possible that among those cast out were people who had pleaded for a lessening of tension with Russia and for more temperate domestic and foreign policies. Chou En-lai remained the one stable factor insofar as foreign policy was concerned amidst China's turmoil. The nimble veteran evidently survived the threat to his position and retained Mao's trust. It is almost exclusively through him that the rare Sino-Soviet contacts took place during those troubled years. But the regular diplomatic, not to mention inter-Party, channels of communication fell during those years into complete disuse.

In the late 1960's, then, the Brezhnev-Kosygin regime became an indirect beneficiary of the difficulties attending the two other giants whose actions and potential moves along with those of Russia preoccupied the attention of the world. The recent reverses and discomfitures of Soviet foreign policy became, at least partly, obscured in view of America's continuing inability to "solve" Vietnam and the consequent seepage of America's prestige in the world. China's bid to seize the leadership of the world Communist movement could not have succeeded in the 1960's anyway: the U.S.S.R. was so much richer and more powerful. But now, whatever inroads Peking had made into Soviet influence over other Communist parties, they were almost totally undone through the fatal effects of the Cultural Revolution. True, Soviet *power* over foreign Communists would never be the same as it had been prior to 1960, not to mention 1950. But again, Soviet *influence* became dominant even in places like North Korea, even over the Japanese Communists where prior to 1966 it had been clearly inferior and declining vis-à-vis that of Communist China.

The troubles of both China and the United States tended to promote the image of the U.S.S.R. as a "normal" peaceful state, no longer a threat to Europe. This enhanced respectability of the U.S.S.R. brought dividends in the increased diplomatic traffic between Moscow and powers that previously were hostile or felt threatened by it. Who could have foretold in 1917, or 1950, that the chief of state of the Soviet Union would in 1966 pay a visit to the Pope? Or that the Soviet Prime Minister would dine at Buckingham Palace?[29] Visits to Moscow by such potentates as the Shah

---

[29] The progress of Soviet influence and respectability (or conversely the decline of the British empire) can be judged by the following sequence: George V would never agree to receive the Soviet Ambassador; Khrushchev and Bulganin went only to tea at Windsor Palace; and then Kosygin, to be sure, in a dark business suit rather than evening dress, went to Buckingham Palace for dinner.

of Iran or the King of Afghanistan became too frequent to be noticed. How blasé the Soviet leaders had become over their country's being visited by the world's statesmen, and how drastically the world had been transformed since the days of Russia's diplomatic quarantine, may be judged from the following incident: the British Prime Minister was asked to hasten his arrival by a few hours. Premier Kosygin would be bidding farewell the same day to Prime Minister Indira Gandhi, and it would be such a nuisance for him to come to the airport, go away, and then come again to greet Harold Wilson. Britain's leader obliged.

The Western united front vis-à-vis the Soviet Union became one of the casualties of the late 1960's. It is difficult to determine what was more in-strumental in causing this change: whether it was the more moderate tone of Soviet foreign policy and hence the lessened sense of danger among the West Europeans or America's overcommitment in Southeast Asia, hence enhanced doubts and nervousness in Europe's capitals about Amer-ica's leadership.

In any case, the U.S.S.R. was capable of drawing solid diplomatic gains from this situation. The Brezhnev-Kosygin leadership, in contrast to Khrush-chev's of 1956–62, set about to reduce American influence in Europe not through dramatic tactics of threats and ultimatums, but through a more patient and subtle policy intended to emphasize Soviet Russia's new respec-tability as contrasted with America's recently displayed irresponsibility. The threatening Soviet rhetoric has not disappeared—to eschew it *entirely* would obviously weaken the Soviets' bargaining position.[30] But whether from the perspective of Paris, Rome, or even Bonn, the "Russian danger," while still clear, was no longer imminent: no one could visualize Messrs. Brezhnev and Kosygin ordering the Red Army to march on the West (it was to be something of a surprise when they launched it on Prague), as people had readily believed (to be sure erroneously) Stalin might have done, or even creating another Berlin crisis. The danger was now, it was thought, that the Russians might do something drastic in response to an *American* move. The realization that Western Europe was protected by U.S. power was thus balanced by the apprehension that this protection had a negative and dangerous side: a U.S.-Soviet confrontation over some dis-tant area, say in Southeast Asia, might suddenly threaten an Englishman's or a Frenchman's peaceful and prosperous existence.

On balance most governments, America's traditional allies, still felt that the benefits of the alliance with the United States outweighed its potential dangers. But the new posture of Soviet foreign policy, as well as grievances

[30] President Kennedy's injunction that one should never negotiate out of fear is, alas, one of those noble but hardly practical slogans: if the element of fear is *entirely* absent, there is but little reason to negotiate, be it with one's employees, students, or foreign powers.

of long standing against America, led one Western leader to seek a rapprochement with the U.S.S.R.

On their part the Soviets had good reasons to take a new look at General De Gaulle and France, where until 1968 his leadership appeared invulnerable to any challenge. Prior to 1963 he was hardly a favorite in Moscow's eyes. In 1959 and 1960 his opposition to Russia's demands on Berlin and readiness to call the Soviet bluff was clear and uncompromising, more so than the response of Washington. During the Cuban missile crisis the masterful Frenchman unflinchingly stood by the American side. In 1963 France refused to accede to the nuclear test ban treaty, thereby irritating Washington but by the same token enraging Moscow.

By the mid-1960's De Gaulle's policies increasingly diverged from those of the United States. Long skeptical over its ability to lead the West, he now despaired of its statesmen's grasp of world affairs. Determined from the beginning of his new lease on power in 1958 for France to have a more significant voice in the Western alliance, he now decided that his country must pursue a fully independent course rather than let the "Anglo-Saxons," as he quaintly called the United States and Britain, speak on behalf of Europe. He led France out of NATO and blocked Britain's entrance into the Common Market. In June 1966, for the first time since Nicholas II entertained President Poincaré, the head of the French Republic stepped on Russian soil.[31]

The visit, unlike his hardly gracious reception by Stalin in wartime, was a personal triumph for De Gaulle. He was lodged in the Kremlin, addressed a popular gathering, and was given an opportunity to inspect Soviet nuclear research and spaceship-launching facilities. These were unusual honors for a visiting Western leader. But the actual political results of the visit had to be disappointing. Unlike in 1914, France was no longer one of the arbiters of the world's fate. If De Gaulle had any hopes of persuading the Soviet Union to relax its grip on Eastern Europe, he was disappointed. The Soviets in their turn must have wished for French recognition of East Germany. But that far the French leader was unwilling to go. The official communiqué spoke modestly of both sides' agreeing that "European problems should be considered above all within the European frame of reference." The Vietnam problem, it was asserted, should be solved through adherence to the 1954 Geneva agreements. France, even its proud leader must have recognized, no longer possessed sufficient weight to be an equal partner of the Soviet Union in attempting to solve major international problems.

In December 1966, Premier Kosygin returned De Gaulle's visit, and it

---

[31] De Gaulle's wartime visit to the Soviet Union was, of course, in his capacity as leader of the provisional French Government.

was perhaps significant that it was *not* the No. 1 man in the Soviet regime to whom this task was delegated. Again, the concrete results were far from sensational. A Franco-Soviet communiqué once more promised mutual consultations on the problems of European security and emphasized the need for Europeans to solve them. Further steps were taken to ensure economic and scientific cooperation between the two countries. But on Germany, the main stumbling bloc to any European settlement, France and Russia were as far apart as ever.

In 1967 Soviet Russia reached the fiftieth year of its existence. Soviet diplomacy has gone through many stages. From a state which in 1918 by its very principle was opposed to every government then in existence, the U.S.S.R. had become by 1967 an accepted member of the world community of nations. From a devastated, weak, and backward country it had developed into one of the two economic and military superpowers. The Soviet regime, which few people outside or inside Russia had thought in 1918 could survive beyond a few months, has shown amazing resiliency and powers of adaptation. It has been able to continue through a period of bitter internal political crisis following Lenin's death, through domestic oppression and tyranny unparalleled in modern history, and a foreign war where at one point the foe had occupied territory comprising some 40 per cent of the Soviet Union's population. There had been, as a poet sang, "the war against the nation [Stalin's] and wars between nations." And then came the great test of the transition after Stalin's death: the regime, though in a very incomplete fashion, acknowledged the crimes of the past, disbanded *most* of the machinery of terror, and yet was able to preserve the main features of the totalitarian state. The semipopulistic, semidictatorial leadership of Khrushchev then gave way to what really is collective leadership—government by an oligarchy based upon a broad layer of state and Party bureaucracy, which no longer, as in Stalin's day, is vulnerable to the whim of the tyrant or, as under his successor, in a much less threatening sense, to the incalculable moods of a dictator, and hence identifies with and supports the Brezhnev-Kosygin regime as it could not have Stalin's or Khrushchev's. This has been the main element in that rather amazing picture of stability which the Soviet regime has displayed since 1967. There have been no continuous purges of the leadership, not to mention the intermediate and lower ranks of bureaucracy as under Stalin, no attempts at a palace coup as in 1957, and no dramatic splits within the ruling body, which were features of the Khrushchev years.

The story of the 1970's will show some of the negative, from the Soviet point of view, results of this achievement of respectability abroad and of stability at home. It will be seen that the basic dilemmas of both Soviet society and world Communism have in no sense become more tractable, but merely obscured. The erosion of the unity of world Communism has gone on, though in a less dramatic manner; the Sino-Soviet conflict, for all the lessening of violent rhetoric that accompanies it, remains insoluble. Since the new rulers discarded many of their predecessors' methods but none of their major objectives, they will not be able to accommodate even the very modest aspirations among their own people for more freedom, or among their own satellites for more internal autonomy. Hence the more rigid suppression of intellectual dissent, hence the invasion of Czechoslovakia. In the general sphere of international relations, the Soviet Government will work strenuously for the prevention of war but does not identify this task with the need for lessening international tension. Hence it bore some of the responsibility for the Arab-Israeli war of 1967. Hence it would not throw its weight decisively behind a peaceful solution of the Vietnam war until that moment when in Moscow's opinion the continued American involvement threatened to have consequences that would benefit China's interests to the detriment of those of Russia.

XIII

SAFETY FIRST

How can one characterize Soviet foreign policies since 1967? It would be a bold, indeed a reckless man who, writing in the 1970's, would attempt a definitive answer. A *future* historian will probably reach one of two basically different verdicts. He may be able to see the period as one of basic change of directions. The need for coexistence finally prevailed over the impetus for expansion. The Soviet Union relinquished active and militant propagation of Communism throughout the world. Without explicitly giving up its professed historical mission of furthering the cause, it acknowledged that in the nuclear age the growth of the "camp of socialism" must be the result of social and economic forces in the non-Communist world without Soviet power's being directly engaged to speed up this process. From this basic premise the Soviet regime has drawn the conclusion that the policy of coexistence with the West must assume a more genuine and active form. No more has the regime been content to define this policy as prevention of a major war. A general lessening of international tension and achievement of political stability first in Europe, then in other areas were added to Soviet goals. The Soviet-American agreements initialed in May 1972 would thus be seen as the beginning of a new era. Soviet influence was thrown on the side of a peaceful settlement of the Indochina crisis; the U.S.S.R. took steps to reduce the explosive potential of the situation in the Middle East. Above all, it acknowledged that coexistence requires a degree of collaboration and cannot be defined as just rivalry that eschews a nuclear conflict. Hence the collaborative effort with the United States to prevent proliferation of nuclear weapons, and first to freeze, then to reduce the nuclear armaments of the two superpowers.

Hopefully, this future historian will also be able to see the U.S.-Soviet agreement on a joint space project as a modest but significant token of what might be called positive collaboration of the Great Powers: not content with devising techniques for avoiding war and lessening tension, the two countries will seek to help each other in solving problems common to advanced industrial nations and thereby pass from the stage of *détente* into that of friendship, with benefits accruing not only to them but ultimately to the world at large. Such a shift in the Kremlin's approach to foreign policy would also influence its domestic politics. The rigorous drawing of domestic reins and repression of dissent were largely conditioned and always rationalized by the external danger. With the fear of the capitalist world gone, the Soviet regime would be bound to renew the process of internal liberalization arrested by the ouster of Khrushchev. Though its internal policies between 1964 and 1973 represented a step backward and a crackdown on dissent, the logic of the lessened world tension argued for domestic reform and relaxation. Even in the period under discussion the Soviet Government took at least one step indicative of its increased sensitivity to domestic protest and its reverberations amidst world public opinion: it allowed, to be sure grudgingly and not without chicanery, a number of Soviet citizens of Jewish origin to migrate to Israel. Though, in numbers and in proportion to those who would avail themselves of this permission, the outflow has not been impressive, the mere fact of its existence certainly is. Under Stalin no one would have dared to express publicly the aspiration to live under a different system, and prior to 1970 or so no one would have expected the Soviet regime to heed it.

As against the enticing prospects contained in the above, one must, however, contemplate a different verdict by a future historian. The 1967–73 period did not portend a fundamental change in Soviet foreign policy. It was one when for pressing reasons its makers changed their tactics without in the slightest being willing or, what is more important, able to depart from its basic premises and strategy. There have been occasions before, and not only touching on foreign policy. Take, for instance, the NEP, when the regime felt constrained to reverse its course and seek friends where it had seen only enemies. Then the particular configuration of events, the specific danger, would pass, and the Kremlin reverted to hostility and militant rivalry with the non-Communist world. In appraising the late 1960's and early 1970's, one ought to keep in mind the lesson of the middle 1930's and of the war years. The rapprochement with the West was terminated by the Soviet-Nazi pact; the sequel to the wartime alliance was Soviet expansion in Eastern Europe and the ominous isolation decreed for the U.S.S.R. by Stalin. What led the Brezhnev-Kosygin regime to become more tractable and to seek a *temporary* accommodation with the United States is clear. There was the need to liquidate the dangerous consequences of Khrushchev's adventurism. Internal, mainly economic difficulties compelled the U.S.S.R. to seek a reduction in its expenditures on armaments, to procure food from abroad, and to give a boost to the declining rate of Soviet industrial growth through wider commercial and technological intercourse with the West.

On the political side the *détente* with the United States grew mainly out of Soviet fears about China. It is characteristic that the most far-reaching steps in this *détente* were taken following the amelioration of relations between Washington and Peking. The Soviet Union, long apprehensive about such a contingency, now saw the horrendous possibility that, in return for Chinese help in extricating the United States from Vietnam, Washington might go beyond just establishing amicable contacts with Mao's regime and offer it economic and technological help. Hence the eagerness to outbid China and the Nixon-Brezhnev agreements.

As against such maneuvers the period still presented abundant evidence of the unchanging nature of Soviet ambitions. The Arab-Israeli war of 1967 would not have erupted except for the Soviet encouragement to Egypt to put a squeeze on Israel and thus on the U.S. position in the Mediterranean. It was only when Nasser went too far and the Arabs' catastrophic defeat threatened a wider conflict that the U.S.S.R. hastened to plead for a truce. The invasion of Czechoslovakia offered another and even more striking example of how the Soviet tactics of temporary *détente* should not be confused with a permanent shift to a policy of accommodation. The Soviet policy has remained the same: one of general advance interrupted occasionally by a tactical retreat. Once the Chinese danger became alleviated, say with the demise of Mao and a pro-Soviet regime in Peking, Soviet pressure on the West would again assume a blatant and dangerous character.

A pessimistic verdict on the 1967–73 period would buttress its argument with the conclusion that, in view of the basic character of the Soviet regime and its internal policies, it was fatuous to have expected Soviet foreign policy to undergo a basic change. Communism is a dynamic creed. For its devotees to acknowledge that there is no enemy to be thwarted, that no further victories beckon beyond the horizon, would mean to renounce their faith. As a practical consequence the Kremlin after such an admission could no longer aspire to the leadership of the world Communist movement. But even more important is the fact that the whole logic of internal repression has always rested on the real or alleged foreign threat. Admit that not merely coexistence but friendship is possible between the U.S.S.R. and America, and how will you contend with your people's clamor for more rights and benefits for the citizen and the consumer? The 1967–73 period was characterized by a steady reimposition of strict controls over cultural life, by a systematic repression of any sources of dissent. That the regime has not been entirely consistent in this respect (e.g., by allowing some Soviet Jews to emigrate) or that it has not cracked down even harder (e.g., by resorting to outright terror to extirpate the so-called *samizdat*, the underground literature) has been due to the realization that, once Khrushchev had opened Pandora's box of liberalization, it would be too dangerous to reverse direction too suddenly and sharply. But how much more difficult the task of running a tight totalitarian society is if the rulers admit that the *only* external threat comes from a country that shares their basic ideology! And so the period of 1967–73 must be seen as one of an illusory brightening of the international sky. Soviet foreign policy of the period might be characterized as New Foreign Policy, no more capable of being maintained for a long time, no more compatible with the essence of the Soviet system than was the New Economic Policy proclaimed by Lenin in the early 1920's meant "seriously and for a long time"—and by 1928 the NEP was abruptly reversed.

Which verdict will in fact be rendered by a historian writing in, say, 1980? All we can say at this point is that a Western statesman must keep the second eventuality firmly in mind while hoping and working for the first.

The year 1967 was one of great temptations for the Soviet foreign-policy-makers. The prudence of Khrushchev's successors was sorely tried by dazzling opportunities to advance Soviet influence in many areas of the world. The danger of a Soviet-American confrontation over Vietnam had clearly passed. The United States became mired down in Southeast Asia, unable to win the war and unable to cut its losses and extricate itself from it. Soviet material aid to North Vietnam was essential in frustrating American hopes for a quick military victory or forcing Hanoi to desist from feeding the flames of the civil war in the South, and yet it came relatively cheap: the cost of Soviet military supplies came to about $700–800 million per year, as against the $30 billion the United States was spending on the war. The impasse in Vietnam reduced the U.S. Government's ability and, above all, the American public's willingness to counter resolutely Soviet moves in other areas of the world. Instead of precipitating new and risky international crises (as in the past over Berlin), the Kremlin could simply wait for a promising conflict to develop in another part of the world and then throw its support to the side whose victory would spell further discomfiture and loss of influence for the West.

Such areas of trouble abounded in the so-called Third World. In Africa the Russians' expectations of deriving solid benefits from the breakup of the colonial systems had hitherto been frustrated. They had backed the losing side in the Congo. In West Africa Soviet hopes had centered upon Nkrumah. But Ghana's dictator, for whom Russian advisers trained a special bodyguard regiment, managed through his extravagant policies not only to ruin his country's economy but also to alienate his regular military establishment. And so in February 1966, while on a trip to Peking, he was overthrown. Within one week of the coup the new government demanded withdrawal of all Soviet citizens not directly connected with the U.S.S.R. Embassy or working on essential economic projects. Though denouncing the coup as spawned by American and British imperialist circles, the Kremlin acceded to the request and on March 17, 1966, recognized the new Ghanaian regime. Quite likely, Nkrumah's recent courtship of Peking served to soften the blow.

Those setbacks were now obscured by a new and major African crisis. On its achievement of independence in 1960, Nigeria was viewed in the West as the most promising force for stability within the African states and the one most likely to preserve a Western-type parliamentary regime. Within a few years these hopes foundered amidst a succession of military coups and growing conflicts between Nigeria's ethnic regions. Finally, a civil war pitted the central government, dominated by Northern Nigerians, against an attempted secession by the southeast area—Biafra. The conflict divided the West. Thus, though the British Government officially supported the central regime, much of the public opinion in Britain and elsewhere could not but sympathize with the weaker party—Biafra—in its struggle for what could be construed as national independence. The Soviet Government could on the contrary, without any compunction, throw its support and help to the stronger party and garner the dividends of increased influence in Africa's most populous state once the unequal contest ended with the liquidation of Biafra.

The Nigerian crisis illustrates vividly the natural advantages enjoyed by the Soviet Union vis-à-vis the West when it comes to dealing with the travails of what might be called the postimperial situation. In practically every corner of the world, the departure of Western rulers or the eruption of civil strife was followed by the arrival of Soviet advisers, economic "developers," and offers of economic and military aid. In contrast, the U.S. image as a noncolonial power was marred not only by America's intimate ties with former imperial powers like Great Britain but also by what in the eyes of much of the world, including a sizable part of the American public opinion, was its quasi-imperial involvement in Southeast Asia. Even in areas without a colonial past, Soviet interference in a domestic conflict could and was rationalized as support for the "progressive" forces as against the "feudal" and traditionalist one. In Yemen the

Egyptian Army, helping one of the warring factions, found itself unable to defeat hostile tribesmen aided by Saudi Arabia. The republican forces, striving for the control of that primitive land, had to be assisted by Soviet arms, supplies, and instructors. With the British about to move out of neighboring Aden, Soviet influence was reaching to the Red Sea.

By the same token, 1967 showed that the exhilarating game of cashing in on the West's past sins and America's current overcommitment could not be played with complete impunity. In intervening in other countries' internal problems and troubles, the Soviets, as against the Americans, have always enjoyed the advantage of what might be called the superior braking mechanism of their foreign policies. Foreign commitments can be undertaken without worrying about reactions of a free electorate, can be broken off suddenly with little or no concern for political consequences at home. And yet this remains true only up to a point. That intangible but important factor—call it national prestige or, in the current fashion, credibility—is involved in any power's *major* foreign entanglement. The inability of the United States to deal speedily and effectively with the insurrection in South Vietnam has eroded much of American prestige; the Russians' failure to prevent their Arab protégés from suffering a crushing defeat damaged that of the Soviet Union.

We have seen how easy and almost painless the task of building Soviet influence in the Middle East appeared *at first*. All it seemed to require from the Soviet Union was anti-imperialist rhetoric and then, as Britain and France clumsily attempted to hang on to the shreds of their former imperial position as in the 1956 Suez venture, some very vague threats addressed to London and Paris. But then as the Soviet stake in the area grew, so did the costs. The U.S.S.R. expanded its economic and military help to its Arab protégés, not only as at first to Egypt, but also to Syria, Iraq, and Algeria. Given the great economic importance of the region and a chance to deny its wealth to the West, the prospect of losing this great investment became distasteful. The great advantage that Moscow enjoyed over Washington in courting the Arabs was of course the fact that it could not only give them money and military equipment but also support *verbally* the anti-Israeli position. But political conditions in the Arab world did not warrant complete equanimity. A coup could change overnight the political complexion of a pro-Soviet Arab regime and bring into power somebody friendly with the West like, say, Tunisia's Bourguiba. And the Russians soon had an occasion to make the same unpleasant discovery as the American policymakers: excessive rhetoric in politics brings its own dangers; the more extreme among the Arab nationalists were not content to be cheered by Moscow for their campaign against that "outpost of Western imperialism" which was Israel. They wanted the mighty Soviet Union to do something about it.

To protect its by now troublesome as well as remunerative investment in the Middle East, the U.S.S.R. established its "presence" in the Mediterranean. On his visit to Egypt in 1966, Kosygin brought with him the commander-in-chief of the Soviet Navy, and it is unlikely that Admiral Gorshkov came just to admire the pyramids. A sizable Soviet fleet in that hitherto West-dominated sea would obviously have a healthy effect on political stability in the *pro-Soviet* Arab countries and offer interesting possibilities in the event of political upheavals elsewhere.[1] The Soviet Navy in the Mediterranean could be offsetting the presence of the U.S. Sixth Fleet and thus symbolically at least succoring the Arabs' confrontation with Israel. But, as events were to demonstrate, symbolic support was not enough.

One of those frequent political coups in Syria brought to power in 1966 a strongly pro-Soviet regime, some members of the new government being avowed Communists. Syria then stepped up its border warfare with Israel, and here one must conclude that, while the Soviets were not directly responsible for this enhanced bellicosity, they took no determined measures to stop or contain it. As border incidents increased in number and intensity, the Syrian press baited Egypt for its alleged unwillingness to confront Israel and for hiding behind the shelter of the United Nations Emergency Force stationed on Egypt's side of the frontier with Israel. While Syria baited Nasser, the U.S.S.R. continued to provide it with arms and military instructors.

In the spring of 1967 the crisis deepened. Soviet intelligence sources alerted Cairo and Damascus that Israel, in the wake of repeated border incidents with Syria, would deal a major blow to that country. Incautiously the Soviets trumpeted this story also in public. A column in *Pravda* on May 22 claimed the imperialists were up to new tricks in the Middle East: "Their main objective is Syria, whose anti-imperialist policy is disliked by Washington. It cannot be excluded that there would be new provocations against Syria." Were those subordinate Soviet organs that carried on this dangerous game or had the Politburo decided to raise the level of tension in the Middle East? In any case, in view of the rumors and the taunts from Damascus and other Arab capitals, Nasser decided to concentrate troops on Israel's frontier and to request the United Nations to withdraw its Emergency Force. Secretary General U Thant complied with his request rapidly and probably more completely than Egypt's leader had wished. On May 18, the entire U.N. Emergency Force, including the tiny detachment guarding the Strait of Tiran, was withdrawn. The latter's presence enabled shipping

[1] In the 1960's the Soviets expanded vastly their naval building program. There was a new and interesting emphasis on surface ships, e.g., some helicopter carriers were launched. The rationale for such innovations is obvious: in a crisis the salvation of some pro-Soviet regime might well depend on a speedy landing and intervention of a regiment of Soviet marines.

to and from Israel to navigate the Gulf of Aqaba and to reach Eilat, a port of some significance for Israel since it was convenient for trade with Asia and Africa and thus offset partly the Egyptian embargo on Israeli shipping through the Suez Canal. On May 22 Nasser, now carried away by the momentum of his own oratory, declared the Gulf of Aqaba closed to shipping by or to Israel, thus rendering Eilat useless. Were Israel to acquiesce in this step, it was clear, it would become the prey of further Arab encroachments and attacks.

It is at this point that the Soviet leaders clearly foresook their prudence and responded to the temptation to have the Middle East crisis "escalate." Whatever the rationale and the responsibility for Soviet moves and intelligence reports before May 18, after that date the gravity of the situation could not escape the attention of the top leaders. Had the Kremlin desired to relieve the tension, it could have warned Egypt not to institute the blockade and not to indulge in provocative oratory; or if private warnings were not heeded, the Soviets could have made plain their disapproval of the blockade and demanded a Great Powers' conference to head off a war. *Afterward,* as in his speech of June 19 to the United Nations, Kosygin was to say that if Israel had a grievance, it should have come to the Security Council. But between May 22 and June 7, the Security Council was impotent to intervene because of Soviet opposition to such a step. On May 30, during a typically fruitless debate in the council, the Soviet delegate, without specifically endorsing the blockade, still supported the Arab position and warned that the U.S.S.R. stood ready to help Arabs fight any would-be aggressors. And on May 29 the head of the Syrian regime arrived in Moscow. Whatever he heard there clearly did not stop the Arabs' bellicose oratory, typified by Nasser's statement that, whether it would take one or ten years, Israel would have to be completely crushed.

It is obvious that the Brezhnev-Kosygin regime had lapsed from its usual caution. Why not let the crisis "ripen"? After the Suez crisis of 1956 the United States, Britain, and France had pledged to keep free navigation in the Gulf of Aqaba. Now France, anxious to woo the Arab states, pulled out of the agreement. Britain was eager to liquidate its commitments "east of Suez" and could not or would not do anything. It was thus tempting to envisage the United States stumbling into yet another military venture, such as military occupation of the Strait of Tiran, or confessing its impotence, either course destroying what remained of American assets and prestige in the Arab world.

While publicly assailing the imperialists for their alleged machinations in the Middle East, the Soviet Government, through diplomatic channels, was urging Washington to restrain Israel, representing not *entirely* truthfully that it was curbing the Arabs' dangerous enthusiasm. Obviously, what the Kremlin desired and envisaged was not an Arab-Israeli war (there could be no illusions in Moscow on its likely outcome, though the speed and completeness of the Arabs' collapse was to come as a shock), but a diplomatic solution that would represent a setback for Israel and its protector, the United States, and a prestige victory for Egypt and the Soviets. Nasser, after the crisis had ripened, might offer a compromise: he would let shipping through the Gulf of Aqaba to Eilat, provided the ships were not under the Israeli flag. The Soviets would get credit for compelling Washington to compel Israel to acquiesce in this blow to its prestige and interests.

The Israeli attack spoiled this scenario. Indicating how soberly the Arabs' chances were viewed in Moscow, within hours of the news of hostilities the Soviet Government and press called for an *immediate* return to the prewar lines. While decrying the Western powers' "instigation" of the Israeli attack, the Soviet sources did not for a moment lend their support to the gross falsehoods propagated by Egypt and Jordan that American and British fliers were bombing Arab targets. When he received the Egyptian Ambassador on June 7, Kosygin must have had some harsh things to tell him about this disingenuous attempt to draw the U.S.S.R. into the conflict. News of the war was confined to the back pages of the Soviet press. The government was ready to lend its diplomatic support and sympathy to save the Arabs from an utter disaster, but nothing more. The famous "hot line" with Washington sprang into activity; both sides pledged their determination to keep out of the war and to bring about a cease-fire.

The latter was felt to be urgent. The Arabs' defeat was proving more rapid and drastic than had been expected. This was a huge embarrassment: all the military equipment and the work of Soviet military advisers had been wasted. But the embarrassment threatened to turn into a disaster. The pro-Soviet regimes in Egypt and Syria might collapse and be replaced either by hotheads who would seek Chinese help or by moderates who might feel the need for a rapprochement with the West. After some feeble attempts in the Security Council to combine a cease-fire with an order to Israel to withdraw to prewar lines, the Soviets acquiesced just in the former.

The Soviets tried to obscure their discomfiture and diplomatic defeat with a flurry of diplomatic activity. On June 9, leaders of the European Communist countries gathered in Moscow to consider the crisis. The conferees included Marshal Tito, his attendance a vivid proof that nothing startling would emerge from the conference—for all the reconciliation with Yugoslavia, the Soviets would never unburden themselves of secrets or plan some drastic action in conjunction with the prodigal son from Belgrade. And what emerged was a piece of rhetoric, a declaration condemning Israel's aggression and the demand that it evacuate the conquered territory. Even so, the Rumanians refused to sign the declaration. They also refused to break off diplomatic relations with the Jewish state, as did the U.S.S.R. and its more pliant Communist allies.

With the cease-fire and the consequent occupation by Israelis of Egyptian, Jordanian, and Syrian territory, the Soviet Union still continued its belated diplomatic offensive. Podgorny was dispatched to the Arab capitals on the difficult mission of trying to appease Arab bitterness. To New York and a special session of the General Assembly convoked at the Soviet request went a top-ranking delegation headed by Kosygin, joined by the premiers of the Ukraine and Byelorussia. For all the prestige-laden character of the delegation, it was clear that it would accomplish but little: a debate and a resolution by the General Assembly could not make the Israelis budge from the territory they had occupied. Their position then as now was that only direct negotiations with the concerned Arab states and subsequent treaties would make them relinquish any or all of the territorial gains of the Six-Day War. And in turn the Cairo and Damascus regimes, though perhaps not Jordan's, rejected categorically the idea of direct negotiations at the moment of the Arabs' greatest humiliation.

The Soviets' maneuvers were, however, not entirely ineffectual. It was widely believed that the Middle East conflagration had been the closest call since the Cuban missile crisis. Hence the world was relieved and grateful when Russia's Prime Minister agreed to meet the President of the United States. There was some rather childish sparring as to who should take the initiative for the meeting and as to its locale. The Soviet leader was on a visit to the U.N. and not, God forbid, to the United States. So, he could not go to Washington to pay his respects to Mr. Johnson. The latter in turn could not for prestige reasons travel "out of the country" (this is, to the East River!) in search of the Soviet dignitary. Many years before, Napoleon and Alexander I solved a similar problem by meeting on a raft in the middle of a river. And so Kosygin and Johnson agreed to meet at a point equidistant from the U.N. and Washington in Glassboro, New Jersey.

This hastily improvised summit was a few weeks' sensation. But for all the pious wishes and hopes for world peace expressed by the two potentates, Glassboro brought nothing of substance. Far away from the small college town, there were some people who professed to see the meeting as a new stage of a sinister plot: "Through the Glassboro talks, U.S. imperialism and Soviet revisionism have arrived at an over-all coordination and collaboration in their global strategy. They have not only struck deals over this or that issue, but have made a package deal."[2] Alas, such a "package deal," much as it might have been welcomed by the simple Russian and

[2] *Peking Review*, July 7, 1967, p. 23.

American citizens, existed only in the masochistic imagination of the Chinese Communists. To be sure, any meeting between American and Soviet leaders in the wake of a crisis was bound to bring a sigh of relief from millions all over the world. Stocks went up on the New York Exchange. Public opinion polls recorded a brief rise in Mr. Johnson's popularity.

What took place at Glassboro was a cordial *dis*agreement. Kosygin had been given no brief to negotiate with the Americans, and he could only politely rebuff the Americans' hints that the U.S.S.R. should use its good offices to bring the Arabs to the negotiating table and should itself pressure North Vietnam to abandon its support of the insurrection in the South. And for the benefit of the Russian reader, the meeting was represented as a triumph of Soviet diplomacy: Kosygin sternly warned the American President against any further intrigues in the Middle East and read him a lesson about Vietnam.

In fact, had the United States not been mired down in Vietnam, it is quite possible that the 1967 conflict could have been followed by a basic rearrangement in the Middle East. For the moment, the Arabs were profoundly disillusioned by the Soviet Union, the Israelis grateful for the extent of their victory. It is just possible that a prompt and vigorous initiative by Washington might have recouped some of the West's former influence among the Arabs and even brought about some—to be sure, it would have been precarious—agreement betweeen them and Israel. But with the U.S. attention and resources again riveted on Vietnam, the opportune moment soon passed. Things in the Middle East returned to normal, that is, instead of a virulent crisis, a festering one. The Soviets set about to re-equip the Arab armies. Israel, though it won a brilliant victory, was as far as ever from achieving security for peaceful development. And more than half a million Arabs in the conquered territories posed a new internal threat. Though mixed with a disillusionment about Russia, bitterness about U.S. policies became once more the dominant emotion in Cairo and Damascus. There were painful economic consequences for the West (especially Britain) in the wake of the Suez Canal closing and first an interruption of and then continuing threat to the flow of vital oil supplies from the Middle East.

Within the Soviet Union the reverberations of the 1967 imbroglio, though less visible, were still considerable. One member of the inner group criticized his colleagues' restraint in a public speech and paid for it with his job: Nikolai Yegoruchev, the Moscow Party secretary. But if there were others who shared his apprehensions, they were in a minority and remained silent. For the regime the crisis was the occasion of what might be called an agonizing reappraisal of the Soviet Union's commitment in the Middle East. The U.S.S.R. would continue to support the Arabs but would try to exercise a tighter rein on the situation, try to prevent the crisis endemic to the area from escalating to the point where the U.S.S.R. *might* be drawn into fighting or endure the embarrassment of seeing its clients trounced. But such "management" of international tension would prove difficult. The Soviet Union would run into continuous trouble, would endure constant criticism from the more bellicose of its clients. And even the latter would be outpaced in their militancy and threatened by Arab guerrilla movements, which, through anti-Israeli terrorism and constant challenge to regimes like Jordan's, would bring a new element of instability and danger to the unhappy region.

The events in the fall of 1973 provide a demonstration of how difficult, at times impossible, such "management" of international tension can be. An armed clash between allies and clients of the two superpowers may thrust them into a near or actual confrontation and may undo or at least threaten all the groundwork previously laid for a Soviet-American *détente*.

The Middle Eastern crisis and its consequences up to this day demonstrate vividly the dilemma of the Great Powers (which for the moment means Soviet Russia and America) in this what might be called postimperial era: worldwide power and influence have become not only costly but endowed with danger; client states, from being the source of profit and additional strength to their Great-Power protectors, have increasingly tended to become claimants on their resources, have threatened to involve them in conflicts where the Great Powers' *own* interests were not clearly involved. The Soviet Union's policy between roughly 1955 and 1967 was predicated on the assumption that it could play a Great-Power role without the disadvantages and perils accruing to the United States: it could cash in on the lingering anti-Western sentiments in the Third World and create situations of embarrassment and danger to the United States and its allies at but a small cost and no danger to itself. Washington would be put on the spot for its real or alleged support of Israel, Portugal, or South Africa. Moscow, just by exuding anti-imperialist propaganda, by providing arms to the Arab states, verbal (and perhaps some discreet material) support to the Angolan, say, rebels, would go on scoring painless victories. The events of 1967 (as we shall see of 1973) demonstrated that such hopes and stratagems were wildly overoptimistic. The U.S.S.R. was "stuck" in the Middle East, though the cost to it was not nearly as great as that to the United States in Southeast Asia. The flurry of Soviet diplomatic activity following the Six-Day War could not quite obscure this fact, nor the Soviet discomfiture. Those constant kibitzers of Soviet moves, the Chinese, had a ruthless comment on Kosygin's performance at the United Nations: his speech was "odious and hypocritical"—the Soviet Union had egged the Arabs on to take an untenable position, abandoned them at the crucial moment, and was now shedding crocodile tears.

Soon trouble was to strike closer to home. The difficulties attendant on the Soviet relations with the Arab protégés might be compared to those inherent in a concubinage; for all the emotional tensions and dangers, the dominant party may preserve a degree of detachment and disclaim responsibility for its partner's mishaps and misbehavior. But in the case of the Communist states of Eastern Europe, the bond between them and the Soviet Union has been much more binding, indeed, in some respects might be likened to that of matrimony, that is, in its pre–Women's Liberation, in fact, very Victorian form.

The Hungarian Revolution and its sequel dispelled most of the hope evidently nourished at one time by Khrushchev that this relationship could be based just on shared emotion (ideological ties) and mutual self-interest; 1956 vividly demonstrated that superior force and its use or threat of use by the U.S.S.R. remained a vital ingredient. But the more than ten years that elapsed since the tragedy of Budapest tended to obscure this lesson. The Sino-Soviet conflict became a new and important factor. Profiting by it and by its geographic situation, little Albania slipped out of the Soviet sphere. Rumania, by skillful maneuvering between the two Communist giants, secured a degree of independence in its foreign and economic policies. The Soviets were visibly and sometimes publicly unhappy over the course adopted by the Ceausescu regime. But Bucharest was careful not to push its policies to' the point of open defiance of its powerful neighbor: Rumania stayed within both the Warsaw Pact and the Comecon. Most important of all, internally the Rumanian Communists ran a tight authoritarian state. Nothing in their domestic policies could be construed as a bad example to other satellites or as an encouragement to forces of dissent in Poland or Hungary to challenge Communist rule. If the Soviets at any point contemplated military intervention in Rumania (as they probably did), they were dissuaded not only by the fear of a possible reaction from Peking but by the reflection that Rumania did not represent enough of a threat to their over-all position in Eastern Europe to justify the risk of invading a country whose army might fight.

But in the case of Czechoslovakia in 1968, the situation was, from the Kremlin's point of view, quite different. There, the course of events appeared to threaten the stability of other Communist regimes in Eastern Europe and not inconceivably might lead to disturbing reverberations within the U.S.S.R. itself. And when they did undertake their August invasion, the Soviets had reasonable grounds to believe that their soldiers would not be met with armed resistance.

Until 1967–68, Czechoslovakia, if it diverged from the general pattern of politics of other people's democracies, did so by being more immune to forces of liberalization. A gigantic statue of Stalin continued to preside over Prague long after similar monuments in other East European capitals had been discreetly dismantled. The Prague regime also lagged behind in rehabilitating Communist victims of the period of terror, 1949–53, when at Stalin's orders real and alleged Titoists were being hunted all throughout

Eastern Europe. The Czechoslovak Government of Antonin Novotny was thus, in the parlance of Communists, the most conservative of all, unwilling to liberalize its domestic policies even to the extent that the Russians were perfectly willing to permit.[3] Gomulka for a few years after his return in 1956 enjoyed wide popularity as a man who had stood up to the Russians. Hungary's Kadar, for all the opprobrious circumstances of his coming to power, gained some national respect as a reformer. But not only to the people at large but to a number of Party members, Novotny and his henchmen were oppressive relics of the Stalinist era. Why did the Russians allow pressures in Czechoslovakia to build up to such a dangerous point rather than speeding Novotny's exit? Well, after their almost disastrous experiences with Hungary and Poland in 1956, they lost the taste for experimenting with new leaders in East Europe. And so they would not take the initiative in removing such hardened Stalinists as Ulbricht in East Germany or Novotny.

In addition to its other negative qualities, the Czechoslovak regime was inept: in the 1960's the country's economy stagnated. Thus everything indicated that, when the shift in leadership finally came, it would be followed by widespread demands for far-reaching changes in policies as well.

Toward the end, in 1967, Novotny's position grew untenable. In December Brezhnev flew to Prague, but while there he decided that it would not serve Soviet interests to try to preserve the discredited satrap. In January, Novotny was finally removed as First Secretary (his dismissal from the presidency came in April) and replaced by Alexander Dubcek, until then head of the Slovak component of the party. The new leader seemingly met Soviet requirements of the moment: young (forty-six), a Communist since his childhood, he was popular with the rank and file of the Party, and yet his whole background bespoke loyalty to the Soviet Union. It was undoubtedly hoped in Moscow that, like Gomulka in 1956, Dubcek would be able to meet national aspirations and initiate badly needed reforms and yet keep them within safe limits.

But the harm done through Novotny and his Stalinist pals hanging on for so long now became apparent. Whether Dubcek himself was infected by the reforming zeal or not, he proved unable to contain the built-up discontent and the clamor for basic reforms. Demands were voiced for a fuller revelation of the excesses of the period 1949–54 and for exemplary punishment of those responsible, including Novotny. More disquieting from the Soviet point of view was the plea that Czechoslovak Communism be reformed in a "democratic and humanistic" direction and for freer intercourse, especially economic, with the West. By Communist standards

[3] Novotny inherited leadership of the Party on Klement Gottwald's death in 1953. He then buttressed his position by combining the Party post with the presidency of the republic.

political debate in Czechoslovakia became during that spring of 1968 scandalously free and turbulent. By June official censorship of the press and other media had virtually ceased, an unprecedented situation for a Communist country. Far-reaching economic reforms were projected with the implication that Czechoslovakia's excessive dependence on trade with the socialist camp had been harmful to its economy and that it might seek credits in the West. None of the publicly voiced demands questioned the primacy of the Communist Party or the need for a continued alliance with the U.S.S.R. and Czechoslovakia's adherence to the Warsaw Pact. In answer to both public and private criticisms from the Soviet Union, Dubcek kept reassuring Soviet leaders both of his loyalty and of his regime's ability and determination to control the situation, that it would not let "democratization" get out of hand.

Obviously, there were divided counsels in the Kremlin. But as the "Prague spring" wore on, there were insistent voices from the more "conservative" East European regimes, Poland and East Germany, that the Russians curb the Czech "revisionists." Gomulka's, which had long lost both its popularity and sensitivity to national aspirations, had just cracked down on dissenting intellectuals and students. The Warsaw government then launched a thinly disguised anti-Jewish campaign. Party leaders of Jewish origin were dismissed or demoted; many, especially Jewish, intellectuals, even those not involved in any campaign for liberalization, were virtually forced to migrate. Those measures were criticized in Czechoslovakia, and now Gomulka, as well as Ulbricht, had additional reasons for expostulating that the scandalous license rampant in a fraternal socialist country was a most unfortunate example for the people in other Communist-ruled states.

In June the Warsaw Pact armed forces held maneuvers, and some in the West expected the Soviets to strike then. But the Kremlin's mind was as yet not made up: with the maneuvers concluded, foreign troops were withdrawn. But in the same month the Soviets had another cause for alarm. An article published in a Prague journal characterized the reforms since January as incomplete and called for further liberalization. This document, entitled "Two Thousand Words" and subscribed to by a number of public figures and intellectuals, had bitter things to say about the past. "The Communist Party, which after the war possessed great trust of the people, gradually exchanged this trust for offices until it had all the offices and nothing else. . . . The main guilt and the greatest deception perpetrated by these rulers was that they presented their arbitrary rule as the will of the workers."[4] While "Two Thousand Words" expressed

[4] Robin Allison Remington, ed., *Winter in Prague: Documents on Czechoslovak Communism in Crisis* (Cambridge, Mass.: MIT Press, 1970), pp. 196–97.

confidence in and support for Dubcek, it called for popular vigilance and pressure so that the reform movement might continue unabated and *foreign* threats would be unable to stop it: "The great apprehension results from the possibility that foreign forces may interfere with our internal development. Faced with all these superior forces, the only thing we can do is . . . hold our own . . . assure our government that we will back it— with weapons if necessary—as long as it does what we give it the mandate to do."[5] This manifesto was repudiated by the regime, but for Moscow the only convincing repudiation would have been an immediate arrest of its author and signatories.

It is quite likely that, at the end of June on the Kremlin's agenda, invasion of Czechoslovakia was removed from the "possible" category and placed under the heading "imperative unless . . ." On July 15, representatives of the Soviet Union and of the Communist parties of Bulgaria, Hungary, East Germany, and Poland issued from their conference in Warsaw a public letter to the Central Committee of their erring sister party. The language of this warning was quite explicit. "The developments in your country have aroused profound anxiety among us. The reactionaries' offensive supported by imperialism . . . threatens to push your country off the path of socialism and consequently imperils the interests of the entire socialist system."[6] The fact that the obstreperous Rumanians did not choose to associate themselves with the warning increased in the Russians' eyes the gravity of the Czech crisis. If the Czechs did not mend their ways or, failing that, were not disciplined and brought back to the straight-and-narrow path, not only some East European regimes but the dominant position of the Soviet Union in the whole area would be jeopardized. Hence a very blunt threat: "It is not only your task but ours, too, to deal a resolute rebuff to the anti-Communist forces and to wage a resolute struggle for the preservation of the socialist system in Czechoslovakia."[7]

Dubcek's regime was caught between two fires: any attempt to crack down on the movement for further liberalization could conceivably have led to a popular revolt. Were he, however, not to heed the Warsaw warning, it should have been clear to Dubcek and his colleagues (though incredibly enough it was not) that the Soviets would not take it lying down. One hesitates to criticize the courageous and attractive Czechoslovak leader. A more cynical politician, with an insight into the mentality of the Kremlin, still might have found a way out and saved a measure of independence for his country as well as his political power. He would have gone through the motions of cracking down on the burgeoning enthusiasm

[5] *Ibid.*, p. 201.
[6] Quoted in *ibid.*, p. 227.
[7] *Ibid.*, p. 229.

for further democratization and reinstituted, at least formally, censorship.[8] Along with a measure of appeasement, Dubcek could have made it clear to the Russians that an invasion could not be carried out with impunity: the Czech Army and people would fight. Such tactics, compounded of part appeasement and part firmness, might well have succeeded; the Russians were well aware that most foreign Communist Parties were opposed to armed intervention, and even among the loyal satellite regimes the Hungarian leadership pleaded for patience and restraint. The prospect of as much as a few days' fighting would have given the Kremlin pause: there could be unpleasant reverberations elsewhere, from China, in Poland and East Germany. But Dubcek and his closest collaborators were incapable of this kind of maneuvering, which does credit to their emotions but not to their political acumen. He himself was a rare example of a Communist idealist: surely the Russian comrades would believe in the sincerity of his protestations of loyalty and would not betray him. And he refused even to contemplate the prospect of his people engaging in an unequal struggle.

It was probably the need to ascertain the chances of the Czechoslovaks' offering armed resistance that explains the next Soviet move. The Politburo of the Soviet Party offered to meet with its Czechoslovak counterpart. After some sparring as to whether the meeting should take place on Soviet or Czechoslovak soil, it was agreed to confer in the Slovak frontier town of Cierna-on-Tisa. For all the subsequent events the mere fact of the meeting illuminates the great changes that have transpired in the Communist world since Stalin's time. Then, if telephone was not enough, an inferior Soviet official would be dispatched to a satellite country and the local leadership would promptly fall in line. Now the whole Politburo set out to plead (at least ostensibly) with fellow Communists of a small country.

The Cierna meeting lasted from July 29 to August 1. The usual amenities were observed, the Soviet leaders posing smilingly with their Czechoslovak hosts. But it was perhaps significant that, after each day's meetings, the visitors would pile into the train and go over to the Soviet side of the border rather than spend the night as guests of the "revisionists." The final communiqué said little, reflecting the fact that by and large both sides stuck to their previous positions. Cierna was followed by a meeting in Bratislava, where the Soviet and Czechoslovak leaders were joined by those of the other parties, signatories of the Warsaw statement. The

---

[8] It was the abolition of censorship that especially incensed and alarmed the Russians and their conservative satellites. Ukrainian- and German-language publications appearing in Czechoslovakia were banned in Soviet Ukraine and East Germany. Among the Soviet Politburo it was Shelest, the Ukraine's boss, who was reputedly most insistent on the need for invasion: events in the neighboring country were stimulating dissent and local nationalism in the Ukraine.

assembled dignitaries were again photographed smiling amiably at each other. Superficially, it seemed that the moment of danger had passed: the Brezhnev-Kosygin regime had acquiesced in the Czech reforms. Dubcek had convinced the Soviets of his good faith and loyalty.

In fact, the assembled Politburo members had reasons to be satisfied by the Cierna meeting, but for reasons quite different from those imagined by Dubcek. The latter, and again most imprudently, had retained in the highest party body people who, if not out-and-out enemies of democratization, were fearful that it has gone too far and who would not be averse to playing the Russians' game. The Soviet leaders were then able to depart confident that there were high Czech and Slovak officials, such as Presidium members Vasil Bilak and Alois Indra, who could serve their purposes once Dubcek was out of the picture. And if the leadership was not wholeheartedly united behind recent policies, it was at least likely that there would be no armed resistance when the Soviets struck. The Bratislava meeting with all its amiabilities was a gross deception: one needed a smoke screen and some time to complete military preparations so that the Soviet Union's and other "fraternal" countries' armies could move swiftly and decisively.

Some doubts and hesitations must have remained within the Kremlin to the last. During the interval between Bratislava and the invasion, Dubcek was visited not only by Tito and Ceausescu, who urged him to stand firm, but also by Ulbricht and Kadar, who undoubtedly pleaded that he repent and appease the Russians.

On August 21, the forces of the Warsaw Pact countries (with the exception of Rumania) invaded Czechoslovakia, or, more precisely, a Soviet army estimated at 400,000 with token detachments from the other four seized the little country of some 14 million people. Militarily, the occupation proceeded smoothly: there were no organized armed resistance and relatively few clashes between the Russian soldiers and local population (mostly students). But in one respect Soviet expectations were betrayed. The invasion was carried out according to the official Soviet statement in answer to the pleas of unnamed "Party and state leaders" who called for Russian help to save socialism in Czechoslovakia. Yet such was the universal if passive popular resistance to the Soviet coup that, at the time, the would-be Soviet collaborators did not dare to identify themselves. Dubcek and other liberal officials were seized and flown to Moscow. The hastily convened Czechoslovak Party Congress defiantly confirmed Dubcek and other imprisoned leaders in their posts. President of the Republic Ludvik Svoboda refused to appoint a government of Soviet puppets.[9]

[9] A former career army officer septuagenarian, Svoboda had been counted on by the Russians to be more pliable. Hence he was not arrested in the wake of the invasion and was extolled in the Soviet press as a World War II hero.

Partially frustrated, the Soviets altered their tactics. From "revisionist" criminals under lock and key, Dubcek and his collaborators again became "comrades." Released from captivity at Svoboda's insistence, they negotiated a partial surrender to the Kremlin leaders: they would be allowed to go back to their posts, but they would crack down on the "antisocialist forces." And this time, no tricks! The Soviet army would stay in Czechoslovakia until the situation was "normalized." The talks, the Soviet communiqué blandly announced, "proceeded in an atmosphere of frankness, comradeship, and friendship."[10]

Stalin once in a wartime conversation with Harry Hopkins criticized the American slogan "unconditional surrender." It was quite unnecessary, said the great man: you can let the enemy surrender with all sorts of reservations, but once you occupy his country, you can then gradually make this surrender *un*conditional. And in dealing with Czechoslovakia Brezhnev and Kosygin demonstrated how, in this as in so many other cases, they remained Stalin's pupils. Within a few months the prevailing mood in the unhappy country turned from defiance to resignation. Dubcek's and other reformers' positions became untenable. In April 1969, Gustav Husak assumed leadership of the party. Dubcek, after a decent interval, disappeared entirely from public life. Others prominent in the "Prague spring" were also demoted, the most unrepentant advocates of democratization choosing exile or, in some cases, and more recently, being ejected from the party and even imprisoned. The new leader, Husak, answered admirably the Soviets' requirements. Himself a political prisoner in the early 1950's, Husak did not turn the clock back to the Novotny days (nor would the Russians want him to). But he firmly put an end to such "excesses" of the Dubcek regime as freedom of the press and other media and dissolved those organizations which sprang up between January and August to promote further democratization. The Husak regime, while avoiding publicized and systematic purges, has authorized arrests of past and potential troublemakers. And so for the moment Czechoslovakia is back safely within the bosom of the socialist camp.

From today's perspective, the Kremlin must view the Czechoslovak operation as a barely qualified success and its initial nervousness as excessive. This nervousness was expressed in such gestures as a special message to the U.S. Government explaining the invasion as an intra-Communist affair and in no sense threatening interests of the United States and its

---

[10] *Pravda*, August 28, 1968. The word "frankness" in this context is always a euphemism for some disagreement. Interestingly enough, diplomatic talks in which the U.S.S.R. and another Communist regime or party engage and where no major disagreement arises are officially characterized as having taken place in an atmosphere of "warm comradeship and friendship" but seldom of "frankness."

allies. President Johnson then canceled his planned visit to Russia, and that was the extent of American official reaction.

Two governments had to be specially alarmed by the Prague coup. Yugoslavia and Rumania made it abundantly clear that if the Kremlin intended to extend to them its lessons in intrasocialist solidarity, the invading armies would be met with much more than just passive resistance. Tito and Ceausescu conferred. The Yugoslav Communists expressed their "deep indignation." Ceausescu publicly branded the occupation as a "shameful event in the history of the revolutionary movements." But as time went on, the Soviet leaders must have noted complacently that their action in Czechoslovakia had a desirable educational effect even on the Rumanians. *Prior* to the invasion, the Ceausescu regime had indulged in a lot of tough talk vis-à-vis the Russians about the need to reform the Warsaw Pact organization so as to assure the equality of its members (e.g., by rotating its supreme command rather than vesting it always in a Russian general). Following it, the Rumanians, while not yielding any of their autonomy, ceased to demand more.

Elsewhere in the Communist world, reactions varied. The two large Western parties, the Italian and the French, condemned the invasion (the latter rather circumspectly). But since neither coupled its denunciation with any concrete measure (such as breaking off relations, or threatening to, with the Communist Party of the U.S.S.R.), the Kremlin had solid grounds to believe that most of the protestations were designed for the benefit of public opinion in the concerned countries rather than a warning to the Soviet Union. The Cubans and North Vietnamese approved. And equally predictably, the Chinese, while expressing their disapproval of Dubcek's revisionism, were gleefully condemnatory of this latest manifestation of Soviet imperialism. There was no reason, therefore, for the Soviets to appear repentant or apologetic. On the contrary, the leadership reaffirmed its right and obligation to interfere in the affairs of a fellow Communist country whenever in its view the interests of socialism were being threatened. In the West the assertion was dubbed the Brezhnev Doctrine, though in fact it was but a reiteration of Soviet policy of long standing and in no way could be considered a theoretical or practical innovation.

But while the outcome of the Czech affair and the worldwide reaction to it could be viewed by the Soviets with some smugness, the crisis itself was bound to give rise to uncomfortable reflections and long-run apprehensions. A thoughtful Soviet statesman had to conclude that, just as Russia's imperial pretensions in the Middle East, so its imperial position in Eastern Europe (though in a different way) was becoming unduly risky and expensive. Viewed realistically, the Brezhnev Doctrine is not only an expression of Soviet power but also a considerable burden on the U.S.S.R. It requires it to watch constantly the domestic affairs of half a dozen Communist countries, to be always ready to intervene no matter what the risk and cost. An American President justified the U.S. involvement in Southeast Asia by invoking the "domino theory," and we all know how costly the implications of that theory have been for his country. But, for the Kremlin, the East European vassals really are "dominoes": if one totters, they all may collapse. The Czechoslovak operation went off as planned (well, almost). But what if the Czech Army had fought? What if the trouble had spread to other Communist countries? The lesson of 1968 will probably for some years keep other Communist regimes in line, make their peoples "behave." But it is almost inevitable that in time there will be another explosion: national aspirations cannot be repressed or contained indefinitely.

The Soviets, as a matter of fact, had a close call in Poland in 1970. The Gomulka regime had long outstayed its welcome, had increasingly shown itself oppressive and inept. Its main figure, a man of undoubted integrity but of limited intellectual horizons, proposed to rule indefinitely on the capital that accrued to him through his courageous stand in 1956 and did not perceive that the people's gratitude for removing the horrors of the now distant past had been eroded by more recent chicaneries and economic shortages. From a liberal reformer Gomulka has grown into a suspicious and bilious conservative. Once a champion of Polish autonomy, he lent his support and army units to the rape of Czechoslovakia. Himself of an ascetic disposition, he could not understand why his hedonistically inclined people should not put up with all sorts of deprivations for the sake of building socialism. The long-suffering patience of the Polish people gave way when the regime compounded its ineptitude with a spectacular piece of idiocy. *Shortly before Christmas,* it raised prices substantially on all forms of foodstuffs. The workers responded to this Christmas gift by rioting, and in places, especially in the maritime region, they stormed Party headquarters. There was a sizable number of casualties. We know—again, the Chinese Communist press has obligingly informed us—that the Soviets were on the brink of military intervention. Fortunately for them and for the Polish Communists, the crisis was allayed through intra-Party changes. Gomulka was removed, his henchmen demoted. The new leader, a more astute politician, Edward Gierek, rescinded the price increases and personally visited the troubled spots, assuaging passions and promising reforms. For the moment Soviet politicians and marshals could relax, and yet they had another occasion to reflect that imperial glory is not conducive to the peace of mind. Some may have had an additional if very secret thought: wasn't it too bad that the Soviet Union had insisted on foisting Communism on so many states within its sphere of influence. Little Finland has to abide by Soviet wishes insofar as foreign policy is concerned, but because its regime is not Communist the Kremlin rulers do not have to lose any sleep over what is and what is not printed in Helsinki news-papers, over food shortages there, and so forth. Its democratic freedoms and multiparty system are not likely to stir up dangerous ideas in East Berlin or Kiev. Yes, in this day and age the "monolithic unity of the social-ist camp" is not only largely illusory but also increasingly burdensome to the main Communist power.

And costly. Under Stalin the Soviet Union unabashedly exploited other Communist countries. The most flagrant aspects of this exploitation were abolished in the Khrushchev era. Now on balance the Soviet Union may still profit by having a sphere of influence or what once would have been described less euphemistically as an empire in Eastern Europe. But on occasion it has to pay for it. By invading Czechoslovakia the Soviets deprived it of the possibility of receiving Western credits, and then the Russians had to assume the not inconsiderable burden of underwriting the Czech economy to save it from a complete and politically dangerous col-lapse. And similarly in 1970–71, the Soviets had to bail out the Warsaw regime by rushing food into Poland. There is yet another and more basic source of economic waste inherent in the Soviet Union's relationship to its "family" in Eastern Europe. The U.S.S.R. has been reluctant to allow its dependents to emulate its example in seeking extensive commercial ties and credits from the West. Hence a vicious circle: the Soviets provide a guaranteed market for their satellites' goods. Thus Polish, Czech, and other industries, especially those producing consumer goods, have little incentive to become efficient and competitive in the world market while the Russian consumer gets shoddy products. And it is an outright and not inconsider-able Soviet subsidy that keeps the Cuban economy going. The Marxist coalition government that recently was in power in Chile was not slow in pleading for Soviet help. And while politically the Soviets have every reason to be glad over this latest setback to "Yankee imperialism" in Latin America, they have shown no alacrity in moving to buttress Chile's falter-ing economy. As a consumer, the hard-pressed Soviet citizen may have little reason for joy over new accessions to the "camp of socialism" or to the ranks of Russia's allies. And with the rate of the country's industrial growth declining and with Russia's agriculture in chronic crisis, even the government grows weary of providing its clients with what is officially described as "selfless help by the Soviet people."

It would be premature to expect this growing economic burden to lead to a basic reorientation of Soviet foreign policy. Economists tell us that old-fashioned imperialism was, even in its heyday, more often a burden than a source of profit to the imperial power. Yet who can deny that to many citizens of the latter it was also a cause for national pride, an ele-ment favoring social and political cohesion. One must acknowledge that similar benefits accrue to the Soviet regime in view of the U.S.S.R.'s leadership of the Communist camp. Soviet, indeed more specifically, Russian nationalism remains the strongest card at the disposal of the regime. The country's sacrifices on behalf of world Communism and the individual citizen's privation can still be convincingly rationalized as part of the price for Russia's greatness. It would be incorrect to assume that the Soviet Union's intervention in Czechoslovakia was abhorrent to the majority of its citizens. There were individual protests, mostly from intellectuals —something that might be characterized as a minidemonstration by a handful of them took place in the Red Square. But sadly enough, to the Soviet man in the street it was the Czechs' attitude that was incomprehensible. Their country enjoys a higher standard of living than Russia, its citizens' liberties are certainly not more restricted than those in the "fatherland of socialism." So the alleged grievances of Czechs and Slovaks were unreasonable. And a small country should defer to the wishes of its big protector!

At the end of the 1960's various elements of Soviet foreign policy would arrange themselves into a new pattern. In Eastern Europe the Kremlin has made it clear that it is determined to hold its own and will not permit any further loosening of the bonds that hold the socialist camp together. By the same token it has acquiesced in the semi-independent posture of Rumania, and as long as Tito remains at the helm the Russians will *try* to collaborate with rather than dominate Yugoslavia. In the Middle East the Soviet Union will continue, but in a manner more prudent than before 1968, to consolidate and expand its influence over its Arab clients. Elsewhere in the Third World it will also be more cautious in playing the old game of exploiting the backwash of Western imperialism in cashing in on the retreats and discomfitures of the West.

For the Soviet Union the main problém of the early 1970's will be how to redefine what we might describe as the rules of coexistence with its main competitors: the United States and Communist China. It would be a gross oversimplification to visualize the Politburo as assembling at any set point and deciding that the old rules could not guarantee the U.S.S.R. and the world against an accidental disaster, that a future crisis in the Caribbean, Southeast Asia, or the Middle East might on some occasion bring about what it had *almost* brought in the past—a cataclysmic collision between the United States and the Soviet Union. But certainly the logic of past events must have strongly argued such a conclusion. And as Communist China began to emerge from the chaos of the Cultural Revolution, what should have been clear and perhaps was to some Soviet leaders long before became obvious: Sino-Soviet relations could not be divorced from those between the Soviet Union and the United States. Whatever Moscow's intentions, fears, and hopes concerning Peking, the Soviet position vis-à-vis China was bound to be weakened by a continuing high level of tension with the West. A decade has now passed since Khrushchev nourished his grand design: a general settlement with the United States that would enable the U.S.S.R. to keep China from becoming a nuclear, and hence a great, power. That was no longer practicable. The Kremlin's ambitions have of necessity become more modest, and its apprehensions on account of China more vivid. To get any handle on the problem, Russia needed a more throughgoing *détente* with the United States. And there was a harrowing possibility that Peking might anticipate that Soviet gambit by itself seeking a rapprochement with America. After all, as early as February, 1964, Suslov said at the Plenum of the Central Committee: "It is quite clear that they [the Chinese] would not refuse to improve relations with the United States, but as yet do not see favorable circumstances for such an endeavor."[11]

The need for a rapprochement with the West was and still is nicely balanced by the Soviet leaders' fear of appearing too eager in the eyes of their antagonists. Their attitude has been similar to that of Khrushchev, who in 1961 acknowledged in a public speech that the new weapons have made a major war too horrible to contemplate, and they added: "But if you and I come up to the imperialists carrying a cross and praying and on our knees, begin to implore them to be humane, they would laugh at us, they would see in this our weakness and their strength."[12] Well, Khrushchev's approach to a *détente* was so oversubtle that it almost plunged the world into war. But if the new leaders learned from his mistakes and proposed to be more straightforward, they were still not going to reveal and publicize their desperate need for a *détente* in the West so that they could cope with the danger in the East. They have been only too conscious that any friendly overture on their part would be interpreted in the West as due to Moscow's fear of China and/or serious domestic troubles within the U.S.S.R. And so, while seeking a *détente*, the Soviet Union would not appear to be pleading for it, would never appear to be negotiating out of fear rather than in pursuance of the immutable goals of Soviet foreign policy.

Fortunately from Moscow's point of view, its "agonized reappraisal" of foreign relations coincided with that in the West; its need to lower the level of tension in the world was no greater than that felt in Washington and other Western capitals.

It would be superfluous to discourse at length on how much Vietnam has affected that picture. But we must note some of the conclusions that Soviet policy-makers derived from America's overcommitment and failure in Southeast Asia. By the end of the 1960's it was obvious that, barring

11 See above, p. 691, at note 158.
12 *Pravda*, December 10, 1961.

some very drastic reversal of the trend, the U.S. original objective in Vietnam, that is, extirpation of insurgency in the South, was not going to be accomplished. The growing social and political disarray in America compelled Washington to embark upon the policy of gradual withdrawal of U.S. troops, to suspend the bombing of the North, and to enter upon negotiations for a political solution of the war. This then endowed the U.S.S.R. with a powerful asset for negotiations with the United States. It could advance or delay any political settlement of the Vietnam tragedy, could throw its powerful weight on the scales to press for, if not to force, a solution that would enable the United States to emerge from the conflict without too great a blow to its prestige or, conversely, could encourage Hanoi in its intransigence and insistence to exact a virtual capitulation.[13] The Soviets were too subtle to play this card openly. Indeed, Soviet diplomats bemoaned in public their alleged inability to influence Hanoi's decisions. But it is clear that the American policy-makers were made to realize that their tractability on other issues dividing the two Great Powers might help to extricate the United States from an intolerable impasse.

The other positive, from the Kremlin's perspective, effect of the war was its impact on America's European allies. They viewed with disapproval the ever greater U.S. absorption in the affairs of a distant Asiatic country. And their disapproval turned to consternation when the war visibly weakened America's economy and social cohesion and brought increasing questioning of that world role which the United States has assumed ever since 1945. The resentment of America's preponderant power was replaced by exasperation at its unintelligent use; the irritation at American presence gave way to fears on account of neo-isolationism, which seemed to be gaining ground across the Atlantic. De Gaulle even before then had decided on an independent posture for France. And now, though none of the remaining European allies would or could afford to emulate the imperious French leader's example, they would seek a reinsurance against the possibility that the United States might at some point weaken its commitment to or even withdraw entirely its protection from Western Europe. The recent and insistent talk in Congress about the need to pull out some U.S. troops from overseas so as to reduce the dollar drain has served to fortify

[13] The precise extent of Moscow's influence on North Vietnam must remain a matter of conjecture. Yet it is obvious that beginning with 1965 the Hanoi leadership, while anxious not to offend China, grew increasingly dependent on the U.S.S.R., the main supplier of war matériel both for the military operations in the South and for defense against American air attacks. And with the Cultural Revolution and the consequent chaos in China, it was obviously the Soviet Union that had to be viewed by the North as its main protector against the possibility of the Americans' drastically escalating the war.

the resolution of West European statesmen to prepare themselves against a contingency that only a few years ago seemed unimaginable.

This resolution received its concrete expression in the new "Eastern policy" of the government of Chancellor Brandt, which came to power in September 1969. Even before then, there had been voices among West German politicians arguing for a new approach toward the U.S.S.R. and the need for formal acquiescence in the *status quo* in Germany as established by the Potsdam agreements of 1945. Bonn, it was argued, no longer stood to gain anything by insisting that the German Democratic Republic was illegitimate and that Poland's annexation of one-time German territories should be undone. More than a generation has passed since the political map of Central Europe assumed its present configuration. The old Adenauer-Dulles policy, which assumed both the possibility and the need to reverse the Potsdam settlement, was no longer practical. As a matter of fact, it received its death blow as early as 1961 when the Americans acquiesced in the erection of the Berlin Wall. Now the German Federal Republic faced the danger of eventual diplomatic isolation. The French no longer supported Bonn's position in its entirety; as part of their rapprochement with the Soviet Union and in pursuance of De Gaulle's vain attempt to recoup some of France's former influence in Eastern Europe, they recognized Poland's western frontier. Washington's support of a policy that for twenty-five years has rendered no concrete results but only led to recurrent crises could no longer be taken for granted. On the contrary, American policy-makers, beset by a multitude of troubles and with fearful memories of the past confrontations over Berlin, gave every indication that they would not hesitate to acknowledge the facts of life in Central Europe, if by doing so they could induce the Soviets to help them out of their predicament in Southeast Asia.

By 1969 the Soviets were more than willing to enter into a diplomatic dialogue with the German Federal Republic. The German danger as perceived by the Kremlin was no longer acute. At one time it was feared that a rearmed Germany would act as a cat's paw of American imperialism in Eastern Europe, become a constant threat to the Communist regimes there. Then, danger was perceived in the possibility of Bonn's acquiring its own nuclear armament. By the end of the 1960's, it was clear that, though rearmed, the Federal Republic was far from willing or able to pursue a militant anti-Communist policy. Then, with its signing of the nuclear nonproliferation treaty, the specter of Western Germany's becoming a nuclear power ceased to agitate the Russians. German "revanchism" remained for Soviet diplomacy and propaganda a convenient bogeyman. The threat of the "Hitlerite generals" (though by this time the surviving ones were getting to be of venerable age) and their sinister designs was invoked as one of the rationalizations for the invasion of Czechoslovakia. It was and is convenient for the Russians to keep reminding the Poles and Czechs that there are elements in Western Germany that have not reconciled themselves to the loss of Pomerania, Silesia, and even the Sudetenland. But against the still lingering propaganda advantages of the alleged German danger there were concrete benefits to be gained by establishing more friendly relations with Bonn.

First, it was hoped, they would lead to further reduction of American influence in Europe. What Stalin and Khrushchev had aimed to accomplish through threats and ultimatums centering on West Berlin, the Brezhnev-Kosygin regime has set out to gain through patient diplomacy. Western Germany would grow accustomed to thinking of the U.S.S.R. as a good neighbor and no longer an enemy, that is, if the Soviet Union's reasonable requests and aspirations are not being thwarted (one would not want the Europeans to lose *entirely* a certain nervousness about the Soviets!). Bonn's dependence on and deference to America's wishes, whether in the military or economic sphere, would be gradually eroded. Dividends from such a new image of the Soviet Union would not be confined, the Kremlin must expect, just to German-Soviet relations. The French and Italian Communist Parties would gain in respectability and popular support: with Russia no longer feared, other left-wing forces in their countries would not balk at the idea of Communists as potential partners in government.[14]

The economic benefits of the European *détente* also promise, in fact have already proved, to be considerable. The Soviet regime has been perplexed by the declining rate of the country's industrial growth and by its inability to keep up with America's and Western Europe's technological advance. It is clear that it hopes to improve this picture by, among other things, increased trade and technological and scientific exchange with the West. In his speech to the Twenty-fourth Party Congress, Kosygin painted a vista of vast projects of economic cooperation, such as a united electric grid, collaboration in transportation networks, and so forth. The Soviets contracted with an Italian firm to construct a huge automobile factory on Russian soil. Once more, as during the initial industrialization drive, the help of Western capitalists is solicited to enable the U.S.S.R. "to catch up with and overtake" the West. And needless to say, all this would hardly be possible in an atmosphere of European tensions, of threats and alarums over Berlin, and the like. By becoming a good neighbor and customer, the Soviet Union may also hope to undercut the possibility that Western expertise and credits might help Communist China unduly in its thrust to become an industrial power.

[14] Thus Socialists and Communists concluded a mutual assistance agreement for the 1973 French parliamentary elections.

At present it is difficult to assess how permanent this shift in the Soviets' European policy is[15] or how far its results will justify the Soviets' expectations. But it must be instructive to note how issues that only a little more than a decade ago threatened to bring about an armed conflict have been resolved by quiet negotiations, how agreements that once would have been greeted by the whole world with vast relief and as a monumental step toward permanent peace were now received as thoroughly unsensational. For at least fifteen years between 1948 and 1963, Western statesmen lived with the apprehension that yet another Soviet challenge to their rights in West Berlin might bring the world to the brink of a nuclear conflict. And during the same period the Soviet citizen was intermittently told by his rulers that the Western powers' refusal to sign a peace treaty and to recognize the German Democratic Republic as a sovereign state threatened an imminent war. It was gravely debated whether it would constitute an intolerable concession by the West to allow its citizens' papers during their passage to and from Berlin to be inspected by East German rather than Russian officials. And on the other side, the presence of a handful of American, British, and French soldiers in West Berlin was portrayed as a sinister threat to the whole Communist camp. By the end of 1972, such fears and fantasies have been laid aside. It would be too much to assert confidently that they will *never* return to haunt the world. But for the present and, hopefully, at least a few years, a new air of realism has pervaded the discussion of the German problem. If for a whole generation, 1945–70, this problem remained in a dangerous impasse, then it must be accounted a miracle of speed that within the next two years the Soviet Union and the West reached an agreement on a complex of treaties and understandings on the key problem of European politics.

Who won and who lost? In answering this question, one might echo *up to a point* Khrushchev's public verdict on the outcome of the Cuban missile crisis: "Prudence, peace, and the world's security have won." But unlike on that occasion, one can also characterize the result of two years' negotiations as an undoubted success of Soviet diplomacy. The Soviet Union secured what it had sought tenaciously since 1945: an official acknowledgment by the West of the territorial *status quo* in Eastern Europe. Poland's territorial acquisitions, declared by the Potsdam Conference to be provisional and subject to a possible modification in a German peace treaty, were now, through formal treaties between Bonn and Poland and the

[15] The Russians would, of course, deny that *they* changed their policies. No, they would argue (and with *partial* justification), it is the others who have seen the error of their ways: Bonn has finally realized the folly and danger of "revanchist" policies; West Germans along with other Europeans became convinced that Soviet aggressive designs existed only in the imaginations of warmongers and troublemakers, and that is what made the rapprochement possible.

U.S.S.R., recognized as permanent. Chancellor Brandt's government's subsequent victory in the parliamentary elections of November 1972 put the seal of popular approval on the virtual renunciation of lands that in many cases have been Germany's for half a millennium. Bonn, with the approval of other Western powers, abandoned its claim to being the only legitimate government of Germany. It has entered upon negotiations with the regime that it had hitherto proclaimed a Soviet puppet and prison guard over 17 million Germans. An agreement in December 1972 between the two Germanys put their relations on a new basis and envisages exchange of representatives, if not full diplomatic relations. A pedant might argue that all those treaties and understandings do not amount to a full, unequivocal recognition of the *status quo,* such as could be provided by a German peace treaty. But in fact they add up to the same thing, and it is the Soviet position which has prevailed.

In exchange for the West's surrendering its claims, which, though rendered unrealistic through the passage of time, have retained considerable moral and legal force and hence some political importance,[16] the Soviet Union solemnly pledged that it will abstain from harassment of the Western rights in and of the status of West Berlin. There is no question that to sorely tried statesmen in Washington and Bonn such a pledge went far in justifying their concessions. A cynic might observe that the West gave up its undoubted rights in exchange for the Russians' promising not to do again what they never had any right to, thus vindicating once again what might be called the Kremlin's technique of bargaining by raising exorbitant demands and abandoning them for substantial concessions.[17] But from the Soviet point of view, harassment of West Berlin has been seen not only as a convenient method of pressuring Russia's one-time allies but also as a legitimate retribution for their original breach of the letter and spirit of the wartime agreements. A written pledge to desist from interfer-

---

[16] The agreements mark a renunciation by the West of its insistence on reunification of Germany under non-Communist auspices. Granted, especially since 1961, not many East Germans could have entertained much hope about an imminent change in their political status. Still, one may speculate about the psychological effect of this definite renunciation. Would it not encourage more active rather than merely outward loyalty on the part of the East Germans toward their regime, make them work harder?

[17] An East European tale recounts the travails of a poor Jewish artisan who, burdened with a numerous family, found living in a small house intolerable. He recounted his plight to the rabbi who urged him to get a goat, the advice which our artisan, though naturally dubious, felt bound to follow. He then stormed into the wise man's presence exclaiming that he now saw suicide as the only solution. "Get rid of the goat," ordered the rabbi. In another week the artisan was back, confessing with tears of gratitude that his house now appeared spacious and life again worth living.

ing with the traffic to and from Germany's one-time capital meant for Moscow to sheathe, at least for the foreseeable future, one of the most convenient weapons in its diplomatic arsenal. Any violation of the written pledge would have to be treated by the West as a basic repudiation of the whole policy of *détente*.

The Four Powers' negotiations on the Berlin problem began on March 26, 1970. The emotions the city had aroused in 1948, 1953, and 1961, when it stood as the symbol of the clash between the free and the Communist worlds, have now largely receded. If the world's attention was once riveted on an American President's declaring before an enthusiastic crowd in the beleaguered city that every free man must feel himself to be one with them, then the more recent news from West Berlin suggested how greatly and ironically the international atmosphere had changed. The Free University was thrown into turbulence through the activities of the New Left, the most militant faction among the students proclaiming themselves to be Maoists.

In September 1971, the Four Powers reached an agreement that became ratified in June 1972 following the Soviet-American summit meeting in Moscow. In the protocol all parties pledged not to attempt unilaterally to change the status of Berlin. "Disputes are to be settled by peaceful means . . . there shall be no use or threat to use force in the area."[18] The U.S.S.R. assumed the responsibility for preserving unimpeded Western access across the intervening East German territory, thus relinquishing the claim that West Berlin was really on the territory of its German satellite. To soothe the sensitivities of the latter, Moscow demanded and obtained the Western powers' admission that West Berlin is not politically a part of the Federal Republic and that the Bonn authorities will refrain from demonstrative gestures such as holding meetings of the Bundesrat there, etc.

The German problem was not solved the way, say, that that of Austria was in 1955 when the Four Powers signed the peace treaty assuring that fortunate land neutrality and freedom from pressures whether from the East or West. Germany is too big, too important not to continue to play an important role in world politics. But the very fact that the issue could be defused of its dangerous potential was symptomatic of the changed balance of forces in the world and hence of the different estimate of opportunities and dangers which prevailed both in Moscow and Washington than had been the case a decade or so before. Both capitals see their main problems and dangers to lie elsewhere than in Central Europe. For the moment, a curtain has descended on the drama of the *original* confrontation between the United States and the Soviet Union, on those conflicts and clashes which had given rise to the cold war.

[18] *New York Times*, September 6, 1971.

In writing an epitaph on this war, one must conclude that, though it was made almost inevitable by the nature of the two systems, it benefited neither the U.S.S.R. nor the United States. What if Stalin's Russia had been more trusting and chose to abide by the Yalta Declaration on Liberated Europe which pledged the Big Three to abide by the free verdict of the nations liberated from the Nazi yoke? What, conversely, might have happened had Truman's America been capable of enough *realpolitik* to concede Eastern Europe to Stalin as his sphere of influence and curb its indignation about free elections not being allowed in Poland, East Germany, Czechoslovakia (after February 1948), etc.? What, and this would have led to the most tolerable solution for the countries concerned—which now might enjoy the status of Finland rather than be under one party dictatorship—if Stalin's fears had been less extravagant, America's moralistic passion more restrained? As it was, a whole generation's time of strife, danger, and suffering, especially for the nations that had been the unwitting cause of the cold war, had to pass before the Soviets' unreasonable fears subsided and the Americans' ineffectual moralism gave way to weary resignation.

The cold war destroyed any possibility of that world order which Roosevelt had believed and Churchill (and perhaps even on occasion Stalin) had hoped would be established in the postwar world. Because when it finally ended, the clock could not be moved back, and a concert of powers enforcing peace could not be resuscitated. Had they even wanted to do so, Nixon and Brezhnev, when they met in Moscow, could not have imposed a solution for *all* the major causes of international strife. For one, their personal power could not compare with that which Roosevelt exercised over *wartime* U.S. policy or Stalin over Russia's at any time. For another, the decades of strife have eroded the fabric of international life to the point where even a concerted effort by the two superpowers could not guarantee a peaceful resolution of problems as vexing as those of the Middle East or Southeast Asia. But most important, there was a new factor, a country that by its potential, if not actual, power makes a Soviet-American dominated world unthinkable.

And so *the* cold war, centered on Germany, though with reverberations as distant as those in Korea or Guatemala, was succeeded not by peace in the true sense of the word but by what might be called a series of brushfire cold wars in many corners of the globe. These are no longer contests between the free world and the Communist one or, to use the other side's rhetoric, between the socialist camp and that of imperialism, but a much more complex series of rivalries that defy a simple formula even for propaganda purposes.

Thus it would be fatuous to expect that the Soviet Union and the United States, even if they synchronized their policies, could bring a prompt and stable peace to the Middle East. The U.S.S.R. finds it difficult, and the United States, impossible, to detach themselves from the cause and interests of their respective allies in the region. Were, by some near miracle, the two superpowers able to agree on a joint course of action, this still could not guarantee an Arab-Israeli settlement. There is another power that, if not yet on the scene, is standing in the wings and making its influence felt —Communist China. Peking's vocal support and quite possibly financial and arms help have for some time been extended to the most militant Arab guerrilla movements, those in whose eyes even the most "progressive" Arab regimes lack fervor and courage in dealing with Israel, while the Soviet Union's position on the issue is seen as pusillanimous.

The Middle East is a prime example of how the Soviet-American rivalry helped to release the genie of international anarchy and of how the belated attempts to repress the dangerous monster have proved unavailing. Had there been a Soviet-American alliance in 1948, it is entirely conceivable that the creation of Israel would have been followed by a resettlement of the exiled Palestinians, the two powers' guarantee both of Israel's and neighboring Arab states' frontiers, and thus in due time the Arab-Israeli truce would have turned into a real peace. As it was in 1948, as in 1956 or 1967, the two Great Powers could agree only on what might be called anaesthetizing the conflict, making sure that it would not spread rather than eradicate its sources.

Following the Six-Day War the Soviet Union resumed massive shipments of war matériel to Egypt and Syria, which in turn led to the Israelis' increased demands for war matériel shipments from the United States. But apart from this now familiar pattern, the depth of their Arab allies' predicament has constrained the Soviets to become even more directly and dangerously involved in the never ending Middle East mess. Israel's lightning victory demonstrated the utter ineffectiveness of the Arab armies, even when equipped with modern Soviet supplies. Its refusal to relinquish conquered territory and the consequent closing of the Suez Canal confronted the concerned Arab governments with an impossible dilemma: to recoup at least some of the lost territories, they would have to negotiate with the Jewish state; to give any appearance of agreeing to such negotiations meant for *any* Arab regime an almost certain overthrow by more militant and fanatic elements. The 1967 cease-fire was thus followed by the threat of another war. For the Soviet Union, such a war would have required a choice: either an acquiescence in the Arabs' even more catastrophic defeat and hence in a definite end to Soviet influence in the area, or open military intervention against Israel with all that that implied. To forestall incalculable risks, the Kremlin felt constrained to assume a calculated one: the Soviets would take over part of the responsibility for Egypt's air defense, thus getting a measure of control over its armed forces as well as conveying a warning to Israel that it would not always have its way in the armed clashes that by 1969 again became endemic along and over Suez.

Small commitments have a way of escalating into large ones. It is instructive, however, to note how the Soviet regime, thrust into a situation not to its liking, could at first obscure the extent of its involvement in a shooting war between Egypt and Israel and then at a given moment cut down drastically on its involvement, the kind of flexibility a democratic regime might well envy. The Soviet share in defending Egypt from Israeli air raids was by 1970 considerable. One source would have some 12,000 Russian troops manning Egyptian missile sites and more than 200 Soviet military pilots flying combat missions.[19] Yet unlike American involvement beginning in the early 1960's in actual fighting in Vietnam, the Soviet Union's in Egypt was not being trumpeted to the world, the average Soviet citizen remaining entirely ignorant that his aviators were flying combat missions and suffering casualties for a foreign state. Officially at least, Soviet prestige was not involved in the fighting, and when in July 1970 the United States proposed a cease-fire along the Canal Zone, the U.S.S.R. could as a disinterested party gravely support the proposal.

The cease-fire agreement reached on August 7, 1970, pledged both sides to refrain from improving their defense positions within the stipulated area on both sides of the canal. It is notorious that this agreement was subsequently breached by the Egyptians, who, undoubtedly with Soviet concurrence, moved into the prohibited zone more than thirty missile batteries. In any case the Soviets' initial aim in rushing pilots and missile crews to Egypt had been accomplished: the country's hinterland received a reasonable measure of protection against the Israeli Air Force; its bargaining position improved.[20]

It is unclear whether and to what extent the next sequence of events reflected Soviet plans or whether the Kremlin simply accommodated itself to an awkward situation. Nasser's sudden death brought into Egypt's presidency Anwar Sadat, reputed to be a moderate, not unalterably opposed to an eventual settlement with Israel. In 1971 he fired some government and army officers reputed to be especially close to the Soviets. Still, just as his predecessors, Sadat had to seek a more thoroughgoing Soviet involvement in Egypt's confrontation with Israel. But here the cautious side of the Soviet approach to the Middle East cauldron came into prominence: Moscow would not provide the Egyptians with the most

[19] Michael Curtis, "Soviet-American Relations and the Middle East, *Orbis*, Spring 1971, p. 406.

[20] The destruction of most of the Egyptian planes on the ground and rendering of the airfields unusable in the very first moments of the 1967 war had been a key factor in Israel's victory.

modern offensive weapons they sought for continuing their confrontation with Israel. On July 18, 1972, Sadat announced his decision to terminate the mission of the Soviet military advisers and ordered their removal from Egyptian soil. In the West this step was interpreted as a blow to the Soviet position and prestige in the Arab world. Yet a suspicion must remain that the Kremlin was at least not too displeased by this turn of events. Its direct military involvement in the danger zone was terminated, and that after at least one of its major objectives had been accomplished. The public character of Sadat's gesture could not have pleased the Kremlin: it would have been better for the Russian "advisers," some 20,000 strong, to depart as they had come—discreetly, with no publicity. Yet the Soviet leaders undoubtedly appreciated the rationale of the Egyptian's gesture: he could now explain to the zealots in his regime and to the country at large why his oft-promised settlement of accounts with Israel again had to be postponed. It was also a badly needed sop to national pride: if Egypt could not move across the Suez Canal, it still peremptorily expelled soldiers of one of the world's superpowers. And since the Soviets, for all their reservations about Sadat, still had a stake in the stability of his regime, they had an additional reason for feeling that the whole imbroglio was far from being a total loss.

The renewal of war in the Middle East in October 1973 brought out vividly both the extent of Soviet involvement in the Middle East and the advantages and dangers accruing to the U.S.S.R. on its account. The U.S.S.R. could not have *wished* for a war at this particular juncture, when it was seeking a further *détente* and development of economic and technological ties with the United States. Yet its rulers obviously felt that they *could not veto* the Egyptian-Syrian attack upon Israel without jeopardizing the fruit of their past political and economic investment in the Middle East: Soviet influence over the Arab states and the virtual eradication of that of the West. Once fighting started, Soviet objectives had to be nicely balanced between the imperative of preventing another catastrophic Arab defeat on the order of 1967 and the one of avoiding a confrontation with Israel's ally and protector. The first dictated the implicit threat to send Soviet troops to the battlefield when Israeli encirclement portended annihilation of an Egyptian army, the second constrained the U.S.S.R. to join the United States in demanding (and in a large measure imposing) an armistice which could satisfy neither of the combatants. The new explosion in the Middle East brought the Soviet Union considerable if indirect gains: the ramshackle system of Western alliances suffered new shocks and strains. America's European partners saw their vitally needed oil supplies, their whole industrial development, threatened by what they felt was Washington's excessive partiality toward Israel. And a strong anti-American feeling now engulfed not only the Arab states (including the hitherto pro-Western regimes like Saudi Arabia and Jordan) but most of the Third World. In the United Nations the United States was virtually isolated almost as much as the U.S.S.R. had been prior to the 1950's.

But if the diplomatic gains were evident, so were the dangers and potential losses. The alert ordered for the U.S. armed forces following the news of a possible dispatch of Soviet troops spelled out once more the incalculable dangers that a local conflict may present in a nuclear age. The whole patiently built groundwork for the *détente*, with its potential economic benefits for the Soviet Union, was threatened. In the wake of the October crisis Soviet diplomacy was faced with an unenviable task: it must demonstrate to the Arabs that it can do more for them than just furnish them with up-to-date military equipment. Hence its Middle Eastern stance has to be "hard" enough to induce America to pressure Israel for at least some territorial concessions. Yet while pressuring the United States the Kremlin must try to avoid not only a new confrontation but also the kind of an American reaction that would undo the Soviet-U.S. *détente* and might besides propel Washington toward a far more extensive one with China! And this intricate game, the calculation of possible risks and gains that each step presents, takes place, the Soviet rulers probably ruefully reflect, vis-à-vis the country whose policies are affected by emotional reactions of the electorate and which finds itself in the midst of a severe political and constitutional crisis.[20a]

The above story provides a vivid demonstration of how, for all the extent of the Soviet Union's involvement in the Middle East, the character of the Soviet regime provides it with a degree of maneuverability and flexibility that the United States cannot enjoy in similar situations. To a degree it can operate clandestinely: how many Soviet citizens are even now aware that in 1970 some Russian pilots were shot down in air fights over the Suez Canal? It is impossible for the Soviet consumer to arrive at a precise calculation of how far his privations are related to the expense his government incurs in arming the progressive Arab states, in subsidizing Castro's Cuba, in bolstering at critical points the Czech and Polish economies to prevent their complete collapse. The citizen of the United States is only too aware of the details of its unhappy liaison with General Thieu's government in South Vietnam, but he, as well as the Russian man in the street, can only speculate about the exact relationship between Moscow and Hanoi. Soviet retreats on the international stage can always be rationalized as *intentional* sacrifices on the altar of peace, the failure of some particular machination abroad always repudiated as not having had the *official* backing of the

---

[20a] History often has a knack of nearly reversing certain truisms. It used to be said that the problem of succession is the Achilles heel of totalitarian governments. Yet as the cases of Khrushchev in 1964 and Lin Piao in 1971 demonstrate, they at times solve them expeditiously and without an *apparent* effect on their foreign policy. Can the same be said of the post-Watergate United States?

Soviet Government, the enterprise being blamed on the unfortunate zeal of the native Communists and/or the local Soviet representative who irresponsibly transgressed his authority.[21]

Alas, when it comes to the main and fundamental dilemma of Soviet foreign policy, these advantages of superior maneuverability do not obtain. Largely concealed from the world until 1960, the Sino-Soviet dispute has been since then an open wound festering in the body of world Communism. And since 1964, when Communist China became a nuclear power, every year has increased the complexity of this dilemma for the Soviet Union and has decreased the freedom of choice the Kremlin has had in dealing with it. The Cultural Revolution had superficially improved the position of the U.S.S.R. versus its Communist rival. The handful of Communist Parties previously sympathetic toward Peking now drew back in the face of the incomprehensible chaos that now engulfed the vast country. Peking itself appeared to lose interest in foreign relations in the strict sense of the word and just exuded violent but formless revolutionary propaganda encouraging militant radicalism of all varieties, from extreme black nationalism in the U.S. to the most terroristic Arab guerrilla movements. There was a comforting, from the Soviet point of view, picture of internal turbulence. Red Guards, fanatical youth detachments, roamed through the country, manhandling and humiliating the highest dignitaries of the Party and state and professing obedience to none but Mao. It could be fondly hoped in the Kremlin that the legacy of the madness would be a relapse to that state of anarchy combined with civil war which prevailed in China between the overthrow of the Manchu Dynasty and the victory of the Communists in 1949.

By 1969 it became apparent that China was emerging from the chaos of the Cultural Revolution, that Mao, having used it to destroy the party and state machinery, which had attempted to wall him in as a divinity symbol deprived of real power, was now set on restoring stability and the resumption of China's world role.[22] A series of armed clashes in 1969 along the Sino-Soviet border, which, unlike previous occurrences of this kind, were publicized by both sides, manifested that while returning to "normalcy" China was not abandoning its anti-Soviet stand.

Though a number of Soviet leaders, political and military, must have been sorely tempted to intervene in China's internal troubles, it is unlikely that the Kremlin ever considered this as a real option. Even prior to the Cultural Revolution such a momentous gamble would have been con-

[21] Thus 1971 saw an unsuccessful coup against the Sudan government of Numeiry. His government then proceeded to execute a number of local Communists.

[22] We do not know whether the curbing of anarchy was primarily due to a decision of Mao himself or to the presence of a handful of the old guard still in power and headed by Chou En-lai.

ceivable only if the U.S.S.R. and the United States had a firm understanding of the subject. Some Soviet air marshals' hands must have itched to take out the Chinese nuclear installations in a neat surgical strike. But the leadership, which would not move against little Czechoslovakia until fairly sure that there would be no armed resistance, would not countenance such fearful risks. The very considerable Soviet military buildup along the Chinese frontier (figures rumored are over half a million soldiers) that has taken place in recent years is for defensive purposes, though should Mao die and in the ensuing civil war one faction call for "fraternal help" the Soviets would quite likely oblige.

In the meantime the main Soviet effort has been aimed at political and diplomatic containment of China. Khrushchev, as we saw, toyed with the idea of having India as a countervailing force in Asia. But the Chinese easily trounced the Indians in frontier fighting in 1962. All that Soviet schemes achieved was to make Mao's regime irreconcilably hostile to Congress-ruled India and to draw close to its enemy Pakistan.[23] Pakistan's hostility neutralized India's military and diplomatic potential and thus rendered vain the Soviet hopes of playing balance-of-power politics in Asia.[24] The Soviets have tried to moderate the hostility of two powers on the subcontinent. In 1965–66 they arbitrated an India-Pakistan clash, which threatened to bring China into the fray. But as long as the basic enmity remained, Soviet hopes for India's power to become a curb on China were bound to be frustrated.

In 1969 Soviet diplomatic activity in Asia became more intense. Rather than seek radical solutions of the outstanding problems through spectacular and risky initiatives à la Khrushchev, the Brezhnev-Kosygin group has tried in a much more circumspect and systematic way to back Peking into a corner, to constrain Mao's regime to agree to abandon its aggressive posture toward the U.S.S.R. or to face isolation.

The post-Khrushchev regime believes in speaking softly while, as witnessed by its hectic armament program, it intends to carry a big nuclear stick. It has avoided threatening rhetoric about Peking's actions and pretensions. At the Twenty-fourth Party Congress in 1971 the representative of the Far Eastern provinces received tumultuous applause when, in an unmistakable reference to the recent border fighting, he exclaimed, "All those who want to seize Soviet land from wherever they may come

[23] Thus neatly reversing the position between 1950 and 1958, when Pakistan as America's ally was an object of Peking's hostility while relations between Nehru's and Mao's regimes were friendly and at times cordial.

[24] One cannot refrain from reflecting on a historical "if." Had the tragedy of partition been avoided when the British were leaving their empire in 1947–48, a united India would have been one of the world's leading powers, with its influence dominating all Southeast Asia, and the tragedy of Vietnam might well have been avoided.

will be dealt a crushing blow." It suits the Soviets to play the aggrieved but patient party to the dispute; again and again Brezhnev and others explain imploringly that, if the Chinese People's Republic wishes sincerely to normalize relations, the Soviets will not be found wanting. Following the flurry of border fighting, the two Communist powers decided, as they have intermittently since 1959, to cool off their dispute at least in public. A joint Sino-Soviet commission was to examine the clashing territorial aims. Diplomatic relations have been patched up through the return of ambassadors to their respective posts.

But the basic quarrel has been at most papered over rather than reduced in intensity. The border dispute obviously transcends in its implications the question of rival claims to a few square miles here and there. The Chinese in the negotiations came up with an offer that was sure, as they knew, to raise the temperature of their Soviet opposite numbers. Yes, they will generously concede that all those vast territories in Soviet Asia that had once been under the Manchu Empire's suzerainty should remain in the U.S.S.R. *for the time being.* But won't the Soviets concede in return that those areas had been secured by their ancestors through force, under "unequal treaties"? That their country's expansion, that selfless bringing of culture and progress to backward areas, was imperialism pure and simple is something no Soviet government will ever concede. Once you grant that, you open up the possibility that some time in the future a Chinese Government will request their return, explaining that, after all, their Russian comrades had conceded the whole matter in principle. But in addition the mere fact of such a request is felt to be a gratuitous insult, a demand that the Russians acknowledge and repent of their imperialist past. Who does the "Mao clique" think the Russians are—the English or the Americans? The Chinese will get this admission when, to quote Nikita Khrushchev's favorite proverb, shrimps learn to whistle!

The Kremlin has been seeking a lever to deal with those impossible people in Peking. It is natural that the Soviets should have canvassed the possibility of Japan's becoming a counterweight to China. But while economically Japan has surged ahead to become the third industrial power in the world, its government until recently has shown no willingness to have the country play a major political role in Asia or at least to have a military establishment commensurate with such a role. The Soviets may ruefully if very privately regret the thoroughness with which American occupation has democratized Japan and contributed to persuade its people to foresake the ancient Samurai ideals in favor of seeking laurels as the world's most efficient industrial producers, feelings which might well be shared by an American businessman. Still, the Soviet Union has persistently tried to improve its relations with the other East Asian colossus. The immediate aim has been to enlist Japanese capital's cooperation in the development of the Soviet Far East. For reasons that do not require elaboration the Soviet Government wants to make its Siberian, especially its maritime part's, domain as strong economically and in terms of population as possible. Japan, it is felt, will not always remain virtually unarmed; to give it a stake in the economic development of Siberia would mean to secure an ally for the time when the Chinese might try to do more than just talk about "unequal treaties."[25]

It is at the other side of China's periphery that the Soviet Union has been able to score a remarkable diplomatic success in recent years. As seen above, after 1962 Soviet expectations of India's becoming a counterweight to China had to be revised. Still, an occasion presented itself in 1971 to demonstrate to the world that Peking, while strong on rhetoric, could not do for its allies what the U.S.S.R. could do for its. The longtime tension between the two parts of Pakistan erupted into a civil war. East Pakistan, more populous, different ethnically and linguistically from its western component, developed a strong nationalist movement, which the central authorities, instead of trying to appease through granting autonomy, proceeded to try to repress through martial law. In the ensuing strife several million Bengali refugees sought shelter on Indian territory. The Delhi government rendered help to the insurgents and prohibited the passage of West Pakistan soldiers and arms through its territory. The Soviets made clear their sympathy for Bengali nationalism. On April 3, President Podgorny gravely admonished Pakistan's leader, Yahya Khan, advising him to seek a peaceful solution to his country's troubles, i.e., to concede East Bengal's independence. The Soviets could doubly relish their role as advocates of national self-determination: Pakistan's crisis was a deep embarrassment to Peking. Usually supporters of all revolutionary movements, the Chinese Communists found themselves on the side of a military regime suppressing what was undoubtedly a popular revolt. But beyond ruffling the feelings of the New Left throughout the world, the Chinese faced the prospect of the virtual disintegration of the regime that was their only major ally in Asia. The situation was scarcely less embarrassing to Washington: its old ties to Pakistan had for some time been strained. Still, the United States had a stake in preserving the integrity of Pakistan. In July, something was revealed that the Kremlin must have known for some time: Yahya's government had acted as an intermediary

[25] It is amusing to note that *both* Communist powers have come to have second thoughts about the desirability of the Americans' removing their air bases from Japan. The Russians, while not publicly altering their position, see them as a curb on Peking's domination of the Far East. The Chinese Communists have come to appreciate their similar effect on the Russians. Also, should the Americans withdraw their military presence and protection from Japan, the latter would have to become a first-rate military power, something that Peking, for all the recent improvement of its relations with Tokyo, is very far from considering desirable.

between its old and its new ally. It was through its good offices that Dr. Kissinger's visit to Peking was arranged with its sensational sequel: the Chinese invitation for President Nixon to visit Peking.

In the past, India's eagerness to move against its neighbor and adversary has always been tempered by the fear of what the Chinese might do. But now the advice from Moscow was that the risk would not be too great. China was recovering from the effects of the Cultural Revolution. There was in addition, and the details still remain a puzzle, another struggle for power within its highest leadership. For some time Marshal Lin Piao, who during the Cultural Revolution was proclaimed Mao's successor and "closest comrade in arms," had disappeared from the news. He reappeared in September as a dead traitor, the plane in which he was allegedly fleeing to his Soviet co-conspirators having allegedly crashed. Whatever the truth of this Chinese version of the "shot while trying to escape" technique of handling political dissidents, it testified to considerable turbulence within China's ruling circles. Following President Nixon's visit, many Americans who visited, or rather were taken on guided tours of, China returned convinced of the Mao regime's stability and strength. But in 1971 at least the Kremlin evidently had reason to feel differently, and presumably so it advised New Delhi.

It would be difficult otherwise to account for the boldness of both Soviet and Indian moves and for the Chinese's passive if verbally furious reaction to them. On August 9, the U.S.S.R. and India signed a treaty of friendship and cooperation which provided for consultation and possible help should one of the signatories be threatened by a third party. This was an open warning to China that its interference with India's moves vis-à-vis Pakistan would incur the danger of Soviet intervention. The summer and fall of the same year saw frequent diplomatic interchanges between Moscow and New Delhi. Mrs. Gandhi thus flew to the Soviet Union in September, and only two days after her return, she received President Podgorny in New Delhi. The fruit of those consultations became apparent in November. The Indian Army moved into East Bengal, where the local insurgents with its help proclaimed the independent republic of Bangladesh. Pakistan, whose armed forces were unable to score any successes even on India's western frontiers, was compelled to plead for a truce.

It had been clear for a long time that post-partition Pakistan was not a viable state, its two parts separated by more than a thousand miles of foreign territory linked only by the tie of religion. But the resolution of the problem at this particular time represented undoubtedly a triumph of Soviet diplomacy. The whole affair left a legacy of India's resentment toward the United States, which felt bound to disapprove of its venture, and of gratitude to the U.S.S.R. China proved incapable of protecting the state that had relied on its support. And it is characteristic that, after at first bitterly assailing Soviet complicity in their country's defeat and partition, Pakistan's leaders felt compelled again to plead for Russia's friendship. The president of the truncated state, Zulfikar Bhutto, set out on a state visit to Moscow in March 1972. It it obvious that his country fears further Indian territorial claims, and that it looks to Moscow rather than to Washington or Peking to restrain New Delhi. The Soviet Union has thus succeeded in becoming the diplomatic arbiter for the Indian subcontinent.

Like most victories, military or political, this one also had costly and dangerous implications. The Soviet Union has assumed the kind of obligation toward India that at some time it may well find quite burdensome. The future orientation, in fact, permanence, of Bangladesh, one of the world's most overpopulated and impoverished areas, remains a question mark. For all of India's success, it still cannot in the foreseeable future offset China's power in Asia. It was a diplomatic skirmish against China that was won by the Soviet Union in the Bangladesh affair and not a war.

The Sino-American rapprochement, which has titillated the world in the last two years, was the logical outcome of the two governments' changing the assumptions that governed their policies. It has been a somewhat naïve tenet of belief of American policy-makers, especially following the Cuban missile crisis and the signing of the nuclear test ban treaty in 1963, that the Soviet Union was now a "responsible" power, while China stood for militant Communism, its leaders bent on "exporting" revolution even at the risk of war. It was but little appreciated that Peking's violent rhetoric was largely the means of pressuring the Soviet Union toward a more anti-American position and thus preventing that accommodation between the United States and the Soviets which is the Chinese Communists' worst nightmare. By the beginning of the 1970's both countries' leaders had a good reason to alter their previous stance. The Soviet Union, unlike what President Johnson's and then Nixon's Administration fondly imagined, showed little sign of helping to extricate the United States from Vietnam. Then perhaps China might help. And in any case an approach to China was bound to have a beneficial educational effect on Moscow.

For their part, the Chinese realized by 1969 that the United States, in view of its domestic situation, was now incapable of achieving the original aims of its Vietnam intervention, much less to threaten China, whether alone or in combination with the U.S.S.R. The danger of Soviet-American collusion now took on in Peking's eyes a different form from before: no longer was there any danger of a joint U.S.-Soviet *action* against Mao's regime. But in their exasperation the Americans might offer the U.S.S.R. a free hand vis-à-vis China if only Moscow would enable them to extricate themselves from the war on less than humiliating conditions. Peking thus realized, if no one else did, that the disenchantment of the United States with the whole course of the foreign policy it has pursued since 1947 threatened to remove that *unwitting* and paradoxical protection which the mere fact of American power and role in the world afforded China vis-à-vis the Soviet Union. There could be but little doubt in Peking that a rapprochement with the United States would be followed by a Soviet attempt to outbid it in seeking a *détente* with Washington. But then at least China could prevent that *détente* from having an outright anti-Peking character. In their own way the Chinese Communists have been quite astute in appraising American foreign policy and its dependence on the public opinion in the United States: it would be simply impossible for the U.S. Government to participate in some Machiavellian plot against a country that most Americans no longer considered an enemy.

The results of President Nixon's visit to China went far to justify both sides' expectations. The U.S. Government declared that the new relations with Peking would in no sense weaken its commitments to America's allies, Japan and Taiwan. But facts speak more strongly than declarations. The U.S. protection of Chiang Kai-shek's domain, if not removed, was certainly attenuated. There must be many in Taiwan, including some in the aged Generalissimo's entourage, who realize that the tide is running against them. And the Japanese, despite soothing American assurances, also drew appropriate conclusions. Premier Tanaka visited mainland China in September 1972. Tokyo followed this up with recognizing the Peking government and dropping its diplomatic links with Taiwan. With American support Communist China entered the United Nations and its Security Council.

On the American side the visit to Peking marked a drastic and fateful reversal of that policy which began in 1950 when President Truman ordered U.S. armed forces to throw a shield around Formosa-Taiwan. The mere atmosphere of the visit suggested an important fact in the eyes of the Chinese and other Asian people, a new international status and prestige for the Peking regime, thus obliterating the fatal impression of the Cultural Revolution. The Great Helmsman did not deign to go to the airport to greet the first American President to set foot on Chinese soil, and only later did Mao receive briefly the leader of the world's greatest power. Few on the American side appreciated the ironic element of the visit. It was to stem what it conceived to be the tide of Chinese-led Communism and to teach Peking that wars of "national liberation" do not pay, that the U.S. Government became involved in the morass of the Southeast Asian wars. And now largely to extricate America from these wars, the President of the United States went to China, thus conferring additional prestige on Mao's regime.

But for all such undertones, the Chinese trip and its amicable result accomplished what was undoubtedly in Washington leaders' minds its main objectives: an invitation to Moscow with its sequels, a prospect of a compromise settlement in Vietnam, and a number of important agreements between the United States and the U.S.S.R.

The Soviet leaders did not mind, as they seldom do when hard pressed to be obvious. The rapprochement between Washington and Peking could not be allowed to proceed too far. They knew this rapprochement was as yet of a very limited and tentative nature. But could one be sure about the future? Always intemperate in their moods about foreign countries, Americans now might embrace as friends those people who, as General Eisenhower told Khrushchev in 1959, were "beyond the pale" insofar as the U.S. Government and public opinion were concerned. They might stake China to industrial and technological development. It was thus advisable to propitiate the Americans and to demonstrate to them that, whether in Vietnam or elsewhere, the Kremlin had much more to offer than "the Mao clique."

There was a tense moment preceding the visit. In the spring of 1972 North Vietnam, undoubtedly spurred by the realization that Chinese and Soviet pressure would soon constrain it to agree to a truce, launched an offensive, this time openly sending regular army units across what for some bizarre reason was still referred to as the Demilitarized Zone between the South and North, as established under the 1954 Geneva agreement. This was obviously a last-ditch effort to overthrow the Thieu regime or, barring that, to secure as much territory for the Vietcong as possible before the belligerents' respective domains became frozen under an armistice. Did this move have the sanction of the Kremlin? Most likely the Russians said, in effect: Try it if you wish, but don't expect us to bail you out if there are unpleasant consequences. President Nixon then ordered stepped-up bombing of the North and—a step the Americans hitherto refrained from precisely because of the fear of the Soviets' reactions— mining of the sea approaches to North Vietnamese ports.

Many expected a repetition of the situation of 1960 when the U-2 episode aborted at the last moment President Eisenhower's visit to Russia. But now the situation was quite different. The U-2 affair was blown out of all proportion by Khrushchev because at the time he realized that the forthcoming summit would not bring the desired result: a solution of the German problem of the kind the Soviets sought. Hence he torpedoed the Big Four meeting in Paris and disinvited the American President.[26] But now the agreements that the Soviet leaders dearly desired—on Germany-Berlin, on nuclear arms, etc.—hung in the balance. Were they to disinvite Nixon, the results of years of patient diplomacy with Bonn and of the Strategic Arms Limitations Talks (SALT) with the United States, which would establish virtual parity of nuclear armaments between the two superpowers, would all be jeopardized. And the United States in its predicament would look to China even more than before. And so the possibility of some Soviet vessels being blown up could not stand in the way of an American-Soviet summit and agreements.

[26] And then began work on his Cuban gambit. See *above*, p. 649.

Was there a split at the highest level about the propriety of inviting Nixon in the wake of his moves against Hanoi? The Western press, helped by some hints from Moscow, seized on one development just on the eve of the President's arrival as evidence that there was such a disagreement on May 23. Pyotr Shelest, member of the Politburo and secretary of the Ukrainian Party organization, was removed from his satrapy to become one of several deputy prime ministers of the U.S.S.R. Yet it is likely that his demotion was due to domestic considerations: Ukrainian nationalism was on the rise. And perhaps for bargaining purposes the Russians were not above giving out that there were hard-liners in the Politburo who might gain the upper hand should the Americans prove obdurate in negotiations.

And despite deep apprehensions in the West,[27] the historical trip was allowed to take place. For the first time the President of the United States visited publicly the Fatherland of Socialism.[28] He was received courteously, and, unlike in Peking, the highest officials of the Party and the state greeted and conferred with him. The President made another historic first, a television broadcast to the Soviet people from the Kremlin. Nothing was spared to impress the Americans with the Soviet leaders' wish for cordial coexistence at the very same time that Soviet-made missiles were bringing down American planes over North Vietnam and American mines were barring the access of Soviet ships to Haiphong.

Indirectly, the summit helped bring about the final ratification of the complex of treaties concerning Germany, of which we already spoke and which took place either just before or following Nixon's visit. Some of the direct results were of what he called a rhetorical or theatrical nature. Thus on May 30 the President and General Secretary Brezhnev affixed their signatures to a declaration on peace: twelve high-minded principles which the two powers have undertaken to observe in their mutual and general international relations. There is to be a joint spectacular venture: in 1975 an American crew is to link its ship in space with one manned by Soviet cosmonauts, the four heroes then to offer a literal demonstration of the principle of coexistence. A number of agreements previously prepared, which could have quietly been signed in the respective capitals—on collaboration on problems of environment and in medicine—were now initialed in the atmosphere of solemn drama, thus impressing the citizens of both countries at how many-sided were the fruits of the historic encounter. President Nixon was a few months away from his bid for re-election. And Brezhnev, while no such test faced him, by taking the spotlight in international negotiations previously occupied by Kosygin, was reasserting and enhancing his dominance of the Soviet political scene.

[27] The *New York Times* in its editorial of May 16 urged a suspension of the bombing and mining so that the visit would not be canceled.

[28] Roosevelt's trip to Yalta in 1945 was under wartime secrecy.

The agreement on nuclear arms limitation, the one supremely important act of the Moscow summit, was thus signed on behalf of the U.S.S.R. by the General Secretary, a breach of protocol, to be sure, but one that nobody in the Soviet Union is likely to bring up (that is, Mr. Leonid Brezhnev is a private citizen to whom the law gives no authority to sign state documents).[29] And somehow Mr. Nixon did not demand to see his co-signatory's credentials![30]

The substance of this agreement, just as of the less important ones, has been hammered out in previous negotiations, the long-drawn-out SALT talks. But unlike them its final conclusion both required and justified this meeting of the top leaders of the two powers.

It is necessary to go back. The goal of limitation of and control over the nuclear race has preoccupied statesmen since the invention of the terrible weapon in 1945. From the beginning, the Soviet attitude has been fairly predictable: the Soviet Union will sign no agreement that would require it to acquiesce in having markedly inferior nuclear armament vis-à-vis the United States. There was, to be sure, an element of paradox in this attitude through 1962. The Soviet leaders believed that for politico-psychological reasons even a small stock of atomic bombs and the means of their delivery in their hands more than neutralized the nuclear superiority of the United States. Thus Khrushchev resorted to what must be called nuclear diplomacy or at least rhetoric on the occasion of the Suez crisis in 1956. Nuclear buildup was *not* pursued by the Soviet Union very vigorously between 1958 and 1962, the period of ultimatums about Berlin and recurrent crises about Cuba, when not only the average citizen in the West but his government lived in dread of a nuclear confrontation and in shock at the Soviet Union's (more specifically Khrushchev's) seemingly almost nonchalant attitude about the prospect. Having stronger nerves, the Soviet leaders believed that they could more than hold their own in the game, even with fewer nuclear chips than the United States.

At the same time there was, beginning at least in 1958, a growing apprehension at the proximity of China's acquisition of nuclear weapons. Khrushchev's intermittent attempts to reach some kind of an agreement with the United States that would bar those arms to Peking as well as Bonn were, as we have seen, so circuitous and oversubtle that instead of the intended results they brought almost war between the two superpowers, notably in 1962. And it is estimated that at the time of the Cuban missile

[29] Stalin, while General Secretary, was more respectful of constitutional *punctilios* and never signed a treaty.

[30] An international law purist would note that the agreement does not contain the usual preamble, "Representatives of X and Y met, and having examined their respective credentials and finding them in good order . . ."

crisis the U.S. superiority in nuclear weapons and means of delivery over the Soviet Union was on the order of six to one.

Soviet leaders, military as well as political, drew two lessons from the Cuban affair: they must increase the number of nuclear chips in their possession, as well as seek, but this time in a more straightforward way, an agreement on their limitation and on nonproliferation of nuclear powers.

The latter lesson was largely belated. Neither the Nuclear Test Ban Treaty of 1963 nor the agreement on nonproliferation reached in 1968 could arrest Communist China's development as an atomic power. Why, somebody in the Kremlin may have well have regretted, did not the Soviet Union make a clean breast of its aims and fears to the United States in the 1950's, when, armed with an agreement with America, it might have prevented or delayed China's getting the bomb?

Still, the nonproliferation agreement subscribed to by most of the world's states, including eventually Bonn, brought the small but substantial comfort that the nuclear club would remain quite small. The Soviets are not unduly worried that Britain and France possess atomic weapons. Along with everyone else they have occasion to be grateful that nuclear arms are not widely dispersed in this explosive world. But they have special reason for satisfaction in the fact that none of the "fraternal states" is equipped with them. Is it conceivable that the invasion of Czechoslovakia would have taken place if Dubcek's government disposed of just a few of those dreaded devices?

The rapid buildup of the Soviet stockpile and delivery systems in the 1960's must then be understood as reflecting the need not only to reduce America's superiority but to establish a crushing Soviet superiority over China's budding nuclear power. And it was to offset the future Chinese threat that the Soviets entered upon the course that puzzled many Western experts, that of erecting ABM (an anti-ballistic missile system) to protect, in the first instance, their capital and then other sites. By purely technical criteria, it has been argued, it makes little sense to install ABM: for all the huge expense it involves, it can provide no protection against a first-rate atomic power. But the Kremlin was not thinking of such a power, i.e., of the United States, in erecting its nuclear defense system. With the enormous degree of centralization that characterizes their political system, the Soviets have to take account of the threat and potential effect of *one* atomic bomb or missile dropped on Moscow.

By the late 1960's there were pressing reasons for both superpowers to take another look at the nuclear race and to consider whether they were increasing their security or just wasting money by adding to their stockpile of warheads, ICBM launchers, nuclear-armed submarines, and intercontinental bombers. Each country had the potential to destroy the other many times over.[31] The essence of deterrence, pundits in these frightful matters agreed, was for a power to possess a "second-strike potential" so that its enemy would not be exposed to the temptation of a surprise attack with but little fear of a substantial retaliation. But now, with many of their ICBM's placed in "hardened" sites, with their nuclear-powered submarines equipped with ballistic missiles and able to cruise indefinitely, both powers appeared to have ample retaliatory potential. No matter how great the element of surprise, an atomic attack would be synonymous with national suicide. Common sense urged an end to the mad race.

Common sense is alas not always the decisive consideration in international affairs. For their part, Soviet policy-makers, with the lesson of 1962 in mind, still aspired to nuclear parity with the United States. For them, as for any sane person, the prospect of an atomic war against a power capable of retaliation is virtually inconceivable. But if one rejects actual employment of atomic weapons, does one have to foreswear their use as a bargaining card? Would the United States, while facing a crisis like the 1962 one, behave the way it did then if it knew that the Soviet nuclear power was now equal to its own? And it is this very same consideration that led some politicians and military people on the American side to argue that the United States could not afford to lose its superiority. There has been another argument employed by American proponents of continuing the nuclear arms race, which may be best summarized by a Russian proverb: "Before a fat one will become thin, the thin one will croak"; the economic burden of the race is likely to be much harder on the U.S.S.R. than on its richer antagonist. But the force of that argument has also declined in recent years: with Vietnam and inflation the U.S. economy has lost much of its fat, and there has been an insistent clamor for more domestic spending. One cannot eat missiles, as Khrushchev said in one of his more "coexistential" moments.

The agreement that Nixon and Brezhnev signed in Moscow on May 26, 1972, was a product of those diverse factors and considerations. It was not an agreement on a measure of *dis*armament, still less one that could be called a decisive step toward the elimination of the specter of nuclear war. It seeks to stabilize the present level of the two powers' nuclear armament, and it was phrased in a way that enables each side to proclaim it has achieved its aims: Russia that it has reached at least parity with the United States, America that it has preserved its lead. As President Nixon declared to the joint session of Congress on his return: "No power on

---

[31] A late 1967 estimate was that the United States could deliver 4,500 warheads, the U.S.S.R. 1,000. Soviet warheads were generally of greater explosive power. See Thomas B. Larson, *Disarmament and Soviet Policy 1964–1968* (Englewood Cliffs, N.J.: Prentice-Hall, 1969), pp. 104–5.

earth is stronger than the U.S. is today. And none will be stronger than the U.S. in the future."[32]

Both sides could adduce substantial arguments to back up their boasts. The agreement freezes the present quantity of fixed ICBM launchers on both sides, and there the U.S.S.R. has an advantage, disposing of 1,618 as against 1,054 for the United States. The U.S.S.R. is permitted to build up to sixty-two modern nuclear missile-equipped submarines, the United States up to forty-four. Yet this apparent Soviet superiority is more than offset by the larger U.S. stockpile of nuclear warheads (estimated at 5,700 to 2,500 for the Soviets) and its *present* superiority in nuclear technology, which enables a single American missile to be equipped with several independently targeted warheads.[33] The treaty[34] does not concern itself with bombers, and there again the United States has an advantage: 460 to 140.

The Interim Agreement (it is supposed to run for five years) on offensive arms was supplemented by a formal treaty defining what the two powers may do in the way of erecting antinuclear ballistic defense. Both sides are limited to two ABM systems—one to protect the capital, another an offensive nuclear installation, neither to be equipped with more than 100 interceptor missiles. This again is aimed at preserving the delicate balance of terror: neither power would be tempted to initiate a nuclear holocaust in the hope or illusion that its cities could enjoy a measure of security against a retaliatory strike. This agreement is also to be subject to review after five years, either side being able to terminate it on six months' notice.

The summit meeting envisaged further strategic arms limitations talks (SALT II) aimed at a more comprehensive agreement. The next five years will thus demonstrate whether what was decided in Moscow was the beginning of an end rather than a respite in the nuclear arms race. And it hardly needs to be added that this momentous conclusion will largely depend not only on mutual relations and intentions of the two powers concerned but also on the future situation and policies of Communist China.

In their present form, experts have hastened to warn, the Moscow agreements do not mark a real end to nuclear arms competition between the United States and the Soviet Union. While placing certain quantitative limits on certain types of nuclear weapons, they do not constrain the signatories from seeking qualitative and technological improvements in

[32] *New York Times*, June 3, 1972

[33] The name for this monster is MIRV, standing for Multiple Independently Targeted Re-entry Vehicle.

[34] On the American side it was an executive agreement, which did not require the Senate's confirmation.

their nuclear and missile arsenals. We may be sure that they will do so—seek that will-o'-the-wisp technological breakthrough to achieve the substance or illusion of nuclear superiority.

Until a few years ago a student of Soviet foreign policy would have been skeptical of the possibility of the U.S.S.R.'s agreeing on nuclear arms limitation, except within the frame of a broader political settlement, if indeed not alliance with the United States. To be sure, the Moscow talks fell considerably short of that. In their joint declaration the leaders of the two states recognized their clashing viewpoints on such areas of international conflict as the Middle East and Southeast Asia. The Moscow summit thus registered a new type of relationship in international affairs: two powers pledge a very close collaboration in certain areas, while recognizing that they remain antagonists on other matters. But this is no more bizarre than some other features of the post–World War II international scene. Who in the classic era of diplomacy could have foreseen the situation under which two countries establish friendly ties while recognizing that their respective commitments do not allow them to have formal diplomatic intercourse, as is the current state of relations between the United States and Communist China? Or two powers "bound" by a military and political alliance which neither has seen necessary to renounce and who yet are in a violent conflict, if not indeed on the brink of war (the U.S.S.R. and China)?

On the American side President Nixon's tours of 1972 marked a definite recognition of the maxim which, if observed before, might well have changed the postwar world: one cannot negotiate with the Communist powers in terms of fixed objectives or principles which one expects them to accept before an agreement can be reached. One must follow the course of flexible bargaining, of give and take.[35] Much has been written in the West on how this policy, whose authorship is sometimes ascribed to Presidential Assistant Henry Kissinger, reflects power politics of the predemocratic era and hence is unsuitable for a country like the United States. But under the conditions of the late 1960's and the 1970's, this policy is not so much the product of an intellectual concept or doctrine as simply an acknowledgment of world realities. True, realism, whether in domestic or foreign policies, does not carry with it an assurance of success. True, there are occasions where a moral stand must be preferred by a democratic society to a calculus of probable gains and losses.[36] But as a rule, realism

[35] Which, of course, need not mean surrendering one's basic principles and interests.

[36] Who can, e.g., fault Churchill for his splendid unrealism in 1940 when, with its back against the wall, Great Britain still refused to accept peace with Hitler?

is a surer guide to stable peace than that ostentatious and ineffectual moralism which has so often warped U.S. policies.

The Moscow accords envisage, hopefully, an enlargement of the area of accommodation between the United States and the Soviet Union. In October 1972 a trade agreement was initialed which when ratified by the U.S. Senate would, it is estimated, lead to a tripling of trade between the two countries within a few years. The chronic ailment of Soviet agriculture has already led the Soviet Union to make vast grain purchases in the United States. Visions of huge mutually profitable trade with Russia have agitated many in the West since 1921, and invariably they have been disappointed: the Soviets have almost always demanded the kind of credit arrangements that would have amounted to a direct subsidy of their economy. But the Soviet Union has reached a stage in its social and economic development where the consumer's plight can no longer be ignored by the regime. Hence there are grounds for cautious optimism on this count.

And they coexisted peacefully ever after? It would be fatuous to see in recent Soviet policies sure evidence of a long-term trend. Or rather, the trend they indicate does not preclude the possibility of future sharp conflicts between the U.S.S.R. and the West. If in the past apparently aggressive policies were often designed to mask Soviet inferiority in power vis-à-vis the United States, then in the future forceful policies may well reflect the Kremlin's feeling that Russia's new status as "second to none" is not sufficiently recognized by the West. Most of the recent East-West agreements are seen through the Kremlin's prism as reflecting the recognition by America of its own reduced power, and never mind whether this recognition is a function of its internal politics or of the changed relationship of forces throughout the world.

Thus the agreement on a truce in Vietnam, arrived at with Soviet behind-the-scenes assistance in January 1973, represents undoubtedly a dazzling success of American *diplomacy*. But it does so because diplomacy had to be called upon to rescue the United States from an untenable military and, most of all, politico-psychological position. The original aims that prompted American intervention—to extirpate insurgency in South Vietnam, to demonstrate the limits of Communist China's power—have been frustrated. The American armed forces will depart from Southeast Asia leaving behind what they came to destroy: enclaves of Communist rule and units of the North Vietnamese Army.

The people who rule Russia are Stalin's pupils who have not forgotten his lessons even if they have learned some new ones. They recognize the imperative necessity of peace, they reject categorically the notion of a world in which there are no basic conflicts and no rivalry between their system and that which somewhat anachronistically is still called "capitalism." The Sino-Soviet conflict has not been a road to Damascus on which the Soviet leaders found the sudden illumination that they must henceforth seek cooperation rather than conflict with the West. It has taught them the necessity of moderation and patience in their methods; it has not punctured the main ideological and nationalist premises on which Soviet policies have rested ever since the treaty of Brest Litovsk. A new generation of leaders may begin to question these premises, but unhappily it is also conceivable that they would retain them while abandoning their predecessors' caution. Will the Soviet Union continue to wait patiently for something to happen in Communist China while that country continues to advance to the status of superpower? Can the Soviet system as presently constituted afford normal coexistence, "friends in peace" with the West? Today, every restriction on Soviet citizens' freedom, every act of suppression of nonobjective art, of an apolitical novel—in brief, of "ideological coexistence" in any form—is still rationalized by the regime as a necessity ultimately due to the capitalist danger. Can Soviet Communism under any leadership dispense with this psychological prop? The Soviet Union has proposed and/or entered preliminary negotiations designed to stabilize the European scene, such as should lead to the reduction in conventional forces between NATO and the Warsaw Pact, and a European security treaty. The *professed* aim of Soviet policy is the eventual simultaneous dissolution of NATO and the Warsaw Pact. But here again the question must be posed: can the Soviet state afford prolonged and far-reaching cooperation with the West if one of the results might well be the erosion of Soviet domination of Eastern Europe?

How those inherent contradictions of Soviet foreign policy will be resolved depends on much more than just a decision by a handful of men in the Kremlin or even the evolution of the Soviet system. Yet if not the present, then the next generation of Soviet leaders faces a choice. They may, mindful of the maxim of their eighteenth-century predecessor—"that which stops growing begins to rot"—seek the phantom of security through even greater power and expansion. Or they may, mindful of the realities of the nuclear age, pursue the goal of a supra-ideological world order without which no state, no matter how powerful, can find security and true greatness.

INDEX